THE NEW DICTIONARY
OF CATHOLIC SPIRITUALITY

The
New Dictionary
of
Catholic Spirituality

Editor: Michael Downey

A Michael Glazier Book
THE LITURGICAL PRESS
Collegeville, Minnesota

Library of Congress Cataloging-in-Publication Data

The New dictionary of Catholic spirituality / editor, Michael Downey.
    p.   cm.
  Includes bibliographical references and indexes.
  ISBN 0-8146-5525-4
  1. Spirituality—Catholic Church—Dictionaries. 2. Catholic Church—Doctrines—Dictionaries. I. Downey, Michael.
BX2350.65.N49 1993
248'.08'822—dc20   92-40959
                                      CIP

CONTENTS

EDITOR'S PREFACE

In 1987 Michael Glazier, Inc., published *The New Dictionary of Theology,* edited by Joseph Komonchak, Mary Collins, O.S.B., and Dermot Lane. This dictionary, as its editorial preface notes, "appears as the Roman Catholic Church observes the twenty-fifth anniversary of the opening of the Second Vatican Council" and "represents the first collaborative attempt in English to take stock of the remarkable developments in the church and in theology since the Council, a purpose which determined the structure, authorship, and intended audience of this work."

The New Dictionary of Theology has been followed by *The New Dictionary of Sacramental Worship,* edited by Peter Fink, S.J., published by The Liturgical Press: Michael Glazier Books. *The New Dictionary of Catholic Spirituality* is intended to be a companion volume to both of these, with a parallel aim and purpose, namely, a collaborative attempt in English to take stock of the remarkable developments in Church and world since the council, but with a specific focus on the reform and renewal of Catholic spirituality that the council set in motion.

For this work, as for its companion volumes, contributors have been solicited from various parts of the English-speaking world. Contributions reflect influences on, and developments within, the English-speaking world, though it must be recognized that the great majority of the contributors are from North America.

In recent years there have appeared, in English, dictionaries and encyclopedias of spirituality that have proven very useful. In addition, there are several worthy dictionaries of spirituality in other languages, most notably the *Dictionnaire de spiritualité.* Each of these has its own strengths and weaknesses and, no doubt, *The New Dictionary of Catholic Spirituality* will be judged to have its own as well. The *NDCS* will take its place alongside these others, but may be distinguished from them by its particular focus and content, which have been shaped by the editor's rationale for the dictionary. This rationale may be outlined as follows:

1. The uniqueness of the dictionary is expressed in the key terms of its title. It is to be a **new** dictionary of Catholic spirituality. The *NDCS* treats the subject of spirituality in light of the reform and renewal that the Second Vatican Council set in motion. It is not intended to be a dictionary of the history of Catholic spirituality. Historical periods, issues, and movements have been selected and treated in light of their significance for Catholic spirituality in the postconciliar period.

2. The *NDCS* is intended to be a **dictionary** that will serve as a reliable theological and pastoral resource. Because of the limits that the genre of dictionary imposes, the *NDCS* does not aim to provide an in-depth treatment of all matters germane to the field of spirituality. Where possible and helpful, the *NDCS* attends to pastoral and practical implications as well as to theological insight.

3. For the most part, contributors to the dictionary are Roman Catholic theologians writing for a readership that is envisaged to be predominantly Roman Catholic. In this sense its focus is **Catholic.** But because of the interdisciplinary character of studies in spirituality today, and because of the importance of the ecumenical and interreligious dialogues, contributors have been invited to attend to these factors as they bear upon their subject.

4. The work is to be a new dictionary of **spirituality,** a rather unwieldy term. In giving shape to the dictionary, several elements central to the editor's understanding of spirituality have been emphasized:

a) Spirituality is concerned with the **human person** in **relation** to God. While this may be said to be the concern of any area of theology or religious studies, it is the specific concern of the discipline of spirituality to focus precisely upon the relational and personal (inclusive of the social and political) dimensions of the human person's relationship to the divine.

b) Earlier distinctions between the *credenda,* what is to be believed (the domain of dogmatic or systematic theology), and the *agenda,* what is to be done as a result of belief (the domain of moral theology), are not always as clear as they may seem. The discipline of spirituality has developed out of moral theology's concern for the *agenda* of Christian living. But the focus in the study of Christian spirituality is on the full spectrum of those realities that constitute **the *agendum* of a Christian life in relation to God,** including the *credenda.* Thus the relationship between spirituality and biblical theology, systematic theology, moral theology, pastoral theology, and liturgical studies is stressed. What differentiates spirituality from, say, systematic theology or moral theology, is the **dynamic** and **concrete** character of the relationship of the human person to God in actual life situations. Moreover, the relationship is one of **development,** of growth in the life of faith, and thus covers the whole of life. Spirituality concerns religious experience as such, not just concepts or obligations.

c) The study of spirituality in the postconciliar period is an **interdisciplinary** enterprise. Though most of the contributors to the volume are Roman Catholic theologians, each has been invited to attend to insights from other disciplines (e.g., psychology, sociology, history, economics) as any one or several of these may contribute to a fuller understanding of the subject at hand. Additionally, the fruits of **ecumenical** and **interreligious** dialogues have been brought to bear on the subject where appropriate.

This rationale has determined the structure, authorship, and intended audience of the *NDCS,* making it a complement to, rather than a duplication of, works in spirituality already in existence.

In planning and organizing the *NDCS,* I have had to decide upon the relative length of the entries, and appropriate authors for each. I have selected several topics that are designated as primary (A entries) because of their importance in Catholic spirituality. But I have departed from the rationale and organization of *The New Dictionary of Theology* and, to a lesser degree, *The New Dictionary of Sacramental Worship.* Rather than designating twenty to twenty-five primary entries that provide orientation and structure for other entries related to them, I have judged it more useful to let each entry, of whatever length, stand alone. Therefore each entry in the *NDCS* is discrete and is not related in any structural or organizational way to the others. However, since even the longest entries in the dictionary cannot provide an exhaustive treatment of a topic, cross-references and bibliographies are provided. To expedite usage, cross-references are listed alphabetically at the end of each entry. A topical index and an index of names are also provided.

The reader will note that there are not separate entries treating significant persons in Catholic spirituality. A new and reliable dictionary of religious biography, or of individual figures in Catholic spirituality, is a task for another editor and another volume.

The reader will also note that there are entries that treat subjects which may seem quite far afield of Catholic spirituality. I have judged it appropriate to include specific treatment of some subjects which fall outside the purview of Catholic spirituality but which will undoubtedly be of import to those interested in Catholic spirituality.

The New Dictionary of Catholic Spirituality is a work of great complexity, and its completion is a testament to the spirit of generosity and collaboration on the part of its contributors. No doubt each one would offer a word of thanks to colleague or friend for assistance and encouragement offered in the completion of his or her individual tasks. However, as editor-in-chief, it falls to me to express gratitude to those who have assisted the project as a whole. The first word of thanks is offered to Michael Glazier, who invited and encouraged me to accept the task of coordinating and editing the *NDCS*. Michael Naughton, O.S.B., Director of The Liturgical Press, remained steady and placid as we navigated the course of this complex undertaking. Mark Twomey, Managing Editor at The Liturgical Press, gave me free rein to take the project in directions I judged appropriate. Above all, I thank John Schneider, in-house editor at The Liturgical Press, who wielded his pen with personal dedication and painstaking care. He has eased my task beyond telling.

Finally, I trust that it will not be judged out of keeping with a spirit of collaboration to dedicate my part in this work to the memory of my father, Edward J. Downey (1932–1990), who died as this project was underway, and to my mother, Margaret Mary McCauley Downey.

MICHAEL EDWARD DOWNEY
Editor

CONTRIBUTORS

M. Clare Adams, O.S.C., Monastery of Saint Clare, Bloomington, Minnesota
Confrontation and protest; Religious life; Tears, gift of

Mary Barbara Agnew, C.PP.S., Villanova University, Villanova, Pennsylvania
Charismatic renewal; Glossolalia; Sacrifice

Tiina Allik, Loyola University, New Orleans, Louisiana
Fundamentalism; Protestant spiritualities

Wilkie Au, S.J., Loyola Marymount University, Los Angeles, California
Holistic spirituality

Gerard Austin, O.P., The Catholic University of America, Washington, D.C.
Baptism; Paschal mystery

James J. Bacik, Corpus Christi University Parish, Toledo, Ohio
Contemporary spirituality; Revelation(s)

Keith R. Barron, O.C.D.S., Duquesne University, Pittsburgh, Pennsylvania
Inspiration; Piety; Quietism; Secular institutes; Third Orders; Unity

Benjamin Baynham, O.C.S.O., Abbey of Gethsemani, Trappist, Kentucky
Examination of conscience; Fidelity; Gratitude; Temptation; Transformation

Dianne Bergant, C.S.A., Catholic Theological Union, Chicago, Illinois
Apocalypticism; Prophecy

Petro B. T. Bilaniuk, University of St. Michael's College and the University of Toronto, Toronto, Ontario, Canada
Eastern Catholic Churches, spirituality of; Eastern Christian spirituality

Michael Blastic, O.F.M. Conv., Washington Theological Union, Silver Spring, Maryland
Franciscan spirituality

John Borelli, Secretariat for Ecumenical and Interreligious Affairs, National Conference of Catholic Bishops,Washington, D.C.
Interreligious dialogue

Joseph A. Bracken, S.J., Xavier University, Cincinnati, Ohio
God

Michael J. Buckley, S.J., Boston College, Chestnut Hill, Massachusetts
Discernment of spirits

Richard Byrne, O.C.S.O., died January 19, 1992.
Journey (growth and development in spiritual life)

Curt Cadorette, M.M., Maryknoll School of Theology, Maryknoll, New York
Third World, spirituality of

Annice Callahan, R.S.C.J., Regis College, Toronto, Ontario, Canada
Heart; Heart of Christ

Denise Lardner Carmody, The University of Tulsa, Tulsa, Oklahoma
Native American spirituality

John T. Carmody, The University of Tulsa, Tulsa, Oklahoma
Ecological consciousness

Michael Casey, O.C.S.O., Tarrawarra Abbey, Yarra Glen, Victoria, Australia
Acedia; Apatheia; Cistercian spirituality; Western (Latin) spirituality

William Cenkner, O.P., The Catholic University of America, Washington, D.C.
Eastern (Asian) spirituality

Joan Chittister, O.S.B., Mount St. Benedict, Erie, Pennsylvania
Vows

Rebecca S. Chopp, Emory University, Atlanta, Georgia
Praxis

Joseph F. Chorpenning, O.S.F.S., St. Joseph's University, Philadelphia, Pennsylvania
Rapture; Salesian spirituality

Andrew D. Ciferni, O. Praem., Washington Theological Union, Silver Spring, Maryland
Intercession

Mary T. Clark, R.S.C.J., Manhattanville College, Purchase, New York
Augustinian spirituality

Joann Wolski Conn, Neumann College, Aston, Pennsylvania
Self

Walter E. Conn, Villanova University, Villanova, Pennsylvania
Self

Michael H. Crosby, O.F.M. Cap., St. Benedict Friary, Milwaukee, Wisconsin
Addiction; Justice

Paul G. Crowley, S.J., Santa Clara University, Santa Clara, California
Enlightenment, influence on spirituality; Opus Dei

Lawrence S. Cunningham, University of Notre Dame, Notre Dame, Indiana
Holiness

James Dallen, Gonzaga University, Spokane, Washington
Forgiveness; Penance, penitence

Cyprian Davis, O.S.B., St. Meinrad Archabbey, St. Meinrad, Indiana
African-American spirituality

Michael Dodd, O.C.D., Institute of Carmelite Studies, Washington, D.C.
Consumerism; Divinization; Materialism; Redemption; Secularism; Vision(s)

Barbara Doherty, S.P., Saint Mary-of-the-Woods College, Terre Haute, Indiana
Providence

Doris Donnelly, John Carroll University, Cleveland, Ohio
Knowledge

Helen Doohan, Gonzaga University, Spokane, Washington
Abba (in prayer); Authority; Beatitude(s); Service

Leonard Doohan, Gonzaga University, Spokane, Washington
Church

Robert M. Doran, S.J., Regis College, Toronto, Ontario, Canada
Affect, affectivity

Michael Downey, Bellarmine College, Louisville, Kentucky
Compassion; Disability, the disabled; Marginalized, the; Postmodernity; Spiritual writing, contemporary; Technology, impact on spirituality; Trinitarian spirituality; Weakness and vulnerability

Elizabeth Dreyer, Washington Theological Union, Silver Spring, Maryland
Love

Michael S. Driscoll, Carroll College, Helena, Montana
Adoration; Celibacy; Chastity; Compunction; Enthusiasm; Friendship; Interiority, interior life; Warfare, spiritual

Stephen J. Duffy, Loyola University, New Orleans, Louisiana
Evil; Sin

Robert D. Duggan, St. Rose of Lima Church, Gaithersburg, Maryland
Parish, parish renewal

Tad Dunne, Marygrove College, Detroit, Michigan
Desire; Experience

Eileen Egan, The Catholic Worker, New York, New York
Catholic Worker Movement

Harvey D. Egan, S.J., Boston College, Chestnut Hill, Massachusetts
Affirmative way; Ignatian spirituality; Negative way

Keith J. Egan, Saint Mary's College, Notre Dame, Indiana
Carmelite spirituality; Darkness, dark night

Chris Nwaka Egbulem, O.P., Inter-African Dominicans, Washington, D.C.
African spirituality

James L. Empereur, S.J., The Jesuit School of Theology, Berkeley, California
Dreams; Leisure; Personality types

George P. Evans, St. John's Seminary, Brighton, Massachusetts
*Cardinal virtues; Deadly sins; Fruit(s) of the Holy Spirit; Gifts of the
Holy Spirit*

M. John Farrelly, O.S.B., De Sales School of Theology, Washington, D.C.
Holy Spirit

Darrell J. Fasching, University of South Florida, Tampa, Florida
Culture

Mary Ann Fatula, O.P., Ohio Dominican College, Columbus, Ohio
Faith

Peter E. Fink, S.J., Weston School of Theology, Cambridge, Massachusetts
Celebration; Petition

Kathleen Fischer, Seattle University, Seattle, Washington
Aging

Austin Flannery, O.P., Dominican Publications, Dublin, Ireland
Vatican Council II

Richard N. Fragomeni, Catholic Theological Union, Chicago, Illinois
*Conversion; Cosmic mysticism; Drugs; Extraordinary phenomena;
Occult, occultism*

Laurence Freeman, O.S.B., Monastery of Christ the King, Cockfosters; World
Community for Christian Meditation, London, England
Meditation; Presence, presence of God

William L. Portier, Mount Saint Mary's College, Emmitsburg, Maryland
American spirituality

David N. Power, O.M.I., The Catholic University of America, Washington, D.C.
Sacraments

Walter H. Principe, C.S.B., Pontifical Institute of Mediaeval Studies, Toronto, Ontario, Canada
Spirituality, Christian; Western medieval spirituality

Sonya A. Quitslund, The George Washington University, Washington, D.C.
Single parent

Boniface Ramsey, O.P., Immaculate Conception Seminary, Seton Hall University, South Orange, New Jersey
Desert; Martyrdom; Teaching; Tradition(s)

Thomas P. Rausch, S.J., Loyola Marymount University, Los Angeles, California
Discipleship; Exorcism; Kingdom of God

John Renard, St. Louis University, St. Louis, Missouri
Islamic spirituality

Richard Rohr, O.F.M., Center for Action and Contemplation, Albuquerque, New Mexico
Masculine spirituality, men's movement

Susan A. Ross, Loyola University, Chicago, Illinois
Body

Janet K. Ruffing, R.S.M., Fordham University, Bronx, New York
Anthropology, theological; Power

Kenneth C. Russell, St. Paul University, Ottawa, Ontario, Canada
Abstinence; Anglo-Catholic spirituality; Ascetical theology; Asceticism; Mystical theology

Don E. Saliers, Emory University, Atlanta, Georgia
Goodness; Joy

James A. Schmeiser, King's College, University of Western Ontario, London, Ontario, Canada
Demon(s), demonic, devil(s)

Sandra M. Schneiders, I.H.M., The Jesuit School of Theology and Graduate Theological Union, Berkeley, California
Feminist spirituality

Robert J. Schreiter, C.PP.S., Catholic Theological Union, Chicago, Illinois
Blood; Trust

Edward C. Sellner, The College of St. Catherine, St. Paul, Minnesota
Lay spirituality; Work

Donald Senior, C.P., Catholic Theological Union, Chicago, Illinois
Adoption as children of God; Covenant; Kenosis; Lord's Prayer

William H. Shannon, Professor Emeritus, Nazareth College, Rochester, New York
Contemplation, contemplative prayer; Future; Humility; Intuition

Philip F. Sheldrake, S.J., Westcott House (Ecumenical Federation of Theological Colleges), Cambridge, England
Interpretation

William J. Short, O.F.M., Franciscan School of Theology, Berkeley, California
Almsgiving; Animals; Stigmata

Richard Sparks, C.S.P., Paulist Press, Mahwah, New Jersey
Suffering

Raymond Studzinski, O.S.B., The Catholic University of America, Washington, D.C.
Feelings; Pastoral care and counseling; Retreat, retreat movement

David M. Thomas, Regis University, Denver, Colorado
Marriage

Terrence W. Tilley, The Florida State University, Tallahassee, Florida
Story

Julia Upton, R.S.M., St. John's University, Jamaica, New York
Consecration; Dance; Mercy; Rheno-Flemish spirituality

Michael Vertin, University of St. Michael's College, Toronto, Ontario, Canada
Freedom; Intention, intentionality; Mind

Paul J. Wadell, C.P., Catholic Theological Union, Chicago, Illinois
Virtue

Janet R. Walton, Union Theological Seminary, New York, New York
Aesthetics; Art; Beauty

F. Ellen Weaver-Laporte, Professor Emerita, University of Notre Dame, Notre Dame, Indiana
Jansenism

Samuel F. Weber, O.S.B., St. Meinrad Archabbey, St. Meinrad, Indiana
Carthusian spirituality

Dick Westley, Loyola University, Chicago, Illinois
Sexuality

Kristopher L. Willumsen, Wheeling Jesuit College, Wheeling, West Virginia
Morality, ethics, relationship to spirituality; Value

James A. Wiseman, O.S.B., The Catholic University of America, Washington, D.C.
Mysticism

Richard Woods, O.P., Institute of Pastoral Studies, Loyola University, Chicago, Illinois; Blackfriars, Oxford, England
Millenarianism; New Age spirituality; Parapsychology; Spirituality, Christian (Catholic), history of; Three ages

John H. Wright, S.J., The Jesuit School of Theology, Berkeley, California
Prayer

Ronald J. Zawilla, Chicago, Illinois
Devotion(s), popular; Dominican spirituality; Hesychasm; Icon(s), iconography

LIST OF ENTRIES

The letters in brackets after the entries in this list indicate the relative importance and length of the entries: A = primary; B = major; C = substantial; D = specific; E = minor; F = definitional.

An asterisk (*) indicates that the topic is treated under the cross-references listed for that entry.

The numbers refer to pages on which the entries are found.

ABBREVIATIONS

AA   Vatican II, decree *Apostolicam Actuositatem* (Laity), AAS 58 (1966) 837–864; Abbott, 489–521; Flannery, 766–798

AAS   *Acta Apostolicae Sedis,* Vatican City: Vatican Polyglot Press, 1909–

Abbott   Walter M. Abbott, S.J., ed., *The Documents of Vatican II,* New York: The America Press, 1966

ABR   *American Benedictine Review,* Richardton, N.Dak., 1950–

AG   Vatican II, decree *Ad Gentes* (Missions), AAS 58 (1966) 947–990; Abbott, 584–630; Flannery, 813–856

CD   Vatican II, decree *Christus Dominus* (Bishops), AAS 58 (1966) 673–701; Abbott, 396–429; Flannery, 564–590

CF   Cistercian Fathers Series, Kalamazoo, Mich.

CIC   *Codex Iuris Canonici,* Vatican City: Vatican Polyglot Press, 1983; *Code of Canon Law,* Washington: Canon Law Society of America, 1983

CS   Cistercian Studies Series, Kalamazoo, Mich.

CSQ   *Cistercian Studies Quarterly,* Vina, Calif., 1966–; known as *Cistercian Studies* prior to 1991

DH   Vatican II, declaration *Dignitatis Humanae* (Religious Freedom), AAS 58 (1966) 929–946; Abbott, 675–696; Flannery, 799–812

DOL   ICEL, *Documents on the Liturgy 1963–1979: Conciliar, Papal, and Curial Texts,* Collegeville, Minn.: The Liturgical Press, 1982

D.Spir.   *Dictionnaire de spiritualité ascétique et mystique. Doctrine et histoire,* ed. M. Viller et al., Paris: Beauchesne, 1932–

DS   H. Denzinger and A. Schönmetzer, *Enchiridion Symbolorum, Definitionum et Declarationum de Rebus Fidei et Morum,* 35th ed., New York: Herder, 1974

DV   Vatican II, dogmatic constitution *Dei Verbum* (Revelation), AAS 58 (1966) 817–835; Abbott, 111–128; Flannery, 750–765

EACW   Bishops' Committee on the Liturgy, National Conference of Catholic Bishops, statement *Environment and Art in Catholic Worship,* Washington: USCC, 1978

EN   Paul VI, apostolic exhortation *Evangelii Nuntiandi,* December 8, 1975, AAS 68 (1976) 5–76; *Evangelization in the Modern World,* Washington: USCC, 1975

Ex.   Ignatius Loyola, *Spiritual Exercises*

Flannery   Austin Flannery, O.P., ed., *Vatican Council II: The Conciliar and Post Conciliar Documents,* Collegeville, Minn.: The Liturgical Press, 1975

GIRM   Sacred Congregation for Divine Worship, *General Instruction of the Roman Missal,* 4th ed., Vatican City: Vatican Polyglot Press, 1975; ICEL, *Documents on the Liturgy 1963–1979: Conciliar, Papal, and Curial Texts,* Collegeville, Minn.: The Liturgical Press, 1982, pp. 465–533

GS   Vatican II, pastoral constitution *Gaudium et Spes* (Church in Modern World), AAS 58 (1966) 1025–1120; Abbott, 199–308; Flannery, 903–1001

ICEL   International Commission on English in the Liturgy

JB   Jerusalem Bible

JTS   *Journal of Theological Studies,* London, 1899–1949; new series 1950

LE   John Paul II, encyclical *Laborem Exercens,* AAS 73 (1981) 577–647; *Origins* 11 (September 24, 1981) 226–244.

LG   Vatican II, dogmatic constitution *Lumen Gentium* (Church), AAS 57 (1965) 5–71; Abbott, 14–96; Flannery, 350–423

MC   Paul VI, apostolic exhortation *Marialis Cultus,* AAS 66 (1974) 113–168; *Devotion to the Blessed Virgin Mary,* Washington: USCC, 1974

MD   Pius XII, encyclical *Mediator Dei,* AAS 39 (1947) 521–595; Washington: National Catholic Welfare Conference, 1947

NA	Vatican II, declaration *Nostra Aetate* (Non-Christians), AAS 58 (1966) 740–744; Abbott, 660–668; Flannery, 738–742
NAB	New American Bible (1970)
NABR	New American Bible with Revised New Testament (1986)
NRSV	New Revised Standard Version
NT	New Testament
OAB	Oxford Annotated Bible
OE	Vatican II, decree *Orientalium Ecclesiarum* (Eastern Churches), AAS 57 (1965) 76–89; Abbott, 373–386; Flannery, 441–451
OP	Sacred Congregation for Divine Worship, *Ordo Paenitentiae,* Vatican City: Vatican Polyglot Press, 1974; ICEL, *The Rite of Penance*, Collegeville, Minn.: The Liturgical Press, 1975
OpT	Vatican II, decree *Optatam Totius* (Priestly Formation), AAS 58 (1966) 713–727; Abbott, 437–457; Flannery, 707–724
OT	Old Testament
OU	Sacred Congregation for Divine Worship, *Ordo Unctionis Infirmorum Eorumque Pastoralis Curae,* Vatican Polyglot Press, 1972; ICEL, *Pastoral Care of the Sick: Rites of Anointing and Viaticum*, Collegeville, Minn.: The Liturgical Press, 1983
PC	Vatican II, decree *Perfectae Caritatis* (Religious Life), AAS 58 (1966) 702–712; Abbott, 466–482; Flannery, 611–623
PG	J.-P. Migne, ed., *Patrologia Cursus Completus: Series Graeca,* 161 vols., Paris, 1857–1866
PL	J.-P. Migne, ed., *Patrologia Cursus Completus: Series Latina,* 221 vols., Paris, 1844–1855
PO	Vatican II, decree *Presbyterorum Ordinis* (Priesthood), AAS 58 (1966) 990–1024; Abbott, 532–576; Flannery, 863–902
PP	Paul VI, encyclical *Populorum Progressio,* AAS 59 (1967) 257–299; *On the Development of Peoples,* Washington: USCC, 1967
RB	*RB 1980: The Rule of St. Benedict,* ed. Timothy Fry, O.S.B., et al., Collegeville, Minn.: The Liturgical Press, 1981
RCIA	Sacred Congregation for Divine Worship, *Ordo Initiationis Christianae Adultorum,* Vatican City: Vatican Polyglot Press, 1972; ICEL, *Rite of Christian Initiation of Adults,* Collegeville, Minn.: The Liturgical Press, 1988

RSV   Revised Standard Version

SC   Vatican II, constitution *Sacrosanctum Concilium* (Liturgy), AAS
           56 (1964) 97–138; Abbott, 137–178; Flannery, 1–36

SCG   Thomas Aquinas, *Summa contra Gentiles*

ST   Thomas Aquinas, *Summa Theologiae*

TDNT   *Theological Dictionary of the New Testament,* ed. Gerhard
           Kittel, trans. and ed. Geoffrey Bromiley, 10 vols., Grand
           Rapids, Mich., 1964–1976

TS   *Theological Studies,* Baltimore, 1939–

UR   Vatican II, decree *Unitatis Redintegratio* (Ecumenism), AAS 57
           (1965) 90–112; Abbott, 341–366; Flannery, 452–470

USCC   United States Catholic Conference

WCC   World Council of Churches

A

ABANDONMENT

Abandonment can be understood in a predominantly active sense (abandonment to God) and in a predominantly passive sense (abandonment by God).

Abandonment to God

In Mt 6:25-34 (Lk 12:22-31) we are told to stop worrying about tomorrow, for God knows our needs. Rom 8:28 and 1 Pet 5:6-8 reinforce that message. Jesus teaches us to pray that God's will be done (Mt 6:10), and in Gethsemane he gives the example: "Not my will but yours be done" (Lk 22:42).

The theme of abandonment to God began its theological development mainly through patristic treatments of God's providence. By the Middle Ages increasing emphasis was being placed on the identification of providence with the divine will and pleasure, and on renunciation of one's own will so as to conform with God's. The use of the term *abandonment* for this specific attitude became more prominent from the late 16th through the early 20th century.

Basic to this evolving understanding was the concept of providence as God's will explicitly directing, or at least permitting, all that is and all that happens, in the life of the individual as well as in the world. This notion of abandonment was discussed most often in reference to the more unpleasant aspects of life—poverty, distress, illness, death—but was usually coupled with the theme of equanimity in the face of either poverty or wealth, distress or joy, illness or health, life or death. It was characterized as essentially a fruit of perfect love, wherein the human will freely and fully embraced the divine will and pleasure (divine pleasure referring to that which cannot be foreseen). It could, of course, admit of stages of surrender along the way, but only with perfect charity would one live in a state of true abandonment.

Abandonment was thus more than mere obedience to God's already perceived will and more than patience or resignation, which still bore elements of fear or coercion. It was for some authors beyond even indifference in the Ignatian sense (*Spiritual Exercises,* no. 23), for when one has fully embraced God's will in all things, indifference loses its reason for being, though Francis de Sales did call abandonment "holy indifference" (*Entretiens spirituels,* II).

This concept of abandonment as total, loving conformity to God's will and pleasure presumed not mere passive acceptance but an active embrace that also cultivated the other virtues. And though suffering sometimes seemed to be glorified as a good in itself, balanced presentations insisted that to desire suffering absolutely was to be less than unconditionally abandoned to God's will. Still, it remained for the late 20th century to develop more fully the aspect of human freedom and responsibility in conformity with the divine will.

1

Vatican II's Pastoral Constitution on the Church in the Modern World revealed this shift when it emphasized the need to pursue fully human solutions to human needs (GS 11). One cannot, for example, in the name of abandonment to God's will, neglect one's health and then rejoice in the resultant illness as a sharing in Christ's cross (except repentantly). One cannot exhort the poor and oppressed simply to embrace their lot as the will of a provident God who will later make up for it in eternity. God's will is inextricably bound up with our freedom and responsibility in bringing creation to its fulfillment.

What, then, remains of the tradition of abandonment? The goal of human life is still conformity with the divine, and this is not realized without the abandonment of our circumscribed, self-centered plots and desires for what we shall be in life or in death. In this sense, abandonment to God remains an essential goal of the spiritual life.

Abandonment by God

The concept of abandonment by God has particular roots in Jesus' cry on the cross: "My God, my God, why have you forsaken me?" (Mt 27:46). Christian spirituality in every age has turned to this cry to discern and interpret the meaning of suffering and desolation.

But most especially in the face of a sense of spiritual abandonment do we find the insistence that what seems to be the absence of God is in fact a particular kind of presence. Catherine of Siena's observation is typical: "I [God] come and go, leaving in terms of feeling, not in terms of grace, and I do this to bring them to perfection. When they reach perfection I relieve them of this 'lover's game' of going and coming back. I call it a 'lover's game' because I go away for love and I come back for love—no, not really I, for I am your unchanging and unchangeable God; what goes and comes back is the feeling my charity creates in the soul" (*Dialogo,* chap. 147).

Ultimately, it is only from the vantage point of abandonment to God that we find meaning in a sense of abandonment by God. And it is out of the depths of the experience of the sense of abandonment by God that we discover the full freedom of abandonment to God.

See also DARKNESS, DARK NIGHT; DETACHMENT; PROVIDENCE; PURGATION, PURGATIVE WAY; QUIETISM.

Bibliography: M. Viller, "Abandon," *D.Spir.*, vol. 1, cols. 2–25. Jean-Pierre de Caussade, *The Sacrament of the Present Moment,* trans. K. Muggeridge (San Francisco: Harper & Row, 1982).

SUZANNE NOFFKE, O.P.

ABBA (IN PRAYER)

Etymology

Used by the Jewish community in everyday life within the family, this Aramaic term from the Hebrew translates as "father." When used within the family, it signifies the father children have in common. As adults and little ones use the term, their tone conveys respect, responsibility, and familiarity. In the period of the Mishnah and the Targum, "our father" and "my father" were the forms used, and *Abba* also existed as a title or proper name. However, *Abba* is never used as an address for God, and rarely is it used to describe the relationship between God and the believer. The meaning of *Abba* seems quite specific as a colloquial expression and as a respectful address for a human father.

Biblical Roots

The OT speaks of the relationship between God and Israel as that of father and firstborn son, indicating a special relationship between God and the community (Exod 4:22; Deut 14:1; Hos 11:1; Jer 31:9). However, when Jesus uses *Abba* as an address for God, he takes a familiar term and indicates something very new about his relationship with the Father. Jesus dares to say *Abba* and, by the term, reveals a dimension of his understanding and experience of God as Father. Confidence, respect, and intimacy are characteristic of Father and Son.

This unprecedented utterance occurs in the Synoptic Gospels only in Mk 14:36, with Matthew and Luke using other expressions in their accounts of the Gethsemane prayer. Paul uses *Abba* in Gal 4:6 and Rom 8:15, expanding the usage from Jesus to the Christian community. The meaning may underlie other NT passages that use "my Father" and "our Father." However, these other designations may imply a different emphasis than the *Abba* meaning, since *Abba* in family usage translates as "father."

Meaning

In Mark's Gospel, Jesus uses *Abba* in a moment of great distress in the garden, praying that the hour might pass from him. Acknowledging that all is possible with God, he expresses full confidence in the Father and obedience to the Father's will. The term *Abba* indicates an aspect of the relationship that Jesus has to the Father; he prays within that Father-Son experience with confidence, trust, and authority.

The Christian community understands this particular prayer as an example and indication of their own relationship to God. We are sons and daughters who share the Spirit of God's Son, and so we can also say *Abba* (Gal 4:6; Rom 8:15). It is the Spirit of the risen Lord who is the dynamic principle of this relationship, and it is through the Spirit that we can use the same formula Jesus used. United with Christ, we enter into a special relationship with God as children and pray in a way characteristically Christian. The early Church seemed to find something special in this original term and so preserved this expression in its unusual context.

The tradition shows the use of *Abba* by Jesus but does not indicate how consistently he used it. The community remembers the term in conjunction with the struggle of Jesus in the garden, when his humanity is poignantly portrayed. In his anguish, Jesus calls upon God as he would a human father, suggesting the quality of the relationship between Father and Son. In his trust and obedience, Jesus becomes the model for believers. Christians, too, cry out *Abba,* indicating a unique relationship with God. However, they too struggle to discern in prayer and faith the will of the Father as they live out their call in difficult situations. Just as the term *Abba* indicates a profound experience for Jesus, it becomes transformational for the Christian, as Paul suggests in his understanding. While Jesus used a variety of forms to address God as Father, the confidence, humility, and intimacy of the term *Abba* expands the possibilities for a mature Christian relationship with the Lord.

See also ADOPTION AS CHILDREN OF GOD; PRAYER.

Bibliography: J. Jeremias, *The Prayers of Jesus* (London: SCM, 1967) 11–65. J. Barr, "Abba Isn't Daddy," JTS 39 (April 1988) 28–47.

HELEN DOOHAN

ABORTION

See PREGNANCY.

ABSTINENCE

Although one may abstain, in the broad sense of the word, from food, drink, excessive laughter, idle talk, etc., abstinence in the Christian context usually refers to the temporary or permanent "holding back from" (*abs-tenere*) the consumption of meat. Milk and eggs, the by-products of animals, may also be avoided. The vision of Peter in which he heard a heavenly voice inviting him to eat from a large tarpaulin holding animals considered unclean by the OT, mixed in with clean animals (Acts 10:9-16), emphasizes that no divinely dictated laws nor any notion of an innate impropriety limits what Christians may eat.

The early monks abstained because they considered meat to be the most nourishing and satisfying food available. Omitting meat from the diet simplified their efforts to establish a tranquil equilibrium between body and spirit. Feeding one's appetite instead of one's need led, they taught, to heaviness of mind and the stirring of sexual passion.

The contemporary awareness of the economic conditions under which the Third World produces certain foods for the West, concern for animal rights, and a reaction against "junk foods" could stimulate a new appreciation of abstinence as a prophetic protest and an affirmation of higher values.

See also ASCETICISM; FASTING; MORTIFICATION.

Bibliography: M. Cawley, "Vegetarianism, Abstinence and Meatless Cuisine," ABR 38 (1987) 320–338.

KENNETH C. RUSSELL

ACCOUNTABILITY

See OBEDIENCE; RESPONSIBILITY.

ACEDIA

Acedia or accidie (from the Greek *akēdeia*) is the lack of commitment to spiritual values, or carelessness, listlessness, unconcern. Ancient monastic authors such as Evagrius Ponticus, John Cassian, and John Climacus have left detailed treatments of this vice. Gregory the Great put the traditional material on acedia under the heading of sadness (*tristitia*), which he included in his list of the seven deadly sins. From the medieval period on, acedia has been discussed mainly by monastic authors, but recently the term has had a minor revival. The ancient texts have been reexamined from a psychiatric viewpoint as indicative of depression, and S. Shoham has suggested *acedia* as a suitable term to describe a common attitude among individuals in Western culture.

Acedia is a chronic state of inability to be committed to a way of life or to a community. It is caused by a failure to appropriate the values of the group or its lifestyle, resulting in an inability to identify with the group and a strong inclination to stand apart from it. It is not open rebellion, since it is characterized by a lack of energy and tends more often toward passive aggression. The individual afflicted by acedia experiences a great deal of unhappiness and disappointment in life, though sometimes this is cloaked by cynicism. If not treated, acedia often leads to depression.

In attempting to ease the burden of acedia, behavioral aberrations may appear. These are described by Cassian (*Institutes* 10). Typical are the following: physical or emotional mobility in an effort to elude any situation of potential challenge; escapist activities, such as daydreaming or idle conversation; a shortened attention span, making it impossible to concentrate on any particular task and bring it to completion. The low level of personal satisfaction yielded by such a life only increases the degree of depression, and the cycle is repeated.

The traditional monastic remedy for acedia was a healthy alternation between prayer and work. The disciplined use of the body in manual tasks was regarded as a means of regaining control over a life that had become too passive. Attending to the needs of others and serving the community were also seen as ways of overcoming a preoccupation with self and of building bridges to the real world.

See also DEADLY SINS; FEELINGS.

Bibliography: C. Folsom, "Anger, Dejection and Acedia in the Writings of John Cassian," ABR 35 (1984) 219–248. J. Driscoll, "Listlessness in *The Mirror for Monks* of Evagrius Ponticus," CS 24 (1989) 206–214. S. Wenzel, *The Sin of Sloth: Acedia in Medieval Thought and Literature* (Chapel Hill, N.C.: Univ. of North Carolina Press, 1967). M. Altschule, "Acedia: Its Evolution from Deadly Sin to Psychiatric Syndrome," *British Journal of Psychiatry* 111 (1965)

117–119. S. Shoham, *Society and the Absurd* (Oxford: Basil Blackwell, 1974).

MICHAEL CASEY, O.C.S.O.

ADDICTION

If alienation is the antithesis of grace, if darkness contrasts with light, if control undermines care, if disease contradicts wholeness, if self-obsession hinders concern for others, and if death stands opposed to life, then addiction represents the polar opposite of spirituality. Alienation, darkness, illusion, control, self-centeredness, and disease leading to death represent dynamics identified with addiction; grace, light, truth, care, concern for others, and wholeness leading to life represent spirituality. Whereas spirituality is grounded in truth, freedom, and detachment, addiction thrives on illusion, compulsion, and disordered attachments. Whereas spirituality ultimately represents a heart steeped in fidelity, courage, and dedication, addiction represents the opposite: a heart dominated by obsessive thinking, anxious feelings, and life that is unmanageable.

This article will examine the etiology or basis of addiction, including its personal and organizational expressions; the relation of addiction to religion and spirituality; and the implications of these considerations for the Catholic Church. It will then show how the founders of Alcoholics Anonymous found in the Twelve Steps a pattern of spirituality for recovering addicts, how the Twelve Steps and Twelve Traditions offer a contemporary spirituality for North Americans, and how these elements contain the best of principles in ascetical spirituality.

The Etiology of Addiction

A proper understanding and treatment of addiction suffers from the proliferation of definitions and models used to diagnose and treat it. At one time addiction was limited to alcoholism and was perceived as a moral weakness. Alcoholism was not identified as a disease by the American Medical Association until the middle of the 20th century. Gradually the notion of addiction moved from being identified with alcohol to abuse of any chemical substance. The World Health Organization defined addiction as "a state of periodic or chronic intoxication produced by the repeated consumption of a natural or synthetic drug for which one has an overpowering desire or need (i.e., compulsion) . . . with the presence of a tendency to increase the dose and evidence of phenomena of tolerance, abstinence and withdrawal, in which there is always psychic and physical dependence on the effects of the drug." Such a notion highlights the difficulties associated with ingesting alcohol or some drug, and the resulting dependency and dysfunctional relationships.

While the cause of alcoholism and other addictions is unclear, contributing factors can include a parental history of addictive behavior; heavy drinking or drug use; biological and ethnic predisposition; unresolved inner and/or outside conflicts; and the phenomenon of codependency, which will be described later. Generally, when people speak of addictive diseases, they consider addiction as a medical problem; when they speak of addictive behaviors, they reveal a social learning or environmental understanding of the problem; and when they use the term "addictive pathologies," they imply a psychological model. Those involved in treating addictions agree that any serious theory of addiction must account for all these variables but would disagree about how they are to be combined and approached. Many others, including the founders of Alcoholics Anonymous, have understood addictions as entailing physical, mental/emotional, and spiritual dimensions.

The addictive cycle begins when one senses the need to act out to alleviate pain or to find more pleasure. In the process preceding the acting-out, a mood change (often called a "rush") takes place. Once the acting-out takes place, the person may fear that pleasure will be diminished or may be even more deeply aware of discomfort or pain; resolution is sought by repeating the cycle. As the cycle continues, an attachment builds. If not stopped, this pattern can lead to obsessive thinking, feelings of anxiety about getting more pleasure or relief, and compulsive behavior to ensure the supply (the "fix"). At some point in the cycle of addiction, cellular and genetic changes take place in such a way that the body develops a craving or dependency. Getting the "fix" becomes the controlling dynamic in one's life (thinking, feeling, and behaving). In alcoholism, intoxication becomes normal; in other addictions, maintaining the supply becomes the norm for functioning.

Because the psychological dependency began to be perceived as preceding any physical addiction, actually launching the addictive cycle, people in the 1980s and 1990s began to attribute the term "addiction" to patterns of thinking, feeling, and acting related not only to substances but to other objects, persons, relations, and institutions insofar as dependency on these result in one's being out of control. Addiction may thus be defined as any object or dynamic that controls behavior, emotions, and thinking in such an obsessive-compulsive way that it leads to increasing powerlessness and unmanageability and, ultimately, death. It can affect persons, groups, organizations, and cultures.

A family-systems model has helped addiction therapists understand that the perceived addict is merely the "identified patient." One person's addiction directly affects at least four others, and their patterns of thinking, feeling, and acting toward the "identified patient" become part of the problem as well. Thus these others can easily become enablers of the identified patient in such a way that they also take on the addictive patterns of the one they perceive to be out of control. In the

process they, too, become out of control and classic "codependents." Given the relational connection to addiction and the need to develop a tri-level approach (individual, interpersonal, infrastructural), codependency may be defined as any obsessive thinking, feeling, and/or acting centered around control. It involves an intellectual, emotional, and behavioral condition that results from the interaction between an individual, group, or institution and relationships and rules (overt or covert) that are ordered to control and/or prevent the open expression of the thinking, feeling, and activity of oneself and others, especially those who may be under the influence of the addictive process. Addictive persons, groups, and organizations, as well as addictive systems, view codependency as normative for members and a sign of loyalty. Because denial is often stronger in codependent people, their disease can be more life-threatening than that of addicts.

"Recovery" is for the addictive process what "conversion" represents in spirituality. Both involve a process of leaving something behind and turning to something else. Thus recovery, like conversion, involves two processes. The first entails stopping the addictive thinking, feeling, and/or behavior; the second demands developing new ways of thinking, alternative ways of feeling, and changed behavior.

In the early days of addiction theory, recovery was perceived to be possible only when someone "bottomed out," or came to feel powerless over the object of the addiction and to admit that his or her life had become unmanageable. Later it became accepted practice to help the addict "bottom out" by providing a "bottoming-up" or "intervention." This occurs when loved ones, peers, bosses, and siblings present the data of one's behavior to the person. In this process the harmful, progressive, and destructive effects of the person's dependency (addiction and/or codependency) are interrupted in a loving way, with the goal that the person will seek recovery.

The Relation of Addiction to Religion and Spirituality

When control constitutes the underlying addictive process, be it of addiction itself or of codependency, and when "letting go" (of control) represents the heart of spirituality, it should be clear that religion and spirituality are not the same. The addictive process undermines spirituality, even though the justification for it can be made in the name of religion. For some, religion itself can function as the addictive substance or dynamic; for others, religion might represent addictive processes.

Bill Wilson, the co-founder of Alcoholics Anonymous, rejected religions but understood the Twelve Steps as a form of spirituality. Despite having taken instructions, he could not accept Catholicism because of its "absolutizing" and "dogmatic" tendencies. Wilson realized that an experience of and relationship with God ("Higher Power") are primary; belief systems (religion) are secondary and, quite possibly, impediments to developing a spiritual life if they revolve around control through articles of faith, rituals, and ministry. When people need these controls, they become codependently attached to the organization and/or its promises, especially its promise of salvation. Consequently, obsessive adherence to religion and its controls can actually make people deviate from a spiritual base. Religion can obstruct spirituality, but spirituality always ennobles religion. The road to recovery for an addict may be a road away from religion (as for "Recovering Catholics"), but one can never be taken on a road to recovery that is not spiritual.

Religion, in its institutional expression, can be the addictive substance one "needs" to alleviate pain or give more pleasure; in its operations it collectively can reveal addictive functioning. According to Ann Wilson Schaef, the loss of spirituality leads to addictive functioning. When an organization, especially a religious organization, takes on the pattern of addiction, it "creates God in its own image and then distorts that image to suit its own purposes. This is an integral part of the delusionary nature of the system. That distortion further separates us from our spirituality and our awareness of ourselves as spiritual beings" (p. 91). It is precisely in religion's functional role as moral legitimator for social conformity in society that it can become addictive.

In the last decade of the 20th century, an increasing number of observers began to analyze the Catholic Church in its organizational expression from the perspective of family systems and addiction theories. A family-systems approach to Catholicism would consider the basic unit of Catholicism—the parish—as (1) a family (2) of families (3) within a larger family (4) served by a priest who came from a family. At any level addictive processes might take place, given the understanding of addiction noted above. With addictive processes in any one of the families, the theory purports, the others are bound to be affected.

In the universal family of Catholicism, because of the control exercised by the hierarchy, and because of the submission the rest of the members are to show to hierarchical authority, the organized expression of the Latin Rite of the Catholic Church came to be seen by an increasing number of people as manifesting addictive patterns. The specific alleged addiction of the Catholic religion was described as the obsession with the preservation of the male, celibate clerical model of the Church to ensure the position and prestige of those in authority. Being a family, its parallel form of codependency was allegedly expressed in those Catholics who accepted this as normative and acquiesced to its control. This was further evidenced, the theory stated, when the primary purpose of the Catholic Church—the celebration of the Eucharist—was unable to take place because only male celibates could be its principal celebrants.

Alcoholics Anonymous and the Twelve Steps

The catalyst for what would become the first Alcoholics Anonymous (A.A.) meeting came during a conversation between a New York stockbroker, William Wilson ("Bill W."), and an Akron physician, "Dr. Bob," in June 1935. Another key person in the early days was Dr. William D. Silworth, a New York specialist in alcoholism, who helped Bill W. understand better the nature of his alcoholism and whose involvement in the Oxford Groups suggested a way of recovery.

The Oxford Groups (not to be mistaken for the Oxford Movement identified with Cardinal Newman) originated among evangelical Christians seeking a deeper way of life in reaction to growing secularism in society. Convinced of the need for small groups of people to gather regularly for sharing, Alcoholics Anonymous borrowed various tenets from the Oxford Groups, such as the need for regular moral inventory, confession of personality defects, restitution to those harmed, helpfulness to others, and the necessity of belief in and dependence on God (later to be called "Higher Power"). These basic principles, offered as a way of ongoing recovery for the addict, came to be known as the Twelve Steps. The Twelve Traditions became the guiding principles for the meetings of the recovering addicts.

The Twelve Steps (here applied to alcohol but also applicable to other addictive substances and dynamics) are essentially a spiritual document centered around the primacy of God in one's life. At least half of the steps refer directly to God; the majority of the steps assume God (or Higher Power) as the source and goal of life. The steps are:

1. We admitted we were powerless over alcohol, that our lives had become unmanageable.

2. Came to believe that a Power greater than ourselves could restore us to sanity.

3. Made a decision to turn our will and our lives over to the care of God as we understand God.

4. Made a searching and fearless moral inventory of ourselves.

5. Admitted to God, to ourselves, and to another human being the exact nature of our wrongs.

6. Were entirely ready to have God remove all these defects of character.

7. Humbly asked God to remove our shortcomings.

8. Made a list of all persons we had harmed, and became willing to make amends to them all.

9. Made direct amends to such people whenever possible, except when to do so would injure them or others.

10. Continued to take personal inventory and when we were wrong promptly admitted it.

11. Sought through prayer and meditation to improve our conscious contact with God as we understand God, praying only for the knowledge of God's will for us and the power to carry that out.

12. Having had a spiritual awakening as the result of these steps, we tried to carry these messages to alcoholics and to practice these principles in all our affairs.

(In using the Twelve Steps for codependency, the word "relationships" is substituted for "alcohol.")

The Twelve Steps can be considered one of the few "spiritualities" to arise from the American Anglo-Saxon culture. A.A., as well as all Twelve-Step programs, are essentially spiritual procedures offering a spiritual way of life. Its core assumption rests on the notion of spiritual experience: "We admitted we were powerless" (First Step), "made a decision to turn our will and our lives over to the care of God as we understood God" (Third Step), and "having had a spiritual awakening as the result of these steps . . ." (Twelfth Step). For the recovering addict, the heart of the process revolves around a daily inventory and making amends (Steps Four to Seven) and seeking to remain in conscious contact with God (Eleventh Step). Its program of evangelizing, like its Eleventh Tradition related to publicity, is based on attraction rather than promotion. With the spiritual awakening that results from fidelity to the steps, the members try "to carry this message to alcoholics, and to practice these principles in all [their] affairs" (Twelfth Step).

As one of the great spiritualities of the twentieth century, the Twelve-Step Program contains elements of other classic spiritualities guiding the mystical/ascetical life. Its centeredness on God speaks of God as the Higher Power, the Absolute in life. Its notion of "spiritual awakening" echoes the essence of Quaker spirituality. Moral inventory on a daily basis becomes the equivalent of the Jesuit particular examen. The need for confession of failings and making amends can be found in the Catholic Church as well as in many contemporary expressions of Protestantism. Its stress on the need for sponsors has parallels in spiritual directors, while its Eleventh Step about keeping in conscious contact with God parallels the need for daily prayer. Its scriptures are "The Big Book" (a "basic text" containing the message of A.A. and its spinoffs for other addictions), the Twelve Steps, and the Twelve Traditions. It has its form of ejaculations: "Let go and let God," "One day at a time," "Turn it over to God." Above all, however, its notion of detachment places it in that group of kenotic spiritualities in the Buddhist and Christian traditions that stress the essential element of disengagement from all that is not spiritual.

Twelve-Step meetings are guided by the Twelve Traditions, which are read at each meeting after the Twelve Steps have been repeated:

1. Our common welfare should come first; personal recovery depends on A.A. unity.

2. For our group purpose there is but one ultimate authority—a loving God whose self-expression may be expressed in our group conscience. Our leaders are but trusted servants; they do not govern.

3. The only requirement of A.A. membership is a desire to stop drinking.

4. Each group should be autonomous except in matters affecting other groups or A.A. as a whole.

5. Each group has but one primary purpose—to carry this message to the alcoholic who still suffers.

6. An A.A. group ought never endorse, finance, or lend the A.A. name to any related facility or outside enterprise, lest problems of money, property and prestige divert us from our primary purpose.

7. Every A.A. group ought to be fully self-supporting, declining outside contributions.

8. Alcoholics Anonymous should remain forever non-professional, but our service centers may employ special workers.

9. A.A., as such, ought never to be organized; but we may create service boards or committees directly responsible to those they serve.

10. Alcoholics Anonymous has no opinion on outside issues; hence the A.A. name ought never be drawn into public controversy.

11. Our public relations policy is based on attraction rather than promotion; we need always maintain personal anonymity at the level of press, radio, and films.

12. Anonymity is the spiritual foundation of all our traditions, ever reminding us to place principles before personalities.

Bill W. declared that the best evidence of the authenticity of one's spiritual experiences is in the "subsequent fruits." Since addiction undermines spirituality, the fruit of a non-addictive way of thinking, feeling, and acting would be ongoing recovery, which involves a cessation of the old patterns and the struggle to develop new patterns. Key to that struggle is the transformation of formerly destructive ways characterized by manipulation and control into wholesome and healthy patterns expressive of compassion and care. These dynamics create a life of sobriety, which is the goal of recovering addicts.

To aid in that recovery, a prayer originally proffered by Reinhold Niebuhr is prayed regularly by recovering addicts and at many Twelve-Step meetings: "God grant me the serenity to accept the things I cannot change, the courage to change the things I can, and the wisdom to know the difference."

See also DETACHMENT; DRUGS; EXAMINATION OF CONSCIENCE; GRACE; POWER; PRAYER.

Bibliography: *Alcoholics Anonymous* ["The Big Book"], 3d ed. (New York: Alcoholics Anonymous World Services, 1976). *Came to Believe . . . : The Spiritual Adventure of A.A. as Experienced by Individual Members* (New York: Alcoholics Anonymous World Services, 1973). M. Crosby, *The Dysfunctional Church: Addiction and Codependency in the Family of Catholicism* (Notre Dame, Ind.: Ave Maria, 1991). A. Schaef, *When Society Becomes an Addict* (San Francisco: Harper & Row, 1986).

MICHAEL H. CROSBY, O.F.M. CAP.

ADOPTION AS CHILDREN OF GOD

The Pauline writings use the metaphor of adoption to characterize the relationship of the Christian to God. In Greco-Roman law the paterfamilias could purchase and legally adopt a son. One of the legal terms used for adoption is *huiothesia* (literally, "the placing of a son"), the same term employed by Paul in several of his letters.

Paul's basic notion is that Israel enjoyed a filial relationship to God through covenant election (Rom 9:4). Gentile Christians could also enter into such an intimate and confident relationship with God through Christ's redemptive death and resurrection. In Romans 8, for example, Paul reminds the Christians that "those who are led by the Spirit of God are children of God. For you did not receive a spirit of slavery to fall back into fear, but you received a spirit of *adoption,* through which we cry *Abba,* 'Father!' " (8:14-15; see also

Gal 4:5-7). As adopted children of God, Christians are joint heirs with Christ of God's promises (Rom 8:17; see also Eph 1:5). The ultimate outcome of adoption is final salvation, which transforms the believer and all of creation (Rom 8:22-23).

Viewing the Christians as the adopted children of God through Christ's redemptive power is, in fact, a strong undercurrent of the NT as a whole. Jesus himself is the unique Son of God; the Christian shares in that intimate relationship through adoption. Thus the Christian has access to the same freedom from fear, the same confidence in prayer, and the same assurance of loving union with God as Jesus does.

See also ABBA (IN PRAYER); BAPTISM; CHRIST.

Bibliography: J. Fitzmyer, "Pauline Theology," *New Jerome Biblical Commentary* (Englewood Cliffs, N.J.: Prentice Hall, 1990), art. 82, pp. 1382ff. D. Stanley, *Boasting in the Lord* (New York: Paulist, 1973).

DONALD SENIOR, C.P.

ADORATION

Adoration, according to the traditional division of prayer into five types, consists in the worship of God alone. Among the Fathers who identify adoration clearly, St. Augustine, in the *City of God* (10, 1), speaks about the absolute worship given to God alone (Latin *latria*), while St. Ambrose, in his *Commentary on Ps. 98,* extends adoration to Christ. Cyril of Jerusalem, in his *Mystagogical Catecheses* (5, 22), writes, "Bow down and in adoration and veneration say Amen"; yet the distinction between adoration and veneration is not clear. Confusion still remained at the Second Council of Nicaea in 787 (DS 601), which dealt with the question of the veneration of icons. This council also used the term *latria,* reiterating that it is worship rendered only to God.

Medieval theology classically distinguished between the supreme worship offered to the Trinity (Greek *latreia;* Latin *adoratio*) and veneration of the angels and saints (Greek *douleia;* Latin *veneratio*). Due to the religious excellence of the saints, they are honored as beings lesser than God. Regarding the veneration of Mary, who has a most privileged place among all the servants of God, the term *hyperdulia* was coined to indicate her superiority among the saints.

Medieval Eucharistic theology, with the doctrinal development concerning the real presence and transubstantiation, underlines the idea of adoration. St. Thomas Aquinas, in his hymns for the feast of Corpus Christi, speaks explicitly of this truth, as seen in the hymn *Adoro te devote,* which is ascribed to him. The Council of Trent, in its thirteenth session, articulated this doctrine as follows: "There is, therefore, no room for doubt that all the faithful of Christ may, in accordance with a custom always received in the Catholic Church, give to this most holy sacrament in veneration the worship of *latria,* which is due to the true God. Neither is it to be less adored for the reason that it was instituted by Christ the Lord in order to be received. For we believe that in it the same God is present of whom the eternal Father, when introducing him to the world, says: 'And let all the angels of God adore him' (Heb 1:6); whom the Magi, falling down, adored (Mt 2:11); who finally, as the Scriptures testify, was adored by the Apostles in Galilee (Mt 28:17)" (chap. 4; see DS 1643).

During the seventeenth century the so-called French School developed a spirituality of adoration. Being strongly Christocentric, this school conceived of the interior life of perfection as a participation in the mysteries of Christ, with the Eucharist playing a dominant role. According to Jean-Jacques Olier, "Christianity consists in these three points . . . to look at Jesus, to unite ourselves to Jesus, and to act in Jesus. The first point leads us to acts of respect and religion. The second leads to union and unity with him. The third leads to action, which is not isolated but rather united to the power of Jesus Christ, whom we have

drawn to us through prayer. The first is called adoration; the second, communion; the third, cooperation" ("Introduction to the Christian Life and Virtues," chap. 4 in *Bérulle and the French School,* ed. W. Thompson, trans. L. Glendon, New York and Mahwah, N.J.: Paulist, 1989, p. 229).

Recent papal documents, Paul VI in *Mysterium Fidei* and John Paul II in *Dominicae Cenae,* restate the rapport between the Eucharist and adoration, making a case for reservation of the holy sacrament as worthy of the cult of *latria.*

See also EUCHARISTIC DEVOTION; FRENCH SCHOOL OF SPIRITUALITY; PRAYER.

Bibliography: *Lettres de M. Olier,* 2 vols., ed. E. Levesque (Paris: J. de Gigord, 1935). M. O'Carroll, *Corpus Christi: An Encyclopedia of the Eucharist* (Wilmington, Del.: Glazier, 1988).

MICHAEL S. DRISCOLL

AESTHETICS

Aesthetics, a word coined by Alexander Gottlieb Baumgarten (1714–1762), typically referred to what is perceptible. As the use and understanding of the word developed, aesthetics came to mean more specifically the branch of philosophy concerned with the nature of art, that which sets parameters for what constitutes beauty, ugliness, the sublime, the foolish, etc. Thus the study of aesthetics offers criteria for artistic judgment.

Aesthetics and Art

The controversial question that has both plagued and stimulated those who think about aesthetics relates to the purpose of art: Does art exist primarily to provide pure delight, or does it have cognitive value (Brown)? The frequently cited saying of Archibald MacLeish, "A poem should not mean / But be," expresses succinctly the widely held opinion that art need not serve any "use" beyond an invitation to an experience; no other application or interpretation is necessary. On the other hand, for some aesthetic philosophers, that understanding of art is too limited. They see art as having cognitive, religious, and moral value as well as providing delight (Brown).

Aesthetic Judgment

Whatever the end of art, it is generally agreed that aesthetic judgment is based on qualities of form (proportion, coherence, and balance in the structure of the work of art) and expressiveness (its capacity to relate emotion). This appraisal presumes the importance of engagement: Does the work of art arrest attention and invite the participant into a process of interaction? Once the latter is established, the controversy about criteria for evaluation begins. Factors of context, experience, need, kinds of available knowledge all influence aesthetic judgment. Though some people hold that there are objective criteria appropriate for universal application, more significant for the relationship of a specific artistic work to spirituality is whether or not it means (communicates) something to persons who encounter it.

Aesthetics and Spirituality

Aesthetics connects with spirituality in that both attempt to disclose the unutterable. Aesthetics is concerned with a wide spectrum of reality, and spirituality with a specific aspect of it—the unfolding of the divine, transcendent and immanent. To the seeker of religious meaning, aesthetic experiences often are occasions of understanding God and divine activity.

The sensuous quality of aesthetic expression offers multidimensional possibilities for this engagement. Perhaps one of the most poignant examples is the use of bread and wine in a Eucharist. These simple, basic foods, when fully explored aesthetically, can convey qualities of God through the senses of smell, touch, taste, hearing, and seeing. No words compare. Similarly, the beauty evident in the lives of wise members of the assembly, felt in their persistence in a search for truth through many

eras of change, symbolizes the faithfulness of God. Aesthetic expressions, such as music, movement, color, light, and design, also convey a sense of God. An aesthetic spirituality suggests a framework for seeing and for acting that identifies God's presence in what is vital, provocative, sensuous, beautiful, honest, passionate, and yearning for justice.

See also ARCHITECTURE; ART; BEAUTY; MUSIC.

Bibliography: F. Brown, *Religious Aesthetics* (Princeton: Princeton Univ. Press, 1989).

JANET R. WALTON

AFFECT, AFFECTIVITY

The role of the affections in the spiritual life is treated by major authors in the tradition, but contemporary developments enable us to attain greater precision.

Bernard Lonergan distinguishes nonintentional from intentional feelings. Nonintentional feelings correspond to what some psychologies call *affects,* as distinct from feelings, while the term *feelings* is used by these psychologies to refer to what Lonergan calls intentional feelings. *Affectivity* is used here to cover both realities, and for the sake of clarity we will employ Lonergan's distinction.

Nonintentional feelings include such states as anxiety and fatigue, which have causes, and such trends as hunger and thirst, which have goals, but they are nonintentional, inasmuch as they do not arise out of an apprehension or representation of their causes or goals or of any object. They occur, and from their occurrence one diagnoses the cause or goal. Intentional feelings, though, are responses to apprehended objects. The major classes of objects to which they respond are, on the one hand, the satisfying or dissatisfying, and, on the other hand, values. The two classes of objects are not mutually exclusive, for what is satisfying may also be truly worthwhile; but they are also not mutually inclusive, for what is genuinely worthwhile may also be disagreeable. What distinguishes value from the merely satisfying is that value carries us to transcend ourselves, and on that basis Lonergan distinguishes vital, social, cultural, personal, and religious values in an ascending order.

Such a link between feelings and values renders feelings of crucial importance in discernment and decision-making. Ignatius of Loyola speaks of three times or moments of election or decision. The times reflect different affective states of the subject, and in each instance affectivity is a criterion of both the method to be employed and of the course of action to be chosen. In one of these times (the second), one is agitated and experiences alternations of consolation and desolation; a decision is reached precisely by monitoring these experiences in the practice of what Ignatius calls the discernment of spirits. In another time (the first), one has been so moved by God as to have no doubt concerning what one is to do. And in the third time, one already is tranquil and so is antecedently disposed to employ more rational means, such as weighing the pros and cons of the various alternatives.

These moments are exhaustive of all possibilities. Either there are no further questions about what is to be done (first time) or there are (second and third times). And if there are, either one is moved affectively in diverse and conflicting directions (second time) or one is not (third time). If a person is in the second time, when affective apprehension is only of *possible* values, one should choose what leads to equanimity. If one is in the third time, a test of the genuineness of a decision is that one preserves and deepens the equanimity that enabled one to employ this method in the first place; and the first time is so clear precisely because it places one in such a state of equanimity that there is no need for further deliberation; the apprehension of values in feelings is, and is known to be,

an apprehension of what is genuinely worthwhile and to be done.

The criterion both of what method is to be employed and of what course of action is to be chosen thus lies in an affective dispositional state referred to by Ignatius as equanimity or equilibrium. When one is in the second time, what *leads to* such a state is to be followed, and what *leads away from* such a state is to be rejected. When one is in the third time, such a state sets the very conditions for employing more rational methods of decision-making, and the choice is to be confirmed by perseverance in such a state; and the first time is one in which one is placed in such a state by the action of grace.

The practice of discernment, of course, is engaged in independently of such moments of decision. Discernment is a matter of noticing constancy in, or departure from, the state of equilibrium that makes affective self-transcendence possible. Self-transcendent affective response, in fact, may be correlated with the dynamic equilibrium that is the criterion for both the method and the object of choice. What calls for further comment, then, is the constitution and origination of this equilibrium of self-transcendent feeling.

Such an equilibrium is constituted by the creative tension or functional interdependence of the linked but potentially opposed principles of (1) limitation rooted in the body and (2) transcendence rooted in the spirit. The human person is an incarnate spirit, and the authenticity of the person is a function of one's perseverance in the tension of matter and spirit. That tension is *felt* in the sensitive psyche, and these feelings are ciphers, indeed criteria, of one's genuineness. What the tradition has called concupiscence is our tendency to distort the tension of matter and spirit in either direction. Sin is capitulation to that tendency. Grace is needed to preserve us in the inner harmony felt in the psyche as equanimity or equilibrium.

The origination of such equanimity is complex, but besides more or less normal favorable circumstances in a person's life, another ground may be found in the experience that St. Ignatius calls consolation without a cause. Karl Rahner has interpreted this expression to mean consolation with a content but without an object. In this sense, consolation without a cause is a peculiar instance of a nonintentional feeling, in that it does not arise from the apprehension or representation of an object but occurs by divine causation without any such apprehension. Its occurrence is a ground or condition of equilibrium, and therefore a factor in the sustained exercise of authentic personhood. It is identified by Bernard Lonergan with the dynamic state of being in love with God, which is the basic fulfillment of our conscious longings. In proportion to the consistency of that state, one's affectivity is of a single piece. Religious and affective development converge in their finality when the goal of each is acknowledged to be a dynamic and habitual state of being in love.

Such a perspective enables the integration of spirituality with a reoriented science of psychology. Many of the techniques discovered by contemporary psychologies can be employed in the spiritual life to enable one to discover, name, and negotiate one's affective dispositions and responses. Under these perspectives, taking cognizance of, and assuming responsibility for, one's affective orientation is partly constitutive of one's development as a spiritual person.

See also COMPASSION; CONVERSION; DISCERNMENT OF SPIRITS; DREAMS; FEELINGS; LOVE; PSYCHOLOGY, RELATIONSHIP AND CONTRIBUTION TO SPIRITUALITY; VALUE; WEAKNESS AND VULNERABILITY.

Bibliography: B. Lonergan, *Method in Theology* (New York: Herder and Herder, 1972), chaps. 2 and 4, and the references given there. W. Johnston, *The Inner Eye of Love* (San Francisco: Harper & Row, 1978) and *Being in Love* (London: Collins, 1988).

ROBERT M. DORAN, S.J.

AFFIRMATIVE WAY

The Fourth Lateran Council (1215) stated that "between the Creator and creature no similarity can be expressed without including a greater dissimilarity" (DS 806). The affirmative way can be understood as a philosophical-theological position, a way of speaking about God, and a contemplative path that emphasize the "similarity" between God and creation.

a) As a philosophical-theological position, the affirmative way stresses what the First Vatican Council (1870) formally declared as a truth of faith, namely, that "God . . . may be certainly known by the natural light of human reason, *by means of created things,* because 'ever since the creation of the world his invisible nature, namely his eternal power and deity, has been clearly perceived in the things that have been made' (Rom 1:20); but that it pleased his wisdom and bounty to *reveal himself* and the eternal decrees of his will to mankind by another and a supernatural way; as the Apostle says: 'In many and various ways God spoke of old to our fathers by the prophets; but in these last days he has spoken to us by a Son' (Heb 1:1-2)" (DS 3004-3005, emphasis added).

St. Thomas Aquinas expresses this philosophical position in the classical arguments for God's existence, in which he concludes: "Hence the existence of God . . . can be demonstrated from those of his effects which are known to us" (ST 1, q. 2, a. 2). His well-known five ways proceed from causality and participation to "what we call God" (ST 1, q. 2, a. 3). The belief of Christian tradition that God has revealed himself in ways that surpass natural reason also find their classic statement in Thomas's theology (e.g., SCG I, chaps. 3–8).

b) As a mode of speaking about God, the affirmative way states that God, as the Creator (efficient cause) of everything that exists, must possess every true perfection found in his creatures. Pseudo-Dionysius' treatise on kataphatic (Greek *kataphatikos* = affirmative) theology, *The Divine Names,* is imbued with a stirring conviction that God truly is manifested in the world. This treatise explains the truths of the faith as proclaimed by the Church and emphasizes that the concepts and images used by Scripture to describe God are analogical. Everything positive in these expressions can and must be applied to God. Thus, despite his underscoring of the inadequacy of all God-language because the "dark" Trinity transcends any and all manifestations and is "distinct from all things," Pseudo-Dionysius nevertheless insists that God does manifest himself in the world and "is therefore known in all things" (*The Divine Names,* VII, 3, 872A). Although God "is not any one thing," nevertheless "every attribute may be predicated of him" (*The Divine Names,* V, 8, 842B).

c) As a mode of contemplative ascent to God, the affirmative way contends that God can be found in all things because all creatures are the overflow and expression of divine fecundity. It sees them as the shadows, echoes, pictures, vestiges, representations, and footprints of the triune God. As St. John of the Cross says, "My beloved is the mountains, and lonely wooded valleys, strange islands, and resounding rivers, the whistling of love-stirring breezes, the tranquil night at the time of the rising dawn, silent music, sounding solitude, the supper that refreshes, and deepens love" (*Spiritual Canticle,* vv. 14-15).

One of the clearest and most profound expositions of the intellectual kataphatic way can be found in Bonaventure's classic work *The Soul's Journey into God.* He contemplates the Trinity as reflected in creation, in sensation, in the soul's memory, understanding, and will, and in the soul's graced faculties. He also contemplates God as Being and as Good. As Bonaventure says, "In relation to our position in creation, *the universe itself is a ladder by which we can ascend into God.* Some created things are vestiges, others images; some are material, others spiritual; some are temporal, others everlasting; some are outside us, others within us. In order to contemplate the First Principle, who is most spiritual, eternal and above us, we must pass through his vestiges, which are material, temporal and outside us. This means 'to be led in the path to God.' We must also enter into our souls, which is God's image, everlasting, spiritual and within us. This means 'to enter in the truth of God.' We must go beyond to what is eternal, most spiritual, and above us, by gazing upon the First Principle" (*Soul's Journey into God,* chap. 1, no. 2, emphasis added). Moreover, in his undeservedly neglected affective work *The Tree of Life,* Bonaventure meditates and contemplates the life, death, and resurrection of Jesus Christ.

The affirmative way is solidly rooted in biblical spirituality and mysticism. Biblical kataphaticism teaches that "from the greatness and beauty of created things comes a corresponding perception of their Creator" (Wis 13:5). One should be able to know God from "the good things that are seen" (Wis 13:1; see also Ps 148; Ps 145:5; Rom 1:20). That God is the one in whom "we live and move and have our being" (Acts 17:28) and from whose radical presence there is no escaping (Ps 139:7-12) underscores God's immanence. The Scriptures also stress that Israel knows Yahweh through his mighty deeds on its behalf (see Ps 136). Moreover, the Scriptures attest that Yahweh reveals *himself* through his life-giving Spirit (Ps 104:29-30; see Job 34:14; Isa 57:16; Jdt 16:14); the prophetic word (Jer 23:18); heavenly voices (Ezek 1:28); visions (Isa 2:1); angelic visitations (Lk 1:11; 1:26; Mt 1:20; 2:19); and the ecstasies of seers (Acts 10:10; 11:5; 22:17; 2 Cor 12:2-5; Rev 4:2). Paradoxically, the incomprehensible, invisible God made us in his "image and likeness" (Gen 1:26-27; see 1 Cor 11:7).

However, Christ states the most profound dimension of biblical kataphaticism: "He who has seen me has seen the

Father" (Jn 14:9; see also Jn 1:18; Heb 1:1-2). Christ is the very "image of the invisible God" (Col 1:15; see also 2 Cor 4:4). In and through Christ the living God allows himself to be heard, seen, and touched (1 Jn 1:1-2; Jn 20:28). If God's self-communication and self-revelation reach their irreversible highpoint in the risen Christ, it must be emphasized that his history is *confirmed*—not swallowed up or dissolved—in the resurrection. The risen Christ *is* the crucified and suffering one, the Christ who still washes his disciples feet, the Christ who still preaches, cures, and performs miracles, the Christ who is still boy, infant, and fetus. This Christological principle undergirds all genuine kataphatic Christ-centered spirituality and mysticism. Furthermore, the incarnational-Christological dimension of the affirmative way penetrates to humanity's very identity, because "all of us . . . are being transformed into the same image from glory to glory" (2 Cor 3:18; see also Rom 8:29; 1 Cor 15:49).

The *Spiritual Exercises* of St. Ignatius of Loyola offers one of the clearest and most influential expositions of the affirmative way. The exercises are essentially meditations and contemplations on Christ's life, death, and resurrection, interlaced with specifically Ignatian material, to aid one to become free of "all inordinate attachments, and after accomplishing this," to seek and to discover "the divine will regarding the disposition of one's life" (Ex., no. 1). Instead of calling upon persons to forget everything for the sake of the naked love of God, Ignatius guides persons in the progressive simplification of their prayer through a sacramental deepening of meditation upon, and contemplation of, Christ's life, death, and resurrection. The result is an increasing transparency of the images, symbols, and mysteries of salvation history to the mystery of God's self-communicating love.

For example, the "preparatory prayer" for any individual exercise requires exercitants to direct themselves totally "to the service and praise of His divine Majesty" (Ex., no. 46). The "first prelude" usually calls upon the exercitant to create a "mental image of the place" (Ex., no. 47) in the Gospel scene or to use some other way of directing one's imagination and fantasy to the truths of salvation history.

In the "second prelude" (Ex., no. 48), the exercitant asks for a specific grace, a "consolation with previous cause" (Ex., no. 331), consonant with the matter of the exercise—for example, grief with Christ suffering or joy with Christ rejoicing. The exercitants must place themselves *into* the mystery of salvation history as if they were actually present while it occurred (Ex., no. 114).

Even the more laborious "meditations" of the first phase ("first week") of the exercises require the exercitant to seek an "interior understanding and savoring of things" (Ex., no. 2). The exercitant should linger with those aspects of the meditation that are satisfying (Ex., no. 76), never rushing from point to point but following the consolations and the spiritual nourishment. Then Ignatius would have the exercitant repeat previously made exercises in order to dwell especially upon those aspects that brought the most consolation and desolation (Ex., no. 62).

The "résumés" (Ex., no. 64) likewise recall and review intellectually what happened in the previous exercises. The "application of the senses" exercises (Ex., nos. 66-70) require the exercitant to see, hear, touch, taste, or smell in imagination certain aspects of a particular Christian mystery. This greatly condenses, intensifies, and transforms the contemplation begun in the exercises of any particular day. Some commentators link the Ignatian application of the senses to the profound prayer with the "mystical senses" in which the person prays with the "senses" of the soul.

Each exercise ends with a "colloquy" addressed to the Father, Christ, Mary, or others. It should be made "by speaking as one friend speaks to another, or as a servant speaks to his master, now asking some favor, now accusing oneself for some wrong deed, making known his affairs to Him and seeking His advice concerning them" (Ex., no. 54). The colloquy actually carries forward, strengthens, and unifies the movement initiated in the exercises of any particular day. In short, instead of having exercitants forget the mysteries of salvation history, the exercises aid them to experience each mystery in its totality.

The power of Ignatian prayer comes from the ability to initiate the whole body-person in the Christian mysteries. The directives in the *Spiritual Exercises* are meant to ensure that the exercitant fully utilize his or her senses, emotions, passions, fantasy, memory, reason, intellect, heart, and will in order to interiorize the material of any exercise. This holistic process awakens the person's mystical senses and renders the *entire* person connatural to the Christian mysteries.

Apophatic mystics sometimes recommend that a person use a meaningful word in prayer (see, e.g., *The Cloud of Unknowing,* chaps. 36–40), not to concentrate on its meaning but to control distractions while emptying the mind of all created things. For Ignatius, however, at the higher levels of mystical prayer the Christian mystery itself becomes a highly concentrated "word" with which the exercitant mystically resonates. It is a word that draws attention not to itself nor to its "letters" but to what it is in its essence: a sacrament of the healing, transforming presence of God. St. Teresa of Avila teaches the same when she exhorts her nuns to turn to the risen Lord within themselves and to use the mysteries of Christ's life, death, and resurrection as "sparks" to enkindle love (see *Life,* chap. 22).

The key to Ignatius's radical affirmative way, therefore, can be found in the dynamism of his *Spiritual Exercises* that renders the Christian mysteries increasingly transparent. Transparency, not forgetting and unknowing, underpins Ignatius's sacramental, or kataphatic, mysticism. In and

through the increasing simplicity and transparency of the Christian mystery, the exercitant penetrates to its very depths to experience its saving power. In fact, the mystery may become so simplified and transparent that it draws the exercitant "wholly to the love of His Divine Majesty" (Ex., no. 330) through a "consolation without previous cause" (Ex., nos. 330, 336).

It must be emphasized that the affirmative way is inextricably linked to the negative way because God is always ineffable and incomprehensible, even to the blessed in heaven. Also, the risen Christ transcends all images and concepts. Finally, the human person is always "spirit-in-world" (Karl Rahner), one whose proper transcendence is open first and foremost to the ever-greater God. Even the self remains a mystery to itself. Thus, for theological, Christological, and anthropological reasons, no spiritual and mystical path can be purely affirmative.

It should also be emphasized that the affirmative way must always be understood in conjunction with the ways of negation and eminence. The attribution of a perfection to God demands the attribution of it eminently and the negation of every imperfection.

See also AFFECT, AFFECTIVITY; CONTEMPLATION, CONTEMPLATIVE PRAYER; DISCERNMENT OF SPIRITS; IGNATIAN SPIRITUALITY; IMAGINATION; MEDITATION; MYSTICISM; THREE WAYS; UNION, UNITIVE WAY.

Bibliography: H. Egan, "Christian Apophatic and Kataphatic Mysticisms," TS 39 (September 1978) 399–426; *Christian Mysticism: The Future of a Tradition* (New York: Pueblo, 1984); *An Anthology of Christian Mysticism* (Collegeville, Minn.: Liturgical Press/Pueblo, 1991).

HARVEY D. EGAN, S.J.

AFRICAN SPIRITUALITY

The decade of the 1960s witnessed significant developments in the Church in Africa. The celebration of political independence in many African countries during this period brought with it a fresh breeze of cultural and religious revival. Local Churches began to seek ways to better articulate the faith brought by missionaries from other parts of the world, and there was increasing interest in various facets of African life.

Before the Second Vatican Council the official position of the Church with regard to the values of African religion and life was not especially favorable. It is reported that when the Declaration on the Relationship of the Church to Non-Christian Religions was being prepared, a suggestion to mention African traditional religion alongside Islam, Judaism, and the Asian religions was simply brushed aside. In spite of the lack of such specific references to Africa and its peoples, the council did recognize the need for the Church to be open to the history, culture, and traditions of all races and peoples. In Africa this meant an appreciation for a spirituality that is integral, binding the visible and the invisible, life and death, the Creator and creation, in a mutual embrace of unity and harmony.

Understanding African Life

Catholicism was slower than Protestant Christianity to recognize the rich religious reality of African culture. African life and history can only be understood from a religious standpoint. With time, Catholic African theologians helped the Church to better understand the truly religious nature of life on that continent. Their research and writings helped to prepare the way for the first official statement by a Roman pontiff to acknowledge some of the core aspects of African spirituality. Pope Paul VI's message to African peoples, *Africae Terrarum* (1967), recognized their unique spiritual heritage as worthy of respect and valuable for the Church. Subsequent evaluations of African life by theologians and social scientists helped to articulate the values of African life that give meaning to African spirituality.

The following seven concepts can be considered to be the pillars of African life and the essence of African spirituality.

1) *The active presence of the Creator God in the world.* African spirituality gives a most prominent place to the Creator. God is Father and Mother, present, alive, active, and in direct communication and collaboration with creation. God is the beginning without an end. All that exists has its origin and meaning in God and will terminate in God. In a special way African spirituality sees the glory of God made manifest in humanity. Names given at traditional naming ceremonies ordinarily have spiritual references to God or religious connotations.

2) *A unified sense of reality.* For the African, divinity and humanity are not seen in isolation. The sacred and the profane interact, and just as the body is united to the soul, divinity indwells our world. The visible and the invisible likewise interact. All the beings in the universe and beyond exercise influence over one another. The world of the spirits participates in the human world. Spiritual needs are as important to the body as bodily needs are to the soul. All are part of human experience, just as life and death are. The human body is like a capsule, an integral whole, incorporating blood, water, fire, air, soil, and all other symbols of life. In short, dualism has little or no place in African thought.

3) *Life as the ultimate gift.* African spirituality identifies life as the prime gift of the Creator to the creature. It is to be received gratefully, sustained, enhanced, and safeguarded. Life at all levels is sacred. It is for this reason that marriage and procreation play central roles in the social and religious rites of Africans. Rituals of birth and burial are among the most sophisticated in Africa. Between birth and death the rituals of healing fulfill a most important role in endeavoring to sustain life when it is threatened by illness, a hostile environment, or even by the aging process. Traditional healers, therefore, hold a prominent place in

the life of the village. Through the power of the spoken word, incantations, divinations, prayers, sacrifices and offerings, the use of roots, herbs, and other natural substances, the healing ministry continues to be promoted in traditional African life.

4) *The family and community as the place to be born, live, and die.* A vital link exists between an individual and members of the same family, clan, or community. Being born into a family inserts a person into a kind of current, and it is identification with that family and community that determines the nature of one's existence and survival. The life of the individual is therefore lived in participation with other community members. This is equally true of men and women. The position of women in traditional African thought is one of honor and respect, although modern trends have tended to relegate them to the background. That is partly due to the religious and theological positions assigned to women by Christian and Islamic missionaries.

The kinship system, which reinforces the traditional notion of the extended family, is what has kept the predominant style of the African family alive. It could be said that the African is incomplete when alone. The unique style of African hospitality derives from the system of the extended family and community. In the moral order this family system demands the practice of social justice and the promotion of the life and well-being of others.

5) *The active role of ancestors.* Ancestors, sometimes called "the living dead," are those members of the family or community whose lives have left a great heritage to the living and who continue to influence their families from beyond the visible world. The memory of ancestors is invoked in various ceremonies and rituals of African peoples; they are intermediaries between God and the people, in continuation of their earthly function, which combined headship of their families with ritual leadership.

The cult of ancestors is not synonymous with the cult of spirits. Whereas the ancestors are believed to be an integral part of the human community, the spirits are not. The cult of ancestors in African life somewhat resembles the memorial of the communion of saints in Roman Catholic spirituality. It should also be noted that for the first time in Roman Catholicism, the invocation of African ancestors in the liturgy has been approved in the new Liturgy of the Eucharist in Zaire (*Missel romain pour les diocèses du Zaire,* 1988).

Elderly people are accorded special respect in African society. They are believed to be in special communion with ancestors because they lived and worked for a long time under the ancestors' inspiration and because they are close to joining their company.

6) *The sense of oral tradition.* The spoken word has great power in African spirituality for three reasons. First, the spoken word derives from the divine presence in the world. The sounds of nature—thunder and lightning, for example—are some of the ways in which God's voice is actualized. Second, the spoken word proceeds immediately from the most privileged of creation—the human person. Words used to bless or curse are believed to possess the power to be effective. Third, the word is not merely sound; it names, identifies, and describes a subject. It is what makes history real. The word in African thought encompasses the entire system of communication. This is what is generally referred to as oral tradition in African life, and it includes communication in music, song, dance, poetry, proverbs, storytelling, art, and ritual. Prayer involves all of these.

7) *The sacredness of nature and the environment.* Africans see the presence of the divine in creation. The moon and the stars, the rivers and the seas, the hills and the mountains, fish and animals and human beings—all carry the message of God's presence. In other words, created nature and the human environment, visible and

invisible, bear the mark of goodness and godliness. This is the first premise of the African notion of the environment. It is for this reason that human activities are generally considered from the religious point of view. All space is sacred. And in spite of the fact that there may be designated locations for worship and sacrifices, the one who is on the way to worship is considered as already in the act of worshiping. The fruits of the earth produced by the labor of human beings are seen as worthy elements for offerings and sacrifices to God.

The seven concepts described above form the core of the African worldview and African spirituality. How these are expressed in the diverse cultures of Africa may differ in details but not in substance. There may be some isolated instances of discrepancy, such as the case of the Nuer of Sudan, who do not have a cult of ancestors.

Opinion differs as to whether one should speak of African culture or African cultures, of African values or tribal values, of diversity or unity. It can be argued that there are sufficient grounds for holding to what has been called a common Africanness or a basic worldview among Africans. This is true especially for the entire sub-Saharan Africa.

The Continuous Evolution of African Spirituality

The preceding paragraphs have described the content of African spirituality, that is to say, the spirituality that belongs to the mainstream religion of traditional Africans. African life, however, is no longer traditional in the same sense that it was before the arrival of Christian and Islamic missionaries. In addition, African spirituality is being bombarded on all sides by the effects of secularism, science, and technology, and by the constant flux within and between cultures. For example, the sense of family and community did not find much support in the Northern capitalistic models nor in the pre–Vatican II sacramental

theology, which emphasized the individual over the community. And yet, African spirituality has been enriched by its contacts with the outside world. The gospel, for example, helped to broaden the scope of the family and community beyond the kinship system. Neither Christianity nor Islam is indigenous to Africa; both, however, have pitched their tents long enough there. It would be legitimate, therefore, to speak of a Christian African spirituality and an Islamic African spirituality.

Christianity and Islam have been influenced in various ways by the values described above and have used them to articulate new tendencies in their missionary efforts. The basic Christian communities in parts of East Africa—for example, the *ujamaa*—have their basis in the family-community orientation of African life and in the value of corporate endeavors. The liberation movements in parts of Africa flow from the traditional moral demand for the practice of social justice. That is why apartheid has been such a horrendous experience for Africans—it defies traditional values.

The reciprocal relationship between Africa and other cultures, while it began very superficially, is continuing in our time in a more systematic and organized way, especially through inculturation in both Christian and Islamic circles. This development, however, is still in a formative stage. A truly Christian African spirituality will emerge as a result of the inculturation movement in the African Churches today. In the meantime a group of Africans belonging to the so-called Independent African Churches or Indigenous African Christian Churches are introducing a practical approach to inculturation. They have incarnated the African values and incorporated them into their style of worship and organization of life. They have extensive rituals of healing, for example, and spend time seeking practical solutions to social problems. This group may become the true custodian of African spirituality, especially since it now has far more converts in Africa per year than all other Christian groups combined.

The Emerging Catholic African Spirituality

Pope Paul VI's message to the African bishops in Kampala, Uganda, in 1969 said in part: "You may and you must have an African Christianity. Indeed, you possess human values and characteristic forms of culture which can rise up to perfection so as to find in Christianity, and for Christianity, a true superior fullness and prove to be capable of a richness of expression all its own and genuinely African. You have the strength and the grace necessary for this because you are living members of the Catholic Church, because you are Christians and you are Africans."

This Christianity envisioned by Paul VI and based on African spirituality has been emerging since the early 1970s. The Zairian rite of the Eucharist approved for use in 1988 embodies a measure of African spirituality. Pope John Paul II, as of March 1993, had completed ten pastoral visits to African Churches, affirming the now popular belief that the Church of the 21st century will be leaning on the faith of the African Churches. Liberation, inculturation, AIDS, war, drought, apartheid are some of the themes that mingle with the traditional values in the formation of a new spirituality in Africa. This new spirituality is already having much impact as Africans in diaspora, especially African-Americans, reinvent their commitment to history. African theologians are participating in promoting the true meaning of African spirituality and values as these become more and more diffused in the world Church.

See also AFRICAN-AMERICAN SPIRITUALITY; COMMUNITY; CULTURE; THIRD WORLD, SPIRITUALITY OF.

Bibliography: J. Mbiti, *African Religions and Philosophy* (New York: Praeger, 1969). A. Shorter, *African Christian Spirituality* (Maryknoll, N.Y.: Orbis Books, 1980).

CHRIS NWAKA EGBULEM, O.P.

AFRICAN-AMERICAN SPIRITUALITY

African-American spirituality is concerned with the prayer experience and God-conscious experience of black people in the United States. It is also concerned with the notions of piety and the ideals of virtue that are held in high esteem within the black Christian community in the United States. Although *spirituality* is a word rarely encountered in black Christian writers until very recently, notions regarding prayer and expressions of devotion have always been plentiful.

Spirituality, moreover, is expressed in bodily actions, concrete images and symbols, along with ideas that flow out of a given culture and evolve within a historical period. The black Christian community in the United States is formed by four historical realities: sub-Saharan Africa as the original homeland, slavery, racial oppression, and the struggle for liberation as a shared experience. These four realities formed the matrix for a culture that is at times ill-defined but constantly present to black Americans in their self-awareness and self-understanding.

The term *African-American* came into usage in the second half of the 1980s to replace the term *black,* which began to be used in the 1960s as the result of a newly discovered racial consciousness and cultural pride. The term *Afro-American* goes back to the 19th century but never came into popular usage. *African-American* cannot completely replace the term *black,* for it is limited in usage to blacks in the United States. The term *black,* however, is global. It means all those of African heritage, whether in sub-Saharan Africa, Latin America, the Caribbean, or Europe. It means cultural affinities and shared influences between and among the worldwide African communities. Thus black Catholics in the United States forged for themselves a Catholic identity linked with a 16th-century black Sicilian, St. Benedict the Moor, and a 17th-century Afro-Hispanic, St. Martin de Porres, from Peru, and they have continued to forge such links with Africa, the Caribbean, and Latin America.

Thomas Wentworth Higginson (1823–1911), a white Union commanding officer of one of the first all-black regiments in the Civil War, wrote in his autobiography his perceptions of the freed black slaves serving in his regiment, who were mainly from South Carolina and Florida. Hearing the words of the spirituals his soldiers sang nightly around the campfires, he described what was almost certainly a Catholic spiritual in honor of the Blessed Virgin with the refrain "Hail, Mary, hail." Higginson noted that some of his soldiers were Catholics from St. Augustine, Florida.

The earliest record of a black Catholic community in this country is from the Spanish colony of St. Augustine, as indicated by baptismal registers beginning in 1565. Although at present little is known of the interior spirituality of this black settlement, this record witnesses to the historic roots of black Catholicism in this country.

We know more about the spiritual life of a pre–Civil War black Catholic community in Baltimore. Known as the Society of the Holy Family (1843–1845), some two hundred black persons, some of whom may have been slaves, met for devotions each Sunday evening in the cathedral parish hall. They put great emphasis on the singing of hymns, usually unaccompanied, together with occasional spontaneous prayer and traditional Catholic devotions, and had ready access to spiritual books. This group revealed the presence of a spiritual intensity within a black Catholic community in a society dominated by slavery and forced illiteracy.

In their pastoral letter *What We Have Seen and Heard* (1984), the black Catholic bishops of the United States suggested four major characteristics of African-American spirituality: contemplative in terms of prayer, holistic in terms of asceticism, joyful in terms of spiritual atmosphere, and community-based in terms of spiritual values. Recent unofficial surveys of African-American Catholics discussing their own perception of black spirituality suggest strongly that blacks see themselves as a spiritual people with the same characteristics noted in the bishops' pastoral letter.

Prayer is considered to be a normal activity that can and should be carried on everywhere. It is based on a profound sense of God's presence and dynamic power in the world, heightened by the fact that the sacred and the secular are not to be separated and based on a conviction that God can and does intervene in personal lives.

Music and dance are intimately connected with the black prayer experience. Hymns, both spirituals and gospel music, very often involve repetition. This repetitiveness is a cultural expression of monological prayer, similar to the Jesus Prayer or a mantra. Recent compositions by African-American Catholic composers often follow the same pattern. The use of dance, the clapping of hands, the swaying of the body, originally found in the slavery period and in the churches of the Deep South, are now common practice in current African-American Catholic worship. These elements are a survival—and in some places a revival—of African practices that are indigenous to the African-American community.

If there is any one notable characteristic of the African-American contemplative experience, that characteristic would be ecstasy. Traditional African religion and its transplanted forms in the New World were based upon spirit possession. In varying degrees this has had its impact on the development of African-American spirituality. Worship, including Catholic worship, is often characterized by an exuberance and vibrancy that lead to a prayer experience of tremendous joy bordering on what can only be called ecstatic. At the same time, the prayer experience, again often inspired by the music, can become a state of meditation that is kataphatic and immediate—the crucifixion is a lived experience, the Exodus event is yesterday. This brings to mind certain affinities with the Ignatian exercises.

African-American spirituality is Scripture-based for both black Catholics and black Protestants. This use of Scripture emerged because the Bible was encountered first as an oral text, particularly as a dramatic presentation of sacred stories. In most slave states the slaves were forbidden to learn to read or write. Moreover, African civilizations were, with few exceptions, nonliterate in culture. Thus the spoken word as power, oral expression as the medium of artistic expression, and storytelling that always includes audience participation are part of the cultural heritage still operative in African-American society. This heritage has made the Bible less a written text than a living text for religious expression. It is a text that comes alive in the contemporary situation.

The emotional element in African-American spirituality is less a question of affectivity or sentiment than an appreciation of the holistic dimension of the spirituality. The attitude toward the body and the soul is one of complementarity rather than opposition. Emotions are a part of the bodily experience. Thus the emotions of joy, sorrow, yearning, love—in fact, the gamut of feelings—are legitimate human experiences to be expressed and never suppressed. Physical contact, moreover, is a cultural value that denotes warmth and hospitality, and is thus a spiritual expression of the same.

Black saints were not aloof, cold, cut off from human experience. St. Moses the Black (d. ca. 410) was a Desert Father who is described in the apophthegmata as a model of hospitality, a monk who could not participate in the community's condemnation of a brother monk, and a former bandit who became the spiritual father to his brother monks in the desert. St. Martin de Porres (1579-1639) was a one-man charity agency for Lima in the 17th century. Pierre Toussaint (1766-1853) was the friend and confidant of rich and poor, white and black, in antebellum New York. A man of moderate means, Toussaint was generous in almsgiving, going so far as to search out abandoned victims of epidemics and providing shelter for homeless black youths. Always the cheerful jokester and mimic, he played the violin at small gatherings. The loving husband of a wife whose freedom he had purchased, he left the sentiments of his affection in letters and a love poem.

Social concern and social justice are important ethical values for a people who have known and continue to experience racial and economic oppression. Thus the spiritual response of African-Americans has never been otherworldly. Practical charity and political involvement are core elements for black Protestant Churches. The same is true for black Catholics. The Society of the Holy Family in pre–Civil War Baltimore was composed of men and women who had lived in slavery and poverty, yet the disbursement of funds for the poor was an important element of their religious activity. Hence holiness is bound up with practical charity; fighting for justice is bound up with response in love. This was made clear by the statements of the black laity in the Afro-American Catholic congresses at the end of the 19th century. This was true also of the congregations of black sisters whose origins go back to the first half of the 19th century.

The best known African-American spiritual writer was Howard Thurman, university professor, author, and minister, who died in 1981. He left over twenty books of meditations, reflections, and spiritual teachings. Through his preaching, conferences, and writings, Thurman gave a shape and an interpretation to African-American spirituality that is profound. Catholic African-American writers have not yet made a comparable synthesis.

See also AFRICAN SPIRITUALITY; CULTURE; DANCE; ECSTASY; FEELINGS; HOLISTIC SPIRITUALITY.

Bibliography: J. Cone, "Black Worship," *The Study of Spirituality,* ed. C. Jones, G. Wainwright, E. Yarnold (New York: Oxford Univ. Press, 1986) 481–490. C. Davis, "Black Spirituality," *U.S. Catholic Historian* 8 (1989) 39–46; *The History of Black Catholics in the United States* (New York: Crossroad, 1990). J. Phelps, "Black Spirituality," and W. McClain, "American Black Worship: A Mirror of Tragedy and a Vision of Hope," *Spiritual Traditions for the Contemporary Church,* ed. R. Maas and G. O'Donnell (Nashville: Abingdon, 1990) 332–361. A. Raboteau, *Slave Religion: The "Invisible Institution" in the Antebellum South* (New York: Oxford Univ. Press, 1978). *What We Have Seen and Heard: A Pastoral Letter on Evangelization from the Black Bishops of the United States* (Cincinnati: St. Anthony Messenger, 1984).

CYPRIAN DAVIS, O.S.B.

AFTERLIFE

Afterlife concerns the continuity of human existence beyond death. Belief in some form of afterlife is arguably the essential feature of all religions. In a multitude of concepts and images throughout human religious history, there has been depicted a realm of existence beyond the reality of this world whereby the good, the faithful, the redeemed are saved eternally. Thus afterlife constitutes the fundamental goal of every spiritual journey, i.e., victory over death through the divine granting of eternal life. *Homo religiosus* believes that life does not end with death, but rather that death is a birth into a new life, an entrance into another, mysterious realm of being. As such, death is not deemed the final end of existence but is seen as an initiation into an afterlife, a dark passage into the eternal beyond.

Afterlife is the concern of that branch of theology called eschatology—the study of last things. Eschatology has two basic aspects, one focusing on the ultimate destiny of the individual and the other on the collective destiny of humankind, which is concerned with the last things proper: the end of history and the world. These two strands of eschatology must be kept together, but because the subject here is spirituality, the focus will be on the former: the individual's destiny beyond death.

Background

Since the beginning of history, humans have sought an answer to the problem of death. The earliest extant text depicting the human struggle with death and the journey beyond death is found in *The Epic of Gilgamesh.* "Is there something more than death? Some other end to friendship?" asks Gilgamesh. The world's religions and spiritual philosophies have offered various answers to this question. All the basic theories of afterlife that have emerged from this struggle with death have ancient roots: reincarnation in Hinduism and Buddhism, metempsychosis in the ancient Greek mystery cults (Orphism and Pythagoreanism), the immortality of the Pharaoh in ancient Egypt, etc. Based on the two ancient pillars on which it is founded—Greek philosophy and the Hebrew Scriptures—Christianity developed its belief in the afterlife in terms of immortality and resurrection.

The great insight of classical philosophy was that a human being is not a "mortal" but a being engaged in a movement toward immortality. Aristotle called this movement *athanatizein,* the activity of immortalizing, which, as the love of divine wisdom, characterized philosophy itself. It is a spiritual movement consummated only through one's personal death. This breakthrough of the classical philosophers was based on the centuries-long differentiation of the individual soul among the pre-Socratics, who understood the soul as the immanent sensorium of transcendence granting the individual a direct relationship to the divine apart from society. From this Greek tradition emerged a view of humans as embodied spirits. In this view the soul is not only the life force of the body, but it also has a preexistence and a postexistence that frame its incarnation in this life as its wherefrom and whereto.

The portrayal of the immortal soul reached its consummate articulation in Plato's dialogues. Like the later books of the OT, the Platonic myths depict a view of the afterlife grounded in a doctrine of moral retribution in which the lot of the good is distinguished from that of the wicked. The just, the lover, the philosopher will alone reap the heavenly reward.

The biblical notion of resurrection derived from the late Jewish apocalyptic hope that emerged around the 2nd century B.C.E. Like the Greek philosophers, Israel's prophets also discerned a movement in human existence toward a state beyond its present structure, but they experienced it as the promise of Yahweh, who will in the future conquer the forces of evil and restore this world to the righteous and the just. During the Maccabean period there arose for the first time in Judaism the possibility of an afterlife (Dan 12:2; 2 Macc 7:9-14), in contradistinction to the purely this-worldly eschatology of the prophets (although the first appearance of this belief can be found a century earlier in Ezek 37:12-14 and Isa 26:19, where the hope for restoration of the dead to life is linked with the expectation of salvation for the whole nation).

This new hope in some kind of life after death came to fruition around the time of Jesus. Various Jewish groups at the time understood afterlife as some form of resurrection, a hope that was intrinsically connected with the imminent reign of God's kingdom. In proclaiming God's kingdom, Jesus himself sided with the Pharisees in affirming the resurrection of the dead against the Sadducees, who denied it (Mt 22:23-33; Mk 12:18-27).

The definitive historical realization of this eschatological hope was, of course, Jesus' own resurrection, which constitutes the principal teaching of the NT. However, the authors of the NT were of a sufficient Greek mentality as to express obliquely the meaning of resurrection in the language of the immortal soul. Paul, for example, speaks of the movement of human existence beyond its present structure of death (perishing) as a transformation into an immortal state that will succeed it through the grace of God, into the state of *aphtharsia,* or imperishing (1 Cor 15:42-55). Against the Gnostic dualism of his Hellenistic audience, which viewed the body as a prison of the soul and redemption as liberation from this prison, Paul conceived of salvation as the putting on of a spiritual body over our earthly one. Paul's belief in such a transfiguration was based on his vision of the resurrected Christ, the core of his spiritual conversion. This experience assured Paul that the transfiguration of human reality had already begun and would soon be fulfilled by the second coming of Christ.

But with the disappointment in the imminently expected parousia, with Paul witnessing the believers in Christ dying before its arrival (1 Thess 4:13-18), his eschatology was revised to incorporate his concern with the manner of life that must be lived in order to ensure the believer's imperishability. In gist, that manner of life is beautifully described in his famous hymn to love (1 Cor 13), where, of the three theological virtues and all the charisms divinely bestowed on us, *agape* is accorded the highest rank, because as the very essence of God it outlasts the conditions of existence in this world. Love alone brings us into the sphere of perfection and promises us an imperishable body as we enter the glory that will soon be revealed to us (Rom 8).

Although quite distinct in their origins, immortality of the soul (which presupposed a body/soul dualism for the Greeks) and resurrection from the dead (which presupposed the self's indivisible unity, a body/soul dualism being quite foreign to the ancient Hebrews) were unevenly blended throughout the early Christian tradition. Although these two eschatological traditions were kept in some theological balance in the early Church, a pronounced shift occurred in the medieval period. At that time the concrete demands of history outstripped the faraway parousia. The unity of body and soul, present and future, individual and community, began to derail into a dualism. The Greek influence came to predominate. As a consequence, the resurrection of the dead, which for Jesus and his followers had a distinctively communal character, as reflected in the NT, yielded to a strong emphasis on the immortality of the individual soul. A rapprochement with the Greek concept of immortality was attempted in the late medieval dogmas, a trend that reached its peak when the Church, at the Fifth Council of the Lateran in 1513, affirmed the immortality of the soul as a dogma of the faith. The Christian transformation of this idea can be seen as a real breakthrough if we understand resurrection to mean the "immortality of the whole person," the person who suffers the utter dissolution of death but by the saving act of God's love is restored to eternal life.

The contemporary debate on the relationship between immortality and resurrection raises an issue that has never been fully clarified in the history of the Church. In any case, traditional Christianity has long believed that the person is created with a soul whose destiny is one of three realms beyond death: heaven, hell, or purgatory. A brief consideration of each follows.

Heaven

In the OT, heaven is understood cosmologically as the heavens or the firmament, the solid vault that holds back the waters above the sky. Hebrew had no single word to express the concept of world or universe. The phrase "the heavens and the earth" was used to indicate the totality of God's creation (Gen 1:1; 2:4). Religiously, heaven signified the dwelling place of God. Israel looked to heaven as the source of salvation

and divine blessings. The nation longed for the day when God would open the heavens to bring salvation to earth (Isa 45:8; 64:1). This entailed the desire to be lifted up to heaven to experience communion with God, the way of salvation that also consisted in the descent of God to earth (Isa 55:10-11; 64:1).

For Christians, this prophecy was fulfilled in Jesus the Christ, who as God's Son came down from heaven (Jn 3:13), only to return to heaven after his resurrection to sit at the right hand of God (Mt 26:64; Mk 14:62; Lk 22:69). The kingdom of God that Jesus preached became identified in Matthew's Gospel with the kingdom of heaven, and, principally in John's Gospel, with eternal life (Jn 3:15; 4:14; 5:24), the final reward granted to the faithful, who in the end will be reunited with Christ (Jn 14:3).

The imagery of heaven employed in the NT is not so much a place that can be located somewhere (the mythological image adopted by the later Church) as it is the quality of human life in its mode of fulfillment and perfection. As such it is fundamentally tied to the disciples' relation to Jesus, the bringer of salvation. In this way the NT transformed the eschatological hopes of the OT into the vision of God (beatific vision) granted through grace at death by way of Jesus, who alone is the way to the Father (Mt 11:27; Jn 14:6).

In the primary Christian sense, then, heaven is that mode of being realized by Christ, who in his full humanity was taken up into union with God (resurrection). Insofar as this divine gift is the universal destiny of all creation, the reality of heaven will be complete only with the raising of all members of the Body of Christ to God in the universal salvation achieved at the end of history, the future promise anticipated in Christ's own resurrection. Thus, for Christians, heaven has a Christological foundation: union with God is mediated through a relation with Christ. To follow Christ is the way to eternal life. In this regard the Christian doctrine of heaven in its origin is not precisely connected with the notion of immortality of the soul, nor even with that of merely personal salvation. Heaven has a corporate dimension insofar as it truly signifies the fulfillment of all human relations with God. From this emerges the Christian truth that no one is finally saved until all are saved, indeed until the salvific process transfigures the whole cosmos in the eschatological end of history.

Hell

For the ancient Israelites, no one went to heaven after death; all went to Sheol, the underworld or the realm of the dead, which was the counterpart of Hades in Greek mythology. The dead did not return from Sheol, and all human activity and vitality ceased there; therefore, it was not an affirmation of an afterlife but its denial. Eventually, under pressures of moral reflection that upheld retribution for evil and the vindication of the righteous who suffer misfortunes in this world, the abode of the dead came to be differentiated. Given Yahweh's justice, the wicked, who often prosper in this world, were consigned to Gehenna, the place of eternal punishment and unquenchable fire (Mt 5:22; Mk 9:43), from which our traditional image of hell derives. The good on the other hand were granted eternal life in paradise.

In the Church's teaching, hell is the state of everlasting punishment for the unrepentant who die in a state of mortal sin, cut off from the grace of God mediated through the sacraments. It is not only eternal absence from God's presence but the suffering of physical fire and physical torment. The Church has never officially taught that anyone is actually in hell, only that hell is a possibility; nor has it defined the metaphysical nature of the pains and fire of hell. The essence of its teaching is that every creature is destined for God's kingdom, given that God's salvific will revealed in Christ is universal, yet there is no guarantee of universal salvation. The sheep and the goats will be separated on the day of judgment (Mt 25:31-46).

Until recent times the Church's normative doctrine of hell went back to Augustine, whose imaginative picture of the afterlife viewed hell as the place of the damned, who are embodied and burn forever in literal flames (*The City of God*, Bk. 21). Thomas Aquinas turned to describing the essence of the pain of hell as the loss of the vision of God, which did little to curb the horrors of hell in the popular mind. Through the ages the doctrine of hell has often been used for the purpose of deterrence, the fear of eternal punishment being an effective motive for upright behavior. However, servile fear is not sufficient for salvation, which is promised only when self-centered fear is actively conquered by self-transcending love.

Purgatory

Defined by the councils of Florence (1439) and Trent (1545–1563), purgatory envisions the intermediate state between the death of the righteous and the last judgment, a state during which there is expiation for sins already forgiven, thus providing for ultimate restoration of fellowship with God. This teaching is connected with prayers for the dead, intended to assure their complete expiation and final salvation. As often suggested, there is no clear biblical warrant for the teaching of purgatory, although 2 Macc 12:38-46, which speaks of prayers for those killed in battle, is often cited as support. Mt 12:32 also hints that some sins may be forgiven in the next world.

The notion of purgation after death is deeply rooted in the Christian tradition, as attested by the common practice of praying for the departed since the earliest centuries. The Fathers increasingly made use of language that eventually, after Augustine, identified the fire of judgment referred to in 1 Cor 3:12-15 as the purgatorial fire. Nevertheless, the idea of such penance being carried out in the next life in a particular place between heaven and hell for a duration commensurate with the number and gravity of sins committed did not fully emerge until the 13th century. Given the legalist conception of salvation that the Western Church adopted, the doctrine of purgatory was promulgated with heavy penal overtones; the contemplative spirituality of the Eastern Church emphasized the more mystical nature of purgatory as a process of purification and maturation. The Protestant Reformers rejected the doctrine of purgatory, based on the teaching that salvation is by faith through grace alone, unaffected by intercessory prayers for the dead.

The early Church imposed penances for sin upon the contrite, for it was not enough to be forgiven sin, which only alleviated one's guilt; one also had to pay sin's penalty. During the Middle Ages the Church engaged in the practice of drawing upon its treasury of grace to repeal the necessary penalty for sin. It could remit some (partial indulgence) or all (plenary indulgence) of the temporal punishment that a sinner must suffer, if not in this world then in the next. By the 13th century the practice of granting indulgences became separated from the sacrament of penance and became more and more the prerogative of the pope. Much of the Protestant revolt centered on the problem of simony, the medieval Church's corrupt practice of selling indulgences to penitents, a lucrative source of income.

This egocentric, calculating approach to salvation, based as it was on an accumulation of spiritual credits, was a deformation of the essential doctrine of purgatory. Against the common juridical and commercial view, the teaching essentially attempts to induce the faithful to show responsibility toward the dead and the communion of saints. Since the Church has taught that death is not the end of life, then neither is it the end of our relationship with loved ones who have died, who along with the saints make up the Body of Christ in the "Church Triumphant."

The diminishing theological interest in indulgences today is due to an increased emphasis on the sacraments, the prayer life of Catholics, and an active engagement in the world as constitutive of the spiritual life. More soberly, perhaps, it is due to an individualistic attitude endemic in modern culture that makes it harder to feel responsibility for, let alone solidarity with, dead relatives and friends.

Contemporary Perspectives

Because the whole realm of afterlife is, of course, an empirically unknowable reality, to be affirmed only in faith, hope and love, its depiction is ineluctably symbolic and speculative. The human imagination knows no bounds in envisioning its wonders and horrors, as demonstrated in Dante's poetic and allegorical vision in the *Divine Comedy*, the most aesthetically powerful expression of heaven, hell, and purgatory ever composed. However, a literal, mythological portrayal of the afterlife in the Church's teaching led to a confusion in the Christian view of the soul and its destiny, making eschatology one of the least coherent aspects of Christian theology. This literalizing trend was rooted in (a) the biblical and medieval cosmology: the three-layered universe comprised of the heavens, the world, and the underworld; (b) the apocalyptic mentality of early Christians; and (c) the Church's inherent tendency to dogmatically hypostatize the unimaginable. Therefore, contemporary theology, following the dictates of the modern scientific mind, has steered away from traditional Christianity's mythological portrayal of heaven, hell, and purgatory as actual locations in the universe populated by spiritual souls with physical properties.

Today theologians attempt to penetrate to the spiritual meaning behind the doctrinal utterances by distinguishing between symbolic discourse and religious message. Although they continue to see heaven, hell, and purgatory as possible destinies of the soul beyond this world, theologians now understand them more symbolically, in terms of a trajectory of a state of being that one is already experiencing in this life. For example, Karl Rahner sees eschatology as grounded in present experience. Eschatological statements are statements about humans existing *now* in relation to their possible future. God's grace already given to a person in creation is the basis for the Christian hope in the future consummation of the human-divine relationship (K. Rahner, *Foundations of Christian Faith*, New York: Seabury, 1978, pp. 103–104, 431–447).

Consequently, the notions of heaven, hell, and purgatory become concretely intelligible through the experiences in this temporal world that disclose something of eternity and the fulfillment of our ultimate desire. There are certain experiences that teach us that our essential humanity is not intrinsically conditioned by space and time, such as a relation of personal love or intense creativity. Any self-transcending experience opens up for us ultimate meaning and value. Who has not experienced new life and hope beyond tragedy and torment, or a breakthrough to a new way of living after encountering the depths of despair and abandonment? Such experiences disclose our radical incompleteness, our dependence on the mystery of God, to whom we ultimately belong. They reveal our orientation to the future as the end of suffering and the promise of fulfillment. All love desires eternity, and God's love not only desires it but effects it, even in the midst of suffering and loss. Such was the disciples' experience at the cross followed by the breakthrough of Easter.

In contemporary perspective, then, heaven is understood as the finality of the state of grace in which one dwells through the gift of the divine self-communication in love, a love that demands the response of one's own gift of self. It is a relation of intimacy with God effected by communion with others, a communion that confers upon us an insurmountable joy, the fulfillment of our ultimate longing. The heavenly beatitude imparted at death is not the result of a legal pact granted to those concerned with saving their souls as a reward for observing strict rules and rituals; rather, it is the gift bestowed on those who at death complete their life project of self-gift. It is the transformation of the whole being of a person based on the outcome of a total life-orientation.

Accordingly, hell is estrangement from this saving relation, a denial of one's true self, a sinful refusal to respond lovingly to the call of divine grace. Thus, it is utter death and destruction, the consequence of sin, for as Paul taught, "the wages of sin is death" (Rom 6:23). Hell is the abolition of one's essential being through the failure to overcome the disintegration of the temporal conditions of human existence. The everlasting torment of hell symbolizes the total, irrevocable nature of self-damnation, the consequence of one's willful separation from the divine ground of being through the obdurate absorption in one's own self-interests over that of others. It is the closing of one's soul in the free choice to live a godless life. In essence, hell is the eternal loss suffered by the refusal to love.

Finally, purgatory is seen as the process of purification, of self-perfection, by which we become more and more oriented to God's self-giving love. It is indeed a process of suffering inflicted upon us, not so much extrinsically as a punishment for sin, but as an intrinsic pain that anyone who chooses to follow the self-sacrificing, agapic love demonstrated by Christ must bear. Such love requires the purging of our residual egoism, a dying to self, so that God's love may rule our heart and mind and will. In this manner purgatory connotes the spiritual life proper, the existential struggle of working out one's salvation through the self-transcending love that is the law of the cross. In the tension of human existence between birth and death, time and eternity, everyone is called to spiritual perfection through a process of integration and maturation. In this sense, purgatory is the ordeal of becoming one's true self in response to the divine initiative. It is the soul's divinizing journey toward God.

In conclusion, heaven, hell, and purgatory ought not to be dismissed as mythological creations of an earlier, uncritical age long past. They are present realities in our life that intimate what lies beyond this world in the next life. Because our true desires, our true selves, cannot be fulfilled or finally perfected in this life, it is important that heaven, hell, and purgatory maintain their status as transcendent realms of being beyond earthly existence, as the possible final ends of life held out to every soul.

As a final caveat, it would be prudent to learn from the critique of the facile belief in afterlife offered by the hermeneutics of suspicion (Marx, Nietzsche, Freud), where afterlife is viewed as a pious distraction from the pressing problems of this life, a false and selfish substitute for the concerns of this world. Authentic Christian hope, however, does not denigrate the importance of responsibility in this world. Indeed, it understands responsibility in the context of ultimate salvation—not only the salvation of every person but of the world itself. What awaits us after death is unknowable, but those who abide in love may find solace in the words of Paul: "No eye has seen, nor ear heard, nor the human heart conceived, what God has prepared for those who love him" (1 Cor 2:9, NRSV).

See also BEATIFIC VISION; DEATH AND DYING; ESCHATOLOGY; FUTURE; REDEMPTION; RESURRECTION; SOUL.

Bibliography: M. Hellwig, *What Are They Saying About Death and Christian Hope?* (New York: Paulist, 1978). J. Hick, *Death and Eternal Life* (New York: Harper & Row, 1976). M. Simpson, *Death and Eternal Life* (Hales Corners, Wis.: Clergy Book Service, 1971).

MICHAEL P. MORRISSEY

AGING

During the past century, life expectancy in the developed nations has nearly doubled, adding several decades to the normal life span. Increased awareness of the spiritual dimensions of the middle and later years has accompanied this extension of human life. Aging as a process is not restricted to the later decades of life, although it is often viewed negatively then. Judged according to standards of maximum productivity and biological functioning, these later stages can be seen as periods of diminishment and loss, as part of the downward curve of life leading eventually to death. From a spiritual perspective, however, they are periods of potential growth. The Holy Spirit is always renewing us and inviting us to fuller life. A focus on spirituality and aging allows the resources of faith to illumine the challenges and gifts intrinsic to adult growth, clarifying the deeper meaning of middle and late adulthood.

Biblical Perspectives

The OT presents a variety of perspectives on aging and old age. When touched by the Spirit of God, we remain creative and fruitful as we age (Joel 3:1; Ps 92:14). While the incapacities of aging are recognized (Eccl 12:1-7), the old are seen as an integral part of society, offered protection and care, but also opportunities for continuing activity. Old age is appreciated as a blessing, a gift of life reaching its fullness in spite of the frailties of life's last phase. Psalm 90 asks for the ability to make the journey of aging a path toward wisdom. Isaiah 65:20 describes the new age as a time in which all persons will be able to live out the fullness of their days. God is faithful up to the last decades of our lives (Isa 46:4).

NT themes support the conviction that life has a significance that transcends death, that human value is not limited to one's achievements, and that it is possible to find hope in the midst of loss. Jesus' life, death, and resurrection witness to the power of life through death. At the heart of the NT is the affirmation of God's unconditional love; Jesus reminds his followers that God's care for the birds of the air and the flowers of the field is not based on their productivity (Lk 12:4-7). In the final chapter of John's Gospel, the risen Jesus tells Peter that experiences that feel like loss can creatively lead to wholeness (Jn 21:18-19). The beatitudes describe a letting go in faith that paradoxically opens the seeker to the experience of new spiritual horizons (Mt 5:1-12).

Anna and Simeon (Lk 2:22-40) provide models of prayerful aging that is open to the Spirit and looks expectantly to the future. The Eucharistic passages in the NT offer insights into all of life's experiences, including the transitions of aging (Mt 26:26-30; Lk 22:14-20; 1 Cor 11:23-26). The Eucharist is a freedom meal, reminding us that true freedom as we age stems from rootedness in God. It is a meal in which bread is blessed and broken and in which we enter into the meaning Jesus gave to the blessings and brokenness we experience as we age. The Eucharist sums up the NT call to love and compassion, to the expansion, as we age, of our capacity to use our talents responsibly in the service of others.

Psychological Resources

Reflections on spirituality and aging frequently combine the best of the spiritual tradition with the work of developmental psychologists such as Carl Jung, Erik Erikson, and Carol Gilligan, as well as that of psychiatrists such as Robert Butler who specialize in mental health and aging. These thinkers recognize major phases in the life cycle, while allowing as much variation as possible within any of these periods. Adult growth covers several decades of life, and there are marked biological, psychological, and spiritual differences in the way persons age. Developmental thinkers

see maturation as coming about as a result of various crises in the life cycle. A person faces the lifelong choice of growth or stagnation, of realizing ever new possibilities or repeating an earlier history. Each stage of the life journey holds fresh opportunities for growth.

According to Jung, the primary task of the first half of life is the development of the ego, accommodating oneself to the external environment; the full development of the genuine self remains for the second half of life. Jung identifies the midlife crisis as the collapse of inadequate, one-sided definitions of the self, opening one to the core self at the center of the psyche. Erikson proposes several tasks as integral to reaching adult maturity: developing the ability to love and commit oneself to other persons, assuming responsibility for what one has generated, and discovering the meaning and value of one's life. He describes midlife as an invitation to generativity, and old age as a call to integrity.

Butler draws on his work with older adults to emphasize the importance of a person's evaluation of his or her life as meaningful or absurd. He sees life review as a normal and healthy dimension of the later years, a process that can lead to regret and despair or to peace and acceptance. Gilligan challenges the exclusively male standard used in the major theories of development and maintains that women's developmental experience is by way of attachment; women develop identity in relationship with others, by way of intimacy. This concern with maintaining relationships results in awareness of the interconnectedness of human beings and an ethic of care and responsibility.

Major Spiritual Themes

The psychological transitions described by developmental thinkers are also religious passages. Emerging from this integration of psychological and theological insights are several major themes in the spirituality of aging:

Embracing the present moment. Awareness that our life span is limited can lead to the wisdom and wonder that come from opening to the grace of the present moment. Midlife is a time of greater interiority; in old age we come to appreciate the preciousness of time and the elemental in life. Both movements prepare us for learning the art of being rather than doing, for contemplation and centering prayer, and for a spirit of gratitude for simple and ordinary things.

Finding meaning in memory. Much of Scripture recounts how people find strength in positive memories. The belief that God is addressing us out of our lives gives spiritual significance to the unique and cumulative experience of an individual's existence. Practical ways of pursuing reminiscing (a more spontaneous remembering) and life review (a more structured and evaluative process) include keeping a journal; writing or taping an autobiography; reflecting on scrapbooks, photo albums, or old letters; and returning in person or through correspondence to the location of our birth, childhood, youth, or young adult life. Reminiscing and life review are greatly helped by sensitive listeners, persons who bear witness to another person's gifts and struggles. Life review opens new paths for the future and can also be a preparation for death. It is a way of passing on our life and its meaning to the next generation; it encompasses the giving and receiving of a spiritual heritage.

Confronting limitations and death. The fact of aging reminds us of our finitude and raises the fundamental questions of life: What is our end? What purpose guides us? The midlife challenge is often described as a crisis of limits. Persons may experience a sense of emptiness and brokenness, be aware of their lost youth and their mortality, and be afraid to start anew. Old age likewise can be a time of multiple losses— health, job, spouse, friends, home—and a sense that death is near. Moving deeply into the death/resurrection mystery enables us to live with the losses of aging and retain the hope that new gifts are to be found in the midst of this passage.

A renewed appreciation of the sacrament of anointing supports this understanding of aging as a religious passage. This sacrament calls the entire community to an awareness of the deeper meaning of sickness and old age, makes clear that both frailty and strength mark us all, reveals the power of touch and the laying on of hands, enables older persons to witness to the death/resurrection mystery, and invites the community to an ongoing pastoral concern for the older persons in their midst.

Seeking reconciliation and forgiveness. Memories can be painful as well as joyful. When our memories lead to a sense of incompleteness and failure, they need to be embraced by the larger stories of faith, stories of a God who heals and forgives and calls us to forgiveness. This may mean actively seeking reconciliation with others from whom we have been estranged or working on the healing of memories. The spiritual journey in both midlife and later adulthood includes the healing of past hurts, a healing that opens up new energies for love.

Expanding the circle of one's love and compassion. The call to love and to grow does not end at a certain age. Middle and old age are times of continued responsibility to serve others and of commitment to larger causes. A spiritual perspective reveals creative roles as we age. We are called to be transmitters of spiritual traditions, promoters of ecological awareness, arbiters of tolerance amid differences, and advocates of the peaceful settlement of conflicts. This love can be expressed in small ways, even when limitations accompany the later years. Its expression may include prayer for others, grief ministry, visits and letters to those who are ill or alone, as well as giving witness to the power of faith and hope in the face of the mystery of suffering and dying.

Eliminating ageism. Intrinsic to a spirituality of aging is a commitment to countering stereotypes, those negative images of aging that endanger the dignity and uniqueness of aging persons. A faith perspective calls us to eliminate the losses which are not intrinsic to aging but which result from that discrimination based on age that is still prevalent in Church and society. This is linked to the creation of a more cooperative and just society and to the promotion of the dignity and worth of all persons.

Multigenerational Focus

Many women in middle age find themselves caring for both children and aging parents, and their spiritual challenge becomes one of defining the meaning of love and fidelity amid conflicting needs. Reflections on the religious meaning of grandparenting reveal grandparents as storytellers who influence the generations by providing a sense of continuity and immortality, and by being present and attentive to members of other generations. Concern with spirituality and aging has expanded to include intergenerational themes, focusing not simply on the aging individual but on family and caregiving networks. Families now often encompass four and even five generations. We are all part of one life cycle, and our spirituality affects and is affected by all other age groups. Family systems are called to see the dynamic of dependence and independence among the generations as one of mutual giving and receiving.

See also COMPASSION; DEATH AND DYING; DISABILITY, THE DISABLED; FORGIVENESS; HEALING; JOURNEY (GROWTH AND DEVELOPMENT IN SPIRITUAL LIFE); MEMORY; PSYCHOLOGY, RELATIONSHIP AND CONTRIBUTION TO SPIRITUALITY; WEAKNESS AND VULNERABILITY.

Bibliography: J. Brewi and A. Brennan, *Mid-Life: Psychological and Spiritual Perspectives* (New York: Crossroad, 1982). E. Bianchi, *Aging as a Spiritual Journey* (New York: Crossroad, 1982). K. Fischer, *Winter Grace* (Mahwah, N.J.: Paulist, 1985).

KATHLEEN FISCHER

ALCOHOLICS ANONYMOUS

See ADDICTION.

ALMSGIVING

The word *alms* derives from the Greek *eleēmosynē*, meaning "mercy." Almsgiving is a religiously motivated giving of money or other resources to benefit those needing them. Often linked to prayer and fasting, it is a prominent feature in several major religions and holds a special place in Jewish and Christian religious practice.

In the later Hebrew Scriptures *ṣĕdāqâ* means both "alms" and "justice," implying that almsgiving restores God's right order in society. Thus, the Israelites gave one tenth of their produce (a tithe) to support the Levites, immigrants, and the poor (Deut 14:28-29); they let their fields lie fallow every seventh year to benefit the poor (Exod 23:11); Job cared for the poor out of religious conviction (Job 31:16-23).

In the New Testament, Jesus enjoins almsgiving: "Sell your belongings and give alms" (Lk 12:33; cf. Mt 19:21); almsgiving, like prayer and fasting, is to be done without fanfare (Mt 6:2-4); Jesus and the disciples gave alms (Jn 13:29). Early Christian communities practiced almsgiving in the organized distribution of food in the Jerusalem Church (Acts 6); Paul encouraged offerings from Gentile communities for the poor of the Jerusalem Church (Acts 24:17; Rom 15:25-26; 1 Cor 16:1-5; 2 Cor 8:1-15; Gal 2:10). Paul proposed the example of Christ as the motivation for almsgiving: "For your sake he became poor although he was rich, so that by his poverty you might become rich" (2 Cor 8:9).

In later Christian practice almsgiving remained important. Basil of Caesarea (d. 379) affirmed that the excess wealth of the rich is the property of the poor, and failure to give alms is tantamount to theft (PG 31:1154-1167). Ambrose of Milan (d. 397) also affirmed that wealth (property beyond one's needs) belongs by right to those who lack necessities (PL 16:65-74).

Among medieval Christians, monasteries and cathedral churches used alms from the faithful to maintain hospices or food programs for the poor, refugees, and exiles. France's massive shrine of St. Martin at Tours could maintain thousands of needy visitors each year through alms. In medieval penances imposed for sins, almsgiving was frequently demanded of penitents who had defrauded others through unfair business practices or had committed other crimes.

The begging (mendicant) religious orders of the later Middle Ages often sought alms of food, goods, or money to maintain their communities. Francis of Assisi considered living on alms an imitation of the life of Jesus, Mary, and the apostles.

In the modern period almsgiving increasingly supported institutions. Bequests, legacies, and spontaneous freewill offerings financed hospitals for the poor, orphanages, and schools for educating poor children.

In contemporary experience almsgiving has assumed various organized forms: special collections in churches or personal gifts to programs that feed or clothe the hungry or homeless; donations to organizations promoting better economic conditions on a national or international level for those lacking the necessities of human survival. Greater emphasis is now placed on addressing the causes of poverty, in addition to alleviating its effects.

In each period of Christian experience, almsgiving, teamed with prayer and fasting, seeks to participate in God's gracious and continuing gift of self in Christ, the greatest Alms.

See also COMPASSION; FASTING; JUSTICE; MERCY; POOR, THE.

Bibliography: L. Wm. Countryman, *The Rich Christian in the Church of the Early Empire* (New York: Mellen, 1980). M. Hengel, *Property and Riches in the Early Church* (Philadelphia: Fortress, 1974). R. Mullin, *The Wealth of Christians* (Maryknoll, N.Y.: Orbis, 1984).

WILLIAM J. SHORT, O.F.M.

AMERICAN SPIRITUALITY

Spanish and French missionaries to North America brought with them their own religious perspectives and practices. To a limited extent, they interacted with Native American spiritualities they found in the new world. In spite of this early European presence in North America, the adjective *American* is used here to refer to the spiritualities of the organized Catholic community in the United States.

Spiritualities map out places where people expect to find God. Catholics in the United States were the first to live in a political environment designed to offer no shared way to God and no public supports to the practice of any particular religious faith. In this unprecedented circumstance, they learned to experience and respond to God in new ways that were voluntary, and developed in interaction with the spiritual ideals and practices of the culturally dominant Protestant majority.

When contemporary Catholics pray, worship, and engage in mission and ministry, they often remain unaware that they do so not only as members of the Church universal but also as heirs of a pluriform spiritual heritage developed in the unique context of separation of Church and state. This context tends to foster both a certain spiritual dividedness and a simultaneous yearning for more integral forms of holiness.

American Catholic history can be divided into three rough but recognizable phases: (1) republican Catholicism, from the Revolution to 1830; (2) immigrant Catholicism, from 1830 to 1960; (3) contemporary Catholicism, from 1960 to the present. Three forms of spirituality correspond roughly to these three phases: (1) Garden of the Soul Spirituality; (2) Household of Faith Spirituality; (3) World of Grace Spirituality. American Catholics have behaved variously as if they believed God more likely to be experienced in the soul, in the Church, or in the world. Each of these three overlapping types embodies itself in particular forms of prayer, relates in a specific way to separation of Church and state, and finds expression in different styles of sacred space. All coexist in contemporary Catholicism.

Garden of the Soul Spirituality

Republican spirituality began with the Anglo-Catholics of Maryland. As a persecuted Church, their English ancestors had limited access to clergy and public worship. The spirituality they developed was domestic, interior, personal, and easily transposed to the situation of Church-state separation. Anglo-American Catholics experienced the free toleration of the new republic as "a blessing and an advantage" they would not needlessly jeopardize.

The piety of these Catholics found typical expression in Richard Challoner's *Garden of the Soul* (1773). Garden of the Soul Catholics expected to find God in a Christ-centered interior life. John Carroll (1735–1815), a Maryland Catholic and the first American bishop, preached on "transforming into our hearts the sentiments and affections of Jesus Christ" (Chinnici, p. 30). Anticipating her death in the same spirit, St. Elizabeth Seton (1774–1821) wrote in her prayerbook: "O my Lord Jesus Christ who was born for me in a stable, lived for me a life of pain and sorrow, and died for me upon a cross, say for me in the hour of my Death *Father forgive,* and to thy

Mother *behold thy child.* Say to me thyself *this day thou shalt be with me in Paradise* O my Saviour leave me not, *forsake me not,* I *thirst* for thee and long for thee fountain of living water—my days pass quickly along, Soon all will be CONSUMMATED for me—to thy *hands I commend my spirit,* now and forever Amen" (Seton, p. 337).

Such Christ-centered affective prayer would issue, in the manner of St. Francis de Sales and St. Ignatius, in a strong emphasis on moral conduct and a life of concrete imitation of Christ. Garden of the Soul Catholics were Enlightenment people who kept spirituals and temporals separate in both Church and state. Though deeply involved in public life, they participated in terms of what they shared with fellow citizens and Christians. They tended to reserve unnecessary explicitly religious behavior for home and church. They called themselves "Catholic Christians." When it came time to build a fitting church, John Carroll asked Benjamin Latrobe to design it. In its stately, geometric calm, Baltimore's Cathedral of the Assumption is an Enlightenment church. As sacred space, it mediates the simplicity, dignity, and strength of republican Catholic spirituality.

Household of Faith Spirituality
The Devotional Revolution

Maryland Catholicism was an elite spirituality. Catholic immigrants brought more popular forms of Catholic spirituality to the United States. New waves of romantic religious sentiment had swept 19th-century Europe and had been taken up into ultramontane Catholicism's defensive defiance of the modern secular state. American devotionalism reflected this posture but also met the needs of the transplanted immigrants. In their interior exile, they looked for God not primarily in the soul's garden but in the Church, experienced as the household of faith, a communion of solidarity uniting believers in a spiritual family with Jesus, Mary, the angels and saints.

American Catholics in the second half of the 19th century supplied a vast market for prayerbooks and manuals of devotion. In addition to the rosary and Benediction, well known to republican Catholics, these books contained devotions to the Sacred Heart, the Five Wounds, and the Precious Blood of Jesus; to the Sacred Heart, Seven Sorrows, and Immaculate Conception of Mary; to St. Joseph, other saints, and the holy souls in purgatory. Various scapulars and the Miraculous Medal became popular, along with novenas, litanies, and the practice of dedicating months, days, and years to a specific devotion.

As voluntary practices, devotions served as a popular vernacular counterpart to the priest's Latin Mass. The immigrant Church's genius was in the standardization of devotional life and the integration of it into parish structures and liturgy. Sometimes this integration was less than complete, and popular devotions existed in uneasy tension beside clergy-oriented Eucharistic piety. In its emphasis on the doctrines of Tridentine Catholicism, devotionalism tended to separate Catholics from other Americans and give them a strong sense of institutional identity. But the devotional parish also served as a school in which immigrants learned voluntaristic and self-reliant attitudes they would need to participate in the wider society.

Oriented more to gaining favors than to affective union with God, prayer in this period represented "the triumph of the purgative way" (Chinnici, chap. 6). Its calculating, practical spirit reflected the prevailing free-market ethos. Under nativist pressure, the civil republican approach to separation of Church and state gave way to a militant, often confrontational emphasis on Catholic self-definition, as embodied in Archbishop John Hughes (1797–1864) of New York. During the first half of the 20th century, the household of faith expanded into a subculture of schools, hospitals, and organizations. In this parallel universe, rather than in the wider history of which it was a part, most 20th-century Catholics learned to look for God.

Nothing conveys the sensibility of devotional Catholics better than the sacred spaces they built to serve as centers of parish life in the immigrant Church. Statues and other likenesses of Jesus, Mary, and the saints, banks of flickering candles, side altars, shrines, replicas of shrines, stained glass, all perceived in myriad shades of light and color, combined to overwhelm believers' senses and transport them into a different and special world—"as if it were nearer Heaven here than elsewhere" (Taves, p. 124). Set on a hill overlooking the national Capitol, the massive National Shrine (now Basilica) of the Immaculate Conception stands as a symbol of devotional Catholicism's triumph and continuing strength in the United States.

Americanist Spirituality

Alongside, and to some extent within, this exotic world appeared an alternative spiritual path, one that took American culture seriously as a providential place for finding God. Its chief proponent was the Paulist Isaac Hecker (1819–1888). His integrative impulses led him to seek God's presence not only in the soul's garden and the household of faith but also in history. As his Americanist basilica, St. Paul's Church on 59th Street in Manhattan, makes clear, he remained a devotional Catholic, but he rejected devotionalism's world-denying side in favor of an emphasis on finding God in everyday life. *Common Ways to a Perfect Life* and *The Sanctification of Daily Life* were titles he proposed during the 1860s for a book on the spiritual life. He urged Catholics to take seriously their belief that at baptism the Holy Spirit comes to dwell within believers. Hecker's spirituality was based on attentiveness to the Holy Spirit's promptings in the soul and a corresponding openness to the same Spirit at work in the Church and the world.

The twin symbols of Providence and the Holy Spirit served to integrate this three-fold spiritual searching. He democratized both affective prayer and the vocation to Christian perfection in the world.

Hecker dreamed of transforming American culture on the basis of a voluntary relationship between faith and culture made possible by separation of Church and state. Pope Leo XIII's censure of Americanism in his 1899 encyclical *Testem Benevolentiae* put a temporary end to Hecker's dream. The encyclical's sharp distinction between religious Americanism (censured) and political Americanism (uncensured but religiously irrelevant) gave a decisive dichotomous cast to 20th-century Catholic experience of Church-state separation. Soul, Church, and world would remain separate, as they were in John F. Kennedy's speech in Houston in 1960.

World of Grace Spirituality

During the first half of the 20th century, the household of faith grew strong, its piety increasingly Eucharistic and clergy-centered. But the experience of building a subculture had sufficiently Americanized some Catholics that they began to feel integrative impulses similar to Hecker's. The liturgical movement, Dorothy Day's Catholic Worker, the Grail, the Christian Family Movement, and other forms of voluntarism sought to sanctify everyday life and experience God in "worldly" activity outside the household of faith. The Second Vatican Council (1962–1965) reinforced this trend. Its teachings on Protestant Christians, world religions, religious liberty, and the modern world confirmed what many American Catholics had already begun to experience. God is present outside the perceptible boundaries of the household of faith. We live in a grace-filled world.

But such an emphasis raises profound questions about the spiritual meaning of life within the household of faith. Thus devotionalism, clearly identifiable in its Tri-

dentine specificity, still offers to many an attractive spiritual path in uncertain times. Devotionalism's world-denying side probably does more religious harm to assimilated contemporaries than it ever did to uprooted 19th-century immigrants or than it now does to suffering 20th-century exiles.

In the struggle for peace, justice, and human rights around the world, many Christians have experienced God anew as liberator. Liberationist spiritualities challenge the destructive effects of devotionalism's world-denying side. They are equally critical of naive postconciliar embraces of the modern world and American culture. Expectations about God's activity there have been tempered and nuanced. But a market phenomenon reminiscent of the 19th century has created a minor spirituality industry. Cassettes and videos have replaced prayerbooks and devotional manuals. Liberationist, personalist, charismatic, and holistic spiritualities offer competing paths to spiritual wholeness and a witness to contemporary spiritual hunger.

Separation of Church and state still holds out the same threefold set of possibilities. The dream of a voluntary transformation of American culture by Spirit-filled souls stands alongside the imposing edifice of devotionalism, challenging American Catholics to connect their experiences of God in soul, Church, and world. Scripture and liturgy offer a common basis for the kind of "integral holiness" urged by the bishops of the United States in their 1986 pastoral letter "Economic Justice For All." Most contemporary spiritualities include a strong emphasis on serious interior prayer. Future architects have the task of imagining sacred spaces appropriate to a world of grace.

See also CATHOLIC ACTION; CATHOLIC WORKER MOVEMENT; CHARISMATIC RENEWAL; CONTEMPORARY SPIRITUALITY; CURSILLO MOVEMENT; DEVOTION(S), POPULAR; ENLIGHTENMENT, INFLUENCE

ON SPIRITUALITY; HOLISTIC SPIRITUALITY; LITUR-
GICAL MOVEMENT; NATIVE AMERICAN SPIRITUAL-
ITY; PARISH, PARISH RENEWAL.

Bibliography: J. Chinnici, *Living Stones: The History and Structure of Catholic Spiritual Life in the United States* (New York: Macmillan, 1989). A. Taves, *The Household of Faith* (Notre Dame, Ind.: Univ. of Notre Dame Press, 1986). E. Kelly and A. Melville, eds., *Elizabeth Seton: Selected Writings* (New York: Paulist, 1987).

WILLIAM L. PORTIER

ANGELISM

See ANGELS.

ANGELS

Angels in one form or another are found in most religions of the world, but most prominently in religions of the book, such as Zoroastrianism, Judaism, Christianity, and Islam. Whether as messengers, companions, guardians, guides, overseers, or members of the heavenly court, they assist the divine-human encounter, while their malevolent counterparts, demons or fallen angels, hinder it.

Angels appear under all these guises in both the OT and the NT. Modern scriptural exegesis and the comparative study of religions afford us perspectives that were not available to patristic and medieval theology and piety. In light of these perspectives, a contemporary understanding of the angels for the life of faith needs to be both appreciative and suspicious of the patristic-medieval elaboration of the biblical sources. On the one hand, the basic idea that one creature can be a vehicle of God's gracious presence to another lies at the heart of Christianity. There is no good reason, either philosophical or theological, for thinking that angels could not serve as companions to the rest of creation in the realization of a new heaven and a new earth. On the other hand, patristic and medieval thought undoubtedly understood angels in ways which were more Neoplatonic than biblical and which in practice, if not in theory, threatened the centrality of Christ as well as the religious agency of the human person. These initial remarks can be elaborated in three additional observations.

First, where angelic mediation between God and humanity is presented in the Bible, it follows patterns derived from external sources. The angelology of the OT is heavily influenced by Zoroastrianism; that of the NT reflects the gnosticism and apocalyptic thought that grew up alongside later Judaism and early Christianity. The Bible in part imbibed and in part revised these angelologies from surrounding religions and cultures. Consequently, while angels are certainly in the Bible and therefore *in* revelation, it is no longer obvious that their existence is a content *of* revelation, as Roman Catholicism has traditionally maintained. The Bible assumes rather than asserts their existence, much as it assumes ancient astronomical views; and assuming their existence, its real interest is to assert a correct understanding of their place in the economy of salvation.

The few official teachings of Roman Catholicism on this subject follow the same pattern. These teachings, such as that of the Fourth Lateran Council of 1215, assert that God created the angels (as well as all other creatures) and that they were created good. Read out of context, such statements appear to make the existence of angels binding official teaching, and some theologians continue to interpret them in this way. Read in context, however, it becomes clear that the real point of such statements is to assert that all beings other than God are created and that evil has a finite, creaturely origin rather than an origin in God. Thus there is room for legitimate differences of opinion about what these teachings intend to clarify and what they require of the believer.

A second and related point is that the place of angels in the biblical economy of salvation is a relatively peripheral one. Though generally an unquestioned part of the worldview of the Scriptures, the role of angels is greatly relativized by God's self-communication via *human* intermediaries such as the patriarchs, the law and the prophets, Christ and the Church. In contrast to Neoplatonism, which was such a formative force on patristic and medieval angelology, the Bible does not present angels as necessary mediators of the divine-human covenant, as though God's transcendence made a direct approach to humanity impossible. The great temptation of angelology and of every theology of mediation is to imagine that the transcendence of God introduces a gap between God and creatures that must be bridged by a "go-between," whether this be Christ, the angels, a hierarchy, or a sacramental system. This Neoplatonic supposition overlooks the fact that God's transcendence is precisely what makes for God's immanence, both as Creator and in the self-communication that is grace. Even an orthodox Christology cannot understand Christ, the mediator par excellence, as a go-between reality; rather, in Christ the direct presence of God to all creation, and particularly human reality, reaches its supreme expression.

Beneath the surface of distorting Neoplatonic suppositions, patristic-medieval speculation also preserved the original biblical view. Indeed, the tasks the Fathers assigned the angels are transparently those belonging either to the Trinity in its direct gracious presence to human persons or to Christians themselves in their ministry to one another. These tasks range from inner enlightenment of the soul to ministries of the ecclesial community, such as guiding catechumens through the process of initiation. On the whole, then, the angels of the Bible are not so much intermediaries as accompaniments to the divine-human partnership, a position that emerges in polemical response to other views assigning a more decisive role to the angels. This is what lies behind Paul's eloquent statement in Romans 8 that nothing can separate us from the love of Christ—the religious agency of the human subject is not to be alienated by higher intermediary powers.

But the potential for religious alienation perceived by Paul remained. As the Church became more hierarchical in the succeeding centuries and the people who comprised it were themselves ranked in lower and higher orders, angelology took on a similarly rigid hierarchical pattern. A striking parallelism can be discerned here between the mediating functions of the clergy and those of the angels, who were sometimes pictured in priestly garb. As the clergy evolved into a supposedly higher order possessing powers to intercede for the lower and now religiously powerless laity, so too angels were increasingly seen as mediators on behalf of humanity. Theoretically, these mediating functions, angelic and priestly, were subordinated to the one mediating priesthood of Christ—a priesthood in which all baptized believers supposedly have a share.

In practice, however, this exaggerated emphasis upon hierarchy and mediation resulted in an increasingly passive and disempowered laity. It also gave rise to angelism, a distorted view of holiness that continues to plague authentic Christian spirituality to this day. Angelism, which has taken many different forms in the history of the Church, pits spirit against matter and turns legitimate differences and tensions into oppositions. The this-worldly is depreciated in favor of the other-worldly, the temporal is depreciated in favor of the eternal, activism and political responsibility are eschewed in favor of withdrawal from the world, celibacy becomes the ideal and sexual activity a fall into imperfection and sin. This distortion takes ecclesial form in the assignment of all material-temporal matters to the laity, with the implication that these are religiously inferior. Spiritual functions are reserved for a much smaller class of religiously serious people, i.e., clergy and religious.

Vatican II's call for the full and active participation of the faithful inaugurated a reassessment of this disenfranchisement of the ordinary believer in all areas of Church life. As the priesthood of all believers is reasserted and faith as a whole becomes more Christ-centered, the relevance of mediating higher powers (saints, angels, and even Mary) for spirituality recedes more and more into the background. This need not be interpreted as a lack of faith or inattention to tradition; it should rather be seen as a legitimate corrective to imbalances in past theologies and spiritualities.

Finally, "angel" is a much more fluid and subtle symbol in Scripture than patristic and medieval angelology understood it to be. Traditional angelology fastened solely upon the interpretation of angel as an objectively distinct being situated between God and humanity. But this is only one of various shades of meaning in the biblical use of the term. The "angel of Yahweh" from the early OT period, for example, sometimes appears as a distinct figure but sometimes is a circumlocution for God's own gracious presence to the people. Similarly, the winged figures or cherubim of Ezekiel's vision are explicitly presented as symbolic likenesses for an experience that cannot be literally described. These likenesses are not so much distinct beings as component parts of the one "appearance of the likeness of the glory of the Lord" (Ezek 1:28, RSV). That angels in Scripture are often ciphers or symbols of God's own presence is borne out by the fact that the Septuagint, or Greek translation of the OT, often interpolates angels where the Hebrew original has God alone acting directly in human affairs.

If the biblical symbol "angel" sometimes stands for the divine pole in the divine-human encounter rather than an in-between being, it may likewise express the human pole, particularly the transcending possibilities of human spirit and freedom before God. Patristic theology made much of the ancient idea that there are two angels within each person, one of justice and one of wickedness, pulling the soul in opposite directions. In the *Phaedrus,* Plato had used similar language, describing the soul as a charioteer drawn by a team of winged horses, one good and the other evil. At a later stage this type of analysis evolved into "the discernment of spirits" and "the contemplation of the two standards" of Ignatian spirituality.

All such symbolisms record the lived experience of dynamisms within the human spirit that are in one sense this spirit itself and, in another sense, forces impinging upon the spirit from without. The ambiguity that these forces are the expression of one's own freedom or agency and at the same time the impress of forces from without cannot be resolved in either direction without falsification. In this regard, the idea of angels as inner psychic forces that both express and impress the human spirit is analogous to God's self-communication in grace.

Grace creates a choice—for or against community with God and neighbor. But grace is not a third thing or entity coming in between God and the human person, nor is it simply one of the two poles of the divine-human encounter. It is God in distinction from the human person (uncreated grace), and yet it is also the human person ratifying and actualizing the life of God within (created grace). In "Annunciation to the Shepherds from Above" from *The Life of Mary,* the poet Rilke captures this sense beautifully by connecting Mary's complete and unconflicted openness to God with the angel who announces the birth of Jesus to the shepherds. The angel says: "What is a thornbush now: God feels his way into a virgin's womb. I am the ray thrown by her inwardness, which is your guide."

See also CHRIST; DEMON(S), DEMONIC, DEVIL(S); DISCERNMENT OF SPIRITS; DUALISM; GNOSIS, GNOSTICISM; GRACE; SPIRITS.

Bibliography: J. Daniélou, *The Angels and Their Mission,* trans. D. Heimann (Westminster, Md.: Christian Classics, 1982). G. MacGregor, *Angels: Ministers of Grace* (New York: Paragon House, 1988). K. Rahner, "On Angels," *God and Revelation,* Theological Investigations 18, trans. E. Quinn (New York: Crossroad, 1983) 235–274.

BOB HURD

ANGER

See DEADLY SINS; FEELINGS.

ANGLO-CATHOLIC SPIRITUALITY

Since the 1830s, Anglicans who feel strongly that their Church is rooted in the patristic tradition of the early Church have drawn much of their spirituality, beliefs, and liturgical practices from Catholic sources.

Although Anglo-Catholic thought encompasses much more than liturgy, most of the controversy it once provoked sprang from the effort of Anglo-Catholics to emphasize the awe and mystery appropriate to communal worship. Anglo-Catholics moved away from the austerity that had long marked Anglican prayer, and did it, they insisted, out of fidelity to tradition. The readiness of Anglo-Catholics to reach beyond the Reformation to recover the common features of Catholic worship such as vestments and candles, or even to borrow developments such as Benediction from other contemporary Catholic Churches, once guaranteed that Anglo-Catholic parishes, with their crosses and statues, were easily distinguished from other, less ornate Anglican churches. Today, however, the widespread acceptance of the liturgical reforms advocated by Anglo-Catholics and the contemporary tendency toward a simplification of liturgical ceremony have had the effect of blurring the old distinctions.

The Oxford Movement

The birth of Anglo-Catholicism can be traced to a small group of Oxford dons who met to form an action committee in response to a sermon John Keble preached on July 14, 1833, against the government's plans to rearrange the diocesan boundaries of the Church of Ireland. This effort to rationalize the temporal affairs of a neighboring established Church forced the Anglican clergy to ask where authority in the Church of England really rested. Was it with Parliament, which had admitted non-Anglicans to its ranks since earlier in the century, or with the bishops, who traced their succession back to the apostles? Is the Church of England the religious arm of secular government, and as such subject to its whim (Erastianism), or a separate entity whose conduct and faith are governed by its fidelity to the tradition of the Fathers of the Church? And, if the latter be true, is the Church as it now stands fully conformed to that tradition, or have the events of the last centuries dulled its awareness of its Catholic nature?

Like most reform movements, the Oxford Movement began with a return to sources. John Keble, John Henry Newman, Edward Pusey, Robert Wilberforce, and Hurrell Froude diligently searched the Fathers for a consensus on the meaning of baptism, the Eucharist, and other doctrines. They were so convinced of the importance of the patristic sources which bypassed Roman Catholic and Protestant divisions that they edited an extensive series of translations called *The Library of the Fathers.*

The discoveries they made in the Fathers and the impetus for reform that stirred these scholars were spread far beyond the university by the ninety tracts the "Tractarians" wrote between 1833 and 1841. The tracts dealt with fundamental matters such as the sacraments and the place of the Church of England in the larger Catholic community.

The extension of the Oxford Movement's influence to parishes all over England demonstrates that it was never engaged in a purely academic endeavor. It aimed at the reform of the heart as well as at the enlightenment of the mind. In fact, it insisted that the latter could not be achieved without the former. The patristic orientation of Keble, Pusey, and Newman was an effort to break away from the cold intellectuality of the Enlightenment with its proud reliance on a supposedly objective reason. Human beings are not disembodied minds, they proclaimed, but feeling and reflecting beings in a world where nothing in human affairs ever attains the pristine clarity of the abstract sciences. Faith, Newman argued, is not the conclusion of a logical exercise of reason but a decision based on probabilities depending on a multitude of inferences drawn from all dimensions of human existence. "After all, man is *not* a reasoning animal; he is a seeing, feeling, contemplating, acting animal" (*Discussions and Arguments on Various Subjects,* 1899, p. 294). A religion that aims at the head alone misses the mark. However, in the opinion of the Tractarians, the raucous emotionalism that characterized the Evangelical Churches of their time did no better. What the members of the Oxford Movement sought was a growth in understanding that went hand in hand with a growth in holiness. The proof of faith is in the living of it.

In part, at least, the Oxford Movement can be seen as an effort to resist the floodtides of Modernism. Its rejection of the arid rationalism of the previous century, its attention to feeling, and its glorification of the Middle Ages establish its ties to the Romanticism that was such a prominent feature of its time. Anglo-Catholicism, in fact, had been permeated by the Romantic spirit. Its influence is evident in the hymnody, church architecture, and the renewal of the vowed religious life Anglo-Catholicism inspired.

On a deeper level, Romanticism's sense of the world as a magical, translucent place meshed well with the conviction of the Fathers that the world is a window to a deeper reality. This sense of the world as a quasi-sacramental place, which has been blessed by the incarnate presence of the Word itself in Jesus Christ, was of prime importance to the Tractarians and their successors.

The Oxford Movement's relationship to Romanticism is perhaps best exemplified in John Keble's life and work. Keble (1792–1866), who laid aside a brilliant career at Oxford's Oriel College to spend thirty years in a small country parish, had a deep feeling for nature and a profound sense of the inexpressible mystery of God. He, like Newman and several other early members of the movement, was a poet. He is remembered for the popular volume of verse he published in 1827 entitled *The Christian Year.*

Keble found a justification for the Oxford Movement's emphasis on the incarnation, episcopacy, and sacraments in Richard Hooker, a seventeenth-century Anglican divine who had defended the Church against the Puritans. Keble devoted his scholarly life to editing his works.

Keble's poetic efforts were an integral part of his theological reflection on the analogy through which God makes himself known. As time went on, Keble's theology, which had always been concerned with prayer, praise, and purification, focused more and more on the Eucharist. (The conviction that Christ is truly present in the Sacrament and is sacrificed in the Mass would become a characteristic teaching of Anglo-Catholicism, although there was never unanimity on just what these terms meant.) Keble, a quiet, humble man, was highly regarded as a confessor and spiritual guide.

Although the Tractarians were sometimes labeled "Puseyites," Edward Bouverie Pusey (1800–1862), who had been appointed regius professor of Hebrew at

Oxford in 1828, was not really the leader of the Oxford Movement. His position, scholarly reputation, and aristocratic background did, however, make him the most prominent member. Pusey, who had the highest regard for the Fathers' symbolic reading of Scripture because it demonstrates their sensitivity to God's revelation of himself through the image of the world and the communication of his grace through divinely instituted symbols, was the prime mover of the *Library of the Fathers* translation project.

Pusey, a retiring, ascetical individual, has been called the *doctor mysticus* of the movement. He turned back not only to the Greek and Latin Fathers but to the great spiritual writers of the Middle Ages, such as Bernard, Ruysbroeck, and Thomas à Kempis. He also read John of the Cross, Teresa of Avila, and more recent spiritual writers in the Roman Catholic and Orthodox traditions. Pusey made the doctrines of the mystery of transforming grace, the divine indwelling of the Trinity, and our participation in the divine nature, which he saw as the basic teachings of the first four centuries, the center of his own theology. Everything in harmony with these doctrines was integrated into his spirituality.

The conviction of John Henry Newman (1801–1890) that the Church of England had been called to walk a *via media* between the excessive systematization of Roman Catholicism and the individualism of Protestantism turned his attention to the Fathers of the Church. In time, however, he saw that in the controversies of the early Church, it was not the groups that held the middle ground who were in the right. He also had to admit that truth was not with the small groups who stood in opposition to the faith of the larger community throughout the world. The parallel with the patristic Church did not work out to the advantage of the Church of England. Newman also saw that if the larger Catholic Church was right then, it was very likely right now. His efforts to understand how the faith retains its identity while undergoing historical development also led him to believe that the truth of the historical community is protected by the teaching office of the Bishop of Rome. On October 8, 1845, therefore, he was received into the Roman Catholic Church by the Passionist priest Dominic Barberi.

This loss was a great blow to the Oxford Movement. Newman had written twenty-seven of the ninety tracts and had been a tremendous influence on hundreds of young men at Oxford who had crowded into St. Mary's Church to hear him preach on Sunday afternoons. He spoke without rhetorical flourishes, but the force of his sincerity and the sense that he gave his listeners of walking with him in his quest for the truth deeply moved his audience (*Parochial and Plain Sermons,* 8 vols., 1898–1899).

When Newman attempted to read the Thirty-nine Articles of Reformation Anglicanism from a Catholic perspective in Tract Ninety, a number of clergy and bishops had seen this as an attempt to Romanize the Church of England. The "defection" of Newman, Faber, and others in 1845 seemed to confirm their worst suspicions.

Newman, who continued his distinguished scholarship as a Roman Catholic priest of the Oratory at Birmingham, traced his progress toward Rome in his *Apologia pro Vita Sua.* Although his advanced ideas never won him the full confidence of the English hierarchy, he was made a cardinal by Leo XIII in 1879.

Newman's theology, like that of the other Tractarians, was essentially patristic and deeply sacramental. He may have been the intellectual star of the first phase of Anglo-Catholicism, but holiness was his constant theme, and a Church that reached out to hearts was his aim.

Liturgical Revival

Although the Tractarians wanted to restore their Church's Catholic heritage, they did not advocate the liturgical reforms that soon came to be the trademark of Anglo-Catholicism. They thought that introducing liturgical changes would awaken suspicion and distract people from fundamental issues. However, the reaction against the rationalism of the previous era was wider than the Oxford Movement, and, inevitably, the sacramental insights of the Tractarians were linked by their followers to the romantic quest to transform churches from places where the Word was heard into centers where the Transcendent was experienced and worshiped. The movement to design fitting places of worship and the ceremonial accouterments to go with them was actually based at Cambridge University in a group originally called the Camden Society and later named the Ecclesiological Society.

Despite the academic credentials of the Tractarians, the Oxford Movement was always pastorally oriented. Its emphasis on the Incarnation also made it socially aware. Pusey maintained that you cannot perceive Christ in the Eucharist if you do not respond to him in the poor (Rowell, p. 82). In the 1840s many young clergy who had been influenced by the Tractarians turned their attention to the dreadful poverty of the slums, and, with the hope that a more vibrant ceremonial would appeal to the poor, they introduced vestments, candles, incense, etc. The missionary impulse gave these changes a rather more flamboyant character than the earlier antiquarian efforts of liturgists like John Mason Neale (1818–1866), who played a part in the founding of the Camden Society and enriched the English Church with a wealth of translations of ancient and medieval hymnody. How effective these liturgical innovations were at a time when members of the working class rarely even entered a church is in considerable doubt, although the good work of the Anglo-Catholic clergy among the poor is well documented.

The Anglo-Catholic liturgical revival prompted strong opposition to what many

considered "popish" ceremonial. Bishops protested against the addition of a drop of water to the wine at the offertory, making the sign of the cross at the final blessing, and reserving the Sacrament. Although the authority of the bishops was the cornerstone of Anglo-Catholicism, priests were convinced that bishops could not forbid things that belonged to the broad Catholic tradition to which their Church belonged. Riots by parish mobs horrified by the changes were not uncommon in the 1860s.

Parliament attempted to bring liturgical innovation under control by passing the Public Worship Regulation Act in 1874 and establishing a special court to try cases dealing with charges regarding vestments and ceremonial. The vigilant Protestant Church Association brought charges against a number of clergy, none of whom appeared before the court because they rejected its authority. Five were found guilty *in absentia* between 1877 and 1887 and sentenced to jail for an average of five months each. The Royal Commission on Ecclesiastical Discipline set up by Prime Minister Arthur Balfour reported in 1906 that while the Public Worship Act was seriously breached by practices such as the adoration of the reserved Sacrament, prayers to the saints, and Benediction, the act was too restrictive for the feeling of the time. This admission had a great effect on the efforts to revise the Prayer Book in 1927–1928 and on all subsequent updating of the Church of England's liturgical books.

Religious Orders

The Tractarians' emphasis on holiness made it inevitable that they should be involved in the revival of the vowed religious life in the Church of England. Although Newman denied that he was attempting to establish a religious congregation during his last years as an Anglican, he did, in fact, live a prayerful, reflective existence centered on the Divine Office with six young men at Littlemore from 1841 to 1845. W. G. Ward attempted a similar experiment.

Keble, and particularly Pusey, helped found sisterhoods to serve the poor. Their efforts to set up convents were much influenced by the example of St. Vincent de Paul and the Daughters of Charity.

The Sisterhood of the Holy Cross, the first community of religious women in the Church of England since the Reformation, was set up in 1845. It was a troubled, unsettled community, but later efforts to establish active, contemplative, and mixed-life communities were more successful.

Richard Meux Benson founded one of the most successful Anglican orders, the Society of St. John the Evangelist or the Cowley Fathers, in 1865. Another influential order of priests, the Community of the Resurrection, was founded in 1892. The Benedictine monks now established at Prinknash Abbey trace their origin back to Fr. Ignatius (Joseph Leycester Lyne), who started his own eccentric variation of Benedictine life in 1870, and to the remnant from the monastery on Caldey Island who did not follow their founder, Benjamin Fearnley Carlyle, and the majority of the community in its transfer to Roman Catholicism in 1913.

Later Developments

The Tractarians' answer to the challenge posed by rationalism was to scorn its premises altogether and to turn their attention to authority as a source of truth and to faith as a matter of the heart as well as the head. But if the link between faith and reason was not to break down completely, some effort had to be made to reconcile the advances of historical-critical scholarship and the received truths of religion.

In 1889 a group of Oxford clergy at Keble College, known as the "Holy Party" and led by Henry Scott Holland (1847–1918), published *Lux Mundi,* in which they attempted to relate their faith to the thought of the time. This was followed by *Essays Catholic and Critical* in 1926. This book, which owed much to the Roman

Catholic Modernists, was authored by contributors from Cambridge.

If Anglo-Catholicism soon found it necessary to modify the intellectual positions it had inherited from the Tractarians, it remained confident that its liturgical orientation was sound. It continued to explore Catholic liturgical tradition in a series of congresses held in 1920, 1923, and 1927. The centennial celebration in 1933 attracted 70,000 participants. The last such meeting was held in 1948.

The widespread acceptance of the liturgical reforms Anglo-Catholicism had advocated, the influence of the ecumenism it had promoted since Lord Halifax's dialogues with Cardinal Mercier in the 1920s, and the simplification of the liturgy encouraged by Vatican II all affected Anglo-Catholicism. Although it has ceased to exist as a distinctive movement, Anglo-Catholicism has left its imprint on the theology, spirituality, and worship of the Anglican Church throughout the world.

See also ENLIGHTENMENT, INFLUENCE ON SPIRITUALITY; LITURGICAL MOVEMENT; LITURGY; MODERN SPIRITUALITY; PROTESTANT SPIRITUALITIES; RELIGIOUS LIFE.

Bibliography: G. Rowell, *The Vision Glorious: Themes and Personalities of the Catholic Revival in Anglicanism* (Oxford: Oxford Univ. Press, 1983). F. Penhale, *The Anglican Church Today: Catholics in Crisis* (London: Mowbray, 1986). O. Chadwick, ed., *The Mind of the Oxford Movement* (London: Adam and Charles Black, 1960).

KENNETH C. RUSSELL

ANIMALS

Animals function as metaphors, symbols, and examples of spiritual truths in Scripture, in the Lives of saints, and in other Christian religious texts.

Animals reveal divine judgment and providence in the Hebrew Scriptures: lions do not harm Daniel (Dan 6:17-25); ravens bring food to Elijah (1 Kgs 17:4-6). God's protection brings safety from wild animals (Ezek 34:25-28); the reign of peace in

Isaiah (11:6-9) pictures harmony among wolf and lamb, calf and lion, "with a little child to guide them." Eliphaz promises Job: "the beasts of the earth you need not dread . . . and the wild beasts shall be at peace with you" (Job 5:22-23). The bond of peace between animals and humans signals the restoration of paradise.

For early Christian commentators, the text of Mk 1:13 assumed particular importance. At the time of testing in the wilderness, Jesus "was among wild beasts, and the angels ministered to him." Jesus stands in the world populated with animals and angels as the new Adam, restoring the lost harmony of Eden.

The Desert Fathers and Mothers of the third to the fifth century reveal this characteristic in early stories about them. Antony of Egypt receives food from the ravens; Macrina receives the gift of a fleece from a hyena. Perhaps the best expression of the meaning of animals in these stories comes from a saying attributed to Paul of Thebes: "If one possesses purity, all things will be subject to him, as they were to Adam when he was in paradise before he disobeyed the divine command" (PL 73:1002). This theme emerges clearly in the Acts of martyrs: they are not harmed but venerated by wild animals in the arena.

In medieval Christian literature, the respect and obedience of animals became a standard motif identifying holy persons, especially solitaries. Withdrawing from human society, they enjoy the company of other creatures that recognize in them the presence of Christ. Venerable Bede (d. 735) asserted that those who serve the Creator of all will be served by every creature, while those who fail to serve the Creator will lose this gift. Perhaps the most famous example of a holy person who lived in harmony with animals and other creatures is Francis of Assisi (d. 1226). Lives of Francis frequently mention his harmonious relationship with animals, which he calls "brother" and "sister."

Another branch of Christian literature made animals and their behavior metaphors of the spiritual life or of vices and virtues. Deriving from the early Christian beast-book *Physiologus,* commentaries on the story of creation (e.g., the *Hexameron* of Ambrose), and the *Etymologies* of Isidore of Seville (d. 636), this tradition found expression in the medieval bestiaries. In this tradition the deer drinking at a stream may symbolize the faithful imbibing the waters of grace; the lizard basking in the sun represents the contemplative in the presence of God. More elaborate tales of moral instruction (*exempla*) used animal figures to instruct readers about the path of Christian perfection.

A third use of animal figures employs them as symbols in the arts. Drawing on classical literature, the Scriptures, and later Christian literature, artists portrayed Christ as the lion (of Judah) or as a lamb (Gen 49:9; Isa 53:7). Christ's life-giving death was represented by a pelican feeding its young on blood from its pierced side. In reading these symbols in religious sculpture and painting, the believer was invited to meditate on the life of Christ, the sacraments, or the practice of Christian life.

With the modern scientific study of animals, their importance in Christian literature and art receded. A new interest in creation as an important element of Christian spirituality suggests that the world of animals and other fellow creatures can be revelatory of the Creator, a return to an ancient Christian belief in our era.

See also CREATION; ECOLOGICAL CONSCIOUSNESS; SYMBOL.

Bibliography: F. Klingender, *Animals in Art and Thought to the End of the Middle Ages* (Cambridge, Mass.: M.I.T. Press, 1971). A. Linzey and T. Regan, eds., *Animals and Christianity* (New York: Crossroad, 1988). W. Short, *Saints in the World of Nature* (Rome: Gregorian Univ., 1983).

WILLIAM J. SHORT, O.F.M.

ANTHROPOLOGY, THEOLOGICAL

Theological anthropology is an articulation of a vision of human existence within the context of Christian revelation. Characteristically it deals with human self-transcendence, the experience of grace, creaturely limitations, and irreducible qualities and capacities of human persons. Thus it is doctrine about "human nature" or what it is to be "person." Within the theological tradition, this vision of the human was articulated within the discussions of creation and the fall from grace, incarnation, redemption, and the theology of grace. In the post–Vatican II era, theological anthropology has become a theological theme in its own right and has been affected by the social sciences, the biological and physical sciences, Christology, and contemporary philosophical understandings of personhood.

Theological anthropology consistently addresses two questions: (1) What is it about humans that makes it possible for them in their creatureliness to know or experience the infinite God? (2) What is it about humans that makes "fallenness" possible in such a way as to require the redemption offered in Christianity?

Within the history of Christian spirituality, writers of mystical texts have been dependent upon the prevailing theological anthropology available to them. Every spiritual text expresses an implicit theory of human being (persons) and how the human relates to the divine. Thus the study of spirituality requires an adequate anthropology from which to critique and appreciate these historical descriptions of both the distortions in the human implied by conversion and purgation, as well as the experience of grace in the transformations of illumination and union with God.

Classical Formulations

Various theological explanations have been offered to describe how human persons relate to the divine. In the earliest theologies, commentary on Genesis 1 and 2 developed a theology of the image of God. Because the story of the fall from grace immediately follows the original vision of the primordial couple, "In the image of God, he created them," it was believed that the image was distorted, and greater explanation was given to the theology of original sin and concupiscence than to how humans were in the image of God. Various patriarchal interpretations of this text tended to imply that man was more adequately in the image of God than was woman because of a supposed greater rationality in the male. Despite this type of application of the image to the disadvantage of woman, it was consistently held theologically that the soul of both man and woman was in the image of God.

The Greek spiritual tradition richly developed this theme in its mystical theology, especially Origen and Gregory of Nyssa. Deification for the Greeks was the cleansing and repair of the damaged image so that one might enjoy the divine life. Augustine placed the "image" in a Trinitarian theology that identified the rational faculties of intellect, memory, and understanding as the image of God in the human.

The later Western medieval spiritual tradition posited a distinct faculty of the soul as the locus of relation to God. This faculty was variously named the *acumen*, the *scintilla* (spark of the soul), and the *capax Dei*. Each of these metaphors attempts to show that in some way the human person is constitutively receptive to and capable of response to the divine initiative. Traditional Catholic theology recognized this inherent "receptive capacity" in the human person and named it *potentia obedientialis*. Within the theology of grace, the distinction between the natural and the supernatural became increasingly differentiated and tended to emphasize an objective, nonexperiential dimension of grace.

The Turn to the Subject

The most significant philosophical influence on contemporary theological anthropology is the "turn to the subject," a redefinition of the human as person who is a "subject" of consciousness, one who is autonomous, historical, and self-constituting rather than the static human "nature" of the classical formulation. This earlier formulation relied upon the vocabulary of intellect, knowledge, and nature in contrast to will, freedom, and history in the discussion of personhood.

Although various strategies have been adopted in contemporary theological anthropology to accommodate this turn to the subject, both Protestant and Catholic versions tend to exhibit two features in common. First, Adam as the paradigm for the human has been replaced by the story of Jesus, who as an actualized person is the image of God in a human person. Recent ecclesiastical documents (*Inter Insigniores, Mulieris Dignitatem,* and drafts of the U.S. bishops' pastoral letter on women), which neglect this shift from the mythical original couple to Jesus as paradigmatic of the human, seem to ignore the implications of their insistence that Jesus' maleness is more significant than his personhood when they use the single feature of gender to maintain the exclusion of women from ordination. A Christ-centered anthropology of necessity must admit that women as well as men participate in the same graced humanity that Jesus redeemed through his concrete enfleshment.

Second, contemporary anthropologies are unanimous in emphasizing the central theological theme that human subjects are oriented to God and stand in a relationship of radical dependency on God. This emphasis on creaturely dependence tends to collapse the distinctions in classical theology between the human person as "knower of God" and the human person as "sinner redeemed by God" into the single category of the dependence of human subjects.

Contribution of Social Sciences

This second theme emerges strongly from Vatican II's recognition of world religions, its insistence on a universal offer of salvation, and its resistance to structures, systems, and philosophies that justify or foster the dehumanization of persons. The Pastoral Constitution on the Church in the Modern World, especially in its teaching on the dignity of the human person, recognizes the contributions of the sciences and of cultures to the understanding of the human person (GS 44).

While interdisciplinary reflection on the human person began prior to the council, theological anthropology today is in dialogue with the social sciences, especially psychology, sociology, and anthropology. The cultural context in which fundamental theology articulates the faith is shaped by the understandings of the social sciences. These categories of human self-understanding, while limited to those specific aspects of the human amenable to scientific investigation, can neither be ignored nor contradicted by theology as long as their truth claims are valid. Because these social sciences also describe the alienations and distortions in human existence, some of their categories can be used to demonstrate the pervasiveness of sin, suffering, and evil in human existence, which justifies the doctrine of salvation offered in Christ.

Experience of Grace

While philosophical categories are required to articulate a vision or ideal of human existence in its wholeness rather than in its parts, this vision must bear some resemblance to experienced reality. Hence an emphasis on the experience of grace or of its refusal in concrete, historical contexts is a theme in theological anthropology. Reflection on a pluralism of experience of the human condition, e.g., the experience of women, of the poor, or of Latin American or black communities, appears in political or liberation theologies.

In this context, A. Carr makes the claim that "the 'nature' of being human is in human hands and that human being is changing because of the reflection of women on their own experience" (*Transforming Grace: Christian Tradition and Women's Experience,* New York: Harper & Row, 1988, p. 117). Reflection on the experience of women (and the poor, etc.) invites theological anthropology to become less androcentric and genuinely inclusive in its reflection on humanity. For Carr, as for K. Rahner, on whom she draws, human nature is not a static essence that in classical formulations was uncritically derived from a given culture; rather, the unchanging aspects of human beings are consciousness and freedom in a worldly, historical context. Liberation theologies go even further in using various forms of social analysis to uncover the extent to which unjust social structures shape consciousness and severely limit the exercise of self-creating freedom for some and maximize it for those who benefit most from a given structure.

Anthropological Constants

E. Schillebeeckx shares this same view of the indeterminate character of "human nature" and offers what he calls "anthropological constants," a system of seven coordinates with *personal identity* within *social culture* as its focal point as the conditions constitutive of the human within which salvation occurs (*Christ: The Experience of Jesus as Lord,* New York: Crossroad, 1981, pp. 734–743).

1) Being human involves a relationship to corporeality, nature, and the ecological environment. The bodily dimension of human reality is not to be overcome but positively taken into account. Neglect of corporeality, including gender, and lack of reverence for material creation have led to attempts to dominate nature to such an extent that the human life-form currently threatens the life of the planet and all other life-forms with destruction. Contemporary cosmological understandings of the earth as a single life-system call theological anthropology to adopt a more geocentric and less anthropocentric view of the role and place of human persons in the scheme of creation.

2) Being human involves being one with others. Human persons are necessarily social beings. Destined for others, they discover their own identity only in relationship with others.

3) Human persons are not only interpersonal but exist of necessity in relationship to social and institutional structures. While these structures are human creations, they function independently over time and deeply influence the personhood of those who participate in them. Although they may appear to be unchangeable, they are contingent and mutable by persons. This analysis of social structures has added the category of "social sin" to describe the sinful effects of these structures.

4) Human persons and their cultures are conditioned by their historical and geographical situation. This anthropological constant emphasizes the historicity of human experience and human consciousness. The study of spirituality increasingly seeks to situate religious experience and spiritual traditions within their concrete historical and cultural matrix. Recently the much-neglected dimension of geography and landscape is emerging as a methodological category within the field of spirituality.

5) A mutual relationship exists between theory and practice. Human theories have concrete consequences for the survival of the human world as well as of the planet. Praxis has become a key category for critical reflection on theory, including the theological. If orthopraxis does not result from orthodoxy, there is something lacking in the interpretation or mediation of doctrine to a new cultural context.

6) A religious or transcendent dimension is constitutive of the human. This anthro-

pological constant has always been assumed in theological anthropology. However, contemporary cultural analysis discovers what some identify as a secular form of "faith" that is distinct from explicitly theocentric religious visions. A fully developed theological anthropology relates humankind to God, revealed through Jesus, as source and term of human existence. However, insofar as reflection on the human accounts for implicit rather than explicit believers, this reflection must respect the variety of content and expressions of secular faith-forms.

7) The final constant Schillebeeckx offers is that all six of the above constants form a synthesis that cannot be reduced either idealistically (by overemphasizing the spiritual dimension over the interpersonal or corporeal) or materialistically (by focusing on material conditions at the expense of the need for meaning or freedom).

These coordinates offer a helpful schema for critical reflection on the implicit anthropologies encountered in the study of spirituality and their reinterpretation in the light of present experience.

See also ADOPTION AS CHILDREN OF GOD; BODY; CONVERSION; DIVINIZATION; ECOLOGICAL CONSCIOUSNESS; ENVIRONMENT; EXPERIENCE; FEMINIST SPIRITUALITY; GRACE; HOLY SPIRIT; IMAGO DEI; PRAXIS; SELF.

Bibliography: D. Kelsey, "Human Being," in *Christian Theology,* ed. P. Hodgson and R. King (Philadelphia: Fortress, 1982). M. Scanlon, "Anthropology, Christian," *New Dictionary of Theology,* ed. Joseph Komonchak, M. Collins, D. Lane (Wilmington, Del.: Glazier, 1987) 27–41. J. Segundo, *Grace and the Human Condition,* vol. 2 of *A Theology for Artisans of a New Humanity* (Maryknoll, N.Y.: Orbis, 1973). T. Berry, *The Dream of the Earth* (San Francisco: Sierra Club, 1988).

JANET K. RUFFING, R.S.M.

ANXIETY

See FEELINGS.

APATHEIA

Apatheia, from the Greek word meaning "passionlessness," is a term used in the Stoic tradition and given a Christian sense, especially by Clement of Alexandria and the Desert Fathers. Apatheia is not to be confused with apathy. It is the quality of the sage or saint who enjoys substantial freedom from desires and passions. The usage emerged in a climate of thought in which the attitude toward emotion was negative, and so passion became identified with vice and was considered something to be avoided.

A more positive content is given to apatheia by Evagrius, who regularly associated it with *agape.* For him, the avoidance of enslavement to subpersonal desires produces a state of inner harmony and peace in which growth is furthered and love flowers. John Cassian avoided the term *apatheia* and used *puritas cordis* ("purity of heart"), which indicates personal integration, a single-heartedness due to a lack of inner division. Such interior unity means that one is free from radical disturbance and therefore ready for contemplation. This emphasis was followed in the Benedictine tradition and was to some extent institutionalized in the value of stability.

A parallel line of development followed Augustine's view of *ordo* as a constitutive element of virtue. In the twelfth century, which appreciated affective experience, the emphasis was less on avoiding passions than on harnessing them to serve a single end. This is expressed in the theme of the ordering of affections (*ordinatio caritatis*). By subordinating "lower" desires to those that are spiritual, the *ordo* intended by God is maintained, and peace and well-being are secured.

The importance of the theme of apatheia is that it reminds us that an uncritical acceptance of the emotions does not promote spiritual growth. Discernment is needed and a choice has to be made so that some passions will be voluntarily followed and incorporated into a personal lifestyle, whereas others will need to be curtailed or completely left aside.

A spiritual life in which apatheia tends toward the elimination of all feeling is usually associated with a solitary lifestyle and a call to strongly apophatic prayer.

See also ASCETICISM; DISCERNMENT OF SPIRITS; FEELINGS; HEART; PASSION(S); SIMPLICITY.

Bibliography: J. E. Bamberger, *The Praktikos. Chapters on Prayer,* Cistercian Studies 4 (Spencer, Mass.: Cistercian Publications, 1970). M. Colish, *The Stoic Tradition from Antiquity to the Early Middle Ages,* 2 vols. (Leiden: Brill, 1985). O. Chadwick, *John Cassian,* 2nd ed. (Cambridge: Univ. Press, 1968).

MICHAEL CASEY, O.C.S.O.

APOCALYPTICISM

The word *apocalypticism* is derived from the Greek word meaning "revelation" and refers to a divine message about the end of the world. For this reason, in the minds of many it is associated with prophecy. The final events are described in symbolic, sometimes even bizarre, descriptions as found in the books of Ezekiel and Revelation (the Apocalypse).

Apocalypticism is a way of understanding one's place in the movement of time. It looks to the end of history to give meaning to the whole of history. An individual's life is set by God within the temporal scope of the entire human race, indeed, of the whole cosmos. Because of sin, the world and all within it must be purged before it can enjoy that for which God intended it. This purgation will be individual, social, and cosmic, and it will take place before the end of time. One might say that apocalypticism is a type of eschatology (doctrine of the endtime).

What makes apocalypticism different from other eschatologies is its pessimistic evaluation of the present times. It maintains that the existing persecution of the righteous and the good fortune of the wicked are evidence that we are in the midst of the final struggle between the forces of good and the forces of evil. Since history is ultimately under divine control, apocalypticism looks expectantly to the defeat of evil and the triumph of goodness. Then a new age will appear, and God's reign will be victorious and unchallenged.

Some believers turn to the apocalyptic writings of the Bible to give meaning to the events of their lives. Therein they find unfolding what appears to be their own struggle. Thus they are consoled in their suffering and encouraged to be faithful in the face of opposition. They even brave death, believing that in the new age they will be vindicated. Apocalypticism gives people a sense of belonging to a history over which they have no control and of being secure in the thought that God, who is in control, will ultimately set things straight.

See also DUALISM; ESCHATOLOGY; FUTURE; HISTORY, HISTORICAL CONSCIOUSNESS; MILLENARIANISM; PROPHECY.

Bibliography: B. McGinn, trans., *Apocalyptic Spirituality,* Classics of Western Spirituality (New York: Paulist, 1979).

DIANNE BERGANT, C.S.A.

APOPHATIC SPIRITUALITY

See NEGATIVE WAY.

APOSTOLIC SPIRITUALITY

The word *apostolic* has been variously applied over the centuries. As descriptive of spirituality, it is of recent origin. In some sense all Christian spirituality is apostolic spirituality. The Second Vatican Council affirmed that the call to the apostolate is rooted in baptism and confirmation, and that apostolic activity is essential to the Christian vocation.

In a more restricted and proper sense, the term *apostolic spirituality* refers to an understanding and integration of one's life in terms of participation in the saving mission of Jesus, sent by God for the life of the world. It denotes a spirituality based on the conviction that action and involvement in the world constitute a path to holiness and to union with God. As in any spirituality, all elements of the Christian life are affected and ordered by this conviction.

Meaning of *Apostolic*

The adjective *apostolic* comes from the Greek *apostellein,* meaning "to send." In its many occurrences in the Septuagint, *apostellein* implies the sending of a messenger on a special mission, with emphasis on the relationship between the messenger and the sender. The verb appears 135 times in the NT, especially in the Gospels and Acts. In the Gospel of John, which also employs the verb *pempein* to denote sending, the term *apostellein,* used 28 times, tends to accent the responsibility, the particular charge, of the one who is sent in relation to the sender. Jesus is the one who is sent to reveal God, and therefore to give eternal life and to bring believers to God. John the Baptist (Jn 1:6) and the disciples of Jesus are likewise sent (Jn 17:8; see also Mt 28:19; Mk 16:5; Lk 24:49ff.; Acts 1:8).

Until the Middle Ages the word *apostolic* implied either a relationship to the Twelve, called apostles by the Synoptic Gospels and later tradition, or it referred to attachment to the Chair of Peter or to any preacher sent by Rome. As reference to the original disciples of Jesus became more remote, the term *apostolic* became more general and vague. In modern times the term was applied especially to the proclamation of the gospel to those who had not yet heard it. This sense was especially strong in the 16th century, age of the "discoveries," when Christianity was proclaimed to the new nations. The 17th century referred to specific activities and virtues as apostolic when these sprang from certain attitudes and virtues. Charity and zeal, for example, were considered apostolic virtues par excellence. The 18th and 19th centuries extended the term to apply to various initiatives undertaken in favor of the neighbor.

However, it was still thought that a truly apostolic spirit was exemplified by the missionary whose life of charity was expressed in proclaiming the gospel in a foreign land.

During the 19th and early 20th century, both of these meanings developed and were related. Missionary expansion in Africa, Asia, and the Americas was unparalleled. While it was largely priests and religious who were directly involved in work in foreign lands, laypersons were intimately associated with missionary works through apostolates of prayer and through associations for the support of missionary activity. Confraternities and associations were likewise formed to meet the needs of society. Various schools of spirituality—Ignatian, the French School, the tradition flowing from Francis de Sales—accented the unity of the Christian life and regarded action on behalf of the neighbor as a duty of all Christians.

Apostolic spirituality, broadly understood, is intrinsic, therefore, to all forms of Christian life and can be lived in lay life, in a religious congregation, or by ordained ministers. In each of these states of life, it will bear its own specific modalities. In *Lumen Gentium,* Vatican II stated explicitly that ordained ministers find holiness through their apostolic labors (LG 41).

The development of the application of the term *apostolic spirituality* to lay life has been most dramatic. Until the 19th century laypersons were seen as objects of the apostolate of the clergy. The Church was understood to be composed of those who governed, led, and taught (clerics) and of those who were to be governed, led, and taught (the laity). Only in the 20th century, with the establishment of the Catholic Action movement and its many similar groups, were laypersons considered as subjects of the apostolate, and then only in a restricted sense as participating in the apostolate of the hierarchy.

Vatican II, however, recognized that laypersons have "the right and the duty to be apostles" (AA 2) because of their union with Christ through baptism. Lay observers at the 1987 Synod on the Vocation and Mission of the Laity called for the articulation of an apostolic spirituality for and by the laity. Such a spirituality must sustain those laypersons who live their apostolic calling individually or primarily in the context of the family, as well as those who participate in organized movements or associations of an apostolic nature whose focus on bringing all temporal realities under the reign of God is explicit.

Apostolic Religious Congregations

It is within religious congregations that apostolic spirituality has been most clearly articulated, and the evolution of male and female congregations differs in this regard. As early as the 13th century, apostolic religious life was an issue for the Franciscans and the Dominicans. While preaching was their primary work, each group understood apostolic life differently. Franciscan life was to be an imitation of the life of the apostles; Dominicans strove to be "useful" to others.

In the 16th century Ignatius of Loyola founded the Society of Jesus as an apostolic group with neither choir nor habit, a radical departure from monasticism. His intention was to institute in the Church a group of apostles fully available for mission in any part of the world. Their sending was to be explicit, and so in 1538 they put themselves totally at the disposition of the Vicar of Christ. Ignatius understood the unity of the apostolic life and expressed it in the single aim of the Society of Jesus: The glory of God *is* the salvation of humanity.

Women in the 16th century shared this apostolic insight, but cultural and ecclesiastical factors hindered its development. Angela Merici's original vision was a group of consecrated women totally dedicated to the protection of youth. She envisaged them living in the world, principally within their own families. Various factors intervened, however, among them the pressures of Tridentine reform, and in 1612 the Ursulines became a cloistered order with solemn vows.

In 1611 Mary Ward, foundress of the Institute of the Blessed Virgin Mary, adopted the constitutions of the Society of Jesus as the foundational document of her institute. The freedom from cloister and centralized government that are pivotal in those constitutions, however, were unheard of in female congregations. Not only was Mary Ward prevented from realizing her vision, but she herself was imprisoned because of the audacity of her idea. In 1631 the "Dames anglaises," as her congregation was sometimes known, were officially suppressed; they were to receive papal approval only in 1877, more than two centuries later.

In 1607 Jeanne de Lestonnac founded the Company of Mary (official title: Congrégation Notre Dame), likewise modeled on the Society of Jesus, but with necessary adjustments made for a cloistered order. While the sisters did not leave their monasteries, these were to be organized for the apostolate of teaching.

For women, the ecclesiastical legislation requiring cloister as well as the cultural attitude toward women continued to be obstacles to a religious life of service outside a monastery of nuns with solemn vows. The apostolic inspiration persisted, however, and during the 17th and 18th centuries several congregations succeeded in leading an apostolically active life in spite of restrictive canonical legislation. At times this was done by not taking perpetual vows (e.g., Daughters of Charity); at other times, by the discreet nature of the congregation, coupled with local support by the clergy or hierarchy (e.g., Sisters of St. Joseph). The establishment of hospitals, orphanages, and schools also enabled the sisters to live an active life within the confines of their own institutions.

The 19th century can truly be called "the apostolic flowering of religious life." In the wake of the French Revolution, an extraordinary number of religious congregations were founded in France and northern Italy, most often to address the crying needs of a society whose structures and institutions of social service had been destroyed. Catholic women found in these congregations a space where they could not only fully serve others in an ecclesial and religious context, but where they also were able to develop their personal talents and exercise leadership and initiative in a way that was not common in civil society. These religious congregations with simple vows, devoted to various apostolic works, were officially recognized by the Holy See in 1900 in the decree *Conditae a Christo*. Vatican II affirmed that in these congregations apostolic activity is of the very nature of religious life, that is, religious vocation and consecration within these institutes are intrinsically for mission. In asking that their entire religious life be "imbued with an apostolic spirit," *Perfectae Caritatis* urged the development of an apostolic spirituality (PC 8).

In the United States the great majority of religious were involved in apostolic works from their first days on American soil. They responded to the human and religious needs of a largely immigrant Church. The health-care and educational institutions that they established and staffed, as well as the social services they provided, gave eloquent witness to the apostolic spirit that motivated them.

Attitude Toward the World and Action

At the heart of apostolic spirituality is an affirmation of the world as the theater of human activity and holiness, a world that God so loved as to send Jesus to dwell in it and the Spirit of Jesus to animate it. For centuries the dominant Christian spirituality was based on a negative view of the world, of matter, the human body, and temporal reality. It saw the world either as an obstacle to union with God or as a mere springboard to that union. Flight from the world, either to a monastery or to the "cell of the soul," was the Christian ideal. Conversion in such a spirituality implied the transfer of one's desires from material creation to supernatural realities, considered to be the only true ones.

An apostolic spirituality, on the other hand, sees the world not as an obstacle to union but as the very place where God is present and encountered. The world is God's parable, having a meaning that is not evident upon first reading. Each generation must reread it to discover there God's meaning for the human race. Vatican II affirmed that God's design for the world is that it should be renewed and, with all humanity, fully become what it was created to be.

A world in evolution precludes any static notion of life and lends a dynamic character to apostolic spirituality. Questions of ecology, of politics, of science, of the development of cultures become central. Indeed, "nothing that is genuinely human fails to find an echo in [the] hearts" of Christians grounded in apostolic spirituality (GS 1).

The action to be exercised in this world is vast. Certainly the proclamation of the gospel in favor of the oppressed, poor, and marginalized continues to be a sign that the reign of God has come; works of charity continue to be an expression of the compassion of Jesus. Apostolic action includes being a leaven of the gospel in the complex world of politics and economics, of science and culture, and exercising the "action of witness" in a variety of difficult circumstances where explicit action is impossible.

Apostolic spirituality strives for a unity of life based on union with Jesus Christ, the One sent by God. This unity goes beyond the necessary and constant organization of one's time, coordination of one's activities, and discipline in one's choices. It touches the depths of personal identity, one's deepest center, the place where one is truly "called." It is there that fidelity to self and fidelity to God are one and the same, that God's will for me becomes my own deepest desire. It is achieved to varying degrees and is never acquired once and for all. Referring to priests' quest for unity of life, Vatican II states: ". . . unity of life cannot be brought about merely by an outward arrangement of the works of the ministry nor by the practice of spiritual exercises alone, though this may help to foster such unity. . . . Priests will achieve the unity of their life by joining themselves with Christ in the recognition of the Father's will and in the gift of themselves to the flock entrusted to them" (PO 14).

The unity of the apostolic life is found in charity. This love, characterized by self-transcendence, is an expression of the great commandment of Jesus. Love of neighbor is at one and the same time the expression, verification, and sign of one's love for God.

Any spirituality affects all elements of life, ordering them in a certain constellation, a particular architecture. As the organizing axis of apostolic spirituality, this active love for others in union with the One sent by God colors all elements of life. *Prayer* is not a source from which one draws water that will then be dispersed in action; it is rather a contemplation of the face of Jesus in the world, in the sister or brother who is in need. The apostle bears the world in his or her heart and stands before God in an appropriate attitude of praise, petition, thanksgiving, or sorrow. The current of liberation theology coming from Latin America understands that it is among the poor that God is revealed and contemplated in a privileged way. A truly apostolic prayer taps into the biblical tradition that recognizes and praises the action of God in history.

The *asceticism* of an apostolic spirituality is rooted in the events of daily life, in the difficulties and self-transcendence inherent in a life of service. The fatigue, travel, and trials experienced by St. Paul, and especially his "daily concern for the churches" (see 2 Cor 11:23-28), have lost none of their actuality and continue to be a source of asceticism. The rapid pace of cultural and social evolution creates a context of uncertainty that provides an ongoing asceticism, as does a daily choice of simplicity in a consumer society.

Community life, whether in a family, parish, or religious house, is also to be marked by an apostolic spirit. How one looks on the "stranger, the widow, and the orphan" and responds in concrete circumstances is a constant challenge.

Expressions of spirituality vary not only according to one's vocation in life but also according to one's culture. The appropriate response to the other, the most effective means of proclaiming the gospel varies from one situation to another, from one culture to another, from one age to another. Responses in our age, which has a societal and global awareness as well as a holistic consciousness of the person, must take these dimensions into account. The task of the Christian was perhaps validly understood in the past as "the salvation of souls." Today it is much more aptly expressed in *Evangelii Nuntiandi* as the evangelization of the "personal and collective consciences of people, the activities in which they engage, and the lives and concrete milieus which are theirs" (EN 18)—in short, the evangelization of "culture and cultures" (20).

The attitudes fostered by an apostolic spirituality in contemporary society are many. Among those most evident are discernment, justice, and active patience. The Church today faces questions that are new for humanity as a whole. The most loving, truthful, and free response is not always evident. Apostolic action requires a constant attitude of discernment in order to perceive the seeds of the gospel in the various movements and situations of our times. To cultivate a discerning heart includes the discipline of listening carefully and seriously to ecclesial tradition and teaching, to the best aspirations of one's contemporaries, to the Spirit-filled members of the Christian community.

A passion for justice that recognizes the essential equality and dignity of all persons (GS 29) is a grace of the present age. To work to ensure that structures and policies are consistent with this recognition is an apostolic task, one that humanizes and evangelizes the deepest strata of human culture.

The Church exists for the world. The means of social communications daily remind the Church of the extent and complexity of its mission: the extent of hatred and greed; the invisibility, manipulation, and oppression of vast numbers of women and children; the growing threat to the human race from military and ecological disaster. To expend one's finite energies day after day in the face of global needs requires an active and persevering patience based on the conviction that the saving mission of Jesus Christ is confided to the whole Church for all time.

In summary, through an apostolic spirituality Christians participate consciously and explicitly in the mission of Jesus, sent by God to bring the human race to God's intended fulfillment. Concern for human salvation marks all aspects of their lives and provides the prism through which they interpret all of the Christian life.

See also CONTEMPORARY SPIRITUALITY; CULTURE; LAY SPIRITUALITY; MINISTRY, MINISTERIAL SPIRITUALITY; MISSION, SPIRITUALITY FOR MISSION; RELIGIOUS LIFE; VOWS; WORLD.

Bibliography: J. Raitt, B. McGinn, and J. Meyendorff, eds., *Christian Spirituality: High Middle Ages and Reformation* (New York: Crossroad, 1987). J. Sobrino, *The Spirituality of Liberation* (Maryknoll, N.Y.: Orbis, 1988). L. Doohan, *The Lay-Centered Church* (Minneapolis: Winston, 1985).

MARY MILLIGAN, R.S.H.M.

APOTHEOSIS

See DIVINIZATION; IMAGO DEI; PATRISTIC SPIRITUALITY.

APPARITIONS

See EXTRAORDINARY PHENOMENA; MARY; VISION(S).

ARCHITECTURE

As a visitor to the church of Holy Wisdom (Hagia Sophia) in Constantinople in the 6th century, the historian Procopius of Caesarea was dumbfounded by the beauty and mystery of the building. The shimmering golden dome overhead did not seem to be supported by masonry, but rather mysteriously and miraculously suspended from heaven by a golden chain. "Whenever one goes to this church to pray," he observed, "one understands immediately that this work has been fashioned not by human power or skill, but by the influence of God. And so the visitor's mind is lifted up to God and floats aloft, thinking that he cannot be far away, but must love to dwell in this place which he himself has chosen" (Mango, p. 76).

Some fourteen hundred years later, theologian John S. Dunne visited the same building, which had functioned as a Muslim mosque for about five hundred years and is now a state museum. He wrote: "As you come into Ayasofya, you come from the outer to an inner world, you come into an inner space, but more than that, you come into the inner world of the spirit. As you move about inside, you move in the world of the spirit, coming at times to some new illumination of mind, at times to some new inspiration of heart. And as you come to rest, maybe in the center, maybe somewhere off from center, a peace begins to encompass you, a peace that makes you reluctant ever again to leave" (Dunne, p. 27). Although Hagia Sophia no longer functions as a Christian church, Dunne found that the God who "cannot be far away" was indeed an enduring presence in that place. Something about the orientation of the space, its proportions, the radiance of the light within, the beauty of its materials and craftsmanship continue to speak to the visitor of holiness, of the presence of God.

In almost every age the great churches of the era not only reflect the prevailing ecclesiology but invite the visitor into some sort of dialogue, some sort of response. The remarks of Abbot Suger, gazing upon his newly completed church at Saint-Denis and its many precious works of art in the mid-12th century, are justly famous. He wrote: "Thus when—out of my delight in the beauty of the house of God— the loveliness of the many-colored stones has called me away from external cares, and worthy meditation has induced me to reflect, transferring that which is material to that which is immaterial, on the diversity of the sacred virtues; then it seems to me that I see myself dwelling, as it were, in some strange region of the universe which neither exists entirely in the slime of the earth nor entirely in the purity of Heaven; and that, by the grace of God, I can be transported from this inferior to that higher world in an anagogical manner" (Bournazel, p. 57). In structures of differing styles, separated in time by six hundred years, visitors report experiences of being lifted up, transported, embraced by a space that leads them into some kind of new relationship with the presence of God.

In our time architectural form continues to resonate with experiences that evoke holiness. In designing the French pilgrimage church at Ronchamp, France, in the 1950s, architect Le Corbusier noted, "In building this chapel I wished to create a place of silence, of prayer, of peace, of spiritual joy" (Jeanneret-Gris, p. 25). Toward that end he designed a building reminiscent of a cave or womb, a place of silence, stillness, security. The thick, sloping stucco walls enclose irregularly shaped spaces that in the side chapels rise up in towers reaching toward the light. The concrete ceiling sags and hovers mysteriously between the walls. A narrow band of light around the rim of the walls subverts one's presumption that the ceiling rests on the walls. Small random slits punctuating the exterior walls become wide, glowing stained-glass windows in the interior, evoking memories of medieval churches transformed by colored light. The architect deliberately shaped his structure so that it would shape the experience of those who approach and enter.

In a post–Vatican II ecclesial world, Le Corbusier's vision of a church as a place of refuge, a sanctuary for individual prayer, is not adequate for a parish church. But the care with which he articulated his concept for his chapel, and his attention to the evocative power of memory in choosing architectural forms to express and convey his ideas, offer a model for the design of worship spaces.

For today's worshipers, it is as important as ever that one sense a holiness within the place set aside for encounters with God. But that search for the numinous, for the transcendent, is not satisfied simply by appeals to pseudo-Gothic interiors or large expanses of stained glass. Wholesale quotation of the style vocabularies of earlier ages does not produce an architecture for a contemporary spirituality.

Spirituality is admittedly an elusive word. For contemporary church architecture it has to do with the articulation of the identity of the Christian community in such a way that it honors the life of the community in a dignified and reverent way, while at the same time supporting and nurturing the ritual experience of that community. As the American bishops' document *Environment and Art in Catholic Worship* (EACW) puts it, the worship environment is a serving environment which in its design, its centers of action, its seating arrangements, acoustics, lighting, etc., affects the actions of the assembly (EACW 24).

EACW emphasizes that "among the symbols with which liturgy deals, none is more important than this assembly of believers" (EACW 28). For some, such an idea requires a shift from imagining that it is statues or the altar or the tabernacle or stained-glass windows or pews that make a church, to understanding that it is the actions of the assembly that sanctify the place. So the building is not an object unto itself, a museum full of treasures to be admired, but a locus for holy actions by a holy people.

A worship place that supports those holy actions is a place whose conceptual design derives from the identity of the faith community. In our times the understanding of that identity has been considerably expanded from primarily a passive model to a participatory one. The auditorium in which worshipers are seated to watch sacred pageantry performed before them, on their behalf, gives way to a much richer definition of community. To describe a Roman Catholic community as an assembly of the faithful that baptizes, reconciles, and celebrates the Eucharist is to evoke images of journey, sequence, and movement. Articulating the identity of Christian community in this way makes demands on architecture that are quite different from simply inspiring awe or overwhelming viewers with transcendent splendor. A new initiative is necessary.

The new initiative does not reject the past. On the contrary, profound insights from earlier but mostly forgotten periods of our history have begun to reshape our worship spaces. Our reclaiming of the ancient catechumenal formation of those entering the faith community by the rites of initiation for adults (RCIA—the Rite of Christian Initiation of Adults) has made us aware of a whole new dynamic.

The journey from attraction to the community, to formation in the community's life, to entry or reentry into the life of the assembly through baptism or reconciliation, to gathering at the table for the offering of Eucharist requires significant centers of action that in an ongoing way will remind the faithful of the shape of this journey. This means new attention to gathering spaces and thresholds, the crossing of which signify conscious assent to the life

on the other side. It means baptismal fonts that contain enough water to drown in, making clear that baptism is not something that happens to one but a choice freely made to go down into the waters of death in Christ in order to emerge into a new life with the resurrected Christ. It means attention to the relationship between baptism and reconciliation, and the hospitality of a community that stands ever ready to baptize new members or embrace those who have been alienated, for the assembly is diminished by their absence. It requires a relationship between entry rites of baptism and reconciliation and the altar, around which the people gather as symbol of their unity.

To have a place where the entry rites coincide with the physical entry into the building and yet clearly relate to the altar, so that the business of the assembly, its ritual life, can be celebrated within the assembly, requires spaces whose shapes and configuration are different from those of longitudinal medieval churches. They require creative thinking about how to distinguish between the corporate life of the gathered assembly and the devotional needs of individual members. They require designs that will provide the ongoing formation of encounter with the rituals that sustain the life of the Church, and simultaneously respect the need for beauty that comes from the enlisting of artists, a reverence for honesty of materials, and noble simplicity of form (EACW 34 and Mauck, *passim*).

In reality, the challenge of contemporary designers is the same as it has ever been—to express and convey the community's understanding of its identity and its worship. The history of ecclesiastical architecture is one of continual change through the ages. The Byzantine church of Hagia Sophia reflects a quite different concept than Abbot Suger's Gothic cathedral, which in turn cannot be compared with Le Corbusier's pilgrimage church at Ronchamp. Each has its own integrity and beauty because it conveys the ecclesial understanding of its time and met the needs of the worshiping community. In so doing, the buildings both expressed and shaped the spirituality of the faithful.

Attention to the understanding of the 20th-century Church of itself as a baptizing, reconciling community that gathers at the altar to offer Eucharist and then goes forth into the larger world renewed in strength and spirit, only to return again and again, will produce architecture that speaks to this assembly of believers as powerfully as any architecture of the past. This architecture will continue the tradition of forms that impinge both on human memory and experience, renewing people, lifting their spirits, and bringing them into encounter with the God who dwells in their midst.

See also AESTHETICS; ART; BEAUTY; ENVIRONMENT; LITURGY.

Bibliography: E. Bournazel, "Suger and the Capetians," *Abbot Suger and Saint-Denis: A Symposium,* ed. P. Lieber Gerson (New York: Metropolitan Museum of Art, 1987). J. Dunne, *The House of Wisdom* (San Francisco: Harper & Row, 1985). Bishops' Committee on the Liturgy, *Environment and Art in Catholic Worship* (Washington: USCC, 1978). C. Jeanneret-Gris, *The Chapel at Ronchamp* (New York: Praeger, 1957). C. Mango, *The Art of the Byzantine Empire* (Englewood Cliffs, N.J.: Prentice Hall, 1972). M. Mauck, *Shaping a House for the Church* (Chicago: Liturgy Training Publications, 1990).

MARCHITA B. MAUCK

ARIDITY

See DARKNESS, DARK NIGHT.

ART

Throughout history the word *art* has been used to express at least three meanings: the skill of making something, usually with materials, words, sounds, or movements; the product of that endeavor; and the distinctive qualities of the product (something that meets aesthetic standards, however broad the spectrum).

Talent, study, and disciplined practice characterize the creation of art. Not everything that is made is art. The artist, applying both ability and intuitive sensitivity, shapes materials in such a way that they communicate meaning through a nondiscursive modality.

Beyond these basic understandings controversy reigns over any single definition of art. The discussion includes primarily whether art is confined to those products or activities that conform to classical aesthetic standards (such as those exemplified in the Parthenon, Michelangelo's *David,* Beethoven quartets) or whether the criteria for qualification include popular expressions of experience and hard-to-categorize contemporary interpretations.

The issue here is not only taste and experience; it also relates to the purpose of art. Does art exist primarily to express beauty? Then what is beauty? Is the value of art connected primarily to its capacity to move those who interact with it, to stretch us to new perceptions, or to focus our experience? Is it an instrument of history, a testimony to the ideas and skills of particular people at specific times, i.e., a legacy to be admired? Is the purpose of art its capacity to make the past present or the future envisionable?

Purposes of Art

Art in whatever form it appears, whether as decoration, entertainment, indicators of historical roots, expressions of cultural realities and values, or interpretations of age-old or contemporary truths, is a vehicle that expresses a fragment of human experience. Art invites interaction with it. It tells us something about what it means to be alive. Though its meaning often cannot be stated discursively, nonetheless its meaning can be felt. In the experience one knows something, and always in a new way. Among the many purposes of art some are appropriate to a discussion of spirituality:

Particularity

No two people experience life in exactly the same way. Each person is influenced by cultural background, class, religion, gender, race. Art communicates the value of such difference as a primary resource for interpreting human situations. Cynthia Ozick's words about the purpose of literature are valid for art in general: "to tell, in all the marvel of its singularity, the separate holiness of the least grain."

An art form is not conceived *de novo;* rather, it reflects, both in form and content, particularities of history and society. As such, it can connect with other specific human realities beyond these roots. The many illustrations and compositions that convey a sense of the crucifixion of Jesus are an example. They call to mind a particular historical situation affected by the political, religious, and social intricacies of the time. However, the meaning stretches to interpret other experiences as well in which greed wins over truth, a body is taxed beyond its limits, or power is misused at the expense of human lives. A particular experience is honored. It informs many different subsequent ones and sets a tone for interpretation.

Meaning

Art connects with the essence of human experience (feelings, dreams, ideas, imaginings) and discloses its meaning. Art embodies human experience, captures it in a moment of time. Such diverse works as those of Henri Matisse, Elie Wiesel, and Emily Dickinson offer examples. Through both the architecture and the interior designs of the Chapel of the Rosary in Vence, France, Henri Matisse illustrates the illusive mystery of resurrected life. To sit in this place is to discover a sense of its reality. Elie Wiesel turns to stories. What does it mean to live in a world invested in dominance? He unveils the evil incarnated through such an imbalance of power. How does one describe the pain? Emily Dickinson expresses it in poetry, pain "so utter that it swallows being." Meaning emerges through a process: the artist interacts with materials, then the participant interacts with the completed work. The goal is not to locate the "right" meaning, but rather to uncover whatever connects with one's own experience.

Revelation

Art opens a door to a deepening and broadening of understanding. It invites connections between shapes, sounds, textures, and/or movements with lived experience or suspected possibilities. In the connection is found the revelation, a realization of something not grasped before. It may be the repetition of a certain rhythm that brings one face to face with the persistence of God in our midst. It may be the irregularity of a pattern that identifies the unpredictability of divine activity or the surprising qualities of friendship. Similarly, a jagged movement may symbolize the experience of unanticipated pain. Such "seeing" offers revelations about human living and divine relationships that can affect changes in our choices, our activities, our convictions.

Illusion

The purpose of art is not to imitate nature, though some classical thinkers argued for this rationale. In Susanne Langer's words, art is the "bearer of an idea." Though "charged with reality," art points to what is beyond it, the passion, the pain, the love, the hate that lies in the in-between places of artistic composition. Called illusion (not using the most common understanding of the word), this quality, inherent in symbolic communication, invites participants into a world of knowing where literal understanding is enlarged. Added to it is an invitation to probe layers of meaning, such as in between the notes of a symphony, in the blending of movement and music, or in the cutting of marble. Something beyond imitation is discovered; the mystery of art unfolds multiple interpretations, multiple meanings. Divine love can be felt in the boldness of design, in the exaggeration of color in textures, in gentle touch or movements.

Emotion

Art makes emotion tangible. The components of art, its shapes, sounds, movements provide a form for the expression of emotion, the "soul" of human life. In the utterance of emotion, the "heart" of art is known, with its distinctive ambiguity, its compelling power, its innate invitation to wonder, its passion, its holistic embrace. In this articulation and in the interaction with it, human life and divine relationships are more deeply understood and potentially lived. Hymns used in a liturgical context offer an illustration. They affirm faith not through the doctrines they proclaim but primarily through the emotion expressed in verbal images as well as musical lines, rhythms, and harmonies. One feels courage, hope, commitment in the lines of a hymn and is inspired to act.

Awareness Conversion

Clearly art wakes us up and in the waking invites response, though no specific one. Georgia O'Keeffe talks about her intent: "I paint pictures big, so no one will be able to walk by without noticing." Significant art makes a difference. It asks questions, offers insights, or at the very least, enlarges the parameters of our consciousness. It can pierce vagueness and uncover apathy.

Awareness is the first step toward change. Contemporary art often offers clear examples. One such illustration is the work of Paula Turnbull. In Sacred Heart Church, Southbury, Connecticut (built in 1990), she carved stations of the cross using the same brick materials as the walls. To some people they seem indistinguishable from the walls. Though they do not claim attention as immediately as brightly colored icons, their subtlety conveys a particular awareness that the way of the cross is ordinary rather than extraordinary. It is a journey every Christian walks. What one sees is the historical event brought into the present. The art is an invitation not only to make a connection between the path of Jesus that led to both death and life but also to feel and embrace the vision of God embodied both in Jesus and in us.

Memory

Through the simple drawings of events in Jesus' life found in the Dura-Europos house-church, the magnificent painting of the Sistine Chapel, the diary of Anne Frank, and the poetry of Adrienne Rich, human beings are challenged to *remember.* Art keeps alive not necessarily facts (though some information may be conveyed) but rather the spirit embodied in an event, moment in time, or human experience. It points to the reasons for a tragedy or triumph. It underscores the determination that is underneath the struggle to survive. It summons interaction with what is true and good. Art makes present what is, what was, and what might be. Just as the stories of Elie Wiesel move us to scream "Never again," so the poetry of Edna St. Vincent Millay invites us to insist on new visions of possibility and beauty. Such is the power of memory recalled through art.

Values

Inevitably, artists communicate values. As visionaries in the midst of society, artists mirror, interpret, and clarify values ranging from political, personal, aesthetic to universal. In fact, suggests Martha Graham, art finds its roots in human values. What a society cherishes, hates, avoids, condemns, or desires can be felt in its art.

Because art plays such a powerful role in reflecting values, it can be clarifying for some people and at the same time threatening for others. When art is too far removed from values that are commonly acceptable, it is pushed to the periphery at best, and at times considered extreme or unimportant. Yet what horrifies one generation as shocking may turn, within a century, into a classic. Stories of artists abound whose work is evaluated as useless in one period of time and invaluable at another. This situation does not undermine the purpose of art to reflect values; rather, it affirms this power. Art reflects change. It connects with primary human experiences. Art anticipates human longings. Art unmasks, names, criticizes, points to possibilities. It challenges human values and affirms them.

Art and Spirituality

From earliest history art has played a role in understanding life guided by belief in the divine. Art offers us significant information about divine-human relationships. As verbal records became important and available, art offered a complementary perspective critical to the full development of our understanding (for all the reasons cited above). At some historical periods the Church was the primary responsible agent for the preservation and development of art, especially during the Middle Ages.

However, the use of art to express the nature of God, God's collaborative activity with humankind, and human response to God's invitations also has been regularly challenged. Its history is a rhythm of rejection and acceptance. There have been times when the boundaries of what is acceptable are so tightly drawn that the Church has little or no partnership with art. At other times art, clearly expressive of profound faith, flourishes. Restrictions have existed for all forms of art, from the evaluation of visual images to what constitutes "sacred" sound. Grasping the expression of human-divine revelation through the movements of the human body has been the most difficult. Yet given Christian belief in the Incarnation, it is one of the most obviously God-given illustrations.

This erratic relationship between art and spirituality emerges from contrasting beliefs about the function of art vis à vis the divine. The first concern relates to the nature of the divine. How can art or anything else, for that matter, convey what is ineffable? Another basis for judgment springs from the freedom of art, which is inseparable from the creativity that undergirds it. The task of the artist is to speak truth as she or he understands it. Such a responsibility requires the artist to respond to the creative process as it unfolds through the use of materials. Nothing in the creative process suggests that the product will be what anyone predicts or thinks it should be. It may be pleasing, but, just as likely, it may be disturbing. Truth is not always comforting.

Adding to these complications, art has not escaped the pitfalls of excess or manipulation. An appreciation of artistic expression throughout human history has demanded uncommon insight and continues to require both discernment and courage. As an activity connected concretely to the work of God, art enjoins human beings to touch what is deepest in their beings, but with some abandon, and in the interaction to release God within them, whatever form that takes. Such is the essence of the creative process both for the artist and the participant in art.

Art promotes seeing beyond the obvious to what lurks in the crevices of human-divine experience. Art offers an unmatched source of history and experience as well as a resource for transformation. To reap its benefits requires risk, imagination, and courage, qualities felt in art, known through the activity of God with humankind, qualities as well that sustain ongoing development of spirituality.

See also AESTHETICS; ARCHITECTURE; ATTENTION, ATTENTIVENESS; BEAUTY; CONVERSION; FEELINGS; MEMORY; MUSIC; PASSION(S); REVELATION(S); VALUE.

Bibliography: S. Laeuchli, *Religion and Art in Conflict* (Philadelphia: Fortress, 1980). S. Langer, *Feeling and Form* (New York: Scribner's, 1953). M. Miles, *Image as Insight: Visual Understanding in Western Christianity and Secular Culture* (Boston: Beacon, 1985). C. Ozick, *Art and Ardor: Essays* (New York: Knopf, 1983).

J. Walton, *Art and Worship: A Vital Connection* (Wilmington, Del.: Glazier, 1988).

JANET R. WALTON

ASCETICAL THEOLOGY

The conviction that ordinary Christian living consists in nothing more than walking the rock-strewn roads of the valley, where virtuous human striving and discipline, under the impulse and guidance of God's grace, bring souls to a perfection that does not normally include contemplative prayer, prompted theologians in the 17th and 18th centuries to divide the study of spirituality into ascetical and mystical theology. Mystical theology was reserved for the study of the extraordinary gifts of prayer, while ascetical theology became, in effect, the study of ordinary Christian perfection.

Neat and convenient as the division between the two disciplines may seem, the boundaries were never clearly defined or stabilized. In fact, the terminology of a rigidly rationalistic theology rode roughshod over experience, exaggerated the rarity of contemplative prayer, and insisted on separating what God had joined together. Contemporary theologians, therefore, see the ascetical phase and the mystical phase of the Christian life as two moments in a continuous movement and prefer to call the one discipline that studies this progression "spiritual theology."

See also HOLINESS; MYSTICAL THEOLOGY; SPIRITUALITY, CHRISTIAN.

Bibliography: T. A. Porter, "Spiritual Theology," *New Catholic Encyclopedia* 13:588–589.

KENNETH C. RUSSELL

ASCETICISM

When the early Christians referred to the disciplinary practices by which the devout seek to condition themselves for the Kingdom, they borrowed a word from the world of Greek sport: *askēsis,* "practice." The comparison between the Christian effort and the single-minded way in which athletes regulate all aspects of their lives to promote the attainment of their primary goal was an obvious one that St. Paul had already exploited: "Every athlete exercises discipline in every way. They do it to win a perishable crown, but we an imperishable one" (1 Cor 9:25). Like athletes, Christians pummel and master their bodies, and, like athletes, they do these things in order to attain a goal that lies beyond the self. The athlete is not a bodybuilder, nor is the Christian ascetic someone bent on displaying the perfection of human nature.

Asceticism is a goal-oriented activity. The determination to bring all features of life into conformity with the pursuit of a primary goal is reflected, for example, in the readiness of Abram to leave home and family in obedience to God's summons (Gen 12:1-4). To reach the Promised Land, the Israelites had to abandon the pleasures of Egypt and undergo the hardships of the desert journey (Num 11:5-6). A new set of values had to replace the old, and life had to be reoriented accordingly (Deut 8:2-6). Jesus emphasizes how radical this turning is when he insists that those wanting to be his disciples must "deny themselves" in a self-emptying like his own, take up their cross and follow him (Mt 16:24).

Since asceticism is a training program that conditions individuals for the attainment of a spiritual goal, the kind of asceticism practiced in a particular period of the Church's history depends on that era's understanding of the nature and the effect of sin and its vision of holiness.

Asceticism as Therapy

In the first centuries, when the influence of Stoicism was strong, Christians saw the effects of sin in the pressures and anxieties that cloud the perception of things as they are. Their ideal, therefore, was the attainment of *apatheia,* or passionlessness. Although this term has often been thought to imply the harsh suppression of all feeling, it actually means that the irrational urges that disturb the interior life have been brought under control so that the individual is free to focus calmly on God.

These Christians moved away from the multitude of concerns that filled their lives with noise and confusion toward simplicity, frugality, and quiet. They refocused the most fundamental and self-centered drives of human nature by making eating, sleeping, and possessions instruments of attentiveness to God and neighbor through fasting, vigils, and almsgiving.

The collections of the sayings of the Desert Fathers and the writings of John Cassian (ca. 365–435), the principal channel of the ascetical tradition of the Egyptian desert to the West, demonstrate the primarily therapeutic concern of this asceticism that sets out to heal the disorder of sin and to focus the individual on God. In addition to being faithful to the carefully moderated practice of the ascetical regime common to all, desert hermits would reveal the inner workings of their minds and imaginations to their spiritual master so that an appropriate therapy could be prescribed to pacify their interior life.

Asceticism as Punishment

Asceticism had always been associated with reparation for sin, but as time went on this feature almost completely overwhelmed the therapeutic dimension. In sixth-century Irish monasticism, which placed great value on humility, asceticism became primarily punitive. It was a means of keeping the monks conscious of their imperfection. The slightest infraction of the Rule brought a fixed penance. The same quid pro quo mentality shaped the private form of the sacrament of penance the Irish monks made popular in Europe. Before long, handbooks for the use of confessors listed sins and the penance due. Once asceticism was something owed for something done, it was no longer a therapeutic strategy but a matter of setting straight one's account with God. Since penance was punitive rather than healing, one penance could be substituted for another, and a longer one could be replaced by a shorter but more intense punishment.

In the eleventh century Peter Damian, prior of the austere colony of hermits of Fonte Avellana and an influential bishop and cardinal, promoted the use of the discipline (whip) as an ascetical exercise. In his hermitage three thousand strokes of the whip were the equivalent of one year of penance. The use of the discipline, which quickly became popular throughout Europe with both lay people and religious, and which played at least a formal part in the ascetical regime of many congregations until recently, encouraged a sharp dichotomy between the exterior body and the interior self: *I* punish my body.

The discipline was also seen as a means of joining Christ in his passion. Somehow it seemed good to suffer, and though it would be a mistake to be too quick to read masochistic tendencies into the desire of many to symbolize the martyrdom that was not available to them, it is obvious that asceticism had lost contact with its original therapeutic emphasis. On the whole, however, monasticism retained a sound, traditional ascetical program.

When the Renaissance emphasized what a glorious thing it is to be a human being and made the perfecting of human potential an end in itself, spiritual writers tended to see ascetical practices as a means of self-development. Asceticism was shown to be in harmony with this desire to develop one's potential because it taught the self-discipline necessary to achieve it. Attention shifted, therefore, from exterior physical practices to the inner workings of the mind and will. This emphasis is evident in the spirituality of the Ignatian exercises and the *Introduction to the Devout Life* of St. Francis de Sales. It is the will that needs training and correction.

Ascetical discipline may have moved inward to monitor the inclinations of the will, but the notion that physical suffering somehow unites individuals to Christ in his offering of himself for the world remained strong. The devotion to the Sacred Heart promoted by St. Margaret Mary Alacoque encouraged this yearning to make one's ascetical regime an offering to God for others.

Contemporary Practice

A number of factors influence the contemporary practice of asceticism. Chief among these is the negative image asceticism has gained from its association with body-hating acts of self-discipline or gratuitous acts of self-torture. The explorations of Sigmund Freud have made moderns very suspicious of the spiked gloves Henry Suso put on each night or of the chain John of the Cross wore embedded in his flesh. In addition, the modern inclination to read the whole history of asceticism as the reflection of a defective Greek split between body and soul has effectively cut contemporary Christians off from the riches as well as the aberrations of the past. The psychologically complex therapeutic teaching evolved by the men and women who stood alone with God in the Egyptian desert has been all but forgotten. Moreover, despite all the attention the modern world pays to making the body aesthetically pleasing by diet and exercise, there is little appreciation of the role the body plays in the salvation of the individual. Physical asceticism is, consequently, ignored, except as a protest against injustice and a sign of solidarity with the oppressed.

Asceticism, however, is basically the effort Christians "in training" make to conform their lives to the faith they profess. The break with the past has allowed the primary point to come to the fore: Asceticism is a disciplined regime that Christians freely take on in order to fulfill their task. Over the centuries asceticism evolved into a collection of penitential practices. In daily existence it is the willingness to make whatever efforts are necessary to fulfill

God's will, no matter what the cost, so that at the end of life the Christian may join St. Paul in saying, "I have competed well, I have finished the race, I have kept the faith" (2 Tim 4:7).

See also ABSTINENCE; ALMSGIVING; BODY; FASTING; MORTIFICATION; PENANCE, PENITENCE; SIN; SUFFERING.

Bibliography: T. Camelot and others, *Christian Asceticism and Modern Man,* trans. W. Mitchell and the Carisbrooke Dominicans (London: Blackfriars, 1955). P. Brown, *The Body and Society: Men, Women and Sexual Renunciation in Early Christianity* (New York: Columbia Univ. Press, 1988).

KENNETH C. RUSSELL

ATTENTION, ATTENTIVENESS

Whether understood psychologically as a concentration of consciousness or theologically as heedfulness (or unheedfulness) toward God's loving self-communication, attention is clearly a crucial factor in spirituality as well as general human experience. The OT stresses attentiveness to the Lord's commands and to the consequent ethical and religious quality of one's life (see Prov 4:1, 20; 5:1; 7:24; 16:17; Sir 16:22). The NT adds a further eschatological dimension as Jesus challenges his disciples not only to "pay attention" to his teaching (Lk 9:44) but to remain watchful for his return (Lk 12:36), a theme reiterated by Paul and other NT authors. From the patristic era onward, many authors discuss attention in terms of self-knowledge and custody of mind and heart, developing numerous ascetical practices and prayer methods for this purpose, including the daily examen, formal meditation, practice of the presence of God, etc., down to the "centering prayer" movement of our own day.

Praying itself, insofar as it involves awareness of, or communication with, the divine, seems necessarily to require attention in some form. Thus Francis de Sales observes that "the word meditation is ordinarily applied to the attention we pay to the things of God in order to arouse ourselves to love them" (*Treatise on the Love of God,* Bk. 6, chap. 2) and "contemplation is simply the mind's loving, unmixed, permanent attention to the things of God" (ibid., chap. 3). Thomas Aquinas discusses the different kinds of attention possible, and even required, for effective vocal prayer (ST II-II, q. 83, a. 13). And Simone Weil asserts an even more radical equation: "Prayer consists of attention," the "orientation of all the attention of which the soul is capable toward God" (*Waiting for God,* New York: Harper Colophon, 1973, p. 105). This intimate link between prayer and attention helps explain the vast literature on the problem of "distractions," given both the inconstant nature of human consciousness and the Christian obligation to "pray without ceasing" (1 Thess 5:17). Scholastic theologians invoke a traditional distinction between intention and attention to explain the possibility of genuine prayer even when other thoughts intrude; a prior global intent often suffices when one's attention inadvertently wanders.

In more recent years there seems to have been a shift away from excessive preoccupation with distractions and human frailty toward the primary biblical emphasis on attentiveness to God. At the same time, in the postconciliar context of interfaith dialogue, many Christians are borrowing, though sometimes indiscriminately, from Oriental meditation techniques intended to foster greater "mindfulness." Contemporary psychologists are developing a taxonomy of meditative and contemplative states in terms of their causes, contents, degrees of passivity, and so on, while some spiritual theologians are exploring the implications of Lonergan's first transcendental imperative: "Be attentive." Finally, liberation theologians and others remind us that no authentic Christian spirituality can dispense with attentiveness to the cry of the poor.

See also CENTERING PRAYER; CONSCIOUSNESS; CONTEMPLATION, CONTEMPLATIVE PRAYER; EAST-ERN (ASIAN) SPIRITUALITY; EXAMINATION OF CONSCIENCE; EXPERIENCE; INTENTION, INTENTIONALITY; MEDITATION; PRAYER; RECOLLECTION.

Bibliography: R. Vernay, "Attention," *D.Spir.,* vol. 1, cols. 1058–1077. Francis de Sales, *Treatise on the Love of God,* 2 vols., trans. J. Ryan (Rockford, Ill.: TAN Books, 1975). C. Naranjo and R. Ornstein, *On the Psychology of Meditation* (New York: Viking, 1971).

STEVEN PAYNE, O.C.D.

AUGUSTINIAN SPIRITUALITY

Augustine of Hippo was born at Tagaste in Africa in A.D. 354 of a Christian mother, Monica, and a pagan father, Patricius. After a wayward youth he taught at Carthage, Rome, and Milan; he was converted to the Catholic faith in 386 and was baptized by Ambrose in 387. After establishing a monastery for laymen at Tagaste in 389, he became a priest in 391 and auxiliary bishop of Hippo in 395. He died as bishop of Hippo in 430.

Augustinian spirituality derives from Augustine's absorption of the Catholic faith into the living out of his daily life. This spirituality is fundamentally that of conversion to Christ through the *caritas* that unifies all one's human energies. It is a finding of one's home in God and a joy of intimacy with the Father, Son, and Holy Spirit. This is "the eternal Jerusalem for which your people in their pilgrimage sigh from the beginning of their journey until their return home" (*Confessions* 9.13).

Augustine describes his own conversion biographically in Books I–IX of the *Confessions,* psychologically in Book X, and theologically in Books XI–XIII. He understood conversion as a call to relationship with Christ (see Rom 13:13). Since Christ lived in this world to return it to the Father, Augustine knew that Christians are called not only to sigh for the kingdom of God but to help the kingdom come on earth. The kingdom or city of God is established and developed through self-transcending love for God and human persons. Just as artists have portrayed Augustine holding a heart to symbolize love, so the character of Augustinian spirituality is best portrayed as the absorption of the gospel teaching on *caritas* into daily living. A conversion, therefore, is a change in the direction of one's love and is concerned more with the future than the past.

Augustinian spirituality has intellectual, moral, sacramental, mystical, and apostolic dimensions. It is expressed in Augustine's teachings. To consider the main themes of Augustinian spirituality, we shall therefore explore his doctrines of the Trinity, of Christ the Mediator and Physician, of the human person as the image of God, of divine grace as the source of spiritual growth, of human freedom as graced, and of the kingdom of God as the community of those who share God's will for the world's transformation through love and peacemaking.

The Trinity

Through faith Augustine accepted Christ's revelation of God as Father, Son, and Holy Spirit and his call to participate in their life of love. This was not a call to self-alienation but to self-identity, not to a forsaking of the world but to collaboration in its creation and transformation. Through the sacrament of baptism the divine Persons begin to dwell within the human soul. The Holy Spirit's gift of *caritas* originates a likeness to the Trinity: the Father as caring, the Son as compassionate and healing, the Spirit as loving in full freedom. Thus Catholic spirituality originates from an appreciation of the relation, actualized at baptism, to the Persons of the Trinity.

Even before baptism there is a universal divine call to all "restless" hearts. The rationality of the human being constitutes persons to be images of God. By affinity with his spiritual reality, they are *capax Dei*, that is, they have the capacity for communion with God. This capacity is actualized at baptism. Deification or participation in Trinitarian life results from this actualization. The gift of this likeness to God enables one to advance from a simple faith to an ever deeper perception of God (*Homily on John's Gospel* 98.1; *Sermon* 71.18). "As you come closer to likeness to God, so you grow in love, and begin to perceive him" (*Exposition Ps* 99.5). This environment of unconditional love nurtures prayer, which is the union of human freedom with divine freedom. The longing to know and to see God is the prayer of the heart. Love arouses the desire to know God and leads to faith seeking understanding. Faith in Christ opens the believer to the full gospel message. This meditation on Scripture increases one's understanding and promotes the love of God and neighbor.

Christ, Mediator and Physician

A preparation and a purification are necessary for incorporating Trinitarian attitudes and actions into one's life. This requires the admission of one's need for healing by Christ the Physician and accepting his mediation for adoption into Trinitarian life. *Christus medicus,* Christ the Physician, was a theme frequently used by Augustine in his sermons. It recalls his personal experience of being healed by Christ and every Christian's need for humility in accepting the mediation of Christ. The Neoplatonic philosophers lacked humility, for although they knew of God's existence, they scorned the incarnation of God and thereby deprived themselves of the "medicine which could cure them" (*City of God* 10.29). Humility as Christ's outstanding virtue was to be imitated by his disciples. Christ's humility is the remedy for Adam's fall through pride. The human heart will find rest only if it follows the "true physician's invitation: 'Learn of me, because I am meek and humble of heart'" (*City of God* 4.16).

Christians who admit the truth of their condition and their need for the remedy possessed by Christ can be cured and returned to life. One prepares for healing by a meditative reading of Scripture and by prayer and fasting. Purification of the heart is also needed. The heart has to be purified and enlightened if God is to be seen. Faith purifies the eye of the heart; faith working through love provides the light for the eye of the heart to see God.

This faith and this charity are God's gifts. Persons who are filled with love are those who participate in the life of the Trinity. By the love that the Holy Spirit pours into hearts at baptism, one grows in the faith that works through love until, with purified eyes of the heart, one sees God in his images: one's neighbor and one's self. In his spirituality of human response to a Trinitarian God who is love, Augustine makes frequent use of the biblical notion of "heart" as uniting flesh and spirit to signify the affective aspect of faith in God. Augustinian spirituality combines an intensity of religious feeling with a sense of the divine.

Image of God

Christ is the perfect image of the Father, equally God. The human person is an imperfect image of the Trinity, not equal to God but having a capacity for communion with God. The journey to God is by way of becoming a more perfect image of the divine Trinity. The Father's perfect image, his Son, is the only way to likeness with God. This likeness is best achieved through wisdom, the crowning gift of the Holy Spirit. Wisdom is "the love and awareness of him who is always present" (*Exposition Ps* 135.8). On it depends the soul's loving intimacy with the divine Persons. It is the final fruit of a living faith that acts in love (see Gal 5:6). It presupposes an eager search for God, but its proper activity is contemplation, that is, the finding of God and rejoicing in him.

This indirect perception of God will become in heaven a direct face-to-face vision

of God. The contemplation of God is the destiny of every Christian (*City of God* 19.19). Here on earth wisdom expands into loving action. The Christian thereby acts out God's love for all creatures, just as Christ in his actions manifested God's love for them. The source of wisdom, the divine love poured into human hearts by the Spirit arouses in persons the acts of remembering, understanding, and loving God.

Thus Augustine saw the essential process of the spiritual life to be the re-formation of the image of the Trinity in the human person by the grace of Christ freely accepted. Transformed into children of God, human persons enter into union with him not merely as creatures with Creator but as friends. The Father offers this grace of friendship to all through Christ, the universal Way.

So convinced was Augustine of the centrality of the Trinity in the living out of Christian faith that he wrote fifteen books on the Trinity. In the first seven books he examined Scripture to show that God had revealed himself as Father, Son, and Holy Spirit. In the later books he searched for human analogies in order to understand as far as possible what he believed of the Trinity. It was important to find the true image of God so that the Trinity might be contemplated in their images.

"We are certainly seeking a trinity, not any trinity at all, but that trinity which is God, the true, supreme, and only God. . . . We are not yet speaking of heavenly things, not yet of God the Father, Son and Holy Spirit. Rather we speak of this unequal image, an image nevertheless, which is human being. For the mind's weakness perhaps looks upon this image with more familiarity and facility. . . . Let us attend as much as we can and call upon the heavenly light to illuminate our darkness so that we might see, as much as we are permitted, the image of God in us" (*On the Trinity* 9.1.1; 9.2.2). This human imaging of God is a call to authenticity, that is, to truth in word and action. The Son, the Word of God, was made flesh so that we might imitate him in living rightly, having "no lie either in the contemplation or in the operation of our word. Truly, this perfection of this image is for sometime in the future" (*On the Trinity* 15.11.20).

Spiritual Growth

Augustinian spirituality is firmly founded on the created reality of sanctifying grace, whereby human persons are made capable of welcoming the uncreated gift that is God, one and three. Although Augustine did not use the expression "sanctifying grace" and made no clear-cut distinction between created and uncreated grace, he spoke often of the interior and real renewal of the Christian by the action of the Holy Spirit and of the Trinity's presence in the soul. He referred to the Christian as one deified by grace that heals and transforms (*Exposition Ps* 49.2).

The state of grace is a state of charity in the person incorporated into Christ, the head of his Mystical Body (all Christians). Thus, persons are deified by the filiation that the Holy Spirit brings about by pouring love into their hearts. There is then an infused *habitus* in the soul distinct from the indwelling of the Spirit or the Trinity (*On the Wages and the Remission of Sin* 7.9; 8.10; 13.18). This makes possible a life of union with God in three Persons. It presupposes a central devotion to Christ as Savior-Physician and interior Teacher as well as to the Holy Spirit within the soul and within the Church. In the Church and sacraments the Holy Spirit acts generously to build up the Body of Christ. Through baptism and the Eucharist the Spirit pours love into the hearts of the faithful. This created *caritas* restores the likeness of God in them and makes them partakers of the divine nature (*Letter* 98.5).

The mystical aspect of Augustinian spirituality is the emphasis upon God's part in a person's communion with him. The love poured into human hearts by the Spirit grows through a prayer-life centered upon the indwelling Trinity. Intimacy with the divine Persons develops by degrees, as does the likeness to God.

Although Augustine began by trying to ascend to God through intellectual steps as philosophers did, he soon discovered in Scripture a pattern of steps that led from the purgative through the illuminative to the unitive way of approaching God. Souls of good will gradually became virtuous and eventually perfect to the extent that perfection is possible on earth. Scripture taught Augustine that ascent to God took place under the influence of the Holy Spirit. "It seems to me as you too perceive and as we believe, that there is no true and divine sanctification apart from the Holy Spirit. . . . Isaiah says that the Spirit of God will descend upon him who believes, the Christian, the member of Christ—the Spirit of wisdom and of understanding, of counsel and of fortitude, of knowledge and piety, the Spirit of the fear of the Lord" (*Sermon,* Frangipani I.17).

Longing for and opening to the gifts of the Holy Spirit enables the Christian to live the beatitudes. In so doing, the likeness to God increases, the image is re-formed. Communion occurs at the level of understanding and wisdom. But the fear of the Lord is the beginning of wisdom, and so the first step in the ladder of perfection is the fear of God's rightful punishment as one faces one's mortality in true repentance. On the second step of piety one becomes meek in docility to God's commands and to Holy Scripture. On the third step of knowledge one mourns one's own inadequacy, realizing the difference between Christ and oneself. On the fourth step of fortitude one thirsts for justice. On the fifth step of counsel one is enlightened to do merciful acts of love. On the sixth step of understanding one attains the purity of heart to be attentive to God and to see him as in a mirror. On the last step of wisdom, one contemplates God and as a peacemaker one lives in tranquility, seeing all things in God and God in all things.

So in the conversion experience, when fear initiates the ascent, there begins a remote preparation, intellectual and moral, for the stage of wisdom.

In his commentary on the Sermon on the Mount (I.3.10-13; 2.11.38), Augustine enriched these steps in the spiritual life by linking each gift of the Spirit not only with a beatitude but also with a petition of the Lord's Prayer, culminating in the petition for the coming of the kingdom. From the foregoing it is clear that the active and the contemplative life are both aspects of Augustinian spirituality. One seeks God by believing, loving, hoping, and preparing for contemplation by virtuous acts. God cooperates with the believer by conferring the gifts of understanding and wisdom. By love the understanding of God that is a perfection of faith becomes a certain perception of God. The gift of wisdom confers on a human person such likeness to God that by connaturality one experiences God in the act of contemplation. Contemplation occurs by the higher or intuitive reason under the action of the Holy Spirit. The result is union with God, a state called wisdom. This is what Christ came to accomplish and what his Church exists to achieve: the holiness of persons through a loving relationship with their God and with others. Grace is the perfection of relatedness. This is the kingdom desired by all who pray "Thy kingdom come."

This contemplative knowledge of God, an experiential knowledge, results from perfect charity and leads to spontaneous good acts. It is a state of intimacy with the divine Persons. The natural immediate principles of this knowledge are being, the true, the good, which are intuitively grasped by the mind in its first contact with reality and which are the mirror in which a person sees God, when illumined by the light of wisdom. In wisdom the pure of heart see God experientially as they are transformed into his likeness. Contempla-

tive life is a life unified in the love of the Lord and does not exclude the spiritual and corporal works of mercy. "No one should be so much at leisure that in leisure there is no thought of the neighbor's needs; no one should be so active as not to find time for contemplation" (*City of God* 19.19).

Spiritual Freedom

Augustine taught that under grace the will obtained a freedom to choose the good spontaneously and joyfully. He saw this condition of *libertas* as the development and perfection of free choice (*liberum arbitrium*). Under this graced freedom "we confide ourselves absolutely to our Liberator, attributing nothing to our merits. Surrendering ourselves affectionately to his mercy we do not let ourselves be overcome by the delights of bad habits drawing us into sin. Still tempted by their allure, we do not, however, yield to them" (*To Simplicianus* 66.3). This liberty can be lost by the free choice of a merely apparent rather than a true good. This happened to Adam and Eve in paradise.

Augustine's reference to this lost liberty has led some to say that he taught that human beings no longer have free choice because of Adam's sin. On the contrary, he distinguished between free choice (*liberum arbitrium*) and freedom (*libertas*) as between a capacity for spiritual freedom and the actuality of spiritual freedom. Moreover, *libertas* was restored by Christ, who strengthens the human will by charity through the Spirit's gift. In Book X of the *Confessions,* Augustine describes his experience of a developing *libertas.* He opened to the Lord the state of his soul, ". . . rejoicing with trembling in your gifts and grieving for my imperfection and hoping that you will perfect your mercies in me till I reach that fullness of peace which both my inward and my outward self will have with you when death shall be swallowed up in victory" (*Confessions* 10.30).

Freedom on earth evolving into the complete freedom of the risen life is a constant motif in the spirituality of St. Augustine. It requires an education concerning the kind of love that unifies the various psychic levels into a wholeness signified by wholeheartedness, or single-mindedness. Mature freedom is possessed by the authentic human person who is mindful of God, understanding and loving him. "Only from God the Father, through Jesus Christ, with the Holy Spirit do persons have the love of God through which they come to God" (*Against Julian* 4.3.33).

In loving God one makes God's will one's own. Then in doing one's own will one is doing the will of God. Augustine expressed this psychological experience by saying: "Love and do as you please" (*On the Epistle of John* 7.8). "And so with the Holy Spirit, by whose gift we are justified, we take delight in this, that we sin not, and that is freedom; without the Spirit we take delight in sin, and that is slavery" (*On the Spirit and the Letter* 16). Through Christ the Liberator the human person recovers the *libertas* lost in paradise and recovers a likeness to the Trinity, since love is the key that unlocks the door to spiritual freedom. God's love, made visible in Christ, engages human affections for the good.

The Rule of St. Augustine

Augustine's monasteries were intended to be communities wherein the ideal of the Christian life of love could be manifested as a witness to God's kingdom having come with Christ. Love for one another was to animate the monks if they were to be of service to others. "This is how all will know that you are my disciples, if you have love for one another" (Jn 13:35). Rather than being founded for a definite apostolic purpose like teaching or preaching, Augustinian monasteries existed to build up the Body of Christ. In his wholehearted adoption of St. Paul's doctrine of the People of God as the Mystical Body of Christ, Augustine saw the vocation of monks to be

that of acting in Christ's role of physician (*Christus medicus*) and improving the health of that body. There must be a harmony between the way a priest lives and what he teaches. That is why an original monastic order became a mendicant order. If love characterizes the life of Augustinian monasteries, and love cannot be contained within itself, it was inevitable for Augustinians eventually to be called mendicants, going out to give to others.

The Rule of St. Augustine (396–400) is not only the oldest surviving rule for religious in the West but also epitomizes the main orientation of Augustinian spirituality: union with others in a common love of God. It contains few regulations concerning government and penances; the emphasis is on charity, the highest goal of all Christian life. Therefore it admonishes sensitivity to the special needs of individuals. All admonitions are given in view of promoting harmony. The superior is reminded to see his role as that of servant to the community, and the members are encouraged to show mercy to the superior. The capacity to forgive and to be forgiven seems to be the most essential quality of the Augustinian monk.

All who enter the monastery must be "intent upon God." This means that they aspire to the graces of infused contemplation and prepare for them by obedience, reading Scripture, and meditation. They see their life as reproducing the first Christian community, in which all lived with "one heart and mind" for God, and in which all things were held in common and distribution was made according to need (see Acts 4:32, 35). At the end of the Rule, Augustine prayed: "May the Lord grant that you observe all these things in love, like lovers of spiritual beauty, burning with Christ's sweet perfume from your good way of life, not as slaves under the law but as free men established under grace."

The Rule recapitulates the main themes of Augustinian spirituality and also reveals the fact that the emphases in Vatican II documents are a renewal of this spirituality. One can cite here Vatican II's emphasis on the theological virtues as the center of Christian life, so that in Lent Christians should concentrate on increasing their love for God and others. There is also the emphasis on authority as an opportunity for exercising service rather than power and the encouragement of prayer and simplicity in lifestyle.

Who are those following the Rule of St. Augustine today? The Hermits of St. Augustine, loosely associated since the fifth century, were united in 1256 into the Order of St. Augustine. This order honors the Mother of God under the title "Our Mother of Good Counsel." Among others who adopted the Rule were the Canons Regular, the Premonstratensians (1120), the Dominicans (1235), and the Servites (1256). In the 14th century it was adopted by confraternities of hermits (the Pauline Fathers, the Ambrosians, and the Apostle Brothers) and confraternities of laymen (the Alexian Brothers, the Jesuates, and the Voluntary Poor). In the 16th century it was adopted by teaching orders, the Fathers of Christian Doctrine and the Piarists, and, more recently, by the Augustinians of the Assumption of Mary, called the Assumptionists, (19th century).

In addition to branches of these orders formed for sisters, some orders exclusively for women follow this Rule. They are the Bridgettines (1344), Annunciates (since 1500), Ursulines (1535), Salesian Sisters and the Poor Teaching Sisters of Our Blessed Lady (1833), the Magdalene Sisters of the Middle Ages (1224) and their modern counterparts, the Angelicals of St. Paul (1530), the Sisters of Our Lady of Charity of Refuge (1644), and the Daughters of the Good Shepherd (1692). There are also contemplative Augustinian nuns in some countries.

Through the Third Orders of the Dominicans, Augustinians, and Servites, the essentials of Augustine's Rule are practiced by lay people. Many other congregations of tertiaries followed suit. Augustinian spirituality is alive among these religious and lay people. Holiness is everyone's destiny. Augustine never proposed a lay spirituality as distinguished from a monastic one. These are different approaches to God. The level of charity is what makes one Christian better than another. Marriage with humility is better than virginity with pride (*Exposition Ps* 99.13). Clergy, religious, and laity build up the Body of Christ and work for a better life on earth for all as well as for the salvation of all. "There is one commonwealth for all Christians" (*The Work of Monks* 25.33).

In addition to the Order of St. Augustine, the core of the Augustinian family, there are Discalced Augustinians, a 16th-century branch emphasizing contemplation. They became an independent order in 1931. In 1958 another branch calling themselves Augustinian Recollects decided to search out the spiritual heritage of St. Augustine. They became an independent order in 1918. They work with the socially, politically, and culturally deprived. They are especially dedicated to the rapidly growing Spanish-speaking populations in the United States, the "Third World within."

Some of the Augustinian family who wholeheartedly accepted the Christian vocation to holiness have been canonized by the Church. First and foremost is St. Monica, the patroness of wives and mothers, who teaches constancy and confidence in prayer for the salvation of husbands and sons. St. Nicholas of Tolentino followed Christ from early youth. St. Clare of Montefalco received images of the Lord's passion upon her heart. St. Rita of Cascia was a widow who became an Augustinian nun at age thirty-six. She received the stigmata (a thorn in her forehead), and when a wish for a rose from her former garden was fulfilled although it was January, she became the patroness of impossible cases. She lived a life of suffering, and her last words were: Remain in peace and fraternal charity. Her body is incorrupt. St. John Stone died for his faith in 16th-century England, and Blessed Stephen Bellesini, the first pastor beatified by the Church, died of a plague contracted while helping his parishioners. St. Thomas of Villanova, elected archbishop of Valencia in 1544, with great charity reformed his diocese. After building schools for the young, he lavished his time on the poor and was known as the "Beggar Bishop."

Less well known are St. John of Sahagún (1430–1499), Blessed Alfonso de Orozco (1500–1591), and Venerable John Baptist de Moya (1570). In 1975 Pope Paul VI beatified Bishop Ezekiel Moreno, who restored Augustinian Recollect religious life and missionary activity in Latin America during the 19th century. In 1987 Pope John Paul II canonized St. Magdalen of Nagasaki, a Japanese Augustinian Recollect Tertiary, who was martyred by the Japanese in 1634. In 1989 two Augustinians were beatified by Pope John Paul II. Martin of St. Nicholas, born in Zaragoza, and Melchior of Saint Augustine, born in Granada, sailed to Japan in 1632 to assist the persecuted Christians and were burned alive at Nagasaki's Hill of the Martyrs. The causes of beatification of three 20th-century Augustinian priests and one Augustinian nun have been introduced.

The missionary spirit is alive among Augustinians today. They are on every continent, and the American Augustinians have established missions in Peru, Japan, Nigeria, and Ecuador.

Apart from those who live under the spiritual leadership of Augustine in the many religious orders following his Rule today, there have been outstanding individuals who have not only followed Augustine's spiritual direction but have deepened it and expanded its influence through their own study and writing. Belonging to this Augustinian tradition are St. Gregory the Great, St. Bernard of Clairvaux, William of St. Thierry, Hugh and Richard of St. Victor, Jan van Ruysbroeck, and St. Gregory Palamas. St. Bonaventure's spirituality, undoubtedly Franciscan, is nevertheless deeply Augustinian in its Trinitarian emphasis. St. Teresa of Avila said that her reading of the *Confessions,* which taught her to look for God within, was pivotal to her "second conversion." There is also an affinity between St. Ignatius' mysticism of the inner Trinitarian life and Augustinian spirituality. St. Elizabeth of the Trinity must also be included within this spiritual tradition. But because Augustinian spirituality is centered on the Trinity, who manifested their love for all human persons by the sending of Christ into the world, this spirituality is the common heritage of all religious orders and all Christian families.

See also BEATITUDE(S); BODY OF CHRIST; CONTEMPLATION, CONTEMPLATIVE PRAYER; CONVERSION; DIVINIZATION; EARLY CHRISTIAN SPIRITUALITY; FREEDOM; GRACE; HOLY SPIRIT; JOURNEY (GROWTH AND DEVELOPMENT IN SPIRITUAL LIFE); LOVE; MYSTICISM; PATRISTIC SPIRITUALITY.

Bibliography: M. Clark, trans. and intro., *Augustine of Hippo: Selected Writings,* Classics of Western Spirituality (New York: Paulist, 1984). M. Clark, "The Trinity in Latin Christianity," *Christian Spirituality: Origins to the Twelfth Century,* World Spirituality 16, ed. B. McGinn, J. Meyendorff, and J. Leclercq (New York: Crossroad, 1985) 276–290. A. Zumkeller, *Augustine's Ideal of the Religious Life* (New York: Fordham Univ. Press, 1986). G. Lawless, *Augustine of Hippo and Monastic Rule* (Oxford: Oxford Univ. Press, 1987). M. Clark, "Augustine: The Eye of the Heart," in A. Callahan, ed., *Spiritualities of the Heart* (New York: Paulist, 1990). M. Clark, *Augustine, Philosopher of Freedom* (New York: Desclée, 1959).

MARY T. CLARK, R.S.C.J.

AUTHORITY

Exousia in ordinary Greek usage denotes the ability to perform action, and secondly, the right or permission conferred by others. Close to *dynamis,* which connotes external power, *exousia* focuses on the inner reality. The Hebrew has no word for the abstract notion of authority, but the Septuagint uses *exousia* for God's power, which is sovereign, everlasting, and universal (Dan 4:14).

In the New Testament, Jesus receives God's *exousia* and shares it with his disciples. Mt 28:18 speaks of complete authority, the only such occurrence in the NT. Elsewhere Jesus teaches with authority (Mk 1:22; Mt 5:22), forgives sin (Mk 2:9), and shares with his disciples his authority to heal (Lk 9:1), expel demons (Mk 6:7), and proclaim the coming of the kingdom (Mt 10:7-8; Lk 9:2). All Christians participate in the authority of Christ, an authority clearly expressed by Jesus as service. NT authority not only implies ability to act and to decide within the community context but also suggests freedom and responsibility in the community. The Latin *augere,* "to increase" or "to enrich," suggests a relationship between the use of authority and the growth and fulfillment of another.

Authority in the Church comes from the presence of the risen Lord, whose Spirit all Christians share. Equality, freedom, respect, and love are characteristic qualities for the exercise of such authority and integral to building the faith community. The Christian exercise of authority is in service to others rather than in having power over others (Mt 20:25-28; Mk 10:42-45; Lk 22:25-27). Authority shared by all within the community opens us to mutual service and to communal discernment of direction as Church. Integrating freedom and responsibility within the institutional framework of Church and inviting members to full participation in the life, mission, and ministry of Church also correspond to the gospel challenge of authority.

See also FREEDOM; OBEDIENCE; POWER; SERVICE.

Bibliography: W. Foerster, "Exousia," TDNT, ed. G. Kittel (Grand Rapids, Mich.: Eerdmans, 1964) 11:562–575. J. Schutz, *Paul and the Anatomy of Apostolic Authority* (Cambridge: Univ. Press, 1975).

HELEN DOOHAN

AUTOBIOGRAPHY, SPIRITUAL
See SPIRITUAL WRITING, GENRES OF.

AVARICE
See DEADLY SINS.

AWE
See ATTENTION, ATTENTIVENESS.

B

BAPTISM

The term *baptism* comes from the Greek *baptizein,* meaning "to dip." The candidate for baptism is immersed into, or infused by, water three times while the minister of the sacrament in the Latin Church proclaims, "I baptize you in the name of the Father, and of the Son, and of the Holy Spirit."

Since the Second Vatican Council, much more emphasis has been given to baptism in the Roman Catholic Church. Many theologians feel that the post–Vatican II era will be known as an era of baptismal consciousness. The dignity and importance of each and every baptized person have been underscored. This represents a return to an older view of sacraments, favored by the New Testament evidence, where baptism and Eucharist were seen as the two premier sacraments. For centuries the sacrament of baptism had been overshadowed by stress on the sacrament of order, the prominence of the ministerial priesthood almost forcing into oblivion the importance of the priesthood of all the baptized. The earlier baptismal theology that viewed each Christian as "another Christ" gave way to a theology that viewed the ordained priest only as the *alter Christus.* Vatican II reversed this, redefining the Church, not in terms of the hierarchy, but first and foremost in terms of the baptized, the People of God (LG, chap. 2). This represented a return to an older ecclesiology of

communion (based on the baptismal unity of head and members within the Body of Christ) as opposed to a later ecclesiology of powers (based on the power given through the sacrament of order whereby one member, the priest, governed the life of the Church and offered the sacrifice).

The return to emphasis on baptism lies at the heart of much present Church renewal, including the importance of "full, conscious, and active participation" in the liturgy (SC 14). No longer just the priest but the entire gathered assembly, under the leadership of the priest, is viewed as the proper subject of the liturgical action.

The postconciliar renewal has contextualized the sacrament of baptism by clearly defining it as one of the three sacraments of initiation. In this vein the 1983 Code of Canon Law states: "The sacraments of baptism, confirmation, and the Most Holy Eucharist are so interrelated that they are required for full Christian initiation" (CIC, can. 842). Furthermore, post–Vatican II theology of baptism has stressed the sacrament's effectiveness in areas beyond the cleansing from original sin. Thomas Aquinas had stressed inward justification, the remission of sin, as the principal effect of baptism (ST III, q. 66, a. 1; q. 69, a. 1). Twentieth-century theology sees baptism in a larger vision as the sacrament by which the Christian community is constituted as Church, as Body of Christ, as People of God. In this approach baptismal theology is developed, not from the case of infants, but from the case of adults who, moved by the Spirit, embark upon a journey of faith that culminates in the sacraments of initiation. "Baptism is therefore, above all, the sacrament of that faith by which, enlightened by the grace of the Holy Spirit, we respond to the Gospel of Christ" (*Rite of Christian Initiation of Adults,* General Introduction, 3). This accounts more fully for the essential elements of personal faith and conversion.

On the symbolic level, water is key for an understanding of the Catholic spirituality of baptism. The universal role of water is grounded in its symbolizing the whole of potentiality; it is the source of all possible existence. Thus the creation account is grounded in the common image of life being drawn from the waters of chaos. The Book of Genesis begins: "In the beginning, when God created the heavens and the earth, the earth was a formless wasteland, and darkness covered the abyss, while a mighty wind swept over the waters" (Gen 1:1-2). The symbol of water in baptism, as in creation, combines the twofold meaning of water as both life-giving and death-giving. To this is finally added the theme of love. Water in the Hebrew Scriptures is the source of life. The blessed one is "like a tree planted near running water" (Ps 1:3). The soul longs for God as for water: "As the hind longs for the running waters, so my soul longs for you, O God" (Ps 42:2). Blessings and salvation flow from the water of God: "With joy you will draw water at the fountain of salvation" (Isa 12:3). Each and every person is invited to follow the inner pull that leads to drink at this source: "All you who are thirsty, come to the water!" (Isa 55:1).

This thirst is ultimately satisfied in the person of Jesus. The Samaritan woman at the well is invited to drink of a water that will quench thirst forever (Jn 4:14). Water had particular religious significance at the Feast of Tabernacles. On the last day of that feast, "Jesus stood up and exclaimed, 'Let anyone who thirsts come to me and drink'" (Jn 7:37). Jesus is himself the wellspring of life.

At the same time, water can be deathgiving. The great flood that covered the face of the earth in Noah's time was the result of forty days and forty nights of torrential rain (Gen 7). The Egyptians were violently drowned by the closing of the mighty waters of the Red Sea (Exod 15).

It is the third theme of water symbolism—love—that serves as a link between water as life-giving and water as death-giving. This particular aspect of water symbolism provides the greatest insights into the spirituality of baptism. It is ultimately love that conquers death, and the world's greatest act of love was the death of Jesus on the cross. Just as the Israelites of the Exodus were freed unto life by the death of their enemies in the waters, so all Christians have conquered sin and death through the crossover of Jesus. As a sign of love, Jesus washed the feet of his followers (Jn 13), and as a sign of the fruitfulness of his death, blood and water came forth from his pierced side (Jn 19). This water prefigured the water of baptism.

Baptism is at one and the same time a matter of death and life: "Are you unaware that we who were baptized into Christ Jesus were baptized into his death? We were indeed buried with him through baptism into death, so that, just as Christ was raised from the dead by the glory of the Father, we too might live in newness of life" (Rom 6:3-4). This reality was expressed architecturally by the early Christian custom of making baptismal pools in the shape of tombs. Those to be baptized descended the three stone steps representing Jesus' three days in the tomb, and then left by ascending the three steps on the other side.

Just as humankind was expelled from paradise by the sin of Adam, so by the death of the new Adam they reentered that same garden. Baptisteries were decorated

accordingly. Christ was frequently represented as the good shepherd surrounded by
his sheep in a paradisal setting of trees,
flowers, and fountains. The pools themselves were often octagonal, the number
eight representing the new, eschatological
era. The newly baptized were clothed in
white robes and entered into the life of
glory shared by the martyrs.

A final insight into baptismal theology
can be grasped by considering the feminine
image of Church as mother, who through
the waters of the font gives birth to a new
Christian. This feminine image of birthing
can be helpful for understanding not only
Church but also God. The gift of life, both
of nature and of grace, is communicated by
the act of love that giving birth is. The
human fetus is surrounded by amniotic
fluid, which has the composition of water.
It is significant that Jesus' statement to
Nicodemus, "Amen, amen, I say to you, no
one can enter the kingdom of God without
being born of water and Spirit" (Jn 3:5), is
situated in the larger context of the eschatological begetting of the members of the
Church through the pouring out of God's
Spirit.

This Church-mother imagery in the waters of baptism was beautifully expressed
by the 5th-century poem of Pope Sixtus III
that is found on the walls of the baptistery
of St. John Lateran, the cathedral of the
city of Rome:

"Here a people of godly race are born for
    heaven;
the Spirit gives them life in the fertile
    waters.
The Church-mother, in these waves,
    bears her children
like virginal fruit she has conceived by
    the Holy Spirit."

See also BODY OF CHRIST; CHURCH; LITURGY; PAS-
CHAL MYSTERY; SACRAMENTS.

Bibliography: J. Daniélou, *The Bible and the Liturgy*
(Notre Dame, Ind.: Univ. of Notre Dame Press, 1956).

D. Stevick, "The Water of Life," *Liturgy,* vol. 7, no. 1
(1987) 47–53.

GERARD AUSTIN, O.P.

BEATIFIC VISION

Among NT metaphors for eternal happiness, that of vision (Mt 5:8; 1 Cor 13:12;
1 Jn 3:2) has been prominent wherever theological reflection has based itself upon Aristotelian philosophy, which sees the intellect as the highest of human faculties, and
supreme beatitude as the attainment of the
intellect's greatest possible object. Benedict XII defined the beatific vision as the
definitive and unmediated enjoyment of
the very essence of God, totally gratuitous,
beyond faith and hope, overflowing in bodily delight (DS 1000). Karl Rahner explicitly integrated what had been said of
intellectual fulfillment in the beatific vision with the inseparability of the true and
the good. Love, therefore, must be integral
to that face-to-face knowledge of God that
constitutes human fulfillment. And, as
Jesus made clear, love of God in truth implies love for all that God loves.

The happiness metaphorically expressed
as beatific vision is, then, salvation of the
whole person in God, in relationship with
all other persons and all creation. It is a salvation begun in this life, shaped by the
moral decisions made in this life, though
fully realized only after death. It is, moreover, salvation beyond all earthly limits on
spirit and freedom, an intimate encounter
with God as that incomprehensible mystery who is not only the boundary of finite
knowing but its goal, wherein knowledge is
merged forever into ecstatic and all-
embracing love.

See also AFTERLIFE; BEATITUDE(S); ESCHATOLOGY;
FUTURE; HOPE.

Bibliography: K. Rahner, "The Life of the Dead," *More
Recent Writings,* Theological Investigations 4, trans.
K. Smyth (New York: Seabury, 1974) 347–354.

SUZANNE NOFFKE, O.P.

BEATITUDE(S)

Etymology

Makarios ("blessed," "happy") in Greek usage initially referred to the blessedness of the gods and later to freedom from worry or concerns. Aristotle first used "beatitude" (Makarism) in the technical sense. With the development of a set form, themes and usage expanded, but the focus remained on persons blessed or happy because of children, riches, righteousness, etc. *Eulogein,* meaning "to speak well of," "to bless," connotes praise and blessing of the gods in the Greek, or the act of blessing primarily in prayer and cultic forms when developed in Judaism. *Makarios* rather than *eulogein* is the foundation for the biblical understanding of beatitude.

Biblical Roots

Old Testament

Blessedness refers to persons experiencing the fullness of life because of trust in the Lord (Ps 40:4), deliverance (Ps 2:11), prosperity (Ps 127:5), or justice (Ps 146:5-7). The beatitudes recognize in the attitudes and behavior of another something worthy of honor and praise (Ps 1:1). These individuals are happy, fortunate, or blessed. The Hebrew Bible contains forty-five beatitudes used in prophetic-apocalyptic settings with their eschatological focus and in wisdom-cultic settings with their ethical orientation. Thus beatitudes include an aspect of promise with reference to future reward and the presentation of models to emulate with their implicit exhortation. The OT contains the ingredients for the form, content, and promise of NT beatitudes, emphasizing the conditions for and experiences of happiness.

New Testament

The NT contains forty-four beatitudes, twenty-eight of which are in the Gospels of Matthew and Luke. A distinctive feature of the beatitudes is spiritual joy resulting from the gift of salvation and participation in the kingdom of God (Lk 1:48; Mt 13:16; Jn 20:29; Rom 4:6-7). Many beatitudes focus on the paradoxical reversal of human values (Mt 5:3-12; 1 Pet 4:14). Others offer eschatological consolation (Mt 5:11-12; Lk 6:20-23), while still others focus on moral behavior and its rewards (Mt 5:7; 24:46; Jn 13:17; Jas 1:25). Several beatitudes refer to watchfulness and endurance (Mt 11:6; Jas 5:11), and a few come from heavenly voices (Rev 14:13; 16:15; 22:7). Only occasionally does this blessedness refer to God (1 Tim 1:11; 6:15). Beatitudes require openness in faith, which is the appropriate context for understanding their challenge.

The beatitudes contained in Mt 5:3-12 and Lk 6:20-26 provide the foundation for the Sermon on the Mount, the oldest summary of Jesus' teaching. The respective authors draw largely on existing tradition, Q (the source common to Mt and Lk), and OT imagery to interpret Jesus' challenge for their own communities. Strong parallels exist between Matthew's Sermon on the Mount and Luke's Sermon on the Plain. Q provides the basis for the introduction (Mt 5:1-2 // Lk 6:20a), actual beatitudes, and the sermon itself.

Underlying Jesus' pronouncements is the richness of the biblical tradition. The sermon portrays Jesus as Messiah, fulfilling the OT promises and inaugurating a new age through his word and work. Recognizable cross-references include the mountain imagery (Mt 5:1; Exod 3:1; Deut 1:6; 4:15); allusions to Moses and Torah (Mt 5:1-2; Exod 19:20; 34:4; Mal 2:4); mention of the poor (Mt 5:3 // Lk 6:20; Isa 61:1; Zeph 2:3; Lev 19:15); the meek (Mt 5:4; Ps 37:11; Isa 29:19); those who mourn (Mt 5:5 // Lk 6:21; Isa 61:2-3; Ps 126:5; Eccl 3:4); those who hunger and thirst for righteousness (Mt 5:6 // Lk 6:21; Ps 106:3; Ps 107:9; Amos 8:11); the merciful (Mt 5:7; Ps 37:26; Prov 14:21; Mic 6:8); the pure of heart (Mt 5:8; Ps 24:3-4,6; Prov 22:11); peacemakers (Mt 5:9; Isa 27:5; Ps 34:14); the persecuted (Mt 5:10-12 // Lk 6:22; Wis

2:18; Ps 119:86), as well as Luke's contrast of blessings and woes (Lk 6:20; Deut 27-28).

Matthew's Beatitudes

Matthew composes the Sermon on the Mount from sayings Jesus used in different settings, and, in the beatitudes, he alters the sequence of Q, adds phrases, such as "in spirit," "thirst after righteousness," and includes five additional beatitudes. In keeping with his Gospel's emphasis on the kingdom of heaven, used thirty-two times in this form only in his account, the Matthean Jesus promises the kingdom to the poor in spirit (5:3) and to those persecuted for righteousness' sake (5:10), thus bracketing the eight beatitudes with this promise and showing all the other attributes as essential to the kingdom.

With their similar structure, crisp form, and rhythmic sound, these happinesses lead to a culmination in Mt 5:11-12. The ninth beatitude also forms a transition to verses 13-16, using the second person rather than the emphatic third person of the previous eight verses. Mt 5:3, 4, 6 have roots in Jesus' ministry to the oppressed, the poor, the weeping, and the hungry. Additional references to the meek, the pure, the merciful, and peacemakers constitute a formidable platform for action, for Torah must be lived out concretely. While the Twelve comprise the primary audience of Matthew, these disciples represent the larger community, with the crowds as neutral observers. The challenge of righteousness in 5:6 and 5:10 applies to disciples who understand Jesus' message in faith and choose appropriate conduct as part of their response. These references to righteousness form an ending for beatitudes 1-4 and 5-8. The disciples' faith-response eventually separates them from the crowds, who remain astonished (Mt 7:28).

Jesus, as an eschatological figure and moral teacher, uses the beatitudes as the theological basis for his ministry. Matthew does not describe these moral demands as a new Torah but solidly bases them in the biblical tradition that Jesus faithfully interprets. While the author Matthew restates, rearranges, restructures, and reinterprets the material, his purpose is to adapt Jesus' message to the changing needs of his community, a Church now separated from Judaism and the synagogue.

Luke's Beatitudes

Luke's four beatitudes include those traceable to Jesus' ministry to the underprivileged and the culminating beatitude that Matthew adapted from Q. With greater emphasis than Matthew on economic realities and their alienating effects, Luke adds four woes to dramatize his points. He addresses disciples, clearly indicating future reward for what they experience "now." This present/future orientation reflects Jesus' ministry and calls for complete detachment with little spiritualizing of poverty, an approach consistent with Luke's gospel challenge of social justice. Luke also uses the second person plural, creating a personal challenge to his Church to show greater sensitivity to the poor and oppressed. Luke's interest and audience offer variations comparable to Matthew's adaptation of Jesus' message.

In general, these beatitudes are not an ideal but a way of life for believers in Jesus. The attitudes embraced become conditions for salvation, but in their acceptance lies the very energy needed to live the radical teaching of Jesus. Furthermore, the promise of future well-being offers hope to those now helpless and despairing.

Historical Development

Chapters 5–7 of Matthew's Gospel are the three most frequently mentioned chapters of the entire Bible in the early Christian writings, presenting a composite of Christian ethics to guide believers in their daily lives. The understanding of Jesus as offering an ideal of moral perfection surfaces in the writings of many, including Justin and John Chrysostom. Sections of the Sermon on the Mount were used against early heresies, such as those representing Jesus as radically breaking from Judaism and the tradition (Mt 5:17-18). Jesus' relationship to the Torah, therefore, emerges early in interpretations of the sermon. An understanding of the beatitudes lies within the interpretation of the sermon itself.

In the first commentary on Mt 5–7 from the 4th century, Augustine may have been the first to identify it as the Sermon on the Mount, and he viewed it as "the perfect measure of Christian life," containing precepts for the formation of that life. The sermon applies to all Christians, but Augustine uncovered a tension regarding Jesus' demands and the demands of the Torah. While Jesus' fulfillment of the Law demonstrates the integral relationship between the OT and the NT, Augustine raised a major distinction in the contrast of a greater righteousness presented by Jesus and a lesser one given to the Jews. He also saw a connection between the beatitudes and the gifts of the Spirit. Between Augustine and the Reformation, interpretation focused on how these demands practically apply to the believers.

Thomas Aquinas, in his *Summa Theologiae,* set a different tone with his distinction between "precepts" necessary for eternal salvation and "evangelical counsels" as optional approaches toward this end. Obligation or option sets a direction in interpretation that changes both the audience and the forcefulness of Jesus' teaching.

With the Reformation, different perspectives emerged. Martin Luther, in his sermons, took a polemical approach in order to modify extreme interpretations of "papists" and "enthusiasts." The sermon is valid for all Christians, not a select few, and Luther saw Christian life, through grace, producing the effects of the sermon, thus resolving conflict between faith and works. Furthermore, the sermon's challenge affects Christians in every aspect of life—to use Luther's distinctions, one's "office" or work for the kingdom in the world and one's "person" or spiritual relationship to God and others.

John Calvin had little time for distinction between "optimal counsels" and necessary commands, seeing the sermon as applying to all believers. His interpretations considered the teaching in all of Scripture and reflected a concern for the theological questioning regarding Jesus' relationship to the Law.

The Anabaptists represented an extreme approach that led them to a withdrawal from political life and to a rigid separation of Church and state. These varied approaches from Aquinas through the Reformation either limited the audience of the sermon to those following the counsels, demonstrated continuity between all aspects of life, thereby expanding the sermon's impact, or forced a split between the secular and the sacred reminiscent of earlier dualism. The complex interpretations in the contemporary period result from these different emphases. Notable works include those of Schweitzer, Kittel, Dibelius, Bonhoeffer, Jeremias, Davies, and Dupont, with many critical contributions in the last decade.

Meaning

Within the context of the sermon, we can now examine the specific meaning of the beatitudes. In Matthew's Gospel Jesus goes up the mountain, seemingly presenting his disciples with significant teaching. However, Mt 5:1-2 sees closure in Mt 7:28-29, where the audience includes disciples and crowds astonished at the teaching. While Jesus "opened his mouth," only a few "hear" his message, indicating that closeness to Jesus in faith is far more important than the actual audience of the sermon. Matthew conveys the solemnity of the instruction by Jesus' sitting posture, a rule in great Torah schools, by use of the mountain, and by allusions to Moses. Luke conveys similar importance by placing the sermon within the context of prayer and the call of the Twelve (Lk 6:12-16), underscoring faith and following Jesus as prerequisites for understanding. The crowds in both accounts must become disciples to truly respond to the message. Jesus is more than a "teaching master"; he is a "life master" (Meister Eckhart) as he delivers the challenging sermon in the Gospels.

The "poor in spirit" remind Matthew's community of 'anawim, the oppressed who are promised the kingdom of heaven. Jesus fulfills the prophecy of Isaiah 61 in his ministry by bringing promised salvation to those who accept God's initiative through him. "Poor in spirit" represents those empty, rejected, abused, who accept life's difficulties without bitterness, waiting for God's deliverance. They stand without pretense before the Lord, realizing their lack of self-sufficiency. Luke's beatitude, using the original challenge of Jesus, speaks to the blessedness of "the poor." While poverty itself is not considered blessed, physical conditions can reflect the attitudes of persons before God and others. The posture of being poor empowers the disciple for the demands that follow and constitute happiness. Luke's socioeconomic emphasis indicates the quality of detachment and his understanding of true riches, thus providing a basis for his strong social concerns, so integral to the mission of the Church.

"Those who mourn" reflects an attitude of total dependence upon God. The helplessness, insufficiency, and need that result from suffering, loss, hardships, or disappointment lead us to hope in something beyond our own capabilities. This vulnerability suggests the emptiness that opens us to God. Neither mourning nor being poor implies apathy, but a recognition of our need for God's grace and a readiness to receive comfort. Luke uses "weeping" and "laughing," concretizing the beatitude even further.

Being "meek" implies more than being humble, gentle, or trustful; rather, this beatitude refers to those empty before God, who recognize their total dependence. Instead of weakness or softness, it suggests our powerlessness without the Lord. Luke omits this beatitude in his series.

These first three beatitudes proclaim a new reality, namely, that the poor and alienated of society possess blessedness and the kingdom because of their present condition, and this situation has future implications. These beatitudes emphasize God's attitude more than that of the persons or groups in need, a revolutionary message embodied in Jesus, who aligned himself with the poor and outcast during his public ministry. Furthermore, beatitudes clarify the ways that Christians can reveal the kingdom in this world.

"Those who hunger and thirst for righteousness" suggests Matthew's concern for a right relationship with God and others. The language speaks of yearning for the fulfillment of the basic command to love God and neighbor, with the satisfaction of working toward that end. Such attitudes create an energy within believers to live in ways suggested by the beatitudes. For Luke, hunger is as concrete and tangible as his use of the poor and those who weep, aligning his blessings with the actual condition of oppression. In this beatitude Matthew adds "for righteousness," with Luke's account reflecting the earliest tradition.

Being "merciful" results from the mercy already shown us by God, an understanding from the OT, where the act of mercy or pardon is an attribute of God. Because we have experienced mercy, we can practice it (Lk 6:36-42). Furthermore, we extend mercy to those who are in the wrong, reflecting a basic attitude required of the believer, now called to be forgiving, understanding, and quick to relieve the suffering of all others. Judgment and condemnation give way to compassion toward those in need.

The "pure of heart" refers to singleness of purpose and loyalty toward God. The heart is the source of vision, aspirations, and direction, with integrity of purpose and sincerity in attitude challenged by this beatitude. This understanding is more basic than moral purity, for it deals with honesty and integrity in our entire being. Only this attitude leads us to the presence of God.

"Blessed are the peacemakers" implies an active participation in bringing about wholeness, reconciliation, and peace. Rather than pacifism, active engagement in establishing peace, showing love and concern for all, healing the brokenness of society, and dealing with conflict and alienation in positive ways are the beatitude's challenge. Insight for such approaches comes from a contemplative faith that expresses itself in service. Peacemakers are truly sons and daughters of God because of their reflection of attitudes present in Jesus' ministry.

"Those who are persecuted" marks the eighth beatitude in Matthew, and he qualifies the statement, "for the sake of righteousness," reminiscent of the fourth beatitude (Mt 5:6). Dedication to God and others that is visible in a way of life results in persecution, but also in participation in the kingdom. The previous attitudes of mercy, integrity, and peace are specific manifestations of righteousness, contradicting the values of the world. Living according to these mandates because of understanding Jesus' call in faith results in suffering.

The final beatitude in Matthew and Luke speaks more fully of persecution, hatred, and exclusion because of a commitment to Jesus, the Son of Man. These forms of abuse, ridicule, persecution, and slander reflect the prophet's fate, now the lot of disciples. In the midst of such suffering, believers rejoice because they realize the outcome, future reward, and transformational power of suffering. In this beatitude joy and gladness refer to present experiences in both Matthew and Luke. Such a culmination for the beatitudes represents the paradoxical values associated

with Christian life. Furthermore, the blessing is operative when these occasions arise, as opposed to the condition of life implied in the previous beatitudes.

The beatitudes are radical demands that require conversion in order to comprehend their challenge to believers and faith communities. Although we receive these beatitudes from Gospel writers who edit and adapt, they do represent continuity with Jesus' proclamation and ministry. Matthew exhorts, encourages, and challenges the behavior of his Christian community; Luke does likewise. Within the categories of people called "blessed" are those who embody the attitudes and qualities of life dedicated to the Lord. Internal disposition and external action indicate the full meaning of righteousness and ensure the blessedness, salvation, and joy promised by Jesus. While the beatitudes indicate earthly situations and heavenly realities, the eschatological blessings are both present and future, consistent with Matthew's and Luke's eschatology.

Jesus thus embodies the beatitudes in his life and ministry, becoming a model for his followers. While he is not the new lawgiver, he interprets Torah in a fuller way, affirming and developing its teaching. If Jesus fulfills the OT in his ministry, then his followers become the recipients of a similar challenge to radically fulfill his message in their lives as Church. The basis for response lies in the new relationship God establishes through Jesus with all believers. The beatitudes are requirements for all Christians so that the kingdom will be realized in a fuller way in this world. Rather than have us wait patiently, the beatitudes urge a spirituality in which we are peacemakers, comforters, etc. Integrity of purpose and appreciation that suffering accompanies prophetic action have practical implications for Christians striving to live out these gospel and ecclesial challenges.

The beatitudes in the NT assure us of God's acceptance and blessing, and inspire us to commitment and response. They recognize that we need God, and they become a spiritual energy, calling us to spiritual and ethical heights, while advocating qualities that are the antithesis of achievement and success. As with the entire life and message of Jesus, paradox often reveals the message of salvation.

See also BEATIFIC VISION; COMPASSION; HUMILITY; HOLINESS; JUSTICE; PEACE; POOR, THE.

Bibliography: J. Lambrecht, S. J., *The Sermon on the Mount: Proclamation and Exhortation* (Wilmington, Del.: Glazier, 1985). R. Guelich, *The Sermon on the Mount: A Foundation for Understanding* (Waco, Tex.: Word Books, 1982). M. Crosby, *The Spirituality of the Beatitudes* (Maryknoll, N.Y.: Orbis, 1982).

HELEN DOOHAN

BEAUTY

From its etymology and ordinary use, the word *beauty* (from the Latin *bellus,* meaning "pretty," "handsome," "fine") refers to what is pleasing. Such pleasure is associated with objects, experiences, and people.

Things are called beautiful when they embody shapes, colors, textures, or sounds in appealing proportions, expressing harmonious relationships. The word is used to describe a wide range of things, from the sculptured Venus de Milo to a Shaker basket or an Appalachian tune. Experiences are deemed beautiful when they connect with a reality beyond oneself (a sunrise or sunset) or when they make some meaning accessible (a ritual event that symbolizes a rite of passage). People are called beautiful when they are physically attractive or when they manifest a distinctive spirit of courage, determination, commitment. Examples in each of these areas stretch the breadth of the etymological definition, from "what is pleasing" to whatever conveys transcendence in its multiple manifestations to the viewer. However, beauty is an elusive quality and often is judged subjec-

tively, as indicated by the adage "Beauty lies in the eye of the beholder."

Purpose

Beauty can be considered an end in itself and/or a form for disclosure. Every "good" work of art can be called beautiful. What makes it good is the same quality that defines its beauty: the capacity to express something and in that communication to transform the person who encounters it. When some people listen to a Beethoven quartet, they know beauty. For a short time they may feel contained by the music, uplifted by it, changed by it. They may or may not impute further meaning to it. It is enough to appreciate it for what it is and does.

Beauty and Spirituality

Beauty reveals what is invisible. A quality of the divine (along with truth and goodness), beauty discloses God. A clear illustration is the work of medieval artists in sculpting and erecting cathedrals whose purpose is to express the glory of God. The extraordinary use of light, finely carved columns, figures, and decorative features, as well as the utter marvel of the proportions throughout the buildings, testify to this quality of God.

Beauty is a name for God. It not only unveils something about divine nature but also expresses something of the relationship God shares with humankind. Beauty is delight and also compassion. God rejoices in human goodness and suffers with human pain. A poignant example is the Cuzco cross created in Peru. It features a human figure with disproportionately large hands and feet nailed to the cross, connecting the redemptive activity of Jesus with the plight of the worker whose body is stretched beyond its limits. It symbolizes beauty found in truth. Beauty is darkness as well as light. The whole spectrum of creation exposes the breadth of God. Beauty is God's unpredictable activity and faithful partnership. God's beauty is recognized along a wide range of human experience, not the least of which is God's unfailing collaborative presence.

Beauty is much more than what is pleasing, though it is that also. It is an experience beyond words that touches the most profound recesses of our being and awakens us to a world beyond the daily grind. It invites affirmation both human and divine.

See also AESTHETICS; ART; CREATION; GOODNESS; TRUTH.

Bibliography: S. Langer, *Feeling and Form* (New York: Scribner's, 1953). H. Marcuse, *The Aesthetic Dimension* (Boston: Beacon, 1978).

JANET R. WALTON

BENEDICTINE SPIRITUALITY

Methodology

This article will be based entirely on the 6th-century *Regula Benedicti* (RB), which has served as the foundation document for most Western monks. Earlier treatises on Benedictine spirituality usually drew on the Life of St. Benedict found in the *Dialogues* of Gregory the Great, but contemporary scholarship recognizes that the saint presented there is more an expression of the spiritual ideals of the author than of objective biography. Granted that Gregory was a great propagandist for the cult of Benedict, and in spite of the fact that the Benedictines have always claimed him as one of their own, it is now agreed that he did not live under the Rule of Benedict. This example illustrates the difficulty of distilling a Benedictine spirituality from the writings of later monastic writers. There is too much diversity in monastic history to warrant such an enterprise.

The Rule itself seems to promote such pluralism, for it blends many different spiritual currents from the earlier monastic tradition. Modern research has discovered that Benedict depends much in his first chapters on an earlier work, *Regula Magistri* (The Rule of the Master), which

emphasizes an individualistic, anchoretic spirituality. Yet, in his later chapters Benedict leans more on cenobitic masters such as Basil, Pachomius, and Augustine. Although many of the important spiritual principles of RB are enunciated in the early chapters, this article will pay equal attention to the communal chapters of the Rule.

Even though the Benedictine Rule is eclectic, it still has a distinctive spiritual physiognomy, which can be delineated though not systematized. This spiritual core has served as an inspiration to Christians for fifteen centuries.

The Divine Approach
The Presence of God

The God of St. Benedict is essentially a high God, exalted and austere. Many passages of the Rule bear this out, but RB 7.26-29 will serve as one good example: "Accordingly, if the eyes of the Lord are watching the good and the wicked, if at all times the Lord looks down from heaven on the sons of men to see whether any understand and seek God, and if every day the angels assigned to us report our deeds to the Lord day and night, then, brothers, we must be vigilant every hour or, as the Prophet says in the psalm, God may observe us falling at some time into evil and so made worthless."

The reference to God as Judge is not casual. At least a dozen times (e.g., 3.11; 4.44; 7.64), Benedict refers to the Last Judgment, when God will call each one to a final accounting. Even though this image seems to extol the power of God at the expense of mercy, the effect is really the opposite: human authorities, and especially the abbot, are often warned that they will answer for any abuse of their office at the dread Judgment (2.6, 9, 38; 63.3; 65.22). The fierce Judge tenderly protects the weak from tyranny.

For Benedict, Christ has much the same role as God the Father. Nowhere is the earthly name Jesus ever used in RB, nor is any historical event of his life mentioned, except the death on the cross. In providing an etymology for the title *Abba,* RB 2.2 explains that it derives from Christ, who is our father. This surprising Christology was typical in the patristic age, and no doubt Benedict found it useful as a foil against the Gothic Arianism that pervaded 6th-century Italy. RB 27 invokes Christ the gentle shepherd, but more often Christ and God are subsumed in the term *Lord,* the object of reverential awe (Prol 3, 7).

RB locates the divine presence in predictable persons, places, and situations. Thus God is very present at the monastic liturgy of the Divine Office. "We believe that the divine presence is everywhere and that in every place the eyes of the Lord are watching the good and the wicked. But beyond the least doubt we should believe this to be especially true where we celebrate the Divine Office" (19.1-2). Because God is especially present in the liturgy, every aspect of its performance must be done with careful attention. It is a serious matter when human carelessness, such as tardiness, disrupts the service; the majesty of God is offended and due satisfaction must be made (11.11-13; 43.1-12).

Not surprisingly, the person in whom Benedict most concentrates the divine presence is the superior of the monastery, the abbot. Two well-developed chapters, RB 2 and 64, place the abbot on a broad theological base, with the former emphasizing God's sternness and the latter putting more emphasis on the divine gentleness. For the abbot, of course, this is a fearsome responsibility, but for the monk the thing is clear-cut: the will of God comes through the superior. "Almost at the same moment, then, that the master gives the instruction the disciple quickly puts it into practice in the fear of God" (5.9).

The hierarchical bias of RB is to be expected, given its feudal context. Less dependent on culture, though, and more reminiscent of the Gospels is Benedict's insistence that God is to be met in the *least*

likely circumstances and in the most unprepossessing persons. Thus RB 53, on the reception of guests, demands that they be treated as Christ himself, and the biblical text quoted is Mt 25:35: "I was a stranger and you welcomed me." The point of Matthew's parable is that we encounter Christ in those we least expect. It is clear that Benedict finds God in the poorest wayfarer more than in the rich benefactor. That is why the guestmaster must be one "whose soul is seized by the fear of God" (RB 53.21).

The one who cares for the sick must also be God-fearing, for those who are ill may be hard to accept. They, too, are warned to see God in the nurse, but the use of Mt 25:36, "I was ill and you visited me," indicates that the main burden is on the server, not the served. Here, again, faith in the "weak God" is necessary if Christ is to be found in "the least of my brethren." Another unlikely class of persons in whom Benedict sees God secretly at work is the youngest monks. They must be asked their opinion in chapter, "because God often reveals what is better to the younger" (3.3). Finally, a visiting monk should be asked by the abbot for his observations on what he has observed, for "it is possible that the Lord guided him to the monastery for this very purpose" (61.4). In all these cases the danger is that one might miss the Lord's approach in an unlikely guise.

Many of these marginal persons are given over to the charge of the cellarer, who is also described as "God-fearing" (31.2): "He must show every care and concern for the sick, children, guests and the poor, knowing for certain that he will be held accountable for them on the day of judgment." But the task is broadened: "He will regard all utensils and goods of the monastery as sacred vessels of the altar" (31.9-10). Benedict shows in the next chapter that he means this literally: all tools and goods are to be carefully handled by the workers and inventoried by the superiors. Still, to compare jugs and pots (*vasa*) to the sacred vessels is a strong theological statement about the divine presence in the lowliest artifacts. Far from mere bourgeois fussiness, the overall concern of RB that the material world be handled carefully is based on the conviction that it can and does bear divinity. Benedict may fall short of Francis's ecstatic mystical companionship with nature, but he reverences the world as penetrated with divinity.

In order to heighten and sustain awareness of the presence of God throughout the monastery, which is sometimes called "the house of God" (31.19; 53.22; 64.5), various sacralizing rituals are used in ordinary life. The conduct of meals, for example, is carried out in ways reminiscent of the liturgy in church. Table-waiters are blessed at Lauds both on beginning and ending their week of service (35.15-18), as is the table-reader (38.1-4). There is no talking at table lest the word of God be inaudible (38.5-9). The proper amount of food and drink is left to local discretion, but RB 39-40 quotes Scripture for guidance. Finally, those coming late for meals are penalized as much as those who are tardy for the Divine Office (43.13-19). All this is done to make the Lord more palpably present at monastic meals.

The Sovereign Action of God's Grace

Monastic life is a life of arduous spiritual striving. In fact, one of the main causes for the rise of the monastic movement after the Peace of Constantine was the desire on the part of some people to continue the old, rigorous Christian ethos of the persecutions and avoid the easygoing new ways of mass Christianity. Benedict, too, sees monasticism as hard "labor" (Prol 2) and judges the progress of a novice by how strenuously he "seeks God" (58.7).

Nevertheless, Christian life, whether monastic or not, is much more than a matter of merely human striving. Before one can move an inch toward God, God must take the initiative. The primacy of divine grace was taken for granted in the spiritual

writing of the Eastern Church, which always emphasized human ascesis. In the West, however, the Pelagian controversy boiled up about A.D. 400 and raged until the time of Benedict. Just before RB was written, a provincial council (Orange, A.D. 529, ratified by Rome in 534) decided in favor of Augustine and grace over against Cassian and the Lerinian monks, who opposed his extreme disparagements of human efforts. Benedict no doubt wrote with this decision in mind. That is probably why he would say the following: "If you notice something good in yourself, give the credit to God, not to yourself, but be certain that the evil you commit is always your own and yours to acknowledge" (4.42-43).

Other, gentler expressions of the divine sovereignty are expressed in RB Prol 9, where the sleeping Christian is exhorted to wake up to see the "sanctifying light" that is already shining, and in Prol 18, which has the Lord saying: "Even before you ask me, I will say to you, here I am." On the other hand, there are expressions of synergism (cooperation between human and divine) in Prol 4, 21, 35 and 41 that almost certainly would not have met Augustine's standards.

It could be objected, of course, that all these passages have been copied from the Rule of the Master, leaving us to guess how much Benedict really cared about the issue; nor is it reasonable to impose the criteria of systematic theology on a monastic rule, which has other concerns besides order and clarity. Nevertheless, Benedict creates elaborate structures where the transcendent dynamic is acted out on the human level.

The premier symbol of divine initiative is the abbot. He is "believed to hold the place of Christ" (2.2). Clearly his sovereignty lies in the realm of faith and not power politics. Since so many discussions in RB conclude on the note that the final decision is the abbot's, it is easy to get the impression that he has absolute power in the monastery. In fact, a careful reading of the entire Rule shows that there are social checks and balances on the abbot, but the abbatial office is still best understood theologically as a kind of divine ikon.

This is well illustrated by RB 3, on the decision-making process. Benedict wants the whole community to be consulted on matters of importance. In this he is pioneering, for no earlier monastic rule calls for such a thing. This does not quite make Benedict a democrat, however, since the entire initiative remains with the abbot. He alone can call the meeting, set the agenda, hear the "testimony," and make the final decision. This aspect of Benedictine doctrine has been faithfully adhered to by monks through the ages. So has the right of the monks to elect their own abbot, a prerogative often violated in the Middle Ages but honored in our time. Present-day canon law puts restrictions not found in RB on the abbot, but most modern Benedictine constitutions still give the abbot more power than other modern religious superiors have.

Perhaps the Benedictine abbot's most remarkable initiative on behalf of the Lord occurs in the legislation on penalties. RB 23–30 arranges for in-house excommunication for certain offenses, but there is no question of merely getting troublemakers out of the way. Indeed, it seems that the abbot's full attention must then be trained on the excluded person in the interest of conversion, rehabilitation, and reintegration (RB 43–46). RB 27 bids the abbot act toward the excommunicated like the shepherd in Luke 15:5, who leaves the whole flock to search for a single stray sheep, a reference to Jesus' own preference for the neglected and marginal. RB 28 also asks the abbot to act like the Divine Physician in searching for therapeutic remedies. Benedict even slyly advises the abbot to break the rule of ostracism (RB 25) by sending in *senpectae,* brothers skilled in winning over souls. In all this the abbot is to embody the divine preference for conversion over condemnation.

In some passages RB ascribes grace to the effects of Christ's cross, the fount of all blessedness for Christians. Prol 50 points to stability and patience as the best way a monk can participate in the salvific sufferings of Christ. In the third and fourth steps of humility, the obedience of Christ unto death is laid down as the basis for monastic obedience, even in unjust circumstances (RB 7.34–43). Probably the most subtle allusion to the primacy of Christ's saving act occurs in RB 72.11, where we are told, "Prefer nothing whatever to Christ." The complete quote, from Cyprian of Carthage, continues, "for he preferred nothing to us."

The action of the Holy Spirit twice carries out the divine initiative in the scheme of Benedict. At the end of the long "ladder of humility" that the monk must ascend by ascetic effort, the conclusion is: "All this the Lord will by the Holy Spirit graciously manifest in his workman now cleansed of vices and sins" (7.70). Just before this the monk is assured that hard effort will eventually give way to "delight in virtue" (7.69). Here asceticism gives way to true joy, which can only be given by God through the Holy Spirit. At this point morality becomes religious experience, a prolepsis of heaven. The same joy of the Holy Spirit is expected to suffuse the practice of Lent when it is carried out in the right manner (RB 49).

Monastic Response to God
Basic Religious Sentiments

The *reverential awe* that the monk ought to experience in the face of the holiness of God receives strong expression in RB 7.10-11: "The first step of humility, then, is that a man keeps the fear of God always before his eyes and never forgets it. He must constantly remember everything God has commanded, keeping in mind that all who despise God will burn in hell for their sins, and all who fear God have everlasting life awaiting them."

This ferocious passage seems calculated to inspire abject terror, but in fact that atmosphere is far more prevalent in the Rule of the Master than it is in RB. What Benedict wants to inculcate is reverence, the basic religious sentiment that characterizes all genuine religious experience. The fear of the Lord that RB often calls for (Prol 29; 2.36; 65.15; 72.9, etc.) is not so much the rudimentary fear of hell that humility is meant to transcend (RB 7.69), but what Prov 1:7 calls the "epitome of wisdom."

Reverence is an attitude that Benedict invokes in many situations. Sometimes it is demanded during public or private prayer (9.7; 11.3; 20.1). Elsewhere reverence is called for as the motivation for silence (6.7), careful movement (52.2), respect for clergy (60.7), honor for elders (63.12), and delegated authority (65.16). In every case the monk acts reverently because he is mindful that God is present to all these transactions. Remembering (and not forgetting), a stance of religious awareness closely associated with fear of the Lord in RB 7.10-11, is frequently used by Benedict as an introduction to biblical quotations (2.30; 2.35; 64.13; 4.61; 19.3; 31.16). For Benedict, the scriptural word is an especially powerful presence of God. The Rule is shot through with biblical quotes and allusions, some of which are presented as coming directly from the mouth of the living God (Prol 8, 10, 15, etc.).

If reverence is the monk's reaction to the divine majesty, *humility* is the reflex sentiment experienced in regard to the self. Compared to the all-holiness of the Creator, the creature feels the weight of unworthiness and impotence. When low self-esteem is rightly diagnosed as a spiritual problem, RB 7, on humility, can cause serious misgivings. This long, elaborate treatise seems to promote a servile mentality, but it should be remembered that Benedict assumes a mature subject, free and ready to move past mastery to self-gift. No one is expected to express unfelt humility, but once that virtue becomes operative, it will seek expression in certain behavioral signs.

One of the most notable signs of humility in RB, and in many ancient monastic texts, is tears of compunction. For the old monks, to weep freely for one's sins was a privileged gift of God and an infallible index of conversion. Moreover, Benedict takes for granted that heartfelt tears will accompany deep prayer (4.57; 20.3; 49.4; 52.4). This high valuation of contrition is doubtless the reason why the Rule roundly condemns what it takes to be a countersign, namely, laughter (4.53-44 and 7.59-60). Today a sense of humor is considered necessary to spiritual and mental health. It must be recalled, though, that the early writers were more concerned with theology than psychology: laughter to them meant forgetfulness of creaturely indigence.

Yet Benedict still thinks a grim atmosphere is inimical to spiritual health. According to him, *joy* ought to prevail in monastic life. But it is also clear from the contexts where this word occurs (Prol 49; 7.39, 69; 49.7) that this joy is a spiritual state that runs far deeper than mere happiness. The joy that ought to permeate the monastery is a firm sense that despite life's trials, God has not ceased to love us, and our salvation is proceeding apace. For Benedict, true Christian joy can only come through suffering along with Christ.

Clearly, Benedict wants no sadness in his monastery, yet the sadness in question here is not psychological depression but something akin to spiritual despair. Nonetheless, difficult social relations can drive people toward an abandonment of hope. That is why Benedict warns the monks not to sadden one another unnecessarily. This especially applies to those to whom others must have recourse for their daily needs: the cellarer is admonished three times not to sadden the community (31.6, 7, 19). Still, no one is ultimately dependent on others for joy or sadness. Much depends on the state of a person's own heart, so Benedict advises the community not to elect an angry or violent abbot (64.16); he in turn should choose peaceful, joyful cooperators (31.1).

The teaching of RB on joy and sadness shows that Benedict puts great store on a good attitude in his monks. In contrast to the Rule of the Master, where the person is assumed to be an essentially passive object of abbatial direction, Benedict expects that ideals will be fully internalized and implemented. This spiritual maturity is called "good zeal" in RB 72, and it is set in contrast to "evil zeal of bitterness," which is a species of religious fanaticism. Zeal appears elsewhere in the Rule (4.66; 64.16; 65.22) as political intrigue that infuriates the conservative Benedict. Still, he realizes that complete docility is too high a price to be paid for order. There is no substitute for high motivation in the religious enterprise. This is Benedict's good zeal.

It is probably a desire to translate good zeal into action that prompts Benedict to urge the monks to "hasten" here and there, to do things "without delay" (Prol 13, 22, 44, 49; 5.4; 7.5; 22.6). Furthermore, his abhorrence of tardiness (RB 43; 47) should not be set down to a fastidious or impatient personality. This is not to deny that the author has put his personal stamp on the Rule; it is merely to insist that ancient monastic rules were intent on putting into literal practice spiritual ideals that tend to evaporate unless lived out in concrete forms.

When all is said and done, the essential Christian attitude is *love*. This is the only fitting response to God's loving initiative, and it is the basis of human relations. Benedict is well aware that all Christian and monastic virtues are subsumed under the rubric of love, so he devotes the penultimate chapter of his Rule mostly to this topic. RB 72 is a grand finale in which all topics previously discussed are summarized in terms of love. This treatise, which takes the form of aphorisms resembling those in 1 Cor 13, gives a closing unity to the document; it is now seen that all monastic values, whether anchoretic or cenobitic, must serve love.

The love that is preached in RB 72 is not romantic or idealistic but involves concrete interpersonal virtues, such as mutual respect, patience, obedience, and selflessness—precisely the behavior that makes it possible for people to live together in harmony over a lifetime. Considering the lack of privacy in ancient cenobitic life, it becomes obvious how practical this chapter on mutual forbearance was. Today most Benedictines have private rooms and ample social space, but the teachings of RB 72 remain pertinent because of the modern tendency toward individualism, the bane of cenobitic life.

RB 72 is characterized by utter realism about human weakness. In urging monks to "support with the greatest patience one another's weaknesses of body or behavior," Benedict admits that infirmity is found in abundant supply in the monastery. The word *infirmus* ("weak") appears twenty-two times in RB. Because Benedictines often live with the same group of people for life, they become very well acquainted with the faults of one another. The temptation is to think that a change of place and companions will be the solution, but the faults go with the person. The only Christian solution is patience, a virtue that RB often associates with the cross (*passio*) of Christ (Prol 50; 7.35; 36.5; 58.11).

Monastic Practices

Probably the central monastic practice required by Benedict is *obedience*. The first few lines of the Prologue (1-3) describe obedience as a turning back to God from a way of slothful and sinful disobedience. This borrowing from an earlier baptismal homily virtually equates obedience with becoming a Christian and a monk. Other parts of RB, though, reduce the meaning of obedience to something much more specific: subordination to the directives and interests of others.

RB 5 presents what is probably best termed an anchoretic view of obedience. In this perspective, largely borrowed from the Rule of the Master, the individual is taught to distrust his own judgments, which are deemed corrupt. The only way out of the trap of self is total dependence on a spiritual master, the abbot. RB 5 emphasizes the need for cheerful, ungrudging obedience as befits a free person, but Benedict leaves no doubt anywhere that obedience to the abbot is demanded of every monk.

Nevertheless, life in community involves more than a master-disciple relationship. There are many persons to attend to; in fact, no one is beneath consideration. RB 71, on mutual obedience, admits this: "Obedience is a blessing to be shown by all, not only to the abbot but also to one another as brothers, since we know that it is by this way of obedience that we go to God." This is a good reminder that the only religious reason for obedience is to carry out the will of God. But God speaks to the Benedictine monk through many channels: Scripture, tradition, the magisterium. Add abbot and community to this list, and it is evident that the Benedictine must pay attention to many authorities. Cenobitic obedience is polyvalent and not unidirectional.

If *asceticism* is defined as rigorous bodily self-denial, the Rule of Benedict does not seem to be particularly attached to that kind of practice. True, it continues the ordinary monastic exercises from the earlier tradition, but it seems rather reluctant to put as much emphasis on them as was sometimes done by the early monks. The important monastic custom of vigils— prayer in the night—is carried on with no great stress on its penitential aspects. In fact, the Benedictine horarium (RB 48) does not break the night with prayer but merely moves retirement to sunset, with vigils about 2 A.M. (RB 8).

The other ascetical pillar, namely, fasting, is given ample discussion in RB 39–41, but the approach is relatively balanced and mild. Benedict notes wryly that the monks of old did not drink wine at all (40.6), but since his monks insist on it, they must be moderate. The author hesitates to prescribe the amount of food and drink for others (40.2), but he does provide a fairly humane regimen, considering the ordinary diet of that time and place. Overall, Benedict seems to value moderation and good order more than ascesis. This is clear from his chapter on Lent (RB 49), where all special penitential practice must first be cleared with the abbot.

Probably the basic Benedictine asceticism is the *common life* itself. This comes through plainly in RB 34, on the distribution of goods. Here the question of poverty is discussed in purely cenobitic terms and in a manner that shows the author is able to sift the monastic tradition for principles that square with human realities rather than with abstract ideals. The Rule of Pachomius forbids a monk to have anything the others do not have, but Benedict prefers to follow Augustine's principle of distribution according to differing needs. The purpose of this nuanced approach is to produce peace.

Benedict is well aware that there is another whole approach to the question of goods. Indeed, he presents the individual, ascetical teaching of Cassian on avarice in RB 33. In that system, one eschews greed in order to keep the heart pure and free of defilement. But a cenobitic approach to virtue must be centered on the needs of others, as is shown in RB 34. In addition, much attention is paid to interpersonal relations. It is not enough to give some more and some less. Those who need more should feel humble at their weakness, while those who need less will thank God for their strength and feel no envy at their neighbor's abundance. Such is the delicate mechanism of Benedictine common life in peace.

The final Benedictine activity that will be discussed here is also one of the least understood, namely, *lectio divina.* The medieval monastic libraries were repositories for much of the learning of classic culture, and so the monks got a reputation for erudition. Yet learning as such has no place in Benedict's scheme of things. RB 48 seems to promote learning, for it requires the monk to "read" up to three hours a day. But this is not reading for information; it is essentially a program to form the heart and mind with the word of God.

Contrary to our habit of silent, rapid reading, the ancients read aloud even when alone. In this manner the text made a greater impression because more senses were involved in the process of reading. For the monk, Scripture, and especially the psalms for the Divine Office, had to be memorized because of the scarcity of books. But biblical texts were also learned by heart for private use in *meditatio*. This did not mean mental reflection on a passage so much as its verbal repetition from memory. Since daily life in preindustrial monasteries involved much time spent in simple, repetitive tasks, biblical prayer-phrases could be "ruminated" all day long.

It would not be true, though, to claim that Benedict's *lectio divina* was restricted to memorization of Scripture. Certainly some monks, and especially those deputed to teach the rest, were expected to study the Bible in some depth. The old monastic commentaries on the sacred text show that these more learned monks spent long hours confronting the word of God in a systematic fashion. Yet little of what they wrote strikes a modern reader as true exegesis. Often the commentator's mind follows a rather intuitive, meandering path through similar sounding words and phrases from his scriptural memory. Most passages are interpreted rather fancifully as referring to the life of prayer and contemplation. This is to be expected from people who used the Bible in a very practical and personal way as the doorway to prayer. In fact, *lectio divina* was and is a peculiarly Benedictine form of prayer.

Benedictine spirituality, then, is based on the Rule of Benedict, one of the classic expressions of monastic Christianity. It was written for a single community in an age remote from our own, but its evangelical faith and its human wisdom are so profound that it has nourished countless Christians through the ages.

See also ASCETICISM; COMMUNITY; COMPUNCTION; GRACE; HUMILITY; JOY; LECTIO DIVINA; LOVE; MONASTICISM, MONASTIC SPIRITUALITY; OBEDIENCE; TEARS, GIFT OF; ZEAL.

Bibliography: *La Règle de saint Benoît,* ed. and comment. A. de Vogüé and J. Neufville, Sources Chrétiennes 181–186 (Paris: Les Editions du Cerf, 1971–72). *RB 1980: The Rule of St. Benedict in Latin and English with Notes,* ed. T. Fry, I. Baker, T. Horner, A. Raabe, M. Sheridan (Collegeville, Minn.: Liturgical Press, 1981). P. Puniet, "Saint Benoît: III. La Doctrine Spirituelle," *D.Spir.* (Paris: Beauchesne, 1937). T. Kardong, *The Benedictines* (Wilmington, Del.: Glazier, 1988). T. Kardong, *Commentaries on Benedict's Rule* (Richardton, N. Dak.: Assumption Abbey Press, 1987).

TERRENCE G. KARDONG, O.S.B.

BIBLE

See SCRIPTURE.

BIOGRAPHY, SPIRITUAL

See SPIRITUAL WRITING, GENRES OF.

BLACK SPIRITUALITY

See AFRICAN-AMERICAN SPIRITUALITY; AFRICAN SPIRITUALITY.

BLOOD

Throughout the ancient Middle East, blood was understood to be the seat of life for humans and animals. For the Hebrews, the very breath of God, which had given life to the creature (Gen 2:7), resided in the blood. Hence blood was sacred and reserved to God (Gen 9:4; Lev 17:14; Deut 12:23) and could not be drunk by humans. Blood played an important part in sacrifices and any communication with God, since it represented the divine presence in every living creature, thus creating a bond between the divine life and all creation. Blood protected the Hebrews from the destroyer in Egypt (Exod 12:23) and signified the bond of God's covenant with the people (Exod 24:8).

Blood within creatures was a sign of life; blood spilled was a sign of violence and death. There are over four hundred references to blood in the Bible, and many are related to wrath (e.g., Isa 63:1-4), suffering (Rev 6:10), cosmic catastrophe (Rev 6:12; 8:7-8; 16:1-6), and death.

The NT came to understand the death of Jesus as a sacrifice and atonement for sin. The shedding of his blood on the cross became a sign of the continuation and culmination of the tradition of sacrifice as a means of communication with God. Just as the blood of the sacrificed animals purified Israel from its sins, so now the blood of Christ ransomed believers from the bondage of sin (1 Pet 1:19). This theological idea is worked out in greatest detail in the NT in the Letter to the Hebrews. The blood of Christ, then, symbolized God's redeeming and reconciling activity in the world (Col 1:25; Eph 2:13), as well as the vindicating power to rescue those who suffered in Christ's name (Rev 7:14).

The symbolism of the blood of Christ finds its most powerful focus in the celebration of the Eucharist, based on Jesus' offering of the blessing cup at the Last Supper, identifying the wine (the blood of the grape) with his own blood (Lk 22:20 and parallels). The ancient taboo against drinking the blood is lifted; Christians are now enjoined to partake of it, so as to participate in the divine life, even to life eternal (Jn 6:25-71).

The symbolism of the blood of Christ has remained a powerful focus for Christian spirituality throughout history. In the patristic period it centered around martyrdom (shedding one's blood in witness to Christ) and the Eucharist as the very presence of Christ's body and blood in the midst of the community.

The controversies over the nature of the real presence of Christ in the Eucharist led to many "blood miracles," such as hosts bleeding in the hands of doubting priests. These, and the importation of purported relics of the passion of Christ from the Middle East, led to a proliferation of shrines to the blood of Christ throughout Europe. More than two hundred such shrines survive to this day.

The height of devotion to the blood of Christ came in the Middle Ages in the West. The chronic suffering of many, compounded by the onslaught of the Black Death, led to a deep devotion to the suffering Christ. Attention to various aspects of the life of the suffering Christ arose at this time, including devotion to the seven bloodsheddings of Christ. Toward the end of the Middle Ages pious associations or confraternities came to be formed, both for devotion to the passion of Christ and as a vehicle for the reparation of sin.

The 19th century witnessed a revival of interest in the spirituality of the blood of Christ. Fifteen religious institutes were founded in the Roman Catholic Church (and one in the Church of England) with the blood of Christ as a central aspect of their charism and spirituality (often under the title of the "Precious Blood," after the Vulgate rendering of 1 Pet 1:19). Devotion to the blood of Christ was fueled in this period by a reaction to Jansenism; the blood of Christ represented God's unbounded love against the sterner image of God proposed by Jansenist theology. Inasmuch as this reaction coincided with the Romantic period in Europe, it produced a literature that today seems florid and sentimental to many tastes. In the English-speaking world, Frederick Faber's *The Precious Blood* gave the devotion wide propagation.

The devotion to the blood of Christ seemed to be a casualty of the liturgical revival following Vatican II, but it has received new impetus from Latin America, where it has become a vehicle for expressing the suffering witness of the poor and oppressed.

See also EUCHARISTIC DEVOTION; JANSENISM; MARTYRDOM; SYMBOL; WESTERN MEDIEVAL SPIRITUALITY.

Bibliography: F. Faber, *The Precious Blood; or, The Price of Our Salvation* (London: Burns and Oates, 1860). R. Schreiter, *In Water and in Blood: A Spirituality of Solidarity and Hope* (New York: Crossroad, 1988).

ROBERT J. SCHREITER, C.PP.S.

BODY

The body is the physical dimension of existence, the corporeal, material nature of the human being. In writings on the spiritual life, "body" is often distinguished from, or contrasted with, "soul" or "spirit." The body has only recently become a separate object of study for theology and spirituality; formerly the distinctive features of human existence were seen to lie in the rationality of human beings, their self-consciousness, their capacity to know God. The body is what connects human beings to animal life; it has been understood as the "lower" aspect of human life. Yet because of God's word in Genesis that all creation is good, and even more because of the incarnation, Christian spirituality has always condemned attitudes that regard the body as evil (e.g., Gnosticism).

Since Vatican II, a general shift away from dualistic categories has led to a more holistic understanding of the person, with a greater appreciation for the physical and secular dimensions of human life. Recent studies have also demonstrated the complexity of the ways in which the body has been understood in Christian spirituality. Disciplines of the body are often indicative of ways in which Church and society deal with mortality, sexuality, male-female relationships, and power.

Biblical Roots

In the OT the term *basar* is the word most often used to designate the body. Translated both as "body" and "flesh," it denotes both the whole person and the strictly physical dimension. There is no specific term, as there is in Greek thought, for soul as distinct from body, although the terms *nepesh* and *rûaḥ* ("neck" and "spirit," respectively) are also used to designate the person. The body was created by God and was therefore good (Gen 1:31). But the body was also the focus of a set of complex regulations regarding ritual purity (see Lev 12–15; 18). Bodily discharges (e.g., menstruation, childbirth, seminal emissions) rendered a person ritually impure (Lev 18), as did touching a dead body (Lev 21:1). Sexuality was carefully regulated, and severe penalties were imposed on those who disregarded its importance (e.g., in adultery; see Exod 20:14), although it was understood to be fundamentally good. All were expected to marry and produce children. Immortality was connected with the body, in that some Jewish ideas held that one lived on in the blood of one's descendants.

In the NT the story is more complex. While Jesus healed many people of bodily ailments, these healings were always connected with the faith of the one healed (e.g., Mt 8:1–17; Mk 5:21–43; Lk 7:1–10). Jesus also spoke of the relative unimportance of the body in relation to the things of heaven (Mt 10:28; Lk 12:4-5). In Jesus' vision of the kingdom of God, there was an intrinsic connection between the physical and the spiritual, the love of neighbor and the love of God.

It is in the Pauline literature, however, that a distinct theology of the body emerges. The term *body* is one of the most fundamental in Pauline thought and also one of the most complex. In speaking of the body, Paul makes a distinction between two Greek terms for body, *sōma* and *sarx*. *Sōma* denotes the person as a whole. It includes the physical, external dimension of human personhood, including sexuality, but it does not mean *only* the physical. The *sōma* is the basis for human life in the world, but it is ultimately meant for God (see 1 Cor 6:19-20; 2 Cor 5:6-8). *Sōma* is connected with but not identical with *sarx,* which may be better translated as "flesh," in the sense of human weakness and mortality. In Paul's understanding, *sarx* is what separates us from God. This is not to say that human physicality is inherently evil but rather that in their fallen state, human beings are weak, alienated from God, vulnerable to sin. *Sarx* is symbolic of this human frailty. To live "according to the flesh" is not merely to live carnally, but to live according to oneself, the law rather than the gospel, in separation from God (see Rom 7:18; 2 Cor 4:11). Ultimately the body (*sōma,* not *sarx*) will be raised up, as God raised up Christ.

Historical Developments

As Christological doctrine developed in the early centuries of Christianity, the importance of Jesus' human body became central. The doctrines of the incarnation—that the Word became flesh and dwelt among us (Jn 1:14)—and of the resurrection—that the body of Christ was raised up by God—have significance both for Christology and for theological anthropology. For Christology, Jesus' full and complete humanity was affirmed and reaffirmed against those who denied his human bodiliness (e.g., Gnostics). The most complete theological statement of Jesus' humanity was made at the Council of Chalcedon (451), which declared that Jesus Christ was "true God and true man." For theological anthropology, Jesus' human nature became both the model for all humanity and the promise of a glorified humanity. The "body of Christ" became the symbol for the Church.

The importance of Greek thought regarding the body, especially in the early centuries of Christianity, cannot be overstated. Gnosticism, with its dualistic framework of good against evil, soul against body, posed a powerful challenge to Christian ideas of the body. If the body was

evil, created by the evil god of the OT, then one either practiced extreme asceticism or showed one's disregard in hedonism. Irenaeus (ca. 130–ca. 200) defended the Christian idea of the incarnation, unacceptable to Gnostic thought, and its implications for a positive regard for the body. But the Neoplatonic ordering of the cosmos, widely accepted at this time, with material reality existing as the result of a fall from divine grace, and therefore of the body's subordination to the soul, nevertheless exerted a strong influence on Christianity. Consequently a certain suspicion of the body marks much of patristic and medieval spirituality.

With the emergence of Christian monasticism in the 3rd century, asceticism came to be seen as a "higher" form of life than marriage, and practices of bodily mortification took on great importance. The increasing practice of clerical celibacy was one consequence of this development. Writers such as Jerome (ca. 342–420) proclaimed the superiority of virginity over marriage. But no single author had more significance for a theology of the body than Augustine (354–430). While the connection between the body and sin had been made by Paul and in the extreme by the Gnostics, Augustine's interpretation of the Genesis account of sin made an explicit connection between human sexuality and the transmission of original sin. Adam and Eve's sin was *concupiscence,* the desire of the self for its own sake, and was manifested primarily, though not exclusively, in sexuality. Every sexual act was at the same time an act of sin and could only be mitigated by the partners' intent to conceive a child. But it was nevertheless through the sexual act that sin was transmitted to the child. Sexual intercourse for the sake of pleasure alone was sinful. Yet Augustine was not a Gnostic, despite his youthful Manicheanism; the body was not evil but problematic. The body, for Augustine as well as many subsequent thinkers, was the place where the battle against sin was primarily fought. His ambivalence toward the body remains characteristic of Christian spirituality in that the body is seen as both the locus of sin and the means for salvation.

The growth of monasticism in the Middle Ages continued the Neoplatonic emphasis on the subordination of the body to the soul. In addition, the severity of physical life, with the constant threats of disease and natural disasters, contributed to a deemphasis on the physical and an elevation of the spiritual as possessing true reality. Since the 3rd century, groups of men and women had left family and worldly status behind and entered into a life which was devoted to God alone and which stressed bodily mortification. Although many of these early monks were overzealous in their ascetic practices, the *Sayings of the Desert Fathers* (ca. 350) continually stressed moderation. In his Rule, Benedict (ca. 480–ca. 550) describes the ideal monastic life as one balanced by work and prayer.

Throughout the Middle Ages, the emphasis of spirituality was on the discipline of the body through fasting, sexual abstinence (practiced periodically by the laity), and other practices that demonstrated the body's subordination to the spirit. Although at times bodily discipline went to extremes, sometimes with the implicit support of the Church, the prevailing attitude toward the body was that it needed to be controlled by the "higher," spiritual dimensions of the person. The language of "hatred" of the body was frequently used, yet the body was not understood, at least in mainline Christianity, to be intrinsically evil. And while vowed religious life was seen as a nobler form of life than marriage, a major step toward recognizing the importance of the body, sexuality, and marriage was taken when marriage was recognized as a sacrament in the 12th century. Vowed religious life was not so recognized, despite the efforts of some to accord it this status.

Thomas Aquinas's (1225–1274) theology represents another important point in the theology of the body. Instead of the Platonic ideal of the forms, where true reality exists immaterially, Aquinas relied on Aristotle's theory of the dynamic relation between matter and form. Material reality then became a source for understanding the nature of reality itself. Aquinas's development of "natural law" as both a metaphysical and moral category has had and continues to have a profound influence on how the body functions in Catholic theology. Because "nature" is interpreted as a way in which God's will is revealed, the workings of nature, as seen in the body, provide a lens for understanding God's work in the world. Aquinas therefore interpreted bodily and sexual difference as having both metaphysical and moral significance; i.e., men's "active" sexuality rendered them more like God, whereas women's "passive" sexuality was subsequent and subordinate to the male's. In Aquinas's theology, men possessed an "eminence" that women did not; this came from the dynamic relation of body and soul, not from the soul alone. The body's metaphysical significance was thus at the heart of sacramental as well as moral theology.

The association of women with bodiliness and evil had devastating consequences for women, especially in the later Middle Ages as waves of hysteria over witchcraft swept Europe and, later, the American colonies, resulting in the deaths of thousands of women. But the more subtle associations of women with immanence as opposed to divine and male transcendence; with body as opposed to spirit; with sexuality as opposed to purity, have been a constant theme throughout the history of Christian spirituality. The connections of women with bodiliness, and of bodiliness with sin, have inevitably led some of the most prominent Christian thinkers to associate women with sin.

Late medieval spirituality evidenced a number of sometimes contradictory attitudes toward the body. Certain groups, such as the Cathars, revived a dualistic opposition of body and soul, and they were condemned, in large part for their teaching that the body was evil. The courtly love and the mystical traditions, on the other hand, gloried in the use of the body as metaphor for the spiritual. It is impossible to read Bernard of Clairvaux (1090–1153), Hildegard of Bingen (1098–1179), Meister Eckhart (ca. 1260–1327), Julian of Norwich (ca. 1342–ca. 1413), and other spiritual writers of this time without discerning a profound respect for and appreciation of the body as mirror of the soul. In addition, the later Middle Ages refocused attention on the humanity of Christ, especially his infancy and his suffering, in art, in ascetical practices, and in edifying spiritual manuals. The spirituality of Francis of Assisi (ca. 1181–1226) and his concern for nature are one such example.

The Reformation provided an opportunity for a reappropriation of the body by both Protestants and Catholics. Led by Martin Luther (1483–1546), the Reformers rejected the idea that the vowed celibate religious life was superior to marriage. Luther argued that marriage constituted a genuine vocation; most of humanity was called to marriage, and celibacy was a rare gift given to very few. Later Reformers, notably the Puritans, developed a kind of Protestant asceticism that sought to "purify" the faith in its disdain for physical pleasure and concern for austerity in life and worship.

Catholic reformers maintained the pride of place given to vowed religious life, but the tenor of this celibate life turned increasingly toward the world in a more "active" form. Modeled on the Society of Jesus (founded 1540), many congregations of women and men sought to bring the word of God to the world through teaching, nursing, preaching, and missionary activity. The model for Catholic spirituality in the post-Reformation years remained the vowed religious life, and consequently the body's role remained subordinate to the spiritual dimension of life. Fasting and sexual abstinence were models of behavior to which laity as well as religious were encouraged to conform. But the Catholic emphasis on the importance of the incarnation remained significant; the role of the body, as seen in the architecture, music, art, and literature of the period, was an important avenue for knowledge of God. The body remained an ambivalent and ambiguous reality for Catholic spirituality.

The Modern Era

It is worth noting that the Enlightenment, with its empirical and scientific perspective on all reality, transformed the image of the body from an organic to a mechanistic one. Catholic spirituality was generally hostile to these modern developments that celebrated the ideals of individual freedom, separation of Church and state, and the openness of all of reality, including religion, to scientific investigation. The promulgation of the dogmas of the Immaculate Conception (1854) and the Assumption (1950) of Mary raised many issues, including the relation of these dogmas to the biblical tradition, and their credibility within a scientific worldview. But perhaps most significantly, they also raised the question of the role of the body in the economy of salvation. Karl Rahner effectively argued that a contemporary retrieval of the dogma of the Assumption results in the confirmation of the promise of the resurrection of the body: what has been created by God and assumed by Christ will ultimately be raised up in glory.

In the early 20th century the philosophical movements of phenomenology and personalism, as well as developments in the social sciences, exerted a strong influence on Catholic theology and spirituality. Catholic writers on marriage condemned "Victorian" attitudes toward the body and maintained that a positive theology of the body and of sexuality was entirely compatible with Roman Catholic teaching and practice. But it was Vatican II (1962–1965) that has had the most profound effect on a theology of the body. In its concern to reconcile the Church and the world, with its focus on the material as well as the spiritual aspects of human life, the council opened the way to a fuller reintegration of the body into Catholic spirituality.

Challenges in the Present

Vatican II's turn toward the world has had a profound influence on all areas of spirituality. With regard to the body, a number of issues and challenges deserve special attention. These are: the recognition of the historicity of attitudes regarding the body, a reassessment of bodily asceticism, the role of the body in liturgy and prayer, and the challenge of feminist theology.

History and the Body

In the 19th century, biblical scholars and theologians came to recognize the importance of historical context with regard to biblical texts and doctrine. And in recent years, as the body itself has come under increased scrutiny, scholars have come to recognize the central role that the body has played in the history of Christian spirituality. In the early centuries renunciation of bodily pleasures served to distinguish Christians from their pagan counterparts and, in the waning years of the Roman Empire, demonstrated that what was spiritual was what would endure eternally (see Brown). In the Middle Ages the severe fasting practiced by many women provided an opportunity to develop a distinctive form of spirituality that was in concert with their roles as providers of food in a time of frequent food shortages (see Bynum). Both of these examples reveal the complexity of the body's role in history and the danger of reading back present attitudes into the past. Augustine's and Aquinas's interpretation of the body were reflective of the Neoplatonism and Aristotelianism of their times as well as the cluster of circum-

stances that affected the Church, the person, and society.

The historicity of the body challenges contemporary interpreters to look at the multiple influences, religious and secular, on the role of the body in the present. The body's symbolic role as representative of the world, of women, and of sin gives contemporary historians a way of interpreting the past through the ways in which the body is described and portrayed. Devotional literature, with its emphasis on bodily discipline, and religious art, in its portrayals of the body, offer two such opportunities for understanding the role of the body in history.

Reassessment of Bodily Asceticism

The history of Christian spirituality is replete with examples of ascetic practices, ranging from abstinence from meat to self-flagellation. In the wake of Vatican II, however, the emphasis on asceticism has been considerably lessened. Such practices as fasting before receiving Communion, self-denial during Lent, and the emphasis on vocations to vowed religious life have received far less emphasis in the present than in the past as measures of one's piety. With the turn to secular values begun in the Enlightenment and continued in Vatican II's positive assessment of the world, practices of bodily mortification have come to be seen by many as relics of the past, indicative of a negative attitude toward the body.

Late 20th-century Western society has come to glorify the body, especially young, attractive bodies, and to emphasize the consumption of physical pleasures through advertising. Dieting and exercise have in many cases come to take the place of fasting and discipline. While these practices are evidence of a somewhat more positive attitude toward the body, they often fail to take into consideration the spiritual and social contexts of human life and human finitude. Contemporary spirituality is still struggling to restore a needed balance to a theology of the body often characterized by its excessive denigration.

While vowed religious life has undergone a decline in membership, due in large part to the reevaluation of the secular world and of the body, it has also undertaken its own renewal. The vows of poverty, chastity, and obedience have been reinterpreted to focus more broadly on their social significance rather than primarily in terms of their effect on the individual person. Instead of being understood as a rejection of the world and a denial of the body, religious life in contemporary society attempts to stand for the importance of gospel values in a secular and commercial world.

Role of the Body in Liturgy and Prayer

The changes in liturgical practice have been for many the most obvious fruits of Vatican II. The use of the vernacular language, the greater participation of the congregation, and Vatican II's general openness to the world have all affected the way in which the body plays a new part in liturgical celebrations. Use of the vernacular language involves the senses in hearing, speaking, and singing; the renewal of the greeting of peace, the reception of the Eucharist under the forms of both bread and wine and in the hands of the recipients involve the bodily participation of the congregation in enhanced ways. The importance of sacraments and the visible community of the Church in the Catholic tradition have always meant that the body plays a central role in Christian life. The liturgical changes since Vatican II have attempted to underscore this recognition. In addition, such practices as liturgical dance have drawn attention to the multiple ways in which the body can celebrate the presence of God in the midst of human life.

While the loss of awe and mystery attributed to the Tridentine liturgy has been lamented by some, the role of the body in that liturgical context was highly circumscribed, at least on the part of the congrega-

tion. Largely silent, kneeling, and discouraged from touching (except on the tongue) the Eucharist, the congregation's physical role was a small one. Hence the transformation of the Church's attitude toward the world has also affected the way in which the body is involved in liturgy.

The resources of other religious traditions, especially Eastern ones, have been drawn upon in recent years. Such practices as yoga and T'ai Ch'i provide ways of centering the body for prayer and meditation. Contemporary texts on prayer emphasize the importance of the body and its wellbeing. A holistic approach to the person promotes care for the spiritual and material dimensions of the self, with both aspects equally important. Contemporary spirituality has also been deeply influenced by some of the movements in contemporary secular culture. Exercise, vegetarianism, abstinence from alcohol, massage are all practices which begin from the premise that the health of the body is essential to the health of the whole person. Creation-centered spirituality incorporates the body and all of nature into the relationship with God.

The Contributions of Feminist Theology

The development of the women's movement since the mid-1960s has focused attention anew on the ways in which women have been associated with the body. Feminists have shown how this association has blamed women for sin, understood women solely in terms of their biological capacity for motherhood, and regarded both women and the body as occupying a lower rank in the spiritual hierarchy than men and the soul. In reconsidering the role of the body, feminists have turned to embodiment as a central category for the theological understanding of the human person (theological anthropology) and for personal and social ethics.

Being embodied, humans come to experience and knowledge through their senses. While women have traditionally been understood to be more vulnerable to their bodies, recent findings in psychology and medicine have shown how deep the connection is between mind and body for both men and women. Even in science, the primacy of "objective," dispassionate thinking has been placed under scrutiny as the ideal of disembodied rationality is questioned. Rather than being understood as an obstacle to theological and moral reflection, "embodied thinking"—that is, thinking rooted in concrete circumstances and oriented toward practical results—may enable human beings to come to more balanced understandings of God, the world, human relationships, and themselves.

Women have turned to their own bodily experiences as potential sources of insight. Menstruation as a reminder of the cycles of nature created by God and childbirth as symbolic of participation in the divine creativity provide insights from the body into the complexity of divine revelation in human life. The historical association of women with nature, which in the past has been seen to justify male domination of women and nature, has in recent years resulted in a new spirituality of the body and nature. "Ecofeminism" seeks to develop a spirituality of awe and respect for the natural world along with respect for the humanity of women.

Theoretical and Practical Considerations

A number of questions arise concerning the role of the body in Catholic Christian spirituality: How is the body defined? What is the body's role in relation to the whole person? How is Christianity's incarnational emphasis on the goodness of the body to be understood in relation to the secular world's worship of the perfect body? In the light of Vatican II and its new stance toward the world, the nature of the body and its role in spirituality have been redefined. From an object of discipline and control, the body has come to be seen as the basis for human thought and action,

as symbolic of the human connection with the natural world, as intimately involved in the development of an adequate liturgical and prayer life. The sharp distinction formerly drawn between soul and body has given way to a conception of the person as embodied spirit. Yet a number of important issues regarding the body have yet to be fully addressed.

While Roman Catholicism has upheld the importance of the body, it has yet to overcome fully a "physicalist" morality while maintaining the importance of embodiment. That is, the natural law basis for Catholic moral thinking has placed the body in a central role, but it has not always given the body's historical and social role adequate consideration. The tensions surrounding such issues as women's role in the Church, contraception, and sexual morality arise from a concern for the body as symbolic of God's will and a historical-critical understanding of the body as symbolic of sexuality and sin. These tensions are yet to be resolved.

While the complexity of the body's role in history has been recognized, millennia of sexism and excessive denigration of the body and sexuality have yet to be fully exorcised from Catholic spirituality. The positive focus on women's experiences offers an alternative to a disembodied spiritual life that has regarded the body as an obstacle to be overcome. And the reintegration of the body into liturgy and prayer recognizes human embodiment as central to spiritual life and growth.

Contemporary secular society presents a challenge to a Catholic spirituality of the body. In a consumer-oriented culture that worships perfect and youthful bodies, a spirituality of the body recognizes the variety and diversity, fragility and finitude of human bodies. Care for the body recognizes its rootedness in nature. Respect for the aging process, for the cycles of nature in human bodies and in the world, implies a spirituality that cares for the body without idolizing it.

Vatican II's turn toward the world has meant that greater consideration has been given to the material circumstances of human life than in the past. Liberation theology, whose concern is liberation from *all* forms of oppression—material, political, religious, racial, sexual—proclaims that care for the suffering bodies of humanity is central to the mission of Christianity in the world. Liberation spirituality involves the unity of prayer and action and, in its concern for the whole person, means that the corporate suffering of humanity must be addressed first of all in its physical aspects.

As noted above, the body has often been seen as the primary location of sin, especially sexual sin. Other injustices done toward the body, such as domestic violence, economic inequality resulting in both hunger and overindulgence, and substance abuse, have not received as much attention. These, too, are problems that involve a lack of care for the body and have come in recent years to be understood as profoundly religious as well as social problems.

The role of the body in Catholic spirituality has always been a significant one. Theological anthropology, Christology, sacramental theology, ethics, and ecclesiology all rely on an understanding of the embodied person. Yet the ambivalence toward the body found throughout the history of Christian spirituality has not entirely disappeared even in present efforts to develop a positive theology of the body. To what extent spirituality can fully embrace the Word-become-flesh is one of the most profound challenges it faces.

See also ANTHROPOLOGY, THEOLOGICAL; ASCETICISM; CELIBACY; FEMINIST SPIRITUALITY; HOLISTIC SPIRITUALITY; MARRIAGE; MIND; SELF; SEXUALITY; SOUL.

Bibliography: P. Brown, *The Body and Society: Men, Women, and Sexual Renunciation in Early Christianity* (New York: Columbia Univ. Press, 1988). C. Bynum, *Holy Feast and Holy Fast: The Religious Significance of Food to Medieval Women* (Berkeley, Calif.: Univ. of California Press, 1987). P. Cooey, S. Farmer, and M. E. Ross, eds., *Embodied Love: Sensuality and Relationship as Feminist Values* (San Francisco: Harper & Row, 1987). M. Miles, *Augustine on the Body* (Missoula, Mont.: Scholars Press, 1979). J. Nelson, *Embodiment: An Approach to Sexuality and Christian Theology* (Minneapolis: Augsburg, 1978). J.A.T. Robinson, *The Body: A Study in Pauline Theology* (Philadelphia: Westminster, 1952).

SUSAN A. ROSS

BODY OF CHRIST

"Body of Christ" is a privileged way of naming and connecting several central Christian experiences: the physical body of Jesus of Nazareth; the reality of the post-Easter Christ; the community of Jesus' followers in communion with him and with one another; and the presence of Christ in the bread of the Eucharist. These meanings are particularly insightful into Christian spirituality when their essential interconnection is honored.

Of these several meanings, "body of Christ" has one literal first meaning: the human body of Jesus during his brief life in first-century Palestine. The remaining important and interrelated meanings are metaphorical meanings. Before broaching these meanings, we must be clear about the nature of metaphor.

Metaphor, Reality and Meaning

In popular usage, metaphor often names a linguistic artifact: saying that one thing is another because there is a real similarity, even though the two fields of meaning are fundamentally different, e.g., "My friend is a jewel." One is justified in saying in this case that "jewel" is only a metaphor. This is a legitimate meaning of metaphor. It is a naming of meaning after the fact. But the Body of Christ is not this kind of metaphor.

Paul Ricoeur has identified another and deeper function of metaphor. In the white-hot moment of a profound religious experience, metaphor is already there, mediating the very act of experiencing. The metaphor and the experience arise together. This is sometimes called the "originative" or "nascent" moment. Metaphor is there as the event occurs, helping it occur. Such a metaphor does not arise after the fact; rather, it helps constitute the "fact" in the first place. The metaphor is disclosing being that would not be disclosed without it. It is a meaning-maker in the nascent moment. In this instance, to say that something is "only" or "merely" or "just" a metaphor is to falsify the epistemological role of the metaphor in the process of knowing. Body of Christ is an experience-mediating metaphor in nascent Christian moments of religious encounter.

In these reflections on the Body of Christ, we will attend first to some related meanings in the Hebrew Scripture. We will then turn to Paul, in the heart of whose religious experience the metaphor sprang forth. Thirdly, we will borrow the concept of "social system" from the social sciences to elaborate upon the Body of Christ, with particular attention to Paul's First Letter to the Corinthians. And finally, we will relate Body-of-Christ spirituality to pressing Christian agenda at the dawn of the third millennium.

"Corporate Personality" in the Hebrew Scriptures

The language of "body" to name the togetherness of a covenanted people is specifically Pauline. But the sense of things that leads Paul to speak of Christians as being "members of one another" is deeply rooted in Hebrew experience. For example, when Achan secretly disobeys God in the battle at Ai, the entire people of Israel is punished, because in Achan, one son of Israel, all Israel sins (Josh 7). When Achan admits his sin, he and his whole household and even his animals are killed, because of a profound corporate sense of personal reality. When those in Ai stone Achan to death, we are told that Israel took Achan's life. This sense of the corporate personality of Israel sounds strange and perhaps even barbaric to contemporary Western ears. But as H. Wheeler Robinson has shown in his study of the corporate personality of Israel, this perception of how we belong to one another and are parts of a "one" is a remarkable insight into our essential sociality.

The reason why we tend to find the notion of corporate personality tribally naive is that our own U.S. culture interprets reality quite differently. We tend to think of individual human beings as unconnected until they choose to become connected, either because it is useful or because of some natural attraction. But there is an important biblical alternative to this interpretation, in many ways countercultural. We are all children of the same God, with the same earth as our common home. We are interrelated and interdependent. We have no choice about whether we live in relationship. Our only choices are whether we tell the truth about our social existence and whether we live in ways that redeem the relational web that is always and forever the matrix of our becoming.

Because Paul was a Jew, we must presume that this second interpretation of human reality was in his Hebrew genes and facilitated his understanding of the reality he called, and we now call, "the Body of Christ."

The expression so familiar in our own day, "Mystical Body," was not used either by Paul or by the early Christian writers. It began to appear in the 9th century in controversies over the Eucharist, and at that time referred to Christ's Body in the Eucharist. In the latter half of the 12th century, "Mystical Body" began to be used for the people who make up Christ's Body. That ecclesial connotation has remained, but it is instructive about the connection between the two that it began first to refer to the Eucharist.

Paul's Experience of the Body of Christ

Paul recounts his conversion experience in his Letter to the Galatians (1:12-27). This narrative was apparently so central to the early communities' self-understanding that it is retold three times by Luke in Acts (9:1-14; 22:5-16; 26:10-18).

Paul is on his way to Damascus to persecute the followers of Jesus, "with the authorization and commission of the chief priests" (Acts 26:10-18). The language of Acts clearly suggests a white-hot moment of nascent religious experience: "I saw a light from the sky, brighter than the sun." Then a voice asks Paul, "Why are you persecuting me?" To Paul's question, "Who are you?" the voice responds, "I am Jesus whom you are persecuting." The conclusion is clear: The word "Jesus" now names not only the historical personage but the Easter Jesus as a new reality with all the Easter baptized: "Do you not know that your bodies are members of Christ" (1 Cor 6:15). In this new reality, the connection that Jesus' disciples have with him also connects them with one another: "We, though many, are one body in Christ, and individually parts of one another" (Rom 12:5). Being "parts of one another" is a new physical reality. John Haughey writes that after the resurrection we must speak of the "social flesh" of Christ (Haughey, p. 126), and he rightly critiques Christology for having over-pondered the individuated Christ and under-pondered the social Christ (Haughey, p. 109). We only theologize upon what our faith-experience calls us to ponder. The Mystical Body, with all its tenacious and pervasive relational texture, is under-experienced and therefore under-theologized. The Body is a way of being human for which the world has a hunger in our day.

Body is not "merely" or "just" a metaphor, a linguistic artifact that the poetry of the Christ-event invites. Body is a physical reality in the world. The toe does not decide whether it is body. It *is*. It is connected whether it likes it or not, and it had better honor the connectedness. We do not decide whether we shall be connected or not. We *are*. Christianhood redeems the connectedness and deepens it beyond all telling as

Christ's Body. The nascent moment of Paul's conversion is an understanding of connectedness that is not external to us but constitutive of us.

Because the Body of Christ embraces and transforms our sociality, there are some new rules. Baptism means membership in a discipleship of equals. For those baptized into Christ, privilege may never be granted or withheld for reasons of race, gender, or social condition (Gal 3:27-28). The differences in gifts are real but complementary (1 Cor 12:27-30). The body needs all its members. This is in accord with Jesus' teaching in Mt 23:8-12 that we are all siblings and must never let roles and titles make a lie of the brother/sisterhood that God's parenthood engenders. That would violate the Body of Christ.

Body of Christ/Social System and Bread

"Social system" is contemporary language drawn from the social sciences. It names a kind of organic connectedness. Whatever happens to any part of the system has effects upon the whole system; whatever happens to the whole system touches every part. The binding forces in a true social system are values that people believe in together, values they have internalized. The Body of Christ that is community is more than a social system, but truly a social system, and never less than a social system.

When a social system's togetherness is rooted in the Christ-event, it is the Body of Christ. If a social system's togetherness has not been made over in Christ, it is not the Body of Christ; or if it has been barely made over, it is barely the Body of Christ. The Christ-event is already a present reality in the world. The major issue, then, is not about its presence or its absence in the world, but, as Edward Schillebeeckx has written, about the density of presence and about whether it is present or absent in some part of the world. The distinction between presence and absence is not as helpful as Schillebeeckx's notion of the density. Presence is manifested in having effects. How engaging and extensive someone's effects are is a measure of the density of presence. A social system is Christ's Body when the hold of Christ upon the system is a defining hold, not one factor among many, but a factor out of which a community's essential passions arise. Presence is a dialogic notion that involves effects, and it may be a thick presence or a thin presence.

Body as Eucharist and Body as social system (community) are distinct but dialogic. In certain Eastern liturgical traditions, the prayer to God's transforming Spirit (the epiclesis) asks that the bread *and* the community be made over into Christ's Body. To extend a term borrowed from Western theology, the transubstantiations of the bread into the Body and of the social system into the Body are distinct but correlative. The presence of Christ in any sacrament is continuous with the presence of Christ in every other sacrament and with the Body that the baptized are with Christ, for there is but one Christ.

In some scorching comments, Paul names the factions among the Corinthians and their disregard of one another's needs, and he says that because of these behaviors "it is not the Lord's Supper that you eat" (1 Cor 11:20, JB). Their social system is not under the power of the Christ-event, and that impinges upon the liturgical event.

Paul then recounts Jesus' institution of the Eucharist and returns to the condition the Body should be in *before* it eats the bread and drinks the cup: "Everyone is to examine himself and only then eat of the bread or drink from the cup, because a person who eats and drinks without recognizing the body is eating and drinking his own condemnation" (1 Cor 11:28-29, JB). Although "the body" here has sometimes been interpreted vis-à-vis the Eucharistic bread, the context suggests that the Corinthians seem to recognize the bread Body, or they would not have assembled in the first

place. But from their behavior at the meal before Eucharist, it is clear that they do not recognize the social-system Body of Christ. They may know Jesus in a Eucharistic way, but they do not recognize the Body of Christ that they themselves are. There is a profound rupture between social reality and sacramental reality, and Paul calls them to Christ's transformation of themselves into his Body so that the Eucharist may encompass the social flesh of Christ.

The Spirituality of the Body

In Greek thought, spirit contrasts sharply with matter, a tradition that has left massive scars on our experience of bodiliness, including the Body of Christ. In Hebrew, *rûaḥ*/spirit is a metaphor for personhood. The metaphoric meaning of *rûaḥ* is rooted in the air/breath that is moved in and out of the body by the body's lungs. *Rûaḥ* is a physiological metaphor for personhood as it exists in us (like breath) and as it goes out from us in our effects upon others and upon the world. Paul presumes that meaning in his interpretation of our experience of God's *Rûaḥ*/Spirit (1 Cor 2:10-16). When *Rûaḥ* underlies the meaning of spirituality, the physiological moorings of faith are evoked. We can only be in the world as bodied. Christian spirituality is that bodied way of being in the world with others because of what Jesus Christ does and is. It is the *Rûaḥ*/Spirit that gives life to the Body.

Because of the Body, there can be no authentic Christian spirituality that is not radically social, because every Christian individual is radically social. Such a spirituality is not any less personal. It simply denies that individuals should or even can be autonomous entities. The restoration of the Rite of Christian Initiation is a retrieval of that operative instinct: initiation is initiation into a community that is the Body of the Lord and not into a private relationship with the Lord. Our relationship is personal without ever being ontologically private.

In the "open moment" of postconciliar deconstruction/reconstruction, the spirituality of the Body is singularly apt for many reasons, three of which are named here.

First, in parish life as in the Corinthian community, those who assemble regularly for Eucharist are meant to be a social system whose behaviors testify to its bodyhood. Christians are under requirement to be members of one another functionally as well as nominally. We must better recognize the Body that *we* are so as not to eat and drink to our condemnation. How we are (or are not!) Body with one another before we get to church has everything to do with the essential rightness or wrongness of celebrating the Eucharistic Body of the Lord. It is fitting that we celebrate Eucharist, not in the company of strangers, but with those with whom we are behaviorally Body before we get there. Eucharist is still Eucharist, of course, if we are there with others of the Body, even if we do not know them. Yet Eucharist especially belongs to an assembled community that is functionally community before and after Eucharist. We must not neglect the physiological base of the social-system Body.

Second, for over a century and a half, commentators upon U.S. culture have been noting the exaggerated individualism that has us believe that we are autonomous entities who can choose whether to relate or not. But, in fact, we are already and always interrelated and interdependent individuals whose only choice is to redeem our relatedness by our love.

There is a possible redemption of U.S. culture by the Body of Christ. The Body is able to make present a different social construction of reality than the operative one in U.S. culture and to let its gracious instancing of that alternative invite U.S. culture to a social reconstruction of its own reality. To say that is to affirm the sacramental character of the Body of Christ that we are and to link our sacramental being once again to that of the Eucharist. The social system that is Christ's Body is called to be a transformative presence in the social system we know as U.S. culture. Nothing less than a "full-Bodied" spirituality can effect such a transformation, and nothing less than the Bread and the Cup is an adequate ritualization of Christ's hold upon the becoming of human history.

Lastly, we sisters and brothers of planet Earth must reconnect with the far reaches of the larger social system: all things are yours, and you are Christ's, and Christ is God's! The spirituality called for by a thoroughgoing ecology is not merely consistent with the Body of Christ but is implicit in it. Human history cannot continue to give nurture to Christ's Body unless we members of the Body treat our earth home far more benevolently than has been our wont. Our times are giving birth to a new word— *ecospirituality*. The terminology may or may not be passing, but the call to create a world that can support a Body is a call from the Body for the Body. That ecology will be a centerpiece in the spirituality of the third millennium seems undoubtable.

Conclusion

Body of Christ is not "merely" a metaphor. It is a physical reality, a new being brought into existence among the disciples of Jesus in the resurrection of Jesus Christ into which we are baptized. Body of Christ is not a theology. It is a way of being in the world with one another and with Christ because of who God is. The body of Jesus in life, the Body of Christ in the Easter event, the Body of Christ that we are, the Body of Christ in the Eucharist, and the Body of Christ that we become more fully in the resurrection of the body—all these belong together in Body's total meaning.

See also BAPTISM; BODY; BREATH, BREATHING; CHRIST; CHURCH; COMMUNITY; COVENANT; EUCHARIST; SAINTS, COMMUNION OF SAINTS; SOLIDARITY.

Bibliography: J. A. T. Robinson, *The Body: A Study in Pauline Theology* (Philadelphia: Westminster, 1977). J. Haughey, "Eucharist at Corinth: You Are the Christ," in *Above Every Name: The Lordship of Christ and Social Systems* (New York: Paulist, 1980). H. W.

Robinson, *Corporate Personality in Ancient Israel* (Philadelphia: Fortress, 1964). M. Gerhart and A. Russell, *Metaphoric Process: The Creation of Scientific and Religious Understanding* (Fort Worth: Texas Christian Univ. Press, 1984).

BERNARD J. LEE, S.M.

BREATH, BREATHING

The biblical *rûah,* or God's spirit, in the Genesis narrative is imaged first as "moving over the face of the waters" (Gen 1:2, RSV) and then as God's breath: "God breathed into [man's] nostrils the breath of life; and man became a living being" (Gen 2:7, RSV). Life and vigor are synonymous in the biblical tradition with *rûah,* imaged as wind. This Hebrew identification of God's creative presence as breath or breathing recurs throughout the OT. For example, Ezekiel speaks of Yahweh's power over the valley of dry bones: "I will cause breath to enter you, and you shall live"; and "Then the Lord God said to me, 'Prophesy to the breath, prophesy, son of man, and say to the breath, Thus says the Lord God: Come from the four winds, O breath; breathe on these slain, that they may live'" (Ezek 37:6, 9-10, RSV). The OT associates the resurgence of God's life with the spirit given in the prophets, associated with God's word (*dabar*) and not expected again until the eschaton (Kasper, pp. 69–70).

The NT employs similar imagery of *rûah* to identify the power (*exousia*) of Jesus as one who controls the wind as a divine manifestation (e.g., "And he awoke and rebuked the wind, and said to the sea, 'Peace! Be still!'" (Mk 4:39, RSV; cf. Mt 8:26; Lk 8:24). But the most important NT image of *rûah* occurs in the Pentecost experience, which portrays the coming of the Spirit as a new creation: "And suddenly a sound came from heaven like the rush of a mighty wind, and it filled all the house where they were sitting. . . . they were all filled with the Holy Spirit . . ." (Acts 2:2-4, RSV). The post-resurrection narratives image Jesus' empowering the apostles' ministry to reconcile sinners with the new life of breath: "He breathed on them, and said to them: 'Receive the Holy Spirit'" (Jn 20: 22, RSV).

The imagery and ritual gestures of breath and breathing were carried over to early baptismal and initiation rituals, e.g., the portrayal of the Spirit as the dove hovering over the waters of chaos, or death, and creating new life; and the *ephpheta,* at which the minister breathed upon the candidate for initiation. The most compelling modern image of the Spirit as *rûah* is given in Gerard Manley Hopkins' poem "God's Grandeur": "Because the Holy Ghost over the bent/World broods with warm breast and with ah! bright wings."

The Greek Orthodox tradition has cultivated a particular emphasis on spiritual techniques that incorporate breath and breathing in the rhythmic recitation of the Jesus Prayer, "Jesus, Son of God, have mercy on me, a sinner!" As an experience of prayer, it points to an inner experience and seeks silence of the heart. Origins of hesychasm can be detected in Greek authors of the 7th to 9th centuries, but the 14th century evidences creative development of hesychasm in Gregory of Sinai (d. 1346) at Mount Athos and Gregory of Palamas (d. 1359). The physical technique connected with the Jesus Prayer affirms the theological principle that the human person is a single unity; therefore the body as well as the soul has a positive, dynamic part to play in prayer. Body posture, rhythmic breathing to secure calm and concentration, and the inward search for the place of the heart aim to acquire a state of inner simplicity in which the one who prays is free from images and discursive thought.

The return to the Eastern traditions of prayer and meditation, especially the Jesus Prayer, was popularized by J. D. Salinger in his novel *Franny and Zooey.* Charismatic renewal likewise stresses the practice of repetitive, rhythmic prayer and incorporates the Jesus Prayer as central to its experience. The dialogue with Asian spiritualities and comparison with Zen meditation techniques has enabled Christian ascetics to retrieve breathing exercises to facilitate experiences of prayer.

See also BODY; CENTERING PRAYER; CREATION; HESYCHASM; HOLY SPIRIT; MEDITATION.

Bibliography: W. Johnston, *The Still Point: Reflections on Zen and Christian Mysticism* (New York: Fordham Univ. Press, 1971). W. Kaspar, *Jesus the Christ* (New York: Paulist, 1976). A. Kavanagh, *The Shape of Baptism: The Rite of Christian Initiation* (New York: Pueblo, 1978). K. Ware, "The Origins of the Jesus Prayer," and "The Hesychasts," *The Study of Spirituality,* ed. C. Jones, G. Wainwright, E. Yarnold (London: SPCK, 1986) 175–183; 242–254.

GEORGE KILCOURSE

BRIDAL MYSTICISM

Scriptural and patristic traditions used bridal imagery to describe the relationship between Israel and God (Isa 54:5; Hos 2:19; Ezek 16:8) and between the Church and Christ (2 Cor 11:2; Eph 5:25; Rev 10:7-9, 21:2; 22:17). Bridal mysticism (*Brautmystik*), the use of nuptial and erotic imagery to describe the soul's union with God, emerged in Origen's *Commentary on the Song of Songs.* In the 12th century Bernard of Clairvaux borrowed images of human love, sexual experience, and marriage from the Song of Songs, and Richard of St. Victor used the symbolic language of betrothal, marriage, wedlock, and the fruitfulness of the soul to describe the developing union of the soul with God. This imagery was elaborated in the 13th-century lay movement of the Beguines as Hadewijch, Mechtild of Magdeburg, and Gertrude and Mechtild of Hackeborn described their experience of mystical union in terms of ecstasy, erotic sexuality, and passionate, loving devotion.

The author of *The Cloud of Unknowing,* Teresa of Avila, and John of the Cross later likened the loving, transforming union of the soul with God to mystical marriage, in which God and the contemplative become one in spirit and love, rendering the contemplative a parent imparting the divine life to others. Thus contemplation itself becomes apostolically fruitful.

The contemporary renewal of marriage and religious life has modified the use of bridal and marital imagery in the texts and ceremonies of marriage and religious profession to express the experience of these commitments as forms of union with God born of mutual self-giving and lifelong celibacy as a means to living an apostolic commitment in community.

See also CHASTITY; MARRIAGE, MYSTICAL; MYSTICISM; RELIGIOUS LIFE; UNION, UNITIVE WAY; VIRGINITY.

Bibliography: C. W. Bynum, *Jesus as Mother: Studies in the Spirituality of the High Middle Ages* (Berkeley: Univ. of California Press, 1982). H. Egan, *Christian Mysticism: The Future of a Tradition* (New York: Pueblo, 1984). J. Leclercq, F. Vandenbroucke, and L. Bouyer, *The Spirituality of the Middle Ages* (Minneapolis: Winston, 1968). Origen, *The Song of Songs: Commentary and Homilies,* trans. R. Lawson, Ancient Christian Writers 26 (Westminster, Md.: Newman, 1957). E. Underhill, *Mysticism* (London: Methuen, 1930).

SUSAN E. HAMES, C.S.J.

BYZANTINE SPIRITUALITY

See EASTERN CHRISTIAN SPIRITUALITY.

C

CAMALDOLESE SPIRITUALITY

The Camaldolese family of monks and nuns follows the Rule of Benedict and is a branch of the larger Benedictine community. The characteristic element of the Camaldolese is the hermitage, with its possibility of deeper solitude, to the point of reclusion. The Congregation of Camaldoli is part of the Benedictine Confederation and also embraces community life of the cenobium (both in the rural and urban setting), with a variety of possible apostolates, especially that of hospitality with silent retreats. Various convents of Camaldolese nuns are basically cenobitical, with provision for reclusion in some instances.

Thus all the elements of Benedictine life—Divine Office, *lectio divina,* work, etc.—are found in a Camaldolese monastery or hermitage. The Camaldolese also open up to the whole monastic heritage of both the East and West preceding St. Benedict, as does the Rule itself. The specific Camaldolese reform of the 11th century is traced to St. Romuald, but the Camaldolese heritage extends back to the 6th century and St. Benedict. But neither of these great figures is considered the "founder" of the Camaldolese family in the sense that, in later centuries, Franciscans would look to St. Francis or Dominicans to St. Dominic. Rather, the Camaldolese trace their spiritual lineage back to the early Fathers and Mothers of the desert, to the early ascetics before them, to the Essenes, and especially to key biblical figures—the prophets, the sapiential voices, the apostolic community, and above all Christ himself, the archetypal monk as well as the model of every Christian life.

The Camaldolese relate less with the later idea of "religious orders" and "schools of spirituality" and more with the earliest self-understanding of monks East and West (which perdures in the Christian East today). Indeed, Camaldolese believe that "there is something of the monk in every person, a kind of universal monastic archetype." Camaldolese also feel a bond with "the earliest monastic figures ... from India," both Hindu and Buddhist, and with all monks of other religious traditions (Matus, p. 3). Thus the Camaldolese spirit has a universal openness, affirmed by the present constitutions of the Congregation of Camaldoli regarding spiritual ecumenism, also in its widest scope (no. 125). The Vatican has also commended this ministry to the Camaldolese. But this openness extends out from the specific center of Christ and the particular Benedictine Camaldolese heritage that gives rootedness to such dialogue.

The etymology of *Camaldoli* is debated, but it seems to derive from a conflation of *campus Romualdi,* "field of Romuald." Romuald (ca. 950–1027), a nobleman of Ravenna, entered the nearby Abbey of St. Apollinaris in Classe to do penance for his father, who had killed a man in a duel. An Eastern, Byzantine influence was felt in the whole Ravenna area, and the magnificent mosaics of the abbey expressed a deep paschal and paradisiacal spirituality that would always inspire Romuald. After three years in the abbey, Romuald obtained permission to retire into solitude to the west of the Venice lagoon, under the direction of an old hermit, Marinus. Romuald then accompanied the Doge of Venice and Abbot Guarin to the famous Abbey of St. Michael of Cuxa in Catalonia. This was a vital abbey of the Cluniac reform, strongly influenced by Eastern monasticism, which hosted a colony of hermits on its grounds.

Romuald's stay, which lasted perhaps ten years, was decisive. He studied Sacred Scripture and monastic literature, and embraced a monastic life nourished by liturgy, work, and *lectio divina*. He also reflected more deeply on the plurality of monastic expressions, from the cenobitic to the eremitic, and even the missionary. He was ordained priest at Cuixa and returned to Italy in 988. Emperor Otto III appointed him abbot of St. Apollinaris in 998, but because the community did not embrace the seriousness of his reform, he retired the next year.

Romuald was a charismatic figure who defended the poor against the lords. He journeyed throughout Italy, renewing monasteries (including at least two for nuns) and establishing eremitical communities on the ancient model of the laura, with a small number of hermitage cells clustered about a central church. The hermitage of Camaldoli, in the Tuscan mountains near Arezzo, was founded by Romuald around 1023. About two miles below the hermitage a monastic center was established that would develop into the great monastery of Camaldoli, which with the hermitage constitutes one community, a central expression of the pluriform monastic life of the Camaldolese. This hermitage-monastery would become the center of the Camaldolese Order.

A key document for Camaldolese spirituality was discovered only at the end of the last century: *The Life of the Five Brothers* by St. Bruno-Boniface of Querfurt. Written several years before Romuald's death by a disciple, it chronicles the warm, open spirit of the Romualdian reform, the deep friendship among the monks, and the heroic courage of five of its early martyrs. It also reveals the pluriform shape of this monastic life, the "Threefold Good" of missionary, cenobitic, and eremitic observance. This unity in diversity is a key dimension of the Camaldolese charism down through the centuries. It is rooted in Christian anthropology, in the nature of the Church, and indeed in the unity in diversity of the Trinity. The *Life of the Five Brothers* also includes the brief but precious Rule of St. Romuald, which sums up his teaching on prayer: "Sit in your cell as in paradise. Put the whole world behind you and forget it. Watch your thoughts like a good fisherman watching for fish. . . . Realize above all that you are in God's presence. . . . Empty yourself completely and sit waiting, content with the grace of God, like the chick who tastes nothing and eats nothing but what his mother brings him" (Matus, p. 23).

St. Peter Damian (1007–1072), Doctor of the Church, also born in Ravenna, but of a poor, struggling family, received an excellent education in Faenza and Parma. In 1035 he entered the austere monastery of Fonte Avellana. He was decisive in bringing Fonte Avellana and the monasteries founded from it into the ambit of the Romualdian reform. He wrote the charming *Life of St. Romuald,* as well as many other spiritual and ascetical works. His *Dominus Vobiscum,* for instance, profoundly explores the bond of the solitary with the whole Body of Christ: "Indeed, the Church of Christ is united in all her parts by such a bond of love that her several members form a single body and in each one the whole Church is mystically present; so that the whole Church universal may rightly be called the one bride of Christ, and on the other hand every single soul can, because of the mystical effects of the sacrament, be regarded as the whole Church" (Peter Damian, p. 57). A prophetic voice for social justice and against the worldliness of the Church, he was made cardinal and expended much energy for Church reform.

From the end of the 11th century through the first half of the 14th, the Camaldolese Congregation grew rapidly, especially in Tuscany and the north of Italy, with hermitages and monasteries in rural and urban locations. Flourishing monasteries in Venice, Florence, and later in Rome resulted in a significant Camaldolese contribution to Christian spirituality and humanism. Some of the significant documents and figures of this Camaldolese heritage are the following:

1. The early *Constitutions* (now dated to the early 12th century), "of remarkable discretion and breadth of view . . . the effect of the whole is one of balance and sanity and supernatural good sense. It reflects the true spirit of the Gospel of Christ and the wisdom of the greatest Desert Fathers" (Merton, p. 155).

2. Guido of Arezzo (d. 1050), "the father of modern music," whose innovative principles set the foundation for modern notation; no medieval treatise is preserved in so many sources spread over so wide an area as his *De disciplina artis musicae.*

3. Gratian (d. ca. 1179), "the father of canon law," whose *Decretum* gathers together some four thousand patristic, conciliar, and papal decrees regarding all areas of Church discipline, thus documenting its deeper and wider basis. (Dante placed Gratian, along with Romuald and Peter Damian, in paradise!)

4. Lorenzo Monaco (d. ca. 1424), perhaps the most important Florentine artist of the first half of the 15th century, who exercised a significant influence on Fra Angelico and other Renaissance artists. His works are in the Vatican, Florence, the Louvre, London, Cambridge, New York, and Los Angeles.

5. Ambrose Traversari (d. 1439), general of the order, described by Pope Eugene IV as "the light of the Church," a pioneering ecumenist whose tireless efforts strengthened the bond between Catholicism and the Eastern Churches. He translated many of the Greek Fathers into Latin, participated in the Council of Florence, and worked for the renewal of the Catholic Church.

6. Fra Mauro (d. 1459), pioneering cartologist, whose carefully drafted maps of the world significantly aided Columbus and other explorers.

All this creative work took place in monastic communities of serious observance and deep prayer. Consequently, popes such as Callixtus II (d. 1124) and Innocent III (d. 1216), mandated the Camaldolese Congregation to reform many Benedictine houses in Italy. But with the 15th century there was a general decline. The ecclesial abuse of the *commendam,* by which the revenues of abbeys were granted to an ecclesiastic not a member of the Order or to a layman for his own use, played a notable part, negatively affecting the Camaldolese more than any other congregation. In this context of spiritual exhaustion, the creative dialectic of eremitical and cenobitical life, characteristically Camaldolese from the beginning, became strained. In the 16th century a strictly eremitical congregation developed, the Camaldolese Hermits of Monte Corona, influenced by the holy and brilliant Bl. Paul Giustiniani (d. 1528). This congregation still exists as strictly eremitical, without the cenobitic form of monasteries on the one hand, and also without the special institution of reclusion within the hermitage on the other. The Congregation of Camaldoli, however, retains both these forms, along with the hermitage and its regular observance, which combines the solitude of the cell with the common life of the church, recreation, and so forth. The two congregations are bonded in friendship, and both follow, with the

Camaldolese nuns, a common Camaldolese liturgical calendar.

In the 17th century a strictly cenobitical congregation was formed, having as its center the great Venetian monastery of St. Michael. After a flourishing short history (which contributed also a Camaldolese pope—Gregory XVI), it reunited with the Congregation of Camaldoli in 1935. One of its great urban monasteries, St. Gregory the Great in the center of Rome, dating from the 6th century and Pope Gregory the Great (thus one of the most ancient of "living" monasteries), is now the central studentate of the Congregation of Camaldoli.

Since 1950 there has been a new influx of vocations into Camaldoli, along with a spiritual and theological renewal, extended by Vatican II and expressed in the constitutions of 1985. Cyprian Vagaggini, *peritus* at Vatican II, who contributed significantly to the shaping of the three new Eucharistic Prayers, is but one representative of flourishing biblical, liturgical, patristic, monastic, and ecumenical studies, as well as musical and artistic work, among the Camaldolese.

Today, as throughout Camaldolese and Benedictine history, it is the "ordinary" monks who keep the tradition alive. Many come with practical gifts that are particularly important for a community; others come without any pretense of possessing any outstanding gifts whatever, other than a deep desire for union with God. And as always, "in both hermitage and monastery the monks attend to the contemplative life above all else" (*Camaldolese Constitutions*, no. 4).

As of 1990, the two men's congregations of Camaldolese and the Camaldolese nuns were present especially in Italy (19 communities), but also in Poland (3 communities), France (1), Brazil (1), Colombia (1), India (1), Tanzania (1), and the United States (4 communities: New Camaldoli Hermitage, Big Sur, California; Incarnation Priory, residence and studentate of New Camaldoli, Berkeley, California; Holy Family Hermitage [Monte Corona Congregation], Bloomingdale, Ohio; and Transfiguration Monastery [nuns], Windsor, New York).

See also BENEDICTINE SPIRITUALITY; DESERT; EREMITICAL LIFE; MONASTICISM, MONASTIC SPIRITUALITY.

Bibliography: St. Peter Damian, *Selected Writings on the Spiritual Life*, trans. P. McNulty (London: Faber, 1959). T. Matus, *The Monastic Life of the Camaldolese Benedictines* (Big Sur, Calif.: Hermitage Books, 1985). T. Merton, *The Silent Life* (New York: Farrar, Straus & Giroux, 1957).

ROBERT HALE, O.S.B. CAM.

CANON LAW, SPIRITUALITY IN

The term *canon law* broadly refers to all the laws of the Roman Catholic Church, whether of the Latin Rite Church or of the Eastern Catholic Churches, whether instituted by the pope or an ecumenical council, or by synods, plenary or provincial councils, episcopal conferences, or diocesan bishops. The principal sources of canon law are the Code of Canon Law, which applies only to the Latin Church; the Code of Canons of the Eastern Churches; liturgical laws; concordat law between the Vatican and secular states; and other laws promulgated by the authority of the pope in the *Acta Apostolicae Sedis* (AAS), the official journal of the Apostolic See. For further treatment of canon law in general, the reader is directed to the publications in the bibliography. This essay will focus on the spirituality reflected in the Code of Canon Law.

When Pope John Paul II promulgated the new Code of Canon Law in 1983, he stated that its revision was inspired by the same purpose as that of the Second Vatican Council—the renewal of Christian living. According to the Pope, the Code purports to create an order in the Church that facilitates the organic development of faith, grace, charisms, and charity (AAS 75 [1983] vi–xiv). The Code determines legal structures and institutions common to all the local Churches to enable Catholic communities everywhere to fulfill the spiritual mission entrusted by Christ to the Church.

Although the Code is binding on all local Churches of the Latin Rite, few of the spiritual practices found in it are mandatory, even for clergy and religious. Great freedom is allowed the individual members of the Church to adopt those spiritual practices that best conform to their own personality, needs, and culture. Among the basic rights recognized in the Code is the right of all the faithful "to follow their own form of spiritual life consonant with the teaching of the Church" (can. 214). The Catholic Church has a rich spiritual heritage, with new expressions of spirituality emerging in every age. Canon 214 establishes the freedom of all the faithful to acquire a form of spiritual life they find meaningful, provided that it conforms to Church teachings. This right of the faithful to follow their own form of spiritual life is fundamental, a part of the Church's constitutional law, and it cannot be taken away by anyone (cf. can. 199, 3°).

Although canon 214 appears open to a wide variety of spiritualities, there is a kind of "official spirituality" sanctioned by the Catholic Church as seen in the Code of Canon Law. Many canons in the Code are related in some way to the spiritual life of the Church. They reflect a spirituality that is common to Latin Catholics, notwithstanding a diversity of local expressions and variations.

The Catholic spirituality that is manifested in the Code has three general characteristics: (1) it is centered in the official liturgy of the Church; (2) it is organized and promoted by established canonical structures, notably parishes and associations of the faithful; and (3) it is often particularized through a canonical state, or vocation, in addition to the primary commitment of baptism, which state is assumed through the sacraments of holy orders or matrimony, or through membership in institutes of consecrated life and societies of apostolic life.

1. The spirituality seen in the Code is centered in the liturgy, especially the Eucharist. Canon 897, echoing Vatican II (SC 10, 47; LG 3, 11, 17, 26), states in part that the Eucharist "is the summit and the source of all Christian worship and life; it signifies and effects the unity of the people of God and achieves the building up of the Body of Christ. The other sacraments and all the ecclesiastical works of the apostolate are closely related to the Holy Eucharist and are directed to it"; through the Eucharist "the Church constantly lives and grows." The Code exhorts the faithful to hold the Eucharist in highest honor, to take part in its celebration, to receive the sacrament devoutly and frequently, and to venerate it (can. 898).

All the faithful are bound by Church law to participate in the Eucharist every Sunday and holy day of obligation (can. 1248). The law encourages seminarians, clergy, and members of religious and secular institutes to participate in the Eucharist daily (cans. 246, §1; 276, §2, 2°; 663, §2; 719, §2). Eucharistic spirituality outside Mass consists of the reception of Holy Communion by those unable to participate in the Mass, notably the sick and infirm (cans. 918, 921), and the veneration of the Eucharist by means of Eucharistic processions and Exposition and Benediction of the Blessed Sacrament (cans. 941-944).

Also important to the liturgical spirituality found in the Code is the celebration of the sacrament of penance. The purpose of the sacrament is to bring about the conversion of the penitent to God (see can. 987); its effects are God's pardon for sin and reconciliation with the Church (can. 959). The law requires that the faithful confess the number and kind of all serious sins in individual confession before receiving Holy Communion (cans. 988, §1; 916). There are two exceptions to this rule for extraordinary circumstances—general absolution, in which absolution is given to a large number of penitents without individual confession (cans. 961-963), and the provision of canon 916 permitting persons in serious sin to receive Communion if they have a serious reason for wanting to receive, provided they make an act of perfect contrition and have the intention of confessing as soon as possible. Minimally, serious sins must be confessed at least once a year (can. 989).

Although venial sins can be remitted in other ways besides the sacrament of penance, the law recommends that the faithful also confess their venial sins (can. 988, §2). Seminarians, clergy, and members of religious and secular institutes are encouraged to approach the sacrament of penance frequently (cans. 246, §4; 276, §2, 5°; 664; 719, §3). In connection with the sacrament of penance, the Code also treats the practice of indulgences (cans. 992-997).

A third important element of the liturgical spirituality in the Code is the celebration of the Liturgy of the Hours. The Liturgy of the Hours is defined as the prayer of the whole Church, which listens to God's word and memorializes the paschal mysteries, praising God in song and prayer without interruption and interceding for the salvation of the whole world (can. 1173). All members of the faithful are "earnestly invited to participate in the liturgy of the hours inasmuch as it is the action of the Church" (can. 1174, §2). Priests and transitional deacons are obliged by law to celebrate the Hours daily; permanent deacons are bound in accord with the law of the episcopal conference; members of institutes of consecrated life and societies of apostolic life are bound according to the norm of their constitutions (cans. 1174, §1; 276, §2, 3°; 663, §3).

The observance of sacred times is another important part of Catholic spirituality related to the liturgy. Sacred times consist of feast days (Sundays and holy days of obligation) and days of penance (the season of Lent and all Fridays). On Sundays and holy days the faithful must participate in the Eucharist and "abstain from those labors and business concerns which impede the worship to be rendered to God, the joy which is proper to the Lord's Day, or the proper relaxation of mind and body" (can. 1247). Fridays are days of abstinence from eating meat in the universal Church, and Ash Wednesday and Good Friday are days of fast and abstinence (can. 1251). The conference of bishops of each nation may make other determinations regarding the laws of fast and abstinence (can. 1253).

In addition to the sacraments (cans. 840-1165), the Liturgy of the Hours, and sacred times, the Code also treats other matters related to Catholic liturgical spirituality. These are the sacramentals, funeral rites, the cult of the Blessed Virgin Mary and the saints, relics, vows and oaths, and sacred places (cans. 1166-1253). Non-liturgical prayers and pious and sacred exercises of the Christian people are not regulated by the Code but by local ordinaries (can. 839, §2). This decentralized approach to popular piety allows for a great diversity of devotional practices among the Catholic people.

2. The second general characteristic of the spirituality manifested in the Code of Canon Law is that it is lived out in the context of institutional structures. Foremost among these is the parish, which is ordinarily a definite territory in a diocese (can. 518); all Catholics with domicile or quasi-domicile in that territory belong to the parish (can. 107) and have a right to partake of the Church's spiritual ministrations there in accord with the law (cans. 528-530; 213-214; 843).

In addition to the parish, there are many organized groups, generically called "associations of the Christian faithful," that build up the spiritual life of the Catholic people. These associations are established to promote a more perfect life, to foster Christian doctrine or public worship, or to support works of the apostolate, such as evangelization, works of piety or charity, or the animation of the temporal order with the Christian spirit (can. 298). Associations of the faithful are regulated by canons 298-329 and by their own statutes.

3. A third characteristic of the spirituality manifested in the Code is that, for most Catholics, it involves the assumption of a new state in the Church in addition to that of *christifidelis,* a baptized believer. The most frequently chosen canonical state is the marital. The Code defines marriage as a covenant by which a man and a woman establish between themselves a partnership (*consortium*) of their whole life (can. 1055). The sacrament is seen as a mystery of unity and of fruitful love reflecting the unity and love that exist between Christ and the Church (can. 1063, 3°). The effects of the sacrament of marriage include the strengthening of the spouses for the duties and dignity of their state so that day by day they may come to lead holier and fuller lives as a couple and as a family (cans. 1134; 1063, 4°). The law exhorts married couples to maintain their marital state in a Christian spirit and to grow in holiness (can. 1063), and to strive to build up the People of God through their marriage and their family (can. 226).

Another sacrament that entails a permanent commitment and a new status in the Church is holy orders (cans. 1008-1054)—the orders of deacon, presbyter, and bishop. Through ordination to the diaconate a person assumes the clerical state and takes on the rights and obligations incumbent upon that state. Among these are obligations pertaining to the spiritual lives of the clergy (cans. 275-280, 282, 287). The Code also establishes rules for the spiritual formation of candidates for the permanent diaconate and seminarians preparing for the presbyterate (cans. 235, 236, 246, 252, 255, 256).

Another way the faithful can exercise a special form of spirituality in the Church is through the profession of the evangelical counsels of poverty, chastity, and obedience. The principal forms of consecrated life are the religious and secular institutes (cans. 573-730). The law also recognizes two rare forms—the eremitic or anchoritic life and consecrated virginity (cans. 603-604). Consecrated life is defined as "a stable form of living by which the faithful, following Christ more closely under the action of the Holy Spirit, are totally dedicated to God who is loved most of all, so that, having dedicated themselves to His honor, the upbuilding of the Church and the salvation of the world by a new and special title, they strive for the perfection of charity in service to the Kingdom of God and, having become an outstanding sign in the Church, they may foretell the heavenly glory" (can. 573, §1; see LG 42-44; CD 33; PC 1.)

Among the forms of consecrated life, the many religious institutes count the most members. Some religious institutes have their own spiritual traditions and practices, which have enriched the whole Church. Unlike members of religious institutes, those of secular institutes do not acquire a new canonical state but retain their status as laity or secular clergy (can. 711). They "express and exercise their own consecration in their apostolic activity and like a leaven they strive to imbue all things with the spirit of the gospel for the strengthening and growth of the Body of Christ" (can. 713, §1). In addition to the laws of the institutes themselves, the Code contains obligations of a spiritual nature that affect members of all religious institutes (cans. 662-664) and all secular institutes (can. 719).

Akin to religious institutes are societies of apostolic life "whose members without religious vows pursue the particular apostolic purpose of the society, and leading a life as brothers or sisters in common according to a particular manner of life, strive for the perfection of charity" (can. 731, §1). The spiritual life of members is regulated by the constitutions of the societies. Clerical members are additionally obliged to observe the spiritual practices and other obligations that bind clergy in general (can. 739).

See also ABSTINENCE; BAPTISM; EREMITICAL LIFE; EUCHARIST; EUCHARISTIC DEVOTION; LAW; LITURGY; MARRIAGE; PENANCE, PENITENCE; RELIGIOUS LIFE; SACRAMENTS; SECULAR INSTITUTES; VOWS.

Bibliography: J. Coriden, T. Green, D. Heintschel, eds., *The Code of Canon Law: A Text and Commentary* (New York/Mahwah, N.J.: Paulist, 1985. J. Lynch, "Canon Law," *The New Dictionary of Theology*, ed. J. Komonchak, M. Collins, D. Lane (Wilmington, Del.: Michael Glazier, 1988). J. Huels, "Law, Liturgical," *The New Dictionary of Sacramental Worship*, ed. P. Fink (Collegeville, Minn.: Liturgical Press, 1990).

JOHN M. HUELS, O.S.M.

CAPITAL SINS

See DEADLY SINS.

CARDINAL VIRTUES

As the Book of Wisdom (8:7) asserts, "If one loves justice, the fruits of her works are virtues; for she teaches moderation and prudence, justice and fortitude, and nothing in life is more useful than these." These four virtues have been emphasized as central to good moral living by the ancient Greek philosophers as well as by Thomas Aquinas and others in the Catholic spiritual tradition. Among many prized virtues, the four have been termed "cardinal" (from Latin *cardo,* "hinge") since the days of Ambrose, because all other moral virtues have been seen as dependent on what they embrace: the ability to discern (prudence), respect for the rights of others (justice), courage in the face of challenges and frustrations (fortitude), and moderation of bodily appetites (temperance). Christian virtues can be understood as developed capacities of the human will and intellect to accomplish moral good with constancy and joy, even in the midst of obstacles and always under the influence of the grace of Christ. The four cardinal virtues are held to be distinct from the three "theological" virtues of faith, hope and charity, which re-

late more directly to God but constitute the context within which cardinal virtues find their Christian meaning.

Far from bringing about mere self-mastery or self-possession, the cardinal virtues orient people outward toward others and God in loving self-giving. The best-formulated teachings about these virtues presuppose that human life participates in the dying and rising of Christ and entails ongoing conversion away from sin toward fuller union with God. Virtues are not ultimately possessions at all, but rather aspects of a unified quest for a life of openness to God that can only be received as grace. A heritage of careful consideration of separate virtues in the Catholic theological tradition should not obscure the ideas that the Christian life is one pursuit, albeit with many dimensions, and that the four cardinal virtues are intrinsically interrelated.

Aquinas's detailed study of the moral life in the *Summa Theologiae* presupposes that all things come from God (*exitus*) and are oriented back to God (*reditus*). Virtues are important means by which humans can return to God. The moral theology of Aquinas closely considers the cardinal virtues, their component elements, their subsidiary moral virtues, and their opposite vices. In all, over fifty virtues and more than a hundred vices are noted. An important Thomistic principle states that one cannot practice one virtue perfectly unless one possesses all of them. In the spirit of Aquinas, the primary question for the Christian called to live the virtues is not "What shall I do?" but "What kind of person shall I be?" Each of the four cardinal virtues disposes different powers and appetites of one who would strive to be a holy disciple of Jesus Christ.

Prudence

Prudence, the "know how" virtue of the practical intellect, seeks the best way to do the right thing in specific circumstances. Entailing the capacity to translate general principles and ideals into practice, prudence deals with acts that are individual but not isolated, for it must know the singular always in its relation to universal norms. Distorted notions of prudence as undue caution, inactivity, moral mediocrity, or selfishness can hamper a richer understanding of the virtue as oriented ultimately toward the praise and service of God.

Successive steps often recommended in exercising the virtue of prudence are: (1) making inquiry, taking counsel, deliberating; (2) making judgment about application of knowledge to a particular situation; and (3) giving command and doing the action.

Qualities found in the prudent person are many: knowledge of moral principles, ability to profit from life experiences, vigilance, perceptivity, docility, ability to make rational inferences, inventiveness or creativity, foresight, and ability to balance and weigh circumstances. Obstacles to prudence include rashness, hesitation, procrastination, negligence, rationalization, and inconstancy.

The Christian spiritual tradition has dealt with the virtue of prudence largely through themes of prayerful reflection and discernment. Prayer can foster growth in prudence, especially when prayer includes thorough meditation on one's everyday experiences and honest examination of one's motivations. In this vein, Bernard of Clairvaux, in *Five Books on Consideration,* spoke of "consideration" (sustained reflection aimed at greater knowledge of self, others, one's surroundings, and God) as displaying prudence, since it purifies the mind, "controls the emotions, guides actions, corrects excesses, improves behavior, confers dignity and order on life, and even imparts knowledge of divine and human affairs" (VII:8).

The discernment of spirits, a practice long valued in the Christian tradition and central to the Ignatian school, exercises prudence as it brings meditation to bear on concrete decisions that arise particularly within a life of action. Under the influence of faith, hope, and charity, discerning individuals or communities examine the nature of the spiritual promptings they experience, as they aim to choose a course of action that best glorifies God and serves others.

Proper emphasis on prudence as a virtue mediating between theory and practice can help to reinforce the long-neglected interconnection of theology with both spirituality and pastoral life. Pope Paul VI's *Evangelii Nuntiandi* (1975) links the essence of the virtue of prudence with the mission of the Church in the late 20th century: "For the Church it is a question not only of preaching the Gospel in ever wider geographical areas ... but also of affecting and, as it were, upsetting, through the power of the Gospel, mankind's criteria of judgment, determining values, points of interest, lines of thought, sources of inspiration and models of life, which are in contrast with the Word of God and the plan of salvation" (art. 19). While respecting the intrinsic link between being and doing, contemporary Christian moral teaching on prudence puts more stress on the importance of the overall faith vision out of which the moral good is to be perceived than on specific instructions on how to do good and avoid evil.

Justice

Justice is the virtue concerned with giving to others what is their due. Human nature imposes on each one an obligation to tend to one's last end and to conform one's conduct to those things necessary to achieve that end. One cannot have such obligations without the right to fulfill them and the consequent right to prevent others from interfering with their fulfillment. Joined prominently to justice is the separate virtue of religion (Latin *religare,* "to bind"), the honor paid by humans toward God, who has a right to their adoration for having created and redeemed them.

Justice is considered as having three basic forms: commutative justice, in relations of people with one another; distributive justice, in relations of society (family, state, church) to individuals; and legal justice, whereby individuals subordinate themselves to the common good.

Writings of the great spiritual writers speak little about justice in itself but much about love, faithfulness, devotion, obedience, and gratitude, virtues related to justice. They speak clearly about two themes that underpin the human rights tradition: that humans are created in the image of God and that they are called to eternal life with God. Christian spiritual movements over the centuries have exemplified care for the socially deprived, e.g., widows, orphans, prisoners, the sick, the uneducated. The papal social encyclicals of the late 19th and 20th centuries have clearly enunciated the need for a just social order and have urged all to take part in achieving this goal.

Recent spiritualities of liberation have looked to the biblical Exodus theme, to the prophets' pleas for justice, and to Jesus' proclamation of the kingdom to ground a call for justice that extends to social, economic, and political circumstances worldwide.

Fortitude

The virtue of fortitude involves standing firm in hope against all pressures, even death. In situations of suffering, desolation, and controversy, it is fortitude, or courage, that moderates the irascible appetite by strengthening it against the passion of fear and by curbing its immoderate stirrings of audacity and destructiveness.

Since fortitude involves human capacities for powerful action that can be oriented positively or negatively, its practice must be guided by self-knowledge and informed by prudence, lest either foolish temerity or quaking timidity hold sway.

The acts of fortitude have been described in the tradition as two—endurance and attack. Endurance, which is more than mere passive submission to danger and suffering, involves the strong action of holding steadfastly to the good while refusing to yield to fear or pain. Its close ally is the virtue of patience (Latin *pati,* "to suffer"), which involves preserving serenity despite injuries resulting from realization of the good. Attack is that aspect of fortitude that does not hesitate to pounce on evil and to bar its progress if this can reasonably be done. When attack stems from motives that are not selfish or wrong, it has sometimes been called "holy anger." Both aspects of fortitude are allied to the virtue of perseverance, or constancy, which strengthens sustained commitment to a good pursuit that one might be tempted to abandon.

In the Christian tradition, endurance has been assigned higher value than attack, inasmuch as endurance often has called for greater bravery. From the Church's early centuries the endurance of a martyr's death stands as the epitome of brave witness to Jesus Christ and his ways. Later, monks living ascetically in community (as "white martyrs") esteemed patience as a way of ongoing and usually quiet participation in the sufferings and death of Jesus Christ.

The context for much contemporary reflection on the virtue of fortitude in everyday living is the human experience of frustration, in which one's goal-seeking is obstructed by factors having to do with oneself, others, the environment, or even the hiddenness of God. For example, Karl Rahner's spiritual writings contain numerous examples of Spirit-empowered fortitude, as when one's love for a neighbor is steadfast although not reciprocated, or when one prays faithfully even when God seems silent.

Spiritual support groups, many inspired by the twelve-step model practiced in Alcoholics Anonymous, offer members help in being courageous in various conditions. A favorite prayer of these participants combines themes of fortitude and prudence: "God, grant me the serenity to accept the things I cannot change; courage to change the things I can; and wisdom to know the difference."

Temperance

Temperance is the virtue that moderates one's bodily appetites and disposes them for development of the whole person. It fosters what might be called selfless self-preservation, since it treats sensual instincts not as ends in themselves but as means to an end, the fulfillment of the kingdom of God. One who chooses to temper or channel the sources of power that lie under one's control is open to experience that life has another and deeper source—God.

The spiritual tradition has often spoken of temperance in terms of asceticism, the "exercise" of removing obstacles that stand in the way of following Christ more freely, and mortification, the "putting to death" of unbridled passions through discipline and self-denial. A sound approach to these themes would acknowledge that the body is not the enemy of the spirit but a normal channel by which spirit expresses itself. Unfortunately, the Christian centuries have not always witnessed such soundness or balance in all who seek spiritual growth. In fact, the Christian tradition's greatest spiritual teachers have counteracted with calls for moderation in spiritual disciplines and penances.

The Christian spiritual tradition has taught that anyone who becomes the servant of the forces of disintegration within oneself, by yielding every time their drive is experienced, is inevitably more and more impaired in every aspect of life; so one becomes less disposed to see truth, to want it, and to choose it.

Maintaining a balanced, or temperate, rhythm of life has long been recommended as essential to growth in holiness. Each person must discover his or her own spiritual equilibrium, by reflection, experimentation, and ongoing effort. Guided by the insight that God does not call a person in ways that violate personal temperament, some recent spiritual writers have stressed the benefits of linking personality types with fitting ways of praying and structuring spiritual disciplines.

Some contemporary theologians have suggested that these four virtues are actually not the most central to Christian moral living. For example, Bernard Häring has proposed that six others—gratitude, humility, hope, vigilance, serenity, and joy—are more richly based in Scripture and more clearly eschatological. Still, reflection on the cardinal virtues can lead people of any age to ponder some of the most crucial dimensions of a holy Christian life.

See also ASCETICISM; CHASTITY; CONSCIENCE; DISCERNMENT OF SPIRITS; HOLINESS; JUSTICE; MORTIFICATION; PASSION(S); PERSONALITY TYPES; POWER; VIRTUE; ZEAL.

Bibliography: J. Crossin, *What Are They Saying About Virtue?* (New York: Paulist, 1985). J. O'Donohoe, "A Return to Virtue," *Church* 3/1 (Spring 1987) 48–54. J. Pieper, *The Four Cardinal Virtues* (Notre Dame, Ind.: Univ. of Notre Dame Press, 1966).

GEORGE P. EVANS

CARMELITE SPIRITUALITY

The name *Carmelite* derives from the mountain range Mount Carmel in the Holy Land, where the Carmelite Order originated about A.D. 1200. A group of lay penitent hermits at the wadi 'ain es-Shiah received a formula of life from Albert, patriarch of Jerusalem, between 1206 and 1214. This formula of life gave the Carmelites their basic spiritual orientation in the Church. The themes of this formula were solitude (individual cells located around a chapel), silence, continual prayer (chiefly the psalms), with life centered on the following of Jesus and an uncommon eremitic element of daily Eucharist when possible, and a life of the usual asceticism common to hermits. Albert's formula of life did not envisage pastoral ministry to those outside the community. In 1229 Pope Gregory IX imposed corporate poverty on the hermits of Mount Carmel.

The deterioration of the Latin kingdom soon made it imperative for the hermits to emigrate from the Holy Land. The Carmelite hermits began to move westward about 1238. They migrated to Cyprus, Sicily, England, and southern France. Within a short time the Carmelites found that their eremitic lifestyle was ill-suited to contemporary religious life in Western Europe. At the very time that the Carmelites were founding eremitic houses in Europe, the Dominicans and Franciscans were meeting the pastoral challenges of the Fourth Lateran Council with extraordinary success.

Faced with this dilemma, the Carmelites acted expeditiously. They sought from the papacy approval for a revision of their formula of life that would make it possible for them to follow in the footsteps of the extremely popular friars. The Carmelites received from Innocent IV approval for slight changes in the wording of their formula of life. Through Innocent's action the formula became an official Rule (*regula*), and the Carmelites became friars. Minor as were the textual changes in the Rule, they had an enormous impact on Carmelite spirituality. The hermits from Mount Carmel were now allowed to settle in towns as well as in the wilderness locations formerly permitted by the formula of life. They were to live in a dormitory (though still with individual cells), eat together in a refectory, and participate in the choral Office. The once semi-eremitic community thus became more cenobitic.

These changes meant, in effect, that the Carmelite hermits were now mendicants like the Dominicans and the Franciscans. They resolutely and immediately acted as such by making foundations in the towns of Europe where the Dominicans and the Franciscans were already ministering to the new urban dwellers. To prepare themselves for the ministries of preaching, teaching, and administering the sacraments, the Carmelites took steps that made

them, like the other friars, a student order. By the end of the 13th century the Carmelites were well established at the universities of Cambridge, Oxford, and Paris. During the rest of the Middle Ages the Carmelites moved to the other universities of Europe.

The Carmelites became and have remained a major mendicant order in the Church. With constitutions modeled on those of the Dominican Order, the Carmelites were thoroughly appropriated into the friars' way of life with a mendicant spirituality: mobility in place of monastic stability, corporate as well as personal poverty, the following of modified monastic prayers and practices, and a commitment to pastoral ministry. They entered the ranks of the mendicants despite internal and external opposition in the 13th century. Yet, the Carmelite friars retained a memory of their eremitic origins, sometimes vivid, sometimes obscured by other preoccupations. Their eremitic origins and their appropriation of cenobitic mendicancy created the fundamental tension in Carmelite spirituality: solitude and (ministerial) community. Vital Carmelite reforms must always return to this tension in order to recover a form of Carmelite life faithful to the order's origins yet responsive to contemporary circumstances.

Elijah

The prophet Elijah occupies a significant place in Carmelite spirituality. Long before the Carmelites came on the scene, Elijah had been a model for monks and especially for hermits. When the Carmelites settled on Mount Carmel, they were well aware of the association of Elijah with this mountain range. The fountain at their original hermitage on Mount Carmel mentioned in the formula of life was later identified as the fountain of Elijah.

The extant constitutions of the 13th century contain a prologue that saw Carmelite life as modeled on the example of Elijah and Elisha. In the 14th century a literary tradition was initiated that looked to Elijah as the inspiration and the founder of the Carmelite Order. Through the centuries, however, much energy was wasted on a literalist interpretation of this myth. However, the modern retrieval of the Elian tradition emphasizes Elijah as an archetype of Carmelite spirituality. When the French Discalced Carmelites consulted Carl Jung, he assured them that Elijah is, in fact, a genuine "living archetype." The motto on the Carmelite shield is an Elian quotation taken from the Vulgate rendition of 1 Kgs 19:10, 14: "I am zealous with zeal for the Lord God of hosts." Teresa of Jesus and John of the Cross had a profound respect for the tradition that saw Elijah as a primal inspiration for Carmelite life. Both saints refer to Elijah as "our father." The Carmelite liturgical calendar has long celebrated a feast in honor of Elijah (July 20).

Retrievals of the Carmelite tradition must take into account the central role that Elijah has had in shaping Carmelite consciousness. That the Carmelites had no known founder, let alone a charismatic founder like Dominic or Francis, predisposed them to emphasize Elijah and Mary when they were competing with other religious orders for stature. These two figures—one from the Hebrew Scriptures and the other from the Christian Scriptures—have had a fundamental role in the evolution of Carmelite spirituality.

Mary

The chapel around which the hermits on Mount Carmel situated their hermitages was dedicated to Mary, an ancient tradition says, and by the mid-13th century the Carmelite friars bore the title that, in one version or the other, they have preserved since that time: "Brothers of the Blessed Virgin Mary of Mount Carmel." Toward the end of the 13th century, the Carmelites stated that their order had been founded to honor Mary. In the order's struggle for identity during the Middle Ages, Carmelite

literature looked more and more to Mary as the order's claim to preeminence.

In the 15th century, devotion to Mary crystalized around the vision of Mary allegedly accorded in the mid-13th century to Simon Stock, a figure about whom little is known once the late medieval legends about him are discarded. Nonetheless, the wearing of the (brown) scapular became a sign of dedication to Mary and of reliance on her promise to Simon Stock of salvation for those who die wearing the scapular. The scapular has also symbolized affiliation with the Carmelite Order. The wearing of the scapular became especially widespread in the 19th and early 20th century and is still a practice among first, second, and third members of the Carmelite Order as well as among those who belong to the Confraternity of Our Lady of Mount Carmel.

In the 17th century there developed within the Carmelite Order a Marian mysticism. Mary, the mother of Jesus, has been and continues to be a central figure in Carmelite spirituality. Although there have been times when this regard for Mary tended toward devotionalism, the Carmelite saints have nurtured a vigorous dedication to the patroness of the order, whose feast as Our Lady of Mount Carmel is July 16. Teresa of Jesus in various places calls herself "a nun of Our Lady of Mount Carmel," and she speaks warmly of wearing Mary's habit. John of the Cross writes in *The Ascent of Mount Carmel* (3.2.10) of Mary's mystical experience. The Carmelites, in addition, continue the medieval custom of making their profession of vows not only to God but also to Blessed Mary. Carmelite identity has been profoundly shaped by a consciousness of the intimacy with the Blessed Virgin that has pervaded the order's history and literature.

Institution of the First Monks

Second only to the Carmelite Rule, the most important medieval text in Carmelite spirituality was the *Institution of the First Monks*. This document appeared about

1370 among a set of texts which were allegedly from an earlier era but which were, in reality, the work of the provincial of Catalonia, Philip Ribot. Otger Steggink has called the *Institution* "the principal book of spiritual reading" among Carmelites until the 17th century. This text, probably studied by Teresa of Avila (in a Castilian translation) and by John of the Cross, laid the groundwork for the mystical orientation of Carmelite spirituality that would be articulated by the two Spanish mystics and the Touraine Reform. The *Institution* sees the life of the Carmelite as a withdrawal from the usual preoccupations of life, a purification of the heart, and the gift of perceived union with God in love. The Carmelite, moreover, according to this document, lives this spiritual journey in the spirit of the prophet Elijah. An edition of this text is being prepared by Paul Chandler and deserves to be much better known by those who seek inspiration in Carmelite spirituality and who wish to understand the roots of the Carmelite mystical tradition.

Reforms and the Origins of the Carmelite Nuns

Like other religious orders in the late Middle Ages, the Carmelites made numerous efforts to return to a more dedicated way of life. By the early 15th century Carmelites in northern Italy initiated a reform that came to be known as the Congregation of Mantua. This group set aside the mitigation of the Carmelite Rule permitted in 1432 by Eugene IV. The Mantuan reform sought a return to the solitude of the Rule and a restoration of both community life and poverty. The latter two elements were at the time concerns of many religious orders seeking reform. The search for solitude, on the other hand, had special significance for Carmelite renewal.

The most important Carmelite reformer before the sixteenth century was the Frenchman Blessed John Soreth, prior general of the order from 1451 until 1471.

Soreth, like other reformers of the era, fostered a return to the spirit of the Rule; in fact, he composed an important commentary on the Carmelite Rule. After Soreth's death his reform was not sustained. Yet, the late Middle Ages produced other saintly Carmelites, among them Baptist of Mantua, Angelus Mazzinghi, Frances d'Amboise, Aloysius Rabata, Joan Scopeli, Bartholomew Fanti, and Arcangela Girlani. Baptist of Mantua died in 1516, while the rest of these holy women and men died during the 15th century, not a time known for an overabundance of outstandingly holy religious women and men.

From the time of the entry of the Carmelites into the mendicant ranks, lay women and men associated themselves with the order and on a variety of levels shared fellowship with the Carmelite friars. Unlike the Dominicans and Franciscans, however, the Carmelites did not develop a second order of women in the 13th century. In fact, it was not until A.D. 1452 that a papal bull gave approval for the incorporation of women into the Carmelite family as a second order. This new evolution in Carmelite history had a permanent and profound effect on the Carmelite Order and its spirituality. These Carmelite women were not only the predecessors of Teresa of Jesus but also of all women who became Carmelites after this event of the mid-15th century. With Teresa of Jesus in the next century, women assumed a central role in the living and articulation of Carmelite spirituality. Though women came belatedly to this status in the Carmelite Order, they have been at the heart of Carmelite spirituality since the time of Teresa of Jesus. This introduction of nuns into the Carmelite Order was the achievement of Blessed John Soreth.

Like other orders struggling with reform at the end of the Middle Ages and in the early 16th century, the Carmelites encountered one frustration after another. Nicholas Audet, prior general from 1524 to 1562, made valiant and energetic efforts to reform the Carmelites. However, success eluded him and others. Not until Teresa of Jesus did there emerge an inspired reading of the original Carmelite charism, a reading that brought true and lasting reform to the Carmelite family.

Teresa of Avila (1515–1582)

A midlife conversion experience of Doña Teresa de Ahumada, a nun at the Carmelite monastery of the Incarnation in Avila, was the catalyst for the most significant reform in the history of the Carmelite Order. For Teresa it was the beginning of a whole "new life" when God began to manifest a loving divine presence to her. Reform for the Carmelite women and then the men came when Teresa recalled the fervor and solitude of the 13th-century hermits on Mount Carmel. Solitude had not been available for Teresa in the large and crowded monastery of the Incarnation, so she shaped a new model of Carmelite life at her first foundation of San José in Avila, where she limited the number of nuns to a small enough community to support a life of solitude and prayer. From the time of this foundation Teresa symbolized her new life with a change of name. From then on Teresa never used the formal title "Doña" but signed herself simply as Teresa of Jesus.

In response to the requests of her nuns for instruction in prayer, Teresa composed *The Way of Perfection,* in which she explores relationships in community, the prayer of recollection, and growth in prayer. In her *Book of Foundations* Teresa shows herself a gifted storyteller, providing spirited vignettes of the establishment of her foundations and of the lives of those involved in these foundations. For her confessors Teresa wrote her *Life.* Here Teresa, with some autobiographical details as the framework, describes God's mystical manifestations in her life and also the beginnings of her reform. It is in this book, chapters 11 to 22, that her treatise on prayer appears, with its imagery of water to describe God's growing mystical presence. These chapters can be read as a separate tract once the rest of the book is read as a unit. While her *Life* was in the hands of the Inquisition, Teresa wrote her classic exposition of the mystical journey to God, *The Interior Castle.* With her experience of the mystical life, she leads the reader through the seven mansions—the first three as prelude to the mystical life, and the last four as the journey to the mystical union of spiritual marriage.

In her writings Teresa of Jesus, architect of the Carmelite reform that resulted, after the death of John of the Cross, in the creation of the Discalced Carmelite Order, gives classic expression to the mystical fruition of the Carmelite contemplative tradition. What she describes is the limit of human effort and the unlimited scope of God's loving action in a human person willing to let God love one fully. Her exposition of Carmelite mysticism is down-to-earth, a story told with compassion and humor. She is clear that what counts is love of God, but she is adamant that the only genuine sign that one loves God is love of neighbor. Her letters show the earthy context of her interests and activities. Teresa's dying words reveal the ecclesial context of her life of Carmelite spirituality. She died calling herself over and over again "a daughter of the Church."

Teresa of Jesus was beatified in 1614, less than thirty-two years after her death, and she was canonized in 1622. In 1970 she was declared the first woman Doctor of the Church. Her warm personality, so evident in her letters and other writings, attracts people of all faiths.

John of the Cross (1542–1591)

Teresa of Jesus handpicked a friar to be her collaborator in the reform of the Carmelite Order. Her choice was the newly ordained John of Saint Matthias, who consented to collaborate in this reform only if Teresa acted quickly. He was already thinking of transferring to the Carthusians for the sake of greater solitude. With Teresa's guidance, John thoroughly committed himself to the radical living of the Carmelite charism. As Teresa had done, her collaborator symbolized the newness of his life by changing his name to John of the Cross.

John's single-minded, God-centered life earned him the animosity of his brothers, who imprisoned him in a tiny closet at the Carmelite monastery in Toledo. There he composed some of his poems, especially many stanzas of his "Spiritual Canticle." After his escape John shared poetry with his directees, especially the Carmelite nuns, who then wanted him to explain the meaning of the poetry that had emerged from his mystical experience. These explanations constitute John of the Cross's four commentaries. *The Ascent of Mount Carmel* and *The Dark Night* comment on the poem "Dark Night," while the following commentaries explain poems with the same names as the commentaries: *The Spiritual Canticle* and *The Living Flame of Love.*

In the past, too little attention has been paid to the poetry of John of the Cross. To understand the spiritual doctrine of John of the Cross, it is necessary to be thoroughly familiar with the poetry upon which he comments. In addition, his letters provide a way of appreciating his relationships with women and men. A better understanding of the doctrine of John of the Cross is available to one who comes to his texts with a thorough acquaintance with his mystically based poetry, his dependence upon the Bible, especially on the Song of Songs, and some knowledge of his compassionate personality. The principal ministry of John of the Cross was spiritual direction, but he was actively involved in other ministries, including his role as an able administrator.

For John of the Cross, the goal of the contemplative life is the transformation of the soul in God, that is, union with God in love. This intensification of love presumes that one has been liberated from the attachments that keep one unfree. The dark-night experience is God's loving action that liberates one in a way that only God can accomplish. John of the Cross calls for radical freedom so that one may be fully open to God's love and love God and neighbor in return. Freed from disordered attachments, the one who is transformed in God, living in union with God, is now free to embrace others and creation as one was formerly unable to do.

In the late 17th century, fear of quietism pushed the spiritual doctrine of John of the Cross into the background. Scholasticism, moreover, robbed John's doctrine of its poetic, biblical, and experiential foundations. The Spanish poets of the 20th century rediscovered the poetry of John of the Cross and brought him to the attention of a wider modern audience. Presently there is a concerted effort to recover his spiritual teachings.

In 1982 the fourth centenary of the death of Teresa of Jesus was an occasion for focusing on the dynamism of Teresa's Carmelite spirituality. The celebration of the fourth centenary of the death of John of the Cross in 1991 offered the same opportunity for the retrieval of the spiritual doctrine of John of the Cross. The writings of Teresa of Avila and John of the Cross are, in fact, the classical expression of the mystical dimension of Carmelite spirituality. In the post–Vatican II era, especially from the 1980s onward, the emphasis has been on learning how to read the writings of these Spanish mystics on their own terms, in their historical context, and with an appreciation of their importance for the Christian life of mystical experience and mystical theology.

John of the Cross was beatified in 1675 and was canonized in 1726. He was declared a Doctor of the Church in 1926. John's poetry and doctrine offer an important opportunity for the healing of the long-standing divorce between mysticism and theology.

Touraine Reform

With the establishment of the Discalced reform as a separate order in 1593, the original branch of the order had to face the need for reform. A congenial climate for reform was found in the renewed interest in the interior life of 17th-century France. The most lasting and influential reform of the original branch took place in the Carmelite province of Touraine. Spearheaded by Peter Behourt (d. 1633), the reform was led by Philip Thibault. The spiritual inspiration of the reform was the blind laybrother John of St. Samson (d. 1636), who was the source of spiritual guidance for many members of this reform. The Touraine reform was another renewal of the Carmelite contemplative tradition that included a mystical expression of the order's charism. Current research into figures of the reform like John of St. Samson promises a new appreciation of the importance of the Touraine reform, which has had a far-reaching influence on the spirituality of the Carmelite Order down to the 20th century.

Thérèse of Lisieux (1873–1897)

Along with Teresa of Avila and John of the Cross, the most widely known Carmelite is Thérèse Martin, whose name in the monastery was Sister Thérèse of the Child Jesus and of the Holy Face. The popular designation "Little Flower" derives from her love of flowers and her use of flower imagery, especially in her references to herself as a "little flower," but indeed as a "little winter flower" who passed through the harshness of suffering. Despite her use of a spiritual idiom of her day that sounds, at times, coy and sentimental, Thérèse of Lisieux lived and wrote about a spirituality matured in the crucible of suffering. For the last eighteen months before she died, the young nun endured a terrible darkness marked by temptations against faith. Yet, she admitted that it was faith that protected her against suicide.

Though Thérèse never used the phrase "spiritual childhood," she lived and spoke of a little way of trust and love that cut through to the heart of gospel simplicity. Her message, like that of Teresa of Jesus and John of the Cross, has a ring of gospel authenticity, as is evident in the emphasis of all three on the love of God and love of neighbor. For Thérèse, "it is love alone that counts." Thérèse of Lisieux had a playful spirit and an infectious sense of humor. Even amid her sufferings she remained very human, as demonstrated by her request from her sickbed for a chocolate éclair. For Thérèse, God was everywhere or, as she said, "Everything is a grace."

The sources of Thérèse's spirituality were, in particular, the Bible (note the impact of Isaiah's suffering servant texts on her), and especially the Gospels. She was also much influenced by the writings of John of the Cross, which she read avidly over a period of several years and whose doctrine she profoundly appropriated. She looked also to the *Imitation of Christ* and to the Carmelite tradition as it was mediated to her in the monastery at Lisieux.

The Church beatified Thérèse in 1923 and canonized her two years later. In 1927 Pope Pius XI named St. Thérèse, with St. Francis Xavier, principal patroness of the missions. Pius XII in 1944 declared Thérèse to be, with Joan of Arc, the secondary patroness of France. Though she did not write for publication, Thérèse, like Teresa and John, had a gift for expressing her spiritual experience in a telling way. Her *Story of a Soul* quickly became a modern spiritual classic. Moreover, devotion to her was intense and phenomenal until the 1960s, when a waning in her cult took place. Her doctrine and life are presently being recovered with a growing appreciation of the soundness of her spiritual perception.

Modern Carmelite Figures

There are a number of 20th century Carmelites who have lived the Carmelite charism in a gifted way. Three of them have become particularly well known and have been beatified. Blessed Elizabeth of the Trinity (1880–1906), a French Discalced Carmelite nun, died at age twenty-six in the Carmelite monastery at Dijon. Blessed Elizabeth's Trinitarian spirituality offers to contemporary theologians an opportunity to reflect upon the mystery of the Trinity as revealed in the life and prayer of a modern Carmelite woman. Elizabeth's spirituality, like that of Teresa of Avila, John of the Cross, Thérèse of Lisieux, and the *Institution of the First Monks,* is a mysticism of love—a love of God and neighbor lived in the solitude of the monastery but extended to the neighbor everywhere.

The second modern Carmelite chosen for inclusion here is Edith Stein (1891–1942), a Jew who converted to Catholicism and became a Carmelite nun in her native Germany. She was known in her order as Sister Teresa Benedicta of the Cross. Edith Stein was a brilliant philosopher who served as an assistant to the phenomenologist Edmund Husserl. As a Catholic, Edith became a teacher. She lectured and wrote especially about issues concerning the education of women. As a Carmelite nun in Cologne, she published an important study of John of the Cross. Her writings, philosophical and otherwise, are being translated into English. As a Jewish, Catholic, Carmelite philosopher and educator, Edith Stein's life and writings have the potential for drawing together what appear to be the irreconcilable paradoxes of her life and also of her death. She was executed in the Nazi concentration camp at Auschwitz. The naming of Edith Stein as a blessed is, indeed, a puzzle for Jews, who view her as a victim of the extermination of the Jews by the Nazis rather than as a Catholic martyr. As a woman intellectual from the Carmelite contemplative tradition, Edith Stein may yet prove to be an inspiration for the reconciliation of Jews and Christians. The beatification of Edith Stein took place in 1987.

Titus Brandsma (1881–1942), a Carmelite friar of the Ancient Observance, was a professor at the University of Nijmegen and a journalist. In his branch of the order, Titus Brandsma was a pioneer in articulating a modern interpretation of Carmelite spirituality. An institute of spirituality has been named in his honor at the University of Nijmegen. Brandsma's opposition to the Nazis and his work with the Catholic journalists of the Netherlands caused him to be taken to the Nazi camps. He was martyred in 1942 at the concentration camp at Dachau. Pope John Paul II named Titus Brandsma a blessed in 1985.

Conclusion

For almost eight hundred years Carmelite spirituality has been a vital way of following Jesus. This spirituality, which originated with simple hermits on Mount Carmel, places a special emphasis on solitude and prayer. A pastoral orientation was introduced into this spirituality when the Carmelite Order entered the mendicant ranks in the middle of the 13th century. Especially well known and formative has been the contribution of the cloistered Carmelite nuns to the evolution of Carmelite spirituality. However, Carmelite spirituality is the common property of the Christian Churches in a day when there is a widespread desire to retrieve a more contemplative approach to the living of the Gospels.

See also CONTEMPLATION, CONTEMPLATIVE PRAYER; EREMITICAL LIFE; JOURNEY (GROWTH AND DEVELOPMENT IN SPIRITUAL LIFE); MARRIAGE, MYSTICAL; MEDITATION; MYSTICISM; REFORMATION AND CATHOLIC REFORMATION SPIRITUALITIES; SPIRITUALITY, CHRISTIAN (CATHOLIC), HISTORY OF; THREE WAYS; WESTERN MEDIEVAL SPIRITUALITY.

Bibliography: K. Egan, "The Spirituality of the Carmelites," *Christian Spirituality: High Middle Ages and Reformation,*ed. J. Raitt (New York: Crossroad, 1987) 50–62. M. Mulhall, ed., *Albert's Way: The First*

North American Congress on the Carmelite Rule (Barrington, Ill.: Province of the Most Pure Heart of Mary, 1989). *The Rule of Carmel,* ed. and trans. B. Edwards (Aylesford and Kensington, England, 1973). L. Saggi, ed., *Santi del Carmelo: Biografie da vari dizionari* (Rome: Institutum Carmelitanum, 1972). L. Saggi, *Saints of Carmel,* trans. G. Pausback (Westmont, Ill., 1975). J. Smet, *The Carmelites: A History of the Brothers of Our Lady of Mount Carmel,* 4 vols. (Darien, Ill.: Carmelite Spiritual Center, 1975–85).

KEITH J. EGAN

CARTHUSIAN SPIRITUALITY

"God, and God alone, in solitude!" These words were frequently in the heart and on the lips of St. Bruno (1032–1101). In founding the Carthusian way of life, he had no other goal in mind than that the monk should "seek God" and, by daily dying to self, learn to "prefer nothing to Christ."

Bruno's aim was not to begin a new way of monastic living but to reinvigorate the monastic life of his day. This he sought to do by combining the eremitical life of earlier times (as lived in the Near East by desert solitaries) with elements of community life. Thus he hoped to eliminate the dangers of solitude, while at the same time profiting from the advantages of the common life.

In doing this, Bruno introduced no new elements as such. Carthusian spirituality is heir to the common heritage of monastic spirituality. Its elements are the same: a vowed life, in a place apart, lived to a rhythm of personal and liturgical prayer, reading, study, and manual labor, in an atmosphere of external and internal solitude and silence. The organization of these elements, and the stress placed upon the solitary experience of the individual monk, is proper to Carthusian spirituality.

Sources

St. Bruno did not provide a monastic rule of his own for his followers. The way of life of the first Carthusians drew its inspiration from the Rule of Benedict, which set forth principles of monastic living and provided an order for the Divine Office. In addition, the monastic literature of both the East and the West was highly valued and carefully studied, in particular the writings of St. Augustine, St. Basil, the literature of the desert solitaries, and the *Institutes* and *Conferences* of John Cassian.

The Carthusians must be viewed in the context of the larger monastic reform movements of the 11th and 12th centuries. Like the Cluniacs, their spirituality was characterized by a strong sense of the communion of saints. In addition to the canonical Office, they daily recited the Office of the Blessed Virgin Mary and the Office of the Dead. Devotion to the saints was carefully cultivated. From the Cistercians they received the writings of St. Bernard and an appreciation of the Canticle of Canticles as an allegory of the soul's spiritual journey to union with God in prayer. With St. Romuald and the Camaldolese, they combined cenobitical and eremitical monastic living, avoided ecclesiastical offices and dignities, and sought to live a simple life, without power and influence, austere, hidden, and unknown. As was common to the age, they adopted such external signs of devotion to Our Lady as the wearing of the white habit and the dedication of each monastery to the Mother of God.

Central Themes

A Place Apart

"I will . . . bring her into the wilderness, and speak tenderly to her" (Hos 2:14, RSV). The charterhouse (as the Carthusian monastery is called, from *chartreuse,* the lonely site of the first of St. Bruno's foundations) is purposely located in a remote, inaccessible place. Mountainous terrain is preferred, rugged and well-wooded. In the stillness of a mountain retreat, the monk feels closer to God. Contact with those outside the monastery is limited; guests are few.

Life Together

"The community of believers was of one heart and mind" (Acts 4:32). Carthusian solitude is cenobitic solitude. The charterhouse is so arranged that the solitary experience of each individual monk receives support from the Carthusian family as a whole. Common spaces (church, refectory, chapter house, infirmary) are located in close proximity to individual cells. The exercises of the common life are highly valued. Those newly come to monastic life receive formation, the sick and the aged are cared for, there is recreation in common, and once a week the brethren leave the enclosure for a long walk in the woods with conversation. The guidance of the monastic superior and the regular practice of spiritual direction aid the monk in discerning God's will and avoiding the traps of illusion and self-deception. Friendship is encouraged and a warm family spirit is carefully cultivated.

O Blessed Solitude!

"Be still, and know that I am God!" (Ps 46:10, RSV). The statutes of the Carthusian Order state: ". . . all our study and intention is to live in the silence and solitude of the cell." The Carthusian passes the greater part of his life in a little four-room dwelling, more a hermitage than a "cell." A garden plot adjoins it. Here he prays, engages in holy reading and study, performs manual labor (gardening and other work done with the hands leave the mind free for meditative prayer), takes his solitary meals, and enjoys leisure and rest. "Remain in your cell and your cell will teach you all things" is an old monastic adage. The Carthusian spiritual discipline creates time and space for the monk to "cultivate the cell" during the day without interruption. He does not go to the church for the minor Hours of the canonical Office but prays them individually (with full choir ritual) in the small oratory of his cell. All that he needs is at hand, so there is no need for

him to go out. At the appointed time meals are brought.

To what end this silence? What lesson does the solitude of the cell teach? Such questions touch upon the very mystery of human existence. The monk believes that God has a word to speak to each human heart. Only the one who is listening is able to hear it. Only the one whose heart has been emptied is ready to receive it. Becoming empty, being still, listening—this is the work of the cell. Its prayer? The heart of the monk, stilled and quieted, yearns for that spirit of continual prayer commanded by the Gospel (see Lk 18:1; 1 Thess 5:17), a prayer pleasing to God more for its "tears of compunction" than for its many words, a prayer that is a foretaste of that constant communion with God that is the goal of all the baptized: "Taste and see that the Lord is good" (Ps 34:8, RSV). As the monk progresses in the way of true prayer, he comes to "know" in the depth of his being that the promise is true: "Blessed are the pure in heart, for they will see God" (Mt 5:8, RSV).

The Body of Christ

"Now there are varieties of gifts, but the same Spirit; and there are varieties of service, but the same Lord" (1 Cor 12:4, RSV). A measure of silence and solitude is essential to the life of every Christian. The degree to which the Carthusian participates in these is a particular gift of the Holy Spirit, given, ultimately, for the building up of the whole Body of Christ. The Carthusian accepts the gift of solitude as his particular way to die to self in order to rise with Christ. His is a hidden way of gospel living, the value of which can be known in its fullness only to God. The Decree on the Appropriate Renewal of the Religious Life of the Second Vatican Council provides insight into the nature of this gift when it states that those who have given themselves to God alone "in solitude and silence through constant prayer and ready penance . . . offer God a choice sacrifice of praise. They brighten God's people with the richest splendors of sanctity. By their example they motivate this people; by imparting a hidden, apostolic fruitfulness, they make this people grow. Thus they are the glory of the Church and an overflowing fountain of heavenly graces" (PC 7).

Carthusian Writers

From the first days of the order, Carthusians have sought to share the fruits of solitude with those outside the cloister by copying, editing, and composing books of a theological and spiritual nature. It has been said that Carthusians "preach with their hands" because of their labor with pen and ink. With the invention of printing, they were among the first to employ the new technology in order to spread the gospel through the printed word.

The list of Carthusian authors whose writings have enriched the corpus of spiritual literature is extensive. A number have enjoyed wide readership.

The tradition began with St. Bruno himself, whose commentaries on the psalms and on the letters of St. Paul were highly regarded by his contemporaries. Medieval spiritual literature was greatly enriched by the "Meditations" of Guigo II. His treatise, *The Ladder of Monks,* on the ascent of the devout soul toward union with God, is a spiritual classic that has once again come to be known and appreciated in our day.

An abundance of writings on the spiritual life was produced in charterhouses from the 13th to the 18th century. One of the most popular books of the Middle Ages was the *Life of Christ* by Ludolf of Saxony. Devotion to the Sacred Heart of Jesus, long a tradition in the order, was further developed and popularized by Lanspergius in the age before St. Margaret Mary. His writings were also instrumental in furthering devotion to the holy rosary. Spurious produced an extensive *Lives of the Saints,* and his efforts provided a first impetus for the monumental work of the Bollandists.

In our own day, the short essays on solitude, silence, and prayer of Augustin Guillerand have been valued for their profound yet simple language. The books of Thomas Verner Moore have sought to apply to traditional spirituality the findings of modern psychology.

See also BENEDICTINE SPIRITUALITY; CAMALDOLESE SPIRITUALITY; CISTERCIAN SPIRITUALITY; CONTEMPLATION, CONTEMPLATIVE PRAYER; EREMITICAL LIFE; MONASTICISM, MONASTIC SPIRITUALITY.

Bibliography: *The Carthusians: Origin, Spirit, Family Life* (Westminster, Md.: Newman, 1959). Guigo II, *The Ladder of Monks and Twelve Meditations,* E. Colledge and J. Walsh (Garden City, N.Y.: Doubleday Image Books, 1978). A Carthusian [A. Guillerand], *They Speak by Silences,* trans. by a Monk of Parkminster (Huntington, Ind.: Our Sunday Visitor, 1975).

SAMUEL F. WEBER, O.S.B.

CATECHESIS

See PREACHING; SCRIPTURE; STUDY; TEACHING.

CATHOLIC ACTION

Catholic Action began as an Italian lay political arm of popes in the early part of the 20th century. Through the active encouragement of Pius XI, it grew from a Catholic political pressure group to a worldwide movement that aimed to bring Christian witness to bear on the secular world through a spirituality that related to life in the world. Pope Pius XI promoted it aggressively in his speeches, defining it as the participation of the laity in the work of the hierarchy.

A Belgian parish priest, Joseph Cardijn, who worked with young miners, formed the Young Christian Workers, a movement that Pope Pius XI strongly endorsed as an authentic form of Catholic Action. The Young Christian Students was organized in Paris as the student counterpart of the worker movement. These movements, known as specialized Catholic Action, spread quickly around the world with the blessing of successive popes.

The specialized movements came to the United States in the late 1930s by way of England and Australia. The Christian Family Movement, which began in Chicago in the late 1940s, was a distinctive American contribution completing the triad of the specialized movements. Reynold Hillenbrand, rector of Mundelein Seminary, was the patron of North American specialized Catholic Action.

The spirituality of specialized Catholic Action was not based on a personal piety but on a spirituality that saw the world as the arena of the layperson's mission, focusing on institutional change. The theology of Catholic Action as lay involvement in the world, viewed as an extension of the ministry of the bishop, ceased before Vatican II affirmed baptism as the layperson's mandate for Christian witness.

See also APOSTOLIC SPIRITUALITY; CATHOLIC WORKER MOVEMENT; LAY SPIRITUALITY; WORLD.

Bibliography: J. Newman, *What Is Catholic Action?* (Westminster, Md.: Newman, 1958). T. Hesburgh, *The Theology of Catholic Action* (Notre Dame, Ind.: Univ. of Notre Dame Press, 1946). M. Zotti, *A Time of Awakening* (Chicago: Loyola Univ. Press, 1991).

DENNIS J. GEANEY, O.S.A.

CATHOLIC WORKER MOVEMENT

"Our Manifesto is the Sermon on the Mount," announced Dorothy Day in *The Catholic Worker* of January 1942 after the United States had entered World War II. As the co-founder of the Catholic Worker movement, she was reiterating the position of pacifism that had caused a division in the movement and was giving rise to defections from it. "We will print the words of Christ who is with us always even to the end of the world," she continued. "Love your enemy, do good to those who hate you and pray for those who persecute and calumniate you so that you may be children of your Father in heaven" (Mt 5:44-45).

The high resolve of living by the beatitudes with which Jesus began the Sermon on the Mount was shared by the movement's co-founder, Peter Maurin. His principle of Christian living, the very heart of the movement, was "the daily practice of the works of mercy." Mercy was simply love under the aspect of need, love going out to meet the needs of the person loved. The person loved was to be seen as Jesus, who in the parable of the Last Judgment identified with the hungry, the naked, and the homeless (Mt 25:31-46).

A lay program to put flesh on the beatitudes, in particular "Blessed are the peacemakers" (Mt 5:9), "Blessed are the merciful" (Mt 5:7), and on the command to love one's enemy (Mt 5:44), the Catholic Worker movement arose out of the fusion of the gifts of two quite different personalities.

Dorothy Day came from a family of journalists. They moved from the East Coast to the West Coast and later settled in Chicago. Moving from Chicago to Greenwich Village in New York City, Dorothy Day joined with socialists and communists struggling for a new social order. An unwed mother, she became a Catholic after the birth of her daughter, Tamar. It was then that she prayed "that I might find something to do in the social order besides reporting on conditions. I wanted to love my enemy, whether capitalist or communist."

Peter Maurin came from a peasant family in southern France. Abandoning studies to become a Christian Brother, he joined a land-settlement scheme in Canada but later crossed into the United States. During years of Franciscan poverty, he steeped himself in the annals of the Church, its saints, theologians, and philosophers, as well as its social teachings. Dorothy Day was thirty-five and Peter Maurin fifty-seven when they met in 1932 at the suggestion of George N. Schuster, editor of *Commonweal* magazine.

Maurin was ready with a theory for a personalist and communitarian revolution grounded in cult, culture, and cultivation.

Day was ready to accept it and to accept Maurin as her mentor.

Cult encompassed the Word of God, the Mass, and Church rituals. Culture was the wisdom of the ages, of the saints, martyrs, and theologians, as well as Church teachings often ignored, like that on usury. Cultivation meant a return to, and respect for, the land and for all work, especially crafts and manual work.

Maurin and Day agreed that a newspaper would be the means for spreading these ideas. On May 1, 1933, Day moved among the fifty thousand people massed in Union Square, New York City. She had come to distribute a tabloid she had edited, *The Catholic Worker.* Its price was a penny a copy. The communist-led demonstration allowed the speakers to vent their near despair and anger against an economic system responsible for a savage depression. The tabloid's editorial asserted that the paper was written "For those who are sitting on park benches . . . For those who are huddling in shelters trying to escape the rain . . . For those who are walking the streets in an all-but futile search for work. For those who think that there is no hope for the future, no recognition of their plight." The paper pointed to the social program of the Catholic Church as a source of hope and of recognition of the plight of the unemployed. "Blowing the Dynamite," an "Easy Essay" by Peter Maurin, stated his aim of "blowing the lid off" the social program of the Catholic Church. This program, he pointed out, had been hidden by Catholic scholars, who had "wrapped it up/ in nice phraseology/ placed it in a hermetic container/ and sat on the lid." With the distribution of this radical tabloid began a movement that was to have a profound influence on the Catholic Church in the United States.

A triad of practical ideas to meet the needs of the time was proposed by Maurin and Day: Houses of Hospitality in every diocese and possibly in every parish; farming communes or agronomic universities, where workers could be scholars and scholars workers; and roundtable discussions for clarification of thought. Maurin and Day advocated the "finding of concordances" with those who did not share their views, whether in the Church or in political groups striving for human betterment.

The discussions began almost immediately around the kitchen table in an East Side tenement, as students, teachers and the unemployed were attracted to the thinking of Day and Maurin. When neither dioceses nor parishes responded by opening Houses of Hospitality, the Catholic Worker opened its own—first an apartment, then an old building on Mott Street on the lower East Side. No Catholic organization made any sign of starting a farming commune or agronomic university.

Funds came in from readers and from the many groups that invited Day to lecture. A bread line, starting small, grew until over a thousand people were fed daily, often with no more than margarine-smeared bread and hot coffee. Day's appeals, blazing with compassion and reflecting her vision of Christ in his disguise of the poor and suffering, brought in enough funds to purchase a small farm on Staten Island. It offered hospitality to families and served as a gathering place for discussion groups.

Personalism and the Works of Mercy

The Catholic Worker's concept of personalism, a conviction that the freedom and dignity of each person is the focus and goal of all moral life, inspired the volunteers who joined the movement. They found meaning in carrying out the works of mercy at the cost of personal sacrifice. The works of mercy were seen as broader than the soup line or the provision of shelter; they included support for cooperatives, unions, and strikes, and as time went on, for such movements as those of Martin Luther King and Cesar Chavez. The bedrock of all activity was the practice of voluntary poverty on behalf of those involuntarily poor. Day and Maurin, no matter how pressured by events, went to Mass and received the Eucharist daily. Often in the evening they gathered with the volunteers for Vespers. Catholic Worker houses soon sprouted across the land, each autonomous but all offering hospitality and merciful help in the spirit of voluntary poverty.

World War II saw the movement diminished, but at war's end it sprang to new life. After a stroke that rendered him mute, Peter Maurin died in 1949. Until her death in 1980 at the age of eighty-three, Dorothy Day was the luminous center of a movement that grew yearly. Her witness for peace and justice included fasting for peace in Rome at Vatican II and several prison sentences to protest the war policies of the United States. Her last jail sentence was served in California in 1973 in solidarity with Cesar Chavez and the United Farm Workers. Day's inspiration was so powerful that fresh groups of volunteers regularly came forward, eager to join her in performing the works of mercy and in carrying the word of gospel nonviolence.

At the beginning of the decade of the nineties, over eighty Catholic Worker houses serve the homeless and needy. Six farming communes, some tiny but others with substantial acreage, keep alive the Catholic Worker devotion to the land. The newspaper reached a circulation of 96,000. Many other organizations, including the Community Land Trust and Pax Christi USA, owe their inspiration to the Catholic Worker movement.

Sign of Contradiction

The enduring witness of the Catholic Worker movement to peace was a sign of contradiction to a warring world. During World War II its paper was the sole pacifist Catholic publication in existence. Some saw the position of gospel nonviolence as near heresy. Yet the Catholic Worker opened its pages to priests who reminded readers that Jesus' message was "Love as I have loved you," a love that was sealed in self-giving and in suffering. John Hugo, Barry O'Toole, and Michael Deacy of the United States, Franziskus Stratmann of Germany, and Johannes Ude of Austria all preached the peace of Jesus and urged the Church to support those who in conscience were opposed to shedding blood. Whole pages were given over to the testimonies of early Church Fathers against war's bloodshed and to the accounts of the soldier-martyrs of the first centuries of the Christian era.

The prophetic witness of the Catholic Worker movement was validated when the bishops of the world at Vatican II condemned modern indiscriminate warfare, supported conscientious objection, and upheld the position of gospel nonviolence. Aware that modern weapons can be instruments of genocide, the bishops of the United States, in their pastoral letter *The Challenge of Peace: God's Promise and Our Response* (1983), came to an incontrovertible conclusion: "We are the first generation since Genesis with the power to virtually destroy God's creation."

See also BEATITUDE(S); CONTEMPORARY SPIRITUALITY; EARLY CHRISTIAN SPIRITUALITY; HOSPITALITY; INCARNATION; JUSTICE; LOVE; MERCY; PEACE; POOR, THE; POVERTY; SCRIPTURE; WAR, IMPACT ON SPIRITUALITY.

Bibliography: D. Day, *The Long Loneliness: The Autobiography of Dorothy Day* (New York: Harper & Row, 1952; rpt. 1981). P. Coy, ed., *A Revolution of the Heart: Essays on the Catholic Worker* (Philadelphia: Temple Univ. Press, 1988). W. Miller, *Dorothy Day: A Biography* (San Francisco: Harper & Row, 1982).

EILEEN EGAN

CELEBRATION

The term *celebration* usually refers to an event, such as a party, a banquet, or a parade, that marks an occasion of great festivity and rejoicing. Every society celebrates days of memorial and thanksgiving, days that honor persons and days that honor achievements, days of hope and days of new beginnings. It is a human instinct to rejoice in new life and new stages in life, and, even at life's end, to rejoice in the face of grief when a life is well lived and well remembered. Celebration is a human need. At times it arises spontaneously when circumstances call it forth; at times it must be orchestrated to counter what is otherwise humanly painful to face or to remember. A life without celebration is no life at all. A society without celebration is a society devoid of something fundamentally human.

In religious parlance, the term *celebration* likewise names events: religious festivals, religious rituals, religious gatherings of many sorts. Religious societies, no less than their secular counterparts, fill a festal calendar with days of memorial and thanksgiving, days that honor persons and days that honor achievements, days of hope and days of new beginnings. It is the same human instinct and the same human need, focused now on those events that mark the religious society's relationship to that mysterious "Other" to whom it is in some way bound (Latin *ligatum* = "tied or bound to"). These events may be "special events" proper to the lore of the religious society, or they may be basic human events seen in the light of that religious lore.

In the language of Christian prayer, *celebration* is used in many ways. Christians celebrate the Eucharist, the sacraments, the Liturgy of the Hours. It thus refers to the enactment of religious ritual. Christians also celebrate the memory of the saints, ancient and contemporary. It thus refers to the memory of people who are special in Christian history and in Christian life. They celebrate the covenant of God, the memory and presence of Jesus Christ, the activity of the Spirit within each human life, and a promise of a time ahead when all will be fulfilled. It is still the same human instinct and the same human need, focused now on the God named and revealed by Jesus Christ, the deeds which that God has wrought in Jesus Christ, and the relationship that has been established between God and the whole human race by this same Jesus Christ. Some events are proper to the "story" of Jesus; others are these same basic human events seen in light of this story. The term *celebration* is used by Christians in many ways and at several levels at once: it is human, religious, and at the same time peculiarly Christian.

Christian Celebration as Human

On a human level, Christian Eucharist celebrates communion among people. It is both achievement and hope, relationship established and relationship longed for. Food shared among people is a most apt ritual act for such celebration. Eucharist also celebrates the value of each human person, a value announced by the welcome that must be given to each. When all are invited to the table feast, all receive in that invitation a strong statement of their own distinctive human worth.

The other sacraments, each in its own way, point to key human moments in life as worthy of festivity and rejoicing. Some are obvious festal events: birth and membership in the Church's community; human love and commitment; appointment to service which is nonetheless appointment to a position held in high esteem in the community; the healing of wounds and human reconciliation. Some are less obvious as events of celebration: specifically sickness, approach to death, death itself. In these latter the human trappings of festivity must necessarily be toned down. Yet the value of each human person, of each human life, still holds even when life seems to crumble. There is nobility in human suffering and frailty, and every human life, even at its end, is worthy of affirmation. Death is a sacred human event, for humanly it brings us to silence, wonder, and fear, and to the questions that open up human life to its own deep mystery.

The Christian calendar not only announces the value of each human life but, by calling forth the lives of special women and men for remembrance and rejoicing, proclaims the importance to all human life of heroines and heroes who inspire and challenge, and who unveil in their own human lives well lived the rich possibilities present in each human life. At the center of the Christian calendar, as indeed of the Eucharist and the other sacraments, is Jesus of Nazareth, who serves on the human level as primary Hero, foundational figure, principal focus of the community's lore. He is the prime exemplar, whose own life unveils the secret of all life.

Christian Celebration as Religious

Christian celebrations are likewise religious celebrations; they announce and rejoice in the relationship that exists between the mystery of God and humanity. To each human event and each human life they proclaim, "Behold, God's dwelling is with the human race. He will dwell with them, and they will be his people, and God himself will always be with them. He will wipe away every tear from their eyes, and there shall be no more death or mourning, wailing or pain, [for] the old order has passed away" (Rev 21:3-4). They establish the two poles around which the Judeo-Christian religious experience is structured: memory of what God has done and hope in what God will yet bring about.

The Eucharist is the central Christian celebration. It contains in itself all other Christian celebrations and the reason why Christians celebrate at all. The Eucharist announces and makes present the covenant initiated by God, which God will never change, alter, or withdraw. It celebrates and makes present in both word and sacrament the sign of the covenant, Jesus Christ, once dead, now risen and exalted forever. And it holds out to all who celebrate the hope in which each human life may live, the victory and exaltation of Christ as the future of all.

The other sacraments, again each in its own way, bring the hope and promise of God's covenant in Christ to key moments of human life. In those moments, from birth to death, be they moments of obvious festivity and rejoicing or moments of sadness and pain, the faithful presence of God is cited. These key moments in human life, with human value of their own, are unveiled to have an even deeper significance. They are key moments in the human relationship with God as well. To those moments sacraments announce and establish God's faithful and loving presence.

The feasts and festivities of the Christian calendar bring forward the full lore of God's faithful love. The various feasts of Christ portray that love in the one human incarnation who is its most powerful voice. Remembrances of heroes and heroines further enflesh that love with tones and nuances that ordinary women and men can hear and identify with. The noble figures of the human family are not only humanly uplifting; they also bear witness in flesh and blood to the covenant relationship of God with the human family.

Christian Celebration as Christian

While Christian celebrations are both human and religious, because they are Christian, a relationship exists between the human and the religious that is distinctive. It is a relationship rooted in the incarnation of Jesus Christ. In him the human and the religious are not two different realms; they are intimately united in such a way that the most truly human is by that very fact religious, and the most truly religious is the most truly human. This relationship is most notably captured by the famous dictum of Irenaeus of Lyons, "The glory of God is the human person fully alive."

The communion that the Eucharist celebrates and brings about is itself brought about by God's covenantal love and is the fruit of Jesus' own sacrificial death. The key moments of human life that are addressed in Christian sacraments humanly contain both the action of God and the worship of God. Christian baptism/confirmation consecrates human life into the mystery of Jesus Christ and establishes that life in all its humanness as relationship with God. Reconciliation and forgiveness *as human realities* themselves are born of God's own action and in themselves relate women and men to God's own love (reconciliation with the Church *is* reconciliation with God). Sickness and suffering embraced, and even death accepted, as human realities proper to a life that is on a journey toward the source of all life, are themselves surrender into that "Other" who summons the journey forward. And finally, committed love and generous service are the ways in which the mystery of God completes God's own creative/redemptive action in the world. In the incarnation of God's own Son, God has revealed that human life humanly lived and embraced in all its fullness is that full relationship with the mystery of God that is the truest religious act.

The Christian calendar of feasts and festivities celebrates this intimate union between God and God's creation. Its primary hinges of incarnation (Advent-Christmas-Epiphany-Presentation) and resurrection (Lent-Easter-Pentecost with their intense baptismal focus) wed the action of God with human life and human action to such an extent that the religious is proclaimed as the *within* of human life, not an alternative or a parallel project. And the heroes and heroines of the sanctoral feasts are celebrated, not because they opted for something other than human life, but because they embraced, as did Jesus himself, human life in all its religious and human truth.

Festivity and Feriality

The language of celebration has a danger built into it when applied to Christian ritual and life. Used superficially, it can imply that every liturgical event must be upbeat and "swinging." The tradition of Christian prayer knows that this is humanly impossible. That tradition has distinguished among various levels of festivity (solemnity with octave, solemnity, feast, memorial) and between festivity and feriality. There are days when nothing

in particular is brought into focus, and while it is still proper to employ the term *celebration* for such occasions, it is low-key and ordinary. There are even days when negativity is highlighted (e.g., penitential days), and these usually prepare for and are in service to solemnity and festivity. Proper use of the term *celebration* in Christian prayer requires that these rhythms of festivity and feriality be observed.

See also CULTURE; DANCE; LITURGY; MUSIC; RITUAL.

Bibliography: K. Rahner, "The Experience of Self and the Experience of God," *Theology, Anthropology, Christology,* Theological Investigations 13, trans. D. Bourke (New York: Crossroad, 1975) 122–132; "Reflections on the Unity of the Love of Neighbor and the Love of God," *Concerning Vatican Council II,* Theological Investigations 6, trans. K. and B. Kruger (Baltimore: Helicon, 1969) 231–252; "The Eternal Significance of the Humanity of Jesus for Our Relationship with God," *Theology of the Spiritual Life,* Theological Investigations 3, trans. K. and B. Kruger (Baltimore: Helicon, 1967) 35–46. United States Catholic Conference, *The Liturgical Year: Celebrating the Mystery of Christ and His Saints,* Study Text 9 (Washington: USCC, 1985). J. Wilde, ed., *At That Time: Cycles and Seasons in the Life of a Christian* (Chicago: Liturgy Training Publications, 1989).

PETER E. FINK, S.J.

CELIBACY

The discipline of celibacy is the renunciation of marriage in order to live in continence for the implicit or explicit purpose of achieving perfect charity. Celibacy occupies a position of esteem as well as of controversy within the Christian tradition. Throughout the centuries the practice has changed, as has the meaning attached to it. Although the Scriptures do not explicitly formulate ecclesiastical celibacy, there is evidence of a positive evaluation, especially in the letters of St. Paul. Placed within a Gnostic milieu, Christianity had the task of affirming the goodness of the created world while simultaneously advocating abstention from certain aspects of it. Consequently, virginity and chastity were highly cherished (see Tertullian, *De exhortatione castitatis,* PL 2:930).

As a requirement for priesthood, the discipline of celibacy took different forms in the East and the West. In the East, since the Council of Trullo (A.D. 692), the discipline was firmly established whereby bishops were held to continence, while priests, deacons, and subdeacons were allowed to marry before ordination; but if they married, they were denied positions in the hierarchy. In the West the practice of celibacy was prescribed by several councils of the fourth century (Elvira, ca. 300; Rome, 386; Carthage, 390). In the 5th and 6th centuries, candidates for sacred orders promised perpetual chastity (Orange, 441; Arles, 524). In the Carolingian period, regional synods again mandated celibacy as a requisite for holy orders. The Council of Trent in its 24th session pronounced in favor of it. Much debate about celibacy has taken place in the 20th century, especially since the Second Vatican Council (see E. Schillebeeckx, *Celibacy*).

Although the practice of celibacy has survived in the Christian tradition, the meanings assigned to it have varied from age to age. In the early Church, heavily overladen with Gnostic influences, celibacy was a means for renouncing the prison of the earthly body. Based upon the Greek dichotomy between body and soul, chastity was seen as protecting the purity of the body, which housed the soul. An explanation proposed by Pope Pius XI endorsed celibacy as a means of total consecration to God. Within this context the argumentation is based upon the economy of time: celibates have more time to devote to the work of God, since they do not have private lives distinct from their official lives. Similar to this argument is the economic one, namely, that it is less expensive to support a celibate person.

Of the more recent discussions on the subject, the argument that favors celibacy as a complement to marriage seems to find widest acceptance. This notion underlines the full sexuality of all human beings, noting that celibates are not any less sexual beings but that they renounce the genital aspect of human existence "for the sake of the kingdom" (Mt 19:10-12). Pope John Paul II, in his weekly audiences between 1982 and 1983, developed the idea of the complementarity of marriage and the celibate life in the context of a theology of the human body. While reaffirming the superiority of continence in the Pauline perspective (see 1 Cor 7:29-30), he upholds the value of marriage. Both married and celibates, however, are called to continence in their respective states of life.

See also ABSTINENCE; ASCETICISM; BODY; CHASTITY; CONSECRATION; DUALISM; GNOSIS, GNOSTICISM; MONASTICISM, MONASTIC SPIRITUALITY; PATRISTIC SPIRITUALITY; RELIGIOUS LIFE; SEXUALITY; VIRGINITY.

Bibliography: E. Schillebeeckx, *Celibacy* (New York: Sheed and Ward, 1968). John Paul II, *Résurrection, mariage et célibat: L'Evangile de la rédemption du corps* (Paris: Cerf, 1985). D. Goergen, *The Sexual Celibate* (New York: Seabury, 1974).

MICHAEL S. DRISCOLL

CELTIC SPIRITUALITY

Ireland, unlike the other Celtic lands that formed so much of the island of Britain, was not invaded by the Romans. That is an important fact to remember in considering Irish culture and spirituality, for they are often thought to be strange and exotic, whereas they simply differ from the Latin order of things. Yet the Celts have very much in common in spirituality, sometimes at least, through Irish influence.

The Celts in general from pagan times were a religious people, as we know from all accounts of them and their remains. Since they were mostly rural—and altogether so in Ireland—their religion was concerned with all the natural phenomena of sea, hill, forest, water, and sun.

St. Patrick himself was a Celt, the most famous and lastingly influential of all. The religion and spirituality of the Irish may be termed Patrician. His name even stands for the Irish; he himself said as much, identifying himself with those whom he had converted to Christ. Irish monks in the early ages brought his name and devotion to him to the European continent, and emigrants carried his name to many parts of the world. At home his name still lives in the common salutation *Dia 's Muire dhuit is Pádraig* ("May God and Mary and Patrick bless you"). Two unique penitential pilgrimages are closely associated with him: that of Cruach Phadraig, the mountain of Patrick's legendary forty days' penance, and Loch Dearg, famous from medieval times in Europe for his purgatory and still today for its three days of penance, fasting, and all-night vigil.

St. Patrick often spoke of himself as being in exile for Christ in a foreign land. The Celts, and in particular the Irish, regarded exile as perpetual pilgrimage for Christ. As in all things, their inspiration came from Scripture itself—in this case, Abraham, *peregrinator fidelissimus,* "the most faithful pilgrim," as he was called. Pilgrimage, or perpetual exile, was regarded as the highest point of asceticism, the denying of oneself and the leaving of one's native land and all for Christ. St. Patrick himself referred to his own perpetual exile and his longing for his own country. Although so many features of the saint's life were reproduced in the lives of his spiritual children, we cannot be sure that there was a conscious following of him, but certainly Scripture was always the exemplar.

Pilgrims often went to holy places in their own and other lands, and they always had great reverence for their own holy ones and their shrines. Such a place was Ynys Enlli (Bardsey Island) off Wales, the burial place, it was said, of twenty thousand saints. Jerusalem and Rome, of course, were visited and held in the highest veneration. Often, however, pilgrims had no fixed goal but went to some remote place or island, inland or on the sea. So we are told in the Anglo-Saxon Chronicle for 891–892: "Three Irishmen came to King Alfred in a boat without oars from Ireland, whence they had stolen away, because they desired for the love of God to be in a state of pilgrimage, they cared not where. The boat in which they came was wrought of two hides and a half, and they took with them food sufficient for seven nights, and on the seventh night they came to land in Cornwall, and they went straightaway to King Alfred. Thus they were called (in modern spelling, since the names are still extant) Dubhshláine, Mac Beatha and Maolionmhuin."

St. Colm Cille or Columba (521–597), of Doire (Derry) and Iona, the Scottish isle, was the first great exile for Christ, and many poems of exile were later attributed to him. A Life of him, written a thousand years later, includes facts and legends, but there is one passage that sums up the attitude of the Celts to pilgrimage and exile: "When Colm Cille was going into exile to Scotland, this holy child, Mochonna, said that he would go with him. 'Don't go,' said Colm Cille, 'but remain with your father and mother in your own country.' 'You are my father,' said Mochonna, 'and the Church is my mother, and the place in which I can give most service to God is my country,' said he, 'and since it is you, Colm Cille, who have bound me to Christ, I will follow you till you bring me to where he is.' And then he took the vow of pilgrimage."

In Ireland and Scotland the word *Diseart* is found as a placename or as an element of a placename; in Wales it is *Diserth.* The word is obviously from the Latin *desertum,* meaning "hermitage." Edmund Hogan, in his monumental work on Irish placenames, *Onomasticon Goedelicum,* says of the word: "I have circ. 500 references to places of which it forms a part," a tribute to a widespread, prayerful following of Christ. There was great earnestness in pure service of God. What good was a tonsured head if the heart was not also tonsured? Private confession and the diligent use of penitentials, spread greatly by the Irish, and the use of the principle that contraries are cured by their contraries helped in the guidance of souls. So did the practice of *anamchairdeas,* or "soul-friendship." It was a common saying that a person without a soul-friend (*anamchara*) was a body without a head.

Undoubtedly notable corporal austerity was a feature of Celtic, and especially Irish, spirituality, and the age-old pilgrimages still in vogue show that it has not lost its attraction. The austerities of Willie Doyle and the holy layman Matt Talbot have a long ancestry. In ancient times three Lents were celebrated in the year in Ireland, and again we see how alive the influence of Scripture was: the Lent of Elijah in winter, of Jesus in spring, and of Moses in summer. In Wales two other Lents were observed: that of Mary from August 1 to 15 and that of the Apostles from Ascension Thursday to Pentecost Sunday. We read of the father of St. Padarn, one of the Welsh saints, that he came to Ireland to spend his life in vigils and fasting, praying day and night with genuflections.

Walafrid Strabo, abbot of Reichenau on Lake Constance in the year 841, mentioned that the Irish were especially remarkable for their practice, day and night, of genuflections, regularly counted. The *crosfhigheall* or *cossvigil*—outstretched arms in the form of a cross—was a common position in prayer or penance. In Brittany, St. Winwalloc was given to that form of prayer, with continual genuflections during the singing of the psalms. (Since there was constant intercommunication between the monks of the various Celtic lands, we may be sure that there was common practice among them, even though we might have evidence for a particular practice from only one country. In fact, most of our documentation comes from Ireland.) The body was expected to play its part simultaneously with the soul in praise of God. The gestures of the various parts of

the body while at prayer—the raising of the eyes or the hands, the bending of the knees, etc.—were regarded as the words of the limbs.

The faith was planted in Ireland without martyrdom, but there was very high esteem for martyrdom. Frequent mention was made of the three martyrdoms: white, blue, and red. White martyrdom was the leaving of all for love of God, the equivalent of the religious life; blue martyrdom was the practice of a penitential life, not necessarily the religious life; red martyrdom was death itself for Christ's sake. In the Rule attributed to St. Colm Cille we read that the religious should have a mind ready for red martyrdom. Within less than a hundred years after St. Patrick, the Church in Ireland had become overwhelmingly monastic, the abbots of the great monasteries wielding jurisdiction, whereas bishops exercised only their sacramental powers. The great St. Columbanus (ca.540–615) is representative of all the ancient saints and abbots in his severe life and Rule, tender in his austerity and austere in his tenderness. Even the animals obeyed him, we are told.

Celtic spirituality was deeply scriptural. The psalms were held in the greatest reverence, and none more so than Psalm 118 (119), which was known by its first word in the Latin, *Beati* (*Biait* in Irish and *Bwyait* in Welsh). In an Irish poem from about the 10th century, we are told of five fastings that are not pleasing to the King of Kings, one of which is fasting from searching the Scriptures. Even today we have visible evidence of the ancient love of the Scripture in the unsurpassed decoration of the Word, above all in the *Book of Kells,* and after a millennium there still stand the high crosses, portraying the history of salvation till the second coming, all summed up and included in the Cross itself. The great cross in Clonmacnoise is called *Cros na Screaptra,* "the Cross of the Scriptures."

Ireland of old had no central government or towns but was divided into a number of small kingdoms, or *tuatha,* of which there could be a hundred or more. Kinship was of the highest importance. Thus we are related to Christ on his Mother's side. He was commonly known by his Mother's name, *Mac Muire,* "Mary's Son," which may well have come from the corresponding Welsh, *Mab Mair.* The killing of Christ was additionally abhorrent because it was the slaughter of a kinsman (termed *fionghal*). The king of the *tuath* was closely related to many of his subjects. The term did not imply remoteness, even if it carried with it a certain dignity. The most common term for God the Father or Christ was *Rí* ("King") and is still so in the large body of traditional Gaelic prayers that have come down to us in Ireland and Scotland. It is a term of intimacy and loving respect.

From *monasterium* comes the modern Irish *muintir,* meaning "the monastic family." From it we have the current adjective *muineartha,* meaning "intimate," "friendly," etc. The noun *muintearas,* "intimacy" or "familiarity" in its original meaning, describes very well a lasting feature of Irish spirituality. The close-knit community of the *tuath* and the monastery within it made the concept of the Church as the Body of Christ very congenial. The corporate feeling is shown in the popularity of the passage on the Last Judgment in Matthew 25. In particular, the guest was always Christ, and that was long the feature of Irish hospitality. Perhaps we see here the long-term and happy wedding of monastic and lay spirituality. The first person plural is the common form in the traditional Gaelic folk prayers of Ireland and Scotland.

The Trinitarian element, as well as the human element, is prominent in Celtic prayer at all times. God the Father was addressed as *mu chridecán,* "my little heart," in an ancient Irish poem. In a famous poem attributed to St. Íde, when the Child Jesus (*Ísucán*) came to her, the saint uses diminutives such as a mother would use with her baby, one verb even being in an untranslatable diminutive form. Our Lady in another poem is addressed familiarly by the poet as "little bright-necked one," and he speaks of consoling her heart, language not heard commonly in Europe until half a millennium later, in St. Bernard's time. When the medieval texts on the Passion arrived, with the Compassion of Our Lady, they received great welcome in Wales and Ireland, since they were of their very own spirituality. The Franciscan text *Meditationes Vitae Christi* was especially popular in Ireland and inspired a long poem in Irish on the life of Christ at the end of the 17th century. To this day also the medieval *planctus* or plaint *Caoineadh na dTrí Muire,* "The Lament of the Three Marys," is sung.

There is a large body of prayers from the ancient days, chiefly in Latin and Irish. A particular form of prayer that always appealed was the *lorica,* or breastplate prayer, for God's protection against all evil. In pagan times it may well have been a charm against the evil forces of nature, but in Christian times, as in the well-known and still popular "Breastplate of St. Patrick," there is the sinful enemy within, and the power and love of Christ to protect.

A feature of these prayers, in Irish and Welsh, is their endeavor to achieve completeness in enumeration, for example mentioning all the stages of Our Lord's life, as in the Litany of the Saints; of all the members of the body; of all external circumstances; of the members of the heavenly and the earthly Church, represented by the angels and saints. Everything must be under God's sway, and God is all-present. The traditional prayers already mentioned show that trait also. Mostly in verse, like the ancient prayers, they cover all the actions of the day and the great natural events of life. There is frequent mention of "all our fellow-creatures," and it is said that "a mean prayer is not good" and "prayer should be cast wide," meaning first of all that in praying for one's own dead one should pray also for all the dead; but an even more universal significance is intended, as is obvious in so many of the prayers.

In an ancient Irish text that tells of the usages and customs in one of the monasteries, we find mentioned "eagerness for Mass," and one of the monastic rules tells us that "when one goes to Mass, noble is the deed, contrition of heart, shedding of tears, raising of hands." Down the centuries and through the Reformation, the Eucharist was at the center of spirituality, and many suffered martyrdom for the Mass. "Nothing is more precious than the hearing of Mass. Never abandon the Mass, nothing in this world surpasses it." So the ordinary, impoverished people spoke.

During the centuries of persecution in Ireland and Scotland, there was an authentic lay spirituality, quite orthodox, although greatly deprived of clerical guidance and easy access to the Mass and the sacraments. This spirituality is seen chiefly in the great body of traditional prayers in Gaelic (very few found their way into English) and customs connected with local shrines and holy wells, where Our Lord, Our Lady, and the native saints were honored. The prayers, as already mentioned, dealt with all occasions of life. Many were once the common patrimony of Europe; others were of native origin, sometimes quite ancient. A number of such prayers are found also in Brittany.

In the matter of Irish spirituality, of first importance is the rosary. It was known as *Saltair Mhuire* (Welsh *Llaswyr Mair*), "Our Lady's Psalter," consisting as it does of the 150 *Aves*. In Ireland, its popularity dates especially from the times of persecution, when it took the place of the Mass. In the many communal prayers associated with it there is frequent mention of "sharing in the holy sacrifice of the Mass" and of praying "for the intention of the Pope and the holy Catholic Church" and for those in purgatory who have no living relatives to pray for them. Also prayed for are "the unbelievers of the world that they may be converted to the right state and that those who are in the right state may be preserved in it."

See also EREMITICAL LIFE; JOURNEY (GROWTH AND DEVELOPMENT IN SPIRITUAL LIFE); MARY; MONASTICISM, MONASTIC SPIRITUALITY; PENANCE, PENITENCE; SPIRITUAL DIRECTION.

Bibliography: L. Gougaud, *Christianity in Celtic Lands* (London: Sheed and Ward, 1931). M. Maher, ed., *Irish Spirituality* (Dublin: Veritas, 1981). J. Ryan, *Irish Monasticism* (Ithaca, N.Y.: Cornell Univ. Press, 1972).

DIARMUID Ó LAOGHAIRE, S.J.

CENTERING PRAYER

The grace of Pentecost affirms that the risen Jesus is among us as the glorified Christ. Christ lives in each of us as the enlightened One, present everywhere and at all times. He is the living Master who promised to send the Holy Spirit to dwell within us and to bear witness to his resurrection by empowering us to experience and manifest the fruits of the Spirit and the beatitudes both in prayer and action.

Lectio divina is the most traditional way of cultivating the friendship of the risen Christ. It is a means of listening to the texts of Scripture as if we were in conversation with Christ and he were suggesting the topics of discussion. Daily encounter with Christ and reflection on his teaching lead beyond mere acquaintanceship to an attitude of friendliness, trust, and love. Conversation simplifies and gives way to communing, or as Gregory the Great (6th cent.), summarizing the Christian contemplative tradition, put it, "resting in God." This was the classical meaning of contemplative prayer for the first sixteen centuries.

Contemplative prayer is the normal development of the grace of baptism and the regular practice of *lectio divina*. We may think of prayer as thoughts or feelings expressed in words. But this is only one expression. Contemplative prayer is the laying aside of thoughts. It is the opening of mind and heart—our whole being—to

God, the ultimate reality, beyond thoughts, words, and emotions. We open our awareness to God, who we know by faith is within us, closer than breathing, closer than thinking, closer than choosing, closer than consciousness itself. God is the ground in whom our being is rooted, the source from whom our life emerges at every moment.

Contemplative prayer is a process of interior transformation, a relationship initiated by God and leading, if we consent, to divine union. Our way of seeing reality changes in this process. A restructuring of consciousness takes place that empowers us to perceive, relate to, and respond with increasing sensitivity to the divine presence and action in, through, and beyond everything that exists.

Centering prayer is a method designed to facilitate the development of contemplative prayer by preparing one's faculties to cooperate with this gift. It is an attempt to present the teaching of earlier times (see *The Cloud of Unknowing* and the whole apophatic tradition) in an updated format and to give a certain order and regularity to it. It is not meant to replace all other kinds of prayer; it simply puts other kinds of prayer into a new and fuller perspective. During the time of prayer it centers one's attention on God's presence within. At other times one's attention moves outward to discover God's presence everywhere else.

Centering prayer is not an end in itself but a beginning. It is not done for the sake of enjoying spiritual consolation but for the sake of its positive fruits in one's life: charity, joy, peace, self-knowledge, compassion, inner freedom, humility. To benefit from these fruits, centering prayer must be done regularly, preferably twice a day for about half an hour each time. To maximize these fruits, practices for use during one's ordinary occupations can be added, e.g., repetition of a prayer sentence, unconditional acceptance of others, letting go of upsetting emotions as soon as they arise.

Outline of the Centering Prayer Method

1. Choose a sacred word as the symbol of your intention to open and yield to God's presence and action within. The sacred word could be one of the names of God or a word that you feel comfortable with, e.g., presence, silence, peace, stillness, oneness.

2. Sitting comfortably and with eyes closed, settle briefly and silently introduce the sacred word as the symbol of your consent to God's presence and action within.

3. When you become aware of thoughts, return ever so gently to the sacred word. This is the only activity you initiate once the period of centering prayer has begun.

4. The term *thoughts* includes any perception at all, e.g., sense perceptions, feelings, images, memories, reflections, and commentaries. During the prayer time, avoid analyzing your experience, harboring expectations, or aiming at some specific goal, such as having no thoughts, making the mind a blank, feeling peaceful or consoled, repeating the sacred word continuously, or achieving a spiritual experience.

5. At the end of the prayer time, remain in silence with eyes closed for a couple of minutes. This gives the psyche a brief space to readjust to the external senses and a better chance of bringing the atmosphere of interior silence into the activities of daily life.

See also ATTENTION, ATTENTIVENESS; BREATH, BREATHING; CONTEMPLATION, CONTEMPLATIVE PRAYER; LECTIO DIVINA; MEDITATION; NEGATIVE WAY; PRAYER; PRESENCE, PRESENCE OF GOD.

Bibliography: T. Keating, *Open Mind, Open Heart: The Contemplative Dimension of the Gospel* (New York: Amity House, 1986). T. Keating, *The Mystery of Christ: The Liturgy as Spiritual Experience* (Amity, N.Y.: Amity House, 1987). B. Pennington, *Centered Living: The Way of Centering Prayer* (Garden City, N.Y.: Doubleday, 1986).

THOMAS KEATING, O.C.S.O.

CHARISM

Progress in biblical studies, growth in psychological awareness, attention to the role of personal and communitarian experience in religious living, extraordinary responses to the challenges Christian vocation and ministry face in our day, rediscovery of the root inspiration of founders of religious movements and communities, appreciation of the distinctiveness in every good person's life, Pentecostalism in its various forms, tensions between Spirit and structure, tradition and innovation, authority and the governed—all these aspects of Christian living in the second half of the 20th century have accompanied and are related to a renewed, abundant presence of charisms in the Catholic Church as well as in other Christian Churches, and have led to a new understanding, appreciation, and desire of these gifts.

The Greek word *charisma* is a verbal noun from the verb *charidzomai,* "to bestow a gift or favor," and means a free gift, a spiritual capacity resulting from God's grace (*charis*). The word *charisma,* given a religious meaning by Paul and used mostly by him in the New Testament, "refers to a dazzling variety of gifts. They include the Spirit itself in some specific manifestation, changes in physical conditions and/or emotional states and dispositions, 'ordinary' and 'extraordinary' talents. Such gifts may be quite temporary, or they may last for a recipient's whole life. In every case the charisma is consciously received as a gift *from God*" (Koenig, p. 124).

Charisma indicates the total gift of salvation received by all believers (Rom 5:15-16; 6:23: ". . . the *charisma* of God is eternal life in Christ Jesus our Lord"). The Spirit is the primal blessing, dwells in us, but is not owned by us. Indeed, the Spirit is "the chief external Witness to the presence of Christ's reign" and is "a gift which both surrounds and inhabits its recipients" (Koenig, pp. 73, 76). In addition, each person has received a particular gift from God (1 Cor 7:7, 17; 12:7), which should be used for the benefit of others "so that in all things God may be glorified through Jesus Christ" (1 Pet 4:10-11). The Pastoral Epistles consider the office conferred by the laying on of hands to be a charism (1 Tm 4:14; 2 Tm 1:6-7). Paul considers celibacy (1 Cor 7:7) and mutual encouragement through witness to faith (Rom 1:11) to be charismatic gifts. In addition, he offers three lists of charisms (1 Cor 12–14, which passage also contains a lengthy discussion on the attitudes toward, and use of, these gifts; Rom 12:6-8; Eph 4:4-11). Taken together, these lists mention prophecy, wisdom, knowledge, extraordinary faith, discernment, healing and the working of other miracles, speaking in tongues and its interpretation, helping, administration, service, teaching, exhortation, contributing, mercy, evangelizing, pastoring.

In the Synoptics, Jesus promises the special assistance of the Spirit to enable a courageous defense of the gospel (Mk 13:11; Mt 10:19-20; Lk 21:14-15; see Acts 2:4; 4:23-31; 6:8-10).

The Acts of Apostles, sometimes called "the Gospel of the Holy Spirit," describes the charismatic effects of the coming of the Spirit on Pentecost (Acts 2:1ff.) and the special power of the Spirit in Stephen (6:5,8); Philip (8:5-8); the Ephesians (19:5-6). The entire book, although it does not use the word *charisma,* gives many evidences of the gifts Paul mentions. Moreover, Acts mentions that the Spirit is given to the Gentiles even before baptism (Acts 10:44-48; 11:16-17; 15:8-9), a fact that invites us to consider how God offers the indwelling Spirit and gracious gifts to every person who does God's will.

God in sovereign freedom bestows gifts in a variety of ways: through the sacrament of baptism, through response to the spoken Word, in a moment of trial, in answer to humble prayer or loving action. We are urged to desire and seek the charisms in order to better serve God and God's people, but it is not for us to determine whether, how, or when any particular gift will be given to us.

The endurance of suffering can itself be a special gift (2 Cor 4:7-12; Phil 1:29; Col 1:24; Jn 18:11). Since enduring his passion and death with love was the work entrusted to Jesus by the Father for the salvation of the world, what effected in us the gift of reconciliation with God and with one another was a gift to Jesus. When we are called to share in his passion and death, and thus witness to God's saving work and mediate its effectiveness, we are being offered a most precious gift. In addition, "a charisma always involves suffering" (K. Rahner, *The Spirit in the Church,* p. 68), for every charism will at least sometimes be crudely misunderstood by others, unjustly criticized, coldly spurned. And yet the one who bears the gift must continue to exercise it for the good of God's people and wait patiently for the moment of greater acceptance, if that is to come. "Long-enduring patience in face of protracted opposition is one of the qualities of the true charismatic" (Bermejo, p. 371).

In Greek the words *charisma* ("gift"), *charis* ("grace"), and *chara* ("joy") all have the same root. Joy, joined to thanksgiving and praise because of God's gracious gifts, characterizes the communities depicted in the New Testament. These attitudes should be marks of the Christian community of any age and impel it to proclaim the Good News far and wide. During the last decades the appearance of charisms in a greater number of Christian individuals and communities, and the consequent attention to and use of these gifts, contrasts sharply with the preceding period, which could be measured in centuries. While ultimately recognizing that God is sovereignly free to distribute charisms when, where, and in the measure Divine Providence wishes, we might still ask if believing communities and individuals, including Christian leaders, are always as ready to receive the gifts of God as God is ready to confer them.

The saving work of God is accomplished through people whom God has gifted, and so the presence of the Spirit and of the Spirit's gifts has a history. In the Old Testament, emphasis is placed on the gifts given to the leaders of the people. But there is a promise that one day the gifts will be given to everyone (Isa 42:1; 44:1-3; Joel 2:28-29; Ezek 36:26-27; Jer 31:31-33). Paul recognizes that "the gifts and the call of God [to Israel] are irrevocable" (Rom 11:28-29; see 9:4-5). When the fullness of time arrived (Gal 4:4), the gifts of God were especially concentrated in the charismatic par excellence, "Jesus the Nazorean . . . a man commended to you by God with mighty deeds, wonders, and signs, which God worked through him in your midst" (Acts 2:22). ". . . God anointed Jesus of Nazareth with the holy Spirit and power. He went about doing good and healing all those oppressed by the devil, for God was with him" (Acts 10:38).

God has chosen to continue the work of Jesus through his disciples, through the Church, which has the duty to preserve and witness to the faith. Every member of the Church is called to share actively in this work, and therefore each has been empowered by the Spirit with a particular gift. In the first three centuries of the Church's life, the charisms indicated in the New Testament continued to be present and recognized, if not in exactly the same degree as in the initial communities, which, admittedly, had a unique role. From about the beginning of the 4th century, there was a significant change. The effects of the Montanist crisis, which sharply contrasted the hierarchical Church with the "true" Church of charismatics, and the progressive institutionalization of the Church were in part responsible. Other heretical movements, the Protestant Reformation, followed by the Counter-Reformation, a growing centralization and defensiveness, and an increasing influence of the clergy and hierarchy in every aspect of Church life did not favor the flourishing of charisms in the body of the faithful. Nonetheless, at every moment of the Church's history various charisms (e.g., in the founders and some members of religious communities and in heroic attention to social and spiritual ills, etc.) have continued to be a sign of God's presence and activity. Medieval and subsequent theologians reflected on the *gratiae gratis datae* ("the gratuitous graces") listed by Paul (see ST II-II, qq. 171-178).

But it was not until the Second Vatican Council that the magisterium gave extensive treatment to the presence of charismatic gifts as a normal aspect of the Church that concerned each of the faithful: "Allotting his gifts 'to every one according as he will' (1 Cor 12:11), he [the Holy Spirit] distributes special graces among the faithful of every rank. By these gifts he makes them fit and ready to undertake the various tasks or offices advantageous for the renewal and upbuilding of the Church, according to the word of the Apostle: 'The manifestation of the Spirit is given to everyone for profit' (1 Cor 12:7). These charismatic gifts, whether they be the most outstanding or the more simple and widely diffused, are to be received with thanksgiving and consolation, for they are exceedingly suitable and useful for the needs of the Church" (LG 12). "From the reception of these charisms or gifts . . . there arise for each believer the right and duty to use them in the Church and in the world for the good of mankind and for the upbuilding of the Church. In so doing, believers need to enjoy the freedom of the Holy Spirit . . ." (AA 3).

In light of the teaching of Scripture and Vatican II, as well as the experience of the Church, we can conclude about the charisms that "they are not a thing of the past (possible and real only in the early Church), but eminently contemporary and actual; they do not hover in the periphery of the Church, but are eminently central and essential to it. In this sense one should speak of a *charismatic structure* of the Church which embraces and goes beyond the structure of its government . . ." (H. Küng, "The Charismatic Structure of the Church," in Concilium 4: *The Church and Ecumenism,* ed. H. Küng, New York: Paulist, 1965, p. 58).

Therefore, it is reasonable to expect a continued outpouring of the Spirit with ever new forms of life, witness, and service, although it is not for us to say to what extent God will offer gifts and to what degree individuals and communities will gratefully receive them. The more Christians assume their vocation to contribute to building a just and peaceful world, offering witness that will offend the selfish and the powerful, the more they will need to be attentive to their personal and collective experience. They must on the one hand read the signs of the times in the events of contemporary history, and on the other discern the prompting of the Spirit within their own hearts. In the more traditionally Christian lands, much needs to be done to evangelize anew societies that have become post-Christian. Churches emerging from decades of oppression and silence need to learn a new language that will proclaim their faith in a way required by new circumstances. Young Churches, as they grow and mature, will need to evaluate the voices that proclaim new forms of thinking, formulating, celebrating, and living the faith in ways that reflect their developing cultures.

Important, efficacious, and even necessary as more extraordinary charisms are for the development of the life of the Church and its mission, the more ordinary gifts are the substance of the life that most truly characterizes the pilgrim Church: "faith, hope and love, in the longing for eternity, the patience of the cross, heartfelt joy" (K. Rahner, *The Spirit in the Church,* p. 57).

To distinguish authentic gifts from illusory ones and to use charisms well, individuals and communities in the Church, together with the hierarchy, need to exercise discernment. Negative factors to be avoided are well described by one author: "a penchant for the striking and sensational, and a possible neglect of gifts which are less showy but more useful; a certain emotionalism which attaches excessive importance to feelings and personal experience when judging the fruits of the Spirit; elitism, which exaggerates the importance of belonging to the Renewal, and may even tend to despise those who do not belong to it; a certain fundamentalism in the interpretation of scriptural passages, neglecting the results of scientific exegesis; false ecumenism, which tends to play down the doctrinal differences that are still keeping the Christian Churches apart; and a certain self-centeredness which seems to neglect the social dimension in the Church's life" (Bermejo, pp. 386–387).

But we can be confident that the same Spirit who generously bestows the charisms will at the same time grant the wisdom and charity necessary to use them wisely for the building up of the body of the Church and for the effectiveness of its mission to the world.

See also CHARISMATIC RENEWAL; CONFRONTATION AND PROTEST; CONTEMPORARY SPIRITUALITY; DISCERNMENT OF SPIRITS; EARLY CHRISTIAN SPIRITUALITY; ENTHUSIASM; GLOSSOLALIA; GRACE; HOLY SPIRIT; PROPHECY; VOWS.

Bibliography: A. Bittlinger, *Gifts and Graces: A Commentary on 1 Corinthians 12-14* (Grand Rapids, Mich.: Eerdmans, 1967). L. Bermejo, *The Spirit of Life: The Holy Spirit in the Life of the Christian* (Chicago: Loyola Univ. Press, 1989). "Charism," in K. Rahner and H. Vorgrimler, *Dictionary of Theology,* trans. R. Strachan (New York: Crossroad, 1981). "Charism" and "Charismatic Movement," in *The New Dictionary of Theology,* ed. J. Komonchak, M. Collins, D. Lane (Wilmington, Del.: Glazier, 1987) 180–185. "Charisms" and "Pentecostal and Charismatic Christianity," in *The Encyclopedia of Religion,* ed. M. Eliade (New York: Macmillan, 1986) 3:218–222; 11:229–235. W. Harrington, *Spirit of the Living God* (Wilmington, Del.: Glazier, 1977). J. Koenig, *Charismata: God's Gifts for God's People* (Philadelphia: Westminster, 1978). H. Küng, *The Church,* trans. R. and R. Ockenden (London: Burns & Oates, 1967) 171–191. S. Land, "Pentecostal Spirituality: Living in the Spirit," *Christian Spirituality: Post-Reformation and Modern,* World Spirituality 18, ed. L. Dupré and D. Saliers (New York: Crossroad, 1989) 479–499. G. Montague, *The Holy Spirit: Growth of a Biblical Tradition* (New York: Paulist, 1976). K. Rahner, *The Dynamic Element in the Church* (New York: Herder, 1964). K. Rahner, *The Spirit in the Church* (New York: Seabury, 1979) 33–73.

EDWARD J. MALATESTA, S.J.

CHARISMATIC RENEWAL

"Charismatic renewal" is the preferred term for the ongoing effects of the Pentecostal experience (an acute experimental awareness of the presence of God, often expressed in glossolalia and/or baptism in the Spirit) that began to occur in Catholicism in 1967 and in mainline Protestant Churches a decade earlier. Neo-Pentecostalism, as it was first called, took shape in prayer meetings, rallies, and large-scale conferences. It was marked by excellent organizational methods and publications, and was quickly carried overseas. Membership and activities leveled off in the late 1970s after a period of rapid growth; it is credited with helping to restore the importance of experience to the often formalistic worship of Catholicism.

The Catholic origins of the charismatic renewal in the United States are usually fixed at the appearance of glossolalia and baptism in the Spirit during a retreat at Duquesne University. Members of the prayer group involved had been actively seeking a fuller presence of the Spirit for some time; several had already received the gift of tongues in a prayer group organized by a Presbyterian woman.

Since 1951 Pentecostal activities had become familiar and respectable among American businesspeople and professionals through the activities of the Full Gospel Business Men's Fellowship International; similarly, South African David du Plessis, "Mr. Pentecost," had been invited to the World Council of Churches General Assembly at Evanston, Illinois, in 1954, and had lectured at Princeton, Yale, and Union Theological Seminary before 1960.

Pentecostal Churches emerged at the turn of the century, after the appearance of glossolalia in congregations in Kansas and California. These events, in turn, were the result of a tide of interest in the Holy Spirit's activity that had been rising for decades. Pentecostal themes appeared in print in 1858, but as early as 1835 Phoebe Palmer had begun sixty years of preaching, writing, and parlor meetings "for the Promotion of Holiness." She taught full baptism of the Holy Spirit, uniting the perfection and cleansing motifs of the Wesleyan tradition with the theme of power in the Spirit. By the 1890s every branch of Holiness and higher life movements and Reformed revivalism were teaching a variation of the baptism of the Holy Spirit—all the basic themes of Pentecostalism except glossolalia.

The Catholic Church had remained untouched by these forces, but many of the experiential aspects of these movements were present in parish missions conducted by visiting preachers; the "altar call" had its parallel in the long lines at the confessionals in a particularly successful mission. Nevertheless, word of the Pentecostal experience of the Duquesne professors and students spread quickly to the University of Notre Dame and to the parish at Michigan State University. In a few months the "Catholic Pentecostal Movement" was flourishing at the three universities and was spreading; hundreds left Notre Dame's summer school that year carrying the message and experience with them.

Leadership developed rapidly in South Bend, Indiana, and Ann Arbor, Michigan; a National Service Committee, which included Cursillo-trained lay leaders and local theologians, was formed to share information and organize activities. Annual Pentecostal conferences held under its auspices drew 30,000 people by 1976; the still-circulating magazine *New Covenant* began publication in 1971. The interest of the hierarchy was sought; Cardinal Joseph

Suenens attended the 1973 conference and spoke approvingly of the charismatic experience. The 1975 conference, held in Rome, was greeted by Pope Paul VI.

As prayer groups multiplied, the National Service Committee developed a series of preparatory experiences, the Life in the Spirit seminars. As the experience spread and deepened, covenant communities and charismatic parishes developed, South Bend and Ann Arbor being sites of the former. While membership in all groups included Protestants, and while the movement was professedly reformist with respect to the Church, there was neither the desire nor the necessity to separate from the Catholic Church. In contrast to the initial hesitancies of mainline Protestant Churches with regard to the movement, the Catholic hierarchy's first formal response, in 1969, was positive and proved to be a turning point in general Church acceptance. As a result of the shared experience among Christians of different denominations, a grass-roots ecumenism developed, highlighted in a 1976 conference on the Charismatic Renewal in the Christian Churches, which drew 45,000 people. Ongoing international Pentecostal-Roman Catholic conversations, begun in 1972, stem from the charismatic renewal and are an example of what Du Plessis called the "totally unanticipated *penetration* or diffusion of the Pentecostal experience into the 'established' denominations" (Quebedeaux, p. 8).

The National Service Committee responded to the leveling off in the late 1970s in ways indicative of the need for understanding the nature of the charismatic experience: calling it the result of infidelity; shifting attention from the movement itself to its place in the Church; recognizing that religious experience itself is not spiritual maturity; analyzing each decade of its existence as a stage in maturity; acknowledging important and parallel gifts in other Church groups; calling for a "second generation" movement in the nineties. But while the Pentecostal Churches have more experience in dealing with the charismata, the Catholic Church's theological reflection on these gifts has richer resources to draw from than these or any of the Churches of the Reformation have. For example, many charismatic movements have already found a home in the Church: 4th-century monastics, 13th-century Franciscans, 16th-century Jesuits. The strong emphasis on the Spirit's role in the life of the Church in *Lumen Gentium* and the traditions of the miraculous in Catholicism are other contexts within which charismatic activity can be assessed.

The 1974 and 1978 *Malines Documents* contain this kind of critical reflection; other analyses argue that if the Church is constituted by mutually supporting charisms, the public gifts of glossolalia, healing, and prophecy must not be overvalued at the expense of more quotidian charisms of service. Still others treat the charismatic experiences as a call to conversion or to contemplative prayer—calls that require discernment and spiritual direction far beyond that which is usually available in the movement. Comparisons have been made to the Corinthians' infidelity in the midst of their plenitude of spiritual gifts, to wit: warnings that miracles and spiritual power are not to be equated with authentically Christian faith and morality.

The characteristics of charismatic activity include the experience of baptism in the Spirit, reception of gifts of the Spirit, such as glossolalia, prophecy, healings, and deliverance from evil. Catholic groups seem to have less experience of glossolalia than others, and, as in other mainline Churches, they experience that charism without the shouting, dancing, or marching around that has been identified as cultural baggage belonging to the charismata's first appearance among lower-class and black congregations. The long tradition of sacramental grace in the Catholic tradition seems also to moderate the inclination to seek abso-

lute assurance of salvation in the Pentecostal experiences. Other characteristics of Pentecostalism, however, are evident: a democratized leadership, prominence of the laity, acceptance of the authority of Scripture, and a strong sense of fellowship.

The experience of baptism in the Spirit in the highly liturgical and sacramental Catholic Church raises the question of its relation to water baptism and confirmation. At root, this is the question of the meaning of any valid but nonexperiential reception of a sacrament, a question that can be found in Origen and Augustine, at the root of the radical Reformation's rejection of infant baptism, and in the questions of Catholics who experience more power in baptism in the Spirit than they did in their own confirmation. The *Malines Document I* calls baptism in the Spirit a "stirring up of the grace of Christian initiation" (baptism, confirmation, Eucharist); Mühlen speaks of it as a "renewal of confirmation"; Aquinas's statement that there can be nonsacramental impartings of the Spirit is valuable for conversations with nonsacramental Churches. Despite these questions, Catholic charismatics are unquestionably more active sacramental participants as a consequence of their experience.

Weaknesses of the charismatic renewal include a tendency to read Scripture in a fundamentalist fashion and to order prayer and covenant groups in an authoritarian and sexist style not typical of the overall Catholic renewal. In the mid-70s the charge was made that there were two types of Catholic charismatics, with some covenanted communities becoming increasingly sectarian, fundamentalist, and authoritarian. Since a bishops' committee for the renewal was established in 1971, there has been more direct Church influence in many areas; the tendency to sectarianism has thus been offset by the renewal's being inserted into many diocesan structures.

Social scientific studies of the renewal have been made. Kilian McDonnell, a

Benedictine theologian invited to join in early research on the movement, notes that as the psychological structure underlying religious experience can be studied, so can its sociocultural structure be analyzed without invalidating the authentic religious content it may have. There is criticism of some of this research, however, for having been done without control groups or on a "one-shot" basis without follow-up.

Studies are of several areas: on the mechanisms of attraction and retention of members; on the renewal's sect- and cult-like characteristics; on the effects of the organizational and group-dynamics skills of several original members of the National Service Committee, evident in recruitment tactics and in the design of training manuals; and on the charismatic renewal as a response to secularization. In the research on secularization, it has become clear that the renewal, together with other modern religious revivals, challenges the secularization hypothesis. Furthermore, it was admittedly not anticipated by social scientists, and certainly not within the hierarchical, liturgical, and sacramental mainline Churches such as the Catholic Church. Nor was it predicted that a movement which had its origins among the socially and economically deprived would appear in an affluent, university-educated group such as that in which it first appeared among Catholics.

A sociologist has noted that the United States offered optimum conditions for the original rise of Pentecostalism—the individualism, diversity, voluntary associations, and optimism of the 19th century. But these same social conditions have been invoked as indicative of a growing secularity, and some analyses characterize revivals and renewals as a response to this secularity; clearly, however, they are not "caused" by the conditions.

Organizationally, the movement possesses a segmented structure and is wholly decentralized; no one knows all who consider themselves participants, nor can any leader make decisions binding on all. Adherents are linked by criteria that flow from a common experience; leadership is a matter of charisma, evidence of possessing the gifts of the Spirit, and the capacity to lead by personal qualities or preaching. But these characteristics also support the charge that it has failed as a movement: it does not possess permanent structures with which to achieve its purposes. Whatever may be accomplished in the area of sociology's main concern, the individual's relationship to society, will probably occur through the prayer groups' impact rather than through structural social change. Congruent with this analysis, late in the 1980s *New Covenant* broadened its statement of purpose to "a commitment to fostering renewal in the Catholic church, especially the charismatic, ecumenical, evangelistic, and community dimensions of that renewal . . . and to the renewal of the whole Christian people."

As with earlier charismatic movements, there is reason to expect that the charismatic renewal will be absorbed into the existing patterns of Church life, with some of the covenant communities forming new religious orders; a pattern of such lay communities has, in fact, been developing for some time.

See also CHARISM; GLOSSOLALIA; HOLY SPIRIT; PROTESTANT SPIRITUALITIES.

Bibliography: R. Quebedeaux, *The New Charismatics II* (San Francisco: Harper & Row, 1983). D. Gelpi, "Conversion: The Challenge of Contemporary Charismatic Piety," TS 43 (1982) 606–628. K. McDonnell, ed., *Presence, Power, Praise: Documents on the Charismatic Renewal*, 3 vols. (Collegeville, Minn.: The Liturgical Press, 1980).

MARY BARBARA AGNEW, C.PP.S.

CHARITY

See LOVE; VIRTUE.

CHASTITY

Chastity (Latin *castitas*) is the moral virtue referring to the adoption of ethical and moral norms that moderate and regulate the sexual appetite. Since all people are sexual beings with innate sexual desires, chastity oversees the regulation of these desires in both personal and social circumstances. The practice of chastity as a virtue requires self-moderation and self-discipline in sexual matters. Although sexual self-moderation is an absolute value, historical and comparative cultural studies indicate that the practice of chastity has varied in various times and places and that it is subject to differing sociological conditions. The practice is most often regulated by religious codes and social mores.

Chastity is highly regarded in the four principal world religions. In the Christian tradition, chastity and the corresponding virtue of virginity have always held a high place, especially in the early Church. It would be erroneous, however, to consider chastity as uniquely Christian. In Islam, chastity is the state of spiritual and physical cleanliness, and is considered a necessary step on the way to God. It involves purity of thoughts and actions but does not require any form of celibate lifestyle. The veiling of Muslim women is one demonstration of chastity in public life. Privately, Muslim couples are required by religious law to abstain from sexual relations during certain times, such as the annual fasting period of Ramadan and while on pilgrimage to Mecca.

In Buddhism, chastity is associated with the monastic life as well as with the lay life. Buddhist monks practice chastity through celibacy in order to gain insight, knowledge, and miraculous powers. Certain magical characteristics, such as floating in air and expansion and contraction of the body, are attributed to the chaste monk. For the laity, chastity is associated generally with purity. Sexual purity, with certain periods of abstention from sexual intercourse, en-sures the married couple of childbirth and is required if one is to reach the state of nirvana.

In Judaism, chastity has had an ongoing development. In the earliest period of Israel's history, warriors were required to be chaste, observing celibacy until after the time of war. In everyday life, chastity made its demands upon all people. According to Jewish tradition, the high priest was held to the virtue of chastity within marriage, and there were restrictions as to whom he could marry; for instance, he could not marry a prostitute or a divorced woman (Lev 21:7, 13f.). Within Jewish marriage, purity and chastity were vital elements; a chaste marriage was one established by God.

In Judaism, as in the other religions of the ancient Near East, the sphere of sexuality was closely linked to the sacred. Since human sexuality was an imitation of the sexuality of the gods, the custom of sacred prostitution found root in religious practices. Within the Yahwist tradition, the reasons behind this sacralization changed, in that human sexuality was more in accordance with God's word, through which God shares the divine creative power. Eve gave birth through the help of Yahweh (Gen 4:1). The sexual symbolism is prevalent in the analogy of Israel's relationship to God, including the practice of circumcision as a sign of ratification of the covenant (Gen 17:9-14; Lev 12:3). Within the sacralization of the sexual there were specific rites of purification, rituals similar to those of other religions of the Near East. Prescriptions were promulgated to protect the sacredness of the sexual sphere. Therefore, during menstruation or after childbirth a woman was declared unclean, necessitating ritual purifications before entering the sanctuary (Lev 12:6; 15:19-30). Provisions were made for men when nocturnal emission occurred (Lev 15:1-17; Deut 23:11). In all these cases sexuality was not denigrated but rather protected in the sphere of the sacred through ritual ablutions.

The subject of a large number of rules in the OT is sexual morality. This does not indicate any condemnation of sexuality or excessive moral attention given to this subject but rather ensures the sacralization, avoiding unnecessary sexual perversions in the area of religion. The Book of Leviticus catalogs a certain number of sexual abuses condemning fornication, sexual relations with a menstruating woman, adultery, incest, homosexuality, and bestiality (Lev 20:10-21). Nowhere does one find contempt for sexuality in itself.

Christian Chastity

In the NT the notion of chastity is closely linked to that of purity and sincerity. Drawing from the Greek *hagneia,* the word is used in a sexual and moral context in 2 Cor 11:2; Tit 2:5; 1 Pet 3:2, although one finds it used elsewhere in a more general sense of purity and rites of purification. The Greek term *katharos* and its cognates denote the idea of moral purity in a physical or ceremonial sense.

Teaching about the sacredness of marriage, Christ underlines the value of chastity within the married state, forbidding divorce (Mt 19:4). Chastity within marriage consists of the temperate use of conjugal intercourse. Marriage becomes the symbol of the relationship of the people to their God. Departing from the sacralization of sexuality to a new idea of holiness, the Christian is called to a relationship with God through membership in the People of God and the presence of the Holy Spirit, not through the sacred character of the sexual relationship. Although one is not made holy by that which is outside of the body, the Christian is still held bound by the demands of sexual purity: "This is the will of God, your holiness: that you refrain from immorality, that each of you know how to acquire a wife for himself in holiness and honor, not in lustful passion as do the Gentiles who do not know God" (1 Thess 4:3). Sexual purity is the model for the relationship between husbands and wives, analogous to the relationship of Christ to the Church (Eph 5:25).

Paul, in a non-Jewish milieu, is quite specific about the right use of human sexuality. He strongly forbids all forms of evil, such as idolatry, adultery, pederasty, sodomy, thievery, usury, drunkenness, slander, and swindle (1 Cor 6:9) and exhorts his listeners often concerning prostitution (1 Cor 6:13ff.; 10:8; 2 Cor 12:21; Col 3:5). If one is not able to moderate one's life, withdrawal from the world might be necessary (1 Cor 5:10). Speaking to a non-Jewish audience, Paul is not able to rely upon the Law with its minute applications. He warns the Corinthians, a people known for their licentiousness, to go beyond what they consider legal to respect their bodies as temples of the Holy Spirit. One cannot be joined to Christ and joined to a prostitute (1 Cor 5:13ff.). In advising the married, Paul concedes that if one cannot abstain from sexual relations altogether, it is better to be faithful to one's spouse rather than be immoral (1 Cor 7:1-7). Given Paul's soteriological perspective, it is understandable why he counsels people to remain single. He counsels the unmarried and widows to remain single, but if they cannot remain chaste, it would be better to marry than to burn with desire. In general, with the coming of Jesus and the teaching of Paul, sexuality is removed from the sphere of the sacred, making holiness more of an interior affair.

As in many ancient religions, virginity was highly valued, and many of the pagan goddesses were called virgins to accentuate their eternal youthfulness and their incorruptibility. In the Christian tradition, virginity took on the meaning of exclusive fidelity to God's love. The Church is depicted as the virgin spouse of Christ, much as Israel had been portrayed as the virgin of Yahweh (Amos 5:2; Isa 37:23; Jer 14:17; Lam 1:15; 2:13). In the Christian context, virginity is closely associated with fidelity and chastity. Remaining a virgin, as Mary and John the Baptist did, reveals the supernatural character of virginity as a personal call from God. One remains virginal and chaste in one's relations only for the kingdom of heaven (Mt 19:12). For St. Paul, virginity is superior to marriage for eschatological reasons. The NT assesses both chastity and virginity positively, since both give witness to a world that will not pass away. They remain as a permanent sign of the eschatological tension in which the Church finds itself, anticipating the resurrection (Lk 20:34ff.).

Patristic Period

In the postapostolic period a shift occurred favoring virginity and preferring the celibate life to the married state. The early Fathers considered celibacy the purest form of chastity. Due to the prevalent attitudes of Gnostic origin, sexuality was suspect in the early Christian period. Certain patristic writings, especially from the Alexandrian school, endorsed an antisexual position under the influence of Neoplatonic and Stoic ideas. In the writings of Philo the Jew and Josephus, both influenced by the Jewish sect of Essenes, marriage was neglected rather than absolutely forbidden. In strong opposition to the Pharisees, they held that true chastity is to be found in the unmarried state. Total continence was demanded, even for converts up to three years before admission into the sect.

In the writings of Clement of Rome, virginity is extolled as a great virtue ensuring one a high place in heaven. He takes the Greek *hagnos* to be equivalent to the celibate (*Ep. 1 ad Cor.* 38), as Ignatius of Rome identifies chastity with celibacy (*Polyc.* 5). Justin Martyr defends the Christians from the accusation of promiscuity by declaring that they are chaste, many of them remaining virgins at the age of sixty or seventy years (*Apol.* 1, 15). Elsewhere he declares that either Christians married or lived chastely (*Apol.* 1, 29).

In the 2nd century various groups of Christian Encratists taught that chastity required that one refrain from marriage. The Marcionites forbade marriage altogether, for which they were condemned by Irenaeus (*Adv. haer.* 1, 28) and by Tertullian (*Adv. Marc.* 1, 29). One must place this controversy against the backdrop of Gnosticism in order to fully appreciate this position favoring absolute celibacy. The morality in this Gnostic environment was almost exclusively ascetic. Epiphanius recounts a story from his youth of Gnostic women who approached him making sexual advances while quoting Gnostic formulas to him. Resisting temptation, he maintained his chastity (see *Adv. haer.* 27, 17). On the other hand, some Gnostic groups, as described by Clement of Alexandria, treated sex as a divine mystery. Sexual intercourse was called a "mystical communion" or a "sacred religious mystery" (*Stromateis* 3, 27ff.).

Tertullian represents the ascetic view, but one notes a change of position from his earlier writing *Ad uxorem,* where he tolerates chastity within marriage. In his Montanist period, clearly under the influence of Gnostic dualism, Tertullian regarded marriage as a violation of strict chastity and a form of fornication (see *De exh. cast.* 9). Strictly speaking, Tertullian did not reject marriage, but he advocated that one refrain from it. Above all, he was opposed to remarriage, which he found absolutely incompatible with chastity.

Within Christian orthodoxy, however, marriage was held as sacred, but the purest chastity favored the unmarried state. In the dualistic environment, where the material world was denigrated in favor of the purely spiritual, marriage was regarded as a participation in the materiality of the world and thus in the domain of evil. Examples of this attitude abound in both the East and the Latin West (see P. Brown, *The Body and Society*).

In the 4th century a reaction to overstrictness developed among more well-balanced thinkers. There were still those who favored celibate chastity, but others sought a more equilibrated notion, adaptable to those living in the world. At the Council of Nicaea in 325, Paphnutius defended the idea that intercourse within marriage is a form of chastity, opposing the proposed canon that would have forced clergy married before ordination to separate from their wives. In the mid-4th century a group called the Eustathians condemned marriage as evil, for which they were anathematized by the Council of Gangra (see letters and canons 3, 10, and 13 in E. Jonkers, ed., *Acta et symbola conciliorum quae saeculo quarto habita sunt,* Textus Minores 19, Leiden: Brill, 1974). St. Ambrose, in his *De viduis* (4, 23), held for a threefold order of chastity to include marriage, widowhood, and virginity, indicating that the virtue of chastity is required of all people, regardless of their state of life.

In later Latin the word *castitas* came to mean celibacy exclusively. By the time of the Council of Trent, the term was explicitly opposed to marriage. In the twenty-fourth session (1563), provision was made for those who did not have the charism of chastity required for sacred orders or regulars, allowing them to marry (can. 9). Marriage, however, was affirmed in its goodness and as a grace-giving sacrament of the evangelical law (can. 1). The council, though, anathematized anyone who held that marriage was a higher state than virginity or celibacy (can. 10).

Conjugal chastity became a major theme of Francis de Sales, who emphasized its necessity more than any other condition of life for the married couple (*Introduction to the Devout Life,* trans. and ed. J. Ryan, New York: Harper & Row, 1966, Part 3, chaps. 12 and 13). A sort of double chastity is imposed upon the couple: to abstain absolutely from any sexual activity when they are apart and to practice moderation when they are together. St. Francis advocated that Philothea follow the three ascending degrees of chastity as practiced by monks and nuns, namely, to be on guard against any forbidden sensual pleasure; next, to avoid any unnecessary or superfluous de-

lights; and finally, not to attach too much feeling to pleasures to which the heart or the spirit should never be attached. Although he models conjugal chastity after that of religious, his counsel is intended for a married person.

In modern times chastity has once again been incorporated into the treatment of marriage, as evidenced by the papal encyclical of Pius XI entitled *Casti Connubii,* which speaks of the "splendor of chastity." Within the moral order, chastity is concerned with the progressive integration of human sexuality for both celibates and married people. The sexual order established by God and confirmed by Christ must be integrated into every Christian life, avoiding the two extremes of excessive rigorism on the one hand and hedonism on the other. In the moral teachings of the Church, conjugal love is promoted within the call of every person to live chastely.

In the Christian tradition, chastity before marriage or after the death of a spouse is highly esteemed. St. John Chrysostom preached forcefully about the obligation of chastity outside marriage (*Serm.* 2, PG 54:652). In the case of virginity, as in the case of conjugal chastity, one is speaking of the virtue as opposed to the vow of chastity taken in religious life.

Religious Vows

The Council of Trent in the twenty-fifth session declared that chastity is one of the three monastic vows, along with poverty and obedience (chap. 1). Religious vows, or the three evangelical counsels, are an inalienable constituent of the form of the Church, symbolizing the love of God, which transcends the world. Chastity in this case is undertaken for the sake of the kingdom (Mt 19:10ff.). In early Christian monasticism chastity always implied celibacy, as well as an obligation to remain pure from every carnal interest. The Rule of Benedict lists chastity among seventy-two instruments of good works. The principal element of chastity is to avoid lust and to remain pure in thought, word, and deed. Purity of thought is required of all Christians, especially married people. In a special way the idea of purity of thought was stressed in monastic circles as a possible means to perfection, provided that other means to the same end are also recognized. Chastity and celibacy are not virtues in and of themselves, but to the degree that they point to eschatological values, to a world that will never end, they are virtuous (see Pius XII, encyclical *Sacra Virginitas,* DS 3911).

In religious life the three evangelical counsels are obligatory. In the decree on religious life from the Second Vatican Council, *Perfectae Caritatis,* the three counsels are maintained in the up-to-date renewal of religious life. "[Chastity] is an outstanding token of heavenly riches, and also a most suitable way for religious to spend themselves readily in God's service and in works of the apostolate" (PC 12). Religious are encouraged to practice mortification and custody of the senses, as well as to take all natural means for good health in mind and body, rejecting anything that endangers chastity. Promoting the common life, the council held that communities secure the virtue of chastity where perfect continence is observed. In his Apostolic Exhortation on the Renewal of Religious Life, Pope Paul VI reiterated the positive role of the vow of chastity as a sign of God's love and the response to God's call. Consecrated chastity is a gift of self made to God and to others which complements marital love and stands as "the image and sharing of the union of love joining Christ and the Church" (*Evangelica Testificatio* 13). In a world ravaged by eroticism, consecrated chastity stands in witness to the positive love of God and symbolizes the union of the Mystical Body with its Head.

Pope John Paul II restates the classical view of the value of virginity and celibacy for the sake of the kingdom. Basing this assertion on the gospel, he underlines consecrated chastity as a means by which one dedicates oneself exclusively to God (*Mulieris Dignitatem* 20). In this context consecrated chastity is a radical way to live according to the gospel.

See also ABSTINENCE; ASCETICISM; BRIDAL MYSTICISM; CELIBACY; CONSECRATION; GNOSIS, GNOSTICISM; MONASTICISM, MONASTIC SPIRITUALITY; MORTIFICATION; RELIGIOUS LIFE; SEXUALITY; VIRGINITY; VOWS.

Bibliography: P. Brown, *The Body and Society: Men, Women, and Sexual Renunciation in Early Christianity* (New York: Columbia Univ. Press, 1988). R. Grant, ed., *Gnosticism and Early Christianity* (New York: Harper & Row, 1966). F. Maloney, *A Life of Promise: Poverty, Chastity and Obedience* (Wilmington, Del.: Glazier, 1984). A. van Kaam, *The Vowed Life* (Denville, N.J.: Dimension Books, 1968).

MICHAEL S. DRISCOLL

CHILD, CHILDREN

The concept of childhood did not exist in medieval times; children mingled with adults as soon as they were able. By the 16th century it was recognized that children were not yet ready for adult life. Therefore the function of the family merely as an institution for transmitting name and property changed. Parents were now to be spiritual guardians and molders of bodies and souls.

Mark's Gospel (10:13-16) presents Jesus as taking children very seriously as persons, whereas the writings of his time presented them as unreasonable and in need of training. Commentators have pointed out that the phrase "of such is the kingdom of God" indicates that only those who know how to receive can enter the kingdom. For the kingdom is a gift. Children with no physical power or legal status should know how to receive this gift.

The responsibility of raising children has always been great. Today the task is even more difficult. Children today are as needy as they were in Jesus' time. Modern culture often makes them demanding. Parents must distinguish between the needs and the wants of children. Jesus gave children, not material gifts, but gifts of the spirit. Parents, as the primary agents of the development of their children, need to be aware that authentic development is more than physical and intellectual development. It is development of the most human aspects of children—their moral and spiritual life—not only as autonomous individuals but as members of the human family contributing to the common good.

Twentieth-century psychologists have plotted not only the cognitive and moral development of children but also various aspects of their religious sense. Elkind has shown that children under the age of eleven cannot understand abstract religious expressions. Children aged five have only a vague notion of prayer; at seven, their prayers are requests for concrete things; by nine years of age, prayer emerges as a private conversation with God and is recognized as connected with a particular belief system.

Rizzuto sees God as a transitional object formed consciously by the child between the ages of two and three. This image should be continually reconstructed. Essential to the formation of the image of a loving God is the experience of being mirrored back or reflected as good in the eyes of the parents or of some significant other. The self-image develops with the God-image. Eventually, it is hoped, the child will accept God as the one mirroring back the essential goodness of the self.

What is clear from object relations psychologists is that the God-image results from early experiences of significant adults who are both mirror and ideal for the child. The process of creating and finding God continues throughout life together with the developing self-image. This essential early experience of being loved, and therefore of being good and desirable, then opens the child more fully to the action of God's self-communication.

See also MARRIAGE; PSYCHOLOGY, RELATIONSHIP AND CONTRIBUTION TO SPIRITUALITY; SELF; SINGLE PARENT.

Bibliography: P. Aries, *Centuries of Childhood,* trans. R. Baldick (New York: Random House, 1962). D. Elkind, *The Child's Reality* (Hillsdale, N.J.: Lawrence Erlbaum Associates, 1978); A. M. Rizzuto, *The Birth of the Living God* (Chicago: Univ. of Chicago Press, 1979).

MARGARET GORMAN, R.S.C.J.

CHRIST

The Risen Christ

No event in the life of Jesus or in the history of the Christian Church was more significant than the resurrection of Jesus from the dead. After the tragic death to which the ministry of Jesus had led, God's raising of Jesus from the dead vindicated Jesus, validated his life and ministry, and revealed that Jesus had in fact been sent by God, was "of God," was God's Servant.

The resurrection of Jesus was a revelatory event. In it Jesus was made known to his disciples as the Messiah. The Greek word *christos* (Christ) is a translation of the Hebrew word for Messiah, which means "anointed one." *Messiah* had various uses throughout Israelite and Judean history, but the earliest Christians used it in the sense of *the* Messiah, the awaited Savior, and also interpreted it in specifically Christian ways in the light of their experience. Thus, in the light of the resurrection, Jesus was recognized as God's unique Servant, Son, and Messiah—the Christ of God.

Views varied as to when Jesus was understood to have become the Christ. Paul seems to have understood Jesus as having become the Christ, the unique Son of God, as of his resurrection from the dead (Rom 1:1-4). The central focus of Pauline Christology is the death and resurrection of Jesus and Jesus as another Adam. The Gospel of Mark, however, seems to assert that Jesus became the Messiah as of his baptism (Mk 1:11). The infancy narratives of Matthew and Luke, and their theology of the virginal conception of Jesus, suggest that Jesus was the Messiah from the moment of his conception (Mt 1–2; Lk 1–2). The Gospel of John interprets the story of Jesus and Jesus' unique sonship to have begun before he was born or conceived (Jn 1:1–18).

What remains common is that all early participants and writers gave witness to Jesus as raised from the dead and as being the Christ. Jesus was the risen Christ, and the risen Christ was Jesus. However this "Christhood" of Jesus was interpreted or whenever it began, the resurrection of Jesus was the event that clearly disclosed or definitively revealed this fact to Jesus' disciples. The resurrection, implying the totality of events and experiences accompanying it, was a revelatory event.

The resurrection of Jesus was also an eschatological event. It was the transformation, or definitive passing over, of Jesus from his earthly, historical form of existence to his continuing, glorified, eschatological existence. Jesus is still with us, still lives, but not in the same way. The resurrection also led to the expectation among the earliest Christians that Jesus would soon be coming again as the risen Lord. In the beginning the earliest Christologies could be seen as a chapter in the history of eschatology. Jesus, the Christ, would come again. Later, however, eschatology became a chapter in Christology. Jesus became the one to embody our hopes and expectations. It is not so much to the future that we look as it is to Jesus Christ.

The resurrection was not only an eschatological event for Jesus and the early Christian movement, and a revelatory event for Jesus' disciples as well as later history, but also an invitation to faith for all of us. The resurrection demands a decision or response. Was Jesus raised from the dead or not? Do you believe that Jesus is the Christ? The resurrection narratives in the NT bring us face to face with this decision of faith. If one does not believe in the risen Jesus, one may still see him as an inspiring, prophetic, and significant religious figure.

If one does accept Jesus as the risen Christ, however, then he or she is called upon to follow him. Christology implies discipleship. The Gospel of John teaches us that truly knowing Jesus means becoming his disciple. Not to follow Jesus means not knowing who he truly is. The resurrection invites this response of faith, and only faith can proclaim Jesus as raised from the dead. Historical research can lead us in the direction of the risen Christ but cannot scientifically demonstrate that Jesus was in fact raised from the dead. The resurrection also reveals that there is more to history than scientific historical research has access to.

The resurrection gave birth to the Christian faith—no resurrection, no Christian faith. The earliest professions of this faith spoke of Jesus as both Christ and Lord (Acts 2:36). The resurrection of Jesus also came to imply his exaltation, his lordship (Phil 2:6–11). It is, however, difficult to say in what ways the language of exaltation and the language of resurrection imply each other. But the resurrection event gave birth to Christian faith, and thus Christian theology, and thus Christology properly understood. Early Christian theology (NT theology) was Christology. The earthly Jesus as such had not taught a Christology. He taught very little about himself. His frame of reference was always God, not himself. He was in no way self-preoccupied.

The resurrection as an event—historically, theologically, liturgically—cannot be separated from Jesus' gift of the Spirit. Easter and Pentecost are thus tied together, as are the risen Christ and the Spirit of the risen Christ. When one speaks of the resurrection, then, one is talking not only about what happened to Jesus but also about the experiences of the risen Christ as given us in the resurrection narratives, as well as the Pentecostal presence of the Spirit of Christ. Thus the resurrection, in its fullest sense, gave birth not only to Christian faith but also to the Christian Church. We can begin to grasp something of the significance of the resurrection and how it deserves to be the starting point for any reflection on Jesus Christ.

Because of the significance of Jesus' resurrection, it has been a central concern from the earliest Christian writings until our own day. Paul stated it clearly, "If Christ has not been raised, then empty too is our preaching; empty, too, your faith" (1 Cor 15:14). Yet the Christian faith cannot prove the resurrection. It remains a meta-historiographical, historical event apprehended by faith and experience (an event in history or aspect of history that escapes historical research or verification). The resurrection makes it clear that there is more to history, in the sense of what happened, than historical research has access to, in the sense of historiography or the science of history. The resurrection indicates that history requires interpretation if history itself is to be understood. In the resurrection, history and all that surrounds it come together. In the resurrection both history and historiography confront their limits. The resurrection is a historical event that requires theological interpretation. There is more to history than history alone. In order to be fully and adequately understood, history requires theology. The resurrection demonstrates the truth of this. History does not provide us with the meaning of the resurrection; rather, the resurrection gives us the meaning of history.

The NT resurrection narratives themselves are testimonies to the faith and experiences of the disciples. The narratives record both the appearances of the risen Jesus (or the appearance-experiences of the disciples) and events at or in the vicinity of the tomb. The emptiness of the grave itself does not, either historically or in the NT narratives, lead to belief in Jesus as raised; rather, the narratives suggest that the origin of faith in Jesus' resurrection lies in the appearances of Jesus to his disciples. Even for the women, who were more attentive to the tomb, it was the appearance of Jesus to Mary Magdalene in the vicinity of the tomb, not the discovery of the empty tomb itself, that led to her recognition of Jesus and commission by him. Thus, although the historical details may be difficult to formulate, as is the particular nature of the resurrection body, the proclamation of the first disciples, women and men, in Galilee and Jerusalem, gave witness to their experiences of Jesus as alive. As Mary Magdalene expressed it, "I have seen the Lord" (Jn 20:18). "He has been raised" (Mk 16:6). Jesus of Nazareth became the risen Jesus, the risen Christ.

The risen Christ, exalted Lord, glorified Son, continues to be present with us, continues God's presence with us, continues to be Immanuel ("God with us"—Isa 7:14). The Christian comes to God in the risen Christ and through the power of the Spirit. The Christian lives a life in Christ and with Christ, according to Paul, or comes to the Father through the Son, according to the Gospel of John. Christian life thus begins with the risen Christ alive and present, not a dead Christ or even a historical Christ, but rather with the risen Lord present in the proclamation of the Church, in the Eucharist, and among the people, especially the poor and marginalized. Thus the starting point for Christology, for a theology of the Christian life, for preaching, or for a theology of the sacraments is the present Christ, the risen Christ.

Jesus' resurrection from the dead is intimately linked to the more general resurrection of all of us from the dead (1 Cor 15:13). We have all been raised already through our baptism into Christ. The fullness of the glorified, resurrected life, however, is not yet ours until we too undergo the transformation that death brings (1 Thess 4:13-18; 1 Cor 15:51-57; 2 Cor 5:1-5) and until the work of Christ itself comes to completion (1 Cor 15:20-28).

Jesus revealed the resurrection from the dead, and his resurrection is a sign that we too will be raised. Why? Because our God is a God of life, a God of power, and a God of justice. Jesus' resurrection reveals to us as well something about who the God of Jesus Christ is. In the Marcan story of the earthly Jesus' confrontation with the Sadducees, who denied resurrection from the dead, Jesus' own understanding of God is disclosed (Mk 12:18-27).

The Sadducees did not believe in resurrection, because they understood neither the Scriptures nor God. The God of Abraham and Sarah, the God of the prophets and martyrs, is not a God of the dead but of the living. Therefore the holy ones of Israel still live. God is a God of life. God who creates a universe out of nothing can transform those who have died into glory. God is a God of power. The first clear statement of the emergence of the doctrine of resurrection among the Judean people came in the second century B.C. and accompanied reflection on the experience of the Maccabean martyrs (Dan 12:2-3). God's servants are not abandoned by God. If God is a God of justice, at least the servants of God are raised from the dead. And God is a God of love. "What eye has not seen, and ear has not heard, and what has not entered the human heart, what God has prepared for those who love him, this God has revealed to us through the Spirit" (1 Cor 2:9-10). Thus the culmination of the earthly life of Jesus was not tragic and God-forsaken but rather a life vindicated and a source of hope. "God greatly exalted him and bestowed on him the name that is above every name . . . Jesus Christ is Lord" (Phil 2:9-11).

The Incarnate Word

Although the better starting point for understanding Jesus Christ is the resurrection, the doctrine with which the history of Christology became preoccupied was that of the incarnation. Jesus as the incarnate Word is the central Christological concept in the prologue to the Gospel of John (Jn 1:1-18). Many argue that the doctrine of incarnation can be found only in John and not in other NT writings. It is certainly most clearly articulated in John: "The Word became flesh" (Jn 1:14). Apart from the prologue, however, Jesus is primarily interpreted in the Gospel of John as Son. Yet the Johannine theology of Son is distinctive. The Son comes from above (3:31; 6:38; 8:23), is in some sense subordinate to the Father (5:19; 8:28; 12:49; 14:28), but for all practical purposes is equal to the Father (5:17-18; 8:16-18; 10:30; 14:9-11).

The Christology of the Johannine prologue decisively influenced Christian history in two ways: with its doctrine of incarnation and with its theology of the Word (the Logos). From the second century on, Christologies became, more or less, Logos Christologies. The incarnational Christology of the prologue can be succinctly stated: Jesus ultimately *is* the Word. The Word *is* God, is eternal. Jesus is the eternal Word present in history in an incarnate mode. Thus Jesus is both Word (God) and flesh (human). In the Gospel of John heaven and earth are woven together in a profoundly integrated way as the Gospel articulates its understanding of Jesus. From a Johannine perspective, one cannot contrast "faith" and "history." Only faith truly understands history. To not recognize who Jesus truly is, which recognition necessitates going beyond historical categories, is to not yet know Jesus in truth. For the Gospel of John, Jesus *is* God's Word, God's unique Son. The Gospel thus raises for Christian history the important question: Who is this Word/Logos?

The Johannine reference to Logos was a stimulus for further development of the theology of the Logos, such as in Justin Martyr and particularly in the Alexandrian tradition. The Gospel of John necessitated the eventual development of a theology of the Trinity. The Church struggled with subordinationism, then Arianism, and finally formulated the Nicene faith, which defined the Logos as *homoousios* (of the same substance) with the Father. But the preincarnate Logos of the Johannine prologue was not that precise.

The Johannine Logos had its roots in the Book of Genesis, among the prophets, and in Israel's wisdom tradition. Genesis began, "In the beginning," with God speaking. Likewise, the Johannine prologue began, "In the beginning," with divine speech. The prophets did not see themselves as proclaiming their own word but rather God's word: "The word of the Lord came to me" (Jer 1:4). The closest parallels to the Johannine Logos, however, come from the wisdom literature. The Logos is divine *sophia* or wisdom (Job 28; Wis 9:9-18; Prov 8; Sir 24:3-21).

The Word is with God in the beginning. In fact, the Word is God. Yet one can distinguish God (*ho theos*) and God's Word (*ho logos en theos*). The Word is God's agent in creation, or God as creating. The prologue presupposes two faces or dimensions of God: transcendence and immanence. God is unknowable, unfathomable mystery, and yet God is also self-communicating, self-revealing. God is God, but God is also Word. The Word is God as self-expressing, as reaching out, as acting *ad extra,* as coming near. While human speech cannot do justice to the mystery of God, the Hebrew people attempted to do justice to their experience of God. God was one whose personal name ought not be uttered. To do so would be to control God. God was the one who is holy and revered. But God was also the one who is with us, who comes to pitch a tent among us (Exod 3:1-14; Isa 7:14).

God's Word, or God as self-disclosing or self-revealing, is the Creator, and creation itself reveals God. The Word creates all things, especially life, and most especially human life. And within human history, the Word was particularly present to the people of the Word, the Hebrew people, and the history of their salvation and liberation. The story of salvation is caught up in the story of creation, which is nothing other than the story of revelation: the story of God's Word. The Word (God) was continually drawing nearer and nearer to God's people until it finally "became flesh and dwelt among us" (Jn 1:14). The Word had become incarnate, enfleshed, identifiable as one of us, woven into the fabric of human history. The Word who was with God in the beginning and who was coming forth from God and who was creating a people among whom it could make its home, had at last become human itself, a human being, Jesus of Nazareth, the culmination of revelation. Jesus was that Word incarnate.

John 1:14 is the biblical text on which the doctrine of the incarnation was constructed: "And the Word become flesh and made his dwelling among us." Were it not for this text and the Johannine theology of Jesus' sonship, Christianity may well not have developed the concept of incarnation as its primary way of interpreting Jesus. Had there been no doctrine of incarnation, the theology of the Trinity would have been quite different. One's theology of Jesus Christ directly affects one's theology of God, as attested by the relationship between the doctrines of incarnation and Trinity. To know Jesus is to know something of God. One cannot ask, "Who is Jesus?" without eventually asking as well, "Who is the God of Jesus?" or "Who is God?" Jesus poses the question of God. Jesus cannot be understood apart from God, and vice versa.

Likewise, Jesus poses the question, "What does it mean to be human?" One cannot talk about Jesus without talking about us—humanity—and vice versa. Christology and theological anthropology are woven together. These questions are interrelated due to the incarnation.

The incarnate Word is both *Logos* and *sarx.* One is not more strongly affirmed than the other. Jesus is both. Jesus *is* the Logos. The Logos is God. Jesus in some way partakes of the divine nature. The clarification of this was an important task of Christology, especially in the 4th and 5th centuries. But Jesus also *is* sarx, flesh, earthly, human, one of us. The Gospel of

John presents both a very divine and a very human Christ, someone through whom the glory of God shines and someone who washes the feet of his disciples.

The incarnation implies holding together these two affirmations about Jesus. Ultimately the incarnation implies that these two affirmations are not contradictory: that union between the Godhead and the human is possible, and that God and the human are not alien to each other. Thus Docetism and Adoptionism became extremes to which Christology could not go and still be judged to be faithful to the NT. Jesus is God's unique Son. Jesus is also the prophet and sage from Galilee. The Word incarnate *is* the Nazarene.

Johannine Christology profoundly influenced the historical Christian faith. Following upon the Gospel of John, Christologies became three-stage Christologies. They began with the prior existence of the eternal Word who became flesh. This traditional approach to Christology is called today "Christology from above." This is a Christology that begins with the eternal Word or the doctrine of the Trinity. Many 20th-century Christologies begin "from below," with the historical Jesus. More recently the starting point is being perceived as the resurrection. A Christology from above focuses on the incarnation, and whatever one's starting point, one eventually has to take a stand on the incarnation as well. Is it true? What does it mean?

The major modern stumbling block to faith in the incarnation is the assumption of an incompatibility between the divinity and humanity of Christ, such that if one is affirmed, the other is denied. But this is the failure of modern rationalism to understand the true meaning revealed in the incarnation, namely, that the Godhead and humanity are not irreconcilable opposites by nature, even if they are existentially estranged due to sin. Jesus' hypostatic unity with God in no way makes him any less human than grace (the divine life) makes other human beings less human. Jesus' divine nature does not make him less fully human; rather, sin makes us less fully human.

There is no question but that the theology of the hypostatic union has had a long and difficult history, and that it is not easy to steer a course between Docetism and Adoptionism or between "Nestorianism" and Monophysitism. Yet the theology of the incarnation came to a less poetic but more precise articulation at the Council of Chalcedon in A.D. 451.

Alexandrian theology began with a theology of the Logos, with a strong concern for the oneness or unity of Christ, and at times did less than justice to the humanness of Christ. Antiochene theology began more often with theological anthropology, thus with a strong concern for the humanity of Christ, and thus at times did less than justice to the oneness of Christ. Antiochenes could give the impression of two Christs, Alexandrians of one divine Christ. The Council of Chalcedon attempted to resolve the dilemma and the tensions by defining Christ as one *hypostasis* or person (an Alexandrian concern) subsisting in two *physeis* or natures (the Antiochene concern). Although the definition did not resolve all the problems, it became paradigmatic for later discussions, at least among the Chalcedonian Churches. After the Council of Ephesus (A.D. 431), Nestorian Churches took their own path, and after Chalcedon the Monophysite Churches did the same.

The incarnation is not a philosophical problem but a theological mystery. It brings us face to face with the mystery of Christ. It becomes problematic when we approach the mystery with prior conceptions or definitions of God and humanity that make them intrinsically opposed. Rather, in the incarnation God is revealed as the One who is with us and for us, and humanity is revealed as being structured for union with God. The incarnate Word is both God's eternal Son and God's historical presence. Jesus introduces us to both a new understanding of God and a deeper awareness of the meaning of human history.

The Galilean Prophet

The earthly, historical, incarnate Jesus of Nazareth has been the object of extensive critical biblical research. Although such research cannot give us the whole story of Jesus, this Jesus of historical critical research is still significant to Christian faith. This Jesus gives us one dimension of the Jesus of faith. When God broke into history, or entered more deeply into human history in Jesus Christ, what did this incarnate face or image of God look like? Who was this Jesus as history experienced him? This historical Jesus has great significance and symbolic power for many Christians and non-Christians.

Although the pictures of Jesus vary, depending upon the researchers, and although contemporary researchers have no intention of writing Lives of Jesus, given the nature of the biblical material, there are nevertheless some clear themes that emerge, e.g., Jesus in relationship to prophecy and to wisdom, Jesus as a man of prayer, and the centrality of the reign of God in Jesus' mission. Each of these has implications for Christian discipleship or spirituality.

One thing is clear. In order to understand the earthly Jesus, one must understand the Hebrew prophetic tradition. In many ways Jesus is like the prophets of old, whose concerns were God, justice, and the nature of true religion and holiness. In some ways Jesus can be understood as having inaugurated a prophetic movement for the renewal of Judaism based upon his understanding of holiness as compassion. When Jesus asked his disciples at Caesarea Philippi how people perceived him, they responded by saying that Jesus was a prophet like Moses or Elijah (Mk 8:27-30). In other ways Jesus was able to be contrasted to the more recent prophet, John the Baptist, whose ministry was the occa-

sion for Jesus' own baptism and call. Undoubtedly the prophetic mission, ministry, and death of John played a strong role in the life of Jesus, for whom John was something of a mentor (Mt 11:7-15; Lk 7:28-29).

The Gospel of Mark provides evidence for at least two ways in which Jesus referred to himself: as a prophet and as a preacher (Mk 1:38; 6:4). Upon his return to Galilee after his baptism, when his own ministry seemed ineffective in Nazareth, Jesus interpreted the experience as "a prophet is not without honor except in his native place and among his own kin and in his own house" (Mk 6:4). On another occasion Jesus said to his disciples, "Let us go on to the nearby villages that I may preach there also. For this purpose have I come" (Mk 1:38). A primary historical image of Jesus is that of an itinerant, prophetic preacher. His ministry was a ministry of the word.

While we cannot be as precise as we might like, we can be more specific and say that Jesus saw himself more as a prophet like Moses than as a king like David. It was more the Mosaic, prophetic, wilderness tradition of spirituality of the North, focused on the Exodus event, that was formative of Jesus' own vision. This is in contrast to the Davidic, messianic, Zionist tradition of spirituality in the South, with its focus on Jerusalem and the Temple. While Jesus made his annual pilgrimage(s) to Jerusalem and respected the Temple, for him the heart of the Law or Torah was focused elsewhere—on love of God and love of neighbor (Deut 6:4; Lev 19:18). Fulfilling messianic expectations was less important to Jesus than action in accord with the intent of the Torah as Jesus understood it. In Jesus' wilderness experience (Mt 4:1-11; Lk 4:1-13) and continuing experiences of God (Mk 14:26-50), he found himself in the companionship of God like the prophets of old. In the Matthean and Lucan interpretations of the wilderness experience, Jesus' source of strength came from his reflection on Deuteronomy 6–8, the story of Moses, the Exodus, the wilderness experience of his ancestors, and the *Shema* (Deut 6:4).

The earthly Jesus is illumined not only through the eyes of ancient prophecy but also through the glasses of Hebrew wisdom. He was perceived by some as a prophet greater than Moses, Elijah, and Jonah (Mk 9:2-8; Lk 11:32), but also as a sage greater than Solomon (Lk 11:31). Jesus was a preacher, but also a teacher of wisdom. His style of teaching manifested forms from the sapiential tradition: proverbs, parables, and symbolic or prophetic actions. Some examples may help us to understand Jesus the teacher and also his teaching.

The beatitudes in the teaching of Jesus are examples of his proverbial wisdom. Although there are beatitudes elsewhere in the Gospels, we ordinarily think of the eight or nine in the Matthean discourse. Luke gives us four. The first, in its Lukan form, is "Blessed are you who are poor, for the kingdom of God is yours" (Lk 6:20). The saying reflects Jesus' compassion for the poor and God's very own love for the poor, as all the beatitudes exemplify Jesus' ministry to the socially marginal. The saying also manifests the centrality of the reign of God (which is to say God) in the preaching and teaching of Jesus. Essentially Jesus was teaching the people that God was with them (Isa 7:15). The reign of God is not a kingdom like the kingdoms of this earth nor a particular social order, but is rather God as near, present, close at hand. God is a God of people. The beatitude reflects Jesus' own experience and image of God as well as Jesus' solidarity with the poor.

The parables of Jesus are essentially stories or metaphors that also disclose the nature of God. They are not references to an apocalyptic, eschatological kingdom, but disclosures of a God who acts, is coming, is near. Sometimes they console: God comforts the people. Sometimes they challenge: God confronts the people. God is a

wonderful Counselor (Isa 9:6) and also a just Judge (Mt 25:31-46; Lk 18:1-8). God's love extends to everyone, to Israel, to the outcasts of Israel, to the Gentiles, women, and children (Mt 22:1-14; Lk 14:16-24). The parables are narratives that announce the gospel of God (Mk 1:14), which is to say the power, compassion, nearness, generosity, and fidelity of God.

Jesus taught his disciples about God not only in word but even more so in deed. The healings and exorcisms were God's love in action. Jesus gathered children to himself, included women among his disciples, and touched those labeled as unclean. He shared meals with rich and with poor. He stayed in the home of a notorious tax collector. His symbolic action of washing the feet of his disciples (Jn 13:1-11) says more than his saying about servanthood: "The Son of Man did not come to be served but to serve" (Mk 10:45).

Jesus' entire life, as well as his suffering and death, was one dramatic, symbolic action, or parable of God. In spite of all this, Jesus taught, "This generation is an evil generation; it seeks a sign, but no sign will be given it, except the sign of Jonah" (Lk 11:29). Jesus was not drawn into the developing apocalypticism of his day. The only sign he saw himself giving was that which he saw as manifest in the story of Jonah—which was primarily a story about God, the compassion of God. Jonah attempted to refuse his prophetic call because he knew God, because he knew that God was a God of love, because he knew that God would relent and not destroy the Ninevites, and because he knew that he was called to play the role of the fool, or foil, so that God's compassion would be revealed. The sign of the prophet Jonah, the only sign Jesus saw himself giving, was a sign of the compassion of God. In all that Jesus said or did, it was God to whom he referred or whom he revealed. Jesus was a man of the *Shema* (Deut 6:4). He loved God with his whole heart.

Whatever else can be said of Jesus of Nazareth, one can say that his mission, ministry, and consciousness were rooted in God. He was God's servant. He preached and taught about God. He embodied God's nearness and presence, especially for those who were socially marginal. And he was a man of prayer (see Mk 1:35). The Gospels often depict him at prayer. He taught his disciples to pray, and the prayer is a succinct summary of his own teaching.

Abba, hallowed be thy name.
Thy kingdom come.
Our bread for tomorrow, give us today.
And forgive us our debts, as we also here
    and now forgive our debtors.
And let us not fall into temptation (Lk
    11:2-4; Mt 6:9-13).

The prayer weaves together Jesus' God-consciousness and social consciousness—the two significant elements of prophetic consciousness. It was always God's word that the prophet proclaimed, but God's word for these people at this period of history. God's word was not an abstract word but a concrete, contextualized, historical word.

Jesus' filial consciousness and relationship with God are expressed in the way he addressed God in prayer and taught his disciples to address God as well: *Abba* (Mk 14:36; Gal 4:6). Although the Israelite and Jewish people saw God as the Father of their ancestors, of Israel, the Aramaic word *Abba* reflected Jesus' intimate and personal experience of God. Jesus was a Galilean Jew, a man of profound prayer, a man moved by compassion, a man whose passion and compassion embodied God's very own compassion and passion.

There remains a difficulty in any historiographical or scientific study of Jesus—a lack of consensus among scholars on many issues. Such a consensus among scholars may not be forthcoming. But we must remember that the earthly Jesus was not the scholars' Jesus but the Jesus of the people. Whatever the details in a biblical, histori-cal study of Jesus, the humanness of Jesus is very clear (Heb 4:15).

The Crucified Savior

The eternal Word became incarnate as Jesus of Nazareth, who lived, suffered, died on a cross, was raised from the dead and made Lord of heaven and earth. His crucifixion became symbolic of his entire mission and ministry, and thus of the mission of the eternal Word as well. The cross was perceived as revelatory and salvific. The sign of the cross became *the* sign of faith in Jesus Christ.

The tragic death of Jesus by crucifixion became the most difficult and the most urgent datum in the life of Jesus to interpret. How could it be understood? How could God allow it to happen? What did it mean? These were the questions with which the earliest preaching struggled. The cross also made the followers of Jesus increasingly aware that its total significance could not be conveyed through historical analysis alone. Like the resurrection of Jesus, the cross was also a meta-historiographical, historical event. History itself required theology for interpretation. We will mention first some historical factors involved in the death of Jesus—religious, economic, and political—and then the theological significance.

There were various historical, religious factors that contributed to the condemnation and execution of Jesus. Hints of these surface in the passion narratives. Jesus' attitude and teaching with respect to the Temple were provocative. Yet this provocation may have been more of an economic threat than a source of religious outrage. Did Jesus claim to be the Messiah, and was his ministry so understood by his disciples? Yet this would have been more of a political than religious concern. These questions had an urgency to them and were a threat to the Sadducees, or to members of the Jewish Sanhedrin, to the power elite within Judaism, as well as to the Romans occupying Palestine. But these questions had more than only economic and political significance.

Was Jesus a false messiah or the awaited Messiah? This question had tremendous religious significance. In what did Jesus' relationship with God consist? Jesus' sonship? Was Jesus' teaching in this regard blasphemy? It certainly came close to it. Was Jesus a false or true prophet? This was an urgent religious concern. If he was a false prophet, he deserved to die (Deut 13:1-5; 18:20). What was Jesus' attitude toward the priesthood? This may be better answered within the context of the Temple incident. It had economic, political, and religious implications. Contempt for the priesthood also carried with it the death penalty (Deut 17:12). At the least, Jesus' life and mission raised serious religious questions that were not easily answerable. The experience of the risen Jesus would help to answer some of them.

Jesus had gone to Jerusalem often, at least annually, for the great festivals. He had taught in the Temple or its vicinity (Mk 14:49; Lk 19:47; 21:37-38; 22:53; Jn 8:2; 18:20). What did Jesus teach concerning the Temple? Did he envision a Judaism without the Temple? Did he predict its destruction (Mk 13:2; Lk 21:5-6)? Whatever he taught, the wilderness tradition of spirituality gave a less central role to the Temple in the religion of the people.

It is difficult to determine the exact character of the Temple incident to which all the evangelists refer (Mk 11:15-17; Mt 21:12; Lk 19:45; Jn 2:3). Did it occur earlier rather than later in Jesus' public ministry, as the Gospel of John suggests? Whatever its precise character, it seems to have been a symbolic action that relativized the role of the Temple, was perceived as an attack on the high priesthood, and threatened Sadducean interests. At the very least, it was a religious action that had economic implications for a Jerusalem power elite that benefited economically from the presence of the Temple in Jerusalem. The Temple incident opens the door to investigating economic motives that may have played a role in the sentencing of Jesus.

Throughout Jesus' Galilean ministry, the major opponents seem to have been some of the Pharisees. In Jerusalem, however, the enemies of Jesus were the chief priests, scribes, and elders—by and large Sadducees, who constituted a socioeconomic power elite. These became a more formidable foe. The Sadducees were as much a socioeconomic class as a religious sect within Judaism. The elders were landowning, Jerusalem-based families that had emerged after the Exile. Of the twenty-eight high priests between 37 B.C. and A.D. 70, twenty-two came from four Jerusalem families. The two most powerful families were those of Boethus and Annas. They could boast eight high priests each. These facts point to Jesus as a potentially significant economic threat to a Jerusalem aristocracy, a form of opposition he would not have encountered in Galilee.

Just as there were economic factors involved in sentencing Jesus to death, there were also political factors. Whatever the character of the gathering of the Jewish Sanhedrin described in the passion narratives, their members had much to gain by sustaining the status quo in their relationship with Rome. The prevailing arrangement allowed some degree of self-government and was again to their economic advantage. The words of Caiaphas echo a continuous political opinion: It is better for one to die than for the whole nation or for all of us to go under (Jn 18:14).

But the major political actors in the drama were Pilate and Rome. The tendency of the Gospels is to play down the responsibility of Pilate, but other historical sources indicate that Pilate was very much his own man, capable of brutality, and a shrewd governor in Palestine. He ordinarily resided in Caesarea Maritima but came to Jerusalem on the occasion of the great festivals precisely to prevent rebellions. However Jesus himself may have understood his messiahship, or whether he even saw his mission in those terms, a predominant popular understanding of the Messiah was as a historical political figure, a king to come who would be like David of old. Even Jesus' closest followers misinterpreted his mission in this way. Thus Pilate and Rome would have been circumspect about any messiahs or messianic movements, especially during times of great pilgrimage to Jerusalem. Executing a death sentence by crucifixion was a Roman penalty.

Thus complex social, economic, and political factors were at work against Jesus. Galilee was one thing. In Jerusalem Jesus was up against a different system. His threat was more than religious simply because true prophetic religion always did have social and economic implications. So did the gospel Jesus preached and lived and from which he would not back away, given his fidelity to God. Both Pilate and Caiaphas, the Romans and Jewish aristocracy, had much to gain from the death of Jesus. Even Jesus' closest disciples did not come to his defense in Jerusalem; only some of the women disciples remained steadfast.

The death of Jesus by crucifixion, or the cross of Christ, became the primary stumbling block to the early Christian preaching of Jesus as the Christ. More than anything it required explanation or interpretation both for Jews and Gentiles.

The historical fact of the death of Jesus necessitated theological understanding. The true meaning of the event was metahistoriographical, or beyond the capacity of historical research alone. History required theology for its own self-understanding. This is one of the major realizations that comes from reflecting on the death and resurrection of Jesus.

The earliest Christian interpretations of the death of Jesus developed somewhat in the following fashion. (1) Jesus died a prophet's death. He was a martyr. The resurrection was his vindication. (2) Jesus was chosen Servant. Thus God must have been present to the death of Jesus and not absent from it. Therefore the death of Jesus was part of God's plan and in some sense even God's work. God did not and would not abandon his Servant. (3) In accord with the varied theologies of "the Servant of God" (e.g., Isa 42:1-4; 49:1-6; 50:4-11; and 52:13–53:12, among others), Jesus' death had salvific significance or saving efficacy (Isa 52:13–53:12). Thus through the death of this one man we have all been saved. Just as eschatology became Christology with the resurrection of Jesus, so Christology became soteriology as people realized that the Christ whom they had expected was not the Christ who had come. Jesus was Savior in a more profound and comprehensive way than Jewish conceptions of the Messiah had anticipated. Thus both historical—religious, economic, and political—and theological inquiry help us to grasp the full significance of the death of Jesus.

Continued theological reflection on the death of Jesus through the centuries has led to varied profound insights and themes in terms of which salvation has been understood: deification, sanctification, justification, forgiveness of sin, resurrection from the dead, redemption, and liberation. The death of Jesus was not only a salvific event but also a revelatory event. Jesus' intimate solidarity with us even unto death, death on a cross, revealed that God was for us and with us. God is the one who is for us, the one who is with us, the one who belongs to people. Jesus' death also revealed the extent of the crucified God's love for us. The crucifixion discloses God's tremendous love and the pain of that love. The crucifixion became the supreme symbol of God's love, the cross the sign of that love, the embodiment of the gospel of God. The cross, like Jesus, like the sign of Jonah, is a story of the compassion and love and mercy of our God, the one who saves us and gives us life.

The Mysterium Christi

According to the Christian tradition and the Catholic faith, Jesus Christ is one person. He cannot be split into two: a human or historical Jesus and a divine or risen Christ. Yet Jesus Christ exists or subsists in two natures: he is at once both human and divine. The earthly Jesus was both human and divine; the risen Jesus is both human and divine. After philosophical inquiry comes to a close in its search to understand Jesus Christ, after historiographical research reaches its limit in its capacity to interpret Jesus Christ, after faith in Jesus Christ has profitably wrestled with both reason and history, the life, death, and resurrection of Jesus Christ remain in the realm of mystery, though subject to the scrutiny of philosophy and historiography. This is not mystification in a pejorative sense but mystery in the historical Christian sense. We find ourselves in the grips of what we thought we could intellectually grasp.

This mystery of Jesus Christ that was once unfolded in history is rightly called the paschal mystery that is still unfolding in the liturgy, proclamation, and lives of the Christian people, God's Church. We commemorate and celebrate the paschal mystery that Jesus Christ is through our participation in the life of the Church and its ecclesial, sacramental, symbolic actions through which Christ continues to be present with us today through the Spirit.

This *mysterium Christi,* this paschal mystery reenacted and celebrated during the Easter triduum, the Easter season, and Pentecost, calls forth from God's people both worship and discipleship. In the face of the mystery of Jesus Christ, we find ourselves in awe before the mystery of God, and also as followers of Jesus. As the NT reveals, to know Jesus is to become his disciple.

Christian discipleship, a part of the mystery of Jesus Christ, involves not only right worship and right thinking (orthodoxy) but also right living as individuals and as communities of faith (orthopraxis). The divinity of Christ ultimately means that we take with absolute seriousness the life to which Jesus calls us. Our witness to the faith is the life that we live—in our love for one another, as the Galilean prophet, the divine Son, taught us through word and action.

Different images of Christ capture different facets of the *mysterium Christi.* No one image or metaphor by itself alone does justice to the fullness of the mystery that Jesus Christ is. Each cultural or historical or theological image gives rise to a different spirituality or emphasis in spirituality. No one spirituality by itself alone captures the totality of all that the gospel contains or contains the fullness of the gifts of the Holy Spirit, the supreme gift that the risen Jesus bequeathed to the Church. One Jesus Christ, one Holy Spirit, but various Christian spiritualities that need to be seen in their complementarity and call us forth "to imitate Christ," or as we say more readily today, to follow Christ or follow Jesus.

See also ABBA (IN PRAYER); ADOPTION AS CHILDREN OF GOD; BODY OF CHRIST; COMPASSION; DISCIPLESHIP; HOLY SPIRIT; INCARNATION; KENOSIS; KINGDOM OF GOD; LORD'S PRAYER; PASCHAL MYSTERY; RESURRECTION; SCRIPTURE; TRINITARIAN SPIRITUALITY.

Bibliography: L. Boff, *Jesus Christ Liberator,* trans. P. Hughes (Maryknoll, N.Y.: Orbis, 1978). M. Borg, *Jesus, A New Vision* (San Francisco: Harper & Row, 1987). L. Bouyer, *The Eternal Son,* trans. S. Inkel and J. Laughlin (Huntington, Ind.: Our Sunday Visitor, 1978). J. Dunn, *Christology in the Making* (Philadelphia: Westminster, 1980). D. Goergen, *The Mission and Ministry of Jesus* (Wilmington, Del.: Glazier, 1986) and *The Death and Resurrection of Jesus* (Wilmington, Del.: Glazier, 1988). A. Grillmeier, *Christ in the Christian Tradition,* vol. 1, rev. ed.: *From the Apostolic Age to Chalcedon,* trans. J. Bowden (London: Mowbray, 1975). G. O'Collins, *Jesus Risen* (New York: Paulist, 1987). J. Pelikan, *Jesus Through the Centuries* (New Haven: Yale Univ. Press, 1985). P. Perkins, *Resurrection* (Garden City, N.Y.: Doubleday, 1984). E. Schillebeeckx, *Jesus,* trans. H. Hoskins (New York: Seabury, 1979) and *Christ,* trans. J. Bowden (New York: Seabury, 1980).

DONALD J. GOERGEN, O.P.

CHRISTIAN FAMILY MOVEMENT

See AMERICAN SPIRITUALITY; LAY SPIR-
ITUALITY; MARRIAGE.

CHURCH

The Church of the New Testament: Communities with Different Understandings of the Spiritual Life

Paul's vision of the Church resulted primarily from his original encounter with the
risen Lord, in which he experienced the
Lord as identified with all Christians (Gal
1:11-17; 1 Cor 15:8-10; Phil 3:4-11; Acts
9:1-19; 22:4-16; 26:12-18), and from his
experiences of ministering to local communities. His conversion led to his sense of
Church and vocation to spread the gospel
and establish communities to embody it;
conversion and apostolic calling are closely
related (1 Cor 9:23). Paul describes the
Church as a building (1 Cor 3:9-10) to
which all disciples contribute (1 Cor 3:12-
13); a new assembly (1 Thess 2:14; Gal
1:22); the household of God (e.g., 1 Cor
16:15); and the family of the Lord (1 Cor
4:14-15; Gal 4:19). His most systematized
models of the Church are the People of
God (Rom 15:10-11); new creation (Gal
6:15); Body of Christ (1 Cor 10:17; 12:27);
and corporate person (Rom 8:9-11; 1 Cor
6:17).

Paul's vision of Church leads directly to
his challenging call for ecclesial living,
which requires a constant dialogue with
God, an appreciation of the centrality of
Christ in all life, and a common vision of
community. He urges disciples to emphasize prayer, live ethically, imitate the dying
and rising Christ, and selflessly give themselves to the service of others and the
spread of the gospel.

The Acts of the Apostles uses the word
church for the whole universal gathering of
the faithful (Acts 5:11; 15:22), which is
then realized in each local gathering (Acts
9:31; 16:5). The Church is God's community, guided by the Spirit and purchased

with the Lord's blood (Acts 20:28). Later
New Testament writings, such as the letters
to Titus and Timothy, show the beginnings
of organizational concerns and institutional roles rather than the earlier emphases on community, charisms, and collaboration found in Paul and the Gospels.

The word *church* does not occur in ten of
the twenty-seven books of the New Testament, and much of the reality of the community of disciples is found in the concept
kingdom of God. Jesus' first public statement in each of the Synoptic Gospels is a
call to repentance because the reign of
God, the age of the Spirit, is at hand (Mt
4:17; Mk 1:15; Lk 4:18-19). This central
notion in the preaching of Jesus, namely,
the proclamation of the kingdom of God,
implies a call to conversion and renewal of
life, and is motivated by the need to live
differently in a new age inaugurated by
God, an age the chosen people have been
expecting. The early Christian faithful see
their gathering as a way of becoming the
reign of God that Jesus has proclaimed.

Mark uses *kingdom* fourteen times,
identifying it with the power of God alive
in Jesus' life. Jesus' inaugural message is
"The kingdom of God is at hand" (Mk
1:15), and the only speech in his Galilean
ministry deals with membership in the
kingdom (Mk 4:1-34). Mark gives a history
of the kingdom, requirements for entrance
(Mk 10:13-31), and its inauguration with
Jesus' entrance into Jerusalem (Mk 11:9-
10) and with the end of the Temple (Mk
11:12-26; 13; 15:37-38). Mark's most detailed characterization of the kingdom is in
his parable discourse (Mk 4:1-34), which
links living in the reign of God with obedient response to Jesus' message. One's present response to the latter determines one's
future membership in the former.

This community of disciples prove their
belonging to Jesus and their anticipation of
life in the reign of God by their repentance,
faith, openness to all, mutual service, and
childlike trust. Theirs is a pilgrim people, a
community of the endtimes, a ministering

community, and a community that reaches out to the Gentiles.

Matthew uses *kingdom* sixty times, seeing it as the global, sovereign reign of God, realized fully at the end of time but anticipated in Jesus. The Matthean Lord stresses its imminence (Mt 4:17, 23), proclaims the news of its arrival (Mt 9:35), gives the conditions for entry (Mt 5–7), and ministers to others that they might enter it (Mt 4:17; 9:35). Matthew dedicates a whole section of his book to describe the nature of life in the reign of God (Mt 11:2–13:53).

Matthew never identifies the new period in history and the resulting life of the Church with the kingdom, but he certainly sees the Church as anticipating and foreshadowing the kingdom. To prepare for the latter requires a conversion that leads to faith in Jesus, genuine humility, vigilance, compassion, and a higher righteousness based on the personal ethic of individual and communal commitment to Jesus. Matthew, the only evangelist to use the word *church* (Mt 16:18; 18:17), sees the community of Jesus' disciples as constantly in need of ongoing conversion, discipline, and formation, and urges them to practice reconciliation, forgiveness, and sharing as they pilgrimage to the Lord. Matthew insists that Jesus is Emmanuel— ever present to the community in its faith, life, love, and hope.

Luke presents both the origins of the Church and the need to adapt the message in order to make it equally relevant to non-Jewish cultures. He portrays growing community awareness among the disciples after Jesus' ascension, (Acts 1:12-14; 2:41-47; 5:12-14); after Pentecost they see themselves as part of a new reality; as the community of Israel's hopes (Lk 16:19-31; Acts 2:21, 47; 3:25) and the new assembly of Israel (Acts 2:17-41; 5:11; 8:1, 3; 9:31; 11:22, 26). They are the community of the end-times (Acts 2:17) that Moses had foretold (Deut 15:4) and the new gathering founded on the outpouring of the Spirit (Acts 2:17, 33; 4:31; 8:17; 10:44-48; 19:1-

7). This community of disciples has a mission of universal reconciliation (Acts 2:8), reversing the disunity of Babel (Gen 11:1-9).

Membership in this community requires repentance, belief in Jesus, baptism, and reception of the Spirit (Acts 2:38). Belonging to the Christian community is not something achieved once and for all but requires ongoing fidelity to the Word and Spirit (Lk 8:15; 11:28) and a readiness to accept the trials that this quality of life brings (Acts 14:22). Ongoing conversion manifests itself in the heart of the Church by living as a prayerful Church (Lk 24:52-53; Acts 1:14, 24-25; 2:42-45; 4:32-35), a sharing Church (Acts 2:42-45; 4:32), a poor Church (Lk 3:10-11; 12:33; 14:13-14; 16:13), and a joyful Church (Acts 2:46; 5:41; 8:39; 12:14; 16:34).

John's understanding of Church focuses less on the specifics of the Church's life— structures, discipline, rituals, and ministry—and more on the theological vision from which Church flows. John stresses that Church life must reflect one's vision of God; theology leads to Christology; Christology is the basis for ecclesiology; ecclesiology necessitates specific patterns of discipleship. While more reserved in his ecclesiology than the Synoptics, John frequently presumes the existence of an ecclesial community (Jn 4:35, 39-42; 11:52; 12:20-26, 32; 17:1-26; 20:21), uses the images of vine (Jn 15:1-17) and sheepfold (Jn 10:1-18), and hints at possible understandings of covenant (Jn 11:52; 13:1-15) and bride (Jn 3:29). Passing over the specifics of community living, John sees the union between the Father and Jesus as the model for the disciples' union with Jesus and with one another. Church life becomes an ongoing deepening by each believer of his or her union with Jesus: "Remain in me, as I remain in you," and elsewhere "remain in my love" (Jn 15:4, 9).

The Church is always moving toward the reign of God, always struggling to become its own self-realization. Ongoing spiritual renewal authenticates that the Church is what it is called to be and to become. Thus the New Testament directly links the understanding of Church with conversion in lifestyle—ecclesiologies produce spiritualities.

The Church's History of Spiritual Search

Founded on Jesus Christ, the early Church was organized and grew under the leadership of his followers and faced the typical problems of any organization—requirements for membership, consolidation of its structures, and consensus in its beliefs. Clement, writing in 96 from the Roman Church to the Corinthian Church, urged the recipients to maintain unity and cooperation, and reminded them that the Church's hierarchical ministries were divinely instituted. Ignatius of Antioch (ca. 107) told the Ephesians (Prol.) that the Father willed the existence of their Church, that it was maintained in unity because of the Lord's passion, and that the Father predestined their Church to glory. The Shepherd of Hermas (ca. 140–155) spoke of God's eternal plan for the Church (Vision 2:4, 1) and affirmed that it was built up on the waters of baptism (Vision 3:3, 3-5). Later several Fathers spoke of the Church as a fruit of the resurrection, the safeguard of truth, and the embodiment of divine love.

Early Christian spiritual writers, influenced by the dualism of Neoplatonism (founder Plotinus, d. 270), stressed a denial of all that is earthly in order to be united spiritually with God. Others, like Clement of Alexandria (d. ca. 215), either influenced by or reacting to Gnosticism, saw spiritual maturity as contemplative knowledge attained through *apatheia*. Church was a community of believers who strove individually to become Christlike. Throughout these early centuries holiness was most clearly seen in imitation of the suffering Christ by martyrdom. Persecution ended with the victory of Con-

stantine, and thereafter holiness was seen in the symbolic death of the body in the asceticism and virginity of monasticism—at first eremitical (Antony withdrew to the desert in 285), then cenobitic (Pachomius [d. 346] developed a monasticism that was partly eremitic and partly communal), and finally the full community monasticism brought to the West by John Cassian (d. 435) and firmly established by Benedict (d. ca. 550). A further effect within the monastic movement was the spiritual theology of a Syrian monk, known now as Pseudo-Dionysius (d. ca. 500), who understood spirituality as the passive assimilation of the soul in the knowledge of God. In the West, Augustine (d. 430) emphasized self-knowledge linked to the service of others. Spirituality was increasingly seen as monastic life and the ordinary faithful viewed as second-class citizens.

However, neither the Constantinian consolidation of Church structures, with its resulting advantages for unity and missionary expansion, nor monasticism's spirituality, pastoral care, and education focused on the implications for spirituality of membership in, and the community nature of, the Church. In fact, no major document on the Church was produced in the first seven centuries, and no full-scale treatise until the 14th century; rather, the Fathers and theologians saw the Church within the mystery of Christ—it is the result of the preaching of the Word, and then safeguards that same Word, and by reliving it in the sacraments, especially the Eucharist, and in the mutual love and fidelity of local Churches, becomes the channel of grace to humanity. As Church became more a political reality, spirituality became increasingly a matter of private devotions and external popular rituals.

The Church's struggle for freedom from temporal control characterized much of the history from the 8th to the 13th century. Reactions involving a spiritual dedication to simplicity of life and rejection of abuses were seen in Francis (d. 1226) and

Dominic (d. 1221) and the renewal movements they inspired. Later the Renaissance popes, rejecting the call to lead a reform, found themselves challenged from below and eventually had to deal with the fragmenting of the Church and the Tridentine call to reform. The Catholic reform was led by great theologians, including Bellarmine, Suarez, and Cano; by new religious orders, such as the Jesuits and Capuchins; and by saintly reformers like Ignatius of Loyola (contemplation in action), and Teresa of Avila and John of the Cross (union with God through a life of prayer).

Cardinal Pierre de Bérulle in the 17th century emphasized priestly renewal, and Francis de Sales (d. 1622) contributed to seeing spiritual growth as a universal call to holiness. At the same time Cornelius Jansen (d. 1638) introduced a rigoristic doctrine of grace that had a more lasting effect on spirituality in the Church. The 17th and 18th centuries witnessed secularization that evidenced separation of authentic spirituality from Church interests. The French Revolution (1789) further separated the Church from political privileges and intensified the conviction that human nature cannot know God except through authoritative channels of revelation and tradition, authentically interpreted through Church authorities. The human condition, progress, and modern culture were all viewed with suspicion, especially by Pius IX (1846–1878) and Pius X (1903–1914), the former publishing his *Syllabus of Errors* (1864) and the latter attacking Modernism.

Nineteenth-century renewal was principally centered on authority and devotion to the papacy, culminating in Vatican I's definition of papal primacy (1870), even though there were also efforts to rethink ecclesiology based on a return to patristic and medieval writers and a wonderful enriching of the Church's charitable and educational ministries through many new religious congregations. The notion of the Church as the Mystical Body, first discussed in Vatican I, was presented to the universal Church by Leo XIII in his encyclical *Satis Cognitum* (1896), but reached its greatest impact in Pius XII's encyclical *Mystici Corporis* (1943) and the renewal it inspired.

The Church of Vatican II: A Spiritual Experience and Challenge

In 1959 Pope John XXIII announced the Second Vatican Council, with the hope that it would lead to a major renewal of the Church. He opened the council on October 11, 1962, but preparations had been underway for over half a century in the renewal fostered by popes, movements, theologians, and local grass-root groups dedicated to spiritual renewal. The council itself lasted four sessions, discussing the subject matter of its final sixteen documents in each of the four sessions. Participants suggested many modifications to conciliar texts—in fact thousands of changes in each session—and the modifications and amendments expressed the mood of the participants: first session—reckoning; second session—direction; third session—critical analysis; fourth session—maturity.

With the perspective of over a quarter of a century, it is now possible to analyze the developments in the life of the council and see the Church moving through a spiritual renewal, or conversional experience, in the changed attitudes of the four sessions. From sessions one to two the Church became aware of itself as a community; from sessions two to three the Church saw itself as a community called to be in the very heart of the world; from sessions three to four the Church expressed the conviction that it was a community in the heart of the world, called there to serve the world. Thus community, incarnation, and service form three parts of a conciliar conversional experience. Moreover, the focus of the preparatory work of the popes, theologians, movements, and spiritual groups emphasized similar concerns.

The council produced sixteen documents on a wide variety of subjects. However, the central insights of the council are ecclesiological and are found in the Dogmatic Constitution on the Church and the Pastoral Constitution on the Church in the Modern World—the two poles of all the council's work. The chapter headings of these two documents in large measure correspond to the titles of most of the other documents, a correspondence that is not merely accidental but rather reaffirms the central, axial nature of these two. Moreover, the former deductive document and the latter inductive one arrive at remarkably similar goals, showing that conclusions based on principles of faith dovetail with those that arise from human aspirations and hope.

Vatican Council II was one of the greatest spiritual challenges of Church history. Whether we examine the variety of participants, the prior teachings of popes and theologians, the changes in attitudes and spiritual dedication fostered by the various worldwide or local movements, the conversional experience of the council, the swings in emphasis, or its major theological and pastoral insights, we find common trends, the Holy Spirit surfacing the same challenges in varied ways.

The Church in Its Unity and Diversity of Spiritual Life

The catholic unity of the Church has always included varieties in understanding the Church's nature, life, and spirituality, from the pluralism found in Paul and the Gospels to the differences between the communities that produced the four Gospels to the autocephalous Churches—Byzantine, Melchite, Maronite, Coptic, and Roman. As the Western Church tried to impose uniformity after the 4th century, different ways of understanding the Church remained among the Franks, Germans, British, Irish, and Romans, differences that produced different virtues, models of holiness, and relationships be-

tween the people and Church authorities. Monastic reforms and their schools, 13th-century universities, debates between conciliarists and papalists—all evidenced different ways of understanding the Church. While some differences were explorations that proved unacceptable, others coexisted peacefully.

The rich and enriching mystery of the Church is difficult to define, since believers are constantly discovering new aspects of its life. Since Jesus' preaching, it has been common to refer to the Church with images that give a momentary intuition into the rich reality of this community. Thus it is a sheepfold, a flock, a field, the temple of God, Jerusalem (see LG 6). Sometimes particularly significant images do more than give a moment's insight; they also evoke specific responses in the hearts and lives of believers—such images become symbols. Thus, describing the Church as "our Mother" suggests attitudes and courses of action for both leaders and followers; to refer to the Church as "the bride of Christ" or "people of the covenant" reminds believers of their need of fidelity. Now and again some descriptions of the Church become particularly important because they not only give a brief insight into the reality (images) and evoke the very attitudes they portray (symbols), but they can also be used to critically explain the whole Church and the interrelationships of its members—such descriptions are called models.

Models not only propose ways of understanding based on a corporate discernment of spirits and build on believers' inner familiarity in faith, but they require a daily living out of the consequences to which they point. Each model understands differently the mission, membership, leadership, and spirituality of the Church, capitalizes on different strengths, and guards against different weaknesses.

Karl Rahner and Edward Schillebeeckx considered that the description of the Church as "the universal sacrament of salvation" (GS 45), "the visible sacrament of ... saving unity" (LG 9), was the most theologically significant model of Vatican II. Too technical and lacking the broad-based resonance of the faithful, this model has not been the key one. Nor have the proposed models of Avery Dulles (mystical communion, sacrament, herald, and servant) received much support. Rather, the principal post-Vatican II model has been the understanding of the Church as the People of God, to which the Dogmatic Constitution on the Church devoted an entire chapter (chap. 2).

As the People of God, the Church is a community that is intimately linked to humanity, sharing its joys and pains, and interested in everything that is of human value (GS 1). Children of the promise, "they make the most of the present time" (LG 35), expressing their hope within the framework of secular life. Citizens of all the world, this People of God "strives energetically and constantly to bring all humanity with all its riches back to Christ its Head in the unity of His Spirit" (LG 13). As the People of God, "the whole Church is missionary" (AG 35). All sense that they have "a lively awareness of their responsibility to the world" (AG 36) and realize their call to bear witness to the Lord by the lives they live within their local communities (AG 37); thus each individual takes responsibility for the ceaseless renewal of the Church (LG 9). All who are made children of God by faith and baptism "come together to praise God in the midst of His Church, to take part in her sacrifice, and to eat the Lord's supper" (SC 10). The council, emphasizing the model of the People of God, stresses that "the heritage of this people is ... dignity and freedom" (LG 9), a common dignity shared by men and women throughout the world (see LG 13).

The Dogmatic Constitution on the Church originally had chapters on the hierarchy before the chapter on the faithful, but in light of the conversional experience of the council, the chapters were rear-ranged to place the People of God before the hierarchy, and even insists that "everything that has been said so far concerning the People of God applies equally to the laity, religious and clergy" (LG 30). To understand the Church as the People of God, sharing in rights, dignity, and duties; to see this new messianic people as "a chosen race, a royal priesthood, a holy nation, a purchased people" (LG 9, quoting 1 Pet 2:9-10; see also LG 10-13); to read that "each individual part of the Church contributes through its special gifts to the good of the other parts and of the whole Church" (LG 13); and to hear proclaimed that "those ministers who are endowed with sacred power are servants of their brethren" (LG 18) is to see a new understanding of the Church, one that all the faithful can appreciate. This has had a dramatic influence on the post-Vatican II Church and has led the people to live differently, interact with religious and clergy in changed ways, accept their baptismal obligations, and live coresponsibly, clearly giving rise to a multifaceted spiritual renewal among the faithful, who see themselves called to be fully mature adult members of the Church.

In 1985 Pope John Paul II convened an extraordinary synod to evaluate the implementing of the reforms of Vatican II. The synod and its resulting document were very positive about the renewal initiated by Vatican II but viewed negatively the worldwide emphasis on the understanding of the Church as People of God, suggesting it be replaced with the view of the Church as *communio*. While the greater equality, mutuality, and coresponsibility implicit in the People of God model can lead to exaggerations and practical problems, the synod's downplaying of this model has been severely criticized even by moderate theologians.

Furthermore, the suggestion to replace such an evidently important part of the council's teaching with a notion that the council never used once—even though the reality of *communio* is present—has led to amazement among many theologians. The fact that the faithful can readily identify with People of God, while they have little understanding of the theological concept *communio*—even, it has been suggested, "hidden" in Latin—has given rise to severe criticism. *Communio* is an important dimension of the Church and has already been used to redraft the document for the Synod on the Laity (1987) and to help in the rethinking of the roles of episcopal conferences (1989), but like the concept "sacrament of the world" it is hardly ever to gain as widespread use as "People of God" has and will continue to have.

The Church in Relation to the World: Incarnational Spirituality

The early Church very soon identified flight from the world as a component of holiness, and while rejecting heresies that saw all the material world as evil, it was nevertheless tainted with their views. The condemnation of Galileo in 1633 seemed to typify the Church's suspicion of the world. Its religious rejection of the sinful world after the fashion of the Johannine Jesus (Jn 8:23; 12:31; 14:30; 17:9; 18:36) was not always complemented by a sense of mission for the world (Jn 12:46) that God created (Jn 1:10), loved (Jn 3:16), and redeemed (Jn 6:51; 12:46). Although the New Testament never teaches flight from ordinary secular circumstances, otherworldliness was frequently viewed as potential holiness, whereas thisworldliness was not. Monasticism in practice was considered better than secular involvement, poverty better than a responsible use of wealth, chastity better than conjugal life, and obedience more religious than personal responsibility. Canonized saints in the former categories abound but few are found in the latter.

Secular values carried no real worth from a religious point of view but were entirely subordinate to the religious realm, with no value except that which religion indirectly gave them. Thus Innocent III (1198–1216) and especially Boniface VIII (1302) claimed absolute sovereignty over all the world. Several centuries later Gregory XVI condemned Lamennais and Lacordaire, and thirty years later Pius IX issued an encyclical (*Quanta Cura,* 1864) that contained a syllabus of eighty errors of modern civilization.

Theological developments prior to Vatican II led to new ways of understanding the relationship between secular involvement and religious development. The council teaches that the Church serves the world (GS 40) by witnessing to eternal values, making God's love present, healing and proclaiming human dignity, and imbuing daily activity with meaning. The Church helps individuals in their daily efforts to better the world (GS 41) by opening to men and women the meaning of their own existence, their dignity, and the importance of the use of their talents. The Church helps the whole of society (GS 42) by maintaining family unity, promoting and consolidating human unity and community, injecting faith and charity into daily life, cooperating with all just institutions, and being a model of universality. The Church's teaching on the importance of Christians' involvement in bettering our world also aids humanity (GS 43) by urging Christians to do their civil duties, insisting that there can be no split between faith and one's daily life and work, teaching that conscience is inscribed in ordinary life values, and reminding believers of their obligation to contribute to the world's development. The council also acknowledges how much the Church receives and learns from the world (GS 44) through the experience of world history, programs of the sciences, culture, prophetical voices of every age, economic and political progress, signs of the times, and methodologies of other sciences.

The Church's relation to the world is a very positive and mature relationship that avoids extremes of neglect or patronizing and appreciates the mutuality of service and growth. The council teaches that:

—God has a plan for the world (AA 7; GS 57). The world, seen both statically and dynamically (GS 36; 64), is all part of the Father's plan (GS 36; LG 2), and Christian faith helps believers (LG 48; GS 11) appreciate their mandate to develop the world (AA 2; GS 34; 57).

—The world and all temporal activities are affected by sin (GS 25). Sin diminishes a person (GS 13), infecting personal life (LG 42; GS 25), one's attitudes to temporal activity (GS 4; 40), and even creation itself (GS 2; 39).

—In spite of sin, the world retains its own intrinsic value, which is seen in faith (GS 36; AA 4). The world is good because it comes from God (GS 36; PO 22), is a sign of God's love (DV 3; AG 9), and finds its fulfillment in the activities of men and women (GS 12; 15; CD 12).

—The divine plan for the world is now continued in the Church (AG 1). It is now the Church's task to explain God's will for world development (GS 2; AA 24) and to continue Christ's redemptive work of the world (AA 5; LG 17).

Looking at the Church-world relationship from the perspective of spirituality, the council indicates several steps in Christian life that show an intensified relationship to the world:

—Christians ought to be totally dedicated to world involvement (GS 67) to prove their faith in God as Creator (GS 36), to fulfill their own vocation (AA 7), and to show their recognition of the autonomy of the various spheres of life (GS 41; AA 1).

—Christians use the world with detachment (GS 38) to fulfill their responsibilities (GS 33), to use and enjoy the world (GS 37), but to safeguard against misuse (LG 42).

—Christians heal the world of its sin (GS 11) to continue Christ's redemption (AA 5), to participate in the Church's mission (AA 5; GS 2), and to extend the redemption of the cosmos (GS 11; AG 11; LG 36).

—Christians give the world a new soul or spirit (AA 19; AG 8; GS 40; 43) to fulfill the lay apostolate (LG 31; 36; AA 29).

—Christians transform the world into what it is capable of being (GS 2; AA 5) to cooperate with God and his Spirit of love (GS 38; AG 8), to discover all that is noble and good (GS 76), and to do this for the benefit of others (LG 36; GS 38).

—Christians consecrate the world to God in Christ (LG 31) to share in the Lord's priestly ministry (LG 34).

Vatican II began a new era in the Church's relationship to the world; from opposition and neglect we have moved to a spirituality of involvement. Major postconciliar papal and episcopal documents have focused on the family, the economy, work, social justice, women's issues, and peace—all components of a broad commitment to respect the autonomy of the world, to appreciate its importance for integral Christian growth, and to be involved in its betterment for the good of others in addition to one's own religious well-being. Detachment in spirituality now gives way to integration; spiritual writers stress the need of holistic living; religious have reexamined the vows to include an appreciation of the positive values of possessions, sexuality, and community; lay people stress the spirituality of the marketplace; and many groups speak of the religious values of liberation theology, incarnational theology, and inculturation.

Ecclesial Spirituality

Although the biblical call was equally for all, history evidenced elitist approaches to spirituality, whether monasticism, priestly life, virginity, widowhood, or membership in third orders. Almost anything seemed spiritually preferable to the ordinary life of the faithful. In fact, the reforms of Gregory VII (1073–1085) presumed that morality was for the ordinary faithful and spirituality was reserved to the religious and clergy. Much history of spirituality is basically a history of private devotions, even though practiced by a group or movement. Where a genuine group or community spirituality emerged for the faithful, it was drawn under Church control and became a religious order. More recently many faithful have found their renewal in local or internationally organized spiritual movements. Church history infrequently offers examples of spiritual renewal that are parish- or diocesan-based or that stress a spirituality that is ecclesial. However, the second half of the 20th century has seen notable changes in the spirituality of all the baptized.

Contemporary spirituality evidences three major components. First, spirituality today is ecclesial. This thrust includes all those trends that emphasize a sense of Church, community awareness, prayer, life of the People of God, and attitudes or styles of living that portray the group dimension of the Church. Second, spirituality is incarnational. This thrust includes contemporary movements and trends that imply a positive appreciation of the world, that call for dialogue between the Church and organizations and between corporate structures and science, and that lead to an integration of the spiritual and the temporal. The third major thrust is toward service to the world; it includes all forms of ministry to the Church and the world, including the commitment to liberation and justice in self, others, and institutional structures, be they civil or ecclesiastical. These three components of contemporary spirituality prolong the threefold conversional experience of the Vatican Council into modern life.

As faithful search to live as called, gifted, adult members of the Church, they find the community of the Church of which they are part characterized by:

—a humanizing of its structures—new collegial, decentralized structures, such as parish councils, pastoral councils, and even national and international participatory structures, such as those used by the U.S. bishops in drafting their pastorals or the Vatican in its synod preparations.

—a change of emphasis from hierarchy to local Church—the latter seen as foundational for ecclesial growth.

—coresponsibility at all levels of ecclesial life—lived by faithful even when they know it is unwanted by authorities.

—new styles of discipleship—new circumstances and Church interests give rise to commitment in peace movements, right to life, politics, social needs.

—a stronger awareness of vocation in all the faithful—a sense of baptismal vocation and of the universal call to holiness.

—an increased importance of living the community vocation of the Church—accompanied by group practices of asceticism.

—new ways of living out the cross of our Lord—as each one takes responsibility for faith and carries the burdens of the Churches.

As faithful seek to respond to the call to be Church, they can benefit from a series of positive developments:

—The faithful of all ranks, but especially laity and women religious, are more educated than ever before.

—Critical issues emphasized in the post-Vatican II Church are nonvocationally distinct values that can be satisfied by any of the faithful.

—Participation and involvement are not only desired but also encouraged in the contemporary Church.

—The centrality of the family is a highlight of recent decades; more are working at the quality of their family life than ever before, enriching both Church and society with their efforts and success.

—Interrelationship between religion and political and social life. While Roman Catholicism will be a major force, it will not be a unified but a pluralistic involvement.

—The emphasis on prayer and spiritual renewal is like a new Pentecost, and it is frequently a grass-roots renewal.

—Theology of ministry. Never since New Testament times have we seen such an emphasis on ministry that will both contribute to renewal and have a positive impact on ecclesiastical structures.

The faithful's dedication to Church is lived out amid a series of negative features that continue to be of concern:

—the continued divisions in the Church: to ecumenical differences are now added internal polarization and forms of pluralism that do not strive for unity—divisions that call for reconciliation.

—the rebirth of conservatism, pressure, and control: the short-lived openness for which John XXIII appealed soon yielded to fear and insecurity that cling to a primitive notion that authorities must conserve what we have.

—a lack of doctrinal renewal: while there has been a lot of adaptation, we have not seen much serious renewal of doctrine in ecumenical, sacramental, ministry, and authority matters.

The faithful also live amidst many signs of hope:

—Much renewal has been achieved intervocationally, and this kind of working together leads to new styles of leadership and increased mutual appreciation among the vocations.

—Today's vision of Church is one that depends on the grass roots. Foundational churches are strong and offer an ascending understanding of Church.

—There is an extraordinary patience in the Church that leads the faithful to continue to search, struggle, and rebuild.

—Members at all levels of the Church increasingly respect the dignity and vocation of everyone else, realizing that we will only grow if we grow together.

History has brought us by many ups and downs to a period of great interest in the Church and a council that has given excellent insights on a spiritual level. The Most Holy Trinity is the fountain of all holiness (LG 7; 40; 47) and continually renews God's chosen family (LG 7). The Church,

Christ's Mystical Body and the People of God, "is holy in a way which can never fail" (LG 39) and lives out its mission in the sacramental life and charisms of its priestly people (LG 10-12). Every individual member of the Church is "called to the fullness of the Christian life" (LG 40; also 39; 42), which is not some unusual response of an elitist group but rather imitation of Christ's charity, for "it is the love of God and of neighbor which points out the true disciple of Christ" (LG 42). Sharing one and the same baptismal call (LG 7; 32), the faithful display rich variety in living out the same constitutive elements (LG 32; 41). Above all, the faithful foster their holiness and ever-deepening unity through the liturgical and sacramental life of the Church (LG 7; 10-11): one and the same holiness that manifests itself in various states in life—lay (LG 30-38), religious (LG 42-44), and priestly (LG 41). Mutually appreciative of each other's vocation, the faithful dedicate themselves to the continual renewal of the Church (LG 8) as they yearn for the fullness that only God can give (LG 4; 8; 9; 48-51).

See also BODY OF CHRIST; COMMUNITY; EARLY CHRISTIAN SPIRITUALITY; HOLINESS; KINGDOM OF GOD; VATICAN COUNCIL II; WORLD.

Bibliography: G. Alberigo, J.-P. Jossua, and J. Komonchak, eds. *The Reception of Vatican II* (Washington: Catholic Univ. of America Press, 1987). A. Dulles, *Models of the Church* (New York: Doubleday, 1974) and *The Reshaping of Catholicism* (San Francisco: Harper & Row, 1988). A. Dulles and P. Granfield, eds., *The Church: A Bibliography* (Wilmington, Del.: Glazier, 1985). H. Doohan, *Paul's Vision of Church* (Wilmington, Del.: Glazier, 1989). L. Doohan, *The Lay-Centered Church* (San Francisco: Harper & Row, 1984) and *The Laity's Mission in the Local Church* (San Francisco: Harper & Row, 1986). A. Stacpoole, ed., *Vatican II Revisited* (Minneapolis: Winston, 1986).

LEONARD DOOHAN

CISTERCIAN SPIRITUALITY

The Cistercian Order takes its name from the mother abbey, Cîteaux (*Cister-*

cium), founded near Dijon in Burgundy in 1098 as a reform of traditional Benedictine monasticism. At the height of its influence in the early 13th century, it numbered approximately 750 monasteries. Today the Cistercian Order is divided into two main groupings representing nearly 300 monasteries: the Order of Cîteaux (O. Cist.), with about 1,300 monks and 1,200 nuns divided into several quasi-regional congregations and to be found especially in German-speaking and Eastern European countries, and the Cistercian Order of the Strict Observance, or Trappists (O.C.S.O.), with about 2,700 monks and 1,900 nuns, which is strongest in French-, Spanish-, and English-speaking countries, including 26 monasteries in developing countries. The Federation of Las Huelgas in Spain and the Bernardine Sisters also claim the Cistercian patrimony.

General Indications

Two series of books are published by Cistercian Publications, associated with the Institute for Cistercian Studies at Western Michigan University, Kalamazoo, Mich.: the Cistercian Fathers Series (CF), giving modern critical translations of traditional Cistercian texts and the Cistercian Studies Series (CS), which includes monographs on all aspects of the monastic tradition and collections of scholarly papers. *Cistercian Studies Quarterly* (CSQ) is a review devoted to Cistercian spirituality. Relevant periodicals in other languages include *Analecta Cisterciensia* (ASOC), *Cistercienser Chronik* (Cist Ch), *Cistercium* (Cist), *Cîteaux* (CN), and *Collectanea Cisterciensia* (COCR).

The most comprehensive treatment available in English is Louis J. Lekai, *The Cistercians: Ideals and Reality* (Kent, Ohio: Kent State Univ. Press, 1977). There is an excellent entry by Edmund Mikkers in the *Dictionnaire de Spiritualité* under "Robert de Molesmes" (vol. 13, 1988, cols. 738–814). For an overview of Cistercian spirituality see, André Louf, *The Cistercian Way* (CS 76, 1983).

The Founding Ideals

In the 11th century, the period of the reforming efforts of Pope Gregory VII (1073–1085), there were many attempts to renew monastic life, especially with regard to poverty, separation from the world and from a worldly Church, and austerity of life. Some of the more well known of these reformers were Romuald (925–1027), founder of Camaldoli; John Gualberti (995–1073); Peter Damian (1007–1072); Stephen of Muret (1045–1124); and Bruno of Cologne (1030–1101), founder of the Carthusians. [For more information see Bede Lackner, *The Eleventh Century Background of Cîteaux* (CS 8, 1972); Henrietta Leyser, *Hermits and the New Monasticism: A Study of Religious Communities in Western Europe, 1000–1150* (London: Macmillan, 1984).]

These projects and many others that scarcely survived a first generation were usually marked by a high degree of fervor and idealism. In general, their strong negativity did not result in a balanced lifestyle, a factor that inhibited their appeal to potential recruits. In reaction, a renewed appreciation of the possibilities inherent in the Rule of Benedict was generated, provided this traditional monastic text could be liberated from the stifling accretions of subsequent centuries. So the second wave of monastic reform movement switched its attention from the implementation of abstract values to a desire to recover the purity and integrity of Benedict's Rule.

Authentic documents survive regarding the foundation of the New Monastery (Cîteaux) and the establishment of the Cistercian Order, though there is considerable scholarly disagreement about their interpretation. They comprise the following texts: the *Exordium Parvum,* an account of the events of the foundation including relevant official texts, and the *Carta Caritatis,* the constitution of the new order, governing relations between the monasteries; the latter exists in both an earlier and a later form. These texts evolved from primitive versions compiled to win the approval of Pope Callixtus II in 1119. To these were added the *Statuta* or *Instituta,* embodying the decisions of the general chapters and the customaries that developed from the 1130s—one for the monks (*Ecclesiastica Officia*) and one for the lay brothers (*Usus Conversorum*). This juridical collection was fixed by 1175. To complicate matters further, a short version of the basic texts apparently circulated in the Clairvaux line from the 1120s, comprising the *Exordium Cistercii,* the *Summa Carta Caritatis,* and *Capitula.*

Latin texts can be found in Jean de la Croix Bouton and Jean Baptiste Van Damme, *Les Plus Anciens Textes de Cîteaux* (Achel: Abbaye Cistercienne, 1974); J. Marilier, *Chartes et documents concernant l'Abbaye de Cîteaux: 1098–1182* (Rome: Editiones Cistercienses, 1961); Danièle Choisselet and Placide Vernet, *Les Ecclesiastica Officia Cisterciens du XIIème siècle* (Reiningue: La Documentation Cistercienne, 1989). English translations by Bede Lackner of some of these texts are given on pages 443-446 of Lekai, *The Cistercians.*

Cîteaux was founded from Molesme, which had begun as a reformed monastery but, according to Cistercian sources, had declined as its riches increased. Because many of its recruits were not zealous for an austere life, contact with the world and the acceptance of a lower standard of monastic discipline left the more conscientious brothers dissatisfied. Under the leadership of Abbot Robert (who subsequently returned to Molesme), his prior Alberic (who succeeded Robert as abbot of the New Monastery), and Stephen Harding (who followed Alberic, 1109–1133), a small number of monks set out for what was described as the "wilderness" of Cîteaux, although in fact they were only twenty kilometers from Dijon and under the protection of the Duke of Burgundy.

The new foundation was poor and isolated, without many of the material benefits of an established monastery. The monks attempted to live by the Rule quite literally, distancing themselves consciously from many, but not all, customs derived from Cluny and other traditional Benedictine centers. A return to poverty, the desire to be "poor with the poor Christ," was a hallmark of the reform. This was expressed particularly with regard to the liturgy, which was radically simplified in its ritual; revenue, which was limited to the fruits of the monks' work; food; clothing; and style of living. Relations with the outside world were kept to a minimum. The monks ran no schools, and only adult recruits were accepted. Lay brothers (*conversi*) were incorporated into the order as a means of economic viability, and thus the religious life was offered to those who were illiterate or unattracted to the full cloistral discipline. In many monasteries lay brothers outnumbered choir monks; the anecdotal literature leaves us in no doubt that they lived a serious spiritual life and were not merely monastic workmen.

Although poverty was a priority, the Cistercians developed an integral monastic culture. The monastic libraries were generously stocked, much of the work coming from their own scriptoria. From the earliest days of the New Monastery, liturgical books, the Scriptures, and patristic works were copied, sometimes with exquisite workmanship. Great effort was expended on establishing a chant that was "authentic," although this was not at first very felicitous in its outcome. A style of architecture evolved that combined simplicity and austerity with proportion and space to produce buildings that eloquently proclaimed the values on which the reform was based. Many arts and skills evolved to meet the challenge of daily living, from water clocks and methods of accurately computing time to techniques of sanitation, agriculture, fish-hatching and herd-improvement. Cistercian life in the 12th century was more than the sequence of traditional observances within the monastic enclosure; it clearly evoked and engaged the creativity of a large number of monks. It was probably this aura of vitality and purpose that attracted so many recruits.

Two policies ensured the permanence of the reform. The first, clearly evident in the *Exordium Parvum,* was to ensure that every stage of the reform was given official approval by the highest authorities. Within two years of the foundation, Alberic had obtained the "Roman Privilege" from Pope Paschal II. Confirmation of the basic texts was given by Callixtus II in 1119, and final approbation by the former Cistercian Pope Eugene III in 1152.

The second stabilizing factor was the adoption of a system whereby all the monasteries agreed not to deviate from the principles of the reform: "to live together in the bond of charity under one rule and in the practice of the same usages." The responsibility for the maintenance of this "one mind and one heart" was twofold: it rested on the abbot of each founding monastery as far as the houses of his filiation were concerned, hence ultimately on the abbot of Cîteaux; it was also exercised when the "co-abbots" of all the monasteries came together in annual general chapter. These institutions were the means by which autonomous monasteries joined together to form one order; the union was primarily designed to ensure a common fidelity to the principles of the reform. The role of the chapter was to update and revise what no longer served this purpose, to facilitate communion among monasteries, to correct deviations from the standard, and to help any that were in need. Thus the *Carta Caritatis* was a dynamic means of ensuring that the order was able to preserve its charism amid changes resulting from external circumstances and from its own extraordinary expansion.

Molesme had been virtually a double monastery, but no systematic steps seem to have been taken initially to apply the principles of reform to women's monasteries. St. Bernard's sister, Humbelina, became a member of Jully, established under the protection of Molesme in 1113. In 1125 Jully founded Tart, which was accepted by Stephen Harding as a daughterhouse of Cîteaux. It seems at first to have been a private arrangement with Cîteaux rather than a formal relationship with the order as such. In 1147 the monastic congregations of Savigny and Obazine were absorbed into the Cistercian Order; since they had women's monasteries affiliated and nothing was done to exclude them, the nunneries gradually came to be regarded as part of the Cistercian entity. For a time both Tart and Las Huelgas in Spain held general chapters approved as such by the abbot of Cîteaux. From the 1150s the number of women's monasteries following the Cistercian usages increased, although their link with the order was unofficial. In the early 13th century the general chapter of abbots stepped in to regulate the multiplying relationships. In 1213 further incorporation was halted, probably because imposition of enclosure forced the nuns into greater dependence on their sponsoring abbots.

The first period of Cistercian history, from 1098 to 1250, may be considered as its Golden Age; during this time the numbers and influence of the Cistercian Order were at a peak, and it counted within its ranks many spiritual masters and saints. The ideals of the reform and the means chosen to promote them were not unique; they were shared with many contemporary monastic enterprises. What made the Cistercian Order such a force in the 12th century was its correspondence to the aspirations of the age, due chiefly to the quality of its recruits and the spiritual doctrine they generated.

The Cistercian Fathers

Stephen Harding, the third abbot of Cîteaux, was a farseeing but uncompromising visionary with a talent for appropriate practical measures to implement the values he espoused. He seems not to have been a teacher but a doer, one who was content to set high standards by his example. In time he became a father figure in the order, commanding respect but austere and distant. If the challenge inherent in the reform was to be taken up and sustained, a complementary mode of leadership was necessary. This was provided by Bernard of Fontaines, who entered Cîteaux in 1113, became abbot of Clairvaux in 1115, and dominated the monastic world for the next forty years.

Bernard of Clairvaux (1090–1153)

St. Bernard is one of the great mystical Doctors of the Church. Notwithstanding a very active career in the service of the Church and of the order, his writings fill eight large volumes. Some of them, such as his treatises *On the Steps of Humility and Pride* and *On the Necessity of Loving God* and his homilies *In Praise of the Blessed Virgin Mary,* are easily accessible. His extensive register of letters readily yields an accurate impression of his personality and philosophy of life. His major works include hundreds of sermons and sermon summaries; the *Five Books on Consideration,* addressed to the former Clairvaux monk who became Pope Eugene III; and the *Sermons on the Song of Songs,* dictated from 1135 until his death. Most of these are available in English in the Cistercian Studies Series. The letters have been translated by Bruno Scott James (London: Burns and Oates, 1953).

There has been a revival of scholarly interest in Bernard. Etienne Gilson's *The Mystical Theology of Saint Bernard* (London: Sheed and Ward, 1940) set a new standard for Bernardine research. This was reinforced by the publication of many serious studies in connection with the eighth centenary of Bernard's death in 1953. The single most dynamic factor in the renewal of enthusiasm for Bernard has been the work of Jean Leclercq, O.S.B., of Clervaux, who has coedited the critical edition of his works, written scores of books and hundreds of articles, enkindled much interest by his conferences all round the world, and encouraged many in studying the saint.

Bernard was not a particularly original thinker; his work is not abstract or speculative but an example of "monastic theology"—a contemplative response to revelation, eloquently expressed to arouse devotion and bring about behavioral change. Although Bernard addressed himself most often to monks, his prayerful, pastoral approach to theology is attractive and helpful to many outside monastic cloisters. Bernard does not propose new doctrines; his aim is to make the mysteries of faith come alive for his contemporaries. From the number of manuscripts of his works extant, we can tell that he succeeded; his works enjoyed a very wide diffusion in the 12th century and long afterward.

A fundamental characteristic of Bernard's spiritual stance was his confidence in grace. This led him to be optimistic in assessing possibilities for salvation. Although well aware of our proneness to evil, he placed great emphasis on the fact that *by nature* human beings have an orientation toward God. Created in God's image, men and women need only leave behind whatever alienates them from their inner destiny and thus grow in self-knowledge, so that they discover within themselves an energy for spiritual things. This is not achieved through merit but is given by grace in the very constitution of human nature and throughout life. That is why the Augustinian and Gregorian theme of desire for God was so important for Bernard. To be truly human is to uncover one's capacity for God, to experience a longing for union with God, and to be willing to take the practical steps necessary to translate this inward movement into daily life. On this see M. Casey, *Athirst for God* (CS 77, 1988).

A parallel theme supports this anthropological position. Central to creation, redemption, and the final culmination is the figure of Christ. Whatever needed to be done has been done by him for us. This is the theme of Bernard's liturgical sermons. All that is impossible for us has been already accomplished by the incarnate Word. By virtue of his ascension, Jesus Christ is no longer bound by space and time and is, accordingly, accessible to us, present to us. There is a real possibility of our making contact with the Word, of being healed and helped by him, and even of becoming united to him as one spirit.

Bernard's mystical doctrine, as given especially in the *Sermons on the Song of Songs,* is biblical and ecclesial. It is based on the idea of progressive conformity of will, realized over many years. One who gives assent to God's will, first at the level of behavior, then through burgeoning love, will finally experience in prayer not only the love of God but the God of love. It is an approach that is eminently practical, calling for selflessness and dedication rather than concentration on subjectivity and techniques. It is ecstasy—a standing away from all that is not God.

A bare outline of the content of Bernard's doctrine cannot convey the force of his teaching, especially in the original. Bernard wrote lively Latin. His remarks were pitched at an experiential level, and he integrated many scriptural and liturgical allusions into the fabric of his discourse, so that they served as a bridge between revelation and daily life. He was a lateral thinker, and the connections he made are often helpful in throwing light on the dynamics of many complex situations.

William of St. Thierry (ca. 1075–1148)

William was abbot of the Benedictine monastery of St. Thierry and a friend and confidant of Bernard, whose Life he wrote.

Both commented on the Song of Songs; William also compiled a selection of patristic comments on the book, and this he doubtlessly shared with Bernard. In 1135 he resigned his office and became a monk of the newly founded Cistercian abbey of Signy. Translations of his works are found in CF.

William had been a student at Reims before his entry into monastic life, and all his life he maintained a keen intellectual orientation. His spirituality was strongly influenced by Augustine, as has been demonstrated by David N. Bell, *The Image and Likeness: The Augustinian Spirituality of William of St. Thierry* (CS 78, 1984). Following in this tradition, he based his mystical teaching on a firm anthropological base, explicitly stated in his treatise *On the Nature and Dignity of Love.* Made in God's image but having thrown off the likeness through sin, human beings must strive while on earth to recover this lost likeness. The return to God begins with an assent of the will to Christ's love, which, once accepted, continues to grow within the person until all that is done is marked by love, and through wisdom one begins to experience and enjoy the reality of God. William had a penetrating understanding of Trinitarian doctrine, and it was his special gift to see its reflections in all aspects of human spiritual ascent. This is especially true of his treatises *The Mirror of Faith* and *The Enigma of Faith.*

Although William was a careful and perceptive theologian, he conceived his writings chiefly as a prayerful exercise in faith, a *meditatio.* His years of monastic life had made him utterly familiar with the Scriptures and with the great Fathers of the Church, so that words and phrases came to be imbued with a wealth of spiritual meaning—a fact that often makes it necessary to approach his own writings in a leisurely and reflective way. He was a quiet, conservative man, committed to monastic discipline, a lover of prayer and solitude. References to spiritual experience leave no doubt that he was a serious follower of the contemplative way. His most monastic work was the so-called Golden Epistle, a letter about the stages of spiritual progress written for the Carthusians of Mont Dieu. This was widely read and for a long time was attributed to Bernard.

Aelred of Rievaulx (1109–1167)

Aelred came from a priestly family and grew up in the Scottish court, where he received an excellent education. He entered Rievaulx about 1134 and after nine years became master of novices and a trusted adviser to his abbot. It was at this stage, at Bernard's suggestion, that Aelred wrote his major work, *The Mirror of Charity.* In 1143 he was elected abbot of Revesby, and four years later he returned to Rievaulx as abbot. The events of his life and the impact of his personality are known to us from the life written by Walter Daniel, who lived seventeen years as a monk in his community.

Under Aelred's sensitive governance Rievaulx flourished both interiorly and materially. His attitude toward his monks is shown in his *Pastoral Prayer.* He was a deeply spiritual man with great affective gifts. This found expression in his book *Spiritual Friendship.* In it he recapitulated classical and monastic teaching about friendship, with the aim of showing its compatibility with the discipline of Cistercian life. Although his devotion was tender and simple, as evidenced in his meditations *On Jesus at Twelve Years Old,* his *Rule for Anchoresses* showed that he could be firm, and his anthropological treatise *On the Soul* demonstrated his intellectual rigor. His spiritual doctrine is to be found most fully in his *Sermons;* he was a loving, pastorally minded abbot, who calmly accepted the changing situations faced by monks in their journey to God and tried to provide suitable guidance to help them on their way.

Guerric of Igny (ca. 1080–1157)

The "fourth evangelist" of Cîteaux was born at Tournai and educated at its cathedral school, where he also became a teacher. He led a solitary life until the 1120s, when, after visiting Clairvaux, he was advised by Bernard to remain. In 1138 he became the second abbot of Igny. He wrote fifty-four liturgical sermons, which are among the most accessible of all the Cistercian writings of the Golden Age. Guerric seems to have been a lenient abbot, and his writings are marked with mellowness. Rather than promoting monastic discipline, he emphasized Christ being formed in us and the spiritual maternity of Mary. Like the other Cistercian Fathers, Guerric's was a spirituality of light. In the mysteries of Christ celebrated in the liturgical year we see mirrored the plan of our salvation. The sermons aim to help us to allow Christ's life to reach its full expansion within us so that by discipline we may be freed from sin and led to knowledge, which by contemplation and love is transformed into wisdom—a taste for the things of God.

Other Writers

The first 150 years of Cistercian history produced many fine spiritual authors. In England, Gilbert of Swineshead (d. 1172) and John of Ford (d. 1214) continued Bernard's unfinished series *On the Song of Songs.* Baldwin of Ford (d. 1190), who later became archbishop of Canterbury, left a series of *Spiritual Tractates,* written during his years as abbot, a treatise *On the Sacrament of the Altar,* sermons, and other works. Stephen of Sawley (d. 1252) wrote several treatises, including *A Mirror for Novices.* Stephen of Lexington (d. 1258) is chiefly famous for his *Letters from Ireland.*

Clairvaux produced a torrent of writers, including the following. Serlo of Savigny (d. 1158) retired to Clairvaux, where he was often asked to preach to the community. Thirty-four *Sermons* remain.

Amadeus (d. 1159), who became bishop of Lausanne, wrote *Homilies in Praise of the Virgin Mary.* Alcher of Clairvaux (d. 1165) wrote an anthropological treatise entitled *On the Spirit and the Soul.* Geoffrey of Auxerre (d. 1188) had been Bernard's secretary and was responsible for much of the *Vita Prima.* As abbot of Clairvaux, he wrote allegorical sermons and minor works. Henry of Marcy (d. 1189) became a cardinal and wrote an ecclesiological tractate, *On the Pilgrim City of God.* Other writers included Odo of Morimond (d. 1161), who composed many sermons; Isaac of Stella (d. 1169), author of a treatise *On the Soul,* fifty-four sermons, and a commentary on the Canon of the Mass, *De Officio Altaris;* Thomas the Cistercian (d. 1190), who wrote a commentary on the Song of Songs; Arnold of Boheries (d. 1200), who wrote *A Mirror for Monks;* Adam of Perseigne (d. 1221), known for his sermons, letters, and scriptural expositions; Helinand of Froidmont (d. 1235), author of liturgical sermons, a *Chronicle,* and minor works.

There were also works of pious anecdote: chronicles, lives, and collections of miracles and *exempla.* Herbert of Clairvaux (d. ca. 1180) compiled three books of stories that are valuable for the details of daily life they contain and also for a strong sense of monastic values. He was one source for Conrad of Eberbach (d. 1221), who wrote the *Exordium Magnum,* a hagiographical account of the beginnings of the Cistercian Order. This tradition was continued by Caesarius of Heisterbach (d. 1240), who wrote the *Dialogus Miraculorum* and a number of sermons. Joachim of Fiore (d. 1202) had been a Cistercian, although he is more famous for his apocalyptic mysticism and his prophecy that the "Age of the Holy Spirit" was about to begin. In 1215 he was condemned by Lateran IV as a heretic.

In the latter part of the 13th century, as the male branch of the order seemed to lose vitality and its authors tended toward Scholasticism, Cistercian nuns began to publish. Beatrice of Nazareth (d. 1268) left an autobiography and several treatises, including *The Seven Ways of Love.* The German monastery of Helfta, although not officially linked to the order, followed Cistercian observances. From this tradition came Mechtild of Hackeborn (d. 1299) and Gertrude the Great (d. 1302), whose works comprise *The Herald of Divine Love* and the *Spiritual Exercises.* They give some idea of the spirituality of women's monasteries, although there is also some influence from the Rhineland mystics.

Subsequent History

The statutes of the general chapters chronicle a gradual change in the order: its movement away from poverty and the monastic lifestyle in the direction of education and outside involvement. This was partly due to pressure from external causes. The Black Death decimated many monasteries. Richer abbeys suffered from interference by both ecclesiastical and secular authorities. Also, the general decline in fervor was reflected in the monasteries. By the 15th century the Cistercians were no longer a spiritual force in the Church. Later, in England and elsewhere, monasteries were suppressed in the wake of the Reformation.

Soon there were reform movements within the order. This resulted in the division of monasteries into regional congregations, each with responsibility for monastic discipline. Under increasing pressures to be "useful," many houses took responsibility for schools and parishes. In some monasteries, especially in France, there were movements toward a more austere lifestyle, which effectively divided the order into "Common Observance" and "Strict Observance." The most effective of the reformers was Armand-Jean de Rancé (d. 1700), abbot of La Trappe. His followers received the name Trappist. De Rancé was a literate man who entered the cloister at age thirty-seven. Although his severity suited the tenor of the times, it went beyond the Cistercian tradition and was closer to Eastern monasticism. He was especially influenced by John Climacus. Although a firm disciplinarian and a tireless polemicist, he was considered a great spiritual master by his contemporaries and attracted many recruits. His sympathies may have been with the Jansenists, but he never supported them or wavered in his obedience to the hierarchy. See A. J. Krailsheimer, *Armand-Jean de Rancé: Abbot of La Trappe* (Oxford: Clarendon Press, 1974).

With their numbers already depleted by the spirit of the Enlightenment and the prevailing "laxism," and with observance ruined by commendatory abbacies, the monasteries were finally suppressed by the French revolutionary government in 1791. In the next thirty years similar prohibitions were repeated in many countries, and the monks were forced either to disperse or to attempt to found monasteries in safe countries. Among the monastic refugees was Augustin de Lestrange (d. 1827), the last novice master at La Trappe, who led twenty-one monks to a haven in an abandoned monastery in Valsainte, Switzerland. Once established, they began a regime of extraordinary austerity, far beyond the Rule and even beyond the customs of La Trappe. Paradoxically, many recruits came and foundations were made. After being expelled from Switzerland, Lestrange led his community on a two-year pilgrimage all over Europe, eventually returning to La Trappe in 1815. A period of expansion followed. Within forty years there were twenty-three monasteries, including Mount Melleray in Ireland and Gethsemani and New Melleray in the United States. By 1894 this number had doubled, with houses located in Beagle Bay, Australia; Oka, Canada; Peking, China; Latroun, Palestine; Mariannhill, South Africa; as well as throughout Europe.

Dissension about observances and authority within the order accompanied the reestablishment of the monasteries. With the dissolution of Cîteaux, the historical basis of leadership in the order was lost. After various attempts, this was finally solved in 1892 by the amalgamation of three Trappist congregations into an order independent of the Order of Cîteaux.

With legal separation the two orders grew further apart. The Common Observance became more oriented to priestly work and education, while the Strict Observance tended to curtail these activities where they existed. Because of its congregational structure, the Common Observance offered more pluralism, whereas the Trappists attached great importance to uniformity of observance and the enforcement of a high degree of austerity. Both groups increased numerically during the first half of the 20th century.

Whereas the Order of Cîteaux produced many monastic scholars, Trappist or Reformed Cistercian authors tended to write spiritual works of a popular nature. Thus Jean-Baptiste Chautard (d. 1935) wrote *The Soul of the Apostolate.* Vital Lehodey (d. 1948) was the author of the *Spiritual Directory* and *The Ways of Mental Prayer.* Eugene Boylan (d. 1964) wrote *Difficulties in Mental Prayer* and *This Tremendous Lover,* both of which enjoyed wide circulation. Fr. M. Raymond (Flanagan) of Gethsemani produced many books that were popular among religious around the world.

The most significant monastic author of the 20th century was Thomas Merton (d. 1968), whose autobiography, *The Seven Storey Mountain,* became a bestseller. A man of great spiritual and poetic gifts, he was a highly effective communicator. The experience of his own conversion and entry into monastic life gave him a critical stance toward "the world," and as his interests evolved beyond the domestic concerns of monasticism, he became a prophetic witness to the values of peace, justice, and integrity, and, paradoxically, a "superstar" in the world he professed to reject.

Merton was one of the first to understand the need to break out from the tight Tridentine mold of the Church and to find freedom and guidance in the ancient wisdom of the West, Eastern Christianity, and world religions. He was a man who was always open to new ideas. His writings were fresh and he was able to lead many to new insights, even when his arguments were technical. Although many find his early emphasis on silence and contemplation exaggerated and romantic, the fact remains that Merton's teaching can never be understood except as a systematic determination to give priority to the spiritual in everything. With the inevitable human blemishes, this was the way he himself lived. For further information see Michael Mott, *The Seven Mountains of Thomas Merton* (Boston: Houghton Mifflin, 1984) and many volumes of CS and several articles each year in CSQ.

Both Cistercian orders have declined numerically since the Second Vatican Council, especially in the industrial nations. Many vocations exist in the younger Churches, and there is evidence of regrowth in Europe and the United States. Among the fruits of renewal might be included an increasing appreciation of the Cistercian patrimony, a desire for a more authentic community life, an interest in prayer and a willingness to share its fruits through hospitality. Perhaps also there is a recognition of a greater importance due to human values. The great challenge is inculturation: to maintain "one rule and similar observances" while becoming true "lovers of the place"; to renew and adapt the Cistercian life so as to ground it in a culture without losing the riches of the tradition or becoming subservient to dehumanizing elements in the local culture. To some extent the situation is reminiscent of that which gave birth to the order, but the response will inevitably be different and more complex.

See also BENEDICTINE SPIRITUALITY; CAMALDOLESE SPIRITUALITY; CARTHUSIAN SPIRITUALITY; CONTEMPLATION, CONTEMPLATIVE PRAYER; EREMITICAL LIFE; LECTIO DIVINA; MONASTICISM, MONASTIC SPIRITUALITY; SILENCE.

Bibliography: A. Altermatt, "The Cistercian Patrimony: An Introduction to the Most Important Historical, Juridical and Spiritual Documents," CSQ 25 (1990) 287–328. D. Bell, *The Image and Likeness: The Augustinian Spirituality of William of St. Thierry*, CS 78 (Kalamazoo, Mich.: Cistercian Publications, 1984). M. Casey, *Athirst for God: Spiritual Desire in Bernard of Clairvaux's Sermons on the Song of Songs* (Kalamazoo, Mich.: Cistercian Publications, 1988). L. Lekai, *The Cistercians: Ideals and Realities* (Kent, Ohio: Kent State Univ. Press, 1977). A. Louf, *The Cistercian Way*, CS 96 (Kalamazoo, Mich.: Cistercian Publications, 1983). J. Sommerfeldt, *The Spiritual Teachings of Bernard of Clairvaux*, CS 125 (Kalamazoo, Mich.: Cistercian Publications, 1991).

MICHAEL CASEY, O.C.S.O.

COMBAT, SPIRITUAL

See TEMPTATION; WARFARE, SPIRITUAL.

COMMANDMENT(S)

The term *commandments* has various meanings in Christian spirituality. Quite commonly it refers to the Ten Commandments of the Jewish Scriptures, the so-called Decalogue. The complete ten-part text appears in two places (Exod 20:1-17; Deut 5:6-21), neither of which precisely matches the version often taught to schoolchildren. Portions of the text also appear in many other places in Scripture, and similar lists occur in the religious literature of other groups. The implication of this is that the significance of the Decalogue lies less in the prohibitions themselves and more in their connection to the proclamation of the God of Israel, the God of goodness, the God of covenant.

The term can also refer to the so-called New Commandments of the Christian Scripture (see Mt 22:34-40; Mk 12:28-34; Lk 10:25-28). Again, the content of the challenge to love God and neighbor is not particularly noteworthy. Both have roots in the Jewish Scriptures (Deut 6:5 and Lev 19:18). But the preaching of Jesus does universalize these commandments by suggesting that all human persons are our neighbors, and the example of his own life makes clear the depth that this love may attain.

The term also refers to the overall dimension of expectation and challenge that is part of the Christian life. One can speak of God's commandments to all people. One can speak of the commandment of Christ, in the sense both of words spoken by him and of the challenge implicit in his very person.

Finally, one can seek to articulate the personal commandment that is experienced concretely in one's own life. In any case, there is a dimension of "ought" that inevitably follows as a consequence of the gift of love.

See also AUTHORITY; CHRIST; COVENANT; DECISION, DECISION-MAKING; DISCIPLESHIP; GOD; LAW; LOVE; OBEDIENCE.

Bibliography: T. O'Connell, *Principles for a Catholic Morality*, rev. ed. (San Francisco: Harper & Row, 1990). R. Gula, *Reason Informed by Faith* (New York: Paulist, 1989).

TIMOTHY E. O'CONNELL

COMMON GOOD

See BODY OF CHRIST; COMMUNITY.

COMMUNION

See COMMUNITY; EUCHARIST; EUCHARISTIC DEVOTION.

COMMUNITY

The largest meaning of *community* is found in the Latin roots of the noun *communitas*. *Com- (cum)* means "with" and implies "severalness," while *-unity (unus)* means "one." The *-tas* ending of the word gives it an abstract notion, i.e., the character of any "severalness" that is together in some way that makes us want to say that it is also a one, a unit. In this sense

we can speak of a neighborhood as a community (geographical oneness); of a Hispanic or black or Anglo community (ethnic oneness); of a Catholic or Lutheran or Baptist community (oneness from a religious tradition); of the community of Western nations (a political and cultural oneness), etc. The focus of this article is upon the nature and behaviors of a Christian community. That narrows the meanings we will consider but still leaves a breadth.

The examination will begin with a biblical reflection on community, followed by a look at the earliest Christian community experience. Our attention will then be upon the ancient rites of initiation and their restoration, for what they say about community. Then follows a brief interlude while we consult the social sciences and social philosophy. Next our attention will be directed to the basic Christian community movement in our own time. Finally, we will locate the small community movement within the context of U.S. culture, with specific attention to the spiritual rhythms of these communities.

Biblical Community in the Hebrew Scriptures

In the Hebrew Scriptures the root metaphor for the binding of many people into one people is "covenant." The literal meaning in which the biblical metaphor is grounded is the sort of treaty agreement that was typical in Middle Eastern culture during the two millennia before the Common Era. In those ancient days there was no question about whether one was answerable to a ruler—it was only a question of which ruler. When a ruler made a treaty with a people, the ruler agreed to take care of their needs, and they in turn entrusted all they were and had to the ruler. A treatied people's loyalty had to be undivided; it had to be given to one ruler alone and it had to be total.

We know from extant treaty texts that when several lesser lords were connected by treaty with the same king, the treaty brought into existence a new relationship between the lesser lords. They had to honor and not violate one another. That was part of their obligation to the covenanting ruler.

This relational treaty between a nation and a king is the metaphor for the relationship between Yahweh and the Hebrew people. The Shema ("Hear!") of Deuteronomy is its most precious expression: "Hear, O Israel! The LORD is our God, the LORD alone! Therefore, you shall love the Lord, your God, with all your heart, and with all your soul, and with all your strength. . . . You shall not follow other gods . . . for the LORD, your God, who is in your midst, is a jealous God" (Deut 6:4-5, 14-15). This text was so important that a written copy was ritually affixed to the hand, to the forehead, and to the doorpost at the entrance to the home. Covenant with Yahweh, binding people in a single movement to God and to one another, was the basis of community in the Hebrew Scripture.

The covenant that Yahweh made was with a people and with all those who made up the people. It was not with individual Hebrews one by one. Individuals were covenanted because they belonged to a covenanted community. There was a radically social sense of individual reality. There were no private covenants with Yahweh.

Just as the secular notion of covenant developed different forms, so too, and often concomitantly with cultural changes, the covenant between Yahweh and Yahweh's people underwent developments: Yahweh's agreement with Adam and Eve, the revised covenant with Noah, an intensified promise to Abraham, another development with Moses, a revision with David, and still another new covenant announced by Jeremiah.

The spirituality generated by this community's covenant with Yahweh involved becoming holy in the same way that Yahweh was holy. The best clues to Yahweh's holiness were Yahweh's *sedeq* and *hesed,* feebly but not inaccurately translated as "justice" and "mercy," respectively. *Sedeq* is a loving concern that all people have what is needed for a decent, fulfilling human life. It has a distributive quality but is based on God's care and is not "merely" legal. *Hesed* is mercy animated by extraordinary compassion. *Sedeq* is so precious to Yahweh that when it is violated, it is *hesed* that tempers God's anger and lets the world continue.

To summarize, there was a oneness to Hebrew "manyness" that was rooted in covenant. The covenant required the total presence of a people to Yahweh. The fidelity of individual Hebrews was profoundly rooted in the fidelity of a people to God and to one another. All covenanted people were to be holy like Yahweh. Justice and mercy were the structural mettle of this spirituality of holiness. To be in covenant with Yahweh was to be required to be just and merciful, and to make a world that was just and compassionate.

Biblical Community in the Christian Scriptures

When Jesus was asked what the greatest commandment was, he cited Deuteronomy 6, as any faithful Jew would have done: Love God with all you have and are. Also in keeping with his tradition, he indicated that how we treat one another is integral to our relationship with God (the second commandment is like the first!). In the great judgment scene of Matthew 25, *sedeq* and *hesed* are the qualities by which we are judged.

In Matthew 5:48 Jesus is quoted as telling us to be perfect as God is perfect. The word *perfect* does not exist in Hebrew; it is a Greek interpretation in Matthew's text. More probable is the same account in Luke in which Jesus tells us to be compassionate as God is compassionate (probably *hesed*). In a word, the community of Jesus presumes all that community means in the Hebrew Scriptures. How, then, is the covenant initiated by Jesus a new covenant (*testament* is the same word as *covenant*)?

The covenanting king is not the only metaphor for Yahweh in the Hebrew Scriptures, but it is a major image. Jesus' insistent message about the immanence of the kingdom of God is consistent with his Jewish heritage. But Jesus picks up a minor theme and moves it to center stage in the new covenant. While the Hebrew Scriptures sometimes use "parent" metaphors for God, God is directly called "Father" only about a dozen times.

"Father," however, is the controlling metaphor for God in the Christian Scriptures. While "Father" occurs less often in Mark (the earliest Gospel) than in the other Gospels (over 30 times in Matthew, over 170 in John), Mark twice preserves the Aramaic word *Abba,* which most scholars think testifies to its authenticity on the lips of Jesus.

For some time Christian scholars supposed that the use of the very tender, colloquial word *Abba* was unique to Jesus. Jewish scholarship indicates that while the use of the word was not widespread, it did not originate with Jesus. Rabbinic sources indicate that combining "King" and "Father" in prayer address was already occurring in second-temple Judaism: *Abbinu-Malkenu,* "Our Father and our King," was probably gaining prominence as a prayer formula in Jesus' time.

One important new covenant motif, therefore, was modifying the covenanting-king image by juxtaposing it to a Father/parent image. That softened the notion of covenant. This development occurred not through the logic of reason so much as through the poetry of root metaphors. The root metaphor of Christian community arises, of course, from Jesus' own experience of self as God's child. It is no surprise, then, that Jesus taught his disciples to pray "Our Father," and that the Our Father has been from the beginning the titular prayer of Christian communities. Even as we note this, we affirm the historical connection of the "Our Father" to the Judaism of Jesus' time.

Thus, while Jesus speaks centrally of the kingdom of God, he gives the parenthood of God an equally central role in showing the character of a new covenant. He draws out the full implication of God's universal parenthood. What the parenthood of God does is make sisters and brothers of all men and women. The only parent figure allowed is God (Mt 23:8-12). We have one Father, and that one is in heaven. We are not to have father figures in our relational structures on earth. We are always and only siblings. Only God is always parent. A discipleship of equals is the character of the oneness of the many who are the community of Jesus Christ.

There is a further implication of the parenthood of God: it relates us, with or without our choice, to one another. Siblings cannot choose whether to be related as siblings; their only choice is whether to live the relationship redemptively or destructively. That is a perception that goes against the grain of mainstream U.S. culture. In *Habits of the Heart,* Robert Bellah and his co-researchers note a strain of individualism that is widespread in U.S. culture. We tend to believe that we are all autonomous individuals who only become related when we choose to. But that is not the biblical anthropology at all. Biblically, we find ourselves related from the nascent moment of existence. We already belong to one another. Autonomous individuality is a fiction, albeit widespread, popular, and embedded in the U.S. economic system. What baptism into Christ does to our "already relatedness" is transubstantiate us into the Body of Christ. The Eucharist is the primordial concelebration of transfigured community.

The equality that characterizes the discipleship of equals in the communities of Jesus Christ is not an anarchy. Power is an issue whenever two or more persons engage in social interaction—neither good nor bad, just there. What we do with it makes it function creatively or destructively. Christian community is no exception. There will always be in Christian community some structured way that power and leadership function. While Jesus gives no precise structure, he proposes three images for how power is to function among his disciples: steward, shepherd, and servant.

The steward image affirms that the community does not belong to the leader. The community is God's people, and the leader has temporary responsibility on God's behalf.

The shepherd metaphor also emphasizes that the leader does not "own" the community. But Jesus picks out two further characteristics of the shepherd that are displayed in his own life as well: inclusivity and care for the stray. Jesus shocked his contemporaries by his table fellowship with sinners as well as saints. Unlike the exclusive table fellowship of the Pharisees, Jesus' table fellowship was open to all. The shepherd metaphor discloses why the sinner can sit with Jesus. The shepherd leaves the ninety-nine sheep and goes after the stray. A particular concern for the outcast, the marginalized, the stray commands the attention of the leader and the resources of a Christian community.

Finally, the servant metaphor reminds the community leader that his or her agenda comes from the community and is not imposed by the designated leader. Pagan leaders lord it over their communities; leaders in Christian communities lead, as it were, from below. Rank and privilege and caste are wholly inappropriate for power operations in the communities of Jesus Christ.

Thus there is a particular way that power must function in faithful Christian communities. Power does not mean only having effects; it also means receiving effects. A servant's agenda is fashioned out of what the servant receives from the community. Power is to be a relational, interactive function, never a unilateral, dominating function. This, too, is an essential trait of Christian community.

New Testament studies note that there were two social forms of discipleship. The first was the smaller group of people who traveled with Jesus—the itinerants. The community characteristics of this group were specific to it: they traveled light, they were willing to be dependent upon those whom they served, they did not worry beyond today. Christian art has regularly depicted Jesus with twelve itinerant male companions, ignoring the testimony of the Gospels that a number of women were itinerant companions as well (Lk 8:13). Disciples following a master teacher was not surprising to Jesus' contemporaries, but the inclusion of women among them surely was. The logic of a discipleship of equals is apparent here in the makeup of the itinerant community.

There was also a resident form of disciple-community: the followers who lived, and continued to live, in the villages where Jesus preached the Good News. The norms for these communities were different. They remained with their families (immediate and extended) and their jobs. These local sympathizers were the beginnings of the house-church form of discipleship that is so apparent in Acts and in Paul, and was presaged by the local sympathizers in Jesus' own time.

Whether itinerant or resident, communities attended to the needs of one another. But they also always faced outward as servants, stewards, and shepherds of the larger world and its needs. The needs were defined above all by *sedeq* and *hesed,* which John subsumes under one word: "God is love" (1 Jn 4:16). Ministry to self-need and ministry to mission are essential characteristics of Christian communities. There are many good groups that attend to their own needs (e.g., support groups), and many good groups that are gathered by an external task (St. Vincent de Paul Society), but these are not communities in the full Christian sense. A full community has both characteristics: the gathering in faith of people close to one another and caring for one another, and an inclusivity that faces outward in mission: *Go* and preach the Good News!

Finally, there is the element of invitation and choice. One is not a disciple of Jesus because one is a Jew or a Greek but because one intentionally chooses to say yes to the call. The intentional yes to Jesus is also an intentional yes to community, to corporateness. It is a yes that includes the good of others.

Some Important Early History

The English word "church" translates the Greek word *ekklēsia*. Behind the Greek word *ekklēsia* probably stands the Hebrew word *qahal*. The Greek and Hebrew words both name a gathering of people. When Paul greets the "church" at someone's "house," he is greeting the community that assembles there. Today we easily think of church as a building or as an institution. The early churches did not have church buildings; until the fourth century they met in homes. At that time a church building was not called "a church" (*ecclesia*) but "the house of a church" (*domus ecclesiae*), thus making clear that church is truly a gathered people.

These individual house churches of the early centuries were always interconnected with all the other house churches in the area. It is clear from Paul that the various house-church communities also gathered at times, resembling a parish or a diocese. Multiple house churches networked *up* into a larger church community; this contrasts with today's tendency to break a parish *down* into communities. The small house church was the fundamental unit of Church.

At the time of Paul and of Acts, there were no Gospel texts or canonical epistles. The Great Story, the Wonderful Good News, existed only in an oral tradition. The story was told to the gathered community and beyond the community. The storytelling was from the community and by the community. The people who were the com-

munity had the story embodied in their communal and personal lives. What they told was what they had within them, what they had received and kept and refashioned as a living Word. Today we have written scriptural texts, but it still is true that the texts alone, without community living of them, are not yet fully the living Word. The Word of God both enlivens and lives in community. The community is a privileged sacrament of Christ's community-forming News about God. Existentially, therefore, the community-sacrament is the effective Christian school for new members. The rites of the early Church expressed that, and these rites are being retrieved in the contemporary Church.

In the postconciliar Church we have brought back from the early Church the Rite of Christian Initiation of Adults. The profoundly accurate instinct at work here is that Christian identity is formed in a new member through a gradual process of socialization into the community's way of life. The way of life is grasped by the sacred texts. It is reflected in history and doctrine. It is celebrated and acted out in ritual. But finally, all these—texts, history, doctrine, ritual—are in the hands and feet and bellies, in the hearts and minds and nerve endings, of a community. The chief dynamic of initiation in the early Church and again today is that of apprenticeship. A prospective community member is apprenticed to a small Christian community and absorbs and appropriates Christian community through a structured commingling of his or her life with that of a strong community.

Paul Tillich rightly noted that community is the shape of grace in history.

Social Sciences and Social Philosophy

We will invoke several notions from the social sciences and social philosophy to clarify the meaning of Christian community. The first involves the notions of primary and secondary groups. The second has to do with intentionality. The third has to do with how the common bond originates and holds. Finally, we will address the notion of the commonweal. Christian community cannot be reduced to sociological and phenomenological descriptors. Grace outruns those. Christian community is always more than these descriptors, yet never less than what they name.

In their book *Community of Faith* (especially chapter 3), Evelyn and James Whitehead invoke a helpful sociological distinction to clarify the particular meaning of community in the context of Christian life. A primary group's main reason for gathering is the affective bonding that ties them to one another, e.g., families and friends. A secondary group's main reason for gathering is some external reason: a parish team, a Bible study group, a prayer group, a faculty. People in a secondary group may also care for one another, but they do not continue to gather when the task does not summon them. Members of a primary group may also occasionally address some external concern together, but that is not the fundamental binding element.

Sociologically, a Christian community is a hybrid group. It has some characteristics of a primary group, for members of a Christian community always minister to one another's needs. It has some characteristics of a secondary group as well, for it is always in mission. It must go beyond its immediate life to build a new world with the transforming Good News of Jesus Christ. There are Christian primary groups and Christian secondary groups, and they are good and necessary, but it is helpful to retain the term *community* for the hybrid group that is a fuller response to discipleship.

No one can just start a community. Community is analogous to friendship: if you work at it too hard, too directly, and too self-consciously, it is likely not to happen, for its nature as gift is not honored. The best we can do—and it is a lot—is create the conditions without which it cannot happen. It takes time. A community must have accumulated a pool of significant

shared memories, and it must have forged some compelling shared hopes. A secondary group can add on to its life primary characteristics and become community, but that takes time. And a primary group can intentionally take up mission and become community; that too takes time.

Intentional community is also a social scientific notion. In the looser sense of the word, one belongs to an Anglo or black or Asian or Hispanic "community" for ethnic reasons, but without choice. But membership in a Christian community is a fully intentional, deliberate choice. Christian community is intentional community.

Many of us are born into Christian families, but the full power of community requires, at some point, our intentionality. We must intend to be what our families and friends have been before us. Intentional community is more than a gathering—it is a place where identity is willingly formed. We say yes to the demands of membership. Active community membership is demanding and taxing, even as it is fulfilling and graced. People have the energy to function in multiple groups, but few have the emotional energy to commit intentionally to more than two, or at most three, communities. To be what it is and do what it does, community must be an engrossing and deliberate commitment. That is the difference between a small group that is a community and one that is not. True community is not just an activity; rather, it is an environment for the life of faith and the faith of life.

We must note a characteristic of community that does not come easily to many, namely, its willingness to sacrifice for the commonweal or common good. The pressure point where we feel the call of commonweal is when we must postpone or surrender some personal desire or need for the sake of some good for the larger community.

In Lev 25:23 Yahweh tells the people that "the land shall not be sold in perpetuity; for the land is mine, and you are but aliens who have become my tenants." Every forty-ninth year, the Jubilee Year, all property was returned to tribal ownership so that large accumulations would not prevent others from having what they needed. The good of individuals always functions within the context of the life of the whole. The possession of goods is not an absolute right. There is a common good on which private ownership may not encroach.

Lavishness is a sacrament of God's own extravagant love. Yahweh prepares for the people a banquet of rich foods, juicy meats, and fine strained wines—vintage bottles, not table jugs (Isa 25:6). The goodness and beauty of the world unveil God. But there is always a proviso: no surplus is allowed until all people's basic needs for a decent life are met. When Pope John Paul II proclaims the priority of labor over capital, he is radically in touch with this biblical expression of the commonweal or common good.

The Anglo-American philosopher Alfred North Whitehead added to Aristotle's notion of society an important insight pertinent to our discussion of community. Not only is membership constituted by some shared defining characteristic (Aristotle), but it is through human interaction that the characteristic is appropriated from one member to another. Whitehead recognizes that a community's defining character lives in the people who make it up. When we say a relational yes to a community of people, the character of the community imposes itself on us. Whitehead is eager to note the aggressive character of this imposition. If an American lives sensitively in Europe, she or he soon discovers many specifically European ways of getting at things. When people deliberately choose to live *in* Europe, Europe will sooner or later live *in* them. This societal dynamic corresponds to the recognition of the early Church that we become members of a community through an apprenticeship in the life of that community. The rites of initiation express and cause the apprenticing.

One is never a community member once and for all. The membership that apprenticeship initiates needs nurturing relationships to continue. After someone becomes a member of a community, the defining characteristic is able to maintain its hold on that person's life through conditions that impose themselves in the mutuality of community life freely chosen. There is a double dynamic: our yes to other Christians is a yes to the Christ-event that makes them what they are; and our yes to the Christ-event relates us essentially to all other yeses from our sisters and brothers.

Baptism celebrates the fact that community membership has happened. But Christian being needs always to be protected by Christian becoming. Becoming Christian is a lifelong community project.

In sum, every community of Jesus Christ not only cares for its own but directs its social energies beyond itself to the challenges of our larger life upon the earth. Out of their internal connectedness with one another, community members understand the claims of the commonweal upon them. Membership is fully intentional, significant in the claims it makes upon human energies, and rewarding in the nurture it offers to life and love. Our identity in Christian community accrues from our apprenticeship.

The relational dynamics that begin identity formation never stop being the matrix for our continual becoming. These are some of the characteristics of the communities that mediate the abundant grace of the Christ-event.

The Spirituality of Basic Christian Communities

Spirituality, the perspectives that energize and drive the life of Christians, is timebound—it always bears the marks of its age. One of the notable spiritualities in the postconciliar Church is that of basic Christian communities.

In Brazil, in the late 1950s, radio was used for catechesis in regions hard to reach otherwise. Catechists were trained to help local people process the instruction received by radio. The people who met regularly in small groups to process their faith growth often bonded relationally. Not infrequently people became aware of how their own lives suffered from systemic violations of justice—the same justice that they learned was the mark of God's holiness and was meant to be the mark of human history. Energized to bring more justice into being, the faith of these small communities has changed the political and ecclesial landscape of a continent. They have, in the words of Johannes Metz, recognized that there are both mystical and political dimensions to following Christ.

The basic Christian communities of Latin America (*communidades de base*) sometimes call themselves basic *ecclesial* communities. In so doing they are claiming not to be small Church groups but small Church units, not simply groups within a Church but groups that are Church, full ecclesial communities. They appeal to the "dangerous" memory of the early house churches. The memory is not truly dangerous, because it is true remembrance of some other way that it was. But it sometimes feels dangerous because it subverts the notion that the parish structure as we have come to know it is what Church really is—and only that.

Small Christian communities have taken similar but varying shape in many other parts of the world as well: Asia, the Philippines, Africa, Australia, Europe, and the United States. Nowhere do these small communities constitute a majority. But their inner vitality and number are sufficient to bring about a critical mass in many areas. Their presence affects the texture of ecclesial life.

These small Christian communities, wherever they are, tend to share the same dynamic: biblical literacy and social analysis conjoined in community with energy that translates into deepened prayer and effective agency for social change. This

rhythm of biblical literacy and disciplined social analysis is a constitutive feature of basic Christian community spirituality. Paul Hanson is clear about this in his study of biblical community: "Word and world continue to relate in the life of religious communities today. Utmost care must be given to both sides of this two-dimensional exegesis. *As much harm can be done by applying an inadequately understood Word to a well-understood world as in applying a well-understood Word to an inadequately understood world.* In an increasingly complex society, biblical interpretation can be carried out faithfully only as an aspect of a community of faith's mission of justice and mercy . . ." (*The People Called,* p. 529, emphasis added). This emphasis upon Word does not exclude Eucharist. When possible, Eucharist remains a precious and central experience. However, presbyters are not plentiful. But these communities find a real presence of the living God in their breaking open of God's Word in the detailed presence of their own lived experience.

For over a century and a half, informed commentators on the U.S. experience have noted a cultural commitment to individualism that makes commitment to community very difficult. In so doing, this same individualism also creates a cultural loneliness that makes community almost as desperate and strong a need as is the drive toward privatism.

Robert Bellah and those who worked with him on *Habits of the Heart* feel that small biblical Christian communities are one of the possible ways in which U.S. culture might recover some of the soul that it has lost to the ravages of unchecked individualism. The intentional nature of commitment is redemptive of the U.S. cultural loneliness, for it asks of us a responsible connectedness to one another. God is our parent, Jesus is our brother. We are a sibling discipleship of equals, and the primary group dimension of community has huge graced potential. That is a perspective from which a Christian life can be lived. In other words, a spirituality awaits us here. The small Christian community has some needed gifts to make to the American experiment in individualism.

Within U.S. culture there is a second crucial call to basic Christian community spirituality, one that plays upon its secondary group nature, i.e., its call to mission and social transformation, a call issuing specifically from the details of our own economic reality.

In the two-century period following the American Revolution, there has been a patterned (i.e., systemic) redistribution of wealth (P. King et al., *Risking Liberation,* p. 95). In 1776 the top 20 percent held about 68 percent of the nation's wealth, the middle 50 percent had 30 percent, and the lowest 30 percent of people had 2 percent of the wealth. Today the upper 20 percent have increased their share from 68 percent to 85 percent, the middle 50 percent have gone from 30 percent to 15 percent, and the bottom 30 percent have lost even the 2 percent they once had.

The consumerist habits that drive the continuing impoverishment of the already poor and the growing powerlessness of the middle are systematically promoted by the media and by advertising. Advertising beguiles people in the middle into purchasing the symbols of upward mobility. But these purchases, in fact, increase the downward mobility. The statistics from the last half century demonstrate the regularity of this systemic pattern in our own times as well.

Biblical literacy (informed biblical interpretation) reminds us of the justice and mercy that define God in the Old Testament and the message of Jesus in the New Testament. Social analysis reveals the shape and systemic nature of poverty and powerlessness in our culture. Prayerful conversation between them, conducted in the heart of small communities, provides a perspective from which Christian life calls out to be lived, i.e., a spirituality.

This call to address systemic injustice suggests abundant reasons for alliances, for shared community, between the poor and the increasingly disempowered middle. The same dynamics that create poverty at the bottom disempower the middle and send more and more of them to the bottom. But it is not in the interests of a consumerist economy, as it functions in the U.S., for those alliances to be made. Individuals are truly powerless to transform a megasystem. But networks of mediating structures, like small Christian communities, can marshal a critical mass. It is here that the secondary-group characteristics of a community, its sense of mission to remake the world according to God's intentions, are able to ground a community's spirituality. There is always a secondary-group mission to community, and the interplay between Scripture and social analysis is the most likely dynamic of spirituality for disclosing the nature of the mission.

In a word, Christian life is profoundly social. It is communitarian. It happens in and to community. Christians are no less personal persons, but they are always communal persons, never radically private persons, never autonomous individuals. Our spirituality, like our identity, emerges from relationships, of which community is a major, enduring, and necessary form.

See also AUTHORITY; BODY OF CHRIST; CHARISM; CHURCH; COVENANT; EARLY CHRISTIAN SPIRITUALITY; KINGDOM OF GOD; MISSION, SPIRITUALITY FOR MISSION; POWER; SAINTS, COMMUNION OF SAINTS; SELF; SERVICE; SOLIDARITY; STORY; WORLD.

Bibliography: L. Boff, *Ecclesiogenesis: The Base Communities Reinvent the Church* (Maryknoll, N.Y.: Orbis 1986). P. Hanson, *The People Called: The Growth of Community in the Bible* (New York: Harper & Row, 1987). P. Hanson, "The Role of Scripture in Times of Crisis," *Word and World* 1 (1981) 116–127. D. Hillers, *Covenant: The History of a Biblical Idea* (Baltimore: Johns Hopkins Univ. Press, 1969). P. King, K. Maynard, and D. Woodyard, *Risking Liberation: Middle Class Powerlessness and Social Heroism* (Atlanta: John Knox, 1988). B. Lee and M. Cowan, *Dangerous Memories: House Churches and Our American Story* (Kansas City: Sheed & Ward, 1986). G. Lohfink,

Jesus and Community (New York: Paulist, 1984). J. Segundo, *The Community Called Church* (Maryknoll, N.Y.: Orbis, 1973). R. Sider, *Rich Christians in an Age of Hunger* (London: Hodder and Stoughton, 1977). E. and J. Whitehead, *Community of Faith: Models and Strategies for Developing Christian Communities* (New York: Seabury, 1982).

BERNARD J. LEE, S.M.

COMPASSION

Modern usage of the term in Christian spirituality, no doubt influenced by ecclesiastical Latin, identifies compassion with mercy, pity, and tenderness. This can obscure the depth of meaning with which Israel invested this word. Though akin to these terms, the meaning of *compassion* is distinct. The term refers to the very core of one's deepest feelings, much as the term *heart* does today.

The Hebrew word for compassion (*rahamin*) expresses the empathetic attachment of one being to another. This feeling of attachment, in Semitic thought, has its origin in the experience of maternity, in the bowels, the entrails, or, as in common parlance, the "guts." Etymologically the Hebrew word for compassion means "trembling womb" (Trible, pp. 31–59). Thus the mother's intimate physical relationship with her newborn is the prime image for understanding the nature of compassion. The implication here is that the mother's physical and psychological bond with her child provides the basis for the development of the less concrete, indeed more abstract, notions of compassion, pity, mercy, and tenderness.

In this light, compassion may be understood as the capacity to be attracted and moved by the fragility, weakness, and suffering of another. It is the ability to be vulnerable enough to undergo risk and loss for the good of the other. Compassion involves a movement to be of assistance to the other, but it ineluctably entails a movement of participation in the experience of the other in order to be present and available in soli-darity and communion. Compassion requires sensitivity to what is weak and/or wounded, as well as the vulnerability to be affected by the other. It also demands action to alleviate pain and suffering. One's deepest inner feelings should always lead to outward compassionate acts of mercy and kindness.

Though the prime image for understanding compassion is a maternal one, this quality is not exclusive to mothers or to women. Compassion also springs from the heart of a father (Ps 103:13) or a brother (Gen 43:30). It is tenderness readily moved to action. It is remedial action in the face of tragedy (Ps 106:45) or forgiveness of offenses (Dan 9:9).

In the New Testament, Jesus exemplifies God's compassion in his preaching and healing (Mt 9:36; 14:4), in his concern for lost humanity (Lk 19:41), and in his self-sacrificial love on the cross (Rom 5:8). The followers of Jesus are to live lives of compassion as an expression of the love that Jesus enjoined (Mt 5:4-7; Jn 13:34; Jas 2:8-18; 1 Jn 3:18). Jesus provided paradigms of compassion in the parables of the good Samaritan, who had compassion on the wounded traveler (Lk 10:33), and the prodigal son, whose father saw him in the distance and, "moved with compassion," ran to meet him (Lk 15:20).

In the history of Christian spirituality, where preoccupation with pain and suffering has not been uncommon, the term *compassion* has sometimes taken on connotations of a sentimental, pious romanticization of the negative factors in human life and of the tragic reality of Jesus' suffering and death. Even when grounded in a strong Christological base and understood as participation in the redemptive suffering of Christ, approaches to compassion in Christian spirituality have often lacked a keen sense of the importance of compassion as a practical response to suffering and to the consequences of social evil and sin. By and large compassion has been understood as an instinctive movement of the heart in the face of the pain or suffering of other individuals. This has been done in such a way that the individual's feeling of compassion has been untethered in theory and practice from a realization that the compassion which exists preeminently in the heart of God, as this is disclosed in Jesus' outreach into human history, calls for active participation in the work of compassion as a response to the divine initiative.

Contemporary approaches to compassion in Christian theology and spirituality give greater attention to God, Christ, and Christian praxis as foundational in reflection on the nature of compassion. Whatever is to be said of compassion must begin with the recognition that it resides in its fullness in God who is present in creation, participant in history, entering into the human experience in solidarity with human suffering, history, and destiny. From a Christian perspective, the fullness of compassion is known in and through Jesus, who discloses the compassion of God. In his person, God truly enters into creation, into the fabric of human life in all its contingency, frailty, and tragedy. Following Jesus entails an invitation to the praxis of compassion. Christian discipleship brings us face to face with human suffering and pain of enormous proportions, caused in part by social systems and structures born of sin and evil in our world.

The Christian's responsibility to act compassionately does not derive from divine injunction to pious sentiment, though it certainly is rooted in an appeal to the human heart. As a feeling and as appropriate action based on this feeling, compassion entails nonviolence, solidarity, and communion, as well as the activities by which pain and suffering are alleviated, depersonalization is combated, and oppression and injustice are overcome. Finally, it is the response of the human heart which knows its own pain and suffering, which does not stand outside the experience of suffering and instruct like the false consolers in the Book of Job, but which seeks to strengthen and empower through a relationship of identification with what is weak and wounded.

See also AFFECT, AFFECTIVITY; FRUIT(S) OF THE HOLY SPIRIT; HEART; HEART OF CHRIST; LOVE; MERCY; PRAXIS; SOLIDARITY; SUFFERING; WEAKNESS AND VULNERABILITY.

Bibliography: M. Hellwig, *Jesus, the Compassion of God: New Perspectives on the Tradition of Christianity* (Wilmington, Del.: Glazier, 1983). P. Trible, *God and the Rhetoric of Sexuality* (Philadelphia: Fortress, 1978) 31–59. J. Nelson-Pallmeyer, *The Politics of Compassion* (Maryknoll, N.Y.: Orbis, 1986) 7–16.

MICHAEL DOWNEY

COMPUNCTION

The term *compunction* (Latin *compunctio,* from *cum-pungere,* "to puncture with") is found in the works of the Fathers of the Church in a number of different patterns, e.g., compunction of fear, compunction of desire and compunction of the heart. In its original profane use the word is a medical term, indicating attacks of physical pain. The first ecclesiastical usage, toward the end of the second century, transposes the meaning to signify pain of the spirit, a suffering due to the actual existence of sin and human concupiscence, and as a result of our desire for God. The theological connotation is closely parallel to the biblical idea of *metanoia,* rendered in English as "penitence."

In the Scriptures the idea of compunction corresponds to the biblical notion of *katanyxeis,* from the two Hebrew words *tar'êlâ* (Ps 60:5) and *tardêmâ* (Isa 29:10), indicating a lethargic inebriation resulting in spiritual blindness. In the NT the Pentecost speech of Peter (Acts 2:37) employs the notion to express the supernatural shock that leads to conversion, translated in the Vulgate as *compuncti sunt corde.* To this extent, the most common use associates the idea of compunction with a change of heart.

The Fathers of the Eastern Church associate the idea of a permanent pain, experienced as a consequence of one's realization of sin, with the notion of conversion and penitence. For the Desert Fathers, compunction is a sign of valid repentance, the fruit of this conversion being tranquility (*hesychia*), a purity of heart. Origen (d. 253) associates the theme with another scriptural theme, *penthos,* indicating public or private mourning. St. John Chrysostom (d. 407) authored two books on compunction (*De compunctione,* PG 47:391-422), while St. Gregory of Nyssa (d. ca. 394), in his *Third Homily on the Beatitudes* (PG 44:1219-1232) distinguishes between the sadness (*penthos*) according to God and the sadness according to the world. One notes the foundations for the later medieval distinction between contrition (sadness for sin because it offends God) and attrition (remorse for sin out of fear of punishment).

John Cassian (d. ca. 435) and St. Gregory the Great (d. 604) were two of the great doctors of compunction in the Latin West, giving the monastic formulation of compunction as an element of affective prayer. In this case compunction is a kind of grace inflamed by the Holy Spirit, producing strong feelings often accompanied by tears. One finds this idea developed in the Rule of Benedict, where he speaks of *compunctio lacrimarum* (chap. 20) and *compunctio cordis* (chap. 49). Tears of love always accompany those of penitence. Initially the penitent experiences tears of remorse, but in time these tears are dominated by tears of joy.

As a monastic virtue, compunction is found throughout the tradition of the Latin West. For example, in the Carolingian period Alcuin (d. 804), in his *speculum* on virtues and vices, notes that compunction of the heart is born out of the virtue of humility, which ultimately leads to the confession of sins. He insists that compunction makes itself manifest through a profusion of tears and concludes that the penitent has the promise of divine indulgence if the tears of penitence excite the heart (PL 101:620). The theme of tears is often associated with the idea of purification of sins through an ablution. To this end, tears are related to the cleansing waters of baptism, the event of one's first penance (*ablutio lacrymis poenitentiae,* PL 100:575). Further evidence of the gift of tears is found in the Roman Missal and in the writings of St. Teresa of Avila (*Autobiography* 29, 17; *Relations* 8, 16, in *The Collected Works of St. Teresa of Avila,* 3 vols., Washington: ICS Publications, 1976, 1980, 1985).

St. Anselm of Canterbury in his *Prayers* proceeded to the awesome fact that God, who knows human beings as they really are, is ever faithful. The love of God pierces the heart (compunction), leading Anselm to consider the cross and passion of Christ as the cost of the faithfulness and love of God for humanity. Assimilated to the cross, the one who prays is involved with the reconciliation of God in Christ. The "Prayer to Christ" is a clear example of this: "Why, O my soul, were you not there to be pierced by a sword of bitter sorrow when you could not bear to see the nails violate the hands and feet of your Creator? Why did you not see with horror the blood that poured out of the side of your Redeemer? Why were you not drunk with bitter tears when they gave him bitter gall to drink?"

See also BENEDICTINE SPIRITUALITY; CONVERSION; HEART; HESYCHASM; MONASTICISM, MONASTIC SPIRITUALITY; PENANCE, PENITENCE; TEARS, GIFT OF.

Bibliography: J. Leclercq, *The Love of Learning and the Desire for God,* trans. C. Misrahi (New York: Fordham Univ. Press, 1961). I. Hausherr, *Penthos: La Doctrine de la componction dans l'Orient chrétien,* Orientalia Christiana Analecta 132 (Rome: Pontifical Institute of Oriental Studies, 1944). J. de Guibert, "La Componction du cœur," Revue d'ascetique et de mystique 15 (1934) 229.

MICHAEL S. DRISCOLL

CONCUPISCENCE

See DESIRE; SIN.

CONFESSION

See PENANCE, PENITENCE.

CONFIRMATION

The spirituality of confirmation can best be discerned by a careful reading of the liturgical rite for the celebration of the sacrament. In the rite itself, prepared by the Congregation for Divine Worship and promulgated by Pope Paul VI (August 15, 1971), one can discover the Church's present theological understanding of this sacrament and its spiritual significance for Christian living.

For a full understanding of its spirituality, confirmation must be studied in its liturgical context as one of the three sacraments of initiation. The overall purpose of the sacraments of baptism, confirmation, and Eucharist is to lead a person to full ecclesial membership and incorporation into Christ. This formation process, which involves the ecclesial community and the individual, is to bring about both conversion and transformation. As a part of the initiation process of Christian formation, confirmation completes the work begun in baptism and leads the individual to full Eucharistic participation. "The faithful are born anew by baptism, strengthened by the sacrament of confirmation, and finally are sustained by the food of eternal life in the eucharist" (*Documents on the Liturgy,* p. 766).

The NT illustrates the significant central role of the Holy Spirit in the life of Christ and the early Church. The Spirit assisted Christ to fulfill his messianic mission. At his baptism by John, he saw the Spirit descend on him (Mk 1:10) and remain with him (Jn 1:32). Guided and assisted by the Spirit, Jesus undertook his public ministry.

The gift of the Spirit was promised by Jesus to his disciples to be an abiding presence and assistance (Acts 1:8; Lk 24:49). In the power of that gift, received at Pentecost, the early Church was strengthened to witness to the truth (Jn 15:26) and proclaim the mighty works of God. The Spirit was, in fact, the first gift from the risen Lord to those who believed. Thereafter the apostles imparted the gift of the Holy Spirit to the baptized by the laying on of hands. "This laying on of hands is rightly recognized by reason of Catholic tradition as the beginning of the sacrament of confirmation, which in a certain way perpetuates the grace of Pentecost in the Church" (*Documents on the Liturgy,* p. 767).

In the history of the Church, the conferral of the gift of the Holy Spirit, not always clearly distinguished from baptism, has been done by the use of different rituals. Whereas the ritual form (words and actions) has varied over the centuries in both the East and the West, the bestowal of the gift of the Holy Spirit has remained central and constant to the celebration of confirmation. In addition, both in the East and the West, the anointing with chrism, which signifies the spiritual anointing of the Holy Spirit, has been given special ritual emphasis.

The 1971 *Rite of Confirmation* emphasizes the centrality of the Spirit throughout the rite of anointing. Adopting the ancient formula of the Church of the Byzantine Rite, the Church of the West has declared that "the sacrament of confirmation is conferred through the anointing with chrism on the forehead, which is done by the laying on of the hand, and through the words: Be sealed with the Gift of the Holy Spirit" (*Documents on the Liturgy,* p. 770).

Although confirmation has been referred to as a rite in search of a theology, the liturgical texts do offer the Church's present understanding of the spiritual effects of the sacrament. The rite teaches that the sacrament brings about a spiritual transformation that completes the work of baptism. More specifically, confirmation makes one more like Christ, who was also anointed by the Spirit at his baptism. It binds one more closely to the Church in the unity of faith and life. It strengthens the confirmed to be witnesses, by lives of faith and love before the world, to both the paschal mystery and the Good News proclaimed by Jesus Christ. Such a strength is indeed the power of the Holy Spirit, helper and guide, who bestows on the initiated a variety of gifts: understanding, right judgment and courage, knowledge and wisdom, wonder and awe in God's presence.

See also BAPTISM; EUCHARIST; FRUIT(S) OF THE HOLY SPIRIT; GIFTS OF THE HOLY SPIRIT; HOLY SPIRIT; SACRAMENTS.

Bibliography: International Commission on English in the Liturgy, *Documents on the Liturgy 1963–1979: Conciliar, Papal, and Curial Texts* (Collegeville, Minn.: Liturgical Press, 1982). G. Austin, *The Rite of Confirmation: Anointing with the Spirit* (New York: Pueblo, 1985).

THOMAS A. KROSNICKI, S.V.D.

CONFRONTATION AND PROTEST

Confront (Latin *con,* "against" + *frons,* "forehead"), meaning to oppose face to face in hostility or defiance, and *protest* (Latin *protestari*), meaning to declare publicly or to express formally one's objection or disapproval, often with respect to something one lacks power to prevent, change, or avoid, together signify a profoundly personal encounter, verbal or nonverbal, between individuals or groups. It engages both parties psychologically and morally in a process of change aimed at achieving congruence between held values and some state of affairs. The concepts are discussed here first as a social-psychological process and then as a paradigm of Christian conversion.

Social-Psychological Process

Always historically conditioned, confrontation and protest involve three ana-

lytically distinct phases closely related to the development of human persons in their individual, social, and moral reality. These can be described as follows.

A. (1) In the effort to act freely and constructively to meet basic human needs or to promote human development of self or others, one encounters resistance from structural barriers or other persons, a resistance not only powerful but threatening. (2) Such resistance engenders an experience of alienation. (3) This alienation is perceived not only as painful and destructive to self and others but wrong, unjust, morally objectionable. (4) The contradiction between what is and what ought to be moves the protester from an unquestioning acceptance of a state of affairs or relationship to a new level of perception and interpretation of experience, thus effecting a change in consciousness. (5) The moral character of this awareness places the issue in a more universal and objective context, adding the element of moral commitment to a struggle seen as transcending private or individual needs and leading to deliberate expression of opposition.

B. In actively confronting a powerful other and protesting a specific wrong, the confronter often encounters resistance from unexpected quarters that reveals more complex causes of the grievance, e.g., dysfunctional family or institutional systems, vested power interests, systemic injustice in the economic/political sphere. Opposing a specific situation may thus require a commitment to oppose or eradicate the causes of an inequity extending beyond the immediate interaction, e.g., tenants' efforts to provide redress for the neglect of a property owner may require a confrontation with local housing or judicial officials responsible for an ineffectual judiciary system subverted by wealth and power interests.

At each stage both the confronter and the confronted face unavoidable moral choices of consequence. The confrontation threatens not only the protester, whose responsibility demands leaving the security of the status quo, but also the one confronted, who is presented with a challenging new perception of the inherent moral deficiency of that status quo. The protester must act not only for the sake of self but also, from the moral standpoint, for the other, for nonaction perpetuates injustice that is morally destructive for the oppressor as well. Because of this, confrontation, when justified, is a profound act of respect and care for the oppressive other.

C. The outcome of the struggle may be negative: suppression of the protester, physically, psychologically, economically, politically. However, insofar as the protest has brought a truth to the surface or discovered a true state of affairs, this reality cannot be negated by suppressing the protester. The outcome may be positive: the overcoming of resistance through taking over power, e.g., politically or economically, or by the gradual conversion of the oppressor. Both lead by different but often interacting processes to a new integration, a healing of the alienation inherent in the initial stage. Confrontation and protest are thus always social in context and actively engage all parties in a process of change.

Paradigm of Christian Conversion

In Christian spirituality this process recurs as a permanent feature of personal and communal response to the living word of God. Scripture offers vivid examples of confrontation in both the Old and the New Testament. Genesis 3:8-12 pictures God confronting Adam, forcing him to confront the discrepancy between his action and his responsibility to God's word. In obedience to, and armed with, the word of God, Moses confronts Pharaoh (Exod 11). The prophet Isaiah confronts Achaz (Isa 7:11), Nathan confronts King David (2 Sam 12), and in the NT John the Baptist, modeling the self-purification required of the protester, confronts the conscience of religious and political authority even to his death, prefiguring the stance fully exemplified in

Jesus, the incarnate Word (Mt 3:7-12; Lk 3:18-20). Jesus exemplifies the confrontative role with religious leaders in word (Mt 23:13-26) and deed in the cleansing of the Temple (Jn 2:13-17). In Acts 7:51-53 Stephen continues the prophetic confrontation at the cost of his life. Paul confronts Peter face to face (*kata prosōpon autoi antestēn*—Gal 2:11) over the Gentile question, pointing out the contradiction between the proclamation of salvation by faith and the ambiguous behavior diluting that message, and accusing Peter of breaking faith by failing to translate the confession of faith into action (Gal 2:11-14).

Scripture thus provides a paradigm of how persons are called and judged by, respond to or resist, are healed or convicted by, the living word of God, mediated through human, social interactions, revealing the meaning and scope of human life, and inviting all to wholeness in God's saving economy.

Ecclesial Dimensions—Prophetic Challenge

In Christian spirituality, confrontation may take place (A) within the Church: between teaching authority and members or vice versa, as well as between other Christian Churches and the Roman Church; and (B) beyond the Church (1) between Church authority or believers and the secular, political community, e.g., in protest of violations of human rights or by solidarity with efforts already underway to oppose injustice; and (2) between individuals or groups outside the Church that challenge Church teaching or practice as infringing upon perceived rights and Church members.

The foundation of such confrontation is what Karl Rahner calls the Church's own "unambiguous creed and dogma" (*Confrontations 2*, p. 232). Precisely because the Church holds itself accountable to the word of God, it is judged by that word. While in principle a saving and unifying force, the word of God is inevitably a catalyst for change and the divisions that occur in the process of change (Mt 10:34-35; Lk 12:51-53; Heb 4:12-13). In this process it is the word of God that illumines the true character of the believer's experience or even of those who find themselves excluded psychologically or spiritually.

A. The role of confrontation thus belongs to the Church in its teaching mission and can be exercised with authority within the Church (head to members). However, since the notion of protest denotes opposition without power, protest refers more precisely to the role of members than to that of the institutional representatives and will be considered here primarily from this perspective.

1. Within the believing individual or community, this can take the form of a growing sense of contradiction between what is proclaimed and signified in the Eucharistic celebration and what is ignored, rejected, or denied in institutional practice. In the very effort to be faithful to word and sacrament, persons may find human development—emotional, moral, or intellectual—and response to grace diminished or blocked within the Church, and themselves alienated from the persons and rites that mediate and celebrate the mystery of communion with God in Christ, e.g., women's experience or the isolation of rich and poor parishes. This experience of alienation not only reveals the Church, bearer of salvation, as a sinful, human institution but also discloses the profound resistance to grace operative in the human condition.

2. Fidelity to the word received and the sacrament celebrated summons the believer so affected to express formal opposition to whatever structure, use of authority, or blindness distorts and dilutes the gospel or limits and blocks authentic response to it. For if what is professed in word and ritual is not lived, one has, in deed, denied the faith and risks serious irreverence in the sacramental celebration itself (1 Jn 1:5–2:11). Those with special roles and abilities may face additional demands in fulfilling this responsibility, e.g., teachers and theologians with respect to dissent.

If keeping faith demands confrontation, however, the same faith requires commitment to the person(s) whose actions or attitudes are being opposed, since it recognizes them as brothers and sisters in Christ, and commitment to the process itself. One cannot escape the demands of the interaction by rejecting the other in the guise of protest but must remain in relationship. This fidelity causes one to remain vulnerable and open to the disclosure of one's own motives and needs often revealed in negative responses of the other. Thus both confronter and confronted are brought face to face with the need for personal conversion. It is the work of spiritual discernment to uncover such multiple motives and emotions at work, a process which, when undertaken with persevering prayer, brings these complex factors to awareness in the light of faith, thus creating emotional and intellectual space essential for moral freedom.

Only commitment to God's word and openness to sharing in the emptying (*kenōsis*) of Christ make the discernment possible. Only when one perseveres are the various levels of values blocking the situation gradually uncovered (e.g., one person's need for security or power as opposed to another's need for respect), the priority among values recognized, and the presence of more fundamental common ground revealed.

3. The limits of human power and the intrinsic freedom of wills are also revealed. Even in the clearest and most responsible confrontation, the other remains free to say no. In the refusal to respond to truth, however, the person is still changed and now stands somehow convicted of resistance to the word of God. As Kierkegaard remarks, we cannot force others to change, but we can compel them to take notice.

In the process, therefore, both parties are called beyond their starting point to a real *metanoia*, or conversion. There is no guarantee that both will persevere or that there will be sufficient perceived values to provide common ground, but insofar as either party remains open, change and growth occur, and the word of God acts to build up the body in love.

B. Confrontation also can and does originate with other Churches and between those of East and West as integral to the ecumenical endeavor, and relies for its moral authority on the mutual acceptance of, and belief in, the word of God.

1. But confrontation is not limited to interactions between believers. It extends beyond the ecclesial community to the political-social sphere. Here the threat may be loss of political or economical security or even persecution, as witnessed widely today, e.g., the Church in Latin America in its solidarity with the poor.

2. Most challenging is the protest directed at the Church or its representatives by those who see themselves as outsiders, requiring the Church to reexamine its own human understanding of the gospel in light of the signs of the times, a process responded to positively by Vatican II. In both contexts the process involves the same stages and potential outcomes, making proportionate demands on all, particularly on those committed in conscience to the word of God revealed in Jesus Christ.

Conclusion

Christian confrontation and protest are thus both prophetic and contemplative, transcending any active/contemplative dichotomy. Rendered transparent by the word of God, they are essentially nonviolent and involve an act of conscience making both parties vulnerable, requiring perseverance in the obedience of faith, promoting integration of personal and social/political values and relationships, and aimed at achieving true unity and communion in love.

See also CONSCIENCE; DECISION, DECISION-MAKING; DISCERNMENT OF SPIRITS; DISCIPLESHIP; FREE-DOM; HOPE; JUSTICE; OBEDIENCE; RESPONSIBILITY; SIN.

Bibliography: J.-M. Ela, The African Cry (Maryknoll, N.Y.: Orbis, 1986). K. Rahner, Confrontations 2, Theological Investigations 12 (London: Darton, Longman and Todd, 1974).

M. CLARE ADAMS, O.S.C.

CONSCIENCE

The term does not exist in Hebrew and consequently is rarely found in the Old Testament. The closest alternative seems to be the word leb ("heart"), which appears frequently. The Greek term (syneidēsis) appears in the New Testament, but almost exclusively in the writings of Paul. A direct and extensive discussion of conscience occurs in 1 Corinthians 8 and 10.

On the basis of this Pauline presentation, as well as philosophical discussions in Greco-Roman authors, the term entered the Christian tradition. But like many central religious terms, conscience has multiple facets. Distinguishing between them will help to clarify the significance of this concept for Christian spirituality.

Anterior conscience is distinguished from posterior conscience on the basis of whether it precedes or follows the action being considered. Posterior conscience is a characteristically modern notion, referring as it does to feelings of guilt that remain when one has violated standards. Psychological theory makes clear that such feelings have many and mysterious sources. Thus a "guilty conscience" is not necessarily an indicator of true moral failure.

Christian tradition more commonly refers to anterior conscience, the exercise of moral consciousness in the choosing of behavior yet to be done. In describing this reality, however, three different aspects may be noted.

First, conscience can be understood as a characteristic of human persons whereby they experience themselves as accountable for their behavior. This sense of accountability is evident when humans confess and apologize, when they accept responsibility for past actions and seek to make amends. Not all human persons have this characteristic, but those who do not and who do not experience themselves as accountable are understood to be deficient. They are described as sociopaths, as afflicted with "psychic impotence," as the victims of a character disorder. Perhaps it is more accurate to say that possession of this characteristic admits of degrees and that all human persons find themselves somewhere on the continuum.

Precisely because persons experience themselves as accountable, they commonly enter into a process of discernment whereby they attempt to discover whether a particular action ought or ought not to be performed. The word *conscience* also refers to this *process of discernment.* The reality of this process reveals several significant things. First, it indicates that there is such a thing as moral ignorance, that human persons do not know what is right in any innate way. For it is precisely the function of this process to replace ignorance with insight. Second, it suggests the possibility of moral error, for the process has a note of uncertainty about it and seems capable of both success and failure. Third, it affirms that conscience is not an ultimate reality but is in service to something else—moral rectitude. Fourth, it hints at the singular importance of human community, for if others know what is to be done, they can facilitate this conscientious process by providing the resource of their wisdom. Indeed, it is unlikely that human persons ever successfully complete this process without just this sort of human assistance.

Still, there comes a moment when the process of discernment must resolve itself in a conclusion. Life itself demands this when it presents moral dilemmas that must be resolved here and now. This *event,* this *judgment* of right or wrong, is the act of conscience—its third facet.

There is a paradoxical quality to this act. Inasmuch as it is nothing other than the concluding moment of the *process* of conscience, it partakes of all the fragility of that process. It is susceptible to error, is touched with uncertainty, and is subject to later review and revision. But inasmuch as it is rooted in and demanded by the *characteristic* of conscience, it has a quality of imperiousness. It is the "voice of God," as is sometimes said, which demands obedience. To refuse to do what one truly believes one ought to do, whether this belief is actually correct or not, is to contradict one's fundamental human responsibility. Indeed, the act of sin is nothing else than the decision to contradict one's judgment of conscience, and, conversely, fidelity to one's judgments of conscience is a definition of the life of sanctity.

These latter comments further serve to shed light on common phrases such as "rights of conscience," "duties of conscience," and the like. Viewed from the outside, so to speak, conscience exhibits no particular rights. It has no unassailable dignity. The goal of the moral life, after all, is not precisely that one follow one's conscience but rather that one do what is right. That is why Catholic tradition has asserted that the ultimate (i.e., radical) norm of morality is the natural law (the objective order of moral value).

But it is the human person who must acknowledge and embrace that objective value, and conscience is the term for the human person as attentive to, and aware of, such values. So, viewed from the inside, so to speak, conscience presents itself as nonnegotiable and unequivocal. The tradition has described conscience as the *proximate* norm of morality, in that it is the norm nearest to the moral agent. But that very proximity makes conscience an "ultimate" norm in its own way. And the moral person does indeed have the duty of following his or her conscience, and therefore also the right to follow that conscience, at least to the extent that the rights of others are not thereby violated.

One last topic demands attention: the formation of conscience. It is commonly asserted that the only conscience that deserves (or requires) obedience is a "rightly formed conscience." This phrase suggests two lines of thought.

First, it can mean that, to be worthy of obedience, the judgment of conscience must follow upon conscientious pursuit of the process of conscience. And such a conscientious pursuit no doubt includes docility (a willingness to learn), openness to the wisdom of others, and appropriate exploration of the matter at hand. This is surely true, although just as the process itself is susceptible to error and disagreement, so also the assessment of whether a particular pursuit of the process has been conscientious will be open to debate. Still, a rightly formed conscience remains the goal of all efforts at moral discernment.

Second, the phrase can invite us to consider the many ways in which formation, malformation, and reformation of conscience take place. It is all too obvious that many human persons are trapped by moral blind spots, by areas of insensitivity or, at the other extreme, of scrupulosity. Indeed, it is probably the case that all human persons are the victims of some degree of this. So "formation of conscience" is not a matter of the simple transmission of information; rather, it is a much more subtle educational process by which value sensitivities are inculcated.

There is much recent research on this topic. A few general comments will suffice. First, one's conscience is formed by experience. It is life-events that shape one's moral sensibilities as well as hone one's skills of moral discernment. Consequently, to the degree that one's life-experience is limited, biased, or destructive, to that extent will one's conscience be malformed.

Second, it follows from this that moral education is a developmental project that lasts throughout the course of one's life. It is not a once-for-all project. Even less is it a project primarily pursued in formal educational settings.

Third, where ethical deficiencies are discerned, the strategy of choice is not the imposition of information but rather the provision of further experiences. Sensitivity to the needs of the poor, for example, will grow much more from a day in a soup kitchen than from lectures on the moral obligations of charity.

Fourth, the project of conscience formation is radically communal. As one's conscience is formed by past experiences with those around one, so further interactions will shape and develop the conscience. Hence the Church can be viewed not only as a teacher of moral values and a source for moral support (which it is) but also as a community of moral education, a place where conscience-shaping experiences take place and where individuals consequently grow in insight into moral value.

Fifth, the experiences whereby one pursues the formation of conscience may be either immediate or vicarious, that is, they can be genuine, "real live" experiences, or they can be imagined experiences. Psychological research has highlighted the power of human imagination to move and shape a person. Creative visualization is used for everything from the improvement of athletic prowess to the combating of disease. And with notable success. So also in the development of moral sensibilities. Storytelling, and narrative more broadly, is pivotal to the project of moral education for precisely this reason: it engenders imagined, vicarious experiences. And such experiences, no less than immediate ones, have the capability of occasioning moral development and the formation of conscience.

Finally, all this presents obvious implications for the project traditionally known as spirituality. It explains the central role often given to the use of imagination in prayer. It clarifies the life-shaping role of liturgy and other rituals. It names in a new way the central Christian project of discipleship. And it describes from within the human person the dynamics by which is enacted the radical gospel challenge to love God and neighbor.

See also AUTHORITY; DECISION, DECISION-MAKING; DISCERNMENT OF SPIRITS; HOLY SPIRIT; IMAGINATION; INTENTION, INTENTIONALITY; LOVE; PASSION(S); RESPONSIBILITY; SELF; VALUE; VIRTUE.

Bibliography: T. O'Connell, *Principles for a Catholic Morality,* rev. ed. (San Francisco: Harper & Row, 1990). R. Gula, *Reason Informed by Faith* (New York: Paulist, 1989).

TIMOTHY E. O'CONNELL

CONSCIOUSNESS

Consciousness and the Subject

To begin with what is most familiar, consciousness is a personal reality. Only persons and what they do or suffer can be referred to, properly speaking, as conscious. Human persons, however—to prescind from the divine Persons and from angels—are not conscious at all times. Under anesthesia, for example, or while comatose or deeply and dreamlessly asleep, I am alive but not conscious. Nor does everything that goes on in me, even when I am wide awake, go on consciously—not the growth of my hair, for example, or the circulation of my blood.

Activities or operations that are, by contrast, conscious are such as these: dreaming, seeing, hearing, tasting, feeling, imagining, thinking, inquiring, considering, supposing, deliberating, deciding, judging, evaluating, loving, doing. Such acts differ in many respects, but they all have two things in common. In the first place, each is intentional. By this is meant, not that they are deliberate or planned, but that they *intend* in the technical sense, borrowed by phenomenology from Scholasticism, that each makes something present to me. Although these operations are mine, although they are given, they are not merely psychological events. As given, they

disclose or refer to some other. This is not to say that the otherness of the other, as present, has any determined status; and it is not to pronounce, either way, upon the validity of the reference. These are further questions. The one point being made is that dreaming, for instance, makes a dream present, seeing makes color present, and so on. As intended, in this open-ended sense, the dream is defined as the *object* of dreaming. In the same sense, the object of imagining is an image; of tasting, flavor; of deliberating, a course of action, and so on.

All conscious operations of the sort listed above make present objects, so defined, and thus all are intentional. Intentionality is not, however, what makes them conscious. Their consciousness is the second characteristic common to such acts: besides their reference to an as yet indeterminate other, each reveals me to myself. With regard to this primitive self-awareness, Augustine said that when the human mind follows the ancient precept "Know yourself," what happens is not like knowing cherubim and seraphim, which are absent; nor is it like examining one's own face, which can be present for inspection only as reflected in a mirror. Rather the mind knows itself in the very act in which it understands the word "yourself," and this it does for no other reason than that it is present to itself (*De Trinitate* X, ix, 12). This presence-to-self is consciousness properly so called, and what a conscious act as conscious makes present, together with the act itself, is the *subject* of that act.

It is important to distinguish this self-presence, which is consciousness, from the two other kinds of presence that Augustine alludes to, which are not consciousness. One is presence in the sense of vicinity, such as the presence of the jar to the jam; the other is the intentional presence, already discussed, of the objects of conscious acts as intentional, the presence of a sound as heard or of an idea as being considered. My presence to myself is neither of these. It is the presence of the dreamer who is dreaming, as dreaming; of the hearer who is hearing, as hearing; of the thinker who is thinking, as thinking, and so on, as the case may be. Stated generally, it is the presence of the one whose present intentional act is making some object present. Thus I have only to open my eyes in order to become aware that I am seeing something, and my awareness is both of an operation (I *am seeing* something) and of myself as performing it (*I* am seeing something).

To summarize, human operations occur that are at once conscious and intentional. As intentional, they make objects present; as conscious, they are present and they make their subject present. Consciousness is the presence to the subject of the operation, and of the operating subject as intending an object but not as object intended. The subject is conscious, in the sense of being that which is conscious; an intentional act is conscious, in the sense of being that by which the subject is conscious; the object of such an act is not conscious in any sense whatever.

Consciousness as Experience

Consciousness, understood as the presence to oneself of oneself and one's acts, is experiential. It is similar to sense-experience in its givenness; it differs in that what is given is not sensed. While all experiencing is conscious, therefore, not all experience is consciousness. Sensation itself is a conscious operation, since it makes the operating subject present; but the same is true of any number of other, different acts. On the one hand, then, there are data, the experiential givens, of sense—the intended objects of hearing, smelling, touching, tasting, and seeing. On the other hand, there are data, the experiential givens, of consciousness—the intending subject of conscious acts, which may be acts of seeing or hearing but may instead be acts of thinking, believing, understanding, defining, feeling, praying.

Consciousness conceived as experience is to be distinguished from the seemingly compatible but in fact thoroughly opposed notion of consciousness as perception or observation. Variants of this alternative account have had an abiding influence, especially on English-language philosophy and theology, and the analogy they all draw between consciousness and perceiving an object does seem plausible. Its implications, however, do not. To suppose, with Locke for instance, that to be conscious is to exercise a kind of inward vision leads in the long run to skepticism such as Hume's as to whether the conscious subject exists at all. "For my part," Hume declares, "when I enter most intimately into what I call *myself,* I always stumble on some particular perception or other, of heat or cold, light or shade, love or hatred, pain or pleasure. I never can catch *myself* at any time without a perception, and never can observe any thing but the perception" (*Treatise on Human Nature* I, iv, 6). In one regard this is quite correct: never will the kind of introspective spying that Hume describes manage to sneak up on the subject and take it by surprise. It would be like looking at one's own eyes. But what frustrates the attempt is not, as Hume goes on to conclude, that there is no such thing as "what I call *myself.*" It is that the self he is looking for, a subject apart from conscious acts, would be precisely not conscious—not an actual subject, that is, but a merely potential subject, anesthetized, as it were, and incapable as such of looking for anything. Otherwise stated, there is no such conscious act as introspection if the word is meant, as it often is, in the sense of somehow looking at oneself as object.

Consciousness as Infrastructure

There is, however, a different and less simplistic meaning of introspection, connected not with self-observation, which is impossible, but with self-knowledge, which is both a possibility and, for some, a fact. Anyone who is consciously operating in any way already has, by the very fact of being conscious, a preliminary, unpatterned awareness of himself or herself and his or her operating. But this awareness need not have been noticed, acknowledged, explored, distinguished, named, described, interpreted, explained, or understood. Just as outer experiences of sensation are not yet full human knowledge of the intelligible world, so likewise the inner experience that is consciousness is not yet knowledge of consciousness. Human knowing is a matter of raising and answering questions about experience. Such an inquiry, when it regards the data of sense, is direct; when it regards the data of consciousness, introspective.

To raise questions about one's own consciousness is itself a conscious operation. To raise them explicitly and articulately, however, is to make use of some suprastructure of language that is not immediately given but mediated by one's culture. Moreover, conscious data are not experienced in isolation from such a structured flow of words and images any more than sensible data are. Inner and outer experience alike stand to verbal or symbolic objectifications of experience as infrastructure to suprastructure, with pure experience as a limit case approached, perhaps, but seldom if ever reached. This does not invalidate the distinction between experience and knowing in general, or between consciousness and an intelligent account of consciousness in particular, but it does mean that between infrastructure and suprastructure, between inner experience as such and this experience as understood more or less correctly, the relationship is dynamic and reciprocal. Hence what is needed in order to confirm an account or description or definition of consciousness—the present article, say—is not, as Hume supposed, a detached observing or perceiving but a heightening or intensifying of consciousness as infrastructure in and through its engagement with the linguistic suprastructure of the account. An appropriating of oneself as

subject, in other words, can take place only in cooperation with appropriating the meaning of the words and sentences under consideration.

An example of this reciprocal process can be seen in client-centered therapy. Emotions and feelings, as felt, belong to the infrastructure of consciousness. But they may and often do disrupt the polyphonic unity of inner experience, and the resulting discord can be destructive. In that case therapy may provide opportunities for those feelings to emerge without overwhelming, to be recognized, discriminated from other elements of consciousness, named, related, and thereby given a place within an interpretive and evaluative suprastructure. Through a process of what may appropriately be called introspection, the client achieves a measure of self-knowledge that can be the basis for self-acceptance, self-control, and self-determination.

Here it may be noted that, *mutatis mutandis,* much the same process of heightening one's consciousness can be a component of spiritual direction, the discernment of spirits, and directed retreats. In different ways these exercises likewise involve expressing and objectifying the contents of consciousness while at the same time moving from what Newman would call a notional apprehension to a real apprehension of the meaning of statements about consciousness. By making it possible to raise explicit questions about states and occurrences that are conscious, to formulate descriptions, grasp connections, make comparisons, and draw inferences, such practices can promote the conscious subject's knowledge of himself or herself, in and through conversation with that component of culture which is some more or less authentic tradition of spirituality. Assuredly it is better to feel compunction than to define it. Still, a definition may help in deciding whether it is really compunction that is being felt.

Consciousness and
Self-Transcendence

Intentional acts are of different sorts, and the quality of the consciousness that accompanies them varies accordingly. One and the same subject is present throughout, but present in different ways. The inchoate, helpless, minimal consciousness of the dreamer passes over, on waking, into the consciousness that accompanies the impulses and perceptions of the same subject, now concerned with meeting needs and engaged through sensation with an environment. Consciousness of this *empirical* kind may well belong to animals as well as to human beings. In any case, human self-presence is enhanced and takes on a new and different quality with the advent of intelligent activity, of inquiring and investigating, understanding and conceiving, defining and hypothesizing. Different from this *intellectual* consciousness is the *rational* consciousness intrinsic to such activities as testing a hypothesis, weighing the evidence for a bright idea, and discriminating between fact and fiction, the true and the false. Different yet again is the *moral* consciousness associated with the human yearning and drive for what is not just true but truly valuable as well, with freedom, responsibility, commitment, promise, trust, and faithfulness.

The conscious operations that effect transitions from one sort of conscious activity to the next are questions. As conscious, they are also intentional; what they intend is answers, but the answers are not yet formulated or known, and so the infrastructure of questioning is the experience of a tension. Of any experience, sensible or conscious, one may wonder about it, ask what it is and why, and so be drawn through this tension to hit on a more or less intelligent description or definition or explanation. Of any such idea or viewpoint or theory, one may ask whether in fact it is true, and so be drawn toward making a more or less reasonable judgment. Of any

actual or possible state of affairs, one may ask what good it is or would be, and so be drawn to a more or less responsible evaluation and beyond that, perhaps, to a personal decision and commitment.

As presented in prose, this outline of four successive spheres or levels of intentional consciousness—empirical, intellectual, rational, moral—belongs to a suprastructure, and a very bare and schematic one at that. It could be and has been refined and illustrated in greater concrete detail. The important point at present, which the metaphor of levels does serve to suggest, is that the conscious human subject who is self-present through different families of operations—present as intending the sensible, the understandable, the verifiable, or the valuable, as the case may be—is no static entity. Human being is a becoming, and each of us is a subject by degrees. My exercise of intelligence in response to my own wonder and curiosity moves me beyond a merely biological habitat into the human world of meaning; at the same time, it is a moving beyond myself. My exercise of reasonable judgment in response to further questions likewise moves me beyond speculation and idea into knowledge of how things really are; at the same time, it is a further achievement of self-surpassing. And not only do I transcend myself; I thereby constitute myself as well, in the sense that I effect my own becoming. I can, as human, be intelligent and reasonable, but it is in the same measure in which I actualize this capacity that I constitute myself as actually a knower, as *homo sapiens*. Even then, however, my self-completing is only cognitive. For I can, as human, be responsible; and the extent to which I actualize this further capacity in my evaluations and moral judgments and decisions is the extent of my real self-transcendence, the measure of my making of myself a genuinely free subject and a doer of genuinely human deeds.

This is the level of consciousness that has been explored and illuminated by existentialist and personalist philosophers. Conscious acts of deciding for or against some action or cause or person certainly have effects on the deed enacted or left undone, the cause promoted or thwarted, the person cherished or disregarded. But their effect on the decider is deeper. Decisions accumulate; the actions they bring about become second nature. And since nobody has the time to deliberate about every deed every day, most of what we do is not deeds but just behavior, the routine result of the ingrained virtues and vices, inclinations and dispositions, that make up and manifest themselves in our character, mentality, and style of life. That is why "not to decide is to decide": in default of deliberate choice, disposition and habit are in control.

Like every other aspect and element of conscious living, the lifelong process of self-constitution goes on as infrastructure whether it is adverted to or not. Never to advert to it is to be content with being and doing what in Kierkegaard's term "the public," or some segment of it, is being and doing. One drifts with the current, unaware of having appropriated unquestioningly the suprastructure of meanings and values that one's culture has to offer. On the other hand, there can come a point at which the conscious subject is not only self-constituting but knowingly and deliberately self-constituting. It is at this point that consciousness becomes conscience. Not that self-transcending then comes to an end. In this life it never does. Mortals are always taking responsibility for who they are and are to be; they are always negotiating the transition from inauthentic to authentic becoming. But the subject who is conscientiously as well as consciously making this transition is, to the same extent, becoming a person in the fullest sense.

Religious Consciousness

To this highest or deepest or most intensely personal level of consciousness, the *apex animae,* or "peak of the soul," what is called religious experience most directly pertains. As experience, it belongs to the infrastructure of consciousness properly so called. Like other conscious contents, it need not be recognized or named or even attended to, much less understood and known. Even when noticed, its being as yet unknown makes it an experience of mystery, of what is beyond one's achieved knowledge, and an experience of awe, of what is above one's acknowledged values. As such it may be that religious experience is, as it has been persuasively argued to be, fundamentally the same, irrespective of the linguistic, cultural, and historical circumstances in which it occurs. But while it may be but a single voice, difficult to discern within the contrapuntal chorus of conscious intentionality, no more than other conscious events does religious experience occur "neat"; and the more specific the words and concepts are that come to be associated with the infrastructure of religion, the more likely it is that they belong to some particular historical tradition.

Often, and perhaps most appropriately, religious experience is spoken of as love. In relation to the preceding section here, this love may be characterized as a complete actuation of the human capacity for self-transcendence. One is most truly oneself, that is, when loving another—when self-surpassing and self-completing become self-surrender. Some such paradoxical expression is all but inevitable in the case of religious experience, inasmuch as here especially the state or condition of fulfillment and integration that is being in love comes not as an achievement, not as the product of one's own intellectual or even moral self-transcendence, but as a gift. It is not something one does but something one undergoes. The metaphor of "falling" in love is very apt.

Such general descriptions would perhaps be deemed acceptable by persons who have no explicit acquaintance with Christianity, perhaps even by some who would not count themselves religious at all. Using specifically Christian terms, however, the awe and mystery of religious consciousness can be identified with the love of God, a love which engages all one's heart, soul, mind, and strength (Deut 6:5; Mk 12:30) and from which "neither death, nor life, nor angels, nor principalities, nor present things, nor future things, nor powers, nor height, nor depth, nor any other creature will be able to separate us" (Rom 8:38-39). On this love there is neither inner restriction (*all* one's heart) nor outer condition (nor any other creature). Consequently, in the same way that human love in friendships and families can and does direct and redirect the conscious living of friends and spouses, parents and children, so the unbounded love of God can and does transform the whole of one's feeling, thinking, and choosing, and with it one's total outlook and attitude toward the world that conscious acts relate to the conscious subject.

Again, following Rom 5:5, the love of God may be identified with the gift of the Holy Spirit and thus, to use theological terms, with sanctifying grace. Within the framework of an older theology that conceived grace in metaphysical terms as an entitative habit, there could be reasonable doubt whether grace is conscious. But one advantage of the present account is that— unlike the soul, its potencies, and its habits—the subject, its acts, and the dynamic states they define can all be found among the data of one's own experience. It follows that for a theology which derives basic terms and relations from introspective inquiry, in the sense of self-appropriation mentioned above, there is in principle no objection to affirming that grace is experienced in and as consciousness. Accordingly, religious consciousness as gift, as dynamic state of unstinting love, might be identified with operative grace and, as the ground of the conscious subject's acts of "love, joy, peace, patience, kindness, generosity, faithfulness, gentleness, self-control" (Gal 5:22), with cooperative

grace. Acceptance of the gift of "love divine, all loves excelling" becomes the basic meaning of conversion. Like the gift, the process of conversion is conscious, but not, for that reason alone, understood or known or chosen. Not uncommonly it is recognized retrospectively, as the emergence of a shift in the pattern and texture of one's attitudes, outlook, beliefs, approvals, prayers. Insofar as religious consciousness suffuses every level of intentional activity, the experience of conversion, the fruit of God's grace, will be as wide as the experience of life.

See also CONSCIENCE; CONVERSION; EXPERIENCE; FREEDOM; GRACE; INTENTION, INTENTIONALITY; MIND; SELF.

Bibliography: B. Lonergan, *Collection* (New York: Herder and Herder, 1967), chaps. 14–16, and *A Third Collection* (New York: Paulist, 1985), chaps. 5, 8–10. K. Rahner, *Theology and the Spiritual Life,* Theological Investigations 3 (Baltimore: Helicon, 1967), chap. 6, and *More Recent Writings,* Theological Investigations 4 (Baltimore: Helicon, 1966), chap. 7.

CHARLES C. HEFLING, JR.

CONSECRATION

Consecration indicates the total dedication of a person or thing to God. The most common application of this term is to the bread and wine that is transformed into the Body and Blood of Jesus at Eucharist. The term is also used to designate the ordination of a priest as bishop. When cemeteries, church buildings, and sacred vessels are blessed, they are spoken of as having been consecrated.

Baptism is the fundamental sacrament of personal consecration. Vows taken in a religious community further dedicate a person to the service of God's people in a particular congregation ratified by the authority of the Church.

Individual and personal consecrations to the Blessed Virgin Mary, the Sacred Heart, or St. Joseph common in the recent past, for example, were intended to draw one into a deeper relationship with the Lord Jesus.

See also BAPTISM; EUCHARIST; VOWS.

Bibliography: J. Lozano, *Life as Parable: Reinterpreting the Religious Life* (New York: Paulist, 1986).

JULIA UPTON, R.S.M.

CONSUMERISM

Consumerism is a worldview in which consumption of material goods is understood as the source of personal and social good. The result of ongoing technological advances, consumerism views individuals primarily in terms of what they consume. It depends on a vast advertising endeavor to convince people to consume more and different items by steadily increasing demand for immediate sensory pleasure. In this sense, consumerism is related to materialism and secularism. With little or no view of the human person as a spiritual being, consumerism focuses entirely on the perceived physical realities of this world. In its worst forms, it exploits the weakest and most vulnerable in society, encouraging alcoholism, chemical abuse, and depersonalized and compulsive sexual behavior, at least indirectly.

Besides being the most recent manifestation of the vice of avarice or greed, consumerism has other serious effects on spirituality. Evangelical simplicity is not valued; instead, consumers are encouraged to concern themselves with accumulating and using more and more goods. Note the replacement of the value "good" by the object "goods." Unlike the admonition of 1 Pet 3:4, "Your adornment [should be] rather the hidden character of the heart, expressed in the imperishable beauty of a gentle and calm disposition . . .," consumerism values things that will fade and need to be consumed again and again. Things possessed replace "the hidden character of the heart." An obsession with the appearance of youth replaces "the imperishable

beauty of a gentle and calm disposition." Since dispositions and character are not marketable commodities, they have no meaning in a consumer society.

Consumption becomes the source of identity. Instead of finding one's personal reality in the experience of interiority, in one's capacity to know, to feel, and to love, one finds it in possessions. In a consumer society, "I am because I consume or possess." This is devastatingly apparent among children unable to distinguish what they want from what they need, unable even to distinguish what they want from what advertisers have told them they want. Various groups have expressed grave concern over exploitation of children in this way by television advertising. Studies indicate, however, that adult consumers are equally nondiscriminating.

Nonreligious meditation and relaxation techniques are marketed to replace a personal relationship with the spiritual dimension of reality. The depersonalization of relationships and their replacement by things manifest themselves in a breakdown of a sense of solidarity with the rest of the human family. Because consumerism depends on those with the resources to purchase, it exalts the powerful and wealthy and ignores the poor and marginalized. For wealthy members of a consumer society, the ready availability of immediate gratification helps mask the suffering of those outside the system. For those without resources, consumption becomes the one thing most desired. Dominical sayings about the blessedness of the poor are ignored or are incomprehensible within this framework.

Consumerism ultimately loses contact with the reality of the human person. Persons, like things, become expendable. Gospel demands for justice fall on deaf ears, drowned out by the louder demands of the advertising industry, which serves to keep the endless cycle of consumption turning. Because the media are dependent on the advertising industry for most of their income, journalism itself is controlled by the consumerist agenda. Thus society controls the flow of information, especially information that would undermine commercial interests. Governments have often shown themselves ineffective in dealing with the issue, although social justice activists make their voices heard.

Consumerism is a pervasive element in First World nations and represents an attractive though strongly anti-evangelical culture. That it should appear as a concern in Pope John Paul II's first encyclical, *Redemptor Hominis,* as well as in the writings of those considered liberal social activists, testifies to its importance as a part of the spiritual landscape of the latter part of the twentieth century.

See also DEADLY SINS; JUSTICE; MATERIALISM; POVERTY; SECULARISM; SIMPLICITY; VIRTUE.

Bibliography: J. Kavanaugh, *Following Christ in a Consumer Society* (Maryknoll, N.Y.: Orbis, 1981).

MICHAEL DODD, O.C.D.

CONTEMPLATION, CONTEMPLATIVE PRAYER

In the history of spirituality the term *contemplation* has been given many different meanings. What is basic is that it has to do with awareness of the presence of God apprehended not by thought but by love. *Contemplation* is often used interchangeably with *mysticism,* though the latter is a more abstract term, applied, somewhat loosely at times, to a number of phenomena that relate human creatures to God. Still, mystical prayer often serves as a synonym for contemplative prayer, though generally for infused or mystical contemplation, the highest form of such prayer. At times *meditation* has been used as a synonym for contemplation. This is an unfortunate usage, because meditation is generally

understood to involve discursive reasoning, something foreign to true contemplation. Reasoning tends to separate, for it involves a subject thinking and an object thought about.

While contemplation has to do with the presence of God, it should not be thought of as making "acts of the presence of God." It is rather a way of making oneself aware of the presence of God who is always there. Awareness, which is central to contemplation, is a very different experience from thinking: it tends always to be unitive. A true sense of awareness reduces the distance between me and that of which I am aware; a very deep sense of awareness closes the gap between us. It brings us together. It unites. In contemplation my subjectivity becomes one with the subjectivity of God, and I as a separate entity seem to disappear. What this means is that in contemplation I put off my false self, my empirical ego, and find my true self in God. While that true self is distinct from God, in the sense that I am not God, it is inseparable from God: it cannot *be* apart from God.

What is true of the self is true of all reality. The contemplative sees everything in unity and therefore rejects any dualism that would separate God from creation. It is this experience of nondualism which, as will be pointed out, resolves the problem so often cited in books on contemplation, namely, the apparent conflict between contemplation and action.

Etymology

Etymologically, the word *contemplation* derives from the Latin *templum,* a diminutive of *tempus.* Generally translated as "time," *tempus* has as its primary meaning "a division or section of time." Among the Romans the *templum* was a space in the sky or on the earth sectioned off for the augurs to read the omens. It came, therefore, to refer to a sacred space, marked off from other space, where the augurs would examine the entrails of birds. Thus the temple was the place where certain sacred persons looked at the "insides of things" (animals) to discover divine meanings and purposes. Contemplation would designate not so much the place but the actual "looking" at the insides of reality. Looking at the insides of reality, we find, if we go deep enough, that of themselves they are nothing. They *are* only because at the level where we discover their nothingness, we discover at the same time a source that is their origin and the ground in which they find their identity. "Looking at" that source, we are "looking at" God.

The Greek word that approximates the Latin *contemplatio* is *theōria,* from the verb *theōrein,* which means "to look at something intently and for a purpose." Some of the Greek Fathers use *theōria* to describe what later came to be called "natural" contemplation, which finds traces of God in created things. They would use the word *theologia* to designate the highest form of contemplation, direct and total awareness of God, in which there is immediate experience of oneness with God.

The New Testament

The New Testament book that speaks most strikingly about the oneness with God which is the meaning of contemplation is the Fourth Gospel. Not without reason is the author called "John the Theologian." The underlying motif of chapters 14 to 17, as of many other sections of the Gospel, is Jesus' oneness with God. He not only *does* what the Father does, but he *is* what the Father is. Moreover, his prayer is that his disciples may be one as the Father is in him and he in the Father. The Fourth Gospel frequently uses the verb *menein,* "to abide," "to live on in," to describe Jesus' oneness with the disciples.

The same theme is found in Paul's teaching on discipleship. For Paul, the community of those who profess that "Jesus is Lord" is made up not of isolated individuals but of persons joined to one another in a series of interlocking relationships that make them one with God in Christ. This oneness in discipleship is what Paul means by the "Body of Christ" and by the oft-repeated phrase "to be in Christ."

History

The history of contemplative prayer, in Eastern and Western Christianity, is too vast and complicated to attempt an orderly presentation in a relatively short space. This entry will try to suggest some highlights, without striving to be complete. First, two important figures from among the Eastern Fathers will be discussed, both for the value of what they had to say and as paradigms for understanding contemplation. Origen and Gregory of Nyssa represent two trends that influenced the subsequent history of spirituality. After showing their influence on later writers and offering a brief look at medieval and post-Reformation thought on contemplation, the article will conclude with a discussion of the contemporary period.

Origen (ca. 185–255), of the school of Alexandria, is the theologian of light. For him, the end of the human being recapitulates his or her beginning. There was first the primitive state of loving contemplation, in which all were in the image and likeness of God. The Fall was the loss of the divine likeness, though not of the image. The goal of redemption was the recovery of the likeness to God and the return to the original state of contemplation.

That return involved three stages, each a movement of increasing illumination. These stages are seen as a journey back to God and to paradise, a journey that Origen compares to the Israelites' journey from Egypt to the Promised Land. First, there is a moral illumination, a movement away from sin and a conversion to the virtues (*praxis*). Then there is the stage of natural contemplation (*theōria*), in which the soul comes to see the created world in God. Finally, there is the contemplation of God himself (*theologia*), which is a return to the beginning and a recovery of the likeness of God. It should be noted that this is progressively a movement toward greater and greater light. Origen knows nothing, or at least says nothing, about a dark night of the soul or of any "knowing through not knowing."

Gregory of Nyssa (ca. 335–395), one of the Cappadocian Fathers, represents a different strain of contemplative understanding. It is found especially in his *Life of Moses*, which speaks, as Origen had done, of three stages. But the stages are reversed: the movement is from light to darkness. The *Life of Moses* is built around this movement. There is, first, Moses' experience of light (*phōs*) in the burning bush episode of Exodus 3. Then there are his two ascents, each time into a deeper darkness: first the ascent into the darkness of the cloud (*nephelē*) in Exodus 19 and then into the thick darkness (*gnophos*) in Exodus 33, in which God is experienced but as unknown.

The two ways of understanding contemplation, represented by Origen and Gregory respectively, have come to be known as the *kataphatic way,* the way of affirmation (in Greek: *kataphasis*), and the *apophatic way,* the way of negation or denial (in Greek: *apophasis*). The kataphatic way is the way of light, such as is seen in Origen. One talks about God by affirming of God all the perfections seen in creatures. The human experiences of motherhood, fatherhood, justice, truthfulness, compassion serve as so many windows whereby one can peer through the created world to the reality of God. Yet these affirmations are limited—they tell us *about* God; they can never reach God's inmost reality.

That is why there is this other way of talking about God (represented by Gregory of Nyssa): the apophatic way, the way of negation. No ideas, thoughts, words, or symbols can reach God as God is in his own reality. To attain to that reality one must go "barehanded," if you will, with all conceptual gloves removed, into the darkness. One puts out the lights of the mind and enters, through love, into the unknown.

Even though the apophatic way is a way of darkness, contemplatives not infrequently speak of the "apophatic light." The tradition abounds in paradoxical expressions such as "dazzling darkness" and "dark light," because there is real knowledge achieved in the apophatic way. But it is knowledge that defies human articulation. Consequently, the apophatic way is often referred to as "knowing by not knowing."

One of the interesting "laws" of the spiritual life, developed by Gregory of Nyssa but having something of a contemporary ring to it, is what the patristic scholar Jean Daniélou has called *epektasis.* This means striving ever more to be perfect, never quite succeeding, yet never ceasing from the striving. For Gregory, a never-ending progress toward perfection replaces the Platonic static unity that represents perfection for Origen's Greek-influenced system.

The three stages of spiritual progress, described by both Origen and Gregory, have continued to find their place in the tradition of spirituality, stylized as the purgative, illuminative, and unitive ways. Likewise, two images they used to describe the path of ascent involved in these three stages have had an enduring influence: (1) the mountain (used later by Dante, John of the Cross, and Thomas Merton) and (2) the ladder, based on Jacob's dream at Bethel (Gen 28:10-15). Guigo II the Carthusian (d. 1188) was one of many who used the image of the ladder. He sums up in his *Scala Claustralium (The Ladder of Monks)* a long-established way of the contemplative life: *lectio divina,* which has fed the spirituality of countless anonymous monks through the centuries. There are but four rungs to Guigo's ladder, yet it is a wondrous ladder, reaching from earth, piercing through the clouds as it reaches for the very secrets of heaven. Guigo describes the rungs of the ladder: "*Lectio* (reading) is a careful study of the Scriptures in which the person's whole attention is engaged; *meditatio* is an action of the mind probing the Scriptures and seeking with reason's help to know the truth hidden therein; *oratio* (prayer) is the intent turning of the heart to God asking him to rid us of evil and obtain for us what is good; *contemplatio* is the devout lifting of the mind to God in such a way that it transcends itself and comes to taste the joys of an everlasting sweetness" (PL 40:998; translation mine).

In addition to Origen and Gregory, another major influence on medieval spirituality was the pseudonymous works written about the 6th century but attributed to Paul's Athenian convert Dionysius the Areopagite. His treatise *The Divine Names* deals with the attributes of God, beginning with his goodness and ending with his unity. It represents the kataphatic approach, making affirmations about God, though insisting that our affirmations always fall short of God, who is essentially unknowable. That is why his final word about Christian prayer comes in another work, *Mystical Theology,* which espouses the apophatic tradition. It begins with a prayer and a word of counsel: "Timothy, my advice to you, as you look for a sight of the mysterious things, is to leave behind you everything perceptible and understandable, all that is not and all that is, and with your understanding laid aside, to strive upward as much as you can toward union with him who is beyond all being and knowledge" (*Pseudo-Dionysius,* trans. Colm Luibheid, Classics of Western Spirituality, Mahwah, N.J.: Paulist, 1987, p. 135).

Dionysius' works became known in the West in the 9th century through the Latin translations of John Scotus Erigena (ca. 810–ca.877) and in 14th-century England through a translation by the anonymous author of *The Cloud of Unknowing.* The latter work was part of the flowering of mysticism in 14th-century England that also saw the writings of Richard Rolle (1300–1349), Julian of Norwich (1343–1415?), Walter Hilton (d. 1396), and the

rather eccentric Margery Kempe (b. ca. 1373). Thomas Merton described these English writers as mystics "whose humility is witty, whose ardor is simple and direct, and whose love for God is the whole offering of their complete self, not divided and destroyed but unified and transfigured in 'self-naughting' and abandonment to his infinite mercy" (*Mystics and Zen Masters,* New York: Farrar, Straus and Giroux, 1967, pp. 135–136).

The 14th century also saw writings on the life of contemplative prayer flourish in the Rhineland and the Netherlands. The most notable perhaps were those of Meister Eckhart (1260–1327), a Dominican preacher and a great speculative mystic whose bold preaching of the dark way to God bore fruit in a lay movement of followers called the "Friends of God." John Tauler (1300–1361), also a Dominican and a respected preacher, was also linked with the Friends of God, as was Henry Suso (1295–1365). Eckhart, whose preaching was the deepest and the most controversial, spoke with passion about the unity of human beings with God. "There is," he said, "something uncreated, something divine in the soul." For Eckhart, above God is the Godhead, the source and end of all things. It is hidden darkness, unknown and never to be known. Yet there is in the human person a divine "spark" that is destined to return to its divine source. After his death several of his propositions were condemned as heretical, though it is doubtful that his accusers really understood what he was saying.

Sixteenth-century Spain produced impressive witness to the life of contemplative prayer. Ignatius Loyola (1491–1556) was a man of deep contemplative prayer; his *Spiritual Exercises* were intended to lead those who made them into such prayer. The exercises exerted an enormous influence on subsequent spirituality. It is a sad fact that after Ignatius' day their meaning was often misinterpreted. It has been left for the 20th century to recover the true contemplative dimensions of his spirituality.

Teresa of Avila (1515–1582) and John of the Cross (1542–1591) worked together to reform the Carmelite Order, and each wrote brilliantly about the life of contemplation. John of the Cross was well trained in Scholastic theology and was a gifted lyric poet. *The Ascent of Mount Carmel* and *The Dark Night of the Soul* are his most influential prose writings. Both works speak of different levels of detachment that must be achieved in making the spiritual ascent. John of the Cross was clearly in the apophatic tradition of contemplative prayer. Teresa, who had little formal education, wrote what she experienced in prayer. She was a practical woman and a highly gifted contemplative. Her *Life, The Interior Castle,* and *The Way of Perfection* are unexcelled in their presentation of the kataphatic tradition. These two Carmelite saints moved in different directions, but their goal was the same: union with God.

The period after the Reformation up until recent times, with a few exceptions and apart from what was happening in the monastic life, must be seen as an arid period for contemplation and a risky time for espousing the apophatic tradition. The specter of Quietism—a heresy that rejected all forms of asceticism and prayer, except for a pseudo-mystical union with God that separated the Quietists from other people—hung uneasily over the lives of people of prayer from the Council of Trent (convened 1545) to the Second Vatican Council (1962–1965). Contemplatives like John of the Cross, Teresa of Avila, and Ignatius Loyola at times found it necessary to tone down what they wanted to say for fear of incurring the ire of the Inquisition, which seemed to sniff the scent of Quietism everywhere.

Contemplation in the 20th Century

Outside the monastic tradition, contemplation received little emphasis in the life of the Christian West until the 20th century. In the early 20th century lone voices like Evelyn Underhill (1875–1941) and Baron Friedrich von Hügel (1852–1925) wrote about mysticism. But it may be said that the contemporary revival of interest in the contemplative way of life came as a result of the spiritual emptiness and the search for the higher values of the spirit that came in the wake of World War II. Some people looked to Eastern religions for the spiritual dimension they felt was missing in their lives. Others came to discover that the spiritual way of life they sought was present, if sometimes hidden, in their own Christian tradition.

Not the only, but perhaps the most influential, leader in that discovery was the Cistercian monk Thomas Merton (1915–1968) of the Abbey of Gethsemani in Kentucky. Some of his early writings, for instance *Seeds of Contemplation* and his bestselling autobiography, *The Seven Storey Mountain,* betray an elitist attitude toward contemplation that would restrict true contemplation to the monastic life. Yet Merton calls people "in the world" to try to become as much like monks as possible. They could at least be "masked contemplatives," persons who experience God in their lives without actually being aware that they are doing so.

Merton has been widely read by people of varied religious backgrounds. Many readers, ignoring the elitist attitude his writings sometimes betray, have "translated" what he says about monastic contemplation into terms more congenial to their own way of life. It must also be said that as he matured in his own understanding of life and shook off the sharp dichotomy between the sacred and the profane, Merton moved toward the more egalitarian view that contemplation is the goal of life for all and therefore must be attainable by all. His position on this matter is not always unambiguous, but it is safe to say that he would have seen the universal call to holiness issued by Vatican II as vindicating the view that all are called to the contemplative life.

Merton's writings consistently express his firm preference for the apophatic way. Thus he writes: "Now, while the Christian contemplative must certainly develop by study the theological understanding of concepts about God, he is called mainly to penetrate the wordless darkness and apophatic light of an experience beyond concepts. . . . Relinquishing every attempt to grasp God in limited human concepts, the contemplatives' act of submission and faith attains to His presence as the ground of every human experience and His reality as the ground of being itself" (*Contemplation in a World of Action,* New York: Doubleday Image Books, 1973, p. 186).

Contemplation and Action

Merton also led the way in overcoming the pseudo-problem of a supposed conflict between contemplation and action. Well known to Merton readers is the contemplative insight that came to him in an experience he had in March 1958 as he was standing in the middle of a shopping district in Louisville. Seeing the many people coming out of the stores, he was suddenly overwhelmed, as he put it, "with the realization that I loved all those people, that they were mine and I theirs, that we could not be alien to one another, even though we were total strangers. It was like waking from a dream of separateness, of spurious self-isolation in a special world, the world of renunciation and supposed holiness. The whole illusion of a separate holy existence is a dream" (*Conjectures of a Guilty Bystander,* New York: Doubleday Image Books, 1966, p. 158).

This experience, which was profoundly contemplative, took place not in the monastery but on a street corner in a busy city. Merton's reflections show how profoundly he came to see the responsibility of contemplatives to understand what is going on in their own times and to respond to historical needs out of a contemplative perspec-

tive. In contemplation Merton discovered God, and in God he discovered people inseparable from God and from one another. The challenge of his writings, especially those on social issues, is to call today's contemplatives to the same discovery.

What resolved the supposed conflict between contemplation and action for Merton was his awareness of his unity in God with all peoples. It is to this awareness that contemplation inevitably leads. In this deep experience of nondualism, contemplatives find that just as they cannot separate God from God's creation, so they cannot separate contemplation from concern for, and engagement in, the needs and problems of the age in which they live. A true experience of contemplation exposes the supposed dichotomy between contemplation and action for the pseudo-problem that it is.

See also AFFIRMATIVE WAY; ATTENTION, ATTENTIVENESS; EXPERIENCE; LECTIO DIVINA; MEDITATION; MYSTICISM; NEGATIVE WAY; PRAYER; PRAXIS; PRESENCE, PRESENCE OF GOD; QUIETISM.

Bibliography: J. Lemaitre, "Contemplation," *D.Spir.,* 2, cols. 1643–1871. C. Jones, G. Wainwright, E. Yarnold, eds., *The Study of Spirituality* (New York: Oxford, 1986). M. Cox, *Handbook of Christian Spirituality* (New York: Harper & Row, 1985).

WILLIAM H. SHANNON

CONTEMPORARY SPIRITUALITY

Given the vast scope of the topic, this entry will concentrate on trends in Catholic spirituality in the United States since the Second Vatican Council, keeping in mind recent changes in society, culture and Church. Since the end of World War II large numbers of Catholics have moved from their urban neighborhoods and parishes into middle-class suburbs, prompting a new search for meaning and community. At the same time poor Catholics, largely African-American and Hispanic, who are concentrated in urban areas long for spiritual and economic liberation. The growing women's movement has spawned a vibrant feminist spirituality that retrieves elements of the prophetic biblical tradition to challenge patriarchal structures, sexist attitudes, and dualistic thinking. The environmental crisis has given birth to a new ecospirituality that stresses the common human responsibility to care for the earth. Finally, world events, including mass starvation in the Southern Hemisphere, the easing of East-West tensions, and the liberation of eastern Europe have prompted a new global spirituality that recognizes the interdependence of all in the one human family.

Cultural changes accompanying the new patterns of social life have also influenced the world of spirituality. The tremendous increase in the numbers of Catholics attending college has produced a more enlightened and self-critical spirituality. The intensification of the spirit of individualism that began in the 1960s has prodded many Catholics to join small intentional communities.

Contemporary spirituality has been affected by a growing recognition of the ambivalence built into our culture. Vietnam and Watergate, racism and sexism, street crime and drug addiction have shattered utopian dreams. Destructive divorces, compulsive behavior, and dysfunctional families have engendered recovery programs and support groups. The plight of homeless persons, abused children, and neglected elderly has moved some to a more compassionate spirituality. Individuals struck by the limitations of the Protestant work ethic have been developing a Catholic spirituality of work and leisure.

At the same time our culture continues to provide marvelous opportunities for spiritual growth. Blessed with freedom, we can explore our faith and find appropriate ways to practice it. Cultural ideals such as self-actualization, cooperation on projects, educational achievement, and community service provide encouragement to live the gospel fully. Individuals and groups working for social change can draw on the inclusive promises of the American Dream.

The Second Vatican Council unleashed major theoretical and practical changes that have had a profound impact on contemporary spirituality. By emphasizing biblical images of the Church, such as the People of God and the Body of Christ, the council prompted Catholics to assume greater responsibility for the Church and their own spiritual development. Changes in the liturgy have fostered a more communal spirituality focused on the Eucharist as the font of Catholic piety. The explicit engagement with the modern world undertaken by the bishops has encouraged Catholics to bring gospel values to the cultural, social, economic, and political spheres of life. The council's positive evaluation of other religious traditions has prompted a remarkable increase in ecumenical and interfaith dialogue and cooperation. By emphasizing the importance of the Bible and espousing important elements of modern biblical interpretation, Vatican II nudged Catholics toward a more scripturally oriented spirituality. Finally, the council has greatly affected contemporary spirituality by reminding laypersons of their importance and dignity, their call to holiness, their essential role in the Church, and their task of humanizing the world. As the laity has gradually assumed its proper role, many priests and members of religious orders are moved to redefine their own positions and to develop new forms of spirituality.

The historical development of spirituality since Vatican II is a complex mixture of conservative and liberal tendencies, of interaction among clergy, religious, and laity, and of new movements designed to respond to the changes in society and culture. During and immediately after the council many Catholics serious about spiritual growth turned from the traditional parish-based organizations such as the Altar Society and the St. Vincent de Paul

Society to transparochial groups like the CFM (Christian Family Movement), which combined a biblically based spirituality with concrete actions to improve life in the family, the neighborhood, and society as a whole. The "see, judge and act" strategy employed by the CFM and other similar organizations gave participants an excellent methodology for continued involvement in the task of promoting justice and peace in the world. Throughout the postconciliar period there has been a tension between those who have stressed transparochial movements as the primary source of renewal and those who insist that vibrant parishes should be the main source of spiritual nourishment.

The promulgation of *Humanae Vitae* in 1968 by Pope Paul VI had a profound effect on Catholic spirituality. Some saw it as an important reaffirmation of enduring values and were strengthened in their traditional piety. Others, bitterly upset because their hopes for change had been frustrated, began to develop a more autonomous spiritual life less dependent on official Church guidance.

By the late 1960s three new movements—Marriage Encounter, Cursillo, and the charismatic renewal—began to grow in popularity. These movements were more concerned with growth in the inner spiritual life than with the social activism encouraged by groups like CFM. All three movements have retained their power and influence because they supply spiritual experiences often not available in the average parish. For example, the charismatic renewal, which began at Duquesne University in Pittsburgh in 1967 and became a powerful worldwide movement, fosters intense Spirit-filled prayer experiences quite different in tone from ordinary parish liturgies.

Beginning in the 1970s the Church experienced a remarkable growth in lay ministry, leading to new efforts to develop a viable lay spirituality. By the 1980s lay ministers constituted 83 percent of the leadership within parishes. As lay people experienced difficulties in these ministries, such as low salaries, unrealistic expectations, and difficulties with the clergy, they found a need to gather together in small groups for support and spiritual nourishment. This pattern of Catholics with similar interests gathering for mutual support extended to other groups and causes. By 1979 it was estimated that there were as many as 15,000 of these intentional communities in the United States.

In the mid-1970s women became more dissatisfied with the patriarchal structures of the Church. Various strategies emerged, ranging from total disaffiliation to working within the system. Some women have adopted the approach of remaining active in their parishes while also participating with kindred spirits in faith-sharing groups that provide spiritual nourishment. In 1976 the "Call to Action" conference was held in Detroit after two years of preparation and consultation with all sectors of the Church. The delegates passed numerous resolutions, including calls for greater understanding for divorced and remarried Catholics, greater sensitivity to the needs of sexual minorities, ratification of the Equal Rights Amendment, and a national commission on economic justice. These resolutions, which combined internal Church reform and action on behalf of justice in the world, serve as a continuing reminder of the need for a contemporary spirituality nourished within the Church but active in the world.

In 1977, the Chicago Declaration of Christian Concern, issued by forty-seven prominent Chicago Catholics, including priests, laity, and members of religious orders, made a plea that laypersons be encouraged to take up their true ministry to humanize the world rather than expend their energies on ministries within the Church. This declaration fueled the continuing effort to develop a marketplace spirituality for laypersons striving to meet their responsibilities in the world. In 1980 the United States Catholic bishops responded to this quest with their statement *Called and Gifted,* which recognized the laity's responsibility to transform the secular world but also extolled lay ministries within the Church. The document spoke of the call to adulthood, which involves a greater understanding and commitment to the faith and a daily struggle to live out Christian values in the family, school, neighborhood, government, and work. It also repeated the Second Vatican Council's insistence that all the members of the Church are called to holiness, a constant theme in contemporary spirituality.

During the 1970s the tendency to form transparochial groups for spiritual growth was balanced by programs to promote spiritual development through the renewal of parish life. One of the most popular, a three-year program called RENEW, which was begun in Newark, New Jersey, in 1978, has been used by thousands of parishes across the country. It represents the growing conviction that vibrant parishes are crucial to the development of a solid and enduring contemporary spirituality.

The bishops greatly influenced the spirituality of Catholics in the United States by publishing their pastoral letters on peace and the economy in 1983 and 1986 respectively. Through these documents the Church entered the public debate on crucial policy questions as a dialogue partner. Thus Catholics were called once more to recognize that a vital spirituality involves responsibility for humanizing the world. The continuing national debate over abortion, as well as other life issues, has also reminded Catholics that their inner convictions cannot be divorced from public policy questions.

Statistical Surveys

Social scientists have provided helpful data on changes in the religious attitudes and practices of Catholics since Vatican II. Especially useful for our purpose is the material collected in the middle 1980s and summarized by Joseph Gremillion and Jim Castelli in *The Emerging Parish: The Notre Dame Study of Catholic Life Since Vatican II* (San Francisco: Harper & Row, 1987), an extensive study of core Catholics who are active parish members. Since the Mass remains at the center of Catholic spirituality, changes in Eucharistic piety are particularly revealing. Broad-based Gallup polls indicate that in 1958 about 74 percent of Catholics attended Mass weekly, while in the 1980s only 53 percent went weekly. Most of this decline occurred between 1969 and 1975, and the percentage has stayed rather steady since then. The Notre Dame Study indicates that 80 percent of those attending Mass receive Communion, a dramatic increase over preconciliar days. Active Catholics have generally accepted extensive liturgical changes that represent a more active communal piety. For example, 67 percent are happy that hymns are sung at Mass, and only 4 percent wish they were omitted. Even the least acceptable change—the introduction of women as Eucharistic ministers—is opposed by only 18 percent. An encouraging sign is that the more college education Catholics receive, the more likely they are to go to Mass regularly. Thus 61 percent of college graduates said they attended Mass within the week, compared to 47 percent of high school graduates. A gender difference is also evident, with 61 percent of women and 44 percent of men reporting that they attended Mass in the last seven days.

The Bible is playing an increasingly important role in Catholic spirituality. This is exemplified in the broader range of readings provided at weekend Masses and by the greater emphasis placed on homilies based on Scripture. Between 1977 and 1986 the numbers of Catholics who said they read the Bible in the past thirty days rose from 23 to 32 percent. Nevertheless, Catholics remain far more likely to turn to private prayer and liturgical celebration for their spiritual nourishment than to Scripture reading.

The sacrament of penance has traditionally been associated with spiritual development. After the council there was a drop of twenty percentage points in the frequency of confession. Since 1971, however, the percentage of Catholics celebrating the sacrament has remained rather constant. Moreover, the more often Catholics participate in communal penance services, the more likely they are to make a private confession. Although the style and frequency of confession have changed, the sacrament remains a viable element in the spiritual life of about 75 percent of the Catholic population.

Since the council the private prayer life of Catholics has changed. Today Catholics are less likely to pray to Mary and the saints and to attend Benediction, novenas, and the Stations of the Cross. The prayer life of Catholics has become more Christocentric. Catholics under the age of forty are far more likely to direct their prayer to God and to exclude Mary and the saints than Catholics over forty. Mary remains an important figure in Catholic piety, even though parish devotions centered on her have declined.

The surveys also corroborate the general perception that postconciliar Catholic spirituality has taken on a greater ecumenical flavor. Around 70 percent of active Catholics support intercommunion. Over a third of parishioners want their parishes to put more emphasis on improving contacts with Protestant churches in their neighborhoods. Moreover, they are more likely to discuss their religious beliefs with non-Catholics who hold similar religious views than with fellow Catholics who have a different outlook.

The surveys done in the 1980s support the perception that developments in society, culture, and Church have produced significant changes in postconciliar Catholic spirituality. In general, Catholic piety has shifted priorities, placing more importance on Christ, Scripture, and liturgy and less on Mary and popular devotions. Catholics have become more open to ecumenical and interfaith dialogue and cooperation. Catholic piety remains heavily sacramental, but there is greater emphasis on the quality of the celebrations rather than the quantity.

Pluralism

One of the results of all these changes is that Catholic spirituality has become more self-consciously pluralistic. Of course, Catholics have traditionally distinguished different styles of spirituality, such as Benedictine, Carthusian, Franciscan, Dominican, Carmelite, and Jesuit. Popular devotion to saints as diverse as St. Augustine and St. Thérèse of Lisieux contained an implicit understanding of diverse forms of Christian discipleship. Today, however, Catholics are more aware not only of a great variety of authentic Christian approaches to the Christian life but also of the possibility of freely appropriating one or more of them. This pluralism appears from many perspectives. The most fundamental distinction is between those who hold to a classical spirituality rooted in a static worldview and the growing number who have adopted a contemporary approach based on a dynamic evolutionary understanding of the world. From a theological viewpoint, some Catholics emphasize the transcendence of God, the divinity of Christ, and the institutional model of the Church, while others stress the divine immanence, the humanity of Jesus, and the communal aspects of the Church. The average parish contains conservatives who prefer traditional forms of piety such as the rosary, Benediction, and Marian devotions and progressives who are more attuned to Scripture reading, liturgical participation, and faith-sharing groups.

Catholics find their primary nourishment from diverse sources, including Scripture reading, liturgical participation, private meditation, and popular devotions. They participate in various groups, ranging from traditional parish organizations and conservative secular institutes to charismatic prayer groups and radical coalitions of peace activists. Within the Church, laypersons, clergy, and members of religious communities are seeking in their own ways a spirituality that fits their distinctive vocations and lifestyles. The feminist spirituality that has blossomed in the last couple of decades has spawned new efforts to develop a viable masculine spirituality. Some Catholics prefer to make the spiritual journey in relative isolation, trusting their own inner compass, and others are more comfortable traveling in groups and seeking direction from spiritual guides. One type of Catholic piety emphasizes the vertical relationship with God, while another stresses the horizontal relationship with people. Catholics experience their religious heritage as tending to be either liberating or constricting.

Many Catholics continue to find their spiritual agenda as well as their support and guidance almost completely from their own religious heritage. At the same time, a growing number are benefiting from dialogue with various other traditions and disciplines, ranging from Orthodox Christianity to humanistic psychology.

Recent surveys add greater precision to our understanding of this pluralism. In the religious realm, for example, 49 percent of Catholics consider themselves to be leaning in a liberal direction, while 34 percent lean to the conservative side. In line with this self-evaluation, 47 percent of Catholics think that non-Christians can go to heaven, while 37 percent say they cannot; 47 percent accept evolution under God's direction, while 38 percent believe in creationism; 53 percent accept or believe that the Bible is the inspired word of God, while 32 percent hold the more conservative position that it is the literal word of God. In terms of fundamental spiritual orientation, 39 percent of Catholic parishioners have an individualistic spirituality, emphasizing their personal relationship with God; 18 percent have a communal spirituality that focuses on the achievement of a peaceful and just social order; and 21 percent have an integrated spirituality that combines both individualistic and communal values. Politically, 55 percent of Catholics describe themselves as right of center, and 33 percent left of center. On particular issues the pattern is mixed: 74 percent favor the registration of all firearms and 26 percent are opposed; 65 percent favor the death penalty for persons convicted of murder, with 34 percent opposed; 69 percent favor the Equal Rights Amendment, while 31 percent are opposed. In the middle 1980s, before the thaw in the Cold War, Catholics were evenly divided on the question of increasing spending for national defense.

Unity

Despite this pluralism, contemporary Catholic spirituality manifests a fundamental unity based on the essential elements of the Christian tradition. The Catholic ideal of unity in diversity is still alive today. Thus Catholics continue to believe in a gracious and merciful God who has been revealed definitively in Jesus Christ and mediated to us through the Church's tradition of Scripture, liturgy, and doctrine. Over 90 percent of Catholics feel that God loves them, and over 80 percent believe that they have a close personal relationship with God. The vast majority of Catholics have no doubt that Jesus was fully God and fully human, and that he is still alive and active today. Despite disagreements with Church leadership, most Catholics remain loyal to the Church. About 85 percent of those who were raised Catholic remain in the Church—a statistic that has remained constant since before the council. Catholic spirituality is still heavily sacramental as large numbers continue to make the Mass the center of their Christian lives and to turn to the sacraments as fitting ways of celebrating major life-events and of meeting spiritual needs.

Catholic morality at its best continues to emphasize the law of love, to accept the reality of sin, to believe in the superior power of grace, and to hope for eternal salvation.

Furthermore, participating in the life of the Church creates a distinctive Catholic imagination and sensibility. Catholics generally have an incarnational spirituality that appreciates the fundamental goodness of God's creation and recognizes the sacramental character of all of reality. For Catholics, God's grace is mediated through created reality, as well as through the Church and its official sacraments. Catholics have a positive sense of human nature, of society, and of the various forms of community life. They respect the rich and diverse Christian tradition and understand the universality of the Church's mission.

At the core of the Catholic imagination are warm and comforting images of God as gracious and intimate, lover and friend, mother and spouse. Based on his research, priest-sociologist Andrew Greeley claims that the prevalence of this distinctive Catholic imagination is not only verifiable but leads to predictable attitudes (see *The Catholic Myth,* New York: Scribner's, 1990). In comparison with Protestants, Catholics are more likely to value social relationships and to be more tolerant of diversity in their communities. They value the virtues of loyalty, obedience, and patience, while Protestants emphasize initiative, integrity, industry, and thrift. Catholics are especially offended by actions that violate the quality of life in the community. Because of their sacramental outlook, they are more likely to advocate social change. Greeley argues that these distinctive Catholic sensibilities have been kept intact since the council, despite the secularization of society and the continuing interaction of Catholics and Protestants in the United States. In fact, his studies show that since the council, younger Catholics have developed an even more positive image of God, suggesting that this focal point of the Catholic imagination will be maintained and even enhanced in the years ahead. If this holds true, then Catholic spirituality will continue to have a solid imaginative and doctrinal foundation as a source of unity in the midst of growing diversity.

Representative Figures

We can gain a better appreciation of important trends in contemporary spirituality by examining two representative figures who have lived out Catholic ideals in the United States: the Trappist monk Thomas Merton and the founder of the Catholic Worker Movement, Dorothy Day.

The original popularity of Thomas Merton (1915–1968) was based on his bestselling autobiographical work, *Seven Storey Mountain,* published in 1946, which described his conversion to Catholicism and his early years as a Trappist monk. His enduring popularity and still growing influence are rooted, however, in his subsequent writings, which reflect the struggles of his fascinating spiritual journey. The questions and tensions that haunted Merton's mind and heart are the abiding concerns of contemporary spirituality: how to relate and balance the life of prayer and action; how to reconcile care for nature and the use of modern technology; how to foster personal relationships that lead to God; how to balance the desire for freedom with the demands of authority; how to enter into fruitful dialogue with other religious traditions; and finally how to relate contemplation and the quest for justice.

Individuals struggling to develop a viable spiritual life today are attracted to Merton, not because he presented clear answers to all these questions, but because he described the questions so accurately, refused easy answers, offered helpful insights, lived out the tensions with great courage, and kept alive the hope that God was present in the search. For some people, Merton's struggles and even his personal failures enhance rather than diminish his credibility as a valuable spiritual guide.

Preconciliar spirituality in the United States had little room for doubt and questioning. The goals and methods of spiritual growth were clear. The real problem was to muster the willpower to follow through. Today the process is less clear and more difficult. Individuals report that the burden of making choices about spiritual goals and methods brings new anxieties and doubts. For many carrying this burden, Merton provides comfort and strength by validating their ambivalent experience.

Thomas Merton also represents those who have found traditional Scholastic theology inadequate for interpreting and guiding their spiritual journey. When Merton converted to Catholicism in 1938, he learned the neo-Thomistic theology espoused by Etienne Gilson and others. In his early writings he tried to work within this traditional system, but as time went on he found that his experiences and insights overflowed the fixed framework and static categories of the so-called perennial Thomistic theology. It seems that Merton never did find a comprehensive theological system that he could appropriate as his own. To his credit, he remained faithful to his own intuitions and was searching till the end of his life for an overarching perspective to encompass his expanding experiences.

In the decades after the council, Catholics trained in traditional Scholasticism, either directly through courses of study or indirectly through the Baltimore Catechism and Sunday sermons, have been challenged to reexamine this theology. Individuals with a strong classical mindset have tended to reaffirm the traditional approach as the authentic guide for their spiritual lives. Some persons who had already adopted an evolutionary worldview have found themselves naturally and comfortably drawn to a more contemporary theology to guide their spiritual journey. Others have experienced various degrees of shock and trauma in facing the inadequacies of the old system and in searching for a theo-logical outlook that adequately interprets their spiritual quest. Merton speaks an especially helpful word of encouragement to these honest but troubled searchers.

The autobiographical style often employed by Merton in his writings represents another feature of contemporary spirituality. Many people today are attracted by personal accounts of the spiritual journey that make the process concrete. Authors such as John Shea (*Stories of Faith*, Chicago: Thomas More, 1980), John Dunne (*The Way of All the Earth*, New York: Macmillan, 1972), and Henri Nouwen (*The Genesee Diary*, Garden City, N.Y.: Doubleday, 1976), who write in a personal narrative style, are popular because their approach illumines the spiritual life of the readers, encouraging them to examine their own stories. Spiritual guides who speak most personally speak most universally, as the continuing power of Augustine's *Confessions* reminds us. Small faith-sharing groups offer average believers an opportunity to tell their stories and to witness to the power of the Spirit working in their lives. Merton's rigorous honesty and his amazing capacity for self-criticism serve as a model for all who hope to grow spiritually by becoming better readers of their own life stories.

Merton longed to combine in his own heart the thoughts and practices of the various branches of the Christian tradition as well as the best insights of the other great world religions. He entered into intensive dialogue not only with Orthodox Christians, Protestants, Jews and Muslims but also with Chinese humanists and Zen Buddhists. He was especially attuned to the mystical element in these traditions. In his later years he became more fascinated with Eastern thought. He died in Bangkok, Thailand, on December 10, 1968, while on an Asian pilgrimage highlighted by an intense religious experience at a Buddhist shrine. Thus Merton epitomizes the ecumenical spirituality that is an important aspect of postconciliar Catholicism. Many

Catholics find nourishment in common worship services as well as ecumenical and interfaith cooperative efforts. Collegians with little sense of historical differences often move easily among various Christian denominations and groups searching for deeper meaning. The tradition of interfaith spirituality represented by Merton is found in other authors such as Raimundo Panikkar (*Myth, Faith and Hermeneutics,* New York: Paulist, 1979); William Johnston (*Christian Zen,* New York: Harper & Row, 1971); and Anthony DeMello (*Sadhana,* Garden City, N.Y.: Image Books, 1984). They have influenced contemporary spirituality by making insights from Eastern religions available to the Catholic world.

As a Trappist monk, Merton struggled to live a life of genuine solitude and prayerful reflection. His writings, such as his popular work *New Seeds of Contemplation* (New York: New Directions, 1972), which explore the nature and importance of contemplation resonate with Catholics who are struggling to maintain a calm heart and a clear mind in the midst of the great demands and stresses of everyday life. By refusing to offer detailed methods of prayer and by honestly admitting his failures to achieve peace of heart, Merton has encouraged serious searchers to find their own practical ways of maintaining a meditative spirit despite the immense pressures of the modern world.

Finally, Thomas Merton is an early forerunner of the continuing effort to combine the mystical and prophetic aspects of the Christian tradition in a viable spirituality that roots the works of justice in a rich inner life. He brought to the attention of a whole generation important representatives of diverse mystical traditions including Origen, Meister Eckhart, and John of the Cross. His own efforts to relate this tradition to the works of justice were signaled by his book *Conjectures of a Guilty Bystander* (Garden City, N.Y.: Image Books, 1968), which addressed important social issues of the times. Throughout the 1960s Merton continued to speak out against racism and the injustices that produce violence and war. Thus Catholic bystanders have an enduring prophetic message from a Trappist monk reminding them that genuine prayer must lead to active concern for the oppressed and suffering.

Most of the concerns of contemporary spirituality are addressed by Merton in his vast and wideranging writings. He did indeed live with the tensions that continue to challenge us today. The growing literature on Thomas Merton indicates his continuing appeal and enhances his role as a representative figure of contemporary spirituality.

Another person who continues to influence and illumine the world of contemporary spirituality is Dorothy Day (1897–1980), called by historian David O'Brien "the most significant, interesting and influential person in the history of American Catholicism." Her life story, recorded up to the early 1950s in her autobiography *The Long Loneliness* (San Francisco, Harper & Row, 1981), is not as well known as Merton's but is important for understanding her influence on contemporary spirituality. Born in 1897 in Brooklyn, she moved to California when she was six and to Chicago when she was nine. After attending the University of Illinois for a couple of years, where she wrote for campus publications, she went to New York in 1916, where she worked as a reporter for a Socialist journal and was active in the women's suffrage movement. After a failed marriage and divorce, she entered a common-law marriage and in 1927 gave birth to a daughter, Tamar. To provide stability for her daughter, she had Tamar baptized a Catholic and then joined the Church herself—a painful move that broke up the relationship with her unbelieving husband and estranged her from her radical Socialist and Marxist friends.

In 1932, after a somewhat aimless period, Day met Peter Maurin, a French peasant who traveled about, expounding the Church's social teaching and a Christian version of personalism. She was captivated by his broad Christian vision, which called for concrete action on behalf of the poor. On May 1, 1922, with Maurin's prodding, Day published the first edition of *The Catholic Worker,* a monthly paper that she edited for the rest of her life. The paper, which reached a circulation of over 100,000 and still sells for a penny a copy, provided a forum for expressing the radical, social demands of the gospel. It also served as the organ for the Catholic Worker Movement, which included not only the well-known hospitality houses in New York and over thirty other cities, where the poor were fed, clothed, and sheltered, but also agrarian Christian communes, which nourished both the soul and the body of those in need.

Through the years, Day took strong positions on a variety of social issues. She supported various causes: the right of workers to unionize, child labor laws, the Castro revolution in Cuba, and the civil rights movement. She fought all forms of prejudice, especially anti-Semitism; risked alienating the Catholic community in the United States by opposing Franco in the Spanish Civil War; adopted a total pacifist position during the Second World War; disputed the political views of Father Coughlin, the popular radio personality; opposed the Vietnam War; and went to jail protesting civil defense practices in New York City.

In great demand as a speaker and symbolic presence, Day traveled extensively, periodically visiting the various Catholic Worker houses around the country, attending rallies and demonstrations, and lecturing at conferences. Her last public appearance before a large audience was in Philadelphia for the Eucharistic Congress in 1976, where she enunciated her usual themes of peace and love of neighbor. After the talk she had a heart attack and spent her remaining years, until her death November 29, 1980, in prayer and in close contact with her daughter and grandchildren.

Dorothy Day lived out and articulated a distinctive American spirituality centered on concrete acts of Christian charity. During her adolescent years she read Dostoevsky's *Brothers Karamazov* and was captivated by Father Zossima's statement that "love in action is a harsh and dreadful thing compared to love in dreams." *A Harsh and Dreadful Love* is the fitting title of William Miller's biography of Dorothy Day, a person who indeed understood the difficult and awesome demands of the law of love. Love takes on a realistic countenance in the life of this dedicated woman. She lived among the poor, who continually intruded on her time and space, treated the countless vagrants who sought her help as unique individuals, and fought to empower the oppressed to take hold of their own lives. Her charity extended to those who vilified and hurt her. She demonstrated publicly and often went to jail in support of particular justice and peace causes. And in the midst of all this activity she still found time and energy for her daughter. Thus Dorothy Day at her best represents the Christian ideal of love in action—an engaged, compassionate, forgiving, courageous, and effective care for human beings in need. This tradition of active charity is exemplified not only by well-known leaders such as Mother Teresa of Calcutta and Jean Vanier, the founder of the communities of l'Arche, but also by countless ordinary Christians who reach out to help others.

From Peter Maurin, Day learned that love in action must be fostered within community life and directed to the well-being of the whole human family. This communitarian personalism formed the theoretical basis for the establishment of the Catholic Worker houses and the agrarian Christian communes. In these communal settings individuals could support one another and develop a rich interior life that would sustain their service of others. By insisting on a communal spirituality, Day not only remained faithful to the Catholic tradition but also provided an important corrective to the individualism dominant in our culture. This communal approach to spirituality continues to operate today in the small-group efforts to revitalize parish life such as RENEW, as well as extraparochial movements such as Cursillo. Dorothy Day's communitarian personalism also stands as a continuing reminder that an integral spirituality always connects interior renewal with active service to others. The small faith-sharing groups in the United States that emphasize mutual support and personal enrichment are challenged by Day's legacy to get more involved in spreading the kingdom of God in the world.

Dorothy Day also exemplifies a viable lay spirituality that combines loyalty to the Church and respect for its leaders with fidelity to personal charism and the courage to take initiative on behalf of the kingdom. In her well-publicized disagreements with Cardinal Spellman she remained firm but respectful. She always insisted that Church tradition be taken seriously within the Catholic Worker Movement. But Dorothy Day did not wait passively for directives from the hierarchy. She listened to the Spirit within prompting her from an early age to show special care for the poor. Regular prayer, periodic retreats, and serious study enabled her to respond passionately and intelligently to her personal charism. Her primary ministry was concentrated on the world and its suffering citizens rather than on the Church and its internal life. She set the style and tone for a whole movement, manifesting in the process a vibrant lay spirituality based on love in action.

Laypersons today continue to search for ways of being faithful to their baptismal call and utilizing their unique gifts. Since the council many well-educated, committed persons have responded by taking on various ministerial roles within the Church, including parish administrators,

pastoral associates, directors of religious education, Communion distributors, and lectors. Catholics reflecting the tradition of Dorothy Day's worldly spirituality have devoted themselves to the task of bringing Christ to the home and marketplace and helping humanize the social, economic, and political spheres.

Finally, Dorothy Day represents the radical spiritual tradition that criticizes the modern industrial world from the perspective of the gospel and proposes alternative forms of organizing human society. Living on the streets of New York, Day was extremely aware of the devastating effect, both physically and spiritually, on those banished to the margins by the economic system. For her, the modern urban world, despite its technological advances, had the effect of diminishing the spiritual life of all the citizens and not just the oppressed. In response to this dehumanizing situation, she sought a community-based third way between capitalism and Marxism. For her, an effective alternative lifestyle must be rooted in an internal conversion to gospel values, including non-violence, voluntary poverty, and solidarity with the poor.

This radical spirituality, which is explicitly countercultural, is carried on by the Catholic Worker Movement, by other peace and justice groups devoted to non-violent approaches, and by committed individuals such as Daniel Berrigan. It is also found among Christian environmentalists, who believe that the biblical mandate to be good stewards of the earth demands a radical change in lifestyle as a response to the ecological crisis.

Dorothy Day has influenced contemporary spirituality through the power of her personal witness and her insightful writings as well as through the thousands of people formed in the ideals and practices of the Catholic Worker Movement. She has made a permanent contribution by demonstrating the power of active love that is nourished in community and directed to those in need.

Theological Influences

Contemporary spirituality in the United States has been influenced by theologians from around the world. Among the most important is the German Jesuit Karl Rahner (1904–1984), who has provided a solid theological framework for the incarnational spirituality adopted by many contemporary Catholics attuned to finding God and living out their faith in the ordinary activities of daily life in the world.

Rahner developed an organic and comprehensive theology that flowed from his central insight that we human beings, in all of our acts of knowing and loving, are positively oriented to the Holy Mystery we call God. Recovering teachings from the Greek Fathers, he insisted that grace is not simply a created reality that functions like a ticket to heaven, but is rather God's gratuitous self-communication that divinizes us in all aspects of our being. God is both the giver and the gift. The whole of human history and all dimensions of human existence are encompassed by this uncreated grace. God's self-communication affects human consciousness, illuminating our intellect and guiding our will. This universal revelation is reflected in the call of conscience and is mediated by our lives in the world. Therefore, all things are potentially revelatory. Every legitimate human effort can bring us closer to the Gracious Mystery and help spread the reign of God. Thus the challenge is to be alert for the clues to the Lord's presence in our daily lives. We must be watchful so that we do not miss the often ambiguous intimations that God is at work in ordinary experience. The Church, through its Scriptures, liturgy, creeds, and doctrines, which witness to Christ and point to the presence of the Holy Mystery, helps believers to achieve a correct and fruitful understanding of their grace-filled experience.

Rahner's fundamental insights are summarized in his difficult but rewarding masterwork *Foundations of Christian Faith* (New York: Seabury, 1978) and applied in his more accessible spiritual writings including *Opportunities for Faith* (New York: Seabury, 1974) and *Prayers for a Lifetime* (New York: Crossroad, 1984). His ideas have filtered down to ordinary people through insightful interpreters and numerous popularizers. Thus many contemporary Catholics have learned to reject a sharp dichotomy between the sacred and the secular in favor of a more integrated incarnational spirituality. They recognize the importance of finding and serving God in all aspects of human existence, even the most ordinary and routine. This is an important corrective to the current cult of the extraordinary, which emphasizes striking and esoteric religious experiences such as speaking in tongues and private revelations. Furthermore, an incarnational spirituality faithful to Rahner's balanced theology retains a strong sense of the ultimately mysterious character of the immanent God, who cannot be controlled or totally comprehended. It also looks to the Church for guidance in interpreting human experience, which is often ambiguous. This balanced incarnational spirituality, made widely available through the immense influence of Rahner, is clearly one of the most important and solid aspects of contemporary Catholic life.

Bernard Lonergan (1904–1984), a Canadian Jesuit who stands with Rahner as a giant of 20th-century Catholic theology, has provided a systematic method for achieving spiritual growth centering on the process of conversion. In his major works, *Insight* (New York: Philosophical Library, 1957) and *Method in Theology* (New York: Herder, 1972), Lonergan describes an invariant pattern in human development through which we begin in experience, gain insights into it, make judgments about these insights, and act on these judgments. To make the process more effective, he offers five guiding principles: Be attentive to the full range of experience; be intelligent by inquiring, probing, and questioning; be reasonable by marshalling evidence, examining opinions and judging wisely; be responsible by acting on the basis of prudent judgments and genuine values; and be in love through wholehearted commitment to God as revealed in Jesus Christ. Thus, integrated growth calls for a process of conversion in the affective, imaginative, intellectual, moral, and religious dimensions of an integrated human life.

Contemporary culture puts great emphasis on personal development through self-actualization. Striking conversion experiences have been an important element in the dominant religious tradition in the United States. Catholic spirituality guided by Lonergan emphasizes that personal development requires systematic effort, that self-actualization is for the common good, and that conversion is a process informed and guided by God's love and the indwelling of the Spirit. With this framework Catholics can fruitfully appropriate insights from the world of psychology: for example, William James on religious experience; Erik Erikson on identity formation; Abraham Maslow on self actualization; and Carl Jung on the process of individuation. Psychologists have helped contemporary spirituality to recognize religious pathology, to understand more about faith and moral development, to appreciate gender differences, and to understand the maturation process. Postconciliar spirituality has been greatly influenced by psychologically oriented spiritual writers, including Eugene Kennedy (*Free to Be Human,* Garden City, N.Y.: Image Books, 1987) and Jack Dominian (*The Capacity to Love,* New York: Paulist, 1985), who draw on their own counseling experience; Bernard Tyrrell (*Christotherapy,* New York: Seabury, 1975) and Sebastian Moore (*Let This Mind Be in You,* London: Darton, Longman and Todd, 1985), who are directly influenced by Lonergan; and John Sanford (*The Kingdom Within,* New York: Paulist, 1970) and Morton Kelsey (*Christo-Psychology,* New York: Crossroad, 1984),

who along with many others are guided by the rich insights of Carl Jung.

Pierre Teilhard de Chardin (1881–1955), who was both a scientist and a mystic, helped impart an optimistic affirmative mood to contemporary spirituality. He enunciated a grand vision, expressed in both scientific and poetic language, of an evolving universe moving toward a personalized center of consciousness, which he called "omega point" and identified with the cosmic Christ of the later Pauline tradition. In his classic work *The Divine Milieu* (New York: Harper & Row, 1960) he celebrates the immanence of God in all creation, the essential goodness of the material world, the intrinsic value of all human activity, and the power of love to unify and personalize our world. These themes combined to create a springtime piety which helped many Catholics to move beyond an otherworldly spirituality that effectively denegrates material reality, human sexuality, and personal activity in the world. Although Teilhard's influence has waned, key elements of his affirmative spirituality, which are solidly rooted in a positive understanding of creation and the incarnation, still play an important role in contemporary spirituality. His optimistic mood is kept alive in the joyful affirmations of the charismatic renewal, which continues to be a powerful witness to the abiding presence of the Holy Spirit. Contemporary spiritualities of work have incorporated his conviction that human activity possesses an intrinsic goodness and helps build the community of love. Finally, Teilhard's celebration of the essential goodness of the material world has been maintained and expanded in the ecospiritualities developed by Thomas Berry (*The Dream of the Earth,* San Francisco: Sierra Club Books, 1988) and Matthew Fox (*The Coming of the Cosmic Christ,* San Francisco: Harper & Row, 1988).

Although the Swiss theologian Hans Urs von Balthasar (1905–1988) has not yet had much direct impact on spirituality in the

United States, he has fashioned a grand synthesis of the Christian faith that gives new coherence and vigor to traditional forms of piety. In his multivolume work *The Glory of the Lord* (San Francisco: Ignatius Press, 1982–1992), Balthasar speaks of God as the Glorious One, the source of all beauty and splendor, and of Jesus Christ the Word Incarnate, who radiates this glory of the Father, especially in his obedient death on the cross. The Spirit establishes an intrinsic bond between Christ and the Church, which as his Body and his Bride manifests the beauty of his form, especially in the celebration of the Eucharist. Through private prayer, which properly begins by listening receptively to the Scriptures, believers can develop a contemplative spirit so that they can worship God reverently in the liturgy and participate wholeheartedly in the Church's mission to redeem the world.

Thus Balthasar offers a new integrated foundation for many themes of classical spirituality, including a strong sense of the transcendence of God, the importance of the redemptive death of Christ, the shaping power of the sacraments, and the role of Mary as the model of total receptivity. In his classic work *Prayer* (San Francisco: Ignatius Press, 1986), Balthasar presents a traditional spirituality that insists on clear priorities: Catholics should gather for Mass primarily to worship God and not to create community; they should read the Scriptures with an open heart and not a critical mind; and they should employ imaginative meditation techniques centered on Christ rather than the imageless methods of the East. This type of classical spirituality, often associated internationally with secular institutes such as Opus Dei and in the United States with the neoconservatives, has remained an important aspect of postconciliar Catholicism.

Through the publication in 1971 of his seminal work, *A Theology of Liberation* (Maryknoll, N.Y.: Orbis, 1988), the Peruvian priest Gustavo Gutiérrez helped to launch a movement that has profoundly affected contemporary spirituality. Gutiérrez and the other liberation theologians, such as Leonardo Boff (*Faith on the Edge,* San Francisco: Harper & Row, 1989) and Jon Sobrino (*Spirituality of Liberation,* Maryknoll, N.Y.: Orbis, 1987), have re-read the Scriptures from the viewpoint of oppressed people. For these theologians, the central problem is not making the faith intelligible to educated people but rather speaking in a credible way of a God who loves the poor. Their dialogue partner is the nonperson rather than the nonbeliever. In the Hebrew Scriptures, the Exodus exemplifies God's desire to liberate his people and to give them social, political, and economic freedom. The full meaning of this saving act is found in Jesus Christ the Liberator, who through his death and resurrection has freed us from sin and strengthened us to fight the injustice it breeds. In order to be faithful to the liberating message of Jesus, the Church must adopt a preferential option for the poor, working to empower the oppressed so that they can overcome injustice and transform society.

In his book *We Drink from Our Own Wells* (Maryknoll, N.Y.: Orbis, 1984), Gutiérrez applies his liberation theology to the area of spirituality. By joining in solidarity with the oppressed, Christians encounter the Lord and follow in his footsteps. Through the power of the Spirit, disciples are called to a process of conversion that reveals the pervasive power of social sin and the need to create institutions that promote justice. Christians who share in the life of the exploited will experience a deep joy, founded on the hope that God will finally triumph over all evil.

In Latin America this spirituality is rooted in the numerous base communities of Christians who gather regularly for prayer and social action. Archbishop Oscar Romero, the celebrated martyr to the cause, represents thousands of others who have suffered for living out a liberation spirituality dedicated to transforming society.

Latin American liberation theology has become well known in the United States both through the translations of the primary authors and the writings of their interpreters. The biblical story of the Exodus and the example of Christ the Liberator have become common themes in the movements for social justice. The method of reading the Scriptures from the viewpoint of the oppressed has been effectively employed by various groups, including women and members of the African-American, Hispanic, and gay communities. New immigrants often bring to the United States extensive experiences with base communities.

Martin Luther King represents an indigenous liberation theology. He enabled a whole nation to hear the Christian message from the viewpoint of African-Americans, who have not shared in the benefits of the American dream. He helped to unmask the social sin that produces racism and fosters the arms race. His nonviolent methods revealed once again the power of Christ's teaching on love and forgiveness. King's genius was to join Christian liberation themes with the highest ideals of the American dream in an effective effort to produce a better life for all citizens of the country.

In the United States today, Catholic liberation spirituality takes its cues largely from Latin America. At the same time some people, especially African-American Catholics, are trying to develop a more indigenous spirituality that will enable them to deal with the specific political and economic situation in the United States.

In her ambitious book *Sexism and God-Talk* (Boston: Beacon Press, 1983), Rosemary Radford Ruether has constructed a systematic theology from the perspective of women and their struggle for liberation. Ruether roots sexism and the evils of patriarchy in dualistic thinking that insists on sharp dichotomies between spirit and matter, soul and body, male and female,

human and nonhuman, grace and nature. In patriarchal societies women inevitably are judged as inferior because they are identified with matter, body, and nature. After disclosing the sexism built into the biblical tradition, Ruether goes on to draw on elements in the Scriptures to further the cause of women's liberation. Thus she speaks of a God who demands that people establish justice in their own society. Her Christology emphasizes that Jesus broke social taboos by speaking with women in public and that he preached the coming of a kingdom in which human relationships would be based on mutuality rather than domination. Ruether believes that this authentic memory of Jesus can be mobilized today to fight oppression of all types, including the domination of women. Other important authors who share this view, such as Elisabeth Schüssler Fiorenza (*In Memory of Her,* New York: Crossroad, 1983) and Anne Carr (*Transforming Grace,* San Francisco: Harper & Row, 1988), have helped provide a foundation for a feminist spirituality that takes women's experiences seriously, especially their struggles for liberation from patriarchal structures. Feminist spirituality tends to emphasize inclusive language and practices, caring relationships, and a positive valuation of bodiliness. Many women find their spirituality nourished by small faith-sharing groups and by prayer services that are feminist-oriented.

Continuing Trends

Within the great diversity of the post-conciliar period, it is possible to discern some important trends as well as continuing challenges.

1. Contemporary Catholic spirituality continues to manifest the traditional ideal of unity in diversity. The pluralism is evident and growing as more and more Catholics feel free to choose among diverse lifestyles and pieties. Nevertheless, an essential unity in faith and religious sensibilities is still in place, even though it is

harder to detect and to define. The enduring challenge is to maintain a solid sense of Catholic unity based on fundamental beliefs and values that will encompass and support the expanding diversity.

2. Since the council the shape of Catholic piety has become simpler and clearer: more Christocentric, more attuned to scriptural themes, and more rooted in liturgical celebrations. Despite these developments, the Catholic imagination continues to be shaped by comforting images of Mary, the example of the saints, and by certain popular devotions. For the future we need a Christocentric spirituality that focuses and expands the Catholic imagination so that it can appropriate the good example of virtuous people and the positive elements in popular piety.

3. Recently Church leaders and spiritual guides have come to a deeper appreciation of the role of the parish in spiritual development. Vibrant parishes create a sense of community, facilitate personal growth, and encourage efforts for justice and peace. It is difficult for parishioners to achieve sustained spiritual growth without this support and guidance. Still the transparochial movements and groups continue to play an important role in meeting particular needs of Catholics. These groups will be more effective in the long run if they encourage and enable individuals to contribute to, and draw on, the resources of parish life.

4. The conciliar insistence on the universal call to holiness has made a great impact. A growing number of Catholics recognize that all the baptized, including laypersons, are called to live up to the highest ideals of the gospel. There is also a growing awareness that authentic discipleship must be practiced in the particular concrete circumstances of life. Thus we face the great challenge of embodying the universal call to holiness in distinctive spiritualities that fit the needs and lifestyles of laypersons, clergy, and members of religious orders.

5. In the postconciliar period many Catholics have grown spiritually by participating in small groups that facilitate mutual sharing, personal witness, and common prayer. Recently spiritual leaders have become more aware of the dangers of privatism and the need to adopt a global perspective that includes collaborative efforts for the common good. The challenge for the future is to develop a global spirituality that encourages small faith-sharing groups to look beyond their own interests and to demonstrate an inclusive concern for the whole human family.

6. Since the council Catholicism has developed a solid incarnational spirituality that is attuned to finding God in the everyday world of ordinary experience. At the same time the contemporary world has generated new religious movements that stress striking religious experiences and esoteric private revelations. The continuing challenge for the Catholic world is to maintain a balanced spirituality that has a proper sense of the transcendence of God and provides an attractive alternative to spiritual fads.

7. Lay spirituality has continued to develop in two directions: one based on an ecclesiology of coresponsibility, which leads to involvement in the internal life of the Church; and another based on an understanding of the Church as instrument of the kingdom, which prompts efforts to humanize the political, economic, and social spheres of life. The Church as a whole must find ways to balance and relate these two trends.

8. In the years since Vatican II, Catholic spirituality has expanded its array of fruitful dialogue partners to include world religions, modern philosophies, and humanistic sciences. At the same time the Catholic community has also reappropriated its own heritage, drawing on biblical insights, the teachings of the Fathers, the experiences of men and women mystics, and the work of contemporary theologians. The enduring challenge is to develop a confident commitment to our own religious heritage that includes a fundamental openness to

the truth, goodness, and beauty found in other traditions and disciplines.

9. Contemporary feminist spirituality, rooted in the experiences of women, has instructed the whole Church in the destructive consequences of sexism and has expanded our perceptions of God and the process of salvation. It has also prompted initial efforts to develop a masculine spirituality that takes seriously the distinctive experience of men in our culture. Our task is to create an integral spirituality that draws on the experience of all people, promoting harmonious interactions between men and women based on mutuality and respect for their distinctive experiences.

10. Involved Catholics, often influenced by leaders such as Thomas Merton and Dorothy Day, have made important strides in creating a spirituality that is both prayerful and prophetic. Some have developed a rich inner life, which leads naturally to efforts on behalf of peace and justice. Others, working diligently to transform society, are thrown back upon the life of prayer for nourishment and strength. In the future, Catholic spirituality must maintain a fruitful tension between prayerful reflection and involvement in the world if it is to avoid falling into individualism or becoming a mere humanism. Catholic spirituality at its best encourages believers to find God in their own hearts as well as in worldly activities.

See also AMERICAN SPIRITUALITY; CATHOLIC WORKER MOVEMENT; CHARISMATIC RENEWAL; CONVERSION; CURSILLO, MOVEMENT; FEMINIST SPIRITUALITY; HOLINESS; LAY SPIRITUALITY; LIBERATION THEOLOGY, INFLUENCE ON SPIRITUALITY; PARISH, PARISH RENEWAL; PSYCHOLOGY, RELATIONSHIP AND CONTRIBUTION TO SPIRITUALITY; VATICAN COUNCIL II; WORLD.

Bibliography: K. Rahner, *Foundations of Christian Faith: An Introduction to the Idea of Christianity* (New York: Seabury: 1978). B. Lonergan, *Method in Theology* (New York: Herder, 1972). H. U. von Balthasar, *Prayer* (San Francisco: Ignatius Press, 1986). G. Gutiérrez, *We Drink from Our Own Wells* (Maryknoll, N.Y.: Orbis, 1984). L. Dupré and D. Saliers, eds., *Christian Spirituality: Post-Reformation and Modern,* World Spirituality 18 (New York: Crossroad, 1989). T. Merton, *Contemplative Prayer* (New York: Image Books, 1970).

JAMES J. BACIK

CONVERSION

Current theological literature devotes significant attention to the explication of the phenomenon of conversion. From a survey of this literature, it becomes clear that this occurrence, in both its personal and communal dimensions, cannot be easily defined. There seem to be several reasons for this difficulty. First, conversion is a complex process of transformation involving various conscious operations of the human person. Second, the phenomenon of transformation influences the personal and cultural dynamics of being and acting within history. These dynamics, such as the distorting power of bias and the clarifying venture of questioning, are themselves complex maneuvers of attention and intellect. In defining the conversion phenomenon, however, the greatest dilemma for Christian spirituality is the understanding of the operation of grace, itself an undefinable reality. Thus conversion is caught up in the mystery of grace operating within human transformation and the potentiality for persons and cultures to become a new creation.

Conversion is comprehensible in glimpses; the whole reality of who we are to become is a journey of discovery. The movements and scope of the conversion process, brought about in grace, therefore, cannot be easily categorized or defined. Nevertheless, certain categories of thought are helpful in understanding the process. This entry will outline four such modes of understanding conversion: the autobiographical, the biblical, the liturgical, and the theological.

The Autobiography

The clearest portrayal and understanding of the phenomenon of conversion are to be discovered within the self-reflective genre of autobiography. Autobiography offers a unique understanding of conversion for several reasons. First, the narrative emplotment of a life, in its various stages and crises, offers insight into the unfolding history of a specific person. Second, the narrative form portrays the experiences and relationships that are worked out in the transformation of the person. Within this context, the autobiography gives an account of the movement of grace and its implications in human life. Third, the autobiography offers symbolic reference to the worldview of a person and how, in the process of conversion, the worldview is entered, integrated, and transformed.

The classic work of this kind is St. Augustine's *Confessions*. Other important autobiographies that attest to the dynamics of conversion and grace are those of Ignatius of Loyola and Teresa of Avila, and *The Story of a Soul* of Thérèse of Lisieux. More recently the self-examination of Thomas Merton in his *Seven Storey Mountain* and of Pope John XXIII in *The Journal of a Soul* has captured the Christian imagination with the vivid conversions of two noted figures.

While autobiography offers the clearest portrayal of the conversion phenomenon, contemporary biblical, liturgical, and theological studies seek to explain this occurrence by developing helpful categories and images.

Biblical Roots

The experience of conversion is central to the biblical and spiritual traditions of both Judaism and Christianity. Although described in other metaphors, this phenomenon seems to be given centrality in other world religions as well. Within the Judeo-Christian writings, conversion means a two-phased turning: first, it is a turning away from alienation and sin, a phase ordinarily called repentance; second, it is a turning toward the living God, a phase sometimes called enlightenment. The Christian Scriptures refer to this process by two Greek words: *metanoia*, a turning from sin, and *epistrophē*, a turning toward God.

Christian spirituality has traditionally placed an emphasis on conversion as repentance. In more recent years, however, a more comprehensive understanding of conversion has sought to include the full depth of the biblical insight into the understanding of the process as a turning from and a turning toward. An emphasis has been placed on the transformational character of the total personality and on the role of God's gift of grace within this process.

In both the Jewish and Christian Scriptures, the call to conversion and repentance is central. Great stories of conversion abound. Characters such as David, Zacchaeus, the Samaritan woman and Paul narrate the importance of this phenomenon. However, the prophetic tradition of the Jewish writings is the classic example of the emphasis placed on conversion. This tradition is a constant reminder of the need for a personal and social turning to the God of the covenant. When Israel forgets the covenant, the prophet voices the need for conversion.

The prophetic ministry is brought forward into the Christian tradition in the figure of John the Baptist, who preaches a radical conversion in preparation for the coming of the Messiah. In the Christian Scriptures the call to conversion finds its clearest voice, however, in the ministry of Jesus, who embodies the very possibility of human transformation. The life and ministry of Jesus incarnate the radical alternative possible in history if discipleship is born anew.

Conversion and Liturgy

The renewal of liturgical rites in the Roman Catholic Church has emphasized the intrinsic relationship between the celebration of the sacraments and the dynamics of conversion. This is most clearly evidenced in *The Rite of Christian Initia-*

tion of Adults (RCIA) and The Rite of Penance (OP).

The Rite of Christian Initiation of Adults

The revised rites of adult initiation, promulgated in 1972, outline a dynamic process of catechesis and liturgical formation. This process leads an adult through stages of conversion to an acceptance of the gospel and the celebration of the sacraments of baptism, confirmation, and the Eucharist. The RCIA clearly acknowledges that conversion is a process by which the grace of God leads persons away from sin into the mystery of love (RCIA 37). The image of journey is employed by the rite to describe the conversion process (RCIA 4). It is explicitly stated as well that the conversion journey is not undertaken alone; rather, new members journey together with others in a community of ongoing conversion and creedal commitment.

The RCIA outlines the conversion process in four periods. This four-part process has been employed by catechists, vocation ministers, and spiritual directors as a paradigm for understanding and encouraging conversion in other settings of Christian formation.

1. The period of the precatechumenate is a time for the first hearing of the gospel and for what the rite calls initial conversion. While the RCIA never specifically defines the meaning of initial conversion, a common meaning seems to have been accepted among those who have implemented the rite in pastoral settings. In this case, initial conversion means a gradual and beginning movement to make sense of one's life and to find the difference for one's existence in the encounter with Christ as proclaimed within the community of faith. Once initial conversion is discerned by the catechumenal ministers of the community, the inquirer is publicly brought forward to profess the desire to journey further in the knowing of God within the community's Liturgy of the Word. The inquirer is signed with the cross on specific parts of the body and is given the name "catechumen."

It is interesting to note at this point that the RCIA marks each stage of conversion with a public ritual and a new name indicating the quality of conversion and membership within the community.

2. The period of the catechumenate is marked by various rites that focus on the hearing of the word of God. The word proclaimed is understood in the RCIA as the premiere sacrament of God's grace inviting the catechumen into a deepening of the initial conversion. Together with the word proclaimed, the establishment of relationships within the community, as well as apostolic activity, brings the catechumen into a new affiliation with the household of Christ (RCIA 75). At this point of the journey, the RCIA seems to understand conversion to Christ and membership in the Body as indistinguishable. One comes to know and follow Christ in the community of discipleship. Conversion, therefore, becomes a reorientation of one's relationships with God, with oneself, and with a community of faith for the life of the world.

Following a second deliberation by the pastoral ministers of the community, the catechumen is brought forward to the celebration of the Rite of Election. This rite, celebrated both in the local parish community and at the cathedral with the bishop on the First Sunday of Lent, proclaims God's election of the catechumen and the movement of grace and conversion. The catechumen is now called "elect" and begins a forty-day fast with the Church in preparation for Easter.

3. The period of enlightenment is normally understood as the forty days of Lent. The RCIA conceives of this period as a Lenten retreat of spiritual preparation for the sacraments of initiation. Included within this period are the three scrutiny rites celebrated on the Third, Fourth, and Fifth Sundays of Lent. These rites are an invocation to God to assist the elect in their

final turning away from sin and the power of evil. They celebrate the scrutinizing power of the Spirit and the transforming grace of Christ. In the context of the RCIA, the Lenten season has been offered a new vitality as a season of ongoing conversion for the entire Christian community.

At the conclusion of the forty days, the initiatory sacraments are celebrated during the Easter Vigil. The conversion of the elect is consummated in water and oil and in the sharing of Christ's Body and Blood at the community's table. Sharing at the Eucharist is considered the height of initiation and the chief sacrament of conversion in the Christian community. The newly baptized person is given the name "neophyte" and is offered a place of honor in the community.

4. The fourth period outlined in the RCIA is called *mystagogia,* which means "a savoring of mystery." This period has traditionally been associated with the fifty days of Easter and is a time for sacramental catechesis. The neophyte, along with the rest of the community, probes the presences of the risen Christ in history with the converted eyes of faith. In the revised U.S. edition of the RCIA, the statutes of implementation suggest that the period of mystagogy be extended for one year as a means of supporting the neophyte's continuing journey of conversion.

From the RCIA, and the pattern of initiation that it outlines, several observations about conversion can be gleaned. First, conversion is imaged as a journey of transformation led by the movement of God. Second, it is a communal experience involving the entire community in its witness and encouragement. Third, the RCIA considers conversion as an ongoing process, celebrated in stages and finding its ultimate Christian expression in the celebration of the Eucharist. Fourth, conversion is not a onetime experience but rather a lifetime transformation that is caught up in savoring the mystery revealed in Christ. Fifth, in keeping with ecumenical insights

on the meaning of conversion and the common heritage of baptism, paragraph 2 of the National Statutes for the Catechumenate, an appendix to the RCIA, states that the term "convert," traditionally associated with baptized non-Catholics seeking membership in the Roman Catholic Church, is to be "reserved strictly for those converted from unbelief to Christian belief."

The Rite of Penance

The Rite of Penance (OP), revised in 1973, also offers insight into the meaning of conversion for the Christian community. Penance, sometimes considered a second baptism, has a complex history in the Western Church. Its concern with repentance, contrition, and reconciliation, however, has remained consistent through the centuries.

In the 1973 rite the language of penance is informed by an understanding of conversion. This is evidenced most clearly in OP 6, which, quoting from Paul VI's apostolic constitution *Paenitemini* of 1966, states: "The most important act of the penitent is contrition, which is 'heartfelt sorrow and aversion for the sin committed along with the intention of sinning no more' [see the Council of Trent, DS 1676]. . . . 'We can only approach the kingdom of Christ by *metanoia.* This is a profound change of the whole person by which we begin to consider, judge, and arrange our life according to the holiness and love of God, made manifest in his Son in the last days and given to us in abundance' . . . [Paul VI, *Paenitemini*]. The genuineness of penance depends on this heartfelt contrition. For conversion should affect a person from within toward a progressively deeper enlightenment and an ever-closer likeness to Christ" (DOL, p. 959).

Conversion is understood in *The Rite of Penance* as an inward transformation. This transformation influences the operations of experience, valuing, and deciding, and forms the core of the sacramental celebration of reconciliation. The OP also claims that conversion is not only a personal matter but that conversion, celebrated in various modes of reconciliation within the Church, is the hallmark of the Church's presence in the world. Thus, "the people of God become in the world a sign of conversion to God. All this the Church expresses in its life and celebrates in the liturgy when the faithful confess that they are sinners and ask pardon of God and of their brothers and sisters" (OP 4).

Both the OP and the RCIA envision conversion as central to the sacramental celebrations of initiation and penance. It can be said that these rites are a celebration and an appropriation of the gift of conversion in the life of the individual and the community. This insight has offered a challenge to pastoral sacramental practice, which has often celebrated the sacraments of initiation and penance as a means to mark life stages and transitions without due regard for the dynamics of conversion.

The RCIA and the OP hold the celebration of the Eucharist as the goal of all conversion for the Christian community. Standing together at the common table of apostles and martyrs is the sacramental symbol and promise of transformation in Christ.

Conversion in Contemporary Theology

Contemporary theologians have placed conversion at the heart of the theological enterprise. They have explored the dynamics of conversion and have attempted to explain the phenomenon in clear categories. Various heuristic models have been offered as ways of explaining and understanding the phenomenon of conversion. These explanations have often employed developmental and consciousness theories from modern psychology. Thus the writings of such psychologists as Freud, Jung, James, Erikson, Kohlberg, and Piaget have informed the theological understandings of conversion. The writings of James W. Fowler, for instance, are noted for their analysis of faith development employing the developmental-stage theory of Erik Erikson.

In recent years the work of Bernard J. F. Lonergan, S.J., and his interpreters has gained noted acclaim among Christian theologians. Lonergan's work sets up explanatory categories of the human operations of consciousness. From within this context he explains conversion as a set of judgments and decisions that move the human person from an established horizon into a new horizon of knowing, valuing, and acting. Thus he identifies and explains the operations of human consciousness and identifies three conversions: intellectual, moral, and religious.

Intellectual conversion is understood as a radical clarification of experience and meaning that allows the human person to eliminate stubborn and misleading myths about reality, objectivity, and knowledge. Thus intellectual conversion allows the human person to differentiate various levels of meanings, to grasp the horizon of one's own knowing and not to confuse sense perception with objectivity.

Moral conversion is the shifting of one's criteria for decision-making from the satisfaction of the self as basis of choice to the discovery and pursuit of value. Moral conversion, therefore, allows the person to opt for the truly good. The morally converted person is able to perceive the inherent biases in the self, in culture, and in history, thus allowing for authentic decision-making.

Religious conversion occurs when one is radically grasped by ultimate concern or love. It is a falling in love unconditionally, leading to surrender to the transcendent, and a gracious being-in-wholeness. Lonergan further differentiates the religious conversion and develops the notion of Christian conversion as God's love flooding our hearts through the Holy Spirit given in Christ. Thus a person can experience religious conversion without thematizing the phenomenon in Christian categories.

Interpreters of Lonergan have differentiated other conversions. Of note here is the work of Robert M. Doran, S.J., and his explanation of affective and psychic conversion, based on the writings of Carl Jung.

Conclusion

Conversion is a complex phenomenon that transforms the entire human person. It also has social and cultural implications, which need further research and elaboration. Within a Christian community it is a process of hope whereby persons are caught up into the promise of the new creation and the metamorphosis promised in the covenant. In the end, conversion is riddled in mystery. While autobiography, biblical insights, liturgical texts, theological reflections, and psychological categories are helpful to understand and explain the occurrence, the Christian tradition ultimately stands in silence before the operation of grace, the wonder of surprise, and the movement of a power beyond that of human consciousness and performance.

See also BAPTISM; DISCIPLESHIP; DIVINIZATION; FAITH; JOURNEY (GROWTH AND DEVELOPMENT IN SPIRITUAL LIFE); LITURGY; PENANCE, PENITENCE; PSYCHOLOGY, RELATIONSHIP AND CONTRIBUTION TO SPIRITUALITY; SACRAMENTS; SELF; TRANSFORMATION.

Bibliography: W. Conn, ed., *Conversion: Perspectives on Personal and Social Transformation* (New York: Alba House, 1978). R. Duggan, ed., *Conversion and the Catechumenate* (New York: Paulist, 1984). E. Griffin, *Turning: Reflections on the Experience of Conversion* (New York: Doubleday, 1980). T. Merton, *The Seven Storey Mountain* (New York: Image Books, 1970). K. Wilber et al., eds., *Transformations of Consciousness: Conventional and Contemplative Perspectives on Development* (Boston: New Science Library, 1986).

RICHARD N. FRAGOMENI

COSMIC MYSTICISM

Cosmic mysticism is a mode of human consciousness and creative activity grounded within an experience and understanding of reality in its all-expanding cosmic dimensions. While cosmic mysticism can be likened to nature mysticism and to other mystical traditions involving the human person with creation, its uniqueness rests with the insights, articulations, and implications it draws from the theories and discoveries of modern science, space exploration, and ecological concerns.

Modern astrophysics, the claims of quantum mechanics, modern philosophies, along with contemporary cosmologies that posit a theory of an expanding universe, afford the possibility for a deepened consciousness of cosmic interrelationality with its political and global implications. This consciousness perceives the human person as part of a vast realm of cosmic evolution and mystery. Within this consciousness humanity is perceived as the universe becoming conscious of itself.

A Christian Appropriation

For Christianity, the mystery of Christ and the communion in the Spirit are the foundation of all mystical experience. The cultivation of a cosmic mysticism within a Christian context, therefore, begins with the predication of the cosmic energies to Christ in a cosmic Christology. While there are roots of this predication in the Christian tradition as early as the writings of St. Paul, the formal elaboration of a cosmic Christology that integrates the discoveries of modern science and philosophy is yet to be written. The beginnings of a cosmic Christology and mysticism are clearly evident, however, in the writings of Pierre Teilhard de Chardin, himself a Christian and a scientist.

Teilhard's work develops the understanding of cosmic evolution and expansion in the image of the Omega Point, which he readily associates with the energy of Christ. The transformative energies of the universe, which have their foundations in the noetic dimensions of Christ, include the human energies of consciousness, which can be transformed to harmonize with the cosmic forces. This transformation is realized in the mystical contemplation of persons who associate themselves in the divine energies of love. In mystical awareness, Teilhard posits a dynamic interplay between personal and cosmic consciousness. Thus cosmic mysticism is participation in the Christic energies of evolution.

Cosmic mysticism ensues in human activity, a task that emerges from the realized cosmic interconnection in Christ. This activity is described as building the earth. For Teilhard, this is not mere activism but rather a quality of work that suggests a new paradigm for activity, that is, the quality of compassionate discovery. Compassion is the vigorous drive to discover the depths of the cosmic energy active in the human and in the universe. It is a passionate energy that directs all human activity into a consciousness of the Divine Milieu from which contemplation and creative activity arise. Cosmic mysticism does not turn from the universe in its diversity but rather celebrates it in the human energies by sharing in the evolving impulse of the universe itself. The cosmic mystic becomes the opening for the evolutionary energies of Christ-Omega to become incarnate. Thus the World Council of Churches, in a recent statement concerning the mission of the Christian in the world, clearly asserts that the doing of justice and the pursuit of peace are both incomprehensible without being grounded within the compassionate preservation and respect for the integrity of creation.

The Scientific Appropriation

Apart from the Christian thematization of cosmic mysticism, evident in the work of Teilhard de Chardin and more recently in the works of Thomas Berry and his interpreters, contemporary culture continues to develop a body of literature that can be considered illuminating and encouraging to the experience of cosmic mysticism. This literature appeals to the insights of modern physics and psychology. Among the leading authors, David Bohm, Fritz Capra, Jean Huston, and Ken Wilber are of special importance. In these writings modern physics, astrophysics, and the relativity theories of universal construction open the avenue to imagine the boundary-less nature of existence itself. Cosmic mysticism, therefore, is considered a non-boundary, or new unity-consciousness, in which the interrelationality of all existence is the foundation for human development, achievement, and decision-making. The cultivation of such consciousness is the transpersonal discovery that a person is not separate from the universe in which he or she operates, but rather that the human person is indeed part of the larger reality which, while differentiated, is without boundaries.

In an age of ecological urgency, the deepening of a cosmic mystical sense is not something of trend but must be considered a necessary and vital stage of human and planetary survival. Such a cosmic experience will require an ongoing conversation between science and religion, the imagination to develop metaphors and symbols of cosmic implication and heuristic appeal, and the shifting of the horizons of persons reared in a technological age to the perception of the real as all-encompassing. In the end, cosmic mysticism is an invitation toward a transpersonal relationality within the universe that reaches ever outward to the possibility of transformation.

See also CREATION; ECOLOGICAL CONSCIOUSNESS; ENVIRONMENT; HOLISTIC SPIRITUALITY; MYSTICISM; NEW AGE SPIRITUALITY; WORLD.

Bibliography: T. Berry, *The Dream of the Earth* (San Francisco: Sierra Club, 1988). P. Teilhard de Chardin, *Christianity and Evolution* (New York: Harcourt Brace Jovanovich, 1969). J. Haught, *The Cosmic Adventure: Science, Religion and the Quest for Purpose* (New York: Paulist, 1984). B. Swimme, *The Universe Is a Green Dragon: A Cosmic Creation Story* (Santa Fe: Bear & Co., 1985). K. Wilber, *No Boundary: Eastern and Western Approaches to Personal Growth* (Boston: Shambhala, 1985).

RICHARD N. FRAGOMENI

COUNSEL

See GIFTS OF THE HOLY SPIRIT.

COUNSELS, EVANGELICAL

See VOWS.

COVENANT

The notion of covenant is one of the Bible's most important and pervasive means of describing the relationship between God and the community of faith. The word *covenant* derives from the Hebrew word *berith,* which means "a binding agreement or pact." Such covenants are found throughout the Bible: peace treaties between warring parties, settlements of territorial disputes, etc. Covenants could be drawn up between equal partners or between a more powerful sovereign and lesser vassals, promising them protection in return for loyalty and tribute. Examples of the latter type of covenant are known from other civilizations in the Ancient Near East, such as the Hittite suzerainty treaties, which date to the 14th to 12th centuries B.C.

More formal covenants were sealed with rituals and signs: a recitation of the monarch's benevolence and powerful deeds; a formula expressing the bond between the covenant partners; a list of obligations that flowed from the covenant; and a description of the blessings and sanctions that would result from transgression or fidelity to the terms of the covenant. Ritual signs, such as the sharing of a meal or the slaughter of animals, also accompanied some of these ceremonies. The Hebrew idiom "to cut a covenant," for example, may refer to the practice of dividing an animal in two and having the partners walk between the parts, probably signifying the fate of those who might violate the covenant (see Gen 15:9-11).

The most significant biblical use of the notion of covenant is its application to the relationship between God and Israel. The Bible describes a series of such covenants. God strikes a covenant with Noah at the time of the flood, promising to spare Noah and to make a new beginning of creation (Gen 6:18-22). There is also a covenant with Abraham (Genesis 15), guaranteeing him land and countless descendants. This covenant is renewed with Isaac (Gen 26:2-5) and with Jacob at Bethel (Gen 28:10-22).

The most fundamental covenant is that made with Moses at Sinai, and biblical writers undoubtedly cast Israel's primeval history in the pattern of this covenant. After liberating Israel from the slavery of Egypt, God cuts a covenant with Moses and Israel. The narrative in Exodus 19 includes many of the ceremonial elements of the covenant treaty described above; most noteworthy is the conferral of the Law upon Israel as the expression of the demands of the covenant. Yahweh adopts Israel as a chosen people and gives them the gift of the land and the promise of a long and prosperous future. They become God's children, and God is like a father to them. In turn, Israel must be faithful to the Law and give exclusive allegiance to God. Much of Israel's religious consciousness is shaped in terms of this relationship. God's promises to protect the Davidic dynasty and to give it an everlasting reign are modeled on the covenants with Abraham and Moses (see 2 Sam 7:1-17).

While the explicit term *covenant* is not always in play, the covenant relationship between Yahweh and Israel is close to the surface in many OT theologies. The prophets rail against Israel's infidelities, which are violations of the covenant. National calamities such as invasions or exile are understood as God's sanctions for the rupturing of the covenant by Israel. Hopes for future redemption also draw upon the covenant relationship. Hosea uses marriage imagery to describe God's renewal of the covenant with Israel and, indeed, with the created world itself (Hos 2:16-25). Isaiah evokes both the covenants to Noah and

David in expressing future hope (see Isa 54:9-10; 55:3). Jeremiah foresees a renewed covenant written on the human heart, forged between God and individual believers (Jer 31:31-34; see also Ezek 36:24-32).

The Greek term for covenant is *diathēkē*, which also means "a last testament or will." That etymology also points to the NT interpretation of covenant, which sees the death (and resurrection) of Jesus as covenant. Each of the institution accounts in the Synoptic Gospels interprets Jesus' death as a sign of the new and definitive covenant described by Jeremiah (Mk 14:24; Mt 26:27; Lk 22:20). In 1 Cor 11:25, Paul, too, echoes this same tradition, understanding the blood of Christ to be the sign of a new covenant. The author of the letter to the Hebrews draws out an extended comparison between the "old" and the "new" covenants as a way of interpreting Jesus' death and exaltation as the definitive means of salvation, longed for by Israel, promised by the covenant, but consummated through Christ (Hebrews 8–10).

The notion of covenant, therefore, expresses some of the most fundamental biblical convictions about the relationship between God and the believing community, a relationship that is both personal (comparable to the relationship between parent and child or between husband and wife) and communal (binding a people together in the solidarity of faith). The genuineness of the covenant bond is tested in faithful, loving obedience to God and in the commitment to justice and compassion among the covenant community. The return to biblical categories that has characterized the postconciliar Church has also led to renewed interest in the notion of covenant, because this biblical notion expresses some of the most essential qualities of any sound Catholic spirituality.

See also COMMUNITY; COMPASSION; FIDELITY; JUSTICE; LAW; OBEDIENCE.

Bibliography: J. Bright, *A History of Israel,* 3rd ed. (Philadelphia: Westminster, 1981) 148–162. X. Léon-Dufour, *Sharing the Eucharistic Bread: The Witness of the New Testament* (New York: Paulist, 1987). D. McCarthy, *Old Testament Covenant: A Survey of Current Opinions* (Atlanta: John Knox, 1972).

DONALD SENIOR, C.P.

CREATION

As a technical, theological term, *create* (Latin *creare,* "to bring forth, produce, make, beget") is used only in reference to God to designate the act by virtue of which God alone is the ultimate source of all finite reality. In this sense it is identical with creation *ex nihilo,* which designates the movement from nonexistence into existence through the creative action of God. In a broader sense, especially in the Scriptures, the mighty acts of God in the history of the Jewish people are seen as acts of divine creative power. In this sense God's creative activity includes not only the work of origins but that of salvation and consummation as well.

Old Testament

The classical texts related to creation theology by the tradition are the opening chapters of the Book of Genesis. It is a common view among exegetes that these texts are best seen, not as reportage of specific persons and events at the beginning of history, but as metaphorical and narrative expressions of elements that Jewish reflection found to be widely present in human experience. Theologians such as Karl Rahner see in this material an attempt to name the causes of the historical situation in which humanity finds itself (= etiology).

Aside from these texts, the OT speaks of creation in the prophetic tradition (Amos 5:8ff.; Mal 2:10ff.; Isa 43:1; 51; 54:16; 65:17ff.; 66:22); in the psalms (Pss 19; 33:6, 9; 89:48; 104:30), and in the wisdom literature (Prov 8; Sir 24:3ff.; Wis 7:21ff.). Especially in Deutero- and Trito-Isaiah, the Hebrew word *bara* is used to designate not only God's action as creative origin but also the divine salvific actions in history as well as the eschatological new creation at the end of history.

Some major points in the biblical understanding are:

1) The material world is not a divine principle but is itself the object of the divine creative power and care. Genesis 1 describes the creative action of God by means of the metaphor of speech, thus suggesting what later theological language will describe as God's free and transcendent creative activity.

2) The dignity and distinctive role of humanity in the created realm is described with a subtlety easily overlooked. In Gen 1:26ff. humanity is seen as a noble pair created in the image of God, blessed with a share in the fertility of creation, and entrusted with the task of caring for the wellbeing of the whole created realm (= theology of blessing). Genesis 2:7 sees humanity more clearly in terms of its earthy roots. Yet despite these humble origins, human beings are endowed with an exalted dignity. Genesis suggests that the task of human beings is to reflect God's creative love by caring for the earth as good stewards (Gen 1:27) or as faithful gardeners (Gen 2:15). Created beings, whether living or nonliving, are created to praise God and to enrich human life. But created things are important not only for their possible human use; in God's sight they are valued in themselves as well (Job 38–39; Ps 104).

3) While chapter 1 of Genesis emphasizes human dignity, chapters 2 and 3 underscore the tragedy of human failure (= theology of sin). This etiological account, which lays out the tension between an "original goodness" rooted in God's creative aim and an "original failure" rooted in the mystery of created freedom, sets the stage and themes for a vision of history that constitutes the core of revelation in the biblical tradition. History is marked by an ongoing tension between the gift of life

and its promise as intended by God, and the ever-present experience of tragedy when the gift is taken up by human beings as free, conscious agents of history. Yet despite human failure, God does not turn the world over to a graceless destiny but approaches it always with the promise of forgiveness and new life (Gen 3:15).

4) To say that creation is "good" is to imply that the Creator has a goal in mind in creating, and that the created world is appropriate for the accomplishment of that goal. While evil is a pervasive part of human experience, the biblical tradition does not see evil as an ultimate principle of reality but rather as a distortion of the divinely grounded order of creation. Therefore the world is capable of finding completion and wholeness. In this sense creation theology provides the theological grounding for salvation expectations as well as for the eschatological hopes that develop through biblical history.

New Testament and Early Christianity

For Christians, the story of creation is told not simply by repeating the OT texts but by reflecting on these texts in the light of the Christian experience of God's salvific action in Jesus Christ. The preaching and other activities of Jesus seem to presuppose the existing tradition of creation theology without developing it in new directions. Jesus recognizes the Creator as a loving parent who cares for humanity as well as for other created beings (Mt 6:25-35) and who is concerned for the good as well as for the evil (Mt 5:43ff.). In the parables the world of nature becomes a rich resource for preaching the kingdom of God. In general, the scriptural presentation of the ministry of Jesus seems to suggest no specifically Christian insight into the mystery of creation.

There are levels of reflection elsewhere in the NT in which the Christian experience of Christ is related expressly to God's original plan in creating. In this sense the mystery of Christ is "with God" from eternity and is intrinsically related to God's purpose in creating. Thus the risen Christ appears as Lord over all creation (Phil 2:5-11). And Paul calls Christ the "last Adam," since the human race created by God has been created anew in Christ (1 Cor 15:45ff.).

Texts such as 1 Cor 8:6; Eph 1:3-14; Col 1:15-20; Heb 1:1-13; and John 1 represent an early form of specifically Christian reflection on creation. They provide the textual basis for the later development of a tradition of cosmic Christology that sees the mystery of God-in-Christ as basic to the meaning of the created universe. Both John and Paul see the creative activity of Christ as extending to all humanity and reaching even to the cosmic realm (Rom 8:18-25). This tendency to link creation and salvation has its historical antecedent in Deutero-Isaiah and in the wisdom literature.

Elements of this cosmic, Christological perspective are gathered together in the vision of Irenaeus of Lyons (d. 202), who, in his arguments against historical and metaphysical dualism, developed a theology of creation shaped by his sense of the history of salvation. From the beginning, and despite the presence of evil, the world and its history are moving toward that fulfillment which God intends in creating. More specifically, the fulfillment of created reality and its history is described as a "recapitulation" in the mystery of Christ (*Adv. haer.* II, 22, 4; III, 18, 1-7).

These early materials suggest a far closer relation between creation and salvation than is commonly envisioned later in baroque and modern theologies. In the earlier tradition the language of salvation and fulfillment is language about the creative purpose of God. While existing as a creature (= *esse*) is not formally identical with existing in grace (= *bene esse*), yet created reality never exists without its actual ordering to grace and salvation. Creation is the sphere within which salvation is worked out. In fact, salvation is the final, life-

giving relationship between the Creator and the world of created reality.

Creation and Christian Neoplatonism

For centuries in Western Christianity, the thought of Augustine played a decisive role in shaping the understanding of creation. His use of an exemplaristic metaphysics set the tone for centuries of theological tradition. Augustine situates the Platonic world of Ideas in the inner life of God and identifies it with the divine Word of Trinitarian theology. The Word, therefore, contains the divine archetypes after which everything in the created world is formed. Creatures are seen to embody divine Ideas in the limited form of finite realities. From this perspective the created world, in all its parts and in its basic unity, is the external expression of the inner Word of God in something that is not divine, namely, the finite world. In this style of theology, therefore, the world appears as intimately related to God and as a vast symbolic language-system that mediates to the finite spirit the reality of the divine.

Creation and the Modern Experience

From the time of the Galileo controversy onward, creation theology became deeply isolated from the development of the sciences. Science was often thought of as the enemy of faith, and the created world was perceived as remote from God. At the present time a more positive relation is sought between theology and the positive sciences. The work of Teilhard de Chardin (d. 1955) was significant in moving toward a more complementary relation between the disciplines. Today there is a tendency to see certain analogies between evolution and the theological concept of continuous creation, between cosmic history and the history of salvation, between the sense of radical contingence and the notion of divine freedom and grace, and between the process of evolution by which humanity emerges from the chemistry of the cosmos and the concept of human fulfillment in the transformation of resurrection.

Creation Theology in Vatican II

Vatican Council II addressed the question of creation on a number of significant points. Concerning the relation of creation theology to the positive sciences, the council reaffirmed the longstanding conviction, common among the Scholastics and affirmed by Vatican I (DS 3017), that there need be no contradiction between theology and science, provided the proper methods and limits of the disciplines are taken into account (GS 36). The council spoke clearly of an "autonomy of earthly realities" that corresponds to "the will of the Creator." Related to this principle is the implication that the relation between theology and science should be one of complementarity, and that questions about ultimate meaning fall properly to the disciplines of philosophy and theology.

The council taught also that humanity possesses a certain preeminence among created realities, and that this preeminence involves a responsible role in bringing creation to its God-intended fulfillment. But this should not lead to reckless disregard for the natural environment from which humanity emerges and in which it remains rooted. Human activity in and on the world is to lead the world into a life-giving relation with God through human endeavor. Such activity is to be regulated by the values of "justice and holiness." The basic norm for such activity is that "in accord with the divine plan and will, it should harmonize with the genuine good of the human race, and allow human beings as individuals and as members of society to pursue their total vocation and fulfill it" (GS 34-35).

Creation Theology and Spirituality

Creation theology provides the basis for an understanding of human reality and the network of relations within which human life is to be worked out. In contrast to all ni-

hilistic philosophies, creation theology affirms the gracious character of existence; created existence is not a mere fact nor a curse, but a gift from the loving source of reality. Therefore created existence is to be accepted, affirmed, nurtured, and brought to fulfillment. As an intelligent, free, conscious creation, humanity (human nature) is created as an open receptacle for the life-giving self-gift of God (grace). This potentiality of human nature (obediential potency) has been brought to its fullest realization in the mystery of Jesus Christ. The success of God's grace in Jesus is the decisive realization of the divine aim in creating. It is likewise the anticipation of the God-intended destiny of all humanity. Thus, while the proximate ground of hope is to be seen in what God has done in Christ, the remote ground of hope is found in creation theology. It is in the gracious character of existence that the possibility of hope is grounded.

The human spiritual project is carried out in the context of other human persons and the world of nature. Viewed from a Christian perspective, this entire network of relations is to be shaped in the light of the Christian mystery of agape, which lies at the heart of the Christ-mystery, and hence at the heart of the Christian perception of the Sacred. Only if we are aware of the degree to which we have failed in our historical task can we sense how deeply the world is in need of healing and of a wholeness that does not yet exist. And because we perceive the world as the good creation of a faithful God, we trust that, finally, the world is capable of being healed. But God does not bypass the free actions of creatures in bringing the world to its final fulfillment.

This is the kind of world in which our spiritual journey is to be carried out. When seen from this perspective, Christian spirituality is not a way out of this world to God, but a way in and with the world to God. God is the mysterious abyss into which human history pours and in which that history ultimately finds its fulfillment.

See also ANIMALS; COSMIC MYSTICISM; ECOLOGICAL CONSCIOUSNESS; ESCHATOLOGY; EVIL; FREEDOM; GRACE; IMAGO DEI; REDEMPTION; SIN.

Bibliography: Z. Hayes, *What Are They Saying About Creation?* (New York: Paulist, 1980). A. Lonergan and C. Richards, eds., *Thomas Berry and the New Cosmology* (Mystic, Conn.: Twenty-Third Publications, 1987). L. Scheffczyk, *Creation and Providence*, trans. R. Strachan (New York: Herder, 1970). M. Schmaus, *Dogma 2: God and Creation* (New York: Sheed & Ward, 1969).

ZACHARY HAYES, O.F.M.

CREATION-CENTERED SPIRITUALITY
See CREATION.

CREATIVITY
See AESTHETICS; ART; CREATION; MUSIC.

CROSS
See CHRIST; DEVOTION(S), POPULAR; SUFFERING.

CULT(S)
See DEVOTION(S), POPULAR; OCCULT, OCCULTISM.

CULTURE

To ask about the relation between spirituality and culture is to ask a very "modern" question. What distinguishes modern consciousness from all premodern forms is socio-historical consciousness, that is, an awareness of "culture" as a humanly created realm distinct from the order of nature and subject to historical transformation. Premodern individuals had no distinct consciousness of culture in this sense; rather, culture was experienced as part of the divinely created order of nature. However, by the 19th century, with the development of the social sciences, societies were compared historically and geographically.

As a result, it became clear that despite significant differences between cultures, each considered its own order as the sacred embodiment of the true order of nature. This led to the obvious conclusion that our very concepts of "nature" are culturally constructed human interpretations. We became conscious that we do not dwell directly in "nature" but in language, the realm of mediated meaning. Culture is a linguistically constructed "second nature" that mediates our relation to the world. When we ask about the relation between spirituality and culture, then, we presuppose a modern historical consciousness of the diversity of spiritualities and cultures.

The very asking of this question illustrates the power of spirituality in relation to culture, for it is no accident that socio-historical consciousness arose in Western civilization. Western civilization is uniquely a product of the desacralizing power of religious traditions that give primacy to the *word* and to *history,* rather than to nature, as the mediators of transcendence. Speaking theologically, if we understand Christian "spiritualities" as the patterns of personal and social existence formed by Christians in response to the divine self-disclosure as word and power (i.e., Spirit or enabling presence) within history, then we are asking about the ways in which the Word becomes flesh in the ecclesial community of the Body of Christ so as to disclose God's covenant intention for humanity within particular cultural times and places. Spirituality is the concrete mediation of transcendent meaning. It is the way in which divine transcendence enters into a culture to assume and transform its patterns of personal-communal existence so as to anticipate God's new creation.

From a history of religions and sociological perspective, spiritualities reflect diverse modes of religious experience that tend to assume one of two social forms: either that of a "sacred society" or that of a "holy community." Throughout history most religious spiritualities focused on developing patterns of life that integrated one into the sacred (and usually hierarchical) order of society, in which allegiance to the sacred required allegiance to the established "sacred" order of society. The way the four yogas as the foundational pattern of Hindu spirituality link the self to Brahman (sacred reality) and the caste system (sacred society) comes to mind as an especially clear example.

The holy community, in comparison, represents a far rarer type of spirituality. Holy communities, as the Hebrew *kadosh* suggests, are communities that have separated themselves from the larger society and developed an alternative way of life in response to an experience of transcendence as Wholly Other than society and the natural order. Using the terms as antonyms rather than synonyms, we can say that the experience of the "sacred" absolutizes the finite order of a culture, whereas the experience of the "holy," responding to transcendence as an experience of the infinite, calls into question every finite order. The holy community must be in but not of the world, maintaining that delicate balance whereby transcendence becomes enculturated in the patterns of life appropriate to its cultural time and place without limiting either "the infinite" or "the human" to the existing horizon of culture. Sacred order is critiqued from the perspective of the holy by insisting that religion/society is made for humans who are open to the infinite—humans are not made for the finite horizon of a sacral religion/society.

The pattern of the holy community seems to have emerged independently only twice in the history of religions: in the Buddhist Sangha in India and the Jewish Synagogue in the Mediterranean. Christian spirituality is decisively shaped by its emergence from the latter. The spiritualities of holy communities are distinctive in the history of religions for their iconoclastic ability to shape patterns of living that offer a critical alternative to the sacred order of the dominant culture in the name of a transcendence manifested through human dignity. Such spiritualities give rise to an ethic of hospitality, e.g., the Buddhist welcoming of the outcast or the Jewish and Christian emphasis on welcoming the stranger and the downtrodden.

It it no accident that the single most decisive postbiblical influence on Christian spirituality, the development of monasticism, took the form of a holy community that gave prominence to an ethic of hospitality. Christian monasticism arose at a time when Christianity, having become the religion of the Roman Empire, was abandoning its status as a holy community to become the religion of a sacred society. Monasticism arose as a spirituality or pattern of Christian existence intent on preserving Christianity as a holy community. Unlike other more sectarian movements, however, it set itself apart without breaking its ties to the larger institutional Church and so was able to act as a catalytic influence for the reform of the Church and society throughout the Middle Ages.

Not only did the Benedictine pattern of spirituality, through repeated self-reform, bring reform to the Church during this period, but it also acted as the catalyst in the transformation of European cultures into a civilization that advanced art, learning, science, and technology. At the heart of Benedictine spirituality is the formation of small holy communities shaped by the discipline of prayer and mutual correction, and the conviction that work itself is a form of prayer. This formula has been central to all those forms of Western Christian spirituality, both Catholic and Protestant, that have had the greatest impact on culture. It was the sociologist Max Weber who demonstrated, in *The Protestant Ethic and the Spirit of Capitalism,* that when the monastic pattern of spirituality was turned loose upon the world—a world that it had helped to create—through the Calvinist wing of the Protestant Reformation, it dramatically reshaped Western European and

American culture. Like the mendicant orders of the late Middle Ages, the Calvinist and later Methodist communities created new urban-oriented communal spiritualities deeply indebted to the Benedictine tradition, and likewise showed themselves capable of transforming not only personal lives but whole cultures. This entire history is ample evidence for the fact that spirituality as the incarnation of the Word in the concrete pattern of Christian life is capable of bringing about profound transformations of culture.

We now live at a unique point in history, one that offers perhaps the greatest challenge yet to Christian spiritual patterns of life. We live in a time of the meeting of the world's religions in an emerging world culture. It is a time when Christian patterns of spirituality are encountering their counterparts in other religions. The spiritual adventure of our time, says theologian John Dunne, is one of "passing over" into other religions and cultures in order to "come back" with new insight into our own. It is not a matter of amalgamating all spiritual traditions into one, but rather of being mutually enriched by shared insights. The biblical warrant for this sharing of spiritual insight is the obligation to welcome the stranger, for in doing so, people have often welcomed angels (Heb 13:2), God (Gen 32:23-32), or Christ (Mt 25:35) without knowing it.

It is likely that the most productive sharing of patterns of spiritual life will occur in the dialogue of the Christian Church with the two other great holy communities in world history, the Jewish Synagogue and the Buddhist Sangha. Probably no greater pioneer of this kind of spiritual adventure has emerged in this century than the Trappist monk Thomas Merton. His vision for the future of Christian spirituality was global—cross-cultural and interreligious. The point of convergence for this new order of spiritual patterns of life, for all their diversity, will surely lie in a common commitment to extending hospitality to

the stranger. Such a spirituality of hospitality is appropriate to the emerging global culture of the coming millennium. Its failure would only increase the chance of the global nuclear annihilation of the whole human race even as the transforming power of such a convergence of spiritual traditions might bring about nothing less than a new order of creation—a global culture of unity-in-diversity.

See also ASCETICISM; BENEDICTINE SPIRITUALITY; COMMUNITY; EASTERN (ASIAN) SPIRITUALITY; HISTORY, HISTORICAL CONSCIOUSNESS; HOSPITALITY; INTERRELIGIOUS DIALOGUE; WORLD.

Bibliography: J. Dunne, *The Way of All the Earth* (Notre Dame, Ind.: Univ. of Notre Dame Press, 1972). T. Merton, *Contemplation in a World of Action* (New York: Doubleday, 1971) and *The Asian Journal of Thomas Merton* (New York: New Directions, 1973). M. Weber, *The Protestant Ethic and the Spirit of Capitalism* (New York: Scribner's, 1958).

DARRELL J. FASCHING

CURSILLO MOVEMENT

A cursillo is a three-day spiritual renewal for lay men and women. The weekend is marked by an atmosphere of joy, humor, and deep sharing as the participants model Christian community. Singing and jokes at mealtime set the cursillo apart from the monastic-type retreat that emphasizes being alone with God. The cursillo is a clear statement that Christianity without community is a contradiction. The talks, followed by discussions, speak to the participants' experience of life at home, at work, and in the community.

The cursillo movement began on the Spanish island of Majorca during World War II. In the official structure of the Church, the cursillo was a branch of Spanish Catholic Action. It became a recognized Church group under the guidance of Bishop Juan Hervas of Majorca. Today it is a worldwide movement with centers in nearly all South American and Central American countries. It has literally spread to every corner of the earth where the Catholic Church is established.

The first cursillo in the United States was held in Waco, Texas, in 1957. It was first given in English in the United States in 1961 and quickly spread to dioceses across the country. In many American dioceses a diocesan office and staff coordinate the movement.

The cursillo has been continually challenged to bring its theology into the mainstream of Vatican II developments. In many ways the cursillo anticipated these developments and has had a remarkable longevity in contrast to lay movements that were unable to move with the Church and the culture beyond the sixties.

See also CATHOLIC ACTION; CELEBRATION; JOY; LAY SPIRITUALITY.

Bibliography: J. Hervas y Benet, "*The Cursillos de cristianidad:* A Magnificent Instrument of Christian Renewal and of Apostolic Conquest," *Christ to the World* 7 (1962) 161–178; 312–324.

DENNIS J. GEANEY, O.S.A.

D

DANCE

Dance is the clearest expression of the body at prayer. God created us as embodied beings, so it is most appropriate that our relationship with God be embodied as well. Rather than being simply an intellectual exercise, prayer is a physical experience of our love for, and gratitude to, God our Creator, Jesus our Redeemer, and their Holy Spirit, who continues to breathe their life in us.

In *Environment and Art in Catholic Worship,* the 1978 statement by the Bishops' Committee on the Liturgy, it is stated that "Christians have not hesitated to use every human art in their celebration of the saving work of God in Jesus Christ." This would include the dance, from its early liturgical expression in Judaism to the present day.

There are two principal ways in which dance functions in religious worship: as cultural or folk expression and as classical or interpretive expression.

Postures for prayer are the most common cultural use for dance at worship, as people kneel, bow, stand, or genuflect in reverence to a deity. Processions and circle dances are also idiomatic communal expressions of shared religious feelings. Similarly, in Christian worship we find the dance of the priest lying prostrate on Good Friday and the dance of deacons lying prostrate as the rite of ordination begins.

Less common is the use of classical or interpretive expression in worship. Rather than springing from the basic culture of a people, this use of dance originates as an overlay of physical and intellectual expression, in which an individual choreographer uses dance movement as a medium for relating or interpreting a religious story or truth.

Throughout the world and down through the centuries, sacred dance has taken various forms: ecstatic, ritualistic, and liturgical. It can, for example, take the form of ecstatic movement, bringing the dancer into an altered state of consciousness, as in the case of the whirling dervishes of Islam. When dance constitutes the entire ceremony, it is regarded as ritualistic, for the dance itself is the ritual. Cultural examples of this form abound throughout the world in the religious expression of tribal peoples. Finally, when dance forms part of a larger ritual structure, it is seen as liturgical, deepening and focusing the awareness of the entire community.

Because dance transcends the limits of verbal expression, it has the power to erase the boundaries language imposes on religious people. Dance can also communicate realities for which mere words are insufficient, making it a significant element of ritual worship.

See also BODY; CELEBRATION; RITUAL.

Bibliography: Bishops' Committee on the Liturgy, National Conference of Catholic Bishops, *Environment and Art in Catholic Worship* (Washington: USCC, 1978). R. Gagne, T. Kane, and R. VerEecke,

Introducing Dance in Christian Worship (Washington: Pastoral Press, 1984).

JULIA UPTON, R.S.M.

DARKNESS, DARK NIGHT

Darkness has been a constant theme in the literature of world religions and has frequently been paired with its antithesis light, images often expressed as night and day. Darkness, like night, has been a description of the time between sunset and dawn, but it has also been a manifestation of cosmological, moral, and religious events, often, but not always, with a negative connotation. Thus in the ancient world darkness was a time for the activity of demons.

In the Hebrew Scriptures as well as other Near Eastern literature, darkness was an image for danger, death, and the underworld. But darkness also characterized the day of the Lord. Genesis 1 saw darkness as preceding creation, but elsewhere, e.g., Isa 45:7, God created darkness. Darkness and night were also times for dreams through which God communicated a message (Gen 28:11; Mt 1:20-21). The darkness of night was also a time for visions (Dan 7:7).

In the Christian Scriptures darkness was to mark the last days (Mk 13:24), just as darkness preceded the death of Jesus (Mk 15:33). In John's Gospel and the Dead Sea Scrolls, darkness was contrasted with light, as evil was with good. But in the new Jerusalem there will be no night (Rev 21:25).

Darkness has been a widespread theme in Christian spiritual literature, especially in the mystical tradition. Memory of Moses drawing near to "the thick darkness where God was" (Exod 20:21, RSV) passed into the tradition through Gregory of Nyssa and a host of other mystical writers.

Particularly influential in the mystical tradition has been the theme of divine darkness taken from the *Mystical Theology* of Pseudo-Dionysius. Here the imagery of darkness celebrated the incomprehensibility of God. As with other themes from the tradition, Meister Eckhart elaborated the theme of darkness in a unique way. Tauler and Ruysbroeck also found this theme crucial to their mystical doctrine. The author of *The Cloud of Unknowing* gave directions for responding to the cloud of forgetting and then to the cloud of unknowing as the darkness of God.

John of the Cross made the most memorable contribution to the theme of darkness through his use of the symbolism of the dark night. For John of the Cross, the whole human journey to God is night: night's purification of attachments, night as a journey of faith, and finally night as the encounter with the God of mystery. John has said that his poem *Noche Oscura* ("Dark Night") was composed from the vantage point of union with God in love, and that it also explored the purification of the senses and the spirit, as well as the blessings of spiritual enlightenment and loving union with God.

For directees John composed commentaries on this poem: *The Ascent of Mount Carmel* and *Dark Night,* both incomplete. In each of these books John recounted his now classical signs for the transition from meditation to contemplation (*Ascent,* 2.13; *Dark Night,* 1.9). Here one experiences the impotence of human effort and the sheer gift of what only God can do. Dark night as contemplation is a flowing of God's love into the soul. The loving presence of God liberates the person from imperfections and attachments as nothing that human effort can effect. This dark night is God's work. For John of the Cross, night is for the sake of light and love, since the dark night prepares the soul for union with God in love. John's use of the symbol of the dark night and his subtle understanding of this spiritual experience have profoundly influenced subsequent Western spirituality, though at times his doctrine has been narrowly applied and superficially understood.

In a way different from John, Thérèse of Lisieux used the night to describe her trial of faith, which lasted for almost two years before she died. Modern spiritual writers like John Chapman and Thomas Merton have explored the theme of the dark night, and John of the Cross's treatment of the dark night affected the poetry of T. S. Eliot. Some modern writers have appropriated the dark night symbolism of John of the Cross to corporate experiences.

See also CARMELITE SPIRITUALITY; EVIL; LIGHT; MYSTICISM; NEGATIVE WAY; PURGATION, PURGATIVE WAY.

Bibliography: *The Collected Works of St. John of the Cross*, trans. K. Kavanaugh and O. Rodriguez (Washington: Institute of Carmelite Studies, 1991).

KEITH J. EGAN

DEAD, PRAYER FOR THE

See INTERCESSION; PETITION; SAINTS, COMMUNION OF SAINTS.

DEADLY SINS

The deadly, or capital, sins are now usually listed as seven: pride, envy, anger, sloth, avarice, gluttony, and lust. Traditionally they have been classified as sins, not because they necessarily involve conscious and voluntary choices, but because they are basic tendencies toward evil, dangerous sources of sin, and habits of vice. The list suggests a complex of emotions, attitudes, desires, and ways of acting which pervert good, useful impulses and which stand in the way of love for God, self, and others. Though called "deadly," these sins have not been viewed as inevitably "mortal," especially when considered apart from the character and motivations of their subjects. At its best, the spiritual tradition's reflection on the deadly sins has been situated positively within the context of the possibility of conversion from sin to virtue.

History

Scripture, while listing sins and mentioning each of the sins later called "capital" (Latin *caput*, "head" or "chief"), is not properly the origin of the list. The notion of particular sins being sources of other sins derives from the experience of the Egyptian desert monks, themselves influenced by Hellenistic ideas. Evagrius Ponticus (d. 399), steeped in desert wisdom and probably familiar with Origen's Alexandrian allegorizing of Deut 7:1-2 (seven enemy nations of the Hebrews) and Lk 11:24-26 (seven wicked spirits), gave the earliest systematic treatment when he wrote of eight vicious thoughts, sinful drives that a monk had to battle. John Cassian (d. ca. 425), writing for monks in community, brought the teaching to the West. Gregory the Great (d. 604) rearranged the list, especially by singling out pride as the root of all the other sins. His classification strongly influenced instruction of monks and laity during the Middle Ages. John Climacus (d. 650) and John Damascene (d. ca. 749) carried the tradition forward in the East.

Throughout the Middle Ages, the sins were listed usually either as eight or as seven, a sacred number, but there was no fixed or authorized list. Under the influence of medieval penitential literature of Celtic monks, an eightfold Cassianic scheme gained prominence over other lists. The capital sins proved a popular theme in the Middle Ages, especially in preaching, art, drama, literature, and spiritual writing, but also in the thought of major theologians (e.g., Hugh of St. Victor, Peter Lombard, Thomas Aquinas, Bonaventure). Along with the Creed and the commandments, the sins provided a handy and clear-cut framework for catechesis.

In their various formulations throughout the Middle Ages, the listed sins were often mentioned within the Pauline theme of spiritual warfare: the battle of the vices against the virtues or against the person.

This pitting of vices against virtues (as in Chaucer's "The Parson's Tale") and the matching of each deadly sin to one element of another list (e.g., Our Father, beatitudes) reveal a medieval penchant for contrasts and parallelisms in an effort to give a rational meaning to the universe. Because the lists of deadly sins had origins independent of the other lists, however, the matchings often were overly contrived.

Theologians of the Protestant Reformation avoided classification of sins, on the grounds that all sins are equally hateful in God's sight. Little attention went to the capital sins, a theme without explicit scriptural basis and with origins in a postbiblical, monastic context.

In the modern period, the Roman Catholic manuals of spiritual life treated the moral effort of combating deadly sins among the challenges facing beginners on the spiritual journey, or those in the "purgative way." These manuals usually agreed in placing the number of sins at seven; however, they differed in their ways of clustering and interrelating the sins, as well as in their naming and grouping derivative sins around each of the seven. With confidence that individuals could cooperate with God's grace to make spiritual progress, writers and preachers urged them to act against sinful tendencies by striving for opposite virtues (*agere contra*). Remedies were prescribed, not as easy solutions, but as possible ways toward growth. Various published examinations of conscience offered the capital sins as reference points for assessing spiritual life in preparation for confession.

In the spiritual tradition generally, the most common metaphor for portraying the interconnection of the seven sins is the tree and its branches, an image that underscores pride's place as the trunk of the tree from which the other sins emerge. The theme of the deadly sins is featured prominently among a few of the most widely read writers of the Christian spiritual tradition. For example, Walter Hilton (d. 1396), in

The Scale of Perfection, stresses love as the way of conquering strong enemies of humanity, the deadly sins. In directives to devout Christians faced with their own distorted self-love, Hilton analyzes each capital sin and describes the seven through various metaphors: streams running from the river of self-love, parts of the body of the devilish beast, separate evil animals. In a less typical way of describing the capital sins in spiritual writings, John of the Cross (d. 1591) in *The Dark Night* describes how the sins show themselves differently in persons who are more advanced in the spiritual life and are challenged with the beginnings of "the passive night of the senses." He stresses that even their earnest efforts at mortification will fall short and that only God can wean them from their imperfections.

Individual Deadly Sins

The sin of *pride* is widely viewed as the "root of all the other sins" (Eccl 9:15). It is marked by a self-aggrandizement that clouds not only God's sovereignty and others' worth but also an appreciation of one's true self. Distinct from healthy self-esteem and from a justifiable pride in one's own God-given talents and achievements, the sin of pride often involves disregard or contempt for ideas and judgments other than one's own. A chief aspect of pride is vainglory, which comprises the inordinate effort to show one's own excellence and the insatiable need for approval. A strong force for self-deception, this aspect was often set off as a separate deadly sin in early lists. Suggested helps for turning from pride include self-abandonment to God's providence, a stance of respectful listening to others, an admission of one's own need for being saved in Christ, and an acknowledged need to be supported by the gifts of others.

Envy, rooted ordinarily in a radical difficulty in trusting that God loves one uniquely and personally, moves the self-doubting person to covet what others seem to be or have. There is sadness or displeasure at the spiritual or temporal good of another. For many people, envy threatens if an atmosphere of competitiveness and comparison degenerates into an environment of stifling jealousy. Then the good of another becomes an evil to oneself, inasmuch as it seems to lessen one's own excellence. From envy can follow hatred and resentment, calumny and detraction. An individual plagued by envy usually needs to be helped to move toward a deeper sense of God's love for oneself and to appropriate concern and compassion for others.

Anger diverts a good capacity for strong action destructively toward self and others, when that action should be used constructively to attack evil and to serve good. This sin often shows clear social consequences. "From anger," wrote Gregory the Great, "are produced strifes, swelling of mind, insults, clamor, indignation, blasphemies." The sin of anger must be distinguished from a "holy wrath," anger which attacks evil bravely and which can be virtuous and praiseworthy. Different personality types experience and express anger differently. It can explode or seethe. Unbridled anger can lead to vengeful actions that are disproportionate to the injury or insult suffered. Movement away from anger usually entails progress in reflectivity and gentleness, so that as truth combines with love, one may act less impulsively than when under sinful anger's influence.

The sin of *sloth,* not to be reduced to bodily laziness, usually shows in the inertia of a deadened spirit. This sin combines two related sins separately mentioned on some early lists: *acedia,* lack of care for duties and obligations to God, which gives rise not only to rancor, passivity, and sluggishness but also to restless activity and aggression; and *tristitia,* melancholy, weariness, or dissatisfaction. Nowadays factors engendering sloth will include insufficient or poorly used leisure time, narrow horizons of worldview, overly high expectations, aversion to love that de-

mands sacrifice, and dependence on counterfeit satisfactions for life's deepest yearnings. Growth toward greater commitment and zeal profits from regular consideration of ideals and values, a search for creativity amid the given factors in life, and provision for truly restorative leisure.

Avarice (greed) is an insatiable or inordinate longing for the possession of something. In a complex, competitive society, avarice can be especially alluring. It shows itself when trust in God is so fragile that worldly supports are grasped too tightly in order to ensure security for an uncertain future. Love of possessions in themselves or for purely selfish reasons leads to self-absorbing preoccupations. Avarice also embraces shame at receiving charity from others and inability to give to others without experiencing self-deprivation. This sin can masquerade as healthy frugality and independence. Progress toward generosity may involve appropriation of a healthy awareness of death's finality, acknowledgment of interdependence and vulnerability, and practice of charitable acts.

Gluttony is typically associated with excessive eating and drinking, but it is not limited to these. Indulging the body at the expense of the mind and the soul, it can sap energy as it partakes of two closely related sins, avarice and lust. More broadly described, gluttony entails excessive and narrowing absorption in the immediate appetitive pleasures of the self, and it may show in insatiable desire for any activity. Culpable gluttony may be difficult to distinguish from the sickness of addiction. True gluttony is related to acts that arise when choice is free, when one may decide whether to indulge or abstain. Recent considerations of the sin of gluttony have raised issues of world hunger and sharing of goods, excessive care for personal appearance, and even dangers of overindulgence in exercise and dieting. Progress in moving away from gluttony will likely involve self-knowledge, self-restraint, and a balanced rhythm of life.

Lust, an excessive desire for sexual pleasure, threatens a striving for calm, gentle self-control. The sin of lust often develops when there is a lack of human wholeness, a pace of life that is hectic, and a lack of respect for self or others. The challenge of chaste living involves not only acknowledging that genital sexual drives and affections are normal and spontaneous but also channeling energies into appropriate levels of interest and occupation. Growth toward chastity can come through quieting one's pace of life, entering into wholesome relationships and well-rounded activities, fostering a healthy attitude toward the body, discovering ways in which the temperate satisfaction of bodily needs can support inner life, and recognizing the limits imposed by one's major commitments in life.

Contemporary Developments

The "turn to the subject" in culture and theology has brought with it increasing sophistication in viewing the capital sins. A contemporary stance would look not only at the sin but at the character and situation of a person faced with it. Deeper and more widespread knowledge of psychology has informed understanding of motivations and manifestations behind displays of capital sins.

Advances in understanding the gradual nature of growth in faith have helped Christians to realize more than ever before that basic tendencies toward evil are seldom conquered once and for all but often through ongoing struggle. For many, a particular vice may recur frequently and may seem to be met with little noticeable progress.

It has now become common to consider the capital sins not only as personal vices affecting individuals but also as social evils with corporate fault, manifestations, and effects. There has been increasing sympathy for the position that corporate, cul-

tural, and national climates can foster sinful attitudes.

In recent decades it has been observed that some of the seven deadly sins have acquired a certain respectability in society (e.g., the sin of pride seen as self-esteem, anger as assertiveness). If the workplace once served as a moral context, keeping the worker from temptations of the deadly sins, now perhaps the modern corporation has neutralized sin and freed its employees from moral responsibility.

Feminist critique has questioned whether the list of deadly sins identifies the worst personal and social evils. Some critics would propose alternative chief sins, e.g., cruelty, hypocrisy, snobbery, treachery, self-negation, and aimlessness. It has been suggested that classifications of sin produced by any society reflect that society's preoccupations, distortions, and self-delusions.

Conclusion

For each person, the movement away from the threat of enslavement to the capital sins will involve growth in some basic virtues: humility that recognizes God as the primary healer; patience with one's own gradual but steady journey toward holiness; and compassion for the weaknesses of others. Although the complex reality that is sin cannot easily be fit into seven specific categories, the survival of the capital sins as a spiritual theme points to the presence of patterns of evil that threaten to dissipate human life in any age.

See also ACEDIA; ASCETICISM; CONSUMERISM; EVIL; FEELINGS; HUMILITY; LEISURE; MATERIALISM; MONASTICISM, MONASTIC SPIRITUALITY; PASSION(S); POVERTY; PURGATION, PURGATIVE WAY; SEXUALITY; SIN; TEMPTATION; VIRTUE; WARFARE, SPIRITUAL.

Bibliography: M. Bloomfield, *The Seven Deadly Sins* (East Lansing, Mich.: Michigan State Univ. Press, 1967). H. Fairlie, *The Seven Deadly Sins Today* (Notre Dame: Univ. of Notre Dame Press, 1978). D. Lowery, *Choosing Virtue in a Changing World* (Liguori, Mo.: Liguorian Publications, 1990).

GEORGE P. EVANS

DEATH AND DYING

Death raises the ultimate question about the meaning of human existence and the relationship of persons to God. As Vatican II noted in the Pastoral Constitution on the Church in the Modern World, human beings are "tormented not only by pain and by the advancing deterioration of [the] body, but even more so by a dread of perpetual extinction" (art. 18). This dread of death, as well as the process of dying, has had a direct impact on the spiritual and pastoral life of the Church.

Experience

The spiritual life has often been conceived of and practiced as a preparation for death and final judgment. One indication of this is the depiction of saints contemplating a human skull, one of the few items among their personal possessions. Death and life-threatening circumstances have been a prime occasion for prayers of petition and deliverance, including many of the psalms. Behind these prayers is a sense of human powerlessness coupled with the image of a powerful God who might intervene and rescue the faithful from death. As a further inducement to God's favor, people have called upon the intercession of saints and undertaken acts of personal mortification for themselves or for the deceased, presumed to be in the interim state of purgatory. When death has occurred despite these efforts or when death occurs unexpectedly, prematurely, or extremely painfully, faithful people have sought to make sense of their experience by invoking the providence and plan of God.

Death as a pervasive and troublesome experience has been traced to the very beginning of human existence, being counted as one of the chief effects of the original sin of Adam and Eve. In this view sin and death are causally connected, and the burden of human labor, the pain of childbirth, and other forms of human suffering are included (Gen 3:16-19), suggesting that the real punishment of death is not the mere physical termination of life on earth but the unnatural emotional and psychic trauma accompanying it.

The experience of dying has posed a major challenge for the Church's pastoral practice. Knowing that all people must eventually die and understanding the dread of death caused by sin do not respond adequately to the anxiety of a person facing death or grieving over the death of a beloved. More compassionate and supportive pastoral care is needed. The pastoral care of the Catholic Church has been channeled primarily through the sacraments, especially anointing, penance, and Eucharist (as Viaticum). Even these liturgical resources have not always matched people's fear of death and feeling of helplessness against it. Some have prepared for or compensated for death by engaging in excessive acts of penance and mortification, or by falling victim to unwarranted assurances claimed for certain prayer formulas or pious devotions, sometimes bordering on superstition or manipulation.

The experience of death and dying in modern times has undergone some major modifications. The primary influence has been the advance in medical knowledge and technology. A cure has been found for many previously terminal illnesses, and the average life span has been extended, at least where such medical technology is available. Where this is the case, people think differently about when to marry, how large a family to have, what career to pursue, how to care for their aging parents, when to take their own retirement. They also become more aware of their aging process and might even develop a sense of confidence about the human capacity to postpone death. In addition, medical advances have generated their own set of unprecedented ethical and legal questions pertaining to the definition of death, the use of life-support systems, experimental drugs, biotechnology, and genetic engineering.

On a different level the "near death" experiences of many people have been recently recorded and correlated with both empirical data and parapsychological phenomena. This cluster of evidence is assumed by some to give a glimpse into the initial phase of the transition from life to death and has altered the way people may feel about dying. On the other hand, information about these phenomena, as well as the availability of modern medical technology, typifies only a small portion of the human race. Most people still live in precarious medical, social, and political circumstances. Disease, malnutrition, infant mortality, genocide, terrorism, civil war, and the specter of nuclear annihilation are the forms death takes for most people in the world. And overriding all personal perspectives is the prospect of an actual death of the planet through technological disasters or the irreversible destruction of the ecosystem.

The insights of modern psychology and studies of human behavior have reshaped the pastoral response to those who are dying, equipping those who provide pastoral care with the skills to attend to human emotions more directly and to interpret the spontaneous expression of those emotions more accurately. This understanding is now the framework for an explicit sacramental ministry whereby prayers and rituals are integrated into human experience rather than being imposed upon it or used to avoid stressful situations. The psychological phases of dying are more fully understood as personal, but not private, experiences over which the dying person should have control. This awareness has been translated into practice through the hospice movement, the living will, and the involvement of family and faith community in the rituals of dying. Likewise, the stages of grieving (for individuals, families, and communities) are more clearly identified, giving rise to support groups and better care of those who mourn.

This accumulation of changes in modern times confronts people with an increased capacity and responsibility regarding death and dying. Human beings are not able to eliminate death, but at the end of the 20th century they are much more aware of their complicity in the causes of some types of death and their conquest of the causes of other types of death. Still, death remains a mystery, confronting the human person with threats and questions to which faith is expected to respond, both theologically and pastorally.

Theological Reflection

Christian faith responds to death out of the paschal mystery of Jesus. This Christological standpoint leads to an eschatology that professes hope for personal immortality and the transformation of creation. Connecting these two poles is ecclesiology, the life of the pilgrim people of God on earth who journey in the company of the communion of saints.

Christology

The central mystery of Jesus' death and resurrection was first proclaimed, and has been preserved in tradition, with elements from both a Jewish worldview (resurrection of the body, general judgment, transformation of the world) and a Hellenic worldview (immortality of the soul, immediate personal judgment, otherworldly heaven). Spiritually, Jesus' death provides a model that his followers may imitate in their own lives. They may adopt his attitude of trust in the power and providence of God, thereby drawing closer to the hidden but effective presence of God in their life; they may subsume their suffering into hope for the personal, immortal happiness he promised, thereby integrating the present with the future, and the material with the spiritual; or they may imitate his freedom and self-determination in the face of forces conspiring against him, thereby sharing in his sacrificial offering of life for the sake of others.

Any of these aspects of Jesus' death can deepen a person's spiritual life, but they can also run the risk of turning the experience into a private relationship with Jesus. This can happen when a person overidentifies with Jesus and withdraws from those who want to offer support or share their own feelings of separation and loss. It can also happen when a person appropriates the death of Jesus solely as a guarantee of one's own immortality rather than as a witness to the primacy of God—as Jesus' own resurrection was. An authentic Christology is unquestionably personal, but it is not individualistic or selective. As Vatican II noted in its Pastoral Constitution on the Church in the Modern World (art. 22), by his incarnation (and death-resurrection) Jesus has united himself in some way with all people. And with all times.

Eschatology

Just as Jesus' death was not the end of his life but its fulfillment, so his death was not the end of history but the fulfillment of history. And yet, the implications of his death have to be lived out in every age and in every situation through his followers. Thus, for Christians, death is not the destruction of everything they have become and accomplished, it is the culmination. Death puts a definitive stamp on the particular quality of each person's life and makes it a permanent contribution to the ongoing development of history mediated through Jesus. This conviction is asserted in the description of the communion of saints (LG 49). This community of holy women, men, and children centered on Jesus is a living community whose legacy is not confined to what they did while alive on earth but extends to what they continue to do now and how they represent a more blessed and permanent community still being formed.

The communion of saints takes on a fresh meaning today in light of the modern awareness of interdependence and wholeness. On an individual level, when persons understand themselves as an integral whole of matter and spirit rather than a combination of two separable elements (body and soul), and when they grasp that the very constitution of their existence is intertwined with others, their approach to spirituality and their reflections on death change dramatically. Spirituality embraces all dimensions of human being and seeks their full interaction rather than suppressing one (sexual, social) for the sake of another (contemplative, private). Likewise, spirituality embraces relationships with others, not just interior experiences; it includes productive activity, not just introspection. Similarly, death affects the whole person, not just the body; and the transition from this life to the next affects the whole person, not just the soul.

On the historical level, the same inclusiveness appears. Although it is Christian belief that time is linear and human life is unrepeatable (LG 48), each person remains part of the future development of history, even after death. In light of Jesus' life and chosen associations, the members of the communion whose impact on the future is most decisive are the poor, the neglected, the outcast. Their lives constitute an abiding, dangerous memory that confronts people with the destructive results of the past and challenges them not to repeat that history in their present decisions. In this eschatological context, spirituality becomes a form of public service, conversion is a commitment to improve society, and asceticism is the discipline and self-sacrifice needed to bring about a new social order. From this same eschatological perspective, death is not so much closure on a private story but a contribution to public history. All these dimensions of Christology and eschatology come together in the understanding of the Church.

Ecclesiology

In the eschatological view of Vatican II, the Church is a pilgrim people, sharing simultaneously in the passing of time and the permanence of God's kingdom, living already the death of Christ but not yet fully sharing the glory of his resurrection (LG 48). This pilgrim people is a sacramental union of the past and the future, of the particular and the universal, of the living and the dead, of the human and the divine. It is a symbol of the whole of humanity in its relation to God and the world. It lives in expectation of that death through which it will cross the threshold to a life that is no longer hemmed in by death.

Spiritually all these themes come together in the liturgy, especially the Eucharist. Here the centrality of Jesus' death and resurrection is proclaimed and enacted; the communion of all the saints is gathered; the impetus toward the future is renewed. From this core experience of liturgy, other forms of devotion, especially to the saints, can flow (SC 13). Likewise, new sources of energy are tapped for the continual effort to transform and perfect the world in which the pilgrim people live. Just as the mystery of death embraces all people, so too the mystery of liturgy embraces all, either directly or indirectly, through the mediation of the Church, carrying in its members the experience of life and death from individual to communal to sociopolitical to cosmic circles of meaning.

Pastoral Praxis

Christological, eschatological, and ecclesiological reflections on death and dying have helped shape a new pastoral praxis that is found both in the training for pastoral care ministry and in the revision of the sacramental rites.

Pastoral care is a specialized, professional ministry. It requires training in the skills of listening, feeling, and responding. It takes seriously the life story of a person and uses it to discover with the person God's unique presence in the person's life. This is quite different from inserting ready-made exhortations or offering well-intentioned assurances about a person's recovery or share in everlasting life. Entering deeply into another person's story is a sacred journey that can be a source of spiritual richness for the minister, the person cared for, and others who share the experience. All are drawn into communion with one another and encounter the living Lord through the mediation of one another. Such experiences, pivoting around the ultimate mystery of death, draw people close to the very source of life and put everything into the perspective of faith.

These values are incorporated into the revision of the *Rite of Anointing and Pastoral Care of the Sick,* which views the occasion of serious illness as a time of special pastoral care, involving the whole community of the sick person as much as possible (General Introduction, 1-7). The aim of the rite is to enable the sick person and those in support to feel the presence of God and to experience God's spiritual strength (if not physical healing). Structuring this ministry sacramentally, the rite clarifies the purpose of each sacramental response: anointing for the seriously ill, Eucharist (Viaticum) and commendation for the dying, prayers for the dead. All three mediate the Christological, eschatological, and ecclesiological dimensions of Christian life in ways that correspond to the condition of the person cared for.

Even with a renewed theology and revised sacramental rites, the pastoral praxis of the Church faces some awkward situations. The ordinary minister of anointing is an ordained priest, even though others, not ordained, may have provided the actual pastoral care up to the point of anointing. Eucharistic ministers, who may also offer Viaticum, are often called upon by the nature of the situation to extend pastoral care but have not been trained to do so. Pastoral care of the dying often occurs without the presence and participation of the person's faith community; this tends to isolate the person's relationship with God and neglect the community's need for mourning the death of its members.

Despite these problems, the praxis of the Church is more consistent theologically and effective pastorally because of Vatican II. With the council it faces death precisely as a mystery and relies on that faith which enables people "to be united in Christ with his loved ones who have already been snatched away by death [and] arouses the hope that they have found true life with God" (GS 18).

See also AFTERLIFE; AGING; CHRIST; ESCHATOLOGY; HISTORY, HISTORICAL CONSCIOUSNESS; LITURGY; PARAPSYCHOLOGY; PRAXIS; SAINTS, COMMUNION OF SAINTS; WEAKNESS AND VULNERABILITY.

Bibliography: R. Kinast, *When a Person Dies: Pastoral Theology in Death Experiences* (New York: Crossroad, 1984). H. Küng, *Eternal Life? Life after Death as a Medical, Philosophical, and Theological Problem* (Garden City, N.Y.: Doubleday, 1984). L. O'Donovan, "Death as the Depth of Life: A Rereading of Eschatology in *Gaudium et Spes*," *Vatican II: The Unfinished Agenda*, ed. L. Richard (New York: Paulist, 1987) 203-223.

ROBERT L. KINAST

DECISION, DECISION-MAKING

The Christian is one who is called to discipleship, that is, to following Christ in the worship of God and the service of neighbor. The acts by which this discipleship is enacted are decisions, and the process can be described as decision-making. The goal of decision and its shape will be considered here.

Put simply, the goal of Christian discipleship is to do what is right. The character of that "rightness," however, is not always clear. At times rightness has been understood as legality, and the goal has been understood as conformity of the person's acts to some law. The Catholic religious tradition has always rejected this view, however. In what was called the natural law tradition, it was held that right behavior is that which accords with the reality of the self (one's *nature*) and responds to the needs of the other in a way that is truly constructive (the *nature* of reality).

The pertinence of law was always acknowledged, of course. Note, for example, that this was called the natural *law* tradition. But the natural law was described as a law promulgated in the very act of creation; that is, it was the inner reality of creation asserting itself and not some arbitrary regulation added on.

Similarly, other laws have genuine value, but only as pathmarks to the truly helpful behavior. Civil law, for example, justifies itself if it guides citizens to acts supportive of the common good and deters evildoers from doing destructive acts. Church laws, and even more Church teachings, justify themselves when they articulate in a helpful manner the truth about behaviors and their objective significance. Even the demands of Scripture are to be understood, not as the arbitrary impositions of despotic authority, but as challenges from a loving God to live in a way that is truly in one's best interest.

Still, it must be acknowledged that a tendency to reduce the challenges of discipleship to legalism has been visible in Christian tradition. There is a temptation to view the center of the Christian life as obedience, when in fact it is love. The temptation has several causes. Personal immaturity is one. Children are formed by an ethic of obedience. In adulthood persons are expected to go beyond this and pursue an ethic of understanding and commitment. But the process of maturation can easily be aborted. The result is a chronological adult living-out of an ethic—and a view of discipleship—that is appropriate for children.

Another cause of legalism is the inappropriate use of legal language on the part of leaders. The exercise of leadership is no doubt simplified if subjects are discouraged from questioning and dialogue. Over the centuries both civil and ecclesiastical authorities have indulged in unexplained commands that call for unquestioning obedience. This has, in turn, led ordinary Christians to misunderstand discipleship, to adopt a legalistic view that sees commands as arbitrary and minimal, and a literal response as sufficient. Thus the challenge of discipleship is robbed of its inner core.

Legalism is also caused by the fact that love, when it is genuine, rightly expresses itself in a yielding of the self to the beloved. Hence obedience, as a manifestation of love, is both common and appropriate. This fact explains the central role of law in the Jewish Scriptures and the "doing of God's will" in Christian spirituality. These are not themselves indications of legalism, but when the behaviors of obedience are not continually reconnected to their roots in love, legalism can easily develop.

Periodically, attempts are made to extricate Christian discipleship from legalism. But sometimes the reaction leads to an opposite distortion: relativism. Relativism understands the goal of decision as nothing more than the conformity of one's behavior to one's own inner vision, and decision-making as nothing else than the sincere following of one's conscience. Relativism has taken various forms, some quite conscious and theoretical. Contemporary moral philosophy, for example, includes an approach known as situation ethics, which amounts to a form of relativism. But more commonly this distortion is manifested in practice rather than in theory. Individuals settle for their preestablished prejudices and remain settled in habitual ways of acting but do not attempt to transcend this subjectivistic bias and attend to the complexity of the concrete world.

All the more is this so in a culture that has elevated the individual to such an unequaled status that dialogue, moral disagreement, and interpersonal challenge are viewed as affronts rather than forms of service. Relativism is also encouraged by a political context that sees religion as an altogether private affair that should not make public demands.

Once again, the distorted view incorporates a note of truth, since the following of conscience is an essential component of Christian living. But it is not everything. Indeed, the function of conscience is precisely to alert the person to those behaviors that are truly helpful and therefore truly right. To put this in the language of traditional Catholic theology, while conscience is the proximate norm of morality, the natural law is the ultimate norm.

While these insights are usually associated with moral theology, their implications for spirituality are obvious. Since the goal of spirituality is wholehearted commitment to God and neighbor, the proper understanding of the relationship of one's inner self to the objective reality of neighbor and world can greatly assist the effort to grow in the spiritual life.

If, then, the goal of decision is behavior objectively helpful to the neighbor, what can be said about the shape of the decision-making process? Two assertions will focus two conclusions.

First, all human decisions are made in the context of conflict. The human person is finite, a being who in choosing one thing necessarily forgoes another. Thus election always involves selection. It follows that the concrete decisions by which one attempts to enflesh love of God and neighbor always involve the choosing among goods in such a way as to do the best one reasonably can.

Second, all human decisions are made in the context of change. The human world is a world in motion and subject to the laws of change. It follows that choices that are appropriate in one context are not necessarily appropriate in another. From one place to another, from one time to another, changes in context may result in the fact that a behavior that was once truly helpful is no longer so. Hence a decision that was once right has become wrong. The proper use of money, for example, will change as a person moves from the single state to the married, as children are born, as professional success increases income, and then as children leave home to take up life on their own. And this susceptibility to change is not expressive of that relativism discussed above. It is simply an acknowledgment that objective morality takes place in a changing world.

These twin facts of conflict and change suggest that proper decision-making is a complex skill. It requires, indeed, skills of the Christian life, otherwise known as virtues. In particular, it requires the skill of good judgment in human matters, otherwise known as the virtue of prudence.

Indeed, our first conclusion involves retrieving the conviction of Catholic theology whereby prudence has been understood as that virtue most central to the living of the Christian life. Love as a virtue is the heart of discipleship, the source of its energy, so to speak. But prudence is the faith-filled skill of expressing love in wise and helpful action.

This is not some abstract or academic skill; rather, it is the ability to deal with the concrete dimensions of life, acknowledging that not all good things are simultaneously possible, sorting through the available alternatives, and choosing the best that can be done in the objective circumstances that present themselves. But this cannot be done alone. The realities of conflict and change, and the decision-making complexity that they suggest, are sufficient to make one humble about one's ability to discover the good. It is only with the help of others that this process can succeed. It is only in community, a place of moral support and moral wisdom, that successful decision-making can take place. The centrality of community, then, is our second conclusion.

The achievement of this sort of moral community is not easy. The American tendencies toward individualism and the privatization of religion militate against it. But by the same token, to the extent that they encourage relativism and imply that the project of seeking the objectively right choice is unnecessary, to that extent do they render moral community superfluous. But it is not.

In a strangely paradoxical way, the institutional use of legalistic approaches also militates against the development of genuine moral community. For such community must be open, honest, dialogical. It must be the expression of adults in sincere and forthright communion.

Still, it is only in community that the goal of decision, the discovery of genuinely helpful ways for love to incarnate itself in behavior, can be achieved. And it is only when this successful decision-making takes place that the goal of discipleship can be achieved.

See also COMMANDMENT(S); COMMUNITY; CONSCIENCE; CONSCIOUSNESS; DISCERNMENT OF SPIRITS; DISCIPLESHIP; LAW; LOVE; OBEDIENCE; RESPONSIBILITY; SELF; VIRTUE.

Bibliography: T. O'Connell, *Principles for a Catholic Morality,* rev. ed. (San Francisco: Harper & Row, 1990). R. Gula, *Reason Informed by Faith* (New York: Paulist, 1989).

TIMOTHY E. O'CONNELL

DEIFICATION
See DIVINIZATION.

DEMON(S), DEMONIC, DEVIL(S)

The place of the devil and of demonic forces in Catholic thought has moved to the periphery at the same time that the popular culture has developed a certain fascination with matters of the occult, possession, and exorcism. Vatican II made succinct references to the reality of "personified evil," at whose urgings we have abused our liberty (GS 13) and whose power was broken by the risen Christ (GS 2). Through the preaching of the word and the celebration of the sacraments, the devil's domain is overthrown (AG 9). When the historical significance given to demonology by the Church is considered, this modest affirmation is quite remarkable. Part of this is due to the shift of focus from the centrality of sin to the omnipresence of God's grace. Also, the reexamination of Scripture has led to nuances that are still subject to ongoing debate.

The word *devil,* from the Greek *diabolos,* means an accuser, a slanderer, or a perjurer. *Satan,* which originally meant an accuser or adversary, came to mean "the evil one" in later Hebraic thought and was used synonymously with *diabolos* in the NT. There is a very important distinction between the devil (Satan), a personal being, and the demons, who are harmful powers or evil spirits causing all sorts of illnesses that could not otherwise be explained.

It is argued by Cortes and Gatti (p. 231) that possession by demons was used as a literary form to express unknown, mysterious, and incomprehensible occurrences and illnesses; they concluded that in the Gospels there are no cases of diabolical possession attributed directly to the devil. This position is more acceptable when it is remembered that sin, illness, and death were ultimately attributed to the devil. Unfortunately, many translators did not exercise sufficient care in distinguishing between the devil, a personal being, and demons.

The accounts of Jesus' healings, whether of those suffering from recognizable illnesses or of those possessed by demons, indicate that he used the same method for both: his presence, touch, word, and authority. This is true also of the exorcisms performed by the apostles. In addition, the Old and New Testaments are filled with references to the angels of God and the angels of Satan (devils). Both are seen as spirits—the former as benevolent spirits who play an important role as intermediaries between God and human beings, the latter as harmful spirits of evil who belong to Satan. Exegetical analyses and traditional positions acknowledge the obscurities of these texts, always affirm-

ing, however, the extraordinary events in life that appear to go beyond human understanding.

As was the case during Vatican II, the doctrine of the Church is quite sparse when compared with popular mythologies. It confirms that initially all creation was good and that the devil is evil by choice. The devil encouraged and encourages human beings to separate themselves from God (DS 800).

Liturgical reform since Vatican II has reflected a change in perspective. In 1969 all explicit elements of exorcism for infant baptism were removed; in 1972 references to original sin and the domination of the world by Satan were removed from the Rite of Initiation for Children of Catechetical Age. Furthermore, the prayers of exorcism in the Rite of Christian Initiation of Adults do not signify an adjuration to a possessing devil, as was the case traditionally.

Since Vatican II, Pope Paul VI and Pope John Paul II have made only a few general comments in their general audiences of November 15, 1972, and August 13, 1986, respectively. Pope Paul affirmed the reality of the devil but prefaced his comments by affirming the beauty of all creation as a work of God. Pope John Paul commented on the devil in the context of the mystery of freedom and its possible abuse. The latter neither affirms nor denies diabolical possession but acknowledges that it is possible.

Today it is postulated that possessions in the biblical narratives could have had different possible causes, ranging from psychological or mental illnesses to organic brain disorders and similar illnesses to the presence of the devil. Those scholars who do not accept diabolical possession do not necessarily challenge the existence of the devil and the devil's angels; they do, however, question the tradition of exorcisms as commonly understood. Other scholars, after careful analysis of both Scripture and tradition, argue that the few doctrinal statements that do exist presuppose rather than affirm the existence of the devil (see Kelly, *The Devil, Demonology and Witchcraft,* p. 123). However, the more general consensus is that the existence of the devil is part of Catholic teaching.

In the development of spirituality, it is important to remember that ultimately all creation is of God and in its origin is a blessing. Sin, division, destructiveness, and death are also part of our lives, realities that have their source, in Catholic tradition, in "the father of lies," the devil. We are counseled to proceed cautiously, not with a view of excessive evil in this world or with an attitude of personal invincibility. We are called to be hopeful, knowing that we are nurtured by the word and the sacraments of God, and that by living a life of love, evil will ultimately be vanquished and complete unity with God will be realized.

See also ANGELS; CREATION; EVIL; EXORCISM; OCCULT, OCCULTISM; SIN; SPIRITS; TEMPTATION.

Bibliography: J. Cortes and F. Gatti, *The Case Against Possessions and Exorcisms* (New York: Vantage, 1975). H. Kelly, *The Devil at Baptism* (Ithaca, N.Y.: Cornell Univ. Press, 1985) and *The Devil, Demonology and Witchcraft* (Garden City, N.Y.: Doubleday, 1968). J. Russell, *The Prince of Darkness* (Ithaca, N.Y.: Cornell Univ. Press, 1988).

JAMES A. SCHMEISER

DEPRESSION

See ACEDIA; FEELINGS.

DESERT

This entry will deal with the desert from two perspectives—that of its religious meaning and that of its physical place in the history of monasticism.

The Religious Meaning of the Desert

Although the desert is first of all a kind of geographical place, it can, like other such places (e.g., the sea, mountains, valleys), be given a religious meaning; indeed,

for millennia it has been endowed with special meaning in religious literature. This is, of course, due to the nature of the place itself. By definition the desert is barren and inhospitable, often the abode of wild animals and subject to extremes of temperature; it is an environment where most human beings find themselves either with reluctance and fear or with some strong and set purpose. For those who must experience it, it is a place not to stay in but to pass through. As a symbol, then, the desert represents for the human being the site of a test of endurance with two possible outcomes—emerging victorious or succumbing.

Translated into religious and more specifically Christian terms, the desert stands for the arena in which one, while submitting to the test, meets one's spiritual salvation or one's spiritual doom. It is life itself in its starkest form. Those who go to the desert for religious reasons do so precisely with the intention of entering this arena and facing the starkness that presents itself there. They seek a barren physical environment for the same reason that they seek an undistracted mind, namely, in order to reduce the struggle to its barest and most essential elements. As Antony of Egypt observes, they have cut themselves off from the struggles that are generated by hearing, speaking, and seeing, and they can devote themselves to the evil that arises from within them (see *The Apophthegms of the Fathers,* Antony 11).

If the desert both is and symbolizes a place of struggle, then the garden serves in the role of countersymbol. If the desert represents the painful aspect of life's journey, which many try to avoid even though it is ineluctable, the garden stands for the longed-for goal of that journey. It is a place of repose and refreshment, and sometimes of sensuous enjoyment (garden imagery occurs throughout the Canticle of Canticles). Eden and the land flowing with milk and honey (see, e.g., Exod 3:8) are archetypes of this. The garden ultimately symbolizes nothing less than heaven itself, which is often portrayed as a lush and verdant place in Christian art. It is true that the garden, too, can give rise to spiritual struggle; there is, after all, Eden, however short the combat there may have been. But in the desert the struggle is clearer, for there it is engaged in alone and against the most uncluttered background. And in the desert, for the same reason, the presence of God and of the devil is perceived with heightened awareness.

The fertility and lushness of the garden are a temptation to indulge in those distractions, preoccupations, and pleasures that blunt the acuity of the spiritual senses. Hence Cassian, an early 5th-century monastic writer who was familiar with the Egyptian desert, can compare the garden unfavorably with the desert. After praising the desert in all its harshness and bleakness, he goes on to write: "Therefore, the person who wants to keep constant watch over the purity of the inner man must seek out places that do not draw his mind to the distraction of cultivating them because of their abundant fertility and that do not make him leave the fixed and set location of his cell and force him to work outside, thus scattering his thoughts at large, as it were, and, by all sorts of things, utterly diverting the aim of his mind and that most delicate focus on his goal" (*Conferences* 24.3.1).

But the desert is, in the end, a place of transition, a place to pass through, whereas the garden symbolizes attainment and repose. Thus it is that when the struggle is finally over, the desert will no longer exist, having either disappeared or been transformed: "The desert and the parched land will exult; the steppe will rejoice and bloom. They will bloom with abundant flowers, and rejoice with joyful song" (Isa 35:1-2). And even in the present life, when virtue has triumphed over its opposite and the struggle has effectively been decided, the desert may be said to be transformed and to blossom (see, e.g., Jerome, *Letter* 14.10; Eucherius, *In Praise of the Desert* 40; John Moschus, *The Spiritual Meadow,* preface).

The city, too, is a countersymbol to the desert. It is populated, civilized. But it is less ambivalent than the garden, for it more readily suggests evil, as in fact it does as early as the Babel account of Gen 11:1-9. The sophistication of the city, perhaps innocent enough in itself, is characteristically eyed with suspicion by the unsophisticated folk who, for the most part, populate the desert. Certainly in the Christian literature of the desert, the city of Alexandria—prosperous, bustling, and still quite pagan—stands in contrast to the desert and is viewed as a place of temptation (see Palladius, *Lausiac History* 35.14).

In the OT the desert is a factor of great significance. Not only do the chosen people look upon the exodus from Egypt, the crossing of the desert, and the entry into the Promised Land as the central event of their history, but the desert recurs constantly in other contexts, as an image and as a reality, most notably perhaps in the psalms and in the Elijah cycle (1 Kgs 17ff.). In his *Homily on Numbers* 27, the early Christian exegete Origen finds, for the first time, in the journey across the desert of Sinai, with its various stops, a symbol of the individual Christian journey through trials to the height of virtue, while in other ancient writings Elijah appears as a model for monks (see Athanasius, *The Life of St. Antony* 7).

In the NT, too, the desert plays a role. John the Baptist lives there (see Mt 3:1), and Jesus is tempted there before he begins his public ministry (see Mt 4:1-11). The chosen people's forty years in the desert, Elijah's forty days on the way to Horeb through the wilderness (see 1 Kgs 19:8), and Jesus' forty days in the desert eventually become, by the start of the 5th century, mystical precedents for the forty days of Lent, the period of preparation for baptism, a kind of spiritual retreat akin to the experience of the desert.

The Desert in Monastic History

As an actual place in the postscriptural world, the desert first enters the Christian consciousness with the initiation of the monastic movement sometime toward the beginning of the 4th century. In his *Life of St. Antony* (3), Athanasius tells the reader that although there had been monks before Antony, none of them had ever ventured into the deep desert of Egypt; rather, they practiced ascetic lives at the edge of towns and villages, on the fringe of the desert. It was Antony who first crossed over the frontier of civilization, at the end of the 3rd century, and by the second decade of the 4th century he had gathered numerous disciples around him in the desert (*Life of St. Antony* 15). At about the same time Pachomius founded a monastery at Tabennisi, in the Thebaid near the Nile. By the end of the 4th century many places in the vast Egyptian waste had been peopled by thousands of monks and nuns, whether as cenobites (i.e., persons living in communities) or as solitaries. Probably the most famous of these places were Skete and Cellae (or Kellia), which belonged to the Nitrian desert south of Alexandria, and the Thebaid, a huge area in upper, or southern, Egypt. Also at this time, monasteries were being founded in various desolate spots in Syria, Palestine, and Gaul.

Egyptian monasticism, which served as a paradigm for monasticism elsewhere and with which we shall be mainly concerned in what follows, produced a fairly abundant literature, a considerable portion of it written by persons who had made pilgrimages to the desert, drawn there by its universal reputation for holiness. Among the earliest and most important works are *The Life of St. Antony*, already mentioned, the corpus of Evagrius Ponticus, *The Lausiac History* of Palladius, the anonymous *History of the Monks in Egypt*, the anonymous *Life* and *Rule* of Pachomius, *The Institutes* and *The Conferences* of Cassian, and a whole series of anonymous sayings and edifying tales.

These sources are significant because they tell us what a monk or nun in the desert might have been like. It would appear that the vast majority of such persons were poor peasants, illiterate and inured to hard labor, although among them were also to be found men like Arsenius, a former high official at the court of Emperor Theodosius I. They lived simply and often roughly, able to survive on a frugal diet, with little sleep and few possessions. Even if some of their austerities were exaggerated in the telling of them (although the Egyptians did not have a taste for the excesses that were typical of Syrian monasticism, such as pillar-sitting), their life was certainly not easy.

The same sources also give us insights into what possessed men and women to pursue monasticism in the desert. Some, to be sure, chose this life for other than religious-ascetical reasons. *The Life of St. Antony* (44) suggests in passing that there were those who were fleeing the onerous taxation of the times, which fell heavily upon the poor. There were almost certainly some who simply opted out of society—criminals, misfits, and the like. But the vast majority were men and women who were genuinely seeking God in an environment that tested them to the limit of their capacities. Among these were persons deeply experienced in sin (e.g., Moses the Ethiopian, a brigand and murderer) as well as innocents. Athanasius offers a paradigmatic monastic conversion: it occurs when someone takes the word of God seriously, as being addressed personally and directly to him or her (*Life of St. Antony* 2). By the late 4th and early 5th century, the scriptural call to conversion and to the following of Christ was so interpreted as to be heavily weighted in favor of some form of monastic life.

Finally, from these sources we gain an understanding of the rudiments of the spirituality of the Egyptian desert. It is a spirituality profoundly marked by the austerity and starkness of its place of origin, to the extent, at least, that it views the inner life in terms of combat and the monk or nun as an *athleta,* an athlete or, more properly, a prizefighter. The adversaries in this combat are the demons, who are everywhere in the desert and who fascinate and repel the ascetic. The monks and nuns of the Egyptian desert certainly did not invent demons; they are already spoken of in the OT and the NT, and Origen had theologized about them a century or more before in his treatise *On First Principles* 3.2 and in other works. But the vast solitudes of Egypt, as has previously been suggested, seemed to make demons a present reality as they had never been before: they appeared in all shapes and under all guises, sometimes manifesting themselves as the "angel of light" referred to in 2 Cor 11:14; and they were masters of fear and seduction, although there were those that were relatively harmless and more annoying than dangerous. According to Evagrius and Cassian, each of the eight principal vices was the area of expertise of a particular group of demons; among these the "noonday demon" of Ps 91:6, the demon of *acedia* (a condition that especially afflicted desert dwellers), was probably the best known.

Whether these demons were the projections of minds rendered susceptible by the desert or completely objective beings is, in the last resort, beside the point; as far as the monks and nuns of Egypt were concerned, they were real. It became a matter of prime importance, then, to be skilled in dealing with them—to be able to recognize them, distinguish them from benign spirits (which also populated the desert and which sought to exert their influence), and resist them. The pertinent skill was, classically, called discretion. The first monastic discourse that we possess, in *The Life of St. Antony* (16-43), is devoted almost entirely to this quality, and it is clearly the key virtue in Cassian's *Conferences.*

Discretion was acquired by seeking the counsel of others, for one's own judgment was notoriously flawed and subject to self-deception or to demonic delusion (*illusio*). Hence extremely typical of desert literature are the accounts of younger monks asking the advice of older and presumably wiser ones. This really represents the beginning of the Christian tradition of spiritual direction as we know it at present. The advice given, at least as it has come down to us, is often in the form of the apophthegm—a short and sometimes lapidary statement which conceals a vast experience and which corresponds well to the taciturnity of the desert. And the quality that made it possible for the monk to relinquish his own judgment and seek counsel from others was, of course, humility, which is in some respects the virtue most characteristic of the desert.

In *The Life of St. Antony* (44), Athanasius offers a description of the group of solitaries who gathered around Antony. They passed their time, in Athanasius' words, in psalm-singing, studying, fasting, praying, longing for heaven, working in order to give alms, and preserving harmony among themselves. This brief passage almost constitutes a definition of desert monasticism.

As far as psalm-singing and prayer are concerned, the monks and nuns of Egypt made an effort to fulfill the injunction of 1 Thess 5:17 to "pray without ceasing," and they frequently understood these words in a literal way. Hence the solitude, the vigils, and the work that they regularly took upon themselves, such as the weaving of mats, which would leave their minds undisturbed for prayer. From the desert comes the so-called prayer of the heart, the repetition of a phrase so often that it virtually becomes a part of oneself. Common prayer formed part of the desert regimen in most cases, but not universally. Although even most solitaries would probably gather for the Eucharist and other prayers on Saturday and Sunday, there were some who, on the basis of personal inspiration, did not attend these gatherings and clung to an absolute solitude for weeks and months, and sometimes longer.

The studying of which Athanasius writes is not to be understood in the usual sense of the term. That would have been foreign to most of the monks and nuns of the desert. Instead, it is probably to be taken as reflection or meditation on Scripture.

Fasting was a very important part of desert life, since its purpose was to control the one urge that could not be entirely abolished and whose satisfaction could become, in the barrenness of the desert, an obsession more tormenting than that of genital sexuality. But the monastic diet was scrupulously regulated with a view to controlling not only the desire for food and drink but also sexual desire, since diet and sexual behavior were closely linked in ancient medicine.

Longing for heaven represents the eschatological aspect of monasticism.

Work occupied a significant place because its alternative was the moral collapse whose symptom was a laziness that could masquerade as prayerfulness. If possible, work was arranged, as has been noted, in such a way as to permit prayer, but if a conflict arose between work and prayer, it would almost certainly be resolved in favor of work. Both solitaries and cenobites, however, labored not simply for spiritual reasons but in order to support themselves. The excess from what they earned was customarily given to the poor; the almsgiving of the Egyptian monks and nuns was proverbial.

The final characteristic of Antony's monks, as Athanasius records, was the preservation of mutual harmony. Broadly understood, this not only included the cultivation of patience and mildness but also left room for the development of friendships (Cassian's sixteenth *Conference* is the earliest Christian treatise on the topic). Harmony was sustained, too, by the visits that the monks and nuns made to one another, which manifested charitable concern in an informal way.

These characteristics assume or imply what later came to be the three great vows of religious life: poverty, chastity, and obedience. It is interesting to note that poverty is probably closer to the original inspiration of monastic life in the desert than chastity is, and that Mt 19:21 ("If you wish to be perfect, go, sell what you have and give to the poor, and you will have treasure in heaven. Then come, follow me") is arguably the central monastic scriptural text. It is perhaps for this reason, among others, that the monastic authorities seem to view breaches of poverty with greater severity than they do breaches of chastity.

A final assumed or implicit characteristic might be mentioned, namely, stability or keeping to one's cell. Perhaps the desert ascetic's greatest struggle was simply to face the nothingness which the desert was and which it symbolized and not to try to fill up the awesome and inevitably tedious void with distractions. The cell of the monk or nun, with its relentless sameness, was a desert within the desert, offering little or no possibility for distraction.

The visitor to the desert would perhaps have been struck most by the routine observed there among both cenobites and solitaries. Feats of heroic asceticism, miracles, and extraordinary gifts of prayer, although not unheard of, would have stood out as quite unusual. The desert was a place for stolid folk, such as the Coptic peasants who populated its monastic communities and hermitages; only dogged determination and a deep-seated optimism could enable them to get through, and undoubtedly these qualities mitigated many of the hardships of the place. But what was disseminated of desert life and spirituality throughout the ancient world tended to be the unusual, and Egypt enjoyed an unparalleled reputation as a result. It was seen as a paradise, a heaven on earth. Despite this ephemeral sensationalism, however, the desert left a permanent and positive legacy:

the basic structure of religious life, both cenobitic and solitary; the practice of spiritual direction; an evocative literature; and a sense of eternity and infinity (see Waddell, pp. 23–25).

But there were also the makings of a negative legacy. The peasant origins and the corresponding illiteracy and simplicity of so many monks and nuns contributed to an anti-intellectualism that continues to be a problem in numerous monasteries to this day. This anti-intellectualism would perhaps have been tolerable had it been merely cultural, but it was necessarily theological as well. Here it typically appeared in the form of biblical literalism and also as the inability to grasp theologically complex arguments. The former produced anthropomorphism (i.e., the belief that God has a human body, since Scripture regularly attributes bodily parts such as eyes and ears to him), while the latter resulted in an unnuanced reliance on authority and ended up specifically in Cyrillian fundamentalism (i.e., an unreflecting recourse to the Christological terminology of Cyril of Alexandria [d. 444]) or Monophysitism.

This reliance on authority also manifested itself in the relationship of the monk or nun to his or her spiritual director, the wise man or woman who offered counsel. Ideally the humility and discretion demonstrated by the person seeking guidance was matched by that of the guide, but the latter nonetheless enjoyed a quasi-absolute spiritual authority that could stifle questioning and turn into something like tyranny, however well-intentioned.

The desert likewise passed on, and in so doing almost surely gave further credibility to, an anti-body tendency that it had inherited from Hellenism and Gnosticism. Despite a warning such as can be found in *The Apophthegms of the Fathers,* Poemen 184 ("We have not been taught to destroy our bodies but to destroy our passions"), the austerities of the monks and nuns, and the mere fact of dwelling in the barren waste, far from every bodily comfort, not only clearly signaled that the body was subordinate to the spirit but also, more detrimentally, often made the body appear threatening to the spirit.

Finally, the monasticism of the desert, which was emphatically a lay and charismatic movement in its origins, had difficulty finding its place vis-à-vis the Church of the hierarchy and the sacraments. As previously noted, some monks and nuns absented themselves from the liturgy for weeks and months at a time. There can be no questioning the holiness of those who did this, just as there can be no questioning the holiness of the literalists who insisted on a divine corporeality, but it was an uninformed holiness reminiscent of that described in Rom 10:2 ("I testify with regard to them that they have zeal for God, but it is not discerning"), and it would set an unfortunate example for those less holy who would follow after them.

Yet these negative elements were not of the essence of desert monasticism. And in any event, it is impossible to conceive of Christianity, to say nothing of religious life, apart from its contributions.

See also ACEDIA; ASCETICISM; DEMON(S), DEMONIC, DEVIL(S); DISCERNMENT OF SPIRITS; DISCRETION; EREMITICAL LIFE; FASTING; HESYCHASM; HUMILITY; MONASTICISM, MONASTIC SPIRITUALITY; PATRISTIC SPIRITUALITY; RELIGIOUS LIFE; SILENCE; SPIRITUAL DIRECTION.

Bibliography: D. Chitty, *The Desert a City* (Oxford: Blackwell, 1966). J. Leclercq, "'Eremus' et 'eremita': Pour l'histoire du vocabulaire de la vie solitaire," *Collectanea Cisterciensia* 25 (1963) 8–30. H. Waddell, *The Desert Fathers* (Ann Arbor, Mich.: Univ. of Michigan Press, 1957), esp. pp. 1–25. A. Guillaumont, "La conception du désert chez les moines d'Egypte," *Revue de l'histoire des religions* 188 (1975) 3–21. St. Athanasius, *The Life of Saint Antony,* Ancient Christian Writers 10 (Westminster, Md.: Newman, 1950).

BONIFACE RAMSEY, O.P.

DESIRE

"The hairs on your head are far easier to count than your feelings and the movements of your heart" (St. Augustine, *Confessions* 4.15).

We experience desires, first of all, as psychological events. But their origins are buried in subpsychological events, and their effects extend beyond our psyches to the larger society and to yet unborn progeny. Furthermore, the history we inherit and the history we make are always entangled in sinful desires and yet graced by a doubly self-giving God. So if we are to understand desire in its fullest contexts, we should take into account a number of perspectives: cosmology, psychology, theology of history, theology of grace, and Trinitarian theology. From these perspectives we can give some very practical suggestions about how to deal with desires. These will be helpful either to spiritual mentors in the process of helping others or more directly to ourselves as we try to understand and deal with the desires of our own hearts.

Let us begin with a partial definition that sets desire in its cosmological, historical, and sin-fraught contexts: Desire is our experience of the burgeoning character of the universe in the throes of an uncertain birth. Keep in mind that as we speak of desire we also include aversion, since aversion is simply a desire to withdraw from something.

A fully empirical view of the burgeoning universe in which we live envisions a series of layered plateaus—from physical, to chemical, to biological, to psychological, to intellectual, to reasonable, to responsible, to the affection and love that mold communities and direct history. If we regard these layers as an ongoing process, the transition from what is "material" to what is "spiritual" should be no more disturbing or miraculous than the transition from physical processes to chemical processes. Up through all the layers, there are events that instigate changes, raising the odds that a higher level of controls will emerge, and there are events that consolidate changes, and so preserve any higher level of controls that happened to emerge. Within the human arena, desires are that part of the great hierarchy of events that instigate change. Desires are the drivers of specifically human evolutionary processes insofar as they help make us what we become, but they are also the experienceable part of a continuous creation going on in the universe.

However, what makes the transition to the human so miraculous and unlike any other known reality is the fact that our human nature has a say over what its nature is to be. We live somewhat above mere spontaneity, inherited instinct, and the blind probabilities of evolution. We experience an inner pull to direct our own nature through our intelligence, wisdom, and love, and particularly through our desire to do what is intelligent, wise, and loving.

We experience desires first as mere instinctual events in reaction to our perceptions or to organic functioning, much as animals do. But our minds measure the costs and our hearts weigh the wisdom of following these instincts, so that instinctual desires can be transformed into responsible or irresponsible desires. Unfortunately, our hearts are fickle, and our desires by themselves do not automatically direct themselves to what is responsible. And so, also unlike any known reality in the universe, the pulls of desire are tragically and paradoxically involved in self-contradiction. We ignore loftier desires and embrace baser desires, making our own nature less than human. Thus, in us the universe can give birth to either its own life or its own death.

This disturbing fact of life is the aboriginal possibility of sin, and every man, woman, and child experiences desires both for and against what is good. All "sins" that display themselves in broken promises, broken families, broken economies, and broken civilizations are hatched from these inner throes of the soul. The Bible is full of admonitions against following sinful desires, but it was not until St. Augustine's brilliant *City of God* that Christian literature named this inner tension of desires as the key to understanding the making of human history. A millennium later St. Ignatius Loyola encapsulated Augustine's theology of history in a parable designed to prepare a Christian for making a major, practical life-decision. His "Two Standards" meditation plunges a person deep into the imagery of this inner war of desires going on in all people, of every race, in any place and time. These visions present the individual with a worldview of the essential workings of all historical process. Such a view of history, rooted in the inner struggle of desires, repudiates other views held by Christians and non-Christians alike— for example, that history is governed ultimately by the stars (astrology), by some philosophical or religious secret (gnosticism), by mere chance (fideism), by uncontrollable forces (Buddhism, Taoism, Stoicism, Progressivism), or by any trick of human will that ignores the pull to evil in us all.

Happily, there is more to the dynamics of history than good and bad desires. There is also the gift of God's grace. But what does this ancient dogma of salvation really mean? Our understanding of how God's "grace" redirects errant desire should be consistent with our contemporary, empirical understanding of the universe so that we can collaborate with God more intelligently. So let us sketch out what we have learned about the exact tasks we face as we beg God to flood our souls with that healing grace.

As of the end of the 20th century, we know of three fundamental tasks regarding our desires. First there is the intellectual task of understanding the specific desires and aversions we experience. We are under a double cloud here. On the one hand, we do not always realize that we desire something, even as we are driven by unnoticed urges—jealousy, for example. Or we may claim to desire something when in fact we only fear to differ from our parents, whose patent desires on our behalf have stilled

our own. On the other hand, we may clearly experience desire but be ignorant about its true object. A teenager may claim to want to be a doctor, but he or she may actually desire merely the esteem of others. So the intellectual task, commonly associated with Freudian psychological analysis of the workings of repression, is to clarify whether our feelings are actually desires and what the precise objects of our desires really are.

The second task lies in the moral realm. Once we know our desires and their objects, it is up to us to either allow or suppress them, since not all desires are for good objects. But to one person "good" can mean whatever is merely self-aggrandizing, while to another it can mean what is objectively worthwhile. We are not speaking here of the mere failure of good intentions to produce good results; we are speaking of the difference between the criterion of the merely comfortable and the criterion of the truly good. It is upon this underlying opposition of criteria that we call some people "good" and others "bad." In practice, it is not enough merely to clarify our values, in a liberal tolerance of subjective desires merely because they are subjective. The moral task is rather to choose what is objectively the best of known options, to turn our desires in that direction, and to suppress contrary desires. This is the task commonly associated with seeking counsel, advice, mentoring, or wisdom.

The third task arises when we actually try to take control of our desires for the truly good and find our hearts enmeshed in the sinful heritage of Adam and Eve. We soon discover that we are morally shortsighted about what the truly life-giving alternatives may be. If this is not shameful enough, even when we do recognize the best option, we do not always experience the effective desire to take the steps to accomplish it, particularly when it comes to letting go of our own attitudes of resentment, bitterness, or self-hate. Finally, even when we recognize, desire, and actually do what is good, we have little assurance that our actions will be effective, as anyone can testify who has tried to renovate our cities, give direction to our youth, or provide security to our elderly and handicapped. So we can say that our good desires are debilitated by a triple disease: blindness, impotence, and despair. There is need for a triple moral healing of desire.

Thanks be to God, when we ask for grace, we usually experience the eye of faith to see what is good, the heart of charity to make good desires effective, and the guts of hope to endure uncertain, forestalled, or frustrated outcomes—healing moral blindness, impotence, and despair, respectively. These graces are experienced events. Yet they cannot be had on demand; they are God's powers, not ours. When God gives them, they enter the soul gently, easily, like something coming home where it belongs. St. Ignatius described the movement as a drop of water penetrating a sponge. For all their quiet arrival, they can supercharge otherwise ineffectual desire. They can unleash our greatest powers for turning around a bad situation. These three strengths come easily and often to the person in love with God—more easily when one asks for them directly, pounding on the Father's door under instruction from the Son.

Each of these three fundamental tasks defines a distinct "moment" in spiritual mentoring. In a "truth" moment, it can take some time and talk to uncover what a person's desires and aversions really are. A spiritual mentor, therefore, must be aware of his or her own limits in psychoanalysis and be prepared to recommend a trained psychologist where repression does not release its real, hidden desires. In any case, both the mentor and the person seeking guidance must share not only an acknowledgment that some closets of the heart detest the light but also a commitment to illuminating the truth.

In a second, "moral" moment, once the relevant desires are brought into the light, the question is one of wisdom. Which desire should I follow? This ought not to be conceived as an intellectual task of "finding God's will," as if God's will were a mere fact to discover; rather, it is the moral task of evaluating known alternatives and being ready to take responsibility for one's actions. Practically speaking, it helps to articulate the various voices of one's culture, family, friends, and Church calling this way and that, in an effort to stand apart from them all and to gain as much objectivity as possible. But having said that, we should add that it very often happens that the right path has been clear to a person for a long time, and there is less need to investigate other paths than to make a heartfelt decision to begin walking.

It is in the moral moment that we discover the phenomena of moral blindness, impotence, and despair. This brings us to the third moment of spiritual mentoring— the moment of "grace." Again, the person seeking guidance should be fully prepared to expect these obstacles to making a good choice, to discuss each of them in detail, to humbly admit his or her own concrete fears and weaknesses, and to beg God for the faith, charity, and hope that will overcome them and liberate God-given desires. In this moment a person "discerns the spirits," that is, scrutinizes the origins and the quality of desires and aversions to determine which are most in harmony with one's being in love with God and with feeling God's love for the world. Also in this moment, a person not only makes a decision, but he or she needs to support that decision thereafter with the image and emotion drawn from Scripture, from an imaginal theology of history such as Ignatius's "Two Standards," from the liturgy, and from the feelings and commitments shared with other Christians.

From a theological point of view, and to finish off the partial definition of desire given above, the deployment of our desires is an experience of God's double self-gift. First, insofar as we effectively desire to embody the truth, do what is truly good, and act in love, we are God's incarnate Word with Christ. We are co-creators with the Word of truth, goodness, and love, making this world God's kingdom coming as part of a historical movement that cannot be reversed. We thus embody Christ often at the cost of our own crucifixion. Second, insofar as we experience God's love flooding our hearts with good desires, we share with God's Spirit both the search for, and the welcome of, God's own Word of truth, goodness, and love in the concrete particulars of our lives. In us the Spirit yearns for the fullness of life, crying, "Abba, Father!" Desire, then, is also our experience, at times, of the parenting character of God's Spirit bringing God's perfect Word to birth.

See also AFFECT, AFFECTIVITY; DISCERNMENT OF SPIRITS; EXPERIENCE; GRACE; HEART; INTENTION, INTENTIONALITY; LOVE; MORALITY, ETHICS, RELATIONSHIP TO SPIRITUALITY; VALUE.

Bibliography: B. Lonergan, "Healing and Creating in History," A Second Collection: Papers by Bernard J. F. Lonergan, S.J. (Philadelphia: Westminster, 1974). E. Kinerk, "Eliciting Great Desires," Studies in the Spirituality of Jesuits 16/5 (St. Louis: Institute of Jesuit Sources, 1984).

TAD DUNNE

DETACHMENT

Detachment is separation. When applied to the spiritual life, it indicates a willingness to give up any worldly value for the sake of a higher spiritual good, such as compliance with God's will, or the spiritual development that is often called the pursuit of perfection, or the expiation of sin. The rightly ordered practice of detachment in no way implies that the abandoned created goods are bad in themselves or despised. Detachment is a means to freedom from sin and from the disordered inclinations or attachments that impede one from

giving greater love and commitment to God.

Such detachment is inculcated in the OT, for example, by Abraham's willingness to leave his country or to sacrifice Isaac, and still more cogently in the NT. Jesus taught it by his example of sacrificing his human life to achieve God's redemptive plan of salvation for those who use their freedom wisely, and also by his words. His conditions of discipleship are: "Whoever wishes to come after me must deny himself, take up his cross, and [=in order to] follow me" (Mt 16:24). To the rich official he said: "Sell all that you have and distribute it to the poor, and you will have a treasure in heaven. Then come follow me" (Lk 18:22). This detachment extends to the most sacred human ties: one's parents, relatives, and very self. "There is no one who has given up house or wife or brothers or parents or children for the sake of the kingdom of God who will not receive [back] an overabundant return in this present age and eternal life in the age to come" (Lk 18:29-30).

Paul called detachment by other terms, such as mortification of one's evil tendencies or as "taking off the old self with its practices" of immorality in order to be reclothed with the new self, renovated in the image of its Creator (Col 3:5, 8-12). Furthermore, Christ went through his life, passion, and death to achieve the redemption and the glory of the resurrection; and by baptism Christians are associated closely with him in order that their sorrows or joys, frustrations or achievements, may lead to the glory of the resurrection and all it brings (Rom 6:3-11).

Throughout subsequent Christian spirituality, authors taught the fundamental notion underlying Christ's teaching on detachment by terms or metaphors that increasingly nuanced its various aspects, such as abnegation, renouncement, mortification, stripping off of the old self, renunciation, self-abandonment, forgetfulness of self, self-sacrifice, humility, or, especially in postconciliar times, spiritual freedom, or availability for apostolic work.

A few samples will illustrate these fluctuating terms. Some early Christians, such as Ignatius of Antioch, prepared themselves for martyrdom, a supreme act of detachment from one's very self. From A.D. 400 onward virgins and hermits gave up worldly goods to seek God. St. Benedict urged his monks to "love the Lord God with your whole heart . . . . Renounce yourself in order to follow Christ; discipline your body; do not pamper yourself, but love fasting" (*Rule* 4:1, 10). St. Francis of Assisi stripped himself of everything—his goods and his very self—in order to follow the poor Christ; and he urged his followers to do the same (*Second Rule,* no. 6). St. Thomas Aquinas wrote of stripping off the old man and putting on the new man, the person renewed by grace (*In ep. ad Colossenses* 3, 2). The Dominican mystics Meister Eckhart, John Tauler, and Henry Suso stressed abandonment of, and detachment from, creatures as a means to union with God.

As systematization of the spiritual life and methodical mental prayer grew toward the end of the Middle Ages, detachment was often linked with the purgative way or with the early stages of infused contemplation. The aim of St. Ignatius of Loyola's *Spiritual Exercises* is to help others to order their lives without reaching decisions through disordered attachments. As means to this detachment he presents his doctrine of indifference (Ex., no. 23). God created human beings that they might attain self-fulfillment by glorifying God in the beatific vision. All creatures are means to this and should be used insofar as they further that end or discarded insofar as they hinder it. If we wish to serve God better, when faced with options we should make ourselves indifferent, that is, undecided, impartial, free from disordered inclinations or attachments, until we can learn which option is likely to be more pleasing to God. Then we should choose the option likely to be more conducive to our end—his greater service and praise. The decision should be made with discernment and discretion. This teaching penetrates virtually all Jesuit retreats and spiritual writings and has been widely influential.

For St. Teresa of Avila, the disturbing influences that arise from the body must be brought under control before one can respond freely to God's love in contemplative prayer. For St. John of the Cross, the "night of the senses" is detachment from the things perceived by them, and the "night of the spirit" is detachment from those apprehended by the memory, understanding, and will. Both nights pave the way to simplified or contemplative prayer.

The spirituality of Vatican Council II is world-affirming and includes a stress on freedom and responsibility (GS 2, 5, 17, 31). Christians are exhorted to shape the world more into conformity with God's designs (GS 22, 34, 55-93). Detachment is not explicitly treated, but the traditional doctrine on it is presupposed and its positive aim receives stress. The purpose of religious life is to follow Christ with greater liberty (PC 1), and poverty, chastity, and obedience are viewed as means to this end. Penance "should be fostered . . . in ways that are possible in our own times and in different regions and according to the circumstances of the faithful" (SC 110). Accordingly, many writers now tend to characterize detachment and indifference as spiritual freedom from sin or disordered inclinations in order to commit oneself more completely to God.

See also DISCERNMENT OF SPIRITS; DISCRETION; FREEDOM; IGNATIAN SPIRITUALITY.

Bibliography: R. Oechslin, G. Bardy, H. Martin, "Dépouillement," *D.Spir.* 3, cols. 455–502. J. de Guibert, R. Daeschler, "Abnegation," *D.Spir.* 1, cols. 67–110. J. English, *Spiritual Freedom* (Guelph, Ontario: Loyola House, 1973) 9–55.

GEORGE E. GANSS, S.J.

DEVOTIO MODERNA

See RHENO-FLEMISH SPIRITUALITY; WESTERN MEDIEVAL SPIRITUALITY.

DEVOTION(S), POPULAR

It is common in academic circles, among historians, medievalists, and students of religion, to employ terms like *popular piety, popular religion,* or *popular devotion.* The qualifier *popular* implies a distinction that is often left implicit. The implied contrast is made explicit in the French dichotomy: "foi savante, foi populaire," referring to a learned or sophisticated faith versus popular belief. Since these terms deal with faith and its expression, it must be asked: What is the meaning of popular faith and what relevance does this concept have to the topic of devotion(s)?

Faith is a gift whereby God moves a person through grace to give God assent. If faith is a gift, then it must be essentially the same in everyone who has it. There are no degrees of possession. In relation to the gift of faith, the ordinary believer, the theologian, the religious, the cleric are all on the same level. All believe in the same God who both gives their faith and guarantees its certainty.

At the level of the expression there may indeed be differences. Education, and especially theological education, or the environment of a religious community may afford the individual a greater capacity to understand the gift of faith and its giver, but the gift of faith as such is not greater in a person who can give it theological expression, nor is it less in a person who is unable to articulate it. Even the most learned formulations of the most articulate theologians fall short of the God who is beyond human comprehension. One has only to recall what Thomas Aquinas said near the end of his life: "Everything I have written is straw." On the level of faith and its expression, everyone, regardless of talent or position, is on the same level, a level we might designate as popular, which is to say human and fallible in relation to God.

The same is true at the level of devotion(s). Common usage defines *devotion* as "profound dedication, the ready will to serve God." In the plural the term refers to religious observances and forms of prayer or worship. Thus it may be said that devotion is any attempt to respond to the gift of faith. Even here the dichotomy between worshiping God or praying in a more or less learned or sophisticated way is not very helpful. Particular forms expressing devotion may have little, if anything, to do with the quality, intensity, or sincerity of belief. Indeed, forms of prayer and devotion that might appear inept or even superstitious to some might be more sincere attempts to express faith than those of the learned. The same may be true as people of one historical period or culture attempt to judge the expressions of another time or place.

If devotion is the desire to respond to God with gratitude for God's gift of faith, and devotions are concrete expressions of that desire, then the best way to critique them is to consider them in relation to the liturgy. In the liturgy of the Church, worship is given to God in the spirit of Jesus. There is something universal, something objective, something timeless about the liturgy, above all the Eucharist. The Eucharist realizes in ritual form the response of Jesus to God. It is, from the standpoint of Christian faith, the most perfect sacrifice of praise and thanks that can be offered to God. As the summit of Christian worship, it is the reference point of the other sacraments and the Liturgy of the Hours, which lead to or flow from the Eucharist.

The same faith that expresses itself in and through the liturgy may seek expression alongside the liturgy. Devotions come and go in the history of the Church, arising in particular times and places because of particular needs, falling by the wayside, or giving way to new devotions. They may be public or private, communal or individual, officially sanctioned or not. But because it is the liturgy that is normative and universal, the authenticity of any prayer form can and must be critiqued and judged by its relationship to the liturgy.

Leonard Boyle has suggested the following categories, which may prove helpful in comparing various forms of devotion. Everything that belongs to the liturgy may be classed as liturgical. This may seem redundant, unless it is considered that although the liturgy is a constant, liturgical piety is not. For example, the celebration of the Liturgy of the Hours, in which the people once participated, has become, for all intents and purposes, something pertaining to clergy and religious. Other forms of devotion might be considered semiliturgical, since they are directly related to liturgical worship. Others could be classed as paraliturgical or nonliturgical, since they do not relate directly to the liturgy but are not at odds with its spirit and intent. Finally, some may be characterized as aliturgical, a designation that would be reserved for exercises that may run counter to what is considered authentic.

It remains to discuss some of the more historically important forms of devotion. To begin with, we may speak of the cult of the saints, who are honored, of course, within the liturgy and outside it. The cult of the saints answers the very real human tendency to identify and honor heroes and to consider those who have passed through death to be alive in God. As understood by the Church, the cult of the saints acknowledges the mystery of Christ in human life and gives praise and thanks to God for what was achieved in Mary and the saints through God's grace.

In the course of the 12th century there was an important development in the history of Christian spirituality, namely, the growth of devotion to the humanity of Jesus, Mary, and the saints. This development coincided with, and was probably occasioned in part by, the Crusades. Two significant devotions that came about were the Stations of the Cross and the worship of the Eucharistic species outside Mass. The intent of the Stations of the Cross was to enable the faithful, who could not make a pilgrimage to the Holy Land, to unite more closely with the suffering Christ by following in imagination his journey from judgment to death and burial.

The worship of the Eucharist outside Mass developed historically as the result of the focus on the humanity of Jesus, coupled with the fact that for a variety of reasons regular Communion was no longer the rule. The Eucharistic bread, in particular, was perceived to be the fulfillment of Jesus' promise to remain always with his faithful (Mt 28:20). Through the establishment of the feast of Corpus Christi, there gradually developed the practice of processions in honor of the Eucharist and then the rite of benediction of the Blessed Sacrament in the 16th century.

Finally, mention must be made of the Rosary. The Rosary is a meditation on the mysteries of the incarnation and saving work of Christ using the angelic salutation, the Hail Mary, as a kind of continuous prayer. The Rosary developed as a substitute for active participation in the Liturgy of the Hours. Each Hail Mary stands for the recitation of a psalm. Thus the recitation of the full fifteen-decade rosary substituted for the recitation of the Psalter. The faithful were encouraged to meditate on the mysteries of Christ as they prayed, much as those who prayed the Office associated the words of the psalms with particular events in Christ's life.

See also AFFECT, AFFECTIVITY; EUCHARISTIC DEVOTION; LITURGY; MARY; PIETY, ROSARY.

Bibliography: L. Boyle, "Popular Piety in the Middle Ages: What Is Popular?" *Florilegium* 4 (1982) 184–193. R. and C. Brooke, *Popular Religion in the Middle Ages* (London: Thames and Hudson, 1984). P. Brown, *The Cult of the Saints: Its Rise and Function in Latin Christianity* (Chicago: Univ. of Chicago Press, 1981). E. Delaruelle, *La piété populaire au moyen âge* (Turin: Bottega d'Erasmo, 1980).

RONALD J. ZAWILLA

DISABILITY, THE DISABLED

Referring to a person or group as disabled is a rather recent practice. To whom this term applies is not always as clear as it may seem at first. At one level, persons with disabilities, or the disabled, are those whose capacities of mind or body are diminished in any way during the pre-, peri-, or post-natal period or at some later period in the course of psychosomatic development, so as to necessitate particular attention or special assistance in meeting basic human needs. This definition excludes infants and children, who, in the course of normal development, need the constant attention of others in meeting basic needs. At another level, a person may be disabled temporarily, as when one requires nursing care or the assistance of a wheelchair during a period of recuperation following surgery. More often than not, those who live to old age become disabled in one way or another.

The term is more usually applied to persons who are permanently disabled. In this view the key is the notion of diminishment due to improper development, accident, or injury to the brain, nervous system, or the body, resulting in a disruption or cessation of their normal functioning. Accident or injury to the brain or nervous system in the pre-, peri-, or post-natal period often results in mental retardation or, said in another way, causes the person to be mentally handicapped. Improper development or injury to nervous system or body often results in physical handicap. More often than not, mental retardation is accompanied by some form of physical disability as well.

There is often great resistance to using the term *the disabled*. Such resistance comes from persons with disabilities themselves and/or from their families, friends, and members of support systems or advocacy groups. It arises from the legitimate concern to avoid the problems inherent in assigning a label to any person or group, notably the prejudice and discrimination from which such practice can stem and to which it often gives rise, as well as the disregard for real differences between and among persons in a given category. Alternative terms such as *disadvantaged, special, handicapable,* or *mentally challenged* as well as a host of others have been proposed as substitutes for *disabled, retarded,* or *handicapped*. Though each adjective has its advantage, no one term adequately describes the complexity of this phenomenon.

The resistance to accept such terms is itself expressive of a shift in understanding those who require assistance in meeting basic human needs. Previous approaches tended to be paternalistic or maternalistic, and were often quite patronizing in theory and practice. For example, mentally retarded persons, at whatever age, were and are often thought of and dealt with as children. In this view, the "normal," "healthy," "strong," and "clever" are the caregivers, the ones who have something to give or to offer the disabled person. Such approaches often result in the needs of mentally handicapped adults for intimacy, ecstasy, and fecundity being overlooked.

Contemporary perspectives, some of them shaped by the experience of living in community with mentally and/or physically disabled persons, lend to viewing them, even and especially the most severely and profoundly mentally retarded, as persons with gifts of the heart and profound capabilities for human relationship. Rather than being viewed solely as recipients of care and attention, disabled persons are to be understood as persons with gifts and riches of the heart, with capacities for care, compassion, forgiveness, celebration, joy, all of which are theirs precisely as disabled persons. The gifts and capacities for authentic human relationship found among disabled persons call into question the modes of perceiving and being in the world of the strong and robust, a world in which efficiency and productivity are prized so highly. Indeed, those disabled in mind and body, because of the riches of their gifts of heart, call into question the operative definitions of what constitutes a "normal" human person.

Those who are disabled remind "normal" persons of the contingency, fragility, and vulnerability that are part and parcel of human existence, and of the strategies and defenses adopted to ignore or deny human suffering, diminishment, and death. In the wounds of body and mind, those who are disabled remind of the finitude of the human person and human race. And in the diminishment of the mental and physical capacities that are so easily taken for granted, they remind that all, even the "normal," strong and self-reliant, will suffer diminishment and stand in need of the other, others, and God.

A spirituality that emerges from the experience of disability, and of life with disabled persons, gives great attention to human need, affectivity, suffering, hope, and celebration. It invites the smart and self-reliant to a recognition of one's own finitude, fragility, and dependence upon others and God, because all human beings are disabled in one way or another, i.e., unable to meet the deepest aspirations and needs of the human heart by reliance on one's own strengths and resources. This is a spirituality that gives attention to the preciousness of human life, which is all the more so because it is so fragile. A Christian spirituality that emerges from the experience of disability is attentive to Christ's agony and passion, the cross, and the beatitudes. It is motivated by the conviction that the fullness of Christian life does not rest in doing great things, even under the pretext that they are for God's greater glory, but in doing little, seemingly insignificant things with love.

In conclusion, it may be useful to draw attention to the point that a disability is not always a handicap. That is to say, in terms of Christian spirituality many who have no impairment find themselves quite handicapped in their relationship with God. On the other hand, some who have physical and mental impairment have no handicap in regard to their spiritual growth. In this light it is helpful to remember that the role of caregivers or pastoral workers with disabled persons is chiefly the task of removing those obstacles that the impairment may create for the full spiritual development of those they serve.

See also AGING; COMPASSION; MARGINALIZED, THE; POOR, THE; SUFFERING; WEAKNESS AND VULNERABILITY.

Bibliography: F. Dougherty, ed., *The Deprived, the Disabled and the Fullness of Life* (Wilmington, Del.: Glazier, 1984). M. Downey, *A Blessed Weakness: The Spirit of Jean Vanier and l'Arche* (San Francisco: Harper & Row, 1986). S. Hauerwas, *Suffering Presence: Theological Reflections on Medicine, the Mentally Handicapped, and the Church* (Notre Dame: Univ. of Notre Dame Press, 1986).

MICHAEL DOWNEY

DISAPPOINTMENT
See FEELINGS.

DISCERNMENT OF SPIRITS

The capacity for the discernment of spirits responds to a profound expectation and a pervasive temptation within Christianity. All human beings who search for God want God to guide their lives, and Christians have been taught normatively to expect "to be guided by the Spirit" (Gal 5:18; Rom 8:14). Such expectations, both of a person and of the Church itself, tend to put great emphasis upon religious experience, upon an abiding interaction with God that engages affectivity and awareness, understanding and choice, prayer and action, intimate personal relationships, ecclesial solidarity, and the entire way of life of the community. This emphasis becomes temptation only under the persuasion that the intensity of experience absolves one from discretion, critical reflection, and the doctrinal content of Christian faith, giving experience a priority over the unspeakable Mystery that approaches human beings through experience and transferring the religious guidance of a single person or of an entire community to an unchallengeable subjectivity, to sentimentality or superstition or excited enthusiasms.

This sense of ambiguity, of the tension between longing and temptation, is found in both Pauline and Johannine theology. In the earliest canonical document of the Church, Paul directs the Christian community: "Do not quench the Spirit. Do not despise prophetic utterances. Test everything (*panta dokimazete*); retain what is good. Refrain from every kind of evil" (1 Thess 5:19-22). The First Letter of John counsels: "Beloved, do not trust every spirit but test the spirits (*dokimazete ta pneumata*) to see whether they belong to God, because many false prophets have gone out into the world" (1 Jn 4:1). Religious experience is almost always an equivocal reality, inherently ambiguous. Even Christian freedom, for example, can be twisted into a pretext for evil (see Gal 5:13). All influences need to be tested prayerfully to determine their authenticity. To meet this need, the community must be gifted with the discernment of spirits.

This NT concern comes out of the experience of Israel. Although the Hebrew Scriptures did not systematize a doctrine or even frame a term for the discernment of spirits, the practice of this religious discrimination pervades the OT in the choices that individuals and, indeed, the entire community were called to make. God will guide the upright with divine counsels (Ps 73:24), but human beings are also liable to be deceived under the appearance of great promise (Gen 3:13). Good and evil spirits were said to come upon a human being, and while all spirits remained under the sovereignty of Yahweh, they led in contradictory directions (1 Sam 16:14). The hearts of human beings themselves were the source of enormous ambiguity: "More tortuous than all else is the human heart, beyond remedy; who can understand it?" (Jer 17:9-10).

Prophetic interpretation emerged in the historical development of the chosen people to determine the presence and direction of God in the life of the community, and a corresponding set of criteria evolved among the people for recognizing the soundness of individual prophecy (Deut 18:21ff.). Prophets were to be judged by their own orthodoxy, the fulfillment of their prophecy, the contents of their prophecy, and the morality of their lives; the accurate discrimination by the people would depend upon the living faith of the community, its fidelity to and sense of the covenant, and an openness to be guided and corrected by God (McNamara et al., pp. 3–13).

In the Essene community at Qumran, during the second century before Christ, discernment of spirits as such emerges in the *Manual of Discipline,* the rule of life for this desert community: "For the instructor. Let him instruct and teach all the sons of light, concerning all the categories of men, all the kinds of spirits found in them, and their distinctive signs." These spirits are two—those of "truth and perversity"— and recognizing this, the community determined "to examine their spirit and their works each year in order to promote each one according to his formation and the perfection of his conduct, or to move him back according to his faults" (*Manual of Discipline* 3:13-14; 3:19; 5:24; see 5:20-21; 6:16-17; 9:14). This discernment is neither the OT prophetic interpretation of history nor the community's discrimination among prophecies. It is done by another—either a wise man or the entire community; its criteria are the rules and good order of the community; its goal is the determination whether a candidate should be admitted into the community and in what position. (See Guillet et al., pp. 17–30.)

New Testament Teaching

The concern to test and discern the influences that affected the Christian community preoccupied the early Church. Paul numbered among the important charismata given by the Spirit the discernment of spirits (*diakriseis pneumatōn*—1 Cor 12:10). This gift responded immediately to the need of the primitive Christian community to distinguish among the sources of ecstatic or prophetic utterances—whether from the Spirit of God or demonic spirits. As pastoral requirements indicated, however, Paul formulated a basic criteriology by which one could distinguish among all the agencies brought to bear upon the Church. On the one hand, there was the promised guidance from the Spirit of God, and one must come to recognize this divine initiative (Rom 8:14; Gal 5:18). On the other hand, the community had to be concerned, as was the Matthean community, to distinguish false prophecy from true (Mt 7:15-20; 12:22-35).

Prophecy and leadership were singled out as especially demanding this testing because destructive temptations entered into the Christian community not so much through the immediate attraction to evil as through the deception worked by the apparently good. "Such people are false apostles, deceitful workers, who masquerade as apostles of Christ. And no wonder, for even Satan masquerades as an angel of light. So it is not strange that his ministers also masquerade as ministers of righteousness" (2 Cor 11:13-15). For the early Church, the prophetic and the charismatic were equivocal experiences, either gift or deception, but in no sense immediately self-justifying, for the demonic can enter a person's life as the apparently more intensely religious. It was imperative to determine how a discrimination among these influences could be made.

In elaborating the criteria by which the authentic influence of the Spirit of Christ could be differentiated from its counterfeit, Paul distinguished three relationships possible between Christians or a Christian community and the promised Spirit of God: the absence of the Spirit; the presence of the Spirit; the guidance of the Spirit.

The primitive and most basic criteria were those that indicated that one's actions were determined in the absence of the Spirit and under the influence of the "flesh": "Now the works of the flesh are obvious: immorality, impurity, licentiousness, idolatry, sorcery, hatreds, rivalry, jealousy, outbursts of fury, acts of selfishness, dissensions, factions, occasions of envy, drinking bouts, orgies, and the like. I warn you, as I warned you before, that those who do such things will not inherit the kingdom of God" (Gal 5:19-21; cf. Rom 13:12). The criteria are clear (*phanera*) enough. Whatever the intensity of one's religious emotions and awareness, or whatever the seemingly charismatic experiences of the community, these deeds or outbursts are evil and they indicate the presence of the evil by which one is guided. "While there is jealousy and rivalry among you, are you not of the flesh . . . ?" (1 Cor 3:3).

The second level, the presence of the Spirit, is disclosed by the commitment to the mystery of God as disclosed in Jesus Christ. "Nobody speaking by the spirit of God says, 'Jesus be accursed.' And no one can say, 'Jesus is Lord,' except by the holy Spirit" (1 Cor 12:3). The first Johannine letter repeats this same doctrine: "This is how you can know the Spirit of God: every spirit that acknowledges Jesus Christ come in the flesh belongs to God, and every spirit that does not acknowledge Jesus does not belong to God" (1 Jn 4:2-3). Specifically, this spirit is "of Christ" if it so conforms human beings to Christ that they, like Jesus, are able to address God as "Abba, Father" (Rom 8:12-17; Gal 4:6). But to be renewed, to be "justified," through the presence of the transforming Spirit is still only to "have begun with the Spirit" (see Gal 3:3).

The third level of the gift of the Spirit is the habitual direction by the Spirit, a guidance which emerges organically from the second level and which draws to itself the whole Christian life and development: "If we live in the Spirit, let us also follow [*stoichōmen*] the Spirit. Let us not be conceited, provoking one another, envious of one another" (Gal 5:25-26). This is to "live in the Spirit" or to be "guided by the Spirit" (Gal 5:16, 18), and it follows upon a fundamental understanding of the gospel: "Those who are led by the Spirit of God are children of God" (Rom 8:14).

The Acts of the Apostles presents the life of Paul as embodying this doctrine. By the Spirit, for example, Paul is sent (13:4), is bound to a particular path (20:22), brought to conviction and choice (19:21), and even prevented from some ministries (16:6). This doctrine applies also for the Christian community itself: the Spirit acts in and through the teaching of the Church (15:28), comforts and fosters the Church (9:31), and Paul recognizes that the guardians who care for the Church have been established by the Spirit (20:28). In Galatians, Paul lists criteria for recognizing the guidance of the Spirit, and, like Matthew, he focuses upon the commensurate effect: "The fruit of the Spirit is love, joy, peace, patience, kindness, generosity, faithfulness, gentleness, and self-control" (Gal 5:22-23).

The criteria have changed in subtlety. While the "works of the flesh" are "obvious," the morality of actions, outbursts and deeds, the "fruit of the Spirit" place greater emphasis upon virtuous affectivity; upon such experiences as love and joy, or peace and gentleness; upon the harmony within oneself and within the community—fundamental dispositions that underlie Christian deeds and make them possible. If one confuses these different levels, a monster can emerge. If, for example, one finds peace in party spirit or in fornication, the "peace" or "joy" does not authenticate one's life. The moral quality of the deed judges the health of the affectivity. But one lives by the Spirit if there is a prior Christian order in her or his life, an order indicated by the moral deeds of the Christian and the commitment to the reality of God

disclosed in Jesus Christ. Then what is in harmony with that orientation issues in love and joy, peace and patience, kindness and goodness, etc., and these states of virtuous affectivity indicate the influential presence of the Spirit. Christians learn to serve God in this way. "For the kingdom of God is not a matter of food and drink, but of righteousness, peace, and joy in the holy Spirit; whoever serves Christ in this way is pleasing to God and approved by others" (Rom 14:17-18). But the distinction of the levels and of their corresponding criteria is essential. In a similar fundamental discernment, the Letter to the Ephesians distinguishes "the works of darkness" from the "fruit of light" (Eph 5:9-10).

There are in Paul, then, three levels of discernment of spirits governed by three commensurate criteria. Even more, there is an organic development from one level to another: from sin through conversion into a life of sanctification, as the Spirit of God penetrates human life more deeply: "Do not conform yourself to this age but be transformed by the renewal of your mind, that you may discern (*dokimazein*) what is the will of God, what is good and pleasing and perfect" (Rom 12:2; see 1 Jn 2:23-24).

Hence one can speak of the discernment of spirits, both a charismatic gift given by the Spirit of God for the common good of the whole community and a developed Christian capacity to discriminate among the various spiritual states that are being experienced—the "spirits"—in order to determine which lead toward God and which lead away from God. The radical source of such discernment is the Spirit, giving a love and a knowledge that transform the Christian into a "spiritual person" (Rom 5:1-5; 1 Cor 2:12). Connaturally, this enables one to "judge (*anakrinei*) all things." The goal of discernment is "God's wisdom, mysterious, hidden" to which a person comes, for "we have not received the spirit of the world but the Spirit that is from God, so that we may understand the things freely given us by God"

(1 Cor 2:7, 12). For the good of the Church, various gifts go together, each paired with another as the completion of its nature: the gift of tongues and the interpretation of tongues; healing and miracles; prophecy and discernment of spirits.

Christian Tradition

The early Church took up and developed out of its own experience the teaching it had received on the discernment of spirits. In his great work in systematic theology, *De principiis,* Origen (184–254) traces human thoughts back either to interior subjectivity or to three sources other than oneself: God, good and evil spirits. He further elaborates criteria by which each may be recognized. Particularly the monastic tradition developed the more individual side of this doctrine. Its classic development is found in the conferences of Abbot Moses in the works of John Cassian (ca. 360–435). "We ought, then, carefully to notice this threefold order, and with a wise discretion (*sagaci discretione*), to analyze the thoughts which arise in our hearts, tracing out their origin and cause and author in the first instance, that we may be able to consider how we ought to yield ourselves to them" (*Conferences* 1:20).

Cassian cites, as did Origen and Jerome, the most quoted apocryphal saying attributed to Jesus: "Become shrewd (*probabiles*) moneychangers," noting that their highest skill is to differentiate what is pure gold from what has been made to look like it, to distinguish true coins from counterfeits, and to determine what is the proper weight of each. Similarly, human beings are taught to examine carefully "whatever has found an entrance into our hearts," whether that be religious doctrine, the interpretation and use of Scripture, the urging to some work of piety or apostolic zeal (*Conferences* 1:20), and the spirit in which something is undertaken and done (*Conferences* 1:22). Any of these can begin a moment of deception whose internal contradiction leads eventually to religious disintegration.

"We should then constantly search all the inner chambers of our hearts, and trace out the footsteps of whatever enters into them with the closest investigation" (*Conferences* 1:22).

Cassian does not elaborate a criteriology for distinguishing among religious influences; he rather suggests a pattern of spiritual discipleship. Discernment can only come out of a humility that will allow a monk to disclose his thoughts and deeds to the elders, "for a wrong thought is enfeebled at the moment that it is discovered" (*Conferences* 2:10). This self-disclosure makes spiritual direction by the elders possible. One learns discernment through this pattern of a continual self-revelation and of an obedience conceived among the monks primarily as a dimension of spiritual direction. (See *Nicene and Post-Nicene Fathers,* 2nd series, 11:304–316).

In the 6th century John Climacus, writing for the monks at Raithu, summarized the debt of Christian tradition in discernment to John Cassian: "From humility comes discernment as the great Cassian has said with beautiful and sublime philosophy in his chapter on discernment. From discernment comes insight, and from insight comes foresight. And who would not follow this fair way of obedience, seeing such blessings in store for him?" (*Ladder* 4:105). Climacus built upon the work of Cassian in the twenty-sixth chapter of the *Ladder of Divine Ascent,* outlining a progress in discernment that marked the faithful life and giving it extensive, albeit aphoristic, treatment: "Discernment in beginners is true knowledge of themselves; in intermediate souls it is a spiritual sense that faultlessly distinguishes what is truly good from what is of nature and opposed to it; and in the perfect it is the knowledge which they possess by divine illumination, and which can enlighten with its lamp what is dark in others. Or perhaps, generally speaking, discernment is, and is recognized as, the assured understanding of the divine will on all occasions, in every place and in all matters; and it is only found in those who are pure in heart, and in body and in mouth" (*Ladder* 26:1).

In the subsequent tradition of the Church, "discernment of spirits" (*discretio spirituum*) came to possess a series of distinct but related meanings, one of which is often confused with another, while the emphasis remained more upon the individual experiences or interpersonal relationships than upon the life of the whole community. Discernment ranged over the whole interpretative process in which human beings make decisions.

Different understandings of discernment of spirits were distinguished in terms of the "spirits" being differentiated. In its most limited sense, this discernment designated the ability to distinguish between evil and good spirits as they attempt to inspire human thinking, choice, or prophecy. In a more general sense, it denoted a discrimination among all the factors that influence human choice: states of affectivity, such as consolation or desolation; states of intentionality, such as imagination, fantasies, thoughts, or visions; and all personal—prophetic, angelic, or demonic—and societal structures that enter a person's world and affect judgments and decisions. In still another sense, it indicated an extraordinary gift for reading hearts and foretelling the future. In each of these three senses, this discernment of spirits remains a hermeneutical capacity, the interpretation of the religious meaning of various influences that bear upon human awareness and decisions. This use of discernment must be further distinguished both from the prudential skill of simple "discretion" (*discretio*) and from what is often called the "discernment of the will of God," the knowledge of that finality which lies at the basis of "the drawing of this Love and the voice of this Calling."

Discernment of spirits in each of its understandings could also be distinguished in terms of its source. It was understood as an infused gift of the Spirit or as a connatural sensibility issuing from a committed Christian life or as knowledge learned from study, or an intermixture of all three. It was consequently classified as an art or as a doctrine, and the experiences out of which it issues have historically included the radical and transforming gift of the Spirit, a life of spiritual discipleship, and the disciplined inquiry into the criteria by which diverse religious influences may be recognized. These criteria focus not so much upon the origins of these influences as upon their orientation.

Ignatius of Loyola

In the *Spiritual Exercises,* Ignatius of Loyola outlines his classic "Rules for the Discernment of Spirits." These function critically as the exercitant attempts to respond to the influence of God directing her or his life. The rules unite all of the factors that previous traditions included: good and evil spirits, personal and preternatural influences, thoughts and imagination, and states of affectivity, consolation and desolation. Consolation indicates any movement of affectivity toward God; desolation, any movement of affectivity away from God. These divergent influences are perceived to be causally connected, e.g., evil spirits can cause the kind of thoughts or imagination that effect desolation, or a state of desolation can issue into commensurate thoughts that place one under the personal influence of evil. The fourteen rules for the first week are offered for those who are being tempted "openly and obviously," i.e., either by the pleasure that attracts to evil or by the pain and cost that can deter from discipleship. Ignatius indicates two different subjects of such temptations and frames a matrix by which the influences upon their lives are united and contrasted (1-2). Consolation and desolation are defined (3-4). The subject is counseled how to act directly against desolation (5-6), against the thoughts that arise from desolation (7-11), and against the personal influences of evil (12-14).

The eight rules for the second week are much more subtle and deal with the experience of being deceived or tempted under the appearance of good. At such a juncture it is no longer enough to know how to deal with the attraction to an obvious evil or with the repugnance for the good. These rules distinguish the consolation in which there is no danger of deception—when one is drawn wholly into the love of God without commensurate thoughts or images—from the consolation mediated by ideas and imagination (2-3), in which deception is possible. These latter must be tested for their authenticity. One must attend to the attraction toward the morally good by considering the beginning, middle, and end of the entire process. These rules outline the progress of deception disguised in apparent consolation (4) and frame a procedure by which true and false consolations can be distinguished at the terminus of their influence (5), during the course of their influence (6), or even at the beginning of an integral religious "movement" (7).

Ignatius warns against giving the rules for the second week to those whose temptations are those of the first week—"week" being used not to designate seven days but a stage in the development of the exercitant's prayer. In the first week affectivity is to be judged by its obvious direction, and this direction distinguishes affectivity into consolation and desolation; in the second week the apparent moral worth of what is proposed is judged by the affectivity and thoughts to which it leads over the course of its history, i.e., by the experience of peace and joy, etc. Affectivity is not the criterion in the first week that it is in the second, and between these two moments lies conversion and the reorientation of affectivity worked by the contemplative union with the mysteries of Christ. Only as affectivity is ordered can it in turn become a clue to the influence of God.

Whereas the focus in the *Spiritual Exercises* is upon the influences that come upon an individual's choice, Ignatius expanded the practice of discernment to an important communitarian function through the "Deliberation of the First Fathers" and through the repeated provisions made throughout the *Constitutions* for the discernment that enters in manifold ways into community life and government.

Other Developments

The discernment of spirits has received extensive analysis in the history of Christian spirituality. Mention must be made of three treatments in the West that have become classics: Denis the Carthusian, *De discretione et examinatione spirituum* (ca. 1445–1450); John Cardinal Bona, *De discretione spirituum liber unus* (1671); and Giovanni Battista Scaramelli, *Discernimento degli spiriti* (1753). In the East, the *Philokalia* (1782) collected many of the most important texts in this tradition from the 4th to the 15th century in order to guide the interior or contemplative life.

Major developments in the understanding and applications of the discernment of spirits have occurred in the contemporary Church. Discernment of spirits has retrieved its importance for individual spiritual direction, and, through communal discernment, it has developed its possibilities for the guidance of Christian community. The Second Vatican Council contributed to this with its emphasis upon "reading the signs of the times." New paths have been opened by the liberation theologians, with their insistence that discernment is an essential part of orthopraxis. The capacity for Christian discernment depends upon the prior position one has taken toward the oppressed. Discernment must be brought to bear upon the revelation of the glory of God disclosed in the liberation of the poor. The absolute criterion of orthopraxis becomes that of Mt 25:32ff.: "I was hungry and you gave me food," etc. One's practical discernment originates both within this eschatological horizon of faith and the historical horizons of situations of justice and injustice (strategy) and within the consequent determination among actions that this condition calls forth from the Christian (tactics)—(Dussel, pp. 47–60).

Jesus is the embodiment of Christian discernment. His Spirit makes it possible for Christians to continue his manner of discernment. His passion and death as praxis—to bring the Good News to the poor—offer a set of criteria for discernment conceived as putting into practice the divine will. For one must verify in the social and historic order what has been understood (Sobrino, pp. 14–26).

See also DESIRE; DETACHMENT; DISCRETION; EXPERIENCE; FEELINGS; GRACE; HOLY SPIRIT; IGNATIAN SPIRITUALITY; PRAYER; PRAXIS; SPIRITS; SPIRITUAL DIRECTION.

Bibliography: (Classical texts and standard bibliographies are given in the works cited here.) M. Buckley, "The Structure of the Rules for Discernment of Spirits," *Spiritual Exercises: Collected Essays*, ed. P. Sheldrake (London: SPCK, 1990). M. McNamara, J. Sobrino, W. Peters, J. Castillo, E. Dussel, et al., *Discernment of the Spirit and of Spirits*, ed. C. Floristán and C. Duquoc (New York: Seabury, 1979). J. Guillet, G. Bardy, F. Vandenbroucke, J. Pegon, H. Martin, *Discernment of Spirits*, ed. E. Malatesta, trans. I. Richards (Collegeville, Minn.: Liturgical Press, 1970).

MICHAEL J. BUCKLEY, S.J.

DISCIPLESHIP

The concept of discipleship, central to the ministry of Jesus, is expressed in the NT by the verb *akolouthein* and by the noun *mathētēs*. Jesus called men and women to "follow after" (*akolouthein*) him. Those who followed him were known as his "disciples" (*mathētēs*).

Discipleship in the NT

The word *mathētēs* appears more than 250 times in the NT, always in the Gospels and Acts. In secular Greek the word means "one who learns." A *mathētēs* was someone bound to another in order to learn, thus an apprentice to someone in a trade or profession or a student of a philosopher. There is

no *mathētēs* without a *didaskalos*, a "master" or "teacher." The English word "disciple" comes from the Latin *discipulus*, "pupil."

In the OT the master-disciple relationship does not appear; *mathētēs* is not used in the Septuagint. It enters the Jewish tradition with Rabbinic Judaism, probably under the influence of the Greek and Hellenistic philosophical schools.

In the NT *mathētēs* refers most often to the disciples of Jesus. There is no question that Jesus gathered a group of disciples around him and sent them out as his co-workers to proclaim the coming of the reign of God. *Mathētēs* is also used for the disciples of John the Baptist (Mt 11:2) and occasionally for the disciples of the Pharisees (Mt 22:16). But its usage in reference to the disciples of Jesus, along with the verb *akolouthein*, is unique.

Akolouthein, appearing fifty-six times in the Synoptics and fourteen times in John, does not always refer to those who were disciples in the strict sense, as when it is used of the crowds that followed Jesus (Mt 4:25; 8:1). But when used of individuals (Mk 1:18; Lk 5:11; Jn 1:43), it, like *mathētēs*, shows the special characteristics of discipleship in relation to Jesus.

First, unlike the case of discipleship in Rabbinic Judaism, the disciples of Jesus did not choose the master; rather, the master chose and called the disciples. The initiative comes from Jesus (Mk 1:17; 2:14). In Mk 3:13-14 Jesus called those he desired for a twofold purpose: that they might be with him and that he might send them out to preach. The coordinate conjunction *kai* ("and") indicates the equal importance of both aspects.

Second, there is an inclusive element to Jesus' call, even if it is still within a Jewish context. Unlike that of the rabbis, Jesus' call was not restricted to the ritually pure and the religiously obedient. Among those invited to follow him were "tax collectors and sinners" (Mk 2:15). Women also accompanied him as disciples (Lk 8:2).

Third, Jesus' call to discipleship demands a radical conversion, a religious conversion to Jesus often symbolized by leaving behind one's possessions. The story of the rich young man illustrates this requirement of discipleship. To this man, who had kept all the commandments since his youth, Jesus said: "You are lacking in one thing. Go, sell what you have, and give to the poor and you will have treasure in heaven; then come, follow me" (Mk 10:21). The conversion is religious in that it goes beyond the requirements of the law. Discipleship means a clean break with the past (Lk 9:57-62). Those who followed Jesus "left everything" (Lk 5:11). They left behind jobs (Mk 2:14), parents, family and children (Lk 14:26). For some, discipleship also meant celibacy for the sake of the kingdom (Mt 19:11-12).

Fourth, discipleship means following Jesus by sharing his ministry. Unlike the disciples of the rabbis, who were students, concerned with passing on the tradition of their teachers, the disciples of Jesus were called for service. Jesus sent them out to heal the sick, to cast out demons, and to proclaim that the kingdom of God was at hand (Mk 6:7-13; Lk 10:2-12). They shared not just his ministry but his poverty and itinerant life as well (Mt 8:20).

Finally, discipleship means a willingness to love others with a sacrificial love. The disciples are to share whatever they have with others (Lk 6:30). They are to take the last place and serve others (Mk 9:35). Their love of others is to be all-inclusive, placing others first, yielding to them, and being willing to bear insult and injury (Mt 5:38-42). Nowhere is the ideal of sacrificial love more clearly expressed than in John's Gospel, where Jesus says: "This is my commandment: love one another as I love you. No one has greater love than this, to lay down one's life for one's friends" (Jn 15:12-13).

The Gospels distinguish between the Twelve and the disciples who traveled with Jesus, other friends and supporters (Lk 10:38-42; Mk 14:12-16), and the larger group to whom Jesus ministered (Mk 6:34).

After Easter, when the Christological meaning of discipleship became clear, discipleship was understood as including the following of Jesus in his Easter passage from death to life. In his "way" section (8:27–10:52), Mark provides an extended instruction on discipleship. The way of Jesus means taking up one's cross and following him, even being willing to give up one's own life (Mk 8:34-35; cf. Jn 15:13). For Paul, Christian life itself is a following of Christ that involves entering into his paschal mystery (Rom 6:3-5; Phil 3:8-11).

Thus discipleship in the NT means a personal following of Jesus that affects every dimension of human life. It shapes one's attitude toward property and wealth, affects a person's human and erotic relationships, gives a new meaning to love, changes the way one understands success and personal fulfillment, and finally, calls one to enter into Jesus' paschal mystery. At its heart is the *imitatio Christi*.

Discipleship in Christian History

After Easter discipleship became synonymous with Christian faith. All Christians are called to a following of Jesus in the service of God's reign. The Church itself is the community of the disciples. But throughout Christian history the sense of a call to a more literal following of Jesus has been present; it has led to the tradition of Christian asceticism and to distinctive expressions of the Christian life.

The Acts of the Apostles uses the word *disciple* to identify the early Christians, though this usage did not endure. Some feminist scholars see the earliest Christians as constituting a discipleship of equals, a Jesus movement consisting largely of poor, rejected, and marginalized people, prior to the development of a structured and hierarchalized Church.

In the 2nd and 3rd centuries martyrdom was understood as a preeminent expression of discipleship. As early as A.D. 115 Ignatius of Antioch wrote that his approaching martyrdom in the arena would make him "truly a disciple of Jesus Christ" (*Rom.* 4), though he recognized all genuine Christian life as an imitation of Christ.

In the 3rd and 4th centuries a commitment to virginity and the ascetical life was frequently described as a type of martyrdom. Those who joined the early monastic movement understood discipleship in terms of a withdrawal from the world, asceticism, and prayer. Many were influenced by the example of Antony, who, according to his biographer Athanasius, sold his property and withdrew into the desert when he heard in the Gospel the words "If you would be perfect, go, sell what you have, and give to the poor . . . and come, follow me." The image of a white martyrdom, first used by the Desert Fathers for the ascetical life, was common until the Middle Ages.

From the 9th century on, monastic theologians used the concept of the *vita apostolica,* or "apostolic life," to describe their own monastic life. By this they understood a common life, communal prayer, and common ownership of property.

But toward the middle of the 12th century lay people as well as clerics began to claim the vision of the apostolic life for themselves. A new and strongly lay understanding of discipleship that stressed a radical personal poverty and itinerant preaching emerged. From this evangelical awakening came a number of movements, not all of which remained within the boundaries of Church orthodoxy. The Humiliati, the Waldensians, and the Beguines were lay movements. The Franciscan movement began as a lay movement and ultimately became a new religious order. At the beginning of the "Earlier Rule" of Francis, the key image, taken from the Gospels, is leaving one's family and possessions and following Jesus (chap. 1). The penitential associations that later became identified as Franciscan or Dominican third orders were originally lay movements.

The 15th-century book by Thomas à Kempis (d. 1471), the *Imitation of Christ,* was a classic medieval expression of discipleship. No other book was as widely circulated in the Middle Ages.

In the 16th century the Radical Reformation produced a number of communities, among them the Spiritualists and the Anabaptists, which believed that the Church had "fallen" with Constantine, and sought to restore it on the model of the apostolic Church of the NT. They practiced a radical Christianity or discipleship that stressed participating in Christ's suffering, imitating him in his poverty, and sharing a communal life. Similarly, discipleship is at the heart of the *Spiritual Exercises* of Ignatius of Loyola; the exercitant is invited to respond to the call of Christ the King and to pray for an identification with him in his poverty and rejection.

Contemporary Approaches

In the 20th century discipleship has increasingly been associated with simplicity of life and solidarity with the poor and the oppressed. One of the most formative influences has been that of Charles de Foucauld (d. 1916), whose life and writings present discipleship as imitating the hidden life of Jesus at Nazareth. A number of modern efforts to bring together the contemplative life and solidarity with the poor reflect his influence.

Dietrich Bonhoeffer, a German pastor who returned from safety in the United States to be with his people in the struggle against Hitler, stressed the "extraordinariness" of Christian life in his book *The Cost of Discipleship.* His own life was an example of solidarity with people in need. Bonhoeffer was executed in Berlin's Tegel prison just before the end of the war. Contemporary Christian communities like the Catholic Worker, l'Arche, Sojourners, Taizé, the Little Brothers and the Little Sisters of Jesus, and the Missionaries of Charity also model a life of discipleship based on simplicity of life and solidarity with the disadvantaged.

Those writing from the perspective of political or liberation theology emphasize the social and political character of Christian discipleship. Johann Baptist Metz sees Jesus as summoning men and women to a radical messianic discipleship which to some "may look like treason—a betrayal of affluence, of the family, and of our customary way of life" (*The Emergent Church*, New York: Crossroad, 1986, pp. 14–15). Jon Sobrino describes Jesus as calling others to a radical discipleship that would place them at the service of the kingdom. For him, orthodoxy is inseparable from orthopraxis; Jesus' disciples are called to faith in God's future and to cooperation in turning the kingdom they proclaim into a full reality (*Christology at the Crossroads*, Maryknoll, N.Y.: Orbis, 1978, pp. 57–58).

Christian spirituality has sometimes tended to identify discipleship with the pursuit of perfection rather than with the following of Jesus. The religious life in the Church was considered the "state of perfection." Similarly, treatments of religious life in the past have too often presented personal sanctification as the primary end, while the service or ministerial dimension was considered a secondary end. Such approaches can confuse the nature of Christian discipleship and suggest a false tension between consecration and mission in regard to the religious life.

Jesus did not proclaim an otherworldly asceticism for a chosen few. He called all who would listen to be his followers and expected them to live out his teaching in their everyday lives. Modern attempts to understand discipleship seek to restore its inclusive nature by basing it on gospel values rather than on the narrower foundation of the evangelical counsels. Yet there is a radical dimension to the gospel call to discipleship. The contemporary emphasis on simplicity of life and solidarity with the poor is an important reminder that the key metaphor for understanding discipleship is the following or imitation of Christ.

See also CHRIST; EARLY CHRISTIAN SPIRITUALITY; KINGDOM OF GOD; RELIGIOUS LIFE; SERVICE; VOCATION.

Bibliography: M. Hengel, *The Charismatic Leader and His Followers*, trans. J. Grieg (New York: Crossroad, 1981). B. Chilton and J. McDonald, *Jesus and the Ethics of the Kingdom* (Grand Rapids, Mich.: Eerdmans, 1987). J. Sobrino, *Christology at the Crossroads: A Latin American Approach*, trans. J. Drury (Maryknoll, N.Y.: Orbis, 1978).

THOMAS P. RAUSCH, S.J.

DISCRETION

The Latin verb *cernere* means either "to separate" or "to see." The two meanings come together in the compound *discernere:* "to see deeply in order to separate, distinguish, or discern." One meaning of the cognate noun *discretio* is "a separation or distinction." Thus in about A.D. 380 the Vulgate used *discretio spirituum* (1 Cor 12:10) to mean discernment of spirits, a gift of the Holy Spirit; and this meaning was repeated by many later writers, including Ignatius of Loyola (*Spiritual Exercises*, nos. 176, 328). But *discretio* took on a second meaning: moderation, right measure, a disposition for making choices that avoid departure by excess or defect from the proper mean. This sense, too, appears in Cassian, whose Conference 2, "On Discretion," is about preserving the balance between excessive fervor and laxity (PL 49:523–553; see esp. 521); in Benedict (*Rule*, chap. 64); Ignatius (*Constitutions*, forty times, e.g., in 154); and many others. Throughout Christian spiritual literature both these meanings of discretion appear with varying nuances. They also interact upon each other.

When discretion refers chiefly to moderation or judgment, it is an application of the virtue of prudence to the living of the spiritual life. Discretion is a disposition that guides us, in our pursuit of spiritual growth, to avoid departure from the proper mean either by excess or by defect. Discretion regulates all the other virtues by keeping them rightly ordered to God's will for oneself. We must make many choices between various options, such as one virtue or another, the good or the better; and something better in itself may not be better for me. We should serve God as generously as possible but also be guided by discretion so that we do not exceed our personal abilities or the measure of grace that God allots to our individual selves.

Much modern discussion of discretion has sprung from the tradition of St. Ignatius. His *Exercises* guide one to discover God's will for oneself and, in accordance with it, to serve him as generously as possible. In them indifference is a means to detachment or freedom to commit oneself more generously to God (no. 23); and the related discernment of spirits is in turn a means to the discernment of God's will, in order to elect (nos. 169-189) what appears likely to please him more. The criterion (no. 179) for this election is: Which option is likely to bring greater glory (in the sense of praise) to God? This also results in correspondingly greater self-fulfillment in the joy of the beatific vision. All these procedures should be guided by prayerful discretion.

See also DETACHMENT; DISCERNMENT OF SPIRITS; FREEDOM; IGNATIAN SPIRITUALITY; VIRTUE.

Bibliography: A. Cabasu, "Discrétion," *D.Spir.* 3, cols. 1311-1330; M. Gaucheron, "Discrétion," *Catholicisme* 3, cols. 882-884.

GEORGE E. GANSS, S.J.

DISSENT

See CONFRONTATION AND PROTEST; CONSCIENCE.

DISTRACTION IN PRAYER

See CENTERING PRAYER; MEDITATION; PRAYER; TEMPTATION.

DIVINIZATION

Divinization is the process of transformation by grace whereby the human person is raised in union with Christ to live the life of God. This is not meant in a pantheistic sense nor as an actual deification process whereby created human reality disappears or is transformed substantially into the Godhead. The doctrine of divinization that developed in the writings of the early Church and in the Eastern Church's theological and spiritual tradition, in contrast to the use of the term by the surrounding culture, was rooted in Scripture. The letters of St. Paul reflect the fundamental truth that the Christian life consists in sharing in the life of Christ. "I have been crucified with Christ; yet I live, no longer I, but Christ lives in me; insofar as I now live in the flesh, I live by faith in the Son of God who has loved me and given himself up for me" (Gal 2:19-20). The Second Letter of Peter speaks of believers as "sharers of the divine nature" (1:4). In 1 John we read, "Beloved, we are God's children now; what we shall be has not yet been revealed. We do know that when it is revealed we shall be like him, for we shall see him as he is" (3:2). Patristic writers developed these scriptural ideas in terms of divinization and participation in the divine nature.

Divinization understood in the Christian sense is a sharing in God's life, in particular God's Trinitarian life. It is Christocentric, for it is as a member of Christ that the believer is brought to participate in the divine reality. Although writers speak of the impact of divinization in the inner reality of the person, in particular in knowing and in loving, its greatest importance is in the area of entry into divine relationship.

See also CHRIST; CONVERSION; EARLY CHRISTIAN SPIRITUALITY; EASTERN CHRISTIAN SPIRITUALITY; GRACE; HOLY SPIRIT; IMAGO DEI; PATRISTIC SPIRITUALITY; TRANSFORMATION.

Bibliography: H. Rondet, *The Grace of Christ*, trans. and ed. T. Guzie (Westminster, Md.: Newman, 1967). "Divinization," *D.Spir.* 3, cols. 1370–1459.

MICHAEL DODD, O.C.D.

DIVORCE (AND REMARRIAGE)

Over the past three decades an increasing number of divorced American Catholics have been coming out of the shadows, forming parochial, diocesan, and national groups for the mutual support, education, and ministerial care of those devastated by failed marriages. Rejecting their previous marginality, such groups have claimed their Catholicism as a primary way of rebuilding their lives, turning to their Church and pastors for the spiritual support and healing grace of the Body of Christ.

Responding to this demand and to a growing awareness of the inadequacy of a pastoral practice dominated by canonical concerns, American bishops and pastors have abolished the excommunication of Catholics attempting an invalid remarriage, radically improved and simplified the annulment process, and worked with others in the development of better marriage preparation and enrichment programs. Many have gone further, inviting divorced, separated, and remarried Catholics to return to the Church and developing support groups and offices to work with these Catholics and their families.

American Catholicism must bring to the present crisis a spirituality incorporating theologies of mercy and faithfulness, offering the compassionate and healing embrace of Christ to those sisters and brothers suffering in the wake of destroyed marriages, while supporting all Catholic couples struggling to be faithful to the gospel ideal of indissolubility in the face of great difficulties. Particularly for the divorced and separated, a spirituality of compassion steeped in a theology of the Cross would offer the nourishment required for their sojourn through the healing process of forgiveness, reconciliation, and graceful recovery. At the same time, this ministry could ultimately empower them and others in the ongoing struggle for fidelity.

See also COMMUNITY; COMPASSION; HEALING; MARGINALIZED, THE; MARRIAGE; MERCY; WEAKNESS AND VULNERABILITY.

Bibliography: G. Twomey, *When Catholics Marry Again* (Minneapolis: Winston, 1982). J. Young, *Divorcing, Believing, Belonging* (New York: Paulist, 1984).

PATRICK T. McCORMICK, C.M.

DOMINICAN SPIRITUALITY

Dominican spirituality is the legacy of the Order of Preachers, founded by St. Dominic Guzman (1170–1221) and confirmed in 1216 as an order of canons regular devoted to preaching and the *cura animarum*. The Order of Preachers is actually a religious family comprised of the friars, nuns, sisters engaged in the active ministry, and lay people. The order has given the Church a host of saints, including three Doctors of the Church: Albert the Great (ca. 1200–1280), Thomas Aquinas (ca. 1225–1274), and Catherine of Siena (1347–1380).

Dominic and the Order of Preachers

Dominic himself, born in the village of Caleruega, in the diocese of Osma, Spain, belonged to the canons regular of the cathedral. He probably would never have founded an order if it had not been for a decisive encounter while he was enroute to Denmark in 1206 with his bishop, Diego d'Azevedo. Throughout Languedoc large numbers of people embraced or supported the Albigensian heresy. There was large-scale disaffection with the corruption and worldliness of the hierarchy. Passing through Montpellier, Dominic and Diego met the papal legates charged with preaching conversion to the people of the region. Dominic and Diego proposed to the legates that they would be more likely to win souls with an example of poverty than with their large retinues and ecclesiastical pomp. The suggestion was taken, and Dominic and Diego joined the preaching, which enjoyed some initial success.

Pope Innocent III supported the approach taken and, in a letter dated November 17, 1206, granted Dominic the right to preach. From this date Dominic signed himself as "Brother Dominic, Preacher." At this time preaching belonged by right to the bishops alone. It was for this reason that many of the lay movements, such as those of Peter Waldes and the Humiliati, ran afoul of Church authority, because they preached in public. In the case of the Humiliati, Innocent III rendered a significant judgment, distinguishing between preaching that involved the teaching of faith and doctrine and preaching that was moral witness and exhortation. The latter was allowed to the Humiliati and later to the Franciscans. Innocent also sought to organize the Humiliati by distinguishing within the movement three orders: first and second orders of men and women, respectively, living the regular life, and a third order of laity.

Dominic remained in Languedoc even after his bishop returned to Spain. In 1207 he founded at Prouille a monastery for women converted from heresy and served as parish priest at Fanjeaux, near Prouille, settling eventually with a few followers in Toulouse under the patronage of Bishop Fulk. To win papal approbation for an order of preachers, Dominic journeyed to Rome with Fulk at the time of the Fourth Lateran Council (1215). Several of the council's canons had direct bearing on Dominic's purpose. These included canon 10, which called on each bishop to establish a corps of competent men to assist in the ministry of preaching; canon 11, which reasserted earlier decrees calling for a theologian at each cathedral to ensure the education of the clergy; canon 13, which forbade any new religious orders; and canon 21, which decreed an annual confession by the laity to their pastors.

Dominic and his followers adopted the Rule of St. Augustine and were recognized as canons regular in Toulouse by Bishop Fulk. Meanwhile, Innocent III was supportive and encouraging, but he died in the summer of 1216. Approbation came from his successor, Honorius III. First there was the approbation of the community and its holdings: the church of St. Romanus, the monastery of Prouille, and the house in which the friars resided (December 22, 1216); next, in a series of bulls came the recognition of the title "Order of Preachers" (January 21, 1217), the recommendation of the preaching friars to the bishops (February 11, 1218), and the recommendation of the friars as confessors (February 4, 1221).

In 1218 Dominic dispersed his small band of friars, sending one group to Paris, another to Bologna, and a third to Spain. The establishment of priories in Paris and Bologna, the homes of the two major universities of medieval Europe, had as its goal to provide ready access to theological study for brethren and sources for recruitment. On May 17, 1220, Dominic convened the first general chapter of the order at Bologna. There the friars drafted the primitive constitutions, borrowing heavily from the customs of Prémontré. The following year the chapter divided the order into provinces and significantly received the first of a series of confessors' manuals authored by a Dominican, Paul of Hungary. Dominic died on August 6, 1221, and was buried at Bologna. He was succeeded as master of the order by Jordan of Saxony and was canonized in 1234.

The Priority of Preaching

No Christian spirituality is original in the sense of being utterly new; rather, each Christian spirituality draws on elements common to the tradition, emphasizing one or another, blending them into a whole that is distinctive. The elements from which Dominic blended the mix he bequeathed to his order include common life, the choral Office, study and contemplation, penance, and the apostolate of preaching. We shall examine these in turn.

What is perhaps most noteworthy about Dominic is the way in which he went about establishing his order. He left no significant writings, only a few letters. Whereas Benedict left a rule, and Francis both a rule and a profound model to be imitated, Dominic left his order a task, namely, apostolic preaching. This in itself was original in its day, as Humbert of Romans, fifth master of the order, notes in his commentary on the constitutions, saying that whereas all other orders were founded for the salvation of their members, Dominic's order was founded for the salvation of others. Dominic, in a sense, disappeared within the task he left his order.

It is also worthy of note that Dominic did not dictate the customs of the order; they were determined by the brethren gathered in chapter, and only after the community had lived and worked together for a time. It was experience and the exigencies of the apostolate that dictated legislation. When the brethren gathered to draft their customs, Dominic surrendered his authority to the group. This belief in the community and the conviction that the group knew more than any one individual is perhaps Dominic's most striking characteristic. It was realized in the structure of the order, which placed supreme authority in the chapter, whether conventual, provincial, or general.

Moreover, it was Dominic's intention that the Rule and the constitutions should not bind the brethren under the pain of sin, as was the norm. It is reported that Dominic felt so strongly about this matter that when some of the brethren wanted to ensure conformity by making the constitutions bind in conscience, Dominic rose to say that if he believed the Rule and the constitutions bound under the pain of sin, he would take his knife and personally rip to shreds all the copies of the Rule he could lay his hands on. Nothing was to bind the order with respect to its founding purpose.

Thus the originality of Dominic's vision is documented in the primitive constitutions framed under his leadership between 1216 and 1220 and revised after his death by the extraordinary, "most general" chapter of 1228. The primitive constitutions consist of the preamble (1228), the prologue (1220), and the two distinctions that treat respectively of conventual life and the government of the order and its apostolate. Borrowing verbatim from the customs of Prémontré, the prologue to the primitive constitutions asserts that in order to fulfill the precept of the Rule that the brethren should be of one mind and heart, it is necessary to commit to writing the customs pertaining to the observance of canonical religious life. There follows an admonition against adding, deleting, or changing the observances. In 1220 the brethren inserted a paragraph that assigns the superior the right and duty to dispense the brethren of his convent from whatever impedes study and preaching. The reason given is the unique purpose of the order: the salvation of souls. The text goes on: ". . . our study ought to tend principally, ardently, and with the greatest striving to the end that we might be useful to our neighbors' souls."

It is not to be inferred from the superior's right to dispense the brethren from the demands of the common life that the traditional elements of monastic or canonical religious life were perceived to be an obstacle to the apostolate that Dominic might have done away with if he could have, as Ignatius of Loyola was to do later. Rather, it was Dominic's intention that the common life, liturgy, contemplation, and study were to be blended into a whole that would serve rather than hinder preaching. The operative principle is the Lord's command to love God and neighbor, the two being intimately connected, not opposed. Thus the elements of the common life, the so-called monastic side of Dominican life, are not merely a preparation for ministry nor an oasis to provide rest from the demands of ministry, but an integral part of the life. The two sides of Dominican life are the expressions of a single love—the love of God and neighbor, the one flowing from the other and vice versa.

Liturgical Celebration

Life in Dominican convents centered on the choral celebration of the Office and Mass. Initially the friars probably followed local liturgical usages, but as the order grew, such diversity proved an obstacle to the unity prescribed by the Rule and constitutions. A clause in the primitive constitutions, "We confirm the whole Office, nocturnal and diurnal, and we ordain that it be uniformly observed by all, so that no one is permitted to add anything new," suggests that a uniform rite was already in place by 1228, if not earlier. The work of revision continued until 1254, when Humbert of Romans produced a definitive prototype. The Dominican Office was not a new creation but a compilation based on models such as those of Prémontré, Cîteaux, and perhaps the liturgy of the Roman basilicas.

In a paragraph devoted to the manner of celebrating the liturgy, the constitutions ordain that the Office shall be celebrated succinctly and with brevity lest study or preaching be impeded. Accordingly, Dominican chant was simpler and less melismatic than that of other traditions. Only for Compline, the last Hour of the day, was this rule relaxed. At the end of Compline the *Salve Regina* was sung as the brethren processed to the Virgin's altar.

Contemplation

Although the Rule for Dominican nuns specifies periods of "secret prayer" after Matins and Compline, the friars' constitutions are silent on this point. Yet there is

every indication that the friars generally observed the same custom. Following the tradition of the canons and monks, the friars' secret prayer was a prolongation of liturgical prayer. It was an interior dialogue with the word of God, although not without external expression. A vivid portrait of Dominic engaged in private prayer is to be found in a little work entitled "The Nine Ways of Prayer of Our Holy Father Dominic" (*Early Dominicans*, pp. 94–103). He would remain in choir and recall what was sung in the Office, or he might take up a book and begin to read. After being thus recollected, he was seen to experience an array of emotions and moods, described thus by the anonymous author: "It was as if he were arguing with a friend; at one moment he would appear to be feeling impatient, nodding his head energetically, then he would seem to be listening quietly, then you would see him disputing and struggling, and laughing and weeping all at once, fixing his gaze, submitting, then again speaking quietly and beating his breast" (*Early Dominicans*, p. 101).

This description of Dominic at prayer conforms to what Hugh of St. Victor, a 12th-century canon, says of prayer in a little treatise entitled *De verbo Dei*. There is but one Word of God, Hugh says, the Son uttered by the Father from all eternity. This one Word is to be discerned in every word of Scripture by the stages of reading, meditation, prayer, and contemplation. What is to be noted here is the conviction that God speaks to the person through the words of Scripture; the notion of method in prayer is not as important as the idea of the engagement of the whole person, body and soul, reason and emotions.

That liturgical prayer prolonged and deepened in private contemplation was related directly to preaching is indicated by the last of the nine ways of prayer, which describes Dominic's custom on the road. It was prescribed in the constitutions that when traveling the friars should recite the Office as best they could, which probably meant reciting the psalms by heart. In another passage they are exhorted to speak only of God or to God. Dominic would often quote Hos 2:16: "I will lead her into the desert and speak to her heart," then lag behind his companion or move ahead, engaged in animated meditation. The author comments that "the brethren thought that in this kind of prayer the saint acquired the fulness of sacred scripture and the very heart of the understanding of God's words, and also a power and boldness to preach fervently, and a hidden intimacy with the Holy Spirit to know hidden things" (*Early Dominicans,* p. 102).

Study

Dominican spirituality may be characterized as a spirituality of the Word incarnate, understood first as a communal and personal engagement of the Word, and secondly as a prolongation of the incarnate Word's preaching ministry. An important dimension of the friar's personal engagement of the Word was his study. Dominic's vision made study a religious exercise, putting it in the place of the monk's manual labor. Every priory was to have a lector in theology, whose task it was to lecture daily on the Scriptures, to hold regular disputations, and to provide expert advice on issues of pastoral concern. All the friars were required to attend the daily lectures, and it was in this way that the majority of the friars received their preparations for preaching. Those selected to be lectors were sent to the universities, and the constitutions stipulated that they should be provided with their own copies of the Bible, the *Sentences* of Peter Lombard, and the *Historia scholastica* of Peter Comestor.

Dominican study, however, was not a pursuit of learning for its own sake. The constitutions make it clear that study was for the sake of preaching. Until 1254 the brethren were even forbidden to pursue secular studies or to get involved in philosophical debates. It must also be remembered that in the Middle Ages theology was

never a purely academic pursuit. To be a theologian meant first and foremost being a person of prayer. Thus study was not merely the acquisition of knowledge but a penetration of the mystery of faith through the exercise of reason. That is why logic and the art of dialectic were so important and why, in time, the friars began to appreciate the value of philosophy. For the friar, study and prayer merged. It was said of Thomas Aquinas that he had as much recourse to prayer as to logic in the resolution of enigmas.

Preaching

History often remembers Dominicans in connection with the Inquisition and so tends to see Dominic and his friars as zealous defenders of orthodoxy. This is unfortunate, for it is clear from the testimony of the canonization process that Dominic devoted much of his prayer to fervent petition for the salvation of souls. Even his penance and ascetical practice were understood as making reparation for sins, not only his own but those of others. The motivation of preaching, then, is not the defense of abstract truth but love of neighbor.

It is here, in relation to the apostolate, that Dominican poverty can be mentioned. Poverty was not embraced by Dominic as an end but as a means to give his preaching credibility. From the beginning Dominic recognized corporate ownership of the friars' churches, houses, and the land on which they stood. What was rejected was ownership of revenue-producing property in the feudal manner.

Dominican Teachers

There were, strictly speaking, no Dominican spiritual writers until the 14th century. Dominicans wrote biblical commentaries, made sermon collections, and wrote theological commentaries and syntheses. If they wrote no spiritual treatises, it was because they were satisfied with the traditional sources. Indeed, Dominic was said to have valued the writings of Cassian and

Bernard of Clairvaux, and it is works such as these, along with the writings of the Church Fathers and the writings of the 12th-century canons, that we find in the inventories of medieval Dominican libraries. It must also be noted that even with the rise of Scholasticism, theology and spirituality were not yet seen as separate disciplines or approaches. Thus it may be said of men like Albert and Thomas that their spirituality is expressed in and through their theological writings.

Thomas Aquinas

Thomas Aquinas gave Dominic's vision a systematic theological expression in his extensive writings. Although he held a chair in theology twice at the University of Paris, he spent most of his career as a lector in Dominican houses. It is most likely that his *Summa Theologiae* was written for his confreres who were trained in their priories. Such training tended to be both haphazard and narrowly focused on the practical—haphazard because the lectures on Scripture given by conventual lectors treated theological topics as they arose in the biblical text; narrow because issues related to hearing confessions were treated by means of a case-study approach (not to be confused with casuistry). In the *Summa Theologiae* Thomas treats all of theology with a brevity that conveys the essential while avoiding excessive detail. The second part, in which he outlines a moral theology, is not a catalogue of sins but a systematic treatment of the principles of moral judgment.

The themes stressed by Thomas in his theology and repeated in his few extant sermons express a rich spirituality based on Scripture and tradition. Central to his theology is his conviction that the intellect is primary, that love flows from knowledge. Affirming the incomprehensibility of God, Thomas nevertheless holds that through revelation God has expressed the will to lead humankind to fulfillment and a share in the divine beatitude. The final human goal is to participate in the vision of God, knowing God to the extent the human intellect can, but even here a direct, intuitive knowledge of God is possible. For Thomas, all being is good, because it is a share in the divine being. Yet God endows creation with a being that is its own and a goodness that is its own. His emphasis on the goodness of creation is most clearly shown in his anthropology, which stresses that humans are made in God's image, which means that they possess minds to know and freedom to act. Speaking of persons being created in God's image, Thomas uses the interesting phrase *ad imaginem Dei* ("toward God's image"), the meaning of which is explored in the second part of the *Summa,* in which he considers the principles of human action by which men and women grow toward, or away from, God's image.

Far from being static, Thomas's theology recognizes that universal principles cannot be applied to individual circumstances without discernment. Law and grace are given as guides; human moral life is a process of character development realized in the acquisition of virtue. For Thomas, obedience to law is through understanding, while grace builds upon nature. There is no sharp division between the realms of grace and nature. He presupposes a created world suffused by the Spirit and open to grace.

Perhaps Thomas's most revolutionary stance was his adoption of the Aristotelian view that the soul is the form of the body, thus departing from the Platonic position that sees the human person as a soul using a body. Thus he also parts company with those who disparage the body or see body and soul as necessarily at odds. Among medieval writers, Thomas has the most integrated view of the human person and the most positive view of the body, the emotions, and human sexuality.

The same attitude toward human nature is to be found in his Christology, which accords to the humanity of Christ a positive contribution to salvation. For Thomas, the motive of the incarnation and saving work of Christ is love for sinners. The value of Christ's passion and death is not measured by the quantity of his suffering but by the depth of his love. Drawing upon the theology of the Letter to the Hebrews, Thomas characterizes Christ's death as a sacrifice of love offered in worship to God. This theology bridges the distance between Christ's life and that of the Church. The Christian people are members of Christ's Body by baptism, and through his priesthood they offer God perfect worship and are made one by the Eucharist.

Eckhart, Tauler, and Suso

Following the death of Aquinas and the condemnation of some propositions associated with his teachings, the hegemony lay with the Franciscan schools of Duns Scotus and William of Ockham. At issue was God's sovereignty, since for many the intellectualism of Aquinas and his optimistic view of human nature were seen to threaten God's sovereign freedom. Dominicans remained faithful to the teaching of St. Thomas, with the spirit of the times. Meister Eckhart, John Tauler, and Henry Suso were German Dominicans who combined some of Thomas's insights with the tradition of German mysticism.

Meister Eckhart (ca. 1260–1328) spent his early years in Erfurt and Cologne, receiving the masterate at Paris in 1302. There he defended the primacy of the intellect, maintaining with Thomas the essential equality of being and knowing in God. His own career was similar to that of Thomas: the majority of his years were spent teaching in Dominican houses, with two sojourns in Paris. More than Thomas, Eckhart seems to have had an important role as preacher and spiritual advisor. His German sermons were taken down in outline and summary form by his auditors: Dominican, Benedictine, and Cistercian nuns and Beguines. He was influenced not only by Thomas but also by Bernard of Clairvaux, Maimonides, Pseudo-Dionysius, and Neoplatonism. Central to Eckhart's teaching is the idea that there is no other being but God. In the highest part of the intellect there is something both uncreated and uncreatable, the ground of the soul, the seat of the divine life, which in the human person is equal to God. To arrive at mystical union, one must leave behind all created reality to stand naked before God. In the uncreated ground of the soul the birth of the Word takes place and the human person becomes one with God. In 1326 Eckhart was called upon to defend himself against charges of heresy in Cologne. He appealed to the Holy See but died in 1327, before the matter was finally resolved. In March 1329 a number of propositions were condemned, though it was acknowledged that with considerable explanation they could be understood in a Catholic sense. It is clear that politics were involved; it is equally clear that Eckhart used bold language and pioneered in using the vernacular as a vehicle of theological expression.

John Tauler, of whom little is known, was born around 1300 and entered the Friars Preachers in his native Strasburg, where he knew and was influenced by Eckhart. He was not a theologian but rather exclusively a preacher and spiritual advisor for monasteries of Dominican nuns. He died in 1361 without leaving behind any writings except for his sermons, which were taken down by auditors. In doctrine Tauler was very close to Eckhart, but he was more prudent in expression. His sermons display a love of examples drawn from everyday life.

Henry Suso was a contemporary of Tauler's, born about 1300 in Constance, and, like Tauler, perhaps knew Eckhart at Strasburg and Cologne. He too was a preacher and advisor to nuns but seems, more than the other two, to have written on the basis of his own mystical experience. In his principal work, *The Little Book of Truth,* he attempts to present and clarify

Eckhart's thought in more prudent language. According to Suso, when the soul reaches the point where it loses the sense of being distinct from God, it arrives at union without distinction. For him, the Christian life is a transformation into Christ, which he describes as a birth, but, unlike Eckhart, he emphasizes that the birth is a human birth and not that of the Word. The supreme union with God, which is beyond all comprehension, is arrived at by means of a stripping of self, which results in a knowing that is direct and intuitive.

Catherine of Siena

Catherine of Siena, a lay Dominican, was born in 1347. Her biographer, Raymond of Capua, says that she was seven years old when she vowed her virginity to God, fifteen when she cut off her hair, defying attempts to marry her off, and eighteen when she took the Dominican habit. She belonged to the Mantellate, a group of women associated with the Dominican Order who, while remaining at home, wore the habit and worked among the poor and sick. For several years she lived as a recluse in her parents' home, going out only for Mass, until 1368, when she sensed a call to join in the work of her sisters. This activity among the sick and destitute won her notoriety. People sought her out, and from hours of conversation she learned theological argument and biblical interpretation, and taught what she knew of God from her experience. As her fame became more widespread, Catherine was called upon to mediate in the intense politics of 14th-century Italy. She wrote letters and traveled, serving as a mediator between Florence and the papacy. She also worked diligently preaching a crusade, which she believed would divert the energies of Christians from internecine strife, strove to reform the clergy, and urged the Pope to return to Rome. Her last journey brought her to Rome at the order of Pope Urban VI, who found himself embroiled in schism. Catherine set up her household there,

meeting with the Pope and cardinals and directing her disciples. She died on April 29, 1380.

The Pursuit of Truth

Catherine, perhaps more clearly than any other Dominican except Dominic, exemplifies the dynamic of contemplation and action. As she herself expresses it: "A soul rises up, restless with tremendous desire for God's honor and the salvation of souls. She has for some time exercised herself in virtue and has become accustomed to dwelling in the cell of self-knowledge in order to know better God's goodness toward her, since upon knowledge follows love. And loving, she seeks to clothe herself in it" (*Dialogue*, p. 25). It is not that action follows upon seclusion nor that prayer is an oasis in the midst of activity; rather, the dynamic exemplified by Catherine and Dominic consists essentially in a dedication to truth, truth that is a "who," not a "what." The Dominican vocation to truth (the order's motto is "Veritas") is indeed intellectualist, in the sense that knowledge is primary. What can be lost sight of is the other side of the coin, namely, love. This is Aquinas's insight that knowledge begets love. Aquinas himself, who in a life span of barely fifty years produced a library of writings, lived a life filled with activity.

This assiduous pursuit of truth, centered in liturgy and common life, nurtured by friendship and prayer, is the hallmark of all the luminaries of the order. If the focus has been on the Middle Ages, it is because the renewal of Dominican life in the 20th century has been achieved by returning to its authentic roots. The great Dominicans of this century—Sertillanges, Lagrange, Chenu, Congar, and Schillebeeckx—have all lived lives of intense activity marked by scholarship and a lively interest in their neighbors' good.

See also ASCETICISM; CONTEMPLATION, CONTEMPLATIVE PRAYER; LECTIO DIVINA; LITURGY;

PREACHING; RELIGIOUS LIFE; ROSARY; STUDY; TEACHING; TRUTH; WESTERN MEDIEVAL SPIRITUALITY.

Bibliography: *Constitutiones antiquae ordinis fratrum praedicatorum (1215–1237),* ed. A. H. Thomas (Leuven: Dominikanenklooster, 1965). W. Hinnebusch, *Dominican Spirituality* (Washington: Thomist Press, 1965); *The History of the Dominican Order,* 2 vols. (Staten Island, N.Y.: Alba House, 1965, 1973). M.-H. Vicaire, *Saint Dominic and His Times,* trans. K. Pond (New York: McGraw-Hill, 1964). Catherine of Siena, *The Dialogue,* trans. S. Noffke, Classics of Western Spirituality (New York: Paulist, 1980). Henry Suso, *The Exemplar, With Two German Sermons,* trans. F. Tobin (New York: Paulist, 1989). Meister Eckhart, *The Essential Sermons, Commentaries, Treatises, and Defense,* trans. E. Colledge and B. McGinn, Classics of Western Spirituality (New York: Paulist, 1981); *Teacher and Preacher,* ed. B. McGinn (New York: Paulist, 1986). Johannes Tauler, *Sermons,* trans. M. Shrady (New York: Paulist, 1985). *Albert and Thomas: Selected Writings,* ed. and trans. S. Tugwell (New York: Paulist, 1988). *Early Dominicans: Selected Writings,* ed. S. Tugwell, Classics of Western Spirituality (New York: Paulist, 1982).

RONALD J. ZAWILLA

DREAMS

Everyone dreams. That has been scientifically established. A great deal of human creativity has found its origins in dreams. Metaphor and symbol make up the language of dreams, a language universal in character. The human sciences have shown that an understanding of dreams is productive of personal insights and clarification of the emotional life. Because dream work can assist in overcoming prejudices, ideologies, and estranging worldviews, it can further involvement in areas of social responsibility. Belonging to a dream group can provide one with a community of support whereby one finds ways to engage in the process of helping others toward a more humane and just life.

Effective dream work is not casual or episodic. One must make a decision to remember one's dreams. One needs to record them and to interpret them. Often this is best done by sharing the dream with someone else. This may be a friend, but sharing them with spiritual directors and therapists can be the most effective. If one finds it difficult to recall dreams, then it is important to prepare oneself by focusing attention on remembering the dreams before going to sleep; they should be jotted down upon awaking. Even dream fragments are very significant. Recalling them can enhance one's ability to recall the full story dreams. Lying in the same habitual body positions one uses in sleep can help the dreaming process. Imagining the face of someone to whom one has a strong emotional connection can bring up dream memories and even trigger full dream recall. Some dream experts recommend vitamin B as a way of strengthening dream memory and lowering stress that might interfere with such recall.

There are many reasons why dreams cannot be remembered. Some of these are physical, some social. The repression of dreams is very often connected with the content of the dreams. This is especially the case when the dream does not conform to a person's present self-understanding. If people find the content repugnant or challenging to the way they see themselves, they may find that it is easier to let the dream return to the unconscious. Another reason for the inability to recall dreams is that they often operate in a different, i.e., timeless, fashion than people do when they are awake. Therefore, the waking experience of ego may not be reduplicated in the dream. (See J. Taylor, *Dream Work,* to which this article is especially indebted.)

Dreams are not only difficult to recall but they are also hard to understand. Many people often find them obscure. This is the case because dreams are multidimensional in meaning. They operate on many different levels. Because dreams are complex experiences, it is not possible to discover one and only one meaning to a dream. One needs to work at a dream, recording it, reviewing it, and titling it. One must approach dream interpretation with an open mind. If one becomes tied to a single interpretation, one will lose the significance of the dream for the dreamer. It is also true that only the dreamer can properly and authentically interpret the dream. There must be some kind of confirmation of a dream interpretation made by the dreamer. This confirmation can take place in many ways, but it is basically that the dreamer experiences some inner resonance with an interpretation given either by the dreamer or someone else. An idea about a dream might be right, but if it is not confirmed by the dreamer, it is not significant for that person.

Dream experts make a number of suggestions for facilitating the use of dreams for personal growth. The most commonly accepted suggestions include making a written record of the dream, noting the date and day of the week on which the dream occurred, recording the dream in the present tense, and titling the dream. Dreamers are also encouraged to draw pictures of dreams, giving different forms of expression to the images, ideas, and energies of the dreams; recording dream fragments, since they may be clearer symbolic statements; being open to the many possible interpretations of dreams and not staying with the first one that seems most attractive. If one does not experience the inner knowledge of the truth of the interpretation, that does not mean that the interpretation is wrong; it may be that the dreamer is not yet willing to be open to such an interpretation. The dreamer should approach the dreams with an active imagination and be in touch with the people in the dream or developing the dream further, imagining what might have happened had the dream continued.

The use of dreams requires a change of attitude toward dreams. One cannot consider them as relatively insignificant or as some kind of epiphenomena. Dreams need to be welcomed. If people look forward to dreams, honoring them and desiring them so that they can have greater contact with the unconscious, dream work will be more successful. It is also helpful to review past dreams, in the hope of discovering something more there. It is profitable to compare the contents of a dream with the significant waking events of the same day. Finally, one of the most productive ways to engage in dream interpretation is to share the dreams with a counselor, a spiritual director, or a friend and to engage in group work on dreams. Dream work should be a communal human endeavor.

There are some points to be kept in mind when working on dreams in a group. It is only the dreamer who can actually know what the dream means. It is important that the dreamer respond positively to the suggestions coming from the group. It is not a question of the group being right and the dreamer being wrong. Dreams have a way of being self-correcting. The atmosphere in the group should be such that the participants are willing to speak about feelings, are centered mentally, and are allowed time to share without interruption. Sharing dreams makes one vulnerable, and what anyone says about another's dreams says a great deal about the speaker. This must be owned and accepted. It is not necessary for the dreamers to fully understand their dreams before they articulate them for others. Dream images that are frightening should not be repressed. This is especially true when death appears in a dream. Death is often a symbol for growth and transformation, and fleeing from death may well be signaling a call to change and further growth. Some find it helpful to share with the group creative expressions of their dreams, such as pictures, sculptures, and songs. When listening to another's narration of dreams, one should listen to the whole person, especially the emotional qualities with which the dream is related and the images used to relate the feelings.

Dreams are multidimensional and so have many meanings. The group cannot hope to interpret a dream exhaustively. Dream groups work on the presupposition of honesty, respect, and attention to the environment and one's body.

The significance of dream work for spirituality and personal integration is based on the conviction that every dream is in the service of wholeness through the integration of the inner and outer lives. This is so because dreams are the way that the unconscious announces itself. In the dream one finds elements of the dreamer's personality, vital energies, sexual desires, the state of his or her physical condition, memories of recent days, some childhood and adolescent reminiscences, speculations about the future, some images in touch with one's archetypal life. One's dreams are the way in which one participates in the common human experience. Dreams are never purely private; there is always an element of universality in them.

Dreams refer to the past, the present, and the future. They commemorate elements of conscious life. They carry elements of constructive self-criticism, and every dream is a source of inspiration and problem solving. Dreams have a religious dimension and have been the source of identifying religious beliefs from many traditions. Because of this comprehensive character of dreams, they serve the waking life in a compensatory role. They correct some imbalance found in normal behavior. A key to effective dream interpretation is to look for the seeming polarities (good and evil, life and death), in order to bring together what appears to be opposed in the conscious life.

Dreams reveal the stages of the evolution of the personality. Every thing, every event, and every person in a dream represents something in the dreamer's interior life. Thus it is important in dream interpretation to pay attention to the connection between the various dreams. They are related. The discovery of the themes in a series of dreams will assist one in understanding the emotional relationships or the lack of them in one's life. It is important to pay attention to the humor and incongruous elements in dreams.

Explicitly sexual and erotic material is an example of the multilevel meaning of dreaming. There are obvious connections with waking experiences and emotional tensions. But beyond this there is a symbolic character to sexual images that refer to deeply spiritual and religious concerns. Enjoyable and gratifying sexual material often refers to the spiritual and moral resolution taking place in one's life, whereas images for which one feels distaste and repugnance refer to repressed concerns and unresolved spiritual issues. Dreams can provide a significant approach to integrating sexuality and spirituality.

It would be difficult to engage in the interpretation of dreams while prescinding from the work of Carl Jung. His naming of the basic patterns of human instinct and development as archetypes has provided a whole vocabulary for dream interpretation. The patterns of myths, cultural beliefs, and social practices are revealed in dreams. Archetypes are both individual and universal, for they embody the basic structure of the human psyche. They belong to individuals while at the same time revealing the psychic patterns of all human beings. Familiarity with the Jungian major archetypes such as the persona, the shadow, light and darkness, animus and anima, death and rebirth, etc., make it possible to identify the ways in which one's basic psychic structure is or is not in balance and is or is not in harmony with the larger universe.

In this regard special consideration must be given to the shadow, that part of us which is usually missing from our conscious development. The shadow side of a person is both social and individual. For instance, for those who live in a white, male-oriented, and highly technological world, the repression of the sensual, the spontaneous, and the relational have caused those elements to be projected onto those who do not share that world. The exploration of the shadow can assist people in the ways in which they participate in such oppression as racism, sexism, ageism, and patriarchy.

Failure on the individual level to bring to conscious light the shadow energies leads to personal fears and hatreds, fueling the collective drives of oppression and evil. Dreams are an important way to admit that people are good as well as evil. If one stays in contact with the shadow, much energy that is wasted in self-defeating, neurotic, and compulsive behavior can be released. It is here that dreams and the area of social justice are intimately bound together.

Acknowledgment of the shadow is a difficult task for most people. It must be done repeatedly throughout life. It is in this area that one can see the clear relation between dreams and spirituality, for spiritual growth involves a spiritual death—death to the fear of change and psychological maturing. But when people let go and die to the old self, the energy that was previously wasted on supporting or fighting those fears is now released for life-giving ventures. Dream work can assist one in touching the source of those energies, and those same energies will make it possible for people to grow in creative ways as they move toward spiritual maturity.

See also EXTRAORDINARY PHENOMENA; IMAGINATION; MEMORY; MIND; PARAPSYCHOLOGY; PERSONALITY TYPES; PSYCHOLOGY, RELATIONSHIP AND CONTRIBUTION TO SPIRITUALITY.

Bibliography: R. de Becker, The Understanding of Dreams (New York: Bell Publishing, 1965). A. Faraday, Dream Power (New York: Berkeley Publishing, 1972). J. Taylor, Dream Work (New York: Paulist, 1983). M. Ullman and N. Zimmerman, Working With Dreams (New York: Delacorte, 1979).

JAMES L. EMPEREUR, S.J.

DRUGS

Drugs of the mind-altering type have been employed in various religious rituals and spiritual quests throughout the centuries. These types of drugs are known by the general term *psychedelic,* derived from the Greek words for "soul" and "manifestation." Such drugs include peyote, a cactus substance employed by the Aztecs and the Plains Indians, and its derivative mescaline, given spiritual acclaim in the work of Aldous Huxley; various types of mushrooms, including the *amantia muscaria,* or the sacred fly-mushroom, linked with the beginnings of Christianity by John Allegro; and other plant substances, such as hemp, from which mind-altering drinks and elixirs are distilled. The use of these various drugs in rituals is considered a portal for religious experience, understood as the expansion of consciousness, communication with spiritual energies, and the discovery of power.

In the United States during the 1960s, synthetic psychedelic drugs were employed in medical research and psychic experimentation. The most popular of these drugs was lysergic acid diethylamide, commonly known as LSD. Timothy Leary's experimentation with the substance in California is the best known case of a seemingly religious usage of the drug. His maxim "Turn on, tune in, drop out" became the motto of an extensive countercultural movement that sought religious identity apart from mainstream religious systems.

In the present era of drug addiction, abuse, and criminal control, the use of psychedelics in religious and spiritual practices has been criticized. Two main questions have emerged. The first is the question of the quality of the reality that arises in the drug experience: Is it simply a substitute dream world that robs creative strength, creates addiction, and lives in illusion? The second concerns the level and staying power of the experience: Does conversion or transformation happen, and is it sustained?

See also ADDICTION; ECSTASY; MIND.

Bibliography: R. E. L. Masters and J. Houston, *The Varieties of Psychedelic Experiences* (New York: Holt, Rinehart and Winston, 1966).

RICHARD N. FRAGOMENI

DRYNESS

See DARKNESS, DARK NIGHT.

DUALISM

Dualism is an understanding of God, the world, and the human person in which two fundamental causal principles are thought to underlie all reality and oppose one another. Often characterized by the antithesis of "good" and "evil" or "spiritual" and "material," the dualistic opposition in religious systems originates on the level of the divinity and is manifested both in cosmology and in anthropology.

Various types of dualism are apparent in the history of religions. In radical versions the two principles are coequal and coeternal, as for example the kingdom of light (good) and the kingdom of darkness (evil) in ancient Zoroastrianism or Manicheism. But dualism may also derive from a monistic or monotheistic base. In this moderate dualism the spiritual or good principle is primary; only after some crisis or fall in the spiritual world does the second, lower principle emerge. The latter is held responsible for the creation of the material cosmos and the embodied human person. This view is typical of Christian Gnostics and extreme Platonists. In a modified form it also influenced some early Christians, such as Origen, who traced the existence of a material creation and an embodied human person back to a fall of the soul.

Dualism can also lead to different evaluations of the material cosmos. In more extreme versions the world is created by a hostile god or angel who is opposed to the supreme deity. This is a classic feature of the ancient Gnostic systems. For moderate dualists, such as Plato and some early Christians, the material world is created by the supreme God, but as a place of toil and chastisement, ultimately to be transcended.

Parallel estimations are made of the human body. Radical dualists see the body as utterly corrupt and alien to the spirit. Moderate dualists understand bodily existence as a salutary training ground for the spirit, temporarily beneficial but ultimately to be discarded. While radical dualism could sometimes lead to an antinomian libertinism, it more often produced an ascetic, body-denying spirituality. Abstention from certain foods (usually meat and wine) and from sexual relations was a typical feature of dualistic asceticism.

As Christianity emerged in the Hellenistic world, it inevitably absorbed elements of the prevailing culture, including dualism. Dualism was essentially a theodicy that offered a persuasive account of the defects of corporeal existence while safeguarding the purity and transcendence of God. It therefore provided early Christians with a framework within which to express their convictions about God and creation, about sin and the need for salvation in Christ. Even orthodox Christian writers, such as Gregory of Nyssa, Ambrose, and the young Augustine, were influenced by a moderate dualism. They preferred to think of God's original creation as sexless; sexual relations were considered a consequence of the fall.

Many Christians, however, were quick to recognize some of the deficiencies of dualism, particularly when it led to doctrinal heresies such as Docetism (the view that Jesus was never truly human). Already in the NT there is a polemic against dualistic errors. The Apostle Paul, for example, criticized Christians at Corinth who claimed that "everything is lawful" (1 Cor 6:12), because they believed that matters of the body were indifferent. The Pastoral Epistles attack Christians who "forbid marriage and require abstinence from foods that God created to be received with thanksgiving" (1 Tm 4:3). The Church's long struggle against Gnosticism in the 2nd and 3rd centuries ensured that radically dualistic interpretations of Christianity would not prevail.

Nevertheless, throughout most of its history Christian spirituality has not escaped the influence of a moderate dualism. Christians have often lacked a positive view of embodied existence and thus have failed to integrate human sexuality and emotions into their understanding of spirituality. While asceticism and celibacy need not be understood in dualistic terms, the tendency to dualism has often affected these practices. Contemporary efforts at holistic and creation-centered spiritualities aim to redress this imbalance in the Christian tradition.

See also ASCETICISM; BODY; CREATION; GNOSIS, GNOSTICISM; HOLISTIC SPIRITUALITY; PATRISTIC SPIRITUALITY.

Bibliography: U. Bianchi, *Selected Essays on Gnosticism, Dualism and Mysteriosophy* (Leiden: Brill, 1978). J. Nelson, *Embodiment: An Approach to Sexuality and Christian Theology* (Minneapolis: Augsburg, 1978). P. Brown, *The Body and Society: Men, Women, and Sexual Renunciation in Early Christianity* (New York: Columbia Univ. Press, 1988).

DAVID G. HUNTER

E

EARLY CHRISTIAN SPIRITUALITY

The chief sources for early Christian (1st century A.D.) spirituality are the books of the NT. What those books teach about God's action in Christ and the appropriate responses to it is the starting point and norm for every genuinely Christian spirituality. Those writings provide the basic elements of Christian spirituality: the kingdom of God as the horizon for spirituality; the death and resurrection of Jesus as the focal event; appropriate action (ethics, prayer, etc.) as the response to Jesus' message of the kingdom; baptism and the Eucharist as participation in his death and resurrection and thus in God's kingdom; and the help and guidance provided to God's pilgrim people by the Spirit-Paraclete. The NT writings challenge Christians in every age and circumstance to develop a spirituality that is faithful to the biblical tradition and sensitive to the needs of particular people. There is enough variety of spiritual perspectives within the NT to have facilitated this process of development and adaptation through twenty centuries. And any program of inculturation in the future must begin in part with the Scriptures if it is to merit the name "Christian spirituality."

There are limits to what we today can know about early Christian spirituality from the NT. We possess only a few written witnesses from 1st-century Christianity. None of these are systematic treatises on the spiritual life; rather, they give spiritual teaching (what God has done in Christ and what responses are fitting) in passing while solving particular problems (as in the Epistles) or telling the story of Jesus and the early Church (as in the Gospels and Acts). They tell us little about important aspects in the spiritual life (prayer, worship, discerning the spirits, spiritual direction, etc.).

The NT writings arose in a cultural milieu different from that of the late 20th-century West. Its authors took for granted the institution of slavery and the subordinate status assigned to women. They wrote in a culture in which novelty was avoided and creativity was defined as rearranging traditional materials in fresh ways. They seldom talked about themselves as individuals, preferring to stress group identity and to think in terms of collectivities. As part of a religious and political minority, they did not imagine a situation in which Christianity would be dominant and could impose its beliefs and ethical standards on society at large.

The center of early Christian spirituality was Jesus' death and resurrection. His death on the cross "for our sins" effected a new relationship with God, and his resurrection served as the decisive anticipation ("the firstfruits of those who have fallen asleep"—1 Cor 15:20) of God's coming kingdom. What is sometimes called the "ethical" teaching of the NT is really instruction about spirituality, that is, how the believer appropriates the Christ-event and puts it into practice ("doing the truth" in the Johannine idiom).

Presuppositions

Early Christian spirituality was shaped to a large extent by assumptions taken over from the Hebrew Bible and early Judaism. Its biblical presuppositions included the following beliefs: God created the world, chose Israel as a special people, and entered into covenant with Israel. These statements assume God's existence and willingness to enter into personal relationship with Israel and individuals within Israel (Abraham, Moses, David, etc.). God's covenant relationship with Israel involved the promise to remain faithful to the people (Davidic covenant) and the people's obligation to respond with appropriate behavior (Mosaic covenant). Failure to respond appropriately within this covenant relation is sin. The ultimate sin is the rejection of God's sovereignty in a kind of practical atheism that is labeled "idolatry," which in turn leads to ever greater sins. But repentance and conversion remain possibilities, though according to the Deuteronomistic philosophy of history, the wicked are inevitably punished for their sins.

These biblical assumptions about spirituality were taken over but modified in early Judaism (that is, from the return from exile to the destruction of Jerusalem in A.D. 70). The exclusive claims of Yahweh over Israel were interpreted as teaching a "philosophical" monotheism (Yahweh is the only God that exists). God's election of, and covenant with, Israel remained firm beliefs. But the present evil state of God's people—successive subjugations to the Persians, Ptolemies and Seleucids, and Romans—meant that God's promises would reach their fullness only with the definitive coming of God's kingdom. Only with the fullness of the kingdom will all creation acknowledge the divine sover-

eignty and Israel be vindicated as God's people.

In apocalyptic circles during the Second Temple period, there developed a "modified dualism" that was presupposed by most NT authors. The God of Israel created all things and remains as sovereign over all. But God has allowed two powers or forces to be at work in the world. The Angel of Light leads the children of light as they do the deeds of light, whereas the Angel of Darkness leads the children of darkness as they do the deeds of darkness. Thus the individual is caught up in the struggle between these powers, and the challenge is to align oneself with the children of light (see the Qumran *Manual of Discipline* 3-4). When God sees fit, the fullness of God's kingdom will be made manifest and the righteous vindicated. Those who have died will be restored to life in the resurrection (see Dan 12:1-3), and in the final judgment the just will be rewarded and the wicked will be punished.

Jewish apocalyptic spirituality retains a firm belief in God's sovereignty and promises to Israel. It defers the full manifestation of that sovereignty and the realization of the promises to the end of human history as we know it. Then all evil will be destroyed. In the meantime the faithful look for signs of the kingdom and pray for its coming, acknowledging that it is God's kingdom and God's task to bring it in. Though their lifestyles may vary from monastic (as at Qumran) to mainline, the faithful take as their guide to behavior in the present the Torah—the instructions from God revealed in the Hebrew Scriptures, especially the Pentateuch. They pray to God not only at the Jerusalem Temple but also at local gatherings (synagogues) where the Scriptures are read and petitions (Eighteen Benedictions) are raised to God. The spirituality of Jewish apocalypticism is summarized in Jesus' own prayer: "Hallowed be your name, your kingdom come, your will be done, on earth as in heaven . . ." (Mt 6:9-13; Lk 11:2-4).

Jesus

The central theme of Jesus' own preaching was the kingdom of God ("Your kingdom come"). Based on the biblical doctrine of God's kingship (celebrated especially in the psalms), the apocalyptic teaching about God's kingdom looked forward to the time when all creation will acknowledge God's sovereignty. Jesus proclaimed the coming of God's kingdom in its future fullness much as his apocalyptic predecessors and contemporaries did. His parables about the kingdom (see Mt 13 parr.) emphasize the greatness and value of the kingdom while holding out the idea of a final judgment accompanying it. Some sayings indicate that God's kingdom will come soon (Mt 10:23; Mk 9:1; 13:30), whereas others suggest that to some extent it is already present or at least inaugurated (Mt 11:12; Lk 11:20/Mt 12:28; Lk 7:20). The kingdom is enough of a present reality that its seed has already been sown.

The kingdom belongs to God, and it is God's prerogative to bring its fullness at the right time. Whereas the God of Jewish apocalypticism was somewhat removed from the ongoing struggle between good and evil, Jesus proclaimed his own relationship of intimacy with God as "Father" (*Abba*) and urged his disciples to share with him in this special relationship with God.

The kingdom of God was also the presupposition of, and context for, Jesus' "ethical" teaching. Those who received this teaching were disciples of Jesus—those who had already accepted to some extent his message about God's future and present kingdom and sought to act in a way appropriate to it. Jesus' ethical teaching was really a response to the kingdom and a challenge to live in accord with hope for God's reign and as witnesses to it. More important than the content of the individual teachings was the theological framework in which these teachings were set. The "good news" of the kingdom was of-fered by Jesus to all kinds of people. But his preaching had its most spectacular successes among the marginal people of Jewish society—tax collectors, sinners, prostitutes, the sick, and so forth. That preaching is aptly summarized in Mk 1:15: "This is the time of fulfillment. The kingdom of God is at hand. Repent, and believe in the gospel."

Jesus' attitudes toward the great religious institutions of Judaism—the Temple and the Torah—were ambivalent. Several sayings attributed to him (Mt 5:23-24; 23:16-22; Mk 1:44; 11:15-18) take for granted the smooth running of the Jerusalem Temple, whereas others carry a threat against the Temple and a contrast between it and one "not made with hands" (Mk 14:58; Mt 26:61; Jn 2:19; Acts 6:14). Jesus surely took a free attitude toward the Jewish traditions surrounding the observance of the Torah on matters such as ritual purity and Sabbath observance (Mk 7:1-23), on the grounds that these traditions were human inventions. In general, he seems to have observed the Torah, though on divorce (Lk 16:18; 1 Cor 7:8; Mk 10:1-12) and oaths (Mt 5:34-37) his teaching seems to contradict what was allowed in the Torah. Jesus' apparent ambivalence toward the Temple and the Torah can be best explained in light of the overriding significance of God's kingdom: in view of the kingdom even the greatest institutions must play a subordinate role and be reshaped to conform to the demands of God's reign. Likewise, Jesus' miracles point to the breaking in of God's kingdom (Lk 7:18-23) and to Jesus as its agent (Mt 12:32-33).

In the twenty years between Jesus' death and the composition of the earliest NT writing (1 Thessalonians), Jesus himself became the focus, if not the center, of early Christian spirituality. The conviction grew that in Jesus God had done something remarkable toward bringing about the fullness of God's kingdom. Jesus not only preached God's coming kingdom but also represented its inauguration.

This perception of Jesus was rooted in aspects of his earthly ministry. His authoritative "I" sayings (Mt 5:21-48; 10:16; Mk 9:25) manifest a special consciousness of mission and personal authority. His address to God as "Father" suggests a special relationship of intimacy with God (Mt 26:42; Mk 14:36; Lk 10:21; 11:2; 23:34, 46; Jn 11:41; etc.), which he invites his followers to share (Gal 4:6). Though his miraculous healings and exorcisms show forth the presence of God's kingdom, Jesus exhibits a remarkable ability to work by his own power and not merely as a petitioner to, or mediator with, God. Jesus' message of God's kingdom and his status as its messenger are intimately related. Whereas Jesus' contemporaries may have viewed him as a prophet, charismatic teacher, or even a political rebel, his disciples recognized him as both the authoritative herald of God's kingdom and its present dimension.

The assessment of Jesus as the presence of God's kingdom expresses itself most dramatically in the proclamation of the resurrection of Jesus. In some Jewish circles (especially the apocalyptists and the Pharisees), resurrection was part of the scenario of end-time events. The idea was that prior to the final judgment the dead would be restored to life, and then the just would be rewarded and the wicked punished (see Dan 12:1-3). In this matter Jesus sided with the Pharisees against the Sadducees (Mk 12:18-27 parr.). The novelty of the Christian proclamation that God had raised Jesus from the dead was twofold: A single person (not all the just and wicked) has been restored to eternal life (resurrection) before the other end-time events take place. Thus God's kingdom has been made present not only in the ministry of the earthly Jesus but also, and even more dramatically, in his resurrection from the dead.

Paul

In summarizing the gospel that he had preached to the Corinthians, Paul placed Jesus' death and resurrection at the center: "Christ died for our sins in accordance with the scriptures . . . he was raised on the third day" (1 Cor 15:3-4). The pre-Pauline confessions of faith show a similar emphasis: "Christ Jesus, whom God set forth as an expiation . . . by his blood" (Rom 3:25); "established as Son of God in power according to the spirit of holiness through resurrection from the dead" (Rom 1:4). The resurrection of Jesus was interpreted by Paul as the "first installment" or "down payment" toward the general resurrection (2 Cor 1:22; 5:5), and the "firstfruits of the Spirit" (Rom 8:23). Jesus' dignity as "the firstborn from the dead" (Col 1:18) provided the context for understanding the titles and images applied to him (Son of God, Messiah/Christ, Lord, etc.).

Paul wrote to give pastoral advice to specific communities in the Greco-Roman world. His theology was in the service of his practical purposes. Rather than exploring the details of Jesus' death and resurrection or the nature of Jesus' dignity or even Jesus' teachings, he focused on the effects or consequences of Jesus' death and resurrection. The basic insight is that through the Christ-event what is expected in fullness at the end of human history has already begun. The Last Judgment is part of the apocalyptic scenario. Then the just will be "declared upright" (or "made upright"), and the wicked will be condemned. Through Jesus' death and resurrection the final judgment has been anticipated, and the righteous "through faith" (Rom 3:25) have had their sins wiped away and now stand in right relationship with God.

The anticipation of the Last Judgment through Christ's death and resurrection is at the root of the other ways in which Paul talked about the effects of the Christ-event: reconciliation (Rom 5:10-11), salvation (Rom 1:16), expiation (Rom 3:25), redemption (Rom 3:24), sanctification (1 Cor 6:11), transformation (2 Cor 3:18), new creation (Gal 6:15; 2 Cor 5:17), and glorification (Rom 8:30). All these conditions that Jewish apocalyptists put off until the end-time were understood by early Christians to have been inaugurated through Christ's death and resurrection. Thus Christians already enjoy the benefits of the fullness of God's kingdom. To some extent God's kingdom has come.

The outline of Paul's Letter to the Romans illustrates the framework of early Christian spirituality. After demonstrating that all people, Gentiles and Jews alike, were under the power of sin (chaps. 1–4), Paul reflects on the results of justification ("since we have been justified by faith, we have peace with God through our Lord Jesus Christ"—5:1): freedom from sin, death, and the Law as the powers ruling one's life (chaps. 5–7), as well as freedom to live life in the Spirit (chap. 8). Paul then looks forward to the reuniting of God's people in the future (chaps. 9–11) and outlines some ways in which Christians live in the Spirit now (chaps. 12–15).

Just as according to Jewish apocalypticism the children of light lived under the guidance of the Angel of Light and did the deeds of light, so through the Christ-event the early Christians viewed themselves as living under the guidance of the Holy Spirit and doing the deeds of the Spirit (Rom 8:1-17; Gal 5:16-26). The present, through the anticipation of God's kingdom, is nevertheless fraught with danger not only with regard to moral choices (Rom 1:29-31; 13:13; 1 Cor 5:10-11; etc.) but also in light of the creation itself as it "awaits with eager expectation the revelation of the children of God" (Rom 8:19). There are certain deeds that one living in the Spirit does and does not do. As in Jesus' preaching, ethics is a response to the present dimension of God's kingdom, not an autonomous philosophical science. In fact, "life in the Spirit" is a far better designation than "ethics" for the paraenetic ma-

terial included toward the end of Paul's letters.

Baptism and Eucharist were early Christian ways of participating in Christ's death and resurrection. Calling upon what had already become traditional in early Christian circles, Paul in Rom 6:1-4 related baptism to the Christ-event and presented it as the presupposition for walking "in newness of life." Likewise, the Eucharist is the memorial of Jesus' Last Supper (at which he interpreted his death) and the proclamation of his death until his second coming (1 Cor 11:23-26). Whereas baptism signified entrance into life in the Spirit, Eucharist maintained and enriched that life and pointed toward even greater fullness at the definitive coming of God's kingdom.

Two controversial topics in the Pauline communities were the status of the Torah and the time of the end. Paul's statements about the Torah are not entirely consistent. Though he often quotes the Torah as an authority and asserts that the Law is holy (Rom 7:12), he also says that it was given because of transgressions and served as a "pedagogue" (Gal 3), and that it helped people to know sin and served as a stimulus to sin (Rom 7). Paul's basic conviction was that Christ, not the Torah, provides the way of access to God. His objection was not to law as such or to the Torah in particular, but to the tendency to attribute to the Torah or to any laws what only God's gracious act in Jesus Christ could do. Thus he also resisted imposing the prescriptions of the Torah upon Gentiles who "turned to God from idols to serve the living and true God and to await his Son from heaven, whom he raised from the dead, Jesus, who delivers us from the coming wrath" (1 Thess 1:9-10).

Keeping a balance between the "already" and the "not yet" was another challenge in Pauline spirituality. When one compares the earliest Pauline letter (1 Thessalonians) with the other letters in their chronological succession (Galatians, 1 and 2 Corinthians, Romans, Philippians, Philemon), it is possible to discern a shift in focus from the "not yet" to the "already." Indeed one of Paul's reasons for writing his first letter was to clear up misconceptions about the end-time and how Christians should prepare for it (1 Thess 4:13–5:11). Some interpret the problems combated in 1 Corinthians as the result of an overemphasis on the present dimensions of salvation in Christ. Nonetheless, throughout his letters Paul never loses sight of both the present and the future aspects of the Christ-event, though he saw more clearly the present implications of some matters in the baptismal slogan in Gal 3:28 ("neither Jew nor Greek") than others ("neither slave nor free person . . . neither male nor female"). In his spiritual teaching and activity Paul's goal was "to know him [Christ] and the power of his resurrection and the sharing of his sufferings by being conformed to his death, if somehow I may attain the resurrection from the dead" (Phil 3:10-11).

The Evangelists

Early Christians wrote Gospels in light of their convictions about Jesus' death and resurrection. Though on a surface level the Gospels look like biographies, the faith-claims made about their hero Jesus put them in a category different even from ancient biographies. Put in final form between A.D. 70 and the end of the first century, the Gospels provide orderly accounts of Jesus' teachings and actions and reach their climax in the narratives of his death and resurrection. Their concern is more with the identity of Jesus than with the consequences of the Christ-event (as was the case with Paul).

The evangelists used traditional material going back to Jesus himself and also transmitted the beliefs of the early Christian communities. They took for granted the various titles applied to Jesus (Messiah, Son of Man, Son of David, Son of God, Wisdom, Lord, etc.). They tell how Jesus gathered disciples who accompanied him during his earthly ministry and bore witness to him after death. They show how Jesus gave the community gathered around him an identity and a mission within the history of salvation. Yet each Evangelist approached the figure of Jesus in a distinctive way, and each presented a distinctive model of discipleship. By attending to their four distinctive approaches to Christology and discipleship, we will discover four kinds of Christian spirituality that nonetheless have Jesus and his gospel of God's kingdom as their center.

Mark presents Jesus as the suffering Messiah. Some of the traditions that Mark used indicate that the idea of Jesus as the miracle-worker was popular in early Christian circles. Mark placed those traditions beside another popular picture of Jesus—the teacher. Without rejecting either image of Jesus, he insisted that Jesus' miracles and teachings be understood in light of the cross. The Marcan disciples provide both positive and negative models of Christian spirituality. In the first part of the Gospel they respond to Jesus' call, abide with him, and even share his mission. But as the story of Jesus unfolds, the disciples misunderstand him repeatedly and eventually betray him in Jerusalem. Only the women remain faithful through Jesus' passion, and they discover the empty tomb on Easter. The male disciples serve as a negative example to the community as it tries to understand the mystery of the crucified Messiah. As the Marcan Christians face opposition and persecution, they have the good example of Jesus the suffering righteous one (Psalm 22) and the faithful women. They too must accept the cross and live under its sign.

Without denying the fundamental significance of the cross, Matthew shows how Jesus brought to fullness the promises of the Scriptures by pointing out how this or that event in Jesus' life corresponded to a biblical text. He portrays Jesus as the authoritative interpreter of the Torah and as the one who reveals God's will. He gives particular attention to those titles with rich Jewish backgrounds: Son of David, Messiah, Wisdom, Son of Man, and Son of God. The same Jesus who is identified as Emmanuel ("God with us") in 1:23 is with the Christian community "always, until the end of the age" (28:20).

Matthew's presentation of the earliest followers of Jesus is more positive than that of Mark: They have "little faith"—some faith but certainly not perfect faith. Peter serves not only as spokesman but also as the exemplary disciple, with all the strengths and weaknesses that involves. The disciples need instruction from Jesus, and so there are five great speeches (chaps. 5–7; 10; 13; 18; 24–25). They need encouragement to entrust themselves to Jesus' power (8:18-27; 14:22-23). They need to recognize that as the community of Jesus Christ they are God's people (21:41, 43) and must share that identity even with those who are not Jewish by birth (Mt 28:19).

Luke's major contribution to Christology comes with his presentation of Jesus as the prophet and martyr. In his first public act at the synagogue in Nazareth (4:16-30), Jesus' mission is defined in terms of Isaiah (Isa 61:1-2; 58:6) and the prophets Elijah and Elisha. Jesus acts as a prophet (7:16, 39) and dies as a prophet (13:33-34) and in accordance with prophecy (24:25-27). Innocent of the political charges against him, Jesus suffers the death of a martyr. On the cross he bears witness to his special relationship with God and remains faithful to his own teachings on forgiveness and love of enemies (23:34, 46). The twelve apostles are the principles of continuity between the time of Jesus and the time of the Church as unfolded in Acts. Those who accompanied the earthly Jesus bear witness to his death and resurrection, and carry the ministry and message that Jesus began "to the ends of the earth" (Acts 1:8)—from Judea to Rome. Yet the circle of Jesus' disciples is not limited to the Twelve. The disciples include figures from the time of the OT (Zechariah and Elizabeth, John the Baptist, Simeon and Anna); from the time of Jesus (the poor, the seventy, the women of Lk 8:1-3, etc.); and from the time of the Church (those who receive the apostles' message). The one character who spans all three periods in salvation history and fulfills the definition of the disciple as one who hears God's word and keeps it (8:19-21; 11:27-28) is Mary. During the time of the Church (from Jesus' ascension to the end-time), the Holy Spirit guides the community of Jesus and guarantees the spread of the gospel—to the point that Acts can be called "the book of the Holy Spirit," and the third period of salvation history can be termed the "time of the Spirit."

Whereas Mark, Matthew, and Luke provide a common view (*synopsis*) of Jesus on the basis of common sources, John uses different sources and offers a distinctive theological perspective. The focus of Jesus' preaching is his task of revealing his heavenly Father and his identity as the revealer. The kingdom of God, which is the center of Jesus' preaching and actions in the Synoptic Gospels, is in the background. Jesus' status as preexistent Son of God, as "I AM," as "God," goes beyond what the other Gospels say about him. Jesus is the definitive expression of God's will for his people, the "man from heaven" sent by the Father. His death was not a defeat; rather, it was the "hour" of his glory in which he began his return to the Father. He invites his followers to share in his relationship with the Father—one characterized by knowledge, love, unity, and mission. He challenges them to be on the side of the "spirit/Spirit" and not on that of the "flesh." Like many others in the Gospel, the disciples often misunderstand the earthly Jesus and thus provide Jesus with the occasion for further teaching. In his physical absence the Spirit-Paraclete will guide and animate and protect the community of Jesus' followers until "the last day."

Pauline School(s)

On the basis of literary style and content, it has become customary to assign certain letters bearing Paul's name (2 Thessalonians, Colossians and Ephesians, and the Pastorals) to the "Pauline school" in the late first century. Disciples and admirers of Paul kept alive his teachings and adapted them to new circumstances. In their letters issued under Paul's name they included traditions and said what they imagined Paul would have said. While it is customary to locate the Pauline school at Ephesus, we need not suppose a formal institution or even a single branch. The so-called Deuteropaulines take for granted the teachings of Paul and show how his insights about Christ and discipleship were reformulated after his death.

The Second Letter to the Thessalonians seeks to provide a balance for early Christians regarding the "already" and the "not yet." It firmly warns against supposing that "the day of the Lord is at hand" (2:2), thus replying to the claims of apocalyptists (who thought that the day was imminent) and/or gnostics (who thought that it was already here). The second coming of Christ remains certain (1:5-10), but in the meantime many events must unfold (2:1-15). Now the challenge facing the Christian is to avoid idleness (3:6-15), either out of fear at the day's imminence or out of complacency because the fullness of God's kingdom is already here. Now is the time for "every good deed and word" (2:17).

In Colossians (and Ephesians) the balance between present and future tips toward the present. While the idea of the second coming of Christ occurs in Col 3:4, the focus is on the Christian's already having been raised with Christ in baptism: "you were buried with him in baptism, in which you were also raised with him" (2:12); "if then you were raised with Christ, seek what is above, where Christ is seated at the right hand of God" (3:1). The whole of Colossians is an expansion and applica-tion of the Christological hymn quoted in 1:15-20. There Christ is celebrated as Wisdom (1:15-17); the firstborn from the dead (1:18); the head of "the body," which is identified as the Church (1:18); and the agent of cosmic reconciliation (1:19-20). The Church is not simply the local community (the Church at Rome or Corinth) but a universal entity, the body of which Christ is the head (1:18, 24; 2:19; 3:15). The spiritual challenge of Colossians is for Christians to live out their share in Christ's death and resurrection now ("think of what is above"—3:2) and to put to death whatever actions and impulses are contrary (3:5-10). The basis and goal of Christian spirituality is that Christ be "all and in all" (3:11).

Though Ephesians is rightly called a compendium of Paul's theology, it also develops ideas first raised in Colossians. There are no explicit references to Christ's second coming or to the imminent end of the world. The emphasis is on Christians sharing in Christ's resurrection in the present. They have been made alive together with Christ and raised up with him (2:6-7). The opening benediction (1:3-14) praises God for what has happened in the Christ-event ("in him we have redemption by his blood, the forgiveness of transgressions"— 1:7) and alludes to baptism as the sealing with the promised Holy Spirit (1:13). The Church is universal and even cosmic (1:21-23; 3:10); it is the body, and Christ is its head (1:22; 5:23). The "mystery of Christ" (3:4) is that through him the division between Jews and Gentiles has been broken down, and now all "have access in one Spirit to the Father" (2:18). The spiritual challenge facing the Christian is to "put away the old self . . . and put on the new self, created in God's way in righteousness and holiness of truth" (4:22, 24). Using the apocalyptic language typical of the Dead Sea scrolls, the writer urges Christians who are now "light in the Lord" to "live as children of light, for light produces every kind of goodness and righteousness and truth" (5:8, 9).

The dilemma of late first-century Christian spirituality in the Pauline tradition appears in the so-called household codes in Col 3:18–4:1 and Eph 5:21–6:9 (see also 1 Pet 2:18–3:7). There the relationships that held society together in the Greco-Roman world (wives-husbands, children-parents, slaves-masters) are taken for granted (with no attention to Gal 3:28). Christians within these relationships are urged to carry out their responsibilities faithfully "in the Lord" and "as to the Lord." To what extent do Christians merely take over the customs and standards of their milieu in order to give good example and be good citizens? That question is answered in one direction by the Pastoral Epistles.

The two letters to Timothy and that to Titus are called the Pastorals because "Paul" gives advice to the pastors Timothy and Titus. While eschatology remains a theme (1 Tm 1:1; 4:1; 6:15; etc.), it is hardly the center of the theology of the Pastorals. Their Christology is expressed mainly in creedal statements and fragments of hymns (1 Tm 1:15; 2:5-6; 3:16; 6:13; 2 Tm 2:8; 2:11-13; Tit 3:4-7) and constitutes the deposit of faith. The Church is "the pillar and foundation of truth" (1 Tm 3:15), and there is great attention to the local Church offices of bishop and deacon (1 Tm 3:1-13; 5:17-22; Tit 1:5-9). Baptism is "the bath of rebirth and renewal by the holy Spirit" (Tit 3:5).

The ideal of Christian spirituality in the Pastorals is faith and a good conscience (1 Tm 1:5, 19; 3:9). Christians are urged to pray for kings and all in high positions so that they can lead a "quiet and tranquil life in all devotion and dignity" (1 Tm 2:2). External respectability is important (1 Tm 3:7, 13; 5:14; 6:1). Women are to perform good deeds, be silent, and bear children (1 Tm 2:9-15). Though Christ came to raise the moral level of human life (Tit 2:11-14), the moral virtues recommended in Tit 2:1-10 are those promoted by moral philosophers of the period. Christians are exhorted to be submissive to rulers and to show courtesy to all people (Tit 3:1-2). An important motive for practical moral action is the respect that such conduct will win from outsiders (Tit 2:5, 8, 10).

Other Perspectives

Every NT writing contains perspectives that are important for Christian spirituality. One could concentrate profitably on the concern for social justice in James, the approach to resolving conflict in the Johannine Epistles, the emphasis on orthodoxy and the apostolic faith in Jude and 2 Peter, and the lively apocalypticism and resistance to the Roman empire in Revelation. But 1 Peter and Hebrews are particularly rich resources for early Christian spirituality, for they give us a sense of what it felt like to be a Gentile Christian and a Jewish Christian, respectively, in the Greco-Roman world of the late first century.

Written in Peter's name in the late first century, 1 Peter shows how largely Gentile-Christian communities in Asia Minor came to understand themselves as "a chosen race, a royal priesthood, a holy nation, a people of [God's] own" (2:9). What led them from darkness to light and made those who were "no people" into "God's people" (2:9-10) was their sharing in Christ's resurrection through baptism: "Blessed be the God and Father of our Lord Jesus Christ, who in his great mercy gave us a new birth to a living hope through the resurrection of Jesus Christ from the dead" (1:3). The addressees seem to be subject to various trials (1:6) and even persecution (4:12), in which they are urged to follow the example of Christ, the righteous sufferer (2:21; 3:18; 4:13-16). They are to give no occasion to their enemies, and so they subject themselves to the political authorities and their domestic masters as in the household codes (2:13–3:7). Their primary missionary strategy is good example. The identity of the Christians addressed in 1 Peter is expressed especially by the phrase "aliens and sojourners" (2:11; see also 1:1, 17). It is possible that this address refers to the social status of many in the communities as resident aliens in their cities, or it may simply be a metaphor, as in Hebrews. At any rate, these "aliens and sojourners" seek a lasting home with God and find a provisional home on earth in the Church. They owe their identity as God's people to the resurrection of Jesus Christ from the dead, on which they also base their hope of "an inheritance that is imperishable, undefiled, and unfading, kept in heaven" (1:4).

The Letter to the Hebrews is a "message of encouragement" (13:22) addressed to Jewish Christians or Gentile Christians who knew a great deal about Judaism. It puts forward Christ as the real key to understanding the OT, as the "leader" of our salvation (2:10), and as superior to Moses as a son is superior to a servant in a household (3:1-6). The dominant Christological image, however, is Jesus the merciful high priest (4:14–5:10) who presides at the heavenly liturgy (8:1-2) as the minister of a new and better covenant. Christ is both priest and perfect sacrifice, and thus does away with the need for all pagan and even Jewish priesthoods and sacrifices.

Those Christians who remain on earth are on a journey or pilgrimage toward fullness of life with God (3:7–4:11). Their goal is "a sabbath rest . . . for the people of God" (4:9). Since according to Ps 95:7-11 the wilderness generation rebelled against and tested God, the old people of God failed to reach its goal of rest in the land of Canaan. The Christians addressed in Hebrews must not fall away from the living God but remain faithful to the end (3:12-19). Faith is the means by which they will enter into rest with God (4:1-2), and their rest is a share in God's own sabbath rest in heaven (4:3-5). Christians must learn the lesson of the disobedience of the Exodus generation and grasp the offer of the true sabbath rest "today" (4:7). The great examples of faith

in the past (Heb 11) recognized that they were "strangers and aliens on earth" (11:13). The real goal of their wandering was the heavenly place where Christ acts as high priest: "they are seeking a homeland . . . they desire a better homeland, a heavenly one" (11:14-16). The spirituality of Hebrews is summarized in 13:14: "For here we have no lasting city, but we seek the one that is to come."

See also CHRIST; DISCIPLESHIP; HOLY SPIRIT; JEWISH SPIRITUALITY; KENOSIS; KINGDOM OF GOD; LORD'S PRAYER; RESURRECTION; SCRIPTURE.

Bibliography: Fundamental for early Christian spirituality are the NT volumes in The Message of Biblical Spirituality series published by Michael Glazier: M. Perlewitz, *The Gospel of Matthew* (1988); K. Barta, *The Gospel of Mark* (1988); P. Van Linden, *The Gospel of Luke and Acts* (1986); J. Wijngaards, *The Gospel of John and His Letters* (1986); T. Tobin, *The Spirituality of Paul* (1987); C. Stockhausen, *Letters in the Pauline Tradition: Ephesians, Colossians, I Timothy, II Timothy, and Titus* (1989); R. McDonnell, *The Catholic Epistles and Hebrews* (1986); S. Kealy, *The Apocalypse of John* (1987).

Other helpful books include R. Brown, *The Churches the Apostles Left Behind* (New York: Paulist, 1984); R. Bultmann, *Theology of the New Testament* (New York: Scribner's, 1955); B. Chilton, ed., *The Kingdom of God in the Teaching of Jesus* (Philadelphia: Fortress, 1984); J. Dunn, *Jesus and the Spirit* (Philadelphia: Westminster, 1975) and *Christology in the Making* (Philadelphia: Westminster, 1980); J. Fitzmyer, *Paul and His Theology* (Englewood Cliffs, N.J.: Prentice-Hall, 1989); L. Goppelt, *Theology of the New Testament* (Grand Rapids, Mich.: Eerdmans, 1981, 1983); W. Meeks, *The First Urban Christians* (New Haven, Conn.: Yale Univ. Press, 1983); P. Perkins, *Resurrection* (Garden City, N.Y.: Doubleday, 1984); E. Sanders, *Jesus and Judaism* (Philadelphia: Fortress, 1985).

DANIEL J. HARRINGTON, S.J.

EASTERN (ASIAN) SPIRITUALITY

Asian spirituality arises within the classical cultures of India and China. Both of these centers of ancient civilization produced religious traditions reflecting a series of unique spiritual experiences. The complexity of cultures and experiences resulted in a plethora of traditions that have had an impact on world spirituality.

Hinduism

Hinduism encompasses the diversity of a spiritual quest over a four-thousand-year period for the peoples of the subcontinent of India. It developed a high religion, a vast culture and social structure, and a variety of spiritual paths. Sanskrit, an Indo-European language and the scriptural language of India, has a cluster of words indicating the spiritual and practical aspect of the Indian quest. All point more to an orthopraxis than to an orthodoxy, namely, a path (*marga*), an integrative method (*yoga*), a spiritual vision (*darsana*) based upon experience, and the actual undertaking of a religious discipline (*sadhana*).

The first sacred literature (Vedas), composed in Sanskrit and considered revealed, contains the earliest religious hymns, prayers, creation myths, ritual texts, meditational reflections, and the first attempt at philosophical speculation (Upanishads). With the composition of this body of literature between 1500–400 B.C.E., the spiritual traditions of classical Hinduism began to emerge. Two controlling concepts, sacrifice (*yajna*) and renunciation (*vairagya*), penetrate this literature. Early Vedic sacrifice was highly ritualistic, with detail as to the building and feeding of the sacred fire, oblations, chants, and hymns. Sacrificial ritual was the unifying factor in early Indian spirituality, since ritual was seen as the creator, preserver, and restorer of cosmic order and life.

The Upanishads, the final composition of the Vedas, advanced another notion of sacrifice as it was interiorized and transformed by meditation and self-renunciation. Here the spiritual quest led to the identification of absolute reality (Brahman) with the most subjective aspect of the self (*atman*) and was summarized in the four great axioms of the Upanishads: "That Thou Art," "I am Brahman," "The Self is Brahman," and "All is Brahman." Medieval Vedanta philosophers gave a wide interpretation to this experience: Sankara (9th cent. C.E.) argued for total identity, nonduality (*advaita*), between the self (*atman*) and absolute reality (Brahman); Ramanuja (11th cent. C.E.) spoke of a qualified nondualism in which the self is one with Brahman but logically distinguishable; Madhva (13th cent. C.E.) took a position of dualism in which the self, Brahman, and the world are really distinct. Different forms of meditation, reflective analysis, and other spiritual practices brought about the variety of spiritual experiences giving rise to the range of philosophical articulation.

Another body of religious literature advanced further the notion of sacrifice and self-renunciation captured in the *Bhagavad Gita,* a small part of the massive Indian epic the *Mahabharata.* Sacrifice became devotional love of the deity, spiritually interiorized but exteriorized in name and form. Likewise, the selfless action taught in the *Gita* became another form of self-renunciation.

In light of the above, the spiritual disciplines of Hinduism can be understood as inclusive and comprehensive: sacrifice as ritual or selfless action-*karmayoga*; sacrifice as self-knowledge and wisdom-*jnanayoga*; sacrifice as devotional love of the deity-*bhaktiyoga*; sacrifice as meditation-*rajayoga*. India's long history of saints and teachers exemplified and directed the spiritual quester with one or a combination of these yogas. The spiritual teacher (*guru*) became indispensable, since it was presumed that such a person (male or female) not only possessed the wisdom to teach but also experienced the sacred in order to lead others to spiritual liberation (*moksa*). The emergence of saints and gurus continued into this century, but only in modern times have they left India to teach throughout the world.

Buddhism

Buddhism, which is a spiritual movement founded in India by Siddhartha

Gotama (563–483 B.C.E.), became the first pancultural tradition of the Eurasian world by establishing spiritual lineages from India to Southeast Asia, China, Korea, Japan, Tibet, and Mongolia. In each instance acculturation and transformations in spiritual development took place.

The life and teaching of a historical figure 2500 years ago who is regarded as a *buddha,* an "awakened one" or an "enlightened one," has structured the liberation process of all followers since his own discovery of the Middle Way between severe asceticism and opulence. He discovered a way of release from the cycle of suffering and rebirth. He entrusted his teaching (*dharma*) to a community of disciples, monastic men and women and lay followers (*sangha*), before leaving the world of phenomena and release (*nirvana*) from the rounds of death and rebirth. Followers take refuge in the Buddha, his teaching, and the community which passes on the life and spirit of those teachings. These are the three jewels or triple treasure advancing Buddhism throughout history.

The spiritual lineages of Buddhism, somewhat discrete in themselves, have in common the threefold practice of morality (*sila*), meditation (*samadhi*), and wisdom (*prajna*). These practices, with modifications from lineage to lineage, form the basis for all spiritual development. Morality includes self-cultivation and a profound compassion for all living beings. Although initially undergone according to negative precepts (not to harm sentient beings, not to take what has not been given, not to lie, not to engage in sexual misconduct, not to consume alcoholic drink), they became positive precepts requiring a restructuring of human life and psyche in order to enter fully into compassionate living. Meditation is the most general term for the domestication of the human mind and psychology. The forms of practice vary from lineage to lineage. At the very least, meditation integrates the calming of the mind with the focusing of the calmed mind

in order to see reality more clearly. Wisdom is study, analysis, and dialectic, and the knowledge that results. No other spiritual tradition has utilized wisdom so integral to the liberation process.

A. *Theravada Buddhism*

No single body of literature is accepted as canonical by all Buddhists. Theravada Buddhism, found in Sri Lanka, Burma, Kampuchea, Laos, and Thailand, possessed the oldest collection of literature written in Pali and containing the Buddha's own discourses, traditional commentary, and monastic rules. The interdependence between the monastic and lay community for spiritual existence and development was especially strong in this lineage. The eight-fold path, offered as the means to overcome suffering inherent in the human condition, structures the enlightenment process: right understanding, right intention, right speech, right action, right livelihood, right effort, right mindfulness, and right concentration. Spiritual growth is firmly based on a moral and compassionate life. Lay people are told to cultivate four conditions: faith, moral virtue, generosity, and wisdom. These conditions form the base for the next stage of development: mental concentration. Although mindfulness is recommended to all Theravadins, the monastic community may alone have the environment and time in which it can lead to insight and the full concentration of the mind necessary for advanced contemplation and ultimately enlightenment. Yet, this meditation tradition (*vispassana*) has been taught to, and pursued by, lay members with success.

B. *Mahayana Buddhism*

India also gave rise to Mahayana Buddhism, with canonical texts written in Sanskrit and early Indian Buddhist thinkers writing in the same language. As this lineage spread throughout East and Central Asia, developing multiple lineages, new literature appeared in the Chinese, Japanese, and Tibetan languages, along with translations of Indian texts. Mahayana Buddhism may be divided into two sociocultural groups: East Asia and Central Asia.

1. *East Asian Buddhism*

Mahayana Buddhism is found in China, Korea, Japan, and regions culturally related to these countries. These cultures brought their own insights to Indian Buddhism whereby a transformation took place in Buddhism itself and the variety of spiritualities within it. The Buddha was raised to ontological reality and sacred status; buddhahood for all became the spiritual ideal; the *bodhisattva* embodied the spiritual figure who vicariously suffers for the liberation of all sentient beings; liberation was now bestowed through grace as a response in faith and devotion to the world of *bodhisattvas* and the Amida Buddha, a savior figure. Elaborate traditions of ritual, festival, prayer, and meditation result. In China the development is contextualized by Taoism and Confucianism, while in Japan by indigenous Shinto and Confucianism. Mahayana Buddhism may be generalized under two forms of spiritual practice: devotionalism and meditation.

The devotional tradition is especially sensitive to the human need for help in the liberation process. The infinite compassion of the Buddha, other buddhas and *bodhisattvas,* is raised to full expression in the most influential text of the lineage, the *Lotus Sutra.* Here the fullness of grace may be conferred in response to simple devotion: an offering of a flower, incense, a song of praise, a bow of the head, or the joining of the hands in reverence. Buddhism became accessible to the masses of people as the invocation "Praise to Amida Buddha," often repeated or said simply once in perfect faith, merited liberation in the Pure Land, the bliss-world of buddhas and *bodhisattvas.*

The meditation tradition had a parallel process of development. Indian meditation (*dhyana*) was transformed by the Chinese Ch'an lineage, influenced by Taoism and China's intimate association with nature, and was further modified by Korean (*Son*) and Japanese (*Zen*) meditation schools. All spiritual practices, such as prayer, ritual, and even methods of meditation, are looked upon as convenient tools to achieve the experience of enlightenment. Such an awakening may take place in the historical life of the practitioner. Regardless of the form meditation may take, the technique is to clear the mind of analytical, logical, and studied efforts to achieve wisdom. From this lineage large communities of monks and nuns gave themselves completely to meditation, each community headed by a master and transmitter of the tradition. One of the primary roles of the master was to authenticate spiritual experience. A succession of meditation masters formed two major schools: Soto and Rinzai. The Soto school is characterized through quiet meditation, sitting and wall-gazing, and fulfilling the ordinary duties of simple monastic life. The Rinzai school makes active use of the *koan* used as a word or phrase of nonsensical language that can be solved not by the intellect but through a new way of seeing reality.

The meditational lineages of China and Japan also nurtured the aesthetic life, whereby an aesthetic spirituality became integral to these cultures. Chinese art forms such as flower arrangement, the tea ceremony, and calligraphy were taken to Japan and further developed along with other forms into spiritual practices, achieving tranquility of mind and body, a Zen achievement.

2. *Central Asian Buddhism*

Mahayana Buddhism of Central Asia is found in Tibet, Nepal, Sikkim, Bhutan, and Mongolia. The wisdom of the Buddhist universities of India (1st to 10th cent. c.e.) and the later forms of Indian Mahayana and Tantric Buddhism were absorbed into Central Asia, especially Tibet, giving to this form of Buddhism an intellectual and scholarly framework. Through the translation of Sanskrit texts into the Tibetan language, Buddhist monastic discipline, wisdom literature, and tantric practices developed within the context of folk religion and shamanism of inner Asia. Buddhist ritual, meditation, and devotion were especially affected by tantric theories. Tantra, either in Buddhism or Hinduism, is a system of practices and meditative discipline releasing the power aspect of reality and polarity within reality. Emphasis is given to elaborate descriptions of divinities set in mystic circles (*mandalas*), use of symbolic gesture (*mudra*), and repetitive sound (*mantra*). Visualized meditation reached a higher form in Tibetan Buddhism than in any other lineage. The symbolic use in meditation of imagined divine forms represents the human personality and the universe on the one hand, and the bondage of phenomenal existence and the perfection of buddhahood on the other hand. In temple ritual the worshiper is faced with a set of divinities, already known in visualized meditation, to whom gifts are offered and from whom blessings are received. Meditation and ritual become one as both integrate the human personality.

Also called the Vajrayana (Diamond Path) lineage, monastic communities of men and women formed in Tibet. Ritual and meditation were contextualized by an intellectual tradition for the entire monastic community. Philosophical analysis and logical debate were essential to the spiritual path. A monastic community spent an equal amount of time and effort in debate and analysis as in meditation and ritual. Multiple lineages exist within Tibetan Buddhism, each with its own emphasis. The Gelug group, to which the Dalai Lama belongs, follows a strict monastic discipline, stresses philosophical study and debate, and gives less emphasis to tantric elements. Entrance into all the lineages is through initiation and strict adherence to a teacher, usually the head of a monastery.

The lay followers exhibit personal devotion through prayer, prostration and *mantra*, pilgrimages to shrines, and support of the monastic community.

Confucianism

The Confucian tradition grew out of the five classics of ancient China: *Book of History, Poetry, Changes, Rites*, and *Spring and Autumn Annals*. It captures the Chinese experience of an all-inclusive harmony of the cosmic and human orders of reality. The relationship between these two orders is cultivated and perfected through ritual/custom which harmonizes both. The early experience captured the rhythms of the universe and developed such in social life through a profound sympathy for and in the created world. Emphasis was given to religious rituals and belief in Providence/Heaven (*t'ien*), a cosmic power or destiny over humanity and all things. The Confucian tradition articulated such experience and vision through a spiritual humanism rooted in social and political life.

Confucius (551–479 B.C.E.) is the Latinized form of the master-sage K'ung Fu-tzu, who is the recognized founder of this tradition. His teachings were collected by his disciples in the *Analects of Confucius*. It can be argued whether he was an ethical rather than a religious teacher, but it cannot be contested that he set the base for a spirituality pervading social life in China and Japan for over two millennia. He spoke of the way (*tao*) of heaven, a path in which the cultivation of human relations holds primary place, namely, the five foundational relationships between parent and child, ruler and minister, husband and wife, older and younger siblings, and friend and friend. The human ideal, the noble person (*chun tzu*), is characterized by human-heartedness (*jen*), filial piety, loyalty, reciprocity, and the harmonious balance of polarities. Such inward goodness is both cultivated and expressed through propriety, decorum, and the observance of ritual (*li*).

Mencius (371–289 B.C.E.) is second only to Confucius as a master-teacher of this tradition. The Confucian canon consists of four books: *Analects of Confucius, Book of Mencius, The Great Learning, Doctrine of the Mean* (the latter two are chapters from the ancient classics). Acknowledged as a social and political thinker, Mencius' central insight is the inherent goodness of human nature, a goodness with potential for actualizing the four major virtues: love, righteousness, propriety, and wisdom. Since every human has this potential, the path of human cultivation is open to all in order to achieve the nobility of the sage. Chu Hsi (1130–1200 C.E.) brought the tradition to its highest expression in a metaphysical synthesis of Neo-Confucian thought and practice. He formulated a spirituality integrating religious reverence, scholarly analysis, ethical practice, and social and political participation. He and Neo-Confucians after him saw the world of change not as bondage to the phenomenal world, as did many Buddhists, but as source of transformation of the cosmos and of all humanity and social institutions. Spiritual discipline cultivated the moral personality in consonance with the greater cosmic change. Moral growth had a cosmic component. Human-heartedness (*jen*) was a source of growth and creativity in both the human person and the universe. The cultivation of this virtue brought about in the individual, in society, and in the greater cosmos "the transformation of things."

A vigorous spiritual discipline was necessary to achieve the harmonization of the human and cosmic orders. The polarization on all levels of reality had to be held in balance: for example, ritual and reverence on the one hand and ethical development and integrity on the other; silent meditation of "quiet sitting" had to be balanced with intellectual investigation and the control of the appetite. An entire ritual system, public and exterior, was harmonized with an interior ritualization that touched the depths of human and cosmic reality. Although spiritual discipline became primary in Neo-Confucian times, emphasis was still placed on reciprocity in human relationships.

Neo-Confucianism spread to Korea, Japan, and Vietnam, where it entered into the formation of those cultures. It must be insisted, however, that in China and elsewhere it never existed as a spiritual path independent of other religious traditions. In China the spiritual seeker could draw upon the insights and practices of folk religion, Taoism, Buddhism, and Confucianism in one and the same spiritual journey; likewise, in Japan, Shinto, Buddhism, and Neo-Confucianism may form the context of an individual's spiritual worldview and life.

Taoism

As a religious movement indigenous to China, Taoism brought together ancient shamanistic and folk cults, alchemy, hygiene and dietary rules, archaic forms of Chinese yoga, and esoteric and petitionary practices to deities in order to realize happiness and the prolongation of life. At an early stage it drew upon the mystical aspects of the Taoist philosophers Lao Tzu and Chuang Tzu.

Taoism, frequently spoken of as nature mysticism by Western scholars but in fact more inclusive, results from the early Chinese experience of the creative and dynamic force immanent in nature, the human order, and throughout the universe, giving meaning, life, and order to all reality. The Confucianists contemplated human nature in order to discover the Tao, while the Taoists contemplated the Tao itself as it brought about change to every order of reality in the universe. For Confucius, the Tao is a way, a spiritual path, while for the Taoist the Tao acquires metaphysical meaning as a governing principle wherein all things are produced and whereto all things return. The genius of Taoist experience was to understand that the simple and spontaneous activity of the

Tao is replicated in the cosmos, nature, and humanity.

Lao Tzu (6th cent. B.C.E.), probably the compiler of the Taoist classic the *Tao Te Ching,* offered the first articulation of this mystical tradition. He wrote that the Tao that can be spoken of is not the eternal Tao; the name that can be named is not the eternal name; the nameless is the beginning, while the named is the mother of all things. The Tao accomplishes without effort as water flows, as the sun shines, as dew gathers. As nature follows this effortless pattern, so human activity should follow the same pattern. Lao Tzu speaks of action-less-activity (*wu-wei*), action without reaction, which returns one to original nature, pure and spontaneous. To return to one's inner nature is to return to the Tao. Chuang Tzu (369–286 B.C.E.), a more creative thinker, advanced the notions of the flux and transformation of reality and the individual seeking inner tranquility along with outer spontaneity. The human ideal is to experience one's own nature in the universal process.

Taoism did not develop a discrete spiritual tradition. Instead, it influenced the development of Neo-Confucianism, provided the terminology for the translation of Buddhist texts into Chinese, inspired the high attainments in Chinese art and literature, and impacted radically upon Ch'an Buddhism in China and Zen in Japan. Any thorough understanding of Chinese or Japanese meditation begins with Taoism. The spontaneous and pulsating power of nature and human life, fundamental to Zen experience, can be viewed as Taoist insight.

Shinto

Shinto as the indigenous tradition of Japan from 5th century C.E. includes folk traditions, shamanism, creation mythology, ancestor worship, ritual purification, and sustaining the Japanese people as a nation. It was reinforced by Confucian social morality and Buddhist religiosity. It has neither creed nor scriptural canon. It does have a priesthood supporting shrine rituals and festivals. The most comprehensive word for the sacred, the powerful, the world of deities in the Japanese language is *kami.* Although it primarily refers to supernatural powers and deities of nature, it also includes superior human beings such as nobility and important national figures. They reward and punish as they dispense good or evil fortune. National, shrine, and home ritual is directed to them.

Shinto's significance as a spirituality is that through national and patriotic rites, loyalty to a people, a nation, and a land is established. It offers to the Japanese a basis for self-identity. Such self-identity is achieved through communion with a land, a nation, nature, and the world of the *kami.*

Asian Spirituality and Christianity

Protestant missionary activity had a significant impact on early 19th-century Hindu renaissance movements with the retrieval of an Indian social consciousness. Even the traditional and saintly figures articulated this; Swami Vivekananda accented a commitment to the betterment of Indian society. Mahatma Gandhi best exemplified the influence of Western movements in his development of nonviolence. On the other hand, Western intellectuals and spiritual seekers took an interest in the spiritual achievements of India. Early 20th-century Catholic thinkers in India tried to bring into synthesis the Vedanta tradition and Thomistic categories.

Yet the monastic encounter between Catholicism and Hindu spirituality may be the most lasting. Henri le Saux, O.S.B. (d. 1973), taking the name Swami Abhishiktananda, along with fellow Benedictine Father Monchanin, established in 1950 a Christian-Hindu monastic center in South India, Shantivanan, in order to bring into dialogue and lived-experiences two world spiritualities. He inspired a whole generation of Christian spiritual seekers to the same task as he entered more deeply into Indian asceticism by adopting Hindu forms of renunciation, prayer, and meditation. He emulated the Hindu *sannyasi* or renunciant in belief that the total self-effacement of the Hindu nondual experience (Advaita Vedanta) was compatible with Christian mystical experience. His *Church of India* (1969) discusses such interfaith experience.

Following upon Abhishiktananda, the English Benedictine Bede Griffiths arrived at a Syrian Rite monastery in Kerala, India, in 1955. In 1968 he established the Saccidananda Ashram, where again Hindu customs and traditional forms of Indian spirituality were incorporated into a Christian salvation process. He articulated his vision in *Christian Ashram: Essays towards a Hindu and Christian Dialogue* (1966). Paralleling these efforts, native Indian Protestant and Catholic ascetics have moved closer to understanding and living out indigenous forms of Hindu spirituality.

Something comparable took place in Japan in this century. Japanese Buddhist philosophers (known as the Kyoto school, in which Nishida may be the most formidable thinker), have articulated Buddhist reality for both a Japanese and a Western audience. At the same time, Western Christians in Japan entered into a profound intellectual and experiential encounter with Japanese Buddhism. The work of Heinrich Dumoulin, S.J., who produced a definitive history of Zen Buddhism, exemplifies the intellectual encounter. His fellow German Jesuit Hugo Lassalle (1898–1990), better known as Enomiya-Lassalle, began Zen training in 1943 and became an authenticated Zen master in Japan. Lassalle believed that Zen practiced properly under a master could be useful in spiritual development, regardless of religious affiliation. His *Zen-Way to Enlightenment* (1966) is a practical guide opening this tradition to Christians.

Asian Spirituality in the United States

The spiritual traditions of Asia first had an influence on American intellectuals through literature introduced by Orientalists. Emerson, Thoreau, Whitman, and the American transcendalists reflect such influence, and along with the Theosophical Society and the work of Helena P. Blavatsky (1833–1893), major Asian insights were introduced for the first time. It was the World Parliament of Religions in Chicago in 1893 where the first Asian spiritual teachers, namely, the Hindu Swami Vivekananda and the Zen master Soyen Shaku, implanted a living tradition. Vivekananda established Vedanta centers in major American cities headed by outstanding Hindu ascetics of the Ramakrishna-Vivekananda Mission. By the early 1920s Swami Paramahansa Yogananda established the Self-Realization Fellowship in Los Angeles with American lay and vowed renunciants. His *Autobiography of a Yogi* remains a classic of esoteric yoga. By the 1930s the First Zen Institute of New York was established. The extraordinary Zen thinker D.T. Suzuki may have made the greatest impact upon American intellectuals and spiritual seekers over a thirty-year period.

Two Americans, Alan Watts and Thomas Merton, continued the development of these spiritualities as part of American intellectual and spiritual life. Watts (1915–1973), with his eclectic and popular studies of Asian spirituality (although *The Way of Zen* [1957] is scholarly), inspired the beat generation of the 1950s with lasting influence on youth culture. His personal quest for individual identity required a radical transformation from a fragmented ego-consciousness to a state of thorough self-awareness.

Merton (1915–1968), the Trappist contemplative and writer, read deeply and widely in Asian religion. He had long correspondence with D.T. Suzuki and consulted frequently Dom Aelred Graham's

Zen Catholicism (1963). His own immersion in Asia is reflected in *Mystics and Zen Masters* (1966), *Zen and the Birds of Appetite* (1968), *The Asian Journal of Thomas Merton* (1973), and *Thomas Merton on Zen* (1976). Much as in Hindu and Zen thought, the discovery of the true self for Merton is the task of spirituality. His influence on American Protestant and Catholic spirituality is lasting, while the spiritual dialogue now going on among Eastern and Western contemplatives is in debt to him.

The theory and practice of nonviolence as envisioned and lived by Mahatma Gandhi is firmly part of the American spiritual movement. First placed in public life by Martin Luther King, who transformed race relations with nonviolence, it was then taken up by the peace movement and more recently by environmentalists.

Parallel to the human potential movement of the 1960s, a wave of Hindu gurus entered the United States with influence on the youth culture. At the same time as the Asian population expanded in the United States, traditional religious leaders established cultural centers, temples, and retreats to aid the new Americans from Southeast Asia, India, and Japan. Some individuals and movements are visibly present and are now a part of the American spiritual scene. Maharishi Mahesh Yogi, although a disciple of a traditional Sankaracarya, taught since the early 1960s a popular meditational technique called Transcendental Meditation (TM), which establishes mental and emotional calm when practiced regularly. Swami Sivananda (1887–1963) sent two of his disciples to the United States: Swami Vishnu Devananda emphasized *hatha* yoga, the physical yoga of postures, breathing, diet, and meditation in established centers of the Sivananda Society; Swami Satchitananda, with greater emphasis on meditation, founded Integral Yoga centers throughout this country. The most visible Hindu guru was Swami Prabhupada Bhak-

tivedanta (d. 1977), who introduced the International Society for Krishna Consciousness (ISKCON) and drew American devotees wearing orange or white robes chanting and dancing ecstatically the "Hare Krishna, Hare Rama, Rama, Rama, Hare, Hare," *mantra.* In recent years the Siddha Yoga Institution, following the teaching of the late Swami Muktananda and now headed by his female disciple Gurumayi Chidvilasananda, has taught meditation that depends upon initiation into yogic and tantric traditions of Hindu Saivism.

Organized Buddhist centers for both Orientals and Occidentals now include American teachers of these spiritualities. American Zen masters such as Richard Baker, Phillip Kapleau, and Robert Aitken have been joined by more recent authenticated *roshis.* A traditional Japanese Buddhist sect, established by Nichiren (1222–1282) and known as the Nichiren Shoshu of America, acknowledges both practical and spiritual benefits through chanting and an active lifestyle. Tibetan Buddhism has been present in the United States through Mongolian immigrants of Eastern Europe now in their second generation. Two Tibetan teachers opened this tradition to American practitioners: Tarthang Tulku in Berkeley, California, and Chogyam Trungpa (d. 1990) in Vermont and Boulder, Colorado. Tibetan canonical literature is being reproduced in the United States and gradually translated into English.

The Second Vatican Council's Declaration on the Relation of the Church to Non-Christian Religions and the consequent establishing of the Secretariat for Non-Christians did much to broaden the dialogue between Asian and Christian spirituality. The dialogue is growing among academics in the United States with such new ventures as the Society for Buddhist-Christian Studies and new journals such as *Buddhist-Christian Studies* and *Bulletin of Hindu-Christian Studies.* The intermonastic dialogue, a work of Aid Inter Monasteres and a subgroup, The North

American Board for East-West Dialogue, has encouraged spiritual exchange between Asian and Christian contemplatives. Catholic European monastics have visited Zen monasteries in Japan, with reciprocal visits by Japanese Buddhist monks; in the United States a similar exchange has been established between Tibetan monastics now living in India and American Catholic monks and nuns. A Vatican document in 1989 from the Congregation for the Doctrine of the Faith, "Some Aspects of Christian Meditation," addressed in broad and cautionary tones the accommodation of Asian meditational methods. Yet Asian apophatic meditation has already renewed to some degree Christian contemplative life.

See also ASCETICISM; INTERRELIGIOUS DIALOGUE; MEDITATION; MYSTICISM; NEGATIVE WAY; WORLD.

Bibliography: R. Ellwood, ed., Eastern Spirituality in America: Selected Writings (New York: Paulist, 1987). W. Johnston, The Still Point (New York: Fordham Univ. Press, 1970). A. Pieris, Love Meets Wisdom: A Christian Experience of Buddhism (Maryknoll, N.Y.: Orbis, 1988). K. Sivaraman, ed., Hindu Spirituality: Vedas Through Vedanta (New York: Crossroad, 1989). J. Stuart, comp., Swami Abhishiktananda: His Life Told Through His Letters (Delhi: I.S.P.C.K., 1989). R Zaehner, Concordant Discord: The Interdependence of Faiths (London: Oxford Univ. Press, 1970).

WILLIAM CENKNER, O.P.

EASTERN CATHOLIC CHURCHES, SPIRITUALITY OF

The Eastern Catholic Churches are the sister Churches of the East. They belong to that confederation which constitutes the one, holy, catholic, and apostolic Church of the Most Holy Trinity, the Mystical Body of Christ united in the Holy Spirit by the same faith, sacraments, and government. These Churches have their own ecclesiastical traditions, liturgical rites, and differing cultures, as well as a rich spirituality and mysticism, all stemming from the apostles and the Eastern Fathers of the Church. The distinctive marks of the East-

ern Catholic Churches are their ancient heritages combined with their union with the Church of Rome and the successor of St. Peter, the Bishop of Rome.

The Churches are divided according to different rites. To the Alexandrian Rite in the East belong the Coptic and Ethiopian Catholic Churches; to the Antiochene Rite: the Malankar, Maronite, and Syrian Churches; to the Byzantine Rite: the Albanian, Bulgarian, Byelorussian, Georgian, Greek, Hungarian, Italo-Albanian, Melchite, Romanian, Russian, Slovak, and Ukrainian Churches; to the Chaldean Rite: the Chaldean and Syro-Malabar Churches; to the Armenian Rite: the Armenian Church.

Vatican II presented Eastern Catholics with the following mandate: to promote "religious fidelity to ancient Eastern traditions" and further "to acquire an ever greater knowledge and a more exact use of [their rites]. If they have improperly fallen away from them because of circumstances of time or personage, let them take pains to return to their ancestral ways" (OE 24 and 6). This is illustrative of an awareness of the distinctiveness of the Eastern Catholic Churches that has often been eclipsed by what has been called the Latinization of the Eastern Catholic Churches in theological, liturgical, canonical, cultural, spiritual, and other respects, from the 10th century onward.

Latinization may be understood as a process of pseudomorphosis (Greek pseudēs, "false," and morphē "form"), which involves an encounter between two disparate cultures. What results from the encounter is a kind of culture that is artificial, lacking organic fusion or growth. The characteristics of one culture become dominant. Many Eastern Catholic Churches came to adopt a pro-Latin, pro-Western orientation in theology, spirituality, liturgical practices, and church art. Thus in many Eastern Catholic Churches there appeared the Italian Way of the Cross; and the Akaphistos and other devotions in honor of the Holy Cross started to recede despite their liturgical beauty, profound theological content, and spiritual significance.

There appeared also the Exposition of the Blessed Sacrament in Latin-type monstrances, which was accompanied by supplication prayers. Those who introduced such practices did so unaware that there always had been a blessing with the Most Holy Eucharistic species during the Byzantine and other Divine Liturgies after Holy Communion. This subtly fostered a certain divorce between the Divine Liturgy and the Adoration of the Blessed Sacrament, something completely alien to the Eastern mentality and spirituality, and the Eastern perception of mystery, especially in its liturgical dimension.

In addition, there appeared the Rosary (of St. Dominic), which soon replaced the *chotki* and the recitation of the Jesus Prayer: "Lord Jesus Christ, Son of God, have mercy on me a sinner (or: on us the sinners)." Furthermore, the devotions to the Sacred Heart of Jesus and to the Immaculate Heart of Mary, and different types of novenas, shifted the devotion of the faithful from emphasis on communal prayers of praise to prayers of personal petition, from the spiritual to the more material realm, and from the liturgical and public worship to private and popular devotions. Thus the qualitative and spiritual perception of sacred reality yielded to quantitative and visible reality. The best example of this was the introduction of the "Gregorian Masses," that is, a series of thirty Masses over a period of thirty consecutive days, with the obligation to start the series again if for any reason the sequence was interrupted. There also emerged an intense interest in indulgences, plenary or otherwise; it became a preoccupation with many Eastern Catholics, both laity and clergy, even to the point of causing dismay to the Orthodox. Latin practices and influences of the Christian West prompted the Eastern Catholics and the Eastern Orthodox to drift apart culturally.

The same phenomenon of Latinization and Westernization occurred in all other areas of culture. For example, Eastern Catholics started to abandon the traditional Byzantine form of architecture and to follow in the footsteps of their Latin counterparts. In the ancient Byzantine style, the church, shaped like a cross and covered with a dome, symbolized earth and heaven, or the cosmos supernaturally transfigured and divinized in the Holy Spirit. The columns, crowned by marvelous capitals, were made of marble and decorated with inlays. The roof was fashioned of cupolas or rotundas, the one in the center being the largest, uniting the whole structure. Inside the main rotunda was a mosaic or fresco of Christ Pantocrator, which constituted the central point of the whole church. Mosaics, frescoes, painted ornamentations, arabesques, and sculptured reliefs created a harmonious whole, presenting a solemn and majestic atmosphere of life in the Holy Spirit and life in its eschatological dimensions. This most noble and aesthetically superb form of architecture began to disappear as Western forms of architecture such as Romanesque, Gothic, and especially Rococo were introduced, leaving generations of Eastern Catholics without the benefit of it.

With these shifts in liturgy, prayer, spirituality, art, and architecture came a diminished sense of the consistency and unity of the natural and the supernatural, of the heavenly and the earthly, of the eternal and the temporal, of the divine and the human. Eastern Catholics changed in cultural and religious outlook, becoming Uniates, that is, Eastern Catholics who culturally are no longer Orthodox and who are influenced by Western and Latin-Rite culture. They are something of a "hybrid," not fully understood by either East or West.

Eastern Christian monasticism ought to be at the core of Eastern spirituality, for it is the struggle to retain the meaning of life and culture by ascetic practices, fasting, silence, work, and worship. This is based on memory and tradition, in continuity with the wisdom of the Fathers of the Church. It is a reenactment of the life of Jesus Christ, the God-man and Savior. Here one must stress the importance of the Jesus Prayer, the inner continuous rhythm of the life of each monk and nun; it is a prayer of the heart based on love and internal discipline.

Today many Western monks and nuns are deeply involved in teaching, publishing, serving the community, peace and justice movements, etc. The calling of the Eastern monk or nun ought, ideally, to be to the "angelic life," that radical openness to the Triune God for the cultivation of the virtues. Eastern monasticism should be free, constantly improvised, and not a strict institution governed by rules and regulations. The search for the presence and glorification of the Most Holy Trinity is the supreme goal and meaning of Eastern monastic existence. This was the central motif in Eastern Christian culture; hence the monasteries formed nuclei in the early Church.

Early Basilian monastic spirituality (from the 4th century) was characterized by the spiritual optimism of the Eastern Fathers of the Church. The members associated to exchange the gifts (charisms) of the Holy Spirit. The deepening of monastic tradition was notably influenced by the ascetical and mystical writing of St. Basil the Great (330–379) and St. Theodore the Studite (759–826). There were no monastic "orders," for monasteries were independent of one another, under the local bishops.

Where the monasteries of the Eastern Catholic Churches have not kept to the fore this central contemplative purpose, they no longer deeply exemplify and emanate that Christian culture in which the sacred meaning of life for the Eastern Catholic person is made clear. Such monasteries are not as influential as they once were: as paradigmatic for the ancient liturgical traditions, as fountains of guidance in the life of virtue, as the homes of thriving creativity in iconography and the sacred arts. Without the primacy of a dynamic heritage of contemplative prayer, the monastery has lost its footing at the center of Eastern Catholic spirituality.

The situation of the Eastern Catholic Churches has begun to change. As a result of Vatican II and its Decree on Eastern Catholic Churches (*Orientalium Ecclesiarum,* November 21, 1964), some of the younger clergy and educated laity have begun a search for renewal in the spirituality and practice that are their ancient heritage.

See also EASTERN CHRISTIAN SPIRITUALITY.

Bibliography: C. Korolevskij, "L'Uniatisme," *Irénikon Collection,* nos. 5-6 (Prieuré d'Amays/Meuse, 1927), pp. 127–190. B. Lyps'kyi, *Dukhovist' nashoho obriadu* (New York: Nakladom Rodyny Pokiinoho, 1974). V. Pospishil, *Ex occidente lex. From the West the Law: The Eastern Catholic Churches under the Tutelage of the Holy See of Rome* (Carteret, N.J.: St. Mary's Religious Action Fund, 1979).

PETRO B. T. BILANIUK

EASTERN CHRISTIAN SPIRITUALITY

Eastern Christian spirituality is the product and synthesis of the theology, liturgical life, culture, ethos, mysticism, and piety that developed and assumed definitive form in the Christian East. The Eastern Christian way of life consists in imitating, glorifying, and participating in the inner life, light, and love of the Most Holy Trinity. This is life in the Mystical Body of Christ; it is imitation of Christ, who is the Pantocrator (All-Ruler) and Suffering Lord; it is life in the Holy Spirit through his gifts and fruits (the charisms). In this life Mary, the Bride of God the Father, is glorified, and her orientation toward the Most Holy Trinity is imitated; she is loved as the Mother of God (*Theotokos*) and as the carrier of the Most Holy Trinity (*Triadophora*) and carrier of the Holy Spirit (*Pneumatophora*).

Orthodox spiritual life takes place in the Church as the family of God, that is, in the doxological-liturgical community, all in the Spirit of love. This spiritual milieu includes the divine Persons, the angels, the saints in heaven, and the human beings on earth. In this milieu the uncreated divine energies are conveyed through the sacraments as the divine sources of grace and mercy, through the holy icons that are venerated, and through the proper use of Church art and music. Hence there is a progressive realization of human beings as divine icons and the immanent theology of beauty, and beauty is engendered. As Christian life deepens and intensifies, there arises monastic life (anachoretic, cenobitic, hesychastic, and idiorrhythmic) with its manifest tending toward the definitive eschatological fulfillment at the end of time in the Most Holy Trinity.

Trinitarian Spirituality

The Christian East has always understood spirituality as an intimate relationship of the individual or the Church with God the Father through the incarnate Son of God, Jesus Christ, and in the Holy Spirit. It has always been a liturgical spirituality, based on the glorification of the Most Holy Trinity through the Divine Liturgy and the holy sacraments.

The Triadic content of this spirituality is based on the teaching that the Trinity is the ultimate beginning (*archē*) of all creatures through the act of creation out of nothing (*triadoarchy*). The whole created cosmos is an icon of the Most Holy Trinity. Therefore it is "triadophoric" reality—bearing the image and seal of the Trinity. Since the visible and invisible cosmos in its entirety exists in the ubiquitous Triadic God who is the ground of its being, it is totally dependent on him for both its existence and its operation. For this reason the total cosmic reality is "triadocentric." Furthermore, the whole cosmos, in its tremendous dynamism, is a "triadoteleological" reality, for it tends toward the Most Holy Trinity as its definitive goal, the Omega Point.

The divine acts of vivification, strengthening, purification, illumination, redemption and salvation, sanctification, transfiguration, divinization, and glorification constitute a great mysterious and inexpressible condescension of God to his creatures. The condescension of each of the divine Persons can be described by a special term bearing a very specific meaning proper to the particular Person of the Trinity in question. The divine acts of God the Father are creation and love for his creatures; furthermore, he attracts them by his grace. This can be called his fatherhood and *basileōsis,* which is that condescension of God the Father whereby he progressively reveals himself as King. This is especially evident in the revealed covenant relationship progressively explained in the OT and culminated in the NT. The believer responds to the Father's attraction by gratitude to the Creator for the created cosmos and for his or her creation as a distinct human person.

The radical condescension of God the Son has been termed *kenōsis,* his emptying and abasement in accepting human nature for the purpose of the purification, redemption, and salvation of the whole world. As a member of Christ, the Christian not only believes with gratitude but embraces and internalizes the kenotic Christ, realizing oneness with him in value-orientation and purposes and in his intuitive responses. This progressively deepens throughout life.

The radical condescension of the Holy Spirit has been termed *episkiasis,* a "coming upon" or overshadowing that invigorates and gives life. Without this energizing, the human person cannot respond to the Father or say "Jesus is Lord." The effective overshadowing of the Holy Spirit brings the human person into contact with the uncreated divine energies, making possible every dimension of the response to the Father and the Son.

The radical condescension of the Triadic God is brought out in the Byzantine Liturgy, as shown in the prayer before the ambo: "O Lord, who blessest those who bless Thee, and sanctifiest those who trust in Thee: Save Thy people and bless Thine inheritance. Preserve the fullness of Thy Church. Sanctify those who love the beauty of Thy house; glorify them in return by Thy divine power, and forsake us not who put our hope in Thee. Give peace to Thy world, to Thy churches, to Thy priests, to all those in civil authority, and to all Thy people. For every good gift is from above, coming down from Thee, the Father of Lights; and unto Thee we ascribe glory, thanksgiving, and worship: to the Father, and to the Son, and to the Holy Spirit, now and ever and unto ages of ages. Amen."

Spirituality focuses on relationship to God the Father, the Son, and the Holy Spirit. The Father is first known as the Creator in whose image human beings have been made (Gen 1–2). The basic pattern is familial; the Father is at once beyond our knowledge (apophatic spirituality) and well known (kataphatic spirituality), and thus to be imitated in deeds of goodness, knowledge, and creativity. The Father is the archetypal householder (Eph 2:13-22; 3:14-15; Lk 15:11-31) who loves his children impartially, and even in spite of sinfulness (see also Mt 5:45-48). The human person must responsibly imitate the Creator-Father in the procreation and education of children, in creative activity, whether prayer, worship, work, political life, or artistic creativity.

The Orthodox Christian is related to the Lord Jesus Christ as to the Good Samaritan who saves and redeems, heals and leads one to the kingdom of God (parousia). Christ is the universal King who governs the whole world. To him the response is made in faith, hope, and love; this means profound prayer and thankfulness both in words and deeds of love and kindness (*diakonia*) to the poor and oppressed—widows, orphans, the aged, the sick, the im-prisoned, etc. Christ is the only Mediator before God the Father; therefore in living the commandments and the beatitudes one comes to the Father. Jesus Christ is the ideal model of life and action. His life and deeds are central to the Eastern Christian worldview and attitudes. He is the Messiah and the primary Image of God (Col 1:15-20). All are in union with him in his Mystical Body.

Eastern Christians feel that they must have a very close interpersonal relationship with the Holy Spirit. The Holy Spirit is the dynamic, divine, and personal Power who is always life-giving, the "Lord and Giver of life" who grants natural and supernatural life, that is, the life of divine grace. Life in the Holy Spirit is the source and foundation of moral, virtuous, and holy life for all orthodox, orthopractical, orthoaesthetical, and orthomystical Christians. The divine action of the Holy Spirit reveals itself as a call or a challenge, a warning, a strengthening, an encouragement, or an illumination. He opens minds and hearts for the reception and understanding of God's word and brings us to a prayerful conversion and repentance (Acts 2:40; Rom 8:28-30; 1 Cor 14:3), and he testifies in us that we are God's children (Rom 8:16; 1 Jn 3:19-24). Orthodox Christianity is actually living *in* the Holy Spirit, which includes all of life in its moral and mystical dimensions. Daily the prayer to the Holy Spirit is: "O Heavenly King, the Comforter, the Spirit of Truth who art everywhere and fillest all things, Treasury of Blessings, and Giver of Life: Come and abide in us, and cleanse us from every impurity, and save our souls, O Good One."

The Role of Mary

The Gospel tradition, especially Luke, portrays Mary as the Virgin, Mother of the Son of God, full of grace, and of Davidic royal lineage, the Queen. The patristic Mariological tradition reaches a high point in St. Ephrem the Syrian (306–373), the minstrel of the Mother of God. As

Theotokos ("God-bearer"), Mary is related to Christ in his every work. St. John of Damascus (ca. 645–ca. 750) exclaimed: "This name contains the whole mystery of the Incarnation." She was the first and archetypal recipient of the God-man, and thus the archetype for everyone's reception of the God-man, Jesus Christ. In this light we have not only an intellectual but also a co-natural understanding of her immaculate conception (see Orthodox texts prior to the mid-19th century), perpetual virginity, universal intercession, bodily assumption, and queenship.

A sense of the role of Mary could be served only minimally through rational exposition; hence the East has used the aesthetic sense with its range of poetic phraseology. For example, on the Feast of the Nativity of the Theotokos (September 8/21) the Irmos reads: "Virginity is foreign to mothers; childbearing is strange for virgins. But in you, O Theotokos, both were accomplished! For this, all the earthly nations unceasingly magnify you!" Here we see paradox, basic to all understanding of the God-man, and hence necessary for appreciating the role of the Theotokos. Many ancient liturgical texts hymn Mary as "Bride of God" or "Bride of God the Father"; for example, on the Feast of the Entry of the Theotokos into the Temple (February 2/15), we read: "O Virgin, fed in faith by heavenly bread in the temple of the Lord, thou hast brought forth unto the world the Bread of Life, that is, the Word; and as His chosen temple without spot, thou wast betrothed mystically through the Spirit, to be the Bride of God the Father" (Matins of the Entry). Thus Mary had the most intense possible relationship to the Father as his Bride, to the Son as Mother, and to the Holy Spirit as Pneumatophora. In many liturgical texts Mary is called Virgin, Ever-Virgin (*aeiparthenos*), Light-bearer, and a whole litany of important and beautiful titles (see *Hymnos Akathistos*).

The Church in Eastern Christianity

Orthodox spirituality is deeply rooted in the mystery of the Church, which is the household of the Father, the Mystical Body of the Son, and the dwelling place of the Holy Spirit. The Church is personally related to the Triadic God in a manner analogous to that of Mary, for Mary is the preeminent member of the Church.

The Church reflects the Triadic God: it is the family of God the Father, a Christ-formed community, and Pneumatophoric reality. Thus the Most Holy Trinity is the prototype of the Church, which in its ultimate fullness and eschatological aspect is of cosmic dimensions. This is reflected even in the ideal iconography of a church. In the central cupola is the icon of Christ Pantocrator; then about him is the world of adoring angels and preeminent saints. On the walls of the church are icons of the saints spanning the whole history of the Church. Within the church are the people who are the living icons of their Creator. Thus in symbol and reality all creation worships God together; and all creation as a family rejoices in its Mother (see the Liturgy of St. Basil the Great). All creation is "recapitulated" (*anakephalaiōsis*) in Christ. The people, in their imitation of God, have as vivid examples around them the saints and the angels. Orthodox spirituality culminates in the "angelic life," that is, the monastic life. Hence an angelic spirit permeates Orthodox life and worship, so much so that the angels are viewed as foremost in the liturgical celebrations.

The Holy Icons

Essential to Eastern Orthodoxy is the veneration of the holy icons. An icon is a channel of divine light, an instrument of prayer and communion with God the Father, through the Son, and in the Holy Spirit. It is a means of contact with the divine life that purifies, illuminates, and elevates the human person; this leads to the ultimate divinization and glorification of people and of the cosmos. The icon, then, is a symbol of hope, and in its liturgical context conveys the unity of the people with God, as living in his divine light, life, and love. Icons are known as "theology in color," "images of the invisible," "windows to eternity," "channels of grace." In them an attempt is made to depict the divine Persons, the angels, and the spiritualized human persons who have become temples of God. Icons are called holy because they try to portray the mysteries of faith and show their relevance to the future eschatological existence in the holiness and glory of God.

The Triadic God is the Archetype and Creator of beauty. His essence is beautiful, and all three divine Hypostases are infinitely beautiful. The Son and the Holy Spirit reveal the splendor of divine holiness and the majesty of the unapproachable light. All created reality is an icon of the Divine; however, created persons, because of their rationality, free will, and aesthetic sense, are very special icons of the Divine, created in the "image and likeness" of God. Therefore created persons, especially the saints, contemplate their own beauty and grasp within themselves the beautiful image of God.

Beauty is the harmony of being, the splendor of form, and the immediate, necessary, and essential property of any true being. Thus unity, goodness, and beauty converge. Inner beauty is spiritual in nature, for it is sublime and superior to outer (physical) beauty. Eastern iconography tries to capture this divine, sublime, inner beauty in its eschatological dimension. Thus Christians are saved not only by belief and goodness but also by their contemplation and creation of beauty. Iconography, art, architecture, music, and poetry converge in the glorious praise of God.

The most obvious feature of Byzantine spirituality is its organic and harmonized unity, without sharp distinctions or even divisions between moral, pastoral, ascetical, and mystical theologies, as has been the case in the Christian West, with its many denominations and sects. Furthermore, in the East there are no sharp divisions between Christian duties and the gospel call to poverty, purity, obedience, or other virtues and practices. Thus Byzantines have aspired toward so-called moral maximalism, that is, to the imitation of the ontological perfection and holiness of the Triadic God, which is the foundation of the morality and holiness of all rational beings. The revealed truths of faith are seen to have a normative character for our actions and for our whole life.

Thus the human being, as a divine icon, strives toward God as the ultimate goal with all his or her being, that is, with the body aspiring to resurrection and the soul striving for salvation. As a person created in the image and likeness of God, the human being has inner strengths, faculties, and possibilities, namely, a mind, or intellect, which is destined to know divine Truth (Church Slavonic: *istyna*) and human truth (*pravda*); a will that strives toward the infinite and highest Good; and feelings and an aesthetic sense that strive toward the infinite divine Beauty. It is not surprising that we find scientists seeking the truth, philanthropists seeking the good, and artists or aesthetes who love and live for beauty. One also finds a very small but very important group, the mystics, who have the gift from God of forming a synthesis between truth, goodness, and beauty, and who strive toward the Most Holy Trinity through all three aspects at the same time. Mystics no longer see God as the infinite Truth separate from the infinite Beauty. They experience the Most Holy Trinity as the absolute source of infinite divine holiness—the best description of the divine essence.

We have *orthodoxy* (*pravoslavia*), which is the correct and lawful worship of the Triadic God, and at the same time the correct and lawful confession of the true faith. Second, we have *orthopraxis* (*pravodiistviie*), which is the correct moral and holy existence and activity of a human being. Third, we have *orthoaesthetics,* which is the correct and lawful reception and creation of beauty, subject to orthodoxy and orthopraxis, that is, in congruence with all the dogmatic and moral precepts of the Church. Finally, we have *orthomysticism,* a healthy, genuine, and all-encompassing mysticism that leads one to the Most Holy Trinity as to the highest Being, the source of holiness, and at the same time the infinite, highest and absolute Truth, Goodness, and Beauty.

Byzantine spirituality is grounded in a wide field of Christian life and experience, which has the Decalogue, or the Ten Divine Commandments (Deut 5:6-21), as its minimal goal, and the Beatitudes (Mt 5:3-12) as its highest goal. This includes the heroic virtues of faith, hope, love, patience, and so forth. Each Christian may freely move about in this range between the minimum and the maximum requirements and choose for oneself the most appropriate and subjectively most feasible moral teaching and practice.

In the Christian East monasticism was the avant-garde of orthodoxy, orthopraxis, orthoaesthetics, and orthomysticism. The roots of monasticism lay in the second and third centuries with the anchorites of the Egyptian desert. The authentic monastic worldview began to be crystallized especially under the influence of the rules and letters of St. Basil the Great (d. 379). The Cappadocians of the fourth century began to appreciate the exchange of the charismata of the Holy Spirit, and for this reason fostered the cenobitic form of monasticism. From that time on not only monks and nuns but also all serious Eastern Christians began to shape their conscience under the guidance of spiritual fathers or elders. Usually these were monks who were recognized as experienced experts in ascetical and mystical matters.

This process gave rise to a whole list of famous teachers of Byzantine spirituality, and they produced extensive spiritual literature. This phenomenon brought about a serious "monasticization" of the spirituality of the Eastern Christian laity. This movement developed significantly with the teaching and practice of Theodore the Studite (759–826) and other teachers of cenobitic or communal monasticism. These teachers taught the secular people fuller Christian practices, social virtues, and responsibilities, as well as how to lead a personal sacrificial life for the good of others.

Alexandria and Antioch

Different schools of spirituality, asceticism, and mysticism originated in the Christian East from two competing schools of theology: the school of Alexandria and the school of Antioch. In the school of Alexandria the philosophical background was based chiefly on Neoplatonic elements of the hierarchical unity of all reality. The pinnacle of this pyramid was the idea of God as the highest Good. In biblical exegesis, under the influence of Philo of Alexandria, the allegorical and typological interpretation was predominant. The mystical and spiritual sense of Scripture was sought and greatly influenced spirituality and spiritual writings. Thus theological methodology was deductive, allegorical explanation in the light of faith. The type of theological thinking was contemplative and dominated by both metaphysical speculation and a profound sense of mystery. Theological principles that were abstract, metaphysical, mystical, spiritual, and supernatural were predominant.

The Alexandrian school developed a direction of speculation that was descending, deductive, "from above to below," an attempt to interpret created reality from God's point of view. Consequently, in Christology the emphasis was on the mystery of the divinity of Christ and the inhominization of the Word of God; but there was also a tendency to minimalize the human nature of Christ. The attendant constant perils were theological irrationalism, uncontrolled mysticism and asceticism, and consequently a contempt for matter, the body, and empirical reality. When this form of thinking became exaggerated, it led to Monophysitism and Manicheism.

In the school of Antioch the philosophical background was predominantly based on Aristotle and Aristotelianism. Reality was approached through the analysis of a particular thing and its truthfulness. There was no strict synthetic view of reality. In biblical exegesis Jewish rabbinical tradition was followed, with a search for the literal sense of the Scriptures and an attempt to establish critical texts. The theological method was inductive and historico-grammatical. Antiochene typology made the historico-salvific facts accessible in the light of reason and faith, and theological thinking was concrete, based on historical investigation. The theological principles used were based on empirical, practical, experiential, and natural reality. Consequently, the direction of Antiochene speculation was ascending, "from below to above"; interpretation of God was from the point of view of created reality, entailing anthropomorphisms, etc. In Christology the reality of the perfect humanity of Jesus was stressed, and there was a tendency to minimalize the divine nature of Christ. Thus the school of Antioch was exposed to the perils of theological historicism and rationalism, which culminated in Arianism, Nestorianism, and Pelagianism.

The two rival schools, Alexandria and Antioch, were instrumental in the production of two different trends of spirituality. Alexandrian spirituality closely followed Alexandrian theology and produced a search for eschatological fulfillment in the mystery of the Most Holy Trinity. The Antiochene school, because of Pelagian tendencies, developed a spirituality based predominantly on asceticism, with very little mystical experience; therefore it tended toward a legalistic type of monastic life.

A happy synthesis between these two rival trends developed gradually in the hesychastic tradition, starting with St. Basil the Great and continuing to the present day. The most important theological foundation of hesychasm was the doctrine of the uncreated divine energies. The uncreated divine energies belong to the three divine Persons. They originate in the transcendent Trinity and are made immanent in the history of salvation for the divinization and transfiguration of human beings and of all extra-divine reality. Between the Trinity and created reality they are the dynamic means of contact. Thus human beings, as icons of God, participate in the divine nature and life, receiving graces from God as icons of God. The unity of the human person with God is not essential or substantial but interpersonal and "energetic" or "synergetic." No creature can act in any way in isolation from the uncreated divine energies.

The second main feature of hesychasm is contemplation of the uncreated divine light emanating from the uncreated divine energies. This light was manifested during the transfiguration of the Lord on Mount Tabor. Hence hesychasts have also been called "Taborites," for they strive to have a participation in this light. Hesychasm is based on the appreciation of both the spiritual and bodily aspects of the human being; therefore the whole human person, body and soul together, is involved in psychosomatic hesychastic practices. The heart and breath and mind all are absorbed in God in the rhythm of the Jesus Prayer.

Byzantine Mysticism

Byzantine spirituality is a social and mystical phenomenon; it gives shape to a specific orthodox ethos, that is, to social morality, sentiment, experience, and response. That is why the Divine Liturgy plays such a crucial and central role. For Eastern Christians the Liturgy has become a school of morals, asceticism, and mysticism; it has become the source of spirituality. Liturgical rites, with their chants, texts, rubrics, movements, and processions, create an atmosphere of piety, worship, prayer, and contemplation. Helpful in building up this atmosphere are the holy icons, church architecture, instruments, and vessels. In this sacred ambience sermons and the readings of Holy Scripture teach and encourage Eastern Christians to attain mystical experience and knowledge. Here the faithful are able to learn the Triadic way to salvation. The first step consists in purification (*katharsis*), illumination (*ellampsis*), and vision (*theōria*). The second step consists in unification (*henōsis*). The third step consists in divinization (*theōsis*).

Purification (*katharsis*) is understood here as a spiritual purification from original sin by baptism or from personal sin by the sacrament of penance or ascetical efforts—prayer, almsgiving, acts of love, self-imposed mortification, especially fasting and abstinence. It is a process of turning away from the abuse of creatures and a conversion to God. The grace of God is experienced as that divine uncreated energy that destroys the work of sin and restores the gift of the divine image and likeness to a person—the true inheritance from the beginning, the original innocence of paradise. This spiritual purification makes one clean in body and soul, that is, in intellect and thoughts, in will and intentions, in feelings and in the perception of beauty, but especially in the exercise of all the virtues, principally faith, hope, and love. Even such crises as war, persecution, calumny, imprisonment, injustice, abuse of authority, sickness, accident, poverty, failure, scandal, ingratitude, the loss of loved ones, conflict, misunderstanding, and even suffering and death may be permitted by God to purify our persons in body and soul.

Illumination (*ellampsis*) means both God's illuminating us and our being illuminated. Here it means a special divine influence of the uncreated divine energies aiding the human person to obtain a certain necessary and universal knowledge.

The mystery of the divine light illuminating the human person is very prominent in the Gospel of St. John, especially in the prologue (Jn 1:4-9): "Through him [the Word] was life, and this life was the light of the human race; the light shines in the darkness . . . . The true light, which enlightens everyone, was coming into the world." All of us remain in the darkness unless we are illuminated by the true light. The whole human being is offered divine illumination of the intellect, will, feelings, and even body. God alone is the true Light who enlightens each individual, the Church, and all humankind. He makes intelligible to them his inner secrets, which are expressed in his self-revelation and appropriated in mystical experience. God and the human person are united in the divine light.

The third moment of the first step of mysticism is vision (*theōria*). It is the result of the first two, that is, of purification and illumination. It is a supernatural perception of truth, of divine wisdom, and finally of the intuitive vision of God. Mystical experience of God is not a vision in the ordinary sense of the word. Ordinary visions are a product of perception with mental images or concepts, but mystical vision, which is a result of purification and illumination, is an intuitive perception without the intermediary of normal concepts or intellectual images originating outside the human being and processed in the mind. Therefore mystics have great difficulty in explaining their mystical experiences to others, for they can only attempt to translate what cannot be adequately rendered in human language into concepts and images. Hence the language of true mystics is poetic in character; they use many descriptive categories from aesthetic perception, inadequately referring them to the infinite and indescribable Beauty, a blue or radiant light, incredibly beautiful music, etc.

St. Gregory Palamas, in his famous *Triads* (New York: Paulist, 1983, p. 58), teaches: ". . . hesychasts know that the purified and illuminated mind, when clearly participating in the grace of God, also beholds other mystical and supernatural visions, for in seeing itself, it sees more than itself: it does not simply contemplate some other object, or simply its own image, but rather the glory impressed on its own image by the grace of God. This radiance reinforces the mind's power to transcend itself and accomplish that union with those better things which is beyond understanding. By this union, the mind sees God in the Spirit in a manner transcending human powers."

The second step in mysticism is unification (*henōsis*). Unification is a process whereby a person undergoes an elimination of inner divisions and inconsistencies, and externally establishes a closer relational bond with other beings, but without a merger or loss of identity. These philosophical ideas are crucial for the correct understanding of mystical union and unification. Through faith a believing person is established in a bond of knowledge with God. Through love a new bond of will and synergetic cooperation comes into existence, for by this the believer starts to participate in the uncreated divine energies and enters into a union with God that is not essential but existential, synergetic, and interpersonal.

The Most Holy Trinity is the most perfect exemplar and creator of true unity of any kind, for the three infinite divine Persons, while remaining infinitely distinct, are perfectly united in one divine essence and nature. This is indicated in Jn 17:21: "that they may all be one, as you, Father, are in me and I in you, that they also may be in us . . . ."

A mystic, by acts of faith, hope, and love, becomes united to God as the Creator, Redeemer, and Sanctifier of reality. Logically, by faith the mind is united to the divine wisdom; by love the will is united to the infinitely benevolent salvific will of God; and by the aesthetic sense, the deeper soul is united to the infinite divine beauty. However, by a convergence of the faculties, the mystic person, with his or her whole being, experiences God's utter closeness to his creatures and God's inhabitation of all just persons. This experience of the unification of the mystic with God is the core of the mystical experience in any religious tradition.

St. Gregory Palamas has the following to offer concerning mystical union with God: "Since the Reality which transcends every intellectual power is impossible to comprehend, it is beyond all beings; such union with God is thus beyond all knowledge, even if it be called 'knowledge' metaphorically, nor is it intelligible, even if it be called so. For how can what is beyond all intellect be called intelligible? In respect to its transcendence, it might better be called ignorance than knowledge. It cannot be a part or aspect of knowledge, just as the Superessential is not an aspect of the essential . . ." (*Triads*, p. 64).

The third and last step of Byzantine mysticism is divinization (*theōsis*). We can offer only a preliminary description of this complex term. *Theōsis,* translated as "divinization" or sometimes even "deification," can be described as the omnipotent and sanctifying divine Triadic activity which, because of the indwelling of the Trinity and grace, and because of the inborn and natural capacity of the creature for transfiguration, induces a process of assimilation to God the Father of the whole human person, of humankind, and of the visible and invisible universe in its totality, through the mediation of the incarnate Logos, Christ the Pantocrator, and in the Holy Spirit.

The good deeds of the person and of the community are the beginning and the *conditio sine qua non* of divinization and mysticism, leading to the more perfect manifestation of the image and likeness of God in the human being. Thus this human being becomes more and more Godlike, or more and more similar to God in thoughts, will and love, deeds and perception of beauty.

True Christian mysticism consists in a new and divinized relationship to the whole uncreated and created reality, that is, to the Triadic God, the Church, humanity, and the whole visible and invisible universe. This is a permanent Triadic experience, given to particular persons and also to the ecclesiastical community. Those persons and the whole ecclesiastical community respond to this loving initiative of God through faith, hope, and love. Genuine Christian mysticism, therefore, does not consist in escaping from the world or merely condemning sinful creation. Mysticism is a contemplation of the world as divinized and a contemplation of God's creation in the state and process of transfiguration.

A monumental influence upon the formation of Byzantine spirituality has come from that monastic spirituality called hesychasm (from *hesychia,* "silence," "peacefulness"). It has long been known as an aesthetico-mystical teaching together with psychosomatic practice, which in many respects calls to mind the practice of yoga. The silent and peaceful meditation and the interior prayer bring the mystic into the presence of God with his uncreated divine energies. The mystic also enters into contemplation of the uncreated divine Light. The whole person prays and is coordinated in prayer. Breath and heartbeat sing the rhythm of an incessant prayer, usually "Lord Jesus Christ, Son of God, have mercy on me, a sinner."

Mystical experience is manifested in the context of prayer. In prayer we can discover the mystery of the human being as a divine icon, for prayer is the most exalted religious activity; it assimilates the human being to the three divine Hypostases and is an outward sign of the mysteries of transfiguration, divinization, and glorification. From an Eastern stance, Christian prayer could be described as a mysterious and loving gift of God the Father through the Son and in the Holy Spirit. It comes to us as a supernatural call in faith, hope, and love,

and develops into an intimate and personal polylogue with the triune God. It includes his praises and our petitions and thanksgiving, and is the expression of a participation in his inner life, light, and love. And finally, prayer ascends from us to God the Father as to the Head of the divine family, through the Son and in the Holy Spirit.

One of the classical examples of an Eastern Christian prayer is the one recited very quietly by the priest during the Divine Liturgy before the gospel reading: "Illumine our hearts, O Master who lovest mankind, with the pure light of Thy divine knowledge. Open the eyes of our mind to the understanding of Thy gospel teachings. Implant also in us the fear of Thy blessed commandments, that trampling down all carnal desires, we may enter upon a spiritual manner of living, both thinking and doing such things as are well-pleasing unto Thee. For Thou art the illumination of our souls and bodies, O Christ our God, and unto Thee we ascribe glory, together with Thy Father, who is from everlasting, and Thine all-holy, good, and life-creating Spirit, now and ever and unto the ages of ages. Amen." This ancient prayer contains the typically holistic understanding of the human person, which understanding is necessary before proceeding with the furtherance of the life of Christian wisdom.

Human wisdom develops as a gratuitous gift from divine Wisdom. This divine Wisdom was poetically described by St. Athanasius of Alexandria (ca. 295–373): "Like a musician who has attuned his lyre, and by the artistic blending of low and high and medium tones produces a single melody, so the Wisdom of God, holding the universe like a lyre, adapting things heavenly to things earthly, harmonizes them all, and, leading them by His will, makes one world and one world order in beauty and harmony" (*Contra Gentes,* 41). Thus the harmony of heaven and earth, the harmony of the cosmos and human life, ecological harmony, and the holistic view of the person—all these have never been seriously called into question. These are deep in Byzantine consciousness and are treasured in ancient prayer, iconography, and architecture.

In conclusion, we can say that the whole of Byzantine spirituality is built on a personal relationship of the believer and the community of believers to each and all of the Persons of the Most Holy Trinity.

See also DIVINIZATION; EASTERN CATHOLIC CHURCHES, SPIRITUALITY OF; HESYCHASM; HOLY SPIRIT; ICON(S), ICONOGRAPHY; KENOSIS; MARY; MYSTICISM; PATRISTIC SPIRITUALITY; THREE WAYS.

Bibliography: P. Bilaniuk, *Studies in Eastern Christianity* (Munich-Toronto: Ukrainian Free University, 1977–1989), 4 vols. H.-G. Beck, *Kirche und theologische Literatur im Byzantinischen Reich* (Munich: C. H. Beck, 1959; rpt. 1977). F. Heiler, *Die Ostkirchen* (Munich-Basel: Ernst Reinhardt, 1971). C. Jones, G. Wainwright, E. Yarnold, eds., *The Study of Spirituality* (New York-Oxford: Oxford Univ. Press, 1986). V. Lossky, *The Mystical Theology of the Eastern Church* (Cambridge-London: James Clarke, 1957). B. McGinn and J. Meyendorff, eds., *Christian Spirituality 1: Origins to the Twelfth Century* (New York: Crossroad, 1985). A Monk of the Eastern Church, *Orthodox Spirituality* (London: S.P.C.K., 1945). J. Raitt, ed. *Christian Spirituality 2: High Middle Ages and Reformation* (New York: Crossroad, 1987). T. Špidlík, *The Spirituality of the Christian East* (Kalamazoo, Mich.: Cistercian Publications, 1986).

PETRO B. T. BILANIUK

ECOLOGICAL CONSCIOUSNESS

"Ecological consciousness" refers to the awareness that has grown in recent decades that how human beings treat the natural environment has crucial implications. Minimally, ecological consciousness calls to mind physical survival, material prosperity, and good stewardship. For present purposes spiritual flourishing is also involved. Christians who have taken to heart the doctrine of creation, according to which everything in existence is a gift of God, should see this clearly.

The natural sciences currently provide a staggering view of the proportions of the physical world. Most astronomers believe that the universe is at least fifteen billion years old, and some think that it is infinitely expansive. Biologists provide an awesome outline of the origins and developments of life, speaking of thousands of species that once populated our planet and are now extinct. Ecologists show how closely interrelated various systems of plants, animals, and human beings are, and they show as well the delicate interactions between the soil, the water, and the air. Be it forests or seas, deserts or mountains, each zone or niche is both complex and delicate. The first goal of an ecological spirituality might well be simply to help people appreciate these wonders of the natural environment.

When one contemplates the effects of human intrusions into the natural environment, matters become only more complex. Since the rise of truly modern technology in the 19th century, human beings have greatly increased their capacity to alter the face, and sometimes the substance, of the environment. Current chemical, biological, and other forms of human impact upon animal, plant, and inanimate life can be so powerful that they change biozones drastically, perhaps even irreversibly. No longer, then, do the biblical or other traditional views of the proportions between nature and human beings obtain. No longer is nature the sovereign force, sweeping all before it, and the human being a tiny creature forced to cower. Certainly earthquakes, tornadoes, and other natural phenomena continue to display powers that human beings cannot match, but on a day-by-day basis human pollution, construction, erosion, and other effects have a great impact on the natural environment. More often than not this impact appears to be for the worse, in the sense of what threatens the survival of the natural environment and so the matrix of all life.

Inasmuch as they have appropriated this state of affairs, people with ecological awareness tend to realize that being fully human in the 21st century will require being intimately involved with caring for the earth. Indeed, the crisis is great enough to speak of a shared destiny, such that if human beings do not change their current technologies, both they and much of nature may perish. This prospect has stimulated considerable reflection on the value that nature, or God's creation, ought to carry in the minds and spirits of human beings. If people could change from a dominative mentality, according to which the earth lies ready to hand as raw material for human beings to subdue and use as they wish, to a conservative or even reverential mentality, according to which people make preserving the natural environment a religious responsibility, the future would look much brighter.

Groups such as the Worldwatch Institute that publish statistics on pollution, deforestation, birth rates, and the consumption of nonrenewable resources make it clear that we are nearing the "carrying capacity" of the earth (the number of human beings it can accommodate). We cannot continue to use natural resources and to consume raw materials at present rates, let alone extrapolate those rates for greatly increased global populations. We need alternatives to our present worldwide dependence on petroleum, automobiles, chemicals, and other products that either consume irreplaceable natural resources or pollute the environment. Those alternatives are not simply different stuffs—renewable resources, products that are biodegradable. They are also different ways of looking at what we require to live full, satisfying, useful, even holy lives. At this point profound questions arise about human existence, and spiritual resources of the world's religions become crucial.

If we limit ourselves to the resources of Catholic spirituality, we find such pregnant yet underdeveloped notions as the presence of God in all of creation and the primacy of contemplation. Inasmuch as all creatures depend upon God for their existence, sharing being from the single divine font, all creatures are presences of divinity. If human beings so wished, they could allow all creatures to enjoy the right to be appreciated and not abused. "Abuse" is wrongful use. The entire population of creatures depends on mutual use, even mutual destruction, but some kinds of use (arguably, many that our current technologies employ) are illegitimate because they harm the matrix of life itself and, unless checked, threaten geocide. Chemical and radioactive pollution appear to fall into this category. A renewed Christian faith in the presence of God in all creatures might give many people salutary pause. Could we recklessly destroy creatures we felt to be holy presences of God?

Contemplation is the nonpragmatic regard of creatures. When we contemplate the sea, we are not interested in its minerals or even its fishes. We are trying to appreciate it as a lovely, God-given whole. When we contemplate the land, we are opening our spirits to the presence of God in its beauty or power. Contemplation is far from the whole of life, but without it, as Scripture says, the people perish. The people perish because they have no nourishment for their souls. They do not know why they are living, what sets their hearts aglow. When people do know these things, they can carry out the pragmatic tasks of survival in good order. Because they know why they are working, what they are trying to accomplish in the overall scheme of things, they are not likely to get sidetracked into abuses of nature.

It is easy to realize that if human beings were to make contemplation the gist of their fulfillment, most of the reasons given for intruding abusively into the natural environment would fall away. If contemplation, in its rich variety of species (play, art, music, scientific research, much teaching and healing), were to take center stage, we human beings would need much less material accumulation. Food, clothing, housing, and possessions could all become integrated with the great love of our lives: finding and serving the meaning and beauty of God. Certainly many practical problems would remain. There has never been an ecological utopia, in which human beings used natural resources with full restraint and reverence. But we now know enough about both the fragility of the planet and the deepest needs of the human personality to mount a twofold attack on the forces of environmental pollution. On the one hand, we know that our present industrial way of life is lethal to nature. On the other hand, we know that material possessions do not give people joy and peace of soul. The confluence of these two streams of knowledge makes plain the task facing those who would raise ecological consciousness around the globe and make it a central force in future spirituality.

For Catholic spirituality, much of what ecological consciousness calls to mind pivots around sacramentality. When people consider God's creation with eyes of faith, they see sacraments—material signs of grace—everywhere. The sacramental materials featured in the primary Catholic rituals—bread, wine, water, oil—are the most prominent, but a little imagination makes it clear that in principle everything made by God refers beyond itself, to its source. So wax, incense, flowers, music, painting, wheat, cotton, palm branches, baby chicks—all carry a lesson. The lesson need not be articulate. It is enough for people to open their hearts to all the good things that come down from their Father of Lights. When they do, they see creation as a cornucopia—a never-failing stream. As well, they see why the Word of God was willing to take flesh and join the great parade of all God's creatures. The proper use of such creatures should be enough to ensure conversion from the ways currently polluting the earth.

When people take ecological instincts to heart, they sign on for a long and painful education. The ways that human beings relate to the land, like the ways that they relate to one another, can be depressing.

Again and again one finds squalor where there might be cleanliness and beauty. Again and again one finds that the problem is the spiritual torpor or ignorance of the people involved. Sometimes this spiritual torpor is a function of self-interest. For example, wanting unlimited electricity, people are willing to overlook the dangers of nuclear energy. Other times it is a function of ambition run amok—for example, developers thinking only of their next shopping mall. Once the economic and political dimensions develop, however, ecological consciousness forces one to rebut a torrent of arguments, most of them specious but many of them popularly effective. Developers chant about "jobs" and "progress." Industrialists warn darkly that pollution controls will threaten local economies. Understandably, people with families for whom to provide become frightened. "Environmentalists" are made to seem their enemies, waiting to snatch the bread from their table.

A major function of Christian spirituality should be to offer people perspectives and resources that can beat down these panicky reactions. In the perspective of Christian faith, nothing happens apart from God's providence, and nothing can separate us from God. Among the main resources that Christian faith offers is a prophetic challenge to those who try to rob others of their peace or turn the land, which should be a common resource, to their own profit. Along this track, it seems clear that a Catholic spirituality of the land, working in the traces of the social encyclicals of Pope John Paul II, would hold little brief for an unbridled capitalism. If the goods of the earth exist for all the earth's people, and if the needs of the many take priority over the wants of the few, then the ecological consciousness that Catholic spirituality should sponsor in the 21st century can be a friend of both the poor and contemplation. Were it to become such, uniting three powerful spiritual trends (concern for the poor, contemplative prayer, and protection of the natural environment), it could be one of the most significant spiritual movements around the globe.

See also CREATION; EASTERN (ASIAN) SPIRITUALITY; NATIVE AMERICAN SPIRITUALITY; PEACE; POVERTY; SACRAMENTS; SIMPLICITY; WORLD.

Bibliography: H. P. Santire, *The Travail of Nature: The Ambiguous Ecological Promise of Christian Theology* (Philadelphia: Fortress, 1985). L. Brown and others, *State of the World 1992* (New York: Norton/Worldwatch Institute, 1992). T. Berry, *The Dream of the Earth* (San Francisco: Sierra Club, 1988).

JOHN T. CARMODY

ECSTASY

Ecstasy is the spiritual experience of "standing outside" one's self in a transcendental, climactic penetration of the mystery of love itself. It is usually associated with the highest mystical stage of perfection—union with God. While some mystics speak of ecstasy as a transient deliverance from the body, contemporary writers emphasize the psychosomatic harmony and elevation of intuitive understanding achieved in an ecstatic moment, which might include sexual intercourse.

Philo of Alexandria (ca. 20 B.C.–A.D. 41) follows Plato's *Ion* and *Phaedrus* to describe ecstasy with the oxymoron "sober intoxication." He suggests that ecstasy involves a suspension of the normal processes of reason and a state of spiritual exaltation. For Philo, ecstasy suggests that for the duration of the experience the natural faculties are muted and replaced by God.

Plotinus (ca. 205–270), on the other hand, speaks of ecstasy as the raising of one's natural faculties (which are already divine) to their most exalted and truest state. This is the fifth and final stage of the spiritual process (awareness, purification, introversion, mind, ecstasy). Ecstasy for Plotinus is a disturbing and exhilarating process, bringing persons into direct relation with the One, a flight of the alone to the Alone (*Enneads* vi.9.11.51).

Dionysius the Areopagite (ca. A.D. 500) profoundly influenced the East and the West with Neoplatonic contributions to Christian mysticism and theology, even using its erotic language to describe the ecstasy in Paul's "I live, yet not I, but Christ lives in me." He develops symbolic and kataphatic theology (the theology of procession) as a celebration of the nature of God that is revealed in God's movement to us in creation and redemption, as our concern with perfecting our praise of God (*The Divine Names*). He contrasts kataphatic theology with apophatic theology, in which we seek to return our concepts to God by ascribing to God what he has revealed of himself.

In his *Mystical Theology* Dionysius relies on Gregory of Nyssa's description of Moses' ascent into the darkness of God. In this darkness the intellect passes beyond any active knowledge from senses or by concepts. This passivity with the unknowable God transcends understanding. The soul submits to God and achieves a "pure and absolute ecstasy," in which the intellect goes beyond itself and is united to "the ray of Divine Darkness that is beyond being." Dionysius emphasizes the positive side of an ecstasy of love as union and deification: "those who are possessed by this love belong not to themselves but to the object of their longing" (*The Divine Names*, III, 13, 712A). He ventures to speak of the ecstasy of God in creation, providence, and incarnation.

With Maximus the Confessor (d. 662), contemplation of God follows the Dionysian description of ecstasy as a transformation, the "sabbath of sabbaths." The intellect is "through ecstasy of love clothed entirely in God alone, and through mystical theology is brought altogether to rest in God." With a pure heart one offers the mind to God free of image and form, ready to be imprinted with the archetypes, by which God is manifest (*Commentaries on Theology and the Incarnation* i.39; ii.8).

Thomas Aquinas (1225–1274) distinguishes three degrees of ecstasy: suspension of the external senses alone; suspension of both the external and internal senses; direct contemplation of the divine essence (ST II-II, q. 175, a. 3).

Finally, in the modern era Francis de Sales (1567–1622) introduced a program of spirituality in his *Treatise on the Love of God* (1616), which sees the love of God as simply "standing outside oneself" rather than in terms of visions. To lose oneself in love of neighbor, with Christ as the neighbor, becomes the true measure of finding God. The paradigm for Francis is the soul in such ecstasy, lost in God.

Carmelite spirituality emphasized delightful ecstasy, as well as violent ecstasy, including flight of the spirit and rapture (Teresa of Avila, *Interior Castle,* Sixth Mansions, chap. 5; John of the Cross, *Dark Night of the Soul,* Bk. 2, chap. 1, no. 2).

In contemporary theology Paul Tillich (d. 1965) employs the term *ecstasy* to describe the shock and experience of revelation in Jesus Christ. He describes the "ecstatic manifestation of the Ground of Being in events, persons, and things. Such manifestations have shaking, transforming, and healing power" (*Systematic Theology,* Chicago: Univ. of Chicago Press, 1951–1963, 2:166–167). For Tillich, "technical reason" (or formal reason) reaches its boundary and becomes "ecstatic reason," overpowered, invaded, shaken by the ultimate concern. In this experience the mind transcends the ordinary situation, its subject-object structure, and achieves a new union with God as the Ground of Being.

Among contemporary writers on spirituality, the Cistercian Thomas Merton has articulated compelling images of ecstasy in terms of a kenotic process for the true or inner self in *The Climate of Monastic Prayer* and other works.

See also ABANDONMENT; AFFECT, AFFECTIVITY; DANCE; EXPERIENCE; INTIMACY; KENOSIS; SEXUALITY.

Bibliography: M. de Goedt, J. Kirchmeyer, et al., "Extase (B), mystique chrétienne," *D.Spir.* 4/2, cols. 2072–2171. T. Merton, *The Climate of Monastic Prayer* (Kalamazoo, Mich.: Cistercian Publications, 1968).

GEORGE KILCOURSE

ECUMENISM, SPIRITUAL

The foundation of the modern ecumenical commitment, distinct from the network of joint biblical and historical studies and from theological dialogues, is the rediscovery of shared Christian experiences as well as common prayer for the Spirit's gift of unity to the Church. The 20th-century liturgical and biblical renewal precipitated among ecumenists a search for spiritual ecumenism as a grounds of truth that transcends historic divisions among the Churches. The Second Vatican Council signaled the Roman Catholic Church's entry into this ongoing ecumenical movement, which had been inaugurated with the World Missionary Conference of 1910, by declaring in its Decree on Ecumenism (*Unitatis Redintegratio*): ". . . change of heart and holiness of life, along with public and private prayer for the unity of Christians, should be regarded as the soul of the whole ecumenical movement, and can rightly be called 'spiritual ecumenism' " (UR 8).

A precursor of this concept of spiritual ecumenism was Paul Watson (1863–1940), founder of the (Graymoor) Society of the Atonement, who in 1908 negotiated the corporate conversion of his Anglican community to Roman Catholicism. He simultaneously established the Church Unity Octave of prayer from January 18, the Feast of St. Peter's Chair at Rome, through January 25, the Feast of the Conversion of St. Paul. The intention to promote other Christians' "return to Rome" through observing this octave received papal approval and sponsorship in 1909.

Abbé Paul Couturier (1881–1953) of Lyons, France, emphasized the fundamental significance of spiritual values in ecumenical life, and in 1934 reconceived the instrument of common prayer by decentralizing Watson's Church Unity Octave and devising a more inclusive and open formula for the Week of Prayer for Christian Unity. This offered all divided Christians the occasion for spiritual ecumenism, "that God will grant the visible unity of his kingdom such as Christ wishes and through whatever means he wishes," while guaranteeing fidelity to their respective Churches. Couturier's pioneering ecumenical ministry in Lyons brought together French-speaking Catholics and Reformed Protestants at the Cistercian monastery at Les Dombes, beginning in 1937. Their emphasis on penitent prayer exposed the scandal of divided Churches. The Groupe des Dombes has consistently contributed important studies of specific issues (e.g., reconciliation of ordained ministries, episcopacy, the Holy Spirit) to the wider ecumenical dialogue. Couturier likewise cultivated spiritual ecumenism with Russian Orthodox emigrés who came to France in the 1920s. Yves Congar described Couturier's method as an emphasis on "doxological soil, a climate of prayer and praise," necessary if theology is to bear fruit in dialogue.

During this same period Cardinal Mercier, archbishop of Malines, Belgium, gave classical expression to spiritual ecumenism with his initiative for a series of "conversations" with Anglican Lord Halifax, the goal and process of which he described: "In order to unite with one another, we must love one another; in order to love one another, we must know one another; in order to know one another, we must go and meet one another." Catholicism's first actual ecumenical institute, the Benedictine community at Chevetogne, Belgium (1926), was stimulated by Mercier's ecumenical initiatives for corporate rapprochement. The emphasis on spiritual ecumenism and theological dialogue at Chevetogne has focused on Russian and other Eastern Orthodox Churches.

The foremost international centers of spiritual ecumenism are the Protestant monastic community at Taizé, France, founded in 1940 by Roger Schutz, and the Tantur Institute, near Jerusalem, founded by the University of Notre Dame in 1972 with an emphasis on Jewish-Christian-Islamic encounters to help reconcile the Middle East conflict.

A particularly important affirmation of spiritual ecumenism came with Vatican Council II's Dogmatic Constitution on Divine Revelation, which affirmed the primacy of Scripture in the life of the Church (DV 10). The same dynamics were contributed by Roman Catholic theologians present at the 1963 World Conference on Faith and Order at Montreal, where they influenced its statement on "Scripture, Tradition and Traditions." The ecclesiological shift in the Dogmatic Constitution on the Church from a Church Militant that made exclusive salvation claims for the Roman Catholic Church to a *koinonia* understanding of the Church as the pilgrim people of God, the "Church always in need of being purified" (LG 8), overlapped with the vision of the Decree on Ecumenism and an emphasis on mutual guilt for divisions and on the obligation to restore full communion in a communion of communions (UR 4).

By returning to the foundational doctrines of Trinity, Christology, and Pneumatology, theologians reconceived the ecumenical context for sacraments and spirituality afforded by contemporary Catholic ecclesiology. The mainspring of the ecumenical advance became a spiritual ecumenism focused on the Pauline and Johannine biblical truths of "one Lord, one faith, one baptism; one God and Father of all, who is over all and through all and in all" (Eph 4:5-6); "All of you who were baptized into Christ have clothed yourselves with Christ. There is neither Jew nor Greek, there is neither slave nor free person, there is not male and female; for you are all one in Christ Jesus" (Gal 3:27-28); and Christ's priestly prayer: ". . . may all be one, as you, Father, are in me and I in you, that they also may be in us, that the world may believe that you sent me" (Jn 17:21). A renewed Pneumatology compelled all Christians to recognize that the Spirit given at baptism empowers an organic unity in the life of the Church. Spiritual ecumenism discovers how God's gift of unity, manifest in the transforming Spirit of the risen Christ, has been concealed by historic divisions between Churches.

Problematic issues in spiritual ecumenism are twofold: (1) structural and canonical realities in the separated Churches; and (2) the relationship of theological dialogues, ministry, and apostolic witness to the experiences of Christian spirituality. The genius of spiritual ecumenism has been an emphasis on God's initiative through the Spirit in the restoration of unity. Every reform in the life of the Church must be authentically rooted in an interior renewal of heart and mind. Thus bilateral and multilateral dialogues have come to be appreciated as moving beyond inherited misconceptions and misunderstandings to a convergence and consensus on truths of faith. The doctrinal language that theologians use to articulate these agreements on apostolic faith must be tested by a broader "reception" in the spirituality and experience of the Churches. A compelling example of this process is offered in the U.S. Lutheran-Roman Catholic dialogue's "test case" of agreement on the doctrine of justification by faith in their study of Mary and the saints. Fundamentally different mentalities and spiritualities separated the histories, doctrine, devotions or pieties of the two traditions. Yet the dialogue members have claimed to find no legitimate obstacles to a wider reception of their theological consensus (*The One Mediator, the Saints, and Mary*).

The most neuralgic issue in spiritual ecumenism remains participation in the sacraments. The affirmation of mutual recognition of baptism has dissolved much of the earlier polemics. However, the trajectory from baptism to Eucharist, "the source and summit" of the Church's prayer, raises unique questions. The Second Vatican Council addressed this difficulty in generally forbidding common worship and intercommunion (*communicatio in sacris*), but at the same time admitted that "grace to be obtained sometimes commends it."

The two principles that give rise to this dilemma are a dialectic at the heart of the Eucharist: it is both a sign ("expression") of the unity that exists and a "means" of sharing the grace of unity (UR 8). Canonists have come to recognize that the 1983 Code of Canon Law incorporates the council's ecumenically revolutionary ecclesiology in addressing the rights of baptized Christians and possibilities for "Eucharistic sharing" (can. 844). A particular pastoral manifestation of such spiritual ecumenism is personified by inter-Church families, whose sacramental marriages have been affirmed since Pope Paul VI's motu proprio *Matrimonia Mixta* (1970). Genuine spiritual ecumenism does not shy away from posing difficult pastoral questions by retreating to rigid denominational boundaries and accepting the ecclesial status quo, but conscientiously serves the Churches by identifying underlying issues such as a common baptism and the unfulfilled commitment of the Church to restore a full Eucharistic communion of all the baptized.

Further insights into the meaning of Eucharist have been assessed and developed by the 1982 study *Baptism, Eucharist, and Ministry* of the Faith and Order Commission of the World Council of Churches, which related justice issues and Eucharist in light of the eschatological meaning of Christ's salvific act. Witness to peacemaking, the elimination of racism and sexism, and the gathered assembly's commitment to human dignity are integrated in the spirituality of the Eucharist. The document admitted that many underlying questions about Eucharist involve issues of mutual recognition of ministry and differences about candidates for ordination. The 1983 Assembly of the World Council of Churches in Vancouver, British Columbia, incorporated the insights of the document by an extraordinary manifestation of liturgical prayer and spiritual ecumenism that has brought worldwide expression of spiritual ecumenism to a new plateau.

Resources in official Catholic teaching that enable spiritual ecumenism include the Vatican's 1969 *Directory Concerning Ecumenical Matters,* the second part of which addresses ecumenism in higher education; and the 1975 document *Ecumenical Collaboration at the Regional, National and Local Levels,* which provides a pastoral theology of spiritual ecumenism. A revision of the Vatican's *Ecumenical Directory* has also been undertaken.

In a broader orbit, spiritual ecumenism is sometimes applied to interfaith and interreligious relationships with non-Christians. The Declaration on the Relation of the Church to Non-Christian Religions (*Nostra Aetate*) states that "the Catholic Church rejects nothing which is true and holy in these religions" (NA 2). It goes further to single out the "spiritual patrimony common to Christians and Jews" and expresses the desire "to foster and recommend that mutual understanding and respect" that have flourished in Jewish-Catholic expressions of spiritual ecumenism (NA 4). The Decree on the Church's Missionary Activity (*Ad Gentes*) likewise discourages proselytizing and recommends ecumenical sensitivity in evangelization (AG 15, 36).

See also BODY OF CHRIST; COMMUNITY; HOLY SPIRIT; INTERRELIGIOUS DIALOGUE; PROTESTANT SPIRITUALITIES; VATICAN COUNCIL II.

Bibliography: J. L. G. Balado, *The Story of Taizé* (New York: Seabury, 1981). G. Cashmore and J. Puls, *Clearing the Way: En Route to an Ecumenical Spirituality* (Geneva: WCC, 1990). R. Davies, "The Spirituality of Ecumenism," *Christian Spirituality: Essays in Honour of Gordon Rupp,* ed. P. Brooks (London: SCM, 1975) 307–328. N. Ehrenstrom, *Confessions in Dialogue,* 3rd ed. (Geneva: WCC, 1975). *A Spirituality of Our Times: Report of a Consultation at Annecy, France, December 1984* (Geneva: WCC, 1985). United States Lutheran-Roman Catholic Dialogue, *The One Mediator, the Saints, and Mary* (Washington: USCC, 1990). M. Villain, *Oecumenisme spirituel* (Tournai and Paris: Casterman, 1963). G. Wainwright, "Ecumenical Spirituality," *The Study of Spirituality,* ed. C. Jones, G. Wainwright, E. Yarnold (New York and Oxford: Oxford Univ. Press, 1986) 540–548.

GEORGE KILCOURSE

EMOTION(S)

See FEELINGS; PASSION(S).

EMPOWERMENT

See POWER.

ENDURANCE

See FRUIT(S) OF THE HOLY SPIRIT.

ENGLISH MYSTICAL TRADITION

The English mystical tradition is generally taken to include the works of five mystics whose lives spanned the 14th century: Richard Rolle, Walter Hilton, the anonymous author of *The Cloud of Unknowing,* Julian of Norwich, and Margery Kempe. However, if one views mysticism as being in continuity with the "ordinary" life of grace, then the study of the Middle English mystics needs to be situated within the broader English spiritual tradition.

The Continental roots of English spirituality are found primarily in the Augustinian tradition, especially as developed by Hugh and Richard of St. Victor, and in the Benedictine tradition, particularly as transmitted by the 12th-century Cistercians, notably Bernard of Clairvaux and William of St. Thierry. It was less strongly influenced by Franciscan and Dominican spirituality. Efforts to trace some direct influence of Rheno-Flemish mysticism on the Middle English mystics have been unsuccessful. Any similarities between the two are probably due to common sources, especially to some contact with Pseudo-Dionysian thought, either through Dominican or Victorine interpretation (predominantly the latter in the case of the English mystics). In addition, Julian of Norwich and Margery Kempe have affinities with Continental women visionaries.

Continental influences were modified by native forces, producing a brand of spirituality that can be described as typically English, with the following characteristics: an appreciation for Scripture and *lectio divina* as the foundation for contemplation; a tender devotion to the humanity of Christ; a consistent harmony and balance between the affective and the speculative; a preference for the concrete over the abstract; an emphasis upon practicality; moderation in ascetical practices; a strong tradition of the solitary life, complemented by loyalty to the institutional Church; and a concern for doctrinal orthodoxy. All these characteristics have individual parallels in Continental spirituality, but there is a consistency of their combination in English spiritual figures that is somewhat distinctive.

These characteristics formed the heritage from which the Middle English mystics drew inspiration. The Venerable Bede and Anselm of Canterbury both represent the affective-speculative synthesis typical of English religious writing. Anselm's prayers and meditations, written in a language restrained yet full of ardor, are early examples of that devotion to the passion of Christ and to the Virgin that would become so celebrated in later English lyrics. Aelred of Rievaulx's *De Institutione Inclusarum* (ca. 1150) and the *Ancrene Riwle* (ca. 1200) give testimony to the English preference for the solitary life, as do the *Lives* of such solitaries as Godric of Finchale (d. 1170) and Christina of Markyate (ca. 1096–1160).

The *Ancrene Riwle,* written for three sisters aspiring to be anchorites, is considered the most influential early ascetical work in the English language. It is not a work of mysticism as such, but a practical guide for the ascetical practices prerequisite to contemplation. There is little original in the subject matter, which reveals the author's thorough knowledge of Augustine, Cassian, Gregory, Bernard, and the Victorines. The author's creativity lies rather in the ability to organize material into a coherent whole, with a delightful gift for concrete, homely illustration. The *Riwle* exhibits an exquisite sense of proportion between essentials and nonessentials.

The *Riwle* actually proposes two rules: one external (found in Parts 1 and 8), regulating the daily life and prayer of the anchorites, and the other internal (Parts 2 through 7), providing guidelines for custody of the senses, resistance to temptation, sacramental confession, and penitential and devotional practices designed to produce that purity of heart necessary for contemplation. The first rule is changeable and exists only insofar as it enables the practice of the second; the author warns against undue emphasis upon regular observance as an end in itself, giving witness to that individuality and preference for the solitary life characteristic of English spirituality. The devotions to the humanity and passion of Christ exhibit the same restrained ardor found in Anselm. The *Ancrene Riwle* circulated widely, in Latin and French translation as well as in the original English, and was likely known by all the Middle English mystics. It thus forms a valuable link between Continental and earlier English spirituality and the English mystical tradition.

The fact that the *Ancrene Riwle* was written in English indicates an effort to make instructional aids for contemplation available to all those desirous of living the contemplative life, an audience that included the relatively uneducated laity as well as traditional religious persons. This effort was shared by the Middle English mystics without exception. However, the frequent assessment of the English mystics as anti-intellectual is surely mistaken. Although Rolle criticized the empty speculation of certain theologians, he himself was trained in Latin and was something of a Scripture scholar, and his works reveal the influence of Western theology. Hilton, Julian, and the author of *The Cloud* all show a respect for theological learning, although they would surely caution against its becoming an end in itself. And while Margery Kempe was illiterate, she was avid for learning, seeking out famous preachers to hear and scholars to read to her.

Beyond the fact that the Middle English mystics wrote in English and shared a common time, heritage, and, for the most part, characteristics typical of the English spiritual tradition, there is little to link them into a definable "school" of mysticism. Each is unique in comparison to the others.

Richard Rolle (ca. 1300–1349)

Richard Rolle was born at Thornton in northern Yorkshire and studied at Oxford until his nineteenth year, when he left abruptly, without a degree, to become a hermit. He lived for a time on the estate and under the patronage of John Dalton, but thereafter wandered from place to place, always engaged in a life of prayer, writing, and spiritual guidance. His last years were spent near a Cistercian convent at Hampole, where he died, possibly a victim of the plague, in 1349. He was venerated for his holiness both during and after his life; soon after his death, miracles were reported to have occurred near his grave, and his cause was advanced for canonization, though without result. A cult of devotion to him flourished well into the 16th century.

Rolle was the most prolific of the English mystics, writing prose and poetry in both Latin and English. *The Canticum Amoris,* a Latin alliterative poem to the Virgin, and *Judica Me Deus,* a transliteration of a pas-

toral manual by William of Pagula, are his earliest works. His last work was probably *The Form of Living,* a guide for the life of an anchorite, written in English and addressed to Margaret Kirkby, who was enclosed as a recluse in the autumn of 1348, a year before Rolle's death. Beyond this the chronology of his works is difficult to establish.

Rolle's writings can be divided into four categories: commentaries, treatises, letters, and lyrics. He wrote partial commentaries in Latin on Job, the Song of Songs, the Lamentations of Jeremiah, and the Book of Revelation, but concentrated his scriptural interpretation on the psalms. He wrote a commentary on the entire Psalter in Latin, as well as a separate treatise on Psalm 20. Believing that those who prayed the psalms often and fervently would eventually be lifted up to contemplation, Rolle thought it important that the Psalter be accessible to those with no knowledge of Latin. Thus he also translated the Psalter into English, to which he added a commentary, completely separate from his own Latin one. In his commentaries Rolle emphasizes the tropological sense of medieval exegesis, interpreting the meaning of the psalms in terms of the human relationship to God, including mystical experience.

Related to the commentaries are the two English *Meditations on the Passion,* a short and long version (Rolle's authorship of these, particularly the long version, has been doubted by some scholars). The details of these are drawn from all four Gospels, and their aim is to provide a graphic picture of the tortures meted out to the suffering Christ in order to awaken compassion and sorrow for sin and to reveal the love of the Savior for sinners. They seem morbid to modern ears but are very much in the tradition of affective piety common to medieval devotional writings.

Rolle's three treatises are *Contra Amatores Mundi (Against the Lovers of the World), Incendium Amoris (The Fire of Love),* and *Melos Amoris (The Song of*

Love). His dependence upon Scripture continues to be evident in these works, which are full of biblical quotations and allusions. The *Incendium Amoris,* written in a highly elaborate, alliterative style of Latin poetry and translated into English early in the 15th century, is perhaps his best known work. In it he describes contemplative union with God in terms of the biblical image of the eschatological banquet, a mystical union accompanied by heavenly music and all that is delightful to touch and taste. The way to this union is the road to the heavenly Jerusalem, and the whole process of spiritual growth along the way is imaged as a homecoming. After certain preliminary penitential practices made possible by the solitary life, each of the stages along the way is represented by a dominant image: the opening of the heavenly door represents the growing awareness of, and longing for, heavenly things; next comes the experience of heat generated by the fire of love, which intensifies the desire for God and burns away all that interferes with it; eventually this experience is accompanied by an incredible sweetness, like honey to the taste, a spiritual delight resembling inebriation; and finally the experience of jubilant song whereby one is in communion with the angels, continually praising God with them. This description of the mystic way is based on Rolle's own experiences in prayer and bears a general resemblance to the classic purgative, illuminative, and unitive phases of the mystic life. There has been a tendency among Rolle's interpreters to understand heat, sweetness, and song as physical experiences, a reading that has won him much negative criticism from his own day onward (both the author of *The Cloud* and Hilton warn against seeking such experiences). However, although some of Rolle's own remarks are ambiguous, it is likely that he intended such descriptions as metaphors for the spiritual senses experienced in mystical prayer. As such, they are no different from the attempts of other mystics to put into words the ineffable experience of union with God.

Rolle's letters are practical spiritual guides for the contemplative life, written for particular individuals. Probably the products of his later life, they are generally more restrained than the treatises, and, as such, more in continuity with the English spiritual tradition. The *Emendatio Vitae* is the only one written in Latin, but it was translated into English by Richard Misyn early in the 15th century and had a wide circulation. The other three, written in English for women desiring instruction in contemplation, are *Ego Dormio, The Commandment,* and *The Form of Living.* These works describe the mystical life in terms of three stages of love, using analogies between human sexual passion and love for Christ, in obvious dependence upon Richard of St. Victor's *Four Steps of Passionate Love,* although Rolle consistently ignored the last of Richard's phases.

Rolle wrote numerous lyrics in both Latin and English, some of which were inserted into his prose works, either as spontaneous outpourings of love for Christ or as sample prayers for those he was instructing. Some of his lyrics have been criticized as unpoetic because they bypass traditional verse styles, but Rolle may have been aiming deliberately at an informal style in order to capture the spontaneity of actual prayer. Others have considered his lyrics, especially those in English addressed to the Crucified, as possessing an artless devotion unparalleled in medieval English poetry.

Rolle has been criticized by modern critics for self-absorption, defensiveness, misogyny, anticlericalism, and lack of depth, but these criticisms need to be balanced by a respect for his unworldliness, his integrity, and his tender concern for those he directed spiritually, especially women. He has often been compared unfavorably with Hilton and the author of *The Cloud.* It is true that he exhibits less of the restraint and intellectual balance characteristic of the English tradition, particularly in his earlier works. He probably owes more to Franciscan influences than the other English mystics do; his emphasis upon song, joy, poverty, detachment from worldly learning, and his affective piety, particularly to Christ's passion and the Holy Name, are reminiscent of Franciscan spirituality. He was above all a poet, a fact that sets him apart from the other English mystics, and might suggest the injustice of comparing him unfavorably with them.

The Author of *The Cloud of Unknowing* (fl. 1380s)

The English mystic who presents the greatest contrast in temperament and outlook to Richard Rolle is the author of *The Cloud of Unknowing.* Beyond the fact that he was a priest, possibly a Carthusian, from the East Midlands, a skilled theologian and a wise spiritual director, we know nothing of his identity. *The Cloud,* his most famous work, was written about 1380 and is addressed to a young man beginning the religious or eremitical life, although it was obviously expected to have wider circulation. The author is also credited with three other original works: *A Letter on Prayer* and *The Book of Privy Counselling,* both written for the same addressee as *The Cloud, The Assessment of Inward Stirrings,* a short account on discernment; and three translations: *The Discernment of Spirits* (from two sermons of Bernard of Clairvaux), *The Pursuit of Wisdom* (a summary of Richard of St. Victor's *Benjamin Minor*), and *Denis's Hidden Theology* (based on Thomas Gallus's Latin translation of the *Mystical Theology* of Pseudo-Dionysius).

Although the author of *The Cloud* is concerned solely with the highest levels of contemplation, his descriptions of the way to reach such heights are simple, clear, and direct. Although he urges the strictest abstraction from thoughts and images, he does so by the use of practical, concrete imagery. As a result, his prose style possesses a vigor and freshness unmatched by the

other English mystics, which probably accounts for *The Cloud*'s enduring appeal. Even while the author emphasizes the rarity and esoteric nature of contemplative union with God, his concrete descriptions make it sound like an attainable experience for those who feel called to leave discursive meditation behind.

While the author of *The Cloud* restricts himself to the explication of apophatic contemplation (the negative way), it would be a mistake to read this as a rejection of the more affirmative Western tradition of spirituality and theology, in which he is thoroughly grounded. He is also strongly biblical; scriptural allusions, particularly to the Pauline corpus, permeate his writings. He presupposes in his addressee a broad background in the tradition of *lectio divina,* a variation of which he proposes as proximate preparation for the graces of apophatic contemplation. He expects that meditation on the sufferings of Christ have led his directee into the experience of compunction, that sorrow for sin accompanied by a strong desire for God that is the necessary foundation for entrance into the "cloud of unknowing." He assumes that participation in the sacramental life of the Church and the practice of Christian virtue are mainstays of his directee's spirituality. Finally, although he advises leaving all creatures behind under a "cloud of forgetting," this pertains to the time of contemplation only, and in no way implies a disregard for them as such.

The dominant imagery of *The Cloud of Unknowing* is drawn from the Dionysian exegesis of Moses' ascent of Mount Sinai in the Book of Exodus, interpreted as the progressive purification from sin and from attachment to all that is not God. Only in the thick cloud at the summit of the mountain, when Moses could see nothing, does God speak. So the aspirant to contemplative union with God sheds an attraction to everything other than God—first sinfulness, then sensual experience, and finally even all mental images or thoughts—until the limits of the human mind are reached. There one must be willing to plunge into darkness in order to encounter God.

Since the intellect is useless at this point, the desire of the will takes over and simply yearns for God. This impulse of love that "beats" upon the cloud of unknowing is described as "naked," that is, stripped of attachment to anything other than God, and "blind," since the activities of the senses, imagination, and reason are stilled. The seeker after God must persevere in this darkness with a single-hearted purpose and not be distracted from it by any attention to thoughts, however holy they might seem. Such perseverance is difficult, and the bulk of *The Cloud* is concerned with practical suggestions about how to resist various kinds of distractions.

As an aid to concentrating the naked intent of the will upon the darkness of God, all creatures, images, and thoughts must be placed firmly under a "cloud of forgetting." When concentration begins to flag, the author counsels, one should constantly repeat a word such as "love" or "God," which acts as a weapon, striking down everything beneath the cloud of forgetting and beating upon the cloud of unknowing. Just as shouting the word "fire" will bring aid in such an emergency, so the repetition of this single word will call down God's grace to help keep one's concentration steady. One must be wary of trying to deal with distractions by one's own effort alone, but rather should take strength from Jesus who endured the cross.

The distractions most likely to pull one away from perseverance are reminders of past sins and temptations to fresh sins. These can engender discouragement over one's weakness, which needs to be distinguished from perfect humility. Awareness of sinfulness is a necessary preliminary to contemplative prayer, but once one is engaged in that prayer, it can be a hindrance to further progress. The true humility of the contemplative means total self-forgetfulness, even of one's sin, for the love of God. It flows from a consciousness of God's majesty rather than from any awareness of self or fear of unworthiness.

If one perseveres in the naked loving intent upon the darkness of God, the author of *The Cloud* is confident that one will experience union with God. While he consistently describes this as a union of wills, in one place he intimates that the intellect may also be graced as a result: God may choose to "send out a ray of spiritual light . . . and . . . show you some of his secrets." However, unlike Rolle, who describes the experiences of mystical prayer with a plethora of images, the author of *The Cloud* is reticent about the effects of mystical union. Aware of the tendency of young contemplatives to become euphoric about such experiences, he constantly warns against seeking them for their own sake.

Walter Hilton (d. 1396)

We know nothing about Walter Hilton beyond the fact that in later life he was an Augustinian canon at Thurgarton Priory in Nottinghamshire, where he died in 1396. Several manuscripts give him the title "master," indicating the possession of a university degree, possibly in canon law, and theological learning is evident in his works.

Hilton's masterpiece is *The Scale of Perfection,* regarded by many as the most complete and balanced treatment of the interior life produced in the Middle Ages. The number of extant manuscripts attests to its popularity: more than forty exist for Book I, and at least twenty-four for Book II; five printed editions were produced by the end of the 16th century. Hilton charts the entire spiritual journey, including the beginning phases of the contemplative life ignored by the author of *The Cloud;* thus his book was meant to have wider appeal. *The Scale* was composed as two separate treatises. Book I, written for an anchorite, is extant in two editions, the second placing added stress on Christological meditation as an integral part of contemplative prayer. Book II traces the continuity of the life of grace from baptism to mystical union.

In Book I, Hilton describes contemplative union with God as the result of a gradual progress along a scale of spiritual experiences. Prerequisite to contemplation are the virtues of humility and faith and the desire to please God in all things. The first degree of contemplation involves the intellectual knowledge of God attained by the study of Scripture and Church teaching. The second degree produces a growth in the love of God, manifested more in feeling than in intellect. Among those absorbed by worldly interests, such experiences of love will be fleeting, but for those dedicated to the regular practice of contemplative prayer, they will be long-lasting, eventually issuing into the third degree of contemplation. Here the intellect will see God, and the emotions will burn with love for God in ecstatic union.

The goal of Christian spirituality is to become conformed to Christ, and Hilton draws upon the *imago Dei* tradition to describe this process. Originally made in Christ's image, humanity lost that likeness through sin, but the grace to regain it has been provided by Christ's redemptive act. By meditating upon Christ's humanity, one becomes aware of the loss of the divine image and conscious of the dark image of sin that has replaced it in the soul. Hilton inserts a long treatment of the seven deadly sins with their effects and suggests concrete ways by which they may be rooted out and replaced by virtue, notably the virtues of humility and charity. As a result of this effort aided by grace, one will see the image of Christ gradually re-formed in one's soul.

Book II further refines the notion of the re-formation of the image of Christ in the soul. Hilton bases his treatment upon Paul's description of the Christian life in Rom 8:30: "Those [God] predestined he also called; and those he called he also justified; and those he justified he also glorified." Hilton adapts this pattern into four stages of spiritual progress. One first experiences a call from a life of absorption in earthly vanities into the desire for the things of God. Justification takes place when one begins to reject sin and advance in the exercise of Christian virtue, a process aided by penitential practices designed to free one from earthly attractions. This is the stage of the "reform in faith" of Christ's image in the soul and is the life necessary for salvation that all the baptized are expected to live. The third stage is "exaltation," Paul's glorification experienced on earth. It consists in the partial "reform in feeling" of Christ's image in the soul and is experienced only by those who dedicate themselves to contemplation. It differs from reform in faith by the fact that the desire for God is intensified to such an extent that the very inclination to sin begins to disappear and one lives only for the love of God. The fourth stage is that glorification attained only by the blessed in heaven, the full "reform in feeling" of Christ's image in the soul when one is eternally united to God. These last two stages indicate that Hilton, like many spiritual writers before him, understood the life of contemplation as the foretaste here on earth of the life of heaven. While there are scattered places in *The Scale* where Hilton describes a kind of apophatic experience of union reminiscent of *The Cloud,* he is less dedicated to Dionysian spirituality than the author of *The Cloud.*

Hilton also wrote several minor works. *The Song of Angels* is a description of the experience of mystical union with a criticism of the kind of demonstrative affectivity characteristic of Rolle. He authored three short scriptural commentaries: *Qui Habitat* on Psalm 90, *Bonum Est* on Psalm 91, *Benedictus* on Zachary's canticle in Lk 1:68-79, and two English translations of Latin works: *Eight Chapters on Perfection,* a short guide outlining the stages of the spiritual journey; and *The Goad of Love,* based on James of Milan's *Stimulus Amoris* but containing much original interpolation. He also wrote several Latin letters to people considering entrance into the religious life. His English letter *The Mixed Life* was written for a man of high social status with important responsibilities who was desirous of leading the contemplative life. It proposes a way of life in which prayer is combined with activity in the world. Hilton suggests that, following the example of Jesus, who was both active and contemplative, one can learn to regard secular duties as a help rather than a hindrance to prayerful union with God, provided they are performed with the desire to please God in all things. This letter enforces the opinion Hilton advanced in *The Scale* that the possibility of reaching the heights of contemplation is not reserved to a select few but is open to all who live the Christian life of grace.

Julian of Norwich (1342–after 1413)

Unlike the mystics considered so far, Julian of Norwich was a visionary—a fact that places her in continuity with the women visionaries who flourished on the Continent during the 13th and 14th centuries. She shares with them the kind of devotion to Christ's passion that inspired her to pray for a vision of the Crucified so as to grow in compassion for him, and to long for a mortal sickness so as to experience the pains of Christ's last agony. Beyond this, however, Julian has little in common with the kind of ecstatic, often erotic mystical experience typical of the Continental visionaries.

In May 1373 Julian fell ill to the point of death. In the course of her illness she received a vision of the Crucified along with sixteen revelations about the love of God for humanity. She recovered and recorded her experience in what has come to be called the Short Text of *Showings,* and twenty years later in a greatly expanded Long Text. At some point she was enclosed as an anchorite in a cell attached to St. Julian's Church at Norwich, where she was still living in 1413. Beyond this we know nothing of her life. Recognized as the first woman writer in the English language, Julian exhibits a degree of learning unusual for women in her day.

Julian's *Showings* is neither a book of spiritual guidance nor a strictly devotional work. The Short Text simply records her visions and revelations and their effect upon her, but the revelations themselves are pregnant with theological meaning. In the twenty years between writing the two texts, through a continual process of prayer and reflection, Julian gradually drew out the implications of the theological seeds present in her revelations. As a result, the Long Text can be considered a work of doctrinal theology in which Julian gives creative expression to all the main areas of Christian doctrine in a way that emphasizes their inner coherence. She thus bears witness to the fact that the experience of contemplation can issue into doctrinal teaching.

Like the other English mystics, Julian was schooled in the *lectio divina* method of Scripture study. Although she rarely quotes Scripture directly, biblical allusions permeate her writing. In the Short Text the foundational symbol of Julian's theology is the crucified Jesus, whose sufferings are described graphically but with more of the restraint characteristic of English spirituality than is found in Rolle's *Meditations.* However, this primary symbol became further elaborated into the Parable of the Lord and the Servant, central to the Long Text. This is the simple story, based upon feudal imagery, of a lord who sent his loyal servant on a mission. Though the servant was eager to obey the lord's will, he fell into a ravine and was powerless to do so. Nonetheless, the lord continued to look upon the servant with love, even though the servant did not realize this and suffered because of his failure. Julian originally understood the parable as an allegory for the Fall, but further reflection revealed that the servant symbolized both Adam and Christ. She gradually understood the parable as an elaborate conflation of many scriptural images, encompassing the whole story of salvation from humanity's creation into the as yet unfulfilled future.

The parable enabled Julian to accept two aspects of her revelations that seemed contrary to Church teaching: the fact that God looks upon humans only with love, even in their sin, and the fact that "all will be well," a promise that hinted at universal salvation. From God's eternal perspective, the fall of Adam is never viewed apart from Christ's fall into humanity in the incarnation, and the whole history of human sin is already overcome by the redemption. Therefore, while God looks upon humans with compassion because sin makes them suffer, God's predominant attitude is joy over the glory to which the atonement has brought all humankind. Julian can thus develop the notion of sin as that "happy fault" in which humans can paradoxically rejoice because of the love of God manifested in the redemption.

Furthermore, since all who will be saved are eternally one with Christ, there is no reason to fear damnation. Julian eventually reconciled the message of her revelations with the teaching of the Church, chiefly by realizing that God is fundamentally incomprehensible and has plans for humanity's future hidden even from the Church's teaching authority. Church teaching about the damnation of sinners serves a useful purpose for human spiritual progress here on earth; without it we would trivialize sin and fall into presumption. But this need not prevent us from trusting that God's love and will for humanity can bring about the salvation even of those considered damned by the Church. These conclusions reveal a sophistication more consistent with contemporary theology than with the prevailing views of the Middle Ages. Nonetheless, they were appropriate words of comfort directed against the fear of eternal punishment that gripped the general populace of Europe toward the end of the 14th century, due in part to the devastation caused by the Black Death.

Though meditation upon Christ was the starting point of Julian's theological reflections, her theology can best be described as Trinitarian. At the beginning of her visions she sees a "little thing" the size of a hazelnut lying in the palm of her hand, representing all that is. In relation to it God is maker, keeper, and lover. In the Long Text, Julian expands this thought into a full-fledged doctrine of the economic Trinity. We receive our being from the operation of God as maker (the work of nature), our increase or re-creation from the operation of God as keeper (the work of mercy), and our fulfillment from the operation of God as lover (the work of grace). Julian then provides titles to describe God's relationship to us through the operations of nature, mercy, and grace. The fatherhood of God is responsible for the work of nature, the motherhood of God provides for our profit and increase, and the lordship of God rewards us, fulfilling and surpassing all that we deserve as creatures. Consistent with classical Trinitarian doctrine, Julian realizes that though it is fitting to appropriate a particular work to each Person, the one and triune God is actually responsible for each of God's works in time. Therefore, the names Father, Mother, Lord properly refer to God's unity of essence, not to the particularity of Persons. This is especially significant for Julian's reference to God as Mother, an image beautifully developed in chapters 59–63 of the Long Text. Many medieval devotional works employed the image of mother as an incidental metaphor to describe Christ's redemptive action toward us, but none took it as seriously as Julian did as a way of describing God's essence.

Julian was influenced by the Augustinian notion that the human soul is made in the image of the Trinity. In the might, wisdom, and love of our own soul, we image God's might, wisdom, and love. However, instead of stressing the natural faculties of the soul as imaging God's Trinitarian essence, Julian describes human likeness to the triune God in terms of God's actions toward humanity in history. We are like God in our nature, but we are meant to become more like God in our re-creation through God's mercy, a work that eventually reaches fulfillment in the triumph of the work of grace. The progress of each individual's life in time mirrors the way God has acted in history through creation, incarnation, and sending of the Spirit.

This Trinitarian focus provides the framework for Julian's description of the spiritual life. God's work of nature makes us aware that we are God's creatures, grounded in a desire for God that is fundamental to the human will. But sin has obscured this, making us blind to that will and too weak to follow its lead. God's work of mercy is twofold: it repairs the damage done by sin, and it enables us to increase in likeness to Christ, the perfect image of God, by meditating upon his life and imitating his example, especially through patience in suffering, humility, and charity. Finally, this leads into contemplative prayer, in which we experience the Spirit's work of grace, receiving the gifts of peace, joy, and love as a foretaste of heavenly bliss.

Margery Kempe (ca. 1373–ca. 1440)

We know more about the life of Margery Kempe than we do about that of any of the other English mystics, because her *Book,* discovered at the home of William Butler-Bowdon in 1934, is an autobiography, the first of that genre in the English language. Though Margery herself was illiterate and her *Book* was dictated to two scribes, she is considered its legitimate author. Her forceful, exuberant personality dominates its pages.

Margery was born in King's Lynn, Norfolk, in 1373, the daughter of a respected citizen, John Brunham, five times mayor of the city. At the age of twenty she married John Kempe, a local burgess, with whom she had fourteen children. After the birth of her first child, she was afflicted by a mental illness from which she was cured by a vision of Christ. After a brief period marked by attachment to material things and several failed business ventures, Margery experienced a mystical conversion that changed her life. She adopted strict habits of prayer and fasting, which drew the hostility of her neighbors, but she found solace in frequent visions of Christ and Mary, who affirmed her intentions and longings. The record of her visions is vividly recounted throughout her *Book* with a charming attention to detail. Always anxious about her spiritual life, Margery habitually consulted well-known spiritual guides, among them Julian of Norwich. She was always on the go, traveling to churches to hear gifted preachers and to the famous shrines of England. After twenty years of marriage, Margery finally won from her husband her long-cherished desire for celibacy, after which they separated, although Margery returned to nurse him through his final illness.

In 1413 Margery, released from her marital duties, made her first pilgrimage overseas, to the Holy Land, where she received the gift of tears, which was to remain with her thereafter. She wept and wailed aloud uncontrollably whenever she encountered a reminder of Christ's passion. Such outbursts incurred the resentment of her fellow travelers, and Margery experienced much misunderstanding and mistreatment as a result. She also traveled on pilgrimage to Rome, Assisi, St. James of Compostela in Spain, Danzig, Wilsnack, and Aachen. Such pilgrimages, filled with seemingly insurmountable difficulties eventually overcome with God's help, are graphically symbolic of Margery's own journey through life. Her behavior was highly unorthodox for a 14th-century wife and mother. She pursued aspirations that did not fit into the narrow confines of her social role, suffering abuse from those who misunderstood her motives and actions. She was several times arrested, imprisoned, and examined for heresy, but was never convicted.

The record of her trials in her *Book* reveals her mettle; her apt retorts to her accusers put them firmly in their place, and Margery always emerged the victor.

Unlike Julian, Margery has a great deal in common with the Continental visionaries. Like them, she practiced rigid bodily penance, accompanied by self-loathing and a desire for humiliation. Like them, she received premonitions about the future salvation of others and had frequent visitations from Christ and Mary, as well as from several saints, which she described in vivid detail. She also experienced visions in which she imaginatively participated in the events of the life of Christ and Mary, especially those surrounding Christ's birth and passion (her record of these is full of delightfully homey details). Margery also possessed a compassionate and apostolic zeal for the physical and spiritual well-being of others. The correspondence between her life and that of the Continental visionaries could well have been conscious imitation, for Margery tells us she was familiar with the *Revelations* of St. Bridget of Sweden. She was probably also familiar with Jacques de Vitry's *Life* of Marie d'Oignies, since her scribe mentions it in reference to Margery's gift of tears. Both Bridget and Marie were married women who struggled to carve out a life of celibacy and contemplation for themselves against the accepted norms of society. Bridget bore eight children before her husband's death freed her for the pursuit of the mystical life. And Marie wept copiously at the thought of Christ's passion, encountering misunderstanding and rejection as a result.

Except for the author of *The Cloud,* with whom she has little in common, Margery was familiar with the English mystics; she mentions "Hilton's book" and she visited Julian. However, she is more like Rolle than the others. The *Incendium Amoris* is cited as one of the works known by her, and she records experiences of heat and song similar to those described there. Also, several passages in her account of Christ's passion repeat details found in Rolle's *Meditations.* Like Rolle, Margery has been the target of much negative criticism. Compared unfavorably with Julian, she has been accused of hypocrisy, self-delusion, self-aggrandizement, and hysteria. But Margery deserves to be appreciated on her own merits. She has provided an intimate picture of the inner life of a 15th-century woman who fought for the chance to practice her religious vocation in the face of tremendous odds. While she may never have reached the heights of the contemplative life as propounded in *The Cloud,* Margery has shared with us an account, unparalleled for its candor, simplicity, and attention to detail, of that tender devotion to the humanity of Christ that was the heart and soul of all medieval spirituality, including that of the other English mystics.

See also AFFIRMATIVE WAY; ASCETICISM; AUGUSTINIAN SPIRITUALITY; BENEDICTINE SPIRITUALITY; CISTERCIAN SPIRITUALITY; COMPUNCTION; CONTEMPLATION, CONTEMPLATIVE PRAYER; DESIRE; EREMITICAL LIFE; FRANCISCAN SPIRITUALITY; IMAGO DEI; LECTIO DIVINA; MEDITATION; MYSTICISM; NEGATIVE WAY; RHENO-FLEMISH SPIRITUALITY; TEARS, GIFT OF; WESTERN MEDIEVAL SPIRITUALITY.

Bibliography: *The Ancrene Riwle,* trans. M. Salu (Notre Dame: Univ. Press, 1955). Richard Rolle, *The Fire of Love,* trans. and ed. C. Wolters (Harmondsworth: Penguin, 1972). Richard Rolle, *The English Writings,* trans. and ed. R. Allen (New York: Paulist, 1988). *The Cloud of Unknowing,* trans. and ed. J. Walsh (New York: Paulist, 1981). *The Pursuit of Wisdom and Other Works by the Author of the Cloud of Unknowing,* trans. and ed. J. Walsh (New York: Paulist, 1988). Walter Hilton, *The Stairway of Perfection,* trans. and ed. M. L. del Mastro (Garden City, N.Y.: Doubleday, 1979). Julian of Norwich, *Showings,* trans. and ed. E. Colledge and J. Walsh (New York: Paulist, 1978). Margery Kempe, *The Book of Margery Kempe,* trans. B. Windeatt (Harmondsworth: Penguin, 1985).

JOAN M. NUTH

ENLIGHTENMENT

See ILLUMINATION, ILLUMINATIVE WAY; LIGHT.

ENLIGHTENMENT, INFLUENCE ON SPIRITUALITY

The Enlightenment, a mid-17th to late-18th century intellectual movement with roots in France, Germany, and Britain, produced tremendous hostility to religion, Christianity in particular. Indeed, "it would be false to tax the Enlightenment with indifference to religion. It would be more discerning to say that it was obsessed with it" (Buckley, p. 37).

Many Enlightenment thinkers were deists, and a number moved beyond that position to a staunch philosophical atheism. The Enlightenment was "ecumenical" in that it crossed confessional boundaries: Kant, Hume, and Leibniz were Protestants. On the other hand, there was a major contribution to Enlightenment thought from Catholic France, where the Enlightenment was in part a reaction against the cultural and religious hegemony of the Catholic Church. Voltaire, Diderot, and Rousseau could only have come from a Catholic culture. In the United States, Paine, Franklin, and Jefferson were deists in the mainstream of Enlightenment thought.

The influence of Enlightenment thought upon spirituality cannot be understood apart from the intellectual foundations of the Enlightenment movement in the newer scientific methodologies represented by Newton and also in bourgeois social and political movements. A faith in critical reason, in individual autonomy, and in various forms of materialism, evinced in much Enlightenment thinking, gave rise to rationalistic forms of religion, scientific theologies, theories of natural religion, a critical approach to the textual traditions of Judaism and Christianity, and to a suspicion and mockery of established religions, especially among the French *philosophes* and *encyclopédistes.* For Kant, *Aufklärung* was emancipation from spiritual tutelage to religious authorities and their political and social allies so that people would dare to think for themselves (*sapere aude!*). Freethinking became institutionalized in such secret societies as the Freemasons, Rosicrucians, and Illuminati.

If the great range of Enlightenment influence upon spirituality can be treated with broad strokes, it can be said that nonatheistic Enlightenment thought supported and led to the development of spiritualities that stressed either providential deism or purely ethical religion. Providence was seen as a concomitant of natural theology, which finds the evidences for the attributes and being of God in the order of creation rather than in revelation. In Newton's *Optiks,* the principal theological attribute of God is domination (*dominatio*), whereby God, the provident governor of the universe, forms matter and associates it according to mechanical laws that are rationally determinable. The order in nature is imposed "in the first Creation by the Counsel of an intelligent Agent" (Buckley, p. 143).

This Newtonian theism was assimilated by Enlightenment-era theologians eager to meet atheists on their own materialist grounds, and there emerged deistic theologies, nominally Christian, which found warrants for God in nature alone. Alongside such deistic theologies there sometimes flourished an ossified scholasticism or, at the other extreme, a critical skepticism. Such theologies led either to an abstracted piety typical of deism, unitarianism, and Socinianism, or to profound religious reactions that stressed the personal experience of God, notably in the development of popular Catholic devotions to Jesus and Mary.

Where supernatural revelation had ceased to claim authority, an ethical religion emerged that encouraged a "spirituality" of piety and good works realized in the civic commonweal. Kant's ethical imperative and moral warrant for the existence of God constitute the most theoretical exposition of this position. But it was also behind Reimarus's portrait of Jesus as a deluded fanatic who had been given cosmetic treatment in the Gospels. Rescued from the corruptions of Christianity, Jesus was restored to his true role—that of a great ethical teacher. In the words of Paine, he "was a virtuous and amiable man," and according to Jefferson, he presented moral precepts that "would be the most perfect and sublime that have ever been taught by man" (Buckley, p. 40). Jesus, understood as the Logos incarnate and giver of grace, was part of the religious tutelage from which Enlightenment thought had freed itself. Ethical portraits of Jesus were not so common in Catholic thought, but a stress on the humanity of Jesus was increasingly evident in popular devotions.

Enlightenment accents upon deistic providence and ethical religion were evident in popular preaching and also in efforts, especially in France and Germany, to strip Catholic churches of the trappings of medieval religion. Vernacular was introduced into the liturgy, pious devotions were curtailed, the churches themselves were simplified. In these outward respects the Enlightenment resembled a Catholic version of the Reformation, with the attendant disorientation and proliferation of spiritualities. The medieval spiritual roots of Europe were upended. "Unbelievers and believers alike had lost the key to the symbolic language of medieval Christendom" (Gay, p. 352).

Not all of Europe was ablaze with the spirit of the Enlightenment, and reactions were varied and deep, as reflected in popular spirituality. Late 17th-century Catholic France saw the rise of Jansenism, an austere form of Augustinianism, but also of spiritualities emphasizing indifference to the will of God (e.g., Fénelon and de Caussade, the latter attempting to chart a delicate course between rationalism and quietism, or Molinism). Later, in the wake of assaults against the Blessed Sacrament, especially during the French Revolution, renewed devotion to the Eucharist became widespread, as well as attachment to the human person of Jesus, as exemplified in the Sacred Heart devotion. After the suppression of the Society of Jesus in 1773, older religious orders were reformed and new orders were founded, many of them dedicated to the corporal works of mercy. Retreat movements, lay organizations, and sodalities proliferated.

There were correlative effects on Protestant spirituality. In Germany, Pietism, an anti-intellectual religious movement especially popular among the poor, women, and marginalized, arose in opposition to rationalist forms of religion that downplayed spiritual experience and the humanity of Jesus. In England, John Wesley's Methodism movement viewed with suspicion Anglican accommodations to deism. Both Pietism and Methodism stressed spiritualities of simple prayer, fellowship, and enthusiasm. In America, the Great Awakening was partly a reaction to Enlightenment rationalism. These, and other spiritualities like them, would not have developed, and cannot be understood apart from, the spiritual conditions set by the Enlightenment itself.

See also ENTHUSIASM; HISTORY, HISTORICAL CONSCIOUSNESS; JANSENISM; MODERN SPIRITUALITY; QUIETISM; SECULARISM; SPIRITUALITY, CHRISTIAN (CATHOLIC), HISTORY OF; WESTERN (LATIN) SPIRITUALITY.

Bibliography: M. Buckley, *At the Origins of Modern Atheism* (New Haven, Conn.: Yale Univ. Press, 1987). P. Gay, *The Enlightenment, An Interpretation: The Rise of Modern Paganism* (New York: Norton, 1966). R. Knox, *Enthusiasm* (New York: Oxford, 1950).

PAUL G. CROWLEY, S.J.

ENNEAGRAM

See PERSONALITY TYPES.

ENTHUSIASM

Derived from the late classical Greek *enthousiasmos* (from *entheazein*, "to be God-possessed"), enthusiasm means to be inspired or even possessed by a god or a divine, superhuman power. It is associated with a psychic excitement whereby one can transcend the purely rational order. Historically, enthusiasm has been regarded with suspicion. In the 17th and 18th centuries both deists and Calvinists sharply contrasted enthusiasm with revelation and inspiration. Due to religious conflict during the English Civil War, Quakers, Ranters, and Oliverians, as well as other splinter groups, were persecuted, much as the Huguenots were pursued in France as false French prophets (Camisards). Jonathan Edwards, for example, alleged that enthusiasts were those who pretended to be inspired by the Holy Spirit as the prophets had been.

In Henry More's brief discourse entitled *Enthusiasmus Triumphatus,* written in 1662 (Los Angeles: Augustan Reprint Society, 1966), enthusiasm is defined in the most pejorative light as a distemper. He compares enthusiasm to false inspiration, indicating that enthusiasm is nothing more than a misconceit of being inspired. True inspiration means to be moved in an extraordinary manner by the power or Spirit of God to act, speak, or think what is holy, just, and true. But enthusiasm is a false persuasion of inspiration (sect. 2). In the 1740s the charge of enthusiasm was the ultimate reproach leveled against the revivalism of the Great Awakening. The period that followed, called the Revival, brought about radical religious expression, involving religious behavior not previously understood or appreciated.

The subject of enthusiasm has been of interest in a more positive way since about 1950, when Msgr. Ronald Knox wrote his lengthy history of enthusiasm. He traces the development of the phenomenon, beginning with the Pauline community at Corinth, through the Montanists and Donatists of the early Church, up to 1820, focusing on certain Protestant sects. Enthusiasm in his perspective is a kind of religious eccentricity associated with people gesticulating wildly, screaming in a religious frenzy. Characteristic of religious enthusiasm are excessive piety, schism, appeal to charismatic authority, ultrasupernaturalism, global pessimism, anti-intellectualism, and millenarianism, among other attributes (see Hitchcock, pp. 16-24).

Knox's definition is closely tied to fanaticism and other pejorative interpretations. In an attempt to explain the phenomenon, Knox decides that the theological foundation of enthusiasm is based upon a theology of grace different from the traditional Scholastic view. Rather than grace building upon nature, where inspiration would be fundamentally a natural human capacity, grace in the case of enthusiasm supplements that which is lacking in nature, making the enthusiast privy to superhuman powers. Therefore new faculties are given to persons so that they can see deeper into the nature of things. Knox detects this idea especially in revivalism and religious groups moved by ecstasy. In a rather precise and technical sense, the term indicates that one relies solely on direct inspiration, ignoring the existing channels of faith. In Knox's assessment, enthusiasm is suspect because of its high emotionalism.

At the root of all enthusiasm is a belief in divine illumination, reminiscent of the gnostic movements throughout history. Gnosticism, believed to have its roots in Persian thought and religion, is based on a dualism whereby anything material is automatically evil, while the purely spiritual is inherently good. Gnosticism makes recourse to divine illumination as a type of purely spiritual knowledge. This interior illumination is of an inspirational kind, but, as Knox attempts to demonstrate, it has led to many religious aberrations in the history of Christianity.

In religious terms, enthusiasm took new form in the amorphous evangelical Christian movements, especially in the fundamentalist Churches. It was largely uneducated segments of the population that were attracted to this kind of religious experience, first called "Pentecostalism." Beginning in 1966, some Catholics were involved in this movement. A growing fear of uncontrolled emotionalism and overzealous frenzy compelled the U.S. Conference of Bishops to oversee this problem, especially as it might influence the charismatic renewal in the United States. Consequently, charismatic piety in the United States tended to avoid the extremes that plagued many of the spiritual movements throughout the history of the Church.

See also CHARISMATIC RENEWAL; FEELINGS; FUNDAMENTALISM; GNOSIS, GNOSTICISM; INSPIRATION; PASSION(S); PROTESTANT SPIRITUALITIES.

Bibliography: J. Hitchcock, *The New Enthusiasts: What They Are Doing in the Catholic Church* (Chicago: Thomas More, 1982). R. Knox, *Enthusiasm: A Chapter in the History of Religion* (New York: Oxford Univ. Press, 1950). D. Lovejoy, *Religious Enthusiasm in the New World: Heresy to Revolution* (Cambridge, Mass.: Harvard Univ. Press, 1985).

MICHAEL S. DRISCOLL

ENVIRONMENT

"Tell me the landscape in which you live," said Ortega y Gasset, "and I will tell you who you are." The role of the environment in forming one's personal and communal identity is a neglected but important dimension of the study of spirituality. One's encounter with God is often inseparably connected with one's experience of place. This could be "sacred space," ritually set apart and identified as such—perhaps a church or shrine, a monastery garden or cemetery. Or it could be an ordinary landscape, understood as holy in a metaphorical sense. The spiritual life has often been described in terms of mountain, river, or desert experiences. Even the earth itself (as land, air, and sea) appears to participate in the spiritual life of human beings. Paul speaks in Romans 8 of the whole creation waiting with eager longing for the redemption of God. To speak of the spiritual life in the Christian tradition, therefore, will require an attention to specific and concrete places that help to shape and even share in that covenantal relationship.

Gabriel Marcel insisted that "an individual is not distinct from his place; he is that place." All of human existence is spatially defined. Important figures in the history of spirituality have often been remembered by association with their places—Clement of Alexandria, Bernard of Clairvaux, Julian of Norwich, Teresa of Avila. Place conveys identity. Martin Heidegger knew that "place is the house of being." One experiences human existence as a matter of "being there" (*Dasein*), dwelling in the world in an anchored fashion—committed to life within specific contexts.

This is why conversion narratives within the history of spirituality have frequently been connected with particular sites. In the effort to recall and describe a vivid encounter of the holy, one necessarily reaches out to the senses, anchoring the experience in the memory of place. Hence Paul's conversion is associated with a particular point on the Damascus Road; Constantine tells of a vision seen in the sky over Milvian Bridge. Augustine's life is changed in a garden of the Villa Cassiciacum outside Milan; Luther's discovery of justification by faith occurs in the monastery tower at Wittenberg; John Wesley's heart is "strangely warmed" at a prayer meeting on Aldersgate Street in 18th-century London. The recounting of spiritual experience can rarely be divorced from such geographical and environmental settings. As a result, sacred places may best be defined as "storied places," locales that are revered because of their role in making palpable the power of sacred narrative.

Interest in questions of place and environment has not always been characteristic of Christian spirituality. Under the influence of Neoplatonic thought, the study of religious experience has frequently tended to dis-"place" the phenomena it has observed, abstracting an experience from its specific context and cataloguing a whole theoretical spectrum of religious affections. Since the Enlightenment, with its effort to reduce all mysteries to problems, the phenomenon of space (and place) has been stripped still further of its earlier importance. Aristotle's conception of place as *topos* (a mere location, an inert container of experience) has come to replace Plato's dynamic view of place as *chora* (that which carries its own generative energy, its unique *genius loci,* or "spirit of place").

Biblical theology itself is marked by a tension between place and placelessness, the impulse toward the specificity of incarnation and the freedom of divine transcendence. In Scripture the divine-human encounter invariably occurs in specific locales—at Sinai or Shechem, on the Temple Mount in Jerusalem, in Bethlehem and Nazareth. One necessarily studies biblical spirituality with map in hand. Yet Old and New Testaments alike reject all efforts to limit the divine presence to "sacred places" narrowly defined. Nathan warns David that Yahweh cannot be contained in any temple built by hands (2 Sam 7), and Stephen repeats the caveat in Acts 7, urging that Christ transcends all spatial bounds.

An ambivalence toward the environment is seen finally in Christian attitudes toward the earth as biosphere. The Judeo-Christian tradition's desacralization of nature and emphasis on human dominion over creation have been blamed for contributing to an ecological irresponsibility in Western thought. Yet calls for a spirituality that embraces the earth have also been heard from Benedict of Nursia and Francis of Assisi to the recent work of Thomas Berry and Matthew Fox.

See also AESTHETICS; ARCHITECTURE; ART; BEAUTY; CREATION; ECOLOGICAL CONSCIOUSNESS; HOSPITALITY; MUSIC; WORLD.

Bibliography: B. Lane, *Landscapes of the Sacred: Geography and Narrative in American Spirituality* (New York: Paulist, 1988).

BELDEN C. LANE

ENVY

See DEADLY SINS.

EREMITICAL LIFE

Human beings are spontaneously drawn to community, but they also require solitude. There is a depth within the human being and within nature that can only be explored in solitude. Thus philosophers from the Pythagoreans and Seneca through Thoreau, the existentialists, and Heidegger recommend withdrawal from the crowd in order to know more profoundly self and nature. The more a society presumes to be able to fulfill every human aspiration, the more urgent it becomes to distance oneself, at least intermittently, from such a collectivity. As countless writers and artists insist, marginality becomes the condition for deeper social criticism, insight, and creativity.

Beyond this basic human need, the religious yearning intensifies the attraction for solitude. Mystics speak of a deep inner space within the human person that only God can fill, and a deep inner space within God that only the human person can fill. All the major religious traditions, i.e., Christian, Jewish, Hindu, Buddhist, and Islamic Sufi, include the component of solitude. It is lived out in different ways: one may live it interiorly only, or also exteriorly, intermittently only, or for extended periods. One may dedicate one's whole life to solitude.

The word *eremitical* is derived from the Greek *erēmia,* meaning "desert." The desert experience had an immense impact on both the OT and the NT. It was in the solitude of the desert that Moses encountered God in the burning bush (Exod 3). It was into the desert that Israel was plunged in order to enter into a covenant with God and to be prepared for entry into the Promised Land. After Israel's infidelity the prophets announced God's saving plan, a new desert courtship: "I will allure her; I will lead her into the desert and speak to her heart" (Hos 2:16). It was while he was alone at the mouth of a cave at Mount Horeb that Elijah encountered God in "a still, small voice" (1 Kgs 19:12, OAB). The prophets proclaimed a desert redemption: "the desert shall rejoice and blossom" (Isa 35:1, NRSV). This foundational and rich desert theme would become key for the later spiritual journey of both Israel and Christianity.

In the NT, John the Baptist, the new Elijah (Mk 9:13), was "a voice crying out in the desert" (Mk 1:3). And Jesus passed forty days of prayer and fasting in the desert, a new exodus that was to prelude the struggles and final victory of his saving ministry (Mk 1:12ff.). Paul's stay in Arabia after his conversion was probably a desert experience (Gal 1:17). And it would be into the desert, "where she had a place prepared by God" (Rev 12:6; see also Rev 12:14), that the mysterious woman would flee the serpent. Paul stressed that Israel's desert experiences were a type of the Christian journey of faith (1 Cor 10:11), as would patristic literature such as Gregory of Nyssa's *Life of Moses.*

In the 3rd century and thereafter, young men and women abandoned the cities for the solitary life of Egypt, Syria, Palestine, Arabia, and Europe. This vast eremitical experience generated a rich spiritual literature, such as the *Life of Antony* by Athanasius, the various collections of the *Sayings of the Fathers,* the writings of Evagrius, the *Conferences* of Cassian, and the *Ladder of Divine Ascent* of John Climacus. This literature greatly influenced all major currents of Christian spirituality.

From the 5th to the 8th century a pilgrim and missionary form of eremitical life flourished in Ireland, Scotland, and Wales. The Rule of Benedict, itself written for cenobites, nevertheless remained open to the possibility of eremitical life, and thus throughout the "Benedictine centuries" up to the present time abbeys and priories would regularly include individual hermitages. Parish churches in the Middle Ages would also sometimes have an anchorage attached. In the Eastern Churches the eremitical life has flourished through the centuries (despite the perplexities of Basil), strengthened by hesychast spirituality of hermits and monks, and by great monastic centers strongly supportive of the eremitical life, such as St. Catherine's in the Sinai and Mount Athos.

In the West there was an explosion of eremitical renewal in the 10th and 11th centuries, also strongly influenced by the East. Romuald, Peter Damian, and the eventual emergence of the Camaldolese Congregation (part of the Benedictine family, but with a distinctive provision for hermitage and reclusion) are a chief example, as are Bruno and the Carthusian Order. In the 13th century Francis of Assisi spent significant periods in solitude and wrote a Rule for Hermitages, so that the solitary life would continue to be an important component of Franciscan life, as it would for John of the Cross and Carmelite spirituality. The 14th century further enriched eremitical contemplative literature with the writings of Richard Rolle, the author of *The Cloud of Unknowing,* Julian of Norwich, Ruysbroeck, and several others.

In recent centuries Christian solitude has been witnessed to in the lives and writings of countless hermits, Eastern and Western, such as Seraphim of Sarov and Charles de Foucauld. In our own time spiritual writers such as Catherine de Hueck Doherty, Thomas Merton, and Henri Nouwen have explored the urgency and centrality of Christian solitude. Merton, for instance, affirms that the wisdom of the Desert Fathers and Mothers "enables us to reopen the sources that have been polluted or blocked up altogether by the accumulated mental and spiritual refuse of our technological barbarism. Our time is in desperate need of this kind of simplicity" (*The Wisdom of the Desert,* p. 11).

See also BENEDICTINE SPIRITUALITY; CAMAL-
DOLESE SPIRITUALITY; CARTHUSIAN SPIRITUALITY;
DESERT; ENGLISH MYSTICAL TRADITION; HESY-
CHASM; MONASTICISM, MONASTIC SPIRITUALITY.

Bibliography: Athanasius, *The Life of Antony and the
Letter to Marcellinus,* The Classics of Western Spirituality, trans. R. Gregg (New York: Paulist, 1980). *The
Wisdom of the Desert: Sayings from the Desert Fathers
of the Fourth Century,* trans. T. Merton (New York:
New Directions, 1960). John Cassian, *Conferences,*
trans. C. Luibheid (New York: Paulist, 1985).

ROBERT HALE, O.S.B. CAM.

ESCHATOLOGY

Until recently, *eschatology* (from the Greek *eschatos,* "the furthest, the last") was understood in theological handbooks to be teaching about the "last things": death, judgment, heaven, and hell for the individual; the second coming, general resurrection, judgment, and the end of the world for the human race as a whole. In the light of recent studies, the term has taken on a fuller meaning. It is now understood to refer to a theology of history, with specific reference to hope for the ultimate fulfillment of God's covenant promise. Thus it includes the themes of the handbook tradition but treats them in a wider theological context.

The Old Testament

As presented in the historical-prophetic tradition of the OT, Israel's history lives from the conviction that God is drawing the people to a future fulfillment of the covenant promise, which, even though promised by God, remains fundamentally unknown and mysterious to the people. What this future fulfillment might be is the object of a series of projections throughout biblical history. The symbols of the tradition suggest a fullness of life, peace, justice, and reconciliation rooted in God's life-giving action.

In the Abraham tradition the future is seen concretely in the form of posterity and a land (Gen 12:1ff.). After the experience of national well-being under the rule of David, the later collapse of the monarchy gave rise to hope for a restoration of the monarchy by a Savior figure from the royal line of David (2 Sam 7; Pss 2:21; 45; 72; 110).

While the expectations of the prophetic tradition were concerned primarily with the destiny of the people as a whole, the influence of Greek thought during the Hellenistic period led to speculation on the destiny of the individual in the wisdom literature, at least in a limited sense (Wis 2:3; 3:1, 4; 9:15). The concept of an immortal soul made it possible to think of some sort of survival after death for the individual person.

In the apocalyptic reflections of the intertestamental period, we encounter the strong hope that despite the tragedy of Israel's historical experience, those powers that are inimical to God will be subdued, and the rule of God will be definitively established. If the prophets, for the most part, looked to a future historical situation as the fulfillment of the promise, apocalyptic raised the question of a future that transcends the framework of any historical experience. In this stage of development the vision of a truly universal and cosmic fulfillment emerges, and with it the possibility of a resurrection of the dead (Dan 12:2-3; 2 Macc).

The OT ends with no uniform vision. Its faith is radically open to the future, but the contours of the future remain basically unknown. The expectations of a God-given fullness of life in a world marked by peace, justice, and reconciliation that run through this history are drawn together in the symbol of a future kingdom of God.

The New Testament

The above remarks set the stage for the appearance of Jesus and the early Christian community. It can be said that Jesus took up the hopes of his people (his kingdom-preaching) and that he transformed those hopes in the light of his own experience of God (the Abba experience).

What the Jewish tradition had hoped for as a future fulfillment Jesus associated immediately with his person and ministry (Mt 11:5; Lk 10:23ff.; 4:21). Thus the Synoptic tradition sees a provisional form of the kingdom in the work of Jesus' ministry, even though the definitive form of the kingdom remains to be realized in the future and is often associated with the appearance of the Son of Man on the clouds of heaven (Mt 26:64; Mk 14:62; Lk 22:69). The sense of the imminence of the end and the decisive coming of God's kingdom is associated with the summons to vigilance and conversion.

If the meaning of Jesus' preaching is called into question by his execution, new light is shed on it from the perspective of the Easter experience of the disciples. A new dimension of eschatological consciousness emerges, rooted in the earlier traditions but now taking a specifically Christian form. The destiny of Jesus with God anticipates the destiny of humanity and, indeed, of God's creation as a whole.

The eschatology of the early Pauline tradition reflects the sense of an imminent end (1 Thess 5:2ff.) and describes the parousia in vivid, apocalyptic terms (1 Thess 4:16-18). The near-expectation of this epistle yields to a more indeterminate expectation in 2 Thessalonians. In other Pauline materials the contrast between present and future yields to a contrast between "above" and "below" (1 Cor 15:35-50; 2 Cor 5:1-10; Phil 3:20-21). This Pauline material offers helpful clues concerning the role of apocalyptic thought and the shifting emphasis placed on the present and future dimensions in early Christianity.

The theology of Ephesians and Colossians moves in the direction of a cosmic, Christological vision according to which Christ is presently at work bringing all cosmic realities, including the demonic powers, into subjection to himself (Eph 3:10; 6:12; Col 1:15; 2:8-15). This vision amounts to a reappropriation of the OT concept of a divine plan, the consumma-tion of which is summed up in the mystery of Christ, who is "with God" from eternity (Eph 1:4; 1:10; Col 1:15).

Exegetes distinguish two patterns of eschatology in the Gospel of John. The dominant pattern has been described as "vertical" and is readily interpreted as a "present" eschatology. Here eschatology relates not so much to a chronological future as to the deep significance of the present experience of faith and grace. Judgment and salvation are realized in our present relation to Jesus (Jn 3:18; 3:36; 5:24). The second pattern has been described as "horizontal" and is more in line with the theology of salvation history commonly associated with the Bible. This pattern situates the final experience of salvation on the "last day" (Jn 6:39-40).

The Book of Revelation is the only book of the NT that is shaped entirely as a work of apocalyptic. Making use of metaphors and symbols of the apocalyptic tradition, including resurrection of the dead and general judgment, the book opens the reader's vision to a "new heaven and a new earth" (Rev 20:11-21:5). The OT traditions are reinterpreted in the light of the Christian conviction about God's decisive action in the person of Jesus. The power of God's life-giving, creative love will be victorious as it brings to completion what it has begun in the resurrection of Christ. Though the scenario is emphatically apocalyptic, the message is a powerful word of hope and consolation to a community that finds itself in dire circumstances.

Tradition

As the mission of the Church moved beyond the context of the early Jewish community to the larger context of the Greco-Roman Empire, the meaning of eschatology and apocalyptic would be a significant problem in a culture that was inclined more toward metaphysical categories than toward historical ones, and that tended to think of the immortality of the soul rather than the resurrection of the body. As Hellenistic thought patterns made their influence felt, the seeds were sown for the later development of a wide range of themes that for many centuries would make up a significant part of eschatological reflection. These included the notion of an interim period between individual death and general resurrection bridged by the notion of the separated soul; prayers for the dead during this interim period; the development of the doctrine of purgatory, which found its high point in the Middle Ages in the context of the highly developed structures of Church authority and the ecclesiastical penitential practice.

Views were divided concerning the appropriate way to read the scriptural texts. When read in a nonmetaphorical manner, the twentieth chapter of Revelation gave rise to millenarianism in a number of early communities. This view involved the conviction that Christ would reign on earth with his elect for a thousand years prior to the end of history. Origen, Jerome, and Augustine championed a metaphorical approach to such texts and rejected millenarian speculation as heterodox. While the main line of Christian theology has followed this lead, the tendency to identify the figures and symbols of the text with historical persons and events has never died out completely. Today it is found among the Adventists, the Jehovah's Witnesses, and above all among the Dispensationalists.

Late medieval and baroque eschatology offered extensive speculations about the nature of the separated soul, the resurrected body, the understanding of heaven as beatific vision, and in general it developed eschatology into an elaborate geography of otherworldly places.

Eschatology and Contemporary Theology

Current directions have moved away from this physical style and have shifted to a more anthropological perspective. Corresponding to this shift is the understanding of eschatological language not as descriptive but as metaphorical. In the aftermath of the Christian dialogue with Marxist philosophy, there is a tendency to cast eschatology in the broad context of a philosophy of hope and to search out the relation between human hope as such and the biblical hope for fulfillment of created reality in God.

These tendencies come together in the focus on the Christ-event as the normative basis for Christian eschatology, and on the understanding of eschatology as a series of analogical extrapolations from that basis. As theology moves in this direction, the following concerns emerge:

1) Since the individual Jesus anticipates the collective destiny of the human race, there must be an individual and a collective dimension in eschatology.

2) At the individual level new approaches to the theology of death, together with analogies with the death of Jesus, have provided insights for current interpretations of judgment, purgation, interim period, etc.

3) At the collective level, in as far as the human history of Jesus is the condition *sine qua non* for the fulfillment of resurrection existence, the need is felt for a more adequate understanding of human history and its relation to the ultimate future anticipated in the resurrection of Jesus. Here emerges the concern for the relation between human, inner-worldly futures and the biblical vision of a future promised by God.

4) Since the ultimate destiny of Jesus is not the escape of a human soul from the prison of a body but the fulfillment of all that makes Jesus to be human—body and soul—eschatology must address the totality of human existence in its bodily as well as its spiritual dimensions. The theological significance of material reality is a concern here.

5) In as far as the future anticipated in the resurrection is not a return into history, it points to an ultimate future that moves

beyond the futures of human, utopian planning and that is appropriately called an *absolute future.* This absolute future is understood to be the ultimate self-gift of God to creation. From the side of creation, the possibility of such a future is understood to involve the self-transcendence of history into God.

6) In view of this understanding of the future, Christian theology expects that there will be a point in the collective history of humanity at which the dialectic of our space-time experience will be brought to a resolution. In this sense, theology expects history to end. Only in view of some such end point can the question of the meaning of history be said to be resolved.

7) If the kingdom of God is taken as a basic symbol of this ultimate future, it becomes clear that the Church cannot be identified with the kingdom. The Church is, in essence, a historical community of faith in the service of the kingdom (see LG 48-51).

See also AFTERLIFE; APOCALYPTICISM; CREATION; FUTURE; HISTORY, HISTORICAL CONSCIOUSNESS; HOPE; KINGDOM OF GOD; MILLENARIANISM; RESURRECTION.

Bibliography: Z. Hayes, *Visions of a Future: A Study of Christian Eschatology* (Wilmington, Del.: Glazier, 1989). B. Hebblethwaite, *The Christian Hope* (Grand Rapids, Mich.: Eerdmans, 1984). J. Ratzinger, *Eschatology: Death and Eternal Life* (Washington: Catholic Univ. of America Press, 1988).

ZACHARY HAYES, O.F.M.

ETHICS, THE ETHICAL

See MORALITY, ETHICS, RELATIONSHIP TO SPIRITUALITY; PRAXIS; VIRTUE.

EUCHARIST

The Eucharist is a liturgical event, a sacramental meal, in which the Church remembers, celebrates, and proclaims Jesus' sacrificial life, death and resurrection.

The Eucharist is a liturgical event in which the Church, assembled in the unity of the Holy Spirit and acting through, with, and in God's Son Jesus Christ, offers all glory and honor to God the almighty Father. It is a sacramental meal in which the simple elements of bread and wine become the body and blood of Christ, to be shared in faith by the participants.

The Eucharist is a memorial of Jesus' entire life, but most especially of its culmination in his passion-resurrection. It is also a celebration, a solemn act of praise and thanksgiving for the signs and wonders God has effected for us throughout the ages, but above all in the mission of his Son Jesus Christ. Finally, it is a proclamation of the Lord's self-offering and death on our behalf until he comes in the fullness of time.

Name, Origins and Meaning

The noun *eucharist* renders the Greek word *eucharistia,* which was in use by the end of the 1st century. Its earliest literary attestation is in the *Didache,* a simple missionary manual developed in the last decades of the 1st century and early in the 2nd. In the *Didache* the term *eucharist* appears in conjunction with baptism and refers to an archaic form of the Eucharistic liturgy (9:1).

Although the term *eucharist* does not appear in the NT, the verb from which it is derived, *eucharistein,* is used quite frequently, notably in the liturgical texts presenting Jesus' Last Supper, but also in other texts influenced by the early Christian Eucharist. In those contexts it forms part of a narrative sequence of verbs describing the action of Jesus.

The Greek verb *eucharistein* and the noun *eucharistia* mean "to give thanks" and "thanksgiving," respectively. They entered early Christian vocabulary as translations of the Hebrew verb *barak* and the noun *berakah,* which are also translated into Greek as *eulogein,* "to bless," and *eulogia,* "blessing." For Jews and Judaeo-Christians, *berakah,* "blessing-thanksgiving," was an act of praise directed to God and the basic expression of all prayer.

In the NT Eucharistic texts the verbs *eucharistein* (1 Cor 11:24; Mk 8:6; 14:23; Mt 15:36; 26:27; Lk 22:17; 24:30; Jn 6:11) and *eulogein* (Mk 6:41; 14:22; Mt 14:19; 26:26; Lk 9:15; 22:19) can be found without significant distinction. However, the fact of having two different Greek verbs does indicate a difference in emphasis. The very use of these verbs in reference to the Eucharistic event highlights its importance as a prayer of praise and thanksgiving.

The oldest attested name for the Eucharist is the Lord's Supper (*ho kuriakon deipnon*—1 Cor 11:20). It designates the Eucharist from the point of view of its relationship to the person of Jesus as risen Lord. Those who participate in the Lord's Supper are expected to reach out to all human beings and welcome them in solidarity with Jesus the Lord of all.

The second name found in the NT is the breaking of bread (*hē klasis tou artou;* Lk 24:35; Acts 2:42). It emphasizes how the Eucharist is a sharing event. Those who break bread are expected to offer their lives for others in the way Jesus the Christ did throughout his life but especially in the passion.

Like the name *eucharist,* which emphasizes the prayer dimension of the Eucharist, the Lord's Supper and the breaking of bread bring out aspects of the Eucharist that are basic in a Christian spirituality. The Lord's Supper draws attention to the way the Eucharist is penetrated through and through by the values and demands flowing from Jesus' risen state. The breaking of bread highlights the quality of sharing and the depth of commitment required of those who participate in the Eucharist.

New Testament

Beyond these names for Eucharist, the Synoptic Gospels make ample use of liturgical texts that were part of the Lord's Supper or the breaking of bread. This practice associated the experience of the early Church with various stories of Jesus, whether as a historical figure, such as in the accounts of the Last Supper (Mk 14:22-26; Mt 26:26-30; Lk 22:14-38) and the miraculous feeding of large crowds (Mk 6:34-44; 8:1-10; Mt 14:13-21; 15:32-39; Lk 9:10-17), or as the risen Lord, such as in the story of the disciples of Emmaus (24:13-35). It enabled the readers of the Gospels to see the implications of the NT events for their lives at later periods of history.

The earliest literary attestation of a liturgical text for the Lord's Supper is in 1 Cor 11:23-25, where Paul quotes it in response to attitudes and practices not in keeping with the nature of the Lord's Supper (1 Cor 11:17-34). The climax of his argument and exhortation comes in 11:26, where he speaks of a genuine Eucharist as being a proclamation of the death of the Lord until he comes.

Unlike Paul's letters and the Synoptic Gospels, John's Gospel does not cite the liturgical text of the Lord's Supper in the account of the Last Supper. Instead, it tells the story of the washing of the feet and adds a long farewell discourse that develops some of the implications of the Lord's Supper for the life of Christians (13:1-17:26). The discourse's main themes are faith, love, peace, unity in Christ, persecution, the Spirit as Advocate, Christian identity, and the universal mission.

Earlier in the Gospel John included another discourse (6:22-71) after an account of a miraculous breaking of bread (6:1-15) and a difficult crossing of the sea (6:16-21). The discourse is particularly rich in biblical spirituality, giving special emphasis to a number of Exodus themes. It refers to Jesus, his word, and the Eucharist as bread come down from heaven. Those who share in the flesh and blood of Jesus abide in him as he abides in them, and they will live forever.

The liturgical texts, the accounts in which they play a role, and the discourses draw upon many of the OT's most basic themes. Particularly noteworthy are the references to the Passover, the covenant, the manna, the messianic banquet, the suffering servant, bread understood as meal, blood as a symbol for life, and remembrance.

Tradition

The subsequent history of the Eucharist and its relationship to spirituality is a multi-party dialogue among the Eucharistic texts of the NT, their background in the OT, the experience of biblical authors, the needs of the Church, and developments in the Eucharistic liturgy. Even a rapid review reveals the extraordinary fruitfulness of this dialogue. Along with the NT, it has marked Eucharistic spirituality into the modern era.

On his way to martyrdom at Rome early in the 2nd century, St. Ignatius of Antioch wrote of the Eucharist as the one bread uniting all the local Churches. Emphasizing the relationship between the Eucharist, hope, and eternal life, he presented the Eucharist as a medicine of immortality, an antidote against death, that we might live forever in Jesus Christ (*Eph.* 20,2).

Later in that century St. Justin described the components of the liturgy and reflected briefly on some of its elements. His description includes the basic outline of the liturgy as we know it today, with a liturgy of the word and the Eucharistic liturgy proper. Within this presentation he stressed the need for prior baptism and rebirth and for living according to the commandments on the part of those who participate in the Eucharist (*1 Apol.* 65-67).

In his *Mystagogical Catecheses* (V, 9-10), St. Cyril of Jerusalem spoke of the Eucharist as part of the process of Christian initiation and highlighted the importance of prayer at Eucharist on behalf of those who have died.

St. Ambrose insisted on the relationship between the Eucharist and the forgiveness of sins. Citing Paul, he presented the Eucharist as a proclamation of the remission of sins because it was a proclamation of the death of the Lord (1 Cor 11:26; *De sacr.* IV, 28).

St. Augustine stressed the role of the Church, which associates itself with Christ the High Priest in offering a universal sacrifice. In the Eucharist the sacrifice of Christ is thus the sacrifice of Christians, who join with Christ in offering themselves even as he offers himself for us (*De civ. Dei* X, 6). In the Eucharist we have been made Christ's body, and "by his mercy we are what we receive" (*Serm.* 229; see also 272).

In the 13th century St. Thomas Aquinas focused on the Eucharist specifically as a sacrament and explored its place in the sacramental system. He saw the Eucharist as a sign which effects what it signifies and in which the Lord is present in a unique way. For Aquinas, the Eucharist is "the summit of the spiritual life and the end to which all the sacraments are ordained (ST III, q.73, a.3).

In response to the Reformation, the Council of Trent placed great emphasis on the reality of the presence of Christ in the Eucharist immediately after the consecration and remaining as long as the Eucharistic species continue to exist (DS 1641). It also stressed the objective value of the Eucharistic sacrifice, which makes present in an unbloody manner the sacrifice Christ offered on the cross in a bloody manner (DS 1740, 1743).

Vatican II and Beyond

Vatican II carried on the dialogue by returning to the biblical tradition, the Fathers of the Church, and the Church's classical theologians. It also drew on prior ecumenical councils and the official teaching of the popes. Its great contribution was to focus on the Eucharist precisely as a liturgical event among others in the context of Christian life. Its Constitution on the Sacred Liturgy has been followed by dozens of official documents aimed at its implementation.

The constitution's contribution to spirituality is clear from the beginning: "Day by day the liturgy builds up those within the Church into the Lord's holy temple, into a spiritual dwelling for God—an enterprise which will continue until Christ's full stature is achieved" (SC 2). The Eucharist is thus a source of personal life and identity for all the members of the Church. The constitution continues: "At the same time the liturgy marvelously fortifies the faithful in their capacity to preach Christ. To outsiders the liturgy thereby reveals the Church as a sign raised above the nations. Under this sign the scattered [children] of God are being gathered into one until there is one fold and one shepherd" (SC 2). The Eucharist is thus a source of power for evangelization and for the Church's mission to the ends of the earth that all human beings might eventually be one in Christ.

The most memorable statement of the Constitution on the Sacred Liturgy is given in article 10: ". . . the liturgy is the summit toward which the activity of the Church is directed; at the same time it is the fountain from which all her power flows." The Eucharist is thus intimately related to the whole of Christian life and is inseparable from it. Christian life finds its summit in the liturgy and flows from it as from a source. The whole of life is thus seen from a liturgical and Eucharistic perspective.

Vatican II thus challenges the Church to view and order Christian life, identity, relationships, prayer, attitudes, and mission from the point of view of the liturgy, and most especially of the Eucharistic liturgy.

See also BAPTISM; BODY OF CHRIST; CELEBRATION; COVENANT; EUCHARISTIC DEVOTION; LITURGY; NARRATIVE; SACRAMENTS.

Bibliography: L. Bouyer, *Eucharist: Theology and Spirituality of the Eucharistic Prayer,* trans. C. Quinn (Notre Dame: Univ. of Notre Dame Press, 1968). X. Léon-Dufour, *Sharing the Eucharistic Bread: The Witness of the New Testament,* trans. M. O'Connell (New York: Paulist, 1987). J. Emminghaus, *The Eucharist: Essence, Form, Celebration,* trans. M. O'Connell (Collegeville, Minn.: The Liturgical Press, 1978).

EUGENE LaVERDIERE, S.S.S.

EUCHARISTIC DEVOTION

Eucharistic devotion refers to a number of religious practices surrounding the Blessed Sacrament outside the celebration of Mass. These practices include private visits to the Blessed Sacrament, processions with the Blessed Sacrament, Exposition of the Blessed Sacrament, and Benediction of the Blessed Sacrament.

Eucharistic devotion presupposes faith in the Blessed Sacrament as well as the reservation of the Blessed Sacrament outside Mass, a practice that can be traced at least to St. Justin in the 2nd century. For centuries the practice inspired respect for the Blessed Sacrament, but it did not give rise to special religious practices until the 13th century, when several factors contributed to their emergence.

Theological controversies over the reality of Christ's presence in the Blessed Sacrament invited private and public expressions of faith. Developments in the liturgy itself encouraged such manifestations by emphasizing the elevation after each consecration. By excluding the faithful from participating in the cup, the liturgy also gave greater prominence to the host.

The earliest Eucharistic devotion consisted in private visits to the Blessed Sacrament. These became popular at the beginning of the 13th century. Later in the same century public processions with the Blessed Sacrament originated in connection with the Feast of Corpus Christi in the city of Liège, and the practice soon spread throughout Europe.

Exposition of the Blessed Sacrament began at the end of the 14th century as an extension of the feast of Corpus Christi in response to popular piety. Benediction of the Blessed Sacrament arose in the 14th century as a conclusion for Compline and Vespers. A precedent for this practice had been set in the Benediction stations that became part of the Corpus Christi processions.

The primary spiritual attitude in all these devotional practices was adoration, but they also invited other basic attitudes inspired by the Eucharistic liturgy, especially faith, charity, hope, thanksgiving, reparation and petition.

In the course of the centuries Eucharistic devotions acquired such importance as to displace the Mass in popular religiosity. This displacement tended to obscure the relationship between the devotional practices and the liturgical celebration from which they had sprung.

Vatican II and the decrees implementing it called for a simplification of the Eucharistic devotions and the elimination of elements that distracted from the Eucharistic sign of bread. It also required that they not distract from the celebration of Eucharist, that the Blessed Sacrament be presented in such a way that its relationship to the Mass would be clear, and that the attitudes of the faithful be inspired by the Eucharistic liturgy and its meaning as presented in Scripture, tradition, and the Church's official teaching.

Accordingly, the expression of Eucharistic devotion has been greatly simplified. Exposition, for example, is done by placing the Blessed Sacrament directly on the altar with little surrounding it that would distract from the Eucharistic signs. The traditional attitudes toward the Blessed Sacrament are complemented by a search to interiorize the significance of the Mass, which the Blessed Sacrament evokes. As a result, Eucharistic devotions have become characterized by contemplation and meditation rather than by specific acts of prayer.

See also ADORATION; DEVOTION(S), POPULAR; EUCHARIST; PRAYER; PRESENCE, PRESENCE OF GOD; SACRAMENTS.

Bibliography: N. Mitchell, *Cult and Controversy: The Worship of the Eucharist Outside Mass* (New York: Pueblo, 1982). "Dévotion eucharistique. A. Esquisse historique" (E. Bertraud); "B. Culte de la présence réelle et magistère" (G. Vassali, E. Nunez, R. Fortin), *D.Spir.* 31–32, cols. 1621–1648.

EUGENE LaVERDIERE, S.S.S.

EVANGELIZATION

See EARLY CHRISTIAN SPIRITUALITY; PREACHING; SCRIPTURE; TEACHING.

EVIL

The mystery of evil raises for Christian theology a challenge unlike any other, for it suggests that faith is ultimately irreconcilable with reason. How affirm at once, without contradiction, that God is all-powerful, that God is absolutely good, yet evil exists? Theodicies battle for coherence in response to the objection that only two of these propositions are compatible, not all three at once. The enigma of evil deepens when made to encompass such diverse phenomena as sin, suffering, death, and "nature red in tooth and claw." Earthquake, death camp, and fallen doe are not the same. Evil as wrongdoing and as suffering belong to heterogeneous categories—blame and lament. Blame names culprits, lament reveals victims. To do evil is always directly or indirectly to make others suffer. Yet boundaries between culprit and victim blur. The guilty experience seduction by dark psychic powers within and entrapment in a history of evil without. This experience of passivity at the heart of evil doing makes culprits also victims. Hence the prayer: "Do not put us to the test."

Theodicies proper appear only after increasingly rational levels of discourse are negotiated in quest of evil's intelligibility. Myth marks the first major transition from experience of evil to language. Telling how the world began, myth tells how the human condition became wretched. The vast field of symbolic narrative structures leaves unexplored no conceivable explanation of evil's whence and why. But myth leaves unanswered "why me?" Thus myth gives rise to thought, and language moves to another register—Wisdom. There lament becomes complaint demanding divinity account for itself.

Myth weaves a story; Wisdom argues. It argues first for a law of retribution. All suffering is punishment for sin, individual or collective, known or unknown. But this penal vision shatters against a wall of disproportionate and innocent suffering. The Book of Job, where tragic theology reappears, is classical argumentative Wisdom. After Job, consolation will not do, only a new wisdom transcending the Adam-Job antithesis. Yet thinking could move from Wisdom to theodicy only because Gnostic speculation postulated a dualism that pits spirit against matter, and forces of good against armies of evil in merciless cosmic struggle to liberate all particles of light held captive by the shadows of evil. Theodicy as such emerges when the problem is framed in propositions intended to be univocal, as are the three above, when the goal of argument is apologetic exoneration of God, and when the means employed meet the logic of noncontradiction and synthesis.

Theodicies of different stripe have entered the lists. Against Manichaean Gnostics, Augustine, learning from Neoplatonists, argued that evil cannot be a substance, for being is intelligible and good. Evil is irrational privation of needed or wanted good. Whence comes wrongdoing? It enters through created wills defecting from God to self or a creature. Evil is not willed by God. God merely permits free agents to do and suffer evil. Augustine's ontotheology shifts the problem of evil to the sphere of volition; his vision is exclusively moral. The deficient cause of evil is a malicious will, incomprehensible choice not to become what one might be. All evil is *peccatum* or *poena,* sin or pain as retributive punishment.

Yet Augustine's anti-Gnostic gnosis is a false clarity. His rationalization of the Adamic myth in terms of original sin leaves loose ends. Why does God permit such deprivation? How can those graced with original justice be attracted to lesser goods? How can sin be inherited? Why so much disproportionate suffering? Augustine's aesthetic corollary, negative and positive working toward final harmony, fails

when it confronts surd evil such as Auschwitz, an excess transcending compensation by any known retribution. Lament and complaint overturn compensation as they did retribution, for neither heals, explains, or rights anything. Yet nescience, meaning deferred, bedevils and narrows human horizons. Is perhaps "all discord harmony not understood"?

These difficulties led some to more Irenaean perspectives. Temptation, sin, and suffering are necessary conditions if egoistic humans are to become loving persons worthy of life with God. History is person-making pedagogy in which the world's rough edges and painful growth are needed if people are to develop virtue and freely turn to a hidden, uncoercive God out of love, not compulsion. God could eliminate evil, but at the price of creating unheroic humanity, a race of pampered children. God is powerful enough to spoil humans, but too wise and good to do so.

But again lament begets complaint. Why explain the obscure by the more obscure, another world? Why does the Master resort to surd evils such as mass death to school us? Why so erratic and unfair in the dosages of pain administered? If sin and suffering are life's necessary conditions, is not God's "permission" a willing of evil? And does not God risk failure? Progress is not inevitable, and many do not seem to be ennobled by experiences of evil but diminished.

This bafflement is attributed to the opacity of God's wise love. Yet such harsh and dreadful love makes sense only if one assumes something so wrong with humanity to begin with that severe therapy is warranted. The divine physician must hurt to heal. But could not God's preventive care have made humans such that these therapies are unneeded? Are humans so botched in the making that only rough handling stanches atrophy and stunted growth?

The response has been that God could have created humans flawless, unspoilable, but did not—not because God was impotent or unloving, but because God intended something far better than perfect human automata, viz., human persons. What distinguishes person from machine is something irreconcilable with a perfect computer or an unspoilable child: freedom. One is what one has become, which depends on what one does and how one chooses. Freedom, humanity's chief dignity, is also its chief peril. Free to choose, humans, individually and collectively, can choose wrongly and produce devastating effects.

More recent process theodicies massively modify the problem of evil by redefining God. Divine power is only the limited power of persuasion as God eternally attempts to lure the world's entities to their greatest individual and collective good. Evil is the cost of this evolution. Such a limited God's success seems dubious, given evil's saturation of the planet. In some instances process theodicies appear insufficiently analogical and eschatological in their God-talk, hence in need of greater sensitivity to the incomprehensibility of the radical mystery stressed by apophatic traditions. Nonetheless, these theodicies more adequately than their classical counterparts articulate the central Christian affirmation that God is love and resonate to a contemporary sense of change, process, and relationship, which they import into the Deity with much success.

The sharpest blow against anguished theodicies was the one struck by Kant against all ontotheology. His dismantling of rational theology as "transcendental illusion" moved the problem of evil to the practical sphere. Even if one does not go as far as Kant, one must soberly admit that theoretical approaches end in blind alleys. Enigma becomes terminal aporia as speculation fails. Faced with this aporia, religion calls upon affect and action, not as solution but as response to render the aporia productive. Evil ought not exist and must be fought against. Myth gives rise to action as

well as thought. The intellectual aporia must be productive, first, by leading to a *docta ignorantia* whereby in not seeing one sees how suffering is not explained, e.g., as divine chastisement. Secondly, the lament of unknowing must be permitted to develop into complaint against the covenant God's "permission" of evil, the too easy expedient of every theodicy. The rage of protest, accusation, and appeal to God against God is the impatience of hope wailing in the psalmist's cry: "How long, O Lord?" Thirdly, the catharsis of lament must lead to awareness that reasons for believing in God have little to do with the need to explain suffering. Suffering truly scandalizes only those who view God as source of all created good, including courage before evil and solidarity with victims. Believers believe despite evil.

Beyond all this, some advance to renounce even complaint and find suffering purgative and educative. Still others advance further to find consolation in the idea that in the crucified suffering becomes a moment in the covenant God. Wisdom may ultimately lead even to renouncement of the very desires whose wounding engenders complaint. Perhaps this is the wisdom of Job, who came to love God for nought and thus escaped the prison of retribution where lament still dwells. Through this mourning process accusation yields to truthfulness, truthfulness to acceptance, acceptance to wisdom and even joy possibly. However, these individual experiences do not exempt from the ethico-political struggle to mitigate suffering inflicted by humans on humans in private and public sectors.

Suffering abounds and evidences little relation to blame or merit. Thus the challenge to work for justice, indeed to go beyond justice to offered suffering. For at a certain level only Christology, God's involvement in human agony, can make the goodness of God credible in a world of caused and suffered evil. New wisdom and transcendence come with the crucified

Ebed. Complaint there is: "My God, my God, why have you forsaken me?" (Ps 22:2). But the evil *undergone* by Jesus became by his embracing it an *action* redeeming evil *committed*. "No one takes my life from me, but I lay it down on my own" (Jn 10:18). The dialectic is resolved as it moves from Adam to Job to Christ; from suffering as penalty to suffering as affliction to suffering as action; from culprit to victim to servant; from evil committed to evil suffered to evil redeemed; from God as lawgiver/judge to God as tyrant to God as advocate and fellow sufferer. Perhaps only when one reaches a capacity for offered suffering does the world cease to be too wicked for God to be good, though there are always the tears of children and the nightmare of the cruel or ineffectual God of tragedy, unthinkable, yet invincible at recurrent levels of experience. Thus always the prayer: "Do not put us to the test; do not meet us with the face of the tragic God."

Juridical theologies, succumbing to rather than inverting retributive patterns, interpret the Christ's active suffering as salvaging the penal vision of history as tribunal. Suffering offered as gift becomes the means by which mercy "satisfies" justice. Offered suffering is absorbed by a quantitative law of retribution instead of wrath by love. Evil triumphs even as it is defeated. Yet if evil is penalty for evil, where is the God of love? The Christian hope is that the active suffering of the Christ can transform evil into redemptive goodness. Nonetheless, vindictiveness, works-righteousness, and the penal vision die hard. Possibility of a hyperethical God beyond accusation and punishment is too much to bear. To entertain transcending the *lex talionis* is to entertain two threatening alternatives: that justice does not rule the cosmos but something less than justice, chaos, or something more than justice, compassionate love. Hence humans are summoned to go beyond vindictiveness, beyond justice, to costly merciful love.

Perhaps only a capacity for voluntary, offered suffering affords wisdom courageous enough to affirm that God is not wickedly chaotic. Perhaps only suffering servants can exorcise the demonic deity. Perhaps the priority is praxis, not argument or even conviction that God is good, but being a redeeming person. Each one is Adam and each one Job, doing and suffering evil as culprit and victim. The challenge and the gift is to be also Ebed, converting the passivity of being victim into the activity of being redemptive servant for others. Adam failed to act wisely or well; Job sank into bitterness and passivity. The Servant transcends both by making of suffering, of evil undergone, an action capable of redeeming evil committed.

See also DEMON(S); DEMONIC, DEVIL(S); FREEDOM; GOD; GRACE; SIN; TEMPTATION; REDEMPTION.

Bibliography: D. Griffin, *God, Power, and Evil: A Process Theodicy* (Philadelphia: Westminster, 1976). J. Hick, *Evil and the God of Love* (New York: Harper & Row, 1978). P. Ricoeur, "Evil, Challenge to Philosophy and Theology," *Journal of the American Academy of Religion* (1985) 635–648. T. Tilley, *The Evils of Theodicy* (Washington: Georgetown Univ. Press, 1991).

STEPHEN J. DUFFY

EXAMINATION OF CONSCIENCE

Examination of conscience, consciousness examen, review of life are all terms for a similar activity approached from differing perspectives. John Henry Newman, in *The Development of Christian Doctrine,* discusses how one idea may be perceived in many ways analogous to the way in which a material object can be described in many ways by persons viewing it from different angles, different sides, differing perspectives. Consciousness examen suffers the same multiplicity of understandings and the consequent plenitude of judgments on its function and efficacy.

Every relationship suffers by neglect. In our spiritual life we seek a wholeness, a path along which we walk in union with

God and others. Headlong passage without a pause now and then to check our position, our companions or Companion can be disastrous. It may be important to know whether we have left others behind or have contrived to halt or even reverse our direction. We may wish to assess whether the territory in which we find ourselves is familiar or strange. This pause and perusal of the territory, of the current interior and exterior situation, is not so much a tallying up of successes and failures as it is an evaluation of the present spiritual "state of the union."

A review of one's present general spiritual health can lead to resolutions concerning the future, a resolve to be more fully human, fully Christian in a particular area of life or relationships. A renewed awareness of the need for encouragement and support can find expression in prayer for grace, mercy, courage, strength, and so on.

The central focus in an examination of conscience should move beyond a simple tally of guilt or the number of sins committed. It is a prayerful reflection on one's relationship with God and with others, as a human being created in love for love, but in need of the support and encouragement of God's presence along the way. As such it can be a powerful aid for a spiritually vital life.

See also CONSCIENCE; CONSCIOUSNESS; RETREAT, RETREAT MOVEMENT; SIN; SPIRITUAL DIRECTION.

Bibliography: G. Aschenbrenner, "Consciousness Examen," Review for Religious 31 (1972) 14–21.

BENJAMIN BAYNHAM, O.C.S.O.

EXERCISE, PHYSICAL FITNESS
See BODY; HOLISTIC SPIRITUALITY.

EXORCISM

Exorcism is the act of driving out an unclean spirit or demon from a person or place believed to be possessed. Jesus fre-quently performed exorcisms during his ministry (Mk 1:39) and gave his disciples the power to cast out demons in his name (Mk 3:15; Mt 10:1; see Acts 16:18).

In the NT period the figure of Satan personified evil and the power of darkness, the ruler of this world. Mental disorders and physical disturbances were assigned to the influence of demonic powers. In Luke's Gospel the close connection between disease, demons, and the devil is evident (see Lk 10:9-20; 13:11-16).

In the patristic period the demons were understood as fallen angels, malevolent spirits still able to act upon the world. There are references to Christian exorcisms in the writings of the Church Fathers. Toward the beginning of the 3rd century exorcisms appear in the rites of Christian initiation; but here exorcism is directed at sinful inclinations and the seduction of evil rather than an indwelling demon.

The Church continues to provide a rite for conducting exorcisms, but they are performed very infrequently. According to the 1983 Code of Canon Law (can. 1172), an exorcism can be performed only by a priest with special permission from the local bishop. The law does not mention any restrictions concerning the religious convictions of the one to be exorcised.

See also DEMON(S), DEMONIC, DEVIL(S); EVIL; PRAYER.

Bibliography: H. Kelly, The Devil, Demonology and Witchcraft (Garden City, N.Y.: Doubleday, 1974).

THOMAS P. RAUSCH, S.J.

EXPERIENCE

Being Christian means embracing an agenda. We are to love the Lord our God with our whole heart, our whole mind, our entire soul, all our strength, and to love our neighbor as ourselves. Ever since Jesus first commissioned us, we have explored the meaning of this agenda in a thousand places, through a thousand epochs. In each locale we have used certain focal words to talk about salvation. Today, as the 20th century slips into history, *experience* has become a focal word for Western understanding of how to live out the gospel.

We must credit William James for raising the category of experience to the level of general discussion in theology, pastoral work, and spiritual mentoring. In *The Varieties of Religious Experience* (1902), he explored the meaning of religion particularly in terms of "conversion" and "mystical" experiences. He gathered many accounts of intense, personal religious experiences and ascribed to them a critical function in religious living. Still, as an admitted atheistic pragmatist, he cut off his own access to the critical functions performed by dogma. That is, he could not allow himself to take as true the statements of people about the God they experienced. For James, their beliefs were merely evidence of a pattern of living, not of a Someone whom they experienced.

This focus on experience as the sole measure of one's relationship with God wormed its way into Christian spiritual preaching. Sad to say, it also imposed on many people a false sense of alienation from God. As spiritual mentors can attest, many Christians believe that they live far from God simply because they never consciously felt any exquisite sense of God. Or there can be found the belief, particularly among Evangelical and Pentecostal Christians, that the spiritual life is a matter of pursuing the poignant religious experience—a belief completely foreign to Scripture. The gospel, after all, is news. It is a proclamation of a truth, not a directive to wait upon experience for personal revelation. The truth is that nothing can separate us from the love of God (Rom 8:35-39), and presumably this includes dry religious feelings.

Karl Rahner and Bernard Lonergan have blazed a more direct trail to understanding the role of experience in the spiritual life. They began from the revealed truth that God exists and acts on our behalf in Christ Jesus and the Spirit. By starting from revealed truth rather than from empirical data alone, they have extended the importance of experience in the spiritual life far beyond what James envisioned. Experience becomes a category within theological anthropology—the study of humanity as graced by God. Experience, therefore, is somehow both human and divine, both immanent and transcendent. It is important to note that theological anthropology is one of the most significant developments in dogmatic theology since the high achievements of Nicaea and Chalcedon. Those early councils defined what God is like, based on Christians' experience of Jesus and the Spirit. Theological anthropology defines what *we* must be like if God's personal Word and Spirit can take up their eternal abode with us. As Vatican II has pointed out, "God has revealed humanity to humanity itself."

So a contemporary study of Christian spirituality should approach experience, not with the expectation that certain religious or mystical experiences are our high roads to God, but with the expectation that all human experiences make up God's humble path to us. Therefore we will examine the role of experience in God's self-gift to us through Word and Spirit. Our guiding question will be: *What divine role does experience play in a Christian's life in the Spirit?* In other words, our subject is not "intense religious experience," but the entire range of experience as it involves us with God.

We will begin by looking at certain features of human experience—in particular, how experience is preconditioned, how it is the source of all meaning, and how it is ultimately ambiguous. After describing the ambiguities of experience, we will then look at how God's gifts of Word and Spirit resolve those ambiguities. Finally, we will describe how human experiences insert us into the life of the Trinity.

Experience Is Preconditioned

Experience is always an interaction of both inner and outer events. The inner events are made up of biological needs, instinctual fears, inherited worldviews, shared biases, and personally developed interests and aversions, loves and commitments. We do not take in life like a vacuum cleaner. We select. We focus our attention on certain experiences and exclude others. Experience has a built-in filtering system, and this filtering always takes place, in every experience. Because these inner events precondition what our five senses see, hear, taste, feel, or smell, there is no such thing as "raw" experience. So there is no such thing as a "pure" religious experience, considered as a look at God without any internal conditioning on our side. Also, the outer events themselves are not simply channeled to our brain through the five senses. Because we take life to be a drama, not a stream of data, meaningful experience is always in the form of a story. The data of the senses are elements of a story, and we are interested in the story, not the data as such.

Most biblical authors wrote their stories in a literary style that did not articulate the inner events that shaped the story. When we hear of Moses seeing the burning bush or of Elijah hearing the sound of a gentle whispering wind, we can forget that besides the visible and audible outer events, there were inner events of belief, hope, desire, and commitment going on as well. Without these inner events of mind and heart, they would never have told the story, because Moses would not have noticed the bush, nor Elijah the breeze.

Each individual shapes his or her experiences in a unique way. Hypochondriacs notice every ache and itch in their bodies rather than practical issues at hand. If philosophers walk into trees, artists stumble into debates, preoccupied by their own concerns. Mystics notice their heart's yearning to be drawn beyond all worldly cares. No doubt the Apostle Matthew was musing on something other than tax records when Jesus invited him to follow. The sight of religious zealots crushing Stephen to death with stones may have profoundly reoriented St. Paul's readiness to experience the initiatives God had in mind for him.

The richness of a person's experience will therefore depend on habits of noticing. A boy in high school may realize that he should apply his mind to understanding the subject he is studying rather than to the clever manipulation of words to impress teachers. He increasingly notices the world presented by his teachers more than his teachers' attitudes toward him. Conversely, many are the tourists who are so preoccupied with taking pictures that they fail to meet the foreigner whose land they visit. They never experienced what they didn't notice.

Some people never fully realize the power they have to enrich their personal experiences. It is chiefly a matter of wanting to notice. Those who want to live in conscious love of God have to take charge of their noticing. They will begin to notice whatever relates to their agenda to love God and neighbor. They start noticing the quiet pull on their hearts to be honest, courageous, and caring. Gradually they grow accustomed to noticing the precise quality of that pull. They learn to taste the difference between a true pull and a false pull. Sometimes they so yearn to see the Source of that pull that they drop the baggage of practical concerns and arrive empty-handed before God in mystical union.

Taking charge of one's own noticing is a prolonged and difficult process. That is because our experience is preconditioned not only by personally developed interests but by biological needs that we can never fully control. Without essential food, water, clothes, or shelter, our experiences will focus merely on the search for survival. Today substance addiction (drugs, alcohol) ravages far more than the bodies of addicts; it narrows the range of their minds and subordinates their friendships, family ties, and jobs to a growing obsession with ingesting a chemical.

One's biological system not only determines needs but shapes a person's values as well. We have become aware that differences in our biological genders have a significant impact on how we each develop morally. For example, some people say that women value personal relations over projects, while men set projects over personal relations. Theorists may argue whether biology or culture ultimately conditions such a preference. But eventually we want to know: How do a man and a woman talk to each other? Are a person's preferences reliable? There is a difference, after all, between bias and perspective. A woman has to distinguish between a threatening male bias and a helpful male perspective in what a man says, as must a man for a woman's statements. It is an unending work.

The work of filtering bias from perspective also applies to race, chronological age, and nationality. Our skin color, age, and provenance are not mere information about us; they confine us within a particular world of both wisdom and foolishness. Most of us take our world as wise and others' as foolish—just as others do about us. To escape that confinement, it is not enough to perceive what others value. The first step in becoming liberated is to perceive that we ourselves experience our world with a mixture of bias and wisdom.

Experience Is the Source of Meaning

Although our experience may be shaped by gender, race, age, and nationality, this does not mean that we do not ask fresh questions. Our uneasiness with old answers that make no sense of new situations liberates us from the confines of the past. But if a liberation from the past is not to be a heavy-handed rejection of everything old, there is something we have to recognize about past achievements: All old answers, when they were fresh, sprung from somebody's experience. Let us put this more strongly: Nothing we hold to be true or valuable entered history outside of somebody's experience. Our beliefs about what makes good parents, about human rights, and about the lifestyles of foreigners have their source in something happening to somebody, somewhere, sometime. The ideas by which we set up our social institutions of language, law, education, health care, economics, technology, and politics spring from people's experience. All the religious practices and liturgical rites that give us ways to express ourselves before God originated in our forebears' experiences in particular circumstances.

To be specific, our beliefs about salvation in Jesus and the Spirit, about the afterlife, about the Virgin Mary, about sin, and so on, were originally someone's understanding of his or her own experience. But we must ask, What kind of experiences raise in us such questions about our relationship to God? Does everyday experience really have such religious meaning? If we look merely at the particular things we want and the grandiose institutions we set up to get them, there is little evidence of anything religious. Yet in all our particular experiences, despite the contradictions and tensions that harass us, we simultaneously experience an abiding yen for harmony, peace, and fulfillment. We feel that each particular experience is a potential step toward that fine goal. Once we begin to notice this transcendental desire in ourselves, we discover that we want ultimate good in everything we do. We want the meaning of the particular passages of our lives to contribute to a single symphony that ultimately resolves all tensions and themes. It is not pious talk that makes us "religious." It is not a deep consciousness of the God we know that defines "religious experience." The authentic religious life develops whenever we notice the transcendent invitation in every experience of wholesome desire. Experience is religious when we recognize that good desires are received, not fabricated, and when we deliberately search out the One who calls us by this gift of desire.

People of genuine faith will nourish that faith by noticing the workings of desire in their ordinary experience. From ordinary experience they will find God. Going in the reverse direction, they will look for the meaning of any traditional doctrine or practice within the data at hand. They will find meaning in doctrines about God by returning to experience. They will turn the other cheek because they believe that this lifestyle made sense out of Jesus' personal experience. They will turn the other cheek also because they tried it and discovered the meaning in their lives. It is important to recognize that Jesus validated his high spiritual principles by his experience. Even when self-sacrificing love drove Jesus to the cross, he did not go out of blind obedience to an abstract principle. Jesus went to the cross because his experience taught him that self-giving is better than self-securing. Likewise, our faith does not just acknowledge the importance of Christian principles; faith also moves us to meditate on how these principles gave meaning to Jesus' experience—and on how they might give meaning to our own.

Our faith, after all, is ultimately built on the faith experiences of the first disciples of Jesus. As the Church began to spread, the lively faith of those who walked and ate with Jesus became the primary evidence for newcomers that the message and style of Jesus are truly life-giving. Throughout history, we know, traditions lost their meaning when people grew oblivious to actual people of faith and merely repeated formulas and performed rituals governed by rubrics. Suddenly a maverick appeared who wanted faith to make sense out of everyday experience. Then a reform of tradition began, because the Spirit in people recognized the cosmic Christ in the flesh of the reformer.

There is an important political significance to the fact that experience is the source of meaning. Precisely because it is *somebody's* originating experience, that somebody becomes an authority. A person who has experienced the Lord at work in history becomes someone whom others want to consult. They want to understand the significance of that engendering experience and to guide the course of its meaning as it develops in different contexts. In Luke's writings, Peter and the apostles form the official center of a larger group of disciples, all of whom have authority to preach and baptize because they experienced Jesus. Paul legitimizes his claim to be called an apostle by appealing to his experience of the risen Christ. In John's Gospel, Mary of Magdala and the Beloved Disciple are the chief spiritual authorities in the Church because of their tender affection for Jesus. But John's Gospel was written long after it dawned on Christians that all the contemporaries of Jesus were going to die, so he advises, "Happy are those who do not see and yet believe." Continuing authority, in other words, depends on the continuing experience of love and fidelity to Jesus, under the guidance of the Spirit. In principle, at least, Christians expect those who hold positions of authority to have earned that authority through experience of life in the pattern of Christ rather than merely to have accepted a title, robe, and ring.

Notice how the thesis that experience is the source of meaning clarifies the purpose of "meditation." Many men and women meditate on mere concepts—how Jesus had the virtue of humility and therefore could lower himself to speak to the woman at the well. Yet real life reveals its meaning through the lens of experience. Therefore meditation should be a matter of gaining the inner sense of another's experience and finding resonances in one's own experience. Much better to meditate on what moved Jesus to overcome Jewish taboos against speaking to a Samaritan woman. Better to consider what religious, national, or gender taboos I experience in my spiritual life and how I might be liberated to overcome them. Again, these are matters of concrete authority, not abstract virtue. When we meditate on how Judith or Jeremiah responded to a divine invitation, it helps greatly to ask ourselves, How did this person accept the call to take charge of a situation? How did they deal with the religious authorities that stood in their way? By meditating on authority, we carry on the tradition of the real saints and reformers in the Church, who were preoccupied with how to mediate God's authority in a world of usurpers.

Experience Is Ambiguous

Experience may provide the basic elements of all meaning. It is another matter to discover what the meaning of any experience may be. Experience by itself, including all the preconditioned meanings and inner attitudes that go with it, remains ambiguous. In other words, experience does not yield up its true meaning easily. Because, as we saw, experience is an interaction of both outer and inner events, we will find the stubbornness of experience both in our psyches and in our stories. On the story side, we find the behavior of others strange, the meaning of everyday talk elusive, our solutions to ordinary problems provisional. Most Christians who read the Bible suffer a hermeneutical shock when they realize that the inspired text is not plain; it is subject to the interpretation of the uninspired. On the psyche side, we find that we sometimes turn away from the meaning of experience. The neurotic, for example, represses certain personal questions that might bring understanding about feelings. The self-centered person cunningly ignores questions about the welfare of the neighbor. Most communities show passionate intelligence about their own welfare but are ploddingly slow to gain insight into the good of other communities and into the larger common good that would benefit a network of communities. Finally, all people seem to suffer an intel-

lectual laziness that refuses to push questions to their limit when short-term answers are patently inadequate. These viruses on the body of meaning infect all of us to some extent. Think of any school, company, or family. Such institutions are always a mishmash of good ideas and nonsense, and the struggle to sift one from the other is unending.

Religious feelings also are ambiguous experiences that beg clarification. When those feelings lift us up to an exquisite sense of God, we still must return to ordinary life and put the lessons of that encounter to the test. Teresa of Avila and Ignatius Loyola experienced intense spiritual consolations that turned out to be untrustworthy. Similarly in the liturgy, the adequacy of specific songs, movements, art and architecture does not depend on the strength of the feelings they evoke; the adequacy of any Christian ritual depends instead on the worth of the gospel values to be celebrated. Sometimes those values call for simple joy rather than high excitement; other times they call for flamboyant celebration rather than sober formulations of contentment.

Nor are religious thoughts exempt from the ambiguity of experience. If the example of the disciples of Jesus tells us anything about faith, it says that it takes great effort and much error to understand Jesus, even though they had already set their hearts on him. What Christian can easily formulate what the "good news" really is? It seems to be a rule that the closer our experience approaches love, the more difficult we find it to understand, even after we have taken the plunge.

In the history of spirituality we find that mystical experience itself is ambiguous. Mystics do not easily explain what happened to them. For most kinds of mystical experiences, a discernment of spirits is necessary to determine whether the experience is truly from God. Also, we should not forget the political side to mysticism. Although works abound on the psychological experience of mysticism, spiritual writers have paid little attention to how it legitimates ecclesial power, despite the common experience of awe that a mystic engenders in the average person. A look at history shows that the mystics honored by Catholics were essentially reformers: Paul, Augustine, Ignatius Loyola, Teresa of Avila, and John of the Cross. Whatever their intentions, their accounts of mystical experiences gave them moral weight in the eyes of anyone who might question the integrity of the reforms they envisioned. Church authorities used St. Margaret Mary's visions of the Sacred Heart of Jesus to legitimate a Catholic, affective response to the Enlightenment, even though she herself lacked the capacity to organize such a reform. The Middle Ages recognized the dangers of mysticism's political power. The visionary teachings of Joachim of Fiore (d. 1202) threatened to demolish the hierarchical structure of the Church, so authorities condemned his writings. Authorities also condemned the mystical teachings of the Dominican Meister Eckhart (d. 1328), more by force of Franciscan envy of his moral power than by rational assessment of his works. So the Church has wisely held, at least in principle, that mystical experience by itself does not unerringly reveal meaning and authorize its recipient.

Besides the ambiguities of our experience of neurosis, egoism, and shortsightedness, besides the ambiguities of our experience of religious feelings, thoughts, and mysticism, there are two further ambiguities present in all experience: the ambiguity of hope and the ambiguity of time. Let us look more closely at each of them.

The Ambiguity of Hope

First we should note that all our experiences occur while we silently nurse a question of hope or despair. Imagine a man who, through no fault of his own, suffers from melancholy, failure, or rejection. His taste for life has departed, and meaning has fled his ordinary experience. Hopelessness shapes the meaning of each everyday experience, and yet something hopeful must be burning within. Why else would he carry on? Imagine a woman who, through personal ambition, has grown wealthy and powerful. Her successes have made her only more rabid about the climb to heights she dreams she will stop and enjoy. But she never stops and enjoys. Every step is part of a hopeful climb that could end in despair.

In either case, it is unlikely that this man and woman could speak unequivocally about their personal hope or despair. Their experience feels like a mixture of both. The only time we can speak with any conviction about a person's hope or despair is at death. Here the final threads of the tapestry of life have been cut, and no further weavings of experience can change the appearance of the whole. Among all the preconditionings of our everyday experience that stem from parents and our culture, one of the most important is the preconditioning that hope or despair brings.

Concretely, we experience hope's ambiguity in the gap between our *hopes* and our *hope*. Our hopes are made up of concrete goals—what we hope for our children, for our health, for our career, for our loved ones. Our hope is another matter. Hope is about what it will mean to realize or fail to realize our individual hopes. A woman can have fulfilled her life's dreams, and yet if she is still unhappy, she finds that success has not sustained her. She fulfilled her hopes but lacks hope. Or a man can fail to achieve his goals and yet discover a quiet expectation in his heart that all shall be well anyway. His hopes are dashed, but he is filled with hope. We must ask, On what do we pin our specific hopes? How can we tell, in everyday experience, that pursuing this or that particular set of hopes is an exercise of hope in life's ultimate meaning? We do not know for sure. Hope is neither certitude nor conviction that our decisions are on target. Hope is rather a felt assurance that even poor decisions will not rob our lives of meaning, in spite of our inability to explain why.

The Ambiguity of Time

The other ambiguity present in all experience regards time. Our experience of the passing of time is unlike our ways of measuring time. When we are bored, "time" passes slowly; when we are active, it passes quickly. We know that the clock hasn't sped up or slowed down. There is something in experience correspondingly slowing down or speeding up. We watch the clock, but we are comparing measured time against some inner timepiece. They say time passes quickly when you're having fun; it also passes quickly when you're working productively. Without meaningful recreation or work, time drags. So our inner timepiece seems to measure the flow of experience by meaning, not by seconds. The more meaning, the faster the flow of experience goes, and vice versa. The human thirst for meaning, therefore, is the inner timepiece that keeps glancing at clocks, not simply to know the hour but to measure the meaningfulness of one's life.

We cannot restrict the meaningfulness of experience to each particular moment of experience. We string our experiences together to form a pattern, to give a direction, to weave partial experiences into something significant and lasting. Whether or not we admit it, we all feel an urgency to make something of ourselves before the death bell tolls. Our experience of time, therefore, finds its meanings in the making of our personal story within history—not written history, but the actual series of experiences about which historians write.

Still, even without a written history, we do live our lives according to a personal image of how our story fits into history. This image is not a written or conceptual philosophy of history. Our image of history is fixed by how we imagine the work of everyday living that everyone is involved in. More significantly, our image of history covertly but powerfully shapes our spirituality. The problem is that our images of history differ from one another, and each person can point to experience for validation. To illustrate, and to demonstrate this ambiguity of our experience of time, let us look at four images of history that everyday experience reinforces.

1. History is cyclic. The image of the circle suggests that the laws that govern the visible universe are essentially the same as the laws that govern history. Thus history is a process of cultures rising and declining, and although specific cultures may appear unique, the same fundamental processes determine their rise and fall everywhere. Children repeat the sins and successes of their parents. Our individual efforts become a somewhat blind contribution to some suprahistorical inevitability concealed from us all. So the author of Ecclesiastes concludes that there is nothing really new under the sun. This vision is preservative in character. It models experience after the orderly cycles of sunrise and sunset. Time is a circle, and we should learn the lesson this time around or there will be trouble on the next turn. All we can do is keep faithful to what we know is good. This preservative spirituality is at its best when not a word of God falls to the ground without being accomplished. This image favors Matthew's Gospel, which downplays the unpredictable gusts of the Holy Spirit and sanctions the stabilizing authority of the apostles. At its worst, spiritual fascists canonize the limpest human opinions, rendering the unexpected work of the Infinite Spirit null.

2. History is random. Here everything is new, special, particular, and surprising. The varieties of sin and grace are infinite. God exercises divine dominion over history by acting without warning and without apology. This vision is interruptive in character. It models experience after the suddenness of lightning and earthquakes, shooting stars and rainbows. Time is a vertical arrow up to eternity. There is only the present moment and both kinds of luck. All

we can do is expect that God will give us sufficient resources in time of trouble. Spirituality is ultimately based on trust. At its best, this vision stands by the rejects of society because each person, each moment, is Christ. It favors John's Gospel, which sanctifies the present moment, making the end-time always the present time. At its worst, it rejects all long-range planning and absents itself from the common struggle to discover the balance between taking and relinquishing control.

3. History is progressing. In this image history is becoming something predetermined, like maple seeds becoming maple trees. Especially in the 20th century, science has marked human life by unprecedented creativity on many fronts, and so the progressive character of history is impressed upon us all. It models experience after the growth of flowers, of children, and after the modern-day sense of evolution. We find it difficult to imagine ever losing the cultural ground gained by science and the arts. Time is an arrow upon whose arc we are gradually rising. God calls us to make the world a better place than we found it. Spirituality is essentially creation-centered. At its best, this vision finds good in all things and seizes every opportunity to bring grace to the world. It favors Luke's Gospel and Acts, which dote on the seed metaphor, following the spread of the Word and Spirit to Jerusalem and then to Rome. At its worst, it ignores human malice, foolishness, and the horrors they spawn. It feels no need for mercy.

4. History is struggle. Here every human event is the result of the collision of contradictory forces. Suffering is the only mother of wisdom. We do not receive life, we fight for it. This vision is dialectical in character. It models experience after the law of the jungle and the battles between opposing desires within the psyche. Time is the bell sounding the end of the final round, when the winner will be announced. God calls us not to create the kingdom but merely to fight for it. Spirituality is centered on the

discernment of spirits. At its best, this vision has uncovered the locus of sin and grace within the arena of human desires. It favors Mark's Gospel and some of Paul's letters, which depict the arrival of God as an inner battle of spirits. At its worst, it justifies hating one's enemy and mounting holy wars against anyone deemed different.

While few people cling exclusively to one of these images of the workings of history, most people favor one over another. Both our experience of nature and our reading of the Bible can find evidence supporting our image. Yet, pushed to its limits, no image alone seems to represent adequately the reality of history as revealed by the gospel. Spiritual mentors can illuminate the spiritualities of the people under their tutelage by asking about their imaginal preconception of the workings of history. This is no small benefit. Yet mentors would fail in their fundamental responsibility if they were unable to state clearly what revelation says about the nature of historical process.

The Experience of Grace

We do not need to rely on the Bible alone to find testimony to the existence of grace. Our own experience and the best fiction bear witness to the phenomenon that when we are at our lowest, we often experience sudden resources. We experience these resources in different ways. I may experience a clarity of moral vision. I may feel the courage to act for the sake of my neighbor. Or I may feel an optimism lifting me above all obstacles. I cannot explain how these resources spurted up from my psyche. I did not decide to experience them. I may have wished for them, but they occurred without my devising.

As experienced, these resources have both an inner and an outer aspect. For example, we suddenly decide to confide in an acquaintance at work. That person appears trustworthy to us. He or she is an outer word to which an inner word in our hearts responds. This is the experience of faith—

no different in structure than the experience of the first Christians seeing in Jesus of Nazareth a person worthy of ultimate trust. Or suppose we discover ourselves making a long-distance call that we promised ourselves we would make to console a lonely friend. Love in our hearts impels us to care for a person whose story beckons us. Think of the times when, say, after the dark nights of despair over the decay of one's city, we awake with an unexpected courage to continue working to bring order out of chaos. The inner word of courage meets the outer word of a city as it might be. This is the experience of hope. It is not a certitude that we will reach our own goals. Hope is a confident desire that in the struggle for integrity, the best goals for all will be reached.

The experience of grace is the experience of faith, charity, or hope, with each kind having one foot in hearts and the other in history. Yet, as we experience these events, we do not necessarily recognize them as grace. Logic cannot deduce that these experiences are anything more than the human spirit responding to human values. It is the event of Christian conversion, sudden or gradual, that leads a person to the conviction that God is at work both in our hearts and in our history. During the first four centuries after Christ, Christians reflecting on their experience could not avoid acknowledging that such experiences are, in reality, the inner expression of God's Spirit welcoming the outer expression of God's Word. No doubt the gift of faith itself leads to this conviction. Faith, the first fruit of conversion, recognizes itself as a gift in experience, and the full horizon of the world opens up to those who believe.

Faith, then, is the door to the truth that resolves the ambiguities of experience. Faith is essentially a judgment of value: It is good to do this; it is good to believe that. Faith is the compass that guides the fickle meanderings of religious feelings and thoughts. No matter how miserable we feel, the truth is that God loves us, and all shall be well. Or no matter to what mystical heights religious fervor lifts us, we return to the realities of daily life to work out our charity in hope. Like the disciples descending the Mount of the Transfiguration, we look up and see only Jesus, and he is yet to be crucified.

Because revelations of values or truths by faith are the fundamental religious experiences, feelings and thoughts play a supportive role. That is why spiritual mentors serve well by dishing up the plain truth without emotional and discursive garnish. The feelings and thoughts of those they guide ought to flow from a personal experience of faith, not from the mentor's enthusiasm. That is also why spiritual mentors should have savored the saving dogmas themselves far more than doting on psychological analysis. The ambiguities of everyday experience are met by judgments of value and fact springing from being in love with God, not from psychology or systematic theology alone. The test of faith, of course, is not belief but action. The test of faith is charity—welcoming the stranger, visiting the imprisoned. So the mentor should direct attention not only to the values and truths revealed in Christ Jesus but also to the everyday experience of being moved to care for others actively.

The experience of hope is somewhat different. Even when God graces us with an eye for what is best and with the determination to act on it, our experience remains ambiguous in the sense that we cannot control outcomes. The outer aspect of hope is a story yet unfinished. We can only act with a faith and charity that rely on hope. Our hope is essentially a confident desire that the kingdom is indeed coming, very likely through the crucifixions behind us and ahead of us. We fix our hope on the truth that in Jesus God has spoken a superabundant Word, a Word that cannot reveal divinity more than it has because the Father has given everything to the Son. We fix our hope also on the truth that in our hearts God-Spirit will personally search and welcome the incarnation of Christ Jesus in everyday life.

Besides speaking to the ambiguity of hope, revelation also speaks to the ambiguity of time. The Spirit in us, cherishing the story of Christ, recognizes that history is predominantly dialectical. Certainly the conservative, interruptive, and progressive routines that stir in our bones and govern much of the world's workings have their place. But we get insight into the *meaning* of nature only by seeing its effect on human beings. The incessant desire we experience to control things—usually through some combination of the conservative, interruptive, and progressive kinds of governance—is ultimately subject to a dialectic of human desires. We experience both an attraction and a repulsion regarding the same people. We want to control situations but know that there is a point at which we should give up control. Even when we are settled within ourselves about the best course of action, there is the neighbor to contend with.

Look at the life of Jesus. The conservative instinct to obey religious laws yielded to inner impulses to cure on a day of rest and to dump the money tables in the Temple. Jesus' advice to trust like the birds of the air and to rely totally on God's interruptive grace was counterbalanced by a canny suspicion of most religious authorities and a wisdom he compared to the wiles of a snake. Jesus delivered his progressive mandate to spread the gospel to the ends of the earth in tandem with his prediction that his disciples would be crucified. Most patent, of course, is the dichotomy between Jesus' assurance that the kingdom is arriving and his agonizing cry, "My God, my God, why have you forsaken me?" (Mt 27:46). We believe in faith that the kingdom arrives, but only through a death and resurrection. The cross, we remember, is a sign of *blessing* that we make upon our bodies and each other, often with little thought of its dialectical significance.

The experience of grace is always an experience of being snatched from some kind of threat. It is essentially dialectical. Practically speaking, we juggle that dialectic by two kinds of discernment. On the inner side of experience, we discern the stirrings in our psyches. For this the classical rules for discernment of spirits have sustained many throughout the centuries. On the outer side, however, there has been a strange lack of rules in the Christian tradition for the discernment of stories. False stories have recognizable features. They tend to eliminate certain groups of people from consideration. They fence out the experiences of people who are demoralized, angry, rejected, or impoverished. They are essentially group propaganda. Or they may glorify some person instead of some action, focusing on who someone is and not what someone does. (For example, look at the vocation ads run by many seminaries.) This glorifying feature usually mystifies the hearer, fostering an admiration that destroys self-esteem and deters taking responsibility. Most importantly, they draw an image of history that either is not dialectical or, if dialectical, is a simplistic pitting of friends against enemies. In any case, discernment of stories is just as important as discernment of spirits in living the shrewd spiritual life.

The Divine Role of Experience

We can now answer our guiding question: What divine role does experience play in a Christian's life in the Spirit? To a great extent, we have answered the question already. Experience is a test of truth; it is a ground of true authority; and it is ambiguous without the further experiences of faith, charity, and hope. When we distinguish immanence and transcendence in human experience, we are only distinguishing aspects of events that are simultaneously earth-bound and heaven-headed. God is at work in all experience that we may think relates only to earthly matters.

Even the experience of sin is experience of sin against the transcendent pull of consciousness. Whether or not we recognize it, all experience is religious experience, although in everyday speech we call "religious" only those experiences whose transcendence we recognize.

To reach the fullest answer to our question, we must look at the role of experience within God's loving purpose. Human experience is God's idea to accomplish a loving purpose. To put it precisely, experience is the double channel of God's gift of self to us. Let us explore this more thoroughly.

God saw fit to share the eternal, divine self with undivine creatures who become what they are over time. This share in the divine self is total. That is, we are able not merely to feel the effects of God; God made us potential recipients of God as God really is. We can become divine, sharing in the divinity of Christ, who emptied himself to share our humanity. If a metaphor be allowed, we are genetically coded to be God's image and likeness, making us real offspring of God. We can act in real collaboration with God, and we experience in time the inner plurality of the eternal Trinity.

One formulation of the inner life of God runs as follows: God eternally utters and welcomes. The Word that God utters is God. The welcome with which God receives the Word is God. The Utterer, the Word, and the Welcome are distinct but meaningless without each other. These distinctions in God do not contradict divine unity. For example, when we appreciate our own wise decisions, we can distinguish the self that decides, the decision, and our appreciation of ourselves having decided. Also, we become better persons, more perfect, more at one with ourselves, having made such decisions. In other words, we can verify in our experience that plurality can enhance and not contradict unity.

The terms *uttering* and *welcoming* in God do not unequivocally illuminate what God is like. They are only our terms for saying something about distinctions in God. They give a good analogy for how the inner plurality in God can account for God's perfection and unity. Yet, given revelation in history, we can go beyond mere analogy to form a *relative* understanding of our own uttering and welcoming that points to God as their ultimate meaning. Besides analogy, we have a method of "indicative signification" to understand the Trinity. We can point to our own uttering and welcoming and say that their full significance, hidden from us in time, lies in a parallel two processions in God. To the extent that we understand the history-bound meanings of God's Word and Spirit, it is the eternal God whom we understand in a partial way.

In a moment of pious reflection, we might thank God for entering our lives through both inner and outer experience. Yet a little further reflection shows this wonderful match to be more than a happy coincidence. The only reason God structured us to encounter reality through inner and outer experiences is to enable us to receive God as God really is—eternally uttering and welcoming the divine self, eternally uttering the Word and eternally loving in Spirit. In other words, we have both inner and outer aspects to our experiences so that God can come to us as Word in our history and as Spirit in our hearts. The double character of human experience is God's kind idea to invent creatures who could share in the intimacy of divine life as it really is.

As God utters the divine self beyond time, our "uttering" consists in incarnating divine values and behavior for others to experience in time. We become part of the divine outer Word to others with Christ, the head of the body of which we are members. We are paragraphs filling out the story of Christ. As God welcomes the divine self beyond time, our "welcoming" consists in searching out and appreciating divine values and behavior whenever we experience them in time.

Yet, because we live in a world of sin, our uttering and welcoming take place in dialectical struggle. We struggle to become the good persons for others to experience. Others will always struggle to discern what part of our story, our conduct and language, is a saving word for them. We writhe in Spirit over the lack of a divine Word in the world. We agonize with God as Spirit in the great act of childbirth to bring life to the world.

Into this world of struggle—not of determinism, not of randomness, not of an automatic progress—we are born to experience God's compassion in us by uttering and welcoming God's Word.

See also AFFECT, AFFECTIVITY; ANTHROPOLOGY, THEOLOGICAL; CONSCIOUSNESS; DESIRE; DISCERNMENT OF SPIRITS; FAITH; GOD; GRACE; HISTORY, HISTORICAL CONSCIOUSNESS; HOPE; INTENTION, INTENTIONALITY; LOVE; MYSTERY; SPIRITUAL DIRECTION.

Bibliography: T. Dunne, Spiritual Mentoring (San Francisco: Harper & Row, 1991); We Cannot Find Words (Denville, N.J.: Dimension Books, 1981). W. James, The Varieties of Religious Experience (New York: Macmillan/Collier, 1961). J. King, Experiencing God All Ways and Every Day (Minneapolis: Winston, 1982). K. Leech, Experiencing God (San Francisco: Harper & Row, 1985). B. Lonergan, "Mission and the Spirit," A Third Collection, ed. F. Crowe (New York: Paulist, 1985) 23–34; "Religious Experience," ibid., 115–128. A. Maslow, Religions, Values, and Peak-Experiences (New York: Viking, 1970). K. Rahner, The Trinity, trans. J. Donceel (New York: Herder, 1970). E. Underhill, Mysticism (New York: Dutton, 1991).

TAD DUNNE

EXTRAORDINARY PHENOMENA

Extraordinary phenomena may be defined as events and experiences that are beyond the explanatory categories of the most current and commonly held scientific theories and cultural perceptions. Thus, beyond the threshold of ordinary explainable occurrences, extraordinary phenomena invite wonder, awe, and a curiosity about the dimension of human reality that has been called the supernatural. These phenomena, therefore, have commonly been associated with the quest for God, the discovery of the sacred, and the human desire to inhabit a world of mystery.

The wonder aroused by extraordinary phenomena may be distinguished from that which accompanies explainable ordinary phenomena, which inspire interest and appreciation. For example, in prescientific cultures, cosmic occurrences, such as the rising of the sun or the eclipse of the moon, were considered extraordinary phenomena, inspiring fear and worship. Although scientific studies now have explained these events, demystifying them of any supernatural claims or intervention, such scientific explanation does not prohibit these events from being experienced as numinous.

The Christian Experience

The Christian tradition, not unlike the Jewish understanding of God's revelation, is founded upon the proclamation of God's work within history. For Christians, God's work finds its apex in the incarnation of the Word and in the life and works of Jesus. The miracles of Jesus, and later those of the apostles in his name, are considered extraordinary events that proclaim the breakthrough of the reign of God into human existence. Although contemporary scriptural studies have sought to demythologize the miraculous works of the Gospels, arguing that Christianity is primarily a matter of morality and not of divine intervention, the texts nevertheless ascribe to Jesus and his apostles extraordinary phenomena that inspire wonder and faith in the community.

The miracles of Jesus as extraordinary phenomena have been categorized in six types: (1) physical and mental healings; (2) exorcisms and expulsions of spiritual forces; (3) communication with the spirit world through dreams, revelations, visions, or prayer; (4) nature miracles, which include walking on water and feeding the multitudes; (5) miracles of telepathic and clairvoyant powers; and (6) the resurrection appearances.

The Roman Catholic tradition, without seeking to explain or defend itself, continues to acknowledge the occurrence of extraordinary phenomena. Some of these phenomena include the liquefaction of powder substances, with the claim of being the blood of Christ or of a martyr; the Shroud of Turin and other relics of unknown origin; apparitions of the saints, the Virgin, or Christ; claims of bilocation; the stigmata, levitation, and various other bodily phenomena; and unexplained physical healings.

For the Christian tradition, a tension continues to exist between the experience of God's revelation in such extraordinary occurrences and the discovery of God's workings in the proclamation of the Scriptures and in the life and history of the community itself. Accordingly, the nature of extraordinary phenomena and its relationship to faith remain a problematic within Christian theology.

Contemporary Cultural Perspectives

There seems to be a natural attraction to, and seeking for, extraordinary phenomena. This is evidenced by the vast history of such events and the responses that they evoke. What is the reason for the attraction to the experience of the extraordinary? Is it a desire to probe the limits of human knowing, and thereby uncover further scientific data; or is it a profound nostalgia to inhabit a world of mystery in which technology and the limits of modern science have no power or control? Whatever the reasons, extraordinary phenomena have become the object of serious scientific and psychological research.

Many modern universities include studies of extraordinary phenomena in their curricula. Over the past decades faculties of parapsychology and psychic research have been developed. Such faculties probe such unexplained phenomena as remote seeing, poltergeists, apparitions, mediumship, clairvoyance, psychokinesis, out-of-body experiences, astral projection, and near-death experiences. These faculties are seeking to move science to a new horizon of reality and an understanding of the possibilities of human consciousness. Recent studies suggest that the occurrence of extraordinary phenomena continues to raise significant questions for Western philosophy and science.

See also DEMON(S), DEMONIC, DEVIL(S); HEALING; PARAPSYCHOLOGY; REVELATION(S); SPIRITS; STIGMATA; VISION(S).

Bibliography: J. Heaney, The Sacred and the Psychic: Parapsychology and Christian Theology (New York: Paulist, 1984). M. Kelsey, The Christian and the Supernatural (Minneapolis: Augsburg, 1976). L. Watson, Supernature: A Natural History of the Supernatural (New York: Bantam Books, 1974); Beyond Supernature: A New Natural History of the Supernatural (New York: Bantam Books, 1988).

RICHARD N. FRAGOMENI

F

FAITH

Used in a Judeo-Christian context, the word *faith* refers to a rich, multidimensional human stance that is inseparably God's gift and our own deepest actualization. In the following considerations we probe various facets of this theological virtue that relates us immediately to God and forms the foundation of our entire life in the Spirit.

Faith in Scripture

Derived from the Middle English *feith* and the Latin *fides* ("trust"), "faith" translates the Greek noun *pistis,* used in the Septuagint and the New Testament. The reality described by *pistis* (from the verb *pisteuein,* "to believe") in turn traces its roots to two verbs used in the Hebrew Scriptures, *aman* and *batah.*

The Hebrew word *aman* ("to be firm, solid"—and thus "true") speaks a personal relationship with the God on whose strength and absolute sureness we can literally stake our lives. This is the God who delivered the chosen people from slavery in Egypt and who continued to work wonders for them throughout history, the God whose immovable love for us evokes our own cry, *amen!* To have faith is to abandon ourselves without reserve into the arms of this God whose faithfulness to us is more sure than our own existence.

The psalmists often use a second Hebrew word, *batah* (e.g., Pss 4:5; 25:2; 55:23; 56:4) to convey the dynamic force of our actively trusting God, confidently expecting every good from the God who cannot fail us: "Steadfast love surrounds those who trust in the Lord" (Ps 32:10, NRSV). Psalm 78, for example, paints a fiery picture of God's mighty deeds and the life-changing faith these deeds are meant to evoke in God's chosen people.

We can understand faith's meaning more deeply if we consider its opposite. "Despite [God's] wonders they did not believe .... Their heart was not steadfast toward God; they were not true to [God's] covenant" (Ps 78:32, 37, RSV). Not to have faith is to live our lives unchanged by God's wonders of love for us, to trust in our own or in others' power instead of on the rock-solid sureness of God's love. Unbelief thus means anchoring ourselves to wind (Ps 78:39).

Isaiah 7:9 proclaims that if we do not stand firm in faith, we shall not stand at all. God alone is the invincible shield and fortress of those who have faith (Ps 91:9-10). Even if mountains could uproot themselves and walk away from us, no power in the universe can make God's rock-solid love leave us (Isa 54:10). To have faith means binding our own lives, through thick and thin, to the God forever bound fast to us in steadfast love.

The Hebrew authors hold before us Abraham and Sarah's story of faith. By faith Abraham trusted God when he was promised the humanly impossible—a new homeland and descendants to outnumber the stars. By faith Sarah bore a child when all past efforts had failed. Asked to let go of everything—their homeland and even their beloved child—and to cling to God alone, they went out in faith, not knowing where they were going. Their trusting surrender to God, and not any deeds of theirs, justified them, put them in right and loving relationship with God (Gen 15:6). Thus the Hebrew authors use the verb *aman,* translated in the Septuagint by *pisteuein,* to describe the entire content of our irrevocable covenant relationship with God.

New Testament authors take up the verb *pisteuein* and apply it to us, members of the Christian community, in our relationship with Jesus. Jesus claims from each of us the total surrender in faith that the Hebrew people gave to Yahweh. Mark focuses on the urgency of our need to respond in faith to Jesus. "The kingdom of God has come near; repent, and believe in the good news!" (Mk 1:15, NRSV). Faith in Jesus means being radically converted to him, and experiencing this conversion as one of unimagined joy, for Jesus and his message are *good news.* Through faith Jesus abides in our boat as our rock-fast shelter against even the most violent storm (Mt 8:23-27; Mk 4:35-41; Lk 8:22-25). Through faith in Jesus miracles happen in our lives and nothing is impossible to us (Mk 9:23; 11:23; see Mk 6:5, 6).

For Paul, this faith, *pistis,* is the very ground of our Christian existence. Like Abraham, we are justified not by our works or by the law but by faith in God's saving grace given to us in Jesus: the just person *lives* through faith (Rom 1:16-17; 3:24). To believe is to accept and receive this gift as real power in our lives, giving us a whole new life in intimate relationship and communion with Jesus (Gal 2:20; 3:26; 2 Cor 4:18; 5:7; 13:5). Clinging to Jesus in our heart through faith means in practice living a new life of faithfulness (Rom 3:3; Gal 5:22; 2 Thess 1:4) and obedience to God (Rom 1:5; 16:26). By faith we profess our belief in Jesus as our risen Lord (Rom 10:9) and enter into his death and resurrection through baptism (Rom 6:4, 6, 8; Gal 2:19; 5:24, 6:14).

The author of John views our faith in Jesus' word as our encounter with the very person of Jesus (Jn 4:50; 5:40; 5:47; 6:35). We come to Jesus himself when we believe the word of those who know him; through faith we experience for ourselves his presence and power (Jn 4:42). Thomas makes an act of faith in Jesus when he is shown signs, but those who believe without seeing are the ones truly blessed (Jn 20:29). For John, faith enables us truly to know God even now: "believe . . . that you may know" (Jn 10:38, RSV). Indeed, the Spirit within us draws us to know and live ever more intimately the truth of God that faith opens to us (Jn 16:13).

When we believe in Jesus, the life of heaven begins for us now (Jn 3:36; 6:40, 47). By participating through faith in Jesus' own communion with the Father, we begin truly to *live* to the full (Jn 10:10), because we experience the very power of the risen Lord in our lives (Jn 14:12). And because faith allows us to share even now in the personal intimacy within God's own heart, it can be God's gift alone: only those whom the Father draws can come to Jesus (Jn 6:44). Faith like this transforms the way we live and shines in the love we bear toward God and one another (Jn 13:34; 15:12).

Faith's Meaning in Subsequent Key Thinkers

The rich biblical understanding of faith includes both trusting surrender to God in Jesus that changes the way we live (the act of faith) and confession of faith in the word and saving mystery of Jesus (content of faith). As Avery Dulles has noted, subsequent thinkers often have stressed one or the other of these two aspects of faith: fiducial, life-changing trust, and intellectual content (Haughey, pp. 14–31).

Following upon the scriptural and especially Pauline understanding of faith, Augustine considers our act of faith as inseparable from faith's content. Influenced by Neoplatonism, Augustine stresses faith as an intellectual knowing, a new way we can see beyond physical appearances into the heart of reality where God abides everywhere. Through this light of faith we can enjoy God even now in a contemplative wisdom that anticipates our unending joy in "seeing" God in heaven.

Thomas Aquinas develops this Johannine and Augustinian understanding of faith as an intimate way of knowing God even now (*Summa Theologiae* II-II, qq. 1-7). By faith our whole person clings to God; our mind, impelled by our will's love and reliance on the God we trust, knows and clings to the truth of God, though in an imperfect and limited way. Yet in and through our faith articulations, we encounter the very reality of the God we confess. As intimate knowing of God, such faith can never be the fruit of simply our own effort. It is sheer gift, dependent not only on God's utterly free self-revelation and bestowal, but also on God's grace enabling us to respond to the divine self-giving. Thus our act of faith is inseparably dependent on the exterior word of the preacher and the interior inspiration of the Holy Spirit, who must anoint both the preacher's words and the hearers' minds and hearts if they are to believe. And while an individual believer's faith conceivably can exist without being informed by charity, faith's fullness as it exists in the Church community is faith always enlivened by grace and charity.

Late medieval nominalists lost this focus on faith as our intimate encounter with God in Jesus and often stressed faith as our blind assent to doctrines we believe simply because God wills us to believe them. Against this conception of faith, which stresses obedience as our human work, the 16th-century Augustinian Martin Luther tried to recapture Paul's understanding of faith as the trusting relationship with Jesus that alone justifies us. Faith frees us from relying on our own works and makes us dependent on God's mercy; doctrines of faith are valid insofar as they articulate the truth of the Scriptures. Luther in this way focuses on faith as our living trust in God's grace given in Jesus, our only way to live in right relationship with God. The Reformer John Calvin stresses faith as our firm knowledge of God's goodness bestowed in Jesus. With Aquinas, Calvin recognizes that our faith depends inseparably on the word of Scripture and the interior action of the Holy Spirit in our hearts.

Participants in the Council of Trent (1545-1560) understood the Reformers as advocating a faith devoid of good works. Trent's response therefore stresses that the trusting (fiducial) faith of our heart is not enough. Faith also requires our good works and our mind's clinging to God through belief in the doctrines proposed to us in Scripture and in the Church's tradition.

Seventeenth-century pietism and romanticism reacted against this focus on the intellectual nature of faith and envisioned faith as our heart's feeling. Eighteenth-century Enlightenment thinkers also rejected faith as a kind of intellectual knowing deeper than what our own minds can deliver to us, and enthroned our power of reason as the highest authority. Faith thus became for many a vague acknowledgment of a highest being.

In this post-Enlightenment context, the 19th-century Protestant Friedrich Schleiermacher (1768-1834) tried to save the centrality of faith by conceiving of it not as a kind of knowing but as a feeling of absolute dependence on God. On the other hand, Søren Kierkegaard (1813-1855) wanted to recapture Paul's focus on the personal nature of the act of faith. For Kierkegaard, faith means total surrender to God, a "leap" and "risk" by which we reject all security except God. Faith is the decision and act of courage we make as a "lonely individual." What we believe—the intellectual content of faith—is secondary and even irrelevant to faith as our personal commitment to God.

Other 19th-century thinkers rejected faith altogether—faith both as a kind of knowing and as the heart's trusting surrender to God—and considered it the enemy of our human wholeness. Ludwig Feuerbach (1804–1872) understood faith as a projection of our own human power and goodness onto a God we create as a figure of our mind's imagination. Karl Marx (1818–1883) interpreted religious faith as the product of our alienation from one another, a way we are kept resigned and passive before the unjust social structures that divide us. Friedrich Nietzsche (1844–1900) understood faith as the way we symbolize our resentment toward our human finiteness and death. And Sigmund Freud (1856–1939) interpreted faith as an illusion, our psyche's way of satisfying wishes that cannot be fulfilled in reality.

In this rationalist context inimical to religious faith and institutions, Vatican Council I (1865–1869) all the more emphasized faith as obedient assent to the doctrines the Church teaches on God's authority. Faith thus seemed to be identified with intellectual content, with propositions offering us theoretical information.

During this same century, however, John Henry Newman (1801–1890) tried to recapture a biblical understanding of faith. In *Grammar of Assent,* Newman writes that we profess beliefs as the intellectual content of faith precisely because faith entails our intimate relationship with the God who is supremely personal. Our believing includes not simply an intellectual assent but our "real" assent to the truth of God, whereby we penetrate more and more deeply into the reality we believe by actually experiencing its power in our lives.

Newman made a key contribution to a contemporary theology of faith by his emphasis on the laity's role as believers in the Church. In his *On Consulting the Faithful in Matters of Doctrine,* Newman pictures the believing community as a dynamic whole, infused by a mutual *conspiratio*—a harmonious "breathing together" of pastors and the faithful. A *sensus fidei,* a "sense of the faith," lives in the baptized as a kind of "instinct deep in the bosom" of the Church. By this instinct the faithful as a whole recognize and receive what is consonant with the faith and reject what is foreign to it. It is not simply the Church hierarchy but the entire believing community, therefore, who are responsible for actively receiving and handing on this faith to others.

In the 20th century, Protestant thinkers such as Dietrich Bonhoeffer and Paul Tillich, influenced by the devastation of World War II, emphasized the significance of Christian faith for our daily lives. In *The Cost of Discipleship,* Dietrich Bonhoeffer (1906–1945), a pastor of the Reformed tradition, focuses on faith as our obedience to God, an obedience that creates a radically new kind of existence for us. True faith entails our courage to be transformed, to participate in the new being and existence of Jesus as the "man for others." Faith lacking this kind of impact in our lives is faith with no integrity, the product of "cheap grace."

Paul Tillich (1886–1965) identifies our deepest modern problem as estrangement from the meaning of our lives. Because we have become strangers to our own selves, we suffer a pervading sense of emptiness and futility. In the face of this anxiety, faith means the courage to surrender to our "ultimate concern." This kind of personal choice constitutes the "dynamic of faith" that takes hold of us in the measure that we continually seek to give meaning to our lives. Faith thus means precisely our search for meaning, our surrender to a matter of "ultimate concern" in our own lives.

For the Protestant Tillich, all those who sincerely seek meaning in their lives, including atheists, are in fact people of religious faith. In an increasingly secularized world, 20th-century Catholic thinkers such as Karl Rahner and Bernard Lonergan, too, tried to regain the relevance of Christian faith even for those who consider themselves unbelievers. Rahner emphasizes faith as our intimate knowing of God. We usually express our faith in beliefs, but true faith can also exist in people without being "thematized" in explicit beliefs. Lonergan, too, saw faith as our knowledge of God "born of religious love." For Lonergan, beliefs are the intellectual affirmations we make as a result of faith, but our faith itself is distinct from, and conceivably possible without, beliefs.

Faith at the Heart of the Believing Community

Following Vatican II and helped by contemporary insights from the social sciences, our understanding of the meaning of Christian faith and its implications for us today continues to deepen. The Second Vatican Council and our reclaiming of the Rite of Christian Initiation of Adults (RCIA) have focused our attention on the essential community context of our Christian faith. We confess and live our faith in Jesus only as members of the believing community. Just as in our daily life we need one another, so too in coming to faith we depend on those who have believed before us. And we truly live our faith only in and with and through the believers who are the Church, the community of the "faithful."

As those involved in parish and family ministry have learned, our living and handing on Christian faith are "absolutely dependent" on our belonging to vibrant faith communities. Forming such communities needs to be a pastoral priority for us, since those who come to faith do so precisely through being touched by the living witness and experience of other believers (Kasper, p. 123). That is why Vatican II's Dogmatic Constitution on the Church stresses that parents are the first heralds of the gospel to their children (see LG 11). The Christian family is meant to be the first, vibrant community nourishing the faith of its members and feeding their life

in the Spirit. For "faith both presupposes the community and creates it; the courage to believe is always born of a pentecostal event" at the heart of a believing community (Rahner, *Practice,* p. 33).

Our initiating new members into the Christian community through baptism and confirmation and our celebrating the Eucharist together are not simply "illustrations" of what we believe. In the sacraments we participate experientially in the very faith we confess. Celebrating with the Church community united in the risen Lord, we begin to encounter the realities we believe, to experience for ourselves the truths we confess (Kasper, p. 109).

Our faith in this way becomes real power for us—the power of the Holy Spirit poured out by the risen Lord to make us and the whole Church and world new. Such a faith is inseparable from hope—hope for a new way to live personally and together. This kind of hope-filled faith becomes the wellspring in us of deeper experiences of personal and community life. Of its very nature, our Christian faith thus urges us to collaboration, to creativity in developing and using our gifts, and in encouraging the gifts of others in and for the Church (J. Comblin, in Cabestrero, p. 40).

Faith and Beliefs

We come to know the risen Lord Jesus only through the witness of the apostolic Church that we encounter through the community's words and life. As Vatican II's Constitution on Divine Revelation stresses, the whole Church community, not only in her teaching but also in her life and worship, continues to hand on to all ages "all that she herself is, all that she believes" (DV 8). Christian faith is born and nourished always at the heart of the Church, in the midst of the community of believers.

"What we have heard . . . what we have looked at and touched with our hands, concerning the word of life . . . we declare to you what we have seen and heard so that you also may have fellowship with us; and truly our fellowship is with the Father and with his Son Jesus Christ" (1 Jn 1:1, 3 NRSV). We enter into fellowship with the triune God and the Christian community through professing at our baptism the one faith of the community. Our faith in this way is inseparably the act and virtue of clinging with our whole person in trusting surrender to God, and also true intellectual content by which we intimately know and confess the God proclaimed to us in the gospel message.

In professing the common faith central to our baptismal commitment, then, we need words to express the essential elements of our faith. Although our propositions can never be adequate to the triune God's mystery, our words as well as the witness of our lives do confess and hand on to others our Christian faith and invite them to experience the full power of God's saving mystery in their own lives. Thus the faith of the Church community supports even those too young to confess this faith at their baptism and lovingly works for the time when they can choose to make the community's faith their own.

These reflections on faith as both trusting surrender and loving assent to God lead us to distinguish between faith, theology, and beliefs. Faith is a graced way of our intimately knowing God even now. But of its very nature faith gives rise to theology—our seeking to understand and penetrate more deeply the loving mystery of the God we cling to in faith. And through beliefs the community articulates its faith in words that express what it has come to experience and know as true.

Karl Rahner stresses that we need to find deeper roots in our daily lives for both our faith and beliefs by clarifying and focusing on what is central to Christian belief—the saving power of the triune God, the healing mystery of Jesus' life, death, and resurrection for us, the transforming power of the Holy Spirit, whom we encounter especially in our sacramental celebrations. In this way we place all our Christian beliefs in

their deepest perspective, that is, within the context of the saving mystery of the triune God (*Practice,* pp. 38–40). So, too, our very unity of faith in these essentials calls us to respect theological pluralism among us if we are to grow in unity rather than uniformity—a uniformity that in its own way is "smallness and frailty of faith" (Schnackenburg, p. 12).

Segundo Galilea speaks of an "anemia of faith" today (Cabestrero, p. 64). So few in the world identify the gospel with good news, with great joy. Perhaps the good news itself has been lost by a stress on propositions that are not central to the gospel. This is why Ladislas Boros urges those responsible for proclaiming the gospel: "Announce, proclaim, hold fast . . . only [to] what you can defend with the sacrifice of your own life" (Cabestrero, p. 19).

Christian leaders and teachers need to convey the good news of Jesus in a way that speaks to people's hopes and deepest hunger. On the other hand, those just coming to faith need time to grow, to assimilate the faith; indeed, they may need to be allowed to go wrong more than once before they are able to make the faith truly their own (J. Segundo, in Cabestrero, pp. 175–176).

At the same time, J. M. R. Tillard notes that a new kind of people is "in gestation" in the world and in the Church. This is a people growing more educated, confident, and responsible, seeking the full development of their freedom and responsibility (Cabestrero, p. 185). Georges Casalis notes that Christian adults may no longer be treated as minors; sincere believers today seek an adult Christianity. They want to belong to a faith community in which they can grow in their own commitment to the Lord. But they seek also a community in which they can contribute to the reformulating of faith and the restructuring of Christian life for a new time so that they can hand on a living faith to future generations (Cabestrero, p. 25).

The gospel's truth thus is infallibly entrusted, with the Holy Spirit's help, "to the totality of believers and to their consensus" (Kasper, p. 120). For the true subject of believing is not simply individuals but the entire community of believers. That is why *Dei Verbum* stresses that the Church itself—the whole community and not simply the hierarchy—hands on the faith to future ages (DV 10).

But we can share with others only what we ourselves personally know and live. As Christians we need to nurture an educated, prayerful faith in ourselves and others, a faith that continually seeks to understand, live, and share more deeply what we believe. Our own faith thus would increasingly gain from, and contribute to, the vigor of our community's faith-life and evangelizing mission.

Our Human Development and Growing in Faith

Thinkers such as Freud and Marx argued that religious faith serves as the enemy of human wholeness. Critiques such as theirs have helped us to focus on Christian faith in the wider context of the developmental tasks that make our very humanness possible and meaningful. In this way we can understand more profoundly how Christian faith is both God's gift and our own deepest human actualization.

As Blaise Pascal (1623–1662) and Søren Kierkegaard (1813–1855) insist, the very structure of our human experience cries out for faith. We literally cannot live without a basic human faith in others' trustworthiness. This faith assures us that we are worthy of faithful love, and is most deeply nurtured by intimate bonding with our parents when we are young. Loved in this way, we begin to base our faith in others not simply on the immediate evidence we perceive with our physical senses, but also on the inherent sense we have gained of their basic trustworthiness.

As we learn to trust others, we learn, too, that we cannot pry from those we love the impenetrable mystery of their uniqueness. We can only receive in loving faith their self-gift to us. This kind of human trust, rather than denigrating our human reason, makes possible our very use of reason. Our own experience in this way shows us that the entire universe, our own life, and the whole of life are a mystery whose "meaning must be dared and believed" (Kasper, p. 46).

When we trust in the essential meaningfulness of life, and of our own life in particular, we make an act of faith that is radically open to reality. Such human faith is, in Tillich's words, the "courage to be." Far from acting as the enemy of our human wholeness, trusting faith is its very condition. And while faith is first and always God's own gift in our hearts, precisely because it is such, faith is also our own deepest accomplishment and human actualization (Kasper, pp. 45–48). Our growing in faith, therefore, is inseparable from our growing in true human wholeness.

Psychologists such as Carl Jung and Erik Erikson have emphasized that human maturing engages us in a continual process of becoming. Erikson, for example, distinguishes eight stages of our psychosexual growing and identifies the critical tasks of each stage. As children grow, they need to develop a sense of trust, autonomy, initiative, and industry. Adolescents, on the other hand, face the task of developing a sense of personal identity. While young adults need to achieve a sense of intimacy, middle-aged and older adults encounter the challenges of generativity and of gaining a sense of personal integrity and hope in the face of death.

Various developmental theories such as Erikson's have helped us to understand that our struggles with religious faith are inseparable from the human-growth tasks we face in our daily lives. The insights of Evelyn and James Whitehead, for example, apply Erikson's stages to our human growth in the context of the Church community and Christian marriage. The work of the Methodist theologian James Fowler has also proved helpful to teachers of the faith. Using insights from Erikson, Jean Piaget's work on child development, and Lawrence Kohlberg's theory of moral development, Fowler has undertaken his own research into the structure of faith. He identifies the following kinds and stages of faith from childhood to maturity: intuitive-protective faith; mythic-literal; synthetic-conventional; individuating-reflexive; paradoxical-consolidative; universalizing faith.

While developmental theories such as Fowler's can focus on a theory of human developing and knowing inadequate for articulating the uniqueness of Christian faith, they nevertheless can aid us in understanding the relationship between our faith-growth and our maturing through basic stages of our human development. Insights of the modern social sciences have helped us to understand how tasks of psychosexual growth often underlie faith struggles. Our evangelization and catechesis, our preaching and teaching thus need to take seriously the developmental nature of our human maturing and of our growing in faith. That is why *Sharing the Light of Faith,* the National Catechetical Directory for Catholics of the United States, adapts Erikson's framework, emphasizing catechists' call and task of helping others grow through these developmental stages to mature faith in Jesus.

Other theologians offer practical insights on the basic faith stages of children, adolescents, adults, and the elderly. Rahner, for example, emphasizes that parents and catechists can feel pressured into treating children as "miniature adults" who need to know every facet of the Christian faith. But precisely because they cannot assimilate the whole of faith's doctrine on a meaningful level, children need, most of all, contact with positive images of God modeled by loving adults who live their Christian faith in a committed way.

Adolescents, on the other hand, struggle through their own social and sexual crises during puberty. Parents and catechists can

help them by refraining from "making the sexual area the all but exclusive battleground of the *religious* decision." Instead of implying that struggles or temporary "non-fulfillment" of Christian mores means a final decision against God, parents and catechists can focus on God's mercy, power, and closeness to us in all of our human struggles (Rahner, *Practice,* p. 126).

Through focusing on how Christian faith answers our deepest thirst for meaning, catechists can help adults also to grow in deeper understanding of their faith as well as in responsible freedom in living it. And those who work with the elderly can illumine the meaning of our loneliness, disappointments, and death itself in the context of the unending joy in which God will wipe every tear from our eyes (Rahner, *Practice,* pp. 127–129).

The God who heals our self-doubt and shame, our guilt and fears, the God who, in Jesus, loves us into personal wholeness thus comes to us at our own level of human maturing. Attending to the developmental stages of human growth in this way can open us and others through us to true faith, or to a deeper, more mature faith.

Faith and Reason, Doubt and Unbelief

Our Christian faith entrusts us to the God we cannot see. For this reason we need to understand how our faith, far from being irrational, gives our rational life its full meaning. But we come to know that our Christian believing is reasonable only when we actually encounter God in our lives. Often, however, experiencing God's presence seems to be impossible in a secularized world that knows evils of overwhelming magnitude. The lines between faith and atheism can seem blurred today; Christians can live like atheists, and atheists can live more lovingly than believers (Kasper, p. 20). For in rejecting what seems to be God, a sincere atheist can be rejecting simply a false image of God. As Boros notes, in today's world the most fearful form of atheism may not be conscious rejection of God but living with an insincere heart (Cabestrero, p. 17).

On the other hand, in the face of great evil even believers cannot escape the experience of doubt and unbelief. The horror of millions of slaughtered innocent people can appear to be the "pitiless contradiction of a merciful God" (Schnackenburg, p. 105). Yet, as Rahner notes, precisely after such atrocities as Auschwitz we must believe in God if we are not to deny those whose suffering seems absurd "their last dignity and significance." The only alternative to such faith is to acknowledge meaninglessness as the final word about our universe (*Our Christian Faith,* pp. 45–47). Countless witnesses throughout history, however, attest to us that far from destroying our faith, mental, physical and emotional struggles and tragedies can occasion in us a spiritual crisis which, by God's grace, can become the womb of true faith in us (E. Dussel, in Cabestrero, p. 49).

This faith often is "naked"; what we feel is not faith but anger and fear, doubt, and bitterness. Yet at times of crisis, what crumbles to pieces in us can be a false or immature system of belief rather than faith itself. As we pass through the "dark nights" that life offers us, what had become in us perhaps self-confidence and self-reliance, or a belief system smug, harsh, and intolerant, can be refashioned into a mature faith that clings not to a system or even to feelings of faith but only to God.

As Rahner says, we know that some realities are true only because we choose to entrust ourselves to them. By opening ourselves to live as if we knew they were real, we come to know through experience that they are real. We discover, for example, that unselfish love makes sense only when we choose to live selflessly. In the same way, we cannot "know" God if we want God's reality to be proved intellectually to us without in some way letting go and surrendering ourselves to God's intimate mystery (*Our Christian Faith,* p. 23).

Intellectual reasons for believing, therefore, cannot prove our faith. Rather, as Newman notes in his *Grammar of Assent,* they give us a rational basis for knowing that our choice to believe is an intelligent decision. Reason alone has no access to the truth of Jesus; only an open heart can embrace his mystery. And yet Christian faith is not irrational. On the contrary, our faith enables us truly to experience the full depth of reality—reality that lies beyond the grasp of our human understanding alone. Indeed, faith itself makes possible our human understanding (Kasper, p. 39).

For faith itself is a light, a way we truly know God and understand more deeply the meaning of life's mystery. Thomas Aquinas asserts that our faith-knowing flowers in an even deeper connatural love-knowing of God intimately through wisdom. Faith thus is a human stance not at all foreign to our humanness, added to our reason as something inimical to it. The supernatural gift of faith itself is the ultimate fulfillment of our reason's infinite thirst to know unbounded truth (Kasper, p. 72).

Finally, however, what draws us to believe is not intellectual reasoning but the compelling power of Jesus' person, the power of his life, death, and resurrection (Schnackenburg, p. 59). We see this "proof" of the Christian faith most radically in the love that shines from believers who know the power of Jesus' resurrection in their own lives.

The God who raised Jesus from the dead thus can raise up faith in us even from the ashes of our unbelief. "God's love in Jesus can sustain us in the abyss of our pain, through all our anxious questioning," supporting us to stare death's horror "squarely in the eyes, and with bold, indeed jubilant and indomitable courage support us to proclaim with the witness of our lives that 'Nothing . . . can come between us and the love of Christ' (Rom 8:35)" (Schnackenburg, pp. 5, 45, 105, 107).

Faith, Prayer, and the Mystical Life

In the daily trials that seem to overwhelm us, we learn that such loving faith in God is beyond our own powers. That is why the Gospels teach us that we grow in faith precisely by praying for it as gift: "Lord, help my unbelief" (Mk 9:24); "Lord, increase our faith" (Lk 17:5). Even our words are unnecessary in this kind of prayer, for the Spirit prays within us with groans too deep for words (Rom 8:26). In this way even our "suffering under the inward incapacity to pray is prayer. Waiting in the presence of God, being silent" in God's presence is prayer (L. Boros, in Cabestrero, p. 9). Indeed, many realities become real for us only because we have prayed over them and struggled with them. As we stay faithful to this kind of prayer, our faith cannot help deepening.

Our faith is meant to feed also in a central way on the communal prayer that is the Church's liturgy. "*Lex orandi, lex credendi*": what we pray we believe, and what we believe we pray. By its very nature, therefore, the liturgy has power to nourish our faith. When we truly celebrate the Eucharist together, for example, we enter into the paschal mystery of Jesus and feed on the very reality that we proclaim. So, too, when we participate in new members' sacramental initiation into the community, we find our own faith deepened by our very sharing in the reality we profess and celebrate.

This kind of prayer in personal and communal settings inevitably draws us to the full flowering of our baptismal faith in what spiritual writers have called the "mystical life." For Thomas Aquinas, our faith as a deepening habit is meant to mature in our becoming more and more docile to the Holy Spirit in our lives. Our faith thus finds its fullness in the gift of understanding whereby, in a connatural knowing through love, we increasingly experience the reality of the mysteries we cling to in faith.

This, then, is the mystical life: to live more and more not from our own resources but from the power of the Holy Spirit within us. Such a mystical life belongs, as Rahner notes, to the very "domain of faith," to the experience of the Holy Spirit given to us in the gift of faith itself (*Practice*, p. 73). Thomas Merton, too, emphasizes that the true purpose of the contemplative life is nothing other than the deepening of our life of faith. Mystical prayer thus increasingly brings us to a wordless experience of the God we cling to in faith, the God intimately present within the depths of our own being (Thomas Merton, *Contemplation in a World of Action* [Garden City, N.Y.: Doubleday Image, 1973], p. 175).

Yet, the mystical prayer to which faith gives rise can be far from what we might expect. St. John of the Cross comments that in mystical prayer, faith itself becomes darkness for us—but a darkness only because of its excessive light. Just as the sun's brightness can actually blind us, so faith can make our reason's light seem like darkness and blindness. Yet, by "blinding" our senses, faith can cause us to see beyond what our physical senses can tell us. We begin then to perceive with deeper vision what Abraham and Paul beheld: in the midst even of tragedies that confuse and overwhelm us, we and the entire world are held in the arms of a God whose steadfast love will never leave us (John of the Cross, *Ascent of Mount Carmel*, II, 3).

In the unfolding of our faith in the mystical life, we may have to pass through stages of spiritual growing that parallel earlier crises of faith. St. John of the Cross, for example, gives a classical description of three ways of the mystical life of faith—the purgative, illuminative, and unitive. Each of these stages begins with a period of darkness and personal upheaval that are meant to open us to even deeper wholeness and intimacy with God.

In our growing in mature faith, we can rarely sidestep the need for undergoing, more than once, a true personal conversion in our lives. Such a conversion can be accompanied by the release of the Holy Spirit that the sacraments of baptism and confirmation are meant to effect in our lives. Often our participating in movements inspired by the Holy Spirit—movements such as the charismatic renewal, cursillo, marriage encounter, Scripture and prayer groups, parish renewal programs, or social justice movements—can bring us to such a personal turning point. We begin to live our faith through a new outpouring of the Holy Spirit's love and power in our own lives. We know a new freedom from fear and self-centeredness; a deepened trust, peace, and intimacy with God; a new power to love; a growing thirst for Scripture and the Eucharist, for community and loving service to others.

However, the light and warmth of this awakening to God's personal love for us often can be followed by darkness, struggles, emptiness, and inner conflicts that seem to rob us of faith and closeness to God. Through these dark nights the Holy Spirit draws us to embrace our weakness and to surrender ourselves to the power of God's love in Jesus. As we grow in this mystical life, the very person of the Spirit prays in us with "inexpressible groanings" (Rom 8:26), drawing us to cling wordlessly to God even when everything and everyone seem to betray us.

By healing our inner wounds the Spirit makes us humble, gentle, and peaceful with all that the Father's will desires for us. In not resisting the trials and temptations that humble us, we are gradually healed of pride and self-reliance, and learn to surrender to the triune God's saving power in our lives (Groeschel, pp. 103–188). Fashioned in this way by the Spirit of love, we begin to experience for ourselves the truth of Paul's words: "It is no longer I who live, but it is Christ who lives in me. And the life I now live in the flesh I live by faith in the Son of God, who loved me and gave himself for me" (Gal 2:20, NRSV).

Faith Committed to Justice in the World

Far from taking us from the world, this kind of mystical life of faith pushes us to its heart. For "surely," Rahner urges, "real faith ought to burn! Ought it not to drive us on to the streets?" (*Our Christian Faith,* p. 1). The Pastoral Constitution on the Church in the Modern World emphasizes that our faith in Jesus makes us responsible for each other and for our human history (GS 55). The gospel itself forbids us to separate our faith from commitment to the world's helpless and poor, with whom Jesus intimately identifies himself: "Just as you did it to one of the least of these who are members of my family, you did it to me" (Mt 25:40, NRSV).

We are called to give "the witness of a living and mature faith" that penetrates our life and commits us to the work of peace and justice in the world (GS 21). Our faith thus gives us eyes to see all of humankind in a new light and inspires us to work for "fully human solutions" to the world's ills (GS 11). Far from taking us away from the world, our faith and its flowering in the mystical life therefore push us to take greater responsibility in and for our world (GS 43).

Liberation theologians have taken these insights of Vatican II still further by stressing the prophetic and critical functions of our faith. In a world whose values grow increasingly atheistic, our faith makes radical demands on us. We face the challenge today of translating our Christian faith into action in the world, of proclaiming it with the witness of our lives. Our very faith calls us to preach the good news in some way to the ends of the earth. Yet our mission demands not simply our words but also a radical life on behalf of the kingdom. In order to preach the gospel in its full power, we must attend not simply to superficial symptoms but to the very "root of social evil." Our Christian faith will become a vital force in our world when we begin to live it in radical love for the most poor, helpless, and marginalized. As disciples of Jesus, we are called to live our faith increasingly as love at the heart of the world (G. Gutiérrez, in Cabestrero, pp. 104, 125).

True faith in this way converts us not only to Christ but also to Christ's members, especially those most weak and poor. Indeed, the mystical life entails living our faith in some way as a true *praxis* on behalf of the poor (G. Gutiérrez, in Haughey, pp. 36–37). Our sacramental celebrations thus are meant to nurture in us the faith that does justice in the world. The Eucharist that feeds us, for example, of its very nature impels us to feed the hunger of others (D. Hollenbach, in Haughey, pp. 250, 258).

Not a few Christians throughout the ages have proclaimed the love of the triune God they have clung to in faith by offering the very witness of their lives. In a world that cries out for a word of truth spoken with conviction, sincere Christian believers today cannot escape taking equally radical stances that fidelity to their very faith inspires. It is this faith itself that makes us responsible for shaping the world and for creating together the Church's future in the world. "The whole community of believers is the sign and instrument of faith. . . . On her face, the light, who is Jesus Christ, must shine in the world" (Kasper, p. 113). Our very faith thus impels us to be co-participants with God in bringing healing to a broken world and in working for the reign of God's kingdom among us (A. Dulles, in Haughey, pp. 11, 32, 13). We may trust that living this kind of biblical faith will make our very lives an act of faith, a living witness to the power of the triune God's love in our world today.

See also CHRIST; COMMUNITY; HOLY SPIRIT; JUSTICE; LITURGY; MYSTICISM; PSYCHOLOGY, RELATIONSHIP AND CONTRIBUTION TO SPIRITUALITY; VIRTUE.

Bibliography: J. Bauer and H. Zimmerman, "Faith," in *Sacramentum Verbi: An Encyclopedia of Biblical Theology* 1, ed. J. Bauer (New York: Herder, 1970). T. Cabestrero, *Faith: Conversations with Contemporary Theologians,* trans. D. Walsh (Maryknoll, N.Y.: Orbis, 1980). G. Chamberlain, *Fostering Faith: A Minister's Guide to Faith Development* (New York: Paulist, 1988). B. Groeschel, *Spiritual Passages: The Psychology of Spiritual Development* (New York: Crossroad, 1984). J. Haughey, ed., *The Faith That Does Justice,* Woodstock Studies 2 (New York: Paulist, 1977). W. Kasper, *Transcending All Understanding: The Meaning of Christian Faith Today,* trans. B. Ramsey (San Francisco: Ignatius Press, 1989). K. Rahner and K.-H. Weger, *Our Christian Faith: Answers for the Future* (New York: Crossroad, 1981). K. Rahner, *The Practice of Faith: A Handbook of Contemporary Spirituality* (New York: Crossroad, 1983). R. Schnackenburg, *Belief in the New Testament,* trans. J. Moiser (New York: Paulist, 1974). United States Catholic Conference, *Sharing the Light of Faith: National Catholic Catechetical Directory* (Washington: USCC Publications Office, 1979).

MARY ANN FATULA, O.P.

FAMILY

See CHILD, CHILDREN; DIVORCE (AND REMARRIAGE); MARRIAGE; SINGLE PARENT.

FASTING

Fasting, the partial or total abstinence from food and drink, has been found in virtually every religion, from primitive to modern times, and practiced for a variety of religious motives. In the Hebrew Scriptures fasting was a means of repentance for sin (1 Sam 7:6; Joel 1:14; Jonah 3:5-9); of remembrance of Yahweh's deliverance from past sin (Lev 16:29-34 [Yom Kippur]; Zech 8:19); of supplication in time of calamity (Judg 2:26; 2 Chr 20:3-4; Ezra 8:21-23); of mourning for the dead (1 Sam 31:13; 2 Sam 1:12); and of preparation for a great undertaking (1 Sam 14:24). In all cases fasting was a symbolic act of prayer and humility before God.

In early Christianity, under Hellenistic influence, the motive for fasting shifted to an emphasis upon bodily discipline, both to avoid the influence of evil spirits that entered the mouth with food and to purify the mind for contemplation and communion with God. Fasting was also viewed as a means of uniting oneself with the sufferings of Christ, a theme that achieved prominence in the Middle Ages. This article will develop one theme in the Judeo-Christian tradition that has the most contemporary relevance: the relationship of fasting to works of justice and charity.

Along with fidelity to the Law, the principal Jewish ideals of piety were almsgiving (Lev 23:22; Deut 24:19-22); prayer (Exod 20:3; Ps 63:6-8); and fasting (see references above). Although the three were seldom mentioned together, the proper practice of each demanded attention to the others. Just as Amos decried ritual worship unaccompanied by justice (5:21-24), so Isaiah defined proper fasting: "Is it not to share your bread with the hungry, and bring the homeless poor into your house?" (Isa 58:7, NRSV; see vv. 3-12).

Matthew 6:1-18 is a catechesis on these three pillars of Jewish piety; the proper practice of almsgiving (vv. 2-4), prayer (vv. 5-6), and fasting (vv. 16-18) for Jesus' disciples is contrasted with that of the "hypocrites" whose sole motivation was gaining the esteem of others. Consistent with the Jewish ideal of fasting, the author emphasizes humility as its essential ingredient. This message reappears in the parable of the publican and the Pharisee, whose practice of fasting fails to justify him because of his pride and disdain for the publican (Lk 18:9-14).

In contrast to John the Baptist and his disciples, Jesus and his disciples do not fast (Mk 2:18-22 par.; Mt 11:16-19; Lk 7:31-35); rather, they feast as a sign of the imminence of the eschatological banquet, at which the poor and marginalized are the most frequent guests. Sharing bread as a sign of solidarity with the poor is more important to Jesus than fasting. His own forty-day fast in the desert, although obviously symbolic of his initiating the new Israel, can also be viewed as an act of solidarity with the hungry and the weak, through which he learned the relative value of bodily comforts, thus being freed for the service of others (Mt 4:1-4; Lk 4:1-4; see Lk 4:16-21).

The relationship between fasting and almsgiving is a prominent theme in patristic literature. The *Shepherd of Hermas* reads: "In the day on which you fast you will taste nothing but bread and water; and having reckoned up the price of the dishes of that day which you intended to have eaten, you will give it to a widow, or an orphan, or to some person in want, and thus you will exhibit humility of mind, so that the one who has received benefit from your humility may fill his own soul" (3.5.3). For John Chrysostom, fasting without almsgiving was not fasting at all (*Homilies on Matthew* 77.6). Origen blessed those who fasted in order "to nourish the poor" (*Homilies on Leviticus* 10.2). For Augustine, fasting was merely avarice unless one gave away what one would have eaten (*Sermon* 208).

While fasting was practiced by both men and women ascetics in the Middle Ages, abstaining from or eating food was more important symbolically for women. The virtually total fast practiced by many women visionaries was complemented by an equally intense devotion to the Eucharist, through which they were united in their own bodily deprivation with the suffering body of Christ. This in turn moved them to exhaust their own bodies in service to the poor and sick through heroic works of charity.

Fasting in the Christian Church was regulated from earliest times (see the *Didache* 8.1), although obligatory fasts varied locally throughout Church history. Obligatory fasting for Roman Catholics was reorganized in 1966 by the apostolic constitution *Paenitemini,* in which Paul VI recommended that forms of fasting be consistent with the economic conditions of each locality and accompanied by prayer and works of charity. Vatican II relegated fasting regulation to national episcopal conferences, and in November 1966 the National Conference of Catholic Bishops limited obligatory fast days in the United States to Ash Wednesday and Good Friday, but strongly recommended voluntary fasting, especially during Lent, accompanied by frequent attendance at the Eucharist and works of charity.

While contemporary fasting practices are not as severe as those of the medieval visionaries, they do link fasting with true celebration of the Eucharist and solidarity with the world's hungry. Besides providing the poor with money saved by abstinence from food (e.g., Operation Rice Bowl, the Oxfam Fast), fasting forms a bond of sympathy with the starving by sharing in their suffering to some degree. This prevents the self-aggrandizement that can result from heroic philanthropic acts and engenders humility, placing one on the same level with the suffering neighbor. Fasting also strengthens the desire to help the poor by restructuring the distribution of this world's goods and teaches one to use the earth's resources with care and respect. Contemporary Eucharistic piety emphasizes the theme that Christians, as Christ's Body, are meant to be bread for the world; it thus logically encourages the practice of fasting by those who have much, so that the needy may have more.

See also ABSTINENCE; ASCETICISM; BODY; BODY OF CHRIST; HOLINESS; JUSTICE; LOVE; PENANCE, PENITENCE; SOLIDARITY.

Bibliography: J. Wimmer, *Fasting in the New Testament: A Study in Biblical Theology* (New York: Paulist, 1982). R. Arbesmann, "Fasting and Prophecy in Pagan and Christian Antiquity," *Traditio* 7 (1949–1951) 1-72. C. W. Bynum, *Holy Feast and Holy Fast: The Religious Significance of Food to Medieval Women* (Berkeley: Univ. of California Press, 1987). P. Clancy, "Fast and Abstinence," *New Catholic Encyclopedia* 5:847–850. J. Lynch, "Fast and Abstinence," *New Catholic Encyclopedia Supplement* 16:180.

JOAN M. NUTH

FEAR OF THE LORD

See GIFTS OF THE HOLY SPIRIT.

FEELINGS

Feelings are subjective sensations in response to internal or external stimuli. They can be powerful experiences, such as those of love or hate, pleasure or pain. In common parlance and in this article, the words *feelings, emotions,* and *affections* are synonymous. However, in some psychological literature (Gaylin), feelings are seen as the subjective side of emotions that are more complex and include the physiological and biochemical components of feeling states. Feelings as subjective experiences have not been the focus of much descriptive analysis in psychology or psychiatry. Still they are recognized by psychologists as having an important role to play in decision-making. They act as signals that direct people away from some things and toward others.

Various groupings of feelings are found in the literature. Gaylin designates three groups and suggests some feelings to be included in each: (1) feelings concerned with individual or group survival—anger, anxiety, guilt, shame, and pride; (2) feelings that signal caution: irritation, tiredness, boredom, envy, and feeling used; (3) feelings that signal success: pleasure, feeling touched, and feeling moved.

Feelings and the Spiritual Life

Feelings have long been recognized as playing a significant part in spiritual development. Through the centuries writers have attended to their precise role in advancing or hindering the spiritual life. Bernard of Clairvaux (1090–1153) develops an affective spirituality in which feelings of love for God and for the humanity of Christ are cultivated. Bernard clearly recognizes the affective dynamics of people's movement toward union with God. His contribution helped to overcome a preoccupation with the spiritual life as primarily an objective contemplation of truths.

Francis de Sales (1567–1622) suggests an appeal to feelings as a way of strengthening the will of those who come for counsel.

Throughout his writings there is a positive appreciation for feelings and how they can lead to a deeper relationship with God and others.

Jonathan Edwards (1703–1758) writes about religious affections, citing love of God as the chief affection and listing hope, joy, fear, zeal, and compassion as other important feelings. He also offers his own manner of grouping the different affections: (1) those related to liking or approval—love, desire, hope, joy, gratitude, complacence; (2) those related to rejection or disapproval—hatred, fear, anger, grief; and (3) those related to both—pity and zeal. For Edwards, the presence of sound religious affections provides the best evidence of the genuineness of religious experience. He believes that true conversion gives an individual a capacity for appreciating the loveliness of God.

Friedrich Schleiermacher (1768–1834) sees religion as consisting of a feeling of absolute dependence on the Infinite. He goes on to enumerate a series of feelings that are connected with one's religiosity: yearning, reverence, humility, gratitude, compassion, sorrow, and zeal. His position on the importance of feelings counters tendencies toward rationalism, formalism, and ritualism in religion.

Rudolf Otto (1869–1937), in *The Idea of the Holy,* elaborates on the feelings that the holy in its various dimensions elicits from human beings. Awe and bliss are singled out by him as primary emotions. He also includes creatureliness, dread, humbleness, and nothingness as other significant feelings. His attention to the nonrational side of religion helped to bring about a more holistic appreciation of the nature of religious experience.

In the history of spirituality feelings have been approached selectively, with some singled out for cultivation, and others, such as bitterness and resentment, for avoidance. Ascetical practices were developed to help control or suppress feelings. Anger and sexual feelings were often the object of such control. Some spiritualities have given considerable attention to the transformation and purification of feelings that occur in the quest for God.

Feelings and Discernment

The important role of feelings in decision-making is acknowledged in writings on discernment. Ignatius Loyola (1491–1556), in his *Spiritual Exercises,* proposes two sets of rules for the discernment of spirits. In the first set a person seeks to discern with regard to choices between good and evil. In the second set the focus is on choices a person has to make between two goods. The process of discernment requires a person to pay attention to the feelings that surface when various choices are considered. Ignatius speaks especially of consolation and desolation as the feelings to be aware of. By taking note of feelings, individuals come to the deep, affective self-knowledge that is essential for conversion.

The foundation for the discernment process that Ignatius describes is an experience of complete openness to God. Ignatius calls it a "consolation without a previous cause." Concrete choices are to be made on the basis of this felt knowledge, this consoling and gifted experience of God's presence. Such an experience presupposes that an individual has achieved a detachment from lesser objects.

Contemporary discussions of discernment approach it as an assessment of inspirations, intuitions, affective states, and impulses in terms of their sources and their congruity with the overall direction of a person's spiritual life. For criteria in evaluating appropriate moral choices, discernment makes use of the central symbols and basic affections found in the Christian tradition, as well as general moral principles. The discerning moral agent in part seeks to follow that course of action which is in harmony with the affections evident in the Scriptures, such as radical dependence on God and repentance.

Contemporary Issues

The source of certain feelings is sometimes a concern in spiritual direction or pastoral counseling. The minister may be faced with the task of distinguishing a genuine experience of the "dark night" from emotional depression. The nights described by John of the Cross (1542–1591) are those periods when persons, despite their commitment to the spiritual life, find themselves without good feelings toward God and without a sense of God's closeness. For John, the night experience is a time for the deepening of faith.

However, someone who is in a state of emotional depression for other reasons could also report feelings of isolation from God. Similarly, individuals with narcissistic disorders describe feelings of emptiness that seem to match the description of mystics regarding stages in their journey toward union with God. Feelings in these cases need to be explored and a careful discernment made. Guilt feelings are another instance where the source is sometimes in question. While moral guilt is related to a failure to exercise proper moral responsibility, guilt feelings can be present when there is no culpability. In some cases, resolving intense guilt feelings may involve the services of both minister and therapist.

Contemporary psychology has made people conscious of the importance of recognizing and owning feelings. Repressed anger, for instance, over perceived or real injuries in one's childhood can pose a block to spiritual development. Spiritual writings today offer guidance in releasing such feelings through the process of forgiveness. In a psychologically minded age the steps in the process are being clearly articulated. Spiritual techniques such as the healing of memories are also available to help people let go of the past.

Anxiety and stress are endemic to contemporary society. Such feelings have led some to seek solace in an intensified spiritual life. The vision of reality that religion offers to these believers provides a buffer against psychic stress even as it leads them to accept all human feelings.

See also AFFECT, AFFECTIVITY; DARKNESS, DARK NIGHT; DEADLY SINS; DISCERNMENT OF SPIRITS; PASSION(S); PSYCHOLOGY, RELATIONSHIP AND CONTRIBUTION TO SPIRITUALITY; SPIRITUAL DIRECTION.

Bibliography: W. Gaylin, *Feelings: Our Vital Signs* (New York: Harper & Row, 1979). P. Pruyser, *A Dynamic Psychology of Religion* (New York: Harper & Row, 1968). M. O'Shaughnessy, *Feelings and Emotions in Christian Living* (New York: Alba House, 1988).

RAYMOND STUDZINSKI, O.S.B.

FEMINIST SPIRITUALITY

Basic Terminology

Feminist spirituality is a term very difficult to define, because the phenomenon to which it refers is both a very recent and a very pluralistic development. Furthermore, both *spirituality* and *feminism* are terms whose meanings are in flux. Consequently, inclusive descriptions are more useful at this point than univocal definitions.

Spirituality was originally a Christian term derived from the Pauline use of *pneumatikos,* i.e., "spiritual" (e.g., 1 Cor 2:14-15), to describe whatever was under the influence of the Spirit of God, and it came eventually (by the 17th century) to denote the interior life of the Christian who was striving for perfection. In recent decades its application has expanded well beyond the Catholic, Christian, or even religious spheres. One hears it used not only for non-Christian religious experience, e.g., in reference to Jewish or Hindu spirituality, but also for inter- or transdenominational (e.g., Twelve Step), nonreligious (e.g., holistic), or even antireligious (e.g., Marxist or secular) experience. A definition of spirituality that can be applied to most of what the term is used to denote today must, therefore, be much more inclusive and open-ended than it would have been thirty years ago.

Spirituality, in this inclusive sense, might be defined as the experience of striving to integrate one's life in terms of self-transcendence toward the ultimate value one perceives. Christian spirituality is specified by the Christian understanding of ultimate value to be God, revealed as Trinitarian mystery by Jesus the Christ, who communicates that mystery to the believer in the gift of the Holy Spirit within the community of the Church. Thus, Christian spirituality is not only theistic but Trinitarian, Christocentric, and ecclesial. As will become evident, all these characteristics present problems for the feminist believer.

Feminism must not be confused with the women's movement in general, nor must the term be applied indiscriminately to women as such. Feminism is a comprehensive ideology that is rooted in women's experience of sexual oppression, engages in a critique of patriarchy seen as the root of women's oppression, embraces an alternative vision for humanity and the earth, and actively seeks to bring this vision to realization. Ideology in this context does not refer to false consciousness or to a mindset uncritically absorbed from one's culture but to a systematic and coordinated body of ideas and aims that constitute a sociopolitical program for social change.

Feminism as a comprehensive ideology is rooted in women's experience of sexual oppression. To become a feminist, one must not only *be* oppressed but *realize* that one is oppressed and correctly identify the source of the oppression. The process of consciousness-raising, so important to all liberation movements including feminism, is the process of analyzing one's experience of oppression and coming to a double realization: that what have seemed to be one's personal problems are not personally but systemically caused and cannot be solved except by structural social change; that one

shares these problems with other members of one's social group and that together the group can effect change. A woman, in other words, comes to realize that her poverty or physical victimization is not due to her personal incompetence but to the sexism built into the socioeconomic system and that she shares these problems with other women precisely because they are all women. Raised consciousness, i.e., feminist consciousness, is the *sine qua non* of feminist commitment.

Feminist analysis of one's experience of oppression leads to the realization that the root of women's oppression is patriarchy, which is both the ideology and the system of social organization based on father-dominance, which underlies the pervasive dichotomous dualism of Western culture. The paradigmatic dominance-subordination dualism is that between husband-father and wife, a dualism that is intrinsically sexual and that dictates the extension of superiority to all that is perceived as masculine and of inferiority to all that is perceived as feminine. Consequently, feminism involves a rejection of patriarchy and a commitment to its demise.

Feminism, however, is not merely critical. It proposes and espouses an alternative vision for humanity and the earth. The feminist vision is characterized by equality, relatedness, and inclusiveness rather than hierarchy, individualistic separatism, and power. It seeks the reintegration of all that has been dichotomized by the patriarchal mindset, and thus the overcoming of the dominative divisions between spirit and body, human and nonhuman creation, transcendence and immanence, culture and nature, the rational and the intuitive, intelligence and emotion—all of which have been genderized as masculine-feminine dichotomies and hierarchized as respectively dominant-subordinate.

Finally, feminism involves a commitment to achieving this alternative vision in the sociopolitical order, i.e., in family, society, and Church. Consequently, feminism is not merely a theory but an activist commitment that is embodied in a variety of projects and organizations as well as in the personal activities of individual feminists.

Feminist spirituality did not arise in any institutionalized religious setting. Rather, it emerged in the United States in the 1970s and in Europe in the 1980s in response to the realization by feminists that the oppression of women is deeply rooted in the spirit/body dichotomy so endemic to patriarchal ideology (Halkes, p. 220). Male control of female sexuality, as it developed over centuries, led to the identification of women with their sexual-reproductive functions and their consequent identification with the realm of body, leading to their gradual exclusion from the realm of spirit. The spiritual realm, presided over by a male God who reigns in heaven, was opposed to the realm of nature, an inferior sphere associated with the reign of the devil. The spiritual realm, including religion, culture, and public life, was assigned to men, and the natural realm of bodiliness, sexuality, the passions, child care, and domestic or servile labor to women.

Feminist spirituality is essentially a reclaiming by women of the reality and power designated by the term "spirit." Feminists quickly realized, however, that to claim spirit to the denigration of body was to accept the patriarchal dualism of body and spirit that is the root of the problem. Thus feminist spirituality involves not only reappropriating the power of spirit but rehabilitating bodiliness as the immanent medium of the transcendent, and finally reintegrating all that has been dichotomized by patriarchal dualism. The term "connectedness" has come to stand for this entire agenda of reclaiming, rehabilitating, and reintegrating (Purvis, p. 509). New images and symbols, such as webs and networks, weaving and dancing, circles and spirals have replaced such classical symbols of patriarchal spirituality as the ladder and mountain, climbing and warfare, and pyramids of power.

Phenomenology of Feminist Spirituality

Before discussing Christian feminist spirituality, and specifically the Catholic version(s), it is necessary to describe feminist spirituality as such, because as women who are members of mainline Churches have come to feminist consciousness and have begun to understand their spirituality in feminist terms, they, of necessity, have had to situate themselves and their spirituality in relation to a larger movement that was already underway. Some Catholic women who are feminists have repudiated certain aspects of post-Christian or nondenominational feminist spirituality and accepted other aspects, while others have found themselves much more in harmony with feminist spirituality than with the traditional spirituality of the official Church.

Relation of Feminist Spirituality to Religion

The relation of feminist spirituality to religion is ambiguous. The feminists who first interested themselves in spirituality were women like Carol Christ, Judith Plaskow, and Rosemary Radford Ruether, who were professionals in the field of theology or religious studies. Because the concern of feminist spirituality is the realm of spirit, it is pervasively religious in its interests and language. However, the areas from which women have been traditionally excluded, precisely because these areas were the shrines of the life of spirit, were Church leadership and the academy, particularly theology. It is still the case that the financial resources and the leadership roles in these two spheres are largely unavailable to women or for women's projects, while the canons of official literature in both Church and university marginalize women's experience when and if they include it at all.

Consequently, feminists concerned with spirituality are, on the one hand, deeply concerned with religion and theology and, on the other hand, often alienated from, or antagonistic toward, the academy and the Church, where the concerns of religion are primarily institutionalized and pursued. While some feminists see their task as the transformation of academy and Church, others see theirs as creating alternatives to these male-dominated and patriarchal institutions.

The Rediscovery of Goddess

Although any discourse about Goddess causes alarm in traditional Christian precincts, it is not possible to understand feminist spirituality without understanding the role the rediscovery of Goddess plays within it. In general, "Goddess" is the term for divine spirit and power imaged in feminine terms, as "God" is the term for divine spirit and power imaged in masculine terms. Religion in the Western world involved worship of Goddess, the Great Mother who was Queen of Heaven and ultimate source of life and death on earth, long before the emergence of patriarchal monotheism.

Gerda Lerner, in *The Creation of Patriarchy* (New York: Oxford, 1986), traces the development of patriarchy in ancient society, the emergence of monarchy as a form of government, and the eventual development of male monotheism as the necessary legitimation of patriarchal monarchy. The important point for our purposes is that, in the Jewish and Christian traditions, the deity who was understood as both personal and unique came to be understood in almost exclusively male terms. Judeo-Christian monotheism is deeply patriarchal and monarchical, even though neither patriarchy nor monarchy is necessarily implied by monotheistic theology. Thus, although "God" is not actually a gendered term or concept, God has been so consistently referred to as "he" and imaged as male that femininity has been effectively excluded from divinity and, in consequence, women from the realm of the divine. The recovery of Goddess is, there-fore, a reassertion of the relation between the divine and the feminine.

The recovery of Goddess has at least three basic forms in feminist spirituality, not all equally compatible with Christian faith, and each signaled by linguistic clues. First, and most radical, is the*alogy in distinction from theology, i.e., discourse about Goddess in contradistinction to discourse about God. It is not always clear whether those speaking of Goddess in this context are referring to a distinct personal entity whom one can worship or to whom one can pray or are using the term as a symbol of sacred power experienced as female rather than male. But a major difference between traditional Christian discourse about God and feminist discourse about Goddess is that the latter is understood as ultimately immanent rather than as ultimately transcendent. More exactly, Goddess is transcendently immanent, thereby not only divinizing the feminine with its life-giving mysteries but also negating the ruinous split between transcendent and immanent, spirit and body, divinity and nature, heaven and earth, and all the Manichean progeny of this hierarchical dualism.

One version of this first form of Goddess religion in feminist spirituality, and one that elicits something close to terror among guardians of patriarchal religion, is Wicca religion. Wicca (the term means "wisdom") is the revitalization of a pre-Christian European tradition of pagan or nature religion through which devotees entered into, celebrated, and were nourished by the great mysteries of nature herself. The deity of these religions is female, and her devotees and priests are predominantly, although not exclusively, women. They come together in "covens," or small, nonhierarchical communities of support and worship, and often call themselves "witches," a deliberately provocative practice that not only signifies their sense of continuity with ancient Wicca but also symbolically expiates the execution of millions of women throughout Christian history on the charge of witchcraft, when their real "sin" was the exercise of personal autonomy and/or spiritual power, which men in their societies regarded as male prerogatives.

Wicca is not "black magic" or nocturnal sexual orgies but ritual participation in the life-giving and healing powers of nature, which are recognized as manifestations of the divine. For Wicca, the universe is not an inert thing but an organic reality in which everything is intimately interconnected. Human beings are the partners and celebrants of creation, not its lords. Spirituality includes sexuality, without being either reduced to it or dominant over it. Life and love are supreme values that are not at odds with truth. Ritual plays a very important role in witchcraft, because it is the place where spirit and nature meet and interact, sacralizing all of reality and uniting people with themselves, one another, and the universe.

A second form of recovery of Goddess in feminist spirituality, and one with which many Christians are much more comfortable, is symbolized by spelling the verbal symbol for deity *God/dess.* Women who refer to the deity this way, as Rosemary R. Ruether explains, are basically appropriating for women all that is true in the theological and religious tradition about God. While repudiating the patriarchal and masculinizing deformation of the God-tradition, they continue to relate to the deity of Judeo-Christian revelation. They emphasize the feminine aspects of the biblical deity, especially as they are elaborated in the feminine personification of God as Holy Wisdom (see Cady, Ronan, and Taussig), insist on a compensatory highlighting of feminine biblical metaphors for Yahweh, demand the use of gender-inclusive language for both divine and human being in prayer and worship, and struggle toward a reimagining for themselves and others of the Christian God in female terms. They see themselves as fully

in the image and likeness of God/dess, not only insofar as they possess the "spiritual" faculties of intellect and will but also because they participate bodily in the great divine work of giving and nurturing life. Thus they attempt to achieve the reappropriation of spiritual power, rehabilitation of the body, and reintegration of the dichotomized spheres of reality without separating themselves from the biblical and sacramental tradition of the Church.

A third form of recovery of Goddess among women involved in feminist spirituality is primarily psychological and therapeutic, and represents a modification of Jungian archetypal theory, which has become important in recent years in developmental approaches to Christian spirituality. Carl Jung recognized the potentiality of transcultural intrapsychic patterns, which he called "archetypes," to constellate the complexes of thought and feeling that are operative in our daily experience. A fundamental pair of archetypes, according to Jung, are the anima, or feminine principle in the male psyche, and the animus, or male principle in the female psyche.

The major problem with Jung's theory, from a feminist perspective, is that he assigned the culturally stereotypical masculine qualities, i.e., those associated with spirit, such as reason, initiative, creativity, leadership, etc., to the masculine principle, and the culturally stereotypical feminine qualities, i.e., those associated with body, such as emotion, instinct, receptivity, passivity, diffusion of mental focus, etc., to the feminine principle. The net result was that men were enabled to draw upon the resources of the culturally inferior and less differentiated "feminine" qualities which, in small doses, enrich the clear, spirit-dominated life of the man without ever having to identify with them. Women, on the other hand, could reach above themselves, out of their natural inferior and matter-dominated sphere, into the higher sphere of mind and spirit in order to draw upon the superior "masculine" qualities that they might need when functioning in such supposedly foreign arenas as the academy or political leadership, but they could never claim these qualities as their own. The feminine (i.e., inferior) qualities remained recessive in the male, and the masculine (i.e., superior) qualities remained recessive in the female.

Despite Jung's effort to valorize both the feminine and the masculine, in which respect he was much less misogynist than his predecessor Sigmund Freud, his dichotomous approach had the effect of canonizing the traditional sexual stereotypes and the cultural hierarchizing of masculine and feminine which alienates women from the realm of spirit. Some feminist Jungian psychotherapists have revised Jung's schema by agreeing that there are feminine and masculine archetypes, but positing that they are multiple and do not function exclusively contrasexually.

Borrowing the personae of the classical Greek gods and goddesses to name the archetypes, these theorists (e.g., Jean Bolen, *Goddesses in Every Woman,* San Francisco: Harper & Row, 1984) propose that there is not a single "feminine archetype" embodying the mother-daughter-wife stereotypical traits (or a single masculine archetype), but a plurality of feminine and masculine inner paradigms. Women have available for realization such inner goddesses as Artemis, the solitary huntress; Athena, the warrior and strategist; Aphrodite, the transformative lover; and Hestia, the contemplative spiritual mentor. Thus a woman who finds herself at home in the role of intellectual, goal-focused achiever, political or religious leader, contemplative, artist, spiritual guide, or any of the other roles traditionally monopolized by men is not an animus-dominated woman but one who has activated one or another of the multitude of feminine archetypes available to her as a woman.

Within this schema women can claim spirit, i.e., inner power and outward influence, not as "borrowed" from the masculine but as their own. The use of goddess language for the multiple archetypes of feminine power emphasizes the spiritual character of the power being claimed and also concretizes and exemplifies the various forms of power through the classical stories of the various goddesses.

Although the recovery of Goddess is often not a primary focus for Christian women involved in feminist spirituality, many of the issues that it constellates are central to Christian feminist concerns. Among these are the effect of the overmasculinization of the God-image; the practical equation of the Trinity with three male persons; the theological interpretation of the maleness of Jesus as a revelation of the normativeness of masculinity as image of the divine, and specifically of Christ; the monopolizing by men of the exercise of spiritual power and the definition of the latter as domination that is implicit in the exclusion of women from ordination and the forced sacramental dependence of women on male ministers; the identification of women with their sexual and reproductive roles through a romantic glorification of motherhood and an elitist understanding of virginity; a dual anthropology which legitimates a doctrine of gender complementarity that functions to subordinate women to men in family, society, and Church.

In short, the spiritual issues that nondenominational feminists often address through reflection, discourse, and ritual around the symbol of Goddess are the issues of women's participation in, and alienation from, spiritual power and their reduction or confinement to the realm of the natural, the bodily, the material. These issues may take different forms among Catholic women who are feminists, but they are equally central.

Major Characteristics of Feminist Spirituality

Certain characteristics distinguish feminist spirituality in general, whether or not it is Church-related. First, feminist spirituality is *rooted in women's experience,* especially their experience of disempowerment and reempowerment. For this reason storytelling, the sharing of the experience of women, which has been largely excluded from the history of mainline religion, is central. Storytelling is both a technique for consciousness-raising and a source of mutual support. By telling their own stories, women appropriate as significant their own experience, which they have been taught to view as trivial. By listening to the stories of other women, they come to see the commonalities and the political power in women's experience, which they have been taught to believe is purely personal and private.

Secondly, because feminist spirituality is concerned with the reintegration of body and spirit, it is concerned with giving voice to and celebrating those aspects of *bodiliness* that religion has covered with shame and silence, particularly those feminine experiences associated with life-giving that have been reduced to sex and those aspects of female sexuality that have been regarded as unclean, such as menstruation and childbirth.

Very closely related with the emphasis on the goodness and holiness of the material and the bodily is a third characteristic: a profound *concern with nonhuman nature.* Feminist theorists have explicated exhaustively the intimate connection between male possessiveness and exploitative violence toward women and toward nature, which men have characterized as feminine and so subject to male dominion. As men have raped women for their own pleasure and utility, so have they raped the environment for the same purposes. Feminists are convinced that only a spirituality that values both women and all those elements of the universe that have been "feminized," including nature, can contribute to a renewed and livable world. However, feminist spirituality is not merely environmentalist, for environmentalism is basically an anthropocentric approach, but ecological in its vision of, and commitment to, a single organic universe.

A fourth characteristic of feminist spirituality is its emphasis on *ritual* that is participative, circular, aesthetic, incarnate, communicative, life-enhancing, and joyful. Feminist spirituality rejects the unemotional, overly verbal, hierarchical, and dominative liturgical practice of the mainline Churches. Furthermore, feminists involved in spirituality choose to organize themselves religiously not in the hierarchical institutional structures of patriarchal religion, with its insistence on obedience and conformity, but in participative and inclusive communities. Consequently, feminists involved in the spirituality movement are committed to a reenvisioning of ministry, liturgy, theology, teaching, community building, and ecclesiastical organization.

A final, but perhaps the most important, characteristic of feminist spirituality is that from the very beginning it has involved commitment to the intimate and intrinsic *relationship between personal spiritual growth and transformation and a politics of social justice.* The feminist rallying cry, "The personal is political," means not only that the problems women have experienced as their personal and private concerns are actually systemically caused and can only be rectified through structural reform, but also that societal transformation is possible only through and on the basis of personal transformation (see Maria Riley, *Transforming Feminism,* Kansas City: Sheed & Ward, 1989). Thus, unlike traditional mainline spiritualities, which constantly (and often unsuccessfully) seek a point of intersection between the process of personal spiritual growth and a commitment to social justice, feminist spirituality starts with a commitment that faces simultaneously inward and outward. The changes and growth that must happen in women if they are to be and to experience themselves as fully human, daughters of divinity and its bearers in this world, are the same changes that must occur in society, namely, the reintegration of what has been dichotomized, the empowerment of that which has been marginalized and abused, the liberation of that which has been constrained and enslaved.

Christian (Catholic) Feminist Spirituality

As has been mentioned, feminist spirituality did not arise within the Churches. However, its originating theorists and practitioners were women who were or had been involved with mainline religions and/or who had professional interests in Jewish or Christian theology or religious studies. Consequently, there has always been a relationship, whether of criticism, antagonism, challenge, or partial continuity, between feminist spirituality and organized religion. As Christian, and especially Catholic, women who were feminists became involved in the feminist spirituality movement, they both assimilated much from the movement and developed their own concerns and approaches. Although there is much common ground among all Christian feminists, what follows is concerned especially with feminist spirituality as it has developed among Catholic women.

At the outset it is important to realize that not all Catholic women, and probably not even the majority, are feminists, and not all feminists have applied their feminist insights and categories to their spirituality. In other words, women's spirituality and feminist spirituality are not synonymous terms. Indeed, some self-designated women's spirituality is antifeminist. Feminist spirituality arises from feminist consciousness, the result of the process of consciousness-raising, when that consciousness becomes operative in the sphere of one's lived faith experience.

Sources of Feminist Spirituality Among Catholics

Catholic women who have embraced a feminist spirituality have done so from a number of different starting points. Some are women, especially members of religious communities, who have been deeply involved in the development of their spiritual lives over a long period of time and, through a process of consciousness-raising as well as involvement with justice issues in society, have become feminists. They have then seen the implications of their feminism for their spiritual lives. The oppressive masculinity of liturgical language, the maleness of the God-image that controls their religious imagination, their domination by men through the sacramental system, the marginality of women in the biblical tradition, the exclusion of female experience and wisdom from the theological and moral tradition of the Church, women's subordination in ministry, and the effective sexual apartheid in the institutional Church have become more and more obvious, painful, and finally intolerable.

A second type of Catholic woman who may be led toward feminist spirituality is one who has suffered personal abuse in and from the Church, e.g., as a member of a religious congregation whose self-determination has been undermined by the Vatican; as a married woman who has suffered under a sexual morality which disproportionately affects women but which has never incorporated women's experience; as the victim, or parent of a victim, of sexual abuse by a priest; as a seminary student or wife of a married deacon whose call to ordained ministry has been dismissed without testing. Such experiences often precipitate a spiritual crisis in which the victim can no longer relate to the God who is represented by those who have abused her. She is forced to find a new approach to God or even a new God to approach.

Finally, some Catholic women began to participate in non-Church related or post-Christian feminist spirituality and gradually came to experience it as more fulfilling of their spiritual quest than the traditional Christian spirituality with which they grew up. They may continue to go to Mass on Sunday and try to pray as before, but they find themselves increasingly overcome with alienating emotions: anger; boredom; discomfort in religious situations that do not reflect feminist values of cooperation, inclusion, holism, and connectedness that are now second nature to them. Thus they tend to gravitate more often to feminist spiritual gatherings, and their spirituality is gradually shaped by the new experience.

No matter how a woman who is a feminist comes to see the connection between her feminism and her spirituality, seeing the connection will present, at the very least, a major challenge in the area of faith and, in most cases, a major crisis.

Areas of Concern

Three areas usually present major problems in spirituality for the Catholic woman who is a feminist: theology, ministry, and personal development.

1. *Theological Concerns.* Obviously, there is a close connection between what one believes, i.e., one's faith, and the lived experience of faith, i.e., one's spirituality. Consequently, the androcentrism (male-centeredness), patriarchy (male dominance), and sexism (male oppression) that are such salient characteristics of Catholic theology present massive problems for feminist women believers. Despite the denial that God, who is pure spirit, is a sexed being, the common teaching and liturgical practice of the Church conspire to present God as three male persons—Father, Son, and Spirit (who is consistently and virtually exclusively referred to as "he").

Jesus, the Savior, was historically a male human being, and his historical sexuality not only completely controls the presentation of the glorified Christ but also has been invoked in recent years, contrary to tradition, to justify excluding women from full sacramental participation in the Church on the grounds that they cannot sacramentally image the male Savior (see Sacred Congregation for the Doctrine of the Faith, "Declaration on the Question of the Admission of Women to the Ministerial Priesthood," 1977, sect. 5).

The Church, according to Catholic teaching, is a patriarchal hierarchy by divine institution. The sacraments of daily life, i.e., Eucharist and penance, can be administered only by males, thus rendering women not only subordinate to, but sacramentally dependent upon, men. Furthermore, women have been declared ontologically incapable of receiving one of the sacraments with the necessary implication that baptism, which renders men subjects, in principle, of all of the sacraments, renders women capable of only some. This baptismal secondary status reflects and sacramentalizes the dual anthropology consistently presented in Church documents on women, according to which women are "different" from men, complementary to them, in ways that virtually always involve an exaltation of femininity in theory and a subordination of women in practice.

The theological impediments to women's experiencing themselves as fully human and fully Christian within the Catholic Church are so overwhelming that many women, like theologian Mary Daly, have come to the conclusion that self-respecting womanhood and Catholicity are incompatible and have moved beyond Catholicism into post-Christian feminist spirituality. Other women, who choose to remain within the Church, face enormous obstacles as they try to both maintain their own spiritual lives and to change the institution. To a large extent Catholic feminist spirituality is characterized by this struggle.

2. *Ministerial Concerns.* Besides the evident difficulties feminist Catholic minis-

ters experience in trying to work with clergy who are not only all male and usually trained in all-male seminary environments but also celibate and often inexperienced in adult relationships with women, these women ministers are increasingly serving in spheres once reserved to the clergy. They are frustrated by their inability to perform those rites, such as Eucharist, penance, the sacrament of the sick, marriages, and funerals, that are intrinsic to their ministries as parish leaders, hospital and prison chaplains, and spiritual directors. While many women have found it impossible to continue to minister in Church settings and have relocated into secular service positions, others continue to try to work within the official ecclesiastical ministries and to bring about change from within.

3. *Developmental Concerns.* As Joann Conn in *Spirituality and Personal Maturity* has shown, traditional Catholic spirituality has conspired with cultural formation to restrict women's psychological development, especially in regard to the achievement of appropriate personal autonomy. The Christian ideal of womanhood, often presented through a distorted Mariology, has encouraged women to remain psychologically and spiritually immature and subordinate to men. As Catholic women's feminist consciousness develops, they often find themselves in conflict with much in the Catholic spiritual tradition, a situation that precipitates uncertainty, guilt, and anger.

Types of Catholic Feminist Spirituality

Basically, Catholic women who are feminists can be divided into two types in terms of their spirituality: those we might call feminist Catholics, *Catholic* being the substantive and *feminist* the modifier, signifying their fundamental self-location in and identification with the Catholic Church; and those we might call Catholic feminists, *feminist* being the substantive, signifying their primary self-location in and identification with the feminist movement, in-

cluding feminist spirituality, within what has come to be called Womenchurch. These are not mutually exclusive categories, because most women Catholics who are feminist actually participate at different times and in different circumstances in both the institutional Church and Womenchurch. However, this typology will allow us to describe two basic types of feminist spirituality that are prevalent among Catholics who are feminists.

1. *Feminist Catholics.* In general, feminist Catholics are women who have developed a deep, personal, Christocentric spirituality, nourished by an intense personal prayer life and sacramental practice, and expressed in energetic ministerial commitment. Even in the midst of profoundly alienating experiences of ecclesiastical sexism, their attachment to the Church as community of believers is too central to their identity to be surrendered.

While no description can do justice to the diversity of the spiritual experience of such women, two features are common to the experience of many: an intense interior struggle with existential anger and a many-faceted effort at ecclesiastical reform. Existential anger, unlike the episodic anger everyone experiences in the face of life's various frustrations, is a continuous state that victims of structural injustice often experience. Feminist consciousness, once activated, makes a person ever more aware of the all-pervasive oppression of women in the Church. The resulting anger, which might begin as passing annoyance with particular affronts, gradually deepens into an abiding and emotionally draining state of anger ranging from towering rage to chronic depression. Such an experience of nearly continuous anger precipitates, for the feminist Catholic, a spiritual crisis of major proportions for which the tradition offers few if any resources. Not only has anger been presented as a sinful passion, but women have been religiously socialized to regard themselves as primarily responsible for preventing conflict in family and

Church. Furthermore, the expression of anger "justifies" male retaliation against modern women, as witchcraft once "justified" the wholesale murder of powerful women in earlier ages of the Church. Such retaliation can take the form of professional reprisals, exclusion from ministry, or personal denigration.

The struggle to integrate into a healthy spirituality justified anger and its effective expression as energy for transformation is a major part of the spiritual agenda of feminist Catholics who are striving to attain an appropriately autonomous maturity, in contrast to the constricted and dependent immaturity to which women have been socialized and for which they have been rewarded, especially in the Church. Many women have found resources for the struggle in the sharing of their personal stories in spiritual direction with feminist women directors (see Kathleen Fischer, *Women at the Well,* New York: Paulist, 1988) and in women's support groups in which feminist ritual plays a major role. Women theologians and psychologists have contributed a variety of theoretical resources for understanding, appropriating, and channeling both the experience of anger and the exciting experiences of self-affirmation and personal integration of women whose spirituality is being refined in the purifying crucible of unjust suffering.

The external face of feminist Catholic spirituality is the active commitment to ecclesiastical reform. Many of these women are energetic members of such organizations as the Women's Ordination Conference, Catholics Speak Out, the Association for the Rights of Catholics in the Church, and Priests for Equality. Feminist Catholic theologians such as Anne Carr and Elizabeth Johnson are involved in a full-scale revisionist criticism of the entire Catholic tradition. The resulting body of feminist theology is increasingly recognized as credible and convincing, even in the male-dominated academy, and its effects are beginning to be felt in the realms of Church teaching and practice. Meanwhile, feminist Catholics involved in pastoral ministry are consistently, and with increasing effectiveness, challenging sexism at the grass-roots level. Feminist Catholics who are parents are striving to inculcate feminist principles and behaviors in the next generation of Catholics, who, they hope, will neither accept the continued oppression of women in family, society, or Church nor participate in any aspect of Church life, including ordained ministry, which discriminates against women.

In short, feminist Catholics are characterized by an abiding affirmation of their Catholic identity and an unwillingness to surrender it despite nearly intolerable suffering from ecclesiastical patriarchy. While they struggle to grow toward spiritual wholeness, including the integration of the existential anger that arises in the face of sexual apartheid in the Church, they channel their energy into transformational involvement in ecclesial life. They continue to hope for the conversion of the institutional Church, and that hope sustains them in membership and commitment.

2. *Catholic Feminists.* The second basic type of woman who is both Catholic and feminist identifies herself primarily not in terms of institutional religion, Catholic or other, but in terms of feminism. These women were among the founders of the movement called Womenchurch, which understands itself as the Church in exodus from patriarchy. Rather than being concerned with reforming the male patriarchal institution, they are concerned with promoting the full personhood of women while being Church in a nonpatriarchal mode. Their criterion for the genuinely religious quality of any experience, project, or process is not whether it is coherent with, or acceptable to, traditional institutional religion but whether it is life-giving for women.

At the present stage of its development, Womenchurch includes members from many religious traditions—Catholic, Protestant, Jewish, Native American, Buddhist, Wicca; from all races and ethnic groups; ordained, lay, and religious women. Many feminists who remain primarily identified with the institutional Church participate in Womenchurch events and find there the nourishment they need to continue their struggle for institutional reform.

The spirituality of Womenchurch members is primarily feminist spirituality rather than Christian or non-Christian. Thus it is characterized by the salient features of feminist spirituality described above. The spirituality of Womenchurch characteristically finds expression in ritual that involves song, dance, poetry, storytelling, and the sharing of meals. The celebration of womanhood is complemented by commitment to social-justice activism because the connection among all forms of oppression is a key insight of feminism.

Catholic feminists, along with religiously committed feminists from other traditions, are not content to await, actively or passively, the reform of the institutional Church. They have undertaken to develop rituals that not only do not oppress them but will give them life and hope. They do not hesitate to rewrite the stories of the biblical tradition from the standpoint of women's experience; to repudiate the stories from the tradition that marginalize, demonize, or degrade women; and to write new stories that carry the nonpatriarchal content of the tradition in ways that are meaningful for women. These feminists are also not waiting for the institutional Church to ask for their opinion about, or to reform the official positions on, moral matters that affect women, and many have publicly taken antiestablishment positions on such issues as contraception, divorce and remarriage, homosexuality, and abortion. Thus, from the standpoint of the institution, Catholic feminists can seem marginal and are often regarded by Church officials as "radical," in the sense of dangerously extremist. The members of Womenchurch, however, see themselves as those who have undertaken to be Church in a new and more authentic way, and they anticipate the distant day when the rest of the Church will join them in the final exodus from patriarchy.

Conclusion

Feminist Catholics and Catholic feminists share feminist consciousness and commitment, but they differ in their primary social location, with the former still primarily situated within the institutional Church, and the latter on the margins of the male institution; in their strategy, with the former still committed to the reform of the institution, while the latter are more concerned with being an alternative Church; in their central spiritual concerns, with the former concentrating on issues of survival, growth, and reform, and the latter on issues of creating a new expression of spirituality. The challenge women face in trying to be both feminist and Catholic is the spring from which Catholic feminist spirituality, still a very young phenomenon, is developing.

See also BODY; CHURCH; CONFRONTATION AND PROTEST; CONTEMPORARY SPIRITUALITY; CREATION; DUALISM; ECOLOGICAL CONSCIOUSNESS; EXPERIENCE; JUSTICE; LIBERATION THEOLOGY, INFLUENCE ON SPIRITUALITY; LITURGY; MARGINALIZED, THE; MYSTICISM; PASSION(S); POWER; PRAXIS; PREGNANCY; PSYCHOLOGY, RELATIONSHIP AND CONTRIBUTION TO SPIRITUALITY; SEXUALITY; SPIRITUAL DIRECTION; TRANSFORMATION.

Bibliography: S. Cady, M. Ronan, and H. Taussig, *Sophia: The Future of Feminist Spirituality* (San Francisco: Harper & Row, 1986). A. Carr, *Transforming Grace: Christian Tradition and Women's Experience* (San Francisco: Harper & Row, 1988). C. Christ and J. Plaskow, eds., *Womanspirit Rising: A Feminist Reader in Religion* (San Francisco: Harper & Row, 1979). J. W. Conn, "Spirituality," *The New Dictionary of Theology* (Wilmington, Del.: Glazier, 1987); *Spirituality and Personal Maturity* (New York: Paulist, 1989). C. Halkes, "Feminism and Spirituality," *Spirituality Today* 40 (1988) 22–36. E. Johnson, "Jesus, the Wisdom of God: A Biblical Basis for a Non-Androcentric Christology," *Ephemerides Theologicae Lovanienses* 50 (December 1985) 261–294. S. Purvis, "Christian Feminist Spirituality," *Christian Spirituality: Post Reformation and Modern*, ed. L. Dupré and D. Saliers, World Spirituality: An Encyclopedic History of the Religious Quest 18 (New York: Crossroad, 1989) 500–519. R. Ruether, "Feminism and Religious Faith: Renewal or New Creation?" *Religion and Intellectual Life* 3 (Winter 1986) 7–20. S. Schneiders, *Women and the Word: The Gender of God in the New Testament and the Spirituality of Women* (New York: Paulist, 1986).

SANDRA M. SCHNEIDERS, I.H.M.

FIDELITY

Whatever faithfulness, whatever trust we may have in God finds its assurance in *God's own fidelity* to us in the love shown us in God's Son. In the covenants God made with Noah and Abraham and Moses, we are given the expression of the extent to which God was committed to the people of Israel and to creation, committed to love and cherish them and it. In the prophets this commitment is expressed in the warm and tender terms of lover and mother (Hos 11:1-4). God's faithfulness to these promises, the promise that we are God's people in Abraham (Gal 3:6-9), is finally and ultimately exemplified in the incarnation of the Son, in which God has become like us in all things but sin.

The message of God's fidelity to love as the basis for our trust in God, and our fidelity to God in turn, is expressed succinctly in the First Letter of John: "In this is love: not that we have loved God, but that he loved us and sent his Son as expiation for our sins" (1 Jn 4:10).

"Fidelity" derives from the Latin *fides*, "faith," and *fidelis*, "faithful." In European history it became a fundamental element of the feudal system in the obligation of *fealty*, or allegiance to one's lord, and in which one's lord also owed allegiance to his vassals. There was mutual reliance, mutual trust. This same mutuality existed in the Near Eastern practice of covenant.

Thus fidelity, or faithfulness, is also trust or confidence in the other, the confidence of a mutual commitment. The message of the prophets was a witness to God's unending love and fidelity to the covenant with Israel. The presence of the Christ, Jesus' witness even in suffering to the unending love of the Father, is the source and the seal of our fidelity to God in our baptismal commitment to live the gospel. Faithfulness to the precepts of the Gospels, to the teachings of Jesus and of the Church, are, then, the outward signs of this inward fidelity to God and trust in God's fidelity to us.

See also COVENANT; FAITH; TRUST.

Bibliography: "Fidelité," *D.Spir.*, vol. 5, cols., 307–332.

BENJAMIN BAYNHAM, O.C.S.O.

FORGIVENESS

Forgiveness refers to the removal of obstacles that lie in the way of intimate union with God and others. Traditionally, forgiveness has been understood as directed first toward guilt for sin (which destroys or weakens the relationship with God and neighbor), and then toward the remnants of past sin (which continue to affect those relationships and which incline the individual to repetition). Forgiveness is thus part of the broader reality of reconciliation with God, others, the world, and even with oneself.

Reconciliation as the context of forgiveness faded near the end of the ancient period. This can be seen in the penitential discipline, where focus shifted from community well-being and individuals' solidarity with the community to an emphasis on experiencing forgiveness, healing, and consolation. Throughout the Middle Ages the penitential system, in close relationship with the understanding of justification, stressed such purification and grace rather than reconciliation with God in the community. It thus became primarily therapeutic, and was often so presented in spiritual writings.

Yet to those born in a world deformed from the image of God in which it was created, God's love comes convincingly as gracious forgiveness. Because God is love, creating out of nothing, insistent love reaches into the depths of creatures who by sin refuse the gift of the divine image. In experiencing that love, they recognize that they have been part of a world alienated from God and have themselves confirmed that condition. Nevertheless, they are loved and transformed—reconciled—by God, who removes the obstacles to such union, not because we are worthy of it but to make us worthy.

The recognition of God's love thus throws light on the human condition. It is a condition of alienation and estrangement—from God, from others, from the world, from oneself. Yet it is not our sin but God's love that is basic. When this love touches us, we see how far we have been from God, others, world, and self, and how that distance has been overcome by God's grace. Many factors, including prior experience and personality, may affect the intensity with which each of these is experienced—and thus the experienced need for forgiveness. But always God's love is a force that draws us into God, and consequently away from our former situation and/or from what could keep us from God.

For this reason a focus on forgiveness is an essential dimension of Christian spirituality and a condition of spiritual growth. This should not be presented in preaching, catechesis, and spiritual direction so as to promote shame, fear, or scrupulosity, particularly with individuals inclined toward an obsessive-compulsive syndrome. Nevertheless, a realization of God's magnificent beauty, of the fears that prevent intimacy among people, of the ways in which we mar the world, of the flaws in ourselves that prevent the full integrity that would image God is a part of the virtue of repentance whereby we recognize our need for forgiveness.

In our society the need for forgiveness, when acknowledged, is generally understood in an individualistic and, consequently, depressing fashion. It is for that reason often denied or avoided. Practically and pastorally speaking, then, individuals should not be encouraged to reflect on their need for forgiveness simply in terms of personal sins but rather in terms of their broader responsibilities to community and thus to God. It is in this way that they move toward Christian perfection.

God's love, experienced as forgiveness, thus moves us in the direction not only of accepting responsibility for the sinfulness of the world but also, and more importantly, of offering resistance to it. Action on behalf of justice and peace is a key effect that follows from the realization of God's love and the human need for forgiveness.

It is in this way that our forgiveness of others is part of spiritual growth. It is shown not only in reaching beyond the faults committed against us and refusing to allow them to become barriers to intimacy but also in seeking to eradicate the obstacles that exist among people, between them and their world, and between them and their God. We forgive as we have been forgiven, and we reconcile as we have been reconciled.

See also COMPASSION; CONVERSION; FRUIT(S) OF THE HOLY SPIRIT; MERCY; PENANCE, PENITENCE.

Bibliography: J. Dallen, *The Reconciling Community* (New York: Pueblo, 1986).

JAMES DALLEN

FORMATION OF CONSCIENCE
See CONSCIENCE.

FORMATION, SPIRITUAL
See JOURNEY (GROWTH AND DEVELOPMENT IN SPIRITUAL LIFE); PSYCHOLOGY, RELATIONSHIP AND CONTRIBUTION TO SPIRITUALITY.

FORTITUDE
See CARDINAL VIRTUES.

FRANCISCAN SPIRITUALITY

Franciscan spirituality describes that approach to God and life in the world characterized by the values and behaviors that have their foundation in the religious experience of Francis and Clare of Assisi and the movement begun by them. This spirituality is expressed in the life and writings of the Franciscan women and men belonging to the First Order, the Second Order, and the Third Order Regular and Secular, as well as countless others who claim the Franciscan spirit as their own.

Francis of Assisi (1182–1226)

Francis of Assisi dictated his *Testament* shortly before his death on October 4, 1226, leaving to his followers for all time a pattern for Franciscan living. While the juridical value of the *Testament* was hotly debated throughout the years following Francis' death, nonetheless it continued to serve as a reminder of both the values and behaviors that defined the Franciscan following of Jesus Christ.

In his *Testament* Francis identified the first moment of his spiritual life with his encounter with the leper: "The Lord granted to me, Brother Francis, to begin to do penance in this way: While I was in sin, it seemed very bitter to me to see lepers. And the Lord Himself led me among them and I had mercy upon them. And when I left them that which seemed bitter to me was changed into sweetness of soul and body; and afterward I lingered a little and left the world" (Armstrong-Brady, p. 154). This encounter with the leper was to mark Francis' religious experience throughout his life: the rich young merchant accustomed to a comfortable lifestyle came face to face with human suffering. And in that encounter with human suffering, Francis came to understand the love of God made flesh in the incarnation of Jesus Christ. As Francis himself remembered it, in that encounter with the leper his values were overturned ("from bitterness to sweetness"),

and his behavior changed as he began to live a life of penance with the lepers from that moment. It is this experience of grace that establishes Franciscan spirituality as the following of the poor and crucified Christ.

This following of the poor and crucified Christ led Francis from life within the social structures of Assisi's communal life to life at the margins of that society with the poor, the outcasts, the lepers—in short, with those who found no place in the world that he had left. As the *Earlier Rule* states in chapter 9, Franciscans "must rejoice when they live among people [who are considered to be] of little worth and who are looked down upon, among the poor and the powerless, the sick and the lepers, and the beggars by the wayside" (Armstrong-Brady, p. 117). While Francis' conversion, expressed by his "leaving the world," did not result in his entrance into a monastery or another existing form of religious life within the Church of his day, it did result in a new social and ecclesial definition that Francis describes in his *Testament* as life "according to the form of the Holy Gospel" (Armstrong-Brady, p. 155).

Francis insists that in this experience of grace it was the Lord himself who showed him what he should do; no human or ecclesial influence determined the path he was to follow. The *Legend of Perugia,* a source that contains the eyewitness remembrances of Francis by his early companions, records Francis himself saying to the brothers gathered in chapter that "the Lord has told me that he wanted to make a new fool of me in the world, and God does not want to lead us by any other knowledge than that" (Habig, p. 1089). The uniqueness and novelty of Franciscan spirituality stem from this fundamental conviction based on Francis' experience. While Franciscan spirituality was influenced by many of the currents of the 12th century and the renewed desire for a more authentic experience of Christian living expressed in the varied historic attempts at reliving the "apostolic life," living according to the "form of the Holy Gospel" indicated something radically new.

One aspect of the novelty of Franciscan spirituality is its focus on the word of God as contained in the gospel, which becomes rule and life, as stated in the prologue to the *Earlier Rule:* "This is the life of the Gospel of Jesus Christ which Brother Francis asked the Lord Pope to be granted and confirmed for him" (Armstrong-Brady, p. 108). But even before Francis was able to hear the word of the gospel, God gave him brothers, as he records in the *Testament.* The word of God is not addressed primarily to individuals but to brothers and sisters, and can be correctly heard and responded to only in brotherhood and sisterhood.

The development of the Franciscan Rule from its initial form in the text presented to Innocent III in 1209 to the form of the *Earlier Rule* as it existed prior to its redaction in the *Final Rule,* which received papal confirmation in 1223, witnesses to the role the word of God played in the life of the early fraternity. Coming together in chapters annually, the brothers reflected together on how they lived the gospel, and on how their concrete experiences of living conditioned their following of the gospel. The *Final Rule* does represent Francis' own religious experience of living the gospel, but it expresses his religious experience only in that it represents at the same time the collective experience of the brothers.

Living in brotherhood and sisterhood is constitutive of life according to the form of the holy gospel, and at the same time a condition for the correct understanding of the word of the gospel. The first version of Francis' *Letter to the Faithful,* written prior to 1215, puts this very succinctly: "Oh, how holy and how loving, pleasing, humble, peaceful, sweet, lovable, and desirable above all things to have such a Brother and such a Son: our Lord Jesus Christ, Who gave up His life for His sheep" (Armstrong-Brady, pp. 63–64). The follow-

ing of the poor and crucified Christ is expressed concretely in a life characterized by relationships of brotherhood and sisterhood in imitation of Christ our Brother and modeled on the word of the gospel.

The centrality of the word of the gospel for Franciscan life is demonstrated in chapter 22 of the *Earlier Rule,* which appears to be a treatise on the following of Christ. Here Francis focuses on the role of the word of God in the life of the disciple. Paraphrasing the Synoptic parable of the sower and the seed, Francis underlines the centrality of the human heart in receiving the word: "But that which is sown on good soil are those who hear the word with a good and noble heart (Lk 8:15) and understand it and (cf. Mt 13:23) keep it and bear fruit in patience (Lk 8:15)" (Armstrong-Brady, p. 128). It is not a fundamentalist, literal understanding of the gospel that Francis urges, but rather a heart open to the inspiration of the Spirit who conforms the person to Christ.

Francis juxtaposes two texts from the Gospel of John to underline the relation of the Spirit to the word: "The words which I have spoken to you are spirit and life (Jn 6:64). I am the way, the truth, and the life (Jn 14:6)" (Armstrong-Brady, p. 129). Both the Spirit and the word lead to Christ. Indeed, as Francis states in the *Final Rule,* "let them pursue what they must desire above all things: to have the Spirit of the Lord and His holy manner of working" (Armstrong-Brady, p. 144). The gospel is not a dead letter or even a voice from the past, but a word that speaks in the present moment to the faithful. It is this dynamic of Spirit and gospel that creates human fraternity conformed to the image of Christ.

Closely linked to Francis' attention to the word of God are his love and veneration for the Eucharist. The first *Admonition* connects both the word and the Eucharist with the activity of the Spirit of the Lord: the Eucharist is "sanctified by the words of the Lord," and it is "the Spirit of the Lord Who lives in His faithful, who receive the most holy Body and Blood of the Lord" (Armstrong-Brady, p. 26). Both the words of the Lord and the Eucharist are visible, concrete, and tangible realities for Francis: as the word is heard with human ears, so the Eucharist is seen by human eyes. For Francis, the experience of the Eucharist is tantamount to the apostles' own experience of the earthly and incarnate Jesus: "See, daily He humbles Himself (cf. Phil 2:8) as when He came from the royal throne (Wis 18:15) into the womb of the Virgin; daily He comes to us in a humble form" (Armstrong-Brady, p. 26).

Francis consistently connects the mystery of the Eucharist with seeing the Lord. In this he is representative of the developing Eucharistic piety of his day, which focused on the seeing of the consecrated host as the way of salvation. But Francis develops this devotion of seeing the Eucharist into a piety that takes flesh in mission. As it is the mystery of the humble Christ that is made present in the Eucharist, so one should respond in a like form of humility. For Francis, this is the core of living according to the "form of the Holy Gospel." As Jesus came in the humble, frail flesh of an infant at Bethlehem, and as he daily comes in the humble form of bread, so one returns to God in humility, in the same form as the God who comes in Jesus. Hearing the word of God in the gospel and seeing the Word in the Eucharist, under the inspiration of the Spirit of the Lord, recreate human identity into its true image, that of Jesus Christ.

Francis' first hagiographer, Thomas of Celano, writing a life of Francis in 1229, presents the spiritual itinerary of Francis in terms of hearing and seeing. Describing Francis' intention to live the gospel, Celano comments that "the humility of the incarnation and the charity of the passion occupied his memory particularly, to the extent that he wanted to think of hardly anything else" (Habig, p. 299). The humility of the incarnation is presented as the fruit of Francis' conversion, which allows Francis to hear the gospel and to discover in that same gospel the deepest longing of his own heart. And what Francis hears he acts on, for he "was not a deaf hearer of the Gospel" (Habig, p. 247) but first practiced what he preached. Celano connects the charity of the passion with Francis' becoming a "visible pattern of the way of salvation" (Habig, p. 305) in the transformation he experiences in the stigmata he received in September 1224. The stigmata are seen by Celano as the fruit in Francis' very flesh of his focus on, and his seeing the presence of, the mystery of Christ. Describing the event of the stigmata, Celano states that "the marks of the nails began to appear in his hands and feet, just as he had seen them a little before in the crucified man above him" (Habig, p. 309). In the stigmata Francis becomes what he sees!

This dynamic of hearing, seeing, and becoming is important to Francis' spiritual progress, according to Celano. Prior to his description of the stigmata, Celano devotes a large section of his narrative to Francis' relation to the poor and to the created world. After recounting how Francis rebuked a brother who doubted the sincerity of a poor man, he comments that Francis was accustomed to saying, "Who curses a poor man does an injury to Christ, whose noble image he wears, the image of him who made himself poor for us in this world" (Habig, p. 293). The poor are sacraments of Christ, for in them Francis sees the poor and humble Christ.

Celano's narrative then turns immediately to Francis' compassion for animals and all creation, especially those things "in which some allegorical similarity to the Son of God could be found" (Habig, p. 293), describing his fondness for lambs and flowers and even for worms. Here Celano describes Francis as "contemplating in creatures the wisdom of their Creator, his power and his goodness" (Habig, p. 296). This is followed by a description of Francis' celebration of the feast of Christmas at Grecchio, where, Celano remarks,

Francis wanted to do something that would "recall to memory the little Child who was born at Bethlehem and set before our bodily eyes in some way the inconveniences of his infant needs" (Habig, p. 300). Celano's focus throughout is on Francis' "seeing" the visible mystery of Jesus Christ in the poor and in all of creation, underlining the connection between Francis as a visible image of the perfection of the gospel as he appeared in his stigmatized flesh and the mystery of Christ, which Francis literally sees everywhere in everyone and everything.

In the winter following his reception of the stigmata, Francis, plagued by increasingly severe illness and almost totally blind, began the composition of his *Canticle of Brother Sun* (Armstrong-Brady, pp. 38–39) while staying at San Damiano. Verses 1 through 9 celebrate the cosmic fraternity of creation, whose elements of moon, wind, water, fire, and earth reflect the brilliant light of Brother Sun. Verses 10 and 11 celebrate pardon and peace, and were written by Francis to settle a dispute between the mayor and the bishop of Assisi. The final verses were written shortly before Francis' death and celebrate the final reconciliation of the human person with God in humility. The *Canticle of Brother Sun* thus synthesizes Francis' own spiritual life. It is his celebration of God's goodness experienced concretely in a world that is seen and received as gift. The canticle expresses Francis' understanding and appreciation of the created world as reconciled space in fraternity. In it he expresses his vision, what he sees, in words: in its brotherhood and sisterhood, in its reconciliation, peace, and humility, creation reflects the poor and crucified Christ. This is the deepest meaning of the dynamic of Francis' life arrived at in the stigmata: his own becoming of what he sees, of living according to the form of the holy gospel.

As Francis wrote the canticle, he had the brothers set it to music so that it could be sung. It was intended by Francis to be the message the brothers and sisters communicated in their preaching both in word and deed. Thus the canticle expresses Franciscan mission in poetic form. In his *Letter to the Entire Order,* written within the last two years of his life, Francis communicates in a direct statement the meaning and purpose he perceives to be the reason for the existence of the Franciscan movement. There he challenges all the brothers to "give praise to [God] since He is good (Ps 135:1) and exalt Him by your deeds (Tob 13:6), for He has sent you into the entire world for this reason that in word and deed you may give witness to His voice and bring everyone to know that there is no one who is all-powerful except Him (Tob 13:4)" (Armstrong-Brady, p. 56). The mission is one of praise to the Creator, echoing the *Canticle of Brother Sun.* After making this statement, Francis further clarifies this mission by focusing on the means to be used, stating that the brothers must show reverence and honor to the Eucharistic Body and Blood of Jesus Christ, "in Whom that which is in the heavens and on the earth is brought to peace and is reconciled to the all-powerful God" (cf. Col 1:20). His experience of the world is celebrated in the Eucharist, which is ultimately the celebration of the mystery of the world becoming the kingdom.

Living according to the form of the holy gospel thus implies mission—a mission of going about the world as pilgrim and stranger, as both the *Earlier Rule* and the *Later Rule* insist (Armstrong-Brady, pp. 120, 141). The focus of Franciscan mission is not in the first place the conversion of sinners and nonbelievers; the focus of mission is for the brothers and sisters to respect the integrity of the created world, which issues forth from the hand of God as fraternal, as gift, as proclaimed in the *Canticle of Brother Sun.* The mission for Franciscans is to give witness in word and deed to the truth that creation is by first becoming that truth in their own lives. Concern for the needs of the suffering, the poor, and the oppressed is a response integral to the life according to the form of the holy gospel, because creation is the gift of God to all people. Concern for the environment is linked to reverence for Christ, whose image creation bears. Interreligious dialogue springs from the conviction that human persons, regardless of their beliefs, and even if these beliefs might be different or incorrect, are brothers and sisters in the eyes of God, as Francis' own mission to Melek-el-Kamel at Damietta in 1219 demonstrates. By the very fact that all persons are brothers and sisters in their very existence as creatures of the one source of all good, the purpose of a mission among the nonbelievers is to first of all express what unites all people in their differences, that is, their common brotherhood and sisterhood. Because creation is fraternal, the Franciscan mission is to make that explicit through relationships of respect and dignity. The contemporary discussion of issues of justice and peace, the crisis of the environment, and the need for respectful interreligious dialogue are thus integral components of Franciscan spirituality as life "according to the form of the Holy Gospel."

From the moment of Francis' encounter with the leper, he describes his life in terms of penance. This life of penance that Francis embarked upon was expressed in his turning away from sin and turning toward God, whom Francis experienced concretely in his embrace of the leper. Franciscan penance implies a life of continual conversion from mere appearance to reality by turning concretely toward others, brothers and sisters, lepers, the poor, the suffering, outcasts, animals, and creation itself. Much more than acts of asceticism, mortification, and penitence, which focus immediately on the self, the life of penance has more to do with receptivity and openness to Christ, which begins not in an activity of introversion and introspection but in looking outside of and beyond oneself to the truth that reality reveals. That truth is the poor and crucified Christ.

This life of penance is ecclesial in its truest sense. Francis insists that his followers be catholic and promises obedience to the Lord Pope, because it is in the Church that the poor and crucified Christ is present. The first prayer that Francis teaches the brothers is an ecclesial prayer: "We adore You, Lord Jesus Christ, in all Your churches throughout the world, and we bless You, for through Your holy cross You have redeemed the world" (Armstrong-Brady, p. 154). It is not the institution that takes first place in Francis' love for the Church, but rather the Church as redeemed creation. This becomes clear in his devotion to Mary the mother of Jesus. Mary is "the virgin made church," the palace, the tabernacle, the servant and mother of Jesus (Armstrong-Brady, pp. 149–150). Mary is redeemed creation.

Part of the prayer that Francis prayed daily before each Hour of the Divine Office addressed Mary in these words: "the daughter and servant of the most high and supreme King and the Father of heaven, you are the mother of our most holy Lord Jesus Christ, you are the spouse of the Holy Spirit" (Armstrong-Brady, p. 82). In her relationship to the Persons of the Trinity and as mother of the Lord, she is truly a creature in that she makes a home for the Word of God and gives to Jesus "the flesh of humanity and our frailty" (Armstrong-Brady, p. 67). This is the Church, the dwelling place of the Word in word and sacrament, in the frail flesh of humanity, realized in the relationships created by and among brothers and sisters of the Lord.

Clare of Assisi (1194–1253)

Moved by the preaching and witness of Francis, Clare began a life of penance on Palm Sunday in 1212. Received by the brothers at the little church of Saint Mary of the Angels, she became the first female member of the Franciscan Order and held tenaciously to the vision of Francis throughout her life and in her struggles with the Roman Curia to win recognition for her ideal of Franciscan life. Both as a follower of Francis and a foundress in her own right, she was acclaimed in the legend written shortly after her canonization in 1255 as "the footprint of the Mother of God, a new leader of women" (Armstrong, p. 189).

In the "form of life" given by Francis to Clare and her sisters soon after her conversion in 1212, Francis summarized the essential elements of the life he saw to be operative in the choices made by Clare and her sisters: "By divine inspiration you have made yourselves daughters and servants of the most high King, the heavenly Father, and have taken the Holy Spirit as your spouse, choosing to live according to the perfection of the holy Gospel" (Armstrong, pp. 243–244). The images that Francis uses to describe the life of the Poor Sisters echo his prayers to the Blessed Virgin Mary. He clearly sees in Clare and her sisters the realization of what it means to live according to the form of the holy gospel as spouses of the Holy Spirit. Thus the command that Francis received from the cross in the church of San Damiano to rebuild the church that was falling down is realized in the life of Clare and her sisters in the enclosure of San Damiano. Indeed, it is the witness of Clare and her sisters that teaches Francis what it means to become and live as spouses of the Lord under divine inspiration, as this is reflected in some of Francis' own writings. Because of this, Francis resolves and promises to Clare for himself and his brothers "to have that same loving care and special solicitude for you as [I have] for them" (Armstrong, p. 244). Both the brothers and the sisters form one family, one religious community, sharing the same ideals, though expressed in different circumstances.

For Clare as for Francis, what defined their manner of life was living according to the perfection of the holy gospel, which found concrete expression in a life of pov-erty. The Fourth Lateran Council, convoked by Pope Innocent III in 1215, refused recognition to any new rules of religious life, so Clare was forced to accept the Rule of Benedict. Unhappy with this Rule's description of monastic possession, Clare requested from Innocent III the privilege of absolute poverty. Her request was granted, and in 1216 Pope Innocent confirmed her "proposal of most high poverty (cf. 2 Cor 8:2), granting you by the authority of this letter that no one can compel you to receive possessions" (Armstrong, p. 84). This was a privilege that Clare would have to cling to and fight for in the face of the many attempts by cardinal protectors, popes, and officials of the Roman Curia to have her accept possessions.

Clare's motivation in the struggle to protect the integrity of her gospel life is found in her understanding of Christ's incarnation. She articulates this understanding in her *Testament,* which she probably wrote soon after the Rule of Innocent IV was promulgated in 1247. Clare remarks that "the Son of God never wished to abandon this holy poverty while He lived in the world" (Armstrong, p. 56). For Clare, the form of the holy gospel demanded imitation of "the God Who was placed poor in the crib, lived poor in the world, and remained naked on the cross" (Armstrong, p. 57). Not an end in itself, the life of poverty was translated into concrete and total dependence on the goodness and generosity of God experienced in the mutual charity of the sisters within the enclosure. As the Poor Sisters would receive spiritual food from the preaching and ministry of the brothers, so they would depend totally on the begging brothers for physical nourishment. While Clare herself practiced a severe form of fasting and mortification, to the point of weakening her own physical health, this was never imposed on the sisters. Her Rule, which was approved by Pope Innocent IV in 1253 as she lay on her deathbed, is moderate and balanced, respectful of individual differences and needs. But in all this, poverty was to be respected.

Poverty created sisterhood. Paraphrasing Francis' Rule, Clare wrote in her Rule that each sister should "confidently manifest her needs to the other. For if a mother loves and nourishes her child according to the flesh, should not a sister love and nourish her sister according to the Spirit even more lovingly?" (Armstrong, p. 71). Clare returns to this theme later in the Rule when she encourages the sisters to strive for this goal: "Let them be always eager to preserve among themselves the unity of mutual love which is the bond of perfection" (Armstrong, p. 74). Evangelical poverty is the sign and condition for spiritual espousal with the Trinity, to which the sisters are called by virtue of the inspiration that stands at the source of their vocation in the Church. It is in mutual love and care that the life of the Trinity is imaged: they are daughters and servants of the Father, mothers of Jesus the Son, and spouses of the Holy Spirit.

The letters of Clare to Agnes of Prague (1205–1282), who founded a monastery of Poor Sisters in Prague in 1234, develop Clare's theology of spiritual espousal through a life of contemplative imitation of Christ. She explains to Agnes in her second letter that in holding fast to the footprints of Christ in poverty, she is joined to Christ as his spouse. The Christ Clare encourages Agnes to espouse is the crucified Christ, who became "for your salvation, the lowest of men, was despised, struck, scourged untold times throughout His entire body, and then died amid the suffering of the Cross" (Armstrong, p. 42). The focus of the evangelical prayer of Clare—the poor and crucified Christ—is described with a succinct formula given to Agnes: "O most noble Queen, gaze upon [Him], consider [Him], contemplate [Him], as you desire to imitate [Him]" (Armstrong, p. 42).

In prayer as in life, the crucified Christ becomes for the Poor Sisters a mirror in which Clare invites Agnes to see her own reflection: "Gaze upon that mirror each day, O Queen and Spouse of Jesus Christ, and continually study your face within it. . . . Indeed, blessed poverty, holy humility, and inexpressible charity are reflected in that mirror, as, with the grace of God, you can contemplate them throughout the entire mirror" (Armstrong, p. 48). For Clare, the cross of Christ clearly shows forth these central virtues in Christ' birth, life, and death: the humility of the incarnation, the poverty of his earthly life, and the charity of the passion shine from "that Mirror, suspended on the wood of the Cross" (Armstrong, p. 49). Gazing on that mirror, one is "inflamed more strongly with the fervor of charity" (Armstrong, p. 49), which is expressed in compassion and mutual love, the bond of perfection. For Clare, contemplation of the crucified Christ is the form that following in the footsteps of Christ takes within the enclosure of the Poor Sisters, expressed there concretely in a life of poverty and mutual love.

As Francis and the brothers went about with their attention focused on the reality of Jesus Christ in the created world, so Clare and her sisters focus their attention in a direct contemplative gaze upon the mirror, Christ crucified. What both Francis and Clare are seeing is the same— the poor and crucified Jesus Christ. Both the friars and the sisters are transformed, through a life of poverty in imitation of Christ, into the very object they lovingly look upon. Far from locking out the world, the enclosure of Clare and her sisters concentrates their attention on the poor and crucified Christ in the frail humanity of each sister and of each person who comes to the door of the monastery. Thus the very enclosure of the sisters becomes a mirror of truth in the midst of the world as a place where the word of God is heard and the presence of the Word is lived. Using the model of Mary, mother of the Lord, Clare expresses her understanding of enclosure to Agnes: "May you cling to his most sweet

Mother who gave birth to a Son whom the heavens could not contain. And yet she carried Him in the little enclosure of her holy womb and held Him on her virginal lap" (Armstrong, p. 45). The life of the sisters in their enclosed place becomes a visible image of the "Son of God who has been made for us the way" (Armstrong, pp. 54–55), as Clare states in her *Testament.*

The mission of the Poor Ladies is the same as that of the friars in their active life: by word and deed, in life, to proclaim that there is no one all-powerful but God. Clare speaks of this mission of the sisters in her *Testament:* "For the Lord Himself has placed us not only as a form for others in being an example and a mirror, but even for our own sisters whom the Lord has called to our way of life as well, that they in turn might be a mirror and example to those living in the world" (Armstrong, p. 55). The impact of the life of Clare and her sisters on the city of Assisi, as well as on all of Europe in her own lifetime, is attested to repeatedly in her *Legend.* In the bull of canonization issued by Alexander IV in September 1255, Clare is celebrated as a light that illuminates the whole world as model and example: "Her life is an instruction and a lesson to others who learned the rule of living in this book of life (Rev 21:27). The remainder learned to behold the path of life in this mirror of life" (Armstrong, p. 180). In being a mirror of life for all people, Clare's spirituality, linked as closely as it is to the spirit and life of Francis, becomes an instruction for all peoples of the truth about human life and the values essential to mature and integrated human living in brotherhood and sisterhood, revealed in the birth, life, and death of the poor and crucified Jesus Christ, and learned from a contemplative gaze upon the mirror of the cross.

The Franciscan Tradition

This spiritual experience of Francis and Clare of Assisi, and the patterns of life deriving therefrom, became the basis for the development of Franciscan spirituality throughout the centuries. With nuancing appropriate to different times and places and the diverse styles of life among the members of the First, Second, and Third Franciscan Orders, the tradition of Franciscan spirituality finds its foundation in the poor and crucified Jesus Christ.

In 1259, two years after his election as general minister of the Franciscan Order, Bonaventure of Bagnoregio (d. 1274) retired to the hermitage on Mount Alverna, the place where Francis received the stigmata, in order to find peace. There on the mountain Bonaventure came to understand that the spiritual itinerary of Francis was itself a model to follow for all who desired union with God. Bonaventure outlines this Franciscan journey in his classic work *The Soul's Journey into God.* The description of Francis' spiritual experience as presented by Thomas of Celano in his *First Life of St. Francis,* as a movement from the created world bearing the traces of God and leading to an understanding of human identity in the poor and crucified Christ to a union with Christ achieved in the stigmata, is reflected systematically in Bonaventure's theology and spirituality. He outlines the journey to God as a progression of six stages beginning in the created world, passing into and through the human person, and arriving at affective union with God through Christ crucified. Bonaventure's Christ-mysticism is modeled on the experience of Francis. He learned from Francis that Christian wisdom is found only "through the burning love of the Crucified. . . . This love also so absorbed the soul of Francis that his spirit shone through his flesh when for two years before his death he carried in his body the sacred stigmata of the passion." This outline of the journey toward God is given flesh in the person of Francis in Bonaventure's *Major Life of St. Francis,* written in 1261.

In addition to Bonaventure's more theoretical works, his *Tree of Life* shows the influence of Francis. Here Bonaventure urges the reader to imagine and picture the cross of Christ as a tree rich with the fruits of the mysteries of Christ's life. By picturing these mysteries in one's mind and becoming present to them through desire, one's life is transformed by Christ into a fruitful source of activity in the world. This Franciscan method of visual meditation is developed in more detail in *Meditations on the Life of Christ*, the work of an anonymous Franciscan written for a Poor Clare and often attributed incorrectly to Bonaventure. Many manuscripts contain illustrations of the events described, as an aid to meditation on the life of Christ. This work was to become a very popular work in the late Middle Ages. The Franciscan James of Milan, who lived in the latter half of the 13th century, deals with the contemplation of Christ's love shown to humans in his sufferings for sin. His work *The Goad of Love* reflects on the "sacred heart" of Jesus as the object of prayer and contemplation, moving the person to transformation into compassion after the example of Jesus.

Jacopone da Todi (d. 1306), the poet of poverty, joined the Franciscan Order in 1278, after living for ten years as a penitent following the death of his wife. A member of the Spiritual observance, he was involved in the conflict between the Spirituals and Conventuals, and was eventually imprisoned for his attacks on the papacy. Jacopone's work *The Lauds* is a poetic diary of his own mystical journey. In Laud 61, Jacopone summarizes the life of Francis in terms of the stigmata, giving poetic voice to the mystery that moved his heart and motivated his struggle to live poverty: "The burning love of Christ, whose depths are lost to sight, / Enfolded Francis, softened his heart like wax, / And there pressed its seal, leaving the marks / Of the One to whom he was united." Jacopone is also credited as being the author of the *Stabat Mater,* a powerful emo-

tional hymn to the sufferings Mary experienced at the cross of her son Jesus.

The penitent-widow Angela of Foligno (d. 1309) is representative of the penitential life and spirituality of Third Order Franciscan women. Received into the Third Order after the death of her husband in 1291, she lived an active life of service to lepers, the poor, and the sick. Her mystical experience is recorded in her *Memoriale,* written down by Brother Arnold, her confessor and spiritual director, as she dictated it to him. She describes her own mystical experience as union with the "All Good," reached through her own sharing in the complete self-emptying of Christ crucified. Her journey into God is described in detail in the thirty steps that lead through suffering, pain, joy, and darkness, as described in her *Memoriale.* In the late 15th century Catherine of Genoa (d. 1510), a married lay member of the Third Order, carried on an active life of service to the sick as a contemplative visionary. Her *Purgation and Purgatory* describes her experience of penitential purgation leading her to union with Christ. This work inspired such diverse persons as Francis de Sales and Cardinal Newman, and sparked a movement toward reform in both Catholic and Protestant circles.

John Duns Scotus (d. 1308) is more appreciated as a theologian than as a master of the spiritual life, and yet his uniquely Franciscan approach to the absolute predestination of Christ, the immaculate conception of Mary, and the primacy of love are direct reflections of Francis of Assisi's spiritual intuitions. For Scotus, the fact that Christ was predestined to become incarnate from all eternity, unconditioned by human sin, is a demonstration of the power and goodness of God who is love. This gives a unique position to Christ, for whom all creation exists and whom all creation mirrors in its very existence. Creation is loved by God in its "thisness" (*haecceitas*), which is Scotus's way of reflecting on Francis' *Canticle of Brother Sun.* The theoretical basis that Scotus provides for the immaculate conception of Mary begins from the love of God, whose activity is not conditioned by human sin. Mary's immaculate conception draws attention not primarily to her as an exception to the human history of sin, but rather to the dignity and created goodness of the human person, inasmuch as she provides a model of God's intention in creating the human person. Mary is not an exception but the rule of human identity.

Hendrik Harphius (d. 1477), a Dutch Franciscan whose works were collected under the general title *Theologia mystica* in the 16th century, was very influential through the 17th century, particularly in the mystical movement of Spain in the 16th century. Describing mystical union as the fruit of love, Harphius describes the path to this union as affective love and the imitation of Christ, which incorporates the human person into Christ, and thus into the very relationship of Christ with the Father and the Spirit.

The influence of Franciscans on the golden age of Spanish mysticism of the 16th century is well documented. Francisco de Osuna (d. 1540), a prolific writer, is representative of the method of prayer called "recollection," practiced in many of the Franciscan houses of Spain at that time. His *Third Spiritual Alphabet* describes this method of prayer, which begins in self-knowledge, passes through the imitation of Christ, and achieves union with God in the soul. It is the way of transformation in love. Teresa of Avila claimed that it was this work of Osuna that taught her how to pray. Other Franciscan authors from this period include Bernardino of Laredo, the author of the *Ascent of Mount Sion,* and Peter of Alcantara (d. 1652), to whom is attributed the influential *Golden Treatise on Mental Prayer.*

Two women of the Second Order stand out in the history of this spiritual tradition. Colette of Corbie (d. 1447), moved by a vision of St. Francis, who spoke to her about relaxations in the order, set out to work for the reform and renewal of the orders that St. Francis founded. She is the author of a Rule for Reformed Poor Clares, echoing St. Clare in her love for poverty as the way to Christ. Veronica Giuliani (d. 1727) is the author of a *Diary* of her mystical experiences. For Veronica, suffering is the expression of love in imitation of the sufferings of Christ. She received in her own flesh the marks of Christ's passion.

Leonardo Boff witnesses to the continuing vitality of the Franciscan spiritual tradition. His work *Saint Francis: A Model for Human Liberation* demonstrates the role of Francis in the development of a contemporary spirituality of human liberation. Boff singles out St. Francis as a fully integrated human being, as a model of poverty, "a way of being by which the individual lets things be what they are . . . . The more radical the poverty, the closer the individual comes to reality" (p. 39). This allows the individual to celebrate the world as a "paradise," which is the way St. Francis and St. Clare lived in the world.

From Francis and Clare of Assisi to Leonardo Boff, the Franciscan spiritual tradition is consistent in its focus on the poor and suffering Christ. Imitating the love and compassion of Jesus Christ, the Franciscan spirit continues to offer the world a way of peace and a model for human life based on the gospel of Jesus Christ.

See also ANIMALS; CHRIST; CHURCH; COMMUNITY; COMPASSION; CREATION; EXPERIENCE; INCARNATION; MARGINALIZED, THE; POOR, THE; POVERTY; STIGMATA; THIRD ORDERS; WESTERN MEDIEVAL SPIRITUALITY.

Bibliography: R. Armstrong and I. Brady, *Francis and Clare: The Complete Works* (New York: Paulist, 1982). R. Armstrong, *Clare of Assisi: Early Documents* (New York: Paulist, 1989). M. Habig, ed., *St. Francis of Assisi: Writings and Early Biographies* (Chicago: Franciscan Herald Press, 1973). R. Manselli, *St. Francis of Assisi* (Chicago: Franciscan Herald Press, 1988). D. McElrath, ed., *Franciscan Christology: Selected Texts, Translations and Introductory Essays* (St. Bonaventure, N.Y.: Franciscan Institute, 1980). W. Short, *The Franciscans* (Wilmington, Del.: Glazier,

1989). L. Boff, *Saint Francis: A Model for Human Liberation,* trans. J. Diercksmeier (New York: Crossroad, 1982).

MICHAEL BLASTIC, O.F.M. CONV.

FREEDOM

Freedom, in the basic sense of the word, is a property of choices and/or the actions proceeding from them. But just what type of property is it, and does it ever actually occur? There are at least five different answers to this twofold question: hard determinism, indeterminism, soft determinism, voluntarist self-constitutionism, and cognitivist self-constitutionism.

Hard Determinism

Hard determinists conceive freedom as the absence of natural necessity. A choice or action is free exactly if it is not related as effect to cause, not under the sway of some exceptionless and irresistible law, not individually predictable even in principle. But any such breach in the fabric of natural necessity is just what hard determinists deny. The grounds for this denial vary. Some persons, for example, argue that such necessity is a logical requirement for the truth of statements about the future. Others see it as an inevitable conclusion of sound metaphysics; others, as the inescapable consequence of a religious belief in the omnipotence of God. For still others, it is an essential presupposition of scientific inquiry or at least a highly probable scientific conclusion. But whatever the precise bases, hard determinists agree that every choice and action, like every other thing and event, is naturally necessitated. Therefore, any appearances to the contrary notwithstanding, no choice or action is free. Properly understood, "freedom" is nothing other than the label for a certain kind of logical contradiction, or for one's ignorance of necessitating factors that in principle can be disclosed by metaphysics or religion or science.

Indeterminism

Like hard determinists, indeterminists equate freedom with the absence of natural necessity. Unlike hard determinists, however, indeterminists maintain that natural necessity is not universal in its scope. Appealing to some metaphysical theory, for example, or to a religious belief that diminishes the omnipotence of God, or to an interpretation of quantum theory in modern physics, or to personal moral experience, indeterminists argue that there is a certain radical spontaneity, contingency, indeterminacy, in nature itself. It is not the case that every individual event is necessitated, related to all other events according to some universal logical or causal law, and thus predictable at least in principle. On the contrary, some events, including at least some of one's choices and actions, just happen. They are purely random, quite simply uncaused, matters of sheer chance. And in just this sense at least some of one's choices and actions are indeed free.

Soft Determinism

Soft determinists stand with hard determinists and against indeterminists in maintaining that every thing and event falls entirely within the sweep of natural necessity. Whatever exists or occurs does so because, whether for logical or metaphysical or religious or scientific reasons, it cannot not exist or occur. But soft determinists disagree with both foregoing groups regarding the notion of freedom itself. Freedom is not the absence of *all* natural necessity; rather, it is the absence of *involuntary* natural necessity. Or, positively, freedom is identical with voluntariness. All of one's choices and actions, like everything else in the universe, are naturally necessitated. But psychology manifests that while some of those actions are necessitated by such factors as external force, fear, passion, and habit, others are necessitated solely by one's choices: I do X

simply because I choose to do *X*. The former actions are involuntary and thus unfree; the latter, voluntary and thus free. On this view, for an action to be naturally necessitated is not always incompatible with the action's being free. Thus the view is often labeled "compatibilism."

Voluntarist Self-Constitutionism

For voluntarist self-constitutionists, freedom has three distinguishing features. First, there is the absence of *natural* necessity, the absence of any logical or metaphysical or religious or scientific factor by virtue of which one's choices and actions in a given circumstance *could* not have been other than they actually are. Second, there is the absence of *moral* necessity, the absence of any ethical standard beyond one's choices and actions themselves, an external standard by virtue of which in a given circumstance they *should* not have been (or else should have been) other than they actually are. Third, there is the presence of unrestricted volitional spontaneity, the ability creatively to determine or constitute one's own choices and actions without referring to anything at all beyond them, and thereby unrestrictedly to determine or constitute one's moral selfhood. Moreover, according to voluntarist self-constitutionists, concrete phenomenological investigation makes clear that the three features do indeed characterize some of one's choices and actions, precisely because they characterize the very structure of one's subjectivity, a structure that the choices and actions reflect. Consequently, any effort to deny either the occurrence or the absolutely basic character of the three features is operationally self-defeating. Hence one cannot but admit that, in exactly the specified sense, at least some of one's choices and actions are free.

Cognitivist Self-Constitutionism

Cognitivist self-constitutionists endorse much of what voluntarist self-constitu-

tionists say, but they also disagree in two important respects. First, freedom is indeed characterized by the absence of *natural* necessity and by the presence of volitional spontaneity, the propensity for creative moral self-constitution. But the absence of *moral* necessity is not a distinguishing feature of freedom. For moral necessity, correctly understood, is nothing other than the body of ethical requirements that follow from one's knowledge of the true order of reality, conclusions about how one ought to choose and act that flow from knowing one's own place in the universe. One is morally bound to observe these requirements but factually at liberty to ignore them. Hence, accordance with moral necessity is the distinguishing feature of the proper use of freedom, the mark of choices and actions that are free and, in addition, morally good. Conversely, nonaccordance with moral necessity is the distinguishing feature of an abuse of freedom, the mark of choices and actions that, though free, are morally evil. Second, cognitivist self-constitutionists maintain that this notion of freedom, together with the associated notions of knowledge, moral goodness, and moral evil, is just the notion that is verified in fact. Concrete phenomenological investigation of one's own conscious performance manifests that some of one's choices and actions are free in just the sense indicated, that their freedom expresses something of the essential freedom of one's subjectivity as such, and that any attempt to deny or relativize this claim inevitably involves one in performative self-contradiction.

See also CONSCIENCE; CONVERSION; DECISION, DECISION-MAKING; MIND; PASSION(S); PRAXIS; RESPONSIBILITY; SIN; VIRTUE; WILL.

Bibliography: B. Lonergan, *Insight: A Study of Human Understanding* (New York: Philosophical Library, 1957); *Method in Theology* (New York: Herder, 1972).

MICHAEL VERTIN

FRENCH SCHOOL OF SPIRITUALITY

Henri Bremond, in his classic treatise (*Histoire du sentiment religieux en France*, 1921, 3:3-4), first popularized the term *French School of spirituality*, although it seems that he did not coin it. Today, particularly in the French-speaking world, the term *Berullian School* is preferred, identifying Pierre Cardinal de Bérulle (1575–1629) as the fountainhead out of which this current of spirituality flowed. Major figures with him were Charles de Condren (1588–1641), Bérulle's successor as superior general of the Oratory; Jean-Jacques Olier (1608–1657), founder of the Sulpicians; and St. John Eudes (1601–1680), founder of the Eudists. Other significant figures were Mother Madeleine of Saint Joseph (1578–1637), disciple of Bérulle and the first French prioress of the Great Carmel in Paris, one of the forty-three monasteries he helped found in France in the years following Teresa of Avila's reform in Spain; St. Jean-Baptiste de la Salle (1651–1719), founder of the Christian Brothers; and Louis-Marie Grignion de Montfort (1673–1716).

The 17th-century French School of spirituality grew out of a number of significant movements of the time. Most important among them were the renewal in biblical and patristic studies; the Catholic Counter Reformation, especially the need for the reformation of the clergy; and a strong reaction to what Bremond calls "devout humanism." These writers had a strong contemplative, apostolic, and missionary spirit. They professed a Trinitarian theology and believed deeply that men and women are called to commune intimately in the divine life of the Father, Son, and Holy Spirit.

As Bérulle and subsequent writers sought to thematize their own religious experience, they evolved a number of major themes that have characterized the faith and formational practices of this spiritual movement for over three and a half centuries. They are theocentrism, Christocentrism, Mary, and the priesthood.

Theocentrism

Cardinal de Bérulle called for a type of "Copernican" revolution in which we would relate to God in Jesus as the sun and therefore the center of our spiritual universe rather than ourselves and our world, which Renaissance humanism seemed to prefer. This fundamental theocentric spiritual attitude was grounded in awe and adoration toward God expressed through what was called the virtue of religion. Denis Amelote, in his life of Condren (1643), wrote that there were many holy and virtuous people in that century but that he saw "more familiarity with God than reverence; there are many people who love God, but few who respect him" (p. 80).

In his *Introduction to the Christian Life and Virtues* (1657), Olier says: "Our Lord Jesus Christ came into this world to bring love and respect for his Father and to establish his reign and his religion. . . . His incessant desire was to open the minds and hearts of the faithful to his religion" (Thompson and Glendon, p. 217).

Integral to this sense of awe before the triune God was the awareness of the nothingness of all creation in itself. Condren, who influenced both Bérulle and Olier, had a transforming vision at the age of twelve in which he saw all creation annihilated before the majesty and wonder of God. This particular type of *via negativa* and the accompanying negative language is a characteristic of the French School and is one of the reasons for its decreased influence in our culture since the Second Vatican Council.

Christocentrism

While Christianity, by its very nature, is in some manner centered on Christ, the French School has its own way of expressing and living this truth. Christ is seen as the incarnate Word, the one who offers perfect religion, i.e., praise, adoration, obedience, and love to God. Therefore we are called to conform ourselves to Jesus Christ, especially in his "states" (*états*), i.e., the interior dispositions through which he faithfully lived out the mysteries of his incarnation, passion, death, resurrection, and ascension. While his actions were transitory, his dispositions are permanent and available to us today; through them we can commune with Jesus and render perfect religion to God. In a strong reading of Gal 2: 20, these authors portrayed the life of the Christian as the life of Jesus in us. John Eudes wrote: "It follows necessarily from this that, just as bodily members are animated by the spirit of their head and live its life, in the same way we must be animated by the spirit of Jesus, and live his life and walk in his ways. We should be clothed with his sentiments and inclinations, perform all our actions with the same dispositions and intentions he brought to his. In a word we should continue and bring to fulfillment the life, religion and devotion with which he lived on earth" (*The Life and Kingdom of Jesus in Christian Souls* (1637), in Thompson and Glendon, pp. 293–294).

Mary

Mary, the Mother of God, occupies a very important theological and affective place in the French School. The poetic and effusive way in which these authors speak of her seems at times foreign and exaggerated to us. It is, however, a natural development of the virtue of religion, which is foundational to their spirituality. For if we contemplate God with awe and reverence, what should be our attitude toward her who was chosen to bring forth the eternal Word into this world? In his *Life of Jesus* (1629), Bérulle speaks of Jesus dwelling in Mary's womb as in a temple: "It is the first and holiest temple of Jesus. The heart of the Virgin is the first altar on which Jesus offered his heart, body and spirit as a host of perpetual praise; and where Jesus offers his first sacrifice, making the first and per-

petual oblation of himself, through which, as we have said, we are all made holy" (Thompson and Glendon, p. 161).

St. John Eudes develops the theme of the heart of Mary, which for him primarily indicates her interior life. She lives so fully in the dispositions and sentiments of Jesus' mysteries that the founder of the Eudists sees her as the icon of Jesus.

While the language is lavish and often archaic, the insights are theologically and spiritually precise. The French School's Marian spirituality conforms fundamentally to the emphasis of the Second Vatican Council, which places Mary's graces and privileges in the context of her unique relationship, as Mother of God, with the Triune God and with the Word Incarnate.

Priesthood

St. Vincent de Paul and Jean-Jacques Olier were involved for a number of years with parish missions in the provinces of France. It became clear to them that the renewal of the faithful would bear fruit only if their pastors were deeply spiritual and learned men. These reformers were concerned with the often lamentable state of the priesthood in 17th-century France. Bérulle and Condren with the Oratory, Olier with the Sulpicians, St. Vincent de Paul with the Vincentians (*Lazaristes*), and St. John Eudes with the Eudists created institutions imbued with the spirit of the French School to train men worthy of the vocation to the priesthood.

While their Neoplatonic view of Church and ordained priesthood was hierarchical, they had a clear sense of both the priesthood of the faithful and the universal call to holiness, themes which appear in the documents of Vatican II and which are the theological basis for the contemporary blossoming of lay ministry in the Church. Some scholars see clear similarities between the French School and the documents of the council in these areas, and especially in some of the themes of the Decree on the Ministry and Life of Priests (see

M. Cancouët, "Traces de la théologie et de la pratique de l'écôle française à Vatican II et au-delà," *Bulletin de Saint Sulpice* 6 [1980] 214–236).

Contemporary Significance

As noted above, the French School connects with a number of contemporary spiritual themes. There are also aspects of its doctrine and practice that seem offensive to contemporary American sensitivities. It is unfortunate that some negative anthropological language, a hierarchical worldview, and at times a lavish style of writing present a major obstacle to many contemporary readers in the English-speaking world. For there are many valid insights that could enrich our efforts at a theologically balanced spirituality. For instance: Among them are:

1. The heightened sense of the transcendence of God has receded from the contemporary collective consciousness as we have reemphasized, for good reasons, the beauty and holiness of the human as spiritual path. However, since the full truth lies in the paradoxical mystery of God as both transcendent and immanent, this spirituality models for us one way of maintaining both aspects of this divine mystery. For the sense of the awe and mystery of God is continually held in balance with a powerful intuition of the mystery of the incarnate Word.

2. The essential connection between the life of prayer and ministry is another strong belief of the French School. The revitalization of the spiritual life was the cornerstone of their efforts to reform the Church of their day. There is a strong emphasis on the communal spiritual life, experienced through the Church, seen as Mystical Body, and the sacraments. At the same time, the French School has always had a profound respect for the unique work of the Holy Spirit in the individual person. This respect has been the life force and dynamism behind the long and rich history of commitment to spiritual direction. As we

experience today a widespread renewal of interest in this *ars artium* and in directed retreats, there are important insights to be gathered from the French School.

For example, Olier offers us an essential practical teaching about spiritual growth. He points out that progress is best nurtured by admitting our own powerlessness (*anéantissement*) and turning our lives over to the Holy Spirit. Our own efforts are doomed to fail unless they flow from the Spirit of Christ. Furthermore, emphasizing our own agenda for spiritual growth can be a most subtle trap that makes us even more self-centered than before. Therefore we are called to commune in the interior life of Jesus Christ as a way to spiritual fulfillment and let God do the work (*Mémoires* 1:44; see also how Olier embodies this strategy in his approach to prayer, Thompson and Glendon, pp. 228–232).

Of course, we need to cooperate with grace, but the point is that it is primarily *grace*. There seem to be many inner psychic similarities between this strategy of the French School and that of Alcoholics Anonymous and other twelve-step programs, in which recovery begins when people admit their radical powerlessness and turn their lives over to a higher power. They both seem to draw on a similar perennial wisdom.

3. Several communities flowing from this tradition have been able to renew their constitutions credibly for today by drawing on the central themes of the French School and the writings of their founders. These documents model well a dialogue between an older spirituality and our contemporary sensitivity, need, and vocation.

The French School offers a powerful spiritual synthesis, blending profound mysticism with zeal and energy for reform. Rarely has such a deep sense of the communion with God in the Spirit of Jesus Christ been expressed and written not only for priests and religious but for the laity as well. It is a spirituality of profound transformation and exquisite adoration. It is lyrical, poetic, and passionate in its love for Jesus Christ and, through his Spirit, in its devotion to the Father.

See also APOSTOLIC SPIRITUALITY; CHRIST; GRACE; MARY; MINISTRY, MINISTERIAL SPIRITUALITY; MODERN SPIRITUALITY; NEGATIVE WAY; SPIRITUAL DIRECTION; ZEAL.

Bibliography: R. Deville, L'Écôle française de spiritualité (Paris: Desclée, 1987). W. Thompson, ed., and L. Glendon, trans., Bérulle and the French School: Selected Writings (New York: Paulist, 1989).

LOWELL M. GLENDON, S.S.

FRIENDSHIP

In the Ancient World

Friendship was held in high esteem in the Greco-Roman world, and consequently the Christian tradition owes much to this influence. Plato, in the *Lysis* and the *Symposium*, develops the famous idea of "Platonic friendship," in which one moves through purely physical attraction (*eros*) to a more spiritual kind of love that unites friends in the purest way possible. Based upon the dualistic notion that the spiritual order is superior to the material order, spiritual love reflects the purest form of love. For Aristotle, friendship means interpersonal and reciprocal love, ordered toward the good. He dedicates two books of the *Nicomachean Ethics* to a discussion of friendship (*philia*), which can be found even in the rapport between parents and children, masters and disciples, or between spouses.

Friendship, strictly speaking, is the mutual good will of two persons who accept each other profoundly in view of reciprocal growth. There are many degrees of acceptance of the other. Friendship can be simple or intimate. Simple friendship happens frequently and does not pose any special problems. It can be simple camaraderie either by choice or by affinity of interests. Intimate friendship is much more rare. Born sometimes by chance happening, it develops in the deepest part of one's personality.

Cicero, in *De amicitia,* follows Aristotle closely, distinguishing between true and false friendship. True friendship must be destined toward the good and involve reciprocal love. False friendship falls under two broad types, namely, friendship for carnal pleasure, common among the young, and friendship for material gain, more common among older persons. Each of these types of false friendship offends against the definition of true friendship by rejecting one of its components: carnal friendship offends against the "good," since reason is subordinated to the passions, while self-seeking friendship offends against reciprocal love, since it simulates an affection toward others that is really felt only toward their goods.

In Scripture

Friendship enjoys a privileged place in the Judeo-Christian tradition. The Book of Sirach says: "A faithful friend is a sturdy shelter; he who finds one finds treasure" (Sir 6:14). A faithful friend is "beyond price . . . a life-saving remedy" (Sir 6:15-16). False friends include "a friend when it suits him, but he will not be with you in time of distress. Another is a friend who becomes an enemy, and tells of the quarrel to your shame. Another is a friend, a boon companion, who will not be with you when sorrow comes" (Sir 6:8-10). Perfect friendship is rare, and it is always a conquest, not a given. One is reminded of the wonderful friendship uniting David and Jonathan (1 Sam 18:1-4), which withstood trial (1 Sam 19–20) and lived on beyond death (2 Sam 1:26).

Like any deep love, friendship refuses the limits of time. The interpersonal encounter creates its own form of duration. An instant in its symbolic fullness is more like an eternal than a temporal passage. Friendship must be more than a simple feeling, and the proof is in its long duration. "A new friend is like new wine which you drink with pleasure only when it has aged" (Sir 9:10).

The greatest form of friendship is the one established between God and humankind, modeled by the rapport between God and Abraham (Gen 18:17ff.) or between God and Moses (Exod 33:11). Fidelity within friendship is the primary goal. From the faithfulness of God, assured one time for all, one moves to human faithfulness, which is fallible and must be constantly renewed. In the NT, Jesus establishes the friendship of God with all humanity (Tit 3:4). Jesus himself is depicted as having many friends. Even the Scriptures attest to the fact that the Lord had a special friendship with John, Lazarus, Martha, Mary Magdalene, and others. Enjoying friendship with Jesus moves one beyond the level of mere servant (Jn 15:15) and requires that one share Jesus' trials, entering the secrets of God. The true friend is depicted as the one who is faithful up to the cross, like the Beloved Disciple (Jn 13:23). Those called to friendship with the Lord share friendship with one another, yet there are moments when this is tested, as seen in Paul's relationship with Barnabas (Acts 15:36-39) or with Peter (Gal 2:11-14). Nonetheless, the ideal of friendship is maintained within the early community (Acts 2:44ff.; 4:32), and from it the Christian can derive strength.

In the Christian Tradition

To Fathers of the Church such as Jerome, Augustine, Gregory, and later Bernard of Clairvaux, friendship is instrumental in achieving Christian perfection. Perfection does not consist in not having friendship but only in having that which is good, holy, and sacred. St. Paul accuses the Gentiles of having been a people without affection, while friendship is linked to virtue. St. Augustine links friendship inseparably to Christian charity. Drawing upon the classic formulation, love is identified in terms of four manifestations: *epithymia,* love driven by lust or sexual desire; *eros,* the desire to be united with the beloved; *philia,* friendship; and *agapē,* charity or selfless love. These four kinds of love are really only one interacting reality, yet they are organized in ascending hierarchical order. For Augustine, one moves from the purely carnal form of love to the more disinterested forms.

Friendship always implies a certain faith in the other person who is befriended. The interpersonal encounter contains the consent of two freedoms as the inviolable core. This consent is susceptible to being constantly called into question. Friendship should therefore avoid short or long separations, lest it experience erosion. For true friendship, there is an act of confidence in the other and in the solidarity of a connection that is fundamentally spiritual. This same solidarity in the freedom of a gift will permit one to overcome all the fluctuations of feelings. In surpassing all the affective stages that tend toward excess, one also overcomes the inexplicable coldness, remaining patient before the small inevitable disappointments, the misunderstandings, or the differences in the affective correspondence. One always returns to the essential core that is the reciprocal gift of two freedoms opening themselves constantly to each other.

Spiritual Friendship

Within the Christian tradition the accent has fallen more on the notion of spiritual friendship, in which there is a reciprocal relationship of mutual sharing between two persons who seek the same spiritual ideals. The expression *spiritualis amicitia* is found already in a letter St. Boniface (d. 754) wrote to a group of nuns (*Epist.* 221.5). Spiritual friendship is more common among members of the same sex, such as in monastic communities, but there are examples of such friendship between members of the opposite sex, for example St. Francis of Assisi and St. Clare. Sharing a common faith, the friends support one another in the search for God. Usually the notion of spiritual friendship involves little or no physical contact, and feelings of passion are translated to a spiritual level. In people who have an intense spiritual life, it ends in a communion of spirits and of hearts that often is consummated in the sharing of prayer. Such a spiritual communion is very open and does not disregard the weaknesses of the other; rather, it understands them, while pursuing its spiritual goal to live in patience and in imitation of Christ.

In the monastic tradition friendship enjoys a privileged place. The Irish monastic tradition identifies the *anmchara,* or "soul friend," who acts as spiritual guide. A perennial tension can be found between the view of friendship as a work of love leading to God and the skeptical view that mistrusts friendship. John Cassian, for example, warns against the dangers of individual friendships in the *Institutions* (Bk. 2, chap. 15). But in his *Conferences* (Vol. 2, no. 16), he gives a more positive evaluation of friendship, seeing it as a means for attaining the monastic ideal of asceticism.

In spite of the many warnings against particular friendships in the monastic milieu, the epistolary tradition attests to their existence. In the late 6th century Gregory the Great developed a language of Christian charity based upon the spiritual life as a kind of pilgrimage toward God. The desire for God is the primary motivation for the Christian pilgrimage, and friendship is a means for sustaining the pilgrims along their way. The monastic ideal of friendship, whose foundations were laid by Benedict of Nursia and Gregory the Great, finds its fullest expression in the monastic writings of Isidore of Seville, Alcuin, Anselm, Bernard of Clairvaux, and especially Aelred of Rievaulx. Monastic letters, rich with affective imagery, are also a valuable source for understanding monastic friendship. These letters, whose sole purpose was to give pleasure to the recipient, are demonstrations of affection, bemoaning long physical separations. They mostly imitate formularies in the epistolary tradition of antiquity, in which rhetorical expression plays a large part, but they demonstrate how the separated friends can seek union through writing.

Characteristic of most of the monastic letters is a more disinterested kind of friendship than is to be found in friendly letters composed in a nonmonastic environment. The great emphasis given to friendship shows how important it was in monastic life itself. The monks contributed most to the rediscovery of a type of friendship that is pure and disinterested, soliciting no favors. This kind of friendship had almost disappeared from literature after the barbarian invasions. With the later expansion of feudalism, relationships took the form of *amicitia* as a kind of juridical bond. Numerous kinds of friends are differentiated according to the services each could be expected to perform. The monks retaught people how to love one another without ulterior motives, writing to one another to give pleasure without seeking material advantages. In the Carolingian period one finds examples of many monks who excelled in this. During the great monastic expansion of the 12th century, a large number of letters, the work of Benedictine and Cistercian writers, attest to this type of friendship. In their letters one notes that the love of God and neighbor imbued their lives, comprising the heart of their doctrine and the subject of their most revealing treatises. (See J. Leclercq, *The Love of Learning and the Desire for God: A Study of Monastic Culture,* New York: Fordham Univ. Press, 1961, pp. 180–181.) In the monastic tradition, friendship exists as a means of achieving an edifying union that symbolizes and points to divine love.

Bernard of Clairvaux (d. 1153) concerned himself with spiritual friendship in the monastic milieu. Drawing upon the courtly tradition of the Troubadors, Bernard describes the four levels of love, leading ultimately to his mystical theology of love. In his correspondence the vocabulary of friendship abounds. Like Augustine and Gregory the Great, Bernard speaks of the spiritual life as a kind of interior pilgrimage whereby the person passes from lower to higher forms of love. In his work *On the Love of God,* Bernard traces the progression in terms of four degrees of love. Beginning with a carnal love of self, one moves toward a more spiritual kind of love, passing through a stage of self-interested love, interested in that which one will receive from God. Progressing then to a third stage, one loves God out of a sense of filial duty. Ultimately the spiritual journey leads to a fourth degree of a sort of nuptial love, in which one loves God selflessly, and in turn one loves oneself because one is loved by God. True friendship becomes more and more disinterested, and spiritual friendship the most disinterested (*De diligendo Deo,* XV). In his *Sermon on the Song of Songs,* Bernard identifies the movement of love from a selfish kind to that which is selfless. Within the context of divine love, one finds human friendship: "Of all the motions, the senses, the affections of the soul, it is love alone in which the creature is able, even if not on an equal basis, to repay its Creator for what it has received, to weigh back something from the same measure." Charity, which engenders all friendship, is a gift of God and leads toward God, passing through human feelings. These affects transform and elevate love without suppressing it. "Since we are carnal, it is necessary that our desire and our love begin through the flesh" (*Epist.* 116). God places in our hearts a love toward our friends that they cannot know unless we show them. This is called affection (*affectio*), a deep and unexplainable attachment, common within human experience, which makes certain demands upon the friendship and establishes certain rights. Friendship can warn, exhort, and give encouragement. But if it must suffer prolonged separation, it makes one want to see the friend again, even if only briefly. The notion of monastic friendship finds its classic expression in Anselm's "A Prayer for Friends" (*Monastic Studies* 3 [1965] 235–236).

In Aelred of Rievaulx (d. 1167) we find one of the clearest expressions of friendship as a monastic ideal. Sometimes called "the Bernard of the North," due to his many Bernardine characteristics, he treats the theme of love and friendship in his *Mirror of Charity* and above all in his treatise *Spiritual Friendship,* patterned after Cicero's *De amicitia.* Through a characteristically Cistercian awareness, he presents friendship as an image of the relationship of the soul with God. Since friendship is mutual, our friendship with God implies the reciprocal love of God for us. One may go so far as to use the idea of friendship to describe the nature of God. Thus Aelred declares, "God is friendship" (*De spirituali amicitia* 1:69).

In his *Mirror on Charity* Aelred describes love as having three parts: attraction, intention, and fruition (*Speculum caritatis* 3.22). Due to original sin, all people are corrupted, and therefore it is possible for any of these three parts to be defective. If one is attracted to the wrong object, one enjoys created goods incorrectly. Love becomes cupidity if any of these corruptions vitiates the goodness of human love. Clearly Aelred is dependent upon Aristotle and Cicero for this idea, whereby true friendship combines the two vital elements of charity and good will.

Beginning with a realistic attitude toward human friendship, Aelred sees true friendship as the perfection of false friendships, not their opposite. Even defective friendship contains some of the essence of true friendship. Identifying the three kinds of friendship as carnal, worldly, and spiritual (*De spirituali amicitia* 1.38), Aelred demonstrates how the first two are defective in form. Carnal friendship has a sort of charity due to natural affection, but it lacks good will. Self-seeking friendship, on the other hand, has the rational choice necessary for good will but lacks charity. It is only spiritual friendship that combines both charity and good will.

Aelred then examines friendship as a virtue, noting from a general anthropological perspective that all people have a need for friendship. In evil people, however, friendship loses its value as a virtue. Due to original sin, very few reach the perfection of friendship. Paraphrasing Jn 15:13, he declares that whoever abides in friendship will abide in God ((De spirituali amicitia 1.70), but imperfect friendship will be perfected at the Last Judgment. To the question whether people can achieve friendship, Aelred replies that true friendship does not require a superhuman degree of goodness. Although human affections are difficult to control, the virtue of friendship still rests within human reach. To renounce friendship as too difficult is to renounce virtue. To be fully human ultimately requires that one have friends. To live without friendship is to live like a beast (De spirituali amicitia 2.52). Although Aelred's theme is spiritual friendship, he allows for friendship in the fully human sense, avoiding some type of overspiritualized, disincarnate notion.

St. Thomas Aquinas (d. 1274) asks in the Scholastic fashion whether charity is friendship, to which he replies that they are one and the same, provided that love is united to benevolence so as to wish well the one loved (ST II-II, q. 23). Simple well-wishing, however, is not sufficient for friendship, since friendship requires a certain mutual love and this well-wishing is founded merely on a kind of communication. Employing the principle of analogia entis, Thomas goes on to speak about human friendship with God, treating friendship as a virtue. Since both virtues and friendship are directed toward the good, friendship must be a virtue. Moreover, since friendship is directed toward another person, it is a part of justice itself. Even though friendship, like justice, sometimes falls short of the mark, it is nonetheless related to the virtue (ST II-II, q. 114).

In the later Christian tradition the idea of spiritual friendship takes on a more ethereal quality and does not tolerate the idea of particular or special friendships. In the letters exchanged between St. Francis de Sales (d. 1622) and St. Jane Frances de Chantal (d. 1641), the idea of spiritual friendship flourishes as a bond leading to human perfection. Within the context of realizing the Christian vocation, spiritual friendship is a means to becoming fully human. Francis de Sales favored a relationship of friendship for spiritual direction, provided that the friendship is wholly spiritual, sacred, holy, and divine. In this context people have been given to each other as spiritual friends, supporting each other in their commitment to fidelity and being of mutual assistance in their search for perfection. The spiritual friendship gives shape to a new spiritual family in the Church.

Most characteristic about the correspondence between Francis de Sales and Jane de Chantal is the role of Jesus to ensure the relationship. This Jesus-centered friendship pervades all the letters that Francis and Jane de Chantal wrote to each other as well as to all their correspondents. Jesus is the foundation for the individual persons, and he himself makes their friendship possible. Their friendship is solidly anchored in their common love of God, and it is friendship that mediates the divine love. There seems to be no propriety for special friendships except through Jesus. Special friendships were therefore forbidden in the cloister. The reason was that without Jesus, friends tend to close in on each other, ignoring other people, but with Jesus friendships open up to the larger world. Exclusive friendship, therefore, was not tolerable.

If intimacy is a deep human desire, one can find this intimacy in God, who gives people to each other in friendship as visible manifestations of divine love. Francis and Jane demonstrate that the deepest intimacy among people is an intimacy that finds its origin and goal in God through Christ. Affection plays a prominent role in their writings and in all their relationships. This deep affection is generously shared with all those with whom they enter into a spiritual relationship. This affection leads one to openness and spontaneity within the relationship, and it is given and received freely and shared generously with all of the spiritual family. In the Salesian context, relationships are central, being neither inimical nor peripheral to one's love of God reflected in relationships between persons.

Together Francis de Sales and Jane de Chantal explored the simultaneous expression of human and divine love. In the midst of a friendship that spanned nineteen years, they both learned what it was to make Jesus live fully. Their friendship widened naturally to a larger circle of friends, allowing for the bond of perfection to be shared in the broader spiritual family. In a letter from Jane de Chantal to her brother, André Fréyot, archbishop of Bourges, dated June 1, 1626, we read: "My very dear and very honored Lord, I thank and praise our good God for the blessing He is pleased to have given us through the exchange made possible by our perfect friendship; for I assure you that if my letters enkindle in you the flame of love for the supreme Good, your very dear letters arouse the same feelings in me and make me wish more and more that our hearts be totally and constantly united to the good pleasure of God which we find so kind and favorable. Let us love this good pleasure, my dearest Lord, and let us see it alone in all that happens to us, embracing it lovingly."

In a more systematic way, St. Francis treats the question of true and false friendship in his *Introduction to the Devout Life,* where spiritual friendship is linked to charity (chap. 19). He warns Philothea to befriend only those with whom one can speak about virtuous things. Among the virtues mentioned are prudence, discretion, fortitude, and justice. The most perfect friendship occurs when there is mutual communication based upon charity, devotion, and Christian perfection. To this degree friendship will be perfected, because it comes from God and tends toward God, God being the link and the assurance of its eternal endurance. Francis clarifies that this is not simple charity but rather spiritual friendship, by which several people communicate their devotion and their spiritual feelings, bringing them into one spirit. God's continuous blessing assures that this friendship is spiritual, and all other friendships stand in the shadow of this type. Citing the example of the great saints, Francis counsels in favor of particular friendship to the extent that it does not distract one's attention or engender envy. He notes the role of particular friendships in the lives of Christ and the great saints without imperiling their perfection. Perfection consists in having friendship that is good, holy, and sacred.

In treating the difference between true and false friendships, Francis cautions Philothea about the poisonous honey of Hercules, which resembles good honey. Even if one mixes the two, the poisonous wins out over the good. One begins with a virtuous love, but if this love is frivolous, it develops into a sensual and carnal love. Even in spiritual love, the worldly overwhelms the holy and the virtuous if one is not on guard. To know whether love is worldly or spiritual, it is sufficient to note the language that is used to support the friendship. If the language is a great mass of words marked by sensuality and false praise, it is worldly. If, on the other hand, the language is simple and frank, then it is spiritual. Francis compares false friendship to a peacock strutting around in search of praise (chap. 20). Like a spiritual doctor, he gives advice and remedies regarding false friendships (chap. 21).

In the main, many of the later Christian writers have tended to separate physical love (*eros*) from spiritual friendship (*philia* or *agapê*), as evidenced in the works of A. Nygren, *Eros et Agapê, la notion chrétienne de l'amour et ses transformations*, 3 vols. (Paris: Aubier, 1944–1952; *Agape and Eros*, Philadelphia: Westminster Press, 1953). Even C. S. Lewis, in *The Four Loves* (New York: Harcourt, Brace and Jovanovich, 1960), draws hard distinctions between the four kinds of love mentioned in antiquity, creating a huge gulf separating human friendship, even in its best form, from divine love. More recently there has once again been an attempt to integrate the various kinds of love, avoiding any hard and fast distinctions that falsely oppose erotic love to friendship. C. Gallagher, G. Maloney, M. Rousseau, and P. Wilczak, in their book *Embodied in Love: Sacramental Spirituality and Sexual Intimacy* (New York: Crossroad, 1989), explore the ideas of sexuality and friendship within the marital relationship. Rather than opposing the various kinds of love, these loves participate in each other and become a means for human development, both spiritually and interpersonally. Currently there is a reemergence of the notion of spiritual companionship as a way of spiritual direction. The model of spiritual companionship fosters the mutuality of spiritual direction, placing two people in a relationship of equality in which they help each other through the pilgrimage of this life.

See also AFFECT, AFFECTIVITY; INTIMACY; LOVE; MARRIAGE; MARRIAGE, MYSTICAL; MONASTICISM, MONASTIC SPIRITUALITY; SALESIAN SPIRITUALITY; SEXUALITY.

Bibliography: Aelred of Rievaulx, *Spiritual Friendship,* trans. M. E. Laker (Kalamazoo, Mich.: Cistercian Publications, 1977). W. Wright, *Bond of Perfection: Jeanne de Chantal and François de Sales* (New York: Paulist, 1985). K. Leech, *Soul Friend: A Study of Spirituality* (San Francisco: Harper & Row, 1980. T. Edwards, *Spiritual Friend* (New York: Paulist, 1980). C. Bernard, *Théologie Affective* (Paris: Cerf, 1984). P. Wadell, *Friendship and the Moral Life* (Notre Dame: Univ. of Notre Dame Press, 1989). J. Leclercq, "L'amitié dans les lettres au moyen âge," *Revue du moyen âge latin* 1 (1945) 391–410. Francis de Sales and Jane de Chantal, *Letters of Spiritual Direction* (New York: Paulist, 1988).

MICHAEL S. DRISCOLL

FRUIT(S) OF THE HOLY SPIRIT

From Gal 5:22-23 comes a list of attributes which characterize Christian life that thrives under the sanctifying influence of the Holy Spirit. Paul names nine qualities as the fruit of the Spirit: love, joy, peace, patience, kindness, goodness (or generosity), faith (or faithfulness), gentleness, and self-control. The Vulgate, accepting duplicate translations of some of the Greek words for the fruit, expands this list to include also modesty, continence, and chastity.

Theologians since St. Augustine have agreed that the list is not meant to be exhaustive but suggestive of the breadth of the Spirit's power to effect good in God's people. (1 Cor 13:4-6 offers a similar list: patience, kindness, humility, gentleness, unselfishness, forgiveness, compassion, tolerance, trust, hope, and endurance. Other concise descriptions of the effects of the Spirit's power in the human character are found in Rom 14:7; Col 3:12-15; Eph 4:2-5; 4:32; 5:9.)

In common parlance, the plural ("fruits") has often been employed to name the list in Galatians. This usage bolsters the ideas that each person's spiritual life has particular strengths, and that these strengths are manifested by many people in different situations and relationships. Use of the singular, however, underscores the idea that the various attributes are interconnected, and that it is the one Spirit of God who activates in each person a single spiritual life. Jn 20:22-23 makes clear that the first fruit of Christ's resurrection is the very gift of the Spirit that brings peace and forgiveness of sins. The singular usage can also point to the predominant position of love, that central quality which all other virtues, gifts, and fruit can be said to radiate and specify. The essence of Christian holiness is the permeating presence of a repentant and sacrificial love that evinces a real sharing in the life of the Trinity; the fruit of the Spirit flows from one's graced acceptance of the Spirit's infused gift of God's own love.

Paul offers the list of the Spirit's fruit as a metaphor of growth, in order to contrast enumerated "works of the flesh" (Gal 5:16-17) with the actions of the Spirit. This contrast is in keeping with a familiar formula of early Christian asceticism, the concept of the "two ways," of light and of darkness (see Rom 13:12; Jn 1:5-11). In the tradition, writers have considered the meaning of "fruit" in two different senses: as product of the Spirit's action or as delight experienced by the one acted upon, or both.

Paul's mention of the fruit should be viewed in light of his theology of humanity renewed through God's grace. Urging his hearers to walk worthy of their vocation, Paul appeals primarily to their status of new creaturehood rather than to moral prohibition, to a "thou art" rather than to a "thou shalt not" (O'Callaghan, p. 289). For a Christian who has "put on Christ" (Gal 3:27-29), identification with Christ ought to increase to the point that the Christian can say, "For to me, living is Christ" (Phil 1:21, NRSV). The New Testament does not teach that the coming of the Holy Spirit will set Christians free from all suffering and conflict; rather, the message is that each follower of Christ is called to self-sacrificing love in the face of struggles occasioned by what the Christian tradition has known as "the world, the flesh, and the devil."

Sound Christian theology has held that the Spirit comes as a free gift of God. Catholic theology has stressed also that the Spirit's power can deeply permeate and transform the lives of those justified in baptism, as it frees them to do their part to cooperate with the Spirit's endowments. So, while holiness is always owing to God's initiative and is God's gift at every moment of its development within the person, those called to holiness are to live up to their calling by living in openness to the Spirit.

Thomas Aquinas, fitting "the fruits of the Spirit" into his view of the justified person's supernatural life as an organic synthesis, offers careful distinctions between virtues, gifts, fruits, and beatitudes. For him, each of the many fruits is linked with the particular virtues and gifts that it serves or directs.

Recent theology offers the possibility for considering the fruit of the Spirit in relation to the experience of conversion of heart, the radical reorientation of one's whole being in response to the gracious gift of God's love. Evidence of the fruit of the Spirit in the life of a Christian can serve as a positive sign of genuine conversion, which involves not only one's outlook but also one's behavior patterns. Specifically, if one has experienced a sense of the living God's closeness in the ordinary events of life, then one will be in a position to grow in self-knowledge and self-acceptance, to acknowledge more freely a personal need to be redeemed and forgiven, to desire to become a disciple of Jesus Christ, and to be open and willing to be taught by God and others. This movement leads to an ever-expanding life of charity, such that the love received as gift from God takes root within oneself, grows more or less steadily, and gradually bears visible fruit in the world. True conversion, though profoundly interior and personal, thus has a way of showing itself and becoming life-giving for others. The fruit of having been forgiven by a loving God is displayed partly in the compassion that the converted have toward others beset with sin. Those truly alive with the fruit of the Spirit act humbly, gratefully, and confidently, for they are aware of the utter giftedness of the Spirit's action.

Noticing the fruit of the Spirit can be crucial also for Christians who enter into a process of discernment of spirits, especially at the point when a decision formulated in prayer needs to be confirmed in a subsequent period of living in the way that has been chosen. As daily duties are undertaken and difficulties in executing the choice are faced, the decision will find confirmation, or not, in its actual effects.

Evidence of the fruit of the Spirit also can be helpful as part of the delicate process of distinguishing God-inspired mystical phenomena from those held to be demonically induced. External phenomena themselves are not sure indications of their origin, but if they are accompanied by love, joy, peace, and other Spirit-given attributes, along with other sound criteria, a clearer sense of their authenticity emerges. The New Testament and the Christian tradition do not encourage any great interest in the acquisition of these special experiences. The mystics have widely held that it is easy for the devil to fabricate them, and that they can lead to pride and elitism. They teach that real growth in the life of the Spirit ordinarily comes in the darkness of faith and through living a life of Christian love that is specified in qualities such as the fruit of the Spirit.

Contemporary Christian spiritual writers, in trying to single out facilitating conditions for spiritual growth in individuals, are apt to combine study of themes in the Bible and the tradition with insights from philosophy and the behavioral sciences. In reflection on the life of the Christian alive with the fruit of the Spirit, consideration might also go, for example, to what the Center for Human Development (Washington, D.C.) offers as nine facilitating conditions for spiritual growth: (1) a developing self-concept, with accurate self-perception and loving self-acceptance; (2) a responsible awareness of one's needs, feelings, and emotions; (3) a sense of autonomy or inner-directedness; (4) an appreciation of genuine authority; (5) a morality based on self-chosen but universally valid principles of love; (6) an orientation toward others as persons, not as objects; (7) a view of spiritual growth as intrinsically related to physical, emotional, and intellectual development; (8) a centeredness on present times and places as avenues of God's activity; and (9) an openness to the transcendent in the reality of self, others, and world (Helminiak, pp. 10–11).

Increased growth in the fruit of the Spirit does not insure a person's attainment of particular degrees of holiness or human maturity. Nevertheless, the fruit produced through the Spirit's action can enliven the human spirit and counteract forces which could draw that spirit downward. While it would be naive to suggest that Christians can be completely immune from fear and anxiety, it is also shortsighted to fail to realize that they have it within their power as recipients of the Holy Spirit to prevent these factors from wholly crushing their human spirits.

See also CARDINAL VIRTUES; CHARISM; CHASTITY; CONVERSION; DARKNESS, DARK NIGHT; DISCERNMENT OF SPIRITS; EXTRAORDINARY PHENOMENA; FEELINGS; FIDELITY; GIFTS OF THE HOLY SPIRIT; GOODNESS; GRACE; HOLINESS; HOLY SPIRIT; JOY; LIGHT; LOVE; PEACE.

Bibliography: D. Helminiak, *Spiritual Development: An Interdisciplinary Study* (Chicago: Loyola Univ. Press, 1987). A. Hughes, *Preparing for Church Ministry: A Practical Guide to Spiritual Formation* (Denville, N.J.: Dimension Books, 1979). D. O'Callaghan, "The Fruits of the Spirit," *The Furrow* 12 (May 1961) 288–295. S. Winward, *Fruit of the Spirit* (Grand Rapids, Mich.: Eerdmans, 1981).

GEORGE P. EVANS

FUGA MUNDI

See DESERT; PATRISTIC SPIRITUALITY; WORLD.

FUNDAMENTALISM

Historically, the term *fundamentalism* is derived from a series of booklets entitled *The Fundamentals: A Testimony to the Truth,* published in the United States between 1912 and 1914. The publication of these tracts was one expression of the effort of some Protestants at the turn of the century to defend the essentials of Christian orthodoxy against liberal theology.

More recently the term *fundamentalism* has been used to describe those Protestant

Christian movements, Churches, and denominations that are characterized by an emphasis on the inerrancy of the Bible and a tenacious insistence that Christians affirm certain basic beliefs: the inspiration and infallibility of the Bible, the divinity of Christ, the Trinity, the vicarious and substitutionary atonement of believers through the death of Christ, and the bodily resurrection and second coming of Christ. These beliefs are not unique to fundamentalists; therefore it is useful to characterize fundamentalism by means of its mindset of tenacious certainty, its hostility toward those who differ, and its use of the teaching of the inerrancy of the Bible as the basis for its certitude.

Fundamentalists object to the use of historical-critical methods to study the Bible. They see the results of such methods—the overturning of traditional beliefs about the authorship, textual integrity, and historical accuracy of some books of the Bible—as an attack on the authority of the Bible, the basic beliefs taught by the Bible, and ultimately the certainty of the personal salvation promised by God through the Bible.

Most fundamentalists object to the label of fundamentalism because of its implications of narrowness, rigidity of beliefs, bigotry, and sectarianism. They prefer to call themselves simply "Christians" or "Bible-believing Christians." Nevertheless, most fundamentalists think that those who do not share their fundamental beliefs cannot be Christians.

A related term is "conservative evangelical," which is the preferred self-description of those Protestants who share the doctrinal beliefs of fundamentalists but resist what they see as the cultural provincialism and anti-intellectualism of some fundamentalists.

The term *fundamentalist* can also be applied to certain Roman Catholic movements and to believers in any religious tradition who object to critical study of their beliefs and authorizing documents.

See also INSPIRATION; PROTESTANT SPIRITUALITIES; REVELATION(S); SCRIPTURE.

Bibliography: J. Barr, *Fundamentalism* (Philadelphia: Westminster, 1977). G. Marsden, *Fundamentalism and American Culture: The Shaping of Twentieth-Century Evangelicalism: 1870-1925* (New York: Oxford Univ. Press, 1980).

TIINA ALLIK

FUTURE

At all times in history men and women have been fascinated by the future: the mystery of that which is not yet, but will be. People want to know what their future will be like. What determines the future? Is it God or fate or the free choices made by human persons? Can the future be predicted? Are there ways of controlling what will be? When we try to peer down the corridors of the future, how far should we look? Is the future restricted to our present existence in this world, or is there a future that transcends this present life?

Jesus came announcing the kingdom of God. That kingdom is presented in the NT sometimes as a reality that is still to come (we are taught by Jesus to pray to God: "Thy kingdom come"), at other times as a present reality (we are told "the kingdom of God is within you"). Thus the kingdom is both "present" and "future." A reality already existing, it will achieve its perfection and fullness in a transcendent, eschatological future.

The kingdom of God moves toward that fulfillment in history. Hence at any given moment the kingdom may be said to have both a historical future and a future that lies beyond history. In the earliest days of the Christian community, it was thought that the historical future would be very brief. The Lord's return, which would usher in the fullness of the kingdom and bring history to its completion, was expected soon. In such a context the attitude toward the future was one of preparedness. Followers of Jesus were to be ready for his imminent parousia. By the time the Gospels came to be written, however, the Church had come to realize that the final coming of the Lord was delayed—indefinitely. This is especially clear in the Lukan writings (the Third Gospel and the Acts of the Apostles). The future and the Church's existence in time became a reality that had to be dealt with in a more serious way. Christians had to face the question: In deciding how we live our lives in the present, what attitude ought we to take toward the future that is in time? Do we take joy in what it offers? Do we expend our energies to help create it? Or do we simply endure it, waiting for the only future that matters, the eschatological future?

Almost at the very time that the Christian Church began to see the need of dealing with questions of this sort, it was plunged into a series of persecutions that it had to endure intermittently for three centuries. During this period the martyr became the ideal of Christian spirituality. Ignatius of Antioch, on his way to Rome as a prisoner, begging the Romans not to interfere with his martyrdom, mirrors the spirituality of the postapostolic age: martyrdom was the goal. The ideal Christian was the martyr. It was not an ideal calculated to produce much concern for the future that belonged to history.

When the persecutions came to an end with Constantine, Christians found the future much more to their liking and rather easily adapted to living in a present with concern for, and commitment to, the historical future. This "secularization" of the Christian community generated a reaction, and a new Christian ideal emerged: that of the monk who withdrew from an overly worldly society to live in solitude with the eschatological future as his or her supreme concern. The monastic movement and the flight from the world (an attitude not always properly understood), which summed up its spirit, were destined to put their stamp on Christian spirituality for centuries.

It could be said that this attitude of fleeing the world, which had its roots in the 3rd-century monastic movement (popularly considered as beginning with St. Antony of Egypt, though he probably had predecessors), tended to dominate Christian spirituality at least until the age of Renaissance humanism and Roman Catholic spirituality as well, probably till the time of the Second Vatican Council. It was a spirituality that saw the world as fallen, and therefore evil or prone to evil. The focus of concern was directed toward the eschatological future. The world and its allurements were to be given a low priority in one's scheme of values. The all-consuming passion was to save one's soul. Very often what it had to be saved from was represented by the "world." This is not to deny that there were those who appreciated the value of the good creation that God had brought into existence. Yet the view that more often prevailed was that creation had been marred by human sin and greed and in its fallenness could lead the unwary (sometimes even the wary) astray. What happened in history was, in ultimate terms, trivial and transitory at best.

One must add, though, that it would be quite wrong to say that Christians were totally indifferent to the concerns of the transitory future. The Church built hospitals and schools. Monks copied manuscripts of classical as well as Christian antiquity. Cistercian monks, in a civilization that lived largely by agriculture, inaugurated new and improved methods of farming. Yet, all this having been said, it still remained that secular activities were considered second-best. They had no lasting meaning. Flight from the world was the surest, the safest, and the best way into the eschatological future.

This spirituality of otherworldliness scarred the Christian way of life with a number of ambiguities and even misrepresentations. Gospel passages such as the story of Mary and Martha or the incident about the rich man who kept all the commandments but could not give up his wealth were interpreted to mean that there were two ways of following Christ: an inferior way (the mere keeping of the commandments) and a superior way (the living out of the "counsels"). This was a classical case of a distinction, already accepted in Christian thought, being "read back into" the Scriptures. Celibate religious were viewed as the authentic signs of the Christian belief in an eschatological future. Exalting the celibate state meant denigrating married life and human sexuality as ways of living out a Christian spirituality. It meant, likewise, that the Eucharist, the high point of the Church's liturgy, could be presided over only by celibate males. It also dealt a deadly blow to what seemed to be the NT trend toward equality of women in the Church. It created an ever-widening gap in the Church between laity and clergy, and a sharp line of demarcation between the sacred and the secular, the holy and the profane.

Such an atmosphere was hardly conducive to the development of a "lay spirituality." The laity could not "flee from the world." Lay life meant living in the world, wherein one's activities were dominated by concern for the historical future—the planting of potatoes, the raising of families, the conducting of affairs of state, and so many other mundane tasks. Lay people had to accept the precariousness of such a situation. They were to say their prayers, try to keep the commandments, be grateful for the clergy's ministry to them and for the intercession of the religious on their behalf. One could hardly speak of a "spirituality of the laity." That is why St. Francis de Sales (1567–1622) appeared to be such an innovator when he wrote his *Introduction to the Devout Life,* in which he tried to show how a life of spiritual devotedness could be achieved without withdrawing from the world.

It was only with the Second Vatican Council that this more incarnational view of spirituality came into its own. The perspective on spirituality adopted in Vatican II's Dogmatic Constitution on the Church (*Lumen Gentium*) and its Pastoral Constitution on the Church in the Modern World (*Gaudium et Spes*) had been prepared for by the *thinking* of Pierre Teilhard de Chardin (expressed in writings that were not allowed to see publication until after his death) and the writings of other theologians, e.g., Yves Congar, Karl Rahner, M.-D. Chenu. It was prepared for also by the social encyclicals of the popes and by the involvement of lay people in the work of Catholic Action in the decades prior to the council.

This incarnational spirituality stresses both the goodness of God's original creation and the influence that the incarnation of the Word of God exerted in bringing us to genuine Christian concern for earthly realities and for human culture. Christians are called to involvement in the world, to assume the responsibility that is theirs to create a just and humane society in which people can achieve their full humanness and realize their openness to the transcendent. What happens in history need not be an obstacle to the growth of the kingdom; in fact, it is the duty of individual Christians and of the Christian community to see to it that a genuine Christian humanism can and does contribute to the building of the kingdom. Constructing the human future for the well-being of all women and men can dispose us for the ultimate transcending of it in the eschatological future.

The opening words of the Pastoral Constitution on the Church in the Modern World are like a trumpet call to involvement in the future of the world: "The joys and the hopes, the griefs and the anxieties of the men [and women] of this age, especially those who are poor or in any way afflicted, these too are the joys and hopes, the griefs and anxieties of the followers of Christ. Indeed, nothing genuinely human fails to raise an echo in their hearts. . . . United in Christ, they are led by the Holy Spirit in their journey to the kingdom of their Father and they have welcomed the news of salvation which is meant for every man [and woman]. That is why this community realizes that it is truly and intimately linked with humankind and its history" (GS 1).

The council Fathers speak of the works produced by human talents and energies that benefit human society: "Christians are convinced that the triumphs of the human race are a sign of God's greatness and the flowering of His own mysterious design.... men [and women] are not deterred by the Christian message from building up the world, or impelled to neglect the welfare of their fellows. They are, rather, more stringently bound to do these very things" (GS 34).

The document insists, moreover, that the ultimacy of the eschatological future does not dispense Christians from their responsibility to the historical future: "... while we are warned that it profits a [person] nothing if he gain the whole world and lose himself, the expectation of a new earth must not weaken but rather stimulate our concern for cultivating this one. For here grows the body of a new human family, a body which even now is able to give some kind of foreshadowing of the new age. Earthly progress must be carefully distinguished from the growth of Christ's king-

dom. Nevertheless, to the extent that the former can contribute to the better ordering of human society, it is of vital concern to the kingdom of God" (GS 39).

It is in the light of these words that we can understand an earlier document issued by the council, the Dogmatic Constitution on the Church, in which it is made very clear that the Church no longer supports an elitist spirituality. The call to holiness of life is a call given equally to all followers of Christ. "In the various types and duties of life, one and the same holiness is cultivated by all . . ." (LG 41). Chapter 5 of this document, entitled "The Call of the Whole Church to Holiness," provides a much needed and long overdue base for a contemporary approach to spirituality that respects the demands not only of the eschatological future but of the historical future as well.

See also AFTERLIFE; ESCHATOLOGY; HISTORY, HISTORICAL CONSCIOUSNESS; HOLINESS; HOPE; INCARNATION; KINGDOM OF GOD; VATICAN COUNCIL II; WORLD.

Bibliography: W. Abbott, *The Documents of Vatican II* (New York: America Press, 1966). Z. Hayes, *Visions of a Future: A Study of Christian Eschatology* (Wilmington, Del.: Glazier, 1989). M. Muckenhirn, ed., *The Future as the Presence of Shared Hope* (New York: Sheed and Ward, 1968).

WILLIAM H. SHANNON

G

GENTLENESS

See FRUIT(S) OF THE HOLY SPIRIT.

GIFTS OF THE HOLY SPIRIT

The gifts of the Holy Spirit traditionally are seven. Isaiah 11:2-3, telling of the spiritual endowment of the promised messianic king, speaks poetically of wisdom, understanding, counsel, knowledge, fortitude, and fear of the Lord. Piety, a rendering of that passage's first mention of fear of the Lord, was added in the Septuagint as a seventh gift, thus according with the biblical number seven and connoting plenitude. While that text is the basis for the traditional list, the teachings of Paul, later theologians, and particularly Thomas Aquinas contributed significantly to the development of the seven gifts as a theme that held central place in the medieval theology of the Spirit.

Paul, never referring explicitly to the Isaian list, observed that God had bestowed irrevocable gifts on the people of Israel (Rom 12:25-29) and noted that the Christians at Corinth lacked no spiritual gift (1 Cor 1:7). 1 Cor 12:4 contains Paul's teaching that "there are different kinds of gifts but the same Spirit" who circulates them among the members of the body of Christ. As do some other New Testament authors, Paul frequently mentions charisms—gifts ascribed to the Spirit that bring grace to concrete expression and enable their recipients to perform specific functions for building up the Church. Paul thus treats God's many gifts in a communal context.

More significant for later theology of the seven gifts is Paul's message about the presence and activity of the Spirit in the justified, a theme found also in Acts and John. For Paul, there is a close connection between being "in Christ" and living "in the Spirit," who, as the great free gift of Father and Son, makes present and extends the reality of Christ. In Paul's mention of "the spiritual person" who has the mind of Christ (1 Cor 2:15, 16), as also in his description of the Spirit's action ("the love of God has been poured out into our hearts through the holy Spirit that has been given to us"—Rom 5:5), as well as in his teachings that all those called by God are predestined to be conformed to the divine image (Rom 8:29) and that only those led by the Spirit can be God's children (Rom 8:14), there is a strong sense that through the Spirit the perfection of Christ is communicable in some measure to the just.

Abundant Greek and Latin patristic writings mention spiritual gifts in many different contexts and variously list them, with no careful distinctions between gifts of the Spirit and graces, charisms, virtues, or beatitudes. Justin Martyr linked each gift from Isa 11:2 to a specific Old Testament hero and attributed the presence of all the gifts in Jesus to the work of the Holy Spirit. Origen added three more gifts to the

Isaian list and taught that only in Jesus is the fullness of the gifts realized. Augustine contrasted the seven gifts with the Ten Commandments. Gregory the Great connected them with the theological virtues, which he saw them as perfecting.

The divinization of the creature was one of the chief themes addressed in patristic theology, especially in the East. Since doctrine was still underdeveloped in this period, however, there were uncertainties about the nature and role of the Holy Spirit. An enduring contribution was made by Augustine. Building on earlier patristic teaching that the Spirit is given to the baptized Christian by God, he advanced that the Holy Spirit is the gift of love proceeding from Father and Son, dwelling in believers and leading them to salvation. It remained for later theology to spell out how the gifts of the Spirit are the consequences and manifestations of this salvific gift. Greek philosophy, investigating how certain people can act heroically, proposed that they are possessed by a higher power and follow an interior instinct; this spurred interest among Christians in considering the effects of the Spirit's action in the justified.

Aquinas's teaching on the seven gifts stems from his basic principle that human nature is open to receiving God's friendship, God's utterly free self-communication (*potentia obedientialis*). He taught that the seven gifts are distinct from other charisms and function as special salutary modifications of that human openness to God; they are created qualities (dispositions, habits) by which one who has received sanctifying grace in baptism can follow the immanent Spirit's promptings with docility, joy, and a certain ease. For Aquinas, those moved by the gifts of the Holy Spirit are aided to act in a way that transcends a merely human mode. With the gifts of the Spirit, the limits of human liberty and love are broadened, not constrained. Under the Spirit's activity, a believer is not merely passive but active in such a way that one's responses to the gift of

the Spirit are at once God's and one's own. With the gifts, God acts not from outside but from within us.

Using Aristotelian categories, Aquinas spelled out an elaborate system in which the seven individual gifts variously perfect faculties of the soul and express specific virtues. The gifts function intuitively and are distinct but derived from the infused virtues, which depend not on intuition but on rational, discursive deliberation. This careful schematization offered precision, even if its connections now appear as somewhat contrived.

The Gifts in the Spiritual Tradition

Most comprehensive manuals of Catholic spiritual teaching, especially if influenced strongly by Aquinas, explained each of the seven gifts at length, in words varying slightly and receiving different embellishments from author to author.

Four of the gifts pertain to the intellect; all four relate to the virtue of faith. *Wisdom,* for Aquinas the greatest of the seven, assists seeing and evaluating aspects of everyday living in relation to God and God's kingdom, according to ultimate principles of faith and aided by the judgment of love. Moving beyond ordinary use of reason, the gift of wisdom involves a process of coming to glean the deeper meaning, hidden treasures, and sublime harmonies of faith truths. *Understanding,* like wisdom, is a gift for comprehending the things of life in relation to God and for achieving deeper insight into the truths held by faith. Self and others are seen as made in the image of God; in creation are discovered the vestiges of God, which point to God the Creator. *Knowledge* aids grasp of divine truths even when they are unsearchable by the human mind. Acknowledgment of the limitedness of the world brings heightened appreciation of the surpassing greatness of God. *Counsel* relates specifically to the practical intellect and thus is connected also to the virtue of prudence. It builds openness to the Spirit's inspiration in the activities of reflecting, discerning, consulting, and advising on matters of teaching or acting.

The other three gifts have to do with the will. *Piety,* associated with the virtue of religion, orients believers to be filially devoted to God, and in turn to be united with brothers and sisters sharing that devotion. It encompasses worship of God, in moments of prayer as well as in lives dedicated to love of God and neighbor. *Fortitude,* dealing with the irascible emotions and with the virtue of fortitude, gives courage to bear sufferings tranquilly, to overcome fears, to resist temptations, and to undertake and carry out difficult tasks for the glory of God and the welfare of others. *Fear of the Lord,* related to the virtues of hope, love, and temperance, brings proper use of pleasures and the senses, on the basis of a sensitivity to the activity of God and reverence for God's majesty. Born of poverty of spirit, this special kind of fear does not block intimate union with God but inhibits offense of God. As an element and not a contradiction of love, it is not to be conceived primarily in terms of human fear or terror. In a healthy spiritual life one fears God out of love instead of loving God out of fear.

Not all Catholic spiritual writers have emphasized the particular gifts of the Spirit as fully as those who closely follow Aquinas. John of the Cross, despite his comprehensive treatment of spiritual life, does not deal with the Spirit's seven gifts as a theme distinct from his decided stress on the theological virtues. For him, "gifts" is a generic designation for God's graces and favors. God adorns with "gifts and virtues" the soul that has achieved the high state of spiritual espousal with the Word, the Son of God (*Spiritual Canticle* 14:2). On the journey to this union, however, the soul will first "feel a withdrawal, deprivation, emptiness, and poverty regarding these blessings" (*Dark Night,* II.9.9). Some later writers mistakenly tried to read a schematization of the seven gifts of the Spirit into John of the Cross's teaching. Francis de Sales, in his *Treatise on the Love of God* (11.15), called the seven gifts of the Holy Spirit "the principal virtues, qualities and properties of charity" and briefly described each one in terms of love. Contrasted with the synthesis of Aquinas, the Salesian treatment is much shorter and omits the clear distinctions between gifts and virtues.

Spiritual teachers have offered some lively imagery to illustrate the working of the Spirit's gifts. Francis de Sales compared charity not only to Jacob's ladder of seven gifts as sacred steps, but also to a lily with six gifts as white flowers surrounding wisdom as the golden central flower. Gregory Nazianzus likened the seven gifts to the strings of a cithara touched by the Divine Artist to produce the most melodious of sounds in harmony. John of St. Thomas (*The Gifts of the Holy Spirit*) proposed a nautical image comparing ordinary efforts with those aided by the gifts of the Spirit: "Although the forward progress of the ship may be the same, there is a vast difference in its being moved by the laborious rowing of the oarsmen and its being moved by sails filled with strong breeze" (1951 ed., p. 56).

Attention to the seven gifts of the Holy Spirit can also be found in the writings of many other prominent Christian teachers, including Philip the Chancellor, Albert the Great, Bonaventure, Jan van Ruysbroeck, Denis the Carthusian, Louis Lallemant, and John Baptist de la Salle.

Contemporary Considerations

Recent theology has focused on the existential unity of the human subject and sees the whole person as affected by the indwelling of the Spirit. Thus, distinguishing among individual human faculties and categorizing the Spirit's gifts count for less than in the past. Two major deficiencies of the medieval theology of the gifts can be singled out: (1) the narrow context of an Aristotelian psychology of the soul and its faculties, and (2) the limited focus on the individual believer rather than on communal considerations.

First, recent thought, especially the theology of Bernard Lonergan, suggests a shift away from viewing the gifts on the basis of a theology of grace that presumes the metaphysical faculty psychology of Aquinas. Rather, it would place the gifts more strongly in the context of grace as a love relationship with a personal God beyond human expression and unrestricted in measure. Not without continuity with the theology of Aquinas, this approach nevertheless emphasizes more strongly a person's "being grasped by ultimate concern" (Lonergan) and experiencing religious conversion, which entails a total reorientation of one's life. There is now more attention given to a believer's growth in conscious relationship with God, whose encounter widens one's horizons of knowing, loving and deciding; this process expands even to the transformation of value systems and the remodeling of structures in the world.

Second, contemporary reflection on the gifts has attempted to take seriously the ecclesial character of Christian life. With a renewed liturgical spirituality, there has been increased emphasis on the meaning of the sacraments of initiation, in which all Christians receive the seven gifts. The Spirit is now readily acknowledged as operative in the shared activities and aspirations of the pilgrim Church, as it moves toward the future fulfillment of the kingdom through the ups and downs of life in the world. Acknowledgment that the Spirit breathes life to all the world, coupled with a reaffirmation of Aquinas's conviction that humans have a natural desire for the vision of God, would imply that the sevenfold gift of the Spirit will be found even beyond the limits of explicitly Christian communities.

See also CARDINAL VIRTUES; CONVERSION; FRUIT(S) OF THE HOLY SPIRIT; GRACE; HOLY SPIRIT; KNOWLEDGE; LOVE; PIETY; PRUDENCE; UNDERSTANDING; VIRTUE; WISDOM.

Bibliography: W. Hill, *The Three-Personed God: The Trinity as a Mystery of Salvation* (Washington: Catholic Univ. of America Press, 1982) 303–307. A. Kelly, "The Gifts of the Spirit: Aquinas and the Modern Context," *The Thomist* 38 (1974) 193–231. J. O'Donnell, *The Mystery of the Triune God* (New York: Paulist, 1989). P. Wadell, *The Primacy of Love* (New York: Paulist, 1992).

GEORGE P. EVANS

GLOBAL CONSCIOUSNESS, GLOBAL SPIRITUALITY

See ECOLOGICAL CONSCIOUSNESS; ENVIRONMENT; WORLD.

GLOSSOLALIA

Glossolalia (Greek *glossa*, "tongue," and *lalia*, "speaking"), or "speaking in tongues," refers to speechlike sounds considered to be a spiritual (but not miraculous) charism of the Holy Spirit for use in private or public prayer. As the behavior described in Acts 2 and 1 Cor 12–14, it was long taught that it was a gift proper only to the early period of Christianity. Glossolalia reappeared in 1901 in Topeka, Kansas, under the preaching of Charles Parham, and in 1906 at the Azusa Street revival in Los Angeles, under the influence of his student William Seymour. Its link with baptism in the Holy Spirit is unclear, but together they were the principal elements in the emergence of Pentecostalism from 19th-century Holiness movements.

Glossolalia appeared in American mainstream Protestant Churches around 1960, where it aroused fear and opposition, but it spread rapidly to Europe and beyond; it began in a Catholic group at Duquesne University in 1967. As a key element in a growing charismatic movement in the Catholic Church, it was less disruptive there than elsewhere. Glossolalia is regarded in Catholic theology as one of many charisms of the Holy Spirit; classical Pentecostals consider it variously as a sign of Spirit baptism, initial evidence of that baptism, or a permanent gift of the Spirit.

Early studies assumed that economic and psychological deprivation were characteristic of glossolalics. With its appearance among mainstream Church members, and with more stringent research methods, the bias in earlier studies has been recognized. Research on its sociological and anthropological aspects is replacing psychological studies. Glossolalic speech is probably neither xenoglossy (speaking in a language unknown to the person) nor a lost archaic tongue, but a new use of the vocal mechanism for prayer under the action of the Spirit. Without prejudice to its graced origin, many consider it to be learned behavior. Older exegesis and many Pentecostals would not agree.

See also CHARISM; CHARISMATIC RENEWAL; ENTHUSIASM; GIFTS OF THE HOLY SPIRIT; HOLY SPIRIT.

Bibliography: C. Williams, *Tongues of the Spirit* (Cardiff: Univ. of Wales Press, 1981).

MARY BARBARA AGNEW, C.PP.S.

GLUTTONY

See DEADLY SINS.

GNOSIS, GNOSTICISM

Gnōsis is a Greek word usually translated as "knowledge." Although the term can be used for any kind of knowledge, it more commonly refers to a special knowledge of God or of the divine world received by revelation, illumination, or initiation. *Gnosticism* is a term not attested in antiquity. It was coined in the 18th century to describe a wide variety of religious sects in the Hellenistic period that made *gnōsis* the basis of salvation.

While the various Gnostic sects differed greatly in their respective myths, certain beliefs were held in common: that the true God is unknown and ineffable; that the material cosmos was created by an inferior deity or angel, often called the Demiurge, meaning "craftsman"; that human beings—at least some of them—have a spiritual part which, though now trapped in matter, really belongs to the divine world; that salvation, understood as escape from matter and ascent to the divine world, is achieved through knowledge of one's spiritual nature. *Gnōsis* of the divine, therefore, is essentially knowledge of self.

Once thought to be of Iranian origin, Gnosticism is now seen as having roots in Hellenistic Judaism. Gnostic ideas exerted some influence on the writers of the NT, but it was only in the 2nd century that well-developed Gnostic systems were formulated by teachers such as Basilides, Valentinus, and Marcion. Gnosticism became a world religion in Manicheism and reappeared throughout the Middle Ages in dualistic sects such as the Cathari and Bogomils.

See also DUALISM; KNOWLEDGE.

Bibliography: B. Layton, *The Gnostic Scriptures* (Garden City, N.Y.: Doubleday, 1987). K. Rudolf, *Gnosis: The Nature and History of Gnosticism,* ed. R. Wilson (San Francisco: Harper & Row, 1987). J. Robinson, ed., *The Nag Hammadi Library,* rev. ed. (San Francisco: Harper & Row, 1988).

DAVID G. HUNTER

GOD

Spirituality as an academic discipline that is in some measure distinct from other branches of theology, such as systematic theology, biblical theology, historical theology, may be defined as "the field of study that attempts to investigate in an interdisciplinary way spiritual experience," that is, "the experience of consciously striving to integrate one's life in terms of self-transcendence toward the ultimate value one perceives" (Sandra M. Schneiders, "Spirituality in the Academy," *Theological Studies* 50 [1989], p. 692). An article on "God" in a dictionary of spirituality, therefore, should logically concentrate on the contemporary experience of God as reflected in new images of the God-world relationship rather than on the more technical concepts of God to be found in current systematic theologies.

In the present article, after a brief summary of the more or less traditional Christian experience of God, four new and quite different experiences of God reflected in contemporary theological writing will be presented. No attempt will be made to correlate them with one another until the very end of the article, when some suggestions for a more comprehensive understanding of God will be set forth. Briefly stated, these new experiences of God would run as follows: the experience of God as a community of divine Persons, and as such the model for all the different forms of Christian community; the experience of God as in dialogue with creatures, and thus as changing in line with the passage of events in the world; the experience of God as female as well as male in relating to creatures; and finally, the experience of God as transpersonal as well as personal. No doubt other experiences of God could be alleged, but these four seem to be the ones most commonly presupposed in contemporary theological writing.

Traditional Experience of God

To begin, then, the traditional Christian experience of God can be summed up as overwhelmingly unipersonal rather than consciously trinitarian. Even though most of the Christian Churches nominally profess belief in God as triune, the implicit focus for worship and belief seems to be on God as generically one. Both public and private prayers are quite often addressed simply to God as Lord and Creator, and only in the concluding words of the prayer does one realize that one is addressing God the Father rather than Christ or the Spirit. Furthermore, the adjectives conventionally attributed to God in forms of public worship have a unipersonal ring to them: for example, *all-powerful, all-knowing, eternal, unchanging*. While all these adjectives in principle could be descriptive of three Persons instead of just one Person, never-

theless the image that is generated by their use is more readily the image of a sovereign ruler vis-à-vis subjects.

Still another feature of the traditional experience of God would seem to be the general conviction that whatever happens is somehow God's will and that God will make sure that our own personal history and the history of the human race will end happily. When tragedy strikes, this belief is sometimes severely put to the test. In some cases this results in a virtual loss of belief in God and divine providence, so that one feels compelled to look out for one's own interests even at the risk of ignoring the legitimate needs of others. In other cases, unexpected reversals simply reinforce the believer's conviction that somehow God will provide.

These remarks are not intended to suggest that the traditional experience of God has been purely negative. On the contrary, it has many positive features that have sustained belief and, above all, trust in God among Christians for roughly two thousand years. But, if we are to judge from the style of theological writing in the years since Vatican II, new experiences of God that call into question various features of the older experience seem to have arisen in great profusion. Here we will discuss only what might be considered the four most widely circulated among these experiences.

Spirit and Community

The first of these experiences is the experience of God as a community of divine Persons. Included in this category would be an experience of God as Spirit, for what is most often meant by this expression is not simply God in a generic sense nor simply the Third Person of the Blessed Trinity, the Holy Spirit; rather, by the expression "the Spirit of God" or "the divine Spirit" one has in mind the Holy Spirit as the bond of love between the Father and the Son within the Trinity, and that same Spirit as the bond of love between Christians within the

Christian community. In both cases, therefore, the Holy Spirit is implicitly linked to the notion of community. Where the Spirit is actively present, there community exists, and vice versa.

The charismatic movement among both Protestants and Roman Catholics in the United States has laid heavy stress both on the influence of the Spirit in the direction of one's personal life and on the workings of that same Spirit within the charismatic community. The honored place given to "prophecy" on the part of inspired individuals within the context of a charismatic prayer meeting is clear witness to the belief that the Holy Spirit does indeed speak to the group periodically through one of its members. At the same time, the leaders of the group feel that it is their responsibility to prayerfully assess the content of the prophecies and the manner in which they are presented, thus giving witness in another way to the presence and activity of the Spirit within the community as well as within the lives of individuals. Finally, it should be noted that many charismatics see their mission within the contemporary Church to be the conversion of all believers to a more charismatic approach to Christian life and worship. The formation of new charismatic communities, accordingly, is not an end in itself but a means to an end: a more Spirit-filled existence for all individuals and all the various communities within the Church (see *The Holy Spirit and Power: The Catholic Charismatic Renewal,* ed. K. McDonnell, Garden City, N.Y.: Doubleday, 1975, pp. 11–33, 119–138).

Still another source for the linkage of the notion of God as Spirit operative in human history with the image of God as a community of coequal divine Persons is to be found in Latin American liberation theology. In *Our Idea of God,* Juan Luis Segundo notes how the Church in Latin America has tended to accept uncritically the distinction between the private and the public spheres of life, with the implied focus for the individual Christian being on the private sphere, where one can truly be oneself (Segundo, pp. 66–69). He himself, on the contrary, argues that only a revived understanding of God as a community of divine Persons will allow Christians to realize that personal fulfillment is to be found in the public sphere, where not only Christians but people of all faiths, and indeed those with no religious beliefs of any kind, must cooperate to achieve a more lasting social order based on principles of justice and equality. Retreat into the private sphere as the place where one can finally be oneself is a tacit acquiescence to the unjust structures of control and domination currently at work in Latin American society. But, cautions Segundo, Church authorities in Latin America may not welcome this new communitarian focus on Christian life and worship, since many of the same structures of domination and control that prevail in secular life are operative within the Church's own system of government (Segundo, pp. 79–84).

This same basic theme was repeated and reinforced a decade later by another Latin American theologian, Leonardo Boff, in *Trinity and Society.* After making a careful study of the historical development of the doctrine of the Trinity in the early Church, he concludes that the most appropriate contemporary model for understanding the doctrine of the Trinity is the notion of *perichoresis* developed by the Cappadocian Fathers and St. John Damascene in the early Greek-speaking Church. According to this model, the three divine Persons reciprocally permeate one another's being and activity. None can exist except in dynamic relationship to the other two. The unique individuality of each divine Person is preserved even as they together co-constitute a perfect communion of being and activity.

Applied to human persons, this model of personhood means that one's personality is constituted by a network of relationships: "relating backwards and upwards to one's origin in the unfathomable mystery of the Father, relating outwards to one's fellow human beings by revealing oneself to them and welcoming the revelation of them in the mystery of the Son, relating inwards to the depths of one's own personality in the mystery of the Spirit" (Boff, p. 149). Applied to human communities and other forms of social, economic, and political organization, this model of common life means that the unity of the group should never be achieved at the cost of negating legitimate differences between individuals. "In the Trinity there is no domination by one side, but convergence of the Three in mutual acceptance and giving. . . . Therefore a society that takes its inspiration from trinitarian communion cannot tolerate class differences, dominations based on power (economic, sexual or ideological)" (Boff, p. 151). Similarly, within the Church there should be great respect for the gifts and talents of individuals, and the Church itself should be seen as a worldwide communion of local churches rather than as an authoritarian power structure.

God and the Problem of Evil

Closely tied into this experience of God as a society of divine Persons who model for their creatures new forms of personhood and community life is the experience of God as responding to events taking place in creation and thus as changing. According to the classical understanding of God as set forth by Thomas Aquinas and others, change in God is unthinkable, since God by nature is the Pure Act of Being (*Ipsum Esse Subsistens*); as such, God simply is, with no possibility of change or alteration (ST I, q. 9, a. 1c). Yet the notion of God as a community of Persons in dynamic interrelationship both with one another and with all their creatures inevitably raises the question whether the divine Persons can be affected in their own essential being and activity by these same relationships. A positive response to this question has been offered by many contemporary

thinkers in North America and in Western Europe. For the ordinary Christian, however, the question whether God changes is focused around the problem of evil. Is God affected by what happens to me and my contemporaries? In short, does God relate to me in a personal way, feeling pain when I suffer and joy when I am happy or at peace?

Perhaps the most dramatic illustration of the pertinence of this question for contemporary Jews and Christians is the enormous popularity of Rabbi Harold Kushner's slim volume *When Bad Things Happen to Good People*. There he argues that in our evolutionary world process many things happen by chance, and even God cannot control their outcome. God's role in our lives, therefore, is not to make something good happen or to prevent something bad from happening, but to help us cope in a creative way with what actually does happen, whether good or bad (Kushner, pp. 113–148). But this commonsense insight, based on Kushner's own family history and his experience in dealing with distraught people as a pastor, conceals a number of theoretical assumptions about the nature of God and the reality of God's dealings with people which, until a few years ago, would have been considered literally incredible. Besides the implication, noted above, that God is susceptible to change rather than immutable, there is the further implication that God is neither omniscient nor omnipotent in the classical sense. That is, apparently God does not have exact foreknowledge of what will take place at every moment of the world process. Furthermore, even if God foresees what is going to happen in the next moment, God is not in a position to alter its outcome simply by divine fiat. God's power, in other words, is not coercive but only persuasive. God can only counsel human beings to do the right thing; the decision for good or evil is the human being's, not God's.

The truly amazing feature of the contemporary experience of God is the fact that so many people now find these unsettling assumptions about the nature of God and God's relationship to human beings both theoretically credible and, in a practical way, true to their own experience. Among professional theologians this attitude might be due to the wide-ranging influence that Jürgen Moltmann's book *The Crucified God* has enjoyed. He argues that in Jesus' cry of abandonment on the cross, not only does Jesus suffer separation from the Father at this critical moment of his life, but the Father grieves over his own separation from the Son (Moltmann, p. 243). Yet what proceeds from this event of supreme self-abnegation between Father and Son is the Holy Spirit, who reestablishes their union with one another, and at the same time is released into human history to offer the hope of salvation to all Godforsaken human beings. Thus all human history, however much it may be determined by guilt and death, "is taken up into this 'history of God,' i.e., into the Trinity, and integrated into the future of the 'history of God'" (Moltmann, p. 246). Accordingly, there is in human life no suffering or joy that does not become part of the unending life of the triune God.

Much of the same idea is to be found in Alfred North Whitehead's description of the "consequent nature" of God in the final part of his masterwork *Process and Reality.* He begins by noting that the ultimate evil in this world of ours "is deeper than any specific evil. It lies in the fact that the past fades, that time is a 'perpetual perishing'" (Whitehead, p. 340 [517]). Especially for a process-oriented thinker like Whitehead, the realization that with the passage of time everything of meaning and value in human life seems doomed for oblivion could be cause for despondency and apathy even now in the present. Yet, if God "prehends" all the events taking place in the world and incorporates them into the divine consequent nature, then the evil of "perpetual perishing" is definitively overcome. "The consequent nature of God is his judgment on the world. He saves the world as it passes into the immediacy of his own life. It is the judgment of a tenderness that loses nothing that can be saved. It is also the judgment of a wisdom which uses what in the temporal world is mere wreckage" (Whitehead, p. 346 [525]).

As noted above, these theoretical reflections on the God-world relationship by Moltmann, Whitehead, and many others have undoubtedly had a significant impact on the thinking of professional theologians and other reflective individuals. But the surprising popularity of Rabbi Kushner's book, which is based more on pastoral practice than on academic theology, indicates that, quite apart from the world of academe, many Christians have come to the conclusion that in an evolutionary world such as ours, where chance and lawlike behavior are inextricably intertwined, God's control over the passage of events is inevitably somewhat limited. Rather than allowing this to be an occasion for despondency or despair, however, many of these same Christians have accepted it as a challenge to assume more responsibility for themselves and their world than in the past. They seem willing, in other words, to give up belief in an all-knowing, omnipotent God if this gives them the freedom to chart their own destinies in a responsible way.

What separates this attitude of Christians from the orientation to life of an agnostic or an atheist is that the Christian continues to believe, in line with Kushner's proposal, that God is active in human life to help human beings cope with the various problems and issues that arise. That is to say, God is not a passive observer of the drama taking place in creation but an active co-participant, albeit in and through the instrumentality of human beings, in the first place, and nonhuman creatures, to the extent that these others can be affected by divine "persuasion."

On this last point, the philosophy of Whitehead seems better positioned than that of Moltmann and other European thinkers inspired by the philosophy of Hegel to offer a coherent explanation for the way in which God influences events taking place in the world without controlling them. According to Whitehead, God, in virtue of the divine "primordial nature," has a vision of possibilities for this world as a whole and for every creature within it. Moreover, God implicitly offers to each creature at every moment of its existence an "initial aim" that embodies what God can see as the range of possibilities, from the best to the worst, for the creature at that moment, together with God's "recommendation" for the best possible choice (Whitehead, p. 244 [373f.]; see also Bracken, pp. 48–50, 62–64). Thus the creature ultimately chooses what it sees as best for itself here and now, but only after it has been exposed to what God proposes as in fact its best possibility. This offer of an initial aim from God is repeated over and over again to the creature as it moves through history, irrespective of whether its past choices have been in line with God's vision for it or not. God, in effect, never despairs of trying to bring order out of chaos, to "save" the creature from its own misguided decisions.

Certainly, this line of thought presents a picture of God in heavily anthropomorphic terms, and perhaps some would prefer the vision of an utterly transcendent God set forth in traditional philosophy and theology. In response, one could argue that the notion of divine initial aims is simply a reworking of the traditional doctrine of grace in process-oriented terms. But, on a deeper level, one could advance the claim that the traditional image of God as totally transcendent has paradoxically given rise to modern atheism as a protest against a God who either doesn't care or doesn't count (see W. Waite Willis, *Theism, Atheism and the Doctrine of the Trinity,* Atlanta: Scholars Press, 1987, pp. 79–107). In other words, with so much evil in the world, perpetrated by entire cultures as well as by individuals, one must conclude that if God is truly omnipotent and does nothing to eliminate these evils, then God does not care about what happens in the world. On the other hand, if such evils exist because God cannot do anything about them, then God does not count. The term *God* becomes then simply a symbol expressing the longing of the human race for a utopian state that in fact will never come to pass. Thus it would seem better to discount the existence of God altogether and to work with other human beings for that more limited state of affairs that appears to be humanly achievable.

The process-oriented theologies of Moltmann, Whitehead, and their respective followers, on the contrary, offer a humanly appealing image of God both as one who resists the spread of evil wherever possible and as one who shows compassion for creatures in pain by accepting the reality of that suffering into the divine being, and thereby finding a way to convert it, paradoxically, into new possibilities for good. In this way they affirm the reality of God in an age when human beings are increasingly inclined to skepticism not only about the existence of God but even about the possibility of human survival beyond the next few generations. The ever-present threat of nuclear war and all the dangers to the environment caused by human greed and indifference to the future pose challenges to contemporary Christians that might well prove to be insurmountable without the accompanying belief in a God who really does care and can be counted on for support in hard times.

Male and Female Images of God

Precisely at this point, however, feminist theologians have set forth the claim that if anthropomorphic imagery is to be used to describe the activity of God in the world, female as well as male images of God should be brought into play. In fact, they would argue, since predominately male images of God were employed in the past to implicitly justify unjust structures of domination and control both in the Church and in society at large, female images of God (such as God the Mother) are needed to restore effective belief in God and divine providence among contemporary Christians. A mothering God, for example, would be seen not only as giving birth to creation out of her own "body" but as anxious to provide nurture and, as far as possible, self-fulfillment for all her children, human and nonhuman alike (McFague, pp. 97–123). Thus, under the influence of a female image of God, a much-needed "ethic of care" exercised by human beings not only toward one another but likewise toward other forms of life within the world might be able to supplant the more rigid "logic of justice" emanating from the male image of God that has indirectly contributed so much to rivalry and division among human beings and to exploitation of the nonhuman environment (McFague, pp. 12f.).

One could, of course, argue that this represents a highly idealized understanding of womanhood and motherhood, pointing out that women can be just as domineering and manipulative in their dealings with men as men have been with women, and that children habitually carry into adulthood negative experiences not only of their dealings with their fathers but likewise of their relations with their mothers. These objections, however, ignore still other facts, namely, that in Western culture, and indeed in most other cultures in the world, there is a bias toward maleness or masculinity as normative for what is generically human; that most women as a result do suffer the adverse effects of social, economic, and political subordination to men; and finally that the so-called Semitic religions—Judaism, Christianity, and Islam—by their largely male representations of God have indirectly contributed to the legitimation of women's secondary place in society as part of the divine plan for the human race.

In particular, within Christianity the maleness of Jesus has been taken to mean that the Second Person of the Trinity, and by implication the two other divine Persons as well, are, if not physical males, at least thoroughly masculine in their dealings with one another and with all their creatures.

There is, then, a problem here that cannot be solved by mentally noting that God is Spirit and that as Spirit the three divine Persons transcend maleness and femaleness, masculinity and femininity. The issue is not whether God is male or female within the divine Being, but rather how God is customarily *experienced* by Christians as a result of indoctrination in Christian life and worship. If the traditional catechesis of the Church and its regular forms of liturgy convey to Christians predominately male images of God, and thereby engender within those same Christians a heavily masculine experience of God, then Christians are, without fully realizing it, being alienated from the full experience of God that in principle should be possible to them. Women, to be sure, will normally feel this alienation more keenly than men, because exclusively male representations of God call into question the authenticity of their own personal identity as female human beings. But men, too, are thereby subtly alienated from the fullness of their own humanity; they are not free to exhibit those character traits and behavior patterns which the culture stereotypes as feminine but which men themselves instinctively recognize simply to be part of what it means to be human. Instead, they must live in "a man's world," where the logic of justice, referred to above, seems generally to prevail over the ethic of care, and where unjust structures of domination and control are frequently sanctioned in the name of natural law and/or the divine will.

There is, therefore, a need for "a therapy of the religious imagination, first in regard to God and then in regard to our relationship with Jesus Christ" (Schneiders, p. 19). The Jewish and Christian Scriptures, for example, are filled with different metaphors to describe the reality of God, some of them personal and others impersonal. Yet, while we "are immediately aware that the personal God is not really a rock or a mother eagle, it is easy enough to imagine that God is really a king or a father" (Schneiders, p. 27). The male metaphors for God, in other words, are for many Christians no longer simply metaphors, imperfect analogies to the reality of God, but pictures, faithful copies of the divine Being. Probably the only effective way to heal the religious imagination of Christians in this regard is to consciously begin using female as well as male metaphors for God, e.g., God as mother (Isa 49:15; Ps 131:2), or God as the housewife searching diligently for the coin she has lost (Lk 15:8-10), or God as the woman kneading yeast into a mass of dough (Mt 13:33; Lk 13:20f.). Interestingly, while everyone recognizes the metaphorical character of female images of God, few advert to the metaphorical character of typical male images of God, e.g., God as Father, as the Good Shepherd, as the sower of the seed, etc. (see Schneiders, pp. 39f.). Yet, precisely for that reason, both male and female images of God should be offered in Christian catechesis and forms of worship. Otherwise there is real danger of idolizing, that is, taking literally, what are only distant metaphors for the reality of God.

Jesus, to be sure, was a male human being. But his behavior toward both men and women was certainly not typically masculine by the standards of his day. In his own words, he "did not come to be served but to serve, and to give his life as a ransom for many" (Mk 10:45). Accordingly, he treated everyone, whether male or female, as his equal, indeed as his potential friend rather than as a rival or opponent. Perhaps, as Sandra Schneiders shrewdly comments, this is the deeper reason why God became human in a male rather than a

female form: God's self-revelation in Jesus as one who willingly serves rather than as one who seeks to be served would quite possibly be overlooked if God became human in a woman. Only if this attitude of willing service is exhibited in a man who consciously set aside the normal behavior patterns for men of his culture in order to set forth a new standard of human behavior for both men and women is there a shock of recognition that this is indeed novel behavior worthy of further consideration (Schneiders, pp. 58f.).

In any event, the physical maleness of Jesus is in itself no argument for the masculinity of God. For that matter, even Jesus' address of God as *Abba* should be seen as an attempt to move away from the thought- and behavior-patterns of the patriarchal society within which he found himself. Not being able, for cultural reasons, to address God directly as both Father and Mother, Jesus chose to use the affectionate form of the address to God as Father. In this way he showed that God, like the father in the parable of the prodigal son (Lk 15:11-32), does not deal with human beings, and indeed with all of creation, by using a highly formalized and exacting logic of justice, but rather by exercising in a deeply interpersonal way an ethic of care. Thus Jesus subverted the institution of patriarchy, with its overtones of control and domination over other human beings, even as he continued to refer to God as Father (Schneiders, pp. 42-47).

Transpersonal Images of God

For many people, however, the struggle to balance male and female metaphors for God in their imagination has apparently proved to be a hindrance to effective prayer, and they have turned in increasing numbers to a new, almost imageless understanding of God as the Ground of Being or the Primal Matrix (see, e.g., Ruether, pp. 47-71). Increased contact with some of the Asian religions, notably Advaita Vedanta Hinduism, Zen Buddhism, and Taoism, have induced many reflective Christians first to think of God in largely impersonal or transpersonal terms, and then through various forms of meditation to seek new experiences of God along these same lines. Men and women who are members of contemplatively oriented religious communities have taken the lead in organizing trips to Hindu-Christian ashrams and to Buddhist monasteries and nunneries in Japan, Korea, and Southeast Asia. At the same time, they have welcomed to their communities in the United States experts on meditation from the various Asian religions. The bulletin of the North American Board for East-West Dialogue, published three times annually at Gethsemani Abbey in Trappist, Kentucky, is normally filled with announcements about conferences and prayer services at which monastics from East and West are gathering to share prayer experiences and to pray for world peace.

Naturally, only a limited degree of insight can be gained from simply sharing prayer experiences with those of another faith. Yet the mutual respect thus engendered among the participants and the trust in the basic integrity of religious traditions other than one's own are an invaluable preparation, if not a precondition, for fruitful dialogue on more theoretical issues connected with belief and practice. Many Protestant and Roman Catholic theologians, accordingly, have traveled to India, Southeast Asia, Korea, and Japan in recent years in search of prayer experiences arising out of Hindu or Buddhist meditation practices; such sharing is seen as providing the necessary experiential grounding for more theoretical discussion of interreligious issues. Likewise, in more limited numbers, religious leaders from Asia have sought philosophical and theological "wisdom" in the universities of Europe and North America.

The Vatican Congregation for the Doctrine of the Faith, under the direction of Cardinal Joseph Ratzinger, issued on De-cember 14, 1989, a "Letter to the Bishops of the Catholic Church on Some Aspects of Christian Meditation," which expressed concern over the injudicious use of meditation practices derived from various Asian religions (*Origins,* Dec. 28, 1989, pp. 492–498). Yet by clear implication it endorsed a judicious use of those same prayer techniques derived from the spiritual traditions of Asia. The first paragraph of the letter, for example, takes note of the keen desire that many contemporary Christians have for "a deeper and authentic prayer life" amid the distractions of contemporary culture and acknowledges that "forms of meditation associated with some Eastern religions and their particular methods of prayer" have been quite helpful to some in achieving "spiritual recollection and deep contact with the divine mystery." Similarly, in paragraph 28, near the end of the letter, the authors concede that meditation practices derived "from the Christian East and the great non-Christian religions" may well constitute "a suitable means of helping the person who prays to come before God with an interior peace, even in the midst of external pressure." Thus Christians are ultimately left free to find a method of prayer suitable to their own needs, provided only that it conforms to the traditional Trinitarian structure of prayer in the Church, that is, directed to the Father through the Son and in the Holy Spirit.

Toward a New Synthesis

Some concluding remarks about a possible conceptual scheme that would bring together into a unity these diverse new experiences of God are in order here. While such a scheme does not exist as yet, its overall contours seem to be already in place; not surprisingly, they are a blend of old and new ways of thinking about and experiencing God. The new emphasis on God as a community of divine Persons, for example, is rooted in the centuries-old doctrine of the Trinity. What is distinctive about the new approach, however, is the shift in focus from a basically "modalistic" to a somewhat more "tritheistic" understanding of the Trinity. Systematic theologians such as Karl Rahner, Bernard Lonergan, and William Hill begin their exposition of the doctrine of the Trinity with the presupposition of the unity of the divine Being in the divine nature, and then offer arguments for the existence and activity of three distinct Persons who share that one nature perfectly (see B. Lonergan, *De Deo Trino,* Rome: Gregorian University Press, 1964, 2:186; Rahner, pp. 133–137; Hill, pp. 241–272). Leonardo Boff, on the other hand, as noted above, begins with the presupposition of the plurality of the divine Persons and conjectures how they can still be only one God, one divine reality. His solution—that the three divine Persons exist in a perfect communion or sharing of life and love—is simultaneously grounded in the doctrine of *perichoresis* among the ancient Greek Fathers and in his own felt need for a new model of community life for Latin American Christians currently engaged in the struggle for economic, political, and social liberation.

A similar blend of old and new themes in theology would seem to be necessary to do justice to the current experience of God as deeply involved in human history, and thus as capable of suffering for and with human beings in their efforts to create a new social order based on justice and equality. Relatively few Christians have ever fully understood, and perhaps still fewer have emotionally accepted, the standard Thomistic doctrine of the eternal immutability of God. The idea that God knows and wills the entire course of human history at the same time as God knows and wills the divine being seems to make petitionary prayer to God here and now rather questionable. Granted that there is a theoretical response to this objection based on God's presentiality to all moments of time as they occur (ST I, q. 14, a. 13c), most Christians, it would seem, in their petitionary prayer

to God, believe that God is indeed mutable in the positive sense, that is, truly compassionate and responsive to their felt needs as they occur. The problem has been that until recently there has been no philosophical justification for this experience of God as engaged in dialogue with human beings. Only with the cosmological schemes of the German Idealists at the beginning of the 19th century and with the evolutionary thinking of Henri Bergson and Alfred North Whitehead in this century have theologians begun to question the traditional immutability of God and to set forth schemes whereby God can be more deeply involved in nature and in human history.

Yet, there are likewise problems for those who accept the process orientation to reality and still wish to remain faithful to traditional Christian dogma, since many of the original process-oriented thinkers like Whitehead were philosophical monotheists who did not incorporate the doctrine of the Trinity into their understanding of the God-world relationship. Hence more work needs to be done to show how the understanding of God as a community of divine Persons undergirds a process-relational understanding of the world of creation (see, e.g., Bracken, pp. 35–60). Still less, of course, did these seminal thinkers of the past have any awareness of the issues raised by contemporary feminist theologians about the gender of God. It was simply taken for granted by them that while God is clearly not male or female, God can and should nevertheless be experienced as masculine by human beings.

The theoretical solution to this new set of gender-related problems is plainly not yet in sight, although it, too, may ultimately be linked with renewed study of the pertinence of the traditional doctrine of the Trinity for contemporary life. If sexuality—maleness and femaleness—is the human way to understand and express relationality as constitutive of one's personhood, indeed of one's entire being, then further study of the Thomistic doctrine of the divine Persons as *subsistent relations* (ST I, q. 29, a. 4c) might well provide clues to the mutual interdependence of the sexes upon one another in human life. Just as Father, Son, and Spirit are each the fullness of what it means to be God and yet are different by reason of the relationality defining their separate personhood, so women and men simultaneously possess the fullness of what it means to be human within their own sexuality and yet are relationally different from one another by reason of that same sexuality or bodily orientation to life.

Still another challenge to traditional thought-patterns about God is presented by those who claim to experience God in a transpersonal or impersonal manner. Here, too, the Thomistic doctrine of the Trinity might prove to be unexpectedly useful. For Aquinas makes quite clear that the divine Persons as subsistent relations are only rationally distinct from the divine nature common to them all (ST I, q. 28, a. 2c)—that is, each of them is the divine nature in a distinctive way. Yet the divine nature is as a result not itself personal but rather transpersonal, since it is the common ground for the existence of all three Persons. Those who claim to be experiencing God as an impersonal or transpersonal reality, therefore, might well be experiencing the divine nature rather than any one of the Persons. But, it may be objected, on what basis would a creature have contact with the divine nature rather than with the three Persons? The only possible answer would seem to be that the divine nature is the ground of the existence and activity of creatures as well as the ground of the existence and activity of the divine Persons. In this sense human beings, in experiencing God as impersonal or transpersonal, would be getting in touch with the ground of their own being.

Much more, of course, would have to be said to make clear that this is not a thinly disguised form of pantheism. At a minimum, one would have to argue that if the divine nature is the common source for

three really distinct Persons within God, then the same divine ground of being could be the dynamic source for the existence and activity of creatures really distinct both from one another and from the divine Persons. At this point, however, it seems best to conclude with the summary statement that in light of the above-mentioned reflections, a rejuvenated doctrine of the Trinity would seem to be the best theoretical frame of reference for integrating the various new experiences of God discussed in this article. Thus, even though the full reality of God will always remain an incomprehensible mystery to the human mind, as Karl Rahner and Bernard Lonergan each in his own way has eloquently argued (see, e.g., Rahner, pp. 44–89; Lonergan, pp. 101–124), the most precious clue for relating this divine mystery to human beings and their increasingly complex lives on this earth would seem to be the ancient doctrine of the Trinity rethought somewhat along the lines suggested above.

See also CHRIST; COMMUNITY; COSMIC MYSTICISM; EASTERN (ASIAN) SPIRITUALITY; EVIL; EXPERIENCE; FEMINIST SPIRITUALITY; HOLY SPIRIT; INCARNATION; INTERRELIGIOUS DIALOGUE; LIBERATION THEOLOGY, INFLUENCE ON SPIRITUALITY; PATRISTIC SPIRITUALITY; SELF; SIN; SUFFERING; TRINITARIAN SPIRITUALITY; WORLD.

Bibliography: L. Boff, *Trinity and Society,* trans. P. Burns (Maryknoll, N.Y.: Orbis, 1988). J. Bracken, *The Triune Symbol: Persons, Process and Community* (Lanham, Md.: Univ. Press of America, 1985). W. Hill, *The Three-Personed God: The Trinity as a Mystery of Salvation* (Washington: The Catholic Univ. of America Press, 1982). H. Kushner, *When Bad Things Happen to Good People* (New York: Schocken Books, 1981). B. Lonergan, *Method in Theology* (New York: Herder, 1972). S. McFague, *Models of God: Theology for an Ecological, Nuclear Age* (Philadelphia: Fortress, 1987). J. Moltmann, *The Crucified God: The Cross of Christ as the Foundation and Criticism of Christian Theology,* trans. R. Wilson and J. Bowden (New York: Harper & Row, 1974). K. Rahner, *Foundations of Christian Faith: An Introduction to the Idea of Christianity,* trans. W. Dych (New York: Seabury, 1978). R. Ruether, *Sexism and God-Talk: Toward a Feminist Theology* (Boston: Beacon, 1983). S. Schneiders, *Women and the Word: The Gender of God in the New Testament and the Spirituality of Women* (New York: Paulist, 1986). J. Segundo, *Our Idea of God,* trans. J. Drury (Maryknoll, N.Y.: Orbis, 1974). A. N. Whitehead, *Process and Real-*

ity: An Essay in Cosmology, ed. D. Griffin and D. Sherburne (New York: The Free Press, 1978).

JOSEPH A. BRACKEN, S.J.

GOODNESS

In the Christian tradition, goodness is both a primary attribute of God and an essential quality of the Christian life. The divine goodness is expressed in the created order itself and is narrated in biblical accounts of the mighty acts of God, especially toward the people of Israel, but supremely in the life, teaching, death, and resurrection of Jesus Christ. In this respect moral goodness flows from the very nature of God and the divine self-revelation. Spirituality is, among other things, the continual practice of acknowledging the goodness of God.

Biblical images of divine goodness begin with the opening chapter of Genesis: "and God saw that it was good." The psalms sing of "the steadfast goodness" of God and invite the faithful to "taste and see the goodness of the Lord." The Neoplatonic strand in early Christianity emphasized the love of the soul insofar as the soul itself reflects the ultimate good. The Idea of the Good is the source of reality and value in the whole pattern of the cosmos and of the individual soul. St. Thomas Aquinas, drawing upon Aristotle and the notion of all creatures' participation in the being of God, gave classical expression to the relation between divine and creaturely goodness: a human being "partakes of good in so far as it is like to the first goodness, which is God" (ScG III, 19). This feature of Thomistic thought articulates a framework in which God is the final end (*telos*) of all things. God's own being is thus "perfect goodness," and various creatures reflect this in accordance with their capabilities for relationship to God.

The status of goodness in various types and schools of Christian spirituality varies in relation to differing theological views of sin, grace, and the "natural" capacities at-tributed to human beings. St. Augustine's polemic against the Pelagians, who were optimistic about human goodness and its accomplishment, claimed that human beings, unaided by divine grace, are incapable of doing the will of God (the good God wills for the creatures). Later Western Christian spiritualities focused upon the development of certain virtues as part of the response of good works flowing from faith. By the eve of the 16th-century Reformation, the notion of good works had been linked with the treasury of merit. Luther and some of the more radical Reformers reasserted the Pauline accent on justification and the Augustinian polemic against the natural human capability for goodness. While it is basic to claim that Christians are justified by grace through faith, and that salvation is not "earned" by good works or by merits of moral virtues, this can lead to the denial of any human activity whatsoever as part of the Christian life of graced response to God's initiative. Quietisms of various sorts have tended in the name of justification by faith to deny such human agency and the role of "good works," whether of mercy or of piety, as part of the spiritual life. Indeed, a suspicion of the very term *spirituality* as a discipline—a seeking of perfection—is deeply rooted in such views.

Goodness in the context of the disciplines of Christian spirituality is best understood by tracing its relatedness to various lists of the "fruits of the Spirit" in the New Testament. In the ninefold list in the Letter to the Galatians ("love, joy, peace, patience, kindness, goodness, faithfulness, gentleness, and self-control"—Gal 5:22-23), emphasis is placed on the charisms (gifts) of the Holy Spirit, which are dispositions belonging to life "in Christ." Goodness here seems particularly related to gratuity, spontaneity, and selflessness. Thus life "in Christ" has these characteristics precisely as charisms and as intention-action patterns for self and for the community of faith.

Views that oppose good works to faith as gift are not adequate to the whole of the biblical witness or to the richness of the spiritual traditions. A way forward in theological reflection on goodness in relation to spirituality is found in the Pauline paradoxes (see Phil 2:12-13), where no claim to inherent or natural goodness is made, yet the faithful are to "grow up into Christ." The goodness of moral character is but one aspect of a graced response to the goodness of the divine creation and redemption. Moral perfection is not the goal of the spiritual life, but rather friendship with God—which is always a gift given that activates the energies of the "gifts of the Holy Spirit."

See also FRUIT(S) OF THE HOLY SPIRIT; GIFTS OF THE HOLY SPIRIT.

Bibliography: S. Hauerwas, *Character and the Christian Life: A Study in Theological Ethics* (San Antonio: Trinity Univ. Press, 1975).

DON E. SALIERS

GOSPEL

See EARLY CHRISTIAN SPIRITUALITY; PREACHING; SCRIPTURE.

GRACE

The term *grace* is one of the most common in the Christian vocabulary. In ordinary Christian speech it points to any freely given gift from God. In Catholic theology, however, the word developed into a technical term in the 5th century and became a classical subject matter of theological reflection. What follows is an explanation of the theology of grace and how it comes to bear on Christian life.

A Definition of Grace

The history of the theology of grace yields no uniform definition of an exact referent of the term. History exhibits a pluralism of theologies of grace. This is partly explained by the diffuse character of

symbol: it is a religious notion that encompasses many experiences and points in many different ways to the mystery of God dealing with human beings. For example, grace is a gift of a personal, benevolent, and loving God; God is gracious, so that grace is God's favor and love poured out generally on humankind and on individuals; God is merciful, and grace is God's forgiveness of sin; grace is the initiative of God's salvation, and salvation is grace; grace is God's indwelling within the person of faith.

No theologian has done more to redefine the concept of grace in the 20th century than Karl Rahner. Following him, grace may be defined as God's personal self-communication to humankind generally and to each individual. Several qualities of grace are implied in this formula. First, grace is totally and absolutely gratuitous. God's self-communication is completely free, unowed, and undeserved, so that there can be no talk of human merit in any strict sense. Whatever is said of merit can be spoken only within the context of God's always prior and initiating grace.

Second, grace is God's communication of God's own personal self. God is present to all creation by the sheer power of God's creating and sustaining activity. But over and above, as it were, this impersonal presence through efficient causality, grace points to God's personal being-present to human existence. This gift of God's self emerges out of the inner freedom of God.

Third, from this one can understand the quality that has often been associated with the theology of grace, namely, that it is doubly gratuitous. Everything that proceeds from God arises out of God's freedom. Thus God freely creates, and in itself creation is free gift. But the grace discussed here is God's personal entering into dialogue with an already created and semi-autonomous free human existence. This does not mean that creation should be viewed independently of grace in the Christian vision of things; rather, from the beginning God intended salvation, and creation is the condition for this free communication of God's self, God's personal dialogue with creation. Grace is God's personal being-present to human existence throughout the course of history. And yet human freedom is such that it can reject this offer of God's communication of self.

Fourth, the idea of supernaturality, which is less used today, simply reinforces the gratuity of grace in this scheme of things. For God's divine life is infinitely and qualitatively different than created human freedom. Thus, although grace fulfills and completes the inner intention of human nature itself, God's presence at the same time transcends it and always comes as gift.

In sum, grace may be defined as God's personal self-communication to every human being, God's being-present within, as the fulfillment and salvation of human nature.

The Significance of Grace

The self-communication of God that is grace should not be conceived in such a way that it falls completely outside human expectation. The gratuity of grace does not mean that it is totally extrinsic to the human condition, without any intrinsic connection to common human experience. On the contrary, grace fulfills human nature. Drawing out the meaning of this axiom in the theology of grace provides an essential rationale for the concept and helps to explain the significance of this doctrine.

The intrinsic human need for grace appears first and most dramatically within the limits and negativities of life itself. Human existence is, like all life on this planet, being-unto-death. One aspect of human finitude is its being bound by time and marked by mortality. Another characteristic of the human condition is the experience of sin and guilt. The evil aspects of the world and nature are taken up into freedom as responsible sinfulness and moral guilt. But the very recognition of these profound negativities implies a desire for their opposite, a longing for permanent and even absolute being, and a need for forgiveness and reconciliation. More positively, but against this negative background, this inner dynamism for permanence and wholeness in being can be found implied in the logic of the human quest for truth, for what is good, and for genuine solidarity with others. From an anthropological point of view, grace comes as a response to the fundamental religious question of salvation. Grace is thus synonymous with salvation; it constitutes union with God.

The history of the theology of grace reflects this underlying logic of the concept. Generally grace is understood within the two different but closely related negative contexts of sin and death. In other words, grace, or God's self-communication, responds to and overcomes sin and death. In relation to sin, God's presence as grace is forgiveness and acceptance of humanity and of each individual. In relation to death, grace is the foretaste of resurrection and the promise of eternal life.

The elemental character of these issues is further underscored by some of the other questions that are considered in the theology of grace. The concept and dynamics of grace respond to the question of how God relates to human existence. What is the character of God's dealing with human beings? In a parallel fashion, the theology of grace characterizes how human beings stand before, and relate to, God. Thus the theology of grace describes the dialogue of God's salvific initiative and the human response, the ongoing interchange between God and human beings that forms the ultimate basis of human life in the Christian vision of things.

The significance of the theology of grace, therefore, is that it defines a Christian anthropology, a characterization of human existence standing before God. As such the theology of grace provides the theological foundation for understanding the Christian life and spirituality.

The Revelation of Grace

Although God's graciousness may be said to be written into creation and nature, it has to be revealed in order to be known explicitly. The notion of grace as defined here is a product of theological reflection on the revelatory experience of grace. That experience has a history that extends back to the formation of Israel, and its foundational record is contained in the Hebrew Scriptures and the New Testament. The reading of this record of the revelation of God's grace should not be limited to scriptural word studies of the Hebrew and Greek equivalents of *gratia*. The whole of the Bible, in its myriad symbols and genres, gives testimony to God's gracious self-communication.

God's creating is for salvation. God's choice of this people Israel is God's grace in its regard. God's entering into a covenant with human beings is a function of God's personal and steadfast love. The liberation of God's people from Egypt through exodus is a manifestation of God's gracious intervention. God's law is God's grace, the communication of God's personal will. God as Spirit is God's being-present to prophets to inspire them, to charismatic leaders so that they may lead, to kings so that they may rule. God's wisdom is God being present in the mind that recognizes the order of God's ways. God's word is God being present in effective sovereignty. Israel's God is a saving God ever present by a faithful love that is manifested in innumerably different historical ways.

For the Christian imagination, Jesus of Nazareth becomes the focal point of God's grace. Jesus Christ is the embodiment of God's self-communication to humankind, the symbol or sacrament that actualizes God's presence in a public way in history. Jesus Christ is grace. The other major symbol in the New Testament expressing God's self-communication is the Spirit of God, depicted as being poured out anew through the risen Christ. As in the Jewish Scriptures, the Spirit is God—God as Spirit at work within the Christian community and experienced in the lives of Christians. The Spirit of God represents God's being-present and bestowing the new life, the salvation, mediated by Jesus Christ. In the climactic words of Paul, "the love of God has been poured out into our hearts through the holy Spirit that has been given to us" (Rom 5:5).

The New Testament contains a remarkable pluralism of conceptions of how God's gracious salvation is to be conceived, as well as of how the self-communication of God affects the lives of Christians. But insofar as grace is conceived as God's self-communication, the substance of grace is most closely linked with Jesus Christ and the Spirit. In the history of the theology of grace, the tradition stemming from Augustine identifies grace with God as Spirit, and the tradition stemming from Luther identifies grace with Christ. But Christ and the Spirit imply each other—Christ identifies the Spirit; the Spirit in us is what God did in Christ.

History of the Theology of Grace

The formal history of the theology of grace as a technical term and a specific locus for theological reflection really begins in the Western Church with Augustine. It was occasioned by the emergence of a number of theological and anthropological problems concerning what grace is and the relation between grace and human nature or freedom. These issues formed the context within which the theology of grace developed. Responses to them shaped the foundations of Christian spirituality. This brief survey of the history of the theology of grace focuses on the shifting conception of grace; the effects of grace will be considered later.

Augustine

Augustine's teaching on grace came to full expression in his exhaustive polemic against Pelagianism during the last twenty years of his life. The Pelagians did not deny grace, but they understood it in such a way that human nature and freedom were not intrinsically damaged by sin. With an external grace, so to speak, human beings could turn to God on the basis of their own resources and gain salvation by obedience to God's commands.

Augustine reacted fiercely against this view. For him, human nature was infected from conception with an inherited sin, with the result that human freedom was a prisoner to itself and to the added bonds of its habits of sin. Grace had to be God's salvific power at work within a person. Grace for Augustine, then, was God's Spirit, who alone could account for the healing of sin and every turning toward God. Augustine's legacy to theology, anthropology, and spirituality consists in the insistence on the universal necessity of God's grace for union with God and the total priority or prevenience of grace to every human initiative toward God. Anything less than this is in some way tinged with the heresy of Pelagianism.

Aquinas

With the advent of the medieval period and the rise of the theology of the university, the concept of grace was radically changed. Grace became something to be explained through the metaphysical categories of Aristotle. In the theology of Thomas Aquinas, grace is understood not primarily in the context of sin, although the Augustinian theme is not forgotten, but against the background of the finitude of natural existence. The term *grace* designated in the first instance a quality of the human spirit, a created modification or ontological habit infused by God, that served as the basis for the theological virtues of faith, love, and hope, and disposed the human person to respond to God. This notion of grace could be regarded as static because it described a state of being. But this would be to ignore Aquinas's idea of a nature as a principle of action. In effect, grace conditioned human nature and was, in Paul's language, a kind of "new creation." It bestowed on human freedom new powers of action leading to the goal of human existence, which is intimate personal union with God. The Thomistic legacy to spirituality is a dynamic life of action according to the theological virtues.

Luther and Trent

The Lutheran contribution to the theology of grace has its basis in a return to scriptural and especially Pauline language. Like Augustine, Luther understood grace against the background of the radically sinful condition of humankind. The key phrase in describing grace is justification through faith. Grace, as God's self-communication, is not, however, identified with God as Spirit but with Christ and the redemption he wrought. Jesus Christ is God's promise of acceptance and Word of forgiveness addressed to each human being. By clinging to Christ in faith, the Christian not only lives within the promise of salvation in the future but is transformed now by the holiness and sanctity of Christ, even while remaining in some measure his or her sinful self. Grace is Christ, who absorbs human sinfulness and guilt into himself and thus negotiates God's own forgiveness and acceptance of the person of faith. Luther's conception of grace corresponded deeply with the experience of Christians at the time and released into the Western Church a distinctive spirituality that is preserved in some measure in the whole Protestant tradition.

Trent's response to Luther, which is found in the Decree on Justification (1547), does not break any essentially new ground beyond the medieval synthesis. Rather, it brings to bear some of the fundamental conceptions of Scholastic theology in polemical contrast to Luther's teaching. The point is to mark out clearly the differences between the teaching of the Roman Church and that of the Reformation. The contrasts in some cases are striking: Beneath Trent's biblical language lies an objective theology of grace, while Luther's language is experiential and descriptive. Trent's language explains systematically; Luther is assertive and paradoxical. For Trent, one cannot both be in and out of a state of grace; for Luther, one is simultaneously a sinner and justified. Trent emphasizes freedom and responsibility within the movement of grace, while Luther emphasizes human passivity before the power of God's Spirit, leading to faith and justification by grace. Trent endorsed a qualified form of the language of merit, while Luther ruled it out completely. Given these points of view, the Catholic cannot be sure of his or her ultimate salvation because of the fallibility of human freedom, while the Lutheran is assured of his or her salvation by faith's absolute reliance on God's self-communication in Christ. The fundamental character of these different anthropologies entails very different Christian spiritualities.

The Modern Period

The period after the Reformation produced no major advance in the theology of grace compared to what has been considered. The end of the 16th century was marked by disputes over the issue of the relation between predestination and human freedom. And from the period of the Enlightenment the theology of grace was expounded in the dry schematic treatises of theological manuals. The category of grace, however, became important in the Modernist movement at the turn of this century. For grace represented how God works in human subjectivity and justified the turn of theology toward an analytical account of religious experience. But Modernism was condemned and exterminated before it could bear fruit. It was only during the thirties and forties that a renewal of the theology of grace began to take shape, ironically through historical study of the patristic and medieval tradition, but within a context of an emergent historical consciousness. Theologians such as Henri de Lubac, Jean Daniélou, Henri Bouillard, and Bernard Lonergan retrieved authentic dimensions of classical theology and brought them to bear against the method and content of the manuals.

Current Theology of Grace

But it was Karl Rahner who most effectively restored the theology of grace to its position close to the center of Christian thought. His theology, or at least many of the conclusions of this thought, are almost presupposed in the theology of grace today. One can see four reversals at work in his reinterpretation of grace. Each one of these will be shown further on to have a direct bearing on Christian life.

First, since the time of Aquinas the term *grace* designated primarily, although not exclusively, "created grace," the habit or quality of the human soul infused by God. Concomitantly with this sanctifying grace, God, who is "uncreated grace," was present to, and dwelt in, the human person. Rahner simply reverses this relationship between created and uncreated grace. Grace is first and foremost God's self-communication and presence to human existence. This simple shift completely reorients one's thinking about grace and opens up the possibility of interpersonal categories to analyze it.

Second, in response to the implied extrinsicism of neo-Scholastic theology, Rahner regards the offer of grace as constitutive of the actual condition of human existence. The supernaturality of grace does not mean that it comes to a purely self-enclosed human nature as an alien, arbitrary, and merely additional factor of the human condition. Rather, God's presence as an offer of salvation is part of the very condition of a human existence whose salvation God wills from the beginning.

Third, against the implication that grace is scarce, then, or that there is no salvific grace outside the Christian sphere, Rahner argued theologically to the universality of grace on the basis of the universality of God's saving will. The implication of this position is dramatic: it means that the whole sphere of human life, even in its most secular aspects, is potentially "graced." This view, which was ratified by the Second Vatican Council (LG 16; GS 22), breaks down barriers separating the Church and the world, and unveils to Christian vision a kingdom of grace beyond the Church.

Fourth, against the Scholastic position that grace cannot be experienced, because it is supernatural, Rahner holds that people do experience grace. This is a qualified view, however, since grace is still not known directly or distinctly as grace but in and as experiences of genuine self-transcendence. But at the same time this conclusion opens the theology of grace to phenomenological and narrative methods of analyzing grace in and through experience.

With these theological moves Rahner has returned the theology of grace to a consideration of the very nature of salvation and how it is experienced in human existence. In some ways Rahner's theology of grace is transitional; he broke open the narrow objectivist treatise on grace and reconceived it in foundational anthropological terms. Yet to a large extent the Catholic theology of grace, even when it moves beyond Rahner, is dependent on him.

The movement beyond Rahner has occurred in several areas. One clear instance of this development lies in the explicit context of ecumenical theology. In an early work Hans Küng succeeded in bringing much closer together the teaching of the Council of Trent on justification and the widely respected neo-Reformation theology of Karl Barth. The work of the Lutheran-Catholic dialogue on the theme of grace charts many areas of agreement while respecting differences of language, theme, and accent.

The significance of the theology of grace has also been expanded by liberation theology. Building implicitly on conclusions shared by Rahner, liberation theology stresses grace as a liberating force in public, social life. It offers a conception of the Christian life of discipleship as participation with Christ in the mediation of grace to society and the building up of social grace.

The concept and theology of grace have also been deepened by the renaissance of scriptural scholarship. Reaching back especially into the New Testament for the foundations of a theology of grace, which of course are prior to Augustine's formulation of the issues, Edward Schillebeeckx, for example, has opened up the rich pluralism of the symbolism of grace. By uniting the theological notion of grace with the very experience of salvation that is expressed in so many different ways by early Church communities, Schillebeeckx has again demonstrated the centrality of this concept.

The Effects of Grace

One should try to distinguish between what is referred to substantively as grace and the effects of grace in the human person. In line with Rahner, grace has been defined as God's self-communication to human existence. The Christian imagination finds the achetype of this self-communication in Jesus; Jesus is the embodiment and definitive realization of God's personal presence to human existence. As such, Jesus is the Christ who reveals and mediates to Christian consciousness how God acts in ourselves. The issue now concerns the effects of God's salvific, personal presence to human life. These effects define in more detail a Christian anthropology and the fundamental principles of the Christian life.

Freedom from Sin

By a logical and psychological priority, the first effect of God's personal self-communication is freedom from sin. All theologies of grace include it, but Luther above all stressed it. God's personal love for each individual person is one that includes forgiveness. God's acceptance of us is an acceptance of the way we actually are, not as what we or others think we are nor as we strive to be. This acceptance is a personal acceptance; it is an interpersonal communication. This is the significance of Luther's biblical language and Rahner's recasting of Scholastic theology into interpersonal terms. By being embraced in God's personal love *for me,* as Luther said, the individual is freed from the negativities that imprison each one and is reestablished or reconstituted with the absolute self-identity that only the love of God can bestow. What is stressed in all this is the priority and gratuity of God's loving self-communication to any possible human achievement as well as the passivity of human freedom in the face of it. God loves human beings first, and all the other effects of this love flow from its priority. This first effect of grace casts the whole of Christian life into a context of fundamental gratitude.

Freedom to Love

Augustine first charted a second effect of grace—the freedom to love. Against the background of the sin of the world and the dynamics of egocentrism, he asked how it could be that there is love in the world. The New Testament says that God is love. Therefore the principle that inspires love wherever it is found must be God's self-communication. But what Augustine argued to, he first experienced. Grace, as God's personal presence and suasive activity, is a stimulus and a lure toward the objectively good and the true; it opens up a human spirit curved in on itself to self-transcendence in the direction of God.

This Augustinian logic underlies Rahner's theology of grace: where there is genuine self-transcendence, there is grace at work. But the mistaken identity between the gratuity and the scarcity of grace is broken; grace abounds. The implication for the Christian life is that this is what grace is for. The teleology of grace is to free from sin, to free freedom from itself, in order that human freedom may transcend itself in love.

Cooperative Grace

One of the distinctions that Augustine makes regarding the effects of grace, one that persists through the medieval period, is between operative and cooperative grace. Operative grace is what God's self-communication accomplishes in us but without us, that is, prior to any response or exercise of freedom. Cooperative grace is God's continuing presence to our freedom and action, sustaining and cooperating with them. The influence of the two cooperating forces here should not be understood as unfolding on the same level nor in competition with each other; rather, God's self-communication does not replace human freedom but respects it and fulfills it by enhancing its own potentiality.

This effect of grace has a new relevance today far beyond what it could have had prior to modernity. For today freedom is recognized as a power that exceeds free choice, consent, or even steady commitment. Human freedom is also a power of creativity that creates new being out of itself and the stuff of the world, or it is a power of destruction. Cooperative grace, in this context, can now be seen as that which enables genuine creativity in this world. Human freedom, empowered by God's self-communication and inspired by the values of God revealed in Jesus' life and teaching, is directed into the world to forge new relationships of love. This is implied in Aquinas's description of what is really the effect of grace in the dynamic terms of a new nature as a new principle of activity.

But it takes on new meaning in the realization accompanying historical consciousness that history is open.

Union with God

All theologies of grace explain how grace unites one with God, and the transformation that this entails. As Aquinas understood it, grace effects the divinization of human existence. Through grace the human person is justified and sanctified, and God dwells within, so that we share in God's divine life. Luther, too, describes this transformation in terms of an interpersonal Christ-mysticism. By faith one so clings to Christ as God's Word of personal address that one is transformed by God's love. The beloved is raised up to the level of the lover, for love when it is genuine bestows equality on the beloved. Thus by our union with Christ we share the qualities of the Son in the eyes of God. The same dynamics are implied in Rahner's personalist theology of God's self-communication and given an ontological basis.

This union with God also has enormous relevance for Christian life in the world. For in the measure that one is conscious of one's union with God, in the same measure is one freed from nature and the world, and especially from fear of the world. Union with God relativizes the world, puts it in its true perspective as creature, and releases one from every fear that can paralyze the action of love. Only on this premise can a person be really free for the world, prophetical and critical in its regard, active in it and for it. Union with God by the dynamics of grace is not escapist, for the effect of grace is freedom from the world in order to be freely immersed in it.

The Wider Dimensions of Grace

These effects of grace, experienced in the Christian community and testified to by the history of the theology of grace, have been expanded in today's theology into a general anthropology. In other words, on the basis of Vatican II's teaching on the universality of grace, the theology of grace is seen as characterizing an anthropology as such. This universal anthropological perspective in turn reveals the wider dimensions of grace.

Nature and Grace

Prior to the Second Vatican Council, the theology of grace of the manuals conceived of human nature as self-enclosed and complete in itself. As a result, grace appeared as extrinsic to human life, that is, coming from outside integral human life and experience in such a way as to bear no intrinsic relation to it. Against this view, Karl Rahner argued that Jesus Christ reveals a God who is from the beginning, and even prior to creation, bent on the salvation of humankind. But this universal and all-encompassing will of God for human salvation cannot be conceived as having no effect at all on actual human existence. Therefore one must consider the actual offer of grace, God's being-present as an offer of self-communication, as an integral dimension of actual human nature.

The consequences of this element of the current theology of grace for spirituality consist in new appraisal of the whole realm of human nature. Although conceptually distinct from grace, everything that is natural about the human is suffused with God's personal presence. The various dichotomies and divisions that Christian theology in the past managed to erect in order to separate the religious and the merely natural sphere are now looked upon as false. The sphere of the natural is not only good but also bears within itself the offer of a personal encounter with God.

The Universality of Grace

The universality of grace is a corollary or a different way of considering the implications of the universal saving will of God. If the grace of God's personal self-communication is the medium of God's will for the salvation of all, it follows that all human beings are from the first moment of their existence born into a sphere of God's offer of grace. All human life in history unfolds within the existential milieu of God's being-present to human freedom. But this expansion of the operation of grace to encompass the whole sphere of historical existence also has dramatic effects on how one conceives the encounter with grace and union with God. The question concerns the way this universally present self-communication of God is concretely encountered.

The theology of grace in the Roman Church has always been closely connected with the sacraments, even as it has been closely related to the theology of the word and preaching in the Protestant tradition. The principle of sacramentality means that for grace to become operative in an explicitly conscious way, it must be mediated by concrete historical events and symbols or sacraments. The sacraments are the explicit mediations of grace, just as is preaching the word of God, for it too conforms to the sacramental principle. The sacraments, then, each in its own way and according to its own intentionality, render concrete and so embody God's self-communication in specific circumstances. Within the Christian community the sacraments are one of the basic foundations of ecclesial spirituality.

In the light of current theology of the world religions, the extension of the sphere of grace also expands and widens the principle of sacramentality. Grace, to become explicitly operative in the lives of all people, must be mediated through the actual historical conditions in which they live. Thus, concretely, the institutions of other religions are the actual mediators and bearers of God's personal self-communication to their members. The Christian must expect to find God's truth and grace within them.

But the sacramental principle extends still further beyond the explicitly religious sphere, because God offers every human being the possibility of responding to God's personal self-communication (GS 22). In the light of this issue of how grace is encountered universally, it becomes apparent how grace is encountered most fundamentally. God's personal self-communication is offered to every person most radically in every situation that calls forth self-transcendence in response to the implicit urging of an ever-present grace. The ordinary dilemmas of human existence, the ordinary historical situations of concrete human life, are the places where God's grace is most fundamentally encountered. Responses to everyday experiences, which together make up the whole of one's life, constitute in turn one's basic response to God's self-communication.

The Breadth of Grace

Much of the development of the theology of grace described thus far can be understood within the context of a personalist or interpersonal anthropology. But liberation theology, political theology, feminist theology, and theological reflection on ecological issues have helped to delineate a more adequate anthropology and thus expand still further the dimensions of grace.

Human nature cannot be described adequately in individual personalist terms, because actual historical human existence is constituted by other this-worldly relationships. Besides being related to itself by reflection and to others by personal contact, the human person is constituted by its being related to the concrete physical world in which it lives. Moreover, the person is also shaped by the specific society in which it participates, by the objective institutions and patterned behavior that form its second nature. Human existence *is* social, and it *is* ecologically a part of nature in the broader sense. Human beings *are* temporal and exist in a solidarity of dependence and responsibility with those who went before and those who will come after. Thus the turn to human nature to find in it the workings of grace cannot be limited to a consideration of an abstracted essence, but must include an examination of actual concrete historical human existence in the many dimensions that make up its reality.

The theologies just mentioned show that grace is revealed in these wider dimensions of human existence just as powerfully as in personal existence and by the same dynamics of negativity and positivity. The human spirit is shocked by the inhuman scandal of the immense deprivation and humanly caused suffering that the world exhibits. It cannot accept the history of the manifest oppression of women. It recoils from the devastation of its own habitat. These negative experiences are simultaneously a potential revelation of God's grace as the power of what should and could be. In this case God's self-communication is specified through Jesus' central message of the rule of the intention and values of God. It is at the same time a summons to combat these evils.

The Response to Grace

The question of the response to grace is where the theology of grace most directly comes to bear on the Christian life. Spirituality is the human response to grace. Traditionally this response to grace has been conceived in terms of the virtues of faith, love, and hope, which are themselves caused by grace.

Faith

Faith has always been considered the first and fundamental human response to grace. The priority of grace and its utter gratuity imply that grace causes faith. Thus the faith that is the response to God's self-communication is not fully in human control but is a function of God's initiative. But the extension of the working of God's grace to the whole sphere of human existence, as well as the issue of whether or not grace can be experienced, has broadened the notion of faith in today's theology.

Faith may be an explicit response to God's grace when, for example, as in the Christian sphere, the self-communication of God is historically identified in Jesus Christ and the Church. Here the object of faith is publicly represented in the history of the Church. But God's grace can also be responded to outside the Christian or any other religious tradition. Karl Rahner showed how grace can be experienced in ordinary secular or profane life, even though what is experienced here is not explicitly identified as grace. Grace is indistinguishable from the stirrings of self-transcendence within the human spirit. A consciousness of grace as a divine summons is thus available in the innumerable limit situations that define historical existence. Whenever a person experiences a call to self-transcendence, to an acceptance of values beyond the self, one is experiencing grace. And whenever a person submits the self to such values by an active commitment to them, one is simultaneously responding implicitly to God in faith.

Love

It has already been shown that grace causes love. Traditionally, beginning with Augustine, the theology of grace and faith has allowed for the separability of faith and love as the effects of grace. One could have faith in God without love of God. But when theology views the response to grace in an existential and historical perspective, this separation is seen to be impossible. Faith without love is neither authentic nor real faith. Theology has come to appreciate the interpenetration of intellect and will, of mind and desire, in a total human response. Although faith and love may be distinct human responses, they are inseparable and imply each other.

Liberation theology further expands the notion of love as a response to grace to form a more integral spirituality. Love of God in the neighbor and love of the neighbor as one beloved of God cannot today be reduced to the interpersonal dimensions of those with whom one comes into personal contact. The sociality of human existence, and the actual interdependence of peoples that now makes up our common history, embodies the Christian imperative of love in a dramatically new way. An integral response to grace entails a concern for the social structures and institutions in which all participate and which have a bearing on the lives of all others.

Action

Liberation theology has developed still further the integral spirituality implied in the anthropology of grace by its retrieval of the pragmatic axiom of the New Testament that the authenticity of any human response lies in action and not in mere words. The reality of faith and love is profound; its deepest roots plunge downward to the core of human personality, beneath human speech and even explicit conviction. The reality of faith and love, one's real commitment that defines who a person is, consists in the fundamental option and direction of one's whole life. This fundamental option is embedded in one's action and can only be fully discerned by an analysis of action.

Action in general, then, bears one's fundamental response to grace. But the general dispositions of faith and love are manifested in a great variety of concrete actions. An integral spirituality must respect the various dimensions of human existence and the various relationships in which the human person stands. The human person relates to the self by reflection, to other individuals personally, to a wider range of human beings through social structures, and stands in a relation of transcendence to God. All these dimensions and relationships intermingle with and influence one another; all must be taken into account in the varieties of action that make up an integral spirituality.

In the end, then, the concept of the Christian life or spirituality that emerges out of the current theology of grace is defined by the praxis of a discipleship of Jesus. The single central symbol in history

that embodies the meaning and the direction of the impulse of grace for the Christian is Jesus of Nazareth. Negatively, the experience of grace is not without its historical criterion or norm that allows for critical evaluation. The experience of God's self-communication must be measured against the New Testament's portrait of Jesus in order to be judged authentic. More positively, Jesus presents the positive guidelines for Christian life. The Christian life is by definition a following of Jesus under the impulse and empowerment of God's self-communication as Spirit. This praxis of discipleship—doing in our world what Jesus did in his world—is the definition of the Christian life.

The End of Grace

The theology of grace today encourages a spirituality of action or praxis. But this raises the question of where this action is headed and what it is worth. What is the teleology of grace? Or better, in a historically conscious world, what is its eschatology?

Hope

Hope is the third theological virtue caused by grace and defines yet another dimension of how human beings respond to God's self-communication. Traditionally hope has been defined as a virtue distinct from faith and love. But a closer existential examination discloses that hope as a human response is scarcely distinct from faith. Faith is hope directed toward the present and the past; hope is faith directed toward the future. The theology of hope points to a basic attitude of trust in being or reality itself, within which faith and love have their roots. Hope is the precondition for faith and love insofar as it consists in that fundamental openness to reality and its ongoing future without which there could be neither faith nor love.

Hope, for the Christian, also finds its defining ground in the life of Jesus. The New Testament presents that life as being confirmed and validated by God in its being raised up into God's own life and reality. Just as the life of Jesus led to new and eternal life, so too the Christian response to God's self-communication is a confidence that Jesus is the firstborn of many, that the destiny of his life in God's Spirit is the destiny not only of the Christians who follow him explicitly but of all who respond to God's self-communication according to the pattern of his self-transcendence.

Eschatology

Finally, what is the end or final goal of God's gracious self-communication to human existence? Once again this question finds its answer in the life of Jesus. For the central message that Jesus preached, and that for which he dedicated his life and action, was the kingdom of God. The kingdom of God is an eschatological idea; it is utopic, referring to something not of this world but of the absolute future. This does not mean that the kingdom of God cannot find fragmentary realization in this world—without that there would be no grounds for hope. But its completion can only be fully realized in another eschatological sphere. And this raises the question of the relation between God's self-communication to human existence in this world and the final kingdom of God.

The theology of grace has always held a strict continuity between God's self-communication to human beings in this world and final salvation. Salvation is being united with God, and the self-communication of God's own self to human existence now is not essentially different from what Catholic theology has called the ultimate self-communication of God that constitutes union with God in beatific vision and love.

But an integral spirituality of action in response to grace is concerned with the spiritual value of all the dimensions of human existence and the potential of the full range of human action to unite one with God. Such a spirituality must ask whether the creative exercise of human freedom in this world really counts. Does human action, which at bottom constitutes one's union with God in this world, also have any final value? Does what human freedom actually accomplishes in this world, initiated by and unfolding within the power of cooperative grace, make any ultimate difference? Or is the creativity of freedom really an illusion, simply a test, or an ultimately indifferent means for individuals passing into eternal life?

Liberation theology, because of its concern for human freedom and for action in the world that corresponds to the action of Jesus engendered by his conception of the kingdom of God, postulates a continuity between the effects of action performed in grace and the ultimate reality of the kingdom of God. In this view of things, by cooperative grace, human beings contribute to the eschatological reality of the kingdom of God, and human action shares the absolute value of the kingdom of God itself. Without some conception such as this, it would be impossible to hold that the creative freedom of human beings within history had any intrinsic and final coherence. It would also be impossible to have an integral spirituality that affirmed the ultimate value of all aspects of human life. Positively, such a continuous eschatology explains the purpose of grace as bestowing meaning on human life in history.

Conclusion

The theology of grace today lays the theological foundations for an integral vision of the Christian life. Stimulated by the Second Vatican Council, especially its Pastoral Constitution on the Church in the Modern World, it has brought its conception of grace into line with Christian life in the world of today. Drawing from the sources for a theology of grace in Scripture and the history of theology, it proposes that grace is God's self-communication to the human person within the full range of human life. Grace touches both the passive

and the active dimensions of human freedom. To human weakness, sin, sickness,
suffering, and ultimate death, God's self-
communication restores wholeness. To
human strength, to invention and creativity, God's self-communication provides
empowerment according to God's values
as revealed in Jesus. An integral Christian
spirituality consists in a human response to
this self-presence of God as Spirit in all the
dimensions of human life. In every case,
however, the summons of God's grace calls
for an active response in whatever measure
is possible, because only in human action is
such a response made real. In the end,
human action in response to God's grace
constitutes union with God.

See also ANTHROPOLOGY, THEOLOGICAL; CHRIST;
DISCIPLESHIP; DIVINIZATION; ESCHATOLOGY; FAITH;
FORGIVENESS; HOLY SPIRIT; HOPE; KINGDOM OF GOD;
LIBERATION THEOLOGY, INFLUENCE ON SPIRITUAL-
ITY; LOVE; PRAXIS; PROTESTANT SPIRITUALITIES; SIN;
TRINITARIAN SPIRITUALITY.

Bibliography: H. G. Anderson, et al., eds., *Justification
by Faith: Lutherans and Catholics in Dialogue VII*
(Minneapolis: Augsburg, 1985). C. Ernst, ed., *The Gos-
pel of Grace* (Oxford: Blackfriars, 1972). W. Oates, ed.,
Basic Writings of Saint Augustine (New York: Random
House, 1948). M. Blondel, *Action: Essay on a Critique
of Life and a Science of Practice,* trans. O. Blanchette
(Notre Dame, Ind.: Univ. of Notre Dame Press, 1984).
R. Haight, *The Experience and Language of Grace*
(New York: Paulist, 1979). H. Grimm, ed., *The Free-
dom of the Christian,* Luther's Works 30 (Philadelphia:
Fortress, 1957). J. Pelikan, ed. and trans., *Lectures on
Galatians,* Luther's Works 26 (St. Louis: Concordia,
1963). K. Rahner, *Foundations of Christian Faith: An
Introduction to the Idea of Christianity,* trans. W. Dych
(New York: Seabury, 1978); "The Order of Redemp-
tion Within the Order of Creation," *The Christian
Commitment,* trans. C. Hastings (New York: Sheed
and Ward, 1963). E. Schillebeeckx, *Christ: The Experi-
ence of Jesus as Lord,* trans. J. Bowden (New York:
Crossroad, 1980). J. Segundo, *The Humanist
Christology of Paul,* trans. J. Drury (Maryknoll, N.Y.:
Orbis, 1986).

ROGER HAIGHT, S.J.

GRAIL, THE

See AMERICAN SPIRITUALITY; LAY SPIR-
ITUALITY.

GRATITUDE

Gratitude and the related idea of thanksgiving are both responses, signs of self-
transcendence in response to life as gift.
Fundamental in both the experience of
gratitude and the expression of thanksgiving are the mature realization of the contingent nature of human existence and a
recognition in that realization of an invitation to a relationship with the other whose
gift is life itself.

Gratitude derives from the medieval
Latin *gratitudo* and the Latin *gratus,* meaning "thankful." It is related to the family of
Latin words that includes *gratia,* meaning
"favor," "grace," or "gift." The word
thanksgiving has Germanic and Anglo-
Saxon origins, and translates the Greek
eucharistia, whose root is *charis,* "gift" or
"grace," from which we derive the word
charism. Thanksgiving implies an active
response to another's favor or gift, a recognition of the other, and a willingness to respond graciously, especially to God.

Gratitude and thanksgiving are both
radically self-transcendent attitudes and
acts by which we orient ourselves toward
another in recognition of the other's freely
given gift, favor, or care. As the ultimate
source of all life and freedom, God is
preeminently worthy of our gratitude and
thankfulness, not only as the object of our
gratitude but as the subject of a relationship that itself gives rise to the feeling of
gratitude and urges acts of thanksgiving. In
the act of giving thanks in gratefulness, the
very contingency under which we labor as
human beings in this world can be transformed. Our hearts and minds and lives
can be opened to an understanding of our
calling to a final transcendence which far
surpasses anything we can imagine here
and now and for which we are prepared by
our present response to God's graciousness
(see Eph 1:16-23).

Our sharing in the table of the Lord, the
eucharist of the Church, is both our response to God's gracious gift of his Son and

the act by which we proclaim our unity in the Body of Christ "until he comes" (1 Cor 11:26).

See also CHARISM; EUCHARIST; GRACE.

Bibliography: G. Kittel, TDNT 9, ed. G. Friedrich (Grand Rapids, Mich.: Eerdmans, 1974), s.vv. *charis* (pp. 372ff.) and *eucharistia* (pp. 407ff.).

BENJAMIN BAYNHAM, O.C.S.O.

GREED

See CONSUMERISM; DEADLY SINS; MATERIALISM.

GROWTH, DEVELOPMENT, PROGRESS IN THE SPIRITUAL LIFE

See JOURNEY (GROWTH AND DEVELOPMENT IN SPIRITUAL LIFE); PSYCHOLOGY, RELATIONSHIP AND CONTRIBUTION TO SPIRITUALITY; SELF; THREE AGES; THREE WAYS.

H

See SPIRITUAL WRITING, GENRES OF.

HAGIOGRAPHY

See SPIRITUAL WRITING, GENRES OF.

HANDICAPPED

See DISABILITY, THE DISABLED.

HAPPINESS

See BEATIFIC VISION; BEATITUDE(S).

HEALING

Experience

Health and wholeness are primary values for human beings. They are considered to be basic conditions for human happiness. Conversely, illness and impairment are undesirable and are considered to be obstacles to human happiness. Human beings sense that their physical, emotional, mental, psychic, spiritual, and social dimensions should be in harmony. Loss or breakdown in these areas is a negative experience, to be overcome or compensated for. Even death is resisted.

When health or wholeness is absent, people seek an explanation, if not a remedy. The more intelligible and demonstrable the explanation, the more credible it is. When such an explanation is not given, people suspect forces or causes that they cannot comprehend. These are often couched in spiritual, mystical, or religious terms and are usually associated with some

notion of sin and evil. This type of explanation can take on the force of truth over a period of time, which makes it difficult for more empirical, alternative explanations to be accepted. This is one reason why science and religion have often been in opposition.

Whatever the explanation of illness, healing is the remedy. The possibilities for healing, however, are directly related to the explanation of what must be healed. Those healers who work exclusively with natural resources have developed the healing professions of medicine, psychology, and social service, supported by research and technology in those fields. Those who use only spiritual resources have developed various forms of faith healing, mediated by prayers, invocations, rituals, and secret formulas. Many combine the two, using scientific skill and resources within a spiritual worldview (the approach favored by Vatican II in the Pastoral Constitution on the Church in the Modern World, GS 36).

The need for healing may be seen at three levels of human existence. The first is basic survival. This pertains mostly to physical well-being and the means for achieving it. Here the hygienic, medical, and therapeutic arts are especially operative, supported by research in cognate fields.

The second level is human dignity. This pertains to a person's acceptance by self and others and the ability to interact with other people and groups. Here the psychological and educational professions are most operative, supported by social institutions like government and organized religion.

The third level is moral and spiritual. This pertains to a person's sense of right and wrong and attitude toward the meaning of life, especially when faced with its termination in death. Here religious and spiritual ministry is distinctively operative, although the psychological and educational professions have major contributions to make as well. All three levels interpenetrate and complement one another. Ultimately the different dimensions of human life cannot be separated from one another, as the current movement of holistic health and wellness advocates.

The desire for health and the need for healing are universal phenomena in human experience. On the one hand, they point to the human capacity to envision alternative situations and to change circumstances as they are found. On the other hand, they point out the human limitations in trying to achieve final or lasting happiness. Christians, of course, share this human condition and have reflected upon, and responded to, it in distinctive ways.

Theological Reflection

Jesus healed. The testimony of the Gospels shows him responding to people at the level of basic need (curing the blind, the lame, the paralyzed); at the level of human dignity (forgiving the adulteress, honoring Zacchaeus); and at the level of morality and the meaning of life (living the beatitudes, raising the dead). All his healings (cures) were done for the sake of the kingdom of God; they were not ends in themselves. He healed in order to remove obstacles to a person's awareness of God's presence and to elicit a new response to God's love.

Jesus' example sets the pattern for Christian healing. There is always a twofold expectation: healing from the immediate illness or problem and healing for a closer union with God in the circumstances of one's life. Both Jesus and the Christian tradition maintain that it is not necessary to have the first in order to have the second, although the desire for both is natural and appropriate. The priority is always the health of one's relationship with God, no matter what other kind of healing may be needed.

Prior to the Second Vatican Council, healing was channeled through two forms in the Catholic Church. One was the sacrament of anointing, and the other was an array of devotions and pious practices. The sacrament possessed an intrinsically greater dignity and value, but in the popular consciousness it often did not address human emotion and need as effectively as other forms of devotion. In addition, anointing was reserved for the last stages of a person's life before death, thus limiting its effectiveness in situations that required healing but were not life-threatening.

Vatican II revised the sacramental rite of anointing, properly locating it within a more comprehensive pastoral care of the sick. The council also clarified the connection that should exist between popular devotions and the liturgy (SC 13). At the same time, the council awakened new interest in the Holy Spirit, whose healing presence among the people of God has become a major postconciliar factor. These changes have led to a new pastoral praxis regarding healing.

Pastoral Praxis

The current pastoral praxis of the Church takes three main forms. The first is sacramental, and the central rite of sacramental healing is the anointing of the sick. As the general introduction to the rite clarifies: "This sacrament gives the grace of the Holy Spirit to those who are sick: by this grace the whole person is helped and saved, sustained by trust in God, and strengthened against the temptations of the Evil One and against anxiety over death" (OU 6). The emphasis is on the healing of the whole person. This is accomplished through the grace of the Holy Spirit, who sustains the person's trust in God. What about physical healing? The rite goes on: "A return to physical health may follow the reception of this sacrament if it will be beneficial to the sick person's salvation." The rite does not claim a causal connection if recovery occurs but clarifies the value of such a recovery in terms of the spiritual well-being of the person. The rite does clarify that "sickness cannot as a general rule be regarded as a punishment inflicted on each individual for personal sin" (OU 2). Nonetheless, anointing can provide for the forgiveness of sin if a person is unable to celebrate the sacrament of penance. It is desirable, of course, that a person be able to experience the special spiritual benefits of sacramental reconciliation.

The second form of pastoral praxis in the Church today is charismatic healing. Like the sacrament of anointing, it is a manifestation of the grace of the Holy Spirit, although it is conveyed in a freer manner and often results in some physical improvement. Charismatic healing usually takes place within a communal gathering arranged with Scripture readings, preaching, prayer, and song. The communal setting is a reminder that the sacrament of anointing is also supposed to be a communal celebration.

The third form of pastoral praxis is counseling. Pastoral counseling is not overtly as spiritual or ritualized as either the sacrament of anointing or charismatic healing. It relies on the insights and methods developed in the various counseling disciplines and usually works in a slower, repetitive, and less dramatic way than the other two. A pastoral counselor helps a counselee achieve wholeness by examining all the parts of one's life in relation to God's desire for human happiness. The counseling relationship itself is an integral part of this process, often leading to a spiritual bonding that is healing for both counselor and counselee.

Spiritual direction, another form of pastoral praxis, uses a method similar to counseling and may occasionally touch on areas needing psychological or emotional healing. Spiritual direction in itself is not aimed at such therapy but may be the occasion for referring a directee to a therapist. In any event, spiritual direction is unlikely to achieve its goal of deepening a person's relationship with God if there are major obstacles to the person's psychic or emotional well-being.

The human person is a complex whole consisting of many dimensions that influence one another. Healing may be focused on one or another aspect of a person's life, but the whole person is healed. In the Christian tradition, such healing is always a sign of God's love and presence and has the spiritual benefit of bringing a person closer to God, even if the expected healing does not occur. As the *Pastoral Care of the Sick* indicates, "Part of the plan laid out by God's providence is that we should fight strenuously against all sickness and carefully seek the blessings of good health, so that we may fulfill our role in human society and in the Church" (OU 3).

See also CHARISMATIC RENEWAL; PSYCHOLOGY, RELATIONSHIP AND CONTRIBUTION TO SPIRITUALITY; SPIRITUAL DIRECTION; SUFFERING.

Bibliography: J. McManus, *The Healing Power of the Sacraments* (Notre Dame, Ind.: Ave Maria, 1984).

ROBERT L. KINAST

HEALTH

See BODY; HOLISTIC SPIRITUALITY; LEISURE.

HEART

The heart symbolizes the center or core of the human person. It is the locus not only of our affectivity but also of our freedom and consciousness, the place where we accept or reject the mystery of ourselves, human existence, and God. The heart is sacred space. There we get in touch with the truth of our being and are open to the presence of God in our lives.

Biblical and patristic writers regarded the heart as a symbol of the whole person. In the OT the word *heart* connotes the principle of our personal life, the depth of our integration and insight, the center of our thinking, feeling, and deciding. This view also underlies the NT notion of the heart.

Augustinian spirituality speaks of "the eyes of the heart," which are enlightened by faith and love of neighbor to see God. The desert writers of the 4th century wrote about "the prayer of the heart," which simplified their desires in their search for God.

In medieval spirituality, for example in the writings of Bonaventure and Thomas Aquinas, there is an emphasis on affectivity as the center of our desire for God. Catherine of Siena saw the heart as the place where truth and love are unified. Martin Luther viewed the believing heart as clinging to God's word of grace. For John of the Cross, the heart is a religious symbol that both instructs and moves.

Contemporary spirituality of the heart tends to be holistic and incarnational, approaching the heart as a reality that is both corporeal and spiritual, a symbol of the mystery of the whole person. A spirituality of the heart invites us to accept our own and others' sufferings and joys as a way of living the paschal mystery. It views the heart as the place of conversion that leads to adoration and compassion. Such a spirituality brings about healing, transformation, and communion, and works in solidarity with the poor and the oppressed to promote peace and justice.

Jean Vanier's spirituality of the heart builds communion through shared vulnerability, in particular with handicapped people. Henri Nouwen's spirituality of the compassionate heart views the heart as home.

Heart language represents a nonconceptual way of knowing. Building on Aquinas's notion of affective connatural-ity, Bernard Lonergan speaks of affectivity as separate from cognition. For him, moral self-transcendence has to do in part with the development of feeling. He calls the heart's reasons feelings that are intentional responses to values. And faith is the loving knowledge of God's love flooding our hearts. Robert Doran, building on Lonergan's threefold schema of moral, intellectual, and religious conversion, has described affective or psychic conversion as a dimension of the conversion of the heart.

According to Karl Rahner, the heart is a primordial word as opposed to a technical word of utility. Like *mother* and *star,* the word *heart* defies definition and points beyond itself to mystery. It refers to the mystery of personal unity in multiplicity, of the whole in the part and the part in the whole. The heart is a symbol, since it causes and contains the reality of love it signifies. It is both the blood-pumping organ of the body and the center of our interiority. The heart is not necessarily a symbol of love; contrary to the sentimental notion perpetuated by Valentine's Day, it can be empty or full of love.

Today we speak of experiences of God, and some call these experiences of the heart. As the place of God's presence in our lives and of our deepest choices, the heart can be considered a symbol of grace and freedom. Native people use the image of the moist heart. Robert Bellah and other North American sociologists have written of "habits of the heart." Others may prefer to talk about desire, affectivity, union with God, or experiences of the Spirit.

See also AFFECT, AFFECTIVITY; COMPASSION; DESIRE; FEELINGS; HEART OF CHRIST; LOVE; MERCY.

Bibliography: A. Callahan, ed., *Spiritualities of the Heart* (New York: Paulist, 1990). A. Díez Macho, "The Heart in the Bible: Symbol of the Person," *With a Human Heart,* ed. E. Cuskelly (Kensington, Australia: Chevalier, 1981) 42–68. T. O'Donnell, *Heart of the Redeemer* (Manassas, Va.: Trinity Communications, 1989).

ANNICE CALLAHAN, R.S.C.J.

HEART OF CHRIST

The heart of Christ symbolizes the center of Christ's humanity. It is the locus of his affectivity, freedom, and consciousness, the place where he surrendered to the mystery of God and of life. It is an unambiguous symbol of love.

Devotion to the Sacred Heart as a means of developing a personal relationship with Jesus has taken several forms in the history of Christian spirituality. The Beloved Disciple expressed his dedication to the Lord by resting his head on Jesus' breast at the Last Supper. The writers of the early Church saw in the outpouring of blood and water from the pierced side of Jesus on the cross the origin of the Church.

In the Middle Ages Christians practiced a devotion to the five wounds of Jesus, in particular to his pierced side, and then more specifically to his heart. Bonaventure and Thomas Aquinas mention the heart of Christ in their scriptural and devotional writings. Mystics influenced by Cistercian spirituality at the convent of Helfta in Germany, including Gertrude the Great, Mechtild of Magdeburg, and Mechtild of Hackeborn, claimed to have experienced revelations of the heart of Jesus. In the account of her tenth revelation, Julian of Norwich records a vision of the heart of Jesus split in two. Catherine of Siena speaks of an exchange of hearts with Jesus.

In the 17th century, devotion to the Sacred Heart became popular in Western Europe. Jane de Chantal and Francis de Sales wrote often about the heart of Jesus. John Eudes promoted the institution of the Feast of the Immaculate Heart of Mary in 1646 and that of the Sacred Heart of Jesus in 1672. Margaret Mary Alacoque, a French Sister of the Visitation, claimed to have received visions of the heart of Jesus between 1673 and 1675, motivating her to encourage frequent Communion, Communion on the first Friday of every month, a Holy Hour on Thursdays, and the annual celebration of a Feast of the Sacred Heart.

The annual liturgical feast of the Sacred Heart was approved for Poland in 1765 and for the universal Church in 1856.

Protestant as well as Catholic spirituality has recognized the heart of Christ as the symbol and center of the person of Christ. For example, Thomas Goodwin wrote a treatise in 1643 entitled *The Heart of Christ in Heaven Towards Sinners on Earth.* Charles Wesley wrote of the heart of Christ in his well-known hymns.

In the 19th century Popes Pius IX and Leo XIII supported the practices connected with the 17th-century form of the devotion. Leo XIII consecrated the whole world to the Sacred Heart of Jesus in 1899.

In the 1950s theologians deemed it imperative to reflect on the technical details about the material and formal object of the devotion to the Sacred Heart in order to decide if its object is Christ's heart as such or the love of God. Pius XII wrote an encyclical entitled *Haurietis Aquas* on the devotion. The Second Vatican Council stated that the incarnate Son "loved with a human heart" (GS 22). In *Redemptor Hominis* Pope John Paul II links the fullness of justice in Christ's heart with the redemption of the world.

Contemporary theologians have contributed significantly to a rethinking of the devotion by disengaging the symbol of the heart of Christ from cultural practices connected with the devotion. Pierre Teilhard de Chardin speaks of the heart of the cosmic Christ as the heart of matter, fire, and energy, the heart of the world in *The Hymn of the Universe.* In *Das Herz der Welt,* Hans Urs von Balthasar deals with the mystery of suffering in God. Bernard Häring has written a book called *Heart of Jesus: Symbol of Redeeming Love.* Rosemary Haughton has focused on the desire of the heart of Jesus that we start living the prophetic vision of a transformed society.

Karl Rahner situates the symbol in the context of Christology, emphasizing the heart of Christ as a symbol of the center of his person rather than as a symbol of love.

He grounds his rethinking of the practice of consoling the Lord in the practice of a Holy Hour of reparation before the Blessed Sacrament in the context of soteriology, observing that Christ now glorified was consoled by our co-suffering with him (*Mit-leiden*). He insists that the heart of Christ contains and mediates the grace it signifies through the life, passion, death, and resurrection of Christ. Furthermore, he thinks that the devotion could be refocused on the love of neighbor in an era marked by an optimism about the possibility of universal salvation, by secularization, materialism, and the need to ask basic questions about God's existence and Jesus' salvific role. Rahner challenges us to become women and men of the pierced heart, willing to be in touch with our own hearts and to let our hearts be pierced by suffering and evil in order to reveal the power of God's love in powerlessness and weakness.

Today reinterpretation of devotion to the Sacred Heart contributes to a contemporary spirituality of the heart of Christ. It shifts the focus from practices connected with the devotion to attitudes underlying a spirituality, for example gratitude, trust, mercy, and compassion. The emphasis is on commitment to the person of Christ and to the service of God's people in faith through the promotion of peace and justice.

See also CHRIST; COMPASSION; DEVOTION(S), POPULAR; HEART; INCARNATION; KENOSIS; LOVE; MERCY; WEAKNESS AND VULNERABILITY.

Bibliography: A. Callahan, *Karl Rahner's Spirituality of the Pierced Heart* (Lanham, Md.: Univ. Press of America, 1985). T. O'Donnell, *Heart of the Redeemer* (Manassas, Va.: Trinity Communications, 1990). J. Stierli, ed., *Heart of the Savior,* trans. P. Andrews (New York: Herder, 1957). R. Vekemans, ed., *Cor Christi: Historia—Teologia—Espiritualidad y Pastoral* (Bogotá: Instituto Internacional del Corazon de Jesus, 1980).

ANNICE CALLAHAN, R.S.C.J.

HEAVEN

See AFTERLIFE.

HELL

See AFTERLIFE.

HERMENEUTICS

See INTERPRETATION; SCRIPTURE.

HERMIT(S)

See EREMITICAL LIFE.

HESYCHASM

The word *hesychasm* derives from the Greek *hēsychia,* meaning "quiet" or "stillness." Although the term *hesychast* can be used to designate a hermit as opposed to a cenobitic monk, it is normally employed more restrictively to designate one who uses the Jesus Prayer and the physical technique connected with it. In its most limited frame of reference, hesychasts were those who supported the position of St. Gregory Palamas (1296–1359) that direct, unmediated experience of God is possible in this life.

The four essential elements that distinguish Hesychasm are devotion to the name of Jesus, a keen sense of sorrow for sin, the discipline of frequent repetition, and a nondiscursive, imageless prayer leading to inner silence. Even though references to all these elements can be found in 4th-century monastic literature, it was Diadochus of Photice (second half of the 5th century) who first connected and presented them as a practical method of prayer. The standard form of the Jesus Prayer ("Lord Jesus Christ, Son of God, have mercy on me") is first found in the *Life of Abba Philemon,* a 6th-century (?) Egyptian monk. More so than Diadochus, he affirms the need for inward grief and repentance. The Jesus Prayer was also recommended by St. John Climacus (7th century) and his followers. In his *Ladder of Divine Ascent,* Climacus teaches that prayer should be simple and thus lead to stillness. He was the first to use the term "Jesus Prayer."

References to the Jesus Prayer in the early literature are scattered, undeveloped, and infrequent. The first significant reference to a physical technique linking the recitation of the Jesus Prayer with the rhythm of breathing is to be found in the writings of Nicephorus the Hesychast, a 13th-century monk of Mount Athos. Nicephorus recommends that the one praying sit with the chin resting on the chest and the gaze focusing on the navel. Next, the rhythm of respiration is to be slowed down. While thus employed, the one praying should focus inwardly upon the place of the heart. Only when the mind and heart have been joined in this manner does the one praying begin to invoke the name of Jesus in the standard form— "Lord Jesus Christ, Son of God, have mercy on me." The invocation of the name serves to keep guard over the heart and to dispel the tendency toward discursive thought.

A generation after Nicephorus, Gregory of Sinai (d. 1346) made the Jesus Prayer central to his spirituality. He used to expand the standard formula to "... have mercy on me, a sinner" and also recommended the use of shortened forms, while cautioning against changing them too frequently. He commends the physical technique favored by Nicephorus, teaching that the object is the control of distracting thoughts. The use of the Jesus Prayer should be continuous as far as possible in order to attain imageless prayer. But although discursive thought is to be resisted, not all emotions are to be rejected. In particular, the practice of the Jesus Prayer ought to lead to a sense of joyful sorrow.

Gregory of Sinai connects the Jesus Prayer with baptism, seeing in it the means whereby the presence of the Holy Spirit given secretly in baptism is made conscious to the one praying. He teaches that when a person becomes consciously aware of the presence of the Holy Spirit, there results a feeling of warmth in the heart, leading to a contemplation of the divine light.

Although he does not talk about this divine light theologically, it is clear that what he has in mind is an immediate experience of God.

It was on this point that the Hesychasts were attacked between 1337 and 1347 by Barlaam the Calabrian (ca. 1290–1348). The Hesychasts' position was taken up and defended by St. Gregory Palamas (1296–1359). The debate centered on the correct interpretation of the writings of Dionysius the Areopagite. For Barlaam, Dionysius wrote as a philosophical theologian, and his doctrine thus excludes any direct knowledge of God in this life. Thus Barlaam held that, contrary to the Hesychasts' claim, seeing the uncreated light of the Godhead is impossible. He further denounced the physical technique they recommended as materialistic and superstitious.

Without denying the incomprehensibility of God, Gregory Palamas, who saw Dionysius as a mystic, drew a distinction between God's inner essence and energies. God's essence remains radically unknowable not only in the present life but even in the life to come. Only God can know God, but Gregory maintained that God is knowable through acts of divine power called "energies," which permeate creation. These energies are not intermediaries between God and creation, but God actually at work in creation. Seeing God at work in creation and in the self, people are seeing God directly.

The real point of dispute between Gregory Palamas and Barlaam was eschatological: Is the vision of God reserved only for the life to come, or is it realized to any extent in the present? It was Gregory's intention to strike a balance between the transcendence and immanence of God in order to uphold the possibility of direct communion with God. In fact, what Gregory terms "uncreated energies" he also calls "grace"; the light seen in contemplation is a manifestation of this grace, the same light seen by the apostles in the vision of Christ's transfiguration on Mount Tabor. The one who beholds this light is caught up in the mystery of the transfiguration and transformed. Much like the experience of the stigmata in the West, the vision of uncreated light is a foretaste of the glorification of the body at the parousia.

This insistence on the glorification of the body at the parousia points to the line of reasoning used to defend the physical technique employed by the Hesychasts. Although Gregory Palamas, and indeed all those who recommended the technique, considered it to be auxiliary and secondary, Gregory maintained the biblical doctrine of the human person as an integrated whole. If body and soul are united, and if the body will experience resurrection and a glorification similar to that of Christ, then it follows that in this life body and soul mutually influence each other, and so the body has an important role to play in prayer.

The position of Gregory Palamas was affirmed by a synod held at Constantinople in 1341, whereupon Barlaam withdrew to Sicily, and again in 1347 and 1351, after the controversy had been raised again by supporters of Barlaam, aided by political opponents. The question raised by Barlaam—whether the distinction of essence and energy in God introduces division into the divine simplicity—and the extent to which it can be maintained that Gregory's doctrine is based on the writings of the Fathers, continued to be discussed both within Orthodoxy and with Western critics.

From the fall of Constantinople to the Ottoman Turks in 1453 until the beginning of the 19th century, Orthodox theology and spirituality clung to a rigid traditionalism. The most significant movement in spirituality during this period was what is known as the Hesychast renaissance in the latter part of the 18th century. Of primary importance is a collection of spiritual texts drawn from patristic writings called the *Philokalia,* which was edited by Nico-

demus of the Holy Mountain (1749–1809) and Macarius of Corinth (1731–1805). The editors, who intended their work for all Christians, emphasized the need for spiritual direction, the link between spirituality and dogma, and the Jesus Prayer as the means of achieving stillness and continuous prayer. It is largely through the *Philokalia,* which was translated from Greek into the languages of the Orthodox peoples and those of the West as well, that the tradition of the Jesus Prayer has become so widely employed in contemporary Orthodoxy and in the Latin West.

See also BREATH, BREATHING; CENTERING PRAYER; EASTERN CHRISTIAN SPIRITUALITY; NEGATIVE WAY.

Bibliography: V. Lossky, *The Mystical Theology of the Eastern Church,* trans. Fellowship of St. Alban and St. Sergius (London: James Clark, 1957). *The Philokalia,* trans. G.E.H. Palmer, P. Sherrard, and K. Ware, 3 vols. to date (London and Boston: Faber, 1979–84). *Writings from the Philokalia on Prayer of the Heart,* trans. E. Kadloubovsky and G.E.H. Palmer (London: Faber, 1951). K. Ware, "The Origins of the Jesus Prayer: Diadochus, Gaza, Sinai"; "The Hesychasts: Gregory of Sinai, Gregory Palamas, Nicolas Cabasilas"; and "The Hesychast Renaissance," in *The Study of Spirituality,* ed. C. Jones, G. Wainwright, and E. Yarnold (New York and Oxford: Oxford Univ. Press, 1986) 175–184; 242–258.

RONALD J. ZAWILLA

HISPANIC-AMERICAN SPIRITUALITY

Any study of Hispanic-American spirituality must take into account the complex expressions of the relationship between the Hispanic American and the transcendent. The complexity stems from the heterogeneity and the richness of the spiritual traditions of the Hispanic-American people in the United States. Hispanic Americans come not only from different countries but also from different social backgrounds, which have been influenced by a variety of cultural factors and indigenous religious beliefs and practices; the latter in turn have been affected by the social, educational, and secular influences of North American culture and the various Christian movements throughout America's history.

In an attempt to understand the living spirit of Hispanic Americans' religious expressions and life, the focus here will be primarily on the common religious grounding of the faith-experience of the ordinary Christian in the United States. From this perspective, the following topics will be treated: religious background, common characteristics, and present challenges.

Religious Background

If religion is the common ground of the many complex cultural values of the Hispanic-American people, spirituality is the key to understanding their unique tradition of a deeply imbedded faith that is inseparable from life. Life is seen as sacred, filled with the presence of the divine. The Hispanic soul is spiritually oriented, and from this spiritual orientation flows the Hispanic-American understanding of the human person and the meaning of life. The uniqueness and thrust of this spirituality derive mainly from the historical encounter of two different religious cultures: the indigenous pre-Columbian culture of the Americas and the Iberian-European culture introduced after Columbus's discovery of America. In addition, some of the Caribbean islands and part of Brazil were influenced by the native African religious experience.

Pre-Columbian American religious beliefs were extremely complex. The native American understanding of the communion between the human and the cosmic reality was rooted in the spiritual world. A sense of mystery and of symbolic meaning in all reality and the importance of life's rituals were an essential part of the native American tradition. As the Indo-American oral traditions demonstrate, the spiritual and transcendent were seen as the essence of the cosmic and human harmony in the life-death cycle.

The arrival of the Spaniards in America brought an encounter between two different worlds with their own religious views and culture. The rational and literal, hierarchical and sacramental Catholicism of the Spaniards would transform, although never completely, the mythic and oral, collective and symbolic indigenous religious culture. The Spaniards identified strongly with the Christian cross, which had stood for eight centuries against the presence of the Muslim crescent within their country.

In the succeeding centuries European missionaries—mainly Franciscans, Augustinians, and Dominicans, followed by the Jesuits—brought to America a Catholicism of sacramental practice, popular devotion, communal participation, dramatic expression, and ascetic and mystical idealism. The Spanish humanism and mysticism of the Catholic Reformation blended with the strong indigenous piety in the newly discovered lands. (The Spanish mysticism of Teresa of Avila and John of the Cross is well known.) The roots of this Spanish Catholicism were grounded in medieval religious thinking and its supernatural vision. The new European humanism of the time also influenced the attempts of the missionaries to establish a Christian civilization in the New World. Bartolomé de las Casas, Antonio de Valdivieso, Bernardino de Sahagún, Toribio de Mongrovejo, Vasco de Quiroga, among many others, are examples of those who attempted to protect the sense of dignity and the religious culture of the native inhabitants of the New World. Post-Tridentine Catholicism, with its doctrinal, disciplinary, and strict sacramental uniformity, prevented a deeper blending with the indigenous religious forms. The process of sacramentalization, pious devotions, festive celebrations, and dramatic plays based on Jesus' life and sufferings flourished. While appreciating the values of this piety and stressing its possible weaknesses, the modern documents of Medellín (1968) and Puebla (1979) inaugurated the post-Vatican II era of an evangelizing and prophetic Church.

Common Characteristics

Hispanic-American spirituality may be characterized as personal and communal, sacramental, and popular. Hispanic humanism reflects a deep appreciation for the dignity of the person and places great value on interpersonal relations within the family and society. The mark of the Creator is on each person, and God cares for all persons, especially children, the poor, the sick, and the elderly. Family relationships, extending even to godparents and close friends, are profound and sacred, and are expressed in terms of reverential respect, protection, and affection. Hospitality and solidarity, especially in times of grief, are cherished. Traditionally, the family more than the parish has been the matrix of Hispanic spirituality and religious traditions—what Virgilio Elizondo has called "homespun religion." The family is the primary transmitter of religious beliefs, values, and traditions.

The Hispanic spirit relates meaningfully to ritual symbolism and sacramentality. Consequently, the sense of the sacred in life and of the divine presence in it calls for festive ritual expressions, which form an integral part of Hispanic-American religious life, despite the modern Anglo-American environment of secularization. This *sensus fidei* is lived creatively and reverently in ways well beyond the Catholic sacraments and is expressed not only in church but at home and in the streets. Traditionally, faith and life have been inseparable in this rich religious-cultural heritage. Art and folklore, processions and festivals, especially in veneration of saints and in the celebration of Christmas-Epiphany, with its pageants and *pastorelas,* and of Holy Week, with its dramas of Christ's passion, have been important components of rituals for the people.

Within this fervent popular piety, adoration of Christ and veneration of the Blessed Virgin Mary are preeminent in Hispanic American spirituality. Christ is worshiped as Savior and Suffering Servant (Santo Christo); as King and Infant God (Niño Dios); as a loving and merciful Person (Sacred Heart); and even as a loving Father (Padre Jesús) who cares for his children and understands human sinfulness. The relationship with the crucified Christ has a strong appeal because his suffering mirrors their own rejection as a migrant and often marginalized people. The Spanish roots are apparent in their Christocentrism as well as in the intense Marian spirituality characteristic of Latin American countries.

Most Hispanic nationalities in the United States celebrate their devotion to Mary as the Mother of Jesus, the Mother of God, and our Mother (Madre Santísima). Guadalupe (Mexico), Altagracia (Dominican Republic), Caridad del Cobre (Cuba), Providencia (Puerto Rico), Luján (Argentina) are among the most popular names of Marian devotion. The Guadalupe event became a central and powerful symbol, not only of religious faith and spirituality but also of human liberation and new life in the history of the Mexican people and in the lives of many Hispanic Americans. Because of Our Lady of Guadalupe's importance for the Americas, a national feast in her honor was approved for the United States in 1988.

Present Challenges

If this richness and depth of spiritual life and cultural values are to be preserved, they must be respected and cherished. A secularized environment, lack of adequate Christian education, and unwelcoming institutions are the greatest concerns. The ever-growing presence of Hispanics presents a great challenge to the Catholic Church, but it also holds great potential for renewal and growth. The Church's official response to these challenges has been clearly stated by the American bishops. The National Pastoral Plan for Hispanic Ministry (1987) summarizes the pastoral strategies for safeguarding and promoting Hispanic-American spirituality in "a model of church that is: communitarian, evangelizing and missionary, incarnate in the reality of the Hispanic people and open to the diversity of cultures, a promoter and example of justice . . . that develops leadership through integral education . . . that is leaven for the kingdom of God in society" (*Origins,* p. 454).

Today many spiritual movements of basic Christian communities and groups demand institutional flexibility and welcoming support, including charismatics, Movimiento Familiar Cristiano, Comunidades Neocatecumenales, and the traditional, popular, and Christ-centered Cursillo de Cristiandad. The biblical renewal has been especially successful and will probably be a more far-reaching spiritual movement in the future of Hispanic spirituality, as Bishop Ricardo Ramirez has pointed out: "Hispanics may be on the verge of a new biblical spirituality" (Ramirez, p. 11). Therein lies the appeal, among many other factors, of evangelical Protestant Churches to Hispanics. Still not fully developed but very promising and necessary is the implementation of the Rite of Christian Initiation of Adults. This is the key to evangelization and a sense of Christian mission beyond routine sacramentalization.

This concern over the need for evangelization, conversion, and religious formation, justified as it is, must respect the Hispanic orientation toward the sacred and the ritual in popular piety. A welcoming, inclusive, and nurturing community environment is also essential. In this regard, the need for full acceptance and incorporation of Hispanics into the wider, culturally sensitive Christian community has been stressed, for, as the National Pastoral Plan for Hispanic Ministry points out, "the great majority of Hispanic people feel distant or marginated from the Catholic Church" (*Origins,* p. 451). However, the same document advises, "integration is not to be confused with assimilation" (*Origins,* p. 451).

Finally, there is urgent need for the formation of leaders and Christian basic communities. The problem of the scarcity of Hispanic clergy and of educated grassroots leaders is compounded by the uprootedness and marginalization experienced by many immigrants, especially in urban neighborhoods. The need for formation and support of basic Christian communities is also very important for ecclesial and cultural reasons; community is very important to the Hispanic spirit. While the present challenges are many, the future of the Hispanic-American community in the United States is promising. The National Pastoral Plan for Hispanic Ministry calls these challenges "a blessing from God" (*Origins,* p. 451). They manifest the evangelical reality that the Church calls us to accept in a spirit of mutual spiritual enrichment: "To evangelize the poor and to be evangelized by them."

See also CELEBRATION; COMMUNITY; CULTURE; CURSILLO MOVEMENT; DEVOTION(S), POPULAR; MARY; PIETY.

Bibliography: A. Deck, *The Second Wave: Hispanic Ministry and the Evangelization of Cultures* (New York: Paulist, 1989). R. Ramirez, "Hispanic Spirituality," *Social Thought* 11 (Summer, 1985) 6-13. "National Pastoral Plan for Hispanic Ministry," *Origins* 17 (1987) 449-463.

GERMAN MARTINEZ, O.S.B.

HISTORY, HISTORICAL CONSCIOUSNESS

For the second half of the 20th century, Roman Catholic theology has been preoccupied with a consciousness of the effect of history on the articulation and interpretation of the doctrines of faith. This represents a radical shift from neo-Scholasticism, the mode of thought which dominated Catholicism from the latter part of the 19th century and which posited the existence of eternal, unchanging, ahistorical truths comprising a divine deposit of faith that it was the theologian's task to preserve and defend.

The current focus upon the historical nature of revelation owes much to 19th-century Protestant scholarship, but Karl Rahner's "transcendental Thomism" articulated the importance of history and human experience for faith in a recognizably Catholic mode. The dialogue he effected between the Aristotelian-Thomistic tradition and the achievements of modern philosophy resulted in a synthesis that allowed for both continuity and change in contemporary Roman Catholic theology. His anthropology and theology of grace, in particular, have also had a tremendous effect upon contemporary spirituality.

According to Rahner, the human being can best be defined as "spirit in world." The human being is spiritual being, which means that there is a basic mystery of human existence that defies precise definition, a freedom to transcend the limits of space and time, possible because of a basic openness in the human to all being, indeed to Being itself, the Mystery Christians call God. Union with that God is the purpose and goal of all human existence. Spirituality can be defined, then, as the progressive development of a person's transcendence and freedom over the course of a lifetime, the development of that basic human capacity to open oneself up and enter into relationship with the Mystery that lies beyond history's limits.

However, human beings exercise this transcendence "in the world." They are limited by space and time even as they transcend them, subject to bodily needs and to the social and cultural contexts of their existence. But such "limitations" ought not to be viewed negatively; they are the raw materials necessary for the exercise of human transcendence. As embodied spirits, the only way humans can meet the transcendent Mystery of God is as it is mediated by the actual situations of their earthly lives. Humans find God through historically conditioned experience, through

the people with whom they engage in relationship, through the events of their personal and communal history, through the needs of the world, and through the choices made in response to these—all of which are regarded as the revelation of God.

Added to this basic description of human nature is Rahner's understanding of grace. Every human being, created with the capacity for God, is also affected by the "supernatural existential," God's offer of grace, which is first and foremost the communication of God's own self. When confronted by the revelation of God in the particular events of one's personal history, one is also aided by grace to accept God as present there, to enter into and grow in relationship with the divine. For Rahner, all of human history is the locus of God's grace. Because of the redemption effected by Christ, in whom nature and grace met in history in an absolute and irrevocable unity, there is no longer any purely "secular" history that is untouched by the offer of grace; all history can therefore be regarded as the history of salvation.

This description of the graced human person situated in a graced history has enormous consequences for spirituality. If the only way embodied spirits can meet God is through bodily experience in history, this calls into question the whole Neoplatonic tradition, so influential in the history of Christian spirituality, which saw the denial of bodily experience and removal from the world as the most ideal ways of coming to a greater knowledge and love of God.

There is still room in Christian spirituality for asceticism, apophatic contemplation, and the monastic life, but their rationale needs a thorough reworking. No longer can asceticism mean simply the rejection of earthly possessions, comforts, or pleasures because they are wrong in themselves or distract one from God; rather, it becomes the process of discerning legitimate human need and enjoyment from superfluity in a consumer-oriented society, with an eye to a more just distribution of goods. No longer can prayer demand the silencing of the senses and the passions in order to attain a purer apprehension of God; rather, prayer essentially involves the active examination of one's inner movements in order to discern therein God's voice. No longer is the time of prayer something divorced from life, but a time dedicated to bringing the events of one's life consciously into relationship with God. When prayer evolves into silent contemplation, the temporary suspension of attention to the involvements of daily life is done so that one may become more conscious of God's presence in them when the time of contemplation is over. No longer can monasticism be viewed as removal from the cares and concerns of the world in order to enjoy a "higher" form of relationship with God; rather, it becomes a unique way of serving that world. In the tradition of Thomas Merton, the contemplative is freed from the noise and business of the world in order to become more attuned to the world's deepest longings and to voice those longings both to God and prophetically to the world itself.

The emphasis upon history in spirituality has cast a new light on the meaning of mysticism, making moot the complicated debates, chiefly between Dominicans and Jesuits at the beginning of this century, regarding "acquired" and "infused" contemplation. If we take human bodiliness and historicity seriously, we can admit of no "direct" experience of God that is unmediated by history. Even the most ineffable mystical experience happens to a particular person in a particular period of history, which has an inevitable effect on the reception of the experience. Rather than viewing mystical experience as an esoteric phenomenon occurring rarely and to a chosen few, it is understood as being in continuity with the "ordinary" life of grace, and indeed, its logical conclusion. All human experiences are "infused" with God's grace;

so constant and pervasive is this divine activity within the human being, so united with natural human thoughts and actions, that it is usually not noticed as something out of the ordinary. However, on occasion a certain experience may point to God's presence with unusual clarity and force, and mystical experience is a particularly strong manifestation of this awareness of the gratuity of God's grace.

If the place of history in human spirituality has cast a negative shadow over the Neoplatonic stream in the Christian tradition, its positive effect has been the development of what might be called "secularized spiritualities." The all-prevailing presence of grace in the world has muted the distinctions between the secular and the sacred. If all history is graced, then the faithful fulfillment of one's daily duties, whatever they might be, becomes the means of progress in the Christian life. Monastic ideals of prayer and asceticism, which have dominated the history of spirituality, are no longer always appropriate or adequate for people involved in the world; at the very least, they need radical modification. Hence, since the Second Vatican Council there has been a burgeoning of different forms of spirituality suitable to the experiences of particular people: family spirituality, lay spirituality, feminist spirituality, and so forth.

One of the most important implications of a historically conscious spirituality is an awareness of one's social nature and responsibility toward others. To be historically conscious is to know how profoundly humans are affected by their social and cultural environment. Human beings are not isolated individuals; their most personal thoughts are colored by the accepted language, images, and concepts of the society that shapes them. This awareness has caused a shift from a spirituality focused upon one's own private relationship with God to a stress on the role of human relationship and community in spiritual growth. It has also led to a renewed awareness of human solidarity and the centrality of Christian love and service, and to a concentrated study and practice of gospel teaching on the kingdom of God.

If history as a whole is graced, then one can seek there for God's will. This is what *Gaudium et Spes* envisioned when it urged Christians to learn from the "signs of the times." It is possible to recognize in the world's efforts for human development, peace, and justice the presence and action of God's grace. But if the world is graced, it is also affected by sin, and part of the Christian call to perfection involves working to eradicate the structures which perpetuate that sin. Since the Second Vatican Council, under the influence of liberation theologies, there has been a tremendous development of the theme that activity on behalf of the poor and oppressed is a constitutive dimension of Christian spirituality. Indeed, activity in the world for peace and justice, informed and energized by a conscious, prayerful imitation of Christ, the man for others, has become the ideal of Christian holiness, replacing the standards of a purely private morality. Committed Christians are conscious as never before that some expression of solidarity with the poor of the world is an essential part of the goal of Christian perfection. One cannot love God without loving God's people and God's world.

Historical consciousness has also had an effect upon the study of the spiritual classics. Each author must be understood against the background of his or her historical milieu, leading to a greater appreciation of the author's motivations and concerns. Such classics are then appropriated for contemporary use, not literally, but by a process of adaptation to contemporary needs and interests. Thus the feudal and military imagery of Ignatius's *Spiritual Exercises,* to cite one example, can be paraphrased into imagery more in keeping with contemporary understanding, while still preserving Ignatius's basic points in using the imagery. Contemporary concerns also

cast new light on works of past history. For example, feminist scholars are beginning to see new value in the writings of medieval women visionaries. Instead of interpreting their extreme asceticism and rapturous experiences as marks of deranged personalities—a common view until now—we can find positive value in their efforts to assert the right to follow their own religious insights. They therefore become inspirations to women today who are engaged in the same effort.

See also BODY; CONTEMPORARY SPIRITUALITY; EXPERIENCE; GRACE; HOLISTIC SPIRITUALITY; JUSTICE; KINGDOM OF GOD; LIBERATION THEOLOGY, INFLUENCE ON SPIRITUALITY; PRAXIS; VATICAN COUNCIL II; WORLD.

Bibliography: K. Rahner, *Foundations of Christian Faith* (New York: Seabury, 1978) 24–43; idem, "History of the World and Salvation History," *Later Writings,* Theological Investigations 5 (London: Darton, Longman & Todd, 1966) 97–114; idem, "Mystical Experience and Mystical Theology," *Jesus, Man, and the Church,* Theological Investigations 17 (New York: Crossroad, 1983) 90–99.

JOAN M. NUTH

HOLINESS

Introduction

Holiness is defined as the state of being set apart for religious purposes or being consecrated for God. The word *holiness* is derived from the Old English word *hālignes,* meaning "without blemish or injury." *Holy,* then, is an English equivalent for the Hebrew word *qds* and the Greek *hagios,* with both the Hebrew and the Greek having the added sense of separation or consecration.

Rudolf Otto's classic study *The Idea of the Holy* describes the Holy as that which is Totally Other (*Ganz Andere*), engendering both awe and fascination. The Holy is absolutely different; it is *mysterium.* It is from analyses like those of Otto and later phenomenologists of religion (Van der Leeuw; Eliade, and others) that the notion of holiness (and its cognates, e.g., the Sacred) takes its most fundamental meaning:

that which is of the transcendent order as opposed to that which is of the finite or limited order.

If the concept of the Holy pertains to that which is ultimate (God/the Sacred), holiness can be applied, by extension, to relationships with that source of the ultimate. Thus St. Thomas Aquinas argues that there is only a rational distinction to be made between religion and sanctity (ST II-II, q. 81). Sanctity, according to the mind of Aquinas, is the virtue by which people apply themselves and their actions to God. In that sense, sanctity or holiness is a dependent notion deriving its meaning only in relation to God.

The Bible, not surprisingly, predicates the word *holy* or *holiness* in the first and fundamental instance of God. God is separate in the sense that God is not to be identified with creation or creature. The great theophanies and hymns of praise of both the Hebrew and Christian Scriptures emphasize the otherness (i.e., the holiness) and singularity of God. "Who," asks Moses in his great hymn, "is like to you, magnificent in holiness? O terrible in renown, worker of wonders ..." (Exod 15:11). In the great prophetic theophany described by Isaiah, the angelic hosts stand between the Temple and God, singing, "Holy, holy, holy is the LORD of hosts!" (Isa 6:3), a hymn that the NT borrows for its own description of the majesty of God (see Rev 4:8). Jesus himself, borrowing the language of the Bible, calls the Father "holy" (Jn 17:11) and instructs the disciples in prayer to "hallow [i.e., make holy] his name" (Mt 6:10; Lk 11:2). When the Bible speaks of "the Holy One," it is a synonym for God, as in the prophetic strophe "God comes from Teman, / The Holy One from Mount Paran" (Hab 3:3).

There are also other words in the Bible (e.g., "glory" = Hebrew *kabod;* Greek *doxa*) that act as synonyms for the holiness of God. When John's prologue confesses, "We saw his glory, the glory as of the Father's only Son" (Jn 1:14), the word "glory" has richly theandric resonances with OT descriptions of the otherness (holiness) of God.

While holiness is a predicate peculiar to God, it becomes an extended quality by reason of proximity to God. Thus the ground surrounding the burning bush becomes holy because of the presence of God (Exod 3:5), as do other sites where God has appeared, such as Bethel (Gen 28:11ff.) and, preeminently, the Temple in Jerusalem. In general, we can say that the places, peoples, rites, etc., that are called "holy" receive that appellation because they are designated as participating in the otherness of God. To use the language of phenomenology, they are sacred as opposed to profane.

This setting apart, however, should not be understood in too spatial or too exclusively a cultic sense. Holiness *derives* from God not only as a designation but as a divine quality that is shared: "But as he who called you is holy, be holy yourselves in every aspect of your conduct, for it is written, 'Be holy because I am holy'" (1 Pet 1:15-16; see Lev 11:44-45). Later theology, as we shall note, saw that sharing as a participation in God's life, i.e., in grace.

By way of summary, we could say that the Bible allows us to understand three kinds of holiness which apply analogously to creatures but which are ultimately rooted in the holiness of God:

1) a *priestly* understanding that emphasizes separation, purity, and segregation for cult;

2) a *prophetic* understanding that underscores the relationship between worship, social justice, and conversion of heart;

3) a *sapiential* holiness that puts emphasis on the need for individual integrity as it develops under the eye of God.

It should be clear, however, that these are not always discrete categories with rigorous divisions, but they do reflect detectable strands within the biblical tradition.

The Holiness of Christ and the Christian

Jesus, as a child of the covenant, was holy in the sense that he was set apart as a member of God's covenanted people, Israel. Luke makes that clear in his description of the presentation of Jesus in the Temple: "They brought him up to Jerusalem to present him to the Lord (as it is written in the law of the Lord, 'Every first-born male shall be designated as holy to the Lord')" (Lk 2:22, NRSV; see Lev 12).

Beyond that the NT calls Jesus "holy" (he does not so describe himself) in a series of set pieces that involve quasi-public professions of faith. A demonic voice distinguishes its own evil from the otherness of Jesus by crying out, "I know who you are— the Holy One of God!" (Mk 1:24; cf. Lk 4:35), while Peter, refusing to abandon Jesus despite the defection of many disciples, cries out, "We have come to believe and are convinced that you are the Holy One of God" (Jn 6:69). That same Peter invokes the psalmist to underscore the resurrection: "You will not abandon my soul to the nether world, nor will you suffer your holy one to see corruption" (Acts 2:27; see Ps 16:10). Similarly, Peter describes Jesus as God's "holy servant" who is anointed (Acts 4:27), so that the notions of holiness and Messiah become conflated in a single phrase. Finally, the holiness of Jesus is communicable to those who follow him, as John's Gospel makes clear: "I consecrate [*hagiazō*, "make holy"] myself for them, so that they also may be consecrated in truth" (Jn 17:19).

Christians, especially in the Pauline literature, are also called "holy." Paul addresses the faithful at Rome as those "who are called . . . to be holy" (Rom 1:7; see also 1 Cor 1:2), while in 2 Corinthians he gives greetings to that congregation and to "all the holy ones throughout Achaia" (1:1). Greetings to the "holy ones" also head the letters to the Ephesians (1:1), the Philippians (1:1), and the Colossians (1:2). As a general term, the "holy ones" or "saints" are those who are set apart by faith in Christ, as opposed to those who are not believers. In this generic sense the word "saint" or "holy one" denotes inclusion rather than exclusion; it is an extension of the Jewish concept of a people beloved and chosen by God. Only in later Christianity will the term take on the meaning of a person publicly venerated in the Church's liturgy. In the mind of the early Church, however, holiness is the state of those who live within the Trinitarian dynamic by which they are connected to the Father through the Son in the Spirit of God, poured out precisely to make us children of God. It is because we possess the spirit of Christ (in faith, in baptism, in communion, in deed) that we are capable of calling out "Abba, Father!" (see Gal 4:6).

Finally, there is a thread in the NT that transposes the cultic notion of the holiness of worship into a spiritual reality by which followers of Jesus are "set apart" for God, as were the gifts of the old dispensation. Paul urges the Roman Christians, "Offer your bodies as a living sacrifice, holy and pleasing to God, your spiritual worship" (Rom 12:1). The First Letter of Peter speaks of Christians as "living stones" that are built "into a spiritual house to be a holy priesthood to offer spiritual sacrifices acceptable to God through Jesus Christ" (1 Pet 2:5; for similar texts, see Phil 2:17 and 4:18; Heb 13:15 and 13:16).

Holiness as a Call

Although there are elements of taboo or cultic understandings of holiness to be seen in the history of Christianity (e.g., an emphasis on the sacred nature of liturgical paraphernalia), Christianity does not understand holiness (except for God's holiness) only as a given condition but also as a call. The New Testament not only calls the followers of Jesus a holy people, but it demands, in the imperative voice, that they become holy. The Corinthians, for example, are "called to be holy" (1 Cor 1:2). In that sense, holiness may be understood as part of the conversion process: a move away from that which is not God (aversion) toward that which makes us closer to God after the manner of Jesus (conversion). To use a traditional vocabulary, the call is the urging *grace* of God, while our conversion to God is a response to that prompting of grace. Holiness, then, involves both a condition and a choice in response to an offer.

This turn to holiness involves decisions that are individual but accomplished within the context of the believing assembly. In the contemporary Church this call to holiness is most solemnly set out in the fifth chapter of the Dogmatic Constitution on the Church (*Lumen Gentium*) of the Second Vatican Council. The title of that chapter, "The Call of the Whole Church to Holiness," is not ornamental but essential. Holiness is not the domain of an elect or cultic group within the Church but the universal vocation of all Christians: " . . . all the faithful of Christ of whatever rank or status are called to the fullness of the Christian life and to the perfection of charity" (LG 40). It may well be—and the conciliar document outlines distinct ways of life in the Church—that people find themselves in various circumstances of life; nonetheless, everyone is called to the same holiness that is rooted in the same bedrock of charity, i.e., the love of God above all things and the love of others for the sake of God (LG 42). Thus a person may have the charism of virginity or the grace of marriage, but the holiness of each is tested by the same rule: Christian charity, by which we love all things in the love of God.

The holiness of the Church, then, is not some abstract quality that adheres to it but the actual presence of this love within its assembly. The Church has a formal holiness in that it possesses the word of God and the sacraments, which, founded on Christ, are holy despite the ill uses made of them or the unworthiness of their ministers. Furthermore, the members of the assembly are a people set apart by God who participate in the priesthood of Jesus Christ (LG, chap. 2). Finally, in every age there are persons who are conspicuous for the generosity of their response to God. They act as signs (sacraments) of the possibility and reality of holiness. They are the *saints,* as we now understand the term.

The place of the saints in the Christian tradition can be variously understood. In the first instance, they are eschatological signs in that they possess what we still look for: fulfillment in God. Second, and closely related to the first, they are part of the Church who are our intercessors before God and, as such, are invoked in the liturgy. Third, they testify to the potentialities of the gospel. As Karl Rahner once wrote, the saints show us that it is possible to be a Christian in *this* particular fashion. They do that in one of two ways. Some saints demonstrate in their lives that the perennial values of the gospel are still pertinent for a new age; thus, for example, the traditional piety of a Mother Teresa of Calcutta demonstrates the perennial value of unrestricted charity. What she and others like her do is essentially no different from what Vincent de Paul did in his age. Other great saints show new and unexpected ways of being holy as responses to the culture in which they live. St. Francis of Assisi, for example, was a saint for the urban culture of his time, when the cloistered life of agricultural Europe no longer touched people in large numbers, just as Ignatius of Loyola provided a mobility for the religious life when the more static forms of the *vita regularis* showed themselves inadequate to the needs of post-Reformation Europe. The saints, in short, serve both as icons of the Gospels and blueprints for new ways of gospel living.

That being said, however, we must also underscore the sinfulness and imperfection of the Christian assembly this side of the *eschaton.* Like the individuals who make up its assembly, the Church must constantly turn away from that which is not God and re-turn to God, since it is "at the same time holy and always in need of being purified, and incessantly pursues the path of penance and renewal" (LG 8). The Church, in short, is not a "sacred object" but an assembly that holds within itself the means of holiness as it re-members, re-calls, and re-creates the saving mysteries of Jesus Christ in time and history. The Church is not a perfectionist sect but a pilgrim people of saints and sinners.

Those in the Church respond to the call to holiness by hearing the word of God preached, sharing in the sacramental life of the Church, and living out those values and insights that we learn from Jesus Christ, "the divine Teacher and Model of all perfection," who "Himself stands as the Author and Finisher of this holiness of life" (LG 40). The holiness of believers, in short, finds its model in Jesus Christ, who mirrors the holiness of God. Vatican II stated it succinctly in its preface to the Decree on the Bishops' Pastoral Office in the Church: "Christ the Lord, Son of the living God, came that He might save people from their sins and that all people might be made holy" (CD 1).

The Paths to Holiness

What has been stated above reflects a somewhat general theological framework for the understanding of holiness. Any brief acquaintance with the history of Christianity, however, will show us that the means by which we utilize the model of Jesus to respond to the call for holiness are manifold and complex. This complexity reflects two important truths that derive from one more basic truth, namely, we do not live as abstractions. On the contrary, (a) we are individuals with all the freedom and gifts that accrue to persons, and (b) we live in definite times with all the particularities of culture, education, and economic or social conditions that derive from that fact. In other words, we are people who live in history.

One clear consequence of our historicity is that our answer to the call of holiness will be as manifold as the complexities of history itself. The very notion that holiness implies a certain setting apart or separation underscores this complexity very well. It also raises questions that have been variously treated over the course of time.

Does holiness, for example, imply a rejection of the profane or, to choose a more biblical usage, must one reject the world when one chooses for God? It is clear that the Bible answers that question in various ways. In both the Johannine and Pauline literature, the word *world* can have such a pejorative sense that one could intuit a rejection of the world in favor of Christ. Yet, at the same time, the Bible provides us with a strong, positive doctrine of creation and ample evidence that the world itself is somehow within the grace of Christ. This follows naturally from the very fact of the incarnation itself, as the prologue to St. John's Gospel, echoing the opening of the Book of Genesis, tells us. Furthermore, John makes clear that the entire dispensation of salvation has a cosmic intent: God sent his Son because he "loved the world" and that Son came into the world, not to condemn it, but that it be saved "through him" (Jn 3:16-17).

It is obvious, then, that the term *world* has different meanings in Scripture, and therefore the relationship of the world to sanctity or perfection will also have different formulations. In fact, when one looks at the history of Christian spirituality, one sees those formulations held at times in tension in the life of the same person, with the word *world* signifying different things, depending on the perspective of the moment. When, for example, a figure like St. Antony of the Desert disposes of his possessions and leaves his village for the desert in order to struggle with Satan, he is clearly opting against the world in order to live a life fully centered on God. He chooses, in the deepest sense of the term, a *holy* life. Paradoxically enough, his rejection of the "world" results in the transformation of the world of the desert in such a fashion that its disharmonies are now graced by his life and that of his disciples. It is "a land all its own—a land of devotion and righteousness. For neither perpetrator nor victim of injustice was there, nor complaint of tax collector" (*Vita Antonii* 44).

Any coherent understanding of the Christian concept of holiness must make sense of that coincidence of opposites (*coincidentia oppositorum*) implicit in a faith that affirms creation and incarnation while calling us to a state that implies a separateness that is for God alone. One sees that tension not always resolved in many discussions in the history of spirituality: the concern for the contemplative life versus the active life, which runs like a thread through ascetic literature. The persistent theme of action/contemplation falls under many different headings: Martha/Mary; desert/city; flight from the world/service to the world; being in the world but not of the world, etc. A proper view of holiness must also recognize that there is an equal tension between what is inherited and what is required for the present moment. The twin extremes in this regard are a traditionalism that turns into mummification, and an experimentalism that is only rationally distinct from faddishness. The history of spirituality testifies both to an extreme rejectionism of rigorist tendencies and to an antinomian strain of "free spirit" spirituality.

A goodly number of the spiritual masters of our time have warned about an excessive reliance or emphasis on either side of the tension. One powerful current operative in the reform movement of the Second Vatican Council, and reflected most openly in the Pastoral Constitution on the Church in the Modern World (*Gaudium et Spes*) was a desire to change an otherworldly Church and a world-denying spirituality into a more incarnational presence in the world itself. In this orientation, holiness is understood not as a rejection of, or separation from, the world but as a way of being in the world.

To understand the concept of holiness, then, two extremes must be avoided. One exaggeration would be to equate holiness with a complete denial of material creatureliness. This was, historically, a persistent temptation in Christian spirituality, aptly called "angelism," to borrow a term from the late philosopher Jacques Maritain, meaning the tendency to denigrate the humanity of a person in order to exalt the "spiritual" nature of a person. The other pole of that exaggeration is to emphasize so completely the necessity of engagement with the world that the transcendent reality of God (and one's relationship to God) is denigrated in the name of activism as illusory at best or, at worst, escapist.

True holiness, like spirituality itself, must do ample justice both to the transcendental axis of the person in relationship to God and, simultaneously, to the immanent reality of a person who lives in the world horizontally as both an individual and a social entity. It is for that reason, among others, that Jesus is the paradigmatic figure for all Christian holiness, since in his life and reality there is the coincidence of opposites that resolves the tensions alluded to above. He is the God-Man; the Word-made-flesh; the Concrete Universal (Rahner), etc.

In the person of Jesus Christ, then, we find both the warrant to respond to the gift of holiness offered by God and the means by which we can grow in that holiness of which he is the model.

Holiness and Christology

The starting point of any Christian concept of holiness would be to stand in a relationship to God that would approximate the ideal set out by Jesus in his life and in his teaching. That, in turn, would mean to live in a relationship with God by which we would see God as a loving Parent, after the manner of the "Abba experience" expressed in the life of Jesus. "Abba" is the favorite term for God on the lips of Jesus, which explains why the Scriptures retain its Aramaic form. It reflects an intimacy with God, who is seen as a caring and compassionate Parent intimately involved with the life of Jesus. The prayer that Jesus taught begins with that phrase (in the original version of the Lord's Prayer), and it is on the lips of Jesus as his agony begins in Gethsemane (see Mk 14:36).

Our capacity to call on God as "Abba" depends on the gift of the Spirit (Gal 4:4-6) and demands, in turn, that our lives, in union with God as loving Parent, reflect the love of God for all of creation. The great Lukan parables of the Good Samaritan (10:25-37) and the prodigal son (15:11-32) reflect that love which is extended when one would ordinarily expect recrimination or neglect. Jesus' doctrine of love is unitary in that love of God and love of neighbor, already hallowed in the Hebrew tradition, are not discrete activities.

In the Gospel portrait(s) of Jesus we see one whose life is theocentric, in the sense that everything Jesus is and does falls under the loving eye of Abba. To keep that in mind is to understand Jesus' insistence that one cannot serve God and mammon (Mt 6:4); that God's providence extends to the smallest detail of the world (Lk 12:6-7); that God provides materially for those whose trust is complete (Mt 6:25-34).

In Johannine theology the theocentricity of Jesus becomes so intimate that a reciprocity is worked out that involves more than mere faith on the part of Jesus: Whatever the Father does, the Son will do also (see Jn 5:19). In the same discourse the Son raises the dead as the Father has done (5:21), just as he judges as the Father judges (5:22). The conclusion is straightforward: "Whoever does not honor the Son does not honor the Father who sent him" (5:23b). This relationship between Son and Father is so intimate that John's Gospel is characterized by a whole series of "I am" sayings (see 6:35; 8:12; 10:17; etc.), which echo God's holy name in the Book of Exodus (3:14).

If, however, Christology meant only a capacity to imitate the God-centered life of Jesus, he would be only another paradigmatic figure worthy of imitation, albeit a God-intoxicated one. There is, though, another strand of the biblical witness of Jesus that insists that his life and work somehow directly affect who we are and what we can be. In this understanding, Jesus is the catalyst for a new form of living that puts us in contact with him and with Abba. Jesus, in short, is the agent of our holiness. In this the experience of the earliest Christian assemblies is paramount. Jesus, according to the most ancient profession of Christian faith, died for our sins and was raised up as the "firstborn" of all who would come after him and believe in him (see 1 Cor 15).

The entire significance of the life, death, and resurrection of Christ was not merely a memory for the first Christians; it was an experience that touched them as they recalled it in baptism and re-called and remembered and re-created it in the breaking of the bread. Indeed, as recent scholars have noted, the earliest Christian assemblies possessed a twofold language by which they summed up who they were and who they were not. The Pauline literature is filled with both inclusionary and exclusionary language: believers versus pagans; the baptized versus the unbaptized; the saints versus the impious, etc. In other words, the early Christian assembly was holy precisely because it was identified with the mysteries of the life, death, and resurrection of Christ kept alive and celebrated in community. At the same time, this community opened itself to everyone who would share that faith in such a way that the exclusionary language defined who a Christian was, but there was an inclusionary motif that welcomed others to be part of that fellowship.

Holiness and Pneumatology

No discussion of holiness would be complete without a consideration of the Spirit of God, which is, in itself, called "holy" and which, in addition, is the source and energizer of holiness. Indeed, the Scriptures so frequently invoke God's Spirit in such different ways that it is difficult to write a systematic biblical pneumatology. The one thing that is very clear is that the Spirit of God is connected, in both the OT and the NT, with the principle of life itself. In that sense, spirit is akin to breath, so that when God breathed life into the first human (Gen 2:7), it was, as it were, the imparting of God's spirit. It is not far-fetched, then, to see the Spirit of God as a vivifying force that links the arena of the world and its inhabitants with the source of life that is God. That link also explains why that Spirit can be called "holy."

Examples describing this vivification abound. John the Baptist promises a new baptism in the Holy Spirit, which will replace his baptism of water (Mk 1:8). Jesus applies to himself the passage from Isaiah (61:1-2) in which the Spirit of God is poured out on the messiah in order that the Good News may be preached to the poor (Lk 4:16-19). Resistance to the Holy Spirit is, for Jesus, more than blasphemy; it is the unforgivable sin (Lk 12:10).

The Spirit that vivifies is at the core of the nascent Christian assembly. Jesus promises them power when the Holy Spirit comes upon them, a power that will permit them to witness to Jesus even to the ends of the earth (Acts 1:8). That promise is fulfilled in the Pentecost experience, when the Holy Spirit, like "a strong, driving wind" and like "tongues of fire," descends on the disciples, empowering them to "speak in different tongues, as the Spirit enabled them to proclaim" (Acts 2:1-4).

Pauline literature is filled with the language of the Spirit as life-giver. Called simply "the Spirit" or "the Holy Spirit" or "the Spirit of Christ," this Spirit is seen by Paul as placing people in dynamic relationship to God. Paul's most dramatic formulation of that relationship is formulated in a series of contrasts that stud his writings. The law of the Spirit sets us free from the law of sin and death (Rom 8:1-2). In that same great chapter it is the Spirit that assures us the right to be called children of God and to cry out "Abba!" (Rom 8:15; see Gal 4:4-6). The Spirit aids us in our weakness at prayer and intercedes with "inexpressible groanings" (Rom 8:26). That contrast between Spirit and non-spirit (i.e., between holiness and non-holiness) takes on moral pungency in Paul's contrast between Spirit and flesh. The latter brings forth all kinds of sin, but the former brings forth the gifts of the spirit: "love, joy, peace, patience, kindness, generosity, faithfulness, gentleness, self-control" (Gal 5:22, 23).

For Paul, it is the Spirit that gives coherence and meaning to the Christian assembly. It is only in the Spirit that one can confess "Jesus is Lord" (1 Cor 12:3). It is that same Spirit that unifies the diverse gifts available to the Church (1 Cor 12:4) while ordering them to the common good (1 Cor 12:7). Finally, the assembly, though diverse in members, is one in Christ, "for in one Spirit we were all baptized into one body, whether Jews or Greeks, slaves or free persons, and we were all given to drink of one Spirit" (1 Cor 12:13). In another place Paul calls this unity a "unity of the spirit through the bond of peace" (Eph 4:3).

It would be left to later generations to clarify the relationship of Abba, the Christ, and the Spirit, but it is clear that in the Scriptures a triadic sense of God's presence in the individual and in the assembly was already present. It is expressed in the ancient (liturgical?) formula of the great mandate, by which the disciples are sent to baptize "in the name of the Father, and of the Son, and of the holy Spirit" (Mt 28:19). In John's Gospel, Jesus promises that the Father will send the Holy Spirit so that the Church will be able both to teach and to remember "all that I told you" (Jn 14:26).

It is clear from a careful reading of the scriptural witness that the Spirit is holy both because it is of God and, further, as a gift, communicates some vital aspect of

God to believers as individuals and communities, invigorating them to be of God and to do God's work. This same Spirit serves as the guide for the believing assembly to seal it in truth and to help it be faithful to the work and words of Jesus (see Jn 14:26).

Holiness and Contemporary Life

Words like *holy* and *holiness* have a certain pejorative ring to them in contemporary demotic speech, as phrases like "holier than thou" or "holy roller" attest. To recover the authentic notion of holiness, one must begin with the fundamental notion that holiness belongs, in the first instance, to God or, to put in more plainly, God as God is holy by definition. To affirm the holiness (i.e., the Otherness) of God does not mean that one so exalts God that God's reality becomes beyond the human ken (this would contradict the biblical notion of God as Abba). It is to say that the truly religious person does not fall into any form of idolatry: "You shall not have other gods besides me" (Exod 20:3).

A person is holy (or seeks holiness) in the most radically authentic sense of the term when that person affirms, by commitment, the reality of God. To be holy means to be nonautonomous; to be holy means to be in relation. While the older, more restrictive notion of holiness as cultic separation/purity is helpful as a phenomenological category, it does not do justice to the broader theological concept of holiness as the term is used both in magisterial statements (e.g., *Lumen Gentium*) and in the tradition of Christian spirituality.

Holiness must not be understood as the single province of those committed by vow to the regular life (*vita regularis*) as it exists within the Church. It would be a deformation to posit a "two-tiered" canon of holiness, with one being superior or open to only an elite few. While the Church has always recognized the special way of the evangelical counsels of poverty, chastity, and obedience, it would be overly restric-

tive to think that these counsels are available only within the regular life of the vowed religious.

Nor is it possible to think of the call of holiness as being restricted to those who are *ex professo* members of the Church. Not only did Vatican II accept the reality of holiness outside the visible bonds of the Church, but it argued that such holiness could be a source of edification for the Church (UR, chap. 1). Indeed, it forthrightly noted that in the non-Christian religious traditions one can find "peoples with a profound religious sense" and, further, that "the Church rejects nothing which is true and holy" in these traditions (NA 2).

Again, the Church reaffirmed, and continues to reaffirm, the value of the contemplative life in its various forms as a legitimate and prophetic charism that provides "institutions of edification" (*seminaria aedificationis:* PC 9) for the entire Church. Nonetheless, the contemplative life is not to be understood as indifferent to the needs of the Church or extraneous to the needs or aspirations of the Christian assembly. The contemplative life testifies to a way (not *the* way) of being for God within the larger parameters of the Christian community.

Again, the Christian ethical life must be viewed in the light of both God's holiness and our common call to holiness. There is no real distinction between the call to be holy and the demands of right behavior; they are of a piece. St. Paul frequently describes the person in Christ as "without blemish." The phrase originally had a cultic ring to it and referred to those animals that could be set apart for sacrifice (hence they were *holy* animals). Paul goes beyond this cultic image in order to envision a person in Christ as set apart to be worthy of God. In Eph 1:4 Paul links the notions: "God . . . chose us . . . to be holy and without blemish [lit.: blameless] before him." Further on in that same letter Paul explicitly links behavior and holiness: "Immorality or any impurity or greed must not even be mentioned among you, as is fitting among holy ones" (Eph 5:3).

For Paul, the way we behave has an essential link with the holiness of God. In the urgent eschatological language of his early writings, Paul prays that the Thessalonians may become "blameless in holiness" in anticipation of "the coming of our Lord Jesus with all his holy ones" (1 Thess 3:13). Later in that same letter Paul says bluntly that the will of God for all of us is our holiness (*hagiasmos*), and he immediately juxtaposes norms of behavior, beginning with abstention from "immorality" (1 Thess 4:3).

The close connection between holiness and ethics has enormous ramifications both for contemporary Christian living and for our conception of theology. Western Christianity has had an unfortunate history of separating belief and practice, so that we have spoken of systematic theology and moral theology as if they were separated by a chasm. More recent attempts to ground ethics theologically and to account for spirituality also as a grounded discipline have had the salutary effect of a more holistic understanding of the Christian life.

That newer understanding is, in essence, a retrieval of the old Augustinian insight "Love God and do what you please." If, to think of the matter in terms of holiness, we belong to God by choice under grace, then that choice carries with it a concomitant demand to act under that same God. Holiness, then, becomes a way of being with God in Christ rather than a mere cultic separation from the world of the "profane" or a sectarian form of spiritual perfectionism. It is, rather, a response to the demand of Jesus that we be perfect as the heavenly Father is perfect.

See also ASCETICISM; CHRIST; DIVINIZATION; GIFTS OF THE HOLY SPIRIT; GOD; GRACE; HISTORY, HISTORICAL CONSCIOUSNESS; HOLY SPIRIT; SAINTS; COMMUNION OF SAINTS; VIRTUE.

Bibliography: "Holiness" in *The Anchor Bible Dictionary* 3 (Garden City, N.Y.: Doubleday, 1992). "Santo" in *Nuovo dizionario di spiritualitá* (Rome: Paoline, 1979). J. Gammie, *Holiness in Israel* (Minneapolis: Fortress, 1989). F. J. van Beeck, *God Encountered: A Contemporary Catholic Systematic Theology* (San Francisco: Harper & Row, 1989). R. Otto, *The Idea of the Holy* (New York: Oxford Univ. Press, 1950). K. Rahner, "The Church of the Saints," *Theology in the Spiritual Life,* Theological Investigations 3 (Baltimore: Helicon, 1960). L. Cunningham, *The Meaning of Saints* (San Francisco: Harper & Row, 1981).

LAWRENCE S. CUNNINGHAM

HOLISTIC SPIRITUALITY

The term *holistic* has in recent years been applied to such diverse fields as medicine, human development, and spirituality. In all these applications the common meaning reflects a concern for wholeness, a desire for integration, and an attempt to understand the connections between the various aspects that constitute a given reality.

What does *holistic* connote when used to describe a spirituality and spiritual formation? Like holistic medicine, which links physical and mental health, a holistic spirituality respects the psychosomatic or body-spirit unity of the person. Holistic prayer, for example, recognizes that bodily calm can engender internal stillness, and external concentration can focus the spirit's awareness. The interior silence needed to hear the often still, subtle voice of the Lord can be induced by the exterior calm and stillness achievable through the various techniques of yoga, Zen, body relaxation, and sense-awareness exercises.

Because the body and the spirit are closely united, bodily expression in prayer can sometimes convey personal concerns and feelings more effectively than words. Examples of such bodily prayer are: expressing a longing for God by inhaling more deeply and drawing in the Spirit which the risen Jesus communicates to all believers, as he did to the disciples in the upper room when he breathed on them (Jn 20:22); expressing a surrender to God by exhaling more fully and pouring one's concerns into God's provident hands; holding out one's hands, palms up, in receptivity to the Spirit; or simply letting one's sorrow, fatigue, and frustration be told by sighs and tears, as Jesus did at the tomb of Lazarus (Jn 11:34-36). These nonverbal ways of praying illustrate the importance placed by holistic spirituality on the imagination, the senses, and on feelings in prayer.

Like holistic human development, which views growth as the lifelong effort to integrate the diverse aspects that constitute the self, holistic spirituality sees the struggle for personal wholeness as an integral part of the journey to holiness. This belief is reflected, for example, in Josef Goldbrunner's *Holiness Is Wholeness* (New York: Pantheon, 1955). To regard the spiritual life holistically is to assert the truth of two central beliefs: (1) the pursuit of holiness is in no way inimical to healthy human growth; and (2) those who strive to be religious are not exempt from the human condition. They must, like everyone else, work out their growth into wholeness in the context of human struggle. Thus those aspiring to be religious persons, whether as professed or as lay people, must continue to invest in their ongoing human growth. Unless they stay open to expanding as persons able to give and to receive love, their quest for religious growth will ironically thwart rather than stimulate their cooperation with God in bringing about the universal society of love envisioned by Jesus. Based on the developmental assumption that maturity comes gradually, stage by stage and not all at once, holistic spirituality sees continual human growth as essential to religious maturation. Barry McLaughlin's *Nature, Grace, and Religious Development* (Westminster, Md.: Newman, 1964), for example, elaborates on the relationship between Erik Erikson's psychosocial stages and religious development. A spiritual life not built on solid human development born of struggle is liable to be superficial and escapist.

Rooted in an incarnational belief in the pervasive presence of God in all reality, holistic spirituality counters the dualism that has plagued spirituality in the Western Christian tradition over the centuries. Platonic devaluation of the world of the senses, Cartesian dichotomization of matter and spirit, and Manichean beliefs that see material things as tainted with sin and the realm of the divine as nonmaterial have separated realities that holistic spirituality insists should be united. In contrast to a dualistic, "either-or" mentality that sees things as irreconcilable opposites, holistic spirituality stresses a complementary, "both-and" attitude that is integrative and inclusive. Specifically, holistic spirituality opposes pitting the sacred against the secular, "this world" against the "next world," the individual against the social, and the spiritual against the material.

Seeing how dualistic thinking has shaped spirituality will further elucidate the contours of a holistic spirituality. In some strains of Christian tradition, for example, spirituality has been equated with the so-called life of the soul, or the interior life. When the spiritual is seen as opposed to the material, spirituality is compartmentalized and set in opposition to other inseparable aspects of human life. In this view of spirituality, the development of one's inner life or the spiritual soul is almost exclusively emphasized; affectivity, sexuality, and whatever belongs to the life of the body are seen as irrelevant to holiness and spiritual development.

Another dualism that is incompatible with a holistic emphasis is the division between the sacred and the secular. A spirituality colored by this dichotomy restricts one's encounter with the holy or the spiritual dimensions of reality to certain times, places, and experiences that are explicitly related to religion or worship. The ordinary experiences of daily life are treated as if they were devoid of God's presence, and therefore irrelevant to divine encounter, discipleship, and spiritual growth. In contrast, holistic spirituality stresses the fact that we live in a divine milieu and that every particle of the created universe is potentially revelatory of God, every bush a burning bush to the eyes of faith (see Exod 3:1-6).

Some strands of traditional spirituality have also been guilty of an imbalanced eschatological outlook caused by a preoccupation with an otherworldly kingdom to come and a resulting neglect of the kingdom of God that has already been inaugurated by the preaching and ministry of Jesus (realized eschatology). When the world is devalued as a transitory valley of tears, worldly affairs are judged to be of little or no consequence; responsible involvement in political and economic matters loses all connection to spirituality. In contrast, holistic spirituality states that discipleship requires commitment to continuing the work of Jesus by working for justice, caring for the homeless, and using the resources of creation in a way that is ecologically and socially responsible. Holding that love of God and love of neighbor are inseparable, holistic spirituality emphasizes the Johannine teaching that those who claim to love God while hating their neighbor are liars (1 Jn 4:20). Thus any spirituality that values a privatized, vertical love relationship with God (a "Jesus-and-me" mentality) at the expense of the communal, horizontal love of neighbor would be inimical to holistic spirituality.

A holistic spirituality is a religious outlook as well as a way of structuring one's life in order to embody religious values. As a religious orientation, it asks the question, "How is God leading and loving me in all aspects of my life?" It is holistic insofar as it acknowledges that all aspects of a person's life must be subjected to the transforming influence of the Spirit. It opposes spiritualities that restrict the scope of the spiritual life to one's relationship to God and the condition of one's soul. A holistic spirituality attempts to embrace the totality of a person's existence, including one's relationship with others, with one's work, and with the material world. Defining the spiritual life as coextensive with life itself, it finds every human concern relevant. God's Spirit can be encountered in all aspects of life and not merely in such explicitly religious activities as prayer and worship. Understanding spirituality holistically involves linking it with every aspect of human development—psychological and spiritual, interpersonal and political.

As a life-structure, holistic spirituality addresses the concrete pattern or design of people's lives. Viewing spirituality as a particular way of being in the world, a way of walking as opposed to merely a way in the mind, a holistic spirituality is concerned with helping people embody in a lifestyle the values that they profess verbally. The concept of life-structure entails the specific choices and decisions people make about the way they spend their money, time, and resources. Issues revolving around work and leisure, prayer and politics, sex and relationships all clamor for attention. Holistic spirituality is concerned with helping people connect and unify the various aspects of their lives in a responsible and coherent manner.

Fulfilling the diverse requirements of Christian living in a balanced fashion, so that no one aspect is overemphasized to the detriment of others, is not an easy task. A holistic spirituality attempts to tackle the tough task of finding an outlook that will integrate people's lives sufficiently to give them a sense of increasing wholeness and guide them in fashioning a concrete way of living out their spirituality. By enabling people to forge a more vital link between their faith and their daily lives, a holistic approach to the spiritual life helps them to heal the dichotomy between the human and the holy, the secular and the sacred—a division that has forced so many to be schizophrenic in living out their religious beliefs. A holistic spirituality helps to develop Christians who can overcome the pernicious schizophrenia between soul and body, brain and heart, and thus become more whole.

See also AFFECT, AFFECTIVITY; BODY; BREATH, BREATHING; CONTEMPORARY SPIRITUALITY; CREATION; DUALISM; HEART; INCARNATION; PSYCHOLOGY, RELATIONSHIP AND CONTRIBUTION TO SPIRITUALITY; SEXUALITY; VATICAN II.

Bibliography: W. Au, *By Way of the Heart: Toward a Holistic Christian Spirituality* (Mahwah, N.J.: Paulist, 1989). J. Carmody, *Holistic Spirituality* (Mahwah, N.J.: Paulist, 1983). A. Wilson, "Holistic Spirituality," *Spirituality Today* 40, no. 3 (Autumn 1988).

WILKIE AU, S.J.

HOLOCAUST

The Holocaust, more commonly known now among Jewish scholars by its Hebrew term, *Shoah* (i.e., "annihilation"), refers first and foremost to the systematic destruction of some six million European Jews by the Nazi government of Germany between 1933 and 1945. It also includes the death through disease, medical experimentation, war, and direct extermination of approximately five million non-Jewish victims, especially the physically and mentally impaired; Polish people, whose nation the Nazis hoped to reduce to slavery status; and Gypsies. The ultimate goal of the Nazis was the creation of a new, supposedly advanced society of totally liberated individuals, biologically perfect and complete masters of their own destiny. For the framers of Nazi ideology, God was dead as an effective force in the universe.

The Nazis would decide who should live and who should die as they saw fit. They were no longer subject, in their minds, to any moral norms beyond the wisdom of their own decision-making. Though they sometimes enlisted the cooperation of churchpeople in their plan of Jewish annihilation, the Nazis were in the final analysis as deeply anti-Christian as they were anti-Jewish. Yet traditional anti-Semitism blinded many Christians to the profoundly anti-Christian outlook of the Nazis.

Jewish religious thinkers who have wrestled with the Holocaust experience generally wind up focusing on one central theme: How do we continue to speak meaningfully of a loving God who seemingly abandoned a covenanted people in their hour of greatest need? Or was God simply too powerless to act? Christian writers have generally followed the lead of their Jewish counterparts in their own reflections on the spiritual significance of the Holocaust, though generally in less radical fashion.

The basic lesson beginning to emerge from both Jewish and Christian Holocaust commentators is the urgent need to develop a spirituality today capable of coping with the newly discovered creative powers of humanity that the Nazis dramatically brought to our attention, although in horribly perverted ways. Modern consciousness is now aware of a depth of human freedom never before imagined. Somehow that freedom must be channeled toward constructive ends. That remains the Holocaust's ultimate challenge to spirituality.

For this to happen in a meaningful way, there is need for people to recover a new sense of a transcendent God. A spirituality will need to take root through which men and women will once more experience contact with a personal power beyond themselves, a power that heals the destructive tendencies still lurking within humanity. Such a spirituality can no longer be grounded in notions of a *commanding God*; rather, it will have to be built upon a vision of a *compelling God*—compelling because people have experienced through symbolic encounter with this God a healing, a strengthening, an affirming that buries any need for them to assert their humanity through the destructive, even deadly, use of human power. This sense of a compelling Parent God who has gifted humanity, who shares in human vulnerability through the cross, is the only viable foundation for a post-Holocaust spirituality.

The Holocaust challenges contemporary spirituality in other areas besides the fundamental issue of imaging God. As Elie Wiesel, Nobel prize writer on Holocaust issues, has reminded us, the Holocaust also forces us to abandon any simplistic notions of human goodness. Post-Holocaust spirituality will have to probe anew the persistence of human sinfulness and how it may be overcome. We cannot fall into the trap of blaming only God for abandoning humanity during this period of *night.* People also failed people. Conversely, we must also examine the example of the righteous Gentiles, the few who often risked everything to save others. What gave them such profound moral courage in a time of crisis, what enabled them to overcome the sinfulness that transformed so many baptized believers into collaborators and bystanders?

The contributions of liturgist David Power also become important for a comprehensive post-Holocaust spirituality. He has written extensively on the need to rekindle within the Churches a spirituality of *lamentation* that will help people through periods such as the Holocaust when God seems especially absent.

Finally, a developed spirituality after the Holocaust will need to highlight the enhanced significance of human cocreatorship in the modern technological world. The Holocaust has made it clear that the human community, not God, must stop massive abuses of human power in our day if they are to be stopped at all. If this is to occur, we shall have to attend also to the nonrational aspects of human consciousness, which the Nazis so skillfully manipulated through their mass public rituals. This means in the end that any adequate post-Holocaust spirituality must have a strong basis in liturgy, for it is liturgical celebration that can best shape the vitalistic side of humanity in a constructive fashion.

See also ENLIGHTENMENT, INFLUENCE ON SPIRITUALITY; EVIL; HISTORY, HISTORICAL CONSCIOUSNESS; INTERRELIGIOUS DIALOGUE; WAR, IMPACT ON SPIRITUALITY.

Bibliography: I. Greenberg, "Cloud of Smoke, Pillar of Fire: Judaism, Christianity, and Modernity after the Holocaust," *Auschwitz: Beginning of a New Era? Reflections on the Holocaust,* ed. E. Fleischner (New York: Ktav, 1977) 7–56. J. Pawlikowski, *The Challenge of the Holocaust for Christian Theology,* rev. ed. (New York: Anti-Defamation League of B'nai B'rith, 1982); idem, "Worship after the Holocaust: An Ethician's Reflections," *Worship* 58, no. 4 (July 1984) 315–329. D. Power, "Response: Liturgy, Memory and the Absence of God," *Worship* 57, no. 4 (July 1983) 326–329.

JOHN T. PAWLIKOWSKI, O.S.M.

HOLY SPIRIT

The Holy Spirit is central to Christian spirituality and to any understanding of it. In fact, the word *spirituality* reflects the realization that Christian life is led in the power and under the guidance of the Holy Spirit; it does not primarily designate this life as dealing with the "spiritual," in the sense of "immaterial." Since Vatican II there has been among Catholics more consciousness of the Holy Spirit in relation to their lives than there was in the earlier modern period. The earlier widespread neglect of the Holy Spirit was due to such historical factors as the defensiveness of the Counter Reformation Church; its isolation from the riches of Eastern Orthodoxy, with its greater concentration on the Spirit; an excessive emphasis on reason in Western culture and Scholastic theology, and on institution in the Church's life.

The context of this reflection on the relation between Christian spirituality and the Holy Spirit is the post-Vatican II era. Here we relate this context briefly and specifically to our theme. People today do not live in a traditional and static culture and society, but in one that is rapidly changing, one in which, at best, they seek to bring about conditions more fitting for the human dignity of all people. These conditions include a greater equality among people, an opportunity for people to have a free and active role in shaping their lives and the societies that affect their lives, and a more positive evaluation of human growth, other Christian denominations, and world religions than the Church at times fostered in the past. People are not objects of history but rather subjects of history, called to take an active role in shaping their individual and social futures, and to do this in the midst of the tensions and conflicts that divide our world (see GS 4-10).

These changed conditions, of course, have an influence on how people see themselves in relation to their Christian life in the Church and call them to reevaluate pre-Vatican II Christian patterns of life. The Church has found that a renewed awareness and theology of the Holy Spirit are uniquely suited to a rearticulation of the Christian life appropriate to these conditions. It is, of course, a sound pneumatology that is needed here. Yves Congar has written that "the soundness of a pneumatology can be judged by a Christological reference to the Word, the sacraments, the ecclesial institution, provided always that such a reference fully recognizes and respects the place and role of the Spirit" (*I Believe in the Holy Spirit,* 1:141).

The theme of the Holy Spirit will be treated (1) by recalling Scripture's teaching on the Spirit as the eschatological gift; (2) by focusing on the Spirit's dynamic impact on Christian life and on the Spirit's indwelling; and (3) by identifying some particular issues of the present day. In treating this theme in Scripture, we shall at times point forward to later developments and Vatican II. The present entry is in agreement with many theologians in referring to the Holy Spirit by the feminine personal pronoun. A rationale for such agreement will be given toward the end of the article.

The Holy Spirit as Eschatological Gift
The Old Testament

The Hebrew word for "spirit" (*rûaḥ*) initially designated the wind, storm, or gentle breeze that brought rain to the fields from the Mediterranean or a sirocco from the desert, and thus life or death to field and flock (Ezek 13:13; 1 Kgs 18:45; 19:12). It also meant the breath in the human person, or life that was thought to be lodged in, or manifested by, breath (Gen 2:7). Human life or breath is a gift of God and belongs to God (Ps 104:27-30); at death it returns to God (Job 34:14f.). In the OT this wind, breath, or spirit was used as a symbol to designate the divine dynamism or force operative in humans to make them capable of exceptional deeds that strengthen the individual and the community in their relation to God, and as such was called "the spirit of the Lord." For example, the spirit of the Lord came upon Samson and he rose up as a defender of Israel (Judg 13:25; 15:14-15). The ecstatic state of the bands of prophets and of Saul when he joined them was ascribed to the spirit of God (1 Sam 10:10); but Saul was also tormented by "an evil spirit sent by the LORD" (1 Sam 16:14). When Samuel anointed David, "the spirit of the LORD rushed upon David" (1 Sam 16:13).

Gradually a more interior empowerment of the person and community in reference to God was ascribed to the spirit of God. Isaiah predicts that the spirit of the Lord will not only come to but "rest upon" the Anointed One who is to save his people, and through this he will receive "a spirit of wisdom and of understanding, a spirit of counsel and of strength, a spirit of knowledge and of fear of the LORD" (Isa 11:2). At the time of the Exile, Ezekiel recognizes that the renewal of Israel to be a faithful people will depend upon God's giving them a new heart and a new spirit (Ezek 36:25-27). This background influenced the psalmist's prayer for personal renewal:

A clean heart create for me, O God,
    and a steadfast spirit renew
        within me.
Cast me not out from your presence,
    and your holy spirit take not from me.
Give me back the joy of your salvation,
    and a willing spirit sustain in me.
(Ps 51:12-14)

Ezekiel also encourages a disheartened people by recounting his vision of a mass of dried bones in the desert being reanimated by the spirit of God (Ezek 37:5-6). Second Isaiah speaks of God pouring out his spirit upon the people like water on thirsty ground (Isa 44:3) and placing his spirit in his servant (Isa 42:1) who will vindicate the cause of Israel. Finally, we hear from the prophet Joel in an apocalyptic vein that on the day of the Lord, a day of judgment and salvation, God will give to the people a far more universal and generous gift of his spirit:

> Then afterward I will pour out
>   my spirit upon all humankind.
> Your sons and daughters shall prophesy,
>   your old men shall dream dreams,
>   your young men shall see visions;
> Even upon the servants and the
>   handmaids, in those days, I will pour
>   out my spirit (Joel 3:1-2).

For context, it should be noted that in the OT, salvation is mediated by different agencies. Specifically, toward the end of the OT period, God's word and spirit were, along with God's wisdom, almost personified as extensions of God by which he acted and was present to his people to save them (Ps 107:20; Wis 18:15; 1:5, 7; 7:22-8:1). God had made his will and commitment known through "the words of the covenant, the ten commandments" (Exod 34:28). God's prophetic word came through the prophets (Ezek 2:9-3:4). Also, creation itself came from God's word (Gen 1:3). God's word and spirit are associated as means by which God creates (Ps 33:6) and saves.

The New Testament

Jesus was himself preeminently a person of the Spirit. (The word *spirit* is capitalized when the NT uses this symbol to refer to a saving influence that is divine and personal, though the multivalent use of the word at times must be preserved.) Luke particularly notes the outpouring of the Spirit in the conception and infancy of Jesus (Lk 1:35, 41, 67; 2:25-27), as he will later note the outpouring of the Spirit in the early Church. Jesus was anointed by the Spirit at his baptism (Lk 3:22) and was filled with the Holy Spirit and led by the Spirit into the desert (Lk 4:1). He returned from the desert in the Spirit and began his public ministry at Nazareth by quoting from Isaiah: "The Spirit of the Lord is upon me, because he has anointed me to bring glad tidings to the poor" (Lk 4:18; Isa 61:1). In Luke's Gospel Jesus ascribes his exorcisms to the "finger of God" (Lk 11:20); in Matthew's Gospel he ascribes them to "the Spirit of God" (Mt 12:28), showing that the early Church associated Jesus' saving power with the Spirit. Luke speaks too of Jesus rejoicing "in the holy Spirit" (Lk 10:21). In short, the whole of Jesus' person and ministry was animated, empowered, and led by the Spirit of the Lord.

It is important to note the relation the primitive Church saw between the salvation it expected through Jesus and the gift of the Holy Spirit. Through his death and resurrection Jesus won salvation for those who believe. The question here is what this salvation means. According to Ernst Käsemann and many other exegetes, the first theological interpretation given to the resurrection of Jesus was apocalyptic. The primitive Church interpreted the resurrection in the line of the OT apocalyptic expectation of God's salvation, exemplified best in Daniel 7 and 12:1-3. Daniel proclaimed to his oppressed people that in the age to come after the present age dominated by evil, God would give his reign to one like a "son of man." This reign to come would be universal and everlasting (Dan 7:13-14, 27), and those forces opposed to God would lose their power and be destroyed. Daniel also prophesied that those faithful to God would rise from the dead to happiness (Dan 12:1-3). This reign of God that included the resurrection of the just is primarily what the first Christians envisioned salvation to be. The fact that the last days or the age to come had begun was shown by the two experiences foundational for, and distinctive of, the Christian community, namely, of Jesus as having already experienced the eschatological resurrection and "experiences of religious ecstasy and enthusiasm recognized as the manifestation of the eschatological Spirit" (Dunn, p. 357). These experiences and the revelation they mediated were an assurance of the promised salvation that those who believed in Jesus and served him in the least of the brothers and sisters would share with him. Early Christians thought that this salvation would be given when Jesus, the Son of Man, came again.

So salvation initially meant that definitive and never-to-be-surpassed deliverance and fulfillment that Jesus would bring with him when he came again. It is future, communal, and transcendent (see Rom 5:9; 8:24; 1 Cor 5:5; Heb 9:28). The kingdom that Christians prayed for was that future reign: "Your kingdom come" (Lk 11:2). And so Christians prayed that Jesus would come again as Lord: "Come, Lord Jesus!" (Rev 22:20; 1 Cor 16:22). The parousia is the fulfillment and liberation of the whole of history as well as of individuals.

Though this salvation is not yet, it is also "already." By this is meant that the salvation that Jesus would effect when he came again is already being given in part and as firstfruits and pledge of the full salvation to come. The age to come has already broken into the present age. Already the forces of evil are being overcome in part, and communion with God and one another in the kingdom is being given in part (see 1 Cor 1:18; 2 Cor 6:2; Eph 2:5, 8).

Through the proclamation of his word, the sacraments, and the Church community, the exalted Jesus is already exercising that lordship which Christians expected him to have when he would come again; and he is sending his Spirit even now. He has already been exalted to the "right hand of the Father." This understanding of Jesus Christ's salvific activity is found in Luke's account of Pentecost (Acts 2:33-34); in John's account of the gift of the Spirit on Easter Sunday, after Jesus had ascended to the Father or been glorified (Jn 20:17, 22; see Jn 7:39); and in Paul's calling the risen and glorified Jesus "a life-giving spirit" (1 Cor 15:45). Thus James Dunn writes: "[T]he Spirit is the future good which has become present for the man of faith—the power of the not yet which has already begun to be realized in his present experience" (Dunn, p. 310). Through the gift of the Spirit, the power of the age to come, we are oriented toward Christ's coming, and indeed "groan within ourselves as we wait for adoption, the redemption of our bodies" (Rom 8:23).

In much of Christian history in the West, the whole of the Christian mystery has been interpreted theologically within a model influenced by Neoplatonism, frequently called the "*exitus-reditus*" model. In this view, all creation was seen to emanate from God and to return to God the Creator through Jesus Christ. There was a descent and an ascent. But in this model there was not sufficient emphasis on our return to God through our orientation to Christ who is to come or to the kingdom as integrating, liberating, and fulfilling history. Christ's second coming was something of an appendix. The *exitus-reditus* model was somewhat appropriate for an agricultural society whose pattern was basically the round of nature's seasons, but it is less adequate for the present age, when people understand themselves as oriented to a historical future.

The recovery of the apocalyptic dimension of the kingdom and the gift of the Spirit in Scripture helps us to present the message of salvation in a way that affirms modern consciousness of orientation to the future. It tends to correct people's fixations on the immediate future or their individual futures, not through discounting the importance of these futures, but through putting them within the horizon of the full future of God's kingdom and calling them to bring about dimensions of this kingdom even in the present.

The Dynamism and Indwelling of the Holy Spirit

In a preeminent sense the Holy Spirit is *the* gift of Christ to his disciples (Acts 2:38; 8:20; 10:45; 11:17; Heb 6:4). The Spirit was given initially to the *whole* community of Jesus' disciples (Acts 1:15; 2:1-3), and given as immediately to all as to the Twelve who exercised a leadership among them. It, or she, was given to others through their inclusion within the community by faith and baptism (Acts 2:38; 10:44-48; 11:16). All are taught by the Spirit (Jn 15:26; 1 Jn 2:27), and all are thus called to be active agents in their Christian life and in the upbuilding of the Church (1 Cor 12) and its missionary activity (Acts 1:8; 2:4; 9:29; 13:2).

Awareness of the dynamic character of the Spirit given to all the baptized has often been lacking in the past, with the result that many Christians considered themselves passive members of the Church, leaving the building of the Church and evangelization to the pope, bishops, priests, and religious. Today, when the dignity of the human person is an essential foundation for social life, it is important to recall this gift of the Spirit to evoke in all Christians a sense of their equal dignity as Christians as well as a movement to genuine Christian adulthood, discernment, and responsibility. The equal dignity of all the baptized is not the only teaching relevant to Christian life, and it can, of course, be misused; but it needs affirmation in our time, and it has been given emphasis by Vatican II (LG 9-12). This belief calls for reflection on the Spirit's dynamic influence in Christian life and the Spirit's personal indwelling.

The Dynamism of the Spirit in Christian Life

In the early Church the dynamism of Christian life was ascribed to God's Spirit or Christ's Spirit, later called the Third Person of the Trinity. The dynamic influence of the Spirit on the Christian's life is treated in the present entry before her indwelling, but it is to be understood that this dynamism is indeed that of a divine Person. The Spirit's influence can be discerned in the teaching of the NT, and particularly of Paul, on the Spirit and the law, the conflict between the Spirit and the flesh, prayer and a sense of God's presence and love, and charisms or gifts and fruits of the Spirit.

The Spirit enables people to do what the law did not: "For the law of the spirit of life in Christ Jesus has freed you from the law of sin and death. For what the law, weakened by the flesh, was powerless to do, this God has done" (Rom 8:2-3). The law is an external principle; it does not give the power to do what it commands, and by telling people what to do, it almost evokes resistance that comes from pride. But the Spirit is an interior principle that gives a new heart; "the love of God has been poured out into our hearts through the holy Spirit that has been given to us" (Rom 5:5). This love is God's love for human beings rather than their love for God. They are given this love by the Spirit, and by the Spirit they can sense the love God has for them. Believers can appreciate through the Spirit what Jesus has done for them: he died for them when they were still sinners (Rom 5:5-8). And so the gift of the Spirit calls people to a response of love to God who first loved them: "we love because he first loved us" (1 Jn 4:19).

God's love and God's humility (Phil 2:5-11) overcome the resistance that comes from pride and show that God wants human beings' union with him as sons and daughters rather than servile obedience. Thus the Spirit gives freedom in the sense that people are enabled to respond to God's call out of an inner will and love. In fact, the love that wells up in them is the Spirit's greatest gift (1 Cor 13). Such a gift of the Spirit enables them to put God first and to fulfill the new commandment of love for neighbor. Love is the fulfillment of the law, because "love does no evil to the neighbor" (Rom 13:10).

The exercise of authority in the Church is to be in accord with this Spirit. Paul did not use his naked authority as an apostle, but rather drew others to Christ by persuasion and gentleness (1 Thess 2:7-11). In the Church "the exclusive purpose of authority is *diakonia* or service" (Bermejo, p. 303). There was tension at times between authority and freedom even in churches established by Paul, but the Spirit is the source of each, and neither can be unlimited. In their freedom, Christians still need the precepts of the law and authority to help them detect the voice of the Spirit. But Paul in freedom also confronted authority (Gal 2:11-14). Christian freedom, then, is paradoxical, and it is a task that is given to all.

A tension exists, then, not only between members of the Church but also within the believer. For, according to Paul, the believer recognizes "that he is a *divided man, a man of split loyalties.* He lives in the overlap of the ages and belongs to both of them *at the same time*" (Dunn, p. 312). Paul expresses this insight clearly in Gal 5:16-17: "I say, then: live by the Spirit and you will certainly not gratify the desire of the flesh. For the flesh has desires against the Spirit, and the Spirit against the flesh; these are opposed to each other, so that you may not do what you want." By "flesh" (*sarx*) Paul means all that is opposed to the Spirit rather than simply carnal impulses (Gal 5:19-21). The gift of the Spirit enables believers to "live according to the spirit" (Rom 8:5), i.e., according to that deepest part of themselves that is particularly apt to receive the Spirit of God (see 1 Thess 5:23 for Paul's distinction in the human person of "spirit" [*pneuma*], "soul" [*psy-che*], and "body" [*sōma*]). Against the Jews, Paul says that Christians have already received the power of the age to come, namely, the Spirit of God and of Christ. But against the early Gnostics, he says that Christians possess this Spirit, or are possessed by it, only in part. The flesh and its impulses are still with us, and so there is the experience of conflict, and Christians cannot do what they want.

Through the Spirit within, Christians have a sense of God's loving dispositions toward them as his sons and daughters, and they respond with confidence in God. "The Spirit itself bears witness with our spirit that we are children of God" (Rom 8:16). There is an inner testimony that the Spirit gives; and thus God's relation to Christians and their relation to God do arise in consciousness and are in some sense an experience, even though this is very elusive, mysterious, and not under human control (1 Cor 2:10-13, 16; Jn 14:17, 26; 1 Jn 4:13). Believers are touched by the Spirit, and Christian prayer is a response to the divine initiative. By the Spirit, Paul tells the Christians of Rome, "you received a spirit of adoption, through which we cry, *Abba,* 'Father!'" (Rom 8:15). By the Spirit, too, they long for "the revelation of the children of God" (Rom 8:19), which will happen when Christ comes again, and they are enabled to pray in a way far beyond what words can convey (Rom 8:26-27).

The author of the Letter to the Ephesians prays that Christians may, by the Spirit, "have strength to comprehend with all the holy ones what is the breadth and length and height and depth, and to know the love of Christ that surpasses knowledge, so that you may be filled with all the fullness of God" (Eph 3:18-19). This prayer is offered within the context of the Christian community, entered through baptism, in which one receives the Spirit (Acts 2:38), for baptism is given "in the name of the Father, the Son, and of the holy Spirit" (Mt 28:19); one receives the Spirit in a special way in what later came to be called confirmation (Acts 3:14-16). Life and its sustenance are given also through the Eucharist, and traditionally the Holy Spirit has been invoked in it (the epiclesis) both to sanctify the bread and wine and to enable the participant to have a full sacramental encounter with Christ. And sins are forgiven by the Twelve, who have been empowered by Christ for this by the gift of the Spirit (Jn 20:21-23).

One manifestation of the Spirit's dynamic influence in the early Church is seen in the *charisms* or gifts given so profusely, particularly in Corinth (see 1 Cor 12-14; Rom 12). Each of these "spiritual gifts" (1 Cor 12:4) is a "manifestation of the Spirit" (1 Cor 12:7), a sort of "brilliant epiphany, like the sparkling reflection of a crystal ball as it rotates in the light" (Montague, p. 148). The charisms are described in 1 Corinthians 12 "less as stable offices than as passing movements of the Spirit" (Montague, p. 148). These gifts are powerful, since they are impulses of the Spirit beyond the simply rational; and they are given for the common good, the building up of the community, and are to be engaged in with that intent, namely, from the motive of love. The Spirit's gifts are sometimes abused, not always used in a way that builds up the community, and so Paul shows that the exercise of the gifts without charity is empty and worthless (1 Cor 13). The Church needs many kinds of gifts, and Paul lists some of these (see 1 Cor 12:8-11). Christians need the mutual services of the community, and Paul generously acknowledges the richness of others' gifts. A hierarchy exists among the ministries for which the gifts equip members: "first, apostles; second, prophets; third, teachers; then, mighty deeds; then gifts of healing, assistance, administration, and varieties of tongues" (1 Cor 12:28). Paul includes the permanent ministry or office of "apostleship" among the gifts, and thus does not give a basis for distinguishing between a "charismatic" Church and an "institutional" Church.

The spiritual gifts that Paul mentions were very evident in the early Church and well into the 2nd century, but many of them, such as speaking in tongues, were not in much evidence later. This decline in the presence of such charisms may have been due in part to the Church's reaction against false claims to gifts of the Spirit by the Montanists in the 3rd century. One of these charisms, discernment of spirits, was discussed at length by writers on spirituality. And, particularly since Vatican II, charismatic gifts have been more widely accepted as normal in the Christian community; their presence has been the basis for one of the most prominent movements in spirituality after Vatican II, namely, the charismatic renewal.

The Fathers of the Western Church and later spiritual writers emphasized the seven gifts of the Holy Spirit, modeled on the gifts that Isaiah prophesied would be fully present in the future Anointed One or Messiah: "a spirit of wisdom and of understanding, a spirit of counsel and of strength, a spirit of knowledge and of fear of the Lord" (Isa 11:2). In the Septuagint and later in the Vulgate, the last-named gift, indicated by one Hebrew word used twice, was translated by two terms—"piety and fear of the Lord"—and so the number of gifts was brought to seven.

The seven gifts of the Holy Spirit were discussed at length by the Scholastics, e.g., Thomas Aquinas (ST I-II, q. 68), and by writers on the spiritual life in the modern age, e.g., Francis de Sales (*Treatise on the Love of God,* Bk. 11, chap. 5). Distinct gifts were related to each of the theological virtues and the four cardinal virtues, though there was not always agreement on which gift was to be attached to which virtue, or how the gifts were to be distinguished from infused virtues. The number seven is now more commonly taken as a symbol of plenitude rather than as indicating seven distinct gifts.

An image used at times to indicate the difference between the practice of the virtues with the gifts and without the gifts is the difference between a boat's movement by wind in the sails and by rowing. The Holy Spirit acts in Christians' lives to inspire them and guide them, illumine them in prayer and move them to action. These gifts of the Holy Spirit are principles both of the Spirit's action and of Christians' docility and free, spontaneous submission to the divine action. It is frequently apparent in the saints' and dedicated Christians' illumination in prayer and boldness in action beyond the common norm, even though these may not be accompanied by any superficial supportive religious feeling. The practice of discernment of spirits was called upon to evaluate these illuminations and impulses. Such practice was evident even in Scripture, where Paul and John used as criteria for these impulses consistency with authentic Christian belief (1 Cor 12:1-3; Jn 16:13-15; 1 Jn 4:1-6), their fruits (Mt 7:16; Gal 5:22-23), and particularly charity (1 Jn 4:12-13).

The Indwelling Spirit

Are the dynamic effects treated above due to God's power acting in the Christian community and individuals, or more definitely due to the person of the Holy Spirit? "Spirit" in Scripture is a symbol, and in the earliest Christian writings it was a symbol of the power acting in Christians and manifesting itself in the attitudes and actions considered above. Many exegetes state that Paul was not clear about the relation between the Spirit and Christ. While this interpretation is true in part, still Paul does at least give bases for the later, clearer Christian insight into the personal character of the Holy Spirit operating in Christian life; and he may give more than this. For example, he uses a tripartite formula: "The grace of our Lord Jesus Christ and the love of God and the fellowship of the holy Spirit be with all of you" (2 Cor 13:13). Furthermore, he understands the Christian

community and the individual Christian to be temples of the Spirit: "Do you not know that your body is a temple of the holy Spirit within you, whom you have from God, and that you are not your own?" (1 Cor 6:19; see 1 Cor 3:16). The Spirit dwells in Christians.

The personal character of the Holy Spirit is clearer in John's Gospel. There Jesus calls the Spirit "another Paraclete" or "another Advocate": "I will ask the Father, and he will give you another Advocate to be with you always, the Spirit of truth" (Jn 14:16-17). The Greek word *paraklētos,* usually translated as "Paraclete," means an advocate in Greek law, a mediator, comforter, helper, or intercessor. Jesus is telling his disciples that though he, their present Paraclete, is leaving them, he will not leave them orphans; he will send them *another* Paraclete, the Holy Spirit. As Jesus was personal, so this other Paraclete is personal. The divinity of this Paraclete is thereby suggested, because it is worthwhile for the disciples to have the substitution of this Paraclete for the visible presence of Jesus (Jn 16:7). The Father and Jesus will send the Paraclete (Jn 14:26; 16:7).

What John emphasizes is not so much the dynamism of the Spirit as the intimate presence of Father and Son she mediates and the affective knowledge or knowledge by experience this presence gives. The disciples will know the Spirit because she "remains with you, and will be in you" (Jn 14:17). The Holy Spirit, "the Spirit of truth," will lead the disciples "to all truth" (Jn 16:13); she will remind them of all Jesus told them (Jn 14:26); she will be with them always (Jn 14:16) and take away their orphaned state (Jn 14:18). Through the Spirit dwelling in the disciple, Jesus and the Father "will come to him and make our dwelling with him" (Jn 14:23); and through the Spirit and the disciples' witness, the world will be convicted of sin because of the way it has treated Jesus (Jn 16:8-11).

Later Christian reflection on the change effected by Christ and the Spirit in the

Christian disciples led to somewhat different emphases in the East and the West. In the West this change was expressed by "grace," a term taken from Paul that primarily meant God's favor or unmerited benevolence toward sinners, but also the effect of that favor within human beings, namely, the justification of sinners, their adoption as sons and daughters of the Father, and sanctification. Though its primary effect in the Christian is in Paul a personal relation to the Father in the Spirit of Christ, in Western theology the emphasis was on a created gift that effected this. In the East the emphasis was more Johannine; that is, what was emphasized was God's gift of the Holy Spirit, God's uncreated gift of himself, and its effect, namely, a divinization of the human being.

In the 20th century there has been an emerging consensus that the primary gift of grace is the uncreated gift that God, Father, Son, and Holy Spirit, make of themselves. This uncreated gift is their indwelling as well as a proper relationship between the believer and each of the divine Persons. Thus they are made sons and daughters of the Father, not simply of the Trinity; they are given a filial relation to the Father that is a participation in that of Jesus Christ; and the sanctity or love that they are given is properly a share or participation in that of the Holy Spirit, the Spirit of the Father and of the Son. Believers are given some consciousness of this. Through this gift and the created gift of grace they are given a new disposition, a new attitude toward, and relationship to, God that changes them, so that they enter into the Trinitarian family.

The Spirit has a certain precedence within this gift of grace, because it is by the Father and the Son pouring the Spirit into the human person that he or she is given the Spirit's relation to the Father through the Son, and the capacity for the life of a disciple that reflects this gift. It is through faith and baptism that this gift is received. As indicated toward the beginning of this entry, the Father sends the Spirit through the risen and exalted Christ (1 Cor 15:45); thus the Spirit is the power of the age to come. The gift of the Spirit is to be continually transforming Christians (2 Cor 3:17-18) into the image of Christ (Rom 8:29), a transformation that is not completed here below.

Some Current Issues

Only a few issues in current reflection on the importance of the Spirit in the Christian life can be taken up here.

Ecclesiology and Spirituality

Christian spirituality is dependent in large part on an understanding of the Church. Vatican II's emphasis on pneumatology in its treatment of the Church is leading to a somewhat new paradigm of being a Christian. The earlier divisions between the Roman Catholic Church and Orthodoxy, on the one hand, and the Reformers, on the other hand, were largely due to different interpretations of the relation between Spirit and institution in the Church. Vatican II and developments in Catholic theology since then have gone far toward overcoming these differences of interpretation. To give just one statement of Vatican II: "It is the Holy Spirit, dwelling in those who believe, pervading and ruling over the entire Church, who brings about that marvelous communion of the faithful and joins them together so intimately in Christ that He is the principle of the Church's unity. By distributing various kinds of spiritual gifts and ministries (see 1 Cor 12:4-11), He enriches the Church of Jesus Christ with different functions 'in order to perfect the saints for a work of ministry, for building up the body of Christ' (Eph 4:12)" (UR 2; see LG 17, 26).

The emphasis here is not on the hierarchy and the word it preaches as sources of unity, though they too are principles of unity, but on the Spirit acting in all the faithful "con-spiring" to build up a community. All the faithful are active subjects in the Church. The local Church is a full manifestation of the Church of God, as long as it is keeping a living communion with the other local Churches. The Spirit brings about a communion of local Churches to form the whole Church, while preserving, purifying, and perfecting the goods proper to the local Churches, for these too enrich the whole. Babel is reversed by Pentecost, but it would not be reversed if unity meant uniformity.

The unity of the Church is modeled on that of the Trinity (LG 4), which embraces to the highest degree both unity and diversity. The charism of leadership in the Church is collegial, in union with the pope, who has a special ministry of unity. Gifts of the Spirit are distributed to Christians as the Spirit wills; and pastors, who have a ministry of service in the Church rather than over the Church, are called to discern, acknowledge, make use of, and organize such gifts, not to suppress them. According to Scripture (see 1 Thess 5:19-21), it is the whole Church, and not only its pastors, that is called to discern the presence of the Spirit. The Spirit was given first to the Church, and to the individual minister and faithful within the Church. Christians are called to have more trust in the Spirit given to the Church as a whole than in the Spirit within them as individuals or as a particular cultural group. But since even Vatican I asserted that God gave to the successor of Peter *that* charism of infallibility that he wanted the whole Church to be endowed with, the belief of the faithful as a community has an infallibility that takes a certain precedence over that of the pope (also see LG 25). Once more, there may be tension, but there is not contradiction between charism and institution.

Spiritual Growth and the Spirit

Scripture itself speaks of a maturity to which Christians are called (1 Cor 2:6; Heb 6:1). This maturity is lacking in those Christians who are still "fleshly people," "infants in Christ" who need milk and can-

not take solid food, whereas they are called to be animated by the Spirit, to be "spiritual" (*pneumatikoi*—1 Cor 3:1-2). Christians are called to live out their baptismal consecration, to be sanctified, to be holy, to grow above all in love of God and neighbor. This call to maturity implies an anthropology, namely, that there are different dimensions to a human being, some deeper and some more superficial.

A theologian who gave significant attention to this sort of Christian anthropology in our century is Karl Rahner, whose first book, *Spirit in the World,* viewed the human person as characterized by an orientation toward the infinite through the finite, as a dynamic orientation in the world toward the Absolute or God. The later Rahner, in response to criticisms of his earlier position, taught that human transcendence is not one that is timeless but is rather openness to the future, and indeed the absolute future. Human persons' openness to others, their experience of the "human Thou," is an essential inner moment of transcendence toward God. Modern developmental psychology has analyzed human growth as occurring through stages in which the maturing subject interacts with an enlarging environment and at the cost of letting go of earlier structures of growth as dominant forms when they are no longer adequate. Classical Christian spirituality mapped spiritual growth through stages, such as the purgative, illuminative, and unitive, and it studied mysticism in this context. The Christian's growth through these stages even to the deepest experience of God, far beyond the emotional or conceptual level, has at times been ascribed to the Spirit. But the place of the Spirit in this growth has also at times not been sufficiently noted, perhaps in reaction to movements of spirituality that were characterized by unsound pneumatologies (e.g., the Allumbrados in Spain in the 16th century). With the renewed recognition that the Holy Spirit comes to the Church and to Christians from the exalted

Christ gone into his kingdom, the Christian's orientation to the future is a response to an *adventus,* a coming of the Spirit from this future kingdom or salvation, and not primarily a response to a primordial mission of the Spirit from God as Creator.

The Spirit and Social Justice

It may seem, and it has seemed to many, that a spirituality that emphasizes the Spirit tends to interiority and intra-ecclesial concerns, but not to a concern for justice in the larger world. An unbalanced interiority may be tied in with a spirituality that considers the person's return to God in too vertical a fashion, without embracing history and its tasks. But such a view did not characterize the early Church, nor should it characterize the present age. It was precisely the gift of the Spirit that opened the early Church up to the larger world and gave it its missionary impulse (Acts 1:8). This dynamic openness to others included a concern for the poor (Gal 2:10; Rom 15:25-28; 1 Cor 16:1-4; 2 Cor 8 and 9), as Jesus' ministry had (Mt 11:5; *passim*); the Spirit gives us the "mind of Christ" (1 Cor 2:16). The kingdom of God that is the horizon of Christian life is that apocalyptic kingdom where the oppressed will be fully liberated, and the Spirit enables believers to put this kingdom first in their lives (Mt 6:33).

Vatican II speaks of the Church as "the kingdom of Christ now present in mystery" (LG 3). Those who are genuinely oriented to such a kingdom will be concerned to overcome all sorts of oppression in the present world. As the assembled bishops wrote at the Synod of 1971 ("Justice in the World"): "The mission of preaching the Gospel dictates at the present time that we should dedicate ourselves to the liberation of man even in his present existence in this world." The bishops called Christians to accept responsibilities in secular life: "In this way they testify to the power of the Holy Spirit through their action in the service of men in those things which are de-

cisive for the existence and future of humanity." Moreover, in this age when it is clear that the oppression an individual suffers is frequently due to humanly made social, economic, cultural, or political systems, the power of the Spirit moves many to seek changes in these systems and not only to relieve the needs of individuals.

Feminine Symbols and the Holy Spirit

A growing number of theologians are suggesting that it is appropriate to speak of the Holy Spirit by the third person feminine pronoun. There seems to be basis for this in the very symbols that Scripture uses of the Spirit. When these symbols are compared with those by which the Word of God (and above all Jesus) is manifested, they seem to be what most people would accept as feminine symbols. For example, in the theophany at the baptism of Jesus, "he saw the Spirit of God descending like a dove and coming upon him" (Mt 3:16). It is the *movement* of the dove that is the center of this symbol. If one sees this text in the light of Deut 32:11, where God's care for Israel in the desert is compared to that of an eagle *hovering* over its young ones, symbiotically inciting them to risk flying, one may find reason to see this symbol of the Holy Spirit as feminine. It is of even greater interest that Luke changed the tradition he inherited concerning this theophany and wrote: ". . . the holy Spirit descended upon him in *bodily form* like a dove" (Lk 3:22). Perhaps one reason Luke emphasized the form of the dove rather than the movement was that in this way he could emphasize for his Gentile readers the feminine character of the symbol, since they knew that in their world the dove was a symbol of goddesses, such as Atargatis, Astarte, Istar, Venus, and Athene (see "Feminine Symbols and the Holy Spirit," in J. Farrelly, *God's Work in a Changing World,* Lanham, Md.: Univ. Press of America, 1985, pp. 49-76).

Space allows only one other example of these symbols here. In the Book of Revelation, John had a vision of a "river of life-giving water . . . flowing from the throne of God and of the Lamb. . . . On either side of the river grew the tree of life that produces fruit twelve times a year" (Rev 22:1-2). The river of life-giving water appears to be a symbol of the Holy Spirit (see Jn 7:38-39). It is a symbol of immanence and of fertility, and in the culture of that time and place feminine deities rather than masculine ones were the principles of fertility and were associated, as earth deities, with immanence. A growing acknowledgment that the major symbols of the Holy Spirit in Scripture are feminine has significance in redressing the imbalance in the traditional Christian view of God and in reaffirming the equal dignity of men and women; it is only in both together that God is properly imaged (Gen 1:27).

The Holy Spirit and World Religions

In the shrinking world of the present, Christians cannot escape influence by, and interaction with, other major world religions. Vatican II affirmed elements of these religions (NA 2) and acknowledged that the Holy Spirit was operating in the world before the glorification of Christ and the advent of the Church to a specific geographical area (AG 4). As the early Church recognized the Logos already operating in the Mediterranean world and dialogued with that world in part through acknowledging this presence of the Logos, a number of those concerned today with interreligious dialogue (e.g., Raimundo Panikkar, Bede Griffiths) consider that a dialogue with major Eastern religions should center on spiritualities and find a point of contact with them not so much in the Word as in the Spirit and the Father. For example, they find a certain affinity between Hinduism, with its stress on the immanence of deity, its dynamism and the religious goal of a mysticism of union, and the Christian understanding of the Spirit or dimensions of experience appropriated to the Spirit (e.g., unity). This perspective in interreligious dialogue perhaps allows Christians to acknowledge the spiritual riches of Hinduism and some other Eastern religions that similarly stress immanence (e.g., Taoism and Shinto), to relate these to certain scriptural symbols of the Spirit (e.g., the river of life-giving waters in the Book of Revelation), and to more fully integrate an experience of immanence into Christian spirituality.

Still another contemporary basis calling for a renewed emphasis on the Holy Spirit is our need for an enhanced ecological consciousness. Perhaps it is in part a loss in the West of any sense of the sacredness of the physical world that has led to a serious pollution of the physical environment in which we live. Such pollution is one way in which "creation was made subject to futility, not of its own accord but because of the one who subjected it" (Rom 8:20). In part because of environmental pollution, "creation is groaning in labor pains even until now" (Rom 8:22) to "be set free from slavery to corruption and share in the glorious freedom of the children of God" (Rom 8:21). A renewed awareness of God's presence through the Holy Spirit can contribute to a greater respect for all forms of God's immanence in creation, including that necessary to recover an ecological balance so important for the present and following generations.

See also BREATH, BREATHING: CHARISM; CHARISMATIC RENEWAL; CHURCH; DISCERNMENT OF SPIRITS; FRUIT(S) OF THE HOLY SPIRIT; GIFTS OF THE HOLY SPIRIT; GOD; GRACE; KINGDOM OF GOD; SACRAMENTS; SPIRITUALITY, CHRISTIAN; TRINITARIAN SPIRITUALITY.

Bibliography: Y. Congar, *I Believe in the Holy Spirit,* 3 vols. (New York: Seabury, 1983). L. Bermejo, *The Spirit of Life: The Holy Spirit in the Life of the Christian* (Chicago: Loyola Univ. Press, 1989). J. Dunn, *Jesus and the Spirit* (Philadelphia: Westminster, 1975). G. Montague, *The Holy Spirit: Growth of a Biblical Tradition* (New York: Paulist, 1975). L. Bouyer, *Le Consolateur, Saint Esprit et vie de grace* (Paris: Cerf, 1980). J. Farrelly, "Trinity as Salvific Mystery," *Monastic Studies* 17 (1986) 81–100. W. Mills, *The Holy Spirit: A Bibliography* (Peabody, Mass.: Hendrickson, 1988).

M. JOHN FARRELLY, O.S.B.

HOMOSEXUALITY

We are very much aware today of the influence of gender identity on spirituality. Many spiritual directors working with lesbian and gay directees are becoming aware of the special influence of sexual orientation on one's spiritual life; homosexuals, because of their sexual orientation and its implications for their affective life, will relate differently to Christ and to God than will their heterosexual counterparts.

Carl Jung recognized a special spiritual quality that characterized the homosexuals with whom he worked as a therapist: "He [the homosexual] is endowed with a wealth of religious feelings, which help him to bring the *ecclesia spiritualis* into reality, and a spirituality which makes him responsive to revelation" (C. G. Jung, *The Collected Works,* New York: Pantheon, 1959, 9:86–87). Anthropologists note that in many primitive cultures gays and lesbians play a strong role in spiritual leadership. For example, in American Indian tradition the berdache or the heyoehkah who gave spiritual leadership to the tribe were usually drawn from among the gay members of the tribe.

Gay men and lesbian women have also played a leading, if hidden, role in Western monastic tradition. Matthew Kelty, a Trappist monk, speaks of a special spiritual quality in his life as a hermit and contemplative that he attributes to his homosexuality: ". . . the reason [for this special quality], as I have worked it out, is that they [homosexuals] are more closely related to the 'anima' than is usual. The man with a strong anima will always experience some inadequacy until he comes to terms with his inner spirit and establishes communion—no small achievement" (*Flute Solo: Reflections of a Trappist Hermit,* Garden City, N.Y.: Doubleday, 1980).

In his book *We Drink from Our Own Wells,* Gustavo Gutiérrez makes the point that the unique experience of suffering by the poor in the Third World gives rise to a very special type of spirituality. In a similar way, the unique and frequently painful experience of being an exile from family, church, and culture can engender a special spirituality among gay people. John Fortunato spells out that experience and the resulting spirituality in his classic work *Embracing the Exile: Healing Journeys of Gay Christians.* The only healthy spiritual way for gay persons to deal with their exile status, according to Fortunato, is to go through a process of mourning and to let go of their desire to belong to, and be accepted by, all the structures of this world. This mourning process recapitulates the ancient spiritual practice of detachment. One must go through the five stages of mourning outlined by Elisabeth Kübler-Ross: denial, compromise, anger, depression, and finally acceptance.

Many gays and lesbians fail to complete this process. As a result, they can get stuck, for example, at the denial or compromise stage, trying to live out their life as a false self, suppressing or denying their reality as gay persons. Or they can get stuck at the stage of anger or depression, becoming full of bitterness and cynicism. But if gay persons complete the mourning process, they will have already completed the detachment process from this world that most people are challenged to achieve only as they approach death. "What gay people have to give up is the attachment to rejection and the need for people (often incapable or unwilling to do so) to affirm their wholeness and lovableness. If they give up denying, fighting, and wallowing in the depression, they stop being stuck. They begin to see that freedom and a sense of belonging are not to be found in the myth at all. They never were. They begin to understand what Jesus meant when he said: 'My kingdom does not belong to this world' (Jn 18:36)" (Fortunato, p. 91). This spirit of detachment has become especially important during this time of the AIDS crisis. Consequently, by deepening their spiritual life, gays can turn what they see as the curse of gayness, the curse of being in exile, into spiritual gold by realizing that to the degree that they are exiles in this world, they belong ever more deeply in the kingdom of God.

Hans Küng, in his book *Does God Exist?*, makes the point that the essential human psychological foundation and presupposition for faith and a spiritual life is the virtue of trust. Trust is the cornerstone of a psychologically healthy personality; without it a spiritual life is impossible. The principal challenge, then, of our spiritual life is to experience the goodness of creation and its essential trustworthiness.

However, lesbians and gay men face a unique challenge to their ability to trust creation. Since they do not choose their sexual orientation, they experience it as a given, a part of created reality. Insofar as they are taught to see themselves as negative, as created sinful, sick, or evil, they will necessarily experience a deep crisis in their ability to trust the Creator. If they believe that their sexual orientation is part of the created reality and at the same time that it is an "orientation to evil," then they will experience a deep crisis in their ability to trust creation and God. Their only alternative is to begin the development of a deep spiritual life. They must achieve an even deeper trust of self, body, nature, the cosmos, and God. As Matthew Fox asks in his essay "The Spiritual Life of Homosexuals and Just About Everybody Else": "Who knows more about the beauty of creation and the New Creation than those who have been told verbally and non-verbally by religion and society that the way they were created was a mistake and even sinful?" (in Nugent, p. 197).

The spiritual struggle for most gays and lesbians, then, is to achieve trust—first of all self-trust. To achieve that self-trust, they must develop their capacity to hear what God is saying to them directly in their own experiences. They must learn to trust the words of Scripture: "You love all things that are and loathe nothing that you have made; for what you hated, you would not

have fashioned" (Wis 11:24). The presence of homophobia in so many mediated sources, even the translations of Scripture, gives a special urgency to the development of autonomy in gay spiritual life. Gays must learn a new level of spiritual maturity, basing their spiritual life on inner convictions and not on outside expectations. They must develop a personal prayer life and learn how to "discern spirits" so that they can hear what God is saying to them through their hearts and trust what they hear, even when it is in conflict with homophobic authorities.

Finally, gay people have a keen awareness that spiritual life is not a matter of the head but of the heart. Thus a healthy spiritual life must be holistic; it cannot be based on a denial and rejection of the body and its feelings, especially its sexual feelings. There is a necessary sexual component in our search for intimacy with God. To totally suppress that component can place a major obstacle in the path of spiritual growth. Gay people are constantly in a process of discernment about how to integrate their growth in intimacy with God with their search to live out human intimacy in its fullness. Many gays are fully aware of their need for spiritual community in order to successfully carry out this discernment process.

See also FEELINGS; HOLISTIC SPIRITUALITY; INTIMACY; LOVE; MARGINALIZED, THE; SEXUALITY.

Bibliography: J. Boswell, *Christianity, Social Tolerance and Homosexuality: Gay People in Western Europe from the Beginning of the Christian Era to the Fourteenth Century* (Chicago: Univ. of Chicago Press, 1980). J. Fortunato, *Embracing the Exile: Healing Journeys of Gay Christians* (San Francisco: Harper & Row, 1984). J. McNeill, *The Church and the Homosexual,* revised and expanded edition (Boston: Beacon Press, 1988); idem, *Taking a Chance on God: Liberation Theology for Gays, Lesbians and Their Lovers, Families and Friends* (Boston: Beacon Press, 1988). J. Nelson, *Between Two Gardens: Reflections on Sexuality and Religious Experience* (New York: Pilgrim Press, 1988). R. Nugent, ed., *A Challenge to Love: Gay and Lesbian Catholics in the Church* (New York: Crossroad, 1984). M. Thompson, *Gay Spirit: Myth and Meaning* (New York: St. Martin's Press, 1987).

JOHN J. McNEILL

HOPE

Hope is traditionally reckoned the second of the three theological virtues, faith and charity being the other two. These virtues are called "theological" because they are explicitly and directly concerned with one's relationship to God. They are understood to be at the same time God's gift to us and our own activity. The virtue of hope, that is, the attitude and activity of hoping, is a focus of attention, affectivity, and commitment to action toward the future goal of fulfillment in God, the full realization of the reign of God. Often, however, the term "our hope" or "the hope of Christians" refers not to the activity of hoping but rather to the ground of our hope in God's promises or the person of Jesus, or to the object or content of our hope as salvation.

Hope in Scripture

The theme of hope is the dynamic element of the whole Bible, where it is presented primarily as hope for the people of God as a community and for the whole world as God's creation, and secondarily as hope for the individual. The story line of the Scriptures is an invitation to hopeful living. It begins with the thesis that the suffering and injustices of the world are not simply inevitable facts of existence, because the world of God's creating is wholly good. Tragedy and exile have come through creaturely misuse of freedom in independence from, and opposition to, God, but God will not abandon creation and reaches out to redeem. There is to be a journey and a struggle through history toward a new harmony and happiness. This is the thrust of Genesis 1–3.

The same theme is basic to the stories of Exodus, Sinai, and the entry into the Promised Land. God does not tolerate the oppression and enslavement of the people, and therefore both promises and commands their liberation and their shaping of a holy peoplehood in full communion with God and the divine intentions for the world. In this the Law of God and the promised salvation are intimately connected (Exodus and Deuteronomy). This is reiterated in the subsequent recital of the history of Israel, nowhere more forcefully than in the prophets who emphasize that the hope of future well-being and salvation is especially for the poor and downtrodden, for the humble and simple, and for those who are faithful, trusting in God's way and not in their own strength and wealth.

In the NT the preaching of Jesus expresses confidence that salvation (the coming reign of God) is now at hand, and calls therefore for radical generosity in community living, unreserved trust in God for the fulfilling of one's own needs, and total commitment to the welcoming and announcing of the reign of God (e.g., Matthew 5–7, the kingdom parables, especially Matthew 13, and the miracles of healing and restoring to life). The preaching of Jesus also reasserts hope for the individual, picking up the intertestamental theme of resurrection to new life, and the practice of hope by living in the historical present as though God reigned quite simply and none other had power (Mt 22:31-33; Jn 5:27-30).

For an analysis of what is involved in the activity of hoping, the Pauline letters are more explicit than the Gospels. Paul writes that hope is the work of the Spirit (Gal 5:5), that hope permeates all creation as it struggles toward salvation (Rom 8:18-25), that hope is expressed in fortitude in the face of risk and suffering (1 Thess 1:1-3), that it is exercised by covenantal living (2 Cor 3:1-3). Paul also maintains that Abraham is an example of hope because, having put his faith in God's promises, he took drastic steps to live according to those promises (Rom 4:18-:9), and that living by hope, which involves endurance of suffering, has a self-validating quality (Rom 5:4-5); this is so because Christian hope is grounded in the first place in the loving generosity of God, manifested to us constantly and most particularly in the sacrificial death of Christ (Rom 5:6-11). From his many allusions to hope, it is clear that for Paul the content of our hope can safely be left implicit and in God's hands, while the quality of hoping to which we are called must be understood quite explicitly, consisting of the passive element of patient and cheerful endurance under trying and frustrating circumstances, and of the active element of courage in taking risks for the gospel and generosity in living a life in the community of believers which is fully faithful to the covenant of God's redeeming love in Christ.

It is in the Pauline letters that we also find the original listing of faith, hope, and love as the preeminent virtues of Christians (1 Cor 13:13; 1 Thess 1:3), though it is clear that the author does not have in mind the elaborate technical definitions that were later given for these virtues. Paul uses the words in a context of exhortation and encouragement that does not demand Scholastic precision, and this is true also when the subject of hope is raised in the First Letter of Peter (1 Pet 1:3, 21) and in brief references elsewhere in the NT.

Hope in Patristic Literature

What was written in the first three centuries of Christianity about hope reflects the time of intermittent persecutions in which the writers and their communities lived. Authentic Christian hope often expressed itself in a radically countercultural way of life. The letters of Ignatius of Antioch stress Eucharist and community harmony as the principal ways of showing forth the hope of Christians, but they also stress endurance in persecution. The *First Apology* of Justin the Martyr sees the hope of Christians expressed in fidelity to community worship and in law-abiding, civically responsible lives lived calmly and without resentment in spite of calumnies and persecution. Origen of Alexandria, in

First Principles and elsewhere, gives more weight to contemplation and renunciation as the proper expressions of Christian hope, which he sees as referring mainly to an afterlife, while Lactantius, in the seventh book of the *Divine Institutes,* lays stress on properly understanding the plan of God as the basic component of the practice of hope. However, these authors were not concerned with analyzing the virtue of hope but were writing rather generally about the Christian way of life as expressing practically the hope offered by God's promises.

On the other hand, these early centuries offer ample, often divergent testimonies about the content of Christian hope. For instance, the *First Letter* of Clement of Rome and the *Didache* hold out the expectation of the parousia, or triumphant return of Christ, a resurrection of the dead, and general judgment, but they are not explicit about what would follow that judgment. From the 2nd to the 5th century, authoritative voices of the Church from Irenaeus onward rejected emphatically two tendencies, the Gnostic and the voyeuristic, and this rejection seems to have stemmed from a discerning of the true Christian practice of hope. The Gnostic tendency to see salvation as escape from the body, the world, human history, and familial and social responsibilities carries an evident danger. If that were the content of hope, then the practice of hope would largely be by withdrawal from responsibilities, relationships, and commitments to community. The discernment of the Church was that this was false to the gospel.

The voyeuristic tendency presented a similar threat to true Christian life and hope. There were in those early centuries, and have been from time to time since then, attempts or claims to see the final future concretely, calculating the time and place of the *parousia* and the exact manner of the end (seen as a specific point in time). This kind of speculation had already been rejected in the apostolic writings, and it is obvious why. Such preoccupations cater to idle curiosity, have no basis in reality, tend to inspire elitist claims to secret knowledge and power, and deflect attention and effort from an authentic and practical exercise of Christian hope. If such claims to know the future concretely by the reading of signs and codes in the Scriptures or elsewhere were valid, the practice of hope would be reduced to speculation and passive waiting.

One especially interesting view of the content of Christian hope, vehemently denied by the Church in retrospect, was that of Origen of Alexandria. He claimed a symmetry in creation and history that required a final restoration (*apokatastasis*) so complete that damnation could not possibly be eternal or definitive. This the Church also rejected, because such expectation cancels the seriousness of the redemption and obscures the role that human freedom must play in it. The virtue of hope, were Origen right, would not include a necessary component of effort corresponding to the goal envisaged. However, while this aspect of Origen's thought was rejected, the Eastern Churches have continued to the present day to develop another aspect of his understanding of the content of hope. They describe the goal as an intimacy with God through vision of the divine that may be called "deification" (*theōsis*), a term suggested by 2 Pet 1:4 and taken up by Irenaeus, Athanasius, Cyril of Alexandria, Maximus the Confessor, and others. The practice of hope corollary to this understanding of the goal consists largely in patient endurance sustained by an otherworldly detachment from pleasure, possessions, and power, and brought to clarity and focus by perseverance in contemplative prayer.

Meanwhile, however, new currents of thought arose in the interpretation of hope according to the gospel of Jesus Christ. In A.D. 313 the Peace of Constantine put a definitive stop to the persecutions and began a process of civic Church establishment, blending the role of bishops, the calendar of Christian feasts, the buildings used for worship, the confessions of faith, and the received teachings on Christian virtues with the needs of imperial order and administration. Subtle changes can be traced in the treatment of hope in the extant writings. With notable exceptions, such as the socially radical exhortations found in the sermons of Ambrose of Milan, hope turns more toward ecclesial observance and civic obedience in a posture of waiting for Christ to take over in person the emperor's role in what was already seen as a Christian empire. This shift is expressed, for instance, in the apse mosaics of Christ as the heavenly ruler of all (Pantocrator), which became customary in the basilicas. The expectation of further redemption of human society tended to be postponed to some distant and sudden end. Accordingly, more emphasis was being placed on the expectations of the individual beyond death. In fact, from this time in history there seems to have been less attention paid to the dynamic of hope in human existence, and more to the faithful fulfillment of obligations within the established order, which was itself beyond challenge.

One aspect of the changing pattern of concern with the content of hope was the preoccupation with the correct interpretation of the biblical language. Authors such as Jerome, Cyril of Jerusalem, Gregory of Nyssa, Hilary of Poitiers, Ambrose of Milan, and Augustine of Hippo all wrote about the manner of the resurrection and the type of body that would be raised, their answers ranging from very literal to frankly figurative interpretations. Likewise, most of the Christian authors of this time discussed the nature of final blessedness and the need for final judgment. All this had the character of trying to decipher things that were already determined. There was little emphasis on human creativity involved in redemption and transformation.

Hope in Medieval Theology and Spirituality

It was in the medieval period that strong analytical interest in the virtue of hope developed. This trend was initiated by Augustine, whose works were widely and respectfully used in the medieval period. In *The City of God* and elsewhere, he expresses great pessimism about the prospects of human society and civilization in history, and sees Christian life as countercultural, even in an ostensibly Christian empire. But he does see prospects for the growth of a city of God which will come to consummation at the end-time and which the Church to some extent anticipates. Nevertheless, hope is essentially focused on a transcendent heavenly future. Throughout the Middle Ages this more pessimistic outlook was in tension with the new optimism about worldly possibilities that was engendered by the papal coronation of Charlemagne in A.D. 800. This newly initiated symbiosis of Church and state in the West provided a counter-theme of hope for the transformation of human society under the divine rule in history.

Nevertheless, popular expectation during much of the medieval period focused more on fear than on hope. The coming end was portrayed in apocalyptic terms spelling out cosmic disasters and a judgment that was to be dreaded. Death, judgment, hell, and heaven were popular themes in visual arts, drama, and other literature, but hell was depicted more concretely and realistically than heaven. In the later Middle Ages the notion of the refining fires of purgatory helped to move the balance a little more toward hope. Such piety was accompanied by much speculation about when the world would end and a general judgment would take place as preface to the new and final order of all creation.

The popular preoccupation with judgment corresponded with an inclination in medieval theology to see relations between God and human beings in juridical terms.

This is evident, for instance, in the writings of Anselm of Canterbury, especially *Cur Deus Homo,* and it occurs among the writers of the 12th century. By the 13th century a detailed map of the afterlife was commonly accepted. Dante Alighieri described it in *The Divine Comedy,* and Thomas Aquinas assumed it in what he wrote about hope. It was generally held that immediately after death each person would face God's individual judgment, passing as a disembodied soul into a provisional state of salvation, purgation, or damnation. Until the end of the world, the general resurrection, and the general judgment, neither the enjoyment of the beatific vision in heaven nor the suffering of damnation in hell would be quite complete, because it would lack the corporeal dimensions of experience. What Christians hoped for, therefore, was entrance into the beatific vision at death, complemented by resurrection of the body at the end of the world. There was, of course, considerable speculation about the exact nature of the disembodied, provisional experience of salvation and damnation in what was seen as a quasi-temporal interval between death and the end of the world.

In his *Summa Theologiae,* Thomas Aquinas has two sections that are primarily about hope. The first of these (I-II, qq. 1-5) sets out the goal of human life as the happiness of seeing God and defends the attainability of this goal. The other section (II-II, qq. 17-21) discusses hope as the second theological virtue. Aquinas gives several definitions of the word *virtue.* Perhaps the simplest is that a virtue is a disposition to act well (I-II, q. 56, a. 3). Hope is such a disposition that embraces as its object a future good, namely, eternal life or enjoyment of God (I-II, q. 17, aa. 1-2). Hope can also embrace intermediate goals and can look to a good both for oneself and for others (q. 17, aa. 3-4). It both relies on God and is directed to God as a source of fulfillment for oneself, preparing the way for love that is directed to God altruistically (q. 17, aa. 5-8).

Aquinas also discusses the practice of hope by linking it to the beatitudes and to the gifts of the Spirit. Christian piety lists fear of the Lord among the gifts of the Holy Spirit. This kind of fear is known as filial fear, that is, the fear of loss or separation that prompts a child to cling to its parent. Such fear establishes a necessary bond that is a factor in the practice of hope. It is understood as a gift of the Spirit that comes with grace in baptism, which makes the baptized children of God, but it is clear in Thomas's treatment that it is also a disposition to act that must be exercised, and whose close correlate is the virtue of hope, looking as it does to a good not yet attained where the risk of loss exists (II-II, q. 19, aa. 1-11). Similarly, Thomas links the virtue of hope with the beatitude of the poor in spirit by showing the connection between that beatitude and the gift of fear. He takes poverty of spirit to mean total trust in God and renunciation of worldly things, which he sees as the perfection of hope (q. 19, a. 12).

Thomas considers at some length the two kinds of sins against hope that were to play a large role in the literature of modern spirituality before the Second Vatican Council. These two kinds of sins are despair and presumption. Despair is a risk because hope is concerned with an arduous good that is nevertheless possible to obtain. Self-indulgence has a corrupting effect, making ultimate blessedness look less attractive, and failure in self-discipline brings on a kind of listlessness that makes the joy of the blessed look less attainable. Consequently, it is important to keep one's attention on the goal in order to avoid drifting into a listless sadness in which it is no longer possible to imagine ultimate blessedness (II-II, q. 20). Presumption is possible in two ways: one might rely on oneself rather than on God, or one might rely on God to do the inappropriate, as when one would expect to obtain forgive-

ness without repentance (q. 21, a. 1). Finally, Thomas observes that in themselves sins against hope may seem less serious than those against faith or charity, but that in their own way they are more devastating because they lead one to abandon the whole project of the Christian life (q. 20, a. 3).

Side by side, however, with this eminently sensible analysis of Christian hope, there were two other strands of thought that were influential at this time. One of them was a new wave of apocalyptic theology and spirituality initiated in the 12th century by Joachim of Fiore and propagated in the 13th century by the Spiritual Franciscans. The goal of their hope was a new millennium in the divine dispensation for history. This millennium, which was to begin shortly, was to be the third age—that of the Holy Spirit—following on an age of the Father under the old covenant and an age of the Son according to the new covenant. It was to be a glorious age of the Church, an age of saints, characterized particularly by perfect vowed religious. The practice of hope by which they reached out toward this millennium was to be a radical interpretation of evangelical poverty as exemplified in the life of Francis of Assisi. In spite of its rather one-sided view of the Christian task in history and its consequent rejection by the Church, this view was held by some deeply spiritual, prayerful people.

The other strand of thought competing with a careful Scholastic analysis of hope was the continued preponderance of fear as the attitude toward the future. It is exemplified in art and literature, in liturgical texts such as the *Dies Irae* in the Mass for the Dead, in Marian piety, and especially in the growing practice of indulgences, and it appears in the extant sermon literature of the next few centuries. Writings such as those of Catherine of Genoa on purgatory were an attempt to revive trust in a merciful God and to inspire hope as the dominant attitude toward the future beyond death. The referent for both fear and hope was the outcome for the individual beyond death, and therefore outside history and the world of everyday experience.

Hope in Modern Theology and Spirituality

In the Catholic sphere, the received theology of the virtue of hope and of the grounds for, and content of, Christian hope remained essentially that of Aquinas. In the Reformation of the 16th century, the grounds for our hope were in dispute with Luther and his followers, who were inclined to give the Christian believer a more passive role in the dispensation of grace than did the Scholastic tradition of theology. The content of hope was in dispute with Calvin and his followers, who opposed the standard teaching of the universality of the salvific will of God. The practice of hope was indirectly in dispute with the Anabaptists, who, like the Spiritual Franciscans before them, saw the need for a more radically countercultural way of life as the expression of Christian hope, and who based it on the baptism only of adult believers, for whom faith, hope, and charity could be immediately operative. Somewhat later the accepted Catholic teaching on the virtue of hope was in dispute again with the Quietists, who advocated passive tranquillity, renunciation of personal initiative in the spiritual life, and surrender of concern for one's own salvation.

The impact of the Enlightenment on the understanding of what was meant by Christian hope was mainly to intensify the already dominant individualism. This was evident in the popularity among the elite of the spiritual doctrine of Louis Lallemant and later that of Jean Grou. The individualization of hope, and its corollary of fear, is also seen in the subject matter of sermons during recent centuries, for instance those traditionally associated with the Redemptorists and Capuchins. Perhaps most importantly, the individualized understanding of hope was formulated in the standard catechisms.

In pre-Vatican II Catholic theological texts, hope is discussed according to the exposition of Aquinas but is given very little space. The object of hope is presented as simply God, or as the vision of God and all intermediate helps to attaining that vision; but secondary objects are admitted, consisting of the resurrection of the body and of the same happiness for others as for oneself. These others are considered severally, however, and in terms of an otherworldly goal and spiritual means to that goal. Thus attention is focused away from direct concern with redemptive transformation of human society in history. This same pattern can be observed in the standard texts of the early 20th century in the distinct discipline of spiritual theology, as for instance those of Reginald Garrigou-Lagrange, Alban Goodier, Joseph de Guibert, and Adolphe Tanquerey. The last-named, however, in his book *The Spiritual Life,* gives more space and attention to a discussion of what is really involved in the exercise of the virtue of hope, breaking it down into three factors: an effective desire great enough to relativize other wants and wishes; a confident expectation that the object of desire (God, beatific vision, union with God) can be reached; and a commensurate commitment of one's life. In this way Tanquerey maintains the delicate balance that combines the pure gift of God with the total responsibility of human freedom.

Many forces combined in the mid-20th century to bring the virtue of hope into prominence in Christian theology and spirituality, and to give it a this-worldly, active, and communitarian turn. New Testament scholars were able to build on the various 19th-century discoveries and attempts at interpretation and reconstruction, in order to explore the content of the preaching of Jesus in quest of the central issues. It became clear that the promise which Jesus held out to his followers was primarily that the reign or kingdom of God was at hand.

Moreover, this promised reign of God is not given a new definition in the NT; it is taken for granted that the listeners already know what is meant by the term because it is in current usage. That throws the definition back to the Hebrew Scriptures and the scribal teaching in the intertestamental period. But this in turn means that it is not a purely otherworldly reality that is being promised but a full redemption of God's creation, and especially of human society. All the prophetic literature of the OT becomes relevant in the interpretation of the preaching of Jesus, and this literature is preoccupied with issues of social justice and peace as these will be realized when the people of God really live by the Law of God.

Thus it becomes evident that in the preaching of Jesus, the object of hope is not simply God or one's personal intimacy with God on the other side of death. Rather, the object of hope is the coming reign of God, in which all creation will be brought into harmony and human society will be fully reconciled to God, a large component of which is the transformation of human relationships and the structures of society at all levels. This brings the communitarian dimension of hope to the center. The hope for the individual as such is expressed in terms of resurrection, and this is an expression of individual hope that is spontaneously integrated into the hope for the community.

In systematic theology the impact of this development in NT studies became explicit first in *The Theology of Hope* by Jürgen Moltmann, a German Lutheran theologian, who was responding to what he saw as the practical, political hopelessness of Christian theologians in the aftermath of World War II. This hopelessness was in marked contrast to the energetic projection of a sociopolitical future by Marxist thinkers of the time. Moltmann and many other Christian theologians were influenced by the philosophical reflections of Ernst Bloch in *The Principle of Hope,* which drew on both biblical and Marxist sources to analyze the dynamic of human social existence in history. Moltmann and others, such as Wolfhart Pannenberg, began to reformulate the standard expositions of Christian doctrine so as to place the focus of salvation history in the future not yet realized, in the redemption of the human community and of the world.

Among Catholic theologians this shift was taken up particularly by Johann-Baptist Metz in his refocusing of fundamental theology in such a way that it began from the great social questions that suspend contemporary people between hope and despair. Metz's theology, which he named "political theology," brought the themes of the theology of hope to more concrete, practical mediation with some incisive questions about where the institutional Church should stand in particular conflicts of interest in society in order to live by the hope that Jesus held out for his followers. This shift was facilitated by the already widely circulated work of Karl Rahner, which included a penetrating analysis of the interpretational principles that must be brought to bear on eschatological assertions, i.e., on statements expressing the content of Christian hope. For Rahner, those principles were derived from existential analysis of human experience, its limits and possibilities, and its symbolic expressions.

Another post-World War II strand of theological reflection that tended toward a more active, this-worldly, and communitarian appropriation of Christian hope developed out of the mystical writings of Jesuit paleontologist Pierre Teilhard de Chardin. Though not permitted by Church authority to publish these writings during his lifetime, Teilhard rapidly became widely influential when his work was published posthumously. His was a world-affirming spirituality in which all scientific and technical progress was seen as integral to God's plan for human history and as leading to a final integration of all creation in Christ at the end-time. This brought together secular hopes and endeavors with religious hope founded on faith in Christ, thus overcoming the kind of discontinuity in modern life by which religious hope had become individualized, privatized, and entirely otherworldly. Objections to the Teilhardian view raised in retrospect have included a concern that this view did not sufficiently notice and protest the effects of sin in the world, and especially of the social manifestations of sin in injustices, oppression, and every kind of unnecessary mass suffering.

This element of social protest in the name of the challenge and promises of the gospel of Jesus Christ was taken up in a variety of Third World theologies now generally known as liberation theologies. The foremost of these spring from Latin America and are expressed in the writings of Gustavo Gutiérrez, Juan Luis Segundo, Leonardo Boff, and others. These theologies raise very concrete questions about Christian hope in relation to specific problems of mass suffering and destitution in our times. Focusing on the biblical understanding of the ultimate content of hope as being not God simply but God for us, and therefore the reign of God established in creation, these theologies address themselves to the discernment and analysis of the authentic intermediate objects of hope—those transformations in relationships, values, expectations, and structures of society that are steps in the direction of the full realization of the reign of God among us.

Such theologies have been based on the authoritative doctrinal support of the Second Vatican Council, more especially the Dogmatic Constitution on the Church (*Lumen Gentium*) and the Constitution on the Church in the Modern World (*Gaudium et Spes*). These documents turned the attention of Christians to the seriousness of tasks in the world for the establishment of peace, social justice, and adequate material well-being for all na-

tions and peoples, linking these tasks with the Christian message of hope for the world. Moreover, the content of these Vatican II documents was made even more explicit in the statement and instructions issuing from the meeting of the Latin American Bishops' Conference in Medellín in 1967. The Medellín documents linked the practice of Christian hope with the elaboration of a contemporary Christian anthropology and with pastoral strategies appropriate to this anthropology. The anthropology was basically that of Paolo Freire, focused on the development of full and critical consciousness and of assumption of responsibility in the course of human growth to maturity. One outcome of the related strategy has been the ever wider diffusion of basic ecclesial communities, groups that meditate on the Gospels together and try to conform their community lives and relationships to the hope and vision of the Gospels, in the assurance that the grace of God makes this possible through the union of Christians with the risen Christ, and that this grace also offers an anticipation now in some measure of the reign of God yet to come in its fullness.

Contemporary Issues of Hope

Contemporary Christian spirituality still faces the challenge of the twin temptations of despair and presumption. On the one hand, there is in our society a pervasive despair of finding meaning, purpose, and ultimate satisfaction in human existence. This is exemplified, for example, in suicide rates, drugs, street violence, growing demand for psychiatric help, a general lassitude among young people, the lyrics of rap and other popular music, and many other such manifestations. The practice of the Christian virtue of hope, and a pastoral strategy to support it, requires means of cultivating creative imagination based, not on secular entertainment, but on the larger vision of a transcendent future that is gift and invitation of God. Such practice and strategy also require some practical experience of ecclesial communities that give experiential grounds for confidence in the divinely offered future, and the development of disciplined lifestyles focused on the pursuit of the vision and hope of the Christian gospel. There is much in contemporary life that militates against this, and the support of a Christian community cannot be taken for granted but needs to be deliberately cultivated. This in turn requires that the laity assume initiatives rather than seeing their role as a passive one—a change involving some adjustment of expectations and traditional roles in the Church.

Yet it is not only despair but also presumption that constitutes a characteristic contemporary temptation against hope. There are many aspects of contemporary urbanized, industrial society that favor confidence in one's own achievement of wealth, status, and power as the way to total happiness. There are widely disseminated philosophies and strategies of contemporary culture that promote self-centeredness and selfishness on principle as a matter of healthy adjustment, pushing individualism and solipsism to the extremes. This is contrary to Christian hope, because Christian hope, focused on the reign of God, recognizes that human beings are essentially interdependent, and therefore called to love and care for one another, achieving personal happiness by looking beyond themselves. The recent rediscovery and refocusing on the reign of God as the central object of hope, rather than an individualized vision of personal happiness to be attained only after death, has helped to sharpen this understanding that community relations at every level of human organization are appropriate intermediate objects of Christian hope.

Perhaps one of the most pervasive errors in contemporary society's attitudes toward private life is the understanding that sexual promiscuity and license lead to human happiness. This is an expectation that has in it both elements of despair and elements of presumption. It has elements of despair

because it reduces the content of hope to something so fleeting, so fragile, and so shallow in the relationships created. And it has elements of presumption because it assumes that consequences to society in general and relationships with other individuals need not be taken into account, but that somehow the stability and goodness of society will take care of themselves.

At the same time, from a Christian point of view, the most pervasive error in public life seems to be the assumption that mass suffering from war, greed, and the quest for world domination is simply inevitable and is acceptable in the world as long as it does not begin to affect those of us who now have the privileges and advantages. This view also contains elements both of despair and of presumption. It contains despair because it assumes either that God has no further power to save in history or that God is unconcerned with mass suffering in the world. And it contains elements of presumption because it assumes that we who now enjoy all the privileges at others' expense can continue to do so indefinitely without consequences or accountability because we are somehow entitled to enjoy privileges and wealth at the expense of others. On the contrary, Christian hope, focused on the ever-coming reign of God, necessarily looks for transformations of society by which many of us would inevitably lose privileges and wealth but would gain the real peace of experiencing the reign of God coming.

The challenge for Christian spirituality and pastoral strategy in our times is to rediscover in depth the personal and communitarian dimensions of the theological virtue of hope, and especially to keep discerning in changing circumstances the interdependence of the personal and social dimensions of hope for the true quest and welcoming of the reign of God coming among us.

See also AFTERLIFE; ANTHROPOLOGY, THEOLOGICAL; COVENANT; ESCHATOLOGY; FAITH; FRUIT(S) OF

THE HOLY SPIRIT; FUTURE; KINGDOM OF GOD; LIB-
ERATION THEOLOGY, INFLUENCE ON SPIRITUALITY;
LOVE; RESURRECTION; TRUST; VIRTUE.

Bibliography: R. Alves, *A Theology of Human Hope*
(Washington: Corpus, 1969). H. Berkhof, *Well-
Founded Hope* (Richmond, Va.: John Knox, 1969). P.
Berryman, *Liberation Theology* (New York: Pantheon,
1987). J. Bouilloc, ed., *The Hope That Is in Us* (Glen
Rock, N.J.: Newman, 1968). J. Cone, *A Black Theology
of Liberation,* 2nd ed. (New York: Orbis, 1986). W.
Desan, *Let the Future Come* (Washington: Georgetown
Univ. Press, 1987). C. Geffré, *A New Age in Theology*
(New York: Paulist, 1972). B. Häring, *Hope Is the Rem-
edy* (Slough, England: St. Paul Publications, 1971). J.
Moltmann, *Theology of Hope* (London: SCM Press,
1965). G. O'Collins, *Man and His New Hopes* (New
York: Herder, 1969). B. Olivier, *Christian Hope*
(Westminster, Md.: Newman, 1963).

MONIKA K. HELLWIG

HOSPITALITY

The word *hospitality* (Latin *hospitium*)
derives from *hospes,* meaning both "guest"
and "host." Behind this dual connotation
lies the Greek concept *xenos,* a stranger
who receives welcome or who welcomes.
Hospitality implies mutuality and is characterized by sincere graciousness between
strangers. Henri Nouwen writes that hospitality is "the creation of a space where the
stranger can enter and become a friend instead of an enemy" (Nouwen, p. 8).
Friendly encounters between people who
ordinarily perceive one another to be different, and even dangerous, have traditionally held religious and ethical value. Civilized people of the ancient world appreciated hospitality and felt it a sacred duty to
provide for the needs of the stranger
(sojourner).

Hospitality is an essential component of
the Judeo-Christian tradition. Biblical literature develops the theme of the close relationship between God and the sojourner.
The patriarchal stories of the OT (Gen
18:1-15; 19:1-11; 24:14-61) establish the
tone for biblical teaching. God is identified
as both guest and gracious host who befriended the Israelite people while they
were strangers. Because they had been so-

journers once themselves (Deut 10:19), the
Israelites esteemed the sojourner highly.

In the NT, Jesus is identified as both
guest and host. Always solicitous for the
needs of the poor, the marginalized, the
sinner, Samaritans, and Gentiles, Jesus remains a wayfarer who depends upon the
hospitality of others (Mt 8:20; 9:10; Mk
7:24; 14:3; Lk 7:36; 8:3; 9:52; 10:38; 14:1;
19:5; Jn 12:2). He is the supreme host when
he washes the feet of his guests and breaks
bread for them to eat (Mk 6:41-45; 8:6-9;
14:22; Lk 22:27; Jn 13:1-17). He assumes
the customary practices of hospitality in
the commissioning of his disciples (Mt
10:5-15; Mk 6:7-11; Lk 9:2-5; 10:4-11). To
act hospitably is the criterion Jesus gives to
his followers for positive judgment before
God. To all who share possessions and
heart's affection, Jesus promises the kingdom of God (Mt 25:35-42). For Jesus,
"neighbor" is coextensive with "humanity" to such an extent that the stranger becomes the neighbor. Any refusal of food,
shelter, or help is an indictment that merits
condemnation.

Hospitality has changed according to the
ages. In the early Church it was the responsibility of missionaries, bishops, priests,
and deacons. In the Middle Ages its duties
extended into the traditions and rules of religious communities, notably those of
St. Benedict and St. Francis of Assisi. In
the present day, hospitality should be understood within the ecclesial framework established since the Second Vatican Council. In *Lumen Gentium* the Church is
identified as a Mystery and as a community invited to participate in the life of the
Triune God. Communion in God transforms all believers into the People of God,
the Body of Christ, and the Temple of the
Spirit (LG 8).

Two clear contexts result wherein the duties of hospitality can be recognized:

1) *Mutual hospitality shared among Christians.* Hospitality is an extension of the
Eucharistic liturgy, in which Christ, who is
manifested as food, invites and welcomes

humanity to the celebration of its own transformation. All who partake of the Eucharistic meal are challenged to serve others as they have been served. In so doing, Christians serve Christ (Mt 25:40). Christian worship lacks authenticity if love and service do not flow from it. The places where believers gather to worship are defined as Christian, not so much by architecture and art, but by the actions that occur within them. The distinctively domestic hospitality that characterizes these places includes the washing of feet, offers of comfort to sick and afflicted people, a receptivity to strangers, and sharing the Body and Blood of Christ in the forms of bread and wine. From the qualities and attitudes that characterize hospitality emerged specific liturgical offices, including those of lector, acolyte, Eucharistic minister, and doorkeeper.

2) *Christian hospitality extends to all peoples.* Christian hospitality manifests the hospitality of the kingdom of God. In its document *Justice in the World,* the 1971 Synod of Bishops identifies the universal scope of Christian outreach: "Never before have the forces working for bringing about a unified world society appeared so powerful and dynamic; they are rooted in the awareness of the full basic equality as well as of the dignity of all." As catholic, the Church extends itself to every people and culture in order to incorporate all into the lordship of Christ and to enrich itself through sharing in the traditions of the various peoples.

Directed toward the peoples and problems of the world, hospitality is realized not only by individuals but also by groups and communities. According to the Decree on the Apostolate of the Laity, the family fulfills the mission of being the "first and vital cell of society . . . if it provides active hospitality and promotes justice and other good works for the benefit of all the brethren in need" (AA 11). In *Populorum Progressio,* Pope Paul VI insists upon the social and political character of the Church's mission. He regards as a "duty imposed by human solidarity and by Christian charity, . . . incumbent upon families and educational institutions of host nations" the responsibility of "giving foreigners a hospitable reception" (PP 67).

Dispositions for hospitality include a willingness to listen to the needs of the world, to acknowledge a preference for the poor and the stranger, and to maintain an openness that is conditioned by attentiveness, humility, kindness, readiness to meet and to be with the other. In continuity with this long tradition, Christians remain both guests and hosts in a world in short supply of hospitality.

See also FRIENDSHIP; LOVE; SERVICE; SOLIDARITY.

Bibliography: A. Böckmann, "Openness to the World and Separation from the World According to the Rule of St. Benedict," *American Benedictine Review* 37 (September 1986) 304-322. H. Nouwen, "Hospitality," *Monastic Studies* 10 (1974) 1-28. D. Power, *Gifts That Differ: Lay Ministries Established and Unestablished* (New York: Pueblo, 1980).

KEVIN GODFREY, O.F.M. CONV.

HUMAN BEING

See ANTHROPOLOGY, THEOLOGICAL; SELF.

HUMILITY

Humility is rooted in the truth of reality. Grounded in a deep awareness of our limitations and shortcomings in the presence of the divine perfection, and of our sinfulness in the presence of the all-holy God, it leads us to a profound sense of total dependence on God and to an ardent desire to do God's will in all things. It means, therefore, grasping the truth about ourselves and about God.

The word *humility* is derived from the Latin *humus,* which is translated as "ground" or "soil"; its meaning, therefore, is "lowly." In classical Latin the word is always used in a pejorative sense: applied to things, it means undistinguished, unimportant, insignificant; in reference to persons, it suggests lowly birth, lack of resources, weakness of character. In an ancient culture that prized freedom, power, and self-aggrandizement, humility, far from being a quality to be admired, was viewed with condescension and contempt.

In the OT, humility is the attitude of the 'anawim, the poor of Yahweh, who have no resources of their own but submit themselves wholly to the will of God, who always hears the cry of the poor. Lowly in the eyes of the worldly-minded, they are seen, in the biblical perspective, to be the special objects of God's solicitude. Their humility involves a sense of total dependence on God in gratitude for his goodness.

In the NT, the disciple of Jesus, faced with the reality of the loving condescension of God—expressed initially in creation and then, when the fullness of time had arrived, in the incarnation of the divine Word—must be humble as a little child (Mk 10:15) in order to enter the kingdom that Jesus Christ brought into human history. Disciples must have the mind of Christ Jesus, who promises the kingdom to the poor in spirit (Mt 5:3), who extends the invitation: "Learn from me, for I am meek and humble of heart" (Mt 11:29), and who gives the deepest expression of humility in his own willing acceptance of the cross: "He humbled himself, becoming obedient to death, even death on a cross" (Phil 2:8).

The humility of Christian discipleship must be expressed not only toward God but also to sisters and brothers in the Christian community, and indeed to all who carry the image of God. The humility of Jesus is once again a model. In washing the feet of his disciples, he gave an example: "If I, therefore, the master and teacher, have washed your feet, you ought to wash one another's feet. I have given you a model to follow, so that as I have done for you, you should also do" (Jn 13:14-15).

In Mary's *Magnificat* (Lk 1:46-55), which incorporates OT themes, a woman who has profoundly assimilated the spirit of the 'anawim gives praise to God for the regard God shows for the humility (*tapeinōsis,* meaning "abasement" or "lowliness") of God's servant (*doulē,* "slave"). She is the humble woman who rejoices in the wondrous condescension of God. Her humility gives her insight into the humility of God revealed in Jesus Christ.

Humility is closely linked with love (see Paul's description of *agapē* in 1 Cor 13). It is lowliness become selflessness.

The Fathers of the Church extol the excellence of humility and point to Christ as the archetype of this virtue. Gregory the Great (540–604) echoes a long tradition when he describes humility as "the mistress and mother of all the virtues" (*Moralia,* xxiii, 13, 24; PL 76:265b). Elsewhere in the *Moralia* he calls the humility of human persons "true wisdom," and the humility of God "the instrument of our redemption."

Humility played a key role in the spirituality of the Fathers of the Egyptian desert, whose ideas were brought to the West by Cassian (ca. 360–ca. 432). There is a long, continuous tradition, going back to the Desert Fathers, of enumerating various degrees of humility. Cassian (360–ca. 435), Benedict (ca. 480–ca. 547), Bernard of Clairvaux (1090–1153), and Ignatius Loyola (1491–1556) are a few examples, among many, of that ongoing tradition.

Humility continues to occupy a central role in contemporary spirituality. It is seen not as self-depreciation but as self-honesty. Thomas Merton (1915–1968), walking in the tradition of St. Thomas Aquinas, who linked humility with magnanimity, sees the humble person as one who can achieve great things for God and for others, because, "living no longer for himself . . . the spirit is delivered of all the limitations and vicissitudes of creaturehood and contingency, and swims in the attributes of God, Whose power, magnificence, greatness and eternity have, through love, through humility, become our own" (*New Seeds of Contemplation,* New York: New Directions, 1961, p. 181).

See also DETACHMENT; FRUIT(S) OF THE HOLY SPIRIT; KENOSIS; POVERTY; VIRTUE.

Bibliography: P. Adnès, "Humilité," *D.Spir.,* vol. 8, cols. 1136-1187. A. Huerga, "Humility," *Sacramentum Mundi: An Encyclopedia of Theology,* ed. K. Rahner et al. (New York: Herder, 1969) 3:79–80. B. Häring, *Free and Faithful in Christ* (New York: Seabury, 1978) 1:202–205; 446–447.

WILLIAM H. SHANNON

HUMOR

See HUMILITY; LEISURE; PEACE.

I

ICON(S), ICONOGRAPHY

There is evidence that representational art and images have been associated with Christian worship almost from the beginning. The oldest known Christian church, discovered at Dura Europos in the 1920s and dated to the 240s, contains frescoes of biblical scenes in the assembly hall and the adjoining baptistery. The synagogue unearthed at the same site likewise has frescoed biblical scenes. The catacombs at Rome, some of which are dated as early as the 2nd century, are also decorated with biblical scenes, as well as with images of Christ. When Constantine granted toleration to the Church in 313, churches on a grand scale began to be built throughout the empire, many with fully developed iconographical programs. Frequently representations of historical figures or episodes from the OT were juxtaposed with scenes from the life of Christ, illustrating the type-fulfillment pattern found in the NT, in patristic exegesis, and in the liturgy.

The sudden appearance of such fully developed iconographical programs has led scholars to hypothesize the existence of narrative sequences in Jewish monumental art and manuscript illumination, to which the discovery of the synagogue at Dura Europos lends support. But if the early Christians relied on Jewish sources—and indeed the greater number of references in the catacombs are to the OT—they also drew on secular sources, sometimes depict-

ing Christ as Orpheus (Catacomb of Domitilla) or as Apollo driving the chariot of the sun (Vatican Grotto). The mosaics found in churches built after Constantine often rely on imperial iconography. Christ, seated on an imperial throne, wears the garb of the emperor, while the apostles appear as Roman senators (Santa Pudenziana). Even in their composition, in which the builder of the church or its patron saint is presented to Christ by Peter and/or Paul, as well as in other details, these mosaics reflect court protocol and etiquette (SS. Cosmas and Damian).

Thus it would appear certain that the early Christians, like their Jewish contemporaries, interpreted the prohibition of images in the Decalogue to exclude only direct attempts to depict God. Nevertheless, at various times some Christians have exhibited a reserve toward representational art in general that has led to iconoclastic movements, as for example in 8th-century Byzantium and during the 16th-century Reformation, or to a critical reserve, as for example in 12th-century Cistercian art. The iconoclasts of 8th-century Constantinople leveled charges of idolatry against their opponents, the iconodules, who held that it was not unlawful to reverence images of Christ, the Mother of God, and the saints.

The controversy raised important theological issues that went far beyond the scope of reverence given to images. The Orthodox cause was led by John of

Damascus and Theodore the Studite. First, the distinction was made between *latreia,* the worship given rightly to God alone, and the honor given to created persons and images. The issues that were the most hotly debated, however, concerned the incarnation, material creation, and the human person. It was argued that refusing to allow icons of Christ is tantamount to a denial of the reality of the incarnation. Icons thus serve as testimony to the historicity of the incarnation. Icons likewise attest the presence of the Spirit in all of creation. Matter, according to John Damascene, is not to be despised, because it was created by God and, moreover, salvation was wrought in and through matter. Thus Christians are not saved from matter but with matter, and through humankind the entirety of material creation is to be transformed and redeemed.

This has further implications for the human person created in God's image. According to Theodore the Studite, the fact that God is an image-maker renders the making of images a divine activity, in which human beings are privileged participants by sharing the divine image. To be an image-maker, an iconographer, belongs to the royal priesthood of the people of God, and to make an icon and use it in God's worship is to call down the divine blessing on everything of human making.

The Iconoclastic controversy was settled by the seventh ecumenical council (Constantinople, 787), which declared that the consensus of the Fathers, who expressed delight in the icons seen in the churches, attested that the iconographic tradition derived from them and was not an invention of artists. Thus the council affirmed that the use of images, as well as the content of the images, is a part of ecclesiastical tradition in the same way as the liturgy and the gospel itself.

Although the content of sacred art belongs to tradition, and the artist may not tamper with it, the style can and does vary. Indeed, the style(s) associated with Byzan-tine art derived originally from the contemporary culture, especially the stylized funeral portraits that have been found on coffins in Egypt, and from the often stylized, hieratic representations of the emperors, which in secular usage symbolized the imperial presence in public buildings and temples.

In Orthodoxy, then, the making of images is a liturgical art. Icons are not merely decorations in churches nor merely reminders of sacred history, but they fulfill a sacramental function. According to John of Damascus, upon seeing an image of the Crucified, for example, people are reminded of the work of redemption and fall to their knees to worship not the image but the one represented by the image. Through icons the worshiper enters sacred time and space and is led to communion with the mystery signified. And according to the Council of Constantinople, when people venerate icons they receive sanctification.

The church itself is considered to be one great icon, its walls covered with representations of Christ, the angels, the mysteries of Christ's earthly life, the Mother of God, the apostles, and all the saints. To enter a church is to enter a representation of the heavenly kingdom. When the people gather for the Eucharistic liturgy, the icons testify that Christ and the entire communion of saints are present celebrating with them.

Orthodoxy knows two ways of praying: the one with the use of the imagination, the other without. In the former, at both the communal and individual level, icons play an important role. The other, associated with Hesychasm and the Jesus Prayer, seeks union with God without the mediation of images and discursive thought. It should be pointed out, however, that the two ways are by no means to be seen as mutually exclusive but rather as complementary.

The Iconoclastic controversy did not have the same impact in the West as it did in the East, and thus the impact of the theology of images was not as great either. Churches, it is true, were seen to be portals of heaven, and images of Christ, Mary, and the saints were reverenced. Until the Renaissance of the 16th century, artists generally adhered to traditional iconography. This was probably due more to the fact that clerical patrons dictated the iconographic programs of churches, as well as to the fact that respect for antiquity urged the artists to follow models. Western artists looked to Byzantium for inspiration. During the Renaissance, when art came to be seen as a personal expression of the artist's genius, artists began to depart freely from the iconographic tradition.

Western Christianity has tended to emphasize the didactic, rather than any sacramental, quality of sacred art. Today there is evidence of renewed interest in the visual arts on the part of Western Christians, both Roman Catholic and Protestant. This can be seen as a by-product of the liturgical movement, which has led to a radical revision of the liturgical rites and a reevaluation of liturgical practice and spirituality. Through the study of the history of liturgy and the role of ritual and symbol, there is increased interest in early Christian and medieval art, as well as in traditional iconography. In addition, there is valid criticism of religious art that is overtly didactic or overly sentimental. This has led to a new appreciation of icons and the art of Third World countries, which often expresses a primal vision, and thus can challenge historically limited and culture-bound images of the incarnation and saving work of Christ.

See also AESTHETICS; ARCHITECTURE; ART; BEAUTY; DEVOTION(S), POPULAR; EASTERN CHRISTIAN SPIRITUALITY; IMAGO DEI; SAINTS, COMMUNION OF SAINTS.

Bibliography: J. Dillenberger, *A Theology of Artistic Sensibilities: The Visual Arts and the Church* (New York: Crossroad, 1986). A. Grabar, *Christian Iconography: A Study of Its Origins* (Princeton, N.J.: Princeton Univ. Press, 1980). L. Ouspensky and V. Lossky, *The Meaning of Icons* (Crestwood, N.Y.: St. Vladimir's Seminary Press, 1982). K. Ware, "The Spirituality of the Icon," *The Study of Spirituality*, ed. Cheslyn Jones, Geoffrey Wainwright, and Edward Yarnold (New York: Oxford Univ. Press, 1986) 196–198.

RONALD J. ZAWILLA

IDEAL(S)

See HOLINESS; VALUE; VIRTUE.

IGNATIAN SPIRITUALITY

St. Ignatius of Loyola (1491–1556) began his "worldly" career as a courtier, a gentleman, and a soldier. In 1521 he suffered a severe leg wound while defending a fortress against French forces at Pamplona, Spain. During his recuperation the thirty-year-old soldier experienced a profound religious conversion and became a wandering ascetic for the sake of Christ. After a short time in the Holy Land "to help souls" and to visit the holy places where his new Lord had lived, died, and risen, he decided to study for the priesthood for a more effective apostolate.

By means of extraordinary experiences of the Trinity, Christ, and Our Lady, through visions and other mystical phenomena, God purified, illuminated, and transformed Ignatius from a knight in the service of a temporal lord to a knight under Christ's banner in the service of the Trinity. Ignatius gathered together a group of companions in Christ (thus, "Society of Jesus"), which became a renowned religious family. He established colleges, universities, and charitable institutions, yet always kept his hands in direct pastoral activity. He had an extraordinary love of the poor, the sick, and the dying, and was deeply concerned about the religious education of youth. He directed a vast missionary network and undertook sensitive diplomatic appointments. Moreover, he authored the highly influential *Spiritual Exercises,* the *Constitutions* of the Society of Jesus, and thousands of letters that demonstrate his far-reaching, religiously motivated, sociopolitical involvement.

In a vision at La Storta near Rome in 1537, the Eternal Father placed Ignatius with Christ in order to serve. The Eternal Father promised Ignatius and his companions that he would be "favorable" to them in Rome. Hence Ignatius's union with the triune God in Christ fostered a mystical community of love in service to the pope, Christ's vicar on earth. Ignatius's mysticism and spirituality are thus communal, ecclesial, and "hyperpapal" (Hugo Rahner), but also Christ-centered, Eucharistic, and priestly. "To be with the Trinitarian Christ in prudent and loving apostolic service to the entire world" may well serve as a summary of his spirituality.

Saints, even religious founders, can be ephemeral. Their person, mysticism, and spirituality may have value only for their region or only for a particular period of time. Yet, through genius and mystical graces, Ignatius left behind a universal message and source for the spirituality of ages to come. His mysticism significantly shaped Catholic spirituality after the 16th century and has fed the spiritual lives of countless Jesuits, men and women of other religious orders whose spirituality is Ignatian, and all who have come into contact with this radical form of spirituality. Ignatius is a creative prototype—his person, writings, and heritage can and should form the subject of contemporary and future spirituality and theological reflection. Yet the key to understanding Ignatian spirituality must ultimately be the person of the mystic, Ignatius of Loyola.

Ignatius's spirituality is first and foremost Trinitarian. He experienced the Father *as Father,* the Son *as Son,* the Holy Spirit *as Holy Spirit,* and the "Essence" of the inner-Trinitarian life. In other words, Ignatius experienced the triune God, the divine community united in ineffable oneness, which loves the world to the point of the Son's death on the cross and bodily resurrection.

Ignatian spirituality can lead persons at any level of spiritual development into ever-deeper realms of the spiritual life. Ignatius can speak to those both in the premystical and the strictly mystical stages of the mystical journey. His richly incarnational, kataphatic (Greek *kataphatikos* = affirmative) mysticism finds God in all things and all things in God. His sacramental, affirmative mysticism and spirituality never separates love of God, neighbor, and world. It is a mysticism and spirituality of joy in the world, an Easter spirituality that loves the earth because the Trinitarian God creates, redeems, and loves it. Ignatius's Trinitarian and Christocentric mysticism and spirituality are incarnated in a community of love for effective apostolic service, service that includes social and political dimensions.

The *Spiritual Exercises*

The *Spiritual Exercises* blend not only Ignatius's personal mysticism and spirituality but also his pastoral experience. The exercises can be called the school of prayer created for, and taught by, the Society of Jesus. Ignatius composed them as a manual for the person giving them. They are to be experienced, not read or studied, by the one making them.

The exercises initiate a dialogue between the person making them (the exercitant) and the person giving them (the retreat director); between the exercitant, the director, and the text itself; between the exercitant and the "true essentials" of the Christian faith; between the exercitant and God, who will work directly with him or her; and between the exercitant and the "signs of the times."

The *Spiritual Exercises* are meditations and contemplations on Christ's life, death, and resurrection, interlaced with specifically Ignatian material and organized into four "weeks." This designation is based not on seven chronological days but on the specific graces sought and granted as a result of each week's exercises. In fact, "the time should be set according to the needs of the subject matter" (Ex., no. 4). The first week corresponds to the purgative way (Ex., no. 10); the second week, to the illuminative way (Ex., no. 10); the third and fourth weeks, to the unitive way. The last two weeks also deepen, in the light of Christ's passion and resurrection, the election or decision concerning one's state or reform of life made at the end of the second week.

For St. Ignatius, "by the term 'Spiritual Exercises' is meant every method of examination of conscience, of meditation, of contemplation, of vocal and mental prayer, and of other spiritual activities that will be mentioned later. For just as taking a walk, journeying on foot, and running are bodily exercises, so we call Spiritual Exercises every way of preparing and disposing the soul to rid itself of all inordinate attachments and, after their removal, of seeking and finding the will of God in the disposition of our life for the salvation of our soul" (Ex., no. 1).

Ignatian spirituality is versatile. The exercises are open to "every method" and to "every way" that removes disordered loves and attachments, thus enabling one to seek and find God's will. Ignatius urged that the exercises "be adapted to the requirements of the persons who wish to make them . . . according to their age, their education, and their aptitudes" (Ex., nos. 18, 72). In fact, the exercises teach almost twenty different ways of praying.

Ignatius makes two astounding claims in the exercises: (1) that one can actually seek and find God's specific will for oneself; and (2) that God will "communicate Himself to the devout soul" and "deal directly with the creature, and the creature directly with his Creator and Lord" (Ex., no. 15). Ignatius concludes many of his letters with the prayer "I beg God our Lord to give us all His bountiful grace ever to know His most holy will and perfectly to fulfill it."

Thus Ignatius does not stress prayer and religious experience for its own sake but as a means to seek, find, and accomplish God's will. The link between prayer, abnegation, and reformation of life, and seeking, finding, and executing God's will (see Ex., nos. 170-189, esp. no. 189) is a distinctive feature of Ignatian spirituality. Ignatius seeks to convert the exercitant into a living and acting incarnation of the divine will. For this reason commentators have distinguished his "service" spirituality from the "bridal" spirituality of other saints and mystics, in which the divine-human intercourse at the soul's center is valued above all else.

The *Spiritual Exercises* begin with the "Principle and Foundation" exercise (Ex., no. 23), which focuses on the ties linking God, all created things, and the exercitant. Ignatius states that "man is created to praise, reverence, and serve God our Lord, and by this means to save his soul" (Ex., no. 23). The exercitant is exhorted to "use" or "rid himself" of "all other things on the face of the earth" insofar as they aid or prevent this. Passionate love of God renders the person "indifferent to all created things" and able to choose "what is more conducive to the end for which we are created"—God's greater praise and service.

This exercise illustrates Ignatius's spirituality of reverential love toward both God and creatures. Reverential love of creatures flows from a theocentric view of creation, in which creatures are seen as traces of God and as ordered to God. Thus one "uses," or refrains from using, creatures in order to attain the praise, reverence, and service of God. Only reverential love for creatures, however, discloses the meaning of this "use." Ignatius's use of creatures is not an "end justifies the means" philosophy or an early form of American pragmatism. A person with the Ignatian view of loving reverence uses creatures as God meant them to be used and thus brings them to their fulfillment.

The First Week

The first week contains material on the particular examination of conscience (Ex., nos. 24-31); the general examination of conscience (Ex., nos. 32-43); general confession and holy Communion (Ex., no. 44); and so-called "additional directions" (Ex., nos. 73-90). However, the focus of the first week is on the mystery of sin and evil. The exercitant meditates on the sin of the angels, Adam and Eve's sin, the mortal sin of a damned person, his or her own sins, and hell (Ex., nos. 45-71)—but all under the shadow of Christ crucified (Ex., no. 53). Every exercise concludes with a "colloquy," a conversation with the Eternal Father, Christ, or Mary, "made by speaking as one friend speaks to another" (Ex., no. 54). Sometimes the colloquy takes place before "all the saints of [the] heavenly court" (Ex., no. 98).

The first week illustrates several important features of Ignatian spirituality. Ignatius spends so much time on the examinations of conscience because he demanded the correction of faults and the acquisition of solid and perfect virtues. Rooting out faults and cultivating virtues even when one does not "feel good" about the undertaking is characteristic of Ignatius. This hardy asceticism demands a pitiless struggle against self-love, comfort, and one's own will and judgment. Ignatius insists that "in all that concerns the spiritual life ... progress will be made in proportion to ... surrender of self-love and of [one's] own will and interests" (Ex., no. 189).

The joining of prayer and reformation of life is another feature of Ignatian spirituality. Ignatius preferred a "mortified" person to one who spends long hours in prayer—he felt that the former progresses more in fifteen minutes of prayer than the latter does in several hours. Ignatius valued mental prayer and saw it as an indispensable means to "familiarity" with God. Nonetheless, he emphasized prayer for the apostolic service of love, and for his own followers he subordinated contemplation to apostolic service. For those called to the strictly contemplative life, however, Ignatius appreciated the apostolic value of prayer in itself. Moreover, Ignatius and Jesuits after him never hesitated to teach the subordination of service to prayer for *some* persons they directed.

The union of the personal interior life with liturgical life is perhaps the principal characteristic of Ignatian spirituality. His spirituality insists upon a deep sacramental life, especially confession and frequent Mass and Communion. Jesuit spiritual writers were also the first to bring daily mental prayer within the framework and formulas of the Church's liturgy.

Like the great artists, who were necessarily great at their crafts and knew the tricks of the trade, Ignatius offers minute instructions on how to pray. To place a person fully in God's hands, he recommends use of the weather, light and darkness, fasting, penances, posture, and recollection just before falling asleep and immediately upon rising, and the like (see Ex., nos. 73-90, 210-217). However, once the person attains "intimate understanding and relish of the truth" (Ex., no. 2), he or she should "remain quietly meditating upon the point in which I have found what I desire, without any eagerness to go on till I have been satisfied" (Ex., no. 76). Thus technique is simply a means to deepen one's experience of God.

Ignatius exhorts the one giving the exercises to "narrate accurately the facts of the contemplation or meditation" so that the exercitant may have "the solid foundation of facts" (Ex., no. 2). This assures penetration of Christian essentials based more on conviction than on emotion. More practical than speculative, and with an emphasis upon *fundamentals*, Ignatian spirituality is both robust and rustic. Nonetheless, it accommodates itself both to simple, rugged souls and to the most profound and delicate.

The first week illustrates Ignatian spirituality's empirical nature and strong scriptural-doctrinal foundation. In general, it is not attracted to the lofty and impenetrable doctrines, but to those that are more easily grasped. Nor does this scriptural-doctrinal spirituality focus upon sentiments or personal experience, but on the fundamental doctrines that are the official teaching of the Church. Ignatius's emphasis upon "safe doctrine" ensures a spirituality that is solid and strong rather than brilliant and striking.

The first week reveals the concreteness of Ignatian spirituality. The mystery of evil is not discussed abstractly; instead the focus is on the cosmic sin of the angels, the sin of Adam and Eve, the mortal sin of one damned person, one's own personal sin, and hell. This week also underscores the Christ-centeredness of Ignatian spirituality. The intimate conversation with Christ crucified (Ex., no. 53) permeates the week. Thus the full horror of the ultimate consequences of sin is disclosed. Sin murders God's personal gift of Love, the incarnate Word.

The first week illustrates Ignatius's mediator spirituality. The *Spiritual Diary* reveals that Ignatius often asked Christ or Mary to intercede with the Eternal Father for a particular grace. Throughout the exercises the exercitant is advised to speak intimately with Christ, *the* mediator, and Mary. Of course, Ignatian spirituality has a profound Marian dimension.

The Second Week

The second week provides material "to contemplate the life of the Eternal King" (Ex., no. 91) and takes us to the heart of Ignatian spirituality. During this week one begs for the grace "not to be deaf to His call, but prompt and diligent to accomplish His most holy will" (Ex., no. 91) and for "an intimate knowledge of our Lord, who has become man for me, that I may love Him more and follow Him more closely" (Ex., no. 104). Just as the Eternal

Father placed Ignatius under Christ's banner through mystical graces at La Storta, the exercitant begs for the same grace (Ex., no. 147).

The "Kingdom of Christ" exercise (Ex., nos. 91-100) expresses the soul of Ignatian spirituality by depicting Jesus as the "Eternal King" who calls all "to conquer the whole world and all my enemies, and thus to enter into the glory of my Father. Therefore, whoever wishes to join me in this enterprise must be willing to labor with me, that by following me in suffering, he may follow me in glory" (Ex., no. 95). The exercitant discovers in the "Kingdom" exercise that he or she was created to serve the triune God. One does so by sharing in Christ's redemptive work through radical imitation of Christ poor, suffering, and humiliated.

The "Two Standards" exercise (Ex., nos. 136-148) expands upon, and forms an inner unity with, the "Kingdom" exercise by contrasting Christ's standard with Satan's. Ignatius depicts Christ as the "true life," and Lucifer as "the enemy of our human nature" who seduces with riches, honor, and pride. With striking symbolism, this exercise reveals the basics for the discernment of spirits.

These two key exercises of the second week emphasize *being called* to serve the Trinitarian Christ. The exercitant begs not to be deaf to this call (Ex., no. 91), to answer with a good knight's disposition (Ex., no. 94), to be chosen to imitate Christ in bearing injuries and insults (Ex., no. 98), and to be placed under Christ's standard either in perfect spiritual poverty or in actual poverty (Ex., no. 147). The "Three Classes of Men" exercise (Ex., nos. 149-157) helps the exercitant sound out just how indifferent he or she actually is to everything except God's greater service. The deeply personal logic of these three exercises should lead to a decision during the subsequent exercise on the "Three Degrees of Humility" (Ex., nos. 165-168) to choose that which will make the exercitant more like Christ poor, suffering, and despised. This *desire* to serve Christ in his redemptive work dominates the entire Ignatian perspective.

However, the poor, suffering, humiliated Christ to be thus imitated is still "the Eternal Lord of all things" (Ex., no. 98), the "Eternal King" (Ex., no. 95), the "eternal Word incarnate" (Ex., no. 109), and the "Second Person," who became "man to save the human race" (Ex., no. 102). This view of the Trinitarian Christ gives Ignatian spirituality its decisive orientation and places even the contemplations on Christ's life, death, and resurrection in a Trinitarian context. This Trinitarian perspective permeates all the contemplations of the second week: the incarnation (Ex., nos. 101-109), the nativity (Ex., nos. 110-117), and the mysteries of Jesus' life from childhood up to and including Palm Sunday (Ex., nos. 132, 134, 158-163).

All the exercises of the second week focus upon the "election" of a particular state of life or the reformation of one's present state of life (Ex., nos. 135, 163-164, 169-189). As a result of his own mystical life, Ignatius realized that the discernment of spirits must be embodied in a concrete decision—the election. This election, moreover, must be congruent with the "hierarchical Church" (Ex., no. 170) and "within the bounds of the Church" (Ex., no. 177).

At La Storta, Ignatius experienced mystically that he had been placed with the Trinitarian Christ to serve, but to serve under the direction of Christ's visible representative on earth. His decision to be totally at the pope's disposal flowed mystically from the same unreserved attitude toward Christ. He experienced mystically that in this way he could be *more certain* of *the Holy Spirit's guidance.* His generous, ardent, reverential, loving service of Christ necessarily included everything that was an intimate part of Christ, that is, his Mother (her flesh is in that of her Son), his Church (his very Body), and his vicar on

earth. Thus mystical experiences united Ignatius not only with the triune God and Christ but also with the "true Spouse of Christ our Lord, our Holy Mother, the hierarchical Church" (Ex., no. 353).

The full sacramental expression of Ignatius's felt knowledge (*sentir*) of Christ is his "Rules for Thinking and Feeling with and in the Church" (Ex., nos. 352-370). These rules stress a mystical felt knowledge of, and of being at home in, the visible, tangible, historical community of Jesus Christ, not the purely invisible Church of some reformers. Moreover, Ignatius emphasized that "between the Bridegroom, Christ our Lord, and the Bride, His Church, there is but one spirit, which governs and directs us for the salvation of our souls, for the same Spirit and Lord who gave us the Ten Commandments, guides and governs our Holy Mother Church" (Ex., no. 365). This quotation points out that his ecclesial spirituality resulted not only from his Christ-centered spirituality but also from his spirituality of the Holy Spirit (which is somewhat understated in the *Spiritual Exercises*). Some rules may now be antiquated, but not the pneumatic, incarnational, and ecclesial mysticism that grounds them. In fact, Ignatius's loyalty to Church authority, doctrines, teachings, practices, and customs is essential to his spirituality, as it is to all genuine Christian spirituality.

As mentioned above, the matter of the election dominates the second week and is the key to understanding the exercises. Ignatius discovered the intrinsic relationship between consolation, desolation, and spiritual movements, and discernment, decision, and confirmation (see Ex., no. 17). The exercises, especially the rules for the discernment of spirits, attempt to provide, and give practice in, a formal, systematic way of discovering the will of God for oneself.

Ignatius based his rules for the discernment of spirits (Ex., nos. 313-336) on the basis of his own mystical life. These "rules for perceiving and understanding to some degree the different movements that are produced in the soul—the good, that they may be accepted; the bad, that they may be rejected" (Ex., no. 313), therefore, must be read and studied carefully in the light of Ignatius's own mystical life.

Ignatius focused upon both affective and intellectual discernment. These rules teach the exercitant to discern the meaning not only in his or her affective states but also to unmask "false reasonings, seemingly serious reasons, subtleties" (Ex., nos. 315, 324), and the thoughts that spring from consolation and desolation (Ex., no. 317). Ignatian spirituality realizes that the evil spirit *counsels* during desolation (Ex., no. 318); that God gives "true knowledge and understanding" (Ex., no. 322); that the evil one may suggest "good and holy thoughts" (Ex., no. 322) that lead to "something evil . . . or less good than the soul had previously proposed to do" (Ex., no. 333).

The rules for the discernment of spirits highlight another aspect of Ignatius's spirituality of service: discreet love. He interlaced his passionate love of Christ with a steady and accurate perception of the end and the means to it. He mistrusted spontaneous impulses and valued well-considered action that was the fruit of mature thought. Affective love must always be *effective,* for "love ought to manifest itself in deeds rather than in words" (Ex., no. 230). Ignatius demanded both magnanimity and sage prudence. He was not one to be deceived by appearances.

The Third and Fourth Weeks

The exercises integrate the exercitant into the great Christian mysteries and induce the person to participate in them. The third week immerses the exercitant in Christ's passion, crucifixion, death, and entombment. Ignatius calls upon the exercitant to ask for "sorrow, compassion, and shame because the Lord is going to His suffering for my sins" (Ex., no. 193). One must ponder "how the divinity hides itself"

and "leaves the most sacred humanity to suffer so cruelly" (Ex., no. 196).

During the fourth week the exercitant participates in the risen life of Jesus Christ (Ex., no. 4). One must contemplate "the divinity, which seemed to hide itself during the passion, now appearing and manifesting itself so miraculously in the most holy Resurrection in its true and most sacred effects" (Ex., no. 223). During this week the exercitant seeks intense joy and gladness for the great glory of Jesus Christ (Ex., no. 221, 229). In fact, Christ *is* the exercitant's consolation during this week (Ex., no. 224). Moreover, this week, along with the third, stabilizes, deepens, and confirms the person's election (see Ex., no. 183).

Ignatius's rich affirmative spirituality focuses a person's intellect, memory, fantasy, emotions, and desires on individual Christian mysteries to render the exercitant connatural with them. In this way the mysteries are also interiorized and their sacramental depths made transparent to the exercitant. Ignatius insists that the exercitant's *intellect* needs to be converted to God's saving truth by having the "true essentials" (Ex., no. 2) of salvation explained carefully by the one giving the exercises. One must frequently summarize previous exercises and have "the intellect, without any digression, diligently think over and recall the matter contemplated in the previous exercise" (Ex., no. 64).

This intellectual grounding flows from Ignatius's own mystical experience on the banks of the river Cardoner, in which he grasped the unity in diversity of all the Christian mysteries. He knew that intellectual clarity in penetrating the truths of salvation history is necessary for an ordered affective-volitional life. Of course, Ignatian spirituality insists more on "an interior understanding and savoring of things" (Ex., no. 2) than on "an abundance of knowledge." Nonetheless, this spirituality recognizes how important the truths of salvation history are for stability in God's service and for grounding discreet love.

The exercises also focus upon purifying, reordering, and centering the exercitant's *desires* so that decisions will not be made under the influence of the "flesh or any inordinate attachment" (Ex., no. 172). At the beginning of every exercise, the exercitant prays for "the grace that all my intentions, actions, and works may be directed purely to the service and praise of His divine Majesty" (Ex., no. 46). Ignatius particularizes this general orientation through the second or third "preludes" ("what I want and desire" [Ex., no. 48]) which ask for a particular grace consonant with the contemplation at hand: for example, sorrow with Christ suffering and joy with Christ risen. God's saving history guides the particular "what I want and desire." By becoming connatural with the truths of salvation history, the exercitant's deepest desires are evoked and more superficial desires redirected.

Ignatian spirituality also seeks to purify two unruly human faculties: *memory* and *imagination*. The exercises steady both faculties by having the exercitant recall the history of the present mystery (Ex., nos. 2, 50-52, 111, 137, etc.). One must examine one's conscience twice daily through a methodical use of memory (Ex., nos. 25-31). One must repeat an exercise in order to "dwell upon the points in which I have felt the greatest consolation or desolation, or the greatest spiritual relish" (Ex., nos. 62, 118, 227, 254, etc.). The exercitant is instructed to make a "mental image of the place" (Ex., nos. 47, 65, 91, etc.) and to see, hear, taste, smell, and touch in imagination what is occurring in the particular Christian mystery (Ex., nos. 66-71, 92, 103, etc.).

Ignatius's *Autobiography* and *Spiritual Diary* reveal a mystic who knew the importance of religious *emotions*. Therefore, he instructs the exercitant throughout the exercises to ask for ("what I want and desire") tears, shame, sorrow, confusion, horror, detestation, amazement, affectionate love, joy, gladness, peace, and tranquillity. The needs one feels should control the direction of prayer (Ex., no. 109). One should give vent to spontaneous feelings and desires in the colloquies (Ex., nos. 53, 54, 63, 109, etc.). When desires contrary to the particular exercise are discovered, Ignatius again uses his direct approach: "We should insist that we desire it, beg for it, plead for it, provided, of course, that it be for the service and praise of the Divine Goodness" (Ex., no. 157).

Some of the exercises set in motion all the exercitant's faculties. However, the contemplations strive for less active, deeper, and simpler ways of praying. The exercitant must linger on, stay with, and fully satisfy himself or herself with the particular mystery before moving on (Ex., nos. 2, 76, 89, etc.). Frequent repetitions return the exercitant to those points of greatest consolation and desolation (Ex., nos. 62, 188). In summation exercises, "the intellect . . . is to recall and to review thoroughly the matters contemplated in the previous exercises" (Ex., no. 64).

The "Application of the Senses" exercise (Ex., nos. 66-71, 121-125) plays a great role in this process. One is to make this exercise before the evening meal almost daily by seeing, hearing, tasting, smelling, and touching in imagination the essential aspects of the mystery contemplated during that day. This exercise carries forward the simplification process initiated in the preparatory prayers, the "what I want and desire" preludes, and the "interior understanding and savoring" (Ex., no. 2) of the various exercises. This dynamic method may even awaken the mystical senses in the soul's center, thus enabling the exercitant to participate in the healing and transformative power of the mystery. In fact, the mystery may become so simplified and transparent that it draws the exercitant "wholly to the love of His Divine Majesty" (Ex., no. 330) through a "consolation without previous cause" (Ex., nos. 330, 336).

The exercises conclude with the "Contemplation to Attain the Love of God"

(Ex., nos. 230-237). Ignatius reminds the person that love "ought to manifest itself in deeds rather than in words" (Ex., no. 230) and that "love consists in a mutual sharing of goods" (Ex., no. 231). Thus effective love is preferred to merely affective love. One contemplates God's gifts in creation and redemption, how God indwells all creatures, and "how God works and labors for me in all creatures upon the face of the earth" (Ex., no. 236). One prays in this exercise for "an intimate knowledge of the many blessings received, that filled with gratitude for all, I may in all things love and serve the Divine Majesty." The appropriate response is Ignatius's prayer: "Take, Lord, and receive all my liberty, my memory, my understanding, and my entire will, all that I have and possess. Thou hast given all to me. To Thee, O Lord, I return it. All is Thine, dispose of it wholly according to Thy will. Give me Thy love and Thy grace, for this is sufficient for me" (Ex., no. 234). This contemplation is a summary of Ignatian spirituality: transforming awareness of God's many gifts that evokes gratitude, reverential love, service, and total self-oblation to God's will. It is the key to Ignatius's finding God in all things, to finding all things in God, and to being with the Trinitarian Christ to serve.

See also AFFIRMATIVE WAY; APOSTOLIC SPIRITUALITY; BRIDAL MYSTICISM; DECISION, DECISION-MAKING; DETACHMENT; DISCERNMENT OF SPIRITS; DISCRETION; EXPERIENCE; MEDITATION; OBEDIENCE; PRAYER; REFORMATION AND CATHOLIC REFORMATION SPIRITUALITIES; RETREAT, RETREAT MOVEMENT; SPIRITUAL DIRECTION; TRINITARIAN SPIRITUALITY.

Bibliography: *A Pilgrim's Journey: The Autobiography of Ignatius of Loyola*, trans. J. Tylenda (Wilmington, Del.: Glazier, 1985). *The Spiritual Diary of Saint Ignatius of Loyola*, trans. J. Munitiz (London: Inigo Enterprises, 1987). *Letters of St. Ignatius of Loyola*, selected and ed. W. Young (Chicago: Loyola Univ. Press, 1959). *The Spiritual Exercises of St. Ignatius*, trans. L. Puhl (Chicago: Loyola Univ. Press, 1951). W. Bangert, *A History of the Society of Jesus* (St. Louis: Institute of Jesuit Sources, 1972). H. Egan, *Ignatius Loyola the Mystic* (Wilmington, Del.: Glazier, 1987). C. de Dalmasas, *Ignatius of Loyola: Founder of the Jesuits*, trans. J. Aixala (St. Louis: Institute of Jesuit Sources, 1985). J. de Guibert, *The Jesuits: Their Spiritual Doctrine and Practice*, trans. W. Young (St. Louis: Institute of Jesuit Sources, 1964). A. Ravier, *Ignatius of Loyola and the Founding of the Society of Jesus*, trans. M. Daly, J. Daly, C. Daly (San Francisco: Ignatius Press, 1987). A. Poulain, *The Graces of Interior Prayer*, trans. L. Yorke Smith (Westminster, Vt.: Celtic Cross Books, 1978).

HARVEY D. EGAN, S.J.

ILLUMINATION, ILLUMINATIVE WAY

The illuminative way is the framework used by spiritual authors in describing the prayer experiences that mark proficients in the journey to spiritual maturity. An individual often passes almost imperceptibly from the prayer of simplicity, which characterizes the culmination of the active and passive purification of the purgative way, to the prayer of infused recollection, which is the first contemplative prayer experience of the illuminative way.

The difference between the prayer of simplicity and the prayer of infused recollection is that the former is a contemplative experience acquired by cooperation with God's ordinary grace, while the latter is a contemplative experience resulting from the infusion of a special grace. The prayer experiences of the illuminative way are sometimes referred to as diverse stages of conforming union. Since the goal of all prayer is union with God, the purifying work of the night of the senses has now brought the individual to a place in the spiritual journey where the Holy Spirit increasingly assumes a more active role in conforming one to the mystery of Christ crucified and risen.

In conforming union the Holy Spirit draws the individual into ever-deeper experiences of the divine presence. The prayer of infused recollection flows from the activity of the gifts of knowledge, understanding, and counsel, which bring great enlightenment to the mind of the believer and cause him or her to experience God's presence in a new way and to know the meaning of the divine attributes at a deeper level of experiential understanding.

The spiritual insights gained from experiences of the prayer of infused recollection have a significant impact upon daily activity because they enable a person to look at her or his life in a totally new way and to understand more fully the truth of God's grace-filled presence in their endeavors.

As the Holy Spirit uses the gifts of understanding, knowledge, and counsel to conform the mind of a person more fully to the mystery of Christ in infused recollection, so the Spirit utilizes the gifts of piety, fortitude, and fear of the Lord to draw the will of the individual into greater conformity with the call to holiness in the prayer of quiet. The Holy Spirit enkindles the will with a new experience of the depth of God's love in the prayer of quiet, which leaves one in a state of great peace. Such experiences of infused prayer can last for an hour or more and cause the person to take up the responsibilities incumbent upon him or her in the activities of daily life with a new zeal. The outpouring of the Holy Spirit upon the individual in the prayer of quiet sets his or her will ablaze with the desire to proclaim the Good News in a way that is symbolized in the account of the experience of the first Christian community gathered in Jerusalem as it received the Pentecostal fire.

In the prayer of infused recollection and in the prayer of quiet, the Holy Spirit conforms the two highest human faculties, the intellect and the will, to the mystery of Christ in a new way. In the prayer of union, the final kind of infused contemplation experienced in the illuminative way, the work of conforming love reaches out to embrace the whole person in order to draw her or him into deeper union with God. The imagination and memory are now brought into the process of integration and purification by which the individual is being re-created in Christ.

The renewal of one's whole life in the pattern of Christ by the purifying activity of the Holy Spirit, which marks the illuminative way, continues the purification begun in the purgative way by passing from the exterior aspects of one's personality and life to the interior realm of intellect, will, memory, and imagination. The Holy Spirit's progressive work of freeing the individual from any attachments to sinful patterns of behavior that would hinder deeper union with God now reaches out to heal the wounds of sin and frailty at the very core of human personhood.

The alternation between consolation and desolation continues in the illuminative way amidst the graced experiences of the prayer of infused recollection, quiet and union and the interior purification of the dark night of the soul. Before the Holy Spirit's work of conforming the individual to Christ's death and resurrection can lead to the unitive way and transformation into Christ, the dark night of the soul must accomplish its work of consuming any remaining obstacles to spiritual maturity in the crucible of divine love.

The light of the infused contemplation of the illuminative way and the darkness of the night of the soul are in reality two sides of the same experience of God's drawing the individual more fully into the divine life. For the increasing presence of the transcendent God in the individual's prayer experiences only serves to place in bolder relief all that separates Creator from creature. The darkness of the night of the soul is the experience of the human heart as the light of the divine mind and the fire of divine love, reaching out to embrace the believer, encounter the sinful and broken aspects of the personality.

The goal of the stripping away of the false images of God and one's self in the dark night is new freedom for life with God, but the resistance of sinful attitudes and habits to the purifying fire of love causes the individual to feel that he or she is passing through the valley of death. Although in truth God is closer than ever before, the person experiences a profound sense of loss and abandonment because old and inadequate images and understandings of God are now yielding to a new and truer experience of God's self and activity. The individual feels lost and totally helpless before the new experience of the transcendent, which indicates more clearly than ever before his or her absolute nothingness before the reality of the triune God.

The individual does not yet understand the wonder of divine love that is inviting her or him to share in the fullness of divine life, not by more exterior and interior conformity to Christ, but by a process of total transformation that will make the person a new creation in Christ without the loss of one's own unique individuality. Not everyone experiences the dark night of the soul precisely as it is described by St. John of the Cross and other spiritual writers. Rather, in the illuminative way the Holy Spirit uses whatever means of purification actually correspond to the needs of the individual for freedom and openness in order for him or her to be able to respond to the call to transforming union with the triune God, the next phase of the spiritual journey.

See also JOURNEY (GROWTH AND DEVELOPMENT IN SPIRITUAL LIFE); LIGHT; PRAYER; PRESENCE, PRESENCE OF GOD; PURGATION, PURGATIVE WAY; THREE WAYS; UNION, UNITIVE WAY; VISION(S).

Bibliography: B. Groeschel, *Spiritual Passages: The Psychology of Spiritual Development* (New York: Crossroad, 1983). J. Lozano, *Praying Even When the Door Seems Closed: The Nature and Stages of Prayer* (New York: Paulist, 1989).

THOMAS D. McGONIGLE, O.P.

IMAGES

See ICON(S), ICONOGRAPHY.

IMAGES OF GOD

See GOD.

IMAGINATION

Background and Definition

Imagination is fundamental to all human activity. Without imagination that remembers the past, projects possibilities for the future, and shapes human desire, there can be no action. As the creative, critical, and integrative process central to human becoming, imagination is integral to the discipline of spirituality. Particularly in its hermeneutical applications, imagination serves the call issued by Vatican II for renewal in Scripture, liturgy, and moral theology. A prophetic imagination is needed to meet the challenge expressed by the 1971 Synod of Bishops: action on behalf of justice is a constitutive dimension of the preaching of the gospel. A spirituality that would be faithful to the revelation of God in Jesus of Nazareth needs to recognize the images and stories of the poor and marginalized. According to feminist and liberation theologians, failure to draw upon these sources for a renewal of religious imagination impoverishes the Church and perpetuates a cultural imagination that fosters racism, classism, and sexism.

At its most basic level, imagination is the act or power of forming mental images of what is not actually present. Broadly understood, imagination is "the faculty that permits human beings to imitate, to intuit, to empathize and to create" (J. Noonan, Jr., *New York Times Book Review,* Feb. 25, 1990, p. 28). The potential of imagination for infantile regression, delusion, prejudice, greed, and domination must also be recognized. The history of Christianity is rife with controversy, cautions, and condemnations regarding symbols and images.

The Catholic Analogical Imagination

Three predominant approaches can be discerned in the mushrooming literature on the role of imagination in theology and spirituality. Treatments can be distinguished according to a relative emphasis upon participation, conceptual realism, or liberative action. This article will describe the Catholic religious imagination and then briefly delineate these patterns, citing a few examples of each. The typology developed here is essentially incomplete. Particularly within women's experience, public structures of mutuality that are sustained by vital images and liberative narratives are emerging. These relationships provide an alternative to the hierarchical dualism that prevails in Western society. In the near future it should be possible to develop concepts that are directly tied to these new imaginative patterns.

No author can be placed into only one of the three categories designated above. Catholic spirituality displays a commonality aptly characterized by David Tracy as an analogical imagination in contrast to the more dialogical dynamic operative within Protestantism. Karl Rahner's theology of grace, which has profoundly influenced the post-Vatican II Catholic consciousness, has intensified the traditionally Catholic rapport between the human and the divine. He announced a basic principle of the spiritual life: "All is grace." This fundamental optimism requires a caution. A necessary and critical function of the imagination is to identify sin and illusion, and thereby facilitate conversion.

The three approaches to be examined here are the Neoplatonic (participation), the Thomistic, including transcendental Thomism (conceptual realism), and critical hermeneutics (liberative action), exemplified by the writings of Paul Ricoeur. The first two have their roots in Platonic and Aristotelian categories that have influenced Christian theology and spirituality over the centuries. Both transcendental Thomism and Ricoeur's hermeneutics are indebted to Immanuel Kant's clarification of the activity of the subject in human knowing. This sea change in the understanding of the role of the imagination develops the creative, productive role of the imagination in contrast to a previous concentration upon the more static, reproductive, or fanciful aspects of imagination. Few contemporary artists, philosophers, or theologians are unaffected by this creative turn.

The Neoplatonic Pattern: Participation

Neoplatonic approaches to the imagination stress the participation of the believer in a sacred reality signified by religious symbols and rituals. Whereas Plato (d. 347 B.C.E.) himself distrusted symbols as mere shadows of the eternal ideas, the Neoplatonism of Plotinus (d. 270 C.E.) values symbols, rituals, and images. Through the influence of Augustine of Hippo (d. 430 C.E.) and Pseudo-Dionysius (ca. 500 C.E.), this attitude permeates Christian spirituality both in the West and in the East. For Augustine, the experiences of the senses are the occasion of divine illumination. Symbols and rituals are a part of God's lure. They attract the human to the higher realm of the spiritual and the divine. Participation in divine love activates imagination.

In contemporary spirituality this Neoplatonic thread can be found in the influential categories of Carl Jung. His universal archetypes indicate each human's participation in a collective unconscious. They function much like Plato's eternal ideas. Appropriation of Jungian psychology in spirituality frequently calls for the believer to attend to the symbols, images, and accompanying feelings that come unbidden to one in dreams and prayer. These are revelatory of the broad unconscious and help one come to a discernment of spirits and healing of memories. Through Jungian personality indicators such as the Myers-Briggs, the directee is helped to identify the most personally fruitful form of prayer. The goal of prayer is not so much imageless contemplation as entering into conversion and contemplation through attention to images and the feelings attached to them.

Drawing on the work of Jung, Mircea Eliade's universal myth and symbolism influence Catholic liturgical theology and the integration of the experiences from various world religions into a Christian spirituality. Here one is not dealing with a collective unconscious, but with a conviction that all religions are manifestations of the sacred and possess a commonality of symbolism, ritual, and narrative.

Art is a significant feature of Catholic spirituality. Stephen Happel highlights the intentional structure of creative imagination as it serves to incorporate one into divine mystery. He applies this sense of imagination to all forms of art and to their coalescence in liturgy, and defines religious imagining as "an intentional operation in which symbolic images, gestures, sounds, words, or actions disclose the ultimate horizon of God in human experience" (*The New Dictionary of Theology*, ed. J. Komonchak, M. Collins, D. Lane, Wilmington, Del.: Glazier, 1987, p. 502).

From a different vantage point, the creation-centered spirituality of Matthew Fox is at home with the Neoplatonic emphasis upon mystical participation. The liberation theology of Leonardo Boff stands squarely in the Augustinian tradition of liberating grace and cherishes the popular religion of the Brazilian poor as a genuine encounter with God.

The Thomistic Emphasis: Conceptual Realism

The second pattern, conceptual realism, flows from the pervasive influence of Thomas Aquinas (d. 1274) upon Roman Catholic self-understanding. He brought Aristotle's realistic notions of analogy and conceptualization into a critical relationship with theology. Aquinas modified but did not discard the notion of participation.

For Aquinas, the imagination is one of four inner senses of the soul. Concepts are formed by abstracting from the data of the inner and outer senses. The concepts thus derived indicate being as it really is. All created reality receives its being from God, the one self-subsisting being. All creation then participates in the goodness of God and images this goodness. Reason is a foundation for the supernatural life of faith and indicates the inner intelligibility of the truths of faith.

Imagination is valued primarily for its contribution to realistic conceptual thought. Yet, Aquinas's position is not an unalloyed rationalism. Rather, it embraces profound insight into the gifts of the Holy Spirit and appreciates the nonrational aspects of practical decisions guided by the virtue of prudence.

Thomism has directly impinged upon Catholic consciousness through its application in the field of moral theology. All too frequently this application has ignored the full richness of Aquinas's thought. Nevertheless, Catholic moral theology is clearly marked by a confidence in the contribution of human reason to the discernment of the good. Contemporary Christian ethics struggles to identify and incorporate nonrational dynamics crucial to human experiencing, understanding, judging, and deciding. Philip Keane has explored the resources of imagination for Christian ethics. He values the insights from Rahner's transcendental Thomism and from Ricoeur's hermeneutics but insists that the realism associated with Aristotle and Aquinas provides a more sure and intellectually satisfying ground for moral principles. In his judgment, the role of the agent intellect in Aquinas sufficiently explores the activity of the subject in providing and interpreting sense data and images. The imagination then helps to apply principles creatively in new and complex situations.

Pope John Paul II's appropriation of the Thomistic tradition develops an apt and powerful use of symbols that appeals to the emotions and to the intellect. Vital images enrich the Neo-Scholastic concepts that are the foundation of his analysis. These two features of image and concept are configured by the intensely personal dynamics of phenomenology's intentional analysis. Thomistic realism and Husserlian idealism merge into a deep-felt conviction about the accuracy of the images and concepts thus identified.

In the transcendental Thomism of the Bernard Lonergan, Karl Rahner, and Edward Schillebeeckx, human experience is the basis for reflection upon the meaning of revelation and the believer's personal encounter with the triune God. It encourages believers to recognize how God has been acting in their daily lives. It also provides categories that help relate these personal reflections to the Catholic doctrinal tradition.

Since symbols are the mediators of the meaning of human experience, transcendental Thomism requires the creative contribution of the imagination. Imagination not only shapes the symbolic universe that is constitutive of human experience, but it is essential to interpreting its meaning and sharing that interpretation with others.

Lonergan esteems symbols for their contribution to decisive acts of religious, moral, and intellectual conversion, to critical rationality, and to the communication of the faith tradition. Rahner presents reality itself as symbolic expression. Schillebeeckx highlights the importance of narrative for mediating the revelation of God that comes through human experience, especially the contrast experiences of poverty, suffering, and discouragement.

Despite the effort to incorporate nonrational aspects of human experience, Thomism remains locked in a primarily conceptual approach to the imagination. Conceptual realism does help to identify illusion and delusion. However, it risks losing sight of the experiences and images that gave rise to the concepts, and thus may unwittingly become an instrument that ignores or oppresses the reality of others.

The Hermeneutics of Paul Ricoeur: Liberative Action

Paul Ricoeur's application of his critical hermeneutics to the interpretation of Scripture constitutes a Christian anthropology in which imagination, animated by the gospel vision of liberative hope, fosters a continual conversion of the self. He assigns a privileged place to experiences of negativity and to the symbols of evil as the starting point for meaningful reflection leading to a fundamental affirmation of God's gracious justification. Catholic scholars in several theological disciplines, including Keith Egan and Constance FitzGerald in the field of spirituality, look upon the writings of this Calvinist French philosopher-theologian as a major resource.

Ricoeur's interpretive theory explores the metaphorical properties of narrative in order to specify and unlock the integrative and creative functions of story. The meaning and role of imagination for Ricoeur can be described by considering how imagination serves the interpretation of the Gospel parables.

Parables are narrative metaphors. Like all metaphors, they bring together opposites in a creative tension. Parables display the narrative function of configuring time. They reveal the extraordinary of the kingdom of God precisely in and through the ordinary of everyday experience. Parables frequently follow a pattern of event, reversal, and engagement or decision. One finds a pearl, sells all one's possessions, then purchases the field with the pearl. This merchandising extravagance is likened to the kingdom of God (Mt 13:45). Parables appeal to the poetic imagination. They stimulate a new self-understanding in the light of Jesus' proclamation. Jesus' life, death, and resurrection can themselves be interpreted as a parable.

Imagination facilitates every step of interpretation. The shock of unlikely combination, the metaphoric impertinence, functions to engage the imagination. The interpreter is helped to abandon preconceived notions and destructive feelings and enter into the possible world of belonging projected by the parable. The imagination then must first exert a certain discipline to distance the interpreting subject from the mystifications of vanity, greed, and domination that fascinate human consciousness. Then imagination opens the subject to the interplay of images and configuration of time presented in the parable. Metaphor stimulates the subject to rethink relationships and to bring images to this emerging meaning. Intellectual explanation and imaginative understanding interweave in this task. Ultimately the interpreter appropriates the world projected by the text as a new way of being in the world. Feelings accompany this process and are structured by it to give rise to hope and action.

All narrative displays the metaphoric quality of a yoking of unlikes. Disparate activities are configured into a plot. Hence history, particularly Scripture as the history of God's saving deeds, is to be interpreted according to the pattern of a metaphoric narrative. In the work of interpretation, imagination creatively orients human existence to the past as memory, to the present as possibility, and to the future as hope.

In comparison with the Thomistic predilection for conceptual realism, Ricoeur's is a philosophy of *praxis* in which conceptualization is subject to critical analysis and subordinated to desire, imagination, and liberating action. In contrast to the appreciation for all forms of symbolism (art, music, dance, etc.) found in the Neoplatonic trend, Ricoeur's critical approach locates the domain of imagination in language. For him, the final act of interpretation is not so much a participation in divine reality as an interior affirmation of God as the source of human hope and freedom.

Unleashing the creative forces of the imagination is a fearsome charge. Dorothy Day frequently drew upon a saying from Tolstoy: "Love in action is a harsh and dreadful thing compared to love in dreams." And yet it is precisely our dreams that bring love into action and continue to give birth to hope.

See also AESTHETICS; ANTHROPOLOGY, THEOLOGICAL; ART; CELEBRATION; DREAMS; ICON(S), ICONOGRAPHY; LITURGY; MEMORY; NARRATIVE; PRAXIS; RITUAL; SACRAMENTS; STORY; SYMBOL.

Bibliography: M. Collins, *Women at Prayer* (New York: Paulist, 1987); "Imagination and Images," *The Way* 24 (April 1984). P. Keane, *Christian Ethics and Imagination* (New York: Paulist, 1984). B. Lane, *Landscapes of the Sacred: Geography and Narrative in American Spirituality* (New York: Paulist, 1988). D. Power, *Unsearchable Riches: The Symbolic Nature of Liturgy* (New York: Pueblo, 1984). P. Ricoeur, "Biblical Hermeneutics," *Semeia* 4 (1975) 29–148; "Imagination in Discourse and in Action," *Analecta Husserliana* 7 (1976) 3–22. P. and S. Scharper, eds., *The Gospel in Art by the Peasants of Solentiname* (Maryknoll, N.Y.: Orbis, 1984).

SALLY ANN McREYNOLDS, N.D.

IMAGO DEI

The symbol *imago Dei* ("image of God") is at once one of the most fundamental anthropological symbols in the Jewish-Christian tradition and one of the most problematic. At the root of the difference in spirituality and theology between the classic Reformation traditions and the Catholic and Orthodox traditions is a fundamentally different evaluation of the effect of sin on humanity. While the Reformation traditions emphasize that original sin radically distorted or even destroyed the image of God in humanity, the Catholic and Orthodox traditions have seen more continuity between creation and incarnation/redemption, and have argued that sin does not destroy the fundamental goodness of creation nor the openness in humanity for the divine.

The "image of God" is the most basic symbol of human dignity that undergirds the social teachings of the Roman Catholic

Church, yet at the same time the effective history of the symbol has served to legitimate structures of domination and subordination in terms of both gender and the relationship of human beings to the rest of creation at various points in the tradition.

Biblical scholars themselves are far from agreement on the meaning of the symbol of creation in the divine image in Gen 1:26-28, although it is usually correlated in some fashion with the specific mention of the creation of humankind as "male and female" (v. 27) and/or with the mandate to subdue the earth and have dominion over all living things (v. 28). In both the Jewish and Christian traditions, Genesis 1 was often interpreted in light of Gen 2:18-24, which in turn was interpreted as the divine legitimation of the subordination of woman to man as part of the divine creative plan, a view reinforced for Christians by Paul's rabbinical exegesis in 1 Cor 11:7-9. More recent biblical scholarship (notably Phyllis Trible's rhetorical analysis in *God and the Rhetoric of Sexuality,* Philadelphia: Fortress, 1978, pp. 72–143) has established that the biblical narratives of creation offer a vision of harmony and equality, and that domination and subjugation enter the narrative as part of the alienation and discord that results from sin (Genesis 3).

A related concern from a contemporary perspective is the relationship between creation in the divine image and the commission to "subdue [the earth]" and "have dominion over . . . all the living things" (Gen 1:28). While critics have attributed the present ecological crisis in large part to the misunderstanding of this mandate, which has led to "the rape of the earth" and a hierarchical anthropocentrism rather than an authentic sense of the interdependence of all of creation, contemporary scholars have emphasized that the designation of human beings as "the divine image" calls for exercise of the kind of "dominion" that God exercised in relation to creation, i.e., compassionate stewardship rather than domination.

The patristic tradition reflected its Platonic and Neoplatonic cultural context in tending to subordinate the material to the spiritual and woman to man in discussions of the image of God. Thus the image of God was located solely in the human soul ("for it is wrong that what is mortal be made like what is immortal"), and arguments were proposed that women image God less than men or not at all (as in Diodore of Tarsus or Ambrosiaster). Many (Irenaeus, Clement of Alexandria) maintained the strong Christocentric focus of the Pauline writings, arguing that Adam is not the truth about humanity—Christ is.

Interpreting the Scriptures with an allegorical hermeneutic, Irenaeus distinguished "image" from "likeness," observing that image refers to our human nature as rational, free beings; hence the image cannot be lost with the fall, yet the "likeness" refers to original justice, the right relation with God and all of creation lost by sin and restored only in Christ (grace/redemption). Athanasius represents an alternate strand of interpretation in the Eastern tradition, identifying the image of God with the ontological relationship with God through grace that is lost through sin.

Preferring the Trinitarian analogy, Augustine, and later Aquinas, located the image of God primarily in the human soul, paralleling the faculties of knowing and willing (loving) with the Trinitarian processions of Word and Spirit and arguing that in this primary way women and men image God equally. Relying on the Pauline interpretation of Genesis 1–2, which emphasized woman as man's helpmate ("created from man and for man"—1 Cor 11:8-9), and on the "natural inferiority" of woman to man (*De continentia,* 1:23; ST I, q. 92), Augustine and Aquinas both argued that in a secondary sense (with regard to embodiment and/or social order), "God's image is found in a man in a way in which it is not found in woman" (ST I, q. 93, a. 4; see Augustine, *De Trinitate,* 12.7.10).

Aquinas describes three stages of the development of God's image in humanity, locating it in the natural aptitude to know and love God (creation), in the habitual knowing and loving of God (re-creation/grace), and in knowing and loving God perfectly (likeness of glory—ST I, q. 93, a. 4), thus recalling the Pauline reminder that only Christ is the perfect image of God; the rest of humanity is created toward (or after) the image of God (*ad imaginem;* ST I, q. 93, a. 1).

Contemporary efforts have been made to locate the image of God in some aspect of human personality (e.g., creativity), or more fundamentally in the mystery of the human person as openness to the divine (K. Rahner), and therefore directed toward the future (W. Pannenberg). Recent writings paralleling other developments in creation theology and anthropology, moral theology, and Trinitarian theology emphasize the eschatological, social, and relational dimensions of the symbol (J. Moltmann, E. Schillebeeckx), as well as its foundational role in Catholic ethical teaching (M. Farley, D. Tracy, W. Kasper).

See also ANTHROPOLOGY, THEOLOGICAL; CREATION; DIVINIZATION; ECOLOGICAL CONSCIOUSNESS; GOD; GRACE; PATRISTIC SPIRITUALITY.

Bibliography: D. Cairns, *The Image of God in Man* (London: SCM, 1953; rev. ed., Fontana Library of Theology and Philosophy, 1973). D. Tracy, "Religion and Human Rights in the Public Realm," *Daedalus* 112 (1983) 237–254. J. Moltmann, *God in Creation* (San Francisco: Harper & Row, 1985). D. Hall, *Imaging God: Dominion as Stewardship* (Grand Rapids, Mich.: Eerdmans, 1986).

MARY CATHERINE HILKERT, O.P.

IMITATION OF CHRIST

See CHRIST; DISCIPLESHIP.

IMMANENCE

See ANTHROPOLOGY, THEOLOGICAL; EXPERIENCE; GOD; GRACE; SPIRIT.

INCARNATION

Christian spirituality is rooted in the doctrine of the incarnation, which affirms the twofold mystery of (1) the history of God's self-communication (Trinity), and (2) the history of humanity's self-transcendence. In the person of Jesus the Christ, God's gracious self-communication achieves an absolute and irrevocable, concrete historical manifestation. The hope and self-abandonment in love that constitute the history of human self-transcendence is a history of freedom made possible by the humanity of Jesus the Christ. Classical Christology defined this mystery in terms of *divinization:* the divine became human in order that the human might become divine.

The NT Christologies include both descending and ascending patterns. While the Pauline and Johannine Christologies (Gal 4:4; 1 Cor 2:8; Phil 2:5-11; Col 2:9; Heb 1:3; Rom 1:3f.; Jn 1:14) emphasized the preexistent Son of God (*Logos,* the Word of God) coming in the flesh (*sarx*) and manifest in the resurrection, this high Christology can be contrasted with the low Christology of the Synoptic Gospels, which emphasized the humanity of Jesus manifest in his ministry, teaching about the reign of God, passion (cross), and death. The infancy narratives, along with the use of various Christological titles (e.g., Lord, Messiah, Son of God, Savior) evidence attempts in the Synoptic Gospels to reveal the eschatological identity of Jesus as the Christ at the time of his birth, his baptism in the Jordan, and throughout the historical ministry. But the passion narratives counterbalance this tendency by placing a central emphasis on the human Jesus' passion and death.

Patristic Theology

By the 4th century the Church was struggling with new questions and developing dogmatic formulas to articulate an understanding of the history of salvation, or what Jesus did for us (soteriology) and who Jesus was (Christology). The question focused on what kind of person is this Jesus, who embodies both humanity and divinity? This interrogation led to a new emphasis on the nature of the self of ordinary Christians, an anthropology (*anthrōpos*). The two were invariably connected in patristic theology, which developed the soteriological questions by Christological expressions.

The late 1st-century Gnostic denials of Jesus' humanity provoked an initial reaffirmation by Ignatius of Antioch (d. 110) of the orthodox position that Jesus was truly God and truly human. Two schools of thought gave rise to the classical Christology that provided a dialectic for the early Christological controversies. At Alexandria in the East, the *Logos-sarx* (Word-flesh) theory of incarnation offered an early model of the person of Jesus that emphasized divinity to combat the Docetists, who had reduced Jesus to a mere man. Athanasius (d. 373) contributed the initial term *homoousios* ("same substance") to defend the divine presence in Jesus as identical to the Father. He was reacting to Arius (d. ca. 336), who had denied the divinity of Jesus, and the Adoptionist claim that only at his baptism or resurrection was Jesus "adopted" as Son of God. In 325 the Council of Nicea proclaimed Jesus *homoousios* with God. While Apollinaris (d. ca. 390) would exaggerate this position to the point of denying the human soul (intellect and will) of Jesus (Monothelitism, or "one will"), a position condemned by the First Council of Constantinople (381), Athanasius, in effect, failed to do justice to Jesus' human soul. Therefore, at Antioch in the West, a school of theology led by Theodore of Mopsuestia (d. ca. 428) introduced a *Logos-anthrōpos* (Word-human) model of incarnation: the truly (fully) human Jesus (flesh and soul) was integrated in the divine Word.

These two schools were further distinguished by the controversy between Nestorius (d. ca. 451), patriarch of Constantinople, and Cyril (d. 441), bishop of Alexandria. Nestorius distinguished carefully between the divinity and humanity of Jesus. Cyril stressed the oneness of Jesus' person, without clarifying the distinction between the divine and the human in Jesus. As a result, the Alexandrians with their *Logos-sarx* understanding continued to distinguish Jesus' human nature from his divine nature. And the Antiochians with their *Logos-anthrōpos* understanding placed the accent on the unity of the person of Jesus as the divine Word of God expressed in human history. In 431 A.D. the Council of Ephesus condemned Nestorius for the apparent denial of the unity of Jesus' person. In a related affirmation, the council taught that Mary was *Theotokos,* the "God-bearer," giving further emphasis to the inseparable unity of Jesus' humanity and divinity.

In a reaction to Ephesus, the Antiochene theologians sought to reassert their *Logos-anthrōpos* theory in the wake of what they perceived as an eclipse of Jesus' humanity. Eutyches of Constantinople (d. 454) articulated an emphasis on the unity of Jesus' person in the divine Word that, in effect, swallowed up Jesus' full humanity. These Monophysite (one nature) and Monothelite (one will) heresies about Jesus led to the resolution of the Council of Chalcedon in 451, that Jesus is two natures (divine and human) in one person. In the event of Chalcedon and its dogmatic terminology of Jesus' dual natures, human and divine, and Jesus' one person (one *hypostasis* and one *prosopon*), the Church had found a moderate orthodoxy between the extremes of Alexandria and Antioch. Two subsequent councils at Constantinople (553 and 680–681) would refine this teaching and conclude that Jesus possesses two fully operative wills, divine and human.

Medieval and Scholastic Developments

The Scholastic synthesis of theology made possible by the rise of the universities posed the soteriological question in a new mode. Foremost among the theologians who attempted to rework an understanding of incarnation was Anselm of Canterbury (d. 1109), whose *Cur Deus Homo* (1098) developed an intricate theory of "satisfaction" in the context of feudal social mores. Describing sin as an affront to God's honor, he affirmed that only a God-Man could uphold God's honor by accepting our sins. While Anselm's theory was distorted by later appropriations that stressed atonement and retribution, he placed the emphasis on Jesus' love and obedience, his loving response to God. Jesus' death makes up for human sins because it is the act of a God-Man.

Devotion to the humanity of Christ developed in the monastic *lectio divina* in the 11th and 12th centuries, with the Cistercian Bernard of Clairvaux (d. 1153) as a major force. He advised that the love of the heart, "the carnal love of Christ," is attracted most toward the humanity of Christ, and therefore we should cultivate this love imaging Christ in the events of his life (*Sermons on the Song of Songs*).

With Thomas Aquinas (d. 1274), Christology is placed in the context of salvation history (soteriology). Only after Aquinas had developed *theologia* as the study of God and God's inner life, and a theology of creation and sin, did he attend to Christological questions. Unfortunately, this lack of a Christocentric focus in Aquinas led some Thomists to consider the incarnation of a God-Man as "fitting" because it remedies the effect of original sin, a modification of Anselm's theory. His theology of incarnation reflected the emphases of the Alexandrian school.

In contrast to Aquinas, John Duns Scotus (d. 1308) emphasized the two natures of Jesus, retrieving emphases of the Antiochian school. His creation-centered theology affirmed that Christ is the highest work of God, the crown of creation, and not merely the remedy for sin. As a paradigm of our humanity, Jesus reveals for us God's love and the goodness of creation. In Scotus's system, incarnation is inevitable because of God's love, not necessary because of sin (*Oxoniense,* 3 sent., d. 20, q. 1). The Franciscan school of theology would keep alive this radically incarnational and sacramental vision.

Modern and Contemporary Theologies

With the advent of 19th-century historical-critical studies of the NT, particularly the Gospels, biblical and systematic theologians began to distinguish later Christological strands of the narratives from the earlier historical core of the Gospel. While the 19th-century quest for the historical Jesus was abandoned in NT research, scholars became more attentive to the nature of the Gospels as confessions of faith. By attending to the passion narrative as the earliest layer of the kerygma, along with the Gospels' preoccupation with Jesus' historical ministry and proclamation of the reign of God, a shift in Christology resulted in greater concern with the human consciousness of Jesus. The Chalcedonian definition, which had effectively insisted on the humanity of Jesus, including his human intellect and will, came to a new fruition in 20th-century theology. Karl Rahner (d. 1984), especially, warned against a practical or crypto-Monophysitism that truncates the humanity of Jesus, and the danger of reducing earlier interpretations of a descending doctrine of incarnation into a mythological thought-form that falsely and insufficiently applies today (Rahner, pp. 289–299). The resulting Christology from below accents the true humanity of Jesus in unity with his divinity.

With the 1500th anniversary of the Council of Chalcedon in 1951, the past four decades have seen a vast reworking of Christology. Major turning points have been away from the abstract metaphysical emphasis on nature (ontology), and attention to Jesus' life, historical ministry, and the narratives of his death and resurrection recorded in the Gospels. Rahner's reinterpretation of incarnation as the supreme fulfillment of God's self-communication in human persons so that they might fulfill themselves in self-transcendence emphasized human freedom and our orientation toward the holy mystery of God. Along the same lines, Bernard Lonergan has reexamined the Chalcedonian terminology and its problematic traditional language of a single divine Person, eclipsing the human person. His turn to the subject in modern philosophy and theology resulted in an appropriation of the Chalcedonian language in terms of human interiority. This affirmed Chalcedon's formula calling for a full human subjectivity in Jesus (human intellect and will) as understood by a contemporary psychological understanding of the meaning of being human. The kenotic motifs in Jesus' experience of agony, alienation, suffering, and temptation to despair redefine the experience of humanity. Edward Schillebeeckx has taken this ascending Christology, or Christology from below, in new directions that highlight the revelatory nature of "negative experiences of contrast." In human "defenselessness" Schillebeeckx finds the abiding presence of God, made paradigmatic in the Jesus experience.

Implications for Spirituality

In the documents of the Second Vatican Council, the pervasive shift from classical consciousness to historical consciousness mirrored the implications of a new incarnational spirituality. Various applications of this current were already apparent in the writing and lives of such diverse Catholics as paleontologist Pierre Teilhard de Chardin (d. 1955), Cistercian Thomas Merton (d. 1968), and Catholic Worker founder Dorothy Day (d. 1980). The conciliar debates on the Church reflect this

development. Early drafts on the "nature" of the Church gave way to a dogmatic constitution (*Lumen Gentium*) that began with the "mystery" of the Church as the pilgrim people of God, immersed in the transformation of history and the world. The opening sentences of the Constitution on the Church in the Modern World (*Gaudium et Spes*) captured this same neo-orthodox affirmation of divinization that moves in and through the truly human: "The joys and the hopes, the griefs and the anxieties of the men of this age, especially those who are poor or in any way afflicted, these too are the joys and hopes, the griefs and anxieties of the followers of Christ. Indeed, nothing genuinely human fails to raise an echo in their hearts" (GS 1).

The Declaration on Religious Freedom (*Dignitatis Humanae*) affirmed the historically conditioned sociopolitical reality, divorcing the Church from privileged concordats that in effect had violated others' religious liberty and human dignity. Subtle but definite shifts to the historical consciousness, a new reverence for the human developmental process, and inculturation were reflected in the Dogmatic Constitution on Divine Revelation (*Dei Verbum*), the Decree on Ecumenism (*Unitatis Redintegratio*), the Declaration on the Relationship of the Church to Non-Christian Religions (*Nostra Aetate*), the Decree on the Church's Missionary Activity (*Ad Gentes*), and the Constitution on the Sacred Liturgy (*Sacrosanctum Concilium*).

Subsequent efforts have implemented this incarnational commitment to human freedom and the transformation of the world. Foremost among these are the liberation theologies, which attend to the human suffering and exploitation of the poor and marginal peoples, particularly in the Third World. Feminist theologies have reappropriated the incarnational principle by integrating the body, bodiliness, and human sexuality into their theological anthropology. The United States Catholic bishops have implemented the incarnational principle in their two pastoral letters, *The Challenge of Peace: God's Promise and Our Response* (1983), which posited the responsibility to work proactively for disarmament and mutual respect among nations; and *Economic Justice for All: Catholic Social Teaching and the U.S. Economy* (1986), which adopted the principle of "the preferential option for the poor"; as well as in their attempt to draft a similar pastoral letter on the role of women in the Church.

See also CHRIST; CREATION; DIVINIZATION; FEMINIST SPIRITUALITY; KENOSIS; LIBERATION THEOLOGY, INFLUENCE ON SPIRITUALITY; RESURRECTION.

Bibliography: B. Besret, *Incarnation ou eschatologie? Contribution à l'histoire du vocabulaire religieux contemporain, 1935–55,* Rencontres 55 (Paris: Cerf, 1964). B. Lonergan, *The Way to Nicea* (Philadelphia: Westminster, 1976). K. Rahner, *Foundations of Christian Faith* (New York: Seabury, 1978) 178–321. E. Schillebeeckx, *Church: The Human Story of God* (New York: Crossroad, 1990). S. Thistlethwaite, *Sex, Race, and God* (New York: Crossroad, 1989).

GEORGE KILCOURSE

INCULTURATION

See CULTURE.

INDIFFERENCE

See DETACHMENT.

INDULGENCES

See AFTERLIFE; INTERCESSION.

INSPIRATION

In general, inspiration, from the Latin *inspiratio,* meaning "in-breathing," is the arousal or infusion of an impulse or illumination that impels a person or group of persons to speak, act, or write under the influence of some creative power. More commonly, divine inspiration is understood as the charismatic supernatural influence that moved and guided the OT prophets in revealing God's will to Israel,

and the sacred authors in writing the word of God in Scripture.

Although the concept of inspiration is not specifically addressed in the OT, it is clear that the Spirit was understood to be profoundly involved in the actions and communications of the prophets who spoke for God (Jer 1:1-4; Ezek 1:3; Hos 1:1; etc.). Divine communications were recorded by OT authors in three main groups of Scriptures—the Torah, the Prophets, and the Writings—which the postexilic Jewish community understood to be the inspired word of God. This understanding of the OT was accepted by early Christians (2 Tm 3:16) and extended to their own NT writings as a sign of the outpouring of the Holy Spirit in "the last days" (Acts 2:16-18; Joel 3:1).

Church doctrine affirms that these authors were incited, moved, and assisted by the Holy Spirit in the faithful conception and transcription of the infallible truth that God called them to write (DS 3293). It is therefore true to say that both God and the inspired writers, in and through whom God acted, are the authors of the sacred texts. This does not mean that God limited the freedom of these authors in a way that might have negated the social and cultural formation of their individual personalities; rather, God spoke through them "in human fashion" according to the particular circumstances and available literary forms of their respective times and cultures (DV 11-12).

Historical critical studies of the Bible have prompted scholars to extend the concept of inspiration to the many anonymous editors and redactors of the various biblical texts. This amplified understanding of inspiration is not incongruent with the Church's understanding of itself as the Body of Christ, one in Spirit with the risen Lord (1 Cor 12:13). The outpouring of the Spirit upon the primitive Church gives to the Church as a whole a share in those gifts given to the followers of Jesus at Pentecost. Among these charisms is the gift of inspiration, which, in a certain respect, has been given to countless persons in the authentic living of their spiritual lives.

Those Christians who are guided or moved by the Holy Spirit to understand more clearly the divine will in their lives may experience what some ascetic writers have called "transitory motions" of inspiration. These are genuine experiences of personal inspiration in the life of grace inasmuch as they provide greater clarity or deeper insight into Christian faith and practice. With such experiences one usually has no direct awareness of being inspired or moved, since grace normally operates beyond the parameters of everyday consciousness. Inspirations of the Holy Spirit are distinguished from visions, locutions, private revelations, or other extraordinary phenomena.

Situations in which one believes one has received a divine inspiration require careful discernment. Masters of the spiritual life (e.g., St. John of the Cross) generally caution against placing too much credence in these or other apparently supernatural phenomena without first having discussed such experiences with one's spiritual director or other knowledgeable persons. In every case, inspiration should be tested against the teachings of the Church and Sacred Scripture. Inspiration—the divine creative impulse at work in the formation of Sacred Scripture and the Church—continues to give life and strength to the Church through the prayerful assimilation of Sacred Scripture in the liturgy, the sacraments, and the teaching of the magisterium.

See also CHARISM; DISCERNMENT OF SPIRITS; REVELATION(S); SCRIPTURE.

Bibliography: R. Collins, "Inspiration," *The New Jerome Biblical Commentary* (Englewood Cliffs, N.J.: Prentice-Hall, 1990), chap. 65. J. Michl, "Scripture," *The Encyclopedia of Biblical Theology: The Complete Sacramentum Verbi* (New York: Crossroad, 1981). K. Rahner, *Inspiration in the Bible* (New York: Herder, 1966).

KEITH R. BARRON, O.C.D.S.

INTELLECT

See MIND.

INTENTION, INTENTIONALITY

The nouns *intention* and *intentionality* and their adjectival, verbal, and adverbial conjugates have three different sets of meanings, based respectively on three different philosophical distinctions. It is convenient to illustrate the characteristic features of each set by showing how each philosophical distinction underlies a different meaning of the word *intentional*.

First, there is the distinction between *two kinds of existence*—the existence of real things and the existence of objects of thought. My mother (whom I write to monthly) exists both in reality and (at least once a month) in my mind. The centaur I read and dream about exists in my mind but not in reality. And there may well be things that exist in reality but (since I never think of them at all) not in my mind. Medieval Scholastics, followed by such modern thinkers as Franz Brentano and Edmund Husserl, label the existence of real things "natural" and the existence of objects of thought "intentional."

Second, there is the distinction between *two properties of mental acts*. Mental acts are other-oriented, the means by which I am aware of contents other than the acts themselves. Thus through sensing I am aware of sense data, through understanding I am aware of intelligible unities or similarities, and so on. But mental acts also are radically self-possessing, the means by which I am primitively aware of the very acts themselves, and, more fundamentally, of myself as actor. Thus through sensing I am primitively aware of my sensing and of myself as sensor, through understanding I am primitively aware of my understanding and of myself as understander, and so on. Bernard Lonergan, like many other modern thinkers, labels mental acts "intentional" insofar as they are other-oriented.

In terminology more distinctively his own, he labels them "conscious" insofar as they are primitively self-possessing.

Third, there is the familiar distinction between *two kinds of human actions.* Some of my actions are deliberate, voluntary, "intentional," performed precisely in order to bring about some anticipated result. Others are "unintentional," either inadvertent or involuntary, done without even anticipating the result or at least without willing it.

See also CONSCIOUSNESS; DECISION, DECISION-MAKING; MIND; SOUL.

Bibliography: B. Lonergan, *Insight: A Study of Human Understanding* (New York: Philosophical Library, 1957); *Method in Theology* (New York: Herder, 1972).

MICHAEL VERTIN

INTERCESSION

Intercession is a theological corollary of mediation. Humanity's full incorporation through baptism into the Body of Christ the eternal High Priest makes this mode of prayer a possibility and a responsibility for all the Church. This truth finds traditional expression in the dismissal from the Eucharistic assembly of all the unbaptized before the general intercessions, which complete the Liturgy of the Word. Petitions for the living and the dead in the Eucharistic Prayers attest to the constitutive role of this prayer form.

The practice of intercessory prayer is evident in the Hebrew Scriptures, where God is seen to raise up great intercessors such as Abraham, Moses, the prophets, kings, and priests who, rooted in God's covenanted fidelity, call the people back to God and intercede for them in their sin. This call often marginalizes the religious leader, and thus the paradigm of intercessory prayer in the Hebrew Scriptures is the Suffering Servant (Isa 53:4–5:12).

Jesus' own earthly prayer and ministry on behalf of others reveal that advocacy in prayer is ultimately for the revelation of God's glory. Many patristic authors, liturgical theologians, and some contemporary writers find in the mystery of Christ's ascension a key to understanding the Christian's duty to intercede in common and individual prayer for the needs of all creation (Rom 8:34). Christ's intercession—and ours in, with, and through him—is a constitutive dimension of his eternal self-oblation (Heb 7:25). In its breadth intercession expresses the nature of the Church's existence for the life of the world. In its particularity it expresses the incarnation of the Church in local communities in all their hopes and sorrows, joys and needs.

Intercessory prayer was a consistent and universal dimension of Judeo-Christian spirituality until the Reformation, when it came under attack because of theological misunderstanding and pastoral abuse in regard to the intercession of Mary and the saints, indulgences, and the Church's intercessory prayer for the dead. Our recourse to the intercession of Mary and the saints and the intercession of the living for those who have died is rooted in our belief that the communion of saints is not fractured by death. Thus the intercession of God's holy ones who interceded for the welfare of all while on earth is rightly held to continue in heaven. The mutual solidarity of all humanity in, with, and through Christ is not destroyed by the grave, and if the salvation of each is affected by that of every other, then our prayerful concern for those who have gone before us in death is legitimate and necessary.

This theory and practice can be maintained only as long as God's absolute sovereignty is maintained. God alone forgives sin. The full process of reconciliation, however, sometimes expressed in terms of the punishment due to sin, demands the prayerful solidarity of saints and sinners. This process of mutual support takes place on earth and in death, and the theory and practice of indulgences, our pleading that the merits of the saints be applied to the full healing of those forgiven by God but still in the process of full reconciliation, can be maintained only insofar as the absolute sovereignty of God and the all-pervasive mediation of Christ is not compromised in any way. Contemporary liturgical renewal often seems intent on addressing these issues by returning to an earlier euchology in which the example and virtue of the saints are stressed as the basis for their ability to intercede for us in Christ.

Other contemporary challenges to intercessory prayer often arise from an ongoing adherence to a Newtonian worldview according to which God is envisioned as a distant and impervious creator of immutable natural laws, from overly rationalistic analyses of prayer in terms of cause and effect (creatures somehow change God's mind by their prayers), and the application to God of our human experience of time (our prayer in the present results in God's future fulfillment of our requests). Intercessor prayer is the object of renewed contemporary ecumenical study and practice.

See also AFTERLIFE; BODY OF CHRIST; DEATH AND DYING; HOLINESS; PETITION; PRAYER; SAINTS, COMMUNION OF SAINTS; SOLIDARITY.

Bibliography: W. J. Grisbrooke, "Intercession at the Eucharist, I. The Intercession at the Synaxis," *Studia Liturgica* 4, no. 3 (1965) 129–155; "Intercession at the Eucharist, II. The Intercession at the Eucharist Proper," *Studia Liturgica* 5, no. 1 (1966) 20–44. P. Molinari, *Saints: Their Place in the Church,* trans. D. Maruca (New York: Sheed and Ward, 1965). M. Perham, *The Communion of Saints,* Alcuin Club Collections No. 62 (London: SPCK, 1980). P. Toon, *The Ascension of Our Lord* (New York: Thomas Nelson, 1984). L. Vischer, *Intercession,* Faith and Order Paper No. 95 (Geneva: World Council of Churches, 1980).

ANDREW D. CIFERNI, O. PRAEM.

INTERIORITY, INTERIOR LIFE

The concept of interiority or the interior life is helpful in the study of spirituality in both Christian and non-Christian contexts. The concept is a familiar one among many of the spiritual writers in both the East and West, especially in the religions of India. Although many of the non-Christian religions speak of the interior life, the context is radically different. For a Buddhist, for example, interiority means retreat from the world into a state of nirvana. For the Christian, the interior life is more a state of prayer than a state of being.

The Interior Life in Scripture

The Scriptures are replete with ideas about the interior life. In the OT, with its accent on holistic anthropology, the human person is considered in its totality; the Greco-Hellenistic dichotomy between body and soul is not apparent. The human body is animated by some kind of spiritual principle, referred to by three Hebrew words (*nephes, ruah, leb*) that give indications of the ancient Hebrews' nuanced understanding of the notion as well as variations in meaning.

The Hebrew word *nephes* (Greek *psychē;* Latin *anima*) is the principle of vitality and is often translated as "soul," but one must remember that the Greek dualistic concept of body/soul was foreign to the Semitic mind. The soul denotes, not something added to the body, but the entire human person. It is necessary to conceive of this as the force of animation closely associated with every living creature, but especially with humans. The term came to be identified with the living individual or the inner feelings associated with a person, such as joy, rest, contentment, love, sadness, pain, bitterness, and anxiety. The wide variety of feelings affects the *nephes* in its relationship with God. For example, the *nephes* wants God (Isa 26:9), thirsts for God (Pss 42:2-3; 63:2), raises itself toward God (Pss 25:1; 86:4), and rests in God (Pss 62:2; 63:9). As the principle of vitality, the *nephes* is the spiritual power of a person and the resonator of one's experience with God.

The Hebrew *ruah* (Greek *pneuma;* Latin *spiritus*), meaning "breath" or "wind," indicates the spirit and is important in the spiritual history of Israel, where it means the spirit both of God and of the human person. It, too, is a force that provides vital energy from God to all living creatures. Death results when God recalls this breath (Gen 6:3; Ps 104:29; Job 34:14). Health and vitality are strictly dependent upon the presence and the dynamism of God's *ruah.* This breath exists in people without belonging to them, as though it were an independent agent. Attached to this concept is the notion of interiority in both the intellectual and affective dimensions. One speaks of the human *ruah* as a stable spiritual disposition, and the biblical expression "a new spirit" (Ezek 11:19; 18:31) indicates a renewal of the spiritual being in humans. The highest spiritual activities are associated with, and individuated in, the human person, joining again to the *nephes* in its personal and interior aspects.

There is a tendency to oppose spirit and flesh, but even the Hebrew notion of flesh (*basar*), because of the psychosomatic unity of the human person, regards the flesh as a spiritual entity. Often the term *flesh* indicates the human person in its fragility and its finitude. To the Semitic mind, the flesh experiences many feelings, such as trembling before God (Ps 119:120) and longing for God like a dry land (Ps 63:2). For the people of the OT, the body is far from being a prison for the soul.

The richest biblical term for indicating interiority is *leb,* meaning "heart" (Greek *kardia;* Latin *cor*). Being the seat of the emotions, the heart was destined to become the symbol of the core of one's being, the most intimate part of the person, where one enters into dialogue with God. To the Semitic mind, the heart is much more than simply the affective center of the person; it is the interior of the person. Besides being the center of feelings, the heart is also the intellectual principle. God gives a heart with which to think (Sir 17:6), and a "hardened heart" can mean a closed mind as well as someone who is embittered and calloused. The heart is the source of one's consciousness and of intelligent and free personality, the place of decision-making,

where the Law is written and where the mysterious actions of God take place.

These Semitic ideas are the backdrop for the NT understanding of interiority. Against the Jewish dietary laws, Jesus insists that it is not something that enters the body from outside that makes a person good, but that which comes from within (Mt 23:27-28). Criticizing the Pharisees, he demands that they look at the interior of the cup and dish, and not simply the exterior (Lk 11:39). The treasure, representing that which is contained within the human heart, and the good earth, which receives the word of God, are images that capture the idea of the interior life.

In the letters of St. Paul further development of the notion of interiority can be noted. His view, often confused with Hellenistic dualism, avoids any opposition between body and soul. Although he distinguishes between those who are under the power of the flesh (*sarkikoi*) and those who are under the influence of the spirit (*pneumatikoi*), he holds for a psychosomatic unity of the human person, maintaining the delicate balance of the constitutive parts of the person (*sarx* and *soma, psychē, nous* and *syneidesis*). Three times Paul uses the expression "the interior person" (*ho esō anthrōpos*—Rom 7), which is not of biblical origin. In describing the fact of interior alienation of the sinner, Paul sees a connection between the interior person and the transforming power of the Spirit (Eph 3:16). The interior person is always in a state of becoming, whereby one becomes interiorized to the degree that one is rooted in the love of God (*agapē*) and knows the love of Christ that surpasses all human understanding. The interior person is someone who is filled with the Spirit of regeneration (Tit 3:5) and who moves toward the fullness of God (Eph 3:19). The dialectic opposing the old Adam against the new Adam is related to the idea of baptism as a progressive change or metamorphosis whereby the believer is identified with Christ as an icon of God.

Interior Life in the Christian Tradition

In the Christian tradition St. Teresa of Avila (d. 1582) is certainly one writer who explicitly mentions the interior life. In her work *The Interior Castle,* the principal source of her mature thought on the spiritual life, she accentuates the life of prayer. The interior castle represents the soul in which the Trinity dwells and where one enters into greatest intimacy with God through prayer. Having passed through the various mansions of the castle, one enters into the most interior chamber, where one is most centered with oneself. In her *Way of Perfection,* written about a decade earlier, Teresa instructs her nuns on the spiritual life and how to pray. Using the Our Father as an instrument, she shows how prayer is a means of getting in touch with one's interiority and of centering oneself in God.

In a similar vein, St. John of the Cross (d. 1591), in his *Dark Night of the Soul,* speaks eloquently of the interior life. In his mystical order the goal of the Christian is to find God who dwells within the soul and to exclude anything that is exterior to the soul. The illumination about which St. John speaks is found in the darkness of one's interiority, which he calls the soul. The task of the mystic is to become passive, allowing God's light to illumine the darkness of the soul.

St. Francis de Sales (d. 1622) identifies interiority with the quiet where prayer originates. In his *Treatise on the Love of God,* he instructs Philothea to actively concentrate on prayer. The spiritual person, rather than seeking mystical passivity, is active in seeking an intimate rapport with God in the interiority of his or her heart.

Psychological Understanding

The notion of the interior life is familiar to the masters of the spiritual life. In the 20th century, psychological reflection has been incorporated into spiritual direction to grasp the interior dimension of human existence. Drawn ostensibly from Jungian psychology, spiritual direction currently takes into consideration the inner workings of the psyche as a constitutive dimension of spiritual development.

Adapted to the psychological principles of human individuation, the question of spiritual interiority identifies the unique personality traits of each individual and attempts to find spiritual forms that correspond to each. Tools such as the Myers-Briggs Type Indicator and the Enneagram deal with the question of temperament and assist persons to conceptualize the interior life. The psychological indicators point to a close relationship between temperament and the type of prayer best suited to the needs of the individual. This is particularly helpful in spiritual direction because it points to the fact that spiritual development is not simply adherence to external forms of spirituality, but rather the identification of forms of prayer that correspond to the unique needs of the individual.

The ancient Greeks recognized four basic temperaments, corresponding somewhat to the four temperaments of Hippocrates, namely: Epimethean (melancholic), Dionysian (sanguine), Promethean (phlegmatic), and Apollonian (choleric). Through study of these four temperaments, one can find an analogous correspondence in the various schools of Christian spirituality, e.g., Ignatian, Franciscan, Thomistic, and Augustinian. This list does not attempt to be exclusive, but rather is descriptive of four types of spiritual approaches to prayer and interior life. The great value in using the psychological approach is that it underlines the invisible, interior dimension of spiritual life and avoids reducing spirituality to a kind of blind adherence to prayer techniques and external spiritual practices.

See also AFFECT, AFFECTIVITY; AUGUSTINIAN SPIRITUALITY; CARMELITE SPIRITUALITY; CENTERING PRAYER; CONSCIOUSNESS; DOMINICAN SPIRITUALITY; FEELINGS; FRANCISCAN SPIRITUALITY; HEART; IGNATIAN SPIRITUALITY; PASSION(S); PERSONALITY TYPES; PSYCHOLOGY, RELATIONSHIP AND CONTRI-

BUTION TO SPIRITUALITY; SELF; SOUL; SPIRITUAL DIRECTION.

Bibliography: P. O'Connor, *Understanding Jung, Understanding Yourself* (New York: Paulist, 1985). C. Michael and M. Norrisey, *Prayer and Temperament: Different Prayer Forms for Different Personality Types* (Charlottesville, Va.: The Open Door, 1984). W. Grant, M. Thompson, and T. Clarke, *From Image to Likeness: A Jungian Path in the Gospel Journey* (New York: Paulist, 1983). X. Léon-Dufour, *Dictionary of Biblical Theology* (New York: Seabury, 1973). K. Healy, *Entering the Cave of the Heart* (New York: Paulist, 1986).

MICHAEL S. DRISCOLL

INTERPRETATION

Serious consideration of historical and textual interpretation, and of their complexity, is a major development in the study of spirituality. Traditional approaches to the history of spirituality tended to pay little attention to the historical context of spiritual traditions or to the contingency of their religious and cultural values and theological assumptions. In general, the approach to history was an old-fashioned narrative, one that reinforced a deterministic view of development and a sense that the historical process was simple rather than complex, monolithic rather than plural. In the case of classical spiritual writings, problems of interpretation were not a major issue in a world where many Christians had little sense of historical distance from the perspective and even the language of the author. The tendency, therefore, was to assume that the meaning of a text was confined to the literal sense of the words, which always remained the same, and to the intentions of the original author.

One important reason why the study of spirituality now pays greater attention to the complexity of historical interpretation lies in an important theological shift provoked by the Second Vatican Council. The use by Pope John XXIII of the phrase "signs of the times" and its repetition in council documents recognized that history was not incidental to, but the context for, redemption. Every historical moment has

a dynamic of its own where the presence and power of God may be perceived. Consequently, faith is not opposed to history, and no separation is possible between religious history and the world at large.

Thus, spiritualities do not exist on some ideal plane outside the limitations of history. The origins and development of spiritual traditions reflect the specific circumstances of time and place as well as the psychological state of the people involved, and consequently embody values that are socially conditioned. For example, the emphasis on radical poverty in the spirituality of the mendicant movement of the 13th century was not the result of spiritual insight abstracted from environment and its influences. It was both a spiritual and social reaction to particular conditions in society and the Church at the time.

This does not mean that spiritualities have no value beyond their original context. However, it does mean that to appreciate their riches fully, we need to take context seriously. It also means that spiritualities are not beyond criticism and must be viewed as limited and conditioned. While gospel values clearly play an explicit role in the development of spiritualities and their response to the needs of the Church and world, critical investigation inevitably reveals other forces that control the development of traditions as well as how they are recorded.

A number of questions may helpfully focus attempts to look more critically at the history of spiritual traditions. First, how was holiness conceived? Which categories of people were thought of as holy? What places or things were deemed to be particularly sacred, and, negatively, who or what was excluded from the category "holy" or "sacred"? For example, close association with sexual activity (marriage) or with physical reality (manual labor) has often been difficult to connect with ideas of holiness. Second, who creates or controls spirituality? For example, to what degree does the language of spirituality reflect the interests and experience of minority groups such as clergy or monastics? Third, what directions were not taken? In other words, to what degree has it been assumed that the choices made were automatically superior? For example, what were the real motives for the condemnations of the medieval spiritual movement of women, the Beguines—a genuine concern for the spiritual welfare of people or a suspicion of lay people not sufficiently under clerical control? Finally, where are the groups that did not fit? For example, why was it that until recently, within the Catholic tradition, the experience of lay Christians, and of women especially, was largely ignored in the formulation of theories of the spiritual life?

All historical studies involve choices, and this affects our interpretation of spiritual traditions. First, *time limits* are chosen. In other words, writers decide on the appropriate boundaries within which to date spiritual movements and thus to understand them. For example, our sense of the continuity or discontinuity between the spirituality of the Middle Ages and that of the Protestant Reformation will be affected by an apparently simple matter of how and where authors choose to divide a multivolume history (see Jill Raitt, ed., *Christian Spirituality: High Middle Ages and Reformation,* World Spirituality 17, New York: Crossroad, 1987, pp. xiii–xxii). Second, traditional histories reveal a *geographical bias*. We have assumptions about where "the center" and "the margins" are in the history of spiritual traditions. For example, until recently, Celtic spirituality was usually treated in terms of its eventual subordination to the Latin tradition rather than on its own terms. Third, we choose *certain evidence as significant*. If historical studies concentrate exclusively on mystical texts or monastic culture, the impression is given that spirituality is essentially literary, is to be found in privileged contexts, and is to be distinguished from "popular religion."

The question of interpretation is clearly very important in relation to spiritual texts. The theory of textual interpretation (or hermeneutics) used to be confined to biblical scholarship because the texts are foundational for Christian identity and experience. However, the issue has become increasingly important in scholarly circles when the interpretation of spiritual texts is addressed. This is partly because, for many Christians, certain important spiritual texts (or "classics") have been accorded a kind of normative status at least in a limited sense.

All spiritual texts are historically conditioned, yet some cross the boundaries of time or place and retain their popularity and importance in contexts very different from their own. These are what we may call "classics." They disclose something that remains compelling, and they continue to challenge readers and bring them into transforming contact with what is enduring and vital in the Christian tradition. These have been referred to as "wisdom documents." The nature of a text's literary genre often has an influence on its popularity and effectiveness. In general, the strength of classics is that they do not merely teach but are capable of persuading and moving a reader to respond.

We live in a historically conscious age and are inevitably aware of different perspectives when we read a classical spiritual text. Assuming that interpretation is not simply a matter of purely antiquarian interest, the question cannot be avoided of how far to respect a text's conceptual framework, structure, or dynamic as appropriate for the contemporary spiritual quest. Certain responses would be naive. We may ignore the author's intention and structure and simply use the text as it suits us. The opposite danger is to assume that the author's intention alone is normative. This subordinates our present horizons to the past and, at worst, ignores entirely the context of the contemporary reader. Both approaches assume that to arrive at the "meaning" of a text is a straightforward matter. A more fruitful approach to interpretation would be a receptive yet critical dialogue with the text in order to allow its wisdom to challenge us yet to accord our own horizons their proper place.

If there is to be a dialogue between the horizons of a text and our own, the text's historical context is an important starting point. Spiritual classics were written for specific audiences and addressed specific concerns. The insights of literary criticism also remind us that however familiar words may seem in the first instance, the experiences and assumptions that lie behind the words are different from our own, and consequently give words a different significance. We also need to recall that in reading a text we are not dealing with two quite disconnected moments—our own and that of the author—because we are also dealing with what comes between, that is, the subsequent history of the text and its interpretation. The tradition of interpretation and use of a text over centuries affects our own moment of reading.

While historical knowledge has some normative role in interpreting texts, there are limits to its value. For example, what we encounter in a text is not direct experience of another time but what the text *claims,* for all texts employ the conventional categories of their age, perhaps most notably in their images of holiness. All texts are themselves interpretations of experience, not merely records of it. Some, such as the Long Text of the *Showings* of Julian of Norwich, the 14th-century English woman mystic, are explicitly reflections based on hindsight. However, to allow for the interpreted nature of texts is not to reject the value of what results. Indeed, subsequent reflections by the author may be more relevant to those who seek to *use* a text than the original experience alone. For example, *the* classical Christian texts, the Gospels, are creative reworkings of earlier oral or written traditions about

Jesus that the Gospel writers allowed to interact with the contexts and needs of their audiences. This creative approach is part of the value of the Gospels for readers in subsequent ages.

However, the conventional approach to interpretation from the last century until fairly recently had as its basic principle that the values or experiences that a modern reader brings to a classic text are a problem for correct understanding. More recent developments in hermeneutics have sought a broader approach whereby the possibilities of a text, perhaps beyond the author's original conception, may be evoked in a creative way by the new religious world in which it finds itself.

The interpretation of spiritual classics is not the preserve of scholars but also takes place in the *use* of texts, e.g., Ignatius Loyola's *Spiritual Exercises* in retreat work. Therefore, the example of the performing arts is helpful in understanding the new approach to interpretation. Musicians interpret a text, the score. They may be technically faultless in reproducing the notes and the composer's instructions. A "good" performance is certainly true to the score, because performers cannot do simply anything with Mozart and still call it "his" symphony. Yet, a "good" performance is more than this. It is also creative, because the composer did not merely describe how to produce sounds but sought to create an experience. Thus, there is no single, true interpretation of a text, as new aspects are revealed whenever the text confronts new horizons and questions (for interpretation-through-performance, see N. Lash, *Theology on the Way to Emmaus,* London: SCM Press, 1986, chap. 3).

Modern theories of interpretation assume that texts have an "excess of meaning" beyond the subjective intentions of the author. This is what enables a classic to come alive in the present. There is a dialogue between text and reader in which both partners are, as it were, challenged. The aim is to fuse the horizons of text and reader in an interpretation that is always new. A classic may reveal a genuinely new interpretation, yet the reader is also provoked into new self-understanding because of the encounter. Thus a spiritual classic is not a timeless artifact that demands mere repetition. Understanding the text implies a constant reinterpretation by people who question and listen within their own historical circumstances (a classic expression of the "new hermeneutics" is H.-G. Gadamer, *Truth and Method,* London: Sheed & Ward, 1988). A concrete example would be the way the Rule of St. Benedict has, over the centuries, regularly provoked reforms in monasticism that, while retaining a common core, have produced strikingly different lifestyles.

Contemporary approaches to interpretation would emphasize both a "hermeneutics of consent" and a "hermeneutics of suspicion." In the first case, we "consent" to the text in the sense that its origins, the author's intention, and the consensus of interpretation over time within the "community of capable readers" continue to exert some kind of normative role that prevents us from exploiting the text for our own ends. However, in the second case, we recognize that the questions provoked by our contemporary situation may well be critical of aspects of the text and its theological or cultural assumptions. For example, we are nowadays more aware of the *social* conditioning of texts and of the need to expose the hidden biases against certain ideas or groups of people within the history of spirituality that continue to influence us.

The presentation of the history of spirituality and of the interpretation of texts is of general as well as scholarly concern. Many people associate themselves with spiritual traditions that have a long history, the understanding of which affects their present sense of identity. Equally, other people who seek the spiritual wisdom of the past do so through the medium of clas-

sical texts. The issue of interpretation is therefore a live and critical one.

See also HISTORY, HISTORICAL CONSCIOUSNESS; TRADITION(S).

Bibliography: P. Sheldrake, *Spirituality and History: Questions of Interpretation and Method* (New York: Crossroad, 1992), chaps. 3, 4, 7. D. Tracy, *The Analogical Imagination: Christian Theology and the Culture of Pluralism* (London: SCM Press, 1981), esp. chap. 3. O. John, "The Tradition of the Oppressed as the Main Topic of Theological Hermeneutics," *Truth and Its Victims,* Concilium 200 (1988) 143–155.

PHILIP F. SHELDRAKE, S.J.

INTERRELIGIOUS DIALOGUE

The Beginning

Despite isolated examples from history—Francis of Assisi's journey to the Sultan of Egypt (1219), Nicholas of Cusa's *De pace fidei* (1453), and Jean Bodin's *Colloquium heptaplomeres* (1588)—interreligious dialogue as a means of mutual understanding and spiritual interacting among those who do not share the same faith did not have a major impact on Christians until the Churches were prepared to promote this model. The change came in 1965 with the passage of the Second Vatican Council's Declaration on the Relationship of the Church to Non-Christian Religions (*Nostra Aetate*): "The Church, therefore, urges her [sons and daughters] to enter with prudence and charity into discussion and collaboration with members of other religions. Let Christians, while witnessing to their own faith and way of life, acknowledge, preserve and encourage the spiritual and moral truths found among non-Christians, also their social life and culture" (NA 2, Flannery). One year prior to this, Pope Paul VI established the Secretariat for Non-Christians (after March 1, 1989, known as the Pontifical Council for Interreligious Dialogue) to prepare Catholics for interreligious dialogue, to meet with religious representatives, and to maintain contact with offices and leaders of non-Christian religious traditions.

A similar but later development took place in the World Council of Churches (in existence since 1948). In 1971 a separate sub-unit was formed to promote dialogue between people of living faiths. After several years of bilateral and multilateral discussions sponsored by the new unit, a consultation at Chiang Mai proposed *Guidelines on Dialogue* as the basis for interreligious work in the sub-unit and in the Churches: ". . . the aim of dialogue is not reduction of living faiths and ideologies to a lowest common denominator, not only a comparison and discussion of symbols and concepts, but the enabling of a true encounter between those spiritual insights and experiences which are only found at the deepest levels of human life" (no. 22).

Kinds of Dialogue

In 1984 the Holy See's Secretariat for Non-Christians issued "The Attitude of the Church Towards the Followers of Other Religions (Reflections and Orientations on Dialogue and Mission)." Four forms of dialogue were identified:

1. The dialogue of life, which is the norm and necessary manner of every form of Christian action implying concern, respect, and hospitality toward the others.

2. The dialogue of deeds, which is collaboration with others toward goals of a humanitarian, social, economic, or political nature addressing the great problems with which humanity is struggling.

3. The dialogue of specialists, which is the exchange of views and joint study of those who have developed special expertise allowing the partners to come to mutual understanding, the appreciation of each other's spiritual values and cultural categories, and to promote friendship and association among people.

4. The dialogue of religious experience, which is the sharing of experiences of prayer, contemplation, faith and duty, expressions and ways of searching for the Absolute, leading to mutual enrichment and the promotion of the highest spiritual values (nos. 28-35).

All four kinds of dialogue can influence significantly the spiritual life for Christians. In the words of Pope John Paul II to a plenary meeting of the Pontifical Council for Interreligious Dialogue marking the twenty-fifth anniversaries both of the establishment of that office and of the promulgation of *Nostra Aetate,* "Dialogue is not so much an idea to be studied as a way of living in positive relationship with others" (April 26, 1990). For a discussion of the relationship between dialogue and mission, one should consult "Dialogue and Proclamation: Two Aspects of the Evangelizing Mission of the Church" (May 19, 1991).

Effects of Dialogue on Spirituality

The impact of interreligious dialogue has been felt significantly by Christians in the general area known as inculturation. In the wake of developments within Churches after the establishment of the World Council of Churches and the Second Vatican Council, Christians throughout Africa and Asia have creatively adapted their liturgical, spiritual, and even theological activities to the cultural and religious contexts for their regions. Because certain cultures, particularly African and Native American cultures, are religious cultures, the spiritual values, even of those who are Christians, are mediated through the religious imagery of the cultural context. Ancestor veneration, narration of ancient stories, dance, food offerings, singing and drumming, dream interpretation, purification rites, and vision quests are among the many gifts of indigenous religious cultures to the lives of Christians in those societies. In the United States this is exemplified in the work of the Tekakwitha Conference, an annual meeting since 1939 of those engaged in the evangelization of Native American Catholics. One of its goals is "to empower Native American Catholics to live in harmony with the Catholic and native spirituality."

Improved interreligious relations have resulted in a number of ways for Christians to join with others in the promotion of peace, justice, and the common good. Thus, a public spirituality has emerged that characterizes those who have crossed religious lines to join in special projects to negotiate the end to war, to apply moral pressure for nuclear disarmament and an end to violence as a political and social method, and to meet the needs of those who are oppressed, impoverished, and underprivileged. The member Churches of the World Council of Churches have dedicated themselves to a conciliar process of mutual commitment to justice, peace, and the integrity of creation. This was a result of their Vancouver Assembly (1983). At a WCC world convocation on these three connected themes, held in Seoul in 1990, the delegates agreed that it is "time for the ecumenical movement to articulate its vision of all people living on earth and caring for creation as a family where each member has the same right to wholeness of life. While this vision is spiritual in nature, it must be expressed in concrete action" ("Justice, Peace, Integrity of Creation," World Convocation, WCC, Seoul, March 6-12, 1990, p. 6). It remains to be seen whether the WCC will develop this three-part ecumenical agenda into a genuine interreligious program.

Notable on the international scene is the World Conference on Religion and Peace, which was formed at an assembly in Kyoto in 1970 and has met four subsequent times (Louvain, 1974; Princeton, 1979; Nairobi, 1984; and Melbourne, 1989). Attending these gatherings are religious leaders, institutional representatives, and experts in various fields. These assemblies are marked by open discussion of international and regional problems, public statements, and multireligious celebrations. Between assemblies a general secretariat has functioned in New York (for a period in Geneva), in close affiliation with the United Nations Organization and having non-governmental status with UNO committees. National and regional WCRP chapters exist throughout the world.

Interfaith councils can be found in cities and towns and on the state level in the United States. Once existing as conferences of Churches, with mostly Protestant membership, these have expanded over the years to include other Christians, then Jews, and now Muslims, Buddhists, and others. The Interreligious Council of Southern California, formed in 1969, now has eleven member organizations representing seven religious traditions. The Interfaith Conference of Metropolitan Washington has over thirty member organizations representing six religious traditions. Not only do these councils provide contact among these groups and nurture friendships among local religious leaders, but they also sponsor annual workshops, symposia, cultural and religious events, and ongoing activities of social service. Collectively, these have a significant impact on Christians and their spiritual development.

Deserving special attention among the dialogues of specialists and focusing on religious experience have been the interreligious dialogues of monastics in the past two decades. These dialogues have been promoted by two committees: the North American Board for East-West Dialogue (in the U.S. and Canada) and its counterpart in Europe, Dialogue Interreligieux Monastique. Now called "Monastic Interreligious Dialogue," the North American committee has participated in a number of intermonastic hospitality programs largely involving Benedictines and Cistercians in North American communities and Tibetan Buddhist and Hindu communities in India. These and other activities involving adepts in contemplative methods have led to important contributions in literature and programs of spirituality for Christians. The enrichment of the practice of contemplative prayer has been significant, resulting in a rediscovery of the contemplative heritage of Christianity for many, as well as a sharing of techniques to aid the spiritual journey.

Symbolic Event

The most significant event thus far in the history of interreligious relations was the World Day of Prayer for Peace held in Assisi on October 27, 1986. Responding to an invitation of Pope John Paul II to attend "a special meeting of prayer for peace in the city of Assisi, a place which the seraphic figure of St. Francis has transformed into a center of universal fraternity," religious leaders from various Christian Churches and communions and representatives of other religions gathered to fast, walk together, and pray for peace in the presence of one another. The convener predicted that it would be a day on which the spiritual movement for the unity and peace among all peoples would have one of its most significant and important moments (January 25, 1986). It demonstrated the importance of another principle articulated by the Second Vatican Council, namely, that "there can be no ecumenism worthy of the name without interior conversion" (UR 7, Flannery).

In a reflection after the Assisi day of prayer, Pope John Paul II observed: "The event of Assisi can thus be considered as a visible illustration, a concrete example, a catechesis, intelligible to all, of what is presupposed and signified by the commitment to ecumenism and to the interreligious dialogue which was recommended and promoted by the Second Vatican Council" (December 22, 1986). The Reverend Paul A. Crow, Jr., president of the Council on Christian Unity of the Christian Church, testified in his address at a National Day of Prayer breakfast: "I have never experienced the depth of spiritual prayer and thanksgiving and struggle as I did at Assisi" (May 7, 1987). The Archbishop of Canterbury, during a visit to Rome on September 30, 1990, said of the event: "In Assisi, without compromise of faith, we saw that the Bishop of Rome could gather the Christian Churches together. We could pray together for the peace and well-being of humankind, and the stewardship of our precious Earth. At that initiative of prayer for world peace I felt I was in the presence of the God who said, 'Behold I am doing a new thing.' "

See also AFRICAN SPIRITUALITY; EASTERN (ASIAN) SPIRITUALITY; ECUMENISM, SPIRITUAL; ISLAMIC SPIRITUALITY; JEWISH SPIRITUALITY; NATIVE AMERICAN SPIRITUALITY; VATICAN COUNCIL II.

Bibliography: Pontifical Council for Interreligious Dialogue, "Dialogue and Proclamation: Two Aspects of the Evangelizing Mission of the Church," Bulletin 77 (1991); see also Origins 21:8 (July 4, 1991); and "The Attitude of the Church Towards the Followers of Other Religions (Reflections and Orientations on Dialogue and Mission)," Bulletin 56 (1984). T. Arai and W. Ariarajah, eds., Spirituality in Interfaith Dialogue (Geneva: WCC Publications, 1989). L. Klenicki and G. Huck, Spirituality and Prayer: Jewish and Christian Understandings (New York: Paulist, 1983). North American Board for East-West Dialogue, Bulletin (Trappist, Ky.: Abbey of Gethsemani).

JOHN BORELLI

INTIMACY

Intimacy is the experience of closeness or union between two persons. Human intimacy is first learned in the family and is fostered by the love and devotion of a parent, the sacrifice and thoughtfulness of family members, the affirmation and care of others. Initial experiences of friendship help people to develop bonds of common purpose. Friendship allows them to discover intimacy in silence and conversation, in taking risks and in trusting another. Some friendships last a lifetime. The yearning for intimacy overcomes short-lived or broken friendships and allows a person to risk in order to make new friends.

Human intimacy is learned in experiences of community. Schoolmates and church members build ties of mutual support, shared meaning, and common value. These ties may inspire a person in moments of loneliness, disappointment, and personal anguish.

The awareness of one's sexuality indicates how deeply people desire to love and to be in intimate communion. Sexual desire can teach a person to be giving, altruistic, and caring. It can move one away from isolation, selfishness, and manipulation of others for one's personal gain. One learns to give the gift of oneself and to receive the gift of another.

The most noble expression of sexual intimacy occurs in marriage. Marital intimacy is meant to reflect God's love for humankind. From a Christian perspective, it is a sacramental bond that mirrors the dying and rising of Jesus. The pressures of individualism, the wounds caused by family dysfunction, and the risk of divorce do not detract from the possibility for intimacy in sexual union and love. Sometimes unplanned separations and necessary absence from one another teach partners the depth of their intimacy. Sometimes the death of a spouse shows just how deeply a married couple had lived an intimate life.

Human experiences of intimacy serve as pathways to intimacy with God. Unloved persons seldom discover a loving God. Intimate communion with a triune God is best nourished by experiences of human intimacy. Those who are loved by their family and spouses can understand a God who calls persons to a loving response. The experience of God is mutual love. The nature of God is love. This intimacy was witnessed by the people of Israel, who described God as a loving spouse. Divine love was shown in the incarnation. Through Jesus, God extends an invitation to intimacy, favor, and a gracious Spirit. Something in the nature of humankind, fashioned in the image and likeness of God, indicates that God desires to dwell in the human heart.

Modern men and women question whether intimacy is possible between God and human beings. God may often seem to be absent. Survivors of the Holocaust may wonder whether God cares or is moved by human suffering. In his play *Ani Maamin* ("I Believe"), Elie Wiesel puts God on trial. Abraham, Isaac, and Jacob all ask God to indicate that God cares. But God is silent. They learn that God cares, because God is crying. God is moved by human anguish.

God still desires intimacy with humankind. God's heart is moved by tears. God's tears unite with the tears that stir the human heart. Intimacy with God is a matter of the heart. Is the human heart vibrant and vital? Is it fertile soil for God? Is it open to lament and to praise? Or is it barren, hard, and sclerotic?

The human heart can remain indifferent to God and others; it can reject intimate communion. A person can turn away in guilt, shame, or sin. One can be so focused on oneself that there may be little space for intimacy with another or with God. No one can become a friend unless the heart is emptied of self in order that the Spirit of Jesus can fill human longing.

The nature of intimacy with God is expressed well in the maxim *Ubi amor, ibi oculus,* "Where the heart's love is, there is one's eye." Intimacy with God requires some kind of spiritual vision. Just as the Israelites saw Moses descend Mount Sinai with the tablets of stone, so too Christians need to see signs of God's call to intimacy. Spiritual vision is imagined as four tablets, each one teaching the eye.

The first tablet is nature. The human eye sees God's grandeur in creation. The universe invites a sense of wonder in the human heart.

The second tablet is Sacred Scripture. Scripture indicates what a person is to believe and what one is to do to achieve intimacy with God. The intellect is illuminated and one learns how to meditate, contemplate, and pray.

The third tablet is the love that Christians have for one another. The eye sees intimacy with God connected with the intimacy one experiences with the Body of Christ. Intimacy with others comes from baptism and Eucharist, from ministering to one another and working to fashion God's reign on earth.

The last tablet is unitive and contemplative prayer. Intimacy with God means surrendering to God's love, letting go of our desire to control God through our concepts and reason. Intimacy can happen only if one allows the Spirit to move one's heart. The mind and heart enter into peaceful communion. This level of intimacy is similar to losing one's life for the sake of Jesus in order to find authentic life (Mt 16:25).

Human persons are gifted with two eyes. In the Christian tradition one eye is reason and the other is love. Intimate and affectionate love between God and the Christian requires that one let go of one's reason so that the heart can surrender in love. The heart is the seat of human and divine love. In the depths of one's heart one arrives at the hearth. Here Christians find God's rest and friendship. Here one hears the sounds of desire for human and divine intimacy. Here one cherishes the love of God and others.

See also ECSTASY; HEART; HEART OF CHRIST; HESYCHASM; SEXUALITY; UNION, UNITIVE WAY.

Bibliography: A. Callahan, ed., *Spiritualities of the Heart* (New York: Paulist, 1990). P. Wadell, *Friendship and the Moral Life* (Notre Dame, Ind.: Univ. of Notre Dame Press, 1989). J. Walsh, ed., *The Cloud of Unknowing* (New York: Paulist, 1981); *The Pursuit of Wisdom and Other Works by the Author of The Cloud of Unknowing* (New York: Paulist, 1988).

JOHN J. O'BRIEN, C.P.

INTUITION

Christian tradition has always held that human beings can know God through "the things God has made." The fundamental question is, What kind of knowledge can women and men have of God? Is the only knowledge possible in this life a knowledge *about God* arrived at by natural reasoning or by revelation? Or is it possible to have, even in this life, an intuitive knowledge of God?

The word *intuition* derives from the Latin *intueri,* which means "to consider, look at, gaze at." It can have the meaning "to look someone right in the face." This last usage of the term can introduce us to the meaning that is traditionally given to intuition, namely, instantaneous apprehension or immediate knowing of something or someone without going through any conscious process of reasoning. This is not an uncommon experience in human life. For example, a person can come to a decision that she or he instinctively knows to be right, without having gone through, consciously at least, a reasoning process to reach that decision.

Is such an intuitive process operative in coming to know God? Most systematic theology has been reluctant to give an affirmative answer to this question. It reserves the immediate apprehension of God to the beatific vision that comes only after death. Mystics are not quite so cautious, and some would maintain that an immediate knowing of God, in which the subject-object dichotomy disappears, is possible in the contemplative experience. Thomas Merton puts it well: "In the depths of contemplative prayer there seems to be no division between subject and object and there is no reason to make any statement about God or about oneself. He IS and this reality absorbs everything else" (Merton, *New Seeds,* p. 267).

See also AFFECT, AFFECTIVITY; BEATIFIC VISION; CONTEMPLATION, CONTEMPLATIVE PRAYER; EXPERIENCE; FEELINGS; MYSTICISM.

Bibliography: M. Redle, "Intuition," *New Catholic Encyclopedia* (Washington: Catholic Univ. of America, 1967) 6:562–563. T. Merton, *New Seeds of Contemplation* (New York: New Directions, 1962).

WILLIAM H. SHANNON

ISLAMIC SPIRITUALITY

With its declaration that the Church "rejects nothing which is true and holy" in other religious traditions (NA 2), Vatican

II challenges Catholics to acknowledge and appreciate what Muslims consider true and holy. Islam's nearly fourteen-century history represents a rich tradition of spiritual values and insights into the divine-human relationship. The following summary will discuss the theological foundations of Islamic spirituality, its sources, some major historical developments, and finally several modes of expression of that spirituality.

Foundations: Divine Transcendence and Prophetic Mission

At the heart of Islam's worldview lie the experience and conviction of divine unity and transcendence. The confession that "there is no god but God" comprises the first half of the basic creedal statement. Across late 6th-century Arabia numerous religious currents had come and gone, but most characteristic of the region was a variety of polydaemonism that focused on local sanctuaries devoted to the spirits that indwelt such natural objects as sacred stones. In the trading entrepot of Makka (Mecca) in west central Arabia only a few miles inland from the Red Sea, the ancient sanctuary of the Ka'ba (a roughly cubic building with a black stone in one of its corners) had functioned as a major axis of religious life and a center of pilgrimage since long before the birth of Muhammad (ca. 570 C.E.). Like other sanctuaries, that of the Ka'ba had its chief deity (*allah* = "God," from a contraction of *al-ilah,* "the-god").

During Muhammad's earlier years he had prayed there, but his own spiritual search seems to have moved him to seek God in the quiet of a mountain cave outside the city. There, around 610 C.E., Muhammad experienced the first of a series of chiefly auditory revelations (with sporadic visual elements) via the mediation of the angel Jibril (Gabriel). Earlier auditions centered on God's goodness and power, human responsibility in light of a coming judgment (an eschatology similar to that of Christianity), and the need to share and give thanks for God's bounty.

Within a few years a growing insistence on God's unity became a constant theme in the revelations, and references to stories of earlier prophets multiplied in Muhammad's utterances. Muhammad came to see Abraham, the first *hanif* (seeker after the One God), as his spiritual model: Abraham had repudiated his own father, a carver of idols, and had set out for parts unknown. Under growing pressure from discontented leaders who feared that Muhammad's preaching would disrupt trade and pilgrimage activities, Muhammad, too, would leave home in the *hijra* (emigration) of 622 C.E. from Makka to Yathrib (now Madina—City [of the Prophet]).

Muhammad's sense of his prophetic call deepened with his experience of God's absolute, simple unity, majesty, and sovereignty. Of God's "ninety-nine Names" (on which Muslims meditate as they finger a rosary of thirty-three beads), the most frequently spoken, "Gracious" and "Merciful," appear at the beginning of all but one chapter of the Qur'an (Koran, see below). Clearly the God of Muhammad's experience was no tyrant, even if the demands of the prophetic call often proved burdensome. Muhammad envisioned himself as part of an unbroken chain of messengers beginning with Adam and continuing through Jesus. All the major prophetic personages brought revelations; some, like David, Moses, and Jesus (Mary also plays a significant role), also received a "Book" to communicate to a people. These prophet-messengers sought to unify humankind through belief in One God.

Muslims believe that all the prophets have spoken the same truth, but they regard Muhammad's revelation as final and definitive, correcting whatever misinterpretations may have distorted the earlier messages over the centuries. Though Muhammad was only human, his example epitomizes for all Muslims the best in the divine-human relationship. Three journeys in Muhammad's life are paradigmatic for Muslims. The Prophet's Hijra, marking the beginning of Islam's lunar calendar (622 C.E.), models the need to "leave home" for one's faith. Muhammad's pilgrimage to the Ka'ba in his last year (632 C.E.) established a similar pilgrimage as a ritual requirement for all able to fulfill it without undue hardship. And from earlier in his life, a two-part mystical experience called the "night journey" (isra', from Makka to Jerusalem's Temple mount) and "ascension" (mi'raj, to the throne of God and through the various levels of heaven and hell) has formed the paradigm of the believer's ultimate spiritual journey. On a more mundane plane, Muhammad's example sets the standard for even the simplest actions in everyday life.

Sources: Qur'an and Hadith

Muslims believe that on a variety of occasions between 610 and 632 C.E., Muhammad received and delivered a series of revelations. His utterances were at first preserved in the memories of prominent "Companions" (Muhammad's contemporaries), and were written down only piecemeal while Muhammad lived. Some twenty years after his death, scribes wrote these revelations and arranged them more or less in descending order of length. Since the earlier chapters (sura; pl. suwar) tended to be briefer and more poetic, they generally appear later in the present arrangement. The Makkan suras (610–622 C.E.) contain much apocalyptic imagery and tales of the prophets. Those that date from the Madinan period (after 622) tend to be more concerned with regulating the life of the community, now newly constituted as a prominent force in its newly adopted city and no longer at the mercy of Muhammad's opponents in Makka.

Qur'anic texts range over numerous topics. Individual suras often give new readers an impression of disjointedness. One may attribute that feel to the book's original orality. Readers with opportunity to spend more time with this scripture will ultimately find it rewarding and intriguing. Muslims have always characterized listening to "recitation" (the literal meaning of Qur'an) in one of two chantlike styles as a most profoundly moving spiritual experience. Even if the listener knows little or no Arabic, the audible arabesques punctuated with electric silences immeasurably heighten a Muslim's sense of being enveloped in the living word of God.

Tucked away among the approximately six thousand verses (comparable in length to the New Testament) are stories of how God has worked through his prophets, specific directives concerning some behavioral and ritual matters, and splendid images of God. For example, the "Verse of Light" (Sura 24:35) reads: "God is the Light of the heavens and the earth; his light is like a niche in which is a lamp, in which is a glass like a shining star kindled from a sacred olive tree neither of east nor west, whose oil would well-nigh glow even if no fire touched it. Light upon light, and God guides to his light whom he will." Few texts appear more often as calligraphic ornamentation in architecture. Its allusion to an image like a burning bush, combined with that of an axial tree of cosmic proportions, suggests both divine immanence and transcendence. Other images of God's majesty, such as that in the "Throne Verse," which pictures God dwelling above all things (Sura 2:256), find counterpoints in such references to divine immanence as "God is closer than the jugular vein" (Sura 50:15).

For Muslims, no document equals the Qur'an for sheer beauty, authority, and quotability. Second only to the scripture comes the vast anecdotal collection of Muhammad's words and deeds, known as Hadith. Compiled in a number of trusted anthologies by the late 9th century, the Hadith constitute a treasury of practical guidance for Islamic spirituality. There one hears Muhammad's advice on everything from where to position the hands during ritual prayer to how to detect the presence of Satan in one's thoughts. Taken as a whole, the Hadith comprise the basic reference for the exemplary conduct (*sunna*) of Muhammad.

Historical Considerations

Spiritual Styles and the Mystical Tradition

Immediately upon Muhammad's death, the young Muslim community faced the crucial problem of establishing criteria for legitimacy in leadership. A majority opinion held that the Prophet had appointed no successor (*khalifa,* "caliph"), so the choice was handed over to the council of elders. When they chose Muhammad's elderly father-in-law, supporters (*shi'a*) of the Prophet's son-in-law Ali claimed that Muhammad had indeed "designated" Ali as his successor. The majority called themselves "The People of the Sunna and the Assembly" (Sunni Muslims). Still a minority, Shi'i Muslims espouse a spirituality based on charismatic leadership and hierarchical authority (through familial descent from Muhammad), while Sunni spirituality exhibits a more communitarian tone.

Shi'i spirituality emphasizes the redemptive value of suffering and martyrdom, with much stronger affective dimensions in its religious observances. Annual mourning for the death of protomartyr Husayn (son of Ali by Muhammad's daughter Fatima) in 680 C.E., for example, includes displays of intense emotion and even self-mutilation. For Shi'i Muslims, the suffering of Muhammad's spiritual successors—the imams and their families—at the hands of oppressors and tyrants (such as the late Shah of Iran or President Saddam Hussein of Iraq) has long provided a major paradigm for the interpretation of history.

As suggested earlier, Muhammad's life serves as a spiritual wellspring for Muslims. Though none has ever equaled the Prophet in holiness or virtue, his example of simplicity, prayer, and sincerity has inspired seekers toward greater interiority since the earliest days. During the 7th and 8th centuries C.E., individual ascetics spoke out against both the secularism of dynastic rulers and the dry ritualism of Islamic law. Asceticism gradually gave place to the love poetry of the first great mystic, a woman from Iraq named Rabi'a. Her frankness and familiarity with God shocked many, but she was only the first of many fascinating Islamic mystics. During subsequent centuries two "schools" developed: the sober and the intoxicated. While the former emphasized the inadvisability or impossibility of attempting to give expression to one's experience (apophatic), the intoxicated mystics poured out their souls in ecstatic and paradoxical utterances (kataphatic), sometimes paying with their lives for their indiscretion.

During the 10th and 11th centuries, a number of prominent Muslim theologians took up the challenge of defending these mystical tendencies (by now known collectively as Sufism) against their critics. They produced theoretical treatises and biographical dictionaries of famous holy persons to demonstrate the compatibility of such interiorization with the communal demands of Islamic practice. During the next two hundred years or so, there ensued a remarkable proliferation of formally constituted religious orders (*tariqa,* "path") across the Islamic world, from Morocco to the Indian subcontinent. These orders had charters, religious superiors and aspirants (*shaykh, pir* [Persian] "elder"; *murid,* "seeker," "novice"), elaborate paraliturgical rituals, and the equivalents of "divine office" and *lectio divina.* Some orders were celibate during the Middle Ages; many were mendicant in the technical sense. Most referred to their members as "poor ones" (Arabic *faqir;* Persian *darvish*). Many orders still exist, though they are generally less politically active than they were in the Middle Ages.

Modes of Expression: Ritual, Literary, Political

For the vast majority of Muslims, spirituality finds its primary expression in the "Five Pillars": the profession of faith; ritual prayer five times daily, oriented to Makka; the giving of alms to be distributed to the needy; fasting from sunrise to sundown during the thirty days of the month of Ramadan (ninth lunar month of the liturgical year); and pilgrimage to Makka once in a lifetime (during the twelfth lunar month). Along with a wide spectrum of other communal and personal devotions, these practices embody the essential attitude of "grateful surrender" (*islam*) and the acknowledgment of humanity's servanthood under one transcendent God as a vast community of believers.

In a dozen or more major Islamic languages, from Arabic to Malay, Muslims have produced rich literary descriptions of the soul's journey away from and back to God, of the lover's passionate longing to rejoin the Beloved, of the divine alchemy wrought in the base metal of human nature. Islam boasts some of the world's greatest religious poetry, rivaling that of John of the Cross, and as rich and diverse as Christianity's religious classics.

Finally, since Islam has never conceived of a separation between the religious and civil spheres, its spirituality has always been what most Americans would call "political." Islam envisions a just world order informed by the acknowledgement of God's unity (*tawhid*). One of the major struggles for contemporary Muslims is to try to reconcile their deepest conviction about the unity of all life with the reality of the political, social, and economic fragmentation in which they find themselves.

See also AFFIRMATIVE WAY; FASTING; INTER-RELIGIOUS DIALOGUE; JEWISH SPIRITUALITY; JOURNEY (GROWTH AND DEVELOPMENT IN SPIRITUAL LIFE); LECTIO DIVINA; NEGATIVE WAY; PROPHECY; REVELATION(S).

JOHN RENARD

J

JANSENISM

The term *Jansenism* has come to have a pejorative connotation that it did not at all bear in the 17th and 18th centuries in France. True, the theological battle between the Jansenists and the Jesuits spawned polemical literature on both sides. However, those concerned about serious reform in the spiritual and intellectual life of the Catholic Church tended more toward the "rigorist" moral position of the Jansenists than toward the "laxism" of the Jesuits. Also, the fact that the Jansenists took the "Gallican" political position aligned them with the *parlements* (provincial as well as Parisian) against the throne, and with episcopal authority against papal authority. Theological Gallicanism affirmed their strong belief in the relative autonomy of the local Church.

Jansenism took its name from Cornelius Jansen (better known as Jansenius), professor of Scripture at Louvain and bishop of Ypres, who authored a book on Augustine's theology of grace entitled *Augustinus.* This book was introduced into France by Jansenius's friend and collaborator Jean Duvergier de Hauranne, abbot of Saint-Cyran. Saint-Cyran, who was more interested in spiritual direction and reform of the Church than in theology, turned to Antoine Arnauld, priest and scholar at the Sorbonne, to defend the doctrine of grace in the *Augustinus* when it was attacked by the Jesuits. Through Arnauld

and his brother, Robert Arnauld d'Andilly, Saint-Cyran and his reform became connected with the monastery of Port-Royal, where Jacqueline Arnauld (Mère Angelique) was abbess and many others of the Arnauld family were members. Through this connection with Cistercian monasticism, and Saint-Cyran's direction of retreats for friends and relatives of the Arnaulds—young intellectuals who were members of the rising class of the bourgeoisie, the *noblesse de robe,* in Paris and other urban centers—a unique spirituality was formed.

From the monastic background came a love of the liturgy, especially the Divine Office and the Eucharist. To this love of the liturgy theological Gallicanism added a profound respect for the local Church: the right of the bishop to adapt the liturgy (for example, the calendar) to his diocese, and the role of the laity in the liturgical ceremonies. Theologically, Jansenist spirituality inherited the extreme Augustinian positions on grace and predestination expounded in the *Augustinus,* and this resulted in a pessimistic view of the human condition and a tremendous awe of the holiness and otherness of God.

Another distinguishing feature was bequeathed to subsequent generations by the *messieurs de Port-Royal.* Jansenius and Saint-Cyran believed that reform would come through recovering the spirit of the early Church. Their interest in the early Church led the scholars in this group to do research on ancient texts and to translate or explicate them in order to make this treasure of early Christian theology accessible to the literate public. They also translated liturgical texts. And, of course, the translation of the Bible by Isaac Le Maître de Sacy and others of the Port-Royal group (including Pascal) stands as a classic French text and was the family Bible in many French homes into the 20th century.

Thus, the marks of Jansenist spirituality are: (1) appreciation of the liturgical life, including an ingredient of theological Gallicanism that emphasized more and more the role of the laity in the liturgy; (2) love of Scripture, urged for the laity as well as clerics (one of the one hundred propositions condemned in the bull *Unigenitus* in 1713); (3) a pessimistic view of the human condition and reverential awe of the "Holy," resulting in a very serious and morally rigorous interpretation of Christian life. These marks can still be found in the Church of Utrecht, which traces its origins to the schism of 1726 and its theology and spirituality to the Jansenists in exile in the Netherlands at that time, and in French families whose ancestors were members of Jansenist groups or sympathizers in the 17th and 18th centuries.

See also AUGUSTINIAN SPIRITUALITY; GRACE; LAY SPIRITUALITY; LITURGY.

Bibliography: L. Cognet, *Le Jansénisme* (Paris: Presses Universitaires de France, 1961). F. E. Weaver, "Port Royal," *D.Spir.,* vol. 13, cols. 1931–1952. C. Sainte-Beuve, *Port-Royal,* 3 vols. (Paris: Éditions Gallimard, 1953).

F. ELLEN WEAVER-LAPORTE

JESUIT SPIRITUALITY

See IGNATIAN SPIRITUALITY.

JESUS PRAYER

See HESYCHASM.

JEWISH SPIRITUALITY

Introduction and Historical Background

Religious sensibilities often begin with a sense of the sublime. For both Jews and Christians, the sublime as the starting point for experiencing the presence of God in the world is expressed most dramatically in the Bible. "Look up to the skies and behold; regard the heavens high above you," Elihu tells Job (Job 35:5). The psalmist also looks to nature and experiences God's presence: "The heavens declare the glory of God, and the firmament proclaims his handiwork" (Ps 19:2).

Sensing or experiencing the presence of God, however, is distinct from seeking God. For Jews, the path to God was clearly established at Mount Sinai: "Therefore, if you hearken to my voice and keep my covenant, you shall be my special possession, dearer to me than all other people. . . . You shall be to me a kingdom of priests, a holy nation" (Exod 19:5-6). This exhortation entails a dual obligation. The people of Israel are collectively expected to keep the covenant; at the same time, each individual is commanded to "walk in his ways, and to keep his commandments and his statutes and decrees" (Deut 30:16). Jewish liturgy has retained this dual perspective. Thus the collection of short, independent petitions (the *shemoneh esreh,* or Eighteen Benedictions) that constitute the heart of daily prayer are written in the plural ("pardon us" . . . "grant us . . ."), and Jewish law encourages, but does not require, that prayers be recited in a quorum of at least ten men. Yet prayer is also known as the "service of the heart"—the individual's expression of his or her love of, and trust in, God.

Expressions of Jewish spirituality have evolved historically. In the patriarchal stage of Jewish history, Abraham, Isaac, and Jacob entered into and affirmed an eternal covenant with God. Although the patriarchs built altars and sacrificed animals, no distinct religious institutions emerged until the revelation at Mount Sinai. The exodus from Egypt and the experience at Sinai welded the Israelites into a national unit with a distinctive national code of law. When Kings David and Solomon established Jerusalem as the religious center of the Jewish people, rituals were performed by a priestly caste, and civil law was interpreted by that caste.

The heart of ritual practice during both the First and Second Temple periods consisted of a complex and elaborate sacrificial system. The dual communal and individual obligations mentioned above were fulfilled by two broad categories of sacrifices (*korbanot*) brought to the Temple. The communal sacrifices (*korbanot tzibur*) were offered on behalf of the entire community; in addition, various sacrifices were brought by individuals on their own behalf.

The destruction of the Temple in 70 C.E., the dissolution of the priestly caste, and the Roman occupation challenged the leadership in Palestine and in the large diaspora centers in Babylonia to evolve other forms of spirituality without displacing the heritage of the past. Jewish authority now emanated from Yavneh, on the Mediterranean coast. The Romans allowed Jochanan ben Zakkai to found an academy and to continue the work of the now defunct Sanhedrin (Great Assembly or high court). After the failed revolt against the Romans (132–135 C.E.), the religious leaders fled to the city of Usha in the Galilee, from where they continued to evolve the tradition that is now considered rabbinic or "normative" Judaism. Though written and redacted by many generations of rabbis in both Palestine and Babylonia, it was in the period between Yavneh and Usha that the classical rabbinic texts and sources emerged.

The rabbis understood themselves to be the keepers and interpreters of the law given to Moses at Sinai. "Moses received the Torah at Sinai and handed it down to Joshua; Joshua to the elders; the elders to the prophets; and the prophets handed it down to the men of the Great Assembly," states the Mishnah, the 2nd-century code of Jewish law that is the core of the Talmudic literature. Even the exegetical method used to interpret unclear or ambiguous areas of the Bible was considered part of the Sinai legacy. "Torah" meant not only the five books of Moses but included the entire corpus of law and wisdom received, interpreted, and taught, both in the past and in the future, by the rabbis. God had not only revealed a Written Law (*torah she b'ictav*) but also an Oral Law (*torah sheb'alpeh*), preserved in a vast legal, homiletic, and mystical literature. Within this enormous, vibrant, and original literature, we find the various expressions of Jewish spirituality.

The Centrality of Law in Jewish Spirituality

A homiletic account in the Talmud (the body of Oral Law compiled and written in the 1st to the 3rd century) relates that when God heard the Jewish people say at Sinai, "We will do and obey" (Exod 24:7), a heavenly voice exclaimed, "Who has revealed to my children this mystery, which the ministering angels enact, to fulfill His word before they hear the voice?" (Shabbat 88a). The spiritual development of the Jew does not necessarily depend upon an understanding of religious or theological principles. Rather, it depends upon the fulfillment of religious precepts (the *mitzvot*) and a commitment to live within the corpus of law (the *halacha*) that contains the various precepts.

The centrality of the *halacha* is insisted upon by every current of Jewish thought, both mystical and philosophical. No matter how speculative and bold their expression, Jewish mystics understood themselves as bound to the authority of halachic Judaism. Similarly, Moses Maimonides (1135–1204), the Jewish scholastic par excellence who wrote the most important philosophical work in Jewish history (*The Guide to the Perplexed*), devoted most of his life to systematizing and explicating the *halacha*. His code of law, the *Mishneh Torah* (lit., "repetition of the Torah"), is still considered a standard reference book of Jewish law.

Rabbi Joseph Soloveitchik's distinction between *homo religiosus* and the halachic person (lit., "man") in his essay on the psychology and philosophy of *halacha* brings into sharp focus the effect of law upon the spiritual life of the Jew: "*Homo religiosus* is intrigued by the mystery of existence—and wants to emphasize that mystery.... *Homo religiosus* is eager to cognize natural phenomena and understand them, but knowledge itself for him is the greatest and most difficult riddle of all" (*Halakhic Man*, p. 11). The *homo religiosus* responds to the *mysterium* by attempting to flee from the material, empirical world to a rarefied transcendental reality where existence is eternally holy. Asceticism, renunciation, and self-affliction are often the forms this flight takes.

The halachic person, by contrast, approaches reality "with his Torah, given to him from Sinai, in hand. He orients himself to the world by means of fixed statutes and firm principles. An entire corpus of precepts and laws guides him along the path leading to existence. Halachic man, well furnished with rules, judgments, and fundamental principles, begins near the world with an a priori relation. His approach begins with an ideal creation and concludes with a real one" (*Halakhic Man*, p. 19). In other words, Torah is the blueprint of nature, and through its fulfillment the kingdom of earth is brought to heaven.

The centrality of law for Judaism departs from the Pauline doctrine that a human being is "justified by faith," that is, by baptism the believer is united with Christ. The Jew is, so to speak, "justified by deed," that is, by his or her commitment to *halacha* and the *mitzvah* system that it entails.

Expressions of Spirituality

Jewish history is not a series of discontinuities; neither is it an ahistorical phenomenon. Both the impact of the surrounding intellectual and cultural environment and the internal dialectic of Jewish history have shaped the various forms of spirituality found in Judaism.

The traditional categories of "rational" or philosophical, and "nonrational" or mystical are too artificial to describe Jewish forms of spirituality. Mystical schools of thought, such as Lurianic Kabbalah (16th-century Palestine) addressed traditional philosophical problems such as *creatio ex nihilo* with original speculative approaches. And "rationalists" such as the Talmudist Rabad of Posquieres (12th century) are claimed by the mystics as their own.

Whatever the approach of the particular thinker, Judaism is strongly text-oriented. An ecstatic mysticism such as that of the Christian Hildegard of Bingen is virtually unknown to Jewish mysticism. And the fact that the rabbis understood themselves as both the inheritors and interpreters of the Oral Law given at Mount Sinai acted as a restraint against personal literary expression of spirituality. Spiritual autobiographies in the style of Augustine's *Confessions* are also not found.

Jewish mystics partake in the same exegetical tradition as non-mystics. The parables, theological statements, and homilies of the *aggadic* literature found in the Talmud (and also as a separate body of literature) are often reminiscent of mysticism. Jewish mystics, however, employ a special language and introduce an ontology not found in aggadic literature or in the great Jewish philosophers of the Middle Ages. The particulars of Jewish mysticism are beyond the scope of this entry (see G. Scholem, *Major Trends in Jewish Mysticism*). It is important to note that Jewish mysticism was never considered heretical by the rabbis and that the mystics themselves accepted the authority and centrality of *halacha.* The opponents of Hasidism, the 18th-century Eastern European pietistic movement, (who declared it heretical), were troubled by other factors (such as the central, almost messianic role of the Hasidic leader), rather than by any specific lack of commitment to the *halachic* framework. Within one generation Hasidism was accepted into mainstream rabbinic Judaism.

Jewish mysticism's major contribution to the non-mystic's spiritual outlook was the idea of *avodah be-gashmiut* (lit., "physical worship"), namely, the hallowing of everyday life. Most fully developed by Hasidism, this view entails the idea that the most mundane occupation can be conducted as a sacred ritual if performed with the correct intent (*kavanah*).

The traditional view held that the spiritual redemption of every Jew is achieved through the performance of *mitzvot.* Indeed, the collective redemption of the Jewish people was also said to be dependent upon the acts of the entire Jewish people: "Rabbi Yochanan said in the name of Rabbi Shimon ben Yochai, 'Were Israel properly to observe two Shabbatot (Shabbat; pl., shabbatot), they would immediately be redeemed'" (Talmud *Shabbat* 118b).

Hasidism made explicit the symbiotic relation between the purely physical, material world and the spiritual world. The redemptive process is furthered when everyday activities such as eating, drinking, working, etc., are done in the service of God with a high degree of deliberation and intention. An example from the *Keter Shem Tov,* an early Hasidic collection of sayings by the founder of the movement, the Baal Shem Tov, illustrates this relationship. Eating is described as an opportunity for spiritual awareness with the following words: "When you take a fruit or any other food in your hand and recite the benediction 'Blessed art thou, O God' with intention, your mentioning the holy name

awakens the spark of divine life by which the fruit was originally created.... The benediction awakens the element of divine life in the fruit, the element which is the food of the soul. This applies to all the permitted and kosher foods, since God commanded us to uplift them from a material existence to a spiritual existence" (see *The Teachings of Hasidism,* ed. J. Dan, New York: Behrman House, 1983, p. 132).

The notion of "uplifting" from the mundane to the spiritual permeates Jewish thinking on spirituality. All rituals are regarded as an opportunity for the individual Jew to mend a spiritual wound and to complete the process of sanctifying God's name. The individual's *tikkun,* however, is intimately intertwined with the collective *tikkun* of the Jewish people. For example, the required four cups of wine at the festive meal (*seder*) of Passover not only correspond to the four expressions of redemption from slavery in Exod 6:6-7 but also symbolically complete various spiritual "failures" from the past, specifically Adam's taking from the tree of the knowledge of good and evil (a grapevine in some midrashic accounts), and Noah's abuse of the grape through his drunkenness. Adam's sin consisted in fragmenting the original unity of the Garden of Eden (the cosmos) by introducing metaphysical dualisms. The Jew during Passover raises the material substance (wine) to a spiritual purpose (rectifying Adam's and Noah's sin with wine). For the mystic, this rectifying act actually contributes to the repair of the cosmos, when the human being recognizes no polarities in God's creation, and all the aspects of God are in balance and harmony.

In a work regarded as the classic handbook of Jewish spirituality, Moses Chaim Luzzatto (1707–1746) teaches that human beings must train and even struggle to attain a high level of spirituality. Such struggle is analogous to the effort required for high achievements in the sciences or the arts. There is, however, more at stake in the search for spirituality. Luzzatto explains:

"For if he [i.e., the human being] is pulled after the world and is drawn further from his Creator, he is damaged, and he damages the world with him. And if he rules over himself and unites himself with his Creator, and uses the world only to aid him in the service of his Creator, he is uplifted and the world itself is uplifted with him" (*The Path of the Just,* trans. S. Silverstein, New York: Feldheim, 1987, p. 21). For the Jew, no less than the state of the cosmos depends upon the human being's commitment to attain an authentic spiritual life in the service of God.

See also COVENANT; EARLY CHRISTIAN SPIRITUALITY; LAW; LITURGY; MYSTICISM; RITUAL; SCRIPTURE.

Bibliography: A. Steinsaltz, *The Strife of the Spirit* (Northvale, N.J.: Jason Aronson, 1988). G. Scholem, *Major Trends in Jewish Mysticism* (New York: Schocken, 1961). J. Soloveitchik, *Halakhic Man* (Philadelphia: Jewish Publication Society of America, 1983).

MICHAEL NUTKIEWICZ

JOURNEY (GROWTH AND DEVELOPMENT IN SPIRITUAL LIFE)

Retrieving the Journey Metaphor

The description of the spiritual life as journey has been a constant theme in the tradition of Christian spirituality. Spiritual life is first of all life, and life means movement and growth. From its prenatal origins through all its maturational phases until the dissolution of death, human life is an emergent phenomenon, a mystery that gradually unfolds, a promise in process of realization. To be human is to be a wayfarer.

The spiritual journey is at the heart of human wayfaring. A distinctively human journey is initiated and directed by the dynamism of the human spirit, which is the capacity for a life of communion with the transcendent mystery that pervades all reality. The spiritual journey is, therefore, the distinctively human journey. It is the core of the human adventure.

In Christian terms, the spiritual journey is the lifelong process of disclosing and incarnating in all dimensions of life and world the image of God that each person most deeply and uniquely is in the depths of his or her being, that is, in the human spirit as graced by the indwelling of God's own Spirit. The Christian life is a movement of ongoing conversion or transformation. It is a journey during which the Christian is "being transformed into the image that we reflect in brighter and brighter glory; this is the working of the Lord who is the Spirit" (2 Cor 3:18, JB).

The journey metaphor in Christian tradition has always tried to express and trace the radically dynamic character of Christian experience: its graced beginnings, its movement through the desert of history, its consummation in transforming union with God. Many metaphors are associated with journey in the tradition. Spiritual literature abounds with images of ascent, steps, degrees, ways, and paths of growth. There are ladders to climb, mountains to ascend, deserts to cross, holy places to visit. All these instill in Christian consciousness the simple realization that "Thee, God, I come from, to thee go" (Gerard Manley Hopkins, Sonnet 63). The journey metaphors provide a hermeneutic that interprets the most foundational dynamics and questions of human existence in light of the Christian message.

While the journey theme is constant throughout the tradition, post-Reformation Catholic spirituality tended to lose sight of it in its emphases upon a static ontology of grace, clearly defined structures of the supernatural organism, and an ahistorical approach to spiritual life as a primarily interior relation to God. Various developments in Church and culture, however, have fostered the restoration of the journey metaphor to its vital role in Christian spirituality. Vatican II clearly emphasized the Church itself as the pilgrim people of God, "led by the Holy Spirit in their journey to the kingdom of their Father" (GS 1). As they travel through history, like pilgrims in a foreign land, "nothing genuinely human fails to raise an echo in their hearts" (GS 1).

As a council of renewal, Vatican II called for return to the wellsprings of ecclesial life as well as for dialogue with the changing and pluralistic world. First of all, returning to the sources of its own life, the Church rediscovered in the Bible, the liturgy, early Church writings, and subsequent spiritual classics the power and prevalence of the journey metaphor as a directive image for Christian life. The Church knew itself again as a pilgrim people; it realized anew that the journey of the redeemed human spirit constitutes its deepest vitality and mission.

Secondly, in a spirit of critical and creative dialogue with the postmodern world, many Christians found themselves appreciating the journey theme as an apt metaphor for their spiritual experience. Existential and process philosophies, often incorporated in theological reflection, stressed the concrete, unfolding dynamism of human existence in history in contrast to an unchanging essence of humankind. Insights into the radical evolutionary progression of the universe and humanity came from dialogue with disciplines like quantum physics and the earth sciences. In the realm of the human sciences, from Freud to recent transpersonal psychologies, empirical observation highlighted the developmental phases of human maturity with their roots in the dynamic structure of the unconscious or the vicissitudes of changing social environments. The popularization of these trends in contemporary culture has influenced Christian understanding of spiritual development. Some of it has been conducive to growth; other influences have been questionable. The fact remains that all have contributed to retrieval of the spiritual life as journey.

Thirdly, exposure to Asian and other non-Christian religious traditions has awakened many Christians to an apprecia-tion of the developmental, phasic dynamism in their own tradition. Many of these traditions provide detailed descriptive and prescriptive accounts of the spiritual journey valuable for all seekers.

Central to Buddhism, for example, are the Four Noble Truths. They present the suffering at the heart of all life, trace its source in desire or false attachment, announce the possibility of liberation from desire, and propose the eightfold Path that moves the wayfarer from immersion in the illusions of desire to nirvana, a state of absolute transcendence of conditioned reality. Hinduism describes outward phases of spiritual development—student, householder, hermit, renunciant—that correspond to an interior journey toward God-realization that is the identification of the believer's deepest self (*atman*) with the Absolute (*Brahman*). The Tao or "Way" underlies both Confucian and Taoist Chinese religions. These present spiritual life as a journey of flowing with the progressive mystery of life itself, revealed in nature and the social order, toward complete harmony with the metaphysical Way underlying all reality. Islam's spiritual consciousness is shaped by three paradigmatic journey stories in the life of Muhammad: his "emigration" from Mecca to Medina in 622, the "farewell pilgrimage" to Mecca shortly before his death in 632, and his "night journey and ascension," symbolizing the mystical reunion of the lover with the Beloved.

The retrieval of journey-consciousness in Christian spiritual theology and practice is thus one consequence of Vatican II's own agenda of spiritual renewal that called for *ressourcement* and *aggiornamento*—return to the classic sources of Church tradition and a discerning dialogue with contemporary thought and other religious traditions.

The remainder of this entry will trace instances of the journey theme in the Bible and in the historical development of Christian spirituality. It will then address current developments in the psychological sciences and in contemporary spirituality. Finally, a summary of implications for spiritual formation in today's Church and world will be presented.

Biblical Foundations of the Spiritual Journey

The Scriptures are filled with journey stories that are integral to the story of salvation itself. These journeys are often normative for the Jewish and Christian communities' understanding of their covenant relationship with God. A brief survey of both Testaments indicates the pervasive influence of the journey theme in biblical spirituality.

Old Testament

In Genesis, the Priestly account of creation (Gen 1:1–2:4) portrays the emergence of the heavens and the earth as a redemptive journey from chaos to harmonic cosmos. The word of God is spoken into a formless void. The word becomes a creative event that successively shapes the geosphere, hydrosphere, atmosphere, and biosphere in a journey of resplendent power and movement "from glory to glory." The journey culminates in creation of the noosphere, humanity formed in the image of God and called to fecundity and stewardship in a cosmos made meaningful by the creative Logos.

Judeo-Christian traditions acknowledge Abraham as their father in faith. The history of salvation begins with God's calling him to journey: "Go forth from the land of your kinsfolk and from your father's house to a land that I will show you. I will make of you a great nation" (Gen 12:1-2). The story of Abraham is one of obedience to God's mysterious call. It is an obedience that is willing to let go of the familiar, to set out for the unknown, to journey in trusting faith that God's promises will be fulfilled.

The Exodus is the decisive salvific event in the history of Israel. The Hebrew Scriptures presuppose the Exodus and are written in its light. The journey story of creation and the faith journeys of the patriarchs find their interpretations in the context of the Exodus (*ex-odos,* the "way out") from the oppressive security of Egypt, through the long journey of forty years in the desert, into the land of God's promise. The various stages of the journey are narrated in the Books of Exodus, Numbers, and Deuteronomy. During all phases of the journey, God is experienced as the One with them: "I myself, the LORD answered, will go along, to give you rest" (Exod 33:14). This journey from bondage through wilderness into possession of the Promised Land has served as an archetypal event for understanding the patterns of the spiritual journey throughout Jewish and Christian history.

The prophetic books of the OT recall time and again the desert journey of Israel as a means of rekindling and challenging the faith of a people who must never lose sight of the nomadic origins and meaning of their relationship with a journeying God. What happened during the desert journey must occur throughout Israel's history if the people are to keep covenant faith. For example, in Amos the forty years are the exemplary period of Israel's history, to which the people must turn to find the authentic ideal of Yahwism, away from the ritualism and lack of justice that undermine their covenant responsibilities (Amos 5:21-25). For the prophet Hosea, the vision of the desert journey evokes the freshness of first love, of a covenant wedding, when the faithfulness of Israel responded to Yahweh's tenderness. Despite current and repeated betrayals, these moments can return, and Yahweh's love can transform the adulterous spouse into the bride who gives herself anew in fidelity (Hos 2:16-17). Finally, the Book of Isaiah, chapters 40–55, is addressed to exiles held captive in Babylon. Again, the Exodus will be repeated for them. They will be liberated, led across the wilderness, and return to rebuild Jerusalem. Yahweh, who once "opened a way in the sea" (Isa 43:16) is now doing a new deed by making a road in the wilderness (43:19) so that the people he formed for himself will sing his praises again (43:21).

After the Exodus accounts, the OT's spirituality of journey is most evident in the Psalter, which is the prayerbook par excellence of Jewish and Christian tradition. Walter Brueggemann (*Praying the Psalms,* pp. 16–24) suggests that the life of faith is always a journey that consists in moving with God through a recurring pattern of (1) being securely oriented, (2) being painfully disoriented, and (3) being surprisingly reoriented. This general pattern applies to all areas of life in which people encounter the divine mystery: in relation to self, others, and world. In regard to each, human life is always journeying. Secure orientation, painful disorientation, and surprising reorientation are three foundational moments repeated throughout life's journey.

The psalms are the ideal manna for this journey in all its phases. They nourish and express faith in the midst of security, in suffering and despair, and in moments of victory and peace. The basic pattern of the Psalter, therefore, shapes believers' faith all along the way. In turn, people find in the Psalter the language of prayer that enables them to give honest expression to their deepest human experiences. The entire Psalter is thus a prayerbook that evokes and sustains the spiritual journey. The major literary genres of the psalms correspond to the basic moments of each spiritual journey. There are the wisdom and security psalms (e.g., Psalms 4, 37, 62, 91, 131, 145); the individual and national psalms of lamentation and supplication (Psalms 6, 10, 22, 32, 44, 69, 74, and *passim*); and the hymns and thanksgivings for surprising reorientation (Psalms 9, 18, 30, 41, 65, 76, 89, 103, 117, and *passim*).

New Testament

Remembering the Exodus as God's decisive salvific act in Israel, the NT theologies of journey are central in the interpretation of God's saving deed in Christ. Instances of these will be cited as they pertain first to the saving work of Christ and, second, to the faith response of Christians.

In the Synoptic Gospels, all three evangelists narrate the story of Jesus' temptations in the desert (Mt 4:1-11; Mk 1:12-13; Lk 4:1-13). The accounts of the temptations, occurring during the forty days of fasting, recall the forty years of the Exodus. As Israel, after having been chosen by Yahweh as his son (Exod 4:22), was led into the desert by pillars of cloud and fire, so Jesus, the well-beloved Son, is impelled into the desert by the Spirit who has just been revealed at the waters of the Jordan. Jesus is led into the desert to share the wilderness and temptation experiences of his people. He is remaking, on his own account, the people's spiritual journey, sharing their testing and desolation. Resolutely faithful to God's call and word, Jesus reveals himself to be the obedient one, the faithful and unique Son of God, freed and empowered by the Spirit for his mission to announce the reign of God (Mt 4:17).

Luke's Gospel sets the public ministry of Jesus largely within the context of one great journey from Galilee to Jerusalem (Lk 9:51–19:27). "When the days for his being taken up were fulfilled, [Jesus] resolutely determined to journey to Jerusalem" (Lk 9:51). Jesus chooses a course from which he will not divert. Luke intended to present Jesus as "a model for the spiritual journey of every human being from the Galilee of self-discovery and self-awareness to the Jerusalem of self-sacrifice before God. For the heart of Jerusalem was the temple; and the heart of the temple was the altar of sacrifice. To understand the message of Jesus, according to Luke, is to make this journey with him" (Dumm, p. 71).

The Johannine Gospel, itself structured around journeys of Jesus to Jerusalem for liturgical feasts, is permeated by the realization that Jesus came from God and goes back to God. Salvation occurs in fact through the journey of the Son from the Father into this world, and his journey from the world back to the Father through the cross, death, and resurrection: "I came from the Father and have come into the world. Now I am leaving the world and going back to the Father" (Jn 16:28). This text summarizes John's theology of redemption. Salvation occurs through participation in this passage of Christ. Welcoming the Son through faith evoked by the signs of his glory, believers follow him in his return to the Father so that "where I am you also may be" (Jn 14:3).

Paul's theology likewise situates redemption in the journey of the Son of God, described as a self-emptying passage into suffering humanity, indeed a journey of identification with human sin (2 Cor 5:21), culminating in Jesus' obedient acceptance of death and his exaltation into glory as the source of all salvation (Phil 2:5-11). For Paul, the mystery of Christ is above all a paschal mystery—a passing from the bondage of sin into the freedom of the children of God who walk by the Spirit (Gal 5:1-15).

The NT witness to the saving work of Christ, so widely narrated with metaphors of journey, speaks of the faith response of Christians in similar terms. Christian life is presented as a response to a summons addressed to each individual and the community as a whole: "Follow me" (e.g., Mt 8:22; Mk 2:14; Lk 5:27; Jn 21:22). The spiritual journey for Christians is nothing more and nothing less than the following of Christ himself in a progressive movement from imitation through intimacy toward an identification with Christ in which believers cry out, "I live, no longer I, but Christ lives in me" (Gal 2:20). Baptized into Christ, they are called to participate in his life journey and are enabled to do so by the gift of his Spirit (Rom 6:1-11; 8:9-11). The Christian journey is initiated by the summons of Christ; it is accompanied by the risen Lord (Lk 24:13-30) and energized within by the power of his Spirit (Rom 8:14-17); and it is brought to completion in glory by the same mercy of the Father that raised and glorified Jesus (Eph 2:4-8).

In short, Christ is the Way for believers (Jn 14:6). In his own person and activity, he is the journey itself. Progressively conformed to him, his disciples follow the new "Way of the Lord" (Acts 9:2; 18:25) through life, death, resurrection, and the consummation of personal and cosmic history where God will be all in all (1 Cor 15:28).

Historical Developments in Christian Spirituality

As a field of study and reflection, Christian spirituality focuses on the experience of God's self-communication and upon how believers may prepare themselves for and express this experience in the whole context of their lives and world. Spirituality concerns itself with *how* to appropriate and incarnate the realities of faith. Virtually every spiritual master and classic author in the recorded tradition of spirituality outlines a progressive movement in describing the lifelong process of appropriation and incarnation of the saving event of Christ. We shall cite a few representatives in order to highlight the journey dimension of all spiritual life found throughout the tradition.

In the 2nd century, Irenaeus of Lyons combated the pseudospirituality of Gnostic heresies that taught an ahistorical, purely interior illumination as an achieved state of salvation. By contrast, Irenaeus emphasized the historical and progressive development of Christian life: "See how God differs from humanity. . . . The Creator is always the same, but those who are created must pass from a beginning and through a middle course, a growth, and progression. And it is for this progress and increase that God has formed them, according to the word of Scripture, 'Increase and multiply' " (*Adv. haer.*, 4, 11).

The 3rd-century school of Alexandria was influenced by the Neoplatonic schema of an ascent from purgation and practice of virtue, through a rising beyond the dominance of sense perception by rational thought, toward a reaching beyond thought to union and ecstatic absorption in the One. Revisioning Neoplatonic thought in the light of the gospel, Clement, and especially Origen, the greatest seminal thinker in the systematization of Christian spirituality, described the successive stages of spiritual progress. Sometimes Origen did so in terms of two stages consisting of *praxis* and *theōria. Praxis* is the active life of purification through practice of virtue; it prepares the soul for the grace of the contemplative life or *theōria,* in which the soul knows God through love in a spiritual marriage with the Logos (see Bouyer, pp. 256–302).

At other times the journey assumes for Origen a tripartite form that describes progression in the spiritual life in terms of beginners, proficients, and the "perfect," the latter enjoying a dynamic life of assimilation to the Logos, not a static state of perfection. Origen relates the three stages allegorically to three books of the OT. The Book of Proverbs serves as a guide for the beginner's life of moral effort and purification; Ecclesiastes directs the soul, gradually illumined by faith, to the presence of God in daily life and creation; and the Song of Songs discloses the way of divine union and transformation into the Beloved (*Fragm. in Lam.,* xiv).

Obviously, the distinctions among these three ways are not absolute; they do not serve as chronological categories. They are spiraling movements, often interpenetrating one another, used to describe normative moments in the spiritual journey. Origen's exposition of the movements had considerable influence on the subsequent development of Christian spirituality with its recurrent teaching on the three ways of the spiritual life—the purgative, illuminative, and unitive—each of which is treated elsewhere in this dictionary.

The 4th-century Cappadocian Grégory of Nyssa is the link between the Alexandrian school and much of the apophatic spirituality of medieval times. Gregory is noted for his teaching of *epektasis,* based on Phil 3:12-13, where Paul speaks of still running, trying to capture the prize for which Christ captured him. Forgetting the past, Paul is "stretching forward" (*epekteinomenos*) for what is still to come. Paul concludes, "With regard to what we have attained, continue on the same course" (Phil 3:16). For Gregory, *epektasis* is part of the person's inward drive or eros toward God. When joined with the gift of agape, it sparks the spiritual journey. *Epektasis* is perpetual ascent from the light of reason to the transcendent darkness in which one discovers God, not in clearly perceived, definable experience, but by "stretching beyond" all experience into the depths of God's eternity (*Sixth Homily on the Canticle,* PG 44:885–888).

In the Western monastic tradition, but with universal spiritual implications, the Rule of St. Benedict (6th century) describes progress toward union with God in terms of twelve degrees of humility (chap. 7), which serve as a "ladder of our ascending actions." The first three degrees call for a commitment to mindfulness of God's presence, transcendence of one's egoic will, and obedience to God in life situations. Steps four through seven trace the journey toward radical poverty of spirit that occurs through obedient response to God in the hardships and temptations of daily life. In degrees eight through eleven, the Rule portrays the outward effects of interior progress in terms of being ordinary and not self-aggrandizing in one's life circumstances with others. With the twelfth degree the journey culminates in a participation in the kenosis of Jesus, whereby one is identified in utter poverty of spirit and humility with Christ crucified ("*inclinato capite*": see Jn 19:30), and thereby raised with Christ to "that perfect love of God which casts out fear. . . . All this the Lord will by the Holy Spirit graciously manifest in his workman now cleansed of vices and sins" (RB 7:67, 70).

The Middle Ages and the modern period continued to understand and explain spiritual growth in metaphors of journey, degrees, steps, and stages. Bernard of Clairvaux (12th century) described the journey with reference to four degrees of love. The beginner moves from narcissistic love of self, through love of God for one's own sake, toward love of God for God's sake and love of self for God's own sake (see *Treatise on the Love of God*). Bernard further schematized the spiritual journey in *The Steps of Humility and Pride*, a commentary on the seventh chapter of the Benedictine Rule with rich phenomenological description of the three degrees of truth, inherent in humility, which lead to the contemplative vision of God, as well as the twelve steps of pride, through which one descends into spiritual death.

Bernard's fellow Cistercian William of St. Thierry wrote a brilliant and influential treatise entitled *The Golden Epistle* to map out the spiritual path for those beginning it. William traces the journey through three stages—the animal, the rational, and the spiritual—wherein the seeker moves from domination by sense perceptions and reactions, through direction by Spirit-illumined reason, toward transforming unity with God's Spirit, in which one fulfills the purpose of his or her creation by becoming in truth the very image of God.

Here might be noted a short 12th-century text, *The Ladder of Monks*, by Guigo II, a Carthusian. Guigo speaks of "four degrees of exercises of the spirit" (*Ladder*, II) that comprise the ancient Christian practice of *lectio divina:* reading, meditation, prayer, contemplation. These represent a spiritual ladder, reaching from earth to heaven, connecting the soil of human experience with the transcendence of God's presence. The practice of *lectio divina*, which begins with a reading of the Scriptures or other texts, becomes norma-

tive for the entire spiritual journey, progressing from attentive listening (reading and meditation), through honest response to the encountered Word (prayer), toward contemplative rest in the intimate presence of God. Guigo's treatise is a significant summary of the most authentic approach to contemplation, deriving from the earliest Christian traditions of prayer. It bears relevance for contemporary Christians in their search for methods and spiritual disciplines along their journey.

The 13th-century spiritual theologian Bonaventure wrote systematized treatises with exquisite descriptions of the steps of progress toward divine union. Chief among them are *Concerning the Triple Way* and *The Soul's Journey into God*. The former work charts the purgative, illuminative, and unitive ways, with special attention to the role that affective devotion to Christ occupies in spiritual development. The latter treatise narrates the journey in relation to ascending degrees of contemplation. The seeker moves from awareness of God in the universe and empirical world (the sensible stage), through contemplation of God imaged in the soul (the psychological stage), toward mystical contemplation of the ineffable being and goodness that is the divine mystery revealed in Christ (metaphysical stage). Contemplation of Christ crucified animates the soul's journey throughout the ascent that leads to the experience of the "fire" of the Godhead, in which the soul dies at last to its self-centeredness and enters the divine darkness and silence, passing with Christ into the bosom of the Father (*The Soul's Journey*, vii.6).

The modern period of spirituality (16th–19th centuries) begins with the Spanish school, represented chiefly by the great masters Ignatius Loyola, John of the Cross, and Teresa of Avila. Influenced by post-Renaissance psychological attention to individual human life as well as by the rational analyses of Scholasticism, these writers offer accounts of the spiritual journey that have become widely known in contemporary Christian culture.

Ignatius's *Spiritual Exercises* is a retreat handbook for directors leading exercitants on a four-week interior journey. The exercises are also paradigmatic for the lifelong journey of the soul. In the first week, directees are led from realization of the purpose of their creation into a repentant confrontation with sinful failures to respond to their destiny. From repentance for sin, directees are moved in the second week to contemplate Christ's lordship over the universe and history through meditations upon the saving mysteries of his life. The third and fourth weeks consummate the interior journey by leading directees toward contemplative identification with the passion and death of Jesus and the joy of his resurrection. At the end of the exercises is the "Contemplation for Obtaining Love," which is a description of, and incitement to, authentic mystical life. The remarkable success of the exercises testifies to their balanced wisdom in promoting spiritual growth for those attracted to the Ignatian way.

John of the Cross and Teresa of Avila are unparalleled guides to the theology and practice of spiritual development in the modern era. Complementary images of the journey to God are woven through all their works. For John, the "aim of the spiritual life is the state of perfect union with God through love" (*Collected Works*, p. 45). It is a union of likeness wherein God and the soul appear to be as one. In the ascent to this height of Mount Carmel, beginners are led by grace from a faith and love that are dependent upon sense experience and consolation, through active and passive nights of sensory deprivation that purify the soul and lead it into the illuminative way, marked by a more mature faith and the beginnings of contemplation in an obscure, loving attention to God's presence. From the relative maturity and purified faith of the illuminative way, the soul enters the active night of the spirit, whose goal is detachment from all that is apprehended in the spiritual realm by mere human understanding, memory, and will. Eventually, nearing the summit of the ascent, the passive night of the spirit occurs, initiated and carried out by God alone in the depths of the soul (*The Dark Night*, II.5-8). Completing the work of the active night of the spirit, this is an often prolonged suffering in which the soul feels abandoned by God, because all its former ways of relating to God are stripped away. This night is a participation in the death of Jesus and his descent into hell. Its terminus is the fullest possible experience of being raised with Christ into the phase of transforming union or "perfect holiness" (*The Dark Night*, Prologue) to be consummated in spiritual betrothal and marriage between the divine and the human in the depths of the soul (*The Spiritual Canticle*, xxvii).

Teresa's spiritual theology closely parallels John's but is less philosophical and more grounded in descriptions of experiential unfolding. Her most vivid description of the spiritual journey is found in *The Interior Castle*. In this text journeyers progress through different rooms in the castle of the soul; the rooms correspond to the traditional three phases of spiritual life: (1) a state of grace, but with serious attachment to the pleasures of life and a dominance of self-will; (2) openness to a disciplined spiritual practice through prayer, reading, and other methods; (3) a life of serious virtue and sacrificial love (1-3, the purgative way); (4) the experience of deeper prayer, the prayer of quiet, in which the soul rests in God's love through the will (the illuminative way); (5) the beginnings of transforming union, evidenced in a deeper prayer of union; (6) further growth in divine intimacy with passive purifications and suffering; (7) spiritual marriage, a more or less permanent state of union with God in the center of the soul, its innermost room (5-7, the unitive way).

The modern period of spirituality ends with the close of the 19th century, which contributed, among other significant writings, two simple yet profound legacies that have exerted great influence. These are Thérèse of Lisieux's *Story of a Soul,* and *The Way of a Pilgrim* by an anonymous Russian peasant.

Writing from the crucible of daily life in a small Carmelite cloister, Thérèse named her journey a "little way" for weak souls. It consisted in progress through ordinariness, humility, and self-sacrificial love of others toward a profound abandonment to God in union with Jesus, her Beloved, in the darkness of faith.

The Way of the Pilgrim is a firsthand account of the peasant's wanderings and journeys throughout Russia. But above all it is the pilgrim's spiritual quest that engages the reader. His was a journey of continual prayer, the Jesus Prayer of Orthodox spirituality, nourished by assiduous reading of the Bible and the *Philokalia,* a collection of ancient and medieval spiritual writings from the Orthodox tradition. As with Thérèse of Lisieux, the ordinary encounters of daily life with people met along the way form continual points of departure for prayer and divine theophanies for the pilgrim.

Even with the omission of many great spiritual masters and thinkers, a cursory view of Christian tradition shows that participation in the paschal mystery of Christ, prefigured by the Exodus event of Israel, remains the enduring core of any Christian spirituality. The richness of this tradition lies in its vast and deep expositions of how Christians may concretely appropriate and incarnate the mystery of the Christ in the course of their life journey.

Contemporary Developments

As the science of theology partly develops in dialogue with the philosophies of each generation and culture, so the discipline of spirituality grows in dialogue with the more empirical understandings of human experience in successive cultures. In the 20th century these empirical insights are often found in the human sciences, especially the science of psychology with its many schools and traditions: for example, psychoanalytic theories, social psychologies, learning theories, humanistic and existential psychology, rational-emotive theories, transpersonal psychology, and behaviorism.

The influence of such studies of the human realm filters to the general public through popular literature, the arts, and the media, as well as through the widespread phenomenon of self-help groups, twelve-step programs based on the approach to spiritual formation developed by Alcoholics Anonymous, and other avenues of spiritual and psychological growth. All this has resulted in a growing popular awareness of human life as a journey of development marked by crucial stages, transitions, crises, and opportunities. The climate of contemporary Western culture, therefore, transmits a heightened sensitivity to the psychodynamics of the inner life and its phasic unfolding. This has been a rediscovery of the developmental patterns so evident in the ancient wisdom of religious traditions in all cultures. Among the many influences in the rediscovery, several theories and critiques that may bear significance for the journey dynamism at the heart of spiritual life are noted here.

Contemporary Psychologies

The scientific discovery and analysis of the realm of the unconscious in so-called depth psychologies offer assistance in exploring the intricacies of the spiritual journey. For instance, Freud's theory of the unconscious stresses the hidden influences of sexual/life instincts and aggressive/death instincts, rooted in the unconscious id, upon the development of the conscious ego as center of the personality. In the formation of personality, under the unconscious drives of the id and preconscious superego determinisms, the person passes through stages of psychosexual development—the oral, anal, phallic, latency, and genital phases—in which one moves from infantile narcissism to reality-oriented adult socialization, if all proceeds normally. Many regressions, fixations, and defense mechanisms, however, can distort this journey on unconscious levels and thus seriously impair ego maturation. Therapeutic interventions may be necessary to disclose the contents of the unconscious that interfere with development and thus, by consequence, impair the spiritual journey, which normally requires an ego sufficiently developed that one can transcend it toward deeper levels of spiritual integration.

While Freudian theory dismisses the spiritual dimension of life as illusion and reduces the explanation of all human development to instinctual drives, Freudian and neo-Freudian teachings can make Christians wiser about the challenges and problematics of integrating vital and sexual life into the spiritual journey. Furthermore, they can help people be more realistic and humble in face of the complex unconscious determinants that affect spiritual growth.

Carl Jung has had a widespread impact on contemporary spirituality with his own interpretations of the unconscious and conscious structure of the psyche and its passage from the conscious ego as center of the personality to the individuated self as the deepest ground of personal life. Jung believed that humans are constantly attempting to progress from a less to a more complete stage of development. This involves the emergence of the unconscious self into consciousness through a process of appropriating and expressing archetypes hidden in the depths of the psyche, for example, the anima or animus, the shadow, and "God."

Because of Jung's apparent openness to ego-transcendent and religious experiences and his allusions to the God-archetype in the unconscious, many people find him a congenial companion for insights into the subtleties of spiritual growth. Critics, however, caution that Jung tends toward a gnostic solipsism, a cultivation of the individuated self through a rarefied journey of introspection, rather than the formation of an authentic personhood through real relationships with the human and divine "other."

Spirituality today is also affected by the school of Erik H. Erikson, sometimes called developmental or ego psychology. As Freud explored the stages of psychosexual development, Erikson investigated psychosocial stages. He explains the life journey as a dialogue between the physically and psychologically maturing organism and successive social, environmental influences.

Erikson describes basic ego qualities, either strengths or weaknesses, that emerge during each stage of development, depending upon the success or failure to resolve the life tasks appropriate to each phase (see his *Childhood and Society,* 2nd ed., New York: Norton, 1963, and *Identity: Youth and Crisis,* New York: Norton, 1968). In fact, Erikson names the stages of growth in terms of the essential conflicts that each entails, thereby articulating the inherent suffering and crises that the human journey always involves, e.g., basic trust versus basic mistrust, intimacy versus isolation.

Erikson's theory and its popularizations have awakened in millions of people an appreciation for the developmental phases, transitions, and crises of human life. A major critique of Erikson and other developmental studies has been made by feminist authors, who point out the predominantly male populations upon which these studies have been based. Feminist thinkers also critique their essentially masculine model of the ego as developing above all through the achievement of self-individuation and functional competence in which human relationships are valued in terms of whether or not they contribute to the maturing ego. The feminist critique calls for a revisioning of developmental psychology and the stages of growth with the categories of intimate and generative relationships as central in understanding the journey of maturation on psychological, moral, and spiritual levels (see Gilligan, *In a Different Voice*).

A recent development in the psychological sciences is that of transpersonal or spectrum psychology. Influenced by cultural anthropology and philosophical theories of evolution, transpersonal theories attempt to move beyond the traditional boundaries of psychology that confine the study of the human to the organismic, emotional, and egoic levels of development. This new approach insists that the spiritual dimension of life is critical in the human journey. Representatives of the transpersonal school argue that the basic conventional structures of human development, described by traditional psychology, must be complemented by investigation of contemplative stages that are integral to human maturation. Once the ego is sufficiently formed to serve as a functional center of personal integration, human life must enter upon contemplative/mystical stages of growth in which consciousness is opened to communion with "trans-personal" dimensions of experience, and ultimately with the cosmic mystery that permeates all reality. The transpersonal self thus becomes "an unlimited consciousness of unity which pervades everywhere ... a being who is in essence one with the Supreme Self" (Wilber, Engler, Brown, et al., p. 74).

Transpersonal theories already have considerable impact upon contemporary perception of spiritual growth, sometimes through what is called the New Age movement. While they offer valuable insights, Judeo-Christian spiritualities must critique their tendency to view the realm of the spiritual as an outgrowth and consequence of healthy psychological development, as well as their seeming absorption of the individual into an undifferentiated oneness with the cosmos or the divine mystery.

Contemporary Spirituality

Most contemporaries in the field of Christian spirituality have incorporated the developmental approaches and the journey metaphors into their reflection upon the spiritual life. For example, Teilhard de Chardin's evolutionary vision of the Omega point—the consciousness of Christ toward which all human progress is directed as its fulfillment—offers a panoramic vision of humanity and the cosmos in various stages of their consummation. Thomas Merton's works include both Scholastic descriptions of the spiritual journey (*The Ascent to Truth*, New York: Harcourt, Brace, 1951) and more contemporary explorations that are written from the perspectives of biblical theology and philosophical existentialism (*The New Man*, New York: Farrar, Straus & Cudahy, 1961, and *Life and Holiness*, New York: Herder, 1963).

Other widely read 20th-century authors such as Evelyn Underhill, Simone Weil, Henri Nouwen, Basil Pennington, Joan Chittister, Rosemary Haughton, Gerald May, and Thomas Keating have shared with a wide readership insightful descriptions and explanations of the spiritual journey in today's culture. Keating, for instance, has outlined a detailed map of the spiritual journey in dialogue with evolutionary anthropology, developmental psychology, existential thought, and the wisdom of traditional Christian spirituality (see *The Spiritual Journey: A Guide Book*).

For a scholarly and systematic exploration of the structure and dynamics of the spiritual journey that integrates insights from spiritual traditions, human sciences, and empirical observation, the prolific work of Adrian van Kaam is of particular importance, although not yet popularly known. In his science of distinctively human or spiritual formation and its corresponding Christian formation theory, van Kaam views the person as always in ongoing formation. The self moves from one current form of life to another through a series of "transcendence crises" that van Kaam describes in highly nuanced detail (*The Transcendent Self,* chap. 3 and *passim*). The animating force of this formation journey is the dynamism of the human spirit, which is a "transcendent aspiration" for the fullness of peace and joy found through participation in the all-pervasive mystery of formation—in Christian terms, the Trinitarian life of God. All the dimensions of human life—the sociohistorical, the vital, and the egoic—are grounded in the transempirical energy of the spirit as indwelt, illumined, and empowered by the Holy Spirit. Personal integration is found only through the direction and power of this deepest center of life, which van Kaam calls the transcendent dimension, or in Christian language, the pneumatic dimension of the human life form (*Fundamental Formation,* chap. 16).

Of special note to contemporary spirituality is van Kaam's critical dialogue with an immense range of modern thought and his creative stand within the stream of authentic Christian spirituality. His formation theory is not an eclectic integration of psychology and spirituality, but a comprehensive approach to the human and Christian spiritual journey that critically utilizes appropriate insights from psychology and other sciences.

Summary of Implications for Spiritual Formation

The retrieval of the journey metaphor by means of return to the sources of Scripture and the tradition of Christian spirituality, and through dialogue with other religious traditions and contemporary thought, has profound implications for the spiritual life of Christians. Viewing the person as a configuration of relationships to self, others, world, and the mystery of God, we shall summarize some of the more significant directives inherent in journey-consciousness.

The first relationship we have is to our own self, constituted and called into being as a unique image of God. To accept and cherish one's deepest self as the image of God is a necessary foundation for beginning and sustaining the journey itself. One must, therefore, love oneself as wayfarer in order to grow along the way.

As wayfarers, we are never complete or whole. We are always only on the way. Therefore, for us there is only the trying, one step at a time. The rest is really not our business. Perfectionism, willful striving for spiritual achievement, and expectation of complete spiritual wholeness are major obstacles to the spiritual journey. To journey well is to be patient and compassionate toward one's own self-in-progress.

Secondly, we never journey alone. We move within the community of faith, the "cloud of witnesses" (Heb 12:1) who have gone before us and the struggling pilgrims at our side. Those who have gone before have mapped the journey for us by the witness of their lives and some by the legacy of their writings. Through the witness and the legacies, we have some idea of where we came from, where we are going, and how to get there. However detailed the maps may appear in descriptions of the journey, they are in fact broad outlines offered by our brothers and sisters in faith. We can learn from them and be encouraged by them. But their teachings are not rigid classifications into which we must fit our life journeys; they must be filtered through the prism of our own uniqueness and cultures. While all Christians share in certain common experiences along the way, the freedom and sovereignty of God lead each person uniquely, sometimes into uncharted waters and along mysterious paths.

Progress in the spiritual journey is manifested by unconditional acceptance and effective compassion toward the pilgrims at our side. We can never fully know where they are on the journey, what they are going through, what unconscious or social determinisms are holding them back from progress. The real journey takes place in the depths of the soul, beyond rational observation and even intuitive apprehension. The imperative of the gospel, "Stop judging, that you may not be judged" (Mt 7:1) always applies therefore. Instead of judging and evaluating our sisters and brothers, we must help pick them up and even carry them along the way whenever possible.

Thirdly, though traveling through this world, nothing human fails to resonate in the hearts of Christian pilgrims. The mystery of the incarnation, at the core of our faith, impels us to enter into the full breadth and depth of the human and cosmic journey in all its realms: the psychological, social, cultural, political, economic, ecological, and cosmological evolution of history and world. Our personal and communal spiritual journeys involve a commitment to the betterment of creation, which from the beginning has been groaning in one great act of giving birth (see Rom 8:22). Christians must help disclose and incarnate the kingdom of God and its justice in all these realms of the human and cosmic situation, each according to his or her unique journey and call.

Finally, the spiritual journey is only possible in relation to the ultimate horizon of the divine mystery. The mystery is always Emmanuel, God-with-us. Whether we are moving toward more authentic relation to self, others, or world, the journey is never self-initiated, self-sustained, self-fulfilled —it is a mystery of grace throughout. The journey is from beginning to end accompanied by God who initiates, God who empowers at each step, God who consummates it in face-to-face communion. It is for us to believe in the Word that calls and directs us; to hope in the promise that keeps us going; and to surrender in love to the will of the One who will carry the journey through to completion, right up to "the day of Christ Jesus" (Phil 1:6). As we follow Christ and undergo all that he underwent, we can journey with one assurance: "I am not alone, but it is I and the Father who sent me" (Jn 8:16).

See also AFFIRMATIVE WAY; ASCETICISM; CARMELITE SPIRITUALITY; HISTORY, HISTORICAL CONSCIOUSNESS; HOLY SPIRIT; ILLUMINATION, ILLUMINATIVE WAY; IMAGO DEI; MYSTICISM; NEGATIVE WAY; PASCHAL MYSTERY; PSYCHOLOGY, RELATIONSHIP AND CONTRIBUTION TO SPIRITUALITY; PURGATION, PURGATIVE WAY; THREE AGES; THREE WAYS; UNION, UNITIVE WAY.

Bibliography: L. Bouyer, The Spirituality of the New Testament and the Fathers, trans. M. P. Ryan, (New York: Desclee, 1960). W. Brueggemann, Praying the Psalms (Winona, Minn.: St. Mary's Press, 1982). D. Dumm, Flowers in the Desert: A Spirituality of the Bible (New York: Paulist, 1987). C. Gilligan, In a Different Voice: Psychological Theory and Women's Development (Cambridge, Mass.: Harvard Univ. Press, 1982). U. Holmes, A History of Christian Spirituality (New York: Seabury, 1980). John of the Cross, The Collected Works, trans. K. Kavanaugh and O. Rodriguez (Washington: Institute of Carmelite Studies, 1979). T. Keating, The Spiritual Journey: A Guide Book with Tapes (Colorado Springs, Colo.: Contemporary Publications, 1987). D. Levinson, The Seasons of a Man's Life (New York: Ballantine, 1978). M. Searle, "The Journey of Conversion," Worship 44 (January 1980) 35–55. A. van Kaam, Fundamental Formation (New York: Crossroad, 1983) and The Transcendent Self (Denville, N.J.: Dimension Books, 1979). K. Wilber, J. Engler, D. Brown, et al., Transformations of Consciousness: Conventional and Contemplative Perspectives on Development (Boston: New Science Library, 1986).

RICHARD BYRNE, O.C.S.O.

JOY

In the *Exsultet*, the Easter liturgy sings, "Rejoice, heavenly powers! Sing, choirs of angels!" When St. Paul speaks of joy in the midst of tribulation or admonishes the Philippians to "rejoice in the Lord always" (Phil 4:4), the character and centrality of Christian joy emerge. Far more than a feeling state or a mere heightened sense of pleasure, joy in the Christian life refers to a basic disposition and a fundamental attunement to the self-giving of God in Christ. To rejoice in the midst of suffering puts a strain on our ordinary conception of joy and enjoyment. This is because the joy of which Scripture and the tradition speak takes a peculiar object—the revelation of God in Christ. Thus Mary's *Magnificat* rejoices in "God my Savior." The joy is configured by who is being acknowledged in the singing: the Holy One of Israel now incarnate.

Joy is thus ingredient in the very pattern of life constituted by trust in God, in, with, and through Jesus Christ. Every activity and relationship in service of God and neighbor shares in a joyful quality. Serving the neighbor becomes an "enjoyment," one of the chief ends of human existence. Such joy is not contingent upon fortune, good or bad, but is grounded in faith that God is Creator and Redeemer of the world. Because of God's covenant, the psalmist enjoins the assembly to "sing joyfully to the LORD" (Ps 98:4).

In sum, joy occupies a central place among the Christian affections, yet it is also characteristic of all activities begun and completed in faith. While ecstatic states of joy may be sought after and experienced from time to time, the principal aim of the Christian life is to serve God and neighbor joyfully. In the spiritual life, God is the supreme joy and the greatest delight.

See also FRUIT(S) OF THE HOLY SPIRIT.

Bibliography: C. S. Lewis, Surprised by Joy (New York: Harcourt Brace Jovanovich, 1954). S. Kierkegaard, The Gospel of Suffering and the Lilies of the Field, trans. D. Swenson and L. M. Swenson (Minneapolis: Augsburg, 1948).

DON E. SALIERS

JUNG, INFLUENCE ON SPIRITUALITY

See DREAMS; PERSONALITY TYPES; PSYCHOLOGY, RELATIONSHIP AND CONTRIBUTION TO SPIRITUALITY.

JUSTICE

In the Catholic tradition, justice involves one's experience of justification (internal justice), which is expressed in the promotion of good works or works of justice (external justice). The former stresses God's action in the person; the latter involves one's response to the gift of God's grace. The former relates to the first and greatest command; the latter gets translated into action on behalf of that justice which moves beyond the person to the group, to societal structures, and to the environment itself.

The Foundation for Justice in Catholic Thought

Particularly since the Synod of Bishops on "Justice in the World" (1971) declared that justice is a "constituent dimension" of the gospel, the link between justice and spirituality has become constant. Previous to that, the Catholic approach to justice often separated the issue of relative rights and responsibilities from spirituality. It tended to limit the theological notion of justice to philosophical, moral, and juridical considerations.

Traditional Catholic Approach to Justice

1. *Philosophical.* The philosophical basis for much of the Catholic approach to justice can be traced to the theology of St. Thomas Aquinas (see esp. ST II-II, q. 58). Aquinas Christianized Stoic philosophy and Roman jurisprudence, which held that the immutable and unwritten laws of the heavens are expressed in the universal law of nature. These "natural laws" are equally accessible to all human beings through reason. For Aquinas, the natural moral law is a participation in God's eternal law; human moral actions are to reflect God's mind. Thus justice on earth is to image God's justice. Just human relations reflect divine relations.

Aquinas based much of his approach to justice on Aristotle. For Aristotle, a necessary and sufficient condition for a just situation occurs when all are treated equally, unless relative differences are clearly evident. In the *Nichomachean Ethics,* Aristotle distinguishes between justice as the whole of virtue (general, "legal" justice) and justice as a particular part of virtue (including corrective or commutative justice, distributive justice, and justice in exchange). Embracing these major distinctions, Aquinas defines the virtue of justice as "the strong and firm will to give to each his due." For him, all the moral virtues can be viewed from the perspective of justice. General justice subordinates all legitimate human behavior to the common good; it takes precedence over an individual's good. Particular justice is expressed primarily in commutative (corrective) justice and distributive justice.

Commutative justice, covering relations of a society's members with one another, seeks equality for private persons and groups in two ways. It demands a fair standard for reciprocity—the give and take of human transactions. Next it forbids unnecessary encroachment on others' rights. The one assumes voluntary actions among equals, such as contracts based on consent; the other applies to involuntary situations in which only one party consents, such as theft, fraud, and unjust damage.

Distributive justice, covering all persons insofar as they are members of a community, seeks the good of all people insofar as they participate in community. It demands that all people be given their due and that one's basic rights be recognized and ensured by the community. Given the communitarian nature of distributive justice, special care is to be given to society's weaker members. This principle has served partially as a rationale for that notion of spirituality which stresses solidarity with the poor.

2. *Moral.* A Thomistic consideration of the philosophical notion of justice can be identified as a moral philosophy and the basis of moral reflection insofar as it considers justice as a virtue. As a virtue, justice, like the other cardinal virtues, is shaped and directed by charity. The ground of justice as well as its goal is love of God and neighbor. This more contemporary approach to the moral dimension of justice grounds and discusses justice in light of love. Because love can never be fully realized, neither can perfect justice.

Thus, since absolute justice is never attainable, relative justice, which is less than love, must calculate competing interests and various duties and rights.

Among the first contemporary Catholic moral theologians to stress love as the foundation of justice was Bernard Häring. He insisted that, besides its Christocentric orientations, the complete integration of love and justice is the chief characteristic of Christian moral doctrine. For him, love is the foundation of ordered relations, and justice (right order) is the way to love. In this sense, the basic ontological order is love, then justice. However, he added, in terms of the gradual achievement of order, the order may be justice, then love: "While love is the foundation of justice, in a certain sense, the involvement of justice in creating happy human conditions precedes the works of charity" (*Free and Faithful in Christ*, p. 471).

The moral virtue of justice becomes concretized in the search for objective fairness and right order. Various criteria have been offered for a more objective or rational basis for settling conflicting claims around justice. While the principle "to all according to their due" may be commonly held as the assumption behind the search for justice, the specific, concrete criteria to achieve that goal differ. The difference derives from the varying worldviews represented in differing moral philosophies. A wide range of criteria has included freedom (Nozick), equality (Marx), equal freedom and equality (Rawls), merit and desert (Aristotle), effort (the Puritans), and social utility (Mills).

Increasingly in Catholic social thought the basic criteria for justice revolve around need. These criteria have a strong scriptural foundation in both the Old and New Testaments, especially Mt 25:31-46. Need as the principal rationale for moral activity was further articulated by the U.S. Catholic bishops in their 1986 pastoral letter *Economic Justice for All:* "The fundamental moral criterion for all economic decisions, policies and institutions is this: they must be at the service of all people, especially the poor" (no. 24).

3. *Jurisdictional.* While the main notion related to the implementation of justice refers to the criteria or values that stand above, and are embodied in, the law itself, "procedural justice" refers to the outcome or decision that results from the application of the criteria of justice to existing and accepted laws. Positive law, grounded in the "law behind the law," views justice as the standard to which all human, prescriptive laws must conform. Such is the assumption behind the conclusions contained in the Code of Canon Law (1983).

Contemporary Catholic Approach to Justice

The current notion of "social justice" has moved to the center of Catholic discussion on justice. Indeed, social justice can be considered as the general rubric for all forms of justice previously considered, including general justice and particular justice (commutative and distributive). In their document *To Do Justice* (1978), the U.S. Catholic bishops declared: "In Catholic thought, social justice is not merely a secular or humanitarian matter. Social justice is a reflection of God's essential respect and concern for each person and an effort to protect the essential human freedom necessary for each person to achieve his or her destiny as a child of God" (no. 8).

While seminally contained in Catholic social teaching since 1891 and the encyclical *Rerum Novarum* of Pope Leo XIII, the term *social justice* took on special meaning in and after 1931 with Pope Pius XI's encyclical *Quadragesimo Anno*. Here social justice pertains to the common good of the whole society and, within it, the common good of its various communities, including the distribution of benefits and burdens (distributive justice) and respect for human rights (commutative justice).

Since Pope John XXIII, the proper ordering of society has been perceived as involving three distinct but complementary goals: freedom (liberty), justice (equality), and love (solidarity and participation). The first stresses the dignity of every human person; the second, the right of all people to have access to resources they need; and the third, the right of people to be involved in the decisions that affect their lives and in community itself. Acknowledging the primacy of freedom as a right ensured by the U.S. Constitution, the 1986 letter of the U.S. Catholic bishops, *Economic Justice for All*, called for balanced, if not greater, stress on equality as another basic right necessary to ensure the third value—solidarity.

While never discounting a possible role for traditional natural law arguments in understanding justice, a contemporary Catholic approach to justice stresses the role of experience and social analysis ("reading the signs of the times"), theological reflection based on revelation ("reading the Scriptures"), and pastoral involvement demanding a justice-oriented spirituality ("practicing justice"). This interrelated methodology offers a contemporary Catholic approach to justice.

1. *Experience and Social Analysis.* Although seminally found in much of Catholic social thought of the late 19th- and early 20th-century, and of the last third of the 20th century, particularly beginning with the writings of Popes John XXIII and Paul VI, the basis for reflecting on reality and whether or not it is just has revolved around the concrete situation of the poor and disadvantaged members of the community. This experience-based approach to social analysis and "reading the signs of the times" reached its apogee in the 1971 Synod of Catholic Bishops in Rome—the first congregational meeting of bishops in the contemporary Catholic Church to be composed of a substantial number of bishops from the Third World. Their document *Justice in the World* states: "Even though it is not for us to elaborate a very profound analysis of the situation of the world, we

have nevertheless been able to perceive the serious injustices which are building around the world of men a network of domination, oppression and abuses which stifle freedom and which keep the greater part of humanity from sharing in the building up and enjoyment of a more just and more fraternal world" (Introduction). Within this statement can be found the principal concerns of Catholic moral anthropology: freedom, equality, and solidarity or participation. Furthermore, this analysis led the bishops to the second step in reflection on justice, theological reflection based on revelation: "Scrutinizing the 'signs of the times' . . . we have listened to the Word of God that we might be converted to the fulfilling of the divine plan for the salvation of the world" (Introduction).

2. *Theological Reflection Based on Revelation.* Increasingly the criteria of social justice have not only stressed need but have returned to an understanding of God as a community of Persons relating to one another in such a way that all their resources are shared in such a manner that the fullness of freedom, equality, and participation is realized. The divine community and its ordering thus constitute the goal of all ordering of human life and interaction. This notion of the divine plan for the world is more fully revealed in reflection on the notion of justice as contained in the Old and New Testaments. Given the notion of God as just, and just in all actions, the scriptural perception of divine and human justice can be termed the right ordering and relationship among persons and resources.

a) *Justice in the Old Testament.* Justice is identified with the nature of God (Isa 30:18) as well as with God's activity (Gen 18:25; Ps 9:5). God's revelation to humans—especially in creation, the covenant, and the commandments—relates to the establishment of justice in our lives (Jer 23:6) and in the world (Ps 119:137-144). Humans fulfill their purpose on earth by acting in accordance with God's decrees in

a way that makes them imitate the divine nature and activity (Deut 16:20). The effort to realize God's justice on earth will be completed in the messianic reign of universal justice. All history thus begins and ends with justice. This more generalized notion of justice also includes the more particularized and juridical notion of rights and responsibilities, especially as they relate to rulers and ruled, accusers and accused. Justice will be realized for the accused (Pss 35:24-29; 40:9-13), sin will be punished (Isa 5:13-16; 10:22), and God's oppressed people will be vindicated (Isa 42:6; 46:13; 62:1-2) in ways that will realize God's justice on earth (Ps 140:12).

The two main Hebrew words for "justice," *sedeq* and *sedaqa,* refer to the many-faceted dimensions of both divine and human justice as well as to the works of justice (Exod 9:27; Prov 10:25; Ps 18:21-25). Both words, despite their nuances, articulate various demands related to *relationships.* The experiential and expressive dimensions of a justice spirituality probably are best revealed in the prophetic injunction: To know Yahweh is to do justice (see Jer 22:13-16). To be in relationship with God demands the expression of this experience in the promotion of relationships of interhuman justice.

In the Septuagint, *dikaiosyne* translates the Hebrew notions of *sedeq* and *sedaqa.* While grounded in the notions above, it adds the notion of mercy and covenantal fidelity to God's manifestation of justice (Gen 19:19; 20:13; 21:23; 24:27-29; 32:10). The human response to God's justice is to observe the will of God in a way that pleases God (Isa 5:7).

b) *Justice in the New Testament.* In the Gospels, justice as *dikaiosyne* is never used in Mark and only once in Luke (1:75) and John (16:8). However, probably because Matthew's audience was not poor but was called to a spirituality of wholeness (see Mt 5:48; 19:21) by developing just relationships with the poor, the word is used seven times in his Gospel (Mt 3:15; 5:6; 10, 20;

6:1, 33; 21:32). The first and last uses relate to the message of John the Baptist that sees Jesus as the fulfillment of all justice (Mt 3:15) and the proclamation of the gospel as one of justice (Mt 21:32). The other five uses of *dikaiosyne* can be found in Matthew's Sermon on the Mount. Although Scripture scholars differ as to the meaning of the term as gift and/or responsibility, it can be said that Mt 5:6 and 6:33 seem to be oriented to the first dimension of spirituality: the experience of God's gift of justice in humans. The manifestation of this justice in human relationships involves the Torah (Mt 5:20), almsgiving, prayer, and fasting (Mt 6:1), and the promise of persecution (Mt 5:10).

Until recently, the Pauline notion of *dikaiosyne* suffered from an interpretation highly colored by Reformation notions, especially how individual sinners could be justified by a just God through righteousness. However, much of current exegesis of Paul has moved the understanding of *dikaiosyne* from the intertestamental and Pharisaic concerns about justification for individuals to notions contained in the Old Testament, especially the prophets and apocalyptic literature. While the notion of producing the fruits of justice is clearly evident, the notion of righteousness and being justified before God is never abandoned.

For Paul, the death and resurrection of Jesus Christ is the manifestation of the work of God's justice in an unjust world. As noted of the Servant in the Old Testament, Jesus is the just one who suffers innocently at the hands of unjust people but, in the process, conquers them (Col 2:15) and makes humans reconciled to God's justice (2 Cor 5:21). New Testament scholar John Donahue shows that the death/resurrection of Jesus resulted in redemptive liberation, sanctification, reconciliation, and justification for humans. The consequence of the latter is that righteousness which frees humans from sin, from the Law, and from death (Rom 6-8). Freedom from sin, the Law, and death re-

sults in freedom for a life of grace (Rom 6:15), for the new law of love that fulfills the Law (Rom 13:8; Gal 6:2), and for a new kind of life lived under the power of the Spirit and manifest in the Spirit's gifts (see Rom 12:4-8). Living in between the time of Jesus and the end-times, the followers of Christ are to live as though in the new reality of God's reign. Those buried in Christ's death and brought to life in his resurrection through baptism, which empowers the follower of Christ to walk in a new life (Rom 6:3-4), become instruments of justice (Rom 6:13) and servants of justice (Rom 6:18). For Paul, those who are just live by faith and thus fulfill the gospel (Rom 1:17).

The constant in both Testaments about justice relates to the work of God in human relations and the way humans relate to God, to one another, and to the world itself. This constant, which characterizes the two main thrusts of all spirituality—the inner, experiential dimension of God's justification in the human, and the outer expression of that experience in the promotion of a harvest of justice in the world—brings us to the final consideration of contemporary notions of justice, namely, its pastoral implications and ramifications for spirituality.

3. *Pastoral Involvement and Justice-Oriented Spirituality.* The most-quoted passage from the document *Justice in the World,* issued by the 1971 Synod of Bishops, establishes the theological foundation for justice being at the heart of ministry and spirituality in general, especially if these are to be grounded in the Scriptures: "Action on behalf of justice and participation in the transformation of the world fully appear to us as a constitutive dimension of the preaching of the Gospel, or, in other words, of the Church's mission for the redemption of the human race and its liberation from every oppressive situation" (Introduction).

Just as faith, hope, and love are essential to the life of discipleship, this understanding of justice makes it mandatory as a characteristic of pastoral activity as well as of all spirituality. The effort to work for the dignity of all persons, a greater equity in the way the earth's resources are produced and distributed, and better ways to ensure participative processes and human solidarity can no longer be seen as peripheral to the life of discipleship and Christian spirituality. The option to follow Christ demands identification with the poor and marginalized as well as an effort to overcome those structures and systems that create and/or sustain their oppression and exploitation. For disciples of Christ with an evangelical spirituality, there is no option when the needs of others become evident (Mt 25:31-46). In their letter *The Eucharist and the Hungers of the Human Family* (1975), the U.S. Catholic bishops declared: "The quest for human freedom is not optional for Catholics, nor is it a small part of the Church's mission. Participation in the struggle for freedom and justice is a duty for each one of us, as it is a central element of the Church's mission of redemption and liberation" (no. 12).

If an understanding of the Word demands seeing justice as essential to its proclamation and expression in spirituality, then all balanced ministry and spirituality must involve justice. They also must be lived and witnessed at all levels of the world: the individual, the interpersonal, and the infrastructural. These three levels—the personal, the communitarian, and the public (political, economic, cultural)—are part of that world that must receive the good news contained in the gospel (Mt 28:16-20).

The greatest obstacle to the promotion of pastoral activity on behalf of justice and a so-called spirituality of justice occurs when the pastoral agent or reputedly spiritual person, group, organization, or structure belies the essential definition of justice in its life and/or activity. When this happens, the term that Matthew's Jesus used for violators of justice can be rightfully incurred: *hypocrites* (see Mt 6:2, 5, 16; 7:5; 15:7; 22:18; 23:13, 15, 23, 25, 27, 29; 24:51). This is especially true of the Catholic Church on its institutional level. This realization prompted the 1971 Synod of Bishops to declare: "While the Church is bound to give witness to justice, she recognizes that anyone who ventures to speak to people about justice must first be just in their eyes. Hence we must undertake an examination of the modes of acting and of the possessions and life style found within the Church itself" (*Justice in the World,* II).

See also CARDINAL VIRTUES; EARLY CHRISTIAN SPIRITUALITY; LIBERATION THEOLOGY, INFLUENCE ON SPIRITUALITY; MARGINALIZED, THE; POOR, THE; PRAXIS; SCRIPTURE; SOLIDARITY; VIRTUE; WORLD.

Bibliography: J. Donahue, "Biblical Perspectives on Justice," in J. Haughey, *The Faith That Does Justice: Examining the Christian Sources for Social Change* (New York: Paulist, 1977) 68–112. B. Häring, *Free and Faithful in Christ: Moral Theology for Clergy and Laity* 2 (New York: Seabury, 1978). National Conference of Catholic Bishops, *Economic Justice for All: Pastoral Letter on Catholic Social Teaching and the U.S. Economy* (Washington: USCC, 1986). Synod of Bishops, *Justice in the World* (Washington: USCC, 1972). J. Gremillion, ed., *The Gospel of Peace and Justice: Catholic Social Teaching since Pope John* (Maryknoll, N.Y.: Orbis, 1976).

MICHAEL H. CROSBY, O.F.M. CAP.

K

KATAPHATIC SPIRITUALITY

See AFFIRMATIVE WAY.

KENOSIS

The word *kenosis* is derived from the Greek *kenos,* meaning "empty, without effect," and its verb form, *kenoō,* "to make empty or of no effect." The adjective and verb are used several times in the NT, usually in a negative sense, e.g., "[God's] grace to me has not been ineffective [*kenē*]" (1 Cor 15:10). Attention in biblical interpretation and subsequent theology, however, has fallen mainly on a single verse in which the verb is used to describe the kenosis of Christ: "Who, though he was in the form of God, did not regard equality with God something to be grasped. Rather, he emptied [ekenōsen] himself, taking the form of a slave, coming in human likeness. . ." (Phil 2:6-7).

This text, which many interpreters believe originated as a pre-Pauline hymn, has a rich theology and has provoked numerous debates about the nuances of its meaning. There is a strong consensus among most recent interpreters, however, that kenosis here does not mean that Christ stripped himself of his divine attributes in becoming human, but that "emptying" refers to the manner of self-transcending love that led Christ, not to claim his rightful lordship, but to take on a human existence marked by humility and servanthood, ultimately expressed in his death for others. Paul uses the hymn in part to urge the Philippians to take on the same self-transcending and mutually loving attitude (Phil 2:1-5). For some modern spiritual writers, *kenosis* has been used as a term to refer to the process of self-transcendence called for in authentic conversion of heart.

See also CHRIST; INCARNATION; SERVICE; WEAKNESS AND VULNERABILITY.

Bibliography: J. Fitzmyer, "Pauline Theology," *New Jerome Biblical Commentary* (Englewood Cliffs, N.J.: Prentice-Hall, 1990) 1382ff. R. P. Martin, *Carmen Christi: Philippians 2,5-11 in Recent Interpretation,* rev. ed. (Grand Rapids, Mich.: Eerdmans, 1983).

DONALD SENIOR, C.P.

KINDNESS

See FRUIT(S) OF THE HOLY SPIRIT.

KINGDOM OF GOD

Jesus preached that the kingdom or reign of God was at hand. Though the term occurs most frequently in the NT, its roots are to be found in the OT concept of the kingship of Yahweh.

In Palestinian Judaism at the time of Jesus, the theme of the kingdom of God was most evident among the Zealots, who interpreted it politically. In the NT it occurs over 150 times, most often in the Synoptic Gospels. It functions more as a symbol than as a concept. Jesus does not explain it, but its meaning emerges from his parables, and its coming is illustrated through his ministry.

First, the expression "kingdom of God" (*basileia tou theou*) in the Gospels should generally be translated "reign of God"; it is a dynamic event, not a place. It means that God is exercising saving power among humankind in a new way.

Second, there is an irreducible eschatological tension in Jesus' preaching; God's reign is both present and future. It is present in Jesus' preaching and parables, his miracles and exorcisms, his proclamation of the forgiveness of sins, and in his practice of table-fellowship. The meals that Jesus shared both with his friends and with sinners and others considered outside the law (Mk 2:16-19) show that no one is excluded from God's reign.

At the same time, there is clearly a future dimension to Jesus' preaching of God's reign. He teaches his disciples to pray, "Your kingdom come" (Mt 6:10). The sayings about the Son of Man coming in judgment emphasize the future dimension of God's reign (Lk 12:8-9). The parables of the kingdom—the farmer and the seed, the weeds and the wheat, the mustard seed, the yeast kneaded in the flour, the net cast into the sea (Mt 13:1-53)—bring to light both the present and the future aspect of God's reign.

Finally, Jesus makes a connection between the coming reign and one's personal response. To enter the kingdom, one must become like a little child (Mk 10:15; Lk 18:17). He called those who would listen to a personal conversion (Mk 1:15), to discipleship in the service of God's reign, and taught them to love others with an all-inclusive and self-sacrificial love (Mt 5:38-48). He frequently warned against the danger of wealth (Mk 10:24-25; Lk 12:16-21). The beatitudes describe those who will find fulfillment in the kingdom. Matthew, in his parable of the Last Judgment, makes entrance into the kingdom dependent on one's conduct toward others, especially the poor and unfortunate (Mt 25:34-46).

The death and resurrection of Jesus transformed the disciples' understanding both of Jesus and of their own mission. Along with the good news of God's reign, the NT writers focus on the person of Jesus and his resurrection. Paul sometimes describes the kingdom as present: "the kingdom of God is not a matter of food and drink, but of righteousness, peace, and joy in the Holy Spirit" (Rom 14:17). But in most of Paul's references to God's reign, the emphasis is on the eschatological future (1 Cor 6:9; Gal 5:21). John refers twice (3:3, 5) to the kingdom; more frequently he uses "eternal life" to express salvation in Jesus. Again, it is both present and future (Jn 6:54; 11:26).

The Christian community needs to reexpress the good news of God's reign in every age. At times the kingdom of God has been improperly identified with the Church. An overemphasis on present or realized eschatology can also risk identifying the kingdom with an ideal political or social order. The Second Vatican Council taught that the Church receives the mission to proclaim and to establish the kingdom, and that the Church on earth is its initial budding forth (LG 5).

Contemporary expressions of God's reign proclaimed by Jesus stress God's unconditional love, manifested in human compassion and service to others. For Michael Cook, the kingdom of God is "Jesus' comprehensive term for the blessing of salvation insofar as it denotes the divine activity at the center of all human life" (*The Jesus of Faith*, New York: Paulist, 1981, pp. 56–57). For Edward Schillebeeckx, God's presence and action are made visible in human beings' caring for one another (*Jesus*, New York: Crossroad, 1981, p. 153). Elisabeth Schüssler Fiorenza describes the reign of God as being realized wherever people are being healed, set free from oppression or dehumanizing power systems, and made whole

(*In Memory of Her,* New York: Crossroad, 1985, p. 123).

See also EARLY CHRISTIAN SPIRITUALITY; ESCHATOLOGY; JUSTICE.

Bibliography: N. Perrin, *Jesus and the Language of the Kingdom* (Philadelphia: Fortress, 1976).

THOMAS P. RAUSCH, S.J.

KNOWLEDGE

In the fields of spirituality and mysticism, knowledge has particular significance in three separate but related areas: types of knowledge, self-knowledge, and knowledge of God.

The most obvious form of knowledge involves human persons through the sense organs of sight, hearing, taste, smell, and touch as they encounter objects outside themselves. Sense knowledge, common to both animals and humankind, is different from intellectual knowledge, through which persons grasp beyond surface qualities of something to its core reality or essence. While sensory and intellectual knowledge can be achieved through natural human cognitive powers, there also exists spiritual knowledge. Spiritual knowledge is not achieved through natural cognitive powers but through a gratuitous gift of God's self-disclosure. This occurrence is familiar to the Christian spiritual tradition.

The type of knowledge which is not dependent on personal effort in its acquisition but which is received as gift is designated as infused knowledge. It differs from acquired knowledge gained through the senses or the intellect insofar as God takes hold of the soul and teaches it. Infused knowledge also differs from connatural knowledge because knowledge by connaturality assumes an association with the intellect.

While infused knowledge may explain the usual means by which God offers self-disclosure to humankind, another kind of knowing is associated with self-knowledge. Introspection, intuition, reflective examination of one's intentionality, insight, and experience of one's own existence and/or of one's creatureliness are all important indicators of who one is. There exists a general assumption in the major schools of spirituality that self-knowledge is essential before one can engage at any depth in a relationship with God. St. Benedict in his Rule counsels listening, silence, the stability of a religious community, obedience, and humility as ways to deepen one's self-awareness and to discover who we are. The Franciscan tradition, through St. Bonaventure (*Itinerarium Mentis ad Deum*) accentuates the emptying of the false self to discover the true self connected with all creation. Catherine of Siena (*The Dialogue*) emphasizes the need for self-knowledge that is born when a person recognizes his or her existence as an unmerited gift from the One who is pure Essence and Creator of us all. *The Spiritual Exercises* of St. Ignatius of Loyola are the blueprint whereby an exercitant grows in self-knowledge regarding his or her creatureliness as the weeks of the retreat progress. Teresa of Avila, in *The Interior Castle,* likewise counsels regarding self-knowledge that it is the one set of rooms in which one may tarry for as long as one likes. It is here, after all, that the preparation for the journey to God is accomplished.

Although self-knowledge is a lifelong process, once one has begun the journey and insights begin to flow, there comes simultaneously knowledge of who God is. The possibility of supernatural knowledge is precisely the possibility that God makes known to persons certain truths that they could not discover by themselves. For Karl Rahner, God's revelation of divine being is spoken of as God's self-communication to the world through Christ in the power of the Holy Spirit (*Foundations of Christian Faith,* pp. 116–137). Insofar as we are free, we are possible receivers of God's self-disclosure that occurs concretely through knowledge and love.

In this connection, St. Thomas Aquinas examined the effect of love on knowledge. Love is not satisfied with a superficial knowledge but longs for union with what is known (ST I-II, q. 28, a. 2). The knowledge at stake is connatural: it involves knowing of the whole person through the intellect but also through noncognitive factors such as appetite and will (ST I-II, q. 16, a. 4). In the long run, we can only love what we know, and we really know only those realities that we are able to love.

See also CONSCIOUSNESS; CONTEMPLATION, CONTEMPLATIVE PRAYER; GIFTS OF THE HOLY SPIRIT; GNOSIS, GNOSTICISM; INTUITION; LIGHT; MEDITATION; MIND; STUDY.

Bibliography: J. Maritain, *Distinguish to Unite, or The Degrees of Knowledge,* trans. G. Phelan (New York: Scribner's, 1959). K. Rahner, *Foundations of the Christian Faith,* trans. W. Dych (New York: Seabury, 1978).

DORIS DONNELLY

L

LABOR

See WORK.

LADDER

See JOURNEY (GROWTH AND DEVELOPMENT IN SPIRITUAL LIFE).

LAW

"Law" (*torah*) had various meanings in the OT. Originally it signified direction and instruction from God for a given situation. With the Deuteronomic reform it took on a more general sense to mean the law of God. Deuteronomy itself is called "the book of the law" (Dt 28:61; 29:20; 30:10), and after the Exile the entire Pentateuch is called the Law. In OT theology the Scriptures are divided into the "Law" and the "Prophets." The Law was given by God to Moses on Sinai; the moral demands of the prophets proceeded immediately from God in the present. From Ezra on, the concept of *torah* or *nomos* became understood as the sum total of the Jewish religion or way of life as a whole.

In the Synoptic Gospels Jesus stresses the primacy of the law of love of God and neighbor (Mt 22:34-39; Lk 10:25-28). He rejects self-righteous observance of the letter of the law without regard for its spirit (Mk 2:23-28). In John's Gospel the law is the possession of the Jews, bearing witness to the promises of Christ (Jn 1:17); it is an imperfect stage of revelation whose fulfillment is in Christ. Paul contrasts law and faith, or law and gospel. Paul does not reject the law; indeed, he says that it is just, good, and holy (Rom 7:12, 16). However, he castigates a legalistic attitude that considers the external observance of the Jewish law, without faith in Christ, as sufficient for salvation.

Both Jesus and Paul were highly critical of empty legalism, but they were not antinomian. The necessity of law in society is recognized in both Scripture and tradition. No human group can exist without normative rules for its organization and conduct.

In the Catholic tradition law is distinguished as *divine law,* whether natural or positive, or *human law.* The natural law is the divine order seen in creation by which all things are inclined toward their natural acts and ends. People come to know the natural law by human reason, by reflection on the created order. The divine positive law consists of the laws of God revealed in the Scriptures. Canon law is the law of the Church; it includes elements of the divine law but is for the most part merely ecclesiastical, or human, law.

Human law in one form or another exists in every social group. Law in the broad sense of the term is found in all cultures, including nonliterate societies. However, the English word *law* is usually understood to refer to positive legislation enacted and promulgated by the legitimate authority of the society, whether Church or state.

Thomas Aquinas defines law as "an ordinance of reason for the common good, promulgated by one who has care of the community" (ST I-II, q. 90, a. 4c). (1) A law is an ordinance of reason; it must be reasonable. (2) The purpose of law is chiefly to provide for the common good, and this includes the welfare of the individuals who make up the society governed by law. Good laws seek to foster the harmonious ordering of society in which individual freedoms can flourish. (3) Law must be made and published by the legitimate legislative authority. The role of authority is necessary in society; Christians are obliged to observe the laws and mandates of the secular authority, provided they are reasonable and just.

If a law is unreasonable or unjust, or if it is harmful to the common good, it cannot be considered a true law according to the Thomistic definition. Even if promulgated by legitimate authority, an unreasonable or unjust law is not morally binding, and active or passive resistance to such a law may be justifiable. In some cases there might even be a moral obligation to oppose a law that creates a serious injustice.

The duty to respect and obey human law does not require blind compliance with all laws. The Christian tradition values a critical appraisal of law in light of ethical principles and gospel values. When a human law is opposed to the law of God, Christians should use just and appropriate means to see that it is abolished.

See also CANON LAW, SPIRITUALITY IN; COMMUNITY; CONFRONTATION AND PROTEST; DECISION, DECISION-MAKING; JUSTICE; OBEDIENCE.

Bibliography: B. Häring, *The Law of Christ* (Westminster, Md.: Newman, 1963). K. Rahner, ed., "Law," *Sacramentum Mundi: An Encyclopedia of Theology* 3 (New York: Herder, 1979) 276–299. C. Brown, ed., "Law," *The New International Dictionary of New Testament Theology* 2 (Grand Rapids, Mich.: Zondervan, 1976) 436–456.

JOHN M. HUELS, O.S.M.

LAY SPIRITUALITY

Christian spirituality has taken many forms throughout the centuries. One important form, consistently overlooked and unappreciated, is lay spirituality. This expression of spirituality has been an inherent aspect of Christianity from the beginning, although lay people themselves have frequently been portrayed by Church historians as incompetent in religious matters and lacking in leadership abilities. In the earliest Christian communities, however, there were no categories separating lay people and ordained ministers. All lived as equals, for according to St. Paul, among the baptized "there is neither Jew nor Greek, there is neither slave nor free person, there is not male and female; for you are all one in Christ Jesus" (Gal 3:28).

New Testament Times and Later Emergence of Clergy and Laity

The early Christian communities followed the example set by Jesus, who transcended the dichotomy between priest and layperson as he went about teaching and preaching in the synogogues and the open air, healing the sick and confronting personal and institutional demons, eating at the homes of certain lay people like himself, and establishing intimate friendships with both women and men. His was a ministry characterized by great compassion and a hospitality and inclusiveness that broke many of the religious and cultural stereotypes of his time. He seemed especially critical of those Jewish leaders, ordained and lay, who attempted to play God in people's lives or arrogantly presupposed an intimacy with God that others could not attain. His complaint against the Pharisees and Sadducees who asked of him a sign when they themselves were unable to read "the signs of the times" was a cry for them to open their eyes to the grace of God freely offered to everyone (Mt 16:1-4).

After his death and resurrection, Jesus' followers began calling themselves "saints":

those who were baptized in Jesus' name and who in solidarity with one another sought holiness in God. These saints, found not only in Jerusalem but in Rome, Corinth, and the whole of Greece, shared a common vision and hope in Christ. They also shared a citizenship of the saints that went beyond their local communities and united them into one body throughout the ancient world. St. Paul expresses this citizenship when he sends greetings "to the church of God that is in Corinth, to you who have been sanctified in Christ Jesus, called to be holy, with all those everywhere who call upon the name of our Lord Jesus Christ, their Lord and ours" (1 Cor 1:2).

In those New Testament times, even while the needs of the various communities eventually gave rise to specific tasks, responsibilities, and titles, it was assumed that every baptized person acted in some capacity as a minister. Women in particular made significant contributions to the life of the early Churches. Among those specifically mentioned in the Scriptures are Tabitha of Joppa, who was "completely occupied with good deeds and almsgiving" (Acts 9:36); Mary, the mother of John Mark, who used her house for meetings of the Christian assembly (Acts 12:12); Lydia, "a dealer in purple cloth" who invited Paul and his companions to stay in her home (Acts 16:14, 40); Prisca, who shared with her husband the title of Paul's "co-worker in Christ Jesus" (Rom 16:3); and Phoebe, who acted as a deaconess (Rom 16:1-2). The Church and the spirituality of those times valued the great diversity of personal charisms and considered all of them to have equal value, given for the building up of the community (1 Cor 12:28).

The Greek term *kleros,* from which the word "clergy" is derived, originally referred to an instrument used for drawing lots. In the New Testament it was not applied to a specific group of ministers or ordained persons, but to all believers, who were called "a chosen race, a royal priest-hood, a holy nation, a people of his own" (1 Pet 2:9). With the exception of Ignatius of Antioch, who applied the term *kleros* to the martyrs (the majority of whom were in fact lay people), it was not until the beginning of the 3rd century that *kleros* was used to describe a specific group within the Christian community. At that time the term *laikos,* or "layman," began to appear with greater frequency, although previously it had been found only in certain profane Jewish texts written before Christ's time and designating the local population as opposed to the administration.

Despite emerging distinctions between lay people and clergy, the theology of most Christian writers during the early centuries acknowledged the inherent dignity and priesthood of all Christians and did not even use the word *lay.* Tertullian (ca. 160–225), who did use the term, asked in his writings, "Are we lay people not priests also? It is written, 'He has made us kings and priests' (Rev 1:6)." Origen (ca. 185–254) preached to his congregation, "Do you not recognize that the priesthood has been given to you also, that is to the whole Church of God and the nation of believers? . . . You have therefore a priesthood, being 'a priestly nation.'" John Chrysostom (347–407) stated that the entire people gathered in prayer constitute the "fullness of priesthood," while Augustine (354–430) wrote in his *City of God:* "As we call everyone 'Christians,' so we call everyone 'priests' because all are members of only one priesthood."

Lay Influence on the Development of Christian Spirituality

The priesthood of all Christians and their common call to holiness were eventually submerged in the history of Christian spirituality as the more ordinary aspects of Christian life, along with women's gifts, were denigrated. Christian spirituality has often been revitalized, however, and many of the great reforms of Church life have come about as the result of lay initiatives.

After the New Testament period, the greatest single influence upon the development of Christian spirituality in both the West and East was that of the early Desert Christians. Primarily lay people, such greats as Antony, Pachomius, Evagrius, Theodora, Sarah, Syncletica, and numerous other *abbas* and *ammas* acted as spiritual mentors and have had a lasting effect on all of us regarding our understanding of prayer, contemplation, asceticism, and the discernment of spirits.

Throughout the centuries the great monastic and mystical traditions that brought new spiritualities into the Churches have also been influenced profoundly by the nonordained. Many of the most visionary and creative of these spiritual leaders were women: Catherine of Alexandria, Brigid of Kildare, Hilda of Whitby, Non of Wales and Cornwall, Julian of Norwich, Teresa of Avila, Hildegard of Bingen, Catherine of Siena. The Reformation—both Protestant and Catholic versions—was preceded by the Beguines and Beghards, lay movements of the 12th and 13th centuries that valued a simple lifestyle, ordinary work, and communities of friends, and by the 14th-century *devotio moderna,* which emphasized an educated laity, daily meditation, a vital liturgical life, and the need for spiritual guides. Protestantism, in its many varieties, has been characterized as a "lay religion" that fosters theologically, if not always in practice, the priesthood of all the baptized, and thus a Christian spirituality more inclusive of the laity than that found within the Roman Catholic Church preceding Vatican II.

In the 20th century, such lay leaders and spiritual writers as Simone Weil, Dag Hammarskjöld, Dorothy Day, Peter Maurin, Evelyn Underhill, and C. S. Lewis have awakened many to the significant contributions lay people can make to both society and Church life. In terms of influence, perhaps the co-founders of Alcoholics Anonymous, Bill Wilson and Dr. Bob Smith, are most responsible for developing in contemporary Western culture an awareness of the vital human need for a spirituality that fosters dynamic change, healing, and reconciliation. The principles that those two laymen articulated continue to guide individuals—many of them Christians—and self-help groups throughout the world.

Vatican II and the Laity

For Roman Catholic Christians, the Second Vatican Council was an important institutional turning point, the beginning of a recovery of that earlier vision and spirituality of Church with its universal call to holiness and appreciation of everyone's ministries and gifts. Rich insights were given at that council, which met from October 11, 1962, to December 8, 1965, on the subject of the laity, primarily in its Dogmatic Constitution on the Church (*Lumen Gentium*), the Decree on the Apostolate of the Laity (*Apostolicam Actuositatem*), and the Pastoral Constitution on the Church in the Modern World (*Gaudium et Spes*). Though Vatican II did not attempt to give a final and binding definition of lay people, its statements had profound implications for lay spirituality among Roman Catholics and other Christians.

The Dogmatic Constitution on the Church adopts as its chief theological category the concept of the Church as the entire People of God (no. 9) and states that "all the faithful scattered throughout the world are in communion with each other in the Holy Spirit" (no. 13). It describes lay people as Christians living in the ordinary circumstances of social life, "from which the very web of their existence is woven" (no. 31), and insists that all members of this priestly people, as a result of their baptism, have a certain basic equality and common call to ministry (no. 33). All Christians, too, "of whatever rank or status are called to the fullness of Christian life and to the perfection of charity"; this call to holiness can bring about "a more human way of life . . . in this earthly society" (no. 40).

The Decree on the Apostolate of the Laity reaffirms that lay people share in "the priestly, prophetic, and royal office of Christ" (no. 2). They especially have a responsibility for social outreach and societal transformation: "The apostolate of the social milieu, that is, the effort to infuse a Christian spirit into the mentality, customs, laws, and structures of the community in which a person lives, is so much the duty and responsibility of the laity that it can never be properly performed by others" (no. 13). This document also calls attention to the important ministries of mentoring that married couples offer each other and their children: "Christian husbands and wives are cooperators in grace and witnesses of faith on behalf of each other, their children, and all others in their household. They are the first to communicate the faith to their children and to educate them; by word and example they train their offspring for the Christian and apostolic life" (no. 11). This same decree, while implying that *ordinarily* the laity will seek the reign of God by engaging in temporal affairs, concedes that lay people are also to be actively involved in Church life: "The laity carry out their manifold apostolate both in the Church and in the world" (no. 9).

The Pastoral Constitution on the Church in the Modern World, which contains a powerful opening statement on the solidarity of the Church with the whole human family (no. 1), speaks eloquently of every Christian's need to "decipher authentic signs of God's presence and purpose in the happenings, needs, and desires in which this People has a part along with other men of our age" (no. 11). It also emphasizes how social justice and the equal dignity of persons "demand that a more humane and just condition of life be brought about" in our personal lives and organizations (no. 29). In no. 43, the document challenges every Christian's personal integrity, especially in the area of work, by addressing what it calls "one of the more serious errors of our age": "the split between the faith which many profess and their daily lives. . . . Christians should rather rejoice that they can follow the example of Christ, who worked as an artisan. In the exercise of all their earthly activities, they can thereby gather their humane, domestic, professional, social, and technical enterprises into one vital synthesis with religious values, under whose supreme direction all things are harmonized unto God's glory." Lay people (though not exclusively) are to take their work seriously as offering opportunities for global transformation, and, in particular, they are to act as mentors, attempting "to enlighten one another through honest discussion, preserving mutual charity and caring above all for the common good." Again, as the Dogmatic Constitution on the Church mentions, this transformation is not limited only to secular affairs but to Church life as well: "The laity are called to participate actively in the whole life of the Church; not only are they to animate the world with the spirit of Christianity, but they are to be witnesses to Christ in all circumstances and at the very heart of the community of mankind."

At Vatican II the Roman Catholic Church for the first time in history took up the question of the status and role of the laity, and provided a theological perspective on a Christian spirituality that takes seriously lay experiences, vocations, and ministries. Most importantly, it laid the groundwork for finally redefining, among Roman Catholics at least, lay Christians in more positive terms. More than twenty years later, after broad consultations among thousands of lay people, the 1987 International Synod of Bishops meeting in Rome addressed the topic "Vocation and Mission of the Laity in the Church and in the World." Its deliberations resulted in Pope John Paul II's apostolic exhortation entitled *Christifideles Laici* ("Christ's Faithful People"), published in 1989.

Though still maintaining a dualism emphasizing Church life as primarily the realm of the ordained and religious, and "the world" as the place of lay people's spirituality and mission, along with the subordination of lay people to their pastors, this document reaffirms the positive interpretation of Vatican II regarding lay people's full membership as Church, their vocation to holiness, and their diversity of gifts. It also recommends collaboration that fosters communion among all baptized members, both women and men (no. 52), and an integrated formation that "is not the privilege of a few, but a right and duty of all" (see nos. 59-63).

Lay Ministries and Lay Spirituality After Vatican II

For many lay people, Vatican II had a profound effect on their practice and understanding of spirituality. They began to see themselves for the first time as full members of the Church, a new awareness that sometimes came through an adult conversion experience or perhaps more commonly through a gradual awakening to the reality of being called, being sent, or, as the Apostle Peter experienced, being led to places one least expected to go (Jn 21:18). While countless numbers of lay people, as a result of this awakening, began to take their jobs and careers more seriously as opportunities to serve God and one another in the workplace and home, others wanted to give themselves more explicitly to ministries closely tied to church settings. Many of these are presently serving as teachers, religious educators, theologians, pastoral ministers or associates, coordinators of ministry programs, hospital and prison chaplains, campus ministers, counselors, retreat leaders, parish administrators, liturgists, peace and social justice ministers, and spiritual guides. These professional or career ministers, volunteer and paid, often empower lay people like themselves to recognize the value of their own ministries, whatever they may be.

According to consultations in the United States preceding the 1987 International Synod on the Laity, there seems to be a universal reawakening among Roman Catholic lay people to their gifts and responsibilities to serve wherever they are called, and they recognize that any dualism that splits body and soul, Church and world, ministry and work, laity and ordained is not true to their life experiences. Responding overwhelmingly in a positive way to the teachings of Vatican II, they generally affirmed: (1) that there is only one Christian spirituality, which people live out differently depending on their life situations; (2) that women have a distinct contribution to make to the life of the Churches; (3) that the primary sources for their spiritual growth are Scripture and liturgy; and (4) that small community experiences are an important resource for their spiritual development. Increasingly lay people seem to be identifying themselves as Church, and their mission and ministries as the mission and ministries of the Church itself. For them, being Church in its fullness is their spirituality. Valuing diversity, they at the same time acknowledge how much all Christians have in common with one another.

Lay spirituality in touch with the earliest days of the Church and the rich history of Christian spirituality shows a clear return to common values of all the baptized, and specifically to a reaffirmation of the positive contributions of lay life. Definitely a grass-roots phenomenon, this spirituality is about the presence and action of God in the lives of ordinary people who hear the Word and respond in the ordinary circumstances of their lives. It is a spirituality of the family and the workplace, and is frequently expressed in the life of the local parish communities. Since there are many circumstances and types of lay people, there are a great variety of lay spiritualities related to personal vocations, choices, commitments, and lifestyles. Lacking the structures and institutional support that the ordained or members of religious communities usually have for the development of their spirituality, lay people rely increasingly upon themselves in networks of friends and in relationships of honest self-disclosure with spiritual guides, many of whom are lay people.

Contrary to theological views that arose glorifying the heroic lifestyle of those who chose to be ordained or to live in monastic communities, lay people too have been intimately acquainted with deprivation and human suffering. Their spirituality necessarily has an ascetic dimension to it, for theirs is a daily struggle and discipline to care for their families, maintain careers and jobs, sustain elderly parents and grandparents, contribute volunteer services, find meaning, persist, let go. At the same time, lay spirituality is not about suppressing one's humanity, for, as the early Church Father Irenaeus of Lyons wrote, Christianity is humanity "more fully alive." The spirituality of the Christian layperson is incarnational, enfleshed, and frequently expressed sexually. It is also realistic in its recognition of age-old patterns of sin and sickness, often inherited from family systems, and of the constant need for forgiveness and for reconciling ministries that reveal God's love. A lay spirituality that is Christian acknowledges that spirituality itself is a lifelong process of intimacy not only with God but with all who inhabit the earth, especially those who are poor, neglected, forgotten, or abused. Global in orientation and committed to personal and organizational change, it develops in service to one's family, friends, and political and ecclesial communities.

A Spirituality That Fosters Lay Leadership

Lay spirituality today far exceeds that of any other age of the Church in its scope, inclusive dimensions, and sheer number of educated laity. Lay ministries are bringing new life, talents, and energies to all the Churches, including the Roman Catholic, and women especially have been in the forefront of these good changes. No longer can being a layperson be associated with ignorance or incompetence as lay leaders who are highly educated, talented, and skilled increasingly emerge. One of their chief characteristics today, as the National Conference of Catholic Bishops in the United States identified in the document *Called and Gifted: The American Catholic Laity,* is their growing sense of being adult members of the Church. Prime criteria in discerning how sound any lay spirituality is should be whether it fosters psychological and spiritual maturity, and whether it encourages and supports leadership in the home and workplace, in our societies and churches. An authentically Christian spirituality promotes lay leaders who are knowledgeable and experienced, free and responsible, whose relationships are characterized by mutuality. Such leaders also have other qualities, all rooted in and nourished by their spirituality.

First, such Christian leaders have an appreciation of the living presence of the past, of the continuity of Christian life and prayer through the centuries. This presupposes a commitment to learning about the rich Judeo-Christian spiritual heritage, not out of some antiquarian interest, but because the wise women and men of the past have a great deal to teach about prayer, suffering, compassion, and social justice. They provide spiritual and psychological insights into contemporary problems and conflicts, as well as creative possibilities never before imagined. They help people emerge from the implicit parochialism, limitations, and biases of any age, including the contemporary one. From them can be rediscovered what the early Church already knew: that being a saint is the vocation to which all Christians are called, not just the "greats" who lived long ago; that being a saint is simply centering one's life in God, and, through ministry, helping others discover what for many is the hardest thing of all: the love and compassion of God for all creation, including ourselves.

A second quality that Christian spirituality fosters in us is a commitment to dialogue, prayer, and ministries with people of other Churches and other religious traditions. Convinced of the importance of ecumenism as a fundamental principle of all Church life and ministry, the Christian leader today works for a Church unity based upon an appreciation of diversity and the recognition of common roots. This ecumenism, as Thomas Merton's life and words clearly reveal, begins with every Christian: "If I can unite in myself the thought and devotion of Eastern and Western Christendom, the Greek and Latin Fathers, the Russian with the Spanish Mystics, I can prepare in myself the reunion of divided Christians. From that secret and unspoken unity in myself can eventually come a visible and manifest unity of all Christians."

Third, Christian leaders today need to be immersed in a spirituality of the ordinary, of the everyday, which includes appreciation of, and gratitude for, our families, friends, work, and leisure. For those who are married, this presupposes valuing family life, a commitment to making family members instead of careers alone a priority, and a willingness to bring lay experiences and family spirituality into the forefront of ecclesial life. Whether married or not, all lay leaders can learn from the early Christian Celts, who had a profound sense of God's immediacy, as well as that of Mary, the saints, and angels, as they went about their day-to-day tasks and met their responsibilities. For them, the powerful, healing presence of God was often found in their communion with nature, in their storytelling around the hearth, and in their poetry, song, and dance. God and the awareness of the holy might be found today in those same activities and places.

A fourth quality for lay leaders, men and women alike, is a sense of inclusiveness regarding women. This century has been one of revolutionary change, especially in the perception of the sexes. Old roles and stereotypes no longer apply. While it seems at times that more progress is happening for women in society and the corporate world than in Church life, it is especially in the Churches—if they are to be true signs to the world—where full equality must be found. Criteria in the discernment of Church ministries should not be whether a person is male or female, single or married, but what sort of talents, skills, and competence the community needs to fulfill its mission of bringing into greater reality the reign of God.

Finally, an authentic spirituality nurtures Christian leaders who, like Christ, manifest hospitality and compassion, and are dedicated to collaboration: the committed efforts of working together to accomplish a goal. Such efforts are based upon a deep respect and appreciation for the gifts of all baptized persons. Collaboration is never easy, and it sometimes only starts with the painful discernment of human needs: that a person cannot do everything his or her own way, and that more is accomplished that is worthwhile when done together. Both the human condition and those positive experiences of collaboration speak loudly of how much we as Church need one another as friends.

Genuine Christian spirituality promotes leadership that values the wisdom of the past, the richness of the present, and a vision of the future that calls everyone to respond. It encourages a maturity in adults that is associated neither with gullibility nor with cynicism, but rather with gratitude and serenity, even in the midst of great anxiety, suffering, and pain. Above all, it takes seriously the experiences, gifts, and common call to ministry of every baptized person. Such a spirituality, if it is a vital one, will always be attentive to those experiences, especially those that raise questions about ultimate concerns, such as the meaning of life, the presence of God, and the depth of our love.

See also BAPTISM; CATHOLIC ACTION; CATHOLIC
WORKER MOVEMENT; CONTEMPORARY SPIRITUAL-
ITY; CONVERSION; CURSILLO MOVEMENT; ECUME-
NISM, SPIRITUAL; FRIENDSHIP; MARRIAGE; SEXUAL-
ITY; SINGLE LIFE; SINGLE PARENT; VATICAN COUNCIL
II; WORK; WORLD.

Bibliography: Y. Congar, *Lay People in the Church*
(Westminster, Md.: Newman, 1957). L. Doohan, *The
Lay-Centered Church* (Minneapolis, Minn.: Winston,
1984). A. Faivre, *The Emergence of the Laity in the
Early Church* (New York: Paulist, 1990). John Paul II,
"Apostolic Exhortation on the Laity" (*Christifideles
Laici*), *Origins* 18, no. 35, pp. 261–283. National Con-
ference of Catholic Bishops, *Called and Gifted: The
American Catholic Laity* (Washington: USCC, 1980).
J. and E. Whitehead, *The Emerging Laity* (Garden
City, N.Y.: Doubleday, 1986).

EDWARD C. SELLNER

LECTIO DIVINA

Found most commonly but not exclusively in literature on monastic spirituality
and originally equated with *sacra pagina,
lectio divina* refers to a "holy reading" of
the Scriptures (almost always) or of the Fathers of the Church or other spiritual writing requiring prayerful reflection on the
text leading to communion with God in
prayer. *Lectio divina* is thus distinguished
from scientific exegesis, hermeneutics, and
the study of Scripture for specifically theological purposes.

In much patristic and monastic literature, as exemplified in the Rule of St. Benedict (8:3, 48:23), *lectio* includes reading,
private prayer, and *meditatio,* with "meditation" meaning the memorization, repetition, and prayerful rumination ("chewing
over") of texts as a stimulus to personal
prayer. The desired result of application to
lectio divina is a thorough assimilation of
sacred truth and a life lived according to
this truth. Chapter 48 of the Rule of St.
Benedict begins with the general instruction: "Idleness is the enemy of the soul.
Therefore, the brothers should have specified periods for manual labor as well as for
prayerful reading [*lectio divina*]" and contains specific times for *lectio* in the daily
and Sunday *horarium,* with special attention to Lent.

Contemporary attention to *lectio divina*
beyond monastic circles concerns the importance of an informed yet spiritual interpretation of and reflection on Scripture for
all the baptized and its usefulness for a
preacher's spirituality and ministry (see
Vatican II, Decree on Priestly Formation,
no. 25).

See also BENEDICTINE SPIRITUALITY; MEDITATION;
MONASTICISM, MONASTIC SPIRITUALITY; PRAYER;
SCRIPTURE.

Bibliography: J. Leclercq, *The Love of Learning and
the Desire for God* (New York: Fordham Univ. Press,
1958). A. Louf, *Lord, Teach Us to Pray,* trans. H.
Hoskins (New York: Paulist, 1975). J. Rousse, H.
Sieben, and A. Boland, "*Lectio Divina,* et Lecture
Spirituelle," *D.Spir.,* vol. 9, cols. 470–510.

KEVIN W. IRWIN

LEISURE

Our lives are composed of work and leisure. Leisure is the free time that we experience either rhythmically or sporadically.
Work, a good and necessary part of our
lives, occupies a significant part of almost
every day we live. The attitude of some cultures toward work is summed up in the
phrase "Business before pleasure." But in
fact most people think that pleasure is
equally important. While at work we watch
the clock and look forward to the weekend
and holidays. Recreation ensures that our
lives will be thoroughly human. Much that
advances our humanity takes place in leisure time: the coming together of companions, a needed balance to our usual activities and professions, and the psychological
space to be ourselves. Leisure is the special
time of engagement for husband and wife,
children, and lovers.

Contemporary society is characterized
in terms of a greater amount of free time.
The five-day week is diminishing in many
places. The media invite us to fill up this
free time with sports, news, and romance.
Many people pass their leisure time in that

which is dulling and trivial. The full and integrated person is one who directs this free time so that it becomes the locus for creativity, the developing of skills, and the gaining of insights. The arts and sciences find their origin in free time.

The Second Vatican Council, in its Pastoral Constitution on the Church in the Modern World (*Gaudium et Spes*), reminds us of the importance of leisure for workers so that they may "cultivate their family, cultural, social, and religious life" (GS 67). And the same document states: "May these leisure hours be properly used for relaxation of spirit and the strengthening of mental and bodily health" (GS 61).

Leisure, like liturgy, takes place in the rhythm of time. Rhythmic time is humankind's way of responding to the endless repetition and cyclical meaninglessness of chronological time, which is mere duration. To experience the benefits of leisure, we must halt this endless flow. We celebrate sacred time through festivals. We transform the ordinariness of time and reveal the potency of duration through leisure.

Because we experience something missing in our lives, we both liturgically celebrate sacred time and enjoy ordinary time in order that we may be fully ourselves. Just as we remember our sacred myths in ritual, so in leisure we enter into our lives more fully. Just as sacred time is celebrated differently by the different traditions, so people recapture and rekindle their lives through leisure in an endless number of ways. It is very difficult, if not impossible, for persons to keep sacred festivals if they have little experience of time through leisure. The same tension exists in liturgy and in leisure: how are we to harmonize our interior and exterior worlds? Leisure, like liturgy, can help us discover a balance between presence to self and presence to others. In order to experience the sacredness of time, we must let time in. That is what leisure does.

See also ART; BEAUTY; BODY; HOLISTIC SPIRITUALITY; JOY; LITURGY; MUSIC.

Bibliography: G. Marcel, *Fest: The Transformation of Everyday* (Philadelphia: Fortress, 1976). J. Pieper, *In Tune with the World* (New York: Harcourt and Brace, 1965). H. Rahner, *Man at Play* (New York: Herder, 1967).

JAMES L. EMPEREUR, S.J.

LEVITATION

See EXTRAORDINARY PHENOMENA.

LIBERATION THEOLOGY, INFLUENCE ON SPIRITUALITY

Liberation theology is a movement that emerged in Latin America during the 1960s. It is rooted in the experience of the Latin American poor, especially that of the *comunidades eclesiales de base,* or base ecclesial communities. Comprised primarily of peasants and workers, these communities are centered on the Word of God, providing a context for reading, reflection, and worship. Many clergy and religious, among them liberation theologians, participate actively in base ecclesial communities. Liberation theology represents a systematic theological reflection on that experience.

A fundamental characteristic of such Christian communities is their emphasis on the intrinsic and intimate connection between worship and the everyday lives of their members. Worship is seen as emerging from the daily struggles of day-to-day existence and as impacting those struggles in turn. Reading the Word of God within a context of oppression, the poor come to see the Bible as a source of empowerment and liberation. With its affirmation of the goodness of creation and of God's universal love for humankind, the Bible stands in judgment over the dehumanizing conditions under which the poor live and empowers them to work for that justice which is God's will. Likewise, the Eucharistic liturgy becomes a source of liberation as the poor seek to make real, in their towns, villages, and cities, that unity which the Eucharist symbolizes (see, e.g., Mt 5:23-24; 1 Cor 11:17-34; 1 Jn 1:6). Assured of their inherent dignity as children of God, the oppressed are empowered to work for justice. Often, therefore, these Christian communities have become catalysts for change.

Reflecting on the meaning of Scripture, faith, and tradition from within the context of oppression, liberation theologians understand God's universal and gratuitous love as inseparable from God's special identification with, and preferential option for, the poor (Gutiérrez, *On Job,* pp. xi–xix). In a context of oppression, God's universal love takes on different manifestations, depending upon one's sociohistorical role in the oppressive situation: for the oppressed, God's love will take the form of liberation, but for their oppressors, it will take the form of a call to conversion and disempowerment. God's love for the oppressor takes the form of challenge and confrontation, much as the love of a parent for an unruly child would.

Hence God's love is both universal and preferential; indeed, it is universal because it is preferential. If God did not side with the poor in their struggle, God's love would not be universal, since its "neutrality" would serve the interests of the oppressors. Far from reflecting a universal love, a "neutral" God's refusal to accompany the poor in their struggle for justice, to take sides with the poor, would be a tacit affirmation of the status quo, i.e., the unjust social order, thereby lending support to the oppressors. Consequently, God's love is universal precisely because it gives preference to the poor, the outcast, the powerless, the marginalized.

Liberation theology suggests that Christian spirituality should be grounded in a preferential option for the poor, a solidarity with the victims of history. Such an option is necessary for two reasons, one theological or scriptural, and the other epistemological. Authentic Christian prayer and worship must be grounded in a solidarity with the marginalized, first, because the God of the Scriptures is a God who is identified with and liberates the poor. In the Old Testament, God's chosen people are the Jews, an outcast, nomadic people despised by their neighbors. God chooses a poor, illiterate man, Abraham, to be the father of God's people. When the Jews begin to treat the poor in their communities as they themselves had been treated earlier, the prophets emerge to preach that the criterion of faithfulness to God is less how one worships than how one relates to the poor.

In the New Testament, Jesus Christ is identified with the poor in his birth, life, passion, and death. The *Magnificat,* the beatitudes, and numerous other texts bear witness to Jesus' identification with the poor and his refusal to accept the authority of their oppressors. Refusing to accept the ultimacy of any authority except God's, Jesus, like the poor and outcast, was crucified by a Roman power structure that itself demanded obeisance. In chapter 25 of Matthew's Gospel, Jesus explicitly identifies himself with the hungry, the naked, and the sick, thereby predicating our relationship to him upon our relationship to the poor. God will judge us according to how we have treated the poor.

Secondly, liberation theologians insist, solidarity with the poor is a prerequisite of authentic Christian spirituality, because the experience of marginalization reveals as idolatrous that spirituality which, born in a sociohistorical context of comfort and privilege, legitimates that comfort and privilege. If we hold a privileged position and thus benefit from the status quo or the present structure of society, we are not likely to develop a spirituality that will engender in us a dissatisfaction with the status quo and thus empower us to work for change. Such a spirituality would effectively be legitimating the very social order that sustains poverty and injustice.

Often such a spirituality will eschew involvement in social issues, which are seen as corrupting and undermining the "higher" life of the spirit. Liberation theologians argue, however, that by presuming to remain "above" the sociopolitical conflicts that generate poverty, oppression, and dehumanization, an apolitical spirituality denies the fact that we human beings are historical creatures, whose ideas, theories, images, ideologies, spirituality, and consciousness are influenced by our concrete social and historical location. Our image of the God to whom we pray is influenced, for instance, by our culture, social class, family background, race, gender, personality characteristics, etc. If our society is structured or ordered in such a way that we derive benefits as a result of our particular culture, social class, family background, race, gender, personality characteristics, etc., our theology, spirituality, and image of God will probably not be such that they will challenge the present order. And a theology, spirituality, and God that have nothing to say to the social order are a theology, spirituality, and God that implicitly condone the present injustices.

Since prayer that remains silent or aloof in the face of oppression or that considers such sociopolitical conflicts as beyond its purview is prayer that tacitly condones oppression, the object of such prayer cannot be the liberating God of the Scriptures, the God of life who identifies with the hungry, the naked, the sick, the "least ones." The object of such ahistorical prayer would be a god whose impartiality in the face of present injustices serves as tacit support for those injustices. In short, it would be a god created in our own image, a god whose silence or neutrality in the face of oppression would serve to perpetuate that oppression.

In liberation theology the suffering of the poor becomes the lens through which all implicit identifications of God with domination and injustice are called into question. Any attempt to identify the given social order with the reign of God, or

Christian spirituality with good citizenship, is brought to naught in the presence of the human suffering engendered by that social order. For that reason one's identification or solidarity with the poor becomes, for liberation theologians, the birthplace and criterion of genuine Christian spirituality. That solidarity is what safeguards the transcendence of God, God's nonidentity with our political systems, worldviews, and ideologies. By bearing in their broken bodies the consequences of our injustice, the poor make visible that injustice, thereby subverting our attempts to idolize our (or any) society. The poor thus reveal to us the truth about ourselves and our society in the same way as the crucified Jesus does. They reveal to us the fact that while we may think that our God is the God of the Scriptures, our true god, the god to whom we devote our greatest energies and by whom our lives are governed, is the god of wealth, security, privilege, status, power, and comfort. Thus only a spirituality grounded in the struggle for social justice and life can be identified with the God of life, the God of the Scriptures (Sobrino, p. 127).

The scandal and incomprehensibility that the poor represent for society reflect the "otherness" of the poor vis-à-vis that society which marginalizes and ostracizes them. Consequently, God's own "utter otherness," i.e., God's transcendence, is mediated through the otherness of the poor. Jesus' identification with the poor and the outcast serves notice that God's truth is beyond human comprehension and expectations, for that truth is revealed where we would least expect to find it—among those persons whom we systematically ridicule and condemn. Thus, if one is to remain open to the transcendent God, his or her spirituality must be grounded in that same identification with the powerless and dispossessed of society. That those who, like Jesus, make a preferential option for the poor also arouse the ire and hostility of the powerful groups in society is evidence of those groups' resistance to such a God (Sobrino, p. 127).

Underlying the liberation theologians' image of God is the rejection of both an individualistic and a dualistic view of the human person. We are not first individuals and only secondarily or accidentally social beings; by nature we are intrinsically social beings. Likewise, we do not live in two worlds, one secular and the other spiritual; we live in one world that is both natural and supernatural. The supernatural or spiritual is not another realm of existence, separate from historical existence; rather, the former is the fulfillment and deepest meaning of the latter. We do not come into contact with the spiritual or supernatural except through the concrete, historical, and natural. Consequently, knowledge of the spiritual comes, not through a withdrawal from society, but through an ever greater immersion in the vicissitudes and struggles of our time, there to encounter a God who is involved in, identified with, and thus revealed through those struggles.

A spiritual person is one who lives his or her life in a certain way, who lives "according to the spirit," as opposed to one who lives "according to the flesh" (Rom 8:4; see Gutiérrez, *We Drink from Our Own Wells*, pp. 54–71; *A Theology of Liberation*, p. xxxii). The term *spirituality* thus applies, not to a particular part of a person's life, but to the whole of it. It is in this sense that a truly Christian spirituality is holistic. It reflects the intrinsic unity between love of God and love of neighbor, recognizing that just as we encounter the spiritual not outside but within historical existence, so too do we express our love of God not outside but through our love of neighbor (see, e.g., 1 Jn 4:7-20; Jer 22:13-17). Prayer or worship must not be divorced from a practical commitment to love and justice: "Away with your noisy songs! I will not listen to the melodies of your harps. But if you would offer me holocausts, then let justice surge like water, and goodness like an un-failing stream" (Amos 5:23-24; see also Isa 58:6-7).

For liberation theologians, Christian spirituality is inseparable from solidarity with the poor and a commitment to justice. As explained above, that commitment or preferential option tells us something not so much about the poor as about God. For this reason the poor are themselves called to reject the seductive idols of power, wealth, and security in order to commit themselves to lives of love and justice. The poor are themselves called to make a preferential option for the poor (Gutiérrez, *A Theology of Liberation*, pp. 162–173). Through the base ecclesial communities, the poor of Latin America seek to live out that commitment, which becomes the basis for their prayer and worship. Out of that unity of prayer and action on behalf of justice a liberating, incarnate spirituality is born. It is that spirituality that liberation theologians have sought to articulate.

See also CATHOLIC ACTION; CATHOLIC WORKER; COMMUNITY; CONTEMPORARY SPIRITUALITY; CREATION; DISCIPLESHIP; FREEDOM; HISTORY, HISTORICAL CONSCIOUSNESS; JUSTICE; LOVE; MARGINALIZED, THE; POOR, THE; POVERTY; POWER; PRAXIS; SOLIDARITY; THIRD WORLD, SPIRITUALITY OF; WORLD.

Bibliography: G. Gutiérrez, *On Job* (Maryknoll, N.Y.: Orbis, 1987); *A Theology of Liberation* (Maryknoll, N.Y.: Orbis, 1988); *We Drink from Our Own Wells* (Maryknoll, N.Y.: Orbis, 1984). J. Sobrino, *Spirituality of Liberation* (Maryknoll, N.Y.: Orbis, 1988).

ROBERTO S. GOIZUETA

LIGHT

In the story of creation, light is a manifestation of God's active presence in a world that apart from it is darkness and chaos (Gen 1:3-5). In the Judeo-Christian tradition, the light/darkness theme develops to include all that enlightens human beings on their way to God. Thus in the Hebrew Scriptures the law (Ps 19:9), the wisdom of God (Wis 7:26), and the word of God (Ps 119:105) are light. Light is often associated with God's self-revealing presence in the form of fire (Exod 3:2-3; 13:22; 19:16-18; Dan 2:19; Wis 7:26). It is also a symbol of life, holiness, and joy, in contrast to darkness, which represents death, evil, and misery (Job 30:26; Isa 45:7; Ps 17:15; Isa 8:22–9:1). The Messiah, the Servant of Yahweh, will be light to the nations (Isa 42:6), and those who follow the way of Yahweh doing good to the poor and the oppressed will be light (Isa 58:10-11).

Light symbolism is used throughout the New Testament in relation to both Jesus and his disciples. In Luke's Gospel the light first manifested to Mary and Joseph in the birthing cave spreads gradually to the shepherds through the luminous apparition of the angel of the Lord (Lk 2:9). In Matthew's Gospel the light of a star rising in the east leads wise men from afar to Jesus (Mt 2:2). In John's Gospel Jesus is proclaimed "light of the world" (Jn 8:12). Called forth from darkness, Jesus' followers will not only have the light of life (Jn 8:12) but are called to be the light of the world (Eph 5:8; Mt 5:14). Consequently, they must strive to discern what the Lord wants of them and to live as children of the light (Eph 5:9-12; Jas 1:17).

Light symbolism permeates the prayer of the Church. The morning and evening prayer of the Church (Lauds and Vespers) are rooted in the symbolism of light and darkness. In them the enduring light of Christ is contrasted with the rise and decline of the light of day.

The contrast between light and darkness is one of the primary symbols of the Church year. It is particularly powerful in the season of Advent-Christmas, where the passage through darkness to light is the constant unifying movement. During the Lent-Easter season, with its central symbolic progression through death to life, the light/darkness contrast continues as a secondary motif. Darkness here is manifested as evil, sin, and death (see the Scrutinies of the RCIA). Light overcomes darkness in Christ's victory over death through his glorious resurrection. During the Easter Vigil the elect, also called the "enlightened," are baptized into Christ and presented with lighted candles, symbolic of their new life.

Two frequent allusions to light in the documents of the Second Vatican Council are to the light of faith and to Christians as light of the world. Faith rooted in the word of God and in tradition (DV 10, 19; LG 8) sheds new light on everything. It manifests God's design and points toward fully human solutions to the great questions facing humanity (GS 11; DV 24). The faithful, incorporated into Christ through baptism, confirmation, and Eucharist, are thus called to be light of the world (LG 1; AG 36). It is therefore a primary responsibility of Christians to live in a manner ever more profoundly in harmony with their faith (AA 13; AG 36; SC 9; LG 35). As the People of God, enlightened by the Spirit of God, believers possess within themselves by grace a capacity to shed light on the events of personal and societal life, and to perceive in them signs of the presence of God and of God's will. Thus personal and corporate discernment is of great significance in contemporary spirituality. Through it the baptized are enabled to fulfill their mission in the world, viz., to infuse a Christian spirit and Christian values into the attitudes, customs, laws, and structures of society (AA 13).

In summary, light in Christian spirituality is a manifestation of God's active presence and power. It represents, among other things life, grace, truth, faith, wisdom, holiness, and prophetic witness. In short, light stands for all that enlightens humanity's path to God.

See also DARKNESS, DARK NIGHT; FAITH; ILLUMINATION, ILLUMINATIVE WAY; PRESENCE, PRESENCE OF GOD; REVELATION(S); TRUTH.

Bibliography: O. Piper, "Light, Light and Darkness," *The Interpreter's Dictionary of the Bible,* ed. G. Buttrick (New York: Abingdon, 1962) 130–132. J. Lecuyère, "Lumière," *D.Spir.,* vol. 9, cols. 1142–1183.

BARBARA O'DEA, D.W.

LITURGICAL MOVEMENT

The liturgical movement is the designation given to regularly recurring efforts of scholars and pastors alike to rejuvenate the Church's life of prayer. The modern liturgical movement dates from the work of Dom Prosper Guéranger (1805–1875) of the French Benedictine abbey of Solesmes to reform the Church's worship through the careful choreography of rites and the recovery of chant. While Guéranger's energies tended to be archeological, Dom Lambert Beauduin (1873–1960) of Mont César in Belgium gave the movement a decidedly pastoral emphasis. Inspired by the *motu proprio* of Pius X (*Tra le sollecitudini*, 1903), Beauduin worked for active participation in worship as the fundamental means of deepening the life and faith of the community, the Body of Christ.

The beginning of the North American liturgical movement is generally identified with Virgil Michel, O.S.B. of St. John's Abbey, Collegeville, Minnesota. After studies in Europe, where he met Beauduin, Michel returned to the States in 1926 and founded *Orate Fratres* (later *Worship*), which served as "house organ" for the North American liturgical movement until the Second Vatican Council. Michel is credited with joining liturgy and just living as correlative and indispensable aspects of the Christian life. Through national study weeks, liturgical retreats, clergy education, translation and publication of the best of European scholarship, the establishment of institutes and summer schools of liturgy, and preparation of liturgical-catechetical materials, the liturgical movement swelled to thousands, thanks to the efforts of H. A. Reinhold, Martin Hellriegel, Godfrey Diekmann, O.S.B., Michael Mathis, C.S.C., Gerald Ellard, S.J., Reynold Hillenbrand, Mary Perkins Ryan, William Busch, and others.

The chief goals of the movement—the reform of all the rites to facilitate full, conscious, and active participation within the assembly, each one according to his or her role; the rediscovery of the whole community as co-offerers; the promotion of liturgical education, in the first instance in seminaries—were adopted in the Constitution on the Sacred Liturgy of Vatican Council II. With this official recognition, the liturgical movement as such has ceased to exist, yet future decades will continue to demand understanding and implementation of conciliar reforms, chiefly through catechesis of rites and their underlying theology.

See also BODY OF CHRIST; LITURGY; SACRAMENTS; VATICAN II.

Bibliography: K. Hughes, *How Firm a Foundation: Voices of the Early Liturgical Movement* (Chicago: Liturgy Training Publications, 1990). V. Funk, "The Liturgical Movement," *The New Dictionary of Sacramental Worship,* ed. P. Fink (Collegeville, Minn.: Liturgical Press/Glazier, 1990) 695–715.

KATHLEEN HUGHES, R.S.C.J.

LITURGICAL PRAYER
See LITURGY; SACRAMENTS; SCRIPTURE.

LITURGICAL YEAR
See LITURGY.

LITURGY

Definitions

The Greek term *leitourgia* refers to a work or action performed by a people in public, usually according to a prescribed ritual. The Greek term for "worship," *latreia,* is wider and has a number of meanings, including rites instituted and regulated by predetermined laws, ritual duties, acts of reverence and devotion to acknowledge and offer homage to God (or the gods), divine service, or the offering of self in service to others. The Septuagint uses *leitourgia* to mean public religious service offered to God by priestly officials. The term is not used in the same way in the New Testament, which emphasizes Christ's paschal sacrifice as the once-for-all acceptable offering (Hebrews), interior worship "in Spirit and truth" (Jn 4:24), or the offering of self in service to others (Rom 12:1). Most generally the Scriptures refer to specific rites, e.g., Passover, synagogue worship, baptism, or the breaking of bread, not to liturgy in general. The term will reappear in postapostolic literature, but the usage is not uniform. The *Didache* (14) refers to Eucharist specifically, a usage that continues in many Eastern Rites.

In the Western Church, liturgy includes all the sacraments (including Eucharist), the Liturgy of the Hours (sometimes called the Divine Office), funerals, the rites for religious profession, ordination, the blessing of persons (abbots, abbesses), as well as the consecration of persons (virgins) and things (churches). Liturgy is celebrated during seasons of the year (e.g., Advent, Christmas, Lent, Easter) on special feasts (e.g., solemnities of the Lord, of the Blessed Virgin, the saints, patron saints' days) or throughout the rest of the year (sometimes called Ordinary Time) according to daily (e.g., Morning or Evening Prayer) and weekly rhythms (Sunday Eucharist), most usually in a specified church space (sometimes called the liturgical environment) through the use of texts (biblical and liturgical), symbols, gestures, actions, and appropriate liturgical music. Liturgy is often called the "public or official prayer of the Church." More common at present is the use of the term "Church at prayer," because it designates the communal dynamism inherent in liturgical engagement.

Contemporary Descriptions

The following descriptions of liturgy are drawn from 20th-century Church documents and the contemporary liturgical movement. The strong Christological and ecclesial roots of liturgy are reflected in the writings, among others, of Dom Lambert Beauduin (1873–1960), who defined the liturgy as the cult of the Church, and Dom Odo Casel (1886–1948), who maintained that the paschal mystery itself is experienced through the liturgy, in which Christ himself is present and acts through the Church while the Church acts with him. The Reformed theologian Jean-Jacques von Allmen states that Christ pursues his saving work by the operation of the Holy Spirit through the liturgy, which is the epiphany of the Church. The Lutheran theologian Peter Brunner notes the dialogic dynamism of liturgy by stating that liturgy is God's service to humans and humans' service to God, and that at liturgy the Lord speaks to us through his holy word and we speak to God through prayer and songs of praise. The Methodist theologian James White asserts that, called from the world, we deliberately seek to approach reality at its deepest level by encountering God through Jesus and by responding to this awareness. The Orthodox theologian Alexander Schmemann (1921–1983) states that "the purpose of worship is to constitute the Church . . . to express the Church as the unity of that Body whose Head is Christ . . . and 'with one mouth and one heart' [to] serve God, since it was only such worship which God commanded the Church to offer" (*Introduction to Liturgical Theology,* London: Faith Press, 1966, pp. 19–20). The American Episcopal theologian Marianne Micks emphasizes the anamnetic quality of liturgy (i.e., as remembrance of the paschal mystery) and thus divides her book *The Future Present* (New York: Seabury, 1970) into "summoning the future" and "shaping the present." The American Roman Catholic liturgical theologian Edward Kilmartin states that "liturgy is primarily the exercise of the life of faith under the aspect of being together 'in the name of Jesus' for the realization of communion, the sharing and receiving, between God, community and individual, in a coordinated system of ministerial services [and that] the Christian obligation to worship in common at regular intervals is based primarily on the need to exercise one's faith in an explicit and social way, to affirm one's fidelity to God, to self, and to others in a communal setting, in order to gain the support to maintain this fidelity in the whole of one's life" (*Christian Liturgy*, Kansas City: Sheed and Ward, 1988, p. 77).

The moral and spiritual consequences of liturgical participation are emphasized by a number of authors, including Jean Corbon, who writes that "if the Lord of glory has transfigured us, then we must now radiate him in our kenosis. The power of the Spirit has configured us to the body of Jesus; it must now manifest in our mortal flesh the power of his resurrection" (*The Wellspring of Worship*, p. 139). Much contemporary American writing on an integral notion of the way liturgy influences all aspects of Church life, particularly the intrinsic relationships between liturgy, spirituality, social justice, and mission, receive inspiration and guidance from the work of pioneers in the liturgical movement earlier in this century, such as Virgil Michel (1890–1938).

In his encyclical on the sacred liturgy, *Mediator Dei* (1947), Pius XII declared that the liturgy is the continued exercise of the priestly office of Christ, the public cult that Christ the Redeemer offers to the Father and the Church offers to the Father through Christ, and the public cult of the whole Mystical Body, Head and members (MD 3). The Constitution on the Sacred Liturgy of Vatican II describes liturgy as "an exercise of the priestly office of Jesus Christ. In the liturgy the sanctification of [human beings] is manifested by signs perceptible to the senses, and is effected in a way which is proper to each of these signs; in the liturgy full public worship is performed by the Mystical Body of Jesus Christ, that is, by the Head and His members" (SC 7). Through the liturgical exercise of Christ's priesthood, the liturgy aims toward "the sanctification of [human beings] and the glorification of God" (SC 10). The constitution also states that "the lit-

urgy is the summit toward which the activity of the Church is directed; at the same time it is the fountain from which all her power flows" (SC 10). The document cites the prayer over the gifts from the Evening Mass of the Lord's Supper to assert that through the liturgy "the work of our redemption is accomplished" (SC 2).

The following six elements, which are found in every act of liturgy, may be said to be constitutive of the phenomenon of liturgy. Liturgy is a corporate work done in faith (conversion and ecclesiology are operative here), at which the proclamation of the word of God takes place (through readings, responses, homily, and intercessions), ritualizing communal participation in the paschal mystery of Jesus past, present, and future (thus in both memory and hope), in a patterned experience of ritual prayer (including speaking, listening, movement, song, and silence), according to a calendar rhythm in time (especially feasts and seasons), in a prayer that is essentially Trinitarian in terms of who is addressed and how the Trinity actualizes and effects the liturgical act.

Because the present reformed liturgy contains flexibility within liturgical rites in terms of choices of scriptural and liturgical texts, a wide range of possibilities for music to accompany the rites, and the possibility of composing invitations to pray (as at the penitential rite at Mass), or intercessions (at every Liturgy of the Word, including the Hours), or commentary on what is taking place (among other things), much attention now focuses on preparing and planning liturgical celebrations to enhance a chief aim of the present liturgical reform, namely, that the assembly "be led to that full, conscious, and active participation in liturgical celebrations which is demanded by the very nature of the liturgy" (SC 14).

Relating Liturgy and Spirituality

The scientific study of liturgy is an integrative discipline, since a number of factors come to bear on describing and analyzing it as an experienced phenomenon. The following five approaches taken together comprise important aspects of liturgical study in general and are also important methodologically for establishing the relationship between liturgy and spirituality: pastoral studies, history, theology, spirituality (in the sense of living the Christian moral life), and the influence of social sciences.

1. Liturgy can be regarded as a branch of pastoral theology in the sense that it concerns reflection on enacted faith, that is, on the way the Church articulates and actualizes its faith in the triune God, and as God both actualizes the liturgy and is discovered in liturgical rites. Here a classical description of theology as the articulation of one's reflection on the faith and action of the Church is operative, especially since expressing faith and acting in faith in the Church constitute part of Christian spirituality. Because the postconciliar liturgy aims at active engagement in the rites, this part of liturgical study would include a consideration of planning and the conduct of liturgy in such a way that active participation is realized. In contrast to the highly rubrical approach to liturgy that preceded Vatican II, the shape of the reformed liturgy fosters a spirit of devotion that avoids cultic self-consciousness, rubrical scrupulosity, extrinsicism, or a functional approach to rites. The present rites lend themselves to emphasis on the proclamation of the word, involvement of a variety of ministers, and qualitative participation of the whole assembly, among other things, which factors are oriented toward the assembly's renewed engagement in the mystery of God.

2. Historical study of the evolution of liturgical rites is helpful in order to differentiate what is constitutive from what is peripheral in liturgical forms, to uncover pluriform liturgical usages within the same Roman rite as well as the evolution of various non-Roman, Western liturgical rites (e.g., Gallican, Mozarabic, Ambrosian). In addition, historical study of Eastern as well as Western rites can help to disclose important meanings inherent in the liturgy that may well have been eclipsed in Western euchology or study, e.g., the importance that the East has classically placed on the epiclesis, the invocation of the Holy Spirit, as part of blessing prayers such as the Eucharistic anaphora. A historical study of the relationship between liturgy and spirituality in both the East and the West can help to mark where and how liturgical rites were comprehended and appreciated as privileged means for experiencing God in the Church at communal prayer and in fostering deeper commitment to lead the Christian life as an essential consequence of celebration.

3. A theological explanation of what occurs in the divine-human act of liturgy and how the Church's liturgical prayer provides an important source for articulating its belief about what is accomplished in the liturgy (often called "liturgical theology"). The theological explanation of liturgy, therefore, concerns Christian worship as a phenomenon, as distinguished from other sources of theological inquiry, e.g., conciliar teachings. The classical adage *lex orandi, lex credendi* articulates briefly that what the Church believes is principally derived from what it prays, that is, the rites of the liturgy, especially Scripture and its euchological (i.e., prayer) texts. A proper interpretation of such data and the accompanying general instructions to all the revised rites require that important categories of theological inquiry and theological method influence how such data is interpreted. These categories include ecclesiology (e.g., the local Church at prayer); Christology (principally a soteriological understanding of liturgy); the Trinity (how the three Persons in God are operative in and actualize the act of liturgy); theological anthropology (the rationale for the necessity of liturgy and the meaning of divine grace operative in it); exegesis (scientific interpretation, particularly of biblical

texts); and catechetics (how the liturgy relates to handing on the faith and to Church teaching and vice versa). In addition, the symbols, gestures, music, and environment for liturgy require attention and analysis (see no. 5 below).

4. Reflection on the life commitment inherent in celebrating liturgy and derived from the liturgy serves to draw out implications of liturgical participation where implications mean living the Christian moral life. In particular, this approach draws on an appreciation of the eschatological nature of liturgy, since liturgical celebration always looks beyond itself for its complete realization in the kingdom and implies a requisite challenge to the present status quo because liturgy celebrates and establishes God's kingdom already present. Implicit in liturgy is the notion that communities already converted to the gospel in the Church continually engage in liturgical actions in order to be more fully transformed and to grow more fully in the life of God (deification). Initial conversion to the gospel is thus articulated in rites (of initiation) that lead to deepened conversion (ritualized in Eucharist, penance, anointing of the sick, etc.) and continual transformation in the Christian life. Thus communal and individual self-transcendence is understood to be constitutive of worship. Concomitant with liturgical celebration is growth in the values of the kingdom and in the life of virtue.

5. The comparatively recent influence of patterns of research from the social sciences has aided in determining the pluriform meanings expressed through liturgy, especially but not exclusively through nonverbal means of communication, e.g., symbol, gesture, movement, music. Here insights from sociology, psychology, phenomenology, and ritual studies, among other disciplines, can aid in the interpretation of what occurs in the liturgical community at liturgy (sociology), in exploring the meaning of the many and pluriform images of God inherent in the liturgy and

an appropriation of these images by an individual and a community (psychology), and how the actual experience of liturgy vis-à-vis what the ritual books describe comprises a proper theological source for inquiry (phenomenology). The comparison of Christian liturgy with other forms of ritual behavior (ritual studies) helps to disclose both the similarity and differences between Christian liturgy and the rites of other religions and nonreligious rituals.

Liturgical Year

The Constitution on the Sacred Liturgy of Vatican II states that "Holy Mother Church is conscious that she must celebrate the saving work of her divine Spouse by devoutly recalling it on certain days throughout the course of the year. Every week, on the day which she has called the Lord's day, she keeps the memory of His resurrection. In the supreme solemnity of Easter she also makes an annual commemoration of the resurrection, along with the Lord's blessed passion. Within the cycle of a year, moreover, she unfolds the whole mystery of Christ, not only from His incarnation and birth until His ascension, but also as reflected in the day of Pentecost, and the expectation of a blessed, hoped-for return of the Lord. Recalling thus the mysteries of redemption, the Church opens to the faithful the riches of her Lord's powers and merits, so that these are in some way made present at all times, and the faithful are enabled to lay hold of them and become filled with saving grace" (SC 102). As is true of all liturgy, an understanding of the liturgical year is based on understanding how the paschal mystery is experienced in and through the act of liturgy. While the saving events of Christ's incarnation, obedient life, suffering, death, resurrection, and ascension happened once for all for our salvation, they are also operative for the present Church and are experienced in a unique but not exclusive way through liturgy. By their nature these saving mysteries that happened once in historical time also transcend historical time in the sense that they are able to be experienced here and now. They perdure as saving events; they are not repeated or reenacted in the liturgy. Once-for-all events that occurred in saving history are thus regarded as transtemporal and metahistorical in that they are also annually appropriated and fully experienced at particular feasts and seasons such as Easter and Christmas.

Because the salvation experienced in the present liturgy is of these very same saving mysteries, the term "actualization of the paschal mystery" is particularly useful to describe what occurs at liturgy. The theological and spiritual significance of the liturgical commemoration of the paschal mystery is that these saving mysteries of Christ offer the faith perspective through which believers deal with, and give meaning to, the fundamental mysteries of human life and salvation, particularly the mysteries of vocation, suffering, and death. The actualization of Christ's paschal mystery in the liturgical assembly underscores intrinsic ecclesiological aspects of the liturgical year. Times, feasts, and seasons for celebration are observed so that through the liturgy the Church can be drawn into Christ's paschal mystery. The second memorial acclamation during the Eucharistic Prayer exemplifies this succinctly:

Dying you destroyed our death,
rising you restored our life.
Lord Jesus, come in glory.

The first and original feast day to evolve in the liturgical year when the paschal mystery was actualized in its fullness is Sunday. In the present Sacramentary, Preface IV for Sundays in Ordinary Time appropriately articulates the juxtaposition of the memorial of the paschal mystery with the Church at prayer on the Lord's day:

By his birth we are reborn.
In his suffering we are freed from sin.

By his rising from the dead we rise to
everlasting life.
In his return to you in glory
we enter into your heavenly kingdom.

This understanding of memorial establishes that the liturgical year primarily concerns our experience and continual appropriation of Christ's dying and rising. Thus the liturgical year does not recount a biography of Jesus; rather, in liturgical celebration the Church enters into the saving events that make up the paschal mystery (past, present, and yet to come) and is transformed by them. Thus liturgical memorial is never merely a present experience of Christ's past saving mysteries. It is also future time experienced now ("thy kingdom come") and the eternal future of God invoked to bring chronological time to an end. Celebrations of feasts and seasons concern the impact on the present of redemptive time, both past and future.

The liturgical year comprises a series of commemorations of the paschal mystery in time according to the cycles of nature (seasons), of human life (birth, rites of commitment, death), and of chronological time (year, week, day). The celebration of annual seasons in the liturgical year (Lent-Easter, Advent-Christmas-Epiphany) derive from the annual repetition of the seasons in nature and the cosmic phenomena of solstice and equinox, darkness and light, specifically at Christmas (the sun returns) and Easter day (the date being established by computation based on the moon). Thus the darkness of winter is the essential context for Advent-Christmas-Epiphany, and the renewal of nature in the spring is the essential context for celebrating Lent-Easter. What was accomplished once for all through the paschal mystery is experienced again and again and continually appropriated "in the year of our Lord."

The Church's liturgical celebration of central feasts and seasons consists in the celebration of the Liturgy of the Hours and of the sacraments where sacraments are particularly important means of articulating the full meaning of the observance of the liturgical year. Specifically, Christian initiation at the Easter Vigil articulates how the Church understands itself as the community that derives its identity from the paschal observance. To ritualize this at Easter with sacraments of initiation exemplifies how the paschal mystery is experienced and appropriated by the Church in every age. A central theological and spiritual understanding of Christmas is that the Word became flesh so that the human race could be deified in and through Christ. Specific reference to our experience of the divine-human interchange in the incarnation is aptly expressed in the opening prayer of Christmas day:

> Lord God,
> we praise you for creating man
> and still more for restoring him in Christ.
> Your Son shared our weakness:
> may we share his glory.

In addition, the third preface for Christmas reads:

> Your eternal Word has taken upon himself our human weakness,
> giving our mortal nature immortal value.
> So marvelous is this oneness between God and man
> that in Christ man restores to man the gift of everlasting life.

Yet the liturgical commemoration of the incarnation of the Word occurs both at the Liturgy of the Hours and at the Eucharist, with the Eucharistic celebration underscoring the essentially paschal overtones of the incarnation. Christ's incarnation leads to his death, resurrection, and ascension. The references to the celebration of Christmas as "the beginning of our redemption" (prayer over the gifts, Christmas Vigil Mass) and to "the child born today . . . the Savior of the world" (prayer after Communion, Christmas Day) help to bring out this understanding.

Liturgy of the Hours

The Constitution on the Sacred Liturgy states that Christ continues "His priestly work through the agency of His Church . . . not only by celebrating the Eucharist, but also in other ways, especially by praying the divine Office" (SC 83). (The term "divine Office" originally meant the obligation of clerics, i.e., not monks, to pray the Hours.) This important nonsacramental, liturgical prayer traces its roots to the fundamentally biblical prayer of the Jewish synagogue. Its Christian forms have evolved "by tradition going back to early Christian times . . . so that the whole course of the day and night is made holy by the praises of God" (SC 84). The particular contribution of the Vatican II reform of the Hours is the restoration of their celebration to the whole praying Church, especially the chief Hours of Morning Prayer and Evening Prayer (SC 100), and the restoration of the traditional sequence of the Hours so that "they may once again be genuinely related to the time of the day at which they are prayed" (SC 88).

The Liturgy of the Hours consists of a pattern of scriptural and scripturally inspired prayer that includes the following major elements in the present Roman rite: a hymn; psalms and scriptural canticles, with accompanying antiphons that emphasize some aspect of the particular psalm or canticle to be prayed or the feast being celebrated; Scripture proclamation and response, plus a nonscriptural reading and response at the Office of Readings; the Canticles of Zechariah and Mary at Morning Prayer and Evening Prayer, respectively; intercessions; the Lord's Prayer; collect; final blessing and dismissal.

This form of liturgical prayer evolved over time from the synagogue, through Christian prayers of private devotion, to two related but distinct forms: ecclesiastical (for parish or cathedral celebration) and monastic (proper to monasteries), and then a merging of these two traditions, a codification in the Breviary of the Council of Trent (1568), and the present revision from Vatican II, which allows for adaptation to suit the variety of Church communities that pray the Hours. The Liturgy of the Hours reflects the classic admonition of St. Paul to "pray without ceasing" (1 Thess 5:17). The intent of the Hours is to foster the true spiritualization of one's existence by giving voice to the praise of all creation and the thanks of the believing Church for creation and redemption. The Liturgy of the Hours is best understood as giving shape, voice, and specificity to the inarticulate and hopefully ceaseless praise of God offered by believers throughout their lives. It is a focal but not unique time of offering praise and thanks to God. It is also a privileged but not exclusive time of God's self-disclosure to the community of the redeemed. Thus the celebration of the Hours underscores a fundamentally incarnational approach to prayer and spirituality, an approach that is intrinsic to all liturgy.

The Hours are classically divided into prayer offered seven times a day: the Office of Readings, having the character of a night Office, with more generous portions of Scriptures proclaimed and psalms prayed, formerly called Matins or Vigils; Morning Prayer, formerly Lauds, meaning "praise"; Midmorning, Midday, Midafternoon Prayer, formerly called Terce, Sext, and None, respectively, and now subsumed under the name Daytime Prayer; Evening Prayer, formerly Vespers, meaning "evening"; and Night Prayer, formerly Compline, to signify "completion" at the end of the day.

In both the ecclesiastical and monastic forms, Morning and Evening Prayer are considered "the two hinges on which the daily Office turns; hence they are to be considered as the chief hours" (SC 89). The cosmic symbolism of the dawning of a new day and the setting of the sun is of central importance in emphasizing the meaning of these Hours of prayer. The theological and spiritual themes at Morning Prayer include commemoration of Christ's resurrection, praise for creation and redemption, and the dedication of a new day in the Lord's service. At Evening Prayer the themes include thanksgiving for Christ our light (sometimes ritually expressed in lighting lamps as evening falls), reflection on his passion and burial, thanksgiving for the events of the day, and asking forgiveness for misdeeds.

As early as Hippolytus (ca. 215, at Rome), the Daytime Hours were given the Christological interpretation of recalling the hour when Christ was nailed to the tree of the cross (Terce), when he was fastened to the cross (Sext), and when blood and water flowed from his wounded side (None). Prayed at the end of the day, Night Prayer is usually more meditative in tone and briefer than the other Hours. Traditionally Psalms 4, 91 and 134 were assigned to this Hour, along with other fixed texts, so that, especially in monastic and mendicant practice, it could be prayed by heart. Night Prayer concludes with one of four sung antiphons in honor of the Blessed Virgin.

Contemporary scholarship and liturgical legislation emphasize the nature of the Hours as an important prayer of the whole Church. Like all liturgy, the Liturgy of the Hours is the prayer of those assembled as the Body of Christ, the Church, in order to experience Christ's redemption more fully by the power of the Holy Spirit. Church communities that have utilized the Hours as a major part of their communal prayer include monks in monasteries (e.g., both male and female Benedictines, Trappists, Cistercians, etc.) as well as vowed (male and female) religious of the mendicant traditions (e.g., Dominicans and Franciscans). While ordained diocesan clergy were deputed to pray the Office *for* the Church, a more traditional understanding of this obligation derives from their presiding at the celebration of the Hours for the Church (e.g., parish) community.

Historical scholarship has also emphasized that various forms of Divine Office evolved, reflecting the nature of the communities engaged in praying the Hours. In the present revision of the Hours, this variety is respected within a stability of liturgical structure comprising the component elements of the Hours. Adaptations of the present Liturgy of the Hours include the hymns to be sung at the beginning of each Hour; the distribution of the psalms over a two-, three-, or four-week cycle; the more frequent use of specific psalms at certain Hours (e.g., Psalm 51 at Morning Prayer and Psalm 141 at Evening Prayer); the use of psalm prayers and the distribution of readings at the Office of Readings and Morning and Evening Prayer (with monasteries often composing a *lectio continua* for Morning and Evening prayer and a wider selection of biblical and nonscriptural lessons for the Office of Readings).

As a stable form of ritual prayer, the Hours invite participants to communal self-transcendence in order to reflect the needs of the whole Church in its praying of the Hours and to appreciate the value of a structured, repetitive, biblically based form of prayer. Recourse to this ritual prayer invites communities to proclaim and participate in Christ's salvation for the life of the world. Christians engage in the Hours principally to give voice to what it means to live the Christian life in the world rather than to step out of time to shun the world. This nonsacramental, liturgical prayer offers the praying Church important opportunities to "sanctify time," in the sense of joining and giving voice to Christ's eternal intercession at the right hand of the Father (e.g., through the petitions at Morning and Evening Prayer). The Hours help Christians articulate how God is discovered in all of life and to bring to the celebration of the Hours the needs of the whole world. This prayer is meant to aid Christians to "pray without ceasing" and to avoid a dichotomy that separates experiencing God in common prayer from discovering God outside liturgy and experiencing God in the rest of life. As a communal prayer it also gives expression to the identity of the community of the baptized as the community of the redeemed seeking its fulfillment in the kingdom of God. The Liturgy of the Hours thus stands firmly within the tradition of Christian spirituality in the sense that it is a prayer that derives from human life, uses the Scriptures as its fundamental inspiration, is offered by the believing Church, according to a recognized form of ritual prayer that leads to living life in response to the salvation and sanctification experienced in it.

See also ANTHROPOLOGY, THEOLOGICAL; BAPTISM; BODY OF CHRIST; CELEBRATION; CHRIST; CHURCH; CONVERSION; EUCHARIST; FORGIVENESS; GRACE; JUSTICE; MARRIAGE; PASCHAL MYSTERY; PENANCE, PENITENCE; PREACHING; SACRAMENTS; SCRIPTURE; SYMBOL.

Bibliography: J. Corbon, *The Wellspring of Worship,* trans. M. O'Connell (New York: Paulist, 1988). G. Guiver, *Company of Voices. Daily Prayer and the People of God* (New York: Pueblo, 1988). C. Jones et al., eds., *The Study of Liturgy* (London: SPCK, 1978). J. Jungmann, *Christian Prayer Through the Centuries,* trans. J. Coyne (New York: Paulist, 1978). A.-G. Martimort, ed., *Principles of the Liturgy,* The Church at Prayer 1, trans. M. O'Connell (Collegeville, Minn.: Liturgical Press, 1987); *The Liturgy and Time,* The Church at Prayer 4, trans. M. O'Connell (Collegeville, Minn.: Liturgical Press, 1986). T. Talley, *The Origins of the Liturgical Year* (New York: Pueblo, 1986).

KEVIN W. IRWIN

LITURGY OF THE HOURS

See LITURGY.

LOCUTION(S)

See EXTRAORDINARY PHENOMENA.

LONELINESS

See AGING; FEELINGS; SOLITUDE.

LORD'S PRAYER

The Lord's Prayer is rightly considered the model of all Christian prayer. Two versions of the prayer exist in the NT. In Matthew (6:9–15) the prayer comes in the midst of the Sermon on the Mount, as one example of the authentic piety along with almsgiving and fasting that is to characterize the disciple of Jesus. In Luke (11:2-4) the prayer leads off a longer instruction on prayer that is triggered by the disciples' request: "Lord, teach us to pray just as John taught his disciples" (11:1). Matthew's prayer is longer, consisting of the address ("Our Father in heaven") and seven petitions; Luke has the address ("Father") and five petitions.

It is probable that Luke's shorter, unadorned version is closer to the original prayer form used by Jesus and his early disciples. In any case, the Lord's Prayer in both Gospels gives us an insight into the spirit of the historical Jesus' own prayer. The style and content of the Lord's Prayer has similarities to the Jewish Qaddish and to some of the petitions of the Eighteen Benedictions, prayers used in the daily life of the synagogue and probably already in place at the time of Jesus.

Jesus' prayer is in harmony with the deepest currents of his teaching as presented in the Gospels. Its overall structure—homage to God followed by petitions of need—reflects the God-centeredness of Jesus' own spirit. Addressing God as "Father" was also characteristic of Jesus' piety and may reflect the use of the intimate address *Abba,* a distinctive use of Jesus absorbed by the early community (see Mk 14:36; Rom 8:15; Gal 4:6). The disciples share in this strong, loving bond by now addressing God together as Jesus does uniquely. Both versions praise God's name and pray for the coming of the kingdom. The coming of God's reign or kingdom was a keynote of Jesus' ministry, as each of the Synoptic Gospels portrays (see Mk 1:14–15 and par.). The plea for the coming of the kingdom gives to the Lord's Prayer its strong eschatological flavor.

The petitions of need are direct and basic, particularly in Luke's briefer version: a prayer for "bread," for forgiveness, and for deliverance from satanic evil. The translation of the adjective *epiousion* attached to "bread" in both versions is particularly difficult. It is a rare Greek word, used only here in the NT. It is usually translated "daily" but can also mean "tomorrow's" or "future." The future orientation of the latter two translations might also reflect an eschatological orientation: the prayer asks God to provide the sustenance needed as the day of the kingdom approaches. The petition for forgiveness (or "debts," a word that reflects Aramaic usage) accords fully with the strong reconciling thrust of Jesus' ministry as presented both in Matthew and Luke. The final petition asks God for deliverance from the "test"; the Greek word *peirasmon* is used in the NT several times to describe the "tests" that evil will inflict on the community at the end-time. Jesus himself endures such a "test" at the beginning of his ministry when he confronts Satan in the desert (see, for example, Mk 1:13). In the original prayer, therefore, the petition is not for deliverance from "temptation" in a generic or ordinary sense, but from that overwhelming assault of evil that could destroy the just on the final day. Matthew makes that clear by reinforcing the last petition with: "deliver us from the evil one" (Mt 6:13).

The evangelists absorb the basic contents of the Lord's Prayer into the context and style of their Gospels. Luke presents the prayer as a model for the disciples' own prayer. The directness of Jesus' words coincides with the illustrative parables and sayings that follow, urging the disciples to be trusting and persistent in their prayer, knowing that as a loving parent God will not let the pleas of his children go unheard (see Lk 11:5–13).

Matthew, too, presents the Lord's Prayer as a model, but one that is to stand in contrast both to the hypocrisy of those in the synagogue who pray "so that others may see them" and to the "babble" of the pagans, "who think that they will be heard because of their many words." The disciple is to pray directly, humbly, and "in secret" (Mt 6:5–8). Compared with Luke's version, however, Matthew does present a more elaborate, but still simple, rendition of the prayer. He adds "in heaven" to the address "Father," typical of a more formal address to God throughout his Gospel. The petition calling for the coming of the kingdom is reinforced with "your will be done, on earth as in heaven"; doing the will of God is a recurring Matthean motif and reflects the strong ethical emphasis of this Gospel, and of the Sermon on the Mount in particular. Matthew also intensifies the emphasis on forgiveness, both in the fifth petition and in the sayings appended to the conclusion of the prayer (6:12, 14–15): God's forgiveness of us is linked to our forgiveness of one another. Matthew's theology calls for symmetry between the world of the transcendent and the human arena: God's gracious forgiveness is to be reflected in extraordinary forgiveness and commitment to reconciliation on the part of the disciple. Therefore, the disciple is to leave the gift at the altar and first be reconciled (5:23–24), to love the enemy (5:43–48), to forgive seven times seventy times (18:21) and thereby to avoid the fate of the merciless steward who could not forgive his brother from the heart (18:23–35).

As reflected by its prominence in these two Gospels, it is likely that the Lord's Prayer became a central focus of early Christian worship. The *Didache* calls for recitation of the Lord's Prayer three times daily. From the earliest centuries, in both the Eastern and Western liturgies, the prayer was an integral part of the Eucharist. Its classic simplicity and its forceful distillation of Jesus' spirit and message make it unparalleled as an expression of Christian prayer.

See also ABBA (IN PRAYER); EARLY CHRISTIAN SPIRITUALITY; KINGDOM OF GOD; PRAYER; SCRIPTURE.

Bibliography: J. Jeremias, *The Prayers of Jesus* (Philadelphia: Fortress, 1978). E. LaVerdiere, "The Lord's Prayer in Literary Context," in *Scripture and Prayer,* ed. C. Osiek and D. Senior (Wilmington, Del.: Glazier, 1988). J. Petuchowski and M. Brocke, eds., *The Lord's Prayer and Jewish Liturgy* (New York: Seabury, 1978).

DONALD SENIOR, C.P.

LOVE

And we are put on earth a little space
That we may learn to bear the beams of love.
William Blake

Only by it, by love,
Life holds together and advances.
Ivan Turgenev

Poetry may best express the centrality and grandeur of love. At the least, it provokes one to pause and reflect on the meaning of love. In diverse ways love is a substantive theme informing almost every culture in the history of the world. The idea of love not only affects human behavior and religious thought and experience, but it also fuels the work of philosophers, writers, poets, musicians, and artists in every age. Anyone who presumed to offer a comprehensive and definitive treatment of love would have to be oblivious to its ineffable quality and to the extraordinary diversity of its expression and meaning.

Although Christians often hold Christianity to be the religion of love, the concept, in some form, holds a pivotal position in most world religions. In the ancient Chinese tradition, love or filial piety (*jen, hsiao*) has its roots in the very structure of the universe. This cosmic law (*tao*), in turn, is the foundation and norm for human behavior. Whether in the family or the wider community, adherence to the *tao* brings harmony, unity, and vitality. In Hinduism's *Bhagavadgītā*, the term *bhakti* means "to eat, partake of, enjoy," and by extension, "to revere, love." Arjuna, the hero of the *Gītā,* loves in a passionate and unqualified way the personal deity, Kṛsna. Through this intense love relationship, Arjuna comes to know Krsna, to enter into his nature, become one with him, and receive blessings. In Mahāyāna Buddhism, the *bodhisattva,* model of self-sacrificing love, embodies noble aspects of the Buddha. This figure is the supreme example of infinite compassion, the perfect personification of selfless and unconditioned love. Laying aside concern for his own salvation (*nirvāna*), he enters into the sufferings of others in order to bring them to freedom (see J. B. Long, *Encyclopedia of Religion,* ed. M. Eliade, New York: Macmillan, 1987).

Christian love has its distinctive qualities as well. Along with the meanings of love inherited from Hebrew culture and Hellenism, Christian love points specifically to the love of God revealed in Jesus Christ, who entered history and died out of love for creation. Throughout the history of Christianity, love has been a cornerstone of discourse on the spiritual life. One thinks of Augustine's treatment of *caritas;* Maximus the Confessor's *The Four Hundred Chapters on Love;* Richard of St. Victor's *The Four Degrees of Violent Love;* William of St. Thierry's *The Nature and Dignity of Love;* Bernard of Clairvaux's *On Loving God;* Richard Rolle's *The Fire of Love;* Francis de Sales' *On the Love of God,* not to mention the love poetry of medieval mystics such as Hadewijch of Antwerp and John of the Cross.

Our present task is to grow in our knowledge and appreciation of this noble tradition; to evaluate it critically in terms of contemporary experience; and to broaden our understanding of the meanings of love and their constitutive role in the spiritual life.

Definition and Divisions

Broadly stated, love is an affective disposition toward another person arising from qualities perceived as attractive, from instincts of natural relationship, or from sympathy, and resulting in concern for the welfare of the object and usually also delight in her/his/its presence and desire for the beloved's acceptance and approval. From a religious perspective, love is considered to be preeminently God's benevolent love. Traditionally, theologians such as Thomas Aquinas have made a further specification, attributing the name Love, taken in a personal rather than an essential sense, to the Holy Spirit (ST I, q. 37, a. 1). By association, God's love encompasses human love for God, human love for the neighbor, human love for creation, and self-love. Theologians have analyzed Christian love primarily in terms of the hierarchical *eros/ philia/agape* distinctions. *Eros,* distinguished by Plato in the *Symposium* as "vulgar" (longing for earthly, material pleasures) and "heavenly" (longing for the perfection of love in the world of ideas), comes to be associated in Christian theology with the lowest form of love—the acquisitive, sensual, passionate, sexual expressions of love. This love, characterized as selfish and grasping, has almost always carried a pejorative connotation. *Philia* refers to dutiful love, such as that between parents and children or the love of friendship. Some theologians lament the neglect of this aspect of love and counsel its inclusion as a step toward a more adequate conception of love. *Agape* is seen as the noblest form of love and a distinctive element of the Christian religion. Agapic love, or charity, is associated with God's love. Human love is agapic only to the extent that it imitates divine, agapic love. It is an altruistic, compassionate, and self-sacrificing form of love.

The relationship between *eros* and *agape* has often been one of conflict, tension, and mutual exclusivity. Unlike erotic love, which is said to be elicited by the attractive qualities of the loved object, agapic love is perceived as pure and selfless, a love that loves even enemies and objects or persons that are repulsive to the beholder. In the Christian tradition, erotic appetite for sensual pleasure or sexual union has often been seen as inimical to the spiritual life and incompatible with self-emptying or self-sacrificing love.

We have recently become aware of the narrowing effects of focusing the discussion on love so exclusively on the distinction between *eros* and *agape*. As a result of the given parameters of these terms, Christian "love" has been discussed almost exclusively in terms of "charity." In the *Dictionnaire de spiritualité,* under the entry "Love," one finds two words: "See Charity." The entry on "Charity" receives 183 columns. In addition, there is an entry of 11 columns under "Self-love," in which a legitimate love of self is acknowledged, but which defines "self-love" as an inordinate love for self that is subordinated neither to God nor reason. The reader leaves with a clear idea of the harmful effect of sinful or egotistical self-love on one's spirituality but with little notion of the enhancing function of authentic self-love.

In an attempt to place Christian love over against, and superior to, other ideas of love, e.g., Plato's concept of *eros,* Christian spirituality has often failed to explore adequately the wide spectrum of expressions of love and to capitalize on their connections. Divisions of love such as *eros/agape* or *amor concupiscentiae/amor amicitiae/ amor benevolentiae* (acquisitive love/ friendship/generous love), while helpful in some respects, can camouflage serious problems and contradictions. Such categories are often no longer adequate for an understanding of the spiritual life grounded in a holistic anthropology and a radically incarnational theology.

Biblical Understanding of Love

Old Testament

In the Septuagint, *agapaō* is the preferred word for the Hebrew *'ahab.* While this term refers only secondarily to God's relationship to the people, God is portrayed throughout the OT as the faithful lover of Israel, and the relationship between God and the human person is de-scribed in terms of love. In the OT the term *agapaō* refers primarily to human relationships, especially the mutual urge between the sexes, but also quite broadly to love of family and friends, and as a cornerstone of civic, social, and familial community life. Love (*'ahab*), often seen as the opposite of hate, has a strikingly pragmatic character. One *acts* on behalf of the loved one (Cant 8:6).

Love is the intense desire to see (Prov 8:17), run after (Isa 1:23), and cleave to (Deut 11:22) the beloved. The yearning for physical proximity is fueled by internal emotions of attraction (2 Sam 1:23), affection (Ps 34:13), and desire for unity. There is also a marked ethical dimension to the OT concept of love. Uncontrolled or false love is irresponsible and leads to grief.

The Hebrew valuation of sexual differences and marital love as special blessings is expressed in the creation stories (Gen 2:18ff.) and in the Song of Songs, which celebrates passionate love. The Song is the text par excellence that eschews the separation of human and divine love, and has become the textbook for all who seek to hold the two together (Guitton, p. 25). Here lovemaking conjures up sensual images of perfume, wine, spices, gazelles, honeycombs, pomegranates, candlelight, dancing, and glad songs.

Love imagery is an important motif in the prophets as well. Using the imagery of both husband and wife and parent and child, they portray Yahweh as a zealous, unfailing, and compassionate lover, one who will not withdraw because of infidelity or rejection. They characterize the divine-human relationship as a love affair or marriage, but in a corporate rather than individual sense. Israel is often presented as a faithless bride to whom Yahweh remains loving and faithful (Hos 1–3; 4:18; 11:1; Jer 2:2-25; 3:1-13; Ezek 16; 23:1-49; Isa 54:4-10; 62:4-5).

God's love in the OT is made visible in God's unfailing and loving activity in Israel's life—the Exodus, the gifts of the land, and the Torah. In Deuteronomy, God's love provides the motive for Israel to love and obey God (7:6–11). "You shall love the LORD, your God, with all your heart, and with all your soul, and with all your strength" (Deut 6:5). For Israel, love involved not only sensuality and affection, but also ethical love of neighbor and fidelity to the covenant and the law.

New Testament

In the NT, love continues as a central motif, encapsulating the whole content of the Christian faith. The term *eros* does not appear in the NT, but *philia* is used to refer to various types of love, primarily that between persons who are closely connected by blood or faith. *Agape* points in nearly every case to God's love for the human race or the love of the human race for God. Only one extrabiblical reference has been found (the title *agape* is attributed to the goddess Isis), underlining the innovative and distinctive role this term held in the Christian community. In both the Synoptic Gospels and the letters of Paul, *agape* incorporates and transforms the Hebrew notion of love (*'ahab/ḥesed*) and the various Greek understandings of love (*eros/philia*).

In the Synoptic tradition, *agape* is connected with the preaching of the kingdom that arrives in Jesus and also with the greatest commandment (Mt 22:34-40). Such love inevitably involves suffering (Lk 6:22ff.), and the disciples are asked to follow in Jesus' footsteps to the cross (Mt 10:37ff.).

For Paul, *agape* refers to the love of God in which God's election is made manifest in Jesus Christ's saving work (Rom 5:8). All God's activities as well as the rule for human behavior are described in the song of love in 1 Corinthians 13: "Love is patient, love is kind. It is not jealous, [love] is not pompous, it is not inflated, it is not rude, it does not seek its own interests, it is not quick-tempered, it does not brood over injury, it does not rejoice over wrongdoing

but rejoices with the truth. It bears all things, believes all things, hopes all things, endures all things" (13:4-7). God's love, which is forgiving, compassionate, and ultimately victorious over death, is sealed in its crowning act—the resurrection (see 2 Cor 5:19ff.).

The Johannine material takes the meaning of *agape* to its apogee, equating it with the essential nature of God (1 Jn 4:8, 16). Believers are included in this love that characterizes the nature, activity, and relationships of God (Jn 14). They are invited into the intimacy of love and friendship, into the very heart, of Trinitarian love (Jn 15–17).

In the NT, *agape* describes God's motive for creation; God's activity in the world; the model for divine-human relationships; and by participation, the love of humans for the neighbor, defined as friend and enemy alike (Rom 5:5). Paul's famous phrase "in Christ" describes human existence within the sphere of God's love, an existence in which one becomes a loving person like unto God (Gal 2:20). The innovation in NT *agape* involves a portrayal of God's love, made visible in Jesus, as the source and substance of a new, compassionate, and selfless love offered by Christians to all people (Lk 10:37).

Recent Developments
Vatican II

Pope John XXIII often expressed the desire that Vatican II might be "a spectacle of love." Indeed, it is accurate to say that the entire council was suffused with the spirit of love. Pope Paul VI stressed the Christocentric orientation of all Christian life, focusing the council on Christ, the supreme expression of God's love for creation. The Constitution on the Sacred Liturgy connects liturgical reform with fostering "unity of all who believe in Christ" (SC 1), the consummate goal of Christian love. The Dogmatic Constitution on the Church views the Church as the People of God, the

Mystical Body of Christ, a mystery of love that is related to Christ as bride.

Within this structure, members are to act collegially, creating and honoring bonds of peace, love, and unity. The Pastoral Constitution on the Church in the Modern World exhorts believers to "cherish a feeling of deep solidarity with the human race and its history" (GS 1, Flannery). The world, made free by the love of Christ, is to be embraced with love and compassion. Vatican II reflects the turn from primarily juridic concerns to a more biblical orientation that views love as the heart of ecclesial life.

More specific references to love are found in Chapter V of the Dogmatic Constitution on the Church, which speaks of the universal call to holiness in terms of love. Charity, "poured out into our hearts through the holy Spirit" (Rom 5:5), is the first and most necessary gift by which we love God and neighbor. It is love, "the bond of perfection and the fulfillment of the law" that "rules over all the means of attaining holiness, gives life to them, and makes them work" (LG 42). It is love that marks all true disciples of Christ.

Love is treated most explicitly in the various sections on marriage (LG 35; AA 11; GS 47–52). The Church rejoices that partnerships of love are nurtured in society and celebrates the God-given intimacy of married love. In the Pastoral Constitution on the Church in the Modern World, conjugal love is held up as a visible meeting of human and divine love. Authentic married love is caught up into divine love and models the love of God and of Christ.

In addition to seeing conjugal love as an eminently human, interpersonal love, Vatican II contributes to the battle against dualism by expressing the holistic dimensions of married love. This love enriches and confers dignity on both body and spirit, "ennobling their expressions as special ingredients and signs of the friendship distinctive of marriage" (GS 49).

While the conciliar documents do not enunciate the positive aspects of the erotic dimensions of human love in terms of the spiritual life, they do acknowledge the exalted way in which conjugal love bears witness, by its faithful love in joy and sacrifice, to the mystery of love shown by the Lord's death and resurrection (GS 52).

Perhaps the aspect of love most dominant in the conciliar texts is that of unity. In the Church; in single, married, and celibate life; in ecumenical concerns; in the liturgy; in all forms of ministry, love is experienced as the unifying force par excellence, a powerful gift that overcomes barriers to the unification of all aspects of creation in a love that surpasses understanding.

Moral Theology

St. Augustine's image of the two cities—the earthly city built by self-love and the heavenly city created by love of God—painted in stark opposition, preoccupied moral theology for centuries. Its starting point was the pervasive sinfulness in human life, and particularly in sexuality. Often the negative rather than the positive aspects of human love held pride of place. In the Middle Ages, St. Thomas Aquinas articulated a developed doctrine of the natural and the supernatural, stressing supernatural moral activity as alone sufficient for salvation. Morality became a two-tiered structure in which human, natural, earthly, moral behavior had no significant value for salvation. This schema explains in part the enduring theological emphasis on "charity," to the detriment of human love. With the emergence of a more unitary perspective in the recent past, moral theologians view reality in its totality as created and redeemed by God, and therefore source of divine revelation and bathed in grace. In this more encompassing view, all forms of authentic love are seen as holy because they participate in God's creative, redemptive love.

Moral theology had also been expressed almost exclusively in terms of law, issued and enforced by a God imaged as the supreme legislator. Bernard Häring's *The Law of Christ: Moral Theology for Priests and Laity* (3 vols.; Westminster, Md.: Newman, 1961–1963) is a benchmark that retrieves both the theological virtues as the foundation for the moral life and the importance of interiority over merely external observance. The vital motivating force of moral existence is presented in terms of an intimate relationship with God in Christ. Häring's work reflects a return to biblical sources that employ the imagery of the love of spouses and friends, covenant, and discipleship. In addition, Häring upholds the nobility, strength, and tenderness of natural love with its tendency to inflame and embrace the body-soul affections even as it is imbued, impregnated, and transformed by supernatural love. "Divine charity penetrates nature to its depths, subsumes and exalts it" (*Law of Christ*, 2:92). Häring regards the love of desire (*amor concupiscentiae*) as genuine love if in the object loved, in the *value-for-me*, one recognizes at least obscurely the *value-in-itself* and takes pleasure in it (*Law of Christ*, 2:87). Supernatural love is rooted in ordered, natural, human love. Even the erotic-sexual love of spouses must be animated by the charity that approaches the erotic through the spiritual (*Law of Christ*, 2:356).

Moral theologians continue to develop approaches to the moral life that supplement and correct an earlier overemphasis on law. What are the consequences for moral theology of imaging God as Love as well as Lawgiver? Themes of attraction, call, invitation, co-creation have emerged. We return to the truth that the law of God is above all the law of love that is poured forth and imprinted in our hearts by the Holy Spirit (Rom 5:5). In addition, the retrieval of the spiritual and mystical traditions that preserved the language and imagery of love functions as a corrective to moral theology's former extreme preoccupation with law, commandment, and sin.

Finally, employing the tenets of liberation theology, many feminist ethicists underline the centrality of love in ethics and love's inalienable connection to justice. Beverly Wildung Harrison and others envision love as a mode of action in contrast to past emphasis on static and passive qualities that equate spirituality with noninvolvement and passive contemplation. From this perspective, moral theology would focus on the power humans have to bring one another to life through acts of love, discovering in the process the opposing power one has to thwart another through lovelessness. The most basic works of love would be communication, caring, and nurturance—tending the personal bonds of the communities in which we live.

Psychology

Sigmund Freud (1856–1939) is said to have commented at the end of his career, "We really know very little about love." Many scholars in the fields of psychology and psychiatry continue to lament the paucity of research on a topic so important to human life. Recent work has focused on definitions of the concept and the psychosocial dimensions of love experience, but current methodologies struggle to investigate adequately the phenomenology or inner experience of love.

Freud located all aspects of the emotional life—desire, love, affection, friendship—in the libido, the channel for the projection into the external world of the forces of *eros*. Subsequent research has called into question Freud's reduction of all expressions of love to sexuality. Some point to him as one who robbed love of its multivalent meaning and mystery, and who eclipsed the concept of love as an altruistic act on behalf of the neighbor. But his pioneering work has profoundly affected the understanding of love in the West, especially his exposure of the illusions and misfirings of passionate love.

Carl Jung (1875–1961) provides a contrast to Freud in his appreciation of the importance of human religious needs. Jung recognized both the spiritual and instinctual dimensions of *eros,* identifying sexuality as an indisputably creative power that influences psychic life in profound ways.

In *The Art of Loving* (New York: Harper, 1956), psychoanalyst Erich Fromm examines love in the context of what he calls a universal, existential need for union. He identifies love as action rather than feeling, action that involves giving, care, responsibility, respect, and knowledge. He questions exclusively negative interpretations of self-love and denies any contradiction between genuine love of self (as opposed to narcissism) and love of others. The latter is not possible without the former, in his view.

Psychology has enhanced our understanding of human love, and many of its findings facilitate a more complete understanding of love. It has alerted us to the developmental aspects of human life, describing the movement from infantile or narcissistic love to sexual attraction and intimacy, and finally to a mature, other-centered love. Psychology has also called attention to the ways in which one is able to make responsible choices, thus helping to create and maintain one's existence in positive, loving ways. Most recently we have witnessed a turn from a singular preoccupation with intrapsychic models to those that are more interpersonal, such as object relations theory—a welcome development for the study of spirituality because it understands love as an eminently communitarian reality.

Recovery of the Tradition

An impetus to the recovery of a broader understanding of love in the spiritual life has been the retrieval of the spiritual tradition. Patristic, medieval, and modern texts, many of which are now available in reliable translation, are being studied by scholars and persons interested in spiritual growth. These masterpieces of the spiritual life reveal to modern readers a rich symbolism and profound knowledge of the understanding and practice of love. Especially noteworthy in this regard is the work of scholars such as Carolyn Walker Bynum, Jean Leclercq, Bernard McGinn, Margaret Miles and J. Giles Milhaven, who examine the roles of affectivity and bodiliness in the accounts of religious experience in the patristic, medieval, and modern periods.

Most theologians in the tradition made use of love language from daily life to describe God's love. But perhaps because human love is marred by sin, they emphasized the differences rather than the similarities between the experiences of this world and those beyond it. This lack of connection between human and divine loves is most obvious in the case of physical, sensual, sexual love, whose imagery is a cornerstone of the mystical tradition but whose reality in time has always been a victim of suspicion.

There have been exceptions to such dichotomous thinking. Although Augustine (354–430) feared the intensity of his own love of friends, he also revealed the anatomy of profound and touching relationships (*Confessions,* II.2; IV.4–6). The 11th and 12th centuries are notable for their fresh insights into the place of nature and the human person in the spiritual life. Anselm of Bec (1033–1109) struggled to find words to express his deep love for his friends (*Letters* 5, 11, 68–69). In his *Spiritual Friendship,* Aelred of Rievaulx wrote that "friendship is wisdom" and "God is friendship" in order to express the close relationship between the love of human friendship and the nature of God.

Bernard of Clairvaux (1090–1153) includes many kinds of love in his portrait of the spiritual life. Love of God begins with self-love and progresses through various stages of love of neighbor to love of God (*On Loving God,* 8–10). For Bernard, the spiritual journey is rooted in nature and uses the instruments of natural virtue to reach a supernatural end. From nature itself arises the inclination to turn to God.

Love has been seen throughout the tradition as the energy of the cosmos. Dante writes, "Love is the heartbeat of the whole universe. Everything participates in it according to its own special love, from simple bodies, to composite bodies, to plants, to animals, to man." (*Convivio*, 3.3.2–11). Teilhard de Chardin was one in our own time who raised questions about the separation of human loving from the cosmic plan of God. As human lovers, lost in each other, find themselves, so the loss of the universe in God will bring about its final fulfillment. Historical, embodied, spiritual love not only leads to divine love but actually participates in it. Attention to the many legitimate connections between human, cosmic, and divine love is part of the task of contemporary theology and spirituality.

Love and Spirituality

Language

We look to many arenas of human life in order to enrich and deepen our experience and understanding of love in the spiritual life. If we continue to use terms such as "erotic love," "passionate love," and "love of concupiscence" in an exclusively pejorative sense, we fail to acknowledge the existence of good as well as destructive *eros* and passion in one's love of self, others, and God. These terms no longer carry an exclusively negative connotation; for example, few would deny that the medieval mystics were passionate people, even though their meaning structures constrained them to define "passion" as a negative aspect of human life and to condemn it.

The meaning of love is revealed in different types of language. Biblical language, such as that in the Song of Songs, offers a wide range of images to talk about love. Theological language articulates the connection of all loves to God. Ascetic language alerts us to the risks and dangers of sin in our failure to love well. Philosophical language challenges us to think clearly about love and to argue reasonably for its place in the wider fabric of existence. The language of poetry and literature is often the most multivalent and powerful way to talk about love. Scientific language, such as that of biology and psychology, offers a window onto love that is more exacting and measurable—an important complement to the more evocative language usually associated with love. The error would be to cut off one or the other of these linguistic avenues and so truncate unnecessarily our potential to love well, to speak of love in all its diverse aspects, and to grow in our understanding of its meanings.

In addition, one must note the role of the fine arts—music, dance, sculpture, painting, etc.—in unveiling the power and nuance of love experience. Age-old images such as heart, fire/flame, marriage/spouse, lover, unity, breast and kiss are infused with new life and meaning in every era.

Inclusive Love

Like our forebears in the Christian faith, we are called to make sense of life in the Spirit in the context of our present experience. Any explication of "love" must take seriously the Bible, tradition, and our present circumstances. We are ill-advised to limit our discussion of love to one or even several categories. We might invoke Thomas Aquinas's principle that the more various the species in creation, the more adequately is God praised (ST I, q. 47, a.1). The more types of love we include in our discussion of the spiritual life, the more the total person participates in the life of God. The approach is cumulative or synthetic as well as analytic, inclusive rather than exclusive, horizontal rather than hierarchical.

Affectivity

Neglect of the theme of love stems in part from a skeptical and suspect attitude toward the emotions. Christian theology has too often regarded feelings with fear and ignorance, seeing them primarily as disruptive of the spiritual life. The recovery of a sense of the importance and dignity of emotion in the recent past, due in part to the advance of psychological studies and the women's movement, has contributed to a fuller appraisal of the role of emotion in the spiritual life. Scholars study affectivity as a complement and supplement to reason in cognitive theory. Theologians examine the affective domain as a channel providing access to meaning and value as well as to a kind of loving knowledge (wisdom) that emerges in commitment. Others examine the role of the passions in human life and the ways in which affectivity functions in relation to symbols and myth.

This newfound acknowledgment and appreciation of the role of affectivity in the spiritual life provides fresh insight into the intense emotion, longing, and passionate desire expressed by the mystics. Such study challenges one to become familiar with the "heart" dimension of human and religious experience—the poetic, moving, luring, ebullient side of life. Emotions are at the very core of existence, providing a system of values within which life either develops and grows or starves and stagnates.

Theological Spirituality

What are major theological principles grounding a new approach to the role of love in the spiritual life? The originating principle is found today, as in the past, in the phrase from the First Letter of John, "God is love" (1 Jn 4:8). God is the source, the way, the fullness of love. The intense love of the divine Trinitarian community is a paradigm for the love of all believers.

A second theological principle stems from the story in Genesis that recounts the creation of a good world by a generous, free, and loving God. All reality, though marred by sin, is of and in God. Creation in its myriad expressions is *imago Dei*, reflecting the infinite fullness of God and participating in the divine love that is the source of its creation and continued existence.

Incarnation takes the loving commitment of God to creation a step further. The loving goodness of all reality is revealed in this act of God's self-communication in the person of Jesus who enters creation and history, thereby sanctifying every particle of reality in a radical and definitive way. In the resurrection, love becomes the victor, robbing death of its sting forever.

Fourth, building on this recovery of creation/incarnation themes and recent psychological insight, theologians endorse a holistic anthropology. The German Jesuit Karl Rahner is representative of a way of thinking that draws intimate connections between the divine and the human, thereby undermining a kind of dualism that pits the human and the divine against each other. Spiritualities that exclude certain dimensions of human existence *a priori* are no longer satisfying or acceptable. Tradition has upheld a vision of the human person as *imago Dei*, a vision that continues to be embraced in ever more inclusive ways. The divine reflection in human life is recognized in all forms of goodness and love, whether in the lives of believers of all faiths, atheists, or agnostics. We have become more cautious about placing limits on the loving wisdom, power, and presence of God.

Grounding theology in the experience of community can also bridge the chasm between human and divine love. The stories of Christians reveal again and again how central to our spiritual lives are our many loves. God becomes visible in the love of lovers, of friends, of parents and children. Reciprocally, a theology that is true to this experience will assist us in our quest to find God in all things, to grow in our ability to love the other as other, to celebrate the divine goodness in loved objects or persons, to wish them well, and to set our own lives aside in order to bestow life on the other. Both cosmic and sacramental eucharists provide the communal setting in which to express unending gratitude for the gift of love.

Discernment is a final issue. One needs to distinguish carefully between human love that is authentic and that which is characterized by selfishness. Paul's hymn in 1 Corinthians 13 serves as a guide. One can judge the goodness of love by its fruits. We know that all human acts of love are a mix of altruism and egoism. Since love is relational, one might say that any loving relationship that moves one primarily toward God and toward behavior characterized by peace, patience, kindness, etc., involves love that is "of God." Inversely, relationships that lead primarily away from God and from loving behavior toward self and others may be characterized as sinful and, in a sense, not love at all. Care for this distinction prevents the error of eliminating a priori certain expressions of love as inimical to spiritual growth.

Conclusion

Theologians writing about the spiritual life are beginning to emphasize the connections between all forms of authentic human love and holiness. Because of creation and incarnation, all aspects of created reality, including authentic sensual, erotic, sexual love, are blessed. The experience of human love is the primary basis for all progress in the life of the Spirit. Human love is a prelude, a symbol, a foretaste of the fullness of complete love in God. Further, though incomplete and tainted by sin, human love is a true participation in the very life-giving love of God. We are called to be imitators of God in the fullness of our humanity.

In themselves, these loves are no longer seen as automatic impediments to sanctity, but rather as potential elements through which one may be called to the heights of sanctity. For many Christians, erotic, sexual love is a primary expression of a love that freely chooses to die to self on behalf of the other in imitation of Jesus. Of course, growth in the spiritual life involves growth in one's ability to recognize the inherently holy elements of human love and to discern good from sinful motives. Spirituality no longer regards various expressions of love as good or evil in themselves but rather asks about one's intentions; about whether one's loves lead toward or away from God, toward or away from radical justice for all creation. All love has the potential to enhance our apprehension of the divine and to participate in, and lead to, the infinite fulfillment of love in a God who is Love.

The Christian idea of love has to include both the erotic aspect, i.e., being drawn to desire something or someone precious and appealing, and the agapic aspect, i.e., loving someone whose value lies primarily in his or her relationship to God. Each has its role and is interconnected with the other. Even God's love can be said to involve eros and desire. The Christian God came not only to save sinners but also because this God perceives something valuable and appealing in creation, which, as imago Dei, is an extension of God and therefore attractive. One might say that God is eminently the One-Who-Desires, the One who wishes our happiness and union, the One who was willing to take on flesh and die so that ultimate union might be possible.

Practically, this means that every attempt, every success, at genuine love of any kind, as a human response to God's originating gestures of love, has the potential to be an intrinsic element of one's spirituality and a force for the life of the community. Called to endow existence with meaning, persons are cautioned against excluding any kind of love from one's spiritual life in an arbitrary manner. Rather, we nurture the vision that sees connections, that sees all genuine love as a locus of God's self-communication. Love of the neighbor next door, love of neighbor in distant lands, love of enemies, love of parents and children, sexual love, sensual love, love of kin, erotic love, self-sacrificing love, love of country, love of the earth, love of the cosmos—each has the potential to be godly and to lead us into loving intimacy with a God who calls us lovers and friends.

No doubt the debate about the meaning of love and its connection to the moral and spiritual life will continue to occupy Christian people, theologians, and Church leaders in the decades ahead. It remains to be seen whether the rehabilitation of certain forms of human love such as *eros* will succeed. But the challenge of taking seriously the experience, knowledge, and culture of love for contemporary women and men, and employing these data critically in our theology, is one that cannot be ignored. The profound and all-encompassing nature of love gives it a preeminent place in the Christian tradition. The genuine renewal of Church and society depends on our ability to connect all our loves with God.

See also AFFECT, AFFECTIVITY; BRIDAL MYSTICISM; COMPASSION; DESIRE; FRIENDSHIP; HOLY SPIRIT; IMAGO DEI; MARRIAGE, MYSTICAL; PASSION(S); PSYCHOLOGY, RELATIONSHIP AND CONTRIBUTION TO SPIRITUALITY; SEXUALITY; UNION, UNITIVE WAY; VIRTUE; WILL.

Bibliography: M. D'Arcy, *The Mind and Heart of Love* (New York: Holt, 1947). J. Guitton, *Human Love* (Chicago: Franciscan Herald Press, 1966). B. W. Harrison, *Making the Connections: Essays in Feminist Social Ethics,* ed. C. Robb (Boston: Beacon, 1985). C. S. Lewis, *The Four Loves* (New York: Harcourt, Brace & World, 1960). R. Haughton, *The Passionate God* (London: Darton, Longman & Todd, 1981). A Pieris, *Love Meets Wisdom: A Christian Experience of Buddhism* (Maryknoll, N.Y.: Orbis, 1988). S. Post, *A Theory of Agape* (Toronto: Associated University Presses, 1990). I. Singer, *The Nature of Love,* 3 vols. (Chicago: Univ. of Chicago Press, 1987). A. Soble, *The Structure of Love* (New Haven: Yale Univ. Press, 1989). C. Spicq, *Agape in the New Testament* (St. Louis: Herder, 1963). D. Williams, *The Spirit and Forms of Love* (New York: Harper & Row, 1968).

ELIZABETH DREYER

LUST

See DEADLY SINS.

M

MANTRA

See MEDITATION.

MARGINALIZED, THE

The term *margin* or *the margins* conveys four interlocking meanings: (1) a margin is a border line or limit, demarcating the words on a typed or written page from its edge; (2) its identity is established by way of negation, in and on the terms of its relation to the center; (3) it refers to the periphery, that space which is unimportant due to its distance from the center; (4) the margin is empty, being constituted by nothing.

The *marginalized* are those individuals or groups that have been cast to the edges or fringes of the social-symbolic order, the center, with its prevailing worldview. Those at the margins are not at home or are not in step with the status quo. It is difficult for them to "fit in" due to prevailing modes of being and perceiving in the world. The term is applied socially in relation to the center and to order, because those at the margins—the marginalized—are often viewed as living a borderline existence between order and chaos, usually on the verge of caving into the abyss of chaos.

The *alienated* and the *oppressed* are terms related to the *marginalized*. Alienation may be the result of specifically political dynamics. But *alienation* also bears emotional and affective connotations, as in the example of large segments of the young or the unemployed, who are frequently described as alienated. The oppressed are pushed to the margins by more active forms of violence, which makes of them victims as well.

Describing an individual or group as marginalized is a recent development, though the phenomenon that this nomenclature describes is, of course, not new. Who are the marginalized? Who are the people living at the margins? To these questions there is no simple, clear-cut answer.

The marginalized are those who live at the margins or edges, between the cracks, in the fissures of a society's center. Another word for the *center* is the *mainstream*. There are many reasons why marginalization occurs. It may result from a lack of financial resources, confining one to an economic status lower than that of the "middle," the mainstream. Some are marginalized because of their physical or mental abilities. Persons with mental and physical handicaps are cast to the margins in a world of "normal people," the "sane," and the strong. Individuals and entire groups are marginalized and alienated from the Roman Catholic Church: the divorced and remarried, resigned priests, single persons in parishes where the virtues of marriage and family are extolled in sermonizing week after week. Women in a "man's world" and homosexuals, who are usually viewed as unnatural or abnormal, are marginalized because of gender or sexual identity. Marginalization is often legitimatized on the grounds of differences in race or language.

The distinguishing factor in all such persons and groups is that they are understood to be different. Because of their difference they are "hard to place" in terms of what is judged as acceptable, regular, normal, or status quo. This element of difference often leads to an overwhelming sense of fatalism and powerlessness in the face of economic systems, political structures, or religious institutions. Those at the margins have little or no access to the power exercised by those who live at the center. Any access to power or influence that the marginalized may gain is far more limited than that of those who stand in the center. Consequently, the marginalized have little or no influence upon the "system," the status quo of Church or society, which, nonetheless, affects them even more than those at the center. In this context, many of those at the margins have no voice, no power to speak—at least not in the modes of discourse that prevail at the center.

There are two major approaches to the experience of marginalization from the perspective of Christian spirituality. It can be viewed as transitional and temporary, as a step or stage in the process of assimilation into prevalent cultural patterns, higher strata of the socioeconomic order, and dominant modes of perceiving and being at the center. From this perspective, the Spirit's work is understood to be discerned first and foremost in life at the center of Church and society. Here diversity of experience, multiplicity of context, and alternative perspectives and perceptions give way to what are judged to be more valuable: compromise, cohesion, unity, and the common good. A second approach to the experience of marginalization recognizes marginalization as a permanent factor in the existence of some persons and groups. Together with this there is a recognition of the epistemological priority of the experience of those at the margins. This

rests in the conviction that the life and ministry of Jesus were focused on those at the margins of religious and social institutions to such a degree that he himself identified with them unto death and into hell. In this view, Christ's Spirit is to be discerned in the struggle for liberation among those who have been cast to the margins of Church and society, making it possible to embrace marginalized existence itself as a primary locus of the Spirit's presence and action.

See also DISABILITY, THE DISABLED; POOR, THE; SOLIDARITY; WEAKNESS AND VULNERABILITY.

Bibliography: L. Boff, *Faith on the Edge: Religion and Marginalized Existence* (San Francisco: Harper & Row, 1989). R. Chopp, *The Power to Speak: Feminism, Language, God* (New York: Crossroad, 1989).

MICHAEL DOWNEY

MARRIAGE

Married Christians are invited to, and capable of, the fullest expression of the Christian life. Their spirituality is not of a lesser order than that of the nonmarried. While married people incorporate into their spiritual life many of the traditional disciplines of spiritual growth, e.g., fasting, prayer, and almsgiving, they also strive to embody *within their conjugal relationship* special emphases that contribute to their particular spirituality. Establishing appropriate parameters for describing these distinctive elements of spirituality is rooted in the Dogmatic Constitution on the Church of Vatican II, where we read, "Married couples and Christian parents should follow their own proper path to holiness by faithful love, sustaining one another in grace throughout the entire length of their lives" (LG 41).

For descriptive purposes, marital spirituality can be divided into four moments or phases, which can be seen as having both a chronological and a developmental dimension. But like the seasons of the year, these phases can also be appreciated as each coming in its own time without any priority of importance being assumed. Outlining the four, we note first the rootedness of marital spirituality in solitude or self-determination; second, its being formed or structured through the commitment central to the interpersonal covenant of Christian marriage; third, its fuller expression in the giving of life, or in more general terms, through generativity; and fourth, its fullest expression in gratitude, or to use a more explicitly Christian language, through its Eucharistic meaning.

Solitude

Every Christian stands before God and all other persons as a free, differentiated person who possesses a unique personality, distinctive ideas and feelings, and a purpose for being unlike any other created human being. In a discussion of marital spirituality, it is important to begin with the concept of "being alone," or the condition of solitude, because marriage, more than any other human relationship, demands intense and ongoing relationality—thus the traditional phrase "two in one." Our current understanding of this phrase invites attention to the retention of the "twoness" in the "oneness," giving rise to a creative tension in which neither individual is reduced in personhood into or under the other person. More precise, then, would be the phrase "two and one," which implies the preserving of individuality while affirming duality. This is no small point, for marriages that fail to reach their fullest personal and spiritual potential either "sin" on the side of too much togetherness or on the side of too much individuality. Healthy marital life combines a full measure of personal presence along with a deep, loving relationship with one's spouse. And unless the marriage is healthy for its participants, it will not be holy.

Biblically, marriage is shown as being a mirror image, a symbol, of the relationship between God and humanity. A similar spiritual theme, which applies to the relationship both with God and with a spouse in marriage, is that of maintaining individuality in the context of relationality. In marriage as in the spiritual life in general, individual personhood is not to be sacrificed for the sake of the relationship. Quite the opposite is appropriate: Married persons invest their individuality in the sharing or social structure, and further, they experience a fuller measure of individual personhood as they share. Implied here is relational and personal health. By this is meant the existence of self-possession or autonomy as a condition for the establishment of the relation structure. Healthy individuals make healthy relationships. And spiritual development occurs best when the individual possesses and takes responsibility for, first of all, his or her own spiritual life. A person does not depend on others to provide what he or she can provide. The idea of "giving oneself to the other" has value only when there is an adequate self to offer.

Other principles flow from this insistence on solitude as foundational. First, each marriage partner must respect the distinctive features of the other's personal and spiritual life (the distinction here between "personal" and "spiritual" life is for the purpose of understanding and discussion only; in actuality, the two aspects of the self are inseparable). This respect has both a passive and an active dimension. Passively, it means that one does not interfere with, criticize, question, or stand in the way of the unique spirituality of the other. This has obvious implications for so-called interfaith or ecumenical marriages.

The active side of respect includes an openness or willingness to learn from the spiritual orientation of the other. Assumed is this: If one genuinely loves the other for the sake of the other (a way of describing altruistic love), then one will also find opportunities for one's own growth within the other. We have much to teach each other of the richness of life, and those who may have the most to share are those deeply involved in each other's personal life-journeys. Marriage partners, therefore, are in a unique and privileged position to learn about life, about self, and about God from and through each other. In religious language, it can be said that one will learn about important features of God and the spiritual life through one's spouse. Marital partners can become instruments of God's revelation.

Nor ought this learning be reduced to mere cognitive content. A feature of marital exchange is that it is holistic, involving virtually every dimension of the human person. One's emotions and physical self are fully expressed in a healthy marriage. To put this more concretely, one can be brought to truly feel the love of God through the love of one's spouse expressed in body and spirit. This love of God is felt most when it is sensed that the expression of married love flows from gift rather than need, from choice rather than demand. In this way the communicated "revelation" more adequately symbolizes or embodies the way God relates to the person. Each marriage can be described as a sacrament of God's faithful love for the other. Couples in healthy marriages are healthy both in their aloneness and in their togetherness. Their relationship is entered into with full freedom, a freedom that continues throughout their life together. Marriage partners can give and share freely out of their personal abundance. They are self-possessed and allow the other to possess them. This also implies that there is a "singleness" that is part of their "togetherness." The singleness establishes the uniqueness of each one's personality, interests, and talents. The thought of the poet Rilke is an excellent summary of this aspect of marital spirituality: the goal of marriage is the protection of each one's solitude. This solitude at its depth is a solitude before God, from whom we came and to whom we are heading.

Commitment

The heart of marriage is the mutual commitment of the spouses to share life in all its vicissitudes. Of particular importance is the sharing of the distinctive sexual aspect of one's personhood with the other. Marriage features the joining of differences; it is the connecting of female with male, and it is this focus on difference that is so important to the inner dynamic of marital life. Given our awareness of the pervasive nature of sexuality beyond the narrow range of the genital, we now sense the more global nature of the sexual union. It is a union of bodies to be sure, but it is much more. It is also a joining of minds and spirits, a union of "hearts." This language signifies a curious return to biblical language, where the heart symbolizes that which is deep and central in the person. Of course, we are also demythologizing to some degree the romantic use of the word *heart,* which is often synonymous with or reduced to emotional experience.

A commitment of the heart in the context of spirituality is deep and lasting. It is like God's *hesed,* God's faithful love. It is reminiscent of Jeremiah's description of the new covenant being written on the tablets of the heart (Jer 31:33). This joining of hearts points to the pervasive nature of the covenant. So it is in marriage. Whereas earlier and somewhat legalistic descriptions of marriage focused on the right to each other's bodies for those acts appropriate to procreation, the newer description touches upon all the realms of human life. In that sense marriage indicates a total commitment. It is always assumed, however, that this structure of relating includes deep and abiding respect for the proper autonomy of the other.

Marital spirituality, therefore, is essentially relational. The spiritual disciplines of marriage concern the focusing of one's presence, time, and energy with and for each other, just as they do for our relationship with God.

The marriage vows—promises made by the partners before God and the community to be faithful to each other in good times and bad—are foundational to the spiritual lifestyle of married Christians. One is sensitized to the comprehensive nature of the vows, or as some characterize them, unconditional promises. Cost is not calculated. They are open-ended. The vows also distinguish marriage as a covenant. Contracts deal with an exchange of things or moneys; covenants deal with personhood.

Because of the element of respect and rationality implicit in healthy marriage, there are limits to what can be included in unconditionality. For instance, anything requested that will harm either partner or the relationship cannot be subsumed into Christian marital life. God never wills the destruction of the person. That there will be sacrifice, hard and difficult challenges, and even suffering for the other is not ruled out when these result in the building up of the couple and each individual. Like life in general, the paradox of the gospel mystery of death yielding life is not to be overlooked. There is room for the cross in marriage, not as a masochistic or sadistic part of marriage (and this is not unheard of in marriage), but as an expression of generous love that may exceed the ordinary boundaries of expectation or justice.

Another manner of describing this phenomenon is to speak of self-transcendence, whereby one moves beyond personal, egocentric boundaries and risks offering oneself and one's services to the other. The possibility of rejection or indifference is real, but the love is such that it conquers that deep fear of rejection.

These interpersonal dynamics are like an envelope without content. They can be filled in by virtually any part of life where sharing and self-offering are possible. They can involve the most mundane events of daily life, e.g., the helping with ordinary household tasks, which in marriage is never a small thing. They can demand personal presence and support, especially when the burden of life seems unusually heavy. They can include the requirements of good communication: the sharing of ideas, feelings, and experiences. All in all, the focus is on the genuine sharing of daily life in a manner that indicates that the task of life is shared either physically, emotionally, or spiritually, or in all three ways together.

Spirituality often has a more narrow focus when the area of concern involves those things explicitly labeled religious. These things, too, need attention, but not before the broader topic of sharing the "earthy" side of marriage is noted as part of married spirituality. Once this is done, then we can attend to the more "religious" aspects of marriage.

First, it is important to mention the role of prayer, common religious activities, and growth together in faith, hope, and love as part of the design of married spirituality. Praying with and for each other is highly recommended. Both formal and informal prayers, particularly those that bespeak gratitude for each other, not only turn the spouses' minds and hearts toward God but also serve to deepen the marital bond. The partners can read or listen to Sacred Scripture or other spiritual material together, discuss its meaning, and relate it to their marital life. Attending church services together is another opportunity for sharing spiritual life. Other resources for the spiritual development of the couple are retreats for married couples, joint pilgrimages, and even individual insights and experiences shared in conversation.

A special concern must be addressed when the spouses are not part of the same Christian denomination or the same religious tradition. Here again mutual respect and learning are important. But what about participating in each other's formal religious activities? There is no simple answer, but the overall principle should be this: God intends that religion (recall its original meaning as "binding together") be a part of life that draws people together. This principle is often overlooked when a couple do not share the same religious tradition. This is not to claim that all religions are alike, but it is to state that there is good in all religions, particularly when one enters another religion "through one's spouse." Their common life is comprehensive, so, in principle at least, it touches everything labeled religion.

Another point of consideration is the distinction commonly made between religion and faith. Religion refers to those humanly constructed ways of expressing faith whose sole object is God. A common faith can be assumed, unless it is clear that it is otherwise. There is, after all, only one God, but it is equally clear that there are many ways to experience and express one's relationship with God.

Finally, there is that special expression of marital love, the marital act itself. Sexual intercourse distinguishes the life of the couple in that it uniquely expresses their full love for each other. Obviously, this is not always its meaning either outside or within marriage. Yet when sexual intercourse occurs within marriage with the appropriate dispositions, it can capture in bodily symbolic form an openness and finality equal to the total commitment implied in Christian marriage. It can express the "without reserve" aspect of the marital attitude, and the experience itself, when loving and effective, can "speak" to the marriage partners of a fullness, however temporary, of the completeness of their relationship. In fact, it is temporary and carries all the burdens of finitude with it. But for that special moment it can signal a full measure of human happiness and satisfaction for the couple. Sexual intercourse does not always accomplish this fullness, as the testimony of married couples will show, but there can be times of special ecstasy and revelation, which is one reason why religion will often suggest the connection between the experience of God's love and the human love experienced within marriage.

In its own right, therefore, marital sexual love stands as a special symbol of God's love for us. This is not simply because of its connection with the procreation of new life, but because of what it means for the couple's relationship, which is a part of God's good creation. Thus the sexual aspect of marriage, taken broadly or narrowly as in the case of sexual intercourse, is a constitutive part of marital spirituality. In that sense, spirituality and earthiness join together in affirming the fact that God is deeply present within creation. This may explain why it took so long for the Church to accept the sacramentality of marriage. It was questioned whether sexuality could actually be sacramental and spiritual. Eventually the Church came to affirm that it could.

But given the length of time it took the Church to incorporate sexuality within the parameters of spirituality, it behooves those in pastoral and educational roles in the Church today to remind the faithful of the sacramentality of sex within marriage. To recall a biological principle, ontogeny recapitulates phylogeny (the life of the individual organism passes through the life of the whole history of the species). So if it took the Church so long to capture the insight that marital sex is holy and sanctifying, it may also happen that this insight is not common among the faithful. It should be included among the great spiritual teachings of the Church. To use today's sacramental language, Christian marriage is a sacrament of creation. In other words, the created world is the "stuff" out of which its sacramentality is formed.

Generativity

There was a time when the spiritual life of the married was reduced to a discussion of procreation. Spiritual success was equated with generosity in the number of children brought into the world and the effort parents expended to form them in the life of the Church. Today, while the value of generosity in procreation is generally upheld, this aspect of married life is integrated with other dimensions of spirituality, some of which have already been discussed here.

The theology of the Church often underscores two aspects of ecclesial life: *communio* ("communion") and *missio* ("mission"). *Communio* centers on the relational life within the Church itself, the embodiment of what the Gospel of John calls for when indicating that Christ's own will be known by the love they have for one another. That love is celebrated and expressed at the Eucharistic meal. The other aspect of Church life, its mission, points to the service given to others. Clothing the naked, giving food and drink to those who need nourishment, caring for widows and orphans—these are indicators that the Church is active in mission. Both *communio* and *missio* are essential features of Church life. The theological roots for this duality of life lie in the life of God and God's activity of creating *ad extra*. God's Trinitarian life is, in that sense, God's *communio*, while God's *missio* life is God's creation of the universe.

Taking this paradigm one step further, Christian marriage contains its own *communio* (the love between the spouses) and its *missio* (the life between them results in new life from them). Obviously, this refers to biological children resulting from the love expressed in the sexual union of the couple, but there are other referents worth mentioning, such as adoption, foster care, and the care of children with special needs and of the disabled and the elderly. The primary point is that marriage is not simply a relationship between two persons, but it is also a relationship of creativity and service for others. In other words, Christian marriage itself is essentially altruistic. The so-called unitive and procreative aspect of marriage, which is the cornerstone for Vatican II's description of marriage in its Pastoral Constitution on the Church in the Modern World (GS 47-52), can be seen in light of this distinction between communion and mission as essential aspects of the life of the Church. Marriage, as a sacrament of the Church, participates in this communion and mission in a specific and concrete manner.

Of course, the mere presence of others does not capture the richness included in generativity. The longstanding tradition of the Church is to speak of marriage as oriented to procreation *and* education of children. Education does not fundamentally refer to book earning, but to the whole spectrum of generative acts done by parents to nurture the Christian personhood of their children. It involves the "teaching" of the Christian faith through word and example, along with all those actions that awaken the person's capacity for participating in God's good creation as a grateful and contributing member of society.

To be a Christian parent is to cooperate with God's Spirit as one who mentors another into maturity. Parents do this for God. Children are not owned by their parents, but they care for them for God. Referring to the point made earlier in our discussion of solitude, each person's existence is rooted in God and will find completion only in God. Along the way, however, the agency of other persons plays an essential, God-given role in assisting the person to reach his or her finality. Parents play a major role in this ministry.

Our lives are structured in ways that work with God in accomplishing God's plan for each one's wholeness and holiness. Our spirituality assists us in gaining an awareness of God, unites us with God in a personal relationship, and empowers us to act in accord with God's intent. It is within this framework that our relational life unfolds. It applies to marriage and family life as it does to all other relational settings.

Taking the process of evangelization in the family as an example of this framework in operation, the proclamation of God's word is done both by the "God language" spoken within the family and by the actions of witness that embody God's care and concern for each family member. While the evangelization process usually begins with the parent communicating with the child, it can work the other way around. Pope Paul VI, in his profound treatise on evangelization, *Evangelii Nuntiandi* (1975), describes the parent evangelizing the children and the children doing the same for the parents.

Two thoughts flow from this insight. One, the family itself is an organic system in which activity is going in all directions all the time. Cause and effect are difficult to isolate, because any given cause is usually the effect of another cause, and so forth. Second, the fundamental equality of every person before God, the idea of all persons being brothers and sisters, alerts one to God's acting through people almost in indiscriminate fashion. Thus the educational correlative to procreation is both interesting and complex. But so is God's generativity as the magnificence of creation is grasped by finite human minds.

Two final aspects of the generative role of parents deserve special mention. First, much has been learned in recent years about the process of human attachment. This refers to the very early stages of life, when the newborn is "attached" to the parent, thus gaining a sense of trust and security in the world. Theorists in child development are apt to claim that without adequate attachment to a reliable and loving person, children will fail to reach a needed level of confidence and will have feelings of insecurity and anxiety about their place in the world. This is no small matter. Thus efforts to establish healthy attachment are to be seen as part of the spiritual demands of parenting.

Second, it is important to maintain a healthy balance between the demands of parenting and the demands of marriage. Marriage is a subsystem within the family. Research shows that healthy marriages are needed to ensure healthy family life. Marriage has demands in its own right. Part of the spiritual discernment of the married

will be to create a lifestyle that values both marriage and parenting without compromising either.

Marriage and Eucharist

The fullest expression of marital spirituality comes to light when it is described in relationship to the Eucharistic celebration. Jesus chose a marriage banquet to begin his public ministry, and this is not without meaning. The reign of God present among us is celebrated in the Lord's Supper, at which we share in God's presence and power among us. The establishment of the new covenant in Christ Jesus has its earthly effects, and marriage is one place where this happens.

Like the dynamics of the "now and not yet kingdom," marriage has its eschatological framework. Within the marriage relationship there is a tension of fullness achieved and frustration over its not having been completed. That is why fidelity is so important in Christian marriage. Staying with each other in times of fullness and in times when there is incompleteness mirrors the drama of life itself in these times. But in hope we can still celebrate the promise fulfilled and the promise yet to be achieved.

Marriage stands at the center of the tension inherent in the gospel itself. Jesus has come and will come again. Paul thought that the second coming was imminent and therefore suggested that those not yet married remain unmarried. His reasoning was adequate; his timetable was not.

In light of the Eucharistic framework, we can conclude that marriage as part of the life of the kingdom contains a "play" aspect (fullness achieved) along with a "work" aspect (more remains to be done). Marriage contains a spiritual task: the ongoing development of the marriage relationship. And as the Eucharist is a celebration and sharing in the person of Jesus, so too is marriage, with the primary form of that celebration and sharing being done through and with each other. This is the heart of spirituality for the married.

See also CHILD, CHILDREN; COMMUNITY; DIVORCE (AND REMARRIAGE); ECSTASY; EUCHARIST; FIDELITY; INTIMACY; LAY SPIRITUALITY; SEXUALITY; SINGLE PARENT.

Bibliography: P. Elliot, What God Has Joined: The Sacramentality of Marriage (New York: Alba House, 1990). M. Kelsey and B. Kelsey, Sacrament of Sexuality: The Spirituality and Psychology of Sex (Warwick, N.Y.: Amity House, 1986). M. Lawler, Secular Marriage, Christian Sacrament (Mystic, Conn.: Twenty-Third Publications, 1985). C. Roberts and W. Roberts, Partners in Intimacy: Living Christian Marriage Today (New York: Paulist, 1988). D. Thomas, Christian Marriage: A Journey Together (Wilmington, Del.: Michael Glazier, 1983). J. Vanier, Man and Woman He Made Them (New York: Paulist, 1984).

DAVID M. THOMAS

MARRIAGE ENCOUNTER

See MARRIAGE.

MARRIAGE, MYSTICAL

Greek religion, Judaism, Christianity, and other religious traditions have used the symbolism of marriage or sexual union to describe the relationship between a people or an individual with God, and especially to express the most profound communion with God that a devout person can experience. In the OT the symbol of marriage describes the bond between God and Israel (Hos 2; Isa 54:5-6; 62:4-5; Jer 2:2; 3:20). The NT portrays the Church as the bride of Christ (Eph 5:25-27; 2 Cor 11:2; Rev 19:7-9; 21:2; 22:17). Gradually this imagery was applied to the sacramental experiences of the individual Christian. In baptism one becomes a spouse of the Holy Spirit (Tertullian); Christian initiation is a spousal bonding with Christ (Origen, Chrysostom); reception of the Eucharist is a marriage symbol (Theodoretus). From the time of Origen, the Canticle of Canticles has been interpreted, in a spiritual sense, as describing both the union of Christ with the Church and the loving union of the individual person with Christ or the Holy Trinity.

The term mystical marriage or spiritual marriage has been used, in an almost technical way, since the time of John of the Cross and Teresa of Avila, to designate the highest states of Christian perfection attainable in this life that these authors so movingly described. But more important than the marriage symbolism employed by them is the emphasis they place on the total gift of oneself to God in faith and love, as a response to God's abiding and transforming presence. As in all aspects of the spiritual life, there is a need for objective criteria to determine, as far as possible, the authenticity of experiences one claims to have of intimate communion with God. At the same time, it should be remembered that transforming union with God is the ultimate stage of development for which each person has been created. Many good people, including canonized saints, have never used marriage symbolism to describe their relationship with God. Moreover, the covenant of love between God and each individual person, and the fecundity of that covenant in love toward others, can be lived in a great variety of ways. Profound communion with God and heroic love for others often exist in those whose psychological perceptions or verbal expressions do not reflect adequately the beauty of their lives.

See also BRIDAL MYSTICISM; HOLINESS; LOVE; MYSTICISM; PRESENCE, PRESENCE OF GOD; UNION, UNITIVE WAY.

Bibliography: P. Adnès, "Mariage spirituel," D.Spir., vol. 10, cols. 388–408. H. Egan, Christian Mysticism: The Future of a Tradition (New York: Pueblo, 1984). "Hieros Gamos" and "Mystical Union," in The Encyclopedia of Religion, vol. 6, pp. 317–321, and vol. 10, pp. 239–245. A. Poulain, The Graces of Interior Prayer (St. Louis: B. Herder, 1951), chap. 19: "The Spiritual Marriage." St. John of the Cross, The Spiritual Canticle; The Living Flame of Love. St. Teresa of Avila, Interior Castle, Seventh Mansion.

EDWARD J. MALATESTA, S.J.

MARRIAGE, SPIRITUAL

See MARRIAGE, MYSTICAL.

MARTYRDOM

The term *martyrdom* is derived from the Greek *martyrein,* meaning "to bear witness." In the Christian context it refers to bearing witness to Christ and to the Christian faith that culminates in a death inflicted by others. In the ancient Church, those who had suffered for Christ and for the faith, but not to the point of death, were called "confessors," but this designation is nowadays understood to apply only to nonmartyr saints. Sometimes, too, the title of martyr was conferred on such persons by way of honor. The witness in question takes its validity from the fact of its having been offered rather than from the fact of its having been received, i.e., the martyr's legitimacy and even greatness depend on firmness of conviction in the face of suffering, not on having convinced anyone of the truth of the Christian faith.

Scripture contains three important accounts of martyrdom: that of Eleazar and the seven brothers in 2 Macc 6:18–7:41; that of Stephen in Acts 6:8–7:60; and that of Jesus himself in the passion narratives of the four Gospels. These three accounts, especially that of Jesus, which was considered archetypal, have exerted a significant influence on subsequent descriptions of martyrdom, particularly in the early Church. Scripture also provides an inchoate theology of martyrdom both in these accounts and elsewhere. Thus, Mt 10:17–25, while recommending flight during persecution, nonetheless suggests that some kind of suffering is to be expected by Christians as a matter of course on account of their discipleship, and that they will then receive divine assistance; and 1 Cor 13:3 makes the worth of a given martyrdom depend unconditionally on love. The Church produced martyrs from its inception, and passages such as these undoubtedly represent, at least in part, a reflection on events that had already taken place.

It was in the patristic period (ca. A.D. 100–ca. A.D. 750), however, that extensive reflection on martyrdom initially occurred. The first noncanonical martyrdom account, the anonymous mid-2nd-century *Martyrdom of Polycarp,* in its recounting of the execution of Bishop Polycarp of Smyrna, already suggests several themes that would become classic in the literature of this genre. By far the most important of these is that the martyr imitates the suffering and death of Christ. But the unknown author of the *Martyrdom* also makes it clear that martyrdom is a charism which cannot be seized but which must be given by God, and that thus it is improper to provoke one's own martyrdom (later authors would see in this sort of provocation an uncharitable act because it was inducing others to the sin of murder); similarly, that the moment of one's martyrdom must not be anticipated; that the martyrs enjoy a special relationship with Christ in their suffering, such that they often do not even feel the torments inflicted upon them; and that they are subject to premonitory dreams, visions, and ecstasies as signs of the divine favor that they enjoy.

The Martyrdom of Polycarp, despite its theological richness, is still fundamentally a simple account that does not dwell inordinately on its hero's sufferings. It seems to have been built around the actual official record of Polycarp's interrogation, sentencing, and execution. But later accounts will be more detailed, and as time goes on, it becomes obvious that many of these details are embellishments having little or nothing to do with historical fact. They typically include edifying but improbable speechifying on the part of the martyr, a graphic portrait of the bloodthirsty pagan judge, and a description of torments that no human being could long have contemplated, never mind endured.

Prudentius's lengthy poem in honor of the martyrdom of St. Lawrence in his

Peristephanon, dating from the very beginning of the 5th century (and thus considerably after the martyr's death in 258), is a case in point. Although Lawrence most likely died by the sword, Prudentius continues the tradition, already decades old, that he died by fire and joked with his executioner during the ordeal. And Lawrence's discourses, while granting some space for poetic license, have little or no basis in reality. Yet exaggerations such as these, which were to be the fare of devout Christian readers well into the 20th century, were not without some sort of deeper purpose. A martyr's speeches, for instance, performed an edifying and even instructive function, and a depiction of the gruesomeness of the torments suffered served to emphasize the heroism displayed and to portray irrefragably the fortifying effects of grace on frail flesh and spirit.

Arguably the most important work on martyrdom ever written is Origen's *Exhortation to Martyrdom,* published about A.D. 235. It is a speculative treatise rather than an account of martyrdom, and in it Origen sets out some of the characteristics of martyrs and martyrdom. Martyrs are, first of all, motivated by so great a love that it demands that their soul be separated from every corporeal object, eventually including their own body. They are also moved by a sense of honor and duty, since they wish to repay God for all the favors given to them, and the best way to do this is to drink the cup of salvation mentioned in Ps 116:13, which Origen, basing himself on Mt 20:22 and 26:39, interprets as a martyr's death. Martyrs imitate Christ, which introduces them to knowledge inaccessible to most Christians, and they receive a spiritual reward more than commensurate with their sufferings. The struggle of the martyrs is not merely an event that involves them, their executioners, and the immediate onlookers; it has cosmic ramifications and is observed by the whole invisible universe, angels and demons and God. Martyrdom can serve as a baptism,

but in this Origen repeats an idea which had already appeared in Tertullian's late-2nd-century treatise *On Baptism* and which must have been current even before that. Certainly the most striking notion in the *Exhortation* is that a martyr's death may have value not only for the martyr but also for others: Origen suggests that, just as Christ's blood has ransomed some, so the blood of martyrs may ransom others.

As startling as this last idea of Origen's may seem at present, it was probably not so in antiquity, for early Christians regarded martyrs with a veneration not accorded to anyone else. Tertullian declared that only they experienced the vision of Christ immediately at their death; all others had to wait for the Last Judgment. Hippolytus recounts, as we know from his *Apostolic Tradition,* written about A.D. 215, that martyrs (who had suffered but not died) enjoyed the status of presbyters. There was also a belief that such persons could reconcile sinners to the Church, which was in fact a function normally exercised only by bishops. The letters and treatises of Cyprian of Carthage (d. 258) reveal that the Churches of Rome and Carthage were severely shaken by the demands of some martyrs that they be treated as the bearers of spiritual powers, like reconciliation, which they had unilaterally arrogated to themselves. Cyprian's response to these demands, elaborated particularly in his work *On the Unity of the Catholic Church,* was to locate the charism of martyrdom unequivocally within the institutional Church, thereby nullifying the actions of martyrs at odds with that Church.

The so-called period of persecution in the Church's history, which was actually far less intense and uniform than is popularly imagined, lasted in the Roman Empire until 313 and the "Edict of Milan," with only sporadic outbreaks thereafter. But the spirit or "mystique" of martyrdom, which was as old as the Church itself, was too deeply rooted in Christian consciousness for it to be easily dislodged.

Hence the elaborations of the martyrdom accounts, already mentioned, which continue through the Middle Ages and which bear witness to an enduring fascination with this theme. Hence also the use of the designation "martyrdom" in contexts other than the traditional one of suffering and dying for the faith. Thus monks, beginning with Antony of Egypt, are regularly said to have undergone a sort of martyrdom in their pursuit of the monastic life, as are ascetics of any kind, especially virgins. It also begins to be said of holy persons who were not martyred that they certainly would have been martyred had the opportunity presented itself; as is recounted of Martin of Tours (d. 397) by his biographer Sulpicius Severus, he lacked not the will but the occasion. This martyrdom of desire, as it was later called, has been a notable characteristic of canonized and uncanonized saints throughout the history of the Church.

From this coopting of the martyr's title for other saints, it must be evident that in some sense the martyr is viewed as the archetypal saint, not only because he or she imitates Christ in the supreme moment of his life, namely, in his suffering and death, but also because of the numerous charisms with which the martyr is gifted. Diadochus of Photice (d. before 486) goes so far as to say in his *Gnostic Chapters* 90: "No one, as long as he is in this body, can attain to [the] perfection [of spiritual love] apart from the saints who have achieved martyrdom and a perfect confession." It is not surprising, then, for example, that all the apostles, with the exception of John (who legend says was *nearly* martyred by being boiled in oil), are assumed by Church tradition to have died violent deaths, when in fact very little is known of their ends; it would have been inconceivable to imagine such great saints without the crowning glory of martyrdom.

It is quite unquestionable that the spirituality of the Church's first three centuries, and of some centuries after, was strongly marked by the mystique of martyrdom—perhaps as strongly as it was by the mystery of baptism, with all its implications. Despite the official (liturgical) prominence that martyrdom continues to enjoy, however, and despite the fact that the Church has had its martyrs in every century, martyrdom seems presently to be less a part of Christian consciousness and hence of Christian spirituality, at least in the West. There are several reasons for this. In addition to a noticeable deemphasis on the possible benefits of suffering (which had admittedly been overemphasized in the past), the formerly preeminent role of martyrdom in Christian spirituality has also been adversely affected by a concentration on the subjective and on inner states; martyrdom, on the other hand, is an indisputably objective reality involving body as well as soul. Moreover, even though the contemporary Church has produced its share of martyrdoms, they have occurred "too far away" to make a lasting impression on most Western Christians, although they may have an immediate shock value.

A current problem is the controversy as to whether some deaths qualify as martyrdoms. The issue has arisen in cases where a person seems to have died not for the faith, narrowly understood, but, like Archbishop Oscar Romero, for some social cause. There are, however, numerous precedents for persons being accepted as martyrs who have not died directly for the faith as such. Among these are to be found, e.g., Thomas à Becket, who died in defense of ecclesiastical prerogatives; Maria Goretti, murdered when she refused to yield her virginity; and Maximilian Kolbe, who, in an act of heroic charity, voluntarily substituted himself for someone else who was condemned to death in Auschwitz. The question is, then, whether a given violent death has borne witness to the Church's practice, which implies faith, and not exclusively, if at all, to some proposition included in the Creed.

Martyrdom presents the Church with a paradox of sorts. Although the Church regularly prays for peace, so that it might exercise its sacramental functions unhindered, it nonetheless rejoices in a special way over those who have died in persecution. Experience has taught it that peace often gives rise to temptations that Christians, being human, can only resist with difficulty (cf., e.g., Cyprian, *On the Lapsed,* 4ff.), whereas persecution acts as a refining fire and serves to promote, in some mysterious fashion, the Church's growth. In the words of Tertullian, "The blood of Christians is seed" (*Apology,* 50.13).

See also BLOOD; EARLY CHRISTIAN SPIRITUALITY; PATRISTIC SPIRITUALITY; SACRIFICE.

Bibliography: T. Baumeister, *Die Anfänge der Theologie des Martyriums* (Münster: Aschendorff, 1980). H. Musurillo, ed. and trans., *The Acts of the Christian Martyrs* (Oxford: Clarendon Press, 1972).

BONIFACE RAMSEY, O.P.

MARY

Mary, the mother of Jesus, has played a consistent role in the spirituality of Catholic Christians of the East and West. Devotion to her has taken many different shapes through the ages, and the image of Mary has entered deeply into the Catholic imagination. While this entry will focus principally on Vatican II and post–Vatican II developments in theology and devotion to Mary, it is necessary to evoke, at least briefly, the historical development of Marian spirituality.

Biblical Foundations

Contemporary biblical scholars, using the methods of historical criticism, have uncovered from the pages of the New Testament the picture of a young Jewish woman who is invited to participate in God's plan of salvation and who takes the risk to say yes to this invitation, although not fully understanding what it would entail. The infancy narratives, which recount the events surrounding the conception and birth of Jesus, are Christological in content

and reflect the awareness of the later Church community of the significance and destiny of Jesus. Thus they are less concerned to give us information about Mary than to indicate that the origins of Jesus reflect his saving significance.

In the Synoptic Gospels the mother of Jesus makes few appearances during Jesus' public life. One significant incident is recounted by all the Synoptics. When the family of Jesus come searching for him, Jesus comments to the disciples that his true family is constituted by "those who hear the word of God and act on it" (Mk 3:20–35; Mt 12:46–50; Lk 8:19–21). Each of the Synoptic texts, however, interprets this incident somewhat differently. Mark implies a contrast between the physical family and the eschatological family, so that Mary and the brothers appear as examples of unbelievers in contrast to true believers. Matthew weakens this negative interpretation somewhat, while Luke's Gospel makes Mary and the brothers positive examples of disciples who hear and act on the word of God. This Lukan interpretation anticipates and prepares for Acts 1:14, where Mary is pictured among the gathered disciples on Pentecost, traditionally considered the foundation event of the Church.

Central to understanding John's view of Mary is the account of her role at the foot of the cross (Jn 19:25–27). When Mary is given to the beloved disciple as his mother and he is given to her as her son, she is seen as a model of belief and discipleship, member par excellence of the believing community.

From this rather meager biblical information has grown the complex and sometimes extravagant history of Marian devotion in the Church. Countless artists have taken Mary as their subject, poets have found inspiration in her, and theologians have analyzed her role in the mystery of redemption. The symbolic truth that the Marian tradition reveals about God, ourselves, and the Church far exceeds the limited historical information we possess. Nevertheless, the sober limitations of the biblical material provide a check against the extravagance that has been a permanent temptation of the Marian tradition.

Historical Development

In spite of the scarcity of information about Mary supplied by the Gospels, she very quickly became an object of both interest and devotion. The apocryphal mid-2nd-century *Protoevangelium of James* purported to supply a good deal of biographical information lacking in the orthodox Scriptures, such as the names of Mary's parents, her presentation in the Temple, the choosing of Joseph as her husband, etc. Belief in the virginal conception and birth of Jesus, which became important themes for many of the Church Fathers, was also reinforced by the *Protoevangelium.* This work provided the background for much later popular devotion and artistic imagination. Another early evidence of popular devotion to Mary is found in the prayer *Sub tuum praesidium,* "Mother of God, [hear] my supplications; suffer us not [to be] in adversity, but deliver us from danger," which is thought to date in an early form to the 3rd or early 4th century. Many scholars see in this prayer aspects borrowed from the goddess tradition, especially noting that in it Mary is invoked as a power in her own right.

Theological themes of the patristic period concerning Mary include an increasing tendency to parallel Eve and Mary. Eve is depicted as the woman whose disobedience brought sin into the world, while Mary's obedience, in the words of Irenaeus, became "the cause of salvation both for herself and for the whole human race" (*Adv. haer.,* 3.22). The early dogmas concerning Mary's virginity and motherhood became part of the Church's tradition during this period. Belief in the virginal conception of Jesus has its roots in the infancy narratives of Matthew and Luke. Scripture scholars today remind us that the intent of

the affirmation of virginal conception is Christological: It is an affirmation that Jesus is Son of God and Son of David, conceived by the power of the Holy Spirit. Although this belief reinforced early ascetic ideals, it is reinterpreted today within a different worldview. "Society and religion should not esteem [Mary's] virginity for ascetic reasons; rather, like her motherhood, her virginity points toward service to the poor of Yahweh" (Gebara and Bingemer, p. 108). Belief in Mary's virginity during and after Jesus' birth is postbiblical in origin and is indicative of the growing interest in Mary herself, which eventually developed into Mariology.

The greatest early impulse toward Marian theology and devotion, however, came from the proclamation of Mary as *Theotokos,* or "God-bearer," at the Council of Ephesus in A.D. 431. Although the concern was Christological, the affirmation of both the full humanity and divinity of Jesus led to the conviction that the woman who bore him can appropriately be called not only Mother of Jesus but Mother of God.

The relationship of Mary and the Church, a theme retrieved as a central image at Vatican II, also appeared for the first time in the creative pastoral theologizing of the Church Fathers, especially Ambrose. The official teaching of the Church through the patristic period, exemplified by the Latin Fathers Ambrose and Augustine, although increasing in Marian devotion, continued to emphasize its Christological origin and impetus.

Before moving to the medieval period, it is important to mention the most important Marian hymn of the Greek Church, the *Akathistos,* which is thought to have originated in the 6th century. This hymn celebrating the incarnation and Mary's virgin motherhood is still used in the Byzantine liturgy. It is punctuated by a series of salutations to Mary that celebrate her role as *Theotokos* in the salvation of the world. "Hail, you who carried in your womb / the guide for all who stray. . . . Hail, pardon for those who have repented; / Hail refuge for those who despair." Mary is the receptacle of wisdom, mighty intercessor, and minister of divine goodness. In this very influential hymn, the tendency to attribute to Mary power and activity more properly belonging to God alone is clearly evident. The poetic imagery of this lovely hymn and others of the same genre began to be taken literally and to influence the development of the theological tradition about Mary.

This became very obvious in medieval times, which saw the development of ever-increasing Marian devotion sometimes leaning toward extravagance. Jesus appeared more and more distant in the theology of the period, as well as in the popular imagination, and was often viewed as stern king and judge. Mary became the gentle intercessor, able to change her Son's mind, sometimes even manipulative in the process. Her mercy was often contrasted with Christ's harsh justice. She became a mediator between sinful humankind and a distant and sometimes vengeful Christ, a kind of idealized human, but more than human. No excellence was considered too great to attribute to this powerful intercessor and queen. All virtue and knowledge, as well as beauty and goodness, were in her possession. Her idealized image provided a welcome contrast to the often ugly and dangerous world of daily life. It became a Mariological principle that one could never say too much about Mary.

Prayer to Mary became increasingly popular during this period. The beautiful hymn to Mary, Star of the Sea, the *Ave Maris Stella,* probably dates from the 8th century, and the Marian antiphons still used in the celebration of the Office appeared in the late 11th and early 12th centuries. The best known of these, the *Salve Regina,* calls on Mary as Mother of mercy, advocate for human beings still on their earthly journey, and hope for their final union with her Son. The Hail Mary, the best known of all the Marian prayers, be-

came widespread during this period through its use in the Little Office of Our Lady, although it has earlier roots. This Office, shorter than the Divine Office, involves psalm recitation, antiphons, Marian hymns, and frequent use of the Hail Mary. Many miracle stories and legends became attached to the recitation of this Office, and thus to the Hail Mary influencing its popularity and widespread use.

Marian litanies, influenced in form and content by the *Akathistos,* grew out of the popular imagination as means of both honoring and petitioning Mary. The Litany of Loreto, which dates from the late 12th century, is perhaps the most enduring of these. And finally, perhaps the most popular of all Marian devotions, the rosary, has its early origins in a paraliturgical recitation of the Psalter, in which the psalms were eventually replaced by Hail Marys interspersed with antiphons and, at least by the 12th century, counted on beads.

The exuberant Marian devotion of the medieval period could not but lead to a reaction, and it came with the critique of the 16th-century Reformers. Although there was not initially a rejection of all Marian piety—indeed Luther has a beautiful meditation on the *Magnificat*—the Reformers moved to reassert that there is only one mediator between God and human beings, Jesus Christ. Any devotion to Mary must be placed firmly in that context and must be biblically grounded. Luther counteracted the maximalizing principle of the Middle Ages with a minimalizing approach. One can never say too little about Mary, since God's honor must not be diminished.

In the polemical post-Reformation period, Mary was almost eliminated from the Protestant traditions, while Marian devotion became a rallying symbol of Roman Catholicism. The 17th century, especially in France with the so-called Ecole Française, was a period of particularly intense Marian devotion. Spiritual writers such as

Pierre de Bérulle, founder of the French Oratory; Jean-Jacques Olier, founder of the seminary of St. Sulpice; John Eudes, founder of the Congregation of Jesus and Mary; and perhaps the best known in this connection, Louis-Marie Grignion de Montfort (d. 1716), developed a Mariology that remained influential into the 20th century. Their Marian spirituality, obviously a product of wider theological and cultural trends of the time, now appears often sentimental and exaggerated. Grignion de Montfort suggested, in his very popular *True Devotion to the Blessed Virgin,* that devotion to Mary sweetens and makes easy the difficult road to union with God. In an idea that became a slogan, he proposed that one *must* go through Mary to reach Jesus. Mary's influence is so great that she has power even over God's own self.

Once again this apogee of Marian devotion was followed by a period of decline. The 18th-century Enlightenment, with its emphasis on rationalism, provided little support for the romantic and sentimental devotion of the previous period. With the 19th century, however, marked by the emergence of romanticism, came another period of strong Marian devotion. This period is sometimes framed by the promulgation of the two Marian dogmas of modern times, the Immaculate Conception in 1854 and the Assumption in 1950. The history of the origin and development of these doctrines shows that while belief in Mary's Assumption has been quite consistent from early times, the Immaculate Conception has a more complex and controversial history, at least theologically if not popularly. In consultations done prior to both promulgations, however, almost universal consensus was expressed about the faith and devotion of Catholic people to these beliefs.

This period was notable, too, for a plethora of Marian apparitions, among which Lourdes and Fatima received worldwide attention and became places of pilgrimage

and centers of Marian devotion. Theological discussions of the period, as well as papal teaching, were concerned with underlining the special privileges of Mary as a result of her role as mother of the Redeemer. Primary examples of these privileges were, of course, the Immaculate Conception and the Assumption. In addition to this, especially in the early 20th century there was great debate about the appropriateness of granting Mary the titles Coredemptrix and Mediatrix of all graces. Popular devotion to Mary during the period focused on the Immaculate Conception, veneration of the Heart of Mary, and the increasingly popular May devotions. The forties and fifties of this century saw Marian devotion flourishing. Sodalities abounded, and young women were encouraged to have a Marylike modesty in dress and demeanor. On the eve of Vatican II, Marian devotion was at one of its highest levels. The shrines of apparitions were important places of pilgrimage. Families were encouraged to recite the rosary together. May processions and crownings of the statue of the Blessed Virgin were yearly parish events of great significance.

How to sum up this complex history of Marian theology and devotion? Karl Rahner offers one approach when he suggests that in every age the image of Mary reflects dominant cultural expectations about women (Rahner, p. 212). In the early centuries of the Church, Mary, ever virgin, reflected the ascetical spirit of the period, which exalted bodily restraint on every level. The medieval period honored Mary as Queen of heaven and the beautiful object of romantic courtly love. By the late 19th and early 20th centuries Mary was again seen as the idealized object of romantic admiration. High on a pedestal, she represented a privatized world of beauty and harmony far removed from the crass world of everyday life.

The relationship of the Marian tradition to the situation of women has been complex. On the one hand, the Marian tradition has kept very central to Roman Catholicism the image of a woman as integral to the process of salvation. Protestant communions have tended to become one-sidedly masculine in their images and symbols, and are today beginning a cautious recovery of Mary. The image of Mary also points to a deep intuition that the Deity cannot be imaged adequately in entirely masculine language (Johnson, in Donnelly, pp. 25–68). The tendency to apply quasi-divine attributes to Mary provides an internal critique to the persistently masculine imaging of God throughout the tradition.

On the other hand, however, this idealized image of a woman has often not translated into changed conditions for actual women. In fact, times of most intense devotion to Mary have frequently been those most repressive to women. The image of this perfect woman, singularly blessed by God, without sin or fault, both virgin and mother, has often been presented as an ideal unreachable by real women, who are more often compared to Eve. One might characterize the Marian theology and piety of the early decades of the 20th century as a privilege-centered approach celebrating those privileges granted to Mary that set her apart from the rest of humankind.

Contemporary Developments

The writings of Karl Rahner, among others, signaled a change in this theological approach, a change that was reflected by Vatican II. While the Immaculate Conception and the Assumption had generally been explained as prime examples of privilege-centered Mariology, Rahner reinterpreted them as radically continuous with human life. In his view, the Immaculate Conception refers to the fact that Mary's life was caught up with God's grace right from the first moment of her conception, in virtue of the redeeming action of Christ. The Assumption implies the same about the end of her life. Body and soul, Mary's whole person is with God, her

human life radically accepted, which is, according to Christian belief, the ultimate hope of all humanity. These two dogmas offer us the conviction and the hope that our lives, too, are graced from beginning to end, that ultimately grace will triumph over sin and we, too, will find God's ultimate gracious acceptance. Thus Mary's life offers a paradigm and a hope for all human life. This interpretation pointed the way to the theological shift away from a privileged-centered Marian theology that took place at Vatican II.

The debate on Mary occasioned one of the most heated discussions of the council. It is perhaps simplistic to describe the discussion as a debate between those who favored the maximalizing, privilege-centered Mariology that had characterized the post-Tridentine Church and those who supported a more minimalizing approach. Nevertheless, this at least approximates the situation. There was some hope on the eve of the council that it would result in a new Marian definition of Mary as Mediatrix of all graces or Coredemptrix. Many council Fathers wanted to devote a whole document to Mary herself. In one of the closest decisions of the council, on October 29, 1963, the decision was made to include the material on Mary as Chapter 8 within the Dogmatic Constitution on the Church, *Lumen Gentium.* In this chapter Mary is situated in her theological role within the community of believers.

The concerns of the minimalizers were to a large degree influenced by the atmosphere of ecumenical sensitivity governing the council discussions. For this reason the sole mediatorship of Jesus is asserted continuously throughout Chapter 8. "We have but one Mediator. ... The maternal duty of Mary toward men [and women] in no way obscures or diminishes this unique mediation of Christ, but rather shows its power" (LG 60). All affirmations about Mary are to be read in the light of this hermeneutical principle. One commentator makes the point that although the chapter reflects the compromise and transitional character of many of the conciliar documents, it does attest to "the clear evolution toward a Marian approach that is essentially biblical, christocentric, ecclesiological, ecumenical and pastoral" (DeFiores, p. 471). In Chapter 8, Mary is seen primarily as a woman of faith who responded to God's word and thus "gave Life to the world" (LG 53). It is for this reason that she is "acknowledged and honored as being truly the Mother of God and Mother of the Redeemer. . . . united to Him by a close and indissoluble tie, she is endowed with the supreme office and dignity of being the Mother of the Son of God" (LG 53). Thus Mary's honor and dignity are clearly connected to her relation to Jesus and her faith-filled response to God's call.

Balancing this Christological connection is the ecclesiological motif whereby Mary is seen as a fully human being sharing with all other human beings the need for redemption by Christ. This assertion counteracts the contention that the dogma of the Immaculate Conception places Mary outside the universal human need for salvation by Jesus Christ. "Because she belongs to the offspring of Adam she is one with all human beings in their need for salvation" (LG 53). In this context, then, she is pictured as the preeminent member of the Church, the one who is the model for the Church's pilgrim life of faith.

Mary's place in the whole document on the Church is significant in this regard, for her chapter follows the one entitled "The Eschatological Nature of the Pilgrim Church and Her Union with the Heavenly Church." Mary is depicted as the faithful disciple who has finished the journey and kept the faith. She is the one who offers hope to those of us still on the journey that our pilgrimage through life may result in a similarly joyful outcome. At the same time she is an icon of fidelity for the Church as a whole, a concrete symbol of hope that the Church as a whole may not stray from the path of truth and faithful action in response to the gospel. "Mary shines forth on earth, until the day of the Lord shall come . . . as a sign of sure hope and solace for the pilgrim People of God" (LG 68). She is a prophetic witness to the salvation that God offers to all human beings. Pope John Paul II made this theme of Mary, symbol of eschatological hope for the pilgrim Church's life of faith, central to his encyclical *Redemptoris Mater* (1987) announcing the Marian Year.

The thorny ecumenical problem of Mary's intercession is also treated in this eschatological perspective. Mary's intercession is not viewed as interposed between human beings and a wrathful Christ; rather, Mary, as well as all the saints, is pictured as caught up into the unique mediatorship of Jesus on our behalf. Their cooperation in this mediation is seen as a witness to the belief that death does not destroy the mutual concern and love that bond members of the Church while on earth. In a mysterious way that solicitude lives on even after death. But this in no way undermines the mediatorship of Christ. "The unique mediation of the Redeemer does not exclude but rather gives rise among creatures to a manifold cooperation which is but a sharing in this unique source" (LG 62).

The dominant theme in this brief conciliar treatment of Mary, then, is Mary as type and model of the Church. It is interesting that although the chapter comes very close, it never gives Mary the title "Mother of the Church." In his closing speech, however, Pope Paul VI did refer to her by that title. Chapter 8 represents a clear move away from the privilege-centered Mariology of the past that set Mary apart to an approach that emphasizes continuity. Mary is the model for the Christian disciple's life of faith in response to God's call.

In spite of this new conciliar direction, there was not an immediate renewal in Marian theology and devotion. The decades following the council saw a dramatic eclipse in interest in Mary, at least in Western Europe and North America. Theological work on Mary almost came to a halt, and what was done seemed most often to continue preconciliar directions. Mariology often disappeared from seminary and theological curricula. Contrary to what might have been expected, however, she did not reappear in courses in ecclesiology or Christology. Popular devotion, where it continued, seemed also little influenced by conciliar thought.

Some possible reasons for this hiatus in Marian interest are internal to the council itself. The conciliar document on ecumenism postulates the theory of a hierarchy of truths of Christian belief (UR 11). Within this hierarchy, truths concerning the self-revealing God, Jesus Christ, the Church, and a renewed anthropology commanded the most attention in the immediate postconciliar period. Mary, while important, was considered to belong to a secondary level of truths of faith and thus took a back seat to more central concerns of liturgical and ecclesial renewal.

In addition, Chapter 8, largely a corrective to past problems, does not set much of a creative direction for the future. While indicating the essentially ecclesiological context for a renewed theology of Mary, it does not invest this direction with positive content. It lacks the concrete dialogue with the modern world, with the signs of the times, so characteristic of the spirit of the council and its most consequential documents (DeFiores, p. 474). Popular devotion to Mary, while acknowledged, is treated in a critical rather than constructive way. There is a warning against extremes of emotional exaggeration or excessive rationalism in Marian devotion, but guidelines for authentic devotion are not suggested.

Pope Paul VI's apostolic exhortation *Marialis Cultus* (1974) represents an important step in post–Vatican II theology of Mary, particularly by developing guidelines for the renewal of popular devotion.

Since the council there has been increasing recognition that Marian theology and devotion are not separate concerns. The highly abstract Mariological speculations of some past theologies, as well as the exaggerations of much popular Mariology, have often come from lack of contact between the two. Theology must be informed by the experience of popular piety, while popular piety must be in dialogue with sober theological thinking. Post–Vatican II thought initially tended to dismiss popular piety rather than see it as a bearer of deep religious and cultural values. *Marialis Cultus* attempts to retrieve the values of popular Mariology within guidelines that reflect the emphases of Vatican II. It is more clearly in dialogue with the social and cultural climate of the present than is Chapter 8 and recognizes that "certain practices of piety that not long ago seemed suitable for expressing the religious sentiment of individuals and religious communities seem today inadequate because they are linked with social and cultural patterns of the past" (MC, Introduction). The changed situation of women in society, Pope Paul suggests, is one reality that must be considered in developing a renewed Marian spirituality.

Paul VI recalls the Trinitarian, Christological, and ecclesial principles that should inform responsible Marian devotion (MC 25–28), and within that context proposes four guidelines for devotion to Mary: biblical, liturgical, ecumenical, and anthropological (MC 29–39). First, Marian devotion should be rooted in the biblical texts and reflect the fundamental themes of the Christian message. Second, Marian devotion should harmonize but not merge with or replace the liturgy. It should be inspired by the liturgy and lead toward it. Third, Marian devotion should be ecumenically sensitive, avoiding misleading exaggeration. In today's ecumenical atmosphere it should be possible to search together for images of Mary that unite Christians around the central truths of faith. Fourth,

Pope Paul recognizes that the changed situation of women in society can cause them to be alienated from some devotional images of Mary that glorify a restricted and passive role for women. He suggests that the Gospels themselves offer alternative images that can inspire the hopes and aspirations of women and men today, for example, Mary as the first and most perfect of Jesus' disciples, who heard the word of God and acted on it; as a strong woman who experienced poverty, suffering, flight, and exile; and as spokesperson for the poor and oppressed of society. Paul VI's guidelines have helped to focus the themes and set the tasks for renewing Marian theology and popular devotion in the postconciliar period.

One aspect of popular devotion that is once again receiving significant attention is the phenomenon of Marian apparitions. Lourdes and Guadalupe have been consistent places of pilgrimage and devotion, and most recently the apparitions at Medjugorje in Yugoslavia have been attracting attention. Without passing judgment on these phenomena, which have been for many people sources of consolation and conversion, it is important to recall the Church's official attitude. When the Church, after investigation, approves an apparition for private devotion, it certifies that the apparition involves nothing contrary to faith and morals, and that it supports the public revelation of the gospel, which is always the norm. Those apparitions that have received Church approval may become part of the devotional life of Catholics but are never obligatory (*Behold Your Mother*, 99–100). In the light of Vatican II and its call for world transformation, the privatistic and conservative messages of many of the Marian apparitions are questioned by some. Others, however, suggest that these phenomena are more complex. It is worth noting that the messages of the Marian apparitions have most often been entrusted to the poor and marginalized of society. Our Lady of Guadalupe, in particular, remains a powerful symbol of liberation for an oppressed people.

After the quiescent period immediately following the council, there has been a period of renewed interest in Marian theology. Two of the promising new directions reflect the confluence of the theological direction of Vatican II with the admonitions of Paul VI to take the present historical and cultural situation seriously.

The person of Mary is once again becoming important in two significant theological movements of today: the liberation theologies of emerging countries and feminist theology, which originated in, but is not confined to, North America. Women have made significant contributions to this renewed Marian theology, perhaps giving credence to Karl Rahner's contention that a renewed theology of Mary must, at least initially, be developed by women (Rahner, p. 217).

As liberation theologies, these two approaches share much in common, particularly their starting point in experience. Liberation theologies arise out of the economic and social situation of the oppressed and marginalized of society. In these theologies, until recently dominated by male theologians, it is being brought to consciousness that in any society the poorest of the poor are women, particularly those with children. Feminist theology takes its starting point from the experience of the abuse and exploitation of women even in the most affluent societies. It, too, is beginning to recognize the linkages between all forms of oppression. While both theologies have had significant years of development since Vatican II, the image of Mary has only recently begun to appear as a more than peripheral concern.

Liberation Theologies

Mary's prophetic role in the *Magnificat* has captured the imagination of liberation theology, which has taken it as a central symbol. In it Mary is seen as the spokesperson for the poor and oppressed of society, the *'anawim*. She is viewed as actively engaged in God's plan of liberation. This is a very different image from the silent, submissive maiden so often proposed to women for their emulation. The final document of the Third General Conference of the Latin American Episcopate (Puebla, 1979), *Evangelization in Latin America's Present and Future,* states:

> The *Magnificat* mirrors the soul of Mary. In that canticle we find the culmination of the spirituality of Yahweh's poor and lowly, and of the prophetic strain in the Old Testament. . . . In the *Magnificat* she presents herself as the model for all . . . those who do not passively accept the adverse circumstances of personal and social life and who are not victims of "alienation" . . . but who instead join with her in proclaiming that God is the "avenger of the lowly" and will, if need be, "depose the mighty from their thrones" (Puebla, 297).

The Puebla document pictures Mary as an active coworker in the mission of Jesus. She freely chose to participate by her yes to God's word. Pope John Paul II echoes this theme in *Redemptoris Mater* (37).

Leonardo Boff devotes a chapter of his *Maternal Face of God* (New York: Harper & Row, 1987) to "Mary, Prophetic Woman of Liberation." Within the oppressive situation of Latin America, he writes, "It is our task . . . to develop a prophetic image of Mary as the strong, determined woman, the woman committed to the messianic liberation of the poor from the historical social injustices under which they suffer" (p. 189).

Another important work combines Latin American and feminist liberation theology by rereading the Marian tradition from the perspective of the poor and oppressed of Latin America, particularly women. As proclaimer of the *Magnificat,* Mary speaks God's word in the midst of the people. "The image of the pregnant woman, able to give birth to the new, is the image of God who through the power of God's Spirit brings to birth men and women committed to justice, living out their relationship to God in a loving relationship to other human beings" (Gebara and Bingemer, p. 73). Mary is seen as the symbol of "the people." By receiving God in her womb she images the faithful people as the privileged dwelling place of God (Gebara and Bingemer, p. 42).

Another powerful image of Mary for Latin American liberation theology is Our Lady of Guadalupe. The Puebla document states, "Like the shrine at Guadalupe, the other shrines to Mary on our continent are signs of the encounter between the faith of the Church and the history of Latin America" (p. 75). These shrines, especially Guadalupe, wed national aspirations for freedom from oppression with deeply held religious convictions. There is renewed interest in these shrines as possible foci for a renewal of popular religiosity within a Church newly sensitive to its pluralistic cultural roots, and within a liberation perspective.

These two images of Mary, then—Mary of the *Magnificat* and Our Lady of Guadalupe—point to a beginning of a critical retrieval and renewal of the Marian image as a prophetic symbol of the Church's mission of liberation and salvation for all, calling the Church to make actual God's preferential option for the poor and oppressed.

Feminist Liberation Theology

Feminist theology also is beginning a cautious, tentative, and critical approach to retrieving the Mary tradition as prophetic and liberating for women within the Christian tradition. This theology proceeds by way of both a hermeneutics of suspicion, which reads the Marian tradition aware of its patriarchal biases and its negative effects on women, and a hermeneutics of recovery, which looks for its liberating aspects, since, paradoxically, Mary has also functioned as a symbol of hope and dignity for women.

The negative critique of Mary was initiated in Simone de Beauvoir's *The Second Sex* (New York: Knopf, 1953). In this work de Beauvoir cites the cult of the Virgin as a cause of the oppression of women in countries influenced by Catholicism. Mary Daly introduced these ideas to the U.S. theological scene in her groundbreaking book *The Church and the Second Sex* (New York: Harper & Row, 1968). Many women began to see in the prevalent Marian image of the sweetly submissive maiden the religious legitimation of their stereotypically subordinate role. As women became more aware in the post–Vatican II Church of their historical and contemporary marginalization, the Mary symbol became increasingly ambiguous and problematic. Seen as a product of male projections about the "ideal woman," the eternal feminine, the image of Mary was renounced by many feminist women.

Recently, however, and cognizant of this negative critique, some feminists are very cautiously and tentatively proposing a retrieval and renewal of the Mary tradition to image the new reality of women in our time. Recognizing that Mary herself is in need of liberation from past interpretations, women are beginning to write about her from a feminist perspective. Courses on Mary are reappearing in theology departments and seminaries, many taught by women.

Feminist explorations begin with the insights of Vatican II and contemporary biblical scholarship. Following Vatican II, they see Mary as a type of the Church. Her relationship with Jesus is predicated, not exclusively on her physical motherhood, but on her role as disciple who heard the word of God and kept it. As disciple, she is seen as a model for all Christians, not merely as an example of a certain kind of feminine virtue. Mary's *fiat* is being reunderstood as an expression of her active, conscious choice to participate in God's destiny for her rather than as the paradigm of passive submission, women's "proper" attitude in marriage, Church, and society. Thus the Vatican II insight is pressed for its implications for women.

Most influential in developing a realistic biblical appraisal of Mary has been the collaborative effort sponsored by the United States Lutheran-Roman Catholic Dialogue. Its work entitled *Mary in the New Testament* (Philadelphia: Fortress, 1978) underlines how little we know about the historical Mary. Her few appearances in the pages of the NT are for clearly theological purposes and offer conflicting accounts of her role. Her historical obscurity, however, allows contemporary writers to exercise a certain sober imagination about the continuities between this ordinary woman's life and the lives of many women today. In contrast to the "House of Gold, Tower of Ivory" invocations of the traditional Litany of Loreto, today's litanies call on Mary as "Mother of the homeless, widowed mother, unwed mother, mother of a political prisoner, oppressed woman, liberator of the oppressed, seeker of sanctuary, first disciple … " ("Litany of Mary of Nazareth," Pax Christi, USA). Identification with this woman, who shares our human story and yet was called to play such a key role in God's liberating activity, can lend dignity to the lives of all those devalued by society. The image of Mary of the *Magnificat* joins feminist liberation theology to all other theologies of liberation.

A final approach of feminist theology focuses on the power of the Marian symbol to testify to the inadequacy of exclusively male images of God. "Images of God as female, arguably necessary for the full expression of the mystery of God but suppressed from official formulations, have migrated to the figure of this woman" (Johnson, in Donnelly, p. 26). Some feminist authors focus on the implications of this insight for a renewal of the doctrine of God, whose power and liberating action can be equally disclosed in male or female images. Many of the qualities traditionally applied to Mary, such as compassion, love, warmth, and intimacy, can and should be restored to our impoverished image of God. With female language and imagery restored to our understanding of God, Marian renewal can locate Mary firmly on the human side of the human-divine equation as a model of Christian discipleship. This approach has the advantage also of ecumenical potential, since it concentrates on the very human Mary pictured in the Gospels.

This must, however, be coupled with continued investigation into the disclosive and challenging power of the symbol and myth of Mary. The symbolic meaning of Mary has always far transcended its meager historical foundation to provide insight into the lives, hopes, and aspirations of Christians in every century. Devotion to Mary has often been an implicit popular critique of an overly institutional, highly rational Church. Both liberation and feminist Mariologies see Mary as a potent symbol of their call to take human historical experience seriously. Mary calls us today particularly to listen to the voices of those traditionally marginalized by Church and society, women and the poor.

See also DEVOTION(S), POPULAR; DISCIPLESHIP; FEMINIST SPIRITUALITY; INTERCESSION; LIBERATION THEOLOGY, INFLUENCE ON SPIRITUALITY; PETITION; PIETY; POOR, THE; ROSARY; SAINTS, COMMUNION OF SAINTS; ECUMENISM, SPIRITUAL; VATICAN COUNCIL II; VIRGINITY.

Bibliography: R. Brown et al., Mary in the New Testament (New York: Paulist, 1978). S. DeFiores, "Mary in Postconciliar Theology," Vatican II: Assessment and Perspectives, vol. 1, ed. R. Latourelle (New York: Paulist, 1988). D. Donnelly, ed., Mary: Woman of Nazareth (New York: Paulist, 1989). I. Gebara and M. C. Bingemer, Mary: Mother of God, Mother of the Poor (New York: Orbis, 1989). H. Graef, Mary: A History of Doctrine and Devotion, vols. 1 and 2 (Westminster, Md.: Christian Classics, 1963 and 1965). E. Johnson, "Mary and the Image of God," in D. Donnelly, op. cit., 25–68, and "Reconstructing a Theology of Mary," in D. Donnelly, op. cit., 69–91. John Paul II, The Mother of the Redeemer (Washington: USCC, 1987). Paul VI, Marialis Cultus (Washington: USCC, 1974). National Conference of Catholic Bishops, Behold Your Mother (Washington: USCC, 1973). K. Rahner, "Mary and the Christian Image of Women," Faith and Ministry, Theological Investigations 19, trans. E. Quinn (New York: Crossroad, 1983). A. Tambasco, What Are They Saying About Mary? (New York: Paulist, 1984).

MARY E. HINES

MASCULINE SPIRITUALITY, MEN'S MOVEMENT

The term masculine spirituality is of recent vintage, emerging in North America and Germany. The theme developed rapidly in the early 1990s, not just as a complement to feminist spirituality and the popular "men's movement," but as a serious attempt to rescue a healthy sense of maleness from its identification with patriarchy and the malignant effects of clerical spirituality. Its proponents insist that masculinity is not the same as the domination, rationalism, and functionalism of the male-controlled tradition, which is sometimes referred to as deteriorated maleness or even "neuter" spirituality. Fortunately they have been able to find many favorable examples of healthy masculine soul both in the Bible and in the history of the Church. Patrick Arnold's Wildmen, Warriors, and Kings would be an excellent example of this retrieval.

In its early stages the theme has drawn heavily upon the popularized mythopoetic approach of Robert Bly and the psychosexual language so common in the United States, particularly the masculine-feminine categories of Carl Jung. This has created some problems with those feminists who do not accept such a division of so-called masculine and feminine qualities or energies. Many feminists insist that all human qualities are a result of cultural conditioning and are not gender specific. Jung's understanding of the contrasexual as existing within each of us—the anima as the feminine soul of a man, and the animus as the masculine soul of a woman—is sometimes understood as a way out of such a dualism.

646   MASCULINE SPIRITUALITY, MEN'S MOVEMENT

The mythopoetic approach of Bly draws upon "tradition" with almost the same authority that Christians would draw upon the fonts of Scripture and tradition. It is assumed that the myths, legends, and fairy tales that are found in various cultures hold deep, abiding truths for human consciousness. Since most recent cultures have been patriarchal and males have controlled the literature, myths provide compelling and symbolic truths for the spiritual journeys of men. Homer's *Odyssey,* Virgil's *Aeneid,* Dante's *Divine Comedy,* the medieval *Quest* legends, Grimm's earthy male figures, as well as Joseph, Jacob, and David in the Hebrew Scriptures, have all been drawn upon to great advantage. Joseph Campbell's monomyth of the hero and the tales of King Arthur are being used in ways that should help Scripture studies immensely. If nothing else, masculine spirituality has helped turn the corner in understanding literature as myth, and sacred myth as transformational and "true." In addition there is a new appreciation for symbol and ritual that is quite congenial to Roman Catholics and very instructional for those from nonliturgical traditions. Many find it ironic that masculine spirituality is drawing so much upon the nonrational, the unconscious, animal and nature symbolism as antidote to centuries of cerebral theology and spirituality. Much of our church ritual has in fact been "feminized" (lace, fashion robes, sanitized sanctuaries, church as good manners) in the worst sense, and thus has become ineffective symbols for many males, even destructive for some. Masculine spirituality is quickly creating new symbols and lay-led rituals that will undoubtedly offer a challenge to the clerical state.

The appeal of Carl Jung, while strengthening the Catholic understanding of sacramentalism and the inner or spiritual world, is also leading many men (and women) to a new confidence in their own inner authority and to the necessity of individual, personal journey. As the private dreams and public myths of other world religions become known to many men, there is often a tendency to either denigrate their own Christian/Catholic tradition or discover its universal depth and meaning. Rohr attempts to connect the universal myths with the spiritual tradition of Judeo-Christianity, attentive to the conversion journey of Jesus in particular. In both feminist and masculine spirituality we find a new valuation of the subjective that will no longer be satisfied with mere deductive or overly objective spiritualities that deny the importance of personal individuation. The task for Christians will be to keep such journeys communal, historical, and socially committed. Fortunately, most of the historic myths are strong on these very points, although they are not always presented in such a way by Western individualists.

As a result, much of what is called the men's movement has moved in the direction of "New Age" spirituality and has been roundly criticized by the media as superficial and thought to be inconsequential by the Churches. It might, however, be a real ally to classical Christian spirituality by providing a new appeal to those middle-class, educated men who no longer seek or understand Christian spirituality. Several retreat leaders who work in this area find the response from clergy to be quite fresh and open when remarks are addressed precisely to maleness, manhood, and masculinity. After all, "new age" is a Christian notion (Mt 19:28, Rev 21:1); and what some call the transformational power of archetypes is what Catholic theology has presented through hagiography, statues, icons, and all forms of liturgy and sacred space. Sacramental theology in particular, as well as liturgy and spirituality in general, would seem to have much to benefit from what is being called masculine spirituality, not to speak of its power for group participation on the part of men.

In general, masculine spirituality seems to emphasize the importance of example, heroes, action, and experience over words, theories, and discussions, balancing *logos* with *mythos* and *pathos*. The autonomous *logos* is now seen as deficient masculinity, with too much ego concern for rightness, control, and power. In the new masculine spirituality, focus is on Jesus the Word becoming flesh, embodied and truly sexual instead of merely dutiful, correct, and controlled, now seen to be a Stoic and limited interpretation of Jesus. The terms "wild man," "wise man," and "holy man" present paradigms of Christian maleness that is both hard and soft, obedient and free, civilized and instinctual, disciplined and honest.

In some ways masculine spirituality is a reaction against what is seen as the new matriarchy, women assuming what were traditionally men's roles instead of changing the patriarchal system. Masculine spirituality at its best is striving for the same synthesis, symbiosis, and partnership that healthy feminist spirituality is seeking, but from the starting point of the male. The goal, as in all spirituality, is *union,* but with a new appreciation for the art of separation, boundaries, identity, and historical purpose, which has been missing in so much soft piety and popular religiosity. Men want to trust a God who trusts them. The noninvolvement of men in Church activities and services certainly has a fuller explanation than mere ill will or male worldliness. Men need to have their soul and spirit respected, their journey described in ways that are honest, and they need a God who does not reject them for being passionate, embodied, and engaged, but who walks with them on the human and spiritual journey. They want a God who does not tell them to be womanly but encourages them to honor their own feminine soul and the feminine soul of the outer world, the world of art, music, poetry, worship, and compassion for human pain. Masculine spirituality maintains that there is a masculine way of doing these things that is qualitatively different from the feminine way. There is a masculine way of feel-ing, a masculine way of knowing, a masculine way of being present that is different from, and complementary to, the feminine way of feeling, knowing, and being present. Only in our relatedness do we fully mirror the image of God: "God created humankind in God's image . . . male and female God created them" (Gen 1:27).

See also FEMINIST SPIRITUALITY; JOURNEY (GROWTH AND DEVELOPMENT IN SPIRITUAL LIFE); NEW AGE SPIRITUALITY; PSYCHOLOGY, RELATIONSHIP AND CONTRIBUTION TO SPIRITUALITY.

Bibliography: J. Carmody, *Toward a Male Spirituality* (Mystic, Conn.: Twenty-Third Publications, 1988). P. Arnold, *Wildmen, Warriors, and Kings* (New York: Crossroad, 1991). J. Miller, *Biblical Faith and Fathering: Why We Call God "Father"* (New York: Paulist, 1989). M. Pable, *A Man and His God* (Notre Dame, Ind.: Ave Maria, 1988). R. Rohr and J. Martos, *The Wild Man's Journey* (Cincinnati, Ohio: St. Anthony Messenger Press, 1992).

RICHARD ROHR, O.F.M.

MATERIALISM

Materialism is a theory positing a world consisting only of material reality, that reality which the science of physics asserts to exist. From the 18th century on, several metaphysical theories have developed some form of materialism. Most but not all of these allow of no independent existence of nonphysical realities such as the mind. Deistic materialism acknowledges a spiritual creator who remains uninvolved with creation.

It is materialism as an ethical attitude that has an impact on spirituality. Here materialism is an interest in sensuous pleasures and bodily comfort. In popular understanding, materialism has come to be associated with the excessive desire for material possessions, which are conceived of as bringing about the desired pleasure and comfort. Materialism as a spiritual force is a particular manifestation of selfishness and greed. As such it is contrary to the gospel, not only as a metaphysical theory that denies transcendent realities but also as an unacceptable ethical stance that violates the demands of charity and justice.

The bishops of the United States addressed the issue of materialism in their 1986 pastoral letter *Economic Justice for All,* reminding Catholics that "Christ warned us against attachments to material things, against total self-reliance, against the idolatry of accumulating material goods and seeking safety in them" (no. 328). The bishops point out the social consequences of materialism, which renders one insensitive to the needs of others and erodes social solidarity.

See also ALMSGIVING; ASCETICISM; CONSUMERISM; CREATION; JUSTICE; POOR, THE; POVERTY; SECULARISM; SIMPLICITY; SOLIDARITY; VIRTUE; WORLD.

Bibliography: National Conference of Catholic Bishops, *Economic Justice for All: Pastoral Letter on Catholic Social Teaching and the U.S. Economy,* (Washington: USCC, 1986).

MICHAEL DODD, O.C.D.

MEDIEVAL SPIRITUALITY

See WESTERN MEDIEVAL SPIRITUALITY.

MEDITATION

The roots of the word *meditation* go back to the Greek *meletē* with its meanings of "care, study, exercise." Its Latin roots convey the sense of preparation and practice. The root *med-* occurs in many words (e.g., *medicine*) denoting cure and care. Meditation as a spiritual practice can be understood as a preparatory practice for the reception of the gift of "pure prayer" or "prayer of the heart," as the desert tradition calls it. Meditation, like all aspects of prayer, is therefore not only a means but also, when practiced as a discipline, an end.

The history of the word *meditation* in Christian spirituality sums up the history of spirituality itself. It highlights the marked prejudice of the Western mind to intellectualize both the idea and the practice of prayer. From the 16th century until modern times, meditation was seen primarily as mental prayer involving the systematic reflection on a religious or scriptural idea, using the mental powers as a stimulus to affection and good resolution. This attenuated understanding of meditation contributed to the inadequate spiritual formation of clergy and laity alike, and has led to the prevailing current sense of the need to deepen the life of prayer in the Church. This sense reflects the insight of the Second Vatican Council about the "universal call to holiness" and its repeated reminders of the contemplative dimension of baptismal faith. As a recovery of the full significance of meditation unfolds, we are witnessing the contemplative renewal of the Church, the reconciling of the unnatural and unscriptural dichotomy of contemplative and active vocations, and the emergence of a spiritually maturer laity and a spiritually humbler clergy.

In the early monastic period (5th–12th century), meditation was organically connected with contemplation in a unified vision of prayer. This sense of prayer began with *lectio,* a reading aloud and memorizing of Scripture in a way that integrated body and mind at prayer, as in the Jewish practice. Meditation was a stage of resting on the words of the text that led beyond the imaginative and rationalizing levels of the mind through *oratio,* in which a personal appropriation of the meaning was made, to *contemplatio,* which was a nonconceptual, thought-free state of being in God rather than talking to God or thinking about God. These aspects of prayer only later hardened into methods and stages, notably after the 14th century. Methods meant to organize and facilitate meditation reflected the intellectual obsession for analysis that overwhelmed all areas of knowledge, formed the new idea of "mental prayer," and lost the simple and spontaneous prayer of primitive and monastic Christianity. The idea of stages of prayer also led to the conception of a spiritual elite for whom contemplative experience was a rare privilege and a restriction of the majority of Christians to devotional or mental piety.

The monastic practice of *lectio* inherits the Jewish way of reading Scripture that formed part of an indivisible unity of prayer. The root Hebrew word *haga* is translated as "meditation" in most translations of the Bible and, as the Midrash states, it is the "heart," not the mind, that meditates. *Hagah* denotes both interiorization (Ps 19:15) and repetition or "murmuring" of the sacred words (Ps 35:20; Isa 38:14). This suggests a practice of prayer entirely comparable to the repetition of a mantra in Asian traditions. Now adopted into the English language, *mantra* (*mantram*) is a Sanskrit term meaning "a sacred word or syllable," the continuous repetition of which focuses the attention beyond thought and imagination and leads to a still, wakeful presence to the reality of God.

John Cassian (ca. 360–ca. 432) advises the selection of a single scriptural verse (Latin *formula*) taken from the *lectio* period of prayer but retained permanently in the life of the person as a means for continual recollection (*Conferences,* X). The formula is a mantra meant to be repeated simply and continuously, revolved constantly in the heart, so that in time and by grace the chronic distractions of the mind and instability of the emotions no longer prevent us from receiving the gift of "pure prayer." No other words are necessary while praying in this way, for the mantra "embraces all the feelings of human nature."

Cassian describes, in Christian terms and with scriptural support, a universal spiritual discipline that leads to unity and integration of all levels of consciousness. The tradition is reflected in the hesychastic school, which teaches the unity of mind and heart in the practice of the Jesus Prayer. The continual recitation of the mantra roots the verse or word in the heart, thus gradually leading to the state of continuous prayer enjoined by Christ (Lk 18:1) and by St. Paul (1 Thess 5:17). By leaving behind "the riches of thought and imagination" (Cassian), the mantra leads to poverty of spirit, the condition of letting go, of radical nonpossessiveness, which applies eventually not only to what we have or what we do but even to what we are, in accord with the Lord's command to his disciples to leave self behind (Lk 9:23; 14:33).

In the teaching of the Benedictine monk John Main (1926–1982), this tradition of Christian meditation is both sustained and developed. Having first learned meditation and the mantra from an Indian teacher, he went on to discover its presence in biblical and later Christian practice, as for example in Cassian and the 14th-century English treatise on Christian meditation known as *The Cloud of Unknowing.* John Main, like Cassian and the author of *The Cloud,* teaches the continuous recitation of a Christian word to lead to peace beyond distraction and the self-centered consciousness of the ego. "Fix the word in your mind so that it will be there come what may" (*The Cloud,* chap. 7). For Main, the poverty of the mantra lies in its simplicity. He advises the repetition of the word until the person can no longer say it, because to choose to stop saying it would be to return to the dualistic level of prayer in which the ego once again is observing, choosing, and controlling. At times the mantra may lead into complete silence. Once we have become conscious of the silence in a way that could be expressed as "I am silent," we are no longer silent and need, therefore, to return to the purifying work of the mantra. The mantra is a way of *kenosis,* an emptying of egoism that leads to fullness of being, "the fullness of God" (Eph 3:19).

In some contemporary presentations of meditation, as, for example, in transcendental meditation, an attempt is made to remove the religious meaning from the practice and to reduce it to a technique of self-improvement (e.g., reduction of stress) or self-enhancement (e.g., acquisition of special powers). While tending toward the commercial and trivial, these schools have unarguably helped many to a deeper spiritual life and led many Christians back to a more mature faith after they had despaired of finding a contemplative path in Christianity.

The difference between transcendental meditation and Christian meditation is that between a self-enhancing technique leading to relaxation and a spiritual discipline leading to peace as the gift of Christ. What makes meditation Christian is not, therefore, the "method" employed but the faith of the meditator in Christ's indwelling and guiding presence. Turning the attention off oneself then really becomes possible as an act of love "for my sake" (Lk 9:24) rather than for one's own growth or fulfillment. Thus the mantra allows the meditator to leave desire, "even the desire for God," as St. John of the Cross puts it, and to do so for pure love of God, not as a way of exploiting God. The Christian context in which one meditates, like one's faith, also defines the practice as a Christocentric path. The Eucharist, community worship, cooperative work in the world, Scripture, and study of the tradition create the nourishing ground of Christian meditation. Meditation also returns us to these traditional practices with renewed depth and holiness.

Christian meditation, like all other aspects of prayer, whether vocal, scriptural, or liturgical, turns the consciousness of the person praying off self toward the divine Other. As the Syriac Fathers bravely said, this loss of self involves a letting go of a personally possessive sense of "my" prayer and a deeper awakening to our union with the prayer of Jesus himself in the Holy Spirit. Because the human consciousness of Jesus worships the Father in us (Gal 8:15-16), the Christian meditator realizes the human capacity to be divinized by sharing in the very being of God (2 Pet 1:4; Eph 3:19).

John Main's development of the traditional practice and of the theology of Christian meditation is evident in several ways. A recovery of this tradition by the laity, he believed, would help toward the realization of their full participation in a Church handicapped for centuries by excessive clericalism. Out of the contemplative experience new forms of Christian community, both monastic and lay, could develop in response to contemporary needs. His strong but simple insistence on seeing meditation as a discipline requiring regular daily practice comprising two daily half-hour periods (morning and evening) allowed ordinary people to undertake a spiritual journey that had once seemed reserved for the cloistered religious. A personal commitment to this discipline has led many to form weekly meditation groups in parishes and places of education and work, thus showing both the capacity of contemplative experience to form community and the power of meditation in common to bring the gospel to the unevangelized parts of the modern world.

The recovery of this dimension of Christian prayer also leads the Church into a wider ecumenism. Meditation is a practice in all religions, though it may employ different systems or "objects of attention" and be explained in different terms. But for Christians or non-Christians, the ordinary experience of meditation is in many ways the same.

The elements of this contemplative experience could be described as silence, stillness, and simplicity. Silence is to be understood primarily as interior, the calming of the mind's noise and an awakening to the silent presence of God within. If seen as an interior reality, silence leads not to escape from, or evasion of, the world but to a deeper involvement in it (such as in the ecological crisis) from a sense of God's presence in creation. Stillness in meditation leads to the knowledge of God (Ps 46:10) through the integration of body and mind in the higher unity of the spirit. Simplicity is the most difficult because it involves the unfolding (Latin *simplex,* "an unfolded cloth") of consciousness from its habitual self-conscious and self-reflective state. Meditation leads beyond all thought, including thought of oneself or one's experience or progress. Thus St. Antony of the Desert said that "the monk who knows that he is praying is not truly praying, and the monk who does not know that he is praying is truly praying." This radical quality of simplicity is the fruit by grace of sustained attention away from self (as in saying the mantra) and a discovery of one's true self inseparable from God, "in Christ."

As with all processes or journeys, meditation has its stages. The expansion of meditation today to all forms of Christian life has enabled the teaching of the traditional masters to be absorbed more widely and naturally. All meditators, for example, experience what St. Benedict called the "first fervor of conversion." Beyond this there are the times of *acedia,* spiritual aridity or depression in which the value of a teacher is inestimable. Finally, there is the progressive realization of *apatheia,* health of soul, calmness and true joy, a peace that embraces others. The stages of meditation, as of all spiritual processes, are better conceived in cyclical and recurrent patterns (of death and resurrection) rather than in crudely rational, linear terms of progress. The meditator is traditionally advised not to be too concerned with measuring progress in terms of what happens during meditation periods but to become aware of a new dimension of depth in ordinary living.

Meditation is a foundation of spiritual life rather than another product in a spiritual supermarket. Pointing us toward our incorporation into the prayer of Christ, meditation naturally exemplifies his teaching on prayer. This teaching, expressed concisely in Mt 6:5-13, highlights the interiority of prayer over its external forms (6:6). Babbling in many words is dismissed as unspiritual. The Lord's Prayer (6:9-13), originally a compendium of easily memorizable rhythmic phrases, is presented as the model of vocal prayer. This movement toward verbal economy leads to radical trust in the parental love of God for his children, thus redefining for all time the way we need to consider petitionary prayer (6:8). Anxiety about material needs reveals a lack of trust and a distractedness that prevent true prayer (6:25). The Lord's final word here is to be attentive, single-minded, or as some would put it, mindful (6:33). These qualities of prayer, together with Christ's imagery of wakefulness, perseverance, and inner organic growth, all take on a new and richer meaning when they are known through the personal experience of the meditator. St. Paul's "fruit of the Spirit" (Gal 5:22) describes the changes that meditation evokes in daily life.

Meditation, then, is a spiritual path and discipline that leads to an encounter of our whole person with the redemptive holiness of Christ. It is a way of interior sacrifice (Rom 12:1-2) that allows the person to cooperate with the transforming and enlightening grace of Christ at work in our humanity through his gift of the Spirit of love. Meditation is an act of faith because it requires generous commitment and perseverance. It is an act of love, manifested in the growth of love in our life and in our relationships, because it turns us away from egoism toward the selflessness of the true self in Christ (Gal 2:20).

See also ACEDIA; APATHEIA; BODY OF CHRIST; CHRIST; CONSCIOUSNESS; CONTEMPLATION, CONTEMPLATIVE PRAYER; CONTEMPORARY SPIRITUALITY; DIVINIZATION; HESYCHASM; JOURNEY (GROWTH AND DEVELOPMENT IN SPIRITUAL LIFE); PRAYER; SELF; SILENCE; SIMPLICITY.

Bibliography: John Cassian, *Conferences* (New York: Paulist, 1985). J. Main, *Word into Silence* (London: Darton, Longman & Todd, 1980). I. Hausherr, *The Name of Jesus* (Kalamazoo, Mich.: Cistercian Publications, 1978).

LAURENCE FREEMAN, O.S.B.

MEMORY

Memory is the ability to recall images of events and to recognize them as having happened in the past. Like imagination, memory is linked to the translation of physical objects into the state of mental images and ideas. Memory is marked, however, by the precise awareness that its images are objects that were presented in the past. Animals share with humans certain functions of memory in their ability to recall sense impressions and to act in response to them. This allows animals a capacity for learning skills related to concrete sense behavior.

A Psychosomatic Phenomenon

Memory is a psychosomatic phenomenon, having features that are both mental and bodily. Psychically, memory involves four steps: (a) learning through impressions that fix an experience in consciousness; (b) retention by marking particular images as needed for future use; (c) restoration of past images within the field of awareness; (d) attributing to images the quality of belonging to the past by putting them in their historical setting.

The somatic elements of memory pertain to the functioning of the brain. Lesions of the cortex of the brain or impairment through injury or drug use can prevent both imagination and memory. Memory depends on the brain for the presence of traces or cortical patterns that establish the record of images that constitute memories. In addition, memory depends upon the nervous system, which translates sense contact with physical reality into the sense impressions and the cortical traces that record those impressions.

Memory does not work at random but in the service of organized patterns of interest. Psychoanalysis postulates that memory works according to laws of association, because memory is improved by the formation of associations between memory traces. Research has shown that an emotional link is useful in enhancing recall and recollection. In parallel fashion, a strong emotional link can likewise serve to reinforce the censoring power of reason when a client is searching for explanatory memories of a threatening kind within the context of therapy.

It appears that memory is able to file through the vast accumulation of stored images and, by association, bring to awareness material that can enrich a present search for understanding. Some theorists propose that humans possess almost unlimited recall ability over sense experience from the past, but need to be stimulated to exercise their memory in order to draw from quiescent imagery. Most people have the capacity to greatly enlarge their use of memory.

Uses of Memory

The person's relation to time is mediated through the power of memory. Memory makes possible the recognition that psychic material pertains to the past. Without memory, we would be limited to the present, and our activities would be determined by instinct and by the physical stimuli acting upon us. Through memory we can contextualize, compare, and evaluate, and thus have a basis for choosing. Without memory, many of the functions of intellect and will would not be possible.

Memory reproduces in consciousness experiences that were vivid at a former time but have become unconscious. The retrieval of meaning is bound up with memory. The wholesome estimation of oneself as a loved and treasured being will depend upon a healthy capacity to recollect and savor significant moments of self-affirmation. Some psychologists think that we can have a bias toward a negative self-image because an overly demanding superego urges the obsessive return to moments of failure in the futile hope of obliterating past frustrations. Thus, in both therapy and spiritual direction, a substantive dimension of adult growth entails appropriating a concrete account of one's life as a loved and productive human person.

In spiritual direction, memory can allow the construction of a "salvation history" of the self with a loving, empowering God.

Sometimes persons whose lives are marked by threat, insecurity, hurt, or change need to be repeatedly reinserted back into a psychic context marked by both divine and human affirmation. The retrieval from memory of marker events that effect such a context can become an important step toward growth and decision.

Memory and Church Practice

The Church has traditionally educated children in the memorization of basic creeds and prayers to assure their communion in the foundational beliefs of the community. While many believe that this practice was used to excess in the period before the Second Vatican Council, others recognize that immediate access to such texts through memory can establish a strong emotional link to the objects of faith as well as provide a basic creedal context for religious thinking. It is likely that the memorized religious material that has the strongest impact upon the psychic life of the child is material that has been memorized by repeated exposure to positive events rather than by the imposition of learning chores of memorization.

Christian ritual, especially in the Eucharist, employs memory in a privileged fashion. The Eucharistic Prayer contains the memorial that recalls the event of Christ's self-offering under the form of bread and wine as a sacrament of his redemptive death. This ritual calls Christians to keep in mind that their lives are ordered to this mystery. Here memory serves the function of integrating our present experiences, lived in faith, with the mystery dimension of Christ, who comes to live in us through the Eucharistic meal. This mystery forms the basis for Christian self-awareness in the Catholic tradition. By it the Christological meaning of ordinary life is established through an ongoing analogical reference to Christ's paschal mystery through ritual and memory.

See also CONSCIOUSNESS; DREAMS; IMAGINATION; MEDITATION; MIND; NARRATIVE; RECOLLECTION; SPIRITUAL DIRECTION: STORY.

Bibliography: R. Baron, D. Byrne, and B. Kantowitz, *Psychology: Understanding Behavior* (Philadelphia: W. B. Sanders, 1978) 153–183. R. Hart, *Unfinished Man and the Imagination* (New York: Seabury, 1979) 189–219.

PAUL J. PHILIBERT, O.P.

MENTAL PRAYER

See CONTEMPLATION, CONTEMPLATIVE PRAYER; MEDITATION; PRAYER.

MERCY

Mercy is the compassionate care for others whereby one takes on the burden of another as one's own. It is an active quality of the virtue of charity, motivated by love. While *mercy* is often treated as a rather benign term, its power is conveyed more accurately by looking at it in a scriptural context.

"Mercy" is used as the translation of three Hebrew words, the most common one being *ḥesed,* which has a broad range of meaning. It is the covenanted love between Abraham and Sarah (Gen 20:13), David and Jonathan (1 Sam 20:8), and Yahweh and the people (Exod 20:6). It is mutual and enduring, implying action on both parts.

Rāḥamîm, the plural form of "womb," is also translated as "mercy." God's mercy is a nurturing womb, implying a physical response and demonstrating that mercy is felt in the center of one's body. This dimension of mercy also requires action.

Also translated "mercy" is the Hebrew *ḥēn/ḥānan,* meaning "grace" or "favor." Unlike the other terms, this is a free gift, with no mutuality either implied or expected. Not necessarily enduring, this quality is dependent solely on the giver and usually occurs between unequals.

Taken together, these three roots give us an understanding of God's mercy in the OT. It is best demonstrated by Hosea and

Jeremiah, who use the analogy of marriage between Yahweh and Israel, showing us that mercy is the fruit of the covenant, forgiving as well as caring and nurturing.

Jesus is the most eloquent witness to mercy in the NT. He is never vague in his proclamation of God's mercy, and rather than using parables or discourses, he reveals God's mercy in his everyday relations with people from all strata of society. Jesus is an active agent of God's mercy—confronting the crowd about to stone the woman taken in adultery, meeting the Samaritan woman at the well, weeping with the other mourners at the death of Lazarus, and ultimately taking up the cross laden with the sins of the world and being led to his death.

According to Mt 25:31-46, mercy will be the quality on which the Christian will ultimately be judged. This understanding of the necessity of mercy was also developed in the early Church, particularly in the *Didache,* which went so far as to state that those who have no mercy will be condemned.

Traditionally these dictates of the Gospel have been handed down to us as the corporal and spiritual works of mercy, which should characterize the lives Christians lead. The corporal works of mercy require the follower of Jesus to feed the hungry, give drink to the thirsty, clothe the naked, shelter the homeless, care for the sick, visit those imprisoned, and bury the dead. The spiritual works of mercy include admonishing sinners, instructing the ignorant, counseling the doubtful, comforting the sorrowful, bearing wrongs patiently, forgiving injuries, and praying for the living and the dead. These build on the biblical foundation that one must "do justice, love mercy, and walk humbly with our God" (Mic 6:8).

See also AFFECT, AFFECTIVITY; COMPASSION; LOVE; WEAKNESS AND VULNERABILITY.

Bibliography: John Paul II, *Rich in Mercy* (Washington: USCC, 1980).

JULIA UPTON, R.S.M.

MERIT, MERITORIOUS ACTION

See GRACE; PRAXIS; VIRTUE.

MIDLIFE CRISIS/TRANSITION

See JOURNEY (GROWTH AND DEVELOPMENT IN SPIRITUAL LIFE); PSYCHOLOGY, RELATIONSHIP AND CONTRIBUTION TO SPIRITUALITY.

MILLENARIANISM

Many early Christians centered their belief in the imminent return of Jesus on the peaceful and glorious thousand-year reign of Christ and his saints described in Rev 20:3-6—the "millennium." Most early "millenarians" or "chiliasts," including Justin Martyr, Hippolytus, and Irenaeus, maintained that Christ's reign would follow the parousia. Later, more literal adherents proposed that the millennial epoch of peace and justice would precede and inaugurate the second coming (premillenialism), a difference in interpretation that has continued to the present. OT and apocryphal influences include Dan 7:13-14; Isa 27:13; the Book of Enoch; and 2 Esdras. Possible NT sources include Mt 24:29-30; Mk 13:26-27; Lk 21:25-27; 1 Thess 4:14-17; 2 Pet 3:8-13; and Jude 14-16.

Opposed by Clement and Origen in Alexandria and Augustine in Carthage, the millenarian theme has had a strong appeal to dissident groups, recurring among Gnostics and Montanists in the 2nd century and the Priscillians of 4th-century Spain. Revived throughout Europe by eschatological expectations shortly before the year 1000, and again in the 13th and 14th centuries; after the Protestant Reformation in Germany and Switzerland; in 17th-and 18th century Pietism; in 19th-century America among sects such as Jehovah's Witnesses and Seventh Day Adventists, millenarianism survives today among many Evangelical and Pentecostal groups as part of a larger system of eschatology, and may be expected to increase as the third millennium approaches.

See also APOCALYPTICISM; ESCHATOLOGY; FUTURE.

Bibliography: E. Chamberlain, *Antichrist and the Millennium* (New York: Dutton, 1975). N. Cohn, *The Pursuit of the Millennium* (New York: Oxford, 1970). Z. Hayes, *Visions of a Future: A Study of Christian Eschatology* (Wilmington, Del.: Glazier, 1989).

RICHARD WOODS, O.P.

MIND

The word *mind* derives from an etymological base whose meaning is "to think." In its ordinary sense, it also more broadly suggests spatiotemporal nonextension and radical self-presence, interiority, consciousness, as contrasted with the nonconsciousness and spatiotemporal extension of *matter*. It remains that in reference to human consciousness, the word has at least three mutually exclusive technical senses, ultimately reflecting three divergent philosophical analyses of the human being. It often retains one of these diverse technical senses (sometimes partly modified, sometimes not) when in turn it is employed in reference to divine consciousness.

Material Monism

The first analysis of the human being has a long and venerable lineage in the history of explicit philosophy, a lineage extending from Epicurus of Athens through Thomas Hobbes to J.J.C. Smart. On this, the "material monist" account, the human being is either simply identical with matter or else wholly reducible to it. The familiar features of "spirit" are merely apparent, not real. What appears to be conscious, self-constituting, and free is really determined, other-constituted, and even nonconscious. What appears to be deed or performance is really just event or process. From the ultimate explanatory standpoint, that of metaphysics, "mind" is finally nothing more than a function of matter; "the mental" is at most a mere epiphenomenon of the material.

The difficulty with the material monist account is that one cannot actually assert it without involving oneself in a contradiction, a latent incompatibility between what one asserts and one's act of asserting. This incompatibility may be brought to light by noting five points. First, a critically based (rather than dogmatic) philosophy recognizes that operationally, if not always explicitly, the fundamental cognitional meaning of the word "true" as applied to claims and the word "real" as employed in them is nothing other than "what rationally structured cognitional consciousness anticipates." One cannot even think about truth and reality except by using one's cognitional consciousness; and whatever one thinks or affirms of them is inevitably prefigured in a basic way by the rational structure of that cognitional consciousness itself.

Second, a critically based philosophy goes on to identify the rational structure of cognitional consciousness as an indubitable and unconditional predisposition to proceed always and only on the basis of the evidence one possesses. It is an antecedently given dynamic imperative to assert all and only those claims supported by evidence that one has grasped as sufficient. Perhaps one violates that imperative from time to time, but one can neither deny the imperative nor rest content with the violations.

Third, it follows that from the fundamental standpoint of one's concrete cognitional functioning, as contrasted perhaps with the secondary standpoint of one's professed account of that functioning, true claims are those that one asserts on the basis of evidence grasped as sufficient, and real things are those to which true claims refer.

Fourth, in and through my very act of asserting the central claim of material monism, "Human spirit as such is just apparent, not real," I inevitably experience both the act itself as conscious and self-constituting, and, more fundamentally, myself as a conscious and self-constituting assertor. For my act of seriously asserting that claim or any other claim is not a blind, mechanical, automatic act. On the contrary, even prior to any reflection on it, my assertory act inherently is primitively self-possessing, radically present to itself. Moreover, it is present as constituting itself, attempting to be judicious rather than just reactive, aspiring to respect the antecedently given imperative to operate rationally. Finally, it is present as *my* act. I experience it as a small but significant exercise of my own self-constituting selfhood.

Fifth, my experience of myself as a consciously self-constituting assertor is evidence irrefutably sufficient for a very different claim, namely, "My spirit as such is real, not just apparent." For conscious self-constitution is a characteristic trait of spirit. My very act of asserting the unreality of human spirit embodies indisputable grounds for asserting the reality of my own human spirit. When the latent contradiction between the claim I assert and the claim implied by my act of asserting it is made explicit, the concrete evidential insufficiency of the first claim becomes explicit as well. Material monism, flawed by the uncritical metaphysical perspective it presupposes and by its corresponding insufficient attention to the fundamental epistemic features of concrete consciousness, is manifest as functionally untenable.

Material-Spiritual Dualism

A second analysis of the human being also has a long and venerable lineage in the history of explicit philosophy, a lineage extending (with variations, to be sure) from Plato through René Descartes to Jean-Paul Sartre. On this, the "material-spiritual dualist" account, the human being is a conjunction of two elements that nonetheless remain radically disparate—even (with Descartes) two distinct substances. It is an aggregate of matter and mind, where "mind" means "spirit." Insofar as it is material, the human being is determined, other-constituted, nonconscious, and spatiotemporally extended. On the other hand, insofar as it is spiritual, the human being is spatiotemporally nonextended, conscious, self-constituting, and free. Moreover, the spiritual element, although it interacts with the material element, basically is totally independent of it. Mind is affected by matter but in no way essentially conditioned by it.

As with the material monist account, however, any effort concretely to assert the material-spiritual dualist account of the human being inescapably embroils the assertor in an inconsistency. The character of this inconsistency may be elucidated in three steps. First, as before, a critically based philosophy recognizes that true claims are those that one asserts on the basis of evidence grasped as sufficient, and real things are those to which true claims refer.

Second, in and through my very act of asserting the central claim of material-spiritual dualism, "Human spirit as such basically is totally independent of matter," I unavoidably experience both the act itself and, more fundamentally, myself as an assertor to be conditioned by sensible data in a partial but basic way. For my act of seriously asserting that claim or any other claim is intrinsically an act of self-present spontaneity striving to be rational, an act of conscious self-constitution aiming to be judicious. But directly or indirectly it also presupposes sensible data and thus stands in extrinsic dependence upon them. Like every other serious assertory act, my assertion of the dualist claim regards intelligibilities that ultimately I have grasped as residing either in sensible data or in my acts of sensing such data. Moreover, it aspires to base itself on evidence that ultimately includes either sensible data or my acts of sensing such data.

Third, my experience of myself as an intrinsically self-constituting but extrinsically dependent assertor is evidence indisputably sufficient for a very different claim, namely, "My spirit as such is intrinsically independent of matter but extrinsically dependent upon it." For if conscious self-constitution is a characteristic trait of spirit, the sensible data upon which that self-constitution depends bear the characteristic traits of matter. Though present to consciousness, simply as sensible data they are nonconscious and spatiotemporally extended. My very act of asserting the basic total independence of human spirit from matter embodies irrefutable grounds for asserting my own human spirit's extrinsic dependence upon matter. When the latent contradiction between the claim I assert and the claim implied by my act of asserting it is made explicit, the concrete evidential insufficiency of the first claim becomes explicit as well. Material-spiritual dualism, flawed by the uncritical phenomenological perspective it presupposes and by its corresponding insufficient attention to the fundamental phenomenal features of concrete consciousness, is manifest as operationally untenable.

Material-Spiritual Compositism

Finally, a third analysis of the human being does not lack proponents in the history of explicit philosophy, unless one wishes to discount Aristotle, Thomas Aquinas, and Bernard Lonergan. On this, the "material-spiritual compositist" account, the human being comprises two elements, matter and spirit. Though they may be conceived as distinct, in reality these two elements always occur together as inseparable components of a substantial unity, the integral composite that is a human being. They give rise to three distinct levels of operation within the human composite. First, physical, chemical, and organic processes, other-constituted and nonconscious, are material in the sense

that they are simple manifestations of matter. Second, sensory knowing and passive affection, conscious but other-constituted, are material in the sense that they are conditioned intrinsically by matter. Third, intellectual knowing and choosing are conscious, self-constituting, and sometimes even free operations. They are spiritual in the sense that they are neither simple manifestations of matter nor intrinsically conditioned by it, although, as *human* (rather than angelic or divine) spiritual operations, they are extrinsically conditioned by it. In this tradition one commonly labels operations on the first level "(strictly) material," on the second level "psychic," on the third level "spiritual," and on both the second and the third levels "mental."

By contrast with material monism and material-spiritual dualism, I am able to profess material-spiritual compositism without performative inconsistency. For in and through my act of asserting its central claim, "Human spirit as such is intrinsically independent of matter but extrinsically dependent upon it," I invariably experience myself as an assertor who is intrinsically self-constituting but extrinsically dependent upon sensible data. That is to say, as was just explained in the discussion of material-spiritual dualism, I encounter evidence undeniably sufficient for the claim, "My spirit as such is intrinsically independent of matter but extrinsically dependent upon it." In seriously asserting any claim, I experience in my own case what the material-spiritual compositist claim expresses as the general case. When this fact is brought to light, crucial evidential support for that general claim comes to light as well. Material-spiritual compositism, its metaphysical perspective critically grounded on a thorough (if historically not always articulated) objectification of the fundamental phenomenal features of concrete consciousness, is vindicated as uniquely plausible.

Summary

In its ordinary sense, the word *mind* suggests spatiotemporal nonextension, consciousness, and at least partly the ability to think. The history of explicit philosophy supplements this ordinary meaning with no fewer than three different technical conceptions of human mentality, conceptions which often are extended (with or without modification) to the mind of God. Material monism conceives human mind as wholly reducible to matter or even simply identical with it. Material-spiritual dualism conceives human mind basically as wholly independent of matter. And material-spiritual compositism conceives human mind in its psychic dimension as intrinsically dependent upon matter but in its spiritual dimension as merely extrinsically dependent upon it. It would seem that only the third view is consistent with personal experience of one's own concrete conscious operations.

See also BODY; CONSCIOUSNESS; EXPERIENCE; FREEDOM; GOD; INTENTION, INTENTIONALITY; PSYCHOLOGY, RELATIONSHIP AND CONTRIBUTION TO SPIRITUALITY; REFLECTION; SOUL; TRUTH; WILL.

Bibliography: B. Lonergan, *Insight: A Study of Human Understanding* (New York: Philosophical Library, 1957); *Method in Theology* (New York: Herder, 1972). R. Doran, *Theology and the Dialectics of History* (Toronto: Univ. of Toronto Press, 1990).

MICHAEL VERTIN

MINISTRY, MINISTERIAL SPIRITUALITY

Ministry is the service of the kingdom of God that flows from the call and empowerment of the Holy Spirit through a community of believers. The spirituality of any ministry will always involve living out the call to service in the pattern of Christ's death and resurrection.

In Jesus' ministry of preaching, teaching, healing, and reconciling, the presence of God's kingdom broke in upon human history in a new and definitive way. In his own death and resurrection, Jesus sealed the truth of his ministry by the total gift of himself for the salvation of all those whom he came to serve.

Through the outpouring of the Holy Spirit at Pentecost, the continuance of Jesus' ministry is now committed to the Christian community. The Church is meant to be the sacrament of Jesus' ministry so that his mission for the kingdom of God will be extended to all times and places. Through the outpouring of a variety of gifts, the Holy Spirit seeks to provide the means necessary in order to meet the manifold needs that people have to encounter the merciful love of God in the diverse circumstances of their lives.

The work of service carried out in a variety of ministries renders the saving reality of God's kingdom present here and now. In the midst of any community of believers, the Holy Spirit constantly calls individuals to hear the word of God, inviting them to the service of the kingdom and empowering them, because of their response in faith, through an outpouring of the varied gifts that are requisite to render Jesus' ministry present.

The teaching of St. Augustine that it is Christ who is operative in any ministerial activity must be the horizon within which one reflects upon ministerial spirituality. For the same Holy Spirit who was operative in the ministry of Jesus is now the source of grace for any ministry in the Church that flows from the salvific activity of the risen Lord. The intentionality with which one approaches the ministry is profoundly significant for developing a spirituality that is both contemplative and apostolic. Ministering persons are meant to grow in their understanding that any apostolic activity in which one is engaged is necessarily rooted in Christ's ministry as its source.

Because ministry is the presence of the saving work of Christ in a concrete set of circumstances through the activity of the ministering person, it is important for those who serve to be aware of their own relatedness in any ministerial situation both to those whose needs are being addressed and to Christ who is at work through the gifts that are being exercised. Those engaged in ministry need to open their hearts in faith to the growth in love that is always being offered in different ways to all those involved in any grace-filled encounter with the Lord's death and resurrection. Openness to the Holy Spirit's work of drawing all present in any exercise of ministry into an experience of the new life of mutual loving service that characterizes the kingdom of God should be the horizon for all apostolic activity.

Ministering persons are asked to listen contemplatively in order to hear God's word of mercy and hope that needs to be addressed to their sisters and brothers within the human family in a specific situation. Contemplative listening becomes the context for prayer, preceding, accompanying, and following any apostolic activity. Prayer is not separate from ministry but is the attitude of listening and responding by the power of the Holy Spirit to the mystery of Christ, who is present as preacher, teacher, healer, prophet, and priest in accord with each one's needs in every aspect of one's daily exercise of ministry.

The ministering person prays surrounded by the experience of the needs of God's people and of Christ's gracious response to those needs through one's own efforts in ministry. Growth in spiritual maturity comes from the willingness to commit oneself to a life of ministerial service that is exercised in the power of the Holy Spirit with integrity and intentionality.

The fruitfulness of any exercise of ministry within a community flows from the willingness of those who minister to experience Jesus' own gift of himself unto death for the needs of those whom they serve. Faced with the challenge of service in the pattern of Christ's death and resurrection, the ministering person must draw upon the power of the Holy Spirit, who alone can provide the strength necessary for any sharing in the paschal mystery.

Ministerial spirituality recognizes the sphere of human activity as the locus for experiencing God's gift of new life in Christ. Called by God from the community and empowered by the Holy Spirit for service, the ministering person finds holiness by ever integrating prayer and apostolic activity within the horizon of sharing here and now in Christ's ministry to those in need of God's love and care. Listening to God's word, surrounded by the needs of one's brothers and sisters, those who minister strive ever more fully to conform their minds and hearts to the pattern of Christ's gracious concern for all. Sustained by the presence of the Lord as the one who ministers in every situation and ever graced by the gifts of the Holy Spirit, ministering persons are able, in union with Christ, to lay down their lives in daily service. Through the gift of themselves in faithful love, they believe that those who are served will indeed, by God's grace, come to share in the fullness of the kingdom by experiencing the gift of new life that flows from the paschal mystery.

See also APOSTOLIC SPIRITUALITY; AUTHORITY; CELIBACY; CHARISM; DISCIPLESHIP; FRENCH SCHOOL OF SPIRITUALITY; KINGDOM OF GOD; MISSION, SPIRITUALITY FOR MISSION; POWER; PREACHING; SERVICE; WORLD.

Bibliography: T. O'Meara, Theology of Ministry (New York: Paulist, 1983). E. Schillebeeckx, The Church with a Human Face: A New and Expanded Theology of Ministry (New York: Crossroad, 1985).

THOMAS D. McGONIGLE, O.P.

MIRACLES

See EXTRAORDINARY PHENOMENA.

MISSION, SPIRITUALITY FOR MISSION

A spirituality for mission depends on the times in which we live and the particular problems that we encounter in our modern world. Today we have moved from the age of missions to that of mission, for we recognize that the Church is present everywhere to some degree. As the 20th century comes to a close, three problems are generally emphasized: (1) the incarnation of the faith in the daily lives of all people; (2) the struggle for justice against all kinds of oppression; (3) dialogue with peoples of other faiths and ideologies.

The unknown author of the following lines has well summarized the contemporary approach to mission after many years of searching since the Second Vatican Council:

> Our first task in approaching
> another people
> another culture
> another religion
> is to take off our shoes
> for the place
> we are approaching is holy
> Else we may find ourselves
> treading on another's
> dream. More serious
> still, we may forget . . .
> that God
> was there before our arrival.

The unevangelized percentage of the world population has, according to David Barrett's statistics, steadily dropped in this century to 24.5% in 1989 and a projected 16.6% in 2000, with some two hundred unreached peoples (*International Bulletin of Missionary Research*, January 1989). Christian martyrs have increased from 35,500 in 1900, to 270,000 in 1980, to 325,800 in 1989, with 400,000 projected in 2000. A significant megatrend is the rise since 1980 of an East Asian colossus of 80 million Christians, mostly Chinese, Koreans, and Japanese, of whom 80% are charismatic and who in turn are sending out their own missionaries across the globe. Other megatrends include the spread of charismatics, the rise in ecclesiastical crimes such as embezzlement, and the increasing use of computers in the service of mission.

It is against this background that steps, admittedly tentative, are being made to explore a new spirituality of mission as the new century approaches. The search for a new spirituality has been particularly urgent since the abolition in 1969 of the *Ius Commissionis,* by which, since 1622, various religious societies were entrusted with the staffing and operation of dioceses and vicariates. Hitherto large territories were the province of particular religious orders. Now the local bishops are fully responsible for staffing, policy-making, and financial support in local churches and communities. Foreign missionaries, therefore, are in a radically different position of service and dependence.

Two recent writers have captured the new mood of mission quite well. In *I Believe in the Great Commission* (London: Hodder & Stoughton, 1976), Max Warren, the widely experienced secretary of the Church Mission Society, suggests that a missionary is anyone anywhere who is obedient to the great commission. Such a person should have the seven qualities of inquirer, learner, listener, lover, link, disturber, and sign of the end. Warren notes seven signs of the times: a compassionate society, a passion for justice, a search for meaning, interiorization, a search for belonging, a search for unity, and the ecumenical movement. In his work *Christianity Rediscovered* (Notre Dame, Ind.: Fides, 1978), Vincent Donovan advises a missionary: "In working with people, do not try to call them back to where they were, and do not try to call them to where you are, as beautiful as that place might seem to you. You must have the courage to go with them to a place that neither you nor they have ever been before" (p. vii).

It is increasingly accepted today that any authentic missionary spirituality must be based on a following of Christ, his ministry and teaching, and must take seriously his experiences of mission. For Vatican Council II, the incarnation of Christ is the model of inculturation. At the World Conference on Mission and Evangelism held in Melbourne in 1980, a shift took place from Paul and apostles as models for mission to Jesus himself, the missionary par excellence. Jesus and his mission were "ultimately decisive for the character, the scope, the urgency, and the authority of the early Church's Christian mission" (Senior and Stuhlmueller, p. 157). And so they should be today.

To summarize, one could quote the incisive remark of François Marie Paul Libermann (1802–1852), founder of the Society of the Immaculate Heart of Mary and a courageous pioneer in sending missionaries to Africa: "I fear for that work which is not marked with the sign of the cross." Or as the Maryknoll bishop James Walsh (1867–1936) once put it: "The task of a missionary is to go to a place where he is not wanted, to sell a pearl whose value, although of great price, is not recognized, to people who are determined not to accept it even as a gift."

Mission is a learning experience, not least for the missionaries themselves and for the Churches from which they are sent. This theme of continuing discipleship is increasingly emphasized in recent official documents. Thus in their 1986 letter on world missions, *To the Ends of the Earth*, the U.S. bishops repeatedly insist that the Church in the United States should learn from returning missionaries and be enriched by the faith and experience of Christians throughout the world.

See also APOSTOLIC SPIRITUALITY; CULTURE; INCARNATION; KINGDOM OF GOD; LIBERATION THEOLOGY, INFLUENCE ON SPIRITUALITY; PREACHING; SERVICE; THIRD WORLD, SPIRITUALITY OF; VATICAN COUNCIL II.

Bibliography: M. Collins Reilly, *Spirituality for Mission* (Maryknoll, N.Y.: Orbis, 1978). D. Senior and C. Stuhlmueller, *The Biblical Foundations for Mission* (Maryknoll, N.Y.: Orbis, 1983).

SÉAN P. KEALY, C.S.SP.

MODERATION

See CARDINAL VIRTUES; VIRTUE.

MODERN SPIRITUALITY

The interplay between spirituality and culture that is at work in any age took a distinctive form in the West in the decades between the late 16th and the early 19th centuries. This so-called modern era spanned the end of the medieval world and the beginning of the contemporary one, and registered all the political, religious, economic, and social upheavals of that time (Late Renaissance, national states, Reformation/Counter-Reformation, Enlightenment, Baroque, etc.), which, at least when compared with previous epochs, came quite rapidly. The spiritualities that prevailed both spoke in their own ways to its deep aspirations and at the same time did not engage a number of its secularizing and scientific tenets. Spiritual movements were clear, intense, gospel-centered and reform-minded, but increasingly tended to distance themselves, certainly linguistically, from the cultural matrix.

Precedents

Late medieval times saw the dissolution of an almost mystical interpenetration between Church and society that had provided stable meaning to its members. The search for immediacy in the Rhineland and in England, the rejection of the apparatus of the schools by the "devout moderns," and the preference for positive rather than speculative approaches to theology were initial signals of this growing unease and unloosed the creativities of various geniuses who were to set the religious tone.

Martin Luther was such a breakthrough personality. A general distrust of philosophy and of religious institutions came to a passionate head in his teaching that all human mediations are radically flawed. Before the cross of Christ, the pretensions of method, hierarchy, and syllogism were laid bare and only served to intensify the desire for grace. For Luther, spiritual life required immediacy and individuality. Pursuit of just these qualities drove the spiritual quest through much of the modern age.

Spain

In Spain, Teresa of Avila and John of the Cross set the standard in Catholic circles for articulating this naked cry for the Absolute. Confessing that the approach to God happens only on God's terms, Teresa nonetheless painted the way there in warm and welcoming colors. Her chronicle of the journey through a series of successively enclosed chambers (mansions) is classic among the descriptions of the mystical path. Sparkling as it does with images of emerging butterflies and bubbling artesian wells, it depicts her move from active to passive contemplation. Hardly a passive personality, Teresa initiated a prodigious reform within the Carmelites and thus also testified to the synergy between genuine interior life and effective apostolic action.

If Teresa sketched resting points along the spiritual ascent, her protégé, John of the Cross, fixed his gaze on the summit. Compactly in his poetry but also in interpretive prose, John detailed the melting-down and recasting of human desire as it draws near the Divine. His is a shadowy passage through a twilight of the senses and spirit, an intensely dark nocturne, and out into a dawn streaked with the divine light. Over the course of that night, the darkness that blinded the traveler is revealed as the radiance of God, which at the earlier stage could not be recognized for the light it was.

In fresh and psychologically astute reinterpretations, the two Carmelites chart the course for healthy spiritual development. While John more so than Teresa appears abstracted from the culture, both resonate to that sigh for closeness to a seemingly withdrawing Deity. Contemporary interest especially in John has been stirred by recognition of his surehandedness in a world intuiting God's absence and searching through the glass darkly for its deepest ground.

Ignatius of Loyola took a different tack as he found intimacy with God in the press of active service. As he interacted with his times and circumstances, he discovered certain patterns of divine guidance embedded within his experience and subsequently constructed an imaginatively rich method to help others appropriate theirs. Basic to his logic was a conviction that the Spirit of Jesus is "afoot in the universe," particularly within each individual, and that therefore the Spirit-filled person is able to know by both interior and exterior signs which activities are the genuine works of Christ. Such a mystical perception of the world ties the closest of bonds between contemplative prayer and ministry, prodding the apostle to view all activities in their relation to their divine ground, and conversely to find that source in all things.

The mobility and confidence of Ignatius's approach provided both framework and stimulus for much of the innovative missionary work in the centuries following. In addition, his insistence upon the complementarity between inner spiritual experience and its objectifications in the doctrines, governance, and pastoral projects of the Church helped later followers to steer (not always successfully) between quietist/illuminist interpretations of his thought and moralistic/Pelagian ones, either of which would have narrowed his unique contribution.

France

Spirituality in France of the 17th century reacted in disparate ways to the societal currents. In the one direction, it looked approvingly on human accomplishment, striving to purify it even as it cooperated with it. In the other, through the so-called French School, it distanced itself from an arrogance it saw in the culture's achievements, even while striving mightily for reform within the ecclesiastical culture. The devout humanism of Francis de Sales and the abstract mysticism of Pierre de Bérulle typify the two streams.

Devout Humanism

Sympathetic though critical alignment with the human marks the wisdom of Francis de Sales. He would have all Christians, lay and religious, discover the touch of God within their daily rounds. In charming analogies, he portrayed all of creation as sacramental and looked to personal relationships especially as the clear optic for discovering the love of Jesus at work in the world. His was a gentle initiation onto the path of paschal compassion, a journey, however, requiring the high asceticism needed to rework human desire into perfect love.

In practice if not always in spiritual doctrine, the religious institutes that multiplied through these centuries were other carriers of the world-affirming instinct. In them, an evangelically entrepreneurial spirit intersected with the social consciousness spreading across France at the time. The foreign mission societies, the communities founded by Vincent de Paul and Louise de Marillac to care for the poor and abandoned, and numerous other associations of men and especially of women established explicitly for service were instances of this new species of religious life, the apostolic congregation. They brought the deeds of Christ to a culture whose thoughts were beginning to sprout from a cognitive soil quite different from the one that supported the Christian worldview.

The French School

The opposite face of the French tradition found its most forceful voice in Pierre de Bérulle. Reinterpreting the negating approach of Pseudo-Dionysius, he advocated radical detachment from all images and techniques so that believers might stand empty—more precisely, "annihilated"—before the divine majesty. Bérulle's contemplation of the humanity of Christ soon tempered this initial starkness. For him, the deeds of Jesus on earth were unrepeatable in their historical particularity, but as dispositions were taken up everlastingly into the life of the Trinity and made available to believers of all eras. By attending to these "states" of Jesus, the disciple could be stripped of interior idols and progressively elevated toward mystical union. Contemplatively transformed, this new heart turned outward in works of reform, particularly within the Church. Bérulle's accomplishment was to have incorporated the Dionysian way into a transcendent interpretation of Jesus' humanity in such ways that the bleak abnegation of the *via negativa* was brightened by the light coming from lives progressing toward oneness with Christ.

This more optimistic strain in Bérulle found expression in fruitful spiritualities of ministry developed for lay, but particularly for ordained, Christians. Reformers like Jean-Jacques Olier, John Eudes, Vincent de Paul, and later Louis Grignion de Montfort located the praxis and structures of service in the context of the Trinitarian missions and most especially of the evangelizing work of Jesus. It was the fertile will of the Father shown in Jesus, transmitted by the Spirit and exemplified by the friends of Jesus (notably his holy Mother) that energized the Christian leader. Activity grounded in the contemplatively transformed heart would revitalize the apostolate.

Jansenism

Bérulle's annihilation doctrine figured in still other movements whose forbidding tone has left its mark on the French School. The most stringent of these was Jansenism, a spiritual outlook in itself but also a participant in the wider debate going on since the Reformation over free will and providence. In support of Michel de Bay, Cornelius Jansen interpreted St. Augustine to mean that those individuals predestined for heaven were capable of doing good only if given a special help (efficacious) beyond the general kind bestowed in redemption, and even with it had to practice a severe asceticism to remain in grace. Jansen's rigorous message found a home at the convent of Port-Royale, where the brother and sister Pierre and Marie Arnauld and the Abbé de Saint-Cyran (Jean Duvergier de Hauranne) developed it into a bracing devotional and moral program.

Early on, political considerations began to mix with theological ones as the movement began to symbolize a whole raft of thoughts and positions within the Church and beyond it. Blaise Pascal, an authentic mystic and gifted writer, emerged as its most persuasive voice. The vileness within the human spirit is more than compensated for by the "fiery mercy" streaming from the God of Isaac, Jacob, and Jesus who penetrates the smug minds of the elect to warm and win their hearts. Despite— and in some measure because of—his lyrical defense, Jansenism as an organized movement ended abruptly, condemned as an elitist and one-sided approach because of its penchant for disputation and its stratifications in holiness and disparagement of the human. But the lofty severity of its moral view and its refined sensitivity to the transcendence of God gave it an influence long after its institutional demise.

Quietism

Alike in combining total trust in God with radical distrust in the human, quietism differed from Jansenism by preferring the passive over the active mode of response. Convinced that only the divine indwelling could dispel the darkness in the soul, the quietists preached total surrender to providence as the one viable spiritual option. Theologically, they sided with Miguel de Molinos, whose teaching confined asceticism to the effort simply of establishing that inner silence necessary for complete abandonment.

In less scholarly and more exuberant language, Madame Jeanne-Marie Guyon extolled the quietist virtues. The control of all activity, both inner and outer, was to be given over to the Spirit, who worked through all mediums, including the psychic processes of automatic writing and speaking. Fear of the excesses of this liberated unconscious raised many suspicions. Her protégé, Francis Fénelon, attempted to ground her insights theologically by establishing their patristic precedents and locating them within a scholastic analysis of "pure love." By letting go of all plans, markers, and methods, the perfect disciple grows indifferent to any state except the love of God for God's sake, even to the point of dropping concern about God's intention toward the self. When Fénelon himself was finally censured, it was political embroilment as well as doctrinal objections that moved Rome's hand. But the fundamental unease was stirred up by the rarefied purity he demanded for spiritual acts and intentions. Untainted by the ambiguities of the everyday, quietism smacked, in Louis Dupre's words, of a "too deliberate attempt to leave the ordinary." Indeed, the more down-to-earth version proposed in a later century by Jean-Pierre de Caussade countered the effetist impression and kept alive the quietists' reminder that the Spirit is the one initiator of every graced choice.

Conclusions

Although other figures and movements merit inclusion in this period of Catholic spirituality (e.g., Benedict of Canfield, Louis Lallemont, Baroque art, devotion to the Sacred Heart, etc.), the ones treated here indicate its main currents. An era of intense search for the spiritual, it moved at times in seemingly opposite directions. The humanistic thrust, although critical, extolled the person and regarded the world as God's own house needing to be peopled with saints and beauty. The theandric emphasis, although centered on Christ's humanity, divested itself of human achievement in order to stand empty and expectant before God's majesty. Passive reception of grace and active cooperation with it were counseled; contemplation took on both cloistered and missionary forms. The sense of God's absence from the world existed contrapuntally with an interior awareness of God's loving presence.

It is in this last disjunction that the opposites begin to coincide, at least to some degree. Reacting to the collapse of the medieval synthesis, modern spiritualities, slowly at first and then more rapidly, left the tracks of meaning being laid down in the wider culture and began to construct their own. They led in the direction of interiority, toward a sphere set off from political, scientific, and social developments. They moved toward an increasingly privatized discourse and were concerned with states of perfection at a considerable remove from the daily round of ordinary life. The subtly distinguished stages, the specialized practices, and perhaps most tellingly the subdivision of ascetical and mystical spirituality into a distinct theological discipline indicate the divergence.

Modern spirituality came to a close in the 19th century when Christians began to concern themselves explicitly with the wider culture by attending to evolutionary patterns, historical consciousness, the social effects of belief, personalistic philosophy, ecumenism, and especially the psychological critiques of a supposedly pure interiority. Nevertheless, the legacy of the period lives on. In the refinement it gave to

the art of discernment, in its apostolically fecund synthesis of contemplation and action, and perhaps most relevantly in its sympathy for the Christian on pilgrimage through a spiritually shallow world does the age called modern keep a hand in the present day.

See also ANGLO-CATHOLIC SPIRITUALITY; APOSTOLIC SPIRITUALITY; CARMELITE SPIRITUALITY; ENLIGHTENMENT, INFLUENCE ON SPIRITUALITY; FRENCH SCHOOL OF SPIRITUALITY; IGNATIAN SPIRITUALITY; JANSENISM; NEGATIVE WAY; PROTESTANT SPIRITUALITIES; QUIETISM; REFORMATION AND CATHOLIC REFORMATION SPIRITUALITIES; SALESIAN SPIRITUALITY.

Bibliography: H. Bremond, *A Literary History of Religious Thought in France from the Wars of Religion Down to Our Own Times,* 3 vols., trans. K. Montgomery (London: SPCK, 1928–1936). L. Cognet, "Ecclesiastical Life in France," *The Church in the Age of Absolutism and Enlightenment,* History of the Church 6, ed. H. Jedin and J. Dolan, trans. G. Holst (New York: Crossroad, 1981). H. O. Evennett, *The Spirit of the Counter Reformation,* ed. J. Bossy (Cambridge: Cambridge Univ. Press, 1968).

THOMAS F. McKENNA, C.M.

MONASTICISM, MONASTIC SPIRITUALITY

If there is one note characteristic of monastic life, it is this: monks and nuns are persons who have gone apart to be alone (Greek *monos,* "alone"), one with God. They have gone apart to find silence to pray, to live in communion with God.

Those who embrace the monastic life want to follow Christ and to live the Christian life to the full. This they do with particular attention to the hidden life of Jesus, recognizing his own call to periods of solitude and mindful of his practice of going apart in order to pray. Jesus' years of growth were so hidden that we know little of them; but as a member of a devout Jewish family, it is likely that it was his practice to give time to prayer on a regular basis. After his baptism by John in the Jordan, he went into the desert for weeks of solitude, silence, and prayer (Mk 1:11-13). As the busy years of his healing ministry unfolded, he went apart again and again, alone or with his chosen friends, to pray (Mt 14:13; 14:23; 17:1; 20:17; Mk 6:30).

Monastic life entails a call to go apart in imitation of the Master, to be one with him in communion with the Father. Monks and nuns seek to be alone. Yet they seek the unity with all men and women that is found in communion with God. In baptism they have been made one with the Son. Their whole life is a gradual movement to the Father in the Son through the Holy Spirit. In Christ they are one with all, and this union with Christ has a universal mediatory role.

The monastic life involves a call to go apart to find greater quiet, which springs from a daily routine free of the distractions of secular life. Entrance into the monastic life is no guarantee against distraction, however. Monks and nuns take with them much of the "old self"—all they have ever experienced—when they begin monastic life. They must learn to integrate the totality of their experience, past and present, into the growing harmony that allows the whole of life to speak of God. Solitude allows them to gain such a perspective on themselves and on the rest of creation.

The solitude that the monk or nun seeks most fervently, for which the solitude of the monastery is a preparation, is the solitude that is found in God. This solitude, life in God alone, cannot be adequately described in words. But those deeply committed to the monastic life know that in this solitude they offer their lives to God together with the whole of creation—every man, woman, and child, all of life, animate and inanimate. In entering into God's embrace, they bring all toward the final consummation that comes about through participation in divine creating love.

Historical Development

From the earliest Christian times, men and women have felt the call to go apart in order to find greater freedom to pray to the Father in Christ through the power of the Spirit. When Christianity began to be more closely allied with secular society, some Christians responded to the call to follow Christ more closely by fleeing the cities and going to live in the desert more or less permanently. Some lived a life of complete solitude; others lived in solitude but came together from time to time in loosely connected gatherings; still others lived in communities under the direction of a wise old guide. These latter drew part of their inspiration from the early Christian communities described in the Acts of the Apostles: "All who believed were together and had all things in common; they would sell their property and possessions and divide them among all according to each one's need. Every day they devoted themselves to meeting together in the temple area and to breaking bread in their homes" (Acts 2:44-46). St. Basil of Caesarea, who drew up the monastic rules commonly used among Byzantine and Eastern Christians, as well as some others, contributed to the movement of monasticism from the desert to urban areas. In part because of the influence of Athanasius's *Life of Antony,* one of the great monastic Fathers of Egypt, monasticism spread rapidly in the West.

In due course monasteries could be found throughout the Christian world in a variety of geographical settings: hilltops, valleys, islands, forests. In the Dark Ages, monasteries became havens of peace and safety, centers of culture, education, and trade. Villages and towns grew up around them. The monastery provided a focal point in both the secular and religious life of the people. Such developments gradually led monks to become more and more involved in ecclesiastical and secular affairs.

Great monastic Fathers wrote rules to give direction to the communal life of their followers. St. Benedict's Rule for Monasteries (RB) became paradigmatic for Western monasticism, eventually gaining normative status through the sanction of Charlemagne. Civil and ecclesiastical authorities, as well as monastic reformers, made repeated attempts to support and bolster the diverse, autonomous monasteries through the establishment of bonds of federation. The reform of Cluny (founded in 909), noted for its splendidly rich liturgical life, had widespread influence on monastic life in the West. The Cistercian reform (started in 1098), emphasizing solitude, poverty, and contemplation, sought to preserve the autonomy of the local community by drafting a Charter of Charity, which provided for general chapters and regular visitations. These structures were adopted by all later monastic communities. The Camaldolese and Carthusian Orders (founded ca. 1012 and 1084 respectively) sought to bring renewed support to the more eremitical impulse of monastic life. In later centuries monastic orders gave rise to various national congregations and communities. Under the papacy of Leo XIII, these were united in an international confederation and several international monastic orders.

Monasticism in the United States

Monks first came to the Americas with the Portuguese who colonized Brazil. Cistercians came to New York around 1800 but moved on to Canada. The United States was not to have its first permanent monasteries until the 1840s: Gethsemani Abbey in Kentucky (1848) and New Melleray Abbey in Iowa (1849). St. Meinrad's Abbey was founded in Indiana in 1854 as a refuge for the monks of Einsiedeln in Switzerland. With Conception Abbey, founded in Missouri in 1872, St. Meinrad's Abbey formed the Swiss-American Congregation in 1881. In 1855, St. Vincent's monastery near Latrobe, Pennsylvania, was raised to the status of an abbey and became the source of the American Cassinese Congregation. Monasteries of both the Swiss-American and the

Cassinese Congregations have spread to all parts of the United States. The English Benedictines also sent monks to the United States. St. Louis Priory on the outskirts of St. Louis, Missouri, was raised to abbatial status in 1989, bringing to three the number of English Benedictine abbeys in the United States, the others being St. Anselm's Abbey in Washington, D.C., and Portsmouth Abbey, Portsmouth, Rhode Island.

Benedictine sisters from St. Walburga's Convent in Eichstätt, Bavaria, also answered the call to pioneer in America. They came to St. Marys, Pennsylvania, in 1852; five years later St. Benedict's Convent was established in St. Joseph, Minnesota. Anselma Ferber and four other sisters left Maria Rickenbach in Switzerland, arriving in northwest Missouri in 1874 to begin the Congregation of Perpetual Adoration. This congregation and three major federations of Benedictine sisters—the Congregation of St. Scholastica, the Congregation of St. Benedict, and the Congregation of St. Gertrude—continue to flourish today, along with several independent convents of Benedictine nuns throughout the United States.

Monastic Spirituality
The Monastic Way

"To truly seek God" (RB 58:7)—this, for St. Benedict, is the very essence of monastic life. Indeed, it is the central precept of all human and religious life: "You shall love the Lord, your God, with all your heart, with all your being, with all your strength, and with all your mind" (Lk 10:27). This is the first commandment. Monastic life entails making this the whole of one's life. For those who follow the monastic way, God, and God alone, is the central, unifying reality of their lives. They remain celibate so that they can freely center their whole being and love in God, and in God love every one of their sisters and brothers.

For monks and nuns, this total commitment to God expresses itself in three interrelated concerns: "The concern must be whether the novice truly seeks God and whether he shows eagerness for the Work of God, for obedience and for trials" (RB 58:7). Monks and nuns must be humble, setting aside their own ambitions so that they can offer a complete "yes" to God. They must be obedient so that their whole being may be fully integrated into the divine plan. And the center of their lives must be the work of God, so that God's creation might be brought to its ultimate consummation, and thereby God be glorified.

Often *Opus Dei,* the "Work of God," is taken to mean the Hours of the Divine Office, the liturgy of praise that nuns and monks celebrate daily in choir. But these Hours are properly understood as the key moments when monks and nuns put aside all other activity to fulfill most solemnly their role as mediators of creation, giving voice and heart to the rest of creation's praise of its Maker. The *Opus Dei* reflects back the glory of its Creator. It is in the liturgy that creation attains its focal point and summit. The Hours constitute the high point of the day of monks and nuns. But this is true only to the degree that these times of praise are the expression of the basic attitude and activity of their whole life and the daily round of monastic existence. The whole being of the monk or nun is to be a doxology. The liturgy is a school in which, through sign and symbol, word and music, their minds and hearts are formed in ever-deepening participation in the life of God.

Monastic Obedience

In every human group, even if made up of only two or three members, someone has to be designated, at least temporarily, to make decisions that affect the life of the group; otherwise the group will be paralyzed or border on the chaotic. The richness of human personalities and the multiplicity of possibilities make consensus very difficult if not impossible to attain. Consensus may express itself in willingness to choose or accept a leader and to render obedience to him or her.

But the obedience of which the monastic Fathers speak is not primarily this functional obedience required by organization, however important this may be for the good order of the monastic community. The monastic Fathers are concerned with deeper values here. Because of an inherent dignity, all human persons are essentially equal. It is beneath their dignity to obey another person simply on the grounds that he or she is a person. When one obeys a person, the superior, in a community or organization, it is because he or she freely chooses to cooperate with the group in attaining its goals. One of the goods of obedience is involved here—cooperation as equals with different roles—but not *the* good of obedience of which St. Benedict speaks (RB 71:1). One alone is to be obeyed ultimately—God. Monks and nuns obey their superior because the superior holds the place of Christ in the monastic community and makes God's will known to them. They want to know the will of God so as to fully conform themselves to it. This is the key to happiness in the monastic way. This is *the* good of obedience.

Monastic Silence

Monks and nuns do not take a vow of silence, but they do have important rules and customs regarding silence in the monastery. These are deemed essential if the community is to live together and still have a context in which to seek God. Herein lies the deepest reason for monastic silence, whether it be the "great silence" of the night that enfolds their sleep and their vigils or the spaces and places of silence that they guard in their waking hours. Silence frees a person from listening to others for the moment in order to listen to God. "Be still and know that I am God" (Ps 46:10, NRSV).

In silence the monk or nun hears God, is embraced by God, and delights in God. But they also hear themselves, their true selves. They cannot give themselves in love if they do not know and possess themselves.

The tradition also notes that "where words are many, sin is not wanting" (Prov 10:19). Good communication is relatively rare. Talk quickly degenerates into gossip, detraction, calumny. To be together in silence, listening to the message of divine love that brothers and sisters may be to one another, can unite members of a community and be a more significant and fruitful form of communication than most speech.

Monastic tradition, then, assigns great value to silence (RB 6:2). It is the pathway to all that the monk or nun seeks.

Moderation

Part of the monastic way involves assigning importance to the value of moderation. This is particularly true regarding food and drink. Monks and nuns hold fasting and abstinence in high regard. Mitigations in its practice have occurred throughout the centuries. When relaxations are permitted, often in response to real exaggerations, they are quite legitimate. But "in all matters frugality is the rule" (RB 39:10). Physical emptiness and hunger can evoke a spiritual hunger for God.

Fasting is expressive of an attitude or disposition toward life, one that should be marked by joy. It is a stance toward the Creator and creation motivated by the desire for fulfillment of the longing heart. Such an attitude is foreign to any preoccupation with the picayune. It is not primarily concerned with minor rules and regulations. A monastic commitment to moderation requires communal order and expression. Thus there need to be opportunities for the monastic community as a whole to affirm in a coordinated way its adherence to the values inherent in disciplines of fasting, abstinence, and other practices of mortification.

Lectio Divina

Lectio divina is a process comprised of *lectio, meditatio, oratio,* and *contemplatio.* It is at the heart of the monastic way. St. Benedict gives it ample space in the daily horarium (RB 48-49). *Lectio* itself has a broader connotation than simple reading. It describes the receptivity to the revelation of God's love. The locus par excellence of this revelation is Sacred Scripture. There God reveals himself most intimately. The early followers of the monastic way memorized large portions of Scripture. For the monk or nun, *lectio* might entail calling up Scripture texts from memory. It might involve hearing another read. Frescoes, icons, and, later, stained glass could be a source of *lectio.* Eastern Christian monks and nuns frequently stand before holy icons and "listen" to them. For those committed to the practice of *lectio,* all creation is a book that speaks of God. Monks and nuns seek to hear this word, in the hope that it will live in them and form them. The images of Scripture may rest in the mind's eye, or a word may be repeated again and again on the lips or within the mind until it makes its home in the recesses of the heart.

Traditionally, monastic meditation does not rely on discursive reasoning or on refined techniques. The monastic approach is quite simple. It stresses an attitude of receptivity, allowing God's self-communication to form and call forth the depths of the heart. God's revelation can evoke many different responses, but ultimately it summons a love that longs for communion. This communion takes full form in *contemplation.*

Monastic life is in many ways very prosaic. An established routine is followed day after day. There is little change, diversion, or deviation. There is often a temptation to step out of the routine in an effort to find a shortcut that will provide a surge of divine power in the painfully slow work of purification and sanctification. The temptation to be impatient, to fall victim to listlessness, ennui, or *acedia,* or to force the hand of God is great. Those in the monastic way must learn again and again to let it be done God's way and in God's time, and to respond to grace in the confidence that God will indeed complete the work in them according to the divine promise.

Monastic Peace

Monks and nuns have been advocates of peace, from the days of Antony of Egypt, who returned from the desert to the city, through the days of Peter of Tarentaise, who stood before the Barbarossa, up to the present day. During the turmoil of war in Vietnam, Buddhist monks and their Catholic brothers and sisters from Cistercian communities joined in solidarity as witnesses for peace. Some continue to call men and women of all faiths, cultures, and nations to a true and lasting peace even and especially in the face of the possibility of nuclear annihilation.

St. Benedict, St. Bernard, and other great monastic promoters of peace throughout history were effective precisely because their activities were rooted in a deep source of peace within themselves. This is the primary matrix for creating a world of peace. Nuns and monks are persons of peace because their asceticism frees them from the violence of unbridled passion. The implication here is not that nuns and monks no longer have emotions, no longer experience love and anger, no longer are touched by stirrings of ambition, revenge, or lust. But the discipline of asceticism is to bring about a recognition and acceptance of these dimensions of the self in a lifelong task of personal integration and transformation by grace in Christ.

Conclusion

Monastic life is to engender a deepening faith, a faith that comes from listening. Though they vow to spend their lives in a specific monastic community (*stabilitas*),

monks and nuns also profess the belief that they do not have a lasting dwelling place here; they are en route, they are pilgrims. With death, life is not ended but changed. Thus even in the face of death they can be at peace because they have confidence that a deeper, unending life in the Spirit will be theirs. Giving their time, talent, energies, indeed their very lives, in communion with life's source, they savor life far more fully than does one who clings to it in a spirit of possessiveness and anxiety. Knowing the sacredness of life and its inherent quality and dignity, they seek to promote life and the quality of life. Monasteries are more often than not places of magnificent architecture, environmental beauty, culture, art, music, liturgy, warm hospitality, reverence for God and neighbor, balance of work and prayer, and peace to all who enter.

Earlier notions such as "fleeing the world" in pursuit of the monastic way have been considerably nuanced in the course of the renewal of monastic life in recent decades. Monks and nuns are now more keenly aware of the unity shared with every human person, more particularly with all those baptized in Christ. They know that their own daily struggle to enter more fully into communion with Christ draws them into deeper communion with all the members of his Body, the Church.

See also ACEDIA; BENEDICTINE SPIRITUALITY; CAMALDOLESE SPIRITUALITY; CARTHUSIAN SPIRITUALITY; CISTERCIAN SPIRITUALITY; CONTEMPLATION, CONTEMPLATIVE PRAYER; DESERT; EREMITICAL LIFE; LECTIO DIVINA; MORTIFICATION; OBEDIENCE; PEACE; SOLITUDE.

Bibliography: *RB 1980: The Rule of St. Benedict in Latin and English with Notes,* ed. T. Fry et al., (Collegeville, Minn: Liturgical Press, 1981). A. de Vogüé, *The Rule of Saint Benedict: A Doctrinal and Spiritual Commentary* (Kalamazoo, Mich.: Cistercian Publications, 1983). M. B. Pennington, *Monastic Life: A Short History of Monasticism and Its Spirit* (Petersham, Mass.: St. Bede's Publications, 1989). D. Rees et al., *Consider Your Call: A Theology of Monastic Life Today* (Kalamazoo, Mich.: Cistercian Publications, 1980).

M. BASIL PENNINGTON, O.C.S.O.

MORALITY, ETHICS, RELATIONSHIP TO SPIRITUALITY

Like the divine and human natures united in the one person of Christ, spirituality and ethics must be neither separated nor confused. While the history of their relationship posits virtually every logical possibility, orthodox reflection has resisted two extremes: (1) *separation that divides,* whether disincarnate spiritualities or autonomous ethics, and (2) *confusion that identifies,* an undifferentiated equation of the spiritual and the ethical.

The terms *morality, ethics,* and *spirituality* may denote Christian principles or policies as well as the concrete performance of Christian living. Each term indicates both moments of a theory-praxis relationship. Spirituality and ethics, whether understood as ascetical or reflective responses to Christ's gospel, constitute distinct but interrelated disciplines. They are united at their source in grace; they are differentiated by cultural expressions and by the qualities of their conscious experience.

Before charting the major historical shifts in the relationship between spirituality and ethics, a heuristic grid may be assembled from the possible relationships that exist between religion and morality. There is a scholarly consensus that religion and morality initially form an undifferentiated whole, an ethos. As experience becomes more complex and reflection more dialectical, religion and morality are distinguished. Their relationship may be continuous or discontinuous. If continuous, religion and morality may be intrinsically related as two expressions of one reality or extrinsically related, as when religious authority and values provide moral motivation or legitimation. If discontinuous, either religion or morality may split off. Religion without morality may generate ethically unrestricted gnostic or enthusiastic spiritualities. Morality without religion becomes widespread in modern forms of atheism and secular humanism. A final possibility is manifested in situations where both religion and morality are present but inadequately integrated, as in the case of Pelagianism and the antinomian fideism associated with such figures as Martin Luther and Søren Kierkegaard.

In the Hebrew Scriptures, spirituality and ethics form an indivisible unity in which divine and social interaction are interdependent. Unlike other Near East divinities, Yahweh, who entered into a covenant relationship with Israel, is not ethically capricious. The scriptural record of revelation, consequently, is ethically oriented and historically specified. Laws governing human relationships are no less revelation than the prescriptions for cultic activity. Terms like *sin* and *redemption* suggest the inseparability of religious significance from ethical behavior. Yahweh, Creator and Redeemer, hates injustice and rejects as empty formalism worship that is divorced from ethical living.

While piety and service of neighbor are experientially discrete, Christianity maintains that their meanings are intrinsically related. The Christian categories of metanoia, the kingdom of God, the paschal mystery, and life in the Spirit, precede the distinction into spiritual and ethical experience, as do foundational beliefs like the incarnation, the Church as the Body of Christ, and the parousia. Liturgical praxis, as formative and doxological immersion in the normative narratives of Christian identity, further subvert sacred-profane dichotomies. Responding to Christ's double command to love God and neighbor (Mk 12:28-34), Christians liturgically remember and imitate as disciples a life in which the spiritual is both the ground and goal of the ethical. But what is inseparably linked is not confused. St. Paul's dialectic of faith and works forbids collapsing the moral and the spiritual into an identity.

In the early Christian period, the relationship between spirituality and ethics was implicit in the theological debates for an orthodox Christology and an adequate

Christian anthropology. Later Scholastics distinguished only to unite and maintained the continuity of spirituality and ethics, the compatibility of faith with reason, and the completion of nature by grace. During and after the Reformation, the relationship between spirituality and ethics was affected by debates both within and outside the Church.

Within the Christian community, the relationship between spirituality and ethics was reexamined by Reformation theologians. Returning to the Pauline faith-works distinction, Catholic abuses were critiqued. Counter-Reformation Jesuits reaffirmed an orthodox integration of contemplation in action. Jean-Pierre de Caussade's *Abandonment to Divine Providence* represents a later and accomplished development of this trend. Reflecting both scholastic decadence and the overzealous suppression of quietism, Giovanni Battista Scaramelli distorted Christian spirituality by separating ascetical and mystical theology, in effect creating two types of Christian life.

Outside the Church the guiding value of the Enlightenment program was autonomy. In practice this meant the rejection of tradition and the apotheosis of reason. With reason as the universally accepted criterion of truth, revelation was rejected and morality placed on a purely rational footing. Religion was undialectically negated, and a secularized morality emerged. The Enlightenment's polemic against religion as a coercive system and ideology was developed and mediated to modern consciousness by Karl Marx and Sigmund Freud. It was with Nietzsche's transvaluation of values, though, that the question of why and how morality is possible after the death of God was most acutely posed.

Christian responses to the Enlightenment variously stressed the discontinuity of spirituality and ethics, or more commonly worked to reintegrate them. Kierkegaard's anti-Enlightenment stance is clear in the theocentric ethics of *Works of Love* (1847). Rather than integrate spirituality and ethics, Kierkegaard affirmed the paradoxes of a "teleological suspension of the ethical" in *Fear and Trembling* (1843). This anti-consequentialist ethics was not arbitrary, "the ethical is the very breath of the eternal," but rather a critique of domesticated Christianity. Kierkegaard's discontinuity of spirituality and ethics also resisted both rationalist (Hegel) and affective (Schleiermacher) accommodation of the Enlightenment.

The historical research and typological studies of Friedrich von Hügel and Ernst Troeltsch aimed to recover the spiritual against both the Enlightenment and the contemporary tendencies toward moral reductionism by anti-mystical Liberal Protestantism (Adolf von Harnack). Von Hügel targeted Kant's work *Religion Within the Bounds of Mere Reason* (1793) for critique. Influenced by John Henry Newman, von Hügel, in *The Mystical Element of Religion* (1911), also stressed the value of the mystical and explored the interrelationship of religion and morality. With greater attention to ethics, Troeltsch's types of Christianity explored the social presence of the Church.

Twentieth-century reflection on the relationship between spirituality and ethics has been shaped by modern advances in biblical studies and theology, as well as by the scholarly and grass-roots developments within the liturgical and catechetical movements. Church renewal, coupled with new contributions from the social sciences, has reevaluated the secularization of morality, the privatization of religion, and the spiritual alienation of the autonomous individual from traditional communities and their constitutive meanings. Political, liberation, and emergent contextual theologies suggest new integrations of spirituality and ethics that avoid old Christendom and neo-integralism.

Contemporary integrations of spirituality and ethics may be traced to foundational theological reflection on Christian anthropology before Vatican II, and to growing insight into the political ramifications of a theology of grace since Vatican II.

Conservative Thomists like Juan Arintero and Réginald Garrigou-Lagrange rejected the dichotomized spirituality inherited from Scaramelli and prepared the way for the Second Vatican Council's universal call to holiness. Transcendental Thomists like Karl Rahner and Piet Schoonenberg challenged nature-supernature discontinuities that supported the questionable separations of history from salvation history, natural ethics from specifically Christian ethics, creation from redemption.

At the beginning of the 20th century, grace-nature dualism within Christian anthropology reinforced the secularization of the public realm, the privatization of religion, and the division of spirituality from personal and political ethics. Toward the end of the 20th century, the reformulation and politicization of Christian anthropology has produced integrations that far surpass the extrinsic approaches of popular piety and the manual tradition that reciprocally instrumentalized prayer for moral attainment and ethical behavior for spiritual progress. Today holistic, creation-centered spiritualities and some narrative-based ethics risk the danger of losing the distinction between the spiritual and the ethical.

From a different perspective, Bernard Lonergan confirms the trend toward greater identification of spirituality and ethics, while grounding their irreducible distinction in the differentiation of consciousness. In the unity of the intending subject, spirituality and ethics are integrally related, but distinguishable, as expressing two distinct levels of consciousness: the desire to attain the truly valuable and the impulse to respond to the holy. Both moral and religious conversion create new horizons of meaning with their own proper languages, but what distinguishes moral commitment from religious love is not necessarily the material contents of these experiences, which may be coextensive, but the experienced qualities of self-transcendence in these experiences.

See also CONTEMPLATION, CONTEMPLATIVE PRAYER; PRAXIS; VALUE; VIRTUE.

Bibliography: D. Dorr, *Integral Spirituality* (Maryknoll, N.Y.: Orbis, 1990). E. McDonagh, *Doing the Truth: The Quest for Moral Theology* (Notre Dame, Ind.: Univ. of Notre Dame Press, 1979). G. Outka and J. Reeder, eds., *Religion and Morality: A Collection of Essays* (Garden City, N.Y.: Doubleday, 1973).

KRISTOPHER L. WILLUMSEN

MORTIFICATION

Found in some form in most religious traditions, mortification (Latin *mortificare,* "to kill") is, for Christians, the killing or deadening through ascetic practices (fasting, etc.) the disordered appetites that hinder the full spiritual integration of the human person in free response to the Holy Spirit. There has been a tendency in Christianity, at least from the rise of monastic life in the 4th century, to emphasize the ascetical effort of the individual, centering on the nature and extent of faults and of mortifying practices. But when Paul introduced the term into the NT, he integrated its ascetical aspect into the mystical/unitive context of the incorporation of the Christian into the death of Christ and the rising with him to new life. "By the spirit" the Christian "puts to death the deeds of the body" (Rom 8:13; see also 7:4-6), in union with the Redeemer, who first took on sinfulness in his own flesh and by dying conquered sin and death (Rom 8:2-3, 10-11; see Rom 4–8).

Although the evangelists do not use the term *mortification,* they record similar teachings of Jesus that "if any want to become my followers, let them deny themselves and take up their cross and follow me" (Mt 16:24, NRSV); they must renounce everything for the sake of the kingdom in order to be united to him in discipleship. Luke's "daily" bearing of the cross finds parallels throughout the NT in exhortations to accept the mortifications involved in daily Christian life (Mt 16:24-26; 10:38-39; Mk 8:34-36; Lk 9:23-25; 14:26-39). John records Christ's call to discipleship in terms of losing one's life in this world, of dying with Christ, to bear fruit (Jn 12:24-26).

From NT times to the present, Christians have recognized the need for discernment and spiritual direction in the practice of mortification; in the 20th century these functions have been influenced by modern psychology. Although the late 20th century has seen a lessening of emphasis on mortification, there are indications that the global crises accompanying the dawn of the 21st century may awaken a renewal of the practice of mortifying those human lusts that threaten our world with extinction. To be fully Christian, this renewal should situate mortification within the NT context of the paschal mystery.

See also ABSTINENCE; ADDICTION; ASCETICAL THEOLOGY; ASCETICISM; BODY; DETACHMENT; DISCIPLESHIP; FASTING; PASCHAL MYSTERY; PENANCE, PENITENCE; PURGATION, PURGATIVE WAY; SIN; SUFFERING; WARFARE, SPIRITUAL.

Bibliography: C. Morel, "Mortification," *D.Spir.,* vol. 10, cols. 1791–1799. M. Miles, "Mortification," *Westminster Dictionary of Christian Spirituality* (Philadelphia: Westminster, 1983) 270–271.

CARITAS McCARTHY, S.H.C.J.

MUSIC

Music is a primal reality—as primal as speech, sound, and silence. For this reason it is found at all times and in every culture. Historically, it is intimately connected with the experience of the sacred. Only in modernity does music emerge as a purely secular reality. Yet even here there is much to suggest that it provides experiences that are at least implicitly religious.

Despite this universality, or perhaps precisely because of it, music is nearly impossible to define. As soon as one begins to pin it down or describe its relation to spirituality, one necessarily draws upon some particular cultural tradition, knowing that even within such a tradition there are competing and contradictory views. Within the Judeo-Christian tradition, for example, there has always been an ambivalent attitude toward music. On the one hand, it has played a central role in worship; on the other, it has been depreciated and even shunned as appealing too much to the nonrational and the sensual.

Much of this ambivalence is due to the influence of Platonism and dualism during the formative centuries of Christian theology and piety. Platonism and Neoplatonism opposed the "inferior" material-temporal-sensitive-affective dimensions of experience (equated with the feminine) to the "superior" spiritual-eternal-rational-contemplative realm (equated with the masculine). The sensual character of music clearly allied it with the inferior and potentially dangerous nonrational dimension. To be of value, it had to be "hemmed in," as it were, by reason.

The influence of this depreciating dualism can be detected in the way music was understood and practiced, especially in the medieval era. One example is the early suppression, both in Judaism and Christianity, of instrumental music in favor of unaccompanied singing. Later this suppression gave way to begrudging acceptance of instrumentation, but only so long as it served as a vehicle for the word. In both cases music was seen as valuable only when tamed and informed by word (i.e., reason).

Another example of this depreciating view of music was the attempt to reduce music to number (mathematical reason), which was the common interpretation of music in the Middle Ages. One need not look far to see this ancient dualism reaching into contemporary experience. While there is surely a certain validity in the demand that church music be "reverent," this adjective often masks a repressive, depreciating fear of the affective and bodily dimensions of experience. The same discomfort and mistrust of the body marks the continuing resistance in some quarters to any legitimate role for dance within liturgy.

It is testimony to the disarming mystery of music, however, that despite these negative attitudes, it has occupied and continues to occupy a central place in worship and spirituality. Several characteristics may be noted that account for the unique power of music to evoke the experience of the sacred.

1. Music is as elemental and universal as speech and humor. The distinction between the musician and the nonmusician is a secondary and derivative one. Everyone is musical, though perhaps some people are musicians and some are not. This elemental fact about our shared humanity has been obscured somewhat in modernity by individualism (with its notion of the artist as a lone genius) and the emergence of the entertainment model of music, in which there is a performer and an audience, a product and a consumer. It is "somewhat" obscured because even this model of music presupposes the empathetic participation of the audience. Music, then, is primordially a communal, participatory event just as speech is.

2. Across many diverse cultures and particularly within the Judeo-Christian culture of the West, music is a symbol of the mystery of being. As a flowing, vital stream of reality which sustains and unifies particular temporal moments, and which is able to entertain all the paradoxes of existence—order and spontaneity, variation and repetition, continuous and discrete sound (the infinite and the finite)—music both embodies and evinces the whole of reality as well as our participation in it. As such it becomes the natural medium for story and mythmaking, since each of these forms also attempts to weave a totality within which some meaning or truth is communicated and celebrated. If this is true, it goes a long way toward ex-

plaining why music has such power to evoke experiences of transcendence, even for people with no particular religious allegiance.

Thus, while music is in a way a cultural object, one item among many, it has the sacramental character of all finite things, which, while being finite, can nevertheless become cyphers of the infinite or transcendent whole. From this perspective, music is not so much an object we create or possess or consume as a cosmic-transcendent medium in which we participate. Numerous composers have given eloquent testimony to the fact that all their creative effort is but a prelude to participation in a reality greater than themselves and their creative powers.

3. Not only is music as primal as speech, but it is also the dialectical partner of speech. This is not a reassertion of the dualistic subordination of music to word, but rather a recognition of the mutual interdependence of *logos* and *eros*. Speech as rational discourse needs more than itself to complete its own possibilities of communication and shared meaning. Just as verbal expressions of love achieve their full significance in the "otherness" of nonverbal lovemaking, the communication of meaning in concepts requires the "otherness" of the nonconceptual, affective dimension. Music expresses the affective depths and heights of reality—reality as value, will, and love—and not only knowledge. This is of crucial importance for spirituality. For when the capacity to feel is repressed in communal life and worship, the capacity to perceive and respond to evil and injustice is likewise deadened. Worship bereft of emotion is worship bereft of truth.

In addition to these general characteristics, two developments within Roman Catholicism are of special importance for understanding the relationship of music and spirituality in our time. One is what may be called the postcolonial situation of the Church. Roman Catholic Christianity is no longer a primarily European, monolithic reality expanding outward to re-duplicate European cultural forms—including musical forms. While there are still important liturgical, artistic, and pastoral judgments to be made about the appropriateness of a given piece of music for worship, Vatican II embraced diversity as a positive value and opened up the possibility of a broad range of musical styles and genres for liturgy. In this connection, the traditional European bias in favor of classical over popular forms is no longer normative. This does not mean that classical forms are devalued—only that popular forms are also valued.

A second and related point is that Vatican II effected a paradigm shift in its view of both the liturgy and the role of music in liturgy. For various reasons the liturgy of the Middle Ages gradually devolved into a solely clerical action in which the ordinary worshiper was reduced to a passive and voiceless spectator. This represented a departure from the liturgy's most ancient pattern, in which the whole community or assembly, inclusive of its presider and leading ministers, conducted worship as a communal action. Vatican II sought to redress this deformation of worship into an elite clerical act by calling for the restoration of the full and active participation of the people. This call in turn entailed a radical rethinking of the nature of liturgical music.

It is somewhat staggering to realize that the understanding of liturgical music dominant in the West until just a few years ago developed after the decline of the ancient assembly-centered, participational model of liturgy. This means that until very recently the predominant operative model of liturgical music was one in which a relatively small body of experts provided vocal and musical embellishment for the edification of a passive audience of worshipers. This model, mirroring the medieval conception of the liturgy, presupposed a dichotomy between a few performers and a nonperforming audience. Furthermore,

since the medieval model reduced liturgical agency to the agency of the priest, music could have at best only a secondary, ornamental role in ritual.

By contrast, the reformed liturgy requires music that is essentially participatory. Further, it understands music as integral to the community's performance of ritual and the proclamation of the Word. When the people sing the Eucharistic acclamations, they are performing the Eucharistic Prayer in dialogue with the presider. When they participate in the singing of the responsorial psalm, they are helping to proclaim and open up the meaning of the Scriptures. When they sing the prayer of the faithful, they are exercising their priestly function by interceding for all humankind as the General Instruction of the Roman Missal states (no. 45).

As this brief historical sketch illustrates, the role of music in worship is a telling sign of the ecclesiology of a given period. To put it simply, before Vatican II liturgical music took the form of a recital or a performance, just as the liturgy itself was a kind of intricate performance by the priest in his role as cult-expert. Since the council it has taken the form of a sing-along. The recital form required little or no relationship to the people because it was a solo performed *for* them instead of *with* them. The sing-along form, on the other hand, is essentially relational and requires that one listen for and learn the melodies of the people.

In this contemporary musical form, expressive as it is of a participatory ecclesiology, one can also discern a characteristic theme of present-day spirituality. This is the theme of empowerment and may be summarized as follows: Persons are to be subjects and agents in their own religious histories, and not just objects of someone else's agency. Seen in this light, participatory music is an empowering medium with sociopolitical and not merely aesthetic significance, because it affords an experience of personal and communal agency.

See also AESTHETICS; AFFECT, AFFECTIVITY; ART; BODY; CELEBRATION; CULTURE; DANCE; LITURGY; POWER; SACRAMENTS; SILENCE; VATICAN COUNCIL II.

Bibliography: J. Gelineau, *Voices and Instruments in Christian Worship*, trans. C. Howell (Collegeville, Minn.: Liturgical Press, 1964). Vatican Council II, Constitution on the Sacred Liturgy, chap. 6. Bishops' Committee on the Liturgy, *Music in Catholic Worship* (Washington: USCC, 1983).

BOB HURD

MYERS-BRIGGS TYPE INDICATOR

See PERSONALITY TYPES.

MYSTERY

The concept of mystery centers on the experiential acknowledgment of the absolute transcendence of God whenever one encounters the divine salvific activity within human history. Awe and reverence in the presence of the divine mark all the revelatory experiences that the world's great religions see as crucial to the Creator-creature relationship.

The Bible

The Christian understanding of mystery, rooted in Jewish biblical thought, flows from the belief that God has freely chosen to enter into a covenant relationship with the human family. The salvific nature of God's election is expressed through the historical unfolding of a gracious plan of salvation that seeks to liberate and divinize sinful humankind.

The Greek word *mysterion* is used in the Septuagint to express the hidden counsel of God as it pertains to the historical development of this covenant relationship. In the process of ongoing revelation, the people of God in general and the prophets in particular come to understand in faith the role of Israel in God's plan of salvation through visions and symbolic language. The revelation of saving love manifested to the prophets through visions and symbolic language comes to fulfillment in Jesus Christ, who incarnates God's plan of salva-tion in the paschal mystery of his own death and resurrection.

Col 1:26-27 and Eph 1:10-11 use the concept of mystery to proclaim that Jesus Christ crucified and risen is the fullest expression of God's plan to redeem and divinize humankind. The experiential process by which we come to understand the paschal mystery and its implications for Christian life are described as wisdom. Subsequent theology has sought to understand how believers become sharers in the saving reality of the death and resurrection of Christ and how to describe the sapiential reflective process that seeks to express the meaning of this incorporation into Christ.

The Church Fathers

Both the Greek and Latin Fathers saw the mystery of God's saving work in the death and resurrection of Christ operative in the sacraments of baptism and Eucharist. Through the sacraments of initiation the believer enters into the mystery of God's saving plan and begins a life journey in, with, and through Christ crucified and risen to the fullness of eternal life. However, the Fathers of the Church applied the term *mystery* not only to the sacramental acts of the Church but also to the typological sense of Scripture. Thus the Pauline notion of wisdom as the way of knowing the mystery of Christ was now understood as an exploration of the spiritual sense of Scripture, by which one sought to penetrate more deeply by faith the meaning of the mystery of life in Christ into which the believer had been plunged by his or her own reception of the sacraments.

The mystery of Christ is hidden within the literal sense of Scripture for the Fathers of the Church, just as participation in the mystery of Christ is hidden within the reception of the sacraments. From the patristic perspective, the believer comes to know the transcendent God and to understand in faith the saving plan of God through sharing in the Body and Blood of Christ in the Eucharist and through studying the unfolding of God's plan of salvation in Christ hidden in the spiritual sense of Scripture. The mystery of Christ in the Eucharist is the source of divinization, and the mystery of Christ in Scripture is the source of the wisdom necessary in the journey of faith.

The 4th-century fascination with celebrating the Eucharist at geographical sites associated with specific Gospel texts eventuated in the understanding of individual events in the life of Christ as grace-filled mysteries. The liturgical celebration of these historical events within a yearly cycle of feasts brought the believer through symbol into contact with the salvific reality of a particular mystery.

Medieval and Post-Renaissance Theology

When reception of the Eucharist became less frequent in the Middle Ages, meditation upon the mysteries of the life of Christ became a means of contact with the salvific acts of God in Christ that brought freedom and divinization to humankind. Meditative recreation of Gospel events made possible the participation of the individual in the mysteries of the life of Christ with or without actual reception of the Eucharist. Use of the imagination as the door to experiential sharing in the saving deeds of Christ became ever more real for visionaries who saw themselves as actual participants in the grace-filled events of the Gospel.

The magnificent wall paintings of Romanesque churches and the breathtaking splendor of the stained-glass windows of Gothic cathedrals witness to the way in which believers sought to use visual representations of the mysteries of the life of Christ as meditative gateways to an experience of the transcendent mystery of God. While the faithful were using the imaginative power of the arts as a means of contemplative access to the mystery of God manifest in the life, death, and resurrection of the Incarnate Word, medieval theologians, such as St. Thomas Aquinas, were using reason to investigate the mysteries of faith, *divina mysteria,* understood not only as saving events but as revealed truths about the meaning of the divine plan of salvation known only through faith seeking understanding. The experiential meditations upon the life of Christ contained in the second, third, and fourth weeks of the *Spiritual Exercises* of St. Ignatius Loyola and the all-embracing theatrical splendor of Baroque churches witness to the continuation within Counter-Reformation spirituality of medieval piety's search to encounter the transcendent mystery of God by sharing in some way in the incarnational reality of the life, death, and resurrection of Jesus Christ.

Nineteenth-Century Thought

In the 19th century the concept of mystery encountered the forces of rationalism as well as the growing interest in the study of the mystery religions of the ancient world as they related to nascent Christianity. The Church's opposition to rationalistic epistemology provided the horizon for the shift away from the patristic and medieval understanding of mystery centered in the incarnation, the fullest expression of God's plan of salvation, to the Trinity, the most profound of the revealed truths that constituted the mystery of faith.

Although medieval theologians spoke of *divina mysteria* as truths known only by revelation, they did not emphasize cognitive trancendence to the same extent as did the Fathers of Vatican I when they proclaimed: "For, divine mysteries by their nature exceed the created intellect so much that, even when handed down by revelation and accepted by faith, they nevertheless remain covered by the veil of faith itself, and wrapped in a certain mist, as it were, as long as in this mortal life, 'we are absent from the Lord: for we walk by faith and not by sight' (2 Cor. 5:6)"—[DS 3016 (1796)].

The danger in such an approach is that mystery can lose its experiential character of awe and fascination in the presence of the incarnation in human history of God's loving plan of salvation; it can become identified almost exclusively with the cognitive presentation of a transcendent truth that can be known only through the process of revelation. The work of Karl Rahner in the 20th century has sought to remedy this situation by carefully balancing the experiential and cognitive dimensions of mystery.

Nineteenth-century study of the religious milieu of early Christianity led some scholars to the conclusion that it was simply another expression of the mystery religions of the 1st-century A.D. Greco-Roman world. Subsequent scholarship, especially the discovery of the Dead Sea Scrolls in 1947, has established that the complex thought-world of 1st-century A.D. Judaism rather than pagan Oriental cults is the most probable source of the NT concept of mystery.

Certainly there are related parallels between the mystery religions and early Christianity, such as initiation rites and sacred meals. However, the Christian concept of mystery, incarnate in the weekly celebration of the Eucharist as the anamnesis of the historical incarnation of God's saving activity in the death and resurrection of Jesus of Nazareth, clearly separates it from the mythical and seasonal character of the worship patterns of the mystery religions. The human desire for encounter with the divine through symbol and ritual, common to both Christianity and the mystery religions, can also be seen as the experiential horizon within which God invites all humankind into the mystery of transcendence.

Dom Odo Casel

The work of the Benedictine monk Dom Odo Casel between 1918 and 1941 was an attempt to return to a renewed understanding of the patristic concept of mystery and to link Early Christian developments more closely with the mystery religions of the Greco-Roman world. His goal was both to move away from the overly intellectual understanding of mystery that was present in the work of the Fathers of Vatican I and also to recognize the possible lines of influence between nascent Christianity and the mystery religions. Casel laid out his major hypotheses in his 1932 work *The Mystery of Christian Worship.*

Casel's theory that the Early Church borrowed some aspects of its early forms of worship from the mystery religions was challenged by those who maintained that the evolution of Christian worship could be adequately explained as an organic unfolding of the Pauline appropriation of the Jewish tradition without the need to have recourse to a theory of dependence upon pagan traditions. Subsequent scholarship has tended to support the views of Casel's critics in this regard.

The strongest discussion about Casel's work has centered on his understanding of the nature of the presence of the saving work of Christ in the sacraments. Casel maintained that the historic reality of the mysteries of the life of Christ is truly present in the sacraments as the here-and-now actualization of the mystery of God's plan of salvation. The purpose behind such a theory was to assure that believers truly had access to a real participation in the historical works of salvation through their actual presence in the sacramental signs. In offering this explanation of the mystery presence as the basis for the relationship between the past historical acts of Christ and any subsequent post-Easter celebration of the sacraments, Casel believed that he was restoring the patristic understanding of mystery.

Casel's critics certainly acknowledged the need for a real link between the saving acts of Christ and the celebration of the sacraments, but they could not concur with his explanation that a past historical event, as a mystery of salvation, could now be present in the same way in which it was present in time and space at the moment of its actual occurrence in history. Indeed, the sacraments must offer the real possibility for participation in the saving deeds of Christ, but Casel's critics maintained that that occurs, not because the historical event as such was present in mystery, but rather because Christ the High Priest, whose saving deeds occurred in history, is now present to share with believers the grace-filled participation in the divine life that eventuates from his redemptive work. The risen Christ is able, by the power of the Holy Spirit, to be present to believers with the full reality of the saving work he accomplished in history without the necessity of the contingent reality of past events being reactualized in the present.

Twentieth-Century Theology

Although most theologians rejected Casel's explanation of the how of the presence of the mysteries of Christ's life in the sacraments, they recognized the significance of his refocusing attention on the patristic understanding of the sacraments as the true place of encounter between believers and the salvific plan of God. The enduring contribution of Casel to the development of the concept of mystery is reflected in Pope Pius XII's encyclical *Mediator Dei* (1947) and Vatican II's Constitution on the Sacred Liturgy (1963), which emphasize participation in the paschal mystery of Christ's death and resurrection as the heart of Christian life and worship.

Modern theology distinguishes: (1) natural mysteries; (2) supernatural mysteries in the broad sense; and (3) supernatural mysteries in the strict sense. The first category, natural mysteries, refers to aspects of the natural world around us and dimensions of human experience that remain obscure because they have not yet been fully grasped by human reason. The second category, supernatural mysteries in the broad sense, refers to aspects of the divine plan of salvation that are manifest in contingent historical events but whose meaning for faith can be known only be revelation, e.g., the virgin birth. The third category, supernatural mysteries in the strict sense, pertains to truths of the faith which are accessible to human reason only by divine revelation and which will always transcend the human spirit, even when the latter is graced by the beatific vision. The three great mysteries that fall within the third category include (1) the Blessed Trinity; (2) the incarnation; and (3) the means and process of human divinization through grace.

Contemporary theology, in its concern for the proclamation of the gospel to the modern world, has struggled with the concept of mystery from a linguistic perspective as well as from an experiential perspective. The fact that any presentation of mystery as encounter with transcendence necessarily involves symbolic language does not mean that there is no validity to theological discourse. It does, however, require believers to recognize the inadequacy of all language in the face of mystery and to acknowledge that only faith makes possible a true grasp of the existential meaning of language that seeks to express transcendent reality.

One of the major contributions of Jesuit theologian Karl Rahner to contemporary theology has been his emphasis upon mystery not so much as a cognitive truth known only by revelation, but rather as the absolute horizon within which all the intellectual and conative strivings of the human spirit for transcendence necessarily take place. The great value of this approach lies in its attempt to balance the cognitive and experiential dimensions of the concept of mystery by emphasizing the incarnational dimension of human participation in the historical unfolding of the plan of salvation.

The significance of the concept of mystery for spiritual growth is twofold. First, it bids us to open ourselves in faith to the presence of absolute transcendence at the center of all human knowing and willing. Second, it asks us to trust in the future promised by God, who beckons humankind through the graced transcendence offered by faith, hope, and love, to share in the process of divinization already realized in the death and resurrection of Jesus Christ, who embodies the fulfillment of all human searching and longing for the infinite.

See also EUCHARIST; GOD; LITURGY; MYSTICISM; PASCHAL MYSTERY; PRESENCE, PRESENCE OF GOD; REVELATION(S); SACRAMENTS; TRINITARIAN SPIRITUALITY.

Bibliography: K. Rahner, "Mystery," *Sacramentum Mundi,* ed. K. Rahner et al. (New York: Herder, 1969) 133–136. O. Casel, *The Mystery of Christian Worship* (Westminster, Md.: Newman, 1962).

THOMAS D. McGONIGLE, O.P.

MYSTICAL BODY

See BODY OF CHRIST; CHURCH.

MYSTICAL THEOLOGY

In the 17th century a number of theologians sought to restore the link between life and thought that had been broken by the dryasdust rationalism of decadent Scholasticism in the 14th century. They focused their attention on the itinerary Christians follow in their progression toward God, and since they saw this as leading to contemplative union, they called their systematic reflection on the purgative, illuminative, and unitive ways "mystical theology."

Other theologians in the 17th and 18th centuries considered contemplative prayer a rare gift. Most Christians, they believed, are called to a perfection that does not include contemplation. They therefore divided the study of spirituality into ascetical theology, which traces the normal progression of virtuous human striving toward perfection under grace, and mystical theology, which is concerned with the extraordinary graces by which God brings the passive soul to mystical union.

This division was consecrated by the rigidly intellectualistic manuals published before Vatican II. The contemporary term *spirituality* overcomes the dichotomies and conflicts implicit in the distinction between ascetical and mystical theology.

See also ASCETICAL THEOLOGY; SPIRITUALITY, CHRISTIAN; THREE WAYS.

Bibliography: J. Welch, "Mystical Theology," *New Dictionary of Theology,* ed. J. Komonchak, M. Collins, D. Lane (Wilmington, Del.: Glazier, 1987) 692–694.

KENNETH C. RUSSELL

MYSTICISM

As one of the primary themes of Catholic spirituality, mysticism touches upon a great many subjects treated elsewhere in this dictionary. Because the very term *mysticism* has been understood in radically different ways and so has generated much confusion, the present article will prescind from detailed consideration of related topics, such as prayer, contemplation, and union, and will focus primarily on the fundamental nature of Christian mysticism as originally understood in the Church, on the way a different understanding came more and more to eclipse the original one, and on the retrieval of that earlier conception by some of the leading Catholic thinkers of the postconciliar period. A concluding section of the article will treat some contemporary questions concerning mysticism in other religious traditions.

Divergent Understandings of the Term

An early, major impetus for the modern study of mysticism in the English-speaking world dates from the year 1899, when Dean William Inge published his Bampton Lectures under the title *Christian Mysticism.* In an appendix to that work, Inge listed and critiqued no fewer than twenty-six definitions of *mysticism* and *mystical theology.* The present article need not examine those many different meanings, much less any additional ones that have arisen since the publication of Inge's lectures. It is appropriate, however, to note at the outset that two general tendencies are found among those who have written about mysticism, and in particular about Christian mysticism, the principal concern of this article.

The difference between these two tendencies can be succinctly illustrated by the way two of the most prominent Catholic theologians of the mid and late 20th century—Hans Urs von Balthasar and Louis Bouyer—approached the question of whether St. Thérèse of Lisieux was a mystic. Von Balthasar, in his *Thérèse of Lisieux* (New York: Sheed and Ward, 1954) stated categorically that this saint never "crossed the threshold into what is known as mysticism," and justified his position by noting that her life was free of the presence of, or even the longing for, extraordinary "mystical phenomena" (pp. 252, 254). Bouyer, also fully aware that such phenomena were absent from her life, drew an altogether different conclusion, namely, that Thérèse offers us "the most convincing testimony of the fact that genuine mysticism does not consist so much in the experience of ecstasies or 'visions' . . . but quite simply in total self-abandonment in naked faith, through an efficacious love of the Cross that is one with the very love of the crucified God" (*Mysterion*, p. 322).

It would be pointless to argue that one of those understandings of mysticism is correct and the other simply wrong, for in fact the term has long been used in both these senses. According to the *Oxford English Dictionary,* the first recorded use of the word occurred in 1736, in H. Coventry's *Philemon:* "How much nobler a Field of Exercise . . . are the seraphic Entertainments of Mysticism and Extasy than the mean and ordinary Practice of a mere earthly and common Virtue!" Here mysticism is clearly considered to be something extraordinary, akin to "Extasy" and of an altogether different order from what is "mean," "earthly," and "common." This usage has tended to predominate in the more than two and a half centuries since Coventry penned those lines. During this period mysticism has generally been understood as related to a particular state of mind, a form of consciousness that transcends ordinary experience by reason of felt union with the Absolute (whether or not that Absolute be understood as the God whom Christians worship). It was in this sense that von Balthasar argued that Thérèse was not a mystic. This, however, was not the original understanding of "the mystical" in the Christian tradition, as the following consideration of the relevant terminology in Scripture and the Fathers of the Church will make clear.

Scriptural and Patristic Usage

The adjective *mystical* (Greek *mystikos*) does not appear in the NT, but its meaning in early Christian literature cannot properly be understood apart from the NT term *mystery* (Greek *mysterion*). Both words are etymologically related to the verb *myein* ("to close," e.g., to close the eyes or lips) and accordingly convey a sense of what is hidden or secret. Some scholars have argued that the ancient Greek mystery religions lie behind the NT understanding of mystery, but the careful analyses of Bouyer and others have shown that in those religions what was to be kept secret was only the ritual activity, which is not at all the concern of St. Paul and the other NT authors who use this language.

As Raymond Brown demonstrated in some of his earliest publications, it is the Semitic background of *mysterion* that best elucidates the use of this term in the NT. The ancient Israelites conceived of God as abiding above the solid firmament of the sky with a council of heavenly advisors, variously described as "the sons of God" (Job 1:6), "the council of the holy ones" (Ps 89:8), "the divine assembly" (Ps 82:1), or "the whole host of heaven" (1 Kgs 22:19). This heavenly assembly, analogous to a civic governing body in the human order, would deliberate on the conduct of the universe, with the final decisions being determined by Yahweh alone. These decisions were in themselves hidden from human beings but could be made known to certain persons, the prophets. Indeed, for Jeremiah the distinction between a true and false prophet depended on whether or not one "has stood in the council of the LORD, to see him and to hear his word" (Jer 23:18). A particularly clear instance of this understanding of divine secrets that can be revealed to human beings occurs in the Book of Daniel, where the prophet introduces his interpretation of the Babylonian king's dream with the words: "There is a God in heaven who reveals mysteries [LXX: *mysteria*], and he has shown King Nebuchadnezzar what is to happen in days to come" (Dan 2:28).

Such passages, as well as similar ones from the noncanonical Jewish pseudepigrapha written in the centuries just before or during the rise of Christianity (e.g., the Book of Enoch), provide essential background for understanding the use of the term *mystery* in the NT. When Jesus, after having narrated the parable of the sower, tells his disciples, "The mystery of the kingdom of God has been granted to you" (Mk 4:11; cf. Mt 13:11; Lk 8:10), the "mystery" referred to is God's plan of salvation, now revealed in the teaching and person of Jesus. The same reality, though this time expressed without use of the word "mystery," is proclaimed in Jesus' exultant cry: "I give praise to you, Father, Lord of heaven and earth, for although you have hidden these things from the wise and the learned, you have revealed them to the childlike. . . . No one knows the Son except the Father, and no one knows the Father except the Son and anyone to whom the Son wishes to reveal him" (Mt 11:25-27).

These and similar texts are the Gospels' counterpart to the much more frequent use of the term *mysterion* in the Pauline letters. To the Corinthians, Paul writes that he and his fellow apostles are to be regarded as "servants of Christ and stewards of the mysteries of God" (1 Cor 4:1), for they "speak God's wisdom, mysterious, hidden, which God predetermined before the ages for our glory" (1 Cor 2:7). A central element in this mystery is God's will that all people be saved, Gentile as well as Jew. In Ephesians this is at one point called simply "the mystery of Christ" (Eph 3:4), while in Colossians the note of personal intimacy with Christ is emphasized when "the mystery hidden from ages and from generations past" is said to be "Christ in you, the hope for glory" (Col 1:26, 27). These and the sixteen other references to "mystery" in the Pauline literature have led the distinguished NT scholar Joseph Fitzmyer to write that *mysterion* is so central to Paul's thought that "it conveys for him the content of his gospel" (*New Jerome Biblical Commentary,* Englewood Cliffs, N.J.: Prentice Hall, 1990, p. 1389).

Mysterion was an equally fundamental term for Origen (ca. 185–ca. 253), that prolific early Christian writer who has often been called "the first great theologian." His chief endeavor, whether in his early treatise *On First Principles,* in his extensive commentaries on individual books of the Bible, or in the numerous homilies that have come down to us from the final years of his life, was to comprehend the multifarious ways in which all of Scripture centers on Christ. To do this was precisely to grasp the "mystical sense" (*mystikos nous*) of the text. Success in this endeavor was not primarily a matter of diligent effort on the part of the reader. Whether it was a question of interpreting the OT as a genuine prefiguring of Christ or of properly understanding the NT itself, one was confronted with "an inner meaning, the Lord's meaning," which "is revealed only by that grace he received who said, 'But we have the mind of Christ . . . that we might understand the gifts bestowed upon us by God'" (*On First Prin.* 4.2.3, quoting 1 Cor 2:16, 12). A similar use of the term *mystical* can be found in Origen's fellow Alexandrian of the preceding generation, Clement. For both, the mystical was not a matter of some extraordinary personal experience but of an interpretation of the scriptural text directed toward what St. Paul had already called "the mystery of Christ."

Origen once remarked how improper and inconsistent it was for some Christians to exhibit great reverence toward the Eucharistic species but to show little reverence toward the Bible. His point was, of course, that Christ is just as truly present in the latter as in the former. In both cases this presence is hidden (*mystikos*), able to be ascertained only with the eyes of faith. Origen's remark serves to introduce the next way in which the term *mystical* came to be used in early Christian literature, namely, with regard to the Eucharist and the other sacraments. Only a few of the many possible examples of this usage need be given here: St. Nilus writes that the Eucharist is to be approached "not as simple bread but as mystical bread" (*Epist.* 3.39); Eusebius speaks of baptism as "mystical regeneration in the name of the Father, Son, and Holy Spirit" (*Contra Marcellum* 1.1); and the *Apostolic Constitutions* calls the Eucharist "the mystical sacrifice of [Christ's] body and blood" (6.23.4).

Even these few examples of the use of the term *mystical* in the first four centuries after Christ indicate how far removed this usage was from that which has become prevalent in recent centuries, when mysticism has regularly been associated with visions, ecstasies, locutions, levitation, or similar phenomena. It would be wrong to conclude from this, however, that there was no "mystical experience" in these early Christian writers. Experience, as the American philosopher John E. Smith writes, is always "a product of the intersection of something encountered and a being capable of interpreting the results" (*Experience and God,* Oxford: Oxford Univ. Press, 1968, p. 24). In other words, experience refers to an encounter that is interpreted within human consciousness. At least in that sense,

Origen's quest for the hidden presence of Christ in the Scriptures and St. Nilus's ascertaining in faith the hidden presence of Christ in the Eucharistic bread and wine were mystical experiences, even if unaccompanied by anything approaching the extraordinary manifestations that are often called "mystical phenomena."

But there is something more. Even though the Eastern Fathers did not normally speak of their experiences in an autobiographical way, there are glimpses here and there of a very personal, deeply felt aspect of their experience. One of the best examples of this is found in Origen's first homily on the Canticle of Canticles. Commenting on the way the bride in the Canticle goes about looking for her beloved, Origen writes: "That often happens throughout this song, and only he can understand it who has himself experienced it. Often, God is my witness, I have felt that the Bridegroom was approaching, and that he was as near as possible to me; then he has suddenly gone away, and I have not been able to find what I was seeking. Again I set myself to desire his coming, and sometimes he comes back, and when he has appeared to me, so that I hold him in my hands, once more he escapes me and once more vanishes, and I start again to look for him. He does that often, until I hold him truly and rise leaning on my well-beloved" (#7). Again, in his *Commentary on the Canticle of Canticles,* he speaks as from personal experience of one who "has burned with this faithful love for the Word of God" and "been pierced with the lovable spear of his knowledge, so that he sighs and longs for him day and night, is able to speak of nothing else, wishes to hear of nothing else, can think of nothing else, and is not disposed to desire, seek, or hope for anything other than him" (3.8).

Some have sought to weaken the apparent force of such passages by claiming that they merely express Origen's preoccupations as an exegete (and thus do not show that Origen was a mystic), but such claims are basically beside the point. It was in these very Scriptures that Origen was convinced that he came into the presence of Christ. The same love for Christ that led him to endure excruciating torture in the persecution of Decius near the end of his life also impelled him to seek "the mystery of Christ" in his work as an interpreter of the Bible. In both the more objective and the more subjective senses of the term—that is, both as seeking the real but hidden presence of Christ in the Scriptures and as keenly involved in the adventure of this search—Origen offers us one of the clearest examples of Christian mysticism in the early history of the Church.

Another figure from the patristic era whose writings have been of enduring significance for the understanding of Christian mysticism is Gregory of Nyssa (ca. 335–ca. 395). One of the three Cappadocian Fathers (the others being his brother Basil and their mutual friend Gregory Nazianzen), Gregory's importance is in large measure located in a doctrine which, while certainly not absent in Origen, was not nearly as emphasized by him as it came to be in Gregory's works—the doctrine of God's incomprehensibility. This is especially prominent in Gregory's *Life of Moses,* which follows the Origenist scheme of first presenting the "narrative" of Moses' life and then going back over the same material to find a "spiritual" interpretation of the narrative. When Moses is said in Scripture to have entered the dark cloud on Mount Sinai and to have met God in the darkness, Gregory concludes that the deeper sense of the text is that the true knowledge of what is sought by us in our journey to God "consists in not seeing, because that which is sought transcends all knowledge, being separated on all sides by incomprehensibility as by a kind of darkness" (2.164).

What Gregory here adumbrated was developed still more acutely a century or more later by one of his spiritual descendants, the mysterious figure long believed to have been the Dionysius converted by St. Paul in Athens (Acts 17:34) and now generally reckoned to have been a Syrian monk of the late 5th and early 6th century. It is above all in his short treatise entitled *The Mystical Theology* that Pseudo-Dionysius develops the Nyssan theme of God's utter incomprehensibility, for he writes in its final chapter that "the Cause of all" cannot "be spoken of and cannot be grasped by understanding. . . . It does not live nor is it life. . . . It is neither one nor oneness, divinity nor goodness. . . . It is beyond assertion and denial." Once translated into Latin by John Scotus Erigena in the 9th century, this treatise exerted incalculable influence on the many subsequent mystical writers in the West, such as Meister Eckhart and the author of *The Cloud of Unknowing,* who gave prominence to the so-called *via negativa* or "apophatic way."

What is often overlooked or underemphasized, however, is that this same Dionysius wrote at even greater length on the affirmative way (*via affirmativa* or "kataphatic way"). The treatise *On the Divine Names* treats in meticulous detail what the many names used of God in the Scriptures reveal about God's nature, while *The Ecclesiastical Hierarchy* examines the sacraments of the Church in just the same way that Origen had earlier studied the Scriptures: after describing each rite as it could be observed by anyone present, Dionysius enters upon a "contemplation" of the same rite, in which each detail of the symbolic ritual action is interpreted according to its inner meaning. Throughout, this deeper meaning is described in terms of the most intimate union with God, called "deification" or "divinization," which "consists of being as much as possible like and in union with God" (*Eccl. Hier.* 1.3). For example, the "contemplation" (or "symbolic lesson") of the threefold immersion of baptism "leads the one who is baptized into the mystery that by his triple immersion and emersion he imitates, as far as the imitation of God is possible to human beings, the divine death of one who was three days and nights in the tomb, the life-giving Jesus" (*ibid.*, 2.3.7). In such a text one finds with all possible clarity that aspect of Christian mysticism that could be considered most central of all: incorporation into the life of Christ, what the Letter to the Colossians had called the mystery of "Christ in you, the hope for glory" and what Paul expressed elsewhere as his conviction that "I live, no longer I, but Christ lives in me" (Gal 2:20).

As we turn from these Eastern Fathers to some of the most important mystical writers of the West, certain continuities are evident. In Ambrose, for example, the "spiritual" interpretation of the Scriptures and the sacraments owes much to Origen and his successors in the East. If one change stands out above all, it is that with Augustine (354–430), the greatest of the Western Fathers, there is a more pronounced interest in ecstasy and visions as experiences taking a person beyond the normal bounds of sense perception. It is not just that the *Confessions* includes his account of that dual experience of ecstasy at Ostia when he and his mother momentarily transcended not only "the various levels of bodily things" but even "rose beyond ourselves and in a flash of thought touched the Eternal Wisdom abiding over all" (*Confessions* 9.10). Elsewhere in his writings, Augustine considers at length the nature of ecstasy, what it would mean for someone like Paul to be carried off to "the third heaven" (2 Cor 12:3), and what might be the differences between "corporeal," "spiritual," and "intellectual" visions (*Literal Meaning of Genesis* 12.15-69). The "visionary literature" that came to form so large a part of the corpus of medieval mystical texts (as, for example, in Hildegard of Bingen, Hadewijch of Antwerp, and Julian of Norwich) could find in such a text from Augustine its theoretical basis.

Medieval and Modern Understandings

Bernard of Clairvaux (1090–1153) may serve as a transitional figure for these reflections, for on the one hand he is often called "the last of the Fathers," but on the other hand there are clearly adumbrated in his writings many of the later developments of medieval mysticism. Like Origen and Gregory of Nyssa, he found in the Canticle of Canticles a privileged locus for his reflections on union with Christ, but at times he treated the experience of such a union in a still more personal way than Origen. For Bernard, the coming of Christ was mystical in the literal sense of "hidden," inasmuch as "none of my senses showed me that he had flooded the depths of my being," but there were *interior* signs of an intensely affective nature that nevertheless revealed the divine Bridegroom's presence: "Only by the warmth of my heart . . . did I know that he was there, and I knew the power of his might because my faults were purged. . . . In the remaking and renewing of the spirit of my mind, that is, the inner man, I perceived the excellence of his glorious beauty, and when I contemplate all these things I am filled with awe of his manifold greatness" (*In Cant.* 74.6).

In such a passage one can sense a shift in emphasis from the way the Eastern Fathers usually wrote about union with Christ. More personal, more affective, Bernard is moving toward that modern understanding of Christian mysticism as a state of consciousness surpassing ordinary experience through union with the transcendent reality of God. This became even more pronounced in the 14th century in a work like Henry Suso's *Life of the Servant,* received scholarly definition in the 15th century when Chancellor John Gerson defined mystical theology as "experimental knowledge of God through the embrace of unitive love," and reached classic expression in the 16th century in the writings of Teresa of Avila. This certainly does not mean that writers like Suso and Teresa were unmindful of the objective reality of God's presence, which they experienced in the depth of their being, but, especially with Teresa, the criteria for discerning the different stages of this journey to God became primarily psychological. Thus the "prayer of quiet" differs from lower levels of prayer because in the prayer of quiet "the soul didn't desire to move or stir," (Teresa, *Life* 17.4), and this prayer can in turn be distinguished from still higher levels by such means as examining the activity (or passivity) of the three faculties of memory, intellect, and will in each case. Teresa's analyses are penetrating, and she herself gained ever-increasing clarity by revising her positions from treatise to treatise (as can be seen by comparing the treatments of the prayer of quiet in the *Life* and in *The Interior Castle*). For this reason, if no other, she is rightly regarded as a Doctor of the Church.

But the gains in this kind of approach to Christian mysticism have also brought about, in the eyes of many, corresponding losses. The extended consideration of visions, raptures, locutions, and similar phenomena, especially in the sixth part of the *Castle,* has almost inevitably given many readers the impression that Christian mysticism is something extraordinary, reserved for a chosen few. This impression was given scholarly support in the early 20th century with the publication of the widely read and often reprinted work of Augustin Poulain, *The Graces of Interior Prayer,* for one of Poulain's main contentions was that there is an essential distinction between mystical and ordinary Christian life, the former being an extraordinary way for those specially called to it.

Already in the decades prior to the Second Vatican Council, Poulain's position came under strong criticism from figures like Reginald Garrigou-Lagrange. Since the council, and in large measure precisely because of the council's strong emphasis on the universal call to holiness (see, e.g., LG, chap. 5), the distinction between an "ordinary" and a "mystical" (= extraordinary) way of Christian life has been in full retreat. Thomas Merton (1915–1968), especially in the final years of his life, was among those most insistent on basic continuity in the path that all Christians are called to follow. This is clearly expressed in the following passage from one of Merton's best-known essays, where he emphasizes not so much the differences between various stages of spiritual growth as the basic continuity underlying them all: "To reach a true awareness of [God] as well as ourselves, we have to renounce our selfish and limited self and enter into a whole new kind of existence, discovering an inner center of motivation and love which makes us see ourselves and everything else in an entirely new light. Call it faith, call it (at a more advanced stage) contemplative illumination, call it the sense of God or even mystical union: all these are different aspects and levels of the same kind of realization: the awakening to a new awareness of ourselves in Christ, created in Him, redeemed by Him, to be transformed and glorified in and with Him" (*Contemplation in a World of Action,* Garden City, N.Y.: Doubleday, 1973, pp. 175–176).

Another monastic writer, David Steindl-Rast, makes the same point even more emphatically (and hyperbolically?) by paraphrasing what Ruskin said about being an artist: "A mystic is not a special kind of human being; rather, every human being is a special kind of mystic" (*Gratefulness, the Heart of Prayer,* New York: Paulist, 1984, p. 86).

With greater theological precision, and developed at much greater length over the course of numerous essays, are the reflections of Karl Rahner (1904–1984) on what he was accustomed to calling "everyday mysticism." Because Rahner is widely considered the most important Catholic theologian of the 20th century, and because his reflections on mysticism are so much in accord with the earliest usage of the term *mystical* in the Fathers of the Church (on whose writings he concentrated when embarking on his theological career), this section of the article will conclude with a brief examination of Rahner's position.

A fundamental principle of all Rahner's theology is that our knowledge and freedom always reach out beyond (or "transcend") the individual objects of inner and outer experience, and that the goal toward which such transcendence tends is the boundless mystery that Christians call God. The transcendent experience of this goal in everyday life is normally unthematic and unreflective (i.e., one does not consciously advert to it), but there are also "more intensive realizations which force this experience of transcendence more clearly on the reflective consciousness as well" (Rahner, p. 57). One way in which this might occur is when the individual objects of daily life clearly and intensely indicate the inconceivable mystery of our existence that always surrounds us. Rahner does not go into great detail about this possibility, but he seems to be referring to the kinds of experience reported in a work like William James's *Varieties of Religious Experience,* where, for example, a clergyman recalls "the night, and almost the very spot on the hilltop, where my soul opened out, as it were, into the Infinite and there was a rushing together of the two worlds, the inner and the outer. . . . I stood alone with Him who had made me, and . . . felt the perfect unison of my spirit with His" (James, p. 66).

There might even occur what Rahner calls a "purely nonconceptual experience of transcendence without imagery," an experience of the type that the 16th-century Carmelite mystic John of the Cross describes at several points in his classic texts (see, e.g., *The Ascent of Mount Carmel,* 2.26). This is the kind of experience that Rahner considers mystical in the "specific" sense, described by the Rahner scholar Harvey Egan as "unusually pure and intense psychological experiences of

our graced orientation to the God of love" (Egan, p. 101).

However, Rahner also considers another possibility, which would likewise be genuinely mystical, but in the broader sense of what he calls "everyday mysticism." Among other occasions, this may at times be provoked when "the graspable contours of our everyday realities break and dissolve; when . . . the question becomes inescapable whether the night surrounding us is the absurd void of death engulfing us, or the blessed holy night which is already illumined from within and gives promise of everlasting day" (Rahner, p. 81). If a person holds fast in such a situation, trying to love God even though no response seems to come from the divine silence, seeking to love others even though no echo of gratefulness is heard in return, bearing the freely accepted burdens of responsibility even when this offers no apparent promise of earthly success, then, says Rahner, "*there* is God and his liberating grace. . . . There is the mysticism of everyday life, the discovery of God in all things; there is the sober intoxication of the Spirit, of which the Fathers and the liturgy speak [and] which we cannot reject or despise, because it is real" (Rahner, p. 84).

Rahner's reference to the fear that "the night surrounding us" might be "the absurd void of death" recalls the final eighteen months of the life of the saint named at the beginning of this article. Using the same language of night and darkness, Thérèse wrote frankly of her trial of faith, a torment in which the enveloping darkness seemed to be saying to her: "You are dreaming about the light, about a fatherland embalmed in the sweetest perfumes . . . about the *eternal* possession of the Creator of all these marvels. . . . Advance, advance; rejoice in death which will give you not what you hope for but a night still more profound, the night of nothingness" (*Story of a Soul,* Washington: I.C.S. Publications, 1976, p. 213). Even while experiencing nothing of "the joy of faith," she continued "trying to carry out its works at least," as by treating with special love a particular nun who was "very disagreeable" to Thérèse on a purely human level but who became attractive to her because of "Jesus hidden in the depths of her soul" (*ibid.,* pp. 222–223).

According to the common, modern understanding of mysticism, there could be nothing mystical about such a life, and that is why, as we have seen, some have denied that Thérèse even crossed the threshold of mysticism. But according to Rahner's understanding of "everyday mysticism," which he explicitly relates to the teaching of "the Fathers and the liturgy," and in accordance with Bouyer's studies of the meaning of "the mystical" in those same Fathers, Thérèse's life was a compelling instance of Christian mysticism in its original sense. As Bouyer writes, one of the primary tendencies of much modern thought is to assume that one can have "real experience" of God *only* when that takes the form of immediate and total awareness of God's presence. But, as Thérèse and all genuine Christian mystics have known, the truly important thing is "to be fully convinced that Christ lives within us, and especially to act in accordance with that conviction" (Bouyer, *Mysterion,* p. 348), and not necessarily to experience more or less forcefully the feeling that that is indeed so.

Mysticism in Other Religious Traditions

Thus far this article has focused on Christian mysticism, and from a Catholic perspective. In concluding, it would be proper to consider the broader question of mysticism in other traditions. Two historically important but quite different approaches taken by many Christian scholars in the early and mid-20th century may be singled out. On the one hand, some theologians spoke of Christian mysticism as "supernatural," on the grounds that, in its authentic form, it alone is induced by divine grace and has the triune God of Christian revelation as its object. These theologians generally considered analogous experiences in other religious traditions to be manifestations of "natural mysticism," brought about by human effort and attaining, at best, a deep experience of the self in what the neo-Thomist philosopher Jacques Maritain once called "the abyss of subjectivity" (Maritain, p. 272). Maritain himself considered it probable that there were also some cases of supernatural mystical experience outside Christianity, as in the Hindu path of love (*bhakti*), but he also recognized that however clear the theoretical distinction between supernatural and natural might be, "the contingencies of history and of the concrete present us with every kind and every degree of mixture and juxtaposition of natural with supernatural" (*ibid.,* p. 281). That complication, and the fact that the Catholic Church has taken a much more positive view of other religions since the promulgation of Vatican II's groundbreaking declaration *Nostra Aetate,* are surely among the reasons why contemporary theologians speak much less frequently of natural mysticism than did their predecessors of a generation or two ago.

An approach quite different from the one just described was taken by scholars who, far from making a sharp distinction between Christian and non-Christian mysticism, assumed that the essence of mysticism is the same in all traditions, with differences arising only from variations in doctrine and imagery that color subsequent formulations of one and the same experience. The Anglican author Evelyn Underhill (1875–1941) may be taken as representative of this position. In her widely read and often reprinted work *Mysticism,* she held that even though the expressions of mystical writers might vary from tradition to tradition, the substance of what they seek (and claim to find) is "always the same Beatific Vision of a Goodness, Truth, and Beauty which is *one.* Hence its substance must always be distinguished from the accidents under which we perceive it" (Underhill, p. 96). So convinced was she of this fundamental similarity that at times she went even further in her formulations and claimed that all mystics "speak the same language and come from the same country," so that "the place which they happen to occupy in the kingdom of this world matters little" (ibid., p. xiii).

Although Underhill's books did much to awaken interest in mystical texts on the part of persons outside narrowly academic circles, her expressed aim of providing a synthesis of the doctrine of Christian and non-Christian mystics is now often looked upon with suspicion, based as it was on the unwarranted assumption that experience and interpretation can be easily and neatly separated along the lines of her distinction between "substance" and "accidents." Far more attention is now being paid to important differences between the mystics of various times, places, and traditions (see, e.g., the books edited by Steven Katz in the bibliography to this article).

If mysticism in other traditions is not to be regarded as merely "natural mysticism" and if, on the other hand, significant differences between all these traditions are not to be ignored, how might this issue of comparative mysticism be better addressed? The approach developed in the remainder of this article takes as its point of departure the original Christian understanding of "the mystical," namely, the search for the "hidden" presence of Christ in the Scriptures and the experience of union with Christ with which that search could culminate in persons like Origen and Bernard. Are there parallels to this in other religions? If so, what would this imply about mysticism in those religions? For reasons of space, in answering these questions we will focus only on the two other great monotheistic religions that arose in the Near East: Judaism and Islam.

Important studies of both Jewish and Islamic mysticism have shown conclusively that here, too, as in Christianity, the origi-

nal impetus came from reflecting on the meaning of the canonical scriptures, in this case, the Torah and the Qur'an respectively. Gershom Scholem, the 20th century's pioneering scholar of Jewish mysticism, once noted that "all Jewish mystics, from the Therapeutae ... to the latest Hasid, are at one in giving a mystical interpretation to the Torah; the Torah is to them a living organism animated by a secret life which streams and pulsates below the crust of its literal meaning" (Scholem, pp. 13–14).

Of the Jewish texts in which such interpretation occurs, pride of place goes to the 13th-century Book of Zohar, described by one of its recent translators as "a mystical commentary on the Torah. God is hidden in the Torah, hidden and revealed there, because Torah is God's Name.... The mystic who studies Torah ... sees through the text into the texture of divine life" (D. Matt, Zohar: The Book of Enlightenment, New York: Paulist, 1983, p. 31). In the Zohar itself, it is said that the Torah, like a beautiful maiden, reveals herself to no one but her lover, and even then only gradually. But "once he has grown accustomed to her, she reveals herself face to face and tells him all her hidden secrets, all the hidden ways, since primordial days secreted in her heart" (Zohar, p. 125). This is clearly similar to the way a Christian mystic like Origen understood the Bible as revealing its secrets, its mysteria, only to one who has been "wounded by love" and "has burned with this faithful love for the Word of God."

What Scholem observed about the origins of Jewish mysticism is true also of Islam. Leading scholars of this tradition like Louis Massignon and Annemarie Schimmel have shown that Islamic mysticism developed out of meditation on the Qur'an and faithful imitation of the actions of Muhammad, the Messenger of God. Constant meditation on the Qur'an led the early Muslim mystics (who came to be called Sufis) to "discover unending mysteries behind each and every word of the Holy Book; they lived in it . . . and to read it meant to meet face to face with the Creator and Judge" (A. Schimmel, in Katz, *Mysticism and Religious Traditions,* p. 130).

Moreover, just as within Christianity the term *mystical* came to be applied not only to the presence of Christ in the Bible but also to his presence in the sacraments, so too in Islam an encounter with the Compassionate and Merciful One was experienced by the Sufis not only in the Holy Book but in other areas of life as well. The Sufi Dhu'n-Nun, who lived in Egypt in the 9th century, gave eloquent expression to this when he wrote: "O God, I never hearken to the voices of the beasts or the rustle of the trees, the splashing of the waters or the song of the birds, the whistling of the wind or the rumble of the thunder, but I sense in them a testimony to Thy Unity, and a proof of Thy incomparability, that Thou are the All-Prevailing, the All-Knowing, the All-True" (quoted by Schimmel, *Mystical Dimensions,* p. 46).

Scholars who are wont to emphasize the differences between the various mystical traditions will be quick to point out specifically Muslim overtones in this prayer, such as the reference to the divine unity, but equally if not more striking is the fact that this mystic's experience of the world as transparent to the divine presence has close parallels in the writings of many Christian mystics—and not only Catholic ones like Francis of Assisi or Thomas Merton. Jonathan Edwards (1703–1758), the New England divine who became America's first great theologian, is sometimes recalled only for his sermon on "Sinners in the Hands of an Angry God," but in fact there was a pronounced mystical side to Edwards' life. His *Personal Narrative* contains passages most reminiscent of the prayer of Dhu'n-Nun, not only in references to the trees and water as revealing "the sweet glory of God" but also in Edwards' more detailed reflections on

what the Sufi had called "the rumble of the thunder." Edwards wrote: "I used to be uncommonly terrified with thunder, and to be struck with terror when I saw a thunder storm rising; but now, on the contrary, it rejoiced me. I felt God, so to speak, at the first appearance of a thunder storm; and used to take the opportunity, at such times, to fix myself in order to view the clouds, and see the lightnings play, and hear the majestic and awful voice of God's thunder, which oftentimes was exceedingly entertaining, leading me to sweet contemplations of my great and glorious God" (*Jonathan Edwards: Representative Selections,* ed. C. Faust and T. Johnson, New York: Hill and Wang, 1962, p. 61).

These similarities in the origins and modes of expression of Christian, Jewish, and Islamic mysticism are surely of more than incidental significance. It is often said that our world is becoming more and more a global village, in which religions long suspicious of one another (and at times mortal foes on the battlefield) are necessarily coming into ever closer contact. The challenge of interreligious dialogue has never been more urgent. Part of that dialogue will rightly be carried on by scholars conversant with the doctrines and rituals of their own tradition as well as those of their partners in dialogue. But one may expect that the ones who will do most to foster the mutual understanding and communion that is the goal of such dialogue will be those who have most deeply penetrated the meaning of their own scriptures and have thereby found themselves uniquely prepared to understand their mystically experienced counterparts in other traditions.

It is a fact that those we preeminently consider mystics often feel this kinship keenly. To none of his numerous correspondents did Thomas Merton write more openly about the intimate nature of his own prayer life than to the Sufi scholar Abdul Aziz. In their correspondence, Merton also referred often to all that he had gained from reading the Sufi mystics.

He called Jalalu'l Din Rumi "one of the greatest poets and mystics" and said that he found his words "inspiring and filled with the fire of divine love." Of Sufism itself, he wrote that "there is no question but that here is a living and convincing truth, a deep mystical experience of the mystery of God our Creator Who watches over us at every moment with infinite love and mercy. . . . May He be praised and adored everywhere forever." And in the conclusion to one letter, Merton told Abdul Aziz that "we must be brothers in prayer and worship, no matter what may be the doctrinal differences that separate our minds" (*The Hidden Ground of Love: The Letters of Thomas Merton on Religious Experience and Social Concerns,* New York: Farrar, Straus, Giroux, 1983, pp. 44, 48, 49).

This attitude of deep reverence toward God and one's fellow human beings is surely a fundamental sign of genuine mysticism and one of the reasons why Christian mysticism, for all that makes it distinctive in its own right, ought never be studied in strict isolation from the mysticism of other religious traditions. In whatever settings *homo religiosus* is found, one may also expect appearances of *homo mysticus.*

See also AFFIRMATIVE WAY; CONTEMPLATION, CONTEMPLATIVE PRAYER; DARKNESS, DARK NIGHT; DEIFICATION; EXPERIENCE; EXTRAORDINARY PHENOMENA; MYSTERY; MYSTICAL THEOLOGY; NEGATIVE WAY; PRAYER; UNION, UNITIVE WAY.

Bibliography: Works by many Christian, Jewish, and Islamic mystics are available in the ongoing series Classics of Western Spirituality (New York: Paulist; London: SPCK). Selections from the writings of twenty-five of the most important Christian mystics may be found in L. Dupré and J. Wiseman, eds., *Light from Light: An Anthology of Christian Mysticism* (New York: Paulist, 1988). See also R. Bailey, *Thomas Merton on Mysticism* (Garden City, N.Y.: Doubleday, 1987). L. Bouyer, *Mysterion: Du mystère à la mystique* (Paris: O.E.I.L., 1986); Eng. trans.: *The Christian Mystery* (Edinburgh: T. & T. Clark, 1990). R. Brown, *The Semitic Background of the Term "Mystery" in the New Testament* (Philadelphia: Fortress, 1968). H. Egan, *What Are They Saying About Mysticism?* (New York: Paulist, 1982). W. James, *The Varieties of Religious Experience,* enlarged ed. (New Hyde Park, N.Y.: University Books, 1963, originally 1902). S. Katz, ed., *Mysticism and Philosophical Analysis* (New York: Oxford Univ. Press, 1978). Idem, ed., *Mysticism and Religious Traditions* (New York: Oxford Univ. Press, 1983). J. Maritain, "The Natural Mystical Experience and the Void," in his *Ransoming the Time* (New York: Scribner's, 1948) 255–289. K. Rahner, *The Practice of Faith: A Handbook of Contemporary Spirituality,* ed. K. Lehmann and A. Raffelt (New York: Crossroad, 1984). A. Schimmel, *Mystical Dimensions of Islam* (Chapel Hill, N.C.: Univ. of North Carolina Press, 1975). G. Scholem, *Major Trends in Jewish Mysticism* (New York: Schocken, 1954). E. Underhill, *Mysticism* (New York: New American Library, 1974, originally 1911).

JAMES A. WISEMAN, O.S.B.

MYTH

The Meaning of Myth

A myth is a story possessed of such energy and significance that one stakes his or her entire life upon it. It is a story about the holy, about what is considered most profoundly important. The word *myth* comes from the Greek word *mythos,* suggesting a word or story that is spoken aloud. In Greco-Roman culture it referred especially to stories pertaining to the gods. It came to be contrasted with the word *logos,* which implied a reasoned argument, something more dependable and truer than myth. This connotation of myth as a falsehood, an attractive fiction at best, was prevalent, therefore, in the social milieu of early Christianity. Hence Paul rebuked those with "itching ears," who were drawn to the speculations of "profane and silly myths" (2 Tim 4:3, NRSV; 1 Tim 4:7).

This negative connotation would persist for centuries, but the modern reappreciation of folklore and the oral tradition, along with the work of anthropologists and historians of religion, would help to restore the word to its original vitality. Myth is far more than primitive fable. It is what roots the individual imagination in the collective unconscious (Carl Jung), what connects human beings with a sense of Primordial Time (Mircea Eliade), what echoes a fundamental structure of the human mind (Claude Levi-Strauss). Myth conveys the intensity of living amid a "surplus of meaning," as the world bursts imaginatively into life (Paul Ricoeur).

Given this deep investment of the participant in the story that is told and lived out, it is necessarily the case that one never fully understands the myths by which one lives. Myth understood is no longer myth. All our lives we participate in narrative structures that are taken perfectly for granted. "Living" myths are characterized by an unreflective immediacy. This explains the power that myth exercises in our experience, yet it also indicates the immense capacity for fooling ourselves—for living by the wrong stories—that is possible in human existence. One's reality, for example, can as readily be constructed by commitment to the Nazi myth of racial superiority as by belief in the continuing presence of a risen Christ.

Myth and Interpretation

Myth flourishes in the mystery and awe of incomprehension. It invites people to abandon themselves to its immediacy and transcendence. Yet because of this fact, myth also requires the exercise of critical insight in testing the validity of its claims. Hence mythology is related to critical reflection in the same way as spirituality is related to theology. Spirituality, like myth, is concerned with the absorbing, "lived experience" of truth, whereas theology makes use of discursive reasoning in examining and developing the clarity of truth itself.

Paul Ricoeur speaks of this tension in his discussion of the theologian's hermeneutical task. Everyone begins at the level of a "first naiveté," captured by the power of myth, alive with wonder, viewing the world unreflectively. But one must move on from there, through a "hermeneutics of suspicion," to think critically, subjecting that initially naive experience to the hardest possible questions. This has been the great impulse of the Enlightenment, for example, with its insistent recourse to logic and analytical reasoning. But the quest for

meaning has to move beyond this stage as well, toward a "second naiveté," in which the original power of myth is rediscovered on the far side of reason. Renewed wonder emerges out of the anguish of criticism, though now less subject to self-delusion, less inclined to a primitive escapism. In such a way, myth can be incorporated into the process of theological investigation and related directly to the study of spirituality. The spiritual life is the living out of one's deeply held stories (*mythos*) under the critical awareness provided by theological reflection (*logos*).

Narrative and the Functions of Myth

Narrative is the dominant form by which myth is shared within a community of people. Storytelling is the perennial human act of "making the world," reminding one another of what matters most. As a result, one finds a persistence to certain mythic tales that get told again and again, even in a modern world that imagines itself rid of all dragons. "There are only two or three human stories," wrote Willa Cather, "and they go on repeating themselves as fiercely as if they had never happened before." Joseph Campbell suggests that "the latest incarnation of Oedipus, the continued romance of Beauty and the Beast, stands this afternoon on the corner of Forty-second Street and Fifth Avenue, waiting for the traffic light to change." We are a people whose lives are inescapably molded by stories. The idea that we live in a world come of age, demythologized, no longer dependent upon "childish" tales is itself a myth, yet another story attempting to offer sustained meaning for our lives.

Particularly relevant to the study of spirituality are the various functions that myth serves in the lived experience of human communities. Campbell points to four of these in his effort to demonstrate the significance of myths for our present existence. The first is a mystical function, by which myth helps to open the world to the presence of mystery. It elicits a sense of awe and wonder, even dread—what Rudolf Otto spoke of as "the idea of the holy." Ghost stories and tales of wonder connect us with a deeply inherent impulse to fear and to praise that which we cannot even name.

The second function of myth is cosmological. Addressing the anxieties people feel in the face of a threatening universe, it gives shape to the world, explaining how things came to be as they are. Creation stories provide a sense of comfort in their description of how order has emerged from chaos. Stories of this nature are etiological, going back to the beginnings to explain why mosquitoes buzz or why evil seems to work in such a free-handed way in the world.

Thirdly, myth functions in a sociological manner to support and validate a certain social order. This is a very familiar function, operative in the political arena and advertising, as well as in the stories parents tell to their children. Myth serves to develop conformity, to mold the young. That is why cautionary tales are repeated from one generation to another, telling what to do and what not to do in order to be an accepted member of the community. Claude Levi-Strauss underscores this essentially conservative function of myth. Its aim is the reconciliation of opposites within a given culture. It tries to resolve tensions, restoring order and peace, as it rehearses the tribal tales that give identity to a people. Such myths are able to remind a clan, a tribe, or a nation of its fundamental values, providing dependable routines in times of crisis.

A final function of myth is psychological, seeking to instruct the individual in how to live a truly human life amid the ever-changing circumstances of growth. How does one internalize the conflicting meanings of birth, initiation, maturity, marriage, retirement, and death? In helping one another deal with the difficulties of these life passages, we tell stories about heroes and saints. Most often these tales take the form of a journey, indicating how we can get from here to there—from the inferno to paradiso, from the pilgrim's gate to the celestial city. They teach us by example how to survive and grow. In all these ways, therefore, myth serves to tell us who we are. We become the stories that we tell. That is why we repeat them over and over again.

Myth, Symbol, and Ritual

If myth assumes the character of a story, told for any or all of these varied purposes, it can also be expressed in "shorthand" or gestured form as symbol or ritual. These are important subdimensions of myth, able to powerfully summarize the dynamic events described by the sacred tale. A symbol operates as a "visual trigger" that not only recalls the myth but participates in its power. Like an icon, it contains within it some quality of that which it represents. Ritual, in turn, is a dramatic gesture that vividly reenacts the mythic story, making it contemporaneous with the participants' present experience. Water, for example, is a symbol of the compelling myth of a dying and rising Lord. Passing through the waters of chaos has been a prominent motif of salvation in biblical thought, from the memory of the Exodus to the baptismal theology of Paul in Romans 6. Water's capacity to drown as well as to give life is what makes it such an effective trigger of the imagination. Baptism, then, is the ritual event that retells the story in "mimed" or gestured form, incorporating the symbol in an "acting out" of the tale. Being intimately drawn into the myth in this kinesthetic fashion offers a profound experience of participation in an all-encompassing reality. It is, by the way, what children do naturally—tell stories, engage in theater, "play" in a way that is also intensely serious.

The history of spirituality is rich with symbols that evoke the enduring myths—the life-engaging narratives—of the Christian faith. There is the "dark night" of John of the Cross, the "interior castle" of Teresa of Avila, the "ladder" of John Climacus, the "seven story mountain" of Thomas Merton, the "cloud of unknowing" described by that great anonymous author of the 14th century. Each of these reaches beyond itself to mysteries of the spiritual life in which we are invited to share. They provide a form of shorthand notation used to recall from deep memory our own identification with the painful and joyous experiences of the saints.

The Unity of Myth

One result of the modern study of myth has been an increased sensitivity to the way in which various myths and their symbols come to be shared among different spiritual traditions. Carl Jung was fascinated by the idea that the same stories have a way of repeating themselves in religious communities from India to the Middle East, from China and Japan to South America. He explained this by pointing to certain inherited primordial images or "archetypes" that connect all human beings with a common body of experience. While individuals may tap this reservoir of shared knowledge by means of their dreams, communities do it by means of their myths.

Joseph Campbell went so far as to suggest a "monomyth" or single shared story that is held by everyone as part of the universal experience of humankind. This is the story of the hero in every culture who passes through a pattern of separation, initiation, and return. He or she departs from the routines of daily life, assumes an impossible task full of danger, and comes back, maybe wounded but triumphant, with blessings for the entire tribe. This is the call to adventure, to the fullness of life, that comes to everyman and everywoman, says Campbell. In trying to reduce all myths to one, he seeks to emphasize the unity that all peoples share. His approach may be too simplistic, yet his concern is an important one. As we recognize the power of one another's stories, we grow in respect for one another, even as we enter more fully into the meaning of what we ourselves believe. C. S. Lewis urged that "those who are at the heart of their different religions are closer to one another than those who are at the fringes." The capacity of myth to bring people together is just as great as its power to divide.

Far from being merely "an invented story," therefore, myth is the root narrative by which a people live out their spirituality. Incorporating conceptions of sacred space and sacred time, images of the hero, and patterns of communal identity, it becomes a way of acting out, as well as summarizing, all that is important.

See also CULTURE: IMAGINATION; NARRATIVE; RITUAL; STORY; SYMBOL; VALUE.

Bibliography: W. Beane and W. Doty, eds., *Myths, Rites, Symbols: A Mircea Eliade Reader*, 2 vols. (New York: Harper, 1975). J. Campbell (with B. Moyers), *The Power of Myth* (New York: Doubleday, 1988). C. Jung, *Man and His Symbols* (New York: Dell, 1968).

BELDEN C. LANE

N

NARRATIVE

Narrative is the most characteristic way of articulating any human experience. Throughout the history of Christian spirituality, it has been the dominant literary form used to describe the spiritual life. From the apophthegmata of the Desert Fathers and Mothers to Jonathan Edwards' narrative of conversion, "story" has assumed a central role in the varied tasks of catechesis, preaching, and spiritual direction. In recent years, as biblical study has shifted from historical to literary approaches, narrative theology has attracted considerable interest, especially as seen in the work of Amos Wilder, Hans Frei, Sallie McFague, and John Shea. While propositional theology may be concerned with the systematic analysis of doctrine, narrative theology seeks to appreciate the multivalence and ambiguity of language as expressed in metaphor and other poetic uses of speech. This offers a deeper way of understanding the multiplicity of the human experience of the divine, even as it also helps to recover the communicative power of the oral tradition.

Three characteristics of narrative may be especially relevant to the study of spirituality. The first is that story thrives on the event-character of oral exchange. The Hebrew word *dabar,* meaning "word" or "story," is intimately connected with the immediacy and effervescence of sound. Isaiah 55:11 suggests that the word of Yahweh does not return empty but accomplishes the task for which it is sent. The word bears a life of its own—a power rooted in its dynamism as an unrepeatable, spontaneous oral event. Much of the power of early Christianity derived from the fact that it was first communicated by word of mouth and only later written down. The transmission of narrative, then, is first of all a spoken phenomenon. This explains the recurring emphasis on the oral reading of Scripture found in the history of monastic life. It underlines the importance of Walter Ong's work in studying the oral tradition and accounts for the current revival of interest in the art of storytelling.

A second characteristic of narrative relates to its capacity for carrying a "surplus of meaning," not readily available in discursive language. Story is never exhausted in a single telling. Nor can its meaning be reduced to a single, rational precept. Narrative remains subject to a fluidity of interpretation. Because of this, preachers and Christian educators have often been distrustful of story, even in their frequent dependence upon it. They may be tempted to "explain" the narrative, fearful that their listeners may not get the "point." In the process, however, they slam shut the doors of imagination that might have been opened by the polysemous richness of the tale. In the *Gesta Romanorum,* a collection of stories used by priests in the Middle Ages, a suitable moral lesson was always attached to the tale, suggesting that truth, to be valid, must finally be reduced to propositions. Such a view does violence to the integrity of narrative and distorts the polymorphic character of human experience.

A third important dimension of narrative is its rootedness in the concrete realities of ordinary life. Stories appeal to the senses—they reconstruct a sense of place, create characters, and recount events with which the reader is invited to identify. That is why narrative is the preferred form by which God is disclosed in biblical faith. Emmanuel—God with us—is known, not by reasoning speculatively, but by reciting the stories of God's presence in human affairs. Story connects us with the incarnational heart of Christian faith. As Nietzsche wrote, "The more abstract the truth is that you would teach, the more you have to seduce the senses to it."

Ignatius Loyola expressed this principle very well in his *Spiritual Exercises.* Careful reflection on the Gospel narratives became, for him, the focus of the spiritual life. He emphasized the use of the five senses and the reconstruction of place as basic methods for entering imaginatively into the experience of these biblical tales.

Narrative is a distinctive, imaginative way of shaping truth, one that takes part in God's own creative action. Elie Wiesel said, "God made man because he loves stories." In the history of Christian spirituality, this impulse to repeat the stories of God has been expressed most often in the lives of the saints. From Athanasius' first *Life of Antony,* through Augustine's *Confessions* and Bonaventure's *Life of St. Francis,* the form of storytelling was adopted as a way of sharing one's spiritual encounter. In this way a pattern would be established that dictated the character of all subsequent experiences of the holy.

See also IMAGINATION; MEMORY; MYTH; PREACHING; SCRIPTURE; STORY.

Bibliography: S. McFague, *Metaphorical Theology* (Philadelphia: Fortress, 1982). T. Tilley, *Story Theology* (Wilmington, Del.: Glazier, 1985).

BELDEN C. LANE

NATIVE AMERICAN SPIRITUALITY

Most commentators regard the present-day native inhabitants of North and Latin America as the descendants of peoples who originally migrated from Asia, across what was a land-bridge at the Bering Strait, more than ten thousand years ago. These peoples spread south throughout the two continents, and over the millennia they developed highly diverse cultures. The main reason for such diversity was the variety of ecological conditions in which they had to live. Inuit (Eskimos), living in the far north, faced different challenges than natives living in the forests of the Amazon. Peoples who lived along the seacoast developed cultures that had little in common with peoples who lived on the plains. If a given tribe owed most of its survival to the buffalo, that tribe thought and lived differently from the tribe that depended mainly on the salmon or on corn or on the seal.

The first rule to observe when discussing Native American spirituality, then, is to be as specific as possible. Native Americans have developed so many different languages, technologies, mythologies, and ceremonies that generalizations are perilous. So much of the Native American past lies beyond our reach, in the twilight of prehistory, that we can seldom say how a given myth or ceremony or traditional way of regarding the corn came into being. As much as any other racial group, Native Americans force us to study the interactions between given tribes and their local environments. If there is a single key to a specific tribal culture, it is likely to lie in the environmental conditions out of which the main features of the culture originally arose.

With this said, one may speculate about some recurrent features of Native American life, confident that the result will not be total misunderstanding. For example, there is the inclination of numerous Native American tribes to accredit shamanic ecstasies. Not all tribes sponsored shamans or rooted their key religious convictions in shamanic experience. But leaving ordinary consciousness for trance, so that one could encounter spiritual helpers or travel on important journeys, was common enough among Native Americans to make it noteworthy. Some students of Native American roots conjecture that the shamanism one still finds in native north-Asian cultures came with the original emigrants to the New World. Those emigrants would not have realized that they were entering a new continental area. Their instinct would have been to continue their traditional ways of hunting, gathering, sheltering themselves against the cold, raising their children, curing their sick, and petitioning the powers they considered responsible for their fate.

For matters such as curing the sick, overcoming violations of tribal taboos, or guiding the dead to their resting place, Inuit of the early 20th century still relied on shamans. These figures, who could be either male or female, were able to go into trance and search for the knowledge the current crisis required. Among their several possible techniques for going into trance, observers noted singing, dancing, beating a drum, staring at a skull, plunging into icy waters, and ingesting tobacco. Shamans who made this work their special vocation might have a special costume, decorated with symbols of their trips to the afterworld or the realm of the gods. In Inuit mythology a goddess could hold back the sea animals, usually because the people had displeased her. One of the shaman's jobs would be to negotiate passage around various horrifying obstacles and gain an interview with the goddess at the bottom of the sea. Then, having appeased her and found out what the tribe had done wrong, the shaman could return to ordinary consciousness and arrange for the wrongdoers to confess and repent.

Observers have also noted that shamans sometimes developed paranormal powers in concert with their facility for trance. They might see or hear at extraordinary distances, and so perhaps perceive the game that the goddess had been withholding. In their guidance of the dead, shamans again depended on their ability to leave ordinary awareness and "travel." Though their bodies were in the lodge, surrounded by the rest of the tribe, their spirits were traveling with the spirits of the dead, guiding them to a place of safety and rest.

Numerous native tribes that did not develop an elaborate shamanic ritual or mythology did rely on individual visions. Especially at puberty, males (and sometimes females) could be ordered to go apart from the tribe and gain a spiritual revelation to direct their adult lives. In solitude, fasting, and devout concentration, native youth prepared themselves to see the world in a new way. Typically, an animal would arrive with a message, meaningful to the individual recipient and sometimes useful to the entire tribe. Thenceforth that animal would probably be the special helper of the person visited. (Girls tended to focus on the power that came with puberty, which made them capable of bearing new life.)

The assumption one finds in accounts of both shamanic journeys and less dramatic vision quests is that human beings are part of a whole swarm of creatures, with whom they can communicate. Human beings are as much like as unlike wolves and bears, birds and fishes. In dealing with such fellow creatures, human beings ought to proceed respectfully, even reverently. It is necessary for creatures to live off one another, but that necessity should increase respect. Some tribes, therefore, would counsel speaking to the plants and animals that one had to kill for food, explaining one's sorrow and necessity. Inuit, for example, would set aside the bladders of all the seals they killed during the (limited) hunting season and then return them to the sea to appease the spirits of the seals and ensure good hunting the next season.

Related to the Native American sense of kinship with the plants and animals was a keen sensitivity to the directions and natural elements. The wind, the rain, the sun, the moon, the clouds—all were powerful forces in the Native American world, and all could be personified, addressed as holy persons. For example, in the purification ceremonies of the Lakota, which featured a sweat lodge where one could cleanse the body of impurities and elevate the mind, prayers would ascend to the four directions of the compass. Using a pipe and tobacco, the human participants would send their prayers, their intentions, their good wishes toward the sky, where their Father dwelt. Similarly, they would bless the stones provided by their Mother, the earth, who gave them so many good things. By the end of the purification ceremony, every significant feature of the Lakota world, physical or mental, would have entered into the litany. The ceremony was an occasion to celebrate the confluence of forces and creatures making up the native world, so that all might feel good and live harmoniously.

If there is a single desire that runs across Native American cultures, perhaps it is to live harmoniously with nature. Human beings ought to dwell together in peace, but the larger context of such peace is the sweep of the seasons, the time and pace of nature. Only in the measure that human beings are adjusted to this larger context can they hope to prosper. The tribe is the smaller unit, and the natural environment is the larger unit. The smaller has to fit itself to the larger.

This spiritual outlook explains the relative poverty of Native American culture. Materially, most Native Americans have not sought to pile up possessions or accumulate novelties. For some tribes, a migratory way of life put a premium on carrying only essentials. But even peoples who dwelt on the same land for generations were more interested in attuning themselves to the environment, appreciating the beauty and wisdom of the land in silence, than in gaining possessions or dispersing themselves in constant talk.

One can romanticize these Native American features, but perhaps it is more useful to consider the implications of the contemplative spirit that most tribes' ways of life encouraged. The great text that people had to master, if they were to become wise, was their environment. The more they could know about how the plants, animals, birds, seasons, weather, hills, streams, and all the rest of their surroundings functioned, the better off they would be. Certainly they would be better off practically, in the sense of being better provisioned. But, more importantly, they would be better off spiritually, more at one with their surroundings, better able to commune with the Holy Forces responsible for the world. To appreciate the world, loving its beauty and estimating correctly its dangers, was the acme of Native American achievement. One only learned about oneself and other human beings if one set them in the context of the natural environment. They only gained their depth, their resonance, their third dimension if one was attuned to the wind without and one's own answering breath within.

Nowadays the ecological crisis offers those who appreciate Native American spirituality a new stage on which to display the wisdoms of the native traditions. Because the industrial way of life developed in the modern West is so obviously killing the earth, it is past time to reconsider how Native Americans dealt with nature. To be sure, Native Americans sometimes treated the land badly. On the whole, however, their entire spirituality assumed that the forces one ought to revere, the forces that gave human beings life and plenty, breathed through the land, making it sweet and green. For the land to sicken, corrode, become a source of death would have been horrifying. The most stable reference point in the Native American repertoire was the goodness of the land. Contemplating the land, Native Americans could always reorient themselves, moving back toward harmony. Contemplating the land, their successors can see what has to change.

See also ANIMALS; CREATION; CULTURE; EASTERN (ASIAN) SPIRITUALITY; ECOLOGICAL CONSCIOUSNESS; ENVIRONMENT; HOLISTIC SPIRITUALITY.

Bibliography: L. Sullivan, *Icanchu's Drum* (New York: Macmillan, 1988). J. Brown, *The Spiritual Legacy of the American Indian* (New York: Crossroad, 1982). A. Hultkrantz, *The Religions of the American Indians* (Berkeley, Calif.: Univ. of California Press, 1979).

DENISE LARDNER CARMODY

NATURE MYSTICISM

See COSMIC MYSTICISM; ECOLOGICAL CONSCIOUSNESS; MYSTICISM.

NEGATIVE WAY

The Fourth Lateran Council (1215) stated that "between the Creator and creature no similarity can be expressed without including a greater dissimilarity" (DS 806). The negative way can be understood as a philosophical-theological position, a way of speaking about God, and a contemplative path that stress the "greater dissimilarity" between God and creature.

a) As a philosophical-theological position, the negative way emphasizes that the all-transcendent God is ineffable, incomprehensible, and "wholly other." For Thomas Aquinas, the human mind can attain only that God is, not what God is. Thus, for Aquinas, the ultimate in human cognition is to know that God cannot be known (*De potentia*, q. 7, a. 5, ad 14).

b) As a mode of speaking about God, the negative way denies to God every imperfection found in created things, as well as the circumscription attached to the imperfections of created things that derive from their finiteness. According to Pseudo-Dionysius, the ineffable, incomprehensible, all-transcendent "falls neither within the predicate of nonbeing nor of being."

Thus, "there is no speaking of it, nor name nor knowledge of it" (*The Mystical Theology*, 1048B).

c) As a mode of contemplative ascent to God, the negative way exhorts the seeker to "leave behind . . . everything perceived and understood, everything perceptible and understandable, all that is not and all that is, and, with your understanding laid aside, to strive upward as much as you can toward union with him who is beyond all being and knowledge. By an undivided and absolute abandonment of yourself and everything, shedding all, and freed from all, you will be uplifted to the ray of the divine shadow which is above everything that is" (Pseudo-Dionysius, *The Mystical Theology*, 997B).

Therefore, apophatic (Greek *apophatikos* = negative) spirituality requires complete spiritual poverty and imitation of Christ's self-emptying love. It also demands the abandonment of all concepts, thoughts, images, and symbols—even and especially those of God. God can be experienced and known only through negation, unknowing, and darkness of mind. It must be emphasized, too, that the goal of the negative way is nothing less than full union with God, that is, divinization.

The negative way is solidly rooted in biblical spirituality and mysticism. Biblical apophaticism teaches not only that no one "has ever seen or can see" the "King of kings and Lord of lords" because God is "invisible" (Jn 6:46; 1 Tm 1:17; see Col 1:15) and "dwells in unapproachable light" (1 Tm 6:16; see Jn 1:1; Exod 3:6; 19:10f.; 33:20), but also that the Spirit alone can comprehend God's unsearchable judgments, inscrutable ways, and incomprehensible thoughts (1 Cor 2:10-11; Rom 11:33; see Sir 43:27f.; Eccl 3:11; 11:5; Pss 92:5; 145:3).

The Scriptures underscore God's utter transcendence by stating that he dwells in a "thick darkness" (Exod 20:21, NRSV), in an impenetrable "cloud" (Exod 24:15), and that neither the heavens nor the earth can contain him (1 Kgs 8:27; see Jer 23:23; Rom 9:5). That Yahweh is the "living" God stresses not only his personal, free, active, and purposeful qualities but also his utterly transcendent nature. "Holiness" is another biblical term that expresses Yahweh's "wholly otherness" (see Isa 6; 8:13; 29:23; Lev 10:3; Amos 4:2; Hos 11:9; 1 Sam 2:2).

The negative way finds another biblical warrant in the veneration of Yahweh without images (Exod 20:4f.; Deut 4:15-23, 5:8f.; Lev 26:1). Yahweh is totally different from everything in the visible world. Therefore nothing can represent him. And Israel dramatized this in a special way late in her history through the emptiness in the Holy of Holies.

The risen Christ's "spiritual body" (1 Cor 15:44)—that is, the fully glorified Christ beyond images and concepts—and the Johannine theology of Jesus' going to the Father so that the Spirit can be given (see Jn 7:39; 14:16-17; 19:30; 20:22) provide the Christological justification for the negative way. John's insistence upon not clinging to Jesus' post-Easter appearances because his permanent presence to the Church is now by way of his Spirit (see Jn 20:17) also undergirds the apophatic, or imageless, dimension requisite for genuine Christ-centered spirituality and mysticism. The negative way also has an anthropological warrant: the human person is "spirit-in-world" (Karl Rahner). As spirit-in-*world*, the human person is open to all that exists. However, in its proper transcendence, spirit is open first and foremost to the incomprehensible God.

The Fourth Lateran Council formally defined as a truth of faith God's incomprehensibility and ineffability (DS 804, 837b). Both the Fourth Lateran Council and the First Vatican Council taught, too, as a truth of the faith, that God's essence is incomprehensible even to the blessed in heaven (DS 3001). St. Gregory of Nyssa gives the clearest and most profound expression of this. For him, "the true sight of God consists in this, that the one who looks up to God never ceases in that desire" (*Life of Moses,* no. 233). His view on *epiktasis,* a graced straining toward God (Phil 3:13), is perhaps Gregory's most significant contribution to the Christian mystical tradition. For him, the movement into possession of the incomprehensible God produces no satiety; it results in the continuous discovery of the impenetrable depths of the divine essence, a movement from "glory to glory" (2 Cor 3:18). Thus Gregory speaks of a "satisfied dissatisfaction" even in the beatific vision.

One of the clearest and most profound expositions of the affective negative way can be found in the 14th-century anonymous classic *The Cloud of Unknowing.* The author's main premise states that "no one can fully comprehend the created God with his knowledge; but each, in a different way, can grasp him fully through love" (chap. 4). Thus he prefers to speak about what God is *not* and teaches a way to find God in the depths of the soul emptied of everything except naked love.

The anonymous author recommends lifting up one's heart in love and rejecting *all* thoughts of, and desire for, creatures. One must place everything—even thoughts about God, Christ, Mary, the saints, and heaven—into a "cloud of forgetting" that arises between the contemplative and all created things. This process causes a "darkness," a "cloud of unknowing," to arise between God and the contemplative. One then prays in naked love, that is, in a love devoid of all concepts, images, and thoughts. For the author, only love shorn of all knowledge can "feel and see God in this life."

God may give the grace of apophatic contemplation to anyone from any walk of life. Nonetheless, the author of *The Cloud* emphasizes that the negative way requires a *special* grace that one could not even desire to have "until that which is ineffable and unknowable moves you to desire the ineffable and the unknowable" (chap. 34).

If the tiny dart of love constantly intrudes in one's life and becomes an obstacle to ordinary prayer, and if one is constantly aroused to apophatic contemplation when one hears or reads about it, then—and only then—can one undertake it.

This author stresses not only that God gives the apophatic vocation selectively but also that "the devil has his contemplatives." Because apophatic contemplation is fraught with dangers, the author of *The Cloud* emphasizes the importance of adequate preparation, the gentle attraction of grace, and the presence of the signs requisite to undertake the negative way. The genuine contemplative heeds the advice of a cleansed conscience, common sense, a spiritual director, reason, and the Scriptures.

On the other hand, "pseudocontemplatives" often embrace the way of straining, morbid introspection, facile iconoclasm, or degenerate passivity. By forcing the forgetting of all created things, they end up with an unhealthy otherworldly fixation leading to physical, emotional, and spiritual deterioration. Frenzy, eccentric mannerisms, pride, intellectual conceit, and sensuality are their hallmarks.

When naked love takes hold at the spiritual root of one who is genuinely called to apophatic contemplation, it tortuously causes all the sins of his or her life to arise. Eventually one suffers, not from the painful remembrance of past sins, but from the acute realization that one is a sinner, a "lump of sin." As the tiny flame of love heals the scars of past sins and removes the lump of sin, the contemplative suffers from not being able to forget his or her self and experiences the self as a "cross" between oneself and God. In time, one agonizes over not being able to love as much as one is loved. This entire process cleanses the person of all sinfulness and increases his or her capacity to love.

As this love purges, it also illuminates contemplatives through ecstatic revelations of God's superabundant goodness and beauty. Paradoxically, the splendor of spiritual light blinds, yet it opens the inner eye to an experience of God "as he really is." Moreover, contemplatives experience that "God is their being, but they are not God's being." Naked love effects such a radical union between God and contemplatives that they are as close to God "by grace" as God is to himself "by nature."

Thus, the anonymous author of *The Cloud* presents in a compact and unsystematic way the purgation, illumination, and divinization caused by the "tiny dart of love" in the depths of one's spirit. He also states that naked love may show itself as ecstatic or as the gentle, peaceful, silent love permeating all the contemplative's daily activities. For him, apophatic love heals, integrates, and transforms the human personality as it graciously but firmly directs the person toward God and neighbor. This love may first gently prod the contemplative's heart to do this or that. If resisted, naked love becomes like a needle in the heart that points to, and insists upon, a certain course of action. For this author, contemplative love is in itself apostolic: it is the best thing we can do for ourselves, for our neighbor, and for those in purgatory.

Meister Eckhart proffers one of the clearest expositions of the *intellectual* negative way. His ontological apophaticism (*Wesensmystik*) focuses upon the intimate relationship between God as Being and the person as a being by emphasizing the divine-human unity in the "spark of the soul" and its implications for human living. One of his favorite themes is the creature's mode of existence in the divine "Womb" prior to its actual creation. In its "primal existence," the creature was a "pure being" and so deeply united with God that God was not "god," and the creature could not be conceived of apart from its divine existence.

For Eckhart, the divine-human union existing from all eternity in the divine mind perdures in the "spark of the soul," the Eckhardian icon for the divine-human relationship at its deepest level. In the soul's core, the divine-human intercourse is so intense because, for Eckhart, "the eye in which I see God is the same eye in which God sees me. My eye and God's eye are one eye and one seeing, one knowing and one loving" (Sermon 12). Furthermore, the soul's spark is both "virgin," because empty of all created things, and "wife," because therein does the Father give birth to the Son and the Holy Spirit springs forth.

In order to experience the ineffable divine-human union, the birth of the Son, and the spiration of the Holy Spirit in the spark of the soul, one must be emptied of everything—even "god." One must get rid of "god" for God, and be "too poor to have a god." Thus the person must annihilate self in all created things and become "as untrammeled by humanness as he was when he came from God," for God *must* pour himself into a perfectly empty soul.

Eckhart's radical apophaticism is another reason for his emphasis upon perfect spiritual poverty. "Because God's unconditioned being is above god and all distinctions," only the totally naked soul perceives the uncreated light that sees God directly. Only in perfect self-annihilation does one grasp that God and the soul are one. The fully detached, naked soul bursts forth to meet the naked Godhead in the divine desert, "untrammeled by humanness." When the person is "as he was when he came from God," Father, Son, Holy Spirit, and the divine Essence disappear into the "desert Godhead" from which they came. Then the person experiences that he or she is perfectly one with God.

Eckhart's radical negative way seemingly identifies the soul's spark with God, obliterating the unity-in-difference between God and creatures. His emphasis upon God's radical oneness "beyond all distinctions," and in which Father, Son, Holy Spirit, and divine Essence disappear, seemingly creates the perfect apophatic "god," that is, a totally unknown Godhead that has nothing

to do with the known triune God of revelation. Some commentators correctly view Eckhart's god as a "quarternity," that is, a foursome god comprised of a Trinity and a distinct, totally unknowable Godhead.

It must be emphasized that the negative way is inextricably linked to the affirmative way because the ineffable God has spoken his word and Word (see 1 Jn 1:1f.). The all-transcendent God has stooped down to help his people (Pss 113:5-9; 40:1; 106; 107:41). The transcendent God is also radically immanent (see Ps 139:7-12). Moreover, the invisible God was seen "face to face" by Moses and Jacob, if only in some qualified sense (see Gen 32:30; Exod 33:11; Num 12:7; Heb 11:27). The incomprehensible God has revealed *himself* in salvation history, a history that finds its irreversible high point in Christ's resurrection. Thus Christ's *history* is confirmed, not swallowed up, by his resurrection. Moreover, the human person is *always* spirit-in-*world,* one who will one day be raised bodily as part of the new creation. Thus, for theological, Christological, and anthropological reasons, no mystical path can be purely negative.

It should also be emphasized that the negative way must always be understood in conjunction with the ways of affirmation and eminence. God does possess every true perfection found in creatures (way of affirmation). However, the attribution of a perfection to God demands that it be attributed to him eminently (way of eminence). Of course, every creaturely imperfection must be negated (way of negation). For example, one must state that God is "person"—not person the way we are person, but person in a supereminent way.

For the great exponents of the negative way, the emptiness of apophatic spirituality does prepare the person for the experience of God's loving self-communication in an ecstasy of pure love through which one goes beyond all things and out of oneself in a way beyond analogies, beyond supereminent negations, beyond knowing, and beyond unknowing. Because the outstanding apophatic mystics *worshiped* the ineffable, incomprehensible God, they experienced that the negative way is more than trans-sensual and trans-intellectual negation. As Gregory Palamas says, "There is a participation in divine things, a gift and a possession rather than just a process of negation" (*The Triads,* I.iii.4). The visionless vision of God may transcend the entire body-person; nonetheless, it is one in which the entire body-person participates.

It is this participation in the divine life that renders a person connatural with God. As the mystical tradition avers, this connaturality is the deepest form of knowledge possible. It is a trans-conceptual loving knowledge engendered by God at the fine point of the human spirit, prior to its division into intellect and will. It knows God by loving God and loves God by knowing him. In the words of Richard of St. Victor, "Where there is love, there is seeing."

See also ABANDONMENT; AFFIRMATIVE WAY; CARMELITE SPIRITUALITY; DARKNESS, DARK NIGHT; ENGLISH MYSTICAL TRADITION; MYSTERY; PATRISTIC SPIRITUALITY; PURGATION, PURGATIVE WAY; RHENO-FLEMISH SPIRITUALITY; UNION, UNITIVE WAY.

Bibliography: H. Egan, "Christian Apophatic and Kataphatic Mysticisms," TS 39/3 (September 1978) 399–426; *Christian Mysticism: The Future of a Tradition* (New York: Pueblo, 1984); *An Anthology of Christian Mysticism* (Collegeville, Minn.: Liturgical Press/Pueblo, 1991).

HARVEY D. EGAN, S.J.

NEOPLATONISM

See AUGUSTINIAN SPIRITUALITY; PATRISTIC SPIRITUALITY.

NEW AGE SPIRITUALITY

"New age" spiritualities appeared in NT times in apocalyptic and eschatological literature associated with shifts in religious or historical awareness. Montanism in the 2nd century, medieval and 19th-century millenarianism, and the 20th-century New Age movement typically anticipate an era of peace, love, and prosperity following an interval of social chaos. Contemporary versions reflect the influence of Carl Jung, who predicted that an "Age of Aquarius" dominated by true science and world humanism would succeed the present "Age of Pisces," the violent Christian era.

Strongly gnostic, New Age spiritualities emphasize esoteric knowledge (enlightenment) in attaining salvation or integrity. Both ancient and modern forms incorporate archaic, arcane, and occult beliefs and practices of Asian, African, and other mythical, religious, philosophical, and magical provenance, such as karmic retribution, reincarnation, psychic powers, and nature lore, including paganism (witchcraft). Elements of Hinduism, Buddhism, Sufism, Cabalism, spiritualism ("channeling"), and numerology may also be present.

Characteristic concerns include planetary healing, holistic health, self-improvement, and the rights of women, minorities, and animals. Nonconventional health care favors acupuncture, biofeedback, herbal medicine, hypnosis, massage, organic gardening, vegetarianism, and other alternative therapies using crystals, colors, aromas, etc. Psychological typologies such as astrology and the Enneagram tend to be favored over uniqueness and individuation.

See also APOCALYPTICISM; COSMIC MYSTICISM; GNOSIS, GNOSTICISM; HEALING; HOLISTIC SPIRITUALITY; OCCULT, OCCULTISM; PERSONALITY TYPES.

Bibliography: J. Needleman, *The New Religions* (New York: Pocket Books, 1972). J. Needleman and G. Baker, eds., *Understanding the New Religions* (New York: Crossroad, 1978). D. Toolan, *Facing West from California's Shores* (New York: Crossroad, 1987).

RICHARD WOODS, O.P.

NONVIOLENCE

See CONFRONTATION AND PROTEST; PEACE.

NUCLEAR AGE, IMPACT ON SPIRITUALITY

The nuclear age in which we live has ushered in wondrous scientific and technological advances. It has had particular impact on the energy and defense industries, which affect us all. But the unleashing of atomic energy over forty-five years ago has also issued in an age of untold peril the world has never known before. After Three Mile Island and Chernobyl, we now know the real dangers of nuclear power plants. But with the vast proliferation of nuclear weapons, the threat of nuclear war is the most urgent problem facing civilization today. We are living in an unprecedented time when there exists serious talk of possible human extinction. Thus the nuclear crisis is the chief issue that our generation must face, for if the nuclear disaster ever comes to pass, all other problems immediately become irrelevant.

The kind of finality that the nuclear peril makes possible has no precedent in human history, for it would entail not just the termination of a whole people or nation but the cessation of life itself in the perpetual darkness of a nuclear winter. As such, the nuclear abyss presents itself as an acute spiritual problem in the life of every person, for it is a universal predicament that challenges our faith in divine providence. It transcends all racial, national, and religious boundaries, all regional conflicts and wars. Indeed, nuclear weapons have imposed on all humans a universally shared fate—either survival or extinction; like nothing else, it throws us back on our collective unity as a human species.

The perils of the nuclear age were unanticipated by biblical authors and theologians of the past. We are living in a time that our religious traditions and their spiritualities have not prepared us for. But this does not mean that all past standards, values, and insights must be overthrown. On the contrary, we must reorient ourselves by garnering all the wisdom and insight that our religious traditions can bring to bear, as we move toward total nuclear disarmament. What, then, are the spiritual repercussions of the nuclear age? What impact does this looming peril have on Christian living? And what response does it demand from us as Christians? In reply, the following themes are the most important to consider.

Psychic Numbing

Our age suffers from an apocalyptic terror—the constant threat of cataclysmic destruction of all order, of a future without hope or meaning. The sobering fact is that we live in a world with over fifty thousand nuclear warheads, all of them ready to arm and explode at the push of a button, and each of them capable of killing millions of people. Full attention to this fact must upset one's psychic balance. The paralyzing fear of imminent destruction (which studies have shown afflicts children especially), of "total death," is too great for any of us to bear, let alone imagine. But the memory of Hiroshima and Nagasaki should remind us that the mythical terror once became empirical reality.

As a result of this predicament, many people suffer from what Robert Jay Lifton, in his study of the survivors of Hiroshima, called "psychic numbing" (Lifton, pp. 52–53; 62; 239–240). The thought of what has happened or could actually happen causes such uneasiness that we deal with it by putting it out of our minds, or by declaring that no one is so stupid as to unleash such destruction on the planet. But such is what the masterminds of nuclear warfare prepare for. In this regard, Jesus's warning that "all who take the sword will perish by the sword" (Mt 26:52) has no greater illustration than the insane logic of mutually assured destruction (MAD) that has governed nuclear defense strategy for the past forty years. We repress the despair that mad thoughts engender by repressing the thoughts themselves. This desensitization is due to unacceptable images and stimuli that may be psychologically necessary for a victim of violence but can later lead to despair, depression, and withdrawal. But short of paralyzing us by fear, the existential anxiety caused by the nuclear threat can be indicative of spiritual health, inducing people to actively work toward a peaceful resolution.

Nuclearism

Recent writing on this problem has focused on the sin of nuclearism: the psychological, political, and military dependence on, and faith in, nuclear arsenals as a solution to the problem of national security (see R. Lifton and R. Falk, *Indefensible Weapons: The Political and Psychological Case Against Nuclearism,* New York: Basic Books, 1982). Nuclearism is rooted in the hubris of believing that the political balance of power lies in the technocratic balance of terror. Accordingly, the Bomb gives humans the chance to play God in their quest for unlimited domination of nature. It harnesses a force that humans have arrogated for themselves, one that bestows the idolatrous power to determine the fate of divine creation itself. Indeed, as Ira Chernus has argued, the Bomb, as ultimate protector and destroyer of life, has become a self-invented deity, a modern golden calf that has immanentized divine transcendence in a worldly technological device of awesome power (*Dr. Strangegod: On the Symbolic Meaning of Nuclear Weapons,* Columbia, S.C.: Univ. of South Carolina Press, 1986).

Apocalypse

Humankind has always suffered from the devastation and misery of human evil. Conquering armies, incessant warfare, pogroms, etc., have all left a mass of death in their wake. In our own century the human capacity for evil has been nonpareil, as demonstrated, for example, by the Nazi holocaust and the Cambodian genocide. Such misery in the past has led to the rise of apocalyptic consciousness, the expectation

of the catastrophic end of history. But this expectation was always rooted in an eschatological vision of the future, when the ultimate cataclysm would be succeeded by ultimate salvation, i.e., an intervention of God to bring about a world of ultimate peace and justice. Such an event was something to look forward to with hope—the final judgment that only the wicked would dread in fear—for it would herald God's ultimate triumph over evil, when the faithful remnant alone would be saved.

However, the end of history that the nuclear threat forces us to contemplate is in marked contrast to this eschatological expectation. A nuclear holocaust would not be an act of God but the result of drastic human folly. No one but the most skewed fundamentalist could believe that the nuclear end of history might be an act of divine will, for it would surely be the most radical affront to God's will imaginable. It would not be the fulfillment of all our hopes but their end. Yet the nuclear threat has been linked with the evangelical impulse of world cleansing by doomsday Christians, who are inspired by the prophecies in the Book of Revelation and other biblical texts. This resurgent apocalyptic consciousness has forged a modern spiritual battleground between the forces of light and the forces of darkness, a holy conflict that is really a disguise for another end-time ideology. Though this apocalyptic vision may appeal to many, it is a perversion of spiritual hope. Believers in Armageddon do not bother with preventing nuclear war but only in preparing themselves spiritually for the inevitable day of judgment.

Responsibility

There is a more authentic Christian response to this crisis. Like other practical problems that plague our world, the nuclear crisis has challenged any notion of spirituality divorced from orthopraxis, the concrete engagement of Christian faith in action. Christian spirituality is a sham unless it actively confronts all forms of evil, not just nuclear mass murder and genocide but other concrete causes of human suffering, such as world hunger, overpopulation, poisoning of the environment, just distribution of resources, etc. As Christians we must focus on how we can all resist evil while living productively in peace and justice together on this earth in accord with the principles of mutuality and love.

From a religious viewpoint, the nuclear age reveals to us a God who is not the omnipotent sovereign over history that earlier theologies professed. If anything, it has awakened us to the full responsibility humans have in determining what Jonathan Schell has called "the fate of the earth." It has taught us the inescapable fragility of life, of our radical contingency. Consequently, we must actively seek the transformation of the institutions and policies that have allowed this particular peril to hang over our heads, like a sword of Damocles, every day for the past four and a half decades.

Conversion: The Way to Peace

Ironically, the nuclear age provides an opportune context for authentic spiritual growth, for it affords us the necessary crisis that alone seems to be the fertile soil of real change, of true *metanoia*. But the breakthrough to a new spiritual level of consciousness that the nuclear age kindles in us must entail a break with the old, fragmented, self-destructive humanity that gave birth to such a crisis. This conversion must not remain individual and private; it must take place on the level of community, in society itself. It must not be confined to personal testimony, but rather must lead to public action in the political, social, and cultural world in which we live. For the human race to renounce the unthinkable terror of nuclear annihilation will require the emergence of a new world in which humans learn to put behind them the instruments of destruction produced by the machinery of fear and dread.

The current crisis may force us to realize that the roots of the nuclear madness are inside each of us, insofar as we all have a capacity for violence and evil. If we could honestly face this fact, then we might understand the distortions of our lives that allow such a menace to continue without abatement. Perhaps what the nuclear age teaches us above all is that the real enemy is within, for it has shown us how distorted our notions of strength and security really are. "Better dead than red" and other ideological affirmations mask the insanity of preparing for such a conflagration. Fear of the enemy has a way of concealing the more dreaded fear of self that we narcotize ourselves from feeling. Unless this trend is curbed, our projection of fear, guilt, and dread could ultimately lead to global suicide.

The solution to the real problems of the nuclear age is not merely human and technological but divine and spiritual. As sin provides the opportunity for grace, so peace may grow out of strife and deathly confrontation. A spirituality that avoids the darkness of the world will be blind to the liberating grace that conquers sin. The Christian hope in eternal life must pass through the suffering of the cross, for only the way of the cross allows the necessary transformation we long for. Such is the wisdom of God that is foolishness to most of us.

What is called for, then, is not greater technological action to ensure the constant strong-arming of the world's superpowers, but the conversion of humanity inspired by Christ's self-sacrificing love. Militarism and nuclearism can be confronted only by a moral-political conversion rooted in love of neighbor. Such a conversion would shift our thinking and living away from domination to mutual participation in solving the world's problems. It must be rooted in the belief that through complete disarmament of all weapons of mass destruction, it is possible for us to enjoy real and enduring peace, not just a lessening of tension (which the recent break in the cold war has thankfully created).

Hope

The spiritual response to the nuclear threat lies in hope. Hope does not guarantee a particular outcome for the future. Given the unboundedness of human freedom, a nuclear holocaust is a possibility, but as Christians we live in hope of the full flowering of human nature perfected by grace. As such, the spiritually mature person is not overwhelmed by the potential horror of nuclear devastation. Without this hope in perfection, the thought of nuclear destruction is unbearable. Such a spiritual hope combats the view that, given original sin, war is inevitable, a view that is itself indicative of the sin of fatalism, of accepting humanity as inherently corrupt and unable to be converted by grace. It confines one to a state of paralysis that is closed to the life of the spirit.

Our response as Christians, then, must be to aim for a world without war, for the grave truth is that unless we end war in the future, it will surely end us. Unless the spirit of love and truth is allowed to reign in this world, the nuclear crisis will plunge us ever closer to the ungodly end-time of history. Our cultural "denial of death" reflects our fallen state, our emotional paralysis, which is inadmissible in a world on the verge of self-destruction. Until our hope overrules our fear through the dying in love that alone can save us, there will be nothing to avert the nefarious eve of destruction.

See also CONFRONTATION AND PROTEST; CONVERSION; ECOLOGICAL CONSCIOUSNESS; ENVIRONMENT; HOLOCAUST; HOPE; PEACE; WAR, IMPACT ON SPIRITUALITY.

Bibliography: G. Kaufman, *Theology for a Nuclear Age* (Philadelphia: Westminster, 1985). J. Schell, *The Fate of the Earth* (New York: Avon Books, 1982). R. Lifton, *The Future of Immortality and Other Essays for a Nuclear Age* (New York: Basic Books, 1987).

MICHAEL P. MORRISSEY

O

OBEDIENCE

The common-sense understanding of obedience simply as compliance with the bidding of another (generally of superior status) is inadequate for understanding the role of this much-maligned virtue in the spiritual life. From the Latin *ob* + *audire,* meaning "to hear," obedience in the spiritual life is a matter of receiving and responding appropriately to a message—or Word—from God. This essential connection between hearing and obedient response reflects the remarkable fact that ancient Hebrew contains no specific word meaning "to obey." *Shema,* whether translated as "to hear" or "to obey," implies that to *hear* God is, necessarily, to respond in love and gratitude to the divine initiative. Hearing is thus never neutral or passive. For Israel, to hear is to obey, and not to obey is to rebel.

Since in Scripture the Word of God always requires a decisive response, the requirement of obedience serves as a kind of spiritual test for both the individual and the nation, and is thus closely associated with faith. The only stricture laid upon the progenitors of the human race is a test of obedience: "You are free to eat from any of the trees of the garden except the tree of knowledge of good and bad. From that tree you shall not eat; the moment you eat from it you are surely doomed to die" (Gen 2:16-17). Through their disobedience to this command, sin comes into the world, and the essential unity between the Creator and the creation is ruptured.

The great Old Testament archetype of obedience (and, therefore, of faith) is Abraham, whose trust in God brings him to the point where he is ready to give back to the Lord that which is most precious to him—his future. God asks for Isaac, the long-awaited, rightful heir; and in a way that is impossible for the old man to understand at the time, his obedience paradoxically returns to him what he is prepared, at great personal cost, to give back to God. Because of the patriarch's obedience, the sacrificial cultus is both transformed and relativized. His obedience and, by implication, ours, is "better" than sacrifice (1 Sam 15:22). With the patriarch's obedience, the promise of salvation is set in motion.

In the New Testament it is Mary's youthful obedience, offered despite the painful and even life-threatening social humiliation it entails, that makes possible God's entrance into human history through the incarnation. She, too, has no way of foreseeing the ultimate significance of her act—that it will finally guarantee the future that Abraham believed he was sacrificing—yet she recognizes, in this great invitation of Grace, that her obedience is somehow inextricably connected to the fruition of that same promise of salvation (Luke 1:46-55).

Finally, it is in Christ's obedient surrender to the Father, an obedience "unto death, even death on a cross," (Phil 2:8,

RSV) that the Christian practice of obedience is rooted and derives its true meaning. The humility of God in the work of the atonement reminds Christians that their own obedience, in matters great or small, is always a derivative or "borrowed" obedience. In the same way, all claims to authority, whether religious or civil, derive their credibility from divine authorization and must be tested in terms of this standard of the prior obedience and self-emptying of God.

Along with the evangelical counsels of poverty and chastity, faithful adherence to a vow of obedience became the primary test of Christian commitment in monastic life. Since sin is understood to reside in the will, those who would be proficient Christians disciplined their wills by submitting themselves to the guidance of a superior in the religious life. Widely criticized today as an immature or irresponsible renunciation of personal agency, the practice of obedience in monasticism is properly understood only in the context of the doctrine of Christian perfection, which aspires to a perfect imitation or following of the crucified Christ.

In monasticism, obedience to a spiritual father or mother is an *ascesis* or form of spiritual discipline, just as prayer and fasting are. Painful as it can be, the crucifixion of the will (along with other forms of self denial) is not, therefore, a *negation* of personhood; rather, it leads to the fulfillment of the person through a mystical participation in the sacrificial, self-emptying obedience of Christ and through submission to Christ himself in the office of the religious superior. It therefore behooves the novice, claims John Climacus, to choose a guide wisely so that "there is no mistaking the sailor for the helmsman, [or] the patient for the doctor. . . . [for] having once entered the stadium of holy living and obedience, we can no longer start criticizing the umpire" (*The Ladder of Divine Ascent,* Step 4: Obedience, p. 92). This 7th-century monk echoes the biblical conviction that obedience is grounded in faith when he admonishes religious to "trust [their spiritual guides] completely, even when they order us to do something that looks like being contrary to our salvation. That is the time when our faith in them is tested as in a furnace of humiliation, and the sign of the most genuine faith is when we obey our superiors without hesitation, even when we see the opposite happening to what we had hoped" (ibid., p. 114).

Scholastic theology provided a rational argument to support obedience, arguing that it was necessary for the orderly functioning of society at large and in smaller communities. Aquinas designates obedience as a moral (rather than a theological) virtue, residing in the will. Because it is subordinate to the virtue of justice, obedience is most perfectly and authentically practiced when it proceeds out of justice through love. It is justice, in fact, that requires giving absolute obedience to God; and human happiness is ultimately impossible without such obedience. Human authority also justly claims our obedience when it is exercised within its proper purview; it can never claim our obedience when it conflicts with the law of God (ST II-II, q. 104).

The most highly developed treatments of obedience come out of the tradition of Ignatian spirituality. A former soldier, Ignatius Loyola was inspired by a military model in fashioning the Society of Jesus. For Ignatius, obedience was not primarily a matter of *ascesis* or even the means to peace and good order in the community; it was *the* essential requirement for effective cooperation with the saving work of Christ. Continuing in the tradition that roots the requirement of obedience in Christology, Ignatius specified this adherence to Christ through a vow of direct obedience to the pope, Christ's vicar on earth, and posited three degrees of obedience: (1) when we do what we are commanded (despite our distaste); (2) when we do what we are commanded willingly; and (3) when we conform our own judgment to that of our superior so that we share in his judgment.

The purity of the St. Ignatius's quite mystical vision of ecclesiastical authority is stunningly stark. Insofar as obedience is a manifestation of faith and unifies us with the divine will, it is an absolute good *in itself*. The Ignatian theory of obedience permits a conceptual separation between the command *qua command*—in which Christ resides—and the actual purpose of the command, which may be flawed or misguided. It allows for the possibility that what appears as failure in our eyes may in fact serve God's purposes admirably. In this sense, obedience may, perhaps *must,* be "blind," since we have no absolute vantage point from which to assess God's purposes in an otherwise inscrutable decision. The most famous formulation of this position is in Ignatius's "Rules for Thinking with the Church," where he admonishes his followers that if they wish to proceed "securely in all things," they must put aside all personal judgment and "hold fast to the following principle: What seems to me white, I will believe black if the hierarchical Church so defines. For I must be convinced that in Christ our Lord, the bridegroom, and in his spouse the Church, only one Spirit holds sway, which governs and rules for the salvation of souls. For it is by the same Spirit and Lord who gave the Ten Commandments that our holy Mother Church is ruled and governed" (*Spiritual Exercises,* no. 365).

This kind of humble submissiveness to authority is singularly unattractive to the modern mind, formed as it is in a cultural context where various forms of humanistic and antimonarchical philosophies and values prevail. Apart from military contexts, where the requirements of efficiency and pragmatism dictate a hierarchical chain of command, there is little patience with and much incredulity surrounding such an approach. Yet it needs to be recognized that the Christian values of humility and obedi-ence were equally distasteful to the "secular" and "modern" minds of the citizens of 1st-century Greece and Rome, where the human spirit was elevated as an absolute good capable of triumphing over a fatally flawed world. For the secular mind in any age, the great issues of life are primarily external problems that can only be solved through the application of human resources: heroic effort, ingenuity, and, in some cases, self-sacrifice.

By contrast, the Christian has traditionally seen the great issues of life as primarily interior or spiritual crises for which there is no help apart from the divine resource: grace. And the source of this grace is God's very own obedience, enacted on the cross. Not surprisingly, in the eyes of the world such a basis for authority is dangerous folly. Significantly, many modern theologians, heavily influenced by historical method and social criticism, are equally suspicious and severely critical of Christian obedience as traditionally practiced. What remains hidden from the world and revealed only to faith is the free choice of the individual, first, instinctively to distrust his or her own disordered will and, second, to submit, out of love for Christ, to what is understood to be divinely constituted authority.

At the end of the 20th century, religious orders continue to face a daunting series of problems, including a deep resistance to the tradition's radical vision of obedience. Yet despite the widespread confusion and controversy, there is no evidence in the documents of Vatican II to suggest that obedience should not continue to remain a compelling form of Christian witness and the essential foundation of religious life. What the documents do stress, however, is the heavy responsibility of the religious superior to be "docile to God's will in the exercise of his office." Those who direct must be eminently directable, humble, pliant, and themselves tested in the fiery kiln of obedience: "Let [the superior] use his authority in a spirit of service for the brethren, and manifest thereby the charity with which God loves them. Governing his subjects as God's own sons, and with regard for their human personality, a superior will make it easier for them to obey gladly. Therefore he must make a special point of leaving them appropriately free with respect to the sacrament of penance and direction of conscience" (PC 14).

The clear intention of the Second Vatican Council to take the ecclesial and spiritual status of the laity with much greater seriousness has profound implications for a renewed understanding of Christian obedience. The sacrament of baptism is seen, now more than ever, as conferring not only power and privilege but inescapable obligation. Just as there is *one* holy, catholic, and apostolic Church, so there is *one* holiness to which all Christians, clergy and lay alike, are called. With respect to clergy, the council states: "Since the priestly ministry is the ministry of the Church herself, it can be discharged only by hierarchical communion with the whole body. Therefore pastoral love demands that, acting in this communion, priests dedicate their own wills through obedience to the service of God and their brothers. This love requires that they accept and carry out in a spirit of faith whatever is commanded or recommended by the Sovereign Pontiff, their own bishops, or other superiors (PO 15). So also are the laity called to obedience: "Let laymen follow the example of Christ, who by his obedience even at the cost of death, opened to all . . . the blessed way to the liberty of the children of God" (LG 37).

Thus the council has clarified and reemphasized the biblical teaching that *every* follower of Christ is called not only to obey pastoral authority but, ultimately, to surrender himself or herself totally to God. What is essential is that all of us understand that this obedience, which is required, is not achieved through the sheer force of human effort. It is not a "work" we can perform out of our natural endowments. Both the will and the ability to obey,

even in the humblest and most mundane circumstances, is a gift from God—a grace made possible because God's sacrificial obedience has preceded and anticipated our own.

See also ASCETICISM; AUTHORITY; CHASTITY; POVERTY; RELIGIOUS LIFE; RESPONSIBILITY; VIRTUE; VOWS.

Bibliography: C. Duquoc and F. Casiano, eds., *Christian Obedience*, Concilium 139 (New York: Seabury, 1980). M. Espinosa Polit, *Perfect Obedience: Commentary on the Letter on Obedience of St. Ignatius Loyola* (Westminster, Md.: Newman, 1947). Ignatius Loyola, *The Spiritual Exercises*, trans. L. Puhl (Chicago: Loyola Univ. Press, 1951). John Climacus, *The Ladder of Divine Ascent*, trans. C. Luibheid and N. Russell (New York: Paulist, 1982). B. Leeming, *The Mysticism of Obedience* (Boston: Daughters of St. Paul, 1964). K. Rahner et al., *Obedience and the Church* (Washington: Corpus Books, 1968). J. Walsh, ed., *The Theology of Obedience*, Supplement to *The Way*, no. 5 (February 1968).

ROBIN MAAS

OBLATION
See SACRIFICE.

OCCASION(S) OF SIN
See SIN; TEMPTATION.

OCCULT, OCCULTISM

The word *occult* derives from the Latin *occulere*, meaning "to hide from view." It was first used by the French author Eliphas Levi and brought into English usage in 1881 in the writings of A. D. Sinnett. In contemporary literature, occult or occultism refers to a variety of practices that include astrology, alchemy, Tarot, I-Ching, occult medicine, and secret magical operations. What these occult practices have in common is the claim for the attainment of spiritual power and insight by the knowledge of the hidden operations of reality and the unfolding dynamics of cosmic energies.

A distinction is drawn in sociological and cultural studies between the occult and the esoteric. While *occult* is used to designate certain secret practices, as mentioned above, *esoteric* refers to religio-philosophic belief systems that underlie and inform these occult techniques. Esoteric theories tend to offer a comprehensive and cognitive mapping of the operations of nature and the cosmos. These theories propose maps of ultimate reality and portray the functioning of cosmic energies by way of a hierarchy of spiritual powers and the interpenetration of all visible and invisible entities.

The language of esoteric theory is usually concealed in symbolic images and metaphorical constructions to prevent public and profane dissemination. Thus esoteric lore, not unlike occult practices themselves, is passed on usually by way of an oral tradition to those who have proven worthy of receiving it. Unlike exoteric knowledge, that is, knowledge given to all in a public fashion, the esoteric tradition and the occult practices that ensue from it are usually associated with secret societies.

Modern culture has seen what can be called an occult revival. Interest in fantasy literature and films that describe the irruption of secret worlds into daily life has increased. In what is considered by many to be a "New Age," interest in ancient divinatory practices, which draw on ancient esoteric cosmologies and spiritual powers, has also emerged.

Channeling is among the more popular occult practices of this New Age consciousness. Channeling is a curious phenomenon that claims direct contact with a "spirit world" of enlightened beings. This contact is mediated by persons who are in tune with the subtle vibrations of such entities. These persons are known as "channels." Channels are said to communicate wisdom and practical information from enlightened entities who use the body and vocal cords of the channel to speak. In recent years the popularization of this practice has been critiqued by many who consider this phenomenon contrived. Critics claim that channels invite an unhealthy dependency from their clients and offer an irrational reality perspective to those who avail themselves of the information acquired by channeling.

With the development of depth psychology, many occult practices have found an alternative theoretical base to what in the past has been considered an esoteric system of thought. Among the major writers who have reinterpreted occult practices from the psychological perspective of human consciousness is Carl Jung. His considerations of alchemy, astrology, the cabala, and the occult have opened the possibility of understanding occult practices from a psychological and symbolic matrix. Such a starting point argues that the esoteric theories of a previous age can be replaced by a theory of human consciousness and its transformation. The heuristic use of occult symbols and practices, therefore, would be available to the contemporary quest for human self-understanding. Such is the case discovered in the reinterpretation of astrological symbolism and usage in the writings of Dane Rudhyar, Liz Greene, and others. This is also occurring in the spiritual writings of those who have reinterpreted the symbols and use of the Tarot.

A less-known occult practice being employed for self-understanding from a psychological base is the Enneagram, which is an occult Sufi mystical technique for transformed consciousness. The cabala, an ancient occult Jewish technique of mystical understanding, has also earned a place in contemporary spiritual usage because of the claimed psychological value of its symbolism. The use of occult practices is also found within the women's movement. Various forms of witchcraft called "wicca" are practiced to encourage an alternative consciousness to the earth and to the patriarchal perceptions of reality.

Occult practices and the theories that inform them, whether esoteric or psychological, can be employed to bind human judgment in fear, suspicion, and political ideologies of oppression. (Note Hitler's use of occultism in the spread of his ideology.) While this does not always seem to be the case, as with the reinterpreted use of occult symbolism from psychological theories, a critical method from which to evaluate these practices and their contribution to culture and consciousness is needed.

See also EXTRAORDINARY PHENOMENA; MYSTERY; NEW AGE SPIRITUALITY; PERSONALITY TYPES; PSYCHOLOGY, RELATIONSHIP AND CONTRIBUTION TO SPIRITUALITY.

Bibliography: E. Tiryakian, "Toward the Sociology of Esoteric Culture," *American Journal of Sociology,* vol. 78, no. 3, pp. 491–512. C. Wilson, *The Occult* (New York: Vintage Books, 1971). R. Woods, *The Occult Revolution: A Christian Meditation* (New York: Herder, 1971).

RICHARD N. FRAGOMENI

OFFICE, DIVINE

See LITURGY.

OPTION FOR THE POOR

See LIBERATION THEOLOGY, INFLUENCE ON SPIRITUALITY; POOR, THE.

OPUS DEI

Opus Dei, known fully as the Priestly Society of the Holy Cross and the Work of God, is a personal prelature approved by Pope John Paul II in 1982. The term *Opus Dei* originally referred to the liturgical prayer of monks. The prelature of that name, however, is not a monastic organization.

Conceived by Msgr. José María Escrivá de Balaguer in 1928 as an organization of laypersons inspired to live a clear religious witness to the gospel, it became a canonically recognized pious union in 1941, with a distinct women's section and a highly stratified system of ranks, headed by celibate numeraries, followed by oblates (also celibate), supernumeraries, and cooperators.

In 1943 clerics were officially incorporated, and in 1947 married people were admitted as supernumerary members. In 1950 Opus Dei became the first secular institute, with constitutions updated in 1982 under the title *Codex Iuris Particularis.*

The *Codex* specifies the aim of Opus Dei as the sanctification of its members through the practice of Christian virtue in each member's state of life and profession. The spirituality of Opus Dei is therefore intended to be lived "in medio mundo" [sic] —(*Codex,* p. 4), with the apostolic end of configuring the world into the image of the gospel as interpreted by Opus Dei members. The hidden life of Jesus is recommended as a model for the spirit in which one serves as an apostolic instrument, each in a way appropriate to his or her own talents. Members are urged to lead a life of prayer, sacrifice, humility, and asceticism, and to adhere closely to the teaching of the ecclesiastical magisterium. Great emphasis is placed upon assiduous study in order to acquire the intellectual and professional formation necessary for the spiritual infusion of culture according to the particular Catholic perspective of Opus Dei.

In light of reforms since the Second Vatican Council, reported Opus Dei practices such as severe bodily disciplines and excessive secrecy might seem anachronistic, though these were once common practices among some religious orders. Opus Dei has been criticized for fostering certain practices at variance with those of the larger Church, especially in regard to the relationship between manifestation of conscience and the sacrament of reconciliation; for promoting authoritarian control over its members; and for attempting to insinuate an ideologically conservative program into the life of the Church through secretive means.

José María Escrivá de Balaguer was declared blessed by Pope John Paul II in 1992.

See also AUTHORITY; CONTEMPORARY SPIRITUALITY; HOLINESS; LAY SPIRITUALITY; MORTIFICATION; SECULAR INSTITUTES.

Bibliography: *Codex Iuris Particularis seu Statuta Praelaturae Sanctae Crucis et Operis Dei* (Rome: Collegii Romani Sanctae Crucis, 1982). G. Rocca, *L' "Opus Dei"—Appunti e Documenti per una Storia* (Rome: Edizione Paoline, 1985).

PAUL G. CROWLEY, S.J.

ORTHODOX SPIRITUALITY

See EASTERN CHRISTIAN SPIRITUALITY.

P

PACIFISM

See PEACE.

PARAPSYCHOLOGY

Although extraordinary phenomena have been observed and commented upon from the time of Aristotle, the effort to observe, describe, and explain in a scientific manner human knowledge and behavior that transcend ordinary sensory-motor abilities can be dated from the mid-19th century. As developed in the 20th century by Joseph Banks Rhine, R. A. McDonnell, Celia Green, and other psychologists, *parapsychology* attempts to measure and describe in an experimental, even laboratory setting "quasi-sensory" or "extra-sensory" perception (ESP) such as telepathy, clairvoyance, precognition, out-of-the-body experiences (heautoscopy), etc.; and behavioral anomalies such as psychokinesis (altering physical objects by mental effort—PK), levitation, nonmedical healing, etc.

Psychical research is a wider term embracing investigation into phenomena not easily subject to laboratory conditions, such as apparitions, near-death experiences, reincarnation, and "poltergeist" activity (now generally referred to as "recurrent spontaneous psychokinesis"—RSPK).

Paraphysics refers to the study of unusual (paranormal) natural phenomena that are not necessarily human in origin but may affect human beings or other living organisms.

All three branches of inquiry bear significantly on the study of, and approach toward, religious experience, charismatic spirituality, occult phenomena, extraordinary mystical states, canonization procedures, etc., regarding natural versus supernatural origin, spiritual direction, possible demonic influence, possession states, exorcism, etc.

See also CHARISM; EXORCISM; EXTRAORDINARY PHENOMENA; GLOSSOLALIA; HEALING; MYSTICISM; OCCULT, OCCULTISM; PSYCHOLOGY, RELATIONSHIP AND CONTRIBUTION TO SPIRITUALITY.

Bibliography: R. Haynes, *The Hidden Springs* (London: Hutchinson, 1973). H. R. Neff, *Psychic Phenomena and Religion* (Philadelphia: Westminster, 1971). H. Thurston, *The Physical Phenomena of Mysticism* (New York: Sheed and Ward, 1952).

RICHARD WOODS, O.P.

PARISH, PARISH RENEWAL

The Second Vatican Council encouraged and supported broad forces of renewal that had been at work within the Church for generations. By adopting its own deliberate strategy of renewal, the council set in motion new energies and focused already existing forces in particular directions. Although its concern with ecclesial reform was aimed beyond the local parish, the work of the council has been felt at virtually every level of the Church's life, including that of the parish.

The years since the council have witnessed a proliferation of reform movements aiming at revitalizing individual believers as well as the Church at large. Some of these, such as the officially sanctioned liturgical reforms, have touched immediately all segments of the Church. Other movements of popular origin, such as the charismatic renewal or the cursillo movement, enjoy no official status but seek to promote renewal at every level by calling all members of the Church to deeper holiness. Still others target specific groups for spiritual renewal and support, such as Marriage Encounter, Separated and Divorced Catholics, and so forth. Surprisingly, there have been relatively few efforts that are specifically parish-based or whose aim is explicitly parish renewal. One thinks of Renew, Christ Renews His Parish, and various efforts to promote small faith communities within parishes.

This paucity of initiatives focused on parish renewal is particularly striking in view of the fact that the parish is one of the basic units of ecclesial life in the Catholic tradition. The "Notre Dame Study of Catholic Parish Life" has provided ample documentation that it is within the context of parish that the vast majority of Catholics have their primary experience of Church. Despite the absence of much specific effort aimed at parish, either on the official or unofficial level, the parish remains the ecclesial structure that most immediately affects the spiritual vitality of millions of Catholics. To a large extent, the vast renewal of the Church envisioned at Vatican II will succeed or fail depending on the extent to which parish renewal becomes a reality.

The components of parish renewal, like the renewal of the larger Church of which it is a microcosm, are varied. Ultimately, it is the quality of Christian life present in each believer that matters most of all. To the extent that each and every parish member is open to, and responsive to, the movement of God's Spirit, to that extent will the entire parish community undergo true spiritual renewal. But experience has shown that we are called and saved as a people, and the influence of those around us can be dramatic in determining the quality of our own personal response to the gospel. Hence, in addition to strategies fostering individual renewal, parishes require other efforts aimed at communal renewal.

Revitalized leadership structures are crucial to any effort to call a community to a deeper Christian life. Recent decades have witnessed an enormous amount of attention given to improving the quality of priestly life and ministry. The phenomena of priestless parishes, collaborative ministry teams made up of highly skilled lay and religious professionals, and the increasing involvement of the laity in all areas of ministry will require a corresponding commitment to forms of leadership development no longer restricted to ordained clergy. The emergence of other leadership structures in the parish—some mandated by the revised Code of Canon Law and others evolving according to local needs—is also important for the vitality of parish life and a broad sense of ownership for the common good. Examples of these structures are the parish finance council, the pastoral council, the council of ministries, and many other committees, task forces, and other groups by which leadership is shared broadly and parish life channeled in particular directions. Ongoing efforts are necessary to nurture and strengthen these fledgling structures and to ensure that those who serve in them are deeply imbued with the vision of the Second Vatican Council as well as the requisite personal qualities of holiness and skills for leadership.

In addition to organizational strategies to restructure parishes in ways that foster renewal, other pastoral initiatives are also necessary. The scope of parish activity necessarily embraces five major areas of concern. A variety of terms are used to describe each of these dimensions of a parish's life, but the content of each is fairly consistent:

1) *Prayer and worship.* Vital to parish renewal is an experience of prayer, both personal and communal, that reflects the direction of liturgical renewal set forth at Vatican II and in subsequent legislation. The agenda in this area has been spelled out in great detail in a wealth of official documents and pastoral exhortations. It is not so much a question of what must be done as it is enabling the skills and habits that make possible the revitalized prayer "in Spirit and truth" (Jn 4:23) called for in documents too numerous to count. Parish renewal must include a liturgical life that is vigorous and faith-filled, characterized by full and active participation in all the ways that form the full complement of liturgical ministries. In addition, a flourishing devotional life should support and nourish the community's prayer with a Catholic piety fully congruent with the shape of liturgical renewal.

2) *Christian formation.* This embraces a range of activities described variously as catechesis, religious education, spiritual formation, and so forth. Across the age spectrum from earliest childhood through old age, each succeeding stage in the life cycle meets the challenge to live out life's tasks in ways informed by Christian faith. This requires of a parish a broad repertoire of supportive efforts, such as formal religious education, catechumenal processes for adults and children, sacramental preparation experiences, retreat and renewal opportunities, etc. The contexts and strategies need to be as varied as the people and situations addressed. Parish renewal implies in this area an ongoing commitment to form faith, to inform consciences, to transform lives in every possible way at every stage of life's journey. The aim is a conscious, active, informed faith in each member of the community, to the fullest extent of that person's present potential. As in the previous area, there is an abundance of official and pastoral direction in

this area to guide a parish's efforts and improve its skills.

3) *Community.* This notion is as elusive as it is real. The shape and experience of being a parish community vary enormously, but in some form or another a parish needs to experience itself as a cohesive entity. Often this will be expressed in forms of bonding that are strong and intimate; at other times there will be relatively little intensity of interaction among members, but a strongly shared sense of purpose and mission. Parish renewal, if it is to be complete, must involve building and strengthening the particular form of community that seems most appropriate for a given parish. Instilling in members a clear sense of identity and a strong loyalty to the parish are important elements in this process of community building.

4) *Outreach and service.* An authentic spiritual life manifests itself in various expressions of Christian mission, no less for a parish than for an individual believer. Integral to parish renewal is an expanding horizon of concern for others that takes shape in many forms. Evangelization must be directed at inactive Catholics, at those without a religious tradition of their own, as well as at a parish's own members. Concern for justice and peace must be expressed both in advocacy efforts and in direct service, and the scope of the parish's attention must be international and national as well as local. Parish renewal requires a self-identity for the parish as a community of active hospitality, genuine concern for the poor and alienated, and effective action to promote God's reign in the social, political, and economic spheres of life.

5) *Stewardship.* Comprehensive parish renewal also includes a wise stewardship of material resources. This means that administrative and organizational matters must be handled in a way that reflects the best resources available. Accountability for good fiscal management, just personnel policies and benefit packages, healthy and

wholesome working conditions for all parish employees are as important as defending the human rights of workers across the globe. A commitment to environmental concerns and careful planning to manage and develop parish properties and resources are likewise integral to good stewardship and parish renewal.

All five of these areas must be attended to by a parish that seeks to live out a full response to the gospel as a community of faith. Each area will require renewal through its own appropriate goals, mechanisms, and strategies. Mobilizing the resources of a parish toward renewal in so many facets of its life is a daunting challenge. What seems essential, for an individual parish as for the Church at large, is an explicit acknowledgment of the need for renewal, a commitment to renewal from leaders as well as members at large, and a plan of action. Renewal does not happen by accident. It requires our active cooperation with the Spirit's movements in our midst.

Parish renewal is best served when a community makes a specific set of commitments whose intended aim is renewal. Often crystallized in a parish mission statement or plan of action, what is really at stake in those commitments is a community's vision that renewal is its mandate if it is to be faithful to discipleship and mission as Christ intends.

See also COMMUNITY; LITURGY; RENEWAL, PROGRAMS OF RENEWAL; SACRAMENTS; SERVICE; VATICAN COUNCIL II.

Bibliography: D. Byers, ed., *The Parish in Transition* (Washington: USCC, 1986). J. Castelli and J. Gremillion, *The Emerging Parish* (San Francisco: Harper & Row, 1988). National Conference of Catholic Bishops, *The Parish: A People, A Mission, A Structure* (Washington: USCC, 1980).

ROBERT D. DUGGAN

PASCHAL MYSTERY

The term *paschal mystery* is best understood in connection with the entire gamut of salvation history. Humankind and the cosmos have been redeemed, and the mystery (the "secret") of this divine plan of salvation was revealed and brought to fulfillment in Christ, our Pasch. Christ is the revelation of God's mystery, and in and through him it is finally and fully made manifest (Empereur, p. 745).

Pre-Vatican II theology tended to stress the salvific action of Christ by what was accomplished on the cross. The Constitution on the Sacred Liturgy enlarged that vision to include other elements of the paschal mystery as the resurrection and ascension (SC 5), and the liturgy of Pentecost proclaims: "Today you sent the Holy Spirit on those marked out to be your children by sharing the life of your only Son, and so you brought the paschal mystery to its completion" (Pentecost Preface of the Roman Missal).

In the fullest sense this paschal mystery continues in the lives of the baptized, the members of Christ's Body, the Church. It could be said that a hallmark of post-Vatican II piety is that daily life and worship are once again seen as expressions of the paschal mystery. Since the completion of the Pentecost mystery, the economy of salvation has taken on the form of liturgy (Corbon, p. 34). But liturgy is not divorced from daily life; it receives from it the warp and woof of the continuing paschal mystery: "In the celebration of the Eucharist these [daily actions] may most fittingly be offered to the Father along with the body of the Lord. And so, worshipping everywhere by their holy actions, the laity consecrate the world itself to God" (LG 34, Flannery). This intimate connection between liturgy and life is seen as a way that the paschal mystery continues in time and space, and represents a return to the Augustinian *totus Christus* theology of Eucharist. As Christ gave of himself once and for all, now his members are called to follow suit by bringing the paschal mystery to completion in their lives.

This vision of the paschal mystery was brought about in large measure because of a recently discovered awareness of, and appreciation for, the human nature of Jesus. Vatican II affirmed the recovery of Jesus Christ's humanity: "He worked with human hands, he thought with a human mind. He acted with a human will, and with a human heart he loved. Born of the Virgin Mary, he has truly been made one of us, like to us in all things exept sin" (GS 22, Flannery). Previously many Catholics had hesitated to identify their lives with that of Jesus because they saw his life as something totally otherworldly. A Christology "from below" has brought with it an easier identification of Head and members within the Mystical Body of Christ.

A final recent development in the understanding of the paschal mystery concerns the physical universe. The object of salvation is seen to be not only humankind but the entire cosmos as well. The paschal mystery is placed in the perspective of the doctrine of creation, with human persons being the stewards of that creation, privileged ministers to whom God has entrusted the responsibility of caring for the earth. The covenant forged with Noah and his descendants (Gen 9) is assumed into the new covenant wrought by Jesus Christ. All knowledge comes to the human person through the senses. Women and men by their essence belong to the material world, and in redeeming them, Christ has included the cosmos in which they find their being. Human persons are no longer content to view themselves as simply passing through a material world en route to a better and lasting one. Life on this earth must include both the good stewardship of creation and the striving for a just distribution of the goods of this earth. All this is not something merely extrinsic to the plan of salvation. The paschal mystery will find its completion in the consummation of human history, when the mystery of God's will shall be made known and accomplished "as a plan for the fullness of times, to sum up all things in Christ, in heaven and on earth" (Eph 1:10).

See also BAPTISM; CHRIST; CHURCH; CREATION; LITURGY; REDEMPTION; RESURRECTION; SACRAMENTS; SACRIFICE.

Bibliography: J. Empereur, "Paschal Mystery," *The New Dictionary of Theology,* ed. J. Komonchak, M. Collins, D. Lane (Wilmington, Del.: Glazier, 1987) 744–747. J. Corbon, *The Wellspring of Worship* (New York: Paulist, 1988).

GERARD AUSTIN, O.P.

PASSION(S)

Derived from the Greek *pathos* and the Latin *passio,* the English word *passion* has a variety of significations. Etymologically, its most basic meaning is physical suffering or endurance. In early Christianity it commonly referred to the torture and death of a martyr, and it is still used in this sense today to designate the suffering and death of Christ.

In Scholastic philosophy passions were manifestations of the sensitive appetite, which was divided by Aquinas into two parts: the concupiscible appetite (directed toward pleasure or pain), to which belong love and hatred, desire and aversion, joy and sorrow; and the irascible appetite (directed toward achievement or failure), to which belong hope and depression, courage and fear, and anger. Today the word *passion* is more broadly used to indicate any intense or violent emotion, but the above list is still a perceptive analysis of those passions that affect humans most deeply.

Aquinas understood the passions as naturally good in themselves but needing the guidance of reason, without which they tend to become destructive, upsetting the balance of the psyche. On the other hand, enhanced by grace, they can be strong motivating forces for spiritual growth and apostolic zeal; it is difficult to imagine the achievement of such goals of the Christian life without them.

Aquinas thought it immoral to try to eradicate the passions, but this was not the prevailing view in the practice of prayer and asceticism handed down from the Greek patristic authors. Strongly influenced by Platonic and Neoplatonic thought, early spiritual writers like Origen and Evagrius strove for *apatheia,* complete indifference to, and freedom from, the passions, gained by turning away from all creatures so as to become more like God and therefore open to the *gnōsis* of God attained through contemplation. Nonetheless, while it was desirable to free oneself from attraction to material things that were the natural objects of the passions, these same passions, when directed to God or against evil, were considered virtues. For example, even in the highly apophatic Dionysian mystical tradition, the desire for God is essential to the attainment of contemplative union, and it is expected that such union will result in the experience of joy.

The striving after *apatheia,* when translated to the West, chiefly by Cassian, became modified to a control of the passions rather than their elimination, with the goal of attaining purity of heart with which to encounter God. With Benedict came the emphasis upon *lectio divina,* the reading and meditating on Scripture accompanied by a strong affective element, positively engaging the passions in the search for contemplative union with God. Gerard Sitwell has isolated these two tendencies—the Greek apophatic and the Western affective, kataphatic traditions—as twin streams that influenced the development of medieval mysticism, and they continue to exist today as two different ways to contemplation.

Contemporary spirituality has benefited from the richness of modern psychology in its understanding of the passions and their role in human growth. The psychology of human relationship, including the role the passions play in its development, provides a useful analogy for the relationship between the human and God. If one's relationship with God is to grow, one must be willing to share one's emotional depths with God, and in turn be receptive to the feelings which that relationship can effect or reveal. Thus an important part of spiritual direction involves helping a person learn to notice the emotional reactions, or the lack thereof, that accompany prayer and to place them trustingly into relationship with God. This can happen with ease when those emotions are positive ones, such as love, desire, joy, or hope, although some people find any affective expression difficult. But the negative passions, so long deemed inappropriate in the Western tradition, are often suppressed or denied, setting up an impassible roadblock to further spiritual growth. This is especially common with anger, whether directed at God or others, which is frequently hidden behind experiences of boredom, frustration, or depression in prayer and which is often the result of even deeper hurts to the psyche. Until anger is acknowledged and expressed, healing and further spiritual development are stymied.

The ancient practice of the discernment of spirits can be interpreted today as the careful examination of one's deepest passions, with the awareness that they can either be put to the service of God and others or become obsessively self-serving and destructive.

See also ADDICTION; AFFECT, AFFECTIVITY; APATHEIA; ASCETICISM; DESIRE; DISCERNMENT OF SPIRITS; FEELINGS; HOLISTIC SPIRITUALITY; PSYCHOLOGY, RELATIONSHIP AND CONTRIBUTION TO SPIRITUALITY; SPIRITUAL DIRECTION.

Bibliography: Thomas Aquinas, ST I, q. 81, aa. 1-3. G. Sitwell, *Spiritual Writers of the Middle Ages* (New York: Hawthorn, 1961) 11–21. W. Barry, *God and You: Prayer as a Personal Relationship* (New York: Paulist, 1987).

JOAN M. NUTH

PASSION OF CHRIST

See CHRIST; DEVOTION(S), POPULAR.

PASTORAL CARE AND COUNSELING

Pastoral care designates the broad range of activities carried out by ordained and nonordained ministers in response to people's needs. These activities, including sacramental and social ministries, can be as informal as conversational encounters and as formal as highly structured ritual events. Traditional teaching on pastoral care is found in the classic literature on the *cura animarum*.

Historical studies of pastoral care have highlighted four basic activities: healing, guiding, sustaining, and reconciling (Clebsch and Jaekle). The guiding function of pastoral care is exemplified in the preaching and educating activities of ministers. Healing, sustaining, and reconciling are evident in sacramental ministrations but in other activities as well, such as counseling and visitation of the sick. The goal of pastoral care is to promote the full well-being of people and to assist them in the ongoing conversion that is part of Christian life.

The locus of pastoral care activities is most often the parish. Ideally, in a post–Vatican II parish setting ordained and nonordained ministers collaborate in responding to the sacramental, educational, and situational needs of parishioners and others. Programs are developed for children, youth, young adults, parents, middle-aged adults, and seniors. Pastoral care to youth typically includes providing educational and social opportunities for them. The frequent presence of a youth minister on a parish staff attests to the importance that is given to caring for this group. Young adults are often assisted in vocational discernment; they are also provided with situations for meeting other young adults sharing similar values. Through educational programs and counseling opportunities, adults are supported in their parenting responsibilities and guided through major life transitions associated with children, midlife, and retirement. The aging are an increasing population meriting the attention of pastoral ministers. The religious, economic, and other challenges that elders face invite supportive and compassionate ministerial responses. The sick and the dying have been the focus of pastoral care through the centuries. Today departments of pastoral care are commonplace in hospitals, and parishes have staff that regularly visit the sick. Contemporary pastoral care also reaches out to the unchurched, divorced and remarried, homosexuals, addicts, and singles.

Pastoral Counseling

Since the fifties and sixties, the pastoral care and counseling movement has drawn heavily on the principles and strategies developed in the social sciences and in other helping processes such as psychotherapy. This is especially evident in pastoral counseling, which is one specific modality of pastoral care that has emerged in the 20th century. Pastoral counseling is a structured process for helping individuals, couples, and families respond to a specific problem or concern in the light of a faith tradition. Typically a troubled individual will enter into an agreement to meet with a pastoral counselor over a certain period of time to resolve some identified problem. The distinctive features of pastoral counseling are the involvement of a minister or someone accountable to the Church as the helping professional and the use of a religious framework for illuminating the situation.

Some contemporary commentators have noted that ministers involved in pastoral counseling often forsake religious categories and embrace psychological ones as they set about a diagnosis of human problems. In pastoral counseling there should be place for a properly pastoral diagnosis that seeks to understand people and situations in light of such religious categories as vocation, faith, repentance, and awareness of the sacred. Some pastoral counselors explore what kind of image of God clients have. Research has shown that an individual's psychic image of God can have an important role to play in that person's psychic economy.

The factors leading up to the emergence of pastoral counseling as a specialized ministry are diverse. At the turn of the century researchers such as William James and Edwin Diller Starbuck began to use psychological concepts to understand religious experience and helped launch the psychology of religion. Early pioneers in the psychology of religion were interested in promoting religious development and so contributed to advances in religious education. Application of psychological concepts and approaches to the counseling work of ministers was an appropriate next step. Courses and books on pastoral counseling began to appear in the twenties and thirties. Anton Boisen, along with others, was instrumental in the mid-twenties in launching the Clinical Pastoral Education (CPE) movement. This movement promoted an intense program of supervised training for ministers and seminarians working with people in emotional distress. By the fifties and the sixties pastoral counseling was a flourishing enterprise in America, with a number of training programs in existence and pastoral counseling centers established in various places. A professional association (American Association of Pastoral Counselors) emerged and professional journals (*Journal of Pastoral Care, Journal of Clinical Pastoral Work,* and *Pastoral Psychology*) began publication.

While the pastoral counseling movement started within American Protestant Churches and has developed there, it has had a significant impact on Roman Catholic seminary education in the United States in recent decades and has spread to other continents. Notably, spiritual direction, which has been a feature of Roman Catholic pastoral care and counseling for centuries, is increasingly sought in Protestant Churches. Whereas pastoral counseling is primarily problem-centered, spiritual direction is a helping process that has as its principal focus the ongoing religious development of the one who comes for assistance.

Pastoral counselors use a variety of approaches and therapeutic strategies that parallel approaches found in secular psychotherapy. Pastoral counselors are trained in grief counseling, marital and family counseling, crisis counseling, supportive counseling, and educative counseling. Some recent developments in the field include the use of hermeneutical theory to illuminate the process of pastoral counseling, the application of family-systems theory to the understanding of congregational life, and an addition to the usual counseling strategies of "reframing," a psychotherapeutic technique that involves recasting and relabeling elements in a problematic situation.

See also HEALING; PSYCHOLOGY, RELATIONSHIP AND CONTRIBUTION TO SPIRITUALITY; SPIRITUAL DIRECTION.

Bibliography: W. Clebsch and C. Jaekle, *Pastoral Care in Historical Perspective* (New York: Jason Aronson, 1983). H. Clinebell, *Basic Types of Pastoral Care and Counseling,* rev. ed. (Nashville, Tenn.: Abingdon, 1984). R. Wicks, R. Parsons, and D. Capps, eds., *Clinical Handbook of Pastoral Counseling* (New York: Paulist, 1985).

RAYMOND STUDZINSKI, O.S.B.

PATIENCE

See FRUIT(S) OF THE HOLY SPIRIT.

PATRISTIC SPIRITUALITY

The term *patristic* refers to the thought and writings of the "Fathers" of the Church, that is, those Christian writers who flourished between the end of the apostolic age (ca. A.D. 100) and the death of Pope Gregory the Great in the West (d. 604) or of John Damascene in the East (d. 749). Christianity in this period included persons of many cultures and currents of thought, from indigenous Syriac-speaking communities in Mesopotamia to native Celtic Christians in Ireland. But most Christians lived in the Roman Empire, and therefore patristic spirituality was greatly influenced by the political history of imperial Rome and the cultural legacy of ancient Greece. The period will be treated in three phases: I. The beginnings (2nd–3rd centuries), before the accession of the emperor Constantine; II. the Golden Age of patristic thought (4th–5th centuries); III. the late patristic period (6th–7th centuries).

I. Beginnings

The spirituality of Christians in the 2nd and 3rd centuries was profoundly shaped by several factors: (1) the threat of persecution by Roman officials; (2) the intensely communal nature of Christian liturgical services; (3) the all-pervasive influence of Greek philosophical thought.

Martyrdom and Persecution

While Roman persecution of Christians was neither as widespread nor as constant as once thought, it is undeniable that the danger of suffering arrest and martyrdom was never very far from the Christian mind. One early document, a letter from Pliny, a Roman governor, to the emperor Trajan (ca. 112), reveals that Christians were liable to be executed simply for confessing their faith in Christ. In the eyes of the Romans, Christians were guilty of "obstinacy" (*contumacia*), a refusal to acknowledge the authority of the Roman Empire in religious matters. Christian spirituality in the 2nd and 3rd centuries, therefore, automatically involved a critical stance toward the political authorities, a stance regarded by the Romans as equivalent to treason and deserving of capital punishment.

From the Christian point of view, the issue was more religious than political. Commitment to Christ involved rejection of idolatry and any trace of emperor worship. If necessary, this meant following the example of Christ, even in his death. Martyrdom was seen as a way of becoming especially close to Christ. As Ignatius, bishop of Antioch, exclaimed in a letter written on the way to his martyrdom (ca. 110): "Come fire, cross, battling with wild beasts, wrenching of bones, mangling of limbs, crushing of my whole body, cruel tortures of the devil—only let me get to Jesus Christ!" (*Letter to the Romans* 6).

Christian martyrdom was viewed as a sacrifice to God in a manner analogous to Christ's own sacrifice (*Martyrdom of Polycarp* 14). It was also seen as a direct combat with the devil (*Martyrdom of Perpetua and Felicity* 10). Some argued that the commitment to take up one's cross and follow Christ was contained in the NT and implicit in the baptismal vow; therefore, readiness for martyrdom was considered incumbent on all Christians (Origen, *Exhortation to Martyrdom* 12; see Mt 16:24-25). But Christians differed widely in their strictness regarding martyrdom: some allowed flight during persecution, while others denied it (Tertullian, *On Flight in Persecution*).

Then, as now, readiness for martyrdom was often more an ideal than a reality. In the middle of the 3rd century, when the first widespread and general persecutions began under the emperor Decius (d. 251), large numbers of Christians either fled or denied their faith. Bitter disagreements arose among Christians regarding whether or not, and under what circumstances, apostates should be readmitted to communion. Under the influence of moderate bishops, such as Cyprian of Carthage, the penitential system of the Church gradually took shape, allowing reconciliation to be offered even to those who had committed the most serious sins. Although martyrdom remained a cherished ideal, the Church acknowledged that less rigorous standards were appropriate to most Christians.

A Communal Spirituality

While not all Christians were called to martyrdom, participation in the liturgical rites of baptism and Eucharist was the *sine qua non* of Christian existence. When the governor Pliny wrote to the emperor Trajan describing the activities of Christians in his region, the services of communal prayer and common meals figured prominently in his account. Ignatius of Antioch frequently stressed the importance of attendance at the Eucharist (under the direction of the bishop) to maintain Christian unity when the danger of heresy was present.

Around the year 150, Justin, a Christian apologist, presented the first detailed description of Christian worship. He portrays Christian baptism not only as the remission of sins but also as a "rebirth" and an "illumination" (*First Apology* 61). He goes on to describe the communal prayers, the greeting with a kiss, the Eucharistic meal, and the weekly collection that Christians share each Sunday. He stresses that when the services are over, "we constantly remind each other of these things. Those who have more come to the aid of those who lack, and we are constantly together" (*First Apology* 67). The presider, Justin says, then sees to it that the offering is distributed to orphans and widows, the sick, prisoners, and guests in the community. Christian liturgy, therefore, flowed into Christian charity.

It is clear from Justin's account that participation in the liturgies of baptism and Eucharist was a central feature of early Christian spirituality. Most Christians would have spent a long time in preparation for baptism; a three-year catechumenate is specified in Hippolytus's *Apostolic Tradition* (ca. 215). This period of testing and instruction, along with the elaborate and highly symbolic rites of the baptismal liturgy, would have done much to strengthen the Christian sense of communal solidarity. As Cyprian, the 3rd-century bishop of Carthage, comments in his discussion of the Lord's Prayer, Christians say "*Our* Father," not "*My* Father," because Christ did not want prayer to be offered only individually and privately: "Our prayer is public and common, and when we pray, we pray not for one but for the whole people, because we, the whole people, are one" (*The Lord's Prayer* 8).

It should be noted that in the 2nd and 3rd centuries there were strong forces at work that threatened to undermine the tendencies we have described. Gnosticism was a popular current of thought that denigrated the material world and its Creator and posited a nonmaterial, otherworldly form of salvation. Already in Ignatius's day the bishop had to warn against heretics who denied the humanity of Christ, avoided the Eucharist, and refused to extend charity to the poor (*Letter to the Smyrnaeans* 6-7). The rejection of Jesus' humanity led some Gnostics to devalue Christian martyrdom as well (Irenaeus, *Against Heresies* 3.18.5).

Orthodox Christian writers responded with a vigorous anti-Gnostic polemic. Prominent among these was Irenaeus (ca. 130–ca. 200), a native of Smyrna in Asia Minor, who became bishop of Lyons in Gaul. Against the dualistic, antimaterial spirituality of the Gnostics, Irenaeus stresses the truly material, as well as spiritual, character of human existence. Central to his view is the biblical notion of humanity created in the image and likeness of God. The entire history of salvation, from Adam to the eschaton, is seen as the story of God's attempt to effect a union of matter and spirit. The first human being received the "image" of God in his physical body and the "likeness" of God in his rational spirit (*Against Heresies* 5.1.3; 5.6.1). In the incarnation God once again united flesh and spirit, and made "a living and perfect Man," through whom humanity could be restored to the divine image and likeness. Christian baptism and Eucharist, Irenaeus argues, are the physical means through which this restoration in Christ continues to be extended to the world (*Against Heresies* 3.17.2; 4.18.5; 5.3.3).

Greek Philosophy

As Christianity spread more widely in the Greco-Roman world, the influence of the prevailing philosophies began to be more strongly felt. Foremost among these were Platonism and Stoicism. Plato's theory of the Forms or Ideas as the immutable, eternal, and immaterial ground of all mutable, temporal, material reality was quickly adopted by Christian apologists to explain their adherence to one God and their rejection of idolatry. Plato's famous description of the ascent of the soul from the love of physical beauty, to the love of spiritual beauty, to the love of the divine Beauty itself (*Symposium* 211C) stands behind both pagan and Christian accounts of the stages by which the human person comes to know God as supreme Truth, Beauty, and Goodness. The Stoic ethical ideal of freedom from irrational passions (*apatheia*) was likewise deemed compatible with the Christian moral life. By the early 3rd century at Alexandria in Egypt there appeared two Christian thinkers who produced thoroughly Hellenized versions of Christian spirituality: Clement and Origen.

Clement (ca. 150–ca. 215), a teacher in the school of catechumens at Alexandria, was concerned both to refute Gnosticism, which was especially strong there, and to offer a persuasive view of Christianity to the non-Christian world. Clement saw a deep compatibility between Greek philosophy, particularly Plato, and Christianity. Plato's ideal of human conduct as "assimilation to God as much as possible" (*Theatetus* 176B) was regarded by Clement as equivalent to the Pauline dictum "Be imitators of me, as I am of Christ" (1 Cor 11:1; *Stromata* 2.22). As a result, Clement's view of Christian spirituality was profoundly shaped by the Platonic dualism of matter and spirit.

This is particularly apparent in the prominent role Clement gives to the Stoic concept of *apatheia*. Since God is by Platonic definition "without passion," to become like God or to be "divinized" means to become "passionless." While Jesus is the model of Christian *apatheia,* Clement's Jesus is "inaccessible to any movement of feeling, either pleasure or pain" (*Stromata* 6.9). Even the apostles, according to Clement, after the resurrection mastered not only anger, fear, and lust but also feelings that seem to be good, such as courage, zeal, joy, and desire (*ibid.*). Clement's brand of Platonism appears to be quite foreign to modern sensibilities.

In fairness, however, it should be noted that Clement considers *apatheia* a means, not an end, to the Christian life. The goal is "knowledge" (*gnōsis*), but a knowledge that begins in faith and, by God's grace, is perfected in love (*Stromata* 7.10). In direct opposition to the heretical Gnostics, Clement proposes the true Christian Gnostic, the "lover of God," who, starting from faith, is granted knowledge, love, and finally the gift of contemplation. The first step is faithfulness, that is, submission to God by obedience to his commandments. But, Clement writes, "the person who goes on to return God's kindness to the best of his power by means of love, rises to the dignity of friend" (*ibid.* 7.3). The knowledge "by its own light carries a person through the mystic stages to the crowning place of rest, teaching the pure in heart to look upon God face to face with understanding and comprehension" (*ibid.* 7.10).

Clement's successor as head of the catechetical school of Alexandria was the brilliant scholar Origen (ca. 185–254). The son of a Christian martyr, Origen was well educated in philosophy, particularly under the Neoplatonist Ammonius Saccas. His literary output was enormous, including a massive apology (*Against Celsus*), a comprehensive system of theology (*On First Principles*), and an extensive series of biblical commentaries. He also composed the first technical discussion of prayer and a treatise of exhortation to martyrdom.

Origen's theology and spirituality were at once more biblical and more Platonic than Clement's. On the one hand, most of his work consisted of sermons and commentaries on the Bible, and the language and imagery of the Bible pervade his thought. On the other hand, a Platonic cosmology and anthropology, which Origen articulated in *On First Principles,* thoroughly shaped his understanding of God and the soul's relation to God.

The controlling theme is Origen's (and Plato's) theory of the preexistence of souls. All spiritual creatures, including human souls and demons, were once pure intellects, created to live in rapt contemplation of God. A natural kinship existed between God and the soul that was formed in the divine image and likeness. Out of satiety, however, all but one of the spirits became bored and turned away from God in varying degrees. God then created the material world as a place of salutary punishment and education for these fallen spirits. God's Son, the divine Logos, after fusing with the one faithful spirit, assumed a human body in order to reveal more clearly the path of return.

As a result of this theory, Origen's view of the spiritual life has a decidedly intellectualist cast. God's purpose and the ultimate end of history is the return of all spiritual beings to their pristine state of contemplation. The point at which human beings are most like God and most truly themselves is when they are "minds," who have achieved loving knowledge of God through union with the Logos. Origen sometimes describes the return of the soul to God as a journey in stages by which a person departs from vices and practices virtue, and then leaves behind corporeal thoughts and images about God and comes to grasp God as a simple intellect (e.g., *Homily 27 on Numbers*).

It is difficult to overestimate Origen's influence on subsequent Christian spirituality. In the East the Cappadocian Fathers—Basil of Caesarea, Gregory Nazianzen, and Gregory of Nyssa—kept alive much of his teaching. Evagrius Ponticus laid a theoretical foundation for monasticism in Origenist terms. Through Cassian the teaching of Evagrius and Origen spread to the West and was virtually canonized for Western monks in the Rule of St. Benedict. While Origen's more exotic speculations were rejected in later centuries, the rudiments of his thought remained central to the spiritual traditions of East and West.

II. The Golden Age (4th–5th Centuries)

The early 4th century marked a decisive turning point for Christian spirituality. The conversion of the emperor Constantine and the gradual Christianization of the Roman Empire placed Christians on a much different footing than in earlier centuries. On the one hand, full participation in social and political life was now open and even encouraged. On the other hand, large numbers of Christians began to feel that life "in the world" was incompatible with authentic Christianity. The monastic movement, which originated in the closing decades of the 3rd century, became the rallying point for Christians of a more rigorist bent.

Asceticism and Monasticism

Devotion to a life of virginity or celibacy had been a vital feature of Christian spirituality from its very beginnings. From at least the end of the 2nd century, groups of widows and virgins constituted a semiofficial "order" in the Church, with their specific duties and privileges (Hippolytus, *Apostolic Tradition* 10-12). A number of Christian writers in the 3rd century had composed treatises dealing with the way of life of virgins, among them Tertullian (*On the Veiling of Virgins*), Cyprian (*On the Dress of Virgins*), and Methodius of Olympus (*Symposium*). But until the late 3rd century, male ascetics lived singly and there was no organized form of monastic life.

The early 4th century witnessed an explosion of enthusiasm for various forms of the ascetic life, first in Egypt, then later throughout the empire. "Withdrawal" (*anachōrēsis*) into the desert or nearby countryside led to the development of new modes of social life that were destined to change profoundly the contours of the late ancient world. The old ideal of the Christian martyr was transformed into the new ideal of the Christian monk. Christian perfection now entailed selling one's possessions, giving to the poor, and following Christ in a life of poverty, celibacy, and obedience. Two figures dominate the first generation of monastic heroes, each exhibiting a different way of life: Antony the hermit and Pachomius, founder of monastic communities (*coenobia*).

The life of Antony was immortalized by his biographer, Athanasius, bishop of Alexandria (ca. 296–373). Composed in Greek and quickly translated into Latin and other languages, the *Life of Antony* was intended to present a paradigm of the life of the monk. Athanasius portrays his hero's successive withdrawal deeper into the desert and further from contact with other human beings. Movement into the desert was marked by encounters with demons, whom Athanasius portrays in vivid and dramatic terms. Twenty years in inaccessible solitude rendered Antony's body and spirit perfectly balanced and healthy: "The state of his soul was one of purity, for it was not constricted by grief, nor relaxed by pleasure, nor affected by either laughter or dejection" (*Life of Antony* 14). Paradoxically, however, Antony gained greater fame at each step and became the teacher of large numbers of monks, as well as a healer and wonderworker. A lengthy discussion of discernment of spirits is included in the *vita* (16–44).

A rather different view of monasticism is provided in the literature associated with communities of Pachomian monks. Pachomius was a convert to Christianity who came to the faith after experiencing Christian charity while in prison. After initial attempts at living as a hermit, Pachomius heard a voice calling him to "stay here and build a monastery" (*First Greek Life* 12). Later his vocation was clarified by an angel who said, "The will of God is to minister to the human race in order to reconcile them to himself" (*ibid.* 23). Pachomius founded a number of communities in upper Egypt, organized under a set of monastic rules. Communal meals, work, and liturgies were distinctive features of Pachomian monasteries. The reading and study of Scripture also figured prominently in the daily regimen. In this community setting, the virtues of obedience and humility were highly prized.

In addition to the eremitic and cenobitic ways of life, other, less formal arrangements could be found: for example, groups of ascetics living singly but in close proximity to one or more "elders" or recognized spiritual masters. Numerous collections of "sayings" and "lives" of the desert monks emerged from this environment. Immensely popular throughout Christian history, these collections preserved in brief, anecdotal form wisdom and discernment distilled from a lifetime of ascetic experience. Humility and obedience were always prominent topics; a healthy skepticism toward manifestations of religious enthusiasm (visions, miracles, extravagant asceticism) is also frequently mentioned. Above all, charity and forgiveness were widely regarded as the hallmark of Christian and monastic virtue. As one elder put it: "Bear your own faults and pay no attention to anyone else wondering whether they are good or bad. Do no harm to anyone, do not think anything bad in your heart toward anyone, do not scorn the person who does evil" (*Alphabetical Collection* [Moses 7]).

Although the earliest monks were generally uneducated and not of the highest social classes, the movement quickly captured the allegiance of many of the "best and brightest" among 4th-century Christians. All the great patristic writers of this era—Ambrose, Jerome, and Augustine in the West; Athanasius, Basil, and Chrysostom in the East—had a deep sympathy for, if not some personal experience of, the monastic life. Well-trained in rhetoric and philosophy, they became articulate spokesmen for the ascetic ideal.

Eastern Spiritual Writers

In the East some bishops, such as Basil of Caesarea in Cappadocia (ca. 330–379), attempted to adapt the desert ideal to a less rigorous, urban environment and to channel monastic energy into the service of the Church. Basil composed a set of eighty rules or moral instructions (*Moralia*), each supported by quotations from the NT. He later added two sets of rules written in the form of questions and answers on matters of monastic practice (*Long Rules, Short Rules*). "Faith working by charity" was the mark of the true Christian, according to Basil (*Moralia* 80). He strongly emphasized the benefits of a communal life, arguing that hermits lacked sufficient opportunity to exercise charity toward others (*Long Rules* 7). Basil's legislation remains to this day the principal monastic rule of Greek Orthodox Christianity.

A more mystical interpretation of Christian spirituality was provided by Basil's younger brother, Gregory of Nyssa (ca. 335–395). Well-versed in Platonic philosophy, Gregory was a gifted speculative theologian who introduced several new ideas into Christian spiritual theology. His treatise *On the Life of Moses* presents an allegorical reading of the three encounters of Moses with God: at the burning bush and in the two ascents of Mount Sinai. Unlike Plato and Origen, who both conceived the ascent to God in terms of moving out of the shadows of materiality into the light of true Being, Gregory describes Moses' ascent to God as a reaching into "thick darkness" (see Exod 20:21). Gregory thereby stresses the unknowability of God to a greater ex-

tent than his predecessors. In another work, *On Christian Perfection,* Gregory takes the fact of mutability (long considered by the Platonic tradition as a flaw of created nature) and turns it into a virtue: mutability enables creatures to make infinite progress in the knowledge of God who is infinite.

The tendency of Greek patristic writers to blend Platonic theology with monastic practice reached a high point in the work of Evagrius Ponticus (ca. 346–399). A friend of the Cappadocian Fathers, Evagrius was ordained deacon by Gregory Nazianzen and became a noted preacher at Constantinople. Through a series of personal misfortunes, he found his way to the Egyptian desert of Nitria (382), where he spent the remainder of his life. Evagrius was the first monk to write extensive works on prayer and spirituality; these have exerted profound influence on Eastern and Western monks. Among his works are the *Praktikos* and the *Gnostikos,* a two-part work on the ascetic life; the *Kephalaia Gnostika,* which contains his more speculative ideas; and the treatise *On Prayer.* Though condemned in 553 as an Origenist, many works of his circulated under the name of other writers.

Evagrius shared Origen's theory of the preexistence and fall of the soul. Like Origen, he believed that the goal of the spiritual life is the restoration of the spirit to knowledge and union with God. Like Clement of Alexandria, Evagrius strongly emphasizes the concept of "passionlessness" (*apatheia*), though also like Clement he stresses the element of love. In the preface to his *Praktikos,* for example, Evagrius offers this summary of the spiritual life, which he attributes to his desert teachers: "The fear of God strengthens faith, my son, and continence in turn strengthens this fear. Patience and hope make this latter virtue solid beyond all shaking and they also give birth to *apatheia.* Now this *apatheia* has a child called *agapē,* who keeps the door to deep knowledge of the created universe. Finally, to this knowledge succeed theology and the supreme beatitude."

Evagrius's unique contributions pertain especially to the psychology of asceticism and prayer. He was the first to analyze the eight kinds of passionate thoughts (*logismoi*) that afflict the monk: gluttony, fornication, avarice, sadness, anger, listlessness, vainglory, and pride. Through Western writers such as Cassian and Gregory the Great, Evagrius's *logismoi* became the seven deadly sins. His treatise *On Prayer,* preserved among the works of Nilus of Ancyra, teaches that true prayer involves the contemplation of God without concepts: "When you are praying do not fancy the Divinity like some image formed within yourself. Avoid also allowing your spirit to be impressed with the seal of some particular shape, but rather, free from all matter, draw near the immaterial Being and you will attain to understanding" (*On Prayer* 66).

Western Spiritual Writers

Much of Evagrius's spiritual teaching was preserved for the West by his disciple John Cassian (ca. 360–435). Cassian was a monk from Bethlehem who spent some time in Egypt with Evagrius and then with John Chrysostom in Constantinople. He eventually settled near Marseilles, where he founded two monasteries (ca. 415). There he wrote several books, among them the *Institutes,* which includes a set of rules for monastic life and a discussion of the eight principal vices derived from Evagrius, and the *Conferences,* a collection of twenty-four addresses delivered in Egypt by hermits or cenobites. Cassian's work has been called "the greatest corpus of teaching on spirituality to come out of the age of the fathers" (O. Chadwick). He succeeded in transposing the rigor of desert asceticism and the speculative genius of Evagrius into a more moderate idiom, thereby preserving for the West the riches of Eastern spirituality. One hundred years later, when Benedict of Nursia composed

his Rule for monks, he ranked Cassian second only to the Bible as an aid in finding God (RB 73).

No discussion of Western spirituality would be complete without some attention to Augustine of Hippo (354–430). Augustine is a paradoxical figure in many ways. He himself was influenced both by the ascetic movement and by the traditions of Christian Platonism, though he gave a novel twist to both. He composed a monastic rule, but as a preacher he was profoundly concerned with the spirituality and way of life of ordinary Christians. He defended the goodness of creation against the Manichees, and yet his own pessimistic estimation of human nature under original sin shocked many of his contemporaries, including monastic writers such as John Cassian.

Augustine's spirituality is also inseparable from his own personal history. His ceaseless search for truth, as well as his experience of moral impotence in the face of his own passions, is chronicled in his *Confessions.* On the one hand, his struggle with the problem of evil led him to reject Manichean dualism and to embrace Christian Platonism with its vision of an immaterial God and soul. On the other hand, his confrontation with his own passionate nature convinced him of the overwhelming need for, and efficacy of, God's grace. As a result, there is little in Augustine's theology that did not emerge out of his personal spiritual experience.

As a Platonist, Augustine never ceased to think of God as supreme Truth and Wisdom. In the famous scene of the *Confessions* where he describes a quasi-mystical experience shared with his mother, Augustine charts the ascent of their minds from the vision of material things to meditation upon the soul, to contemplation of divine Wisdom: "At last we passed beyond our souls to that place of everlasting plenty, where you feed Israel forever with the food of Truth. There life is that Wisdom by which all these things that we know are made, all things that ever have been and all that are yet to be" (*Confessions* 9.10). It is even possible in this life, Augustine suggests, to grasp this Wisdom directly, though only fleetingly: "And while we spoke of the eternal Wisdom, longing for it and straining for it with all the strength of our hearts, for one fleeting instant we reached out and touched it" (*ibid.*).

The steps from the material world to spiritual world to God is a pattern often found in Neoplatonic spirituality. What is new in Augustine is his deep grasp of the inscrutability and ambivalence of the human heart. His spirituality is not "intellectualist" in the same way as that of Origen or even of the Cappadocians. Augustine was profoundly aware that the core of the human person is not the mind but the heart. The road to God is a "road of the affections" (*On Christian Doctrine* 1.16). Human beings are impelled by their loves, as if by gravity, he says in the *Confessions* (13.9): "My love is my weight (*pondus meum amor meus*); I am drawn by it wherever I go." Only when inflamed by the fire of the Holy Spirit, Augustine argues, can a person rise to God.

Augustine's sense of the centrality of love and the reality of the divided human heart led him to challenge one of the primary tenets of monastic spirituality and the Greek patristic theology that supported it. Ascetic teachers such as Pelagius stressed the basic soundness of the human will and its ability to make choices for good. Augustine's personal experience, on the contrary, had taught him that all human love is self-love, unless the Holy Spirit, the gift of love, heals and directs the will to its proper object, the love of God. The disordered affections that stemmed from Adam's sin, Augustine maintains, are so pervasive that even the human body is affected. Augustine sees this evidenced most obviously in the unruly concupiscence of the sexual organs.

III. The Late Patristic Period (6th–7th Centuries)

The later patristic period was a time of consolidation and synthesis of the several different traditions of spirituality from earlier generations. But this did not exclude the possibility of creativity; especially in the East, several important figures emerged whose impact on subsequent Christian spirituality was decisive.

In the West, Augustine's influence was preponderant, and it would be several centuries before someone of comparable originality and depth would arise. However, one writer worthy of mention is Gregory the Great (ca. 540–604), monk and bishop of Rome. Dependent on both Cassian and Augustine, Gregory wove their doctrine into a more pastoral and practical synthesis. His *Homilies on Ezekiel* contains teaching on contemplation and the contemplative and active lives that became classic in the West. His largest work was a massive commentary on Job, the *Moralia,* which probably originated in a series of monastic conferences. Its exegesis departs quickly from the literal meaning in order to present Gregory's moral and spiritual teachings.

In the East a collection of writings ascribed to Dionysius the Areopagite, a convert to Christianity mentioned in Acts 17:34, was composed in the late 5th century and "discovered" by Syrian Monophysite Christians in the 6th century. Their allegedly apostolic origins gained for these texts a wide reading, although it is likely that the Dionysian corpus would have succeeded on its own merits. The works were revered in both the East and West; translated into Latin in the 9th century by Erigena, the collection was a popular subject for medieval commentaries.

Heavily influenced by the Neoplatonism of the pagan Proclus, the writings of the Pseudo-Dionysius include the *Celestial Hierarchy,* a discussion of the nine orders of angels who mediate God to human beings, and the *Ecclesiastical Hierarchy,* which treats of the sacraments and the three ways of the spiritual life by which a person is "divinized": purgation, illumination, and union. This triad was to become almost canonical in subsequent spirituality. Another work, the *Divine Names,* examines the attributes of God that can be affirmed in a positive way (kataphatic theology), and the *Mystical Theology* describes the ascent of the soul to union with God.

This last work presents the author's well-known apophatic theology, in which God is known by "unknowing." Borrowing from Gregory of Nyssa's *Life of Moses,* the Pseudo-Dionysius describes Moses' ascent into the cloud as a plunging into the mysterious darkness of unknowing: "Here, being neither oneself nor someone else, one is supremely united by a completely unknowing inactivity of all knowledge, and knows beyond the mind by knowing nothing" (*Mystical Theology* 3). Although the author stresses the importance of denying all God's characteristics in order to gain a proper apprehension, he also makes it clear that neither the affirmations nor the negations capture the transcendent Cause of All: "It is beyond assertion and denial" (*ibid* 5).

One further figure from the Greek world must be mentioned in this survey: Maximus the Confessor (ca. 580–662). Heir to the Origenism of Evagrius, Maximus rejected the theory of the pre-existence and fall of souls. Though he accepts Evagrius's analysis of the eight *logismoi* and the ideal of *apatheia,* he modifies both to emphasize the importance of charity in addition to knowledge. He states that contemplation involves not merely the mind (*nous*) but also *erōs* and *agapē* (*Centuries on Charity* 2.48). Maximus also adopted elements of the teaching of the Pseudo-Dionysius, stressing the ecstatic union of the mind with God in unknowing. Like most of the Greek Fathers, Maximus places "divinization" (*theōsis*) at the center of his spiritual theology, though he never

ceases to emphasize that it was the incarnation, God's becoming human, that enables humans to become divine.

See also ACEDIA; AFFIRMATIVE WAY; APATHEIA; ASCETICAL THEOLOGY; ASCETICISM; AUGUSTINIAN SPIRITUALITY; BENEDICTINE SPIRITUALITY; CELIBACY; DESERT; DISCERNMENT OF SPIRITS; DIVINIZATION; DUALISM; EASTERN CHRISTIAN SPIRITUALITY; EREMITICAL LIFE; GNOSIS, GNOSTICISM; IMAGO DEI; MONASTICISM, MONASTIC SPIRITUALITY; NEGATIVE WAY; WESTERN (LATIN) SPIRITUALITY.

Bibliography: A. Louth, *The Origins of the Christian Mystical Tradition: From Plato to Denys* (Oxford: Clarendon, 1981). C. Jones, G. Wainwright, and E. Yarnold, eds., *The Study of Spirituality* (New York: Oxford Univ. Press, 1986). B. McGinn, J. Meyendorff, and J. Leclercq, *Christian Spirituality: Origins to the Twelfth Century* (New York: Crossroad, 1989). B. McGinn, *The Foundations of Mysticism: Origins to the Fifth Century* (New York: Crossroad, 1991).

DAVID G. HUNTER

PEACE

One of the most significant biblical texts highlighting the meaning of peace in a Christian context is found in the Letter to the Ephesians, wherein Jesus is identified as our peace. "But now in Christ Jesus you who once were far off have become near by the blood of Christ. For he is our peace, he who made both one and broke down the dividing wall of enmity" (Eph 2:13, 14). This text not only mysteriously identifies Jesus as our peace but also relates peace with peacemaking. Through the shedding of his blood, Jesus made peace by breaking down the barrier of hostility.

The "enmity" directly referred to in this Ephesians text was that between Gentile and Jew in those earliest years of Christian life. However, the profound theological understanding of this text situates all Christian peacemaking in the death and resurrection of Jesus—the paschal mystery.

In the various Easter stories of the Gospels, time and again Jesus meets his followers with the greeting "Peace" (Mt 28:9; Lk 24:36; Jn 20:19, 21). In Jesus' own Hebraic understanding, this greeting of peace, of *shalom,* spoke to a fullness of peace and wholeness permeating every facet of a person's life. These Easter stories indicate a special eagerness on Jesus' part to gift his disciples with the *shalom* he had made possible through his sufferings, death, and resurrection.

The Pauline letters continued this beautiful greeting of the risen Jesus. At the beginning of those letters the earliest Christian communities read, "Grace and peace from God our Father and the Lord Jesus Christ" (Rom 1:7; 1 Cor 1:3; 2 Cor 1:2; Gal 1:3; Eph 1:2; Phil 1:2; Col 1:2; 1 Thess 1:1; 2 Thess 1:2; 1 Tm 1:2; 2 Tm 1:2; Tit 1:4; Phlm 1:3).

For those early Christians, receiving the peace of Jesus meant more than personal well-being. Jesus' own peace included Jesus' ways of peacemaking. To be children of God meant a peacemaking way of life, as the Matthean beatitude stated clearly (Mt 5:9). Peacemaking meant forgiveness and love of enemies in the spirit of the gospel (Mt 6:43f.; Lk 6:27f.). Peacemaking also meant a refusal to participate in warfare. For the first three hundred years of Christian life, most followers of Jesus could not reconcile war with Jesus' witness to the making of peace.

In *The Challenge of Peace: God's Promise and Our Response,* the Catholic bishops of the United States pointed out that the Catholic tradition on war and peace, in all its complexities, begins with the Sermon on the Mount (no. 7). The bishops highlighted the text from Ephesians identifying Jesus as our peace (Eph 2:13f.) as an objective basis of a religious vision for peace in the contemporary world of sovereign states (no. 20). Throughout this entire pastoral letter, the intrinsic relation between peace in one's personal life and peacemaking in the social order is emphasized.

One of the most significant sections in *The Challenge of Peace* is the teaching on "The Value of Nonviolence." Strong statements on gospel nonviolence are included

from different periods of Christian life, including references from the Second Vatican Council's Pastoral Constitution on the Church in the Modern World (*Gaudium et Spes*). Although "nonviolence" and "pacifism" are sometimes used synonymously in *The Challenge of Peace,* this pastoral letter makes it clear that nonviolence does not mean nonactivity in the face of injustice and violence. Gospel nonviolence is always very active, but always in a nonviolent way.

In the United States, the 20th century has given us the remarkable Christian nonviolent witness of Dorothy Day, Martin Luther King, Jr., and Cesar Chavez. Both King and Chavez are indebted to Gandhi for their nonviolent action in the social and political orders. Each of these leaders, including Gandhi, is known for a profound spirituality, one nourished by a maturing life of prayer.

The 20th century has also witnessed thousands of Christians joining peace organizations of various kinds. Christian men and women have always been a part of the Fellowship of Reconciliation, an international, ecumenical, and interfaith movement committed to nonviolence. The Christian Peace Conference, begun in Eastern Europe after World War II, has welcomed Christians from all denominations to continue dialogue for the making of peace. Christian women have joined others in the Women's International League for Peace and Freedom, begun during World War I by Jane Addams. Christian women and men have joined other concerned citizens in organizations protesting the escalation of the arms race, particularly nuclear weapons.

One peace movement, Pax Christi International, deserves special mention here because of its significance for Catholic spirituality. Pax Christi International, the Catholic Peace Movement, was begun by French and German Catholics to bring about reconciliation after the horrendous brutality of the Second World War. Today

Pax Christi has fully developed sections throughout Europe and North America. New sections are beginning in Latin America, Asia, and Africa. Programs include national and international conferences and retreats, educational programs and publications, and various nonviolent actions. A prayerful spirit permeates every meeting and action of Pax Christi. Although members are not required to be committed totally to nonviolence, some members do take a vow of nonviolence.

Pax Christi began with a Eucharist at which those first members were reminded that Jesus, who is our peace, made peace possible for us through the shedding of his blood. Reconciling participation in the Eucharist with participation in warfare has always been problematic for Christians. From early Christian times to the present day, many Christians have raised the question of the incompatibility of partaking in the body and blood of Jesus, and then proceeding to destroy the bodies and shed the blood of countless members of the human family. Nuclear war raises this question to an unprecedented urgency.

In the Eucharistic celebrations since Vatican II, every Catholic now has the opportunity to extend Jesus' own greeting of peace and to receive the nourishing strength necessary for genuine peacemaking in the spirit of the gospel. May this Eucharistic awareness bring the entire Church to a new peacemaking stance in this "hour of supreme crisis" (GS 77).

See also BODY OF CHRIST; CONFRONTATION AND PROTEST; NUCLEAR AGE, IMPACT ON SPIRITUALITY; PASCHAL MSYTERY; WAR, INFLUENCE ON SPIRITUALITY.

_____

Bibliography: H. Camara et al., *Peace Spirituality for Peace Makers* (Antwerp: Pax Christi International, 1981). C. F. Jegen, *Jesus the Peacemaker* (Kansas City, Mo.: Sheed & Ward, 1986). R. Powaski, *Thomas Merton on Nuclear Weapons* (Chicago: Loyola Univ. Press, 1988).

CAROL FRANCES JEGEN, B.V.M.

PENANCE, PENITENCE

Penance, also called penitence or repentance, is a dimension of conversion as a dynamic of Christian spirituality. Specifically, it is an attitude or virtue motivating Christians to resist evil and sin and to undo the harm done by sin. Because of the ecclesial character of Christian spirituality, the virtue of penance is closely related to the liturgical celebration of the sacrament.

Spiritual writers of the past often linked the virtue of penance with the virtues of justice (obligations to God) and charity (responsibilities to neighbor). Contemporary writers retain these links but are more likely to deal with social responsibilities as well as reverence toward God.

The call to conversion is prominent in the Christian Scriptures. It was central in the preaching of Jesus (Mt 4:17; Mk 1:15; Lk 5:32; 13:5), as it had been in John the Baptist's and continued to be in that of the apostles (e.g., Acts 2:38). In time, the scriptural understanding of "conversion" was reduced to "penance." The virtue was generally treated individualistically in terms of hatred of sin and atonement for sin. Its practice was often identified with mortification as a means of atoning for one's past sins—doing penance—and regular celebration of the sacrament in the form of private confession. This was largely due to the Latin Vulgate's translation of the scriptural *metanoiete* as *paenitentiam agite* and the medieval emphasis on satisfaction (especially prominent in Celtic, Anglo-Saxon, and Teutonic culture), as well as the individualistic orientation of medieval liturgy and spirituality, and a somewhat materialistic and mechanistic understanding of grace.

Spirituality and spiritual direction have often emphasized penance as sorrow or contrition for one's sins and the effort to atone for them (expiation, satisfaction, reparation), with both motivated by justice (what is due to God and God's punishment of sin) and charity (toward ourselves and others). Works of penance were then often understood as self-purification and self-punishment to satisfy God's justice and escape punishment in purgatory.

Cultural shifts in imaging and language necessitate reinterpretation. The underlying constant is that penance, as a dimension of conversion, is an ever-present dynamic of the Christian life, not a one-time or occasional reality. A sense of individual and ecclesial responsibility for one's actions and for growth in likeness to Christ under the guidance of the Spirit leads Christians to take penance seriously.

Spiritual growth thus requires sensitivity to sin—a consciousness both of our own sins and of others' sins and also of the evil present in society. When this is coupled with a realization of God's love and our relationships with others, it leads, not to shame, fear, and scrupulosity, but rather to a motivation for actively resisting sin and evil in our own lives and in society.

Likewise, making amends for personal sin (or the sin of others) is not self-punishment or payment to God. It is rather the wholehearted acceptance of one's responsibilities and call to holiness, and the difficulties that come with the effort to fulfill these responsibilities and this vocation. It extends to include the willingness to share the responsibilities of others, an element that in the past was also often put in terms of expiation, e.g., through fasting and abstinence or other penitential works.

Contemporary spirituality thus retains the personal or individual element of penance that has been a part of Christian tradition but broadens it to include the relationship to neighbor as well as to God, and responsibility for one another as well as for oneself. Thus, where past spiritual writers dealt with atonement or expiation, writers today will be more inclined to speak of the responsibility to undo harm done to and by others. However, individualism may still be present, even though disguised by psychological terminology; for example, where past writers spoke of a struggle against evil inclinations in order to subject them to the will and thus to God, contemporary writers may speak, in an individualistic or even egotistic fashion, of the effort to achieve self-integration.

Where a significant advance has been made, especially since Vatican Council II, is in the connection between penance and social justice. Although past writers did link penance and justice, it was generally in terms of the individual's obligations to God and consequent responsibility to atone for offenses against God. Without abandoning this element, the Constitution on the Sacred Liturgy (*Sacrosanctum Concilium*), in speaking of Lenten penance, reemphasizes the spirit of baptismal conversion and the social dimension of penance (SC 109).

Pope Paul VI's postconciliar reform of penitential practices, and especially of the discipline of fasting and abstinence, emphasizes the social dimension of conversion and the link between penance and the world's progress. Though his document *Paenitemini* keeps much of the late medieval and post-Tridentine understanding of mortification and self-denial, penitential practices are regarded more as elements of social responsibility and social action than individualistic asceticism. Paul VI's reform of indulgences also reinterprets expiation to highlight the restoration of friendship with God and of the personal and social values weakened or destroyed by sin (*Indulgentiarum Doctrina* 2-3). A similar orientation is found in the addresses and encyclicals of Pope John Paul II. Thus the spirituality of penance has been increasingly correlated with the social teachings and social mission of the Church.

A healthy appreciation of the virtue of penance as a dimension of the spiritual life is the context for recognizing the proper place and celebration of the sacrament of penance. This is now often spoken of as the sacrament of reconciliation in order to emphasize its relational and social character. The reformed rite of penance stresses ongoing conversion or continual repentance as part of everyday Christian life and social responsibility (e.g., OP 3-4). It also stresses the relationship between the sacrament and social justice (OP 5, 7) and the sacrament as part of ecclesial responsibility (OP 4, 8, 11). It emphasizes, too, that the sacrament includes the virtue of penance or repentance both as attitude—contrition—and as action—act of penance or satisfaction (OP 6). Most significantly for appreciating the place of the sacrament in the spiritual life, it recovers the tradition of the sacrament as a proclamation of faith and thanksgiving and as self-offering in service (OP 7). The virtue and sacrament of penance are thus once again closely linked and clearly related to the Church's mission and worship.

Because of this reorientation, the sacrament should not be used as a means of individualistic purification or a perfunctory part of spiritual direction. The frequency of celebration should be related to the rhythms of liturgical time and the life of the community, as well as to the individual's realization of personal needs. The *Rite of Penance* speaks of "frequent *and careful* celebration" (OP 7, emphasis added). Other means of forgiveness are acknowledged. The idea of getting grace or using devotional confession as an ascetic discipline to root out faults is absent. The criterion instead is intensifying the spirit of ecclesial conversion that flows from baptism. Though closer conformity to Christ and greater attentiveness to the Spirit are possible in many ways, it is not possible to celebrate the ecclesial dimension of conversion apart from the Church and its liturgical celebrations.

The rediscoveries and reorientations in recent reforms have not yet been fully incorporated into spirituality. Until they are, they are unlikely to bear the fruit intended. Present tensions regarding the sacrament of penance and the manner of its celebration, particularly the communal forms of celebration, witness to the failure. At the same time, the prominence of penance (both virtue and sacrament) in our tradition shows that spiritual renewal, whether of individuals or of the Church, is unlikely to be achieved without it.

See also ABSTINENCE; ASCETICISM; COMPUNCTION; CONVERSION; DETACHMENT; FASTING; FORGIVENESS; HEALING; MORTIFICATION; PURGATION, PURGATIVE WAY; TEARS, GIFT OF.

Bibliography: J. Dallen, *The Reconciling Community: The Rite of Penance* (New York: Pueblo, 1986).

JAMES DALLEN

PENANCE, PHYSICAL
See ASCETICISM; MORTIFICATION.

PENTECOSTALISM
See CHARISMATIC RENEWAL; ENTHUSIASM; FUNDAMENTALISM; GLOSSOLALIA; PROTESTANT SPIRITUALITIES.

PERFECTION
See HOLINESS.

PERSON
See ANTHROPOLOGY, THEOLOGICAL; SELF; TRINITARIAN SPIRITUALITY.

PERSONALITY TYPES
The classification of human persons into types has a long history. Such typing has been used by the medical, psychological, and religious professions in dealing with people seeking help and direction. The more prominent classifications have been the humoral types, the constitutional types, the Myers-Briggs, and the Enneagram.

Hippocrates in the 5th century B.C. originated the medical approach to human classification. Relying on the four humors of blood, yellow bile, black bile, and phlegm, he categorized persons as sanguine, choleric, melancholic, or phlegmatic. This system of classification lasted through the Middle Ages. The sanguine temperament represents the person who is cheerful, optimistic, charming, playful, generally upbeat, and characterized by quickly changing facial expressions. The choleric temperament describes the person with a quick anger, an ardent, passionate, and impulsive personality, and a readiness to criticize. Such a person is idealistic, decisive, and energetic. The melancholic temperament refers to the type that frequently demonstrates a depressed and pessimistic attitude. Persons with this temperament are overly serious in their personal relationships. They lead guarded emotional lives and are often filled with feelings of guilt and rejection. Finally, the phlegmatic temperament denotes a person with an unemotional, detached, and unsentimental attitude toward life. Such persons have isolated their feelings from the rest of their lives and therefore often present themselves as cold and uncaring. But they also possess a dry humor and an objective view of the world.

The constitutional typing originated in the 18th century with the use of phrenology. Out of this emerged three temperaments: the mental, in which the nervous system predominates; the vital, in which the alimentary system predominates; and the motive, in which the muscular system predominates. The 19th century saw attempts to correlate temperament with bodily proportions, and these correlations have appeared in the 20th century as the three somatypes: ectomorph, the elongated appearance; endomorph, the stout appearance; mesomorph, the balanced appearance. Ectomorphs are usually found to have a high level of nervous energy and tension. They protect themselves from too much stimulation in several ways: by a shy and retiring attitude; a defensiveness toward sexual desires, which are seen as threatening; and a suspicious and superior view of others. Endomorphs are known for their laid-back appearance, predictability,

tolerance for differences, and lack of discrimination in emotional expressions. Mesomorphs are strong-willed, confident, vigorous, and competitive.

The system that has been the most influential in the area of Christian spirituality and prayer had its origin in the thought of Carl Jung. He developed the description of the classes of introverted and extroverted types. Jung's typology has been somewhat modified by Isabel Myers and her mother, Katherine Briggs. The advantage of the Jungian personality typing is that it is determined by means of a psychometric questionnaire, basically devised by Isabel Myers, called the Myers-Briggs Type Indicator (MBTI). Although the instrument was at first met with hostility, it has become the most widely used way of determining personality types outside a psychiatric situation.

Every individual is unique and has a specific personality that differs from other personalities. This is due to the way people prefer to use their minds in the areas of perceiving and judging. People fall into large categories in terms of their processes of being aware and in coming to conclusions. The way they perceive and judge explains the way they evaluate the outside world and act in that world.

For Jung, there are two contrasting ways of perceiving: sensing, that is, operating through the five senses; and intuition, that is, an inner perception or one that works from the unconscious. The point of the distinction is that one is more significant than the other, although both are present. Persons who prefer sensing pay attention to reality outside themselves and have little time for ideas that do not have an obvious origin. For those who prefer intuition, the opposite is the case: they are so engrossed in looking for what is not immediately perceptible that they often pay little attention to the concreteness of their experience of the world outside themselves. People develop their preferred way of perceiving in childhood; the other kind of perception remains in the background and is less focused. As they move into adulthood, their preferred way of perceiving is strengthened, and they develop along divergent lines, some more S (sensing) and some more N (intuition).

The other basic difference arises in the area of coming to conclusions. There is the way of thinking (T) and the way of feeling (F). Thinkers conclude at the end of a logical process; feelers conclude by means of appreciation of things. The T is more impersonal, the F more personal. Although all people make use of both ways of making judgments, a person enjoys and trusts one way more than the other. As people enter adulthood, they become more adult either in handling human relationships (F) or in organizing ideas and facts (T).

The two preferences (TF and SN) are independent and can be combined in different ways, e.g., ST, SF, NF, NT. Each combination has its own character, interests, value systems, ways of paying attention, and external characteristics. Each combination produces a distinct personality. Because it is easier to relate to and work with people of the same personality type, and difficult to understand and predict people of a different type, the MBTI can be a helpful tool for dealing with conflicts, making a choice of work, understanding one's friends, and discovering a personal style of prayer.

Another way that people differ in regard to perception and judgment is indicated by their interest in their outer and inner worlds. Jung pointed to the difference between the introvert and the extrovert (I and E). The introvert perceives and judges with a focus on ideas, while the extrovert performs these functions by focusing on the outside environment. A final preference used by the MBTI has to do with two differing ways of dealing with the outside world. The judging (J) attitude comes to a conclusion by temporarily prescinding from perception, refusing to admit any more evidence. The perceptive (P) attitude withholds judgment and delays until more evidence is received. There are sixteen possible combinations of EI, SN, TF, and JP.

Identifying one's personality preferences, especially the dominant process, has proven to be helpful in the area of spirituality. In a situation of counseling or spiritual direction, an understanding of the classification of psychological types can be effective for guidance in prayer. For instance, an extrovert who is dominantly a sensate (ES) might find books, material aids, and outward details a value in prayer, whereas an introvert who is also sensate (IS) will experience these same externals as symbols of an inner world and will be predisposed to make use of the imagination in prayer to a greater extent. Theological reflection as a way of entering prayer will be the choice of a T, whereas affective forms of prayer will be more appealing to an F. The EN person may be attracted to a spiritual life characterized by outward ministry, while the IN may be more readily called to mystical experiences. (The above summaries are dependent on *Interrater Reliability and Validity of Judgments of Enneagram Personality Types,* W. S. Gamard (1986) and *Gifts Differing.* Material below is dependent on H. Palmer, *The Enneagram.*)

Unlike the Myers-Briggs Type Indicator, which began as a psychological tool and was later employed for spiritual purposes, the Enneagram began as the mapping of a spiritual practice that was psychologized when it was introduced into the West. The origins of the Enneagram are unknown. Some contend that it emerged from the Sufi practice of the master assisting the disciple. Others hold that it has its home in occult practices of Islam.

The Enneagram was introduced into the West through the teachings of George Ivanovich Gurdjieff (1877–1949), who used it in Russia prior to World War I. Gurdjieff, however, did not identify the Enneagram with the nine personality types. His disciples, especially Peter D. Ouspensky and John G. Bennett, elaborated on the system as taught by their teacher. But it was the Bolivian Oscar Ichazo who, through his teaching of the Enneagram at his institute in the city of Arica, Chile, as well as other places, made an enormous contribution to the elaboration of the Enneagram system. To him we owe many of the names associated with the Enneagram. A group from America, including Dr. Claudio Naranjo, a Chilean psychiatrist at the University of California, Berkeley, went to Arica to study with Ichazo. They brought the Enneagram back to the United States, and Naranjo's students and their followers spread it throughout this country and other parts of the world. It has become almost standard fare in growth workshops, retreat houses, and spiritual direction. And what was once a purely oral tradition is now claiming a respectable bibliography.

The word *enneagram* is derived from the Greek words for "nine points." It is usually portrayed in the form of a circle with nine equidistant points and nine interconnecting lines. There are two sets of interconnecting lines: one forms a triangle connecting points (or spaces) six, three, and nine. The other connecting lines form a pattern following the order of one, four, two, eight, five, seven. In Ichazo's language, each of the nine points represents a personality type. These nine points are further divided into what are called areas or centers. Points two, three, and four belong to the feeling center, sometimes also called the heart and social center. These are the people who are preoccupied with excessive role-playing. Points five, six, and seven belong to the mental center, sometimes called the head or sexual center. Here belong those who are trapped by excessive thinking. Points eight, nine, and one constitute the practical center, sometimes called the gut or self-preservation center. These are the people who are caught in diversionary activity.

Each type is described in terms of its preoccupations and the remedy for the fixations that follow from these preoccupa-

tions. On the head level the preoccupation is a kind of mental bias, which is healed by the acquiring of the higher mind. In a Christian framework, higher mind is similar to a proper image of God. For example, for point two the chief feature, or mental bias, is flattery, and the higher mind is will or freedom. Point three's chief feature is vanity, and its higher mind is hope. Melancholy is the chief feature of point four, and originality is one of the words describing the higher mind.

On the heart level the preoccupation is an emotional one. The emotional center, called the passion, is healed or "redeemed" by the higher emotional center, called the virtue. For example, the passions of points five, six, and seven are avarice, fear, and gluttony respectively. The respective virtues are detachment, courage, and sobriety.

On the gut or instinctual level each of the nine spaces or types has three subtypes. These refer to the largely unconscious aspect of the personality and are recognized by the issues that affect our physical survival, our sexuality, and our social lives. Each person has three areas of relationships: the personal, called self-preservation; the one-to-one, called sexual; and others as a group, called social. In early childhood, anxiety develops in one of these areas of relationships, and the person develops a mental preoccupation to lessen this anxiety. Examples of the words describing these subtypes would be those taken from points eight, nine, and one—point eight: sexual = possessiveness; social = social friendship; self-preservation = satisfactory survival; point nine: sexual = union; social = participation; self-preservation = appetite; point one: sexual = jealousy; social = inadaptability; self-preservation = anxiety.

The two adjacent types of any point on the Enneagram are considered that point's neighbors or wings. The wings are a further nuancing of the particular personality. For instance, the space of four, which tends to present feelings in dramatized ways, can be influenced by the five wing and so act in an internalized and depressive way, or the four can lean toward the three and act in a more hyperactive way. Each point on the Enneagram carries the flavor of each of its neighbors, although one will usually be more dominant.

There is an internal dynamic to the Enneagram that is usually presented graphically by means of arrows directing away from one point to another point. For instance, the arrows move in the direction of one, four, two, eight, five, seven. Also, the direction is three, nine, six. The space toward which the arrow points is considered the personality's stress point. For example, four is the stress point of one, two is the stress point of four, etc. The space toward which the personality goes when it goes against the arrow is considered the heart space. For example, the heart space of four is one, of two is four, etc. Stress does not mean that the person is to avoid connecting with that space on the Enneagram, and heart does not mean that the person should move to that space for health. Rather, stress means that when a person, such as a six, is in a situation of stress, there is some helpful energy to be found in the three space, and when six is moving through life on an even keel, there is some energy to be found in the heart space of nine. It is also possible that any point can take on the negative qualities of their heart and stress points.

The Enneagram is a highly nuanced instrument of spiritual and psychological growth. It is a tool of compassion, for not only does it help people to understand those they live with, work with, and love, but it teaches that the truly integrated and holy person is the one who can visit the other eight spaces on the Enneagram at will when necessary. However, persons do not change their place on the Enneagram. Their strongest and original energy comes from their home space.

See also ATTENTION, ATTENTIVENESS; CONSCIOUSNESS; FEELINGS; INTUITION; PASSION(S); PSYCHOLOGY, RELATIONSHIP AND CONTRIBUTION TO SPIRITUALITY.

Bibliography: I. Briggs-Myers, *Gifts Differing* (Palo Alto, Calif.: Consulting Psychologists Press, 1980). M. F. Keyes, *Emotions and the Enneagram* (Muir Beach, Calif.: Molysdatur Publications, 1990). H. Palmer, *The Enneagram* (San Francisco: Harper & Row, 1988).

JAMES L. EMPEREUR, S.J.

PETITION

The prayer of petition, from the Latin *petere* ("to ask," "to beseech") is a fundamental religious stance before the mystery of God. It arises at the intersection of human need (e.g., for a successful harvest, for a cure, for deliverance from some evil) and the religious belief in a caring "Other" who desires what is for human good. Though the requests are usually quite specific (petitions), this form of prayer must wrestle with two realities: the theological concern that the mystery of God not be put under human control, and the experiential awareness that what one requests is often not granted as requested. The prayer of petition must therefore be deeper than specific requests. It must take the form of surrendering oneself, one's needs, and one's human situation to the God of mystery whose care is sought.

For Christians, the warrant for petitionary prayer is given, on a first level, in both the teachings and the actions of Jesus. The care of God, *Abba,* is set forth, for example, in the parable of the lilies of the field (Mt 6:28ff.), and is the context in which the disciples are urged to "ask" with confidence (Mt 7:7, 11). Jesus himself, in countless stories of healing, evokes and responds to confident request (e.g., the Canaanite woman in Mt 15:28: "O woman, great is your faith! Let it be done for you as you wish"). And as the post-resurrection faith deepens, the very name of Jesus becomes for believers the guarantor that their prayer of petition will be answered: "Until now you have not asked anything in my name; ask and you will receive ..." (Jn 16:24).

On a deeper level, the warrant for prayer of petition is the paschal mystery of Jesus Christ, i.e., his own faithful obedience unto death, his resurrection, and the sending of the Spirit to all who believe. In the fullness of that mystery the covenantal stance of God, *Abba,* is proclaimed anew, and the loving response of God, the transforming Spirit, is already given forth. No longer does the prayer of petition arise because of a promise that God will respond; it arises in the face of a response already given. Indeed, it is God's response, this same Holy Spirit, who teaches and enables the believer to pray (Rom 8:26-27).

In the sending of the Holy Spirit, new light is shed on the intersection between human need and the mystery of God. The indwelling Spirit is God's own desires and yearnings for men and women intimately wedded to their own. Even before they take shape as "prayers" of petition, these deep human needs and desires are already the "prayer" of petition, called forth by the mystery of God's own love. They are the human face of that "eager expectation" and that "groaning in labor pains" that God has set at the heart of creation itself; their origin is the One according to whose will creation was subjected in hope (see Rom 8:19-23).

Christian prayer in the West has focused on Jesus Christ as mediator or intercessor before God; the typical ending of Western liturgical prayer is "We ask this through Christ, our Lord." This dominantly Christological focus has tended to keep the prayer of petition on the first level alone, where believers pray "in the hope that" their prayer will be answered. Christians are urged to conform their desires to the desires of God. Prayer in the East has more firmly developed the pneumatic dimension of the paschal mystery, i.e., the Spirit as *dynamis* ("power") who shapes and guides the human approach to God. It is more confident and optimistic. Petition in the West is one with the obedient surrender of Jesus to *Abba;* in the East, it is *epiclesis,* the calling forth of the Holy Spirit who has already been sent "as the first gift to those who believe" (Eucharistic Prayer IV, adapted from the Eastern anaphora of St. Basil).

Contemporary liturgical reform has restored the petitionary prayers of the faithful, which had been replaced by the more narrowly focused "intention" of the Mass. The desires and needs of the gathered assembly are placed with Christ in his own offering to *Abba.* In the new Eucharistic Prayers, the Church's petitions are set in a pneumatic context, following and extending the second *epiclesis* for the unity of the Church. This combined wisdom of both East and West soundly locates the Christian prayer of petition within the context of the full paschal mystery of Christ, where love proclaimed and made present invites surrender and enables confident trust.

See also ABBA (IN PRAYER); INTERCESSION; PRAYER.

Bibliography: K. Irwin, *Liturgy, Prayer and Spirituality* (New York: Paulist, 1984). J. B. Metz, *Poverty of Spirit* (New York: Paulist, 1968). K. Rahner, "The Possibility and the Necessity of Prayer," *Christian at the Crossroads* (New York: Seabury, 1975) 48–61.

PETER E. FINK, S.J.

PIETISM

See PROTESTANT SPIRITUALITIES.

PIETY

As one of the gifts of the Holy Spirit, piety perfects the moral virtue of religion by engendering within the human person a filial affection for God and a loving regard for all people as fellow children of God. The inclusion of piety (*eusebeia*) as one of seven gifts of the Spirit of the Lord bestowed upon the Messiah occurs in Isa 11:2 in the Septuagint, although it is not found in the Hebrew, which names only six gifts. The word *piety* comes from the Latin *pietas,* which means "responsibility" or "a sense of duty and devotion." Piety implies as well fidelity, reverence, obedience, and commitment.

In the Old Testament, relations with others, whether with God or other persons, that are qualified by piety can be described in terms of *ḥesed,* a term that is difficult to translate but is close in meaning to piety. *Ḥesed* is the steadfast loyalty and love that ideally characterize relationships of mutual obligation and responsibility. Pious persons of the Old Testament conformed themselves to the Sinaitic covenant by dutifully observing the Mosaic Law. The formalistic and legalistic observance of the law, however, sometimes encouraged the projection of a mere façade of piety.

In the New Testament, artificial piety becomes the sin of the Pharisee, since it lacks the heartfelt sincerity of right intention. According to Jesus in his Sermon on the Mount (Mt 6:1-18), one's motive in fulfilling responsibilities to both God and one's fellow humans must be pure and free from the external formalism and ostentation of the hypocrite who seeks nothing more than human praise and worldly glory.

The piety, or faith, of the Christian is grounded in the piety of Christ, who reveals the mystery of godliness (*eusebeia*) through his incarnation, teaching, and resurrection unto glory (1 Tm 3:16). To be truly pious is to follow the way of Jesus in humble submission to the will of the Father in complete trust and obedience. Pious Christians are called to live "temperately, justly, and devoutly in this age" (Tit 2:12) while expecting persecution (2 Tm 3:12). Although they must discipline themselves with spiritual exercises in order to live pious lives (1 Tm 4:7-8), a life of piety is nonetheless a free gift from God (2 Pet 1:3). This gift comes through the "knowledge of God and of Jesus our Lord" and finds its authentic expression in care and love for one's neighbor (2 Pet 1:2, 6-7).

The terms *pious* and *piety* are often used in a pejorative way to refer to the insincer-ity of those who are pretentious or sanctimonious in the practice of their religion. These persons might assume an appearance of sullenness and solemnity in order to look pious in the eyes of others. Such affectation and pretension betray a distorted image of the loving God revealed in the life and teaching of Jesus Christ. True Christian piety rejoices in the life of faith and sings praise to God with gladness (Ps 100:2; Jn 15:11). It is the grace of God that enables Christians to embrace piety so that they might look forward in happy expectation to the return of Christ Jesus in the glory of God (Tit 2:11-13).

See also DEVOTION(S), POPULAR; GIFTS OF THE HOLY SPIRIT; VIRTUE.

Bibliography: R. Garrigou-Lagrange, *Christian Perfection and Contemplation* (St. Louis, Mo.: B. Herder, 1951). M.-F. Lacan, "Piety," *Dictionary of Biblical Theology,* 2nd ed. (New York: Seabury, 1973).

KEITH R. BARRON, O.C.D.S.

PILGRIMAGE

See JOURNEY (GROWTH AND DEVELOPMENT IN SPIRITUAL LIFE).

POOR, THE

In the Bible "the poor" are the oppressed, the humiliated, the deprived, the degraded, or the indigent. The Hebrew language contains several words that describe the poor in this way—*'ani, 'anaw, dal,* and *'ebyon*—but none of them is translated exactly as "the poor." In the OT the understanding of the term varies. The poor person is the sinner, and the rich person is blessed by God. However, as OT literature develops, the prophets and the postexilic writers see that the increase of wealth and the spread of poverty indicate a hardening of hearts. Amos blushes over the crimes of Israel (Amos 2:6ff.), and Isaiah proclaims that it will be the task of the Messiah to defend the poor (Isa 11:4). In the psalms the poor appear as the beloved of Yahweh. Yahweh hears their cry and delivers them.

Jesus' inaugural discourse, the Sermon on the Mount, concerns the poor. The beatitudes are foundational for understanding the poor as heirs of the kingdom (Mt 5:3; Lk 6:20). In her *Magnificat,* Mary, the poor handmaid of the Lord, proclaims that the hungry will be filled and the rich will be sent away empty (Lk 1:53). Jesus himself is the poor man of Bethlehem and Nazareth. He warns his disciples about the dangers of riches (Mt 6:19ff.), and he identifies his mission as directed primarily to the poor (Lk 7:21-23). Finally, on the cross he becomes a poor man, deprived even of his own garment (Mt 27:35).

All genuine disciples are destined to be poor and to share the cross. They are to be free from illusions of self-sufficiency and power. They are not to "take gold or silver" (Mt 10:9). The gospel is to be preached without recompense (1 Cor 9:18), and the model of the early Church remains a constant inspiration: "The community of believers was of one heart and mind, and no one claimed that any of his possessions was his own, but they had everything in common" (Acts 4:32). However, the fundamental NT insight into understanding a poor person is found in the very identity of the poor man of Nazareth, "who, though he was in the form of God . . . emptied himself, taking the form of a slave" (Phil 2:6-7).

Christian spirituality, based on the Scriptures, has always developed a conscious relationship to the poor in some way. The Judeo-Christian message is a message of hope for the poor. The rich are called to share their goods. The example and teaching of Jesus show both an attitude of heart and a way of life in which he is numbered among the poor. The Christian experience cannot be conceived apart from the poor.

Early Awareness

Early Christianity experienced an increase in indigents in the great cities in the East and in the rural areas in the West. Disease was rampant among the poor. Churches and monasteries, which made the important contribution of providing hospitals in cities and along major roads, developed their vision of Christian life and practice in the care of the sick and in almsgiving for the poor.

The first centuries of Christian education took into account the reality and the needs of the poor. According to Gregory of Nyssa, to feed and to clothe the poor is to feed and clothe Christ. St. Basil taught that the Christian can be only an administrator of goods for the needs of others. It was St. Jerome who formulated the famous phrase "Follow naked the naked Christ" (*Nudus nudum Christum sequi*). In the nakedness of the poor, one finds the way to follow and to recognize Christ. St. Gregory the Great's *Pastoral Care* says that it is the duty of all Christians to reach out to the poor. Earthly goods are for all and not for the few. St. Gregory encouraged all bishops to be fathers of the poor. In fact, Church property was considered to be the patrimony of the poor. The great model of the early Christian centuries is St. Martin, the Roman equestrian who cut his cape in two with a sword and gave half to a beggar.

The Carolingian renaissance fostered the notion that the good king was a protector of the poor. Developments in hagiography idealized care of the poor as God's deliberate plan of salvation: "God could have made all men rich, but he wanted poor men in this world so that the rich might have opportunity to redeem their sins" (*Life of Saint Eligius,* PL 87:533). Monastic hospitality, as it developed through the customaries applying the rule, was directed primarily to the poor. The monk became a pauper of Christ, and this voluntary asceticism was to open the heart of the monk to the involuntary paupers.

Evangelical Awakening

The Crusades and the founding of new cities in the 12th and 13th centuries awakened a new vision of the humanity of Christ. Christ was no longer simply the Judge and the Redeemer urging almsgiving and charity for the poor. Christ was the poor man, despised and rejected. The poor were no longer the means by which the wealthy were saved, but rather the poor were the bearers of salvation. Imitation of Christ meant joining the ranks of the poor. St. Francis of Assisi captured and expressed the spirit of this age.

The Poverello of Assisi recognized a Christ who was not only the Son of the living God; he was also "a poor man and a transient and lived on alms." Therefore, he says in his Rule of 1221 that his friars "must rejoice when they live among people of little worth and who are looked down upon, among the poor and the powerless, the sick and the lepers, and the beggars by the wayside." His own conversion experience began when, as he himself wrote, "The Lord led me among them [the lepers]."

The poor, in Francis's vision, are no longer the object of alms and works of charity, but they are brothers and sisters to whom Christ brings all who would follow him. The lot and the life of the poor are to be shared by the follower of Christ. Early Franciscan iconography and hagiography present a Francis who, unlike St. Martin, gave his entire cloak rather than only half of it to the poor man. The poor man literally offers the identity of Christ. Upon meeting the poor man, Francis wanted simply to be with him, even to take his place.

St. Bonaventure develops this notion of a poor man in his philosophy and theology. All human persons are poor from the very beginning of their existence because, as he writes in his *Commentary on the Sentences* (11.35), "Every creature depends essentially and totally on the Creator." The poor person is every person, but only the poor acknowledge this basic truth about themselves. They are the ones who alone can worship God in truth, because they are freed from the illusion that they do not need to ask for anything God can provide. Prayer gushes forth from the heart of the poor person.

There is a genuineness about the poor. Aelred of Rievaulx writes in his classic text *Spiritual Friendship* (3.70) that "friendships among the poor are generally more secure than those among the rich, since poverty takes away the hope of gain in such a way as not to decrease the love of friendship but rather to increase it. And so toward the wealthy one acts flatteringly, but towards the poor no one pretends to be other than he is. Whatever is given to a poor man is a true gift, for the friendship of the poor is devoid of envy."

Modern and Contemporary Attitudes

St. Vincent de Paul captures this tradition in a consistent but unique approach. The poor are the members of Jesus, and this vision prompts great attention and charity in the service of the poor. In the poor one finds God. In his *Talks to the Daughters of Charity* (10.595), he encourages them to interrupt their schedule of prayer when the poor call upon them: "If you hear the poor calling you, mortify yourselves and leave God for God. It is not leaving God to leave God for God, that is one work of God for another, or one of greater obligation and merit." No facet of personal privacy or spiritual exercise can be an excuse for separation from the poor.

In early 20th-century America, Dorothy Day stands tall in developing a spirituality that participates in socioeconomic action for the deprived and the oppressed. Her life of advocacy for the poor was articulated in her newspaper, *The Catholic Worker*. She established Houses of Hospitality for the poor and lived a spirituality of the poor that demanded conscious involvement in radical social politics on their behalf, especially workers exploited as cheap labor. She took the Catholic social justice teaching of papal encyclicals seriously.

In her autobiography, *The Long Loneliness* (San Francisco: Harper & Row, 1981), Dorothy Day says: "To help the organizers, to give what you have for relief, to pledge yourself to voluntary poverty for life so that you can share with your brothers is not enough. One must live with them, share with them their suffering too. Give up one's privacy, and mental and spiritual comforts as well as physical." Her years of living in the slums was her way of actualizing the spiritual strength of the Catholic tradition. She asked how Catholics in America could in conscience tolerate the death-dealing machine of a "filthy rotten system." Her harsh love in action for the poor and her compassionate life with the poor find a parallel in the work of Dom Helder Camara of Recife, Brazil.

Although the documents of the Second Vatican Council do not deal specifically with this subject, the windows were opened for the fresh air of a spirituality of the poor: "The spirit of poverty and charity are the glory and authentication of the Church of Christ" (GS 88). The Church "recognizes in the poor and the suffering the likeness of her poor and suffering Founder" (LG 8). This theme was taken up by Pope Paul VI in his 1964 encyclical *Ecclesiam Suam* (nos. 53-54), in which he described the "general lines of the renewal of ecclesiastical life": "The first of them is the spirit of poverty, or rather the zeal for preserving this spirit. . . . It is a fundamental element of that divine plan by which we are destined to win the kingdom of God, and yet it is greatly jeopardized by the modern trend to set so much store by wealth." Four years later Paul VI acknowledged that his vision of renewal of ecclesiastical life had been taken a step further in the final document of the second general conference of Latin American bishops at Medellín. Less than a month later in a general audience (October 2, 1968), he hailed the "pastoral directives

which make this defense a proof of solidarity with the humbler social classes, an exemplary testimony of the style befitting ecclesiastical life and, finally a demonstration of the spirit of service that must characterize the Church's activity." A new spirituality for the renewal of the whole Church was being born.

Yet a further step was taken by the Latin American bishops in 1979 at Puebla, Mexico. In their *Final Document of the Third General Conference of the Latin American Episcopate,* they state: "We affirm the need for conversion on the part of the whole Church to a preferential option for the poor, an option aimed at their integral liberation." The Church seeks out the poor not only for the renewal of ecclesiastical life but for ecclesial conversion. The poor are no longer simply to be served or embraced by the Church; they are to characterize the spiritual life and breadth of vision necessary to be Church.

By the use of the notion of "fundamental option," Gustavo Gutiérrez, a chief architect of Latin American liberation theology, develops a deeper theological interpretation of the Puebla "preferential option" for the poor. The overall thrust or intentionality of the Christian must be focused on solidarity with the poor. This is the condition of an authentic solidarity with anyone. In his *Power of the Poor in History* (Maryknoll, N.Y.: Orbis, 1983, p. 128), Gutiérrez writes: "It is precisely this preference that makes the gospel so hard and demanding for the privileged members of an unjust social order."

In the U.S. Catholic bishops' 1986 pastoral letter *Economic Justice for All,* the notion of the fundamental option for the poor is taken up again. In a country where only a minority are considered the poor, the hermeneutic context is different than in Latin America. Nevertheless, the U.S. bishops acknowledge: "Jesus takes the side of those most in need physically and spiritually. The example of Jesus poses a number of challenges to the contemporary Church. It imposes a prophetic mandate to speak for those who have no one to speak for them, to be a defender of the defenseless, who in biblical terms are the poor" (no. 52). This demands "moral priorities for the nation," and this implies a shift in both ecclesial and political spirituality.

Pope John Paul II, in his addresses to U.S. Catholics during his visits of 1979 and 1987, accented the parable of Lazarus and the rich man (Lk 16:19-31). During his first visit to New York, he stated that "the parable of the rich man and Lazarus must always be present in our memory; it must form our conscience." Eight years later, during his visit to Detroit, he asked Americans: "What have you done with that parable?" prior to demonstrating the global significance of the parable. The interdependence of nations can no longer be ignored: "The continuing existence of millions of people who suffer hunger or malnutrition and the growing realization that the natural resources are limited make clear that humanity forms a single whole. Pollution of the air and water threatens more and more the delicate balance of the biosphere on which present and future generations depend and makes us realize that we all share a common ecological environment." Spirituality of the poor becomes a global and an ecological spirituality. Lazarus is the world.

A spirituality of the poor has been part of the Christian experience from the beginning. In the latter years of the 20th century, spirituality of the poor has become central to a new insight into Christology and ecclesiology. It now forms the basis of global and ecological awareness. Those who would bring this spirituality to bear on their own lives must wrestle with the question raised by St. Catherine of Siena in her *Dialogue* (no. 33): "How can these wretched evil people share their possessions with the poor when they are already stealing from them?"

See also CONSUMERISM; FRANCISCAN SPIRITUALITY; LIBERATION THEOLOGY, INFLUENCE ON SPIRITUALITY; MARGINALIZED, THE; MATERIALISM; POVERTY; WEAKNESS AND VULNERABILITY.

Bibliography: M. Mollat, *The Poor in the Middle Ages*, trans. A. Goldhammer (New Haven, Conn.: Yale Univ. Press, 1986). R. Neuhaus, ed., *The Preferential Option for the Poor* (Grand Rapids, Mich.: Eerdmans, 1988).

J. A. WAYNE HELLMANN, O.F.M. CONV.

POPULAR DEVOTION

See DEVOTION(S), POPULAR.

POSITIVE WAY

See AFFIRMATIVE WAY.

POSTMODERNITY

The modern (Cartesian-Kantian), post-Enlightenment worldview which emphasized individual subjectivity, interiority, and self-subsistent autonomy has given way to the postmodern sensibility which is more fully cognizant that the human person is a relational being who exists toward others and within a tradition or traditions. The term *postmodern* is of rather recent origin and is quite ambiguous. The adjective is used variously to describe and evaluate the current cultural, religious, and political climate as different from that of premodernity and modernity. As a distinctive worldview and sensibility, it is identifiable by way of contrast to the latter. Modernity's bold claims for the idealist self-subsistent rational self and its view of history as inevitably progressive have been unsettled by the "terror of history" which interrupts and disorients, calling into question human conceptions of order, divine providence, indeed the very nature of God.

More than anything else it is the shock of historical events that has shaken modernity's certitude and called into question the ability of modernity to make good on its promise for order, cohesion, coherence in self, community, history, and world. The horror of events such as Hiroshima and

Auschwitz has done the most to dislodge an ordered view of history and of divine providence. Such views of order, unity, and coherence, characteristic of the premodern sensibility carried over into modernity, even in its most atheistic and agnostic froms. But in modernity, the premodern belief in order, unity, and progress according to a preordained divine plan was placed in the human rather than in God, in rationality rather than in providence. But the conviction about order, unity, and coherence remained strongly ingrained in the modern mindset and exercised enormous influence in political and economic affairs. Modern theology witnessed the "turn to the subject," i.e., the individual human person whose ordered cognitive operations were understood to provide a basis for integration and unity in self, as well as the seeds for the ideal human ordering of human relationships, communities, and societies. Events baffle, however. They baffle both the belief in a provident and ordering God and in an ordered human freedom, capable of bettering the world. The violence inflicted upon innocent millions, the massacre of whole races of people, the aggression of powerful nations against the defenseless, the generations-old religious and cultural conflict in Northern Ireland, the horror of the AIDS epidemic, all interrupt tightly knit worldviews and neat-and-tidy systems of order, unity, and coherence. Who would dare answer the question of where such events belong in the order of providence?

Suffering, however repressed, eventually erupts to subvert the most basic and tightly held modern belief that everything makes sense and fits into an ordered, coherent, unified purpose. It defies modernity's most arrogant claim: Through adherence to rationality's imperatives we can think our way through this horror once again.

Though many of the interpretations of the postmodern period are nihilistic, calling for complete "deconstruction," they nonetheless have important consequences for Christian spirituality. Others are more optimistic. Since Christian spirituality is concerned with the cultivation of the deepest reserves of human hope grounded in faith in the resurrection of Christ, even and especially when there seems to be no apparent reason to be hopeful, it is the more hopeful currents in postmodernity that merit attention.

One of the more hopeful currents in postmodernity is the deconstruction of the altogether modern conviction regarding the necessarily progressive nature of history and the truculent and bold claims of the post-Enlightenment subject. The snubbing of religion and tradition (religious and otherwise) that has been characteristic of modernity, as well as the adulation of the self-determined, autonomous, self-subsistent self, is giving way to a critical yet appreciative awareness of the indispensability of relationality, interdependence, community, and traditions. There is a greater measure of humility in the postmodern period, a deeper awareness of the fact that our view of truth is necessarily partial, and that the promises of modernity and rationality gone unchecked in the technological age have failed to satisfy the deepest longings of the human heart. Nowhere is the audacity of modernity more apparent than when considering its pretensions about the transcendence of history. Human persons are historical. Ineluctably in the mix of history, humans remain finite and fragile. The truth claims of postmodernity tend to be more partial, cognizant that any point of view is one view of a point. Discourse about God and God's activity in the world is more tentative. This does not imply that truth is relative or that God is a matter of personal taste and pleasure; rather, it is to suggest that our rather tenuous grasp of truth is relative to the possibilities of our historical situation, and our apprehension of God and God's ways in the world is not to be gauged by Enlightenment canons of certitude but in terms of the premodern sense of knowing and understanding.

The recognition that traditional human conceptions of order and providence are no longer plausible in light of the terror of history, and that promises made by and to modernity's idealist self-subsistent self have failed to satisfy the deepest longings of the human heart does not inevitably entail abandoning faith in God. It does entail the recognition of a more fragile self and of a God of divine vulnerability. The interruptive character of history, the capacity of suffering to disorient and baffle, the discontinuities between expectation and event all render human persons and history precincts of epiphany. The coherent narrative with beginning, middle, and end gives way to the epiphanies in James Joyce, Marcel Proust, and Thomas Mann at the close of modernity. These writers still attempt to fashion a coherence in the narrative order, however. It is with writers such as Samuel Beckett that temporality itself is ruptured altogether and a mythic return to order is no longer acceptable.

Historical relativity is one of the hallmarks of the modern period, to be sure. That is to say that already in modernity it was recognized that perspectives are relative and limited by historical and cultural context. But modernity still affirmed that there was a "givenness" in the world, and that human beings could come to know this givenness, albeit in a partial and limited way. But in postmodern perspective, views of reality are themselves understood to be constructed. Human beings are makers and shapers of worlds of meaning and value.

In postmodern perspective, the world is not understood as a coherent picture, but in terms of a multiplicity of constructs that together constitute a collage. Universal norms and claims no longer persuade. Because of the perpetration of horrible evil through the laws and norms of cultures and societies, postmodernity is suspicious of any claim to objectivity and universality. A postmodern sensibility gives rise to the query: How can one claim that other countries in the world would be better off if they adhered to principles of American democracy? Or to the principles of Christianity?

Postmodern perspectives are suspicious of modernity's effort to construct the self-subsistent self. Such a goal is judged impossible and results in an artificial self which, in turn, constructs institutions and societies that are themselves artificial. As but one example, the contemporary university, with its proliferation of committees and departments all in service of a myriad of specializations, seems to have lost track of its central purpose: the education and formation of the whole person in service of the human community. A postmodern perspective recognizes the holistic nature of persons and societies. That is to say that the person is not purely, or even primarily, a rational being, but rather a being who desires wholeness while at the same time demanding respect for individual differences, historical specificity, and cultural particularity. In the perspective of modernity, wholeness and particularity seem ultimately irreconcilable. In postmodernity they are dialectically inseparable.

In sum, there are three hallmarks of a postmodern sensibility. First, since views of reality are not "given" but constructed, there is suspicion of all universal and normative claims. This is especially because of the reality of historical evil. The interruptive character of history, the suffering and terror perpetrated by powerful elites and ideological victors, calls into question any and all claims to have a complete hold on the truth. Second, there is a suspicion of modernity's tendency toward compartmentalization and specialization. This is true not only of the institutions and societies given shape by modernity. It is also true of the human being, who is not a composite of various components or faculties, the premier of which is reason narrowly understood, but a whole person who desires integration in relation to others in community and tradition. Third, there is the affirmation that particularity and wholeness are not irreconcilable but are dialectically inseparable. Lamentably, modernity has made of them rivals and competitors.

The implications of postmodern sensibility for Christian spirituality are wide-ranging. Above all, there is the recognition that modernity's project of constructing the self-subsistent rational self was wrong-headed and artificial. Consequently, there is greater attention given to other dimensions of the self in understandings of human personhood, especially relationality, community, and the ineluctable necessity of traditions for human flourishing.

Postmodernity's emphasis on interruption, disorientation, and discontinuity evokes the recognition that the God of the Hebrew and Christian Scriptures is not first and foremost a God of order and providence, but a God who is active in history and present to creation. This postmodern sensibility is not inevitably at odds with the gospel of Jesus, who interrupted rather than fulfilled conventional certainties regarding God's plan of salvation for the chosen people. The promises offered by the Christ flew in the face of tightly held expectations. Indeed, his very coming and his cross were discontinuous with all that was judged to be God's way and work in the world.

An authentic Christian spirituality marked by the more hopeful and optimistic currents in postmodernity is willing to relinquish audacious claims about God's permissive will, a preordained order, and a benevolent providence that fly in the face of common sense and sober faith. But this Christian spirituality is buoyed up by the conviction that even and especially in the discontinuities and interruptions of human history, precisely in the midst of those events that boggle and baffle, God comes.

See also CULTURE; ENLIGHTENMENT, INFLUENCE ON SPIRITUALITY; HOLOCAUST; MODERN SPIRITU-ALITY; NUCLEAR AGE, IMPACT ON SPIRITUALITY; WORLD.

Bibliography: D. Tracy, *Plurality and Ambiguity: Hermeneutics, Religion, Hope* (San Francisco: Harper & Row, 1987). R. Kearney, *The Wake of the Imagination: Toward a Post-Modern Culture* (Minneapolis: Univ. of Minnesota Press, 1988). D. N. Power, "Sacrament: Event Eventing." *A Promise of Presence*, ed. M. Downey and R. Fragomeni (Washington: Pastoral Press, 1992).

MICHAEL DOWNEY

POSTURES IN PRAYER

See BODY; CENTERING PRAYER; MEDITATION; PRAYER.

POVERTY

Poverty is a condition in which people are economically disadvantaged, materially deprived, and powerless to support themselves. It affects those who are hungry, who are without housing and clothing, who lack education, medical care, and job opportunities. Poverty means being without the basic goods needed for an authentic human life. Poverty is political. It is perpetuated by systems of injustice that divide people into those who have and those who have not. The poor feel oppressed and exploited. They are often excluded from participating in decisions that affect their lives. Poverty is international. Powerful nations can dominate poorer nations, forcing them into submissive partnership. Poverty is global. It touches the majority of the world's population, especially in Third World countries. Poverty is an evil often beyond the control of individual groups. It lies at the root of classism, sexism, racism, and militarism.

Poverty is also a religious reality. People of faith embrace poverty as a positive value because they reverence the material cosmos and the goods of the earth as God's creations. Christians willingly renounce the inauthentic styles of power, status, or prestige that accompany wealth. Some Christians live a style of simplicity based on the invitation to sell all one's possessions, to give to the poor, and to follow Jesus. Others live in solidarity with the poor, bonding with them and living among them. Still others directly serve the poor and become advocates for them.

When viewed from a Christian perspective, poverty has been embraced as a religious value mainly by those living in communities under religious vows. Poverty is vowed along with celibacy or chastity, obedience, and sometimes with a vow specific to the charism of the religious group. The full meaning of the vow is expressed in the virtue of poverty, which tempers the human drive to acquire material goods. The vow and the virtue of poverty can discipline the drives of avarice, selfishness, and possessiveness.

Poverty is a polyvalent reality. Three historical periods contribute insight into a contemporary spirituality of poverty.

Three Historical Periods

The Gospels and the Beginnings of Religious Life

Jesus was born into a people of faith who had experienced the poverty of the Exodus and the Exile. The Gospels present him as one who espoused the weak in their struggle with the strong. He sympathized with the Hebrew 'anawim, the poor of God. God alone was the source of refuge for those afflicted and those seeking divine deliverance from their plight. The psalms exalted God who delivered the poor out of their destitution (e.g., Pss 22:23; 35:9-10, 27-28; 109:30-31; 140:12-13). The prophets called Israel to act justly, to love tenderly, and to walk humbly with God (Mic 6:8).

Jesus himself was not part of the destitute poor, nor was he a landed farmer. However, he became conscious of the destitute, the oppressed, and the marginalized people of his society. His prayer and his ministry brought him to side with the poor of God. This was evident in his miraculous healings, his preaching, and his proclamation of the reign of God. He invited the poor and powerless to share at table. He reached out to those who were socially marginal, those crushed and meek. His circle of friends included those in debt, widows, orphans, day laborers, those who were blind, deaf, and physically disabled, those afflicted with Hansen's disease, (i.e., lepers), women, tax collectors, shepherds, prostitutes, and fisherfolk. All these were invited to accept the reign of God, even though they were disdained by religious and social standards. He called people of wealth and the poor to a discipleship of equals. He rejected the dominative style of power found in the Roman household. The only one he called Father, *Abba,* was his God.

Jesus offered new life to sinners, not to the righteous (Mk 2:17). If sinners turned and followed him, they would put on his mind. The Sermon on the Mount indicated that the poor in spirit and the meek are blessed with God's special care (Mt 5:10-12). Luke portrays God as benefactor of Israel and the Gentiles, of women and the poor, of Samaritans and beggars. God offers them mercy and compassion. God is on the side of the poor beggar Lazarus, but not on the side of the rich property owner (Lk 16:19-31). God and money cannot both be served (Lk 16:14-15).

The Gospels do not condemn riches. They do not require that riches be relinquished or that the disciples become destitute. Instead they portray Jesus as a poor man on the cross, as one who entrusted his life to God. NT writings encourage Christians to share their wealth generously in order that poorer churches can survive. Sometimes this ideal is utopian (Acts 2:42-47 and 4:32-35); at other times it is practical (1 Cor 1:17-29; 2 Cor 8:1-9, 15). Urban Christians use their wealth to assist defenseless children, widows, and visitors.

When Christianity became the state religion, three approaches to material goods and wealth emerged. First, some Egyptian Christians left the city for the desert. Their poverty was radical. They renounced all possessions in order to follow the Lord totally. Antony lived with the essentials: a mat, a tunic, and a container of water. Second, Pachomius and his community shared essential goods. Third, Italian Christians used money to support scholars and to fund projects. In 386 Augustine retired to an estate to contemplate, to study, and to live the virtuous life. Paulinus of Nola relinquished his fortune in order to seek out a life of holy leisure (*otium honestum*). The originators of religious life did not reject wealth in order to espouse destitution; instead they advocated a sharing of possessions and used wealth to promote human and Christian development.

The Medieval Period

When medieval cities developed and banking and commerce began, a nuanced vocabulary developed in description of poverty. The poor were described as paupers and were objects of pity. They were those without food and clothing. The poor of the 13th and 14th centuries were people who were blind, lame, infirm, disabled, leprous, injured, feeble, mentally impaired, and weak. An ambivalence developed. When adversity left the poor vulnerable, the response was compassion. Poverty became idealized. The naked followed the naked Christ, the paupers followed the crucified Christ. But the poor were disdained as vulgar, dirty, lazy, delinquent, and criminal. They lacked power, strength, wealth, and civic liberty. Poor people became vagabonds and beggars. Poverty left them ill, humiliated, vulnerable, and powerless. Many died uprooted from their families and alone in their poverty. Others revolted.

Christian responses to poverty varied. Monks (9th century), hermits (11th century), and mendicants (13th century) gave direct aid to the poor. St. Francis and his mendicant friars possessed no property and became religious beggars. Their spirituality presented Jesus as one born poor and naked. Devotion to the naked Christ on the cross identified the mendicants with the poor and the powerless. Their solidarity with the poor became the antidote for an avaricious society. The friars assisted the poor and established lay confraternities to feed, clothe, and house the poor. Eventually hospitals became castles for the poor.

The Contemporary Period

By the year 2000 seventy percent of the world's Catholics will live in the Southern Hemisphere. Many of them already know the destitution of poverty. By the year 2000 many will know misery.

The bishops of these regions have already begun to address the poverty of their people. When the bishops of Latin America met at Medellín, Colombia, in 1969, they committed themselves to the poor. When the bishops of Latin America met at Puebla, Mexico, in 1979, they reaffirmed their commitment to a preferential, though not exclusive, option for the poor and the young. Furthermore, they identified the poor in their countries. The poor are native peoples. They are peasants, workers, women, uneducated children, and jobless youth. They are exploited farmers, day laborers, and immigrants. The bishops of Latin America invited the wealthy and the powerful to join in the struggle for liberation and redemption. Since these two meetings of Latin American bishops, the bishops of the United States and Canada have stated their preferential option for the poor.

The poor have become significant in teaching the Churches the memory of the passion (*memoria passionis*) as they develop small church communities. The poor have begun to tell their stories. These stories, which have been neglected, suppressed, forgotten, or denied, now serve to give voice to the victims of past oppression and the survivors of poverty today.

The experience and reflection of the poor have taught them to interpret their lives with the hope of the gospel and the solidarity of their lives together. Theologians of the Second and Third Worlds have begun to listen to the poor and their reflections. Theological reflection now sees the poor as privileged recipients of the gospel and God's special care. Both the poor and the theologians reject a Christian message that is aloof and distant from the plight of those living in poverty.

A Spirituality of Poverty

The voice of the poor is the voice of God. The faces of the poor are the faces of God. A spirituality of poverty demands that Christian communities act on behalf of the poor. This action combines three elements.

First, a spirituality of poverty requires an affective option for the poor. This means that Christians do nothing to oppress the poor. It means that Christian communities let the poor touch their hearts. This is reflected in the ways communities pray, the values they embrace, and the virtues they cultivate. A spirituality of poverty requires that Christians examine their lifestyles, their use of material goods, their hiring and salary policies, and their use of the earth's resources. It is reflected in the spirit of justice, welcome, and hospitality that communities show.

Second, a spirituality of poverty requires indirect effective action for the poor. Christian communities can live and act in ways that transform the structures of society. This can become concrete in five areas: economic action, personal study, advocacy, community education, and cross-cultural experience.

1. *Economic action*. Christian communities, when they have money, can keep their monies in banks that do not oppress the poor or that assist the poor through their policies and investments. Communities can support businesses that hire and train the poor, provide day care for single parents, and employ the disabled. Communities can support boycotts of unjust companies. They can develop a spirituality of poverty by diverting their monies from institutions that promote militarism and that use food as a weapon against poor nations. They can analyze the economic systems of their countries and act to transform those systems.

2. *Personal study*. Christian communities can begin to reflect on the Scriptures from the side of the poor. Members can begin to learn about the causes and experiences of poverty. They can ask themselves: How do the Scriptures teach us about the poor? How do the Scriptures sound when they are heard by the poor?

3. *Advocacy*. Christian communities can act on behalf of the poor by writing their congressional representatives, by joining citizens' action groups that lobby on behalf of the poor, and by contributing to grassroots groups that provide job training, housing, and health care for the poor.

4. *Community education*. Christian communities can learn about poverty and the poor through speakers, videos, and visitors who can inform them about other Christian communities and their struggle for structural transformation.

5. *Cross-cultural experience*. Christian communities can engage in action and in worship with other Christians to promote harmony and unity. This includes clothing drives, opening homes to students from other cultures, and sharing meals and conversation with the poor.

Third, a spirituality of poverty requires direct effective action for the poor. This hands-on involvement can mean community organizing, helping in soup kitchens, volunteering in nursing homes, tutoring poor children, working with the disabled, assisting immigrants, helping the poor obtain health care, and visiting the poor in prison. Christian communities can offer sanctuary and hospitality.

Conclusion

Poverty is an evil condition affecting millions of people and the economic-political systems in which they live. But poverty is also a religious value that motivates people to a simplicity of life, dedicated ministry, and a vision of the world based on the gospel. How poverty has shaped the lives of the poor and how it has motivated religious dedication have varied according to historical circumstances, charismatic insight, and practical action.

A spirituality of poverty will challenge the Churches to analyze the causes of poverty in their midst, to reflect and pray with the poor, and to continue indirect and direct effective action for the poor. A spirituality of poverty will enable them to hear the voice of God, to see the face of God, and to fulfill their vocation to fashion the reign of God.

See also CATHOLIC ACTION; CATHOLIC WORKER; CONFRONTATION AND PROTEST; ENVIRONMENT; FRANCISCAN SPIRITUALITY; LIBERATION THEOLOGY, INFLUENCE ON SPIRITUALITY; MARGINALIZED, THE; POOR, THE; RELIGIOUS LIFE; VOWS; WORLD.

Bibliography: D. Ellwood, *Poor Support: Poverty in the American Family* (New York: Basic Books, 1988). B. Gordon, *The Economic Problem in Biblical and Patristic Thought* (Leiden: Brill, 1989). J. Gonzalez, *Faith And Wealth: A History of Early Christian Ideas on the Origin, Significance, and Use of Money* (San Francisco: Harper & Row, 1990). G. Gutiérrez, *The Power of the Poor in History* (Maryknoll, N.Y.: Orbis, 1983). P. Henriot, *Opting for the Poor: A Challenge for North Americans* (Washington: Center of Concern, 1990). M. Lamb, *Solidarity with Victims: Toward a Theology of Social Transformation* (New York: Crossroad, 1982). M. Mollat, *The Poor in the Middle Ages: An Essay in Social History* (New Haven, Conn.: Yale Univ. Press, 1986).

JOHN J. O'BRIEN, C.P.

POWER

The most common definitions of power include the notion of agency, the ability to produce a change or to have an effect. These definitions of power link it to the correlative concept of authority, which connects the exercise of power to authorization and legitimation in the social process.

Power is understood by the social sciences to be both personal and social. Personal power refers to the capacity to influence another, which is an aspect of human personhood and which cannot be alienated. Societies have various ways of agreeing to specific power arrangements. Contemporary social analysis and critiques of power arrangements from the perspective of the poor, the marginalized, or the oppressed reveal that even these groups are capable of exerting "the powers of the weak," which in turn can influence social processes. When exercised, the powers of the weak result in empowerment and liberation.

Because of the long association of power with dominative authority and its ability to corrupt those who exercise it and coerce those it subordinates, new definitions of power are emerging from the experiences of the "weak." Power is being viewed as a process of interaction between persons rather than as a quality possessed by individuals. Power is further viewed in a differentiated way by the ways these interactions both create or threaten human community and enhance or restrict the growth of persons.

One example of an expanded schema of power as a process has been developed by Rollo May. One can employ this schema as an analysis of both personal power and social power and its effects on persons. May distinguishes five forms of the exercise of power:

1) Exploitative power depends on force and involves power *over* others.

2) Manipulative power relies on psychological means to gain power *over* another. These first two kinds of power involve domination and inequality.

3) Competitive power is a contest among equals and involves power *against* another.

4) Nutrient power involves temporary or permanent inequality of status in the relationship but is power used *for* the benefit of another in such cases as parenting, healing, and some forms of ministry.

5) Integrative power relies on mutual influence and the cooperative freedom of the parties involved and is power *with* others (*Power and Innocence,* New York: Norton, 1972, pp. 105–121).

These definitions and analyses of power coming from the social sciences and Marxist analysis generally consider power to be a fact of social life and morally neutral, if not positive.

Christianity has offered critiques of exploitative and manipulative power as it operates in the social order, particularly in politics and economics. According to the Bible, all power belongs to God and originates in God (Mt 6:13; 26:64). Human power is participation in God's power and confronts us with the choice of using that power in the service of our neighbor and for the care of the earth or for prideful self-assertion. Abuse of this freedom is so common an experience of personal and social sin that theological and spiritual authors frequently assume that any exercise of power is sinful instead of carefully analyzing the way it is exercised. Although the exercise of power is corrupting, according to Lord Acton, so too is the unwillingness to exercise power.

Through Jesus, God reveals how power is to be exercised within the human community and particularly within the Church. In Jesus the power of love is lived out to the death, evoking a community of mutual service and care; by him the destructive and dehumanizing forms of power are dethroned, if not annihilated. Jesus' own ministry takes place in the power (*exousia* or *dynamis*) of the spirit, a suasive and noncoercive manifestation of divine power proclaiming a message of liberation, forgiveness, and healing, especially to those who are abandoned, sinful, sick, and oppressed. All four Gospels clearly indicate that power in the kingdom of God is to replace existing structures of domination and oppression with the power of service and freedom, the power of love and the gifts of the Spirit, even if that means suffering and seeming powerlessness or weakness (Mt 20:20-28; Mk 10:35-45; Lk 12:50; 22:24-27; Jn 13:4-5, 13-17).

Within the history of the Catholic spiritual tradition, the exercise of power was considered at best to be ambiguous and at worst a manifestation of sin and incompatible with the gospel qualities of humility, service, weakness, and patient suffering. Up until the last twenty years, the meaning attached to power and its exercise has been that of domination or coercion, a characteristic of "the world" and an indication of ambition, and therefore to be renounced, abdicated, and avoided by true Christians. In absolute necessity power could be exercised as a burden laid upon those charged with the duty of office. Notable exceptions to this attitude toward power were the knightly orders and the crusades as a form of spiritual pilgrimage in the medieval period.

The 4th-century ascetical movement rejected not only the exercise of civil authority but of ecclesiastical power as well. "The beginning of the thought of the love of command is ordination" (Pachomius). The relationship of neophyte to elder was based on the authority of charism and the experience of the elder. Western monasticism provided a structure for its members to renounce power and authority for those who were not officeholders through the monastic vows. However, the office of abbot or abbess conferred total dominative authority over all persons as well as over all temporalities in the monastery. Cistercian documents attest to the ambivalence such power created for those who found themselves invested with such authority, when they preferred to see themselves as spiritual leaders who had left "the world."

While Christians who had embraced some form of the religious life in these early centuries were clear in their rejection of power and avoided positions of authority, the institutional Church embraced the prevailing models of authority and power with enthusiasm, replicating all the governmental mechanisms of the empire. The institutional Church attempted to Christianize the social role of the knight by consecrating the warring profession to the service of the gospel. At first this took the form of protecting the widow and the orphan, then protecting pilgrims to the Holy Land, and finally conducting the holy war to free the pilgrimage sites. Eventually the crusade was used by the papacy to combat heresy and to extend papal political control. Thus a pervasive ambivalence about the wielding of power is inherent in Christian tradition. One resolution of this tension emphasized the necessity of authority and restricted the formal exercise of power within the Church to clerical elites, while laypersons were to obey this authority and voluntarily relinquish power whenever possible in imitation of Jesus' teaching and example.

Contemporary social analysis and liberation theology serve the ecclesial community through their critique of abuses of power within the Christian community (L. Boff, *Church: Charism and Power,* New York: Crossroad, 1985, pp. 49–56). The exercise of dominative power within the Christian community was largely legitimated through appeals to the household codes, which accepted the current social view of authority. The elaboration of the medieval papacy further consolidated an absolute exercise of power in a central bureaucracy. Hence, virtually all authority and exercise of power were vested in the papacy and its curia by divine right, and the appropriate role of all others in the Church was to submit in obedience, humility, and service. This exalted view of ecclesial authority managed to mystify the actual exercise of power within the Church and maintained within its members an often uncritical acquiescence to this use of power and a flight from the exercise of other forms of power through a spirituality that valued such uncritical obedience and humble service as practically ultimate values in the spiritual life.

Contemporary spirituality, influenced by Vatican II and recent social teachings such as *Justice in the World,* is increasingly embracing a more nuanced view of power. Following the gospel witness, the exercise of power, especially dominative and manipulative power, is subject to critique. Karl Rahner developed a theology of power in which he offered several theses for an understanding of dominative power and the responsibilities of Christians in its exercise. "Power, including physical force . . . is not itself sin but a gift of God, an expression of [God's] power" (Rahner, p. 395). However, our experience of power is often ambiguous. It is affected by concupiscence and therefore is a kind of power that ought never have existed, because it stems from sin and is a form in which guilt manifests itself. Nonsinful power would address itself to the free decision of the other in an appeal to insight and love.

The spiritual task, as Rahner sees it, is that sinful power is "gradually to be overcome, it is something to be fought against by means of spirit, love and grace" (*ibid.,* p. 394). He further sees that power is the condition of possibility of freedom. Power and freedom are mutually and dialectically interdependent. Hence he rejects a principle of absolute renunciation of dominative power. It is permissible and good to exercise even this kind of power in good faith for others in order to achieve a morally justified end. However, this use of power requires great restraint because it is often used to rule rather than serve, to assert oneself at the expense of others, and to deceive oneself as well as others. For Rahner, power "*exists* either as the embodiment of sin, egoism, and rebellion against God . . . *or* as the effort of faith which knows that power is always unreliable and unrewarding, but accepted obediently as a task from God as long as he wills" (*ibid.,* p. 409).

As Christian reflection on power progresses, a variety of responses have appeared within the community. Most people are comfortable with nutrient power as an expression of service. However, even nutrient power can become oppressive when its exercise keeps another in a position of servitude by not allowing temporary inequality to be overcome. Relationships of domination and subordination can result from the abuse of nutrient power when the dominants presume that the subordinates are permanently incapable of overcoming this inequality, as in the relationship of slaveholders to slaves, clergy to laity, men to women, or one race to another. Hence, among adults "power with" is to be preferred to "power for" or "power over" whenever possible.

Some continue to relinquish dominative power voluntarily through reinterpreting the formal vows of religion (poverty, chastity, and obedience) as a preferential option for the poor, sharing the powerlessness of the oppressed, and contributing to their empowerment. Many lay Christians embrace activities of peacemaking, mission work, and other forms of social action that involve gospel-inspired nonviolent action for social change rather than methods that require force.

A critical relationship to one's exercise of power is, moreover, a spiritual task for all Christians. There are many sources of power: wealth, education, elective or appointive office, reputation, organizational skill, control of information, and personal gifts. Each Christian is responsible for his or her exercise of power on behalf of the human community and the enhancement of the personhood of others within his or her spheres of power. All Christians are called to live their lives in the service of the kingdom of God and the values of the gospel regardless of their particular settings. It is through the critical exercise of power that one inhabits more fully one's humanity, empowers others as well as oneself, responds to the power of Jesus' spirit within the community, and effects change in the world.

See also AUTHORITY; CHARISM; CHURCH; LIBERATION THEOLOGY, INFLUENCE ON SPIRITUALITY; LOVE; PEACE; SERVICE; WAR, IMPACT ON SPIRITUALITY.

Bibliography: K. Rahner, "The Theology of Power," *Theological Investigations* 4, trans. K. Smyth (Baltimore: Helicon, 1966) 391–409. Catholic Theological Society of America, "Power as an Issue in Theology," *Proceedings*, vol. 37 (1982). J. Provost and K. Walf, eds., *Power in the Church*, Concilium 197 (Edinburgh: T. & T. Clark, 1988). E. Janeway, *Powers of the Weak* (New York: Knopf, 1980).

JANET K. RUFFING, R.S.M.

PRAXIS

The primacy of the term *praxis* has replaced the importance of the term *existence* or even *experience* in most contemporary theology. Traditionally translated as action or doing, the term *praxis* in recent years has come to signify intentional social activity and the need for emancipatory transformation. The new primacy of the term in theology derives from three sources: first of all, an orientation in much theology to structural and cultural crises such as poverty, the Holocaust, sexism, racism, and psychic destructiveness. Secondly, the primacy of the term *praxis* arises from the influence of various contemporary theories that stress the importance of praxis in terms of the social situatedness of reason, the cultural-structural formation of anthropology and history, and historical aims of freedom. Thirdly, praxis is important due to renewed attention in Christian theology to faith as not only an existential or inward experience but as the embodied activity of Christian faith and its communal character in transforming situations and experiences of suffering into those of freedom.

Praxis is a term with much richness and multiplicity of meaning in contemporary theology and theory. It suggests the horizon of doing or activity, the primacy of understanding intersubjectivity and the structural nature of anthropology and history. Such formal characteristics of praxis are, in the present situation, often combined with a normative claim for freedom in relation to change and transformation both in terms of specific crises in society and the world. The claim for freedom expressing itself through concerns for transformation in terms of social structures, cultural forms, and individual existence forms a structuring horizon of emancipatory transformation in contemporary theology. The formal nature of praxis as the historical situatedness of reason and the emphasis on practical activity combines with the material nature of praxis as emancipatory transformation to make theology a guide to the ongoing transformation of Christian praxis.

Indeed, if there is a current paradigm shift going on in contemporary theology, as much literature indicates, praxis, as well as any other term, signifies this new paradigm. In contemporary theology the term *praxis* achieved popularity through the emergence of liberation theologies. Latin American liberation theology calls for theology to be a critical reflection on liberating praxis, while German political theology examines the priority of praxis over theory, and black theology addresses the embodiment of spirituality and social witness in the civil rights movement. Though the term may have been popularized through liberation theologies, the same concerns and issues appeared in other forms of contemporary theology. The concern for new forms of "practical theology" in the United States and Europe attempts to find new forms of reflection on practice, and various forms of pastoral theology expand the dimensions of pastoral practice to structural relations and concerns for transforming human life.

Revisionist theologies, concerned with correlating contemporary human experience and Christian tradition, have moved both to attend to practical theology and to incorporate a concern for ethics and social transformation in fundamental and systematic theologies. Current phenomenological theologies, such as that represented by Ed Farley, rely heavily upon social phenomenology to inquire into corporate structures and upon phenomenological hermeneutics to interpret and construct structures of meaning. Postliberal theologies, heavily influenced by the work of George Lindbeck, also include a concern for praxis as the understanding of religion in terms of a cultural-linguistic system and interpreting theology as a grammar of faith, thus addressing issues of praxis in terms of the activity of language and culture as symbolic structures. In theologies influenced by the American pragmatic tradition, such as represented by Francis Schüssler Fiorenza, there is great attention to the reconstructing of Christian tradition as the praxis of theology.

Many theologians draw on a variety of these schools of method to construe new ways of doing theology that attend to Christian faith as a liberating praxis addressing the crucial concerns of our day, such as sexism, racism, the threat of nuclear war, and psychic destructiveness. For instance, Elisabeth Schüssler Fiorenza draws upon revisionist, liberation, and pragmatic methods of praxis to offer a new understanding of the Bible as prototype rather than archetype, a new role for the Bible and tradition in theology through the notion of rhetoric as persuasive action, and a new description of theology as working out of pastoral-hermeneutical concerns while addressing the concrete concerns of sexism in the Christian tradition and Church. Cornel West has relied on pragmatism, hermeneutics, and poststructuralism to criticize the symbolic and political structures of racism and to formulate a prophetic tradition of critical inquiry in North America.

History of the Term

The concern for praxis goes back to Greek philosophy and is related to the question "How do we live a good life?" Aristotle may have been the first Greek philosopher to use the term *praxis* to refer to business and political life, or the life of the *polis* as one dimension of the good life. Such activity, for Aristotle, is characterized by purpose, desire, and reasoning related to some end. Since praxis is carried out in the realm of the political and business activities, praxis has to do with things that are indeterminate or "that which could be other." The ability to make the necessary prudential judgments in variable situations Aristotle called *phronēsis*, or practical reasoning. *Phronēsis* is distinct from knowledge as *epistēmē* and knowledge as *technē*. *Epistēmē* is the knowledge of the realm of *theōria*, the domain of science and the contemplation of the unchanging. *Technē* is the knowledge involved in *poēsis*, the production of human artifacts. The term *praxis* has to do with how humans live together in the *polis* with purpose and direction, cultivating a particular type of reason (*phronēsis*) that has to do with judgment, character, and insight.

The meaning of the term *praxis* began to shift from Aristotle's usage with the Neoplatonists in the 2nd to the 4th century, who separated the act of contemplation from theory, allowing a contemplative union with the Absolute. Political life, and thus the realm of praxis, came to be seen as a lesser life. Such life in the *polis* could, at best, for a thinker such as Plotinus, help with the perfection of virtues necessary for the contemplative life.

Christian theology, to some extent, followed the Neoplatonists by elevating the contemplation of God as the good life. Yet the philosophical priority on the contemplation of God did not fit easily with Christian mandates about love of neighbor, charity, and the doing of Christian witness. In general, early theologians decided that most Christians have to live a life of practice in terms of good deeds and specific acts (not the full sense of praxis in determining life together in the *polis*) and hope to achieve contemplation in the afterlife. A certain hierarchy of spiritual positions thus ensued, since those in religious orders had better opportunities to join together for a life of contemplative union and active charity. Augustine, so influential for Western Christian theology, taught that no one way to God is the best, but what matters is the balance of contemplating God and acts of charity, no matter what one's place or activity.

Despite Augustine's teaching that every Christian life requires the balance of contemplation and charity, spirituality came increasingly to refer to the contemplative life of the Christian, while acts of charity were seen as merely the Christian's responsibility while in the world. Thus the role of spirituality and contemplative life from the 5th through the 12th century became increasingly the realm of ascetical and mystical theology. Praxis no longer answered the question of how to live the good life in terms of life in the *polis*, but referred to the demands of faith while on the temporary journey of this world.

With the translation of Aristotle in the 12th and 13th centuries, Christian theologians considered anew the active life, since Aristotle's stress seems so strongly to be not on the saintly life but on all human activities. Duns Scotus explicitly returned to the term *praxis*, defining it to mean intentional human activity that may be morally right or wrong, but outside the realm of ethics. Indeed, Duns Scotus argued that theology should be a practical knowledge, that God is the "doable knowable" (*cognoscibile operabile*), for we should seek God through love and not theory.

Another way praxis is reintroduced in medieval theology is the attention to the relation between theoretical and practical knowledge. Medieval thinkers such as Aquinas began to develop the notion that practical truth is an extension of theoretical truth. Now praxis and theory were related not so much as opposite ways of life or dimensions of human activity as by way of extension, so that praxis is the application of theory. Medieval thinkers strengthened the role of theory as discursive knowledge, largely forgotten since Greek philosophy, and stressed practical knowledge as the knowledge of making and producing.

With the rise of modern science, theory is fashioned along a model of deductive propositions, modeled after mathematical propositions. Knowledge in general is subsumed under this model, including the knowledge of politics and ethics. John Locke, for instance, argued that moral and political knowledge are similar, in shape and status, to the theorems of geometry.

In Kant, the distinction between the theoretical and the practical has to do not with ends but with subject matters. The theoretical in Kant's *Critique of Pure Reason* has to do with the realm of the phenomena, explicating the concepts of nature, while the practical in his *Metaphysics of Morals* and *Critique of Practical Reason* deals with the realm of the noumena, postulating the concepts of freedom. The noumena has to do with that which is beyond our experiences, which takes on the character of an ideal. The practical comes to mean that which ought to be, a normative ideal, rather than the indeterminacy of human situation or the application of the theoretical.

Hegel denies Kant's distinction between the phenomena and noumena, and thus the theoretical and the practical, arguing that reason (*Vernunft*) unfolds and realizes itself in history. The tracing out of the unfolding of reason is the task of philosophy; in a sense for Hegel, theory recognizes in practice the unfolding of realization of reason. In criticizing Kant's understanding of freedom as formally empty, Hegel argues that freedom occurs only in existence, as a form of activity. But because Hegel believes that philosophy is the self-consciousness of completed history, of reason unfolding, practical philosophy is negated.

After Hegel, left-wing Hegelian interpreters criticized Hegel for merely resonating with the status quo and attempted to find ways to understand practice, not as the unfolding of reason, but as an activity of human history. Count August Cieszkowski criticized Hegel for only offering a retrospective interpretation of history, arguing that philosophy ought instead to anticipate and predict the future. Being able to achieve absolute knowledge in theory, Cieszkowski suggested, persons must now govern practice, organizing society around the ideas of absolute knowledge. Ludwig Feuerbach radicalized the left-wing Hegelians by criticizing Hegel for giving priority to predicates instead of subjects, insisting that Hegel absolutized predicates which really belong to the human subject. Indeed, Feuerbach argued that the splitting off of predicates and projecting them onto an Absolute resulted in alienation. Though Feuerbach is little concerned with praxis, his critique of Hegel's idealism and his concern for alienation create the space for reintroducing the social-historical nature of praxis and a new type of concern for the realization of freedom.

Marx, as a young left-wing Hegelian, accepted the radical historical grounding of theory and praxis, but radicalized this to not be based in the human subject, as in Feuerbach, but in the societal foundation of all life and knowledge. In "The German Ideology," Marx argues that humanity produced the first historical act in the production of the means of subsistence. The mode of production is a definite form of the expression of human life. Humanity produces the means to satisfy a need, which in turn creates new needs. Humanity also reproduces the species. The production of life, both of one's own labor and of new life, appears as a double relation in which a certain mode of production is always combined with a certain stage of cooperation. In this way, consciousness is a social product.

For Marx, alienation arises as the force of production, the state of society, and consciousness come into contradiction with one another. Like Cieszkowski, Marx suggests that philosophy's task, to cite his famous thesis number eleven, is not to interpret history but to change it. Yet Marx never leaves his Hegelian roots completely, arguing that history passes through stages of evolution, which would allow philosophy really to only passively bring about what inevitably must happen.

In a sense, Marx summarizes the ideas, at times even contradictory ideas, associated with the concept of praxis in Western thought: purposive action, normative freedom, historical constitutive nature of reason, governing ability of reason, indeterminacy of social praxis, the desire for how the good life ought to be. In some ways Marx returns knowledge, as in *phronēsis,* to history and activity, and explicates history and activity as a way of knowledge. Yet Marx also represents an enormous distance from the original concerns for praxis in Aristotle in his insistence that praxis is where all knowledge begins and to which freedom is directed. For Aristotle, praxis has to do with indeterminacy and thus requires a practical reason plus a virtuous character that can provide appropriate judgment, while for Kant praxis has to do with the real of the ideal, with the normative conception of freedom, which ought then to be applied in particular situations. The history of the term *praxis,* it can be said, provides both a set of concerns and rich resources for the continued construction of intentional historical action.

Contemporary Theories of Praxis

In current philosophical theory, the concerns and resources of praxis enjoy enormous popularity. Indeed, most current theories assume the historical situatedness of reason, a position of nonfoundationalism. Nonfoundationalism is the belief that there is no transcendental term, outside the limits of reason or history, that secures or grounds all knowledge. Rather, we must begin our knowledge the only place we can begin it, in the here and now of praxis, formulating our critique, interpretation, and transformation based on our human, historical reasons and judgments. Yet most theories also suggest that the priority of praxis is not a move to absolute relativism, to a position that anything can be proven or "anything goes." For praxis, the present historical construction of reason and action also provide norms, albeit always already interpreted, for human knowledge, activity, and transformation. Current theories of praxis draw upon a wide range of resources to express a variety of concerns with norms for historical action, the relation of interpretation and transformation, and the understanding of the social and human subjectivity.

Hermeneutics focuses on the importance of tradition as providing us lenses for experiencing the world and criteria for judgment. For Hans Georg Gadamer, hermeneutics is a form of *phronēsis,* practical wisdom, in interpreting the past in light of specific problems or situations. Gadamer argues that hermeneutics names who human beings are, engaged in the ongoing activity of living out of traditions that both provide the perimeters of how humans experience themselves but are themselves continually changed and transformed through history.

Critical theory continues, in some sense, Marx's insistence on the continuing critique of praxis, concentrating on systematic distortion and false ideologies in normative social practices. In the thought of someone like Jurgen Habermas, critical theories are a sort of social therapy of praxis, seeking to move human agents to more advanced dimensions of enlightenment. Some forms of critical theory rely heavily on some type of "quasi" transcendental norms of freedom or interest that are abstracted from and can govern concrete situations. Other forms of critical theory are more contextual, using forms of nonidentity such as contradictions or breaks in cultural norms, social practices, and philosophical ideas to reveal distortions of interests, power, and knowledge.

Pragmatism is a North American philosophical system focusing on philosophy as nonepistemological, that is, not primarily involved in the nature of reason as such and oriented to social issues and problems. Charles Sanders Pierce, John Dewey, and William James, pragmatism's historical figures, stressed in various ways the present and future social effectiveness of ideas and reason. In the contemporary retrieval of pragmatism, philosophy is seen as a form of critical inquiry, set in a community of inquirers and aimed at cultural criticism and transformation.

Neo-Kantianism expresses itself primarily in the discipline of ethics, attempting to continue the concern for morality and normative conceptions of freedom. In the thought of John Rawls, the normative dimension is arrived at through the principle of "impartiality" by assuming that one does not know one's position in history and must make ethical judgments behind an imaginary veil of ignorance of any particular knowledge about oneself. Such disinterested impartiality is seen as the essence of practical, moral reasoning.

Poststructuralism concentrates on the changing meaning of cultural signs and how symbols and language constitute human consciousness. Perhaps one of the greatest contributions of poststructuralists lies in their expanding the indeterminacy of praxis into the dimension of human consciousness and language. Poststructuralists have been especially attentive to how structures of power through cultural mediation constitute human meaning and signification. Praxis in this sense is extended into constituting consciousness and is attended to in the symbolic and linguistic realms.

Theological Signification

The term *praxis* refers to many different issues and concerns in theory and in theology. It is, therefore, impossible to give a precise meaning to the term. What is possible, however, is to discuss the variety of ways, across various theologies, in which the term *praxis* signifies and forms basic theological concepts. These theological concepts all rest on the assumption, in contemporary theology, that Christianity is a praxis, an intentional historical activity that is ongoing and changing, but nonetheless reconstructing or retrieving its rich and varied tradition and working for emancipatory transformation.

Christian faith is itself a doing, not merely a being or an experiencing. The doing of Christian faith occurs in at least three senses. First, faith itself is an activity, a praxis of solidarity with God or a way of following Christ in the world. The basic metaphors for faith are ones of activity and doing in the sense of praxis. The scriptures often cited in contemporary theology underscore the doing of faith, and the relation of salvation and emancipatory transformation such as the doing of faith in 1 Jn 3:16-18, the public announcement of Jesus's liberating ministry in Lk 4:16-19, and the Jubilee traditions in Deuteronomy, Exodus, Jeremiah, and Isaiah.

Second, faith is decentered from individual meanings to communal activity. Clearly in liberation theology, with the stress on women Church, basic Christian community, and the black Church, the community of faith as the place where activity is centered is stressed. But community, the ongoing active life of community, also receives high priority with a phenomenological theologian such as Ed Farley, who speaks of the ongoing interpretation of ecclesial community as the basic task of theology.

Third, much of contemporary theology envisions some type of Christian "orthopraxis" directed toward the realization or constitution of freedom in history. Here praxis invokes not only the concern of how to live the good life as in Aristotle but also concerns for normative freedom, the "what ought to be" of the Enlightenment tradition. Christian praxis is oriented toward transformation of historical conditions for realization of freedom. For instance, Latin American theologian Gustavo Gutiérrez suggests that Christianity is transformed through the movements of liberating praxis among the poor in Latin America, making Christianity into a praxis of liberating activity serving as a sign of God's gratuitous activity in history. North American theologian Schubert Ogden, to take a quite different perspective, offers a Christology of liberation to answer the contemporary existential-historical quest for freedom.

Interpretation of Scripture and tradition demonstrates the full force of the turn to praxis in much contemporary theology. On the one hand, Scripture and tradition are treated formally, not as the repository of unquestionable truths or as containing kernels of existential meanings, but as narratives or prototypes of how the Church has attempted to form a language for its community and to address its life together and its life in the world. On the other hand, a great deal of fresh interpretive and historical work has occurred in recent years through the Scripture and tradition by reading it through the contemporary quests for emancipatory transformation. For instance, black theology has added to the "standard" or "classical" theological tradition in North American Christianity thinkers such as W.E.B. Du Bois, Zora Neale Hurston, Martin Luther King, Jr., and Malcolm X, and has questioned the ways in which the tradition of North American Euro-Anglo theology has contributed to, allowed, or resisted racism. Likewise, the concerns of emancipatory transformation have led to a great deal of new attention to biblical and historical perspectives on the poor and oppressed, on women, on issues of slavery. Scripture and tradition form primary sources for theology and the activity of Christian faith by providing, through ongoing construction, a way of construing identity and a way of disclosing relevance: to use a linguistic metaphor, a sense of grammar and a sense of meaning.

Anthropology and history have radically altered with the turn to praxis. Modern theology followed the anthropological turn

of Enlightenment thought, tending to secure the individual existentially or at least privately with a relationship to God prior to, outside, or underneath the historical activities of the subject. In a way, the present praxis paradigm continues the anthropological turn of modern theology but transforms it through an anthropology that is far more historically constituted and one that is decentered in terms of acknowledging the importance of relationships, social structures, and language in and through which the individual is constituted. For instance, Johannes Baptist Metz, a leading Roman Catholic political theologian and student of Karl Rahner, in some ways took Rahner's fundamental anthropological stance and replaced its implicit idealism with an intentional orientation to praxis. For Metz, the subject has three related characteristics: (1) the human subject is fully constituted in a particular historical situation; (2) the human subject is an active agent in which there is possibility for reflective thought; and (3) freedom has an anticipatory structure in the human subject.

History has, in general, played an important role in Christian theology. In contemporary theology, history is not the arena in which we toil away awaiting "real" Christian salvation after our death, nor is it the stage through which we experience our individual faith relation with God and, in some secondary moment, express it through ethical action or Christian witness. Rather, history constitutes us, it is open to us, and we have responsibility for how our own particular historical situation is structured and experienced. Much of Latin American liberation theology, for instance, stresses the tensive relationship between liberation and salvation in history, arguing that while salvation is never complete in history, it is realized through liberating activity, and indeed history must be seen as itself a project of liberation. Again, it is easy to see the formal claim of praxis operating, in that history is constitutive, that social structures and cultural systems make us who we are; it is also important to see the normative claim associated with praxis: history is open, should be constructed for freedom, and must be transformed always from systems and structures of oppression and destruction.

Spirituality is also being understood through the lens of praxis, with renewed interest in performing spiritual disciplines, in social witness as itself a form of spirituality, with understanding Christianity as a mystical and political faith. Certainly in black theology, and in the work of the black Church, the civil rights movement was seen as an intense form of embodying spirituality. Likewise, in feminist theology the exercise of consciousness-raising, the claiming of one's oppression, and the struggle of women to speak and write their own life with God are intensely spiritual. Rosemary Radford Ruether, for instance, begins and ends her volume in systematic theology, *Sexism and God-Talk: Toward a Feminist Systematic Theology,* with two pieces of spiritual prose—one a feminist midrash on the gospel, and the other an icon of the divine. Ruether's concentrated effort to focus on women's spirituality and liturgy occurs in her book *Women-Church,* where she examines the power of women's spiritual experience despite the strictures of the institutional Church and offers new forms of liturgies for women's experiences.

Increasingly, theologians address the material structural crisis in the world and the spiritual crisis as problems that are co-present and must be addressed. Indeed, for many contemporary theologians spirituality names the fullness of Christian praxis in prayer, liturgy, action, reflection, fellowship, and service.

The purposes, sources, and nature of theology are also transformed through praxis. First, theology is seen as the interpretation and transformation of praxis, that is to say, theory occurs in a tensive relationship to the praxis of Christianity. In the movement of practical theology, the purpose of theology is understood to be the attention to, and transformation of, practices, situations, and events. Political theology defines theology as a critical praxis correlation, with praxis as both the foundation and the aim of theology.

For much theology, its role in reflecting on praxis has meant the addition of social science disciplines, especially sociology, political theory, and economics. Latin American liberation theology has received great notoriety for its dialogue with Marxism. Part of that dialogue has been an effort to find a way to dialogue with sociology appropriate to the Latin American situation. José Miguez Bonino, for instance, though critical of a great deal of Marxism, finds its sociological analysis potentially more illustrative than the functional sociology so popular in the First World. Feminist theology increasingly attends to political theory in terms of how political theory contributed to modern forms of patriarchy in establishing the realms of the public and private, assigning those realms to men and women respectively, and dividing knowledge to men in the public realm and religion to women in the private realm. Black theology in the United States dialogues with economics, especially as racism shifts its locus of oppression from legislative practices to economic practices. Among debates in practical theology the social sciences are used to describe a person's experience and to relate the descriptive analysis of experience to the normative dimensions of religious experience.

The normative claims of praxis concerning emancipatory transformation entail the use of critical theories in theology. Certainly many liberation theologies include a dimension of ideology critique as they call to question prevailing beliefs, attitudes, and structures about racism and sexism. Theologians addressing issues such as nuclear reality, consumerism, and environmental destruction have also found it necessary to employ ideology critiques to help question the relation of interests, power, and knowledge. Likewise, various Christian symbols have become powerful tools of ideology critique as God becomes a way to call to question human usurpation of power to determine life or death. For example, the symbol of creation stands for a view of living with the planet rather than destroying it. In a sense, theology itself is a form of critical theory, a knowledge of freedom, aimed at emancipation and transformation.

Finally, the nature of theology, that is, how theology itself is understood, is defined through praxis. Theology is far more contextual in the contemporary period, more attentive to itself as a particular historical reflection arising in a concrete time and place with all the respective limits and horizons. Much contemporary theology has a "problem" locus, what the pragmatists would associate with addressing particular ills or problems of the public. For instance, Gordon Kaufmann addresses the issue of nuclear devastation, and Sallie McFague addresses the crucial context and issue of ecological deterioration of the earth.

Theology is also much more oriented to a type of practical reason, *phronēsis* or wisdom. Hermeneutical theologians such as David Tracy emphasize, following Hans Georg Gadamer, the role of *phronēsis* in interpreting tradition in light of some particular situation, insisting upon the importance of judgment. Phenomenologists such as Ed Farley speak of the role of *habitus* in theology, accentuating being formed in the wisdom of the Christian tradition. Postliberal theologians such as Charles Wood talk about theology's task as vision and discernment, the vision of the whole of existence and the discernment of particular issues, problems, doctrines.

In sum, praxis serves to speak of a new way of envisioning spirituality and theology, of viewing human subjects and history, of configuring Christian faith and symbols, and of speaking to the crisis of structural and psychic suffering in the contemporary situation.

See also FEMINIST SPIRITUALITY; FREEDOM; HISTORY, HISTORICAL CONSCIOUSNESS; LIBERATION THEOLOGY, INFLUENCE ON SPIRITUALITY; SOLIDARITY; VIRTUE.

Bibliography: R. Bernstein, *Praxis and Action: Contemporary Philosophies of Human Activity* (Philadelphia: Univ. of Pennsylvania Press, 1971). D. Browning, *Religious Ethics and Pastoral Care* (Philadelphia: Fortress, 1983). R. Chopp, *The Praxis of Suffering: An Interpretation of Liberation and Political Theologies* (Maryknoll, N.Y.: Orbis, 1986). E. Schüssler Fiorenza, *Bread Not Stone: The Challenge of Feminist Biblical Interpretation* (Boston: Beacon Press, 1984). F. Schüssler Fiorenza, *Foundational Theology: Jesus and the Church* (New York: Crossroad, 1984). N. Lobkowicz, *Theory and Practice: History of a Concept from Aristotle to Marx* (Notre Dame, Ind.: Univ. of Notre Dame Press, 1967). J. B. Metz, *Faith in History and Society: Toward a Practical Fundamental Theology*, trans. D. Smith (New York: Seabury, 1980). L. Mudge and J. Poling, eds., *Formation and Reflection: The Promise of Practical Theology* (Philadelphia: Fortress, 1987). S. Ogden, *The Point of Christology* (San Francisco: Harper & Row, 1982). C. West, *The American Evasion of Philosophy: A Genealogy of Pragmatism* (Madison, Wis.: Univ. of Wisconsin Press, 1989).

REBECCA S. CHOPP

PRAYER

Etymology and Meaning

The English word *prayer* means literally a petition or request. It comes from the Latin verb *precari*, which means "to entreat or beg." Although the word may be used to mean a petition made to anyone at all, its customary use is both more particular (made to God or some holy person reigning with God) and more comprehensive (every communing with God, whether in explicit petition or in any other way). This more comprehensive use points to the fact that human beings always stand in need before God, even in moments of joyful gratitude or the highest reaches of mystical prayer. Even when petition is not the central activity, it is always implicit in any kind of prayer to God.

In the Hebrew of the OT, the most common verb meaning "to pray" is the reflexive form of *pâlal*, meaning literally "to mediate" or "intercede." But although this means "to pray for another," it is used in the more general sense of simply "to pray," e.g., "Hannah prayed and said, 'My heart exults in the Lord'" (1 Sam 2:1, NRSV). Other Hebrew words that are translated into English as "pray" give some of the flavor of OT prayer. One of these indicates a bodily posture: *tsela,* whose root meaning is "bend" or "bow down" ("Pray for the life of the king and his sons"—Ezra 6:10). A number of other words translated "pray" or "make supplication" mean basically "to ask." They are *bea* ("[Daniel] continued . . . to get down on his knees three times a day to pray to his God and praise him"—Dan 6:10, NRSV); *athar* ("when they entreat you in the land of their captivity"—2 Chr 6:37); and *shaal* ("Pray for the peace of Jerusalem!"—Ps 122:6). (For more information on this, see McKenzie, p. 686.)

In NT Greek the most common word for "pray" is *euchomai* or, more frequently with a prefix, *proseuchomai.* The root meaning of the verb is connected with "wish" or "vow." The prefix *pros* has the force of "toward." The NT also uses *deomai,* meaning "want"; *erōtaō,* meaning "ask"; and *parakaleō,* meaning "call for."

Nature of Prayer as Personal Address

What most fundamentally characterizes the activity of prayer is that we somehow address God in the second person as "thou" or "you," and do not just think about or speak of God in the third person as "he" or "she." Even when no words are spoken, when one's whole conscious attitude is simply attentive openness, God is the term or focus of that attention in a personal relationship of union or communion. It is not just a question of saying "you," for one can seem to address even totally inanimate things in the second person, as John Keats does in his "Ode on a Grecian Urn." Nor is God addressed simply in imagination, as I might mentally carry on a conversation with the author of a book I am

reading. Prayer occurs when in all sober truth and reality my mind and heart are directed toward God, addressing him as a personal center.

Addressing God in this way, we should note, is actually responding personally to one who has already personally addressed us. For in prayer it is God, not we, who takes the initiative. The image of Christ in the Book of Revelation accurately sums up this insight into prayer: "Listen! I am standing at the door, knocking; if you hear my voice and open the door, I will come in to you and eat with you, and you with me" (Rev 3:20, NRSV).

Contemporary Problems

In 1923 Adolphe Tanquerey, S.S., defined prayer as "an elevation of our soul to God to offer Him our homage and ask His favors, in order to grow in holiness for His glory" (Tanquerey, p. 243). Some such understanding has always been behind the practice of prayer; and even when modern difficulties and objections were raised against it, the practice itself was for the most part self-authenticating, and people generally continued to pray as they always had.

But a number of the questions either raised in the modern period or urged in a new fashion do legitimately require answers, even though not much attention has been given to them. Books and other studies on prayer generally set forth the biblical, historical, and phenomenological aspects of prayer, giving much valuable guidance about how to proceed, about kinds, methods, and levels of prayer, but they do not attempt to get behind the metaphors for prayer or to explain how or why praying really makes any difference. That it does make a difference may well be a matter of experience, but how was this experience to be understood and justified?

Dealing with these questions about prayer is a truly crucial area of theology. Here faith in God is finally tested, and theology about God either yields some kind of coherent understanding or fails in its essential task. For in prayer we express what we believe about God and about our relationship to God. If we think that God listens to prayer and responds to it, if we believe that prayer really makes any difference in the way God acts in the world, our faith is consonant with biblical faith and we believe in a God who is personally concerned with creation and answers its cries for help. But if we think that prayer is simply a way of changing ourselves or an expression of frustration or some other kind of psychological urging, our faith is at odds with biblical faith and we believe that God is basically unconcerned about human need and unresponsive to it.

The main source of the difficulties and questions concerning prayer is "secularism," a spirit and an attitude that excludes God from the world (Latin *saeculum*). Secularism has a number of causes and manifestations, most of them good in themselves but subject to some distortions.

1) Most notable is the development of science and technology in the past century. Albert Einstein wrote about science and religion:

> The main source of the present-day conflicts between the spheres of religion and of science lies in this concept of a personal God. It is the aim of science to establish general rules which determine the reciprocal connections of objects and events in time and space. . . .
>
> The more a man is imbued with the ordered regularity of all events, the firmer becomes his conviction that there is no room left by the side of this ordered regularity for causes of a different nature. For him neither the rule of human nor the rule of divine will exists as an independent cause of natural events. To be sure, the doctrine of a personal God interfering with natural events could never be refuted, in the real sense, by science, for this doctrine

can always take refuge in those domains in which scientific knowledge has not yet been able to set foot ("Science and Religion II," *Out of My Later Years,* New York: Philosophical Library, 1950, pp. 27, 28).

But if God is not personal and actively present to us, how can we address God?

Technology is the application of science to controlling the world and bringing about the effects we desire. Successful technology induces an attitude of self-sufficiency, which can be very much at odds with the attitude of need and dependence that prayer implies. Hence the great technological revolution of the past century has caused many to be unwilling to take prayer seriously.

2) Another development that promotes a secularist spirit is the increased problem of evil in our century. World wars, genocide, starvation, oppression, disease, etc., make it difficult to recognize the presence of a God who is caring and powerful, to whom one could pray in praise or petition.

3) Some philosophers and theologians have unintentionally strengthened secularism by presenting a God who is nearly totally irrelevant to us. Divine immutability is taken to mean that God is utterly unaffected by anything we do, even by our prayers. If God is not dead, he certainly seems to be absent.

In these circumstances prayer, if it survives at all, can be interpreted largely as autosuggestion. Or else it is emotional release in intolerable situations, a cry, because one can no longer remain silent. Or since God is not affected by anything, it is just a way of adapting ourselves to what God has already determined to do.

Many people who have intense lives of prayer are not troubled by these problems, but others who desire to have intense lives of prayer are hindered by an inability to deal with them.

The Example and Teaching of Jesus

Before directly addressing these problems, we will consider the example and teaching of Jesus so that we may see what it is that we as Christians wish to affirm about the practice and meaning of prayer in the face of doubts, questions, and objections. For how Jesus prayed is the model for our prayer. What he taught about prayer is the core of our understanding of prayer.

The Example of Jesus

The example of Jesus that the primitive Christian community recalled and enshrined in the Gospels is that of a man of prayer. This in itself is not remarkable, since all the great men and women of the Bible were people of prayer. What is remarkable is the degree to which prayer belonged to the essence of Jesus' life and mission. It was an integral part of his whole way of acting, not just something fitted in if time permitted.

At the beginning of Jesus' public life, when he was baptized by John, when the heavens were opened, when the Holy Spirit descended and the Father spoke words of approval, "Jesus was praying" (Lk 3:21-22). Next, led by the Spirit into the desert, he spent forty days in fasting, prayer, and struggle with the powers of evil, preparing for his public mission (Lk 4:1-13). When his life of preaching and healing drew large crowds, Jesus "withdrew to deserted places to pray" (Lk 5:16). Mark notes an occasion that illustrates Jesus' habitual practice of praying. After preaching in the synagogue at Capernaum, healing Simon's mother-in-law and many other sick people, and casting out demons, Jesus, "rising very early before dawn, left and went off to a deserted place, where he prayed" (Mk 1:35).

At important moments in his public life, Jesus devoted special time to prayer. Before choosing the Twelve, "he departed to the mountain to pray, and he spent the night in prayer to God" (Lk 6:12). While he was praying alone with his disciples, he asked them the question that led to Peter's great profession of faith: "'Who do the crowds say that I am?' ... Peter said in reply, 'The Messiah of God'" (Lk 9:18, 20). Matthew adds, "the Son of the living God" (Mt 16:16). After feeding the multitude in the desert and before preaching the crucial sermon on the bread of life, Jesus once again spent the night in prayer (Mk 6:46; Mt 14:22-23; Jn 6:15). This sermon caused many to turn away from him but led Peter to make another great confession of faith: "Master, to whom shall we go? You have the words of eternal life" (Jn 6:68).

When his disciples returned from a successful missionary journey, Jesus prayed a prayer of gratitude and praise—the first prayer for which the Gospels give us his words: "I give praise to you, Father, Lord of heaven and earth, for although you have hidden these things from the wise and the learned you have revealed them to the childlike. Yes, Father, such has been your gracious will" (Mt 11:25-26; Lk 10:21). Jesus' addressing God as "Father" or "Abba" is noteworthy, for this expressed both Jesus' extraordinary intimacy and union with God and his willing submission to the Father as obedient Son; it was his habitual way of speaking to God. Later, while Jesus prayed on the mount of the transfiguration, preparing himself and his disciples for his passion and death, the Father reaffirmed his solemn approval: "This is my chosen Son; listen to him" (Lk 9:35). In Luke's account, it was after observing Jesus at prayer that one of his disciples asked him to teach them to pray. Jesus then taught them the Lord's Prayer (Lk 11:1-4).

Toward the end of his public life, Jesus prayed and blessed little children brought to him by their mothers (Mt 19:13-15; Mk 10:13-16). He prayed before calling Lazarus from the tomb: "Father, I thank you for hearing me" (Jn 11:41). He prayed on his last day in the Temple: "I am troubled now. Yet what should I say? 'Father, save me from this hour'? But it was for this purpose that I came to this hour. Father, glorify your name" (Jn 12:27-28a). At the Last Supper he referred to a prayer that he had offered for Simon Peter: "Simon, Simon, behold Satan has demanded to sift all of you like wheat, but I have prayed that your own faith may not fail; and once you have turned back, you must strengthen your brothers" (Lk 22:31-32).

The hours of Jesus' suffering and dying were filled with prayer. The Gospel of John gives a long prayer offered at the Last Supper, the so-called high priestly prayer (Jn 17:1-26). Here Jesus prayed first for himself and his glorification, i.e., for the manifestation of himself as Son through his obedience unto death and through the Father's raising him to glory. He prayed next for the apostles, for their preservation, unity, and holiness. He prayed finally for future believers, for their unity, their glorification with him, and God's dwelling in them in love.

Later that evening, in Gethsemane, Jesus begged his Father to remove the chalice of suffering, but he prayed even more that his Father's will, not his own, be done. As he hung on the cross, he prayed for his persecutors (Lk 23:34). In his overwhelming sorrow and pain, he prayed the opening verse of Psalm 22: "My God, my God, why have you forsaken me?" (Mk 15:34; Mt 27:46). At the end he surrendered himself in prayer to his Father: "Father, into your hands I commend my spirit" (Lk 23:46).

The NT writers also present Jesus as now interceding for us in glory. Paul says that Jesus is one "who died, rather, was raised, who also is at the right hand of God, who indeed intercedes for us" (Rom 8:34). The Letter to the Hebrews says, "he lives forever to make intercession" (Heb 7:25). The First Letter of John declares, "We have an Advocate with the Father, Jesus Christ the righteous one" (1 Jn 2:1). In Matthew's Gospel Jesus assures his disciples that where two or three of them gather to pray in his name, he is there among them (Mt 18:19-20). In John's Gospel Jesus prays for the bestowal of the gift of the Spirit: "I will ask the Father, and he will give you another Advocate to be with you always, the Spirit of truth" (Jn 14:16-17a).

Thus Jesus' prayer assumed many forms in the different circumstances of his life. There were prayers of praise, gratitude, submission, and trust. There were petitions for himself and for others. Before the great events of his mission there were special prayers. He spent most or all of the night in prayer before choosing the Twelve and before giving the sermon on the bread of life. He prayed before the apostles' profession of faith, the raising of Lazarus, and his own suffering and death. Jesus constantly employed a way of addressing God that others used seldom if at all; he called God "Abba," expressing both an astonishing sense of intimacy and of obedient surrender to the Father's will.

Jesus' life of prayer revealed his deepest personality. He showed himself before all else the Son of the Father. He was completely obedient to the Father's will, spontaneously grateful for the Father's gifts, full of praise for the Father's deeds, completely trusting in the Father's disposition of his life, intent on carrying out the mission given him by the Father, and closely united with his Father in thought, purpose, sentiment, and affection. This intimate relationship with God in turn determined how he related to other persons. He bore within himself the purpose and the love of God for others, and thus his prayer showed care, concern, forgiveness, and acceptance of his fellow human beings. At the same time he was strong and authoritative in revealing to them the truth of their condition before God and God's abiding love for them. His prayer showed that he was able to draw upon the divine power for their relief and well-being. The prayerfulness of Jesus drew others to him; they asked him to teach them how to pray, and to bless and pray for their children. The prayerfulness of Jesus lies at the heart of the attractiveness of his personality (see Wright, pp. 25–27).

The Teaching of Jesus

Jesus taught about prayer not only by example but also by words. He described the one to whom we pray, the things we are to pray for, the way we are to pray so as to be heard, the effects of prayer, those for whom we should pray, and his own place in our prayers. And finally he gave us a model prayer to guide us.

Both in the Synoptics and in John's Gospel, Jesus tells us to pray to the Father in heaven, his Father and ours: "When you pray, go to your inner room, close the door, and pray to your Father in secret. And your Father who sees in secret will repay you" (Mt 6:6; see also Mt 18:19; Mk 11:25; Lk 11:11; Jn 4:24; 14:13; 15:16; 16:23). The Father is more concerned about us and is better than any earthly father (Mt 7:11; Lk 11:11-13). He cares for both the just and the unjust (Mt 5:45). He knows our needs even before we ask him (Mt 6:7). He forgives us as we forgive others (Mk 11:25).

Jesus' instruction regarding the things we may or should pray for is all-embracing: Pray for anything at all (Mt 18:19; Mk 11:24; Jn 14:13-14; 15:7, 16; 16:23). Pray for any good thing you need (Mt 7:11). Prayer is especially necessary in opposition to what is evil: to drive out demons (Mk 9:29); to be protected in the final trial (Mk 13:17-18; Lk 21:36); to avoid succumbing to temptation (Lk 22:46), since the spirit is willing but the flesh is weak (Mk 14:38). We should pray that laborers be sent into the harvest (Lk 10:2). And, finally, we should pray for the gift of the Holy Spirit (Lk 11:13).

Jesus singles out our enemies and persecutors as those for whom we should pray (Mt 5:44). Only one place in the OT gives this directive. Jeremiah, writing to the exiles in Babylon, tells them to pray for that city, since their own welfare depends on its welfare (Jer 29:7).

The basic directive on how to pray effectively is to pray with faith (Mk 11:22-24). But we are also to pray in secret (Mt 6:6).

This is not an exhortation to avoid praying with others, but to avoid praying just to be seen and praised for it. In the same way, we are to avoid long, empty phrases (Mk 12:40; Mt 6:7-8), but we are to pray perseveringly, not giving up though we seem not to be heard (Lk 18:1). Finally, we are to pray after we are reconciled to our brothers and sisters (Mk 11:25).

In our prayers to God our Father, Jesus has a particular place. He is in the midst of two or three who gather in his name: "For where two or three are gathered together in my name, there am I in the midst of them" (Mt 18:20). We are to ask the Father in his name (Jn 14:12-14; 16:24). This does not mean simply using a formula of words, but being somehow identified with him, bearing his person, sharing his life. He expressed it also by saying that we should pray dwelling or abiding in him (Jn 15:7). He will do what we ask in his name (Jn 14:14), and the Father answers our prayers in his name (16:23b).

In indicating the effects of prayer, Jesus says that praying for our enemies makes us like the Father (Mt 5:44). The one who prays humbly for mercy is justified, i.e., made right with God, as in the story of the Pharisee and the tax collector (Lk 18:14). Finally, those who pray as they ought, i.e., with faith, perseveringly, not with empty phrases or mere show, at peace with others, and in Jesus' name, receive what they ask for.

When the apostles, moved by the example of Jesus (Lk 11:1), asked him to teach them to pray, he gave them the Lord's Prayer (Mt 6:9-13). This prayer expresses the heart of the new covenant. As in every covenant formula, it tells what is the relation between the Lord and the people with whom he makes the covenant and among those people themselves. It also describes their duties and the favors the Lord confers. Jesus expressed the relationship between God and us and among ourselves by saying, "Our Father who art in heaven." He is not merely our God but our Father, and, having the same Father, we are brothers and sisters. He indicates our duties in the first three petitions: to praise God, to work for the establishment of his kingdom, and to do his will. These are our duties, but in our weakness we ask that God help us to fulfill them. Then in the final four petitions Jesus indicates what God will do for us: feed us, forgive us, uphold us in temptation, and preserve us from evil. These too we ask for, acknowledging that they are gifts. There is a condition attached to the gift of forgiveness: we must forgive others.

Four Questions for Today

The example and teaching of Jesus raise questions for us today in our largely secular society: (1) How does God act in a world governed by scientific laws? (2) How does prayer itself make any difference? (3) How can we address God in praise or petition, since his creation contains so much sin and suffering? (4) Is God in any way affected by our prayers?

1) How is God at work in the world?

God is not to be thought of as just one cause among others, more powerful no doubt, but working alongside them to produce changes in the way things relate exteriorly to one another. It was, in fact, this view of God that Einstein rejected in the passage noted earlier. But Christian believers are not concerned to affirm God as a cause "by the side of this ordered regularity" of causes, "interfering with natural events." God is not one particular cause among many, but rather the transcendent cause who sustains the whole "ordered regularity" of causes.

In the 19th century it became popular to think of the "laws of nature" as rigidly determined ways in which the material world operates. But more recent scientific views speak of statistical regularity rather than rigid determinism, so that one particular state of things does not lead to another particular state with absolute necessity, but only with a certain high degree of probability. There is a kind of indeterminism in matter that is shaped by influences of many kinds. This is what makes it possible for a human being to make a free decision affecting how the body is to operate (walk, sit, look around, etc.), without violating any law of nature. The same physical/chemical state of the body can be succeeded by any one of several different possible states.

Teilhard de Chardin distinguished between the "within" and the "without" of things (*The Phenomenon of Man,* 2nd ed., New York: Harper & Row, 1965, p. 56). We directly observe the without of things—their external and objective aspect, their way of relating to one another and influencing one another in their external structure and organization. This is the field studied by the natural sciences. But in ourselves we directly observe another aspect. We see that matter highly organized in an external way (our body) has also a within, an internal and subjective dimension, a conscious center. This holds the whole together from inside, and by our choices influences our body without suspending any law of nature.

Furthermore, what we directly and intuitively observe within the highly complex organization of our bodies we indirectly and deductively recognize as proportionately the case in other less complex things. We can see that animals have a centered within, a consciousness of some sort. We see that plants, too, respond from within as a unity to the surrounding environment; their center is not conscious awareness (so far as we can tell), but they have a unity that is more than a simple juxtaposition of parts. Further, still less complex bodies are centered unities: protozoa, viruses, other molecules, even atoms and subatomic particles. We would not see at the higher level of evolutionary development a fundamental characteristic like the within if it were not somehow present in rudimentary fashion even at the lowest level. Thus, throughout the whole material world, all bodies have a without and a within; the intensity of the within is in proportion to the degree of the complexity of the without.

In somewhat the same way as we consciously operate in the within of matter and influence it without violating any law of nature, so God operates directly and immediately in the within of all things. This is not to say that God is the within of all things, but he operates there. He is not one cause alongside other causes, but from within sustains all things in being, upholds their power of acting, draws them into the future, and makes of them one universe. From within he influences the whole order of created causes, not depriving them of their natural and spontaneous activities, but knitting them together into a vast and ordered complex. Without interfering with their "ordered regularity," God can incline things one way rather than another, as the human will influences the body's acts. For this regularity, as we said, is not a rigid determinism but a statistical probability. God, then, acting in the within of all things within the limits he has set by the natures he has made, may respond to prayers in the ordinary course of his active guidance of the world.

2) How is prayer itself effective?

a) *Kinds of prayer*

In answering this question, we need first to distinguish between two basically different ways of responding to God as he addresses us: one responds to God in view of what he has already done for us, the other in view of what we want God to do for us in the light of his promise to hear us. This distinction gives us four basic kinds of prayer. The first response is chiefly praise and thanksgiving; the second is petition and intercession. The first is a response out of our abundance; the second is a response out of our weakness and poverty. St. Paul indicates that our poverty and our abundance belong together in our prayers:

"Have no anxiety at all, but in everything, by prayer and petition, with thanksgiving, make your requests known to God" (Phil 4:6).

Prayer is first of all praise and thanksgiving, since God addresses us most radically as creating, sustaining, and gifting us within the total context of the universe and history. Psalms of praise acknowledge the greatness and goodness of God in making the world and in guiding the events of history (e.g., Psalm 33). Psalms of gratitude thank God for gifts given to us either individually (e.g., Psalm 30) or collectively (e.g., Psalm 67).

This responding to God from the greatness of his gifts also includes the prayer of adoration—praising the supreme majesty of God in himself; the prayer of faith—acknowledging God's self-communication in the past and in the present; and the prayer of love—acknowledging God's infinite goodness in himself and in his personal concern for us individually and collectively.

Prayer is also response to God as he promises to help us in our weakness and poverty. This is the prayer of petition and intercession. I pray in my sinfulness for forgiveness, in my sickness for health, in my suffering for relief, in my weakness for strength, in my fear for courage and hope, etc. I also pray for others in their need, asking God to help them.

b) *Effective symbolic activity*

In asking how these ways of responding to God are effective, we should note first of all that prayer is symbolic activity. It brings to expression my personal relationship to God, a relationship that he initiates and I accept. The relationship is grounded both in the goodness God has already shown me and in the needs I experience for still further gifts. Prayer is like the symbolic activity of words and gestures by which human beings bring to expression their personal relationships to one another.

But these words and gestures among human beings do not merely express and embody existing relationships; they also initiate, sustain, modify, and intensify them. As symbolic activity, they are effective, they produce a result. Making promises, signing contracts, buying and selling, electing people to political office, getting married, and all the other activities that bind human beings together are symbols or expressions that bring about what they signify.

So, too, prayer accepts, deepens, and intensifies my relationship with God, the relationship he intends and initiates. The power of prayer as symbolic activity comes from the initiative of God, to which it responds. Praising and thanking God, by acknowledging the goodness and greatness of what he has done and continues to do for me, accepts that activity and its purpose into my life: my relationship to God as Father and Mother grows stronger and deeper.

When we respond to God's invitation to ask for what we need, symbolic activity deepens the personal relationship of trust and dependence on him. Whatever else we ask for in prayer, one fundamental request underlies all others: that we may grow in our relationship to God as sons and daughters, and as brothers and sisters of one another and of Jesus Christ. It is in this sense that the prayer of petition is always answered. Any particular thing we ask for is always sought within the context of these personal relationships: we ask for it only as it draws us closer to God, to one another, and to Jesus Christ. The prayer of petition, then, neither informs God of something he doesn't know nor persuades him to act as he would rather not act, but expresses and deepens our relationship of trust and dependence on God. When in addition God grants a particular favor, it is always in view of this relationship. The prayer of intercession that asks something for another deepens the bond between us and the ones we

pray for, a bond that God has first established and continues to uphold.

3) But how can we address God in praise or petition, seeing the enormous amount of sin and suffering in the world?

Much has been written about the problem of evil in the history of Christian thought, and a full treatment is not possible here. But one element is always present in these considerations, one that we can grasp anew in our own day: God creates us to be truly free and responsible sons and daughters. He does not want beings whose actions are concretely determined by the world in which they live or by their natural capacities to act, but beings who out of their own self-possession can decide for themselves how they will relate to God, to the world, and to one another. Their faithfulness in difficulty, their unselfish love, their gratitude and praise, their efforts at personal development and generous self-giving are not inevitable results of blind determinism but come from conscious, free, responsible decisions. God wants us as friends, not as slaves.

But a world in which free, responsible persons can come to be and can exercise their freedom cannot be rigidly determined but must be open to chance and contingency. In such a world, by the very nature of the case, accidents happen. Things and events occur that are not directly intended. Even though the environment favors the emergence of life and has nurtured its development in many forms, still some things happen naturally that are harmful to life, simply because of the openness of the world. Furthermore, beings who are asked to do good freely can do evil. And sometimes they do so, with harmful consequences for themselves and many others. In this situation God continues to will the world and the free beings in the world as he has made them, but he also determines how he may draw good from whatever happens, if only we are willing.

Thus sin and suffering are not reasons for failing to praise God and ask for his help. We do not praise and thank him precisely for the evil we undergo, but for the kind of world that makes it possible for us to be free, and for his presence in every situation to draw good from it.

4) Does prayer affect God in any way?

By loving us, God opens up the possibility of being somehow affected by what we do. For if it is really the case that God loves us and intends that we be his sons and daughters, then we must say that praise and thanksgiving really please God, really rejoice his heart, since what he intends is coming about. Trito-Isaiah describes God's joy in achieving his purpose in creation: "For I create Jerusalem to be a joy and its people to be a delight; I will rejoice in Jerusalem and exult in my people" (Isa 65:18b-19a). This can in a sense be called a "change" in God, not a change that increases or diminishes his goodness, but a change that shares that goodness with creation and rejoices in the sharing.

The reality of this "change" is exactly the same as the reality of the love that God has for us, as individuals and as a community. The "change" that the joy implies cannot be denied without denying the reality of the love. This may pose a question for philosophers, but it is not an insuperable problem for those who affirm the freedom of God as something more than extrinsic denomination derived from the contingency of the created world.

God's love has also led him to promise to hear and answer our prayers of petition. This promise has opened him to being affected by our prayers. These prayers respond to God's invitation to ask for what we need with faith and trust, seeking to deepen our relationship to God as our loving and powerful Father. God personally responds by deepening this relationship and by acting in the within of things, granting what will serve to advance our union with him—either what we have asked or something that in the end is more beneficial.

Methods of Prayer and Growth in Prayer

We have indicated kinds of prayer that are different acts or attitudes by which we respond to God: praise, gratitude, faith, sorrow, petition, etc. Methods of prayer are the different ways of expressing these acts or attitudes: vocally or mentally, privately or communally, etc. Growth in prayer affects both the kinds of prayer (e.g., growth in faith or praise) and methods of prayer (e.g., greater simplicity).

Mental Prayer and Vocal Prayer

We can distinguish two fundamental methods of prayer: mental and vocal. The difference is not that one uses words and the other does not, but that vocal prayer uses a preset formula, whereas mental prayer, if it uses words, is not tied to any set formula but, as in a conversation, makes up the words as it goes along. In the case of vocal prayer, our aim is to mean what we say; in mental prayer we try to say what we mean. Generally speaking, the life of prayer requires both methods: vocal prayer so that we do not overlook important aspects of our relationship with God; mental prayer so that our response to God can fit different circumstances of our lives and the different ways in which God calls us.

Discursive and Affective Prayer

Discursive and affective prayer differ in the way in which thinking and feeling influence the way we address God. Feeling need not mean strong emotion but may be a quiet, almost passive state. In discursive prayer the influence of reason predominates. It is true that our reasoning sometimes precedes our address to God, and then it is more preparation for prayer than prayer itself. But reasoning can be kind of a conversation with God in which we, as it were, discuss something with God. Reasoning should always lead to some kind of affective expression: trust, surrender, gratitude, love, etc. When the feeling or affective expression dominates, we have affective prayer. Then our time is largely spent loving, thanking, sorrowing, rejoicing, or simply resting peacefully in God's presence. A move from more discursive to more affective prayer is a normal development in the life of prayer.

Meditation and Contemplation

The terms *meditation* and *contemplation* are sometimes used interchangeably. But when a distinction is made, it usually refers to the different ways in which the mind functions in prayer. If in our response to God there is an extended pondering of different aspects of God's presence and activity, we are meditating. However, if there is a simple gazing, with our attention fixed lovingly upon just one or two aspects, we are contemplating. Sometimes a distinction is made between meditation and contemplation by saying that in meditation reasoning predominates, and in contemplation imagination predominates. A development from meditation to contemplation is a normal pattern of growth in prayer.

Kataphatic and Apophatic Prayer

The distinction between these methods of prayer is that kataphatic prayer uses words and images, while apophatic prayer is simply silent in the presence of God, using neither exterior nor interior words. *Kataphatic* means literally "affirmative," and *apophatic* means "negative." Apophatic prayer is a kind of contemplation.

Centering Prayer

Centering prayer describes a special method of contemplation that is, to some degree at least, apophatic. The person praying simply attends to the presence of God within, at the center of one's being. A mantra or short phrase may be repeated to keep one's attention centered. (See M.

Basil Pennington, *Centering Prayer,* New York: Doubleday, 1980.)

Mystical Prayer

This term normally designates prayer in which the grace and attractive power of God are more manifest. It is also called "infused contemplation" to distinguish it from "acquired contemplation." In mystical prayer one's mind and heart are directly and powerfully influenced by God to operate in a way that human effort by itself cannot achieve, though with God's grace one can prepare for it. This method of prayer can go through many stages and assume many forms.

Glossolalia

Glossolalia, or praying in tongues, is a way of praying that was particularly treasured in the Pauline churches. From Paul's description in 1 Corinthians 14, it was not praying in a foreign language actually in use somewhere, but rather a spontaneous expression of deep religious experience. The revival of glossolalia in our day may be seen as overcoming a cultural repression of this kind of expression. Just as contemporary Western culture has to a large degree repressed weeping in public by men (but not by women), so it has over a long period repressed this way of expressing religious devotion. Perhaps exaggerated and self-serving uses of this prayer made people uncomfortable. It is, however, as Paul reminded us, a gift of the Holy Spirit that can serve to build up the individual and, to some degree, the community.

Private and Communal Prayer

Private and communal prayer differ fundamentally according to whether a person addresses God alone or a group of persons address God together. Liturgical prayer is the most important form of communal prayer, for here the members of the Church, gathered as the Body of Christ, express together their common faith and worship. In this activity the Church most profoundly actualizes its reality as Church. This is the center of the Church's life, as Vatican II reminded us: "The liturgy is the summit toward which the activity of the Church is directed; at the same time it is the fountain from which all her power flows" (SC 10).

Intensive and Extensive Prayer

A final distinction can be made between particular periods of prayer, whether private or communal (intensive) and prayer that permeates one's whole life (extensive). To the degree that God is personally present throughout the day as somehow "addressed" by me, I am praying always. Normally God cannot always occupy the center of one's attention, but God can always be there at the periphery, as the atmosphere of one's life, to whom one's full attention spontaneously returns when it is released from other things.

Conclusion

We may finally describe prayer as "life with the living God." This life takes many forms and goes through many phases. In the end it becomes beatific vision, in which we see God face to face, as he addresses us with inexhaustible and undying mercy in the gift of himself to each and all of us, and we, individually and together, address him in joyful adoration and unending love, giving ourselves to him in return.

See also ABBA (IN PRAYER); ADORATION; AFFIRMATIVE WAY; CENTERING PRAYER; CONTEMPLATION, CONTEMPLATIVE PRAYER; CREATION; EXPERIENCE; FAITH; FEELINGS; GLOSSOLALIA; GRACE; HESYCHASM; HOLY SPIRIT; INTERCESSION; LITURGY; LORD'S PRAYER; MEDITATION; MYSTICISM; NEGATIVE WAY; PETITION; PROVIDENCE; RECOLLECTION; SECULARISM.

Bibliography: P. Baelz, *Prayer and Providence* (New York: Seabury, 1968). L. Boase, *The Prayer of Faith* (Huntington, Ind.: Our Sunday Visitor, 1976). T. Green, *When the Wells Run Dry* (Notre Dame, Ind.: Ave Maria, 1985). O. Hallesby, *Prayer* (Minneapolis: Augsburg, 1975). J. McKenzie, "Prayer," *Dictionary of the Bible* (Milwaukee: Bruce, 1965) 686–688. C. Mooney, ed., *Prayer: The Problem of Dialogue with God* (New York: Paulist, 1969). A. Tanquerey, *The Spiritual Life: A Treatise on Ascetical and Mystical Theology,* 2nd ed. (Tournai: Desclée, 1930). P. Teilhard de Chardin, *The Divine Milieu: An Essay on the Interior Life* (New York: Harper & Row, 1960). J. Wright, *A Theology of Christian Prayer,* 2nd ed. (New York: Pueblo, 1988).

JOHN H. WRIGHT, S.J.

PRAYER OF THE HEART

See HESYCHASM.

PREACHING

The significance of preaching for the formation of Christian spirituality was captured by Yves Congar when he noted that a number of ancient texts indicate that "if in one country Mass were celebrated for thirty years without preaching and in another there was preaching for thirty years without the Mass, people would be more Christian in the country where there was preaching" ("Sacramental Worship and Preaching," *The Renewal of Preaching: Theory and Practice,* Concilium 33, New York: Paulist, 1968, p. 62). Reflecting a real shift in the position of Catholic theology and spirituality since the time of the Reformation, Vatican II's Constitution on the Sacred Liturgy speaks of the real presence of Christ not only in consecrated bread and wine but in the gathered community and proclaimed word as well (no. 7).

Rooted in a biblical spirituality of the word of God, preaching (announcing the good news of salvation) shares in the mystery of God's word as dynamic, creative, saving, and effective. The Hebrew *dabhar,* meaning "to drive forward" or "to push," conveys a clear sense of energy, derived from the biblical understanding that the power of a word carries the power of its speaker. The first narrative of creation extends the creative power of the divine word to the origins of the cosmos ("God said . . . and so it happened"), a motif reflected also in the psalms: "By the word of the Lord the heavens were made, by the breath of [the Lord's] mouth all their host" (Ps 33:6). Revealing the rich ambiguity of the Hebrew term *dabhar YHWH,* which denotes both the speech of God and God's "mighty acts," the Deuteronomist refers to all of history as the unfolding of God's word. On the other hand, this word that changes the course of history is located within the mystery of the human heart and the human community. God's commands are not mysterious and remote; rather, "[the word] is something very near to you, already in your mouths and in your hearts; you have only to carry it out" (Deut 30:14).

The prophets, often clearly designated as unlikely choices for the mission of proclaiming God's message of judgment and challenge to repentance, as well as promise of consolation and "a future full of hope" (Jer 29:11), emphasized that it was God's word they preached. The call narratives of the prophets reflect the mystery of the vocation to preach, the unique word each was called to speak, and the power of God at work in their own lives. Even the reluctant Jeremiah yielded to the word of God, which he describes as "a fire burning in my heart, imprisoned in my bones" (Jer 20:9). Transformed by a deep consciousness of God's fidelity (often in unexpected ways) to the promises of the past in the community's history as well as in their own unique life story, and keenly sensitive to the injustices, pain, and need for hope in the community to which they were sent, the prophets preached with a passion that Abraham Heschel describes as emerging from an experience of "God's own pathos" (*The Prophets,* New York: Harper & Row, 1962).

Isaiah 55 reflects the biblical conviction that the word of God will bring about the salvation and judgment it promises when the prophet announces God's claim: "So shall my word be that goes forth from my mouth; it shall not return to me void, but shall do my will, achieving the end for which I sent it" (Isa 55:11).

From a Christian perspective, the proclamation of the word of God shares in a unique way in the mystery of the incarnation, in which God's Word "was made flesh." Connecting the mysteries of creation and incarnation, John's Gospel announces that in Jesus, the Word that was in the beginning, the Word that was with God and was God, has "pitched a tent among us" (Jn 1:14, Greek text). The Christian conviction that in and through Jesus one encounters the mystery of God's own self-expression is captured later by the claim of Ignatius of Antioch that Christ is the Word who, in his incarnation, "breaks God's silence" (*Magnesians* 8).

Jesus' proclamation of the reign of God encompasses his life, ministry, death, and resurrection, as well as his parables, teaching, and explicit preaching. In his very person and in all his actions and relationships, Jesus announced the good news of God's compassion for humanity. The Matthean and Johannine portraits of Jesus recall the figure of Wisdom, the prophetic street preacher from the Book of Proverbs who proclaims God's message of judgment and promise in the marketplace, reaches out her hand to the needy, clings to truth, decides for justice, orders all things rightly, and gathers her children at table for a feast of bread and wine.

The depiction of Jesus as preacher in the tradition of the prophets is central to Luke's version of Jesus' ministry and identity as he claims in the programmatic proclamation of chapter four that the words of Isaiah are fulfilled in him: "The Spirit of the Lord . . . has anointed me to bring glad tidings to the poor . . . to proclaim liberty to captives, and recovery of sight to the blind, to let the oppressed go free, and to proclaim a year acceptable to the Lord" (Lk 4:18-19). Jesus' table fellowship with the outcast, his healing touch, his forgiveness of sins, his encounters with women, and his banquets with friends and foreigners are all proclamations of God's will of universal salvation.

Within that broader context of Jesus' life and ministry, the power of "grace come to word" (Rahner's expression) is evident throughout Jesus' preaching ministry. The Synoptic Gospels record repeated amazement at the authority with which this lay man spoke—"not like the scribes and Pharisees." Luke describes the drawing power of the proclaimed word in picturing the crowd as "pushing forward" or "pressing in on him" to hear the word of God (Lk 5:1), and ultimately in the conversion of life and heart of those who accepted the challenge of discipleship. Precisely because the proclamation of the gospel (the good news of salvation) requires repentance and radical change, however, the preaching of Jesus, like that of the prophets before him and the disciples who would follow him, was met with resistance and rejection by the "hard of heart" and eventually led to his death. The Gospel of Mark, in particular, emphasizes the cross as the cost of discipleship for those who would follow Jesus in preaching the reign of God.

Soon after his crucifixion and burial, Jesus' disciples were proclaiming with boldness that he had been raised from the dead by the power of God. The resurrection narratives, whether accounts of the discovery of the empty tomb or appearances of the risen Jesus, include commissions to the disciples—both women (notably Mary Magdalene) and men (Peter, the Eleven)—to spread the good news. Paul, too, claims the authority of his experience of the risen Christ ("as to one untimely born"—1 Cor 15:8, NRSV) as the source of his conversion and the commission to proclaim the gospel of Jesus Christ. He insists that it is God's power at work in his preaching, not his own, and that the wisdom of God is found in Christ crucified and raised rather than in human wisdom. Moral exhortation, while integral to Pauline preaching, is always preceded by proclamation of the power of God's grace in the lives of those who believe. The Letter to the Romans highlights the necessity of preaching for the transmission of the mystery of faith: "But how can they call on him

in whom they have not believed? And how can they believe in him of whom they have not heard? And how can they hear without someone to preach?" (Rom 10:14).

The Church is born of the evangelizing activity of these witnesses to the resurrection, empowered by the Holy Spirit to proclaim the good news to all nations. As Paul VI's 1975 apostolic exhortation *Evangelization in the Modern World* notes: "Evangelizing is in fact the grace and vocation proper to the Church, her deepest identity" (EN 14). In a similar way the Acts of the Apostles repeatedly summarizes the success of the Church's ministry in a specific area with statements such as "The word of God continued to spread" (Acts 6:7).

A variety of ministries of the word were exercised in the early Church by female as well as male prophets, teachers, and apostles within diverse communities of believers, although as disputes arose concerning the authentic tradition of faith, and the hierarchical ordering of ministries developed, emphasis was placed on the bishop as official preacher/teacher of faith, and preaching became gradually restricted to him or his clerical delegates.

The liturgical homily as an integral part of the Christian Eucharist is mentioned specifically in the mid-2nd-century *First Apology* of Justin Martyr. Following the reading of "the memoirs of the Apostles or the writings of the Prophets," the president of the assembly "verbally admonishes and invites all to imitate such examples of virtue" (chap. 67). The earliest clear example of this style of sermon as moral exhortation is found in the *Second Letter of Clement.* By the 4th century, preaching had become more theological (doctrinal sermons explaining the authentic faith of the Church in the face of heresy), catechetical (explanations of the Christian faith for the increasing numbers of catechumens), and mystagogical (further exploration of the mysteries of faith for the newly initiated members of the community).

The mystagogical preaching of the early Church linked the Word of God revealed preeminently in Jesus Christ with the spiritual sense of the Scriptures (thus frequently giving the Hebrew Scriptures a Christological interpretation) and the faith of the worshiping community (the sacraments continue in the present the great works of God recorded in the Scriptures). Typological and allegorical interpretations of the biblical and sacramental symbolism were intended to expand the community's understanding of the pattern of God's fidelity to the promises of the past, and thus encourage the hope that God would also prove faithful in their own day.

While adequate historical development of the relationship of preaching and spirituality is not possible here, mention should be made of several significant medieval developments. During the "evangelical awakening" of the 12th to the 14th century, preaching events included not only traditional liturgical preaching, the instruction given in monasteries and convents, and the commentaries on Scripture of the medieval masters of theology, but also the creative forms of medieval art, drama, and architecture, and street preaching. In addition to the formation of the mendicant orders, the evangelical spirit of the age was evident in the formation of itinerant preaching bands of lay men and women who felt called to imitate Jesus and the apostles through the living of the apostolic life (*vita apostolica*), with particular emphasis on voluntary poverty and the preaching of penance and reform. Concern that preaching regarding faith and the sacraments required knowledge of Scripture and theology emerged in the disputes over granting the lay preaching bands permission to preach (e.g., Innocent III and the Humiliati), in the emphasis of the newly formed Dominican Order on doctrinal preaching, and in the initiation of necessary reforms in clerical education and life by the Fourth Lateran Council (1215).

The Reformation disputes about the efficacy of preaching and the relationship between sacraments and preaching resulted in a distortion of Catholic spirituality that took centuries to dismantle. The 20th-century biblical, liturgical, kerygmatic, and theological renewal movements resulted in a more integrated theology (and spirituality) of word and sacrament, reflected in significant declarations by the Second Vatican Council, such as: "The Church has always venerated the divine Scriptures just as she venerates the body of the Lord" (DV 21). Further, the conciliar documents stress preaching as crucial to the mission of the Church (LG 17; AG 3) and as the Church's chief means of evangelization (AG 6); furthermore, it is necessary as a call to faith and conversion (SC 9) and central to the ministries of bishop (LG 25; CD 12) and priest (PO 4; LG 28), and to the share of all the baptized in the prophetic office of the Church (LG 12; AA 2, 3; GS 43). The Constitution on the Sacred Liturgy restored the ancient liturgical homily as an act of worship, "part of the liturgy itself" (SC 52, 35). The Decree on the Life and Ministry of Priests calls the preached word essential to sacramental celebration, emphasizing that "faith is born of the Word and nourished by it" and insisting that the homily drawn from scriptural and liturgical texts of the day "apply the perennial truth of the gospel to the concrete circumstances of life" (PO 4).

An important shift from earlier ways of viewing the relationship between preaching and spirituality is evidenced in Paul VI's statement in *Evangelization in the Modern World* that while people can gain salvation in other ways by God's mercy even if the gospel is not preached to them, the challenge to the Church is: "Can we gain salvation . . . if we fail to preach it?" (EN 80).

More recent developments hold promise for an even fuller understanding of the relationship between preaching and spirituality. Karl Rahner's fundamental work on word as sacrament opened the way for further theological and linguistic explorations of the power of language (and linguistic forms and genres) to shape human experience and constitute community. Liturgical theologians are pursuing the relationship between word and ritual, how liturgical context influences preaching, and how the entire liturgy is a preaching event. Biblical, systematic, and liturgical scholars continue to probe the meaning of the term *word of God* in rethinking the relationship between revelation and human experience.

The recovery of pneumatology and the Trinitarian dimensions of preaching prompt greater awareness of the role of the Holy Spirit in relation to discussions of "the power of the word." Homiletic attention to creativity and the role of imagination in preaching (e.g., W. Burghardt and W. Brueggemann) further connects theological attention to the role of the Holy Spirit with the concrete "art and craft" of preaching. Developments in communication theory related to theological research in the area of revelation/faith suggest more recognition of the role of hearers/congregation in theologies of preaching and the dialogical nature of the preaching event.

Coming from base communities of Christians in a variety of cultures, liberation theologians raise major questions with regard to inculturation and preaching, and remark that preaching is most effective when members of the community are encouraged to tell their own stories. They also underline the claim of the statement of the 1971 bishops' synod that "action on behalf of justice is a constitutive part of the preaching of the gospel" (*Justice in the World,* Washington: USCC, 1972, p. 34). Feminist theologians and other critical liberation theologians emphasize that the word of God and the symbols of the Church, as well as preaching, must be appropriated critically. All of this suggests not only that preaching is formative of the spirituality of the community but also that the presence of the Spirit in the community should be formative of the preaching event.

See also CONVERSION; DOMINICAN SPIRITUALITY; FAITH; FRANCISCAN SPIRITUALITY; LITURGY; NARRATIVE; PROPHECY; REVELATION; SCRIPTURE; STORY; TEACHING; WESTERN MEDIEVAL SPIRITUALITY.

Bibliography: W. Burghardt, *Preaching: The Art and the Craft* (New York: Paulist, 1987). G. Sloyan, *Worshipful Preaching* (Philadelphia: Fortress, 1984). W. Brueggemann, *The Prophetic Imagination* (Philadelphia: Fortress, 1978) and *Finally Comes the Poet* (Minneapolis: Augsburg Fortress, 1989).

MARY CATHERINE HILKERT, O.P.

PREFERENTIAL OPTION FOR THE POOR

See LIBERATION THEOLOGY, INFLUENCE ON SPIRITUALITY; POOR, THE; SOLIDARITY.

PREGNANCY

Many distinct bodily experiences could be subsumed under the heading of pregnancy: conception, gestation, labor, birth, surrogacy, lactation, contraception, miscarriage, induced abortion, and stillbirth. Each of these related subtopics is spiritually significant and worthy of meditation. However, the focus here will be primarily on childbearing and its refusal, that is, on gestation and abortion.

That which is spiritual permeates all of life's experiences and activities. The Church has always understood that religious questions and reflection about what is ultimate can arise out of bodily events, especially those associated with diminishment, disease, and death. Pregnancy is simply another kind of life passage stemming from embodiment. Though not an illness, each and every pregnancy can generate anew questions for women about their purpose and identity.

Motherhood can occasion much theological reflection and be an experience through which one encounters God. This is especially true when its spiritual dimensions are highlighted and validated. Apart from such illumination and the invitation to meditate upon childbearing, women themselves may be confused by or even deny the spiritual dimensions of pregnancy.

Pregnant women have the capacity to be living signs to the world of God's own incarnate self-giving in Christ. Traditionally, the Church recognized at least one woman's pregnancy as being such a prototype of Christian discipleship. In her very bearing of the Christ, Mary the Mother of God imaged God's own self-gift. Through her willingness to give of her own flesh toward an uncertain future, she bore witness to her experience of God's love for all of creation.

More recently the Church has recognized that every pregnancy can be for the world such a sign of God's self-giving. Through childbearing women share with others God's gift of life. It is one of the few ways in which humans can be physically the bread of life for another. Through the shedding of their blood and the breaking of their bodies, pregnant women and their unborn are united. We encounter an analogous kind of nurture and communion through and with Christ in the Eucharist. Those among us who are great with child invite us into a joyous expectancy. It is a hope quite similar to that out of which the faithful prayerfully and sometimes impatiently await the birth of the reign of God. That Great Feast which we anticipate is experienced like prenatal life, that is, as already but not yet. We are as God's people—men and women and children alike—called like Mary to be the bearers of the Christ Child to the world.

To acclaim and rejoice in the manifold blessings of pregnancy is not to sanctify lifestyles in which women are laid waste and exhausted by an uninterrupted series of pregnancies. To celebrate pregnancy as sacramental is not to endorse attitudes that disparage the lives of those women who for whatever reason do not bear children. Pregnancy is an important but not exclu-

sive or exhaustive source of Christian identity for women. It is a rich spiritual storehouse worthy of exploration, but it is also filled with ambiguity for many women. Some theologians are dangerously romantic about motherhood. They are blind to the fact that many women are still given and taken in marriage, and routinely seized for battery and raped therein. These women often experience their own fertility as a curse. Such romanticism obscures for many the real problems and devastating conflicts pregnant women can face. In our fallen world, self-giving all too often becomes self-sacrifice. Work, delayed gratification, suffering, and sacrifice are part of even planned pregnancies.

If we are to take the experience of these women seriously, childbearing will require carefully nuanced interpretation. Induced abortion may be seen as an analgesic choice, a headlong flight from suffering and an egoistic act. Correspondingly, the willingness to carry a problematic pregnancy to term may be meaningfully understood as a sign of solidarity with the weak. However, it is extremely important that our affirmation of childbearing not reinforce the sense of powerlessness and violation many women feel in such situations. An exhortation to meet the needs of the unborn should be accompanied by an exhortation to meet the needs of the pregnant woman. Appropriate love for others must not be pitted against that self-love appropriate to those called to be daughters of God. Pregnancy itself illumines for us the ultimacy of the interconnections (rather than the tensions) within God's command that we love the neighbor as our self.

See also BODY; BODY OF CHRIST; EUCHARIST; FEMINIST SPIRITUALITY; MARRIAGE; MARY.

Bibliography: John Paul II, *On the Dignity and Vocation of Women* (Washington: USCC, 1988). A. Carr and E. Schüssler Fiorenza, eds., *Motherhood: Experience, Institution, Theology* (Edinburgh: T. & T. Clark, 1989).

PATRICIA BEATTIE JUNG

PRESENCE, PRESENCE OF GOD

Only a personal God can be present to the human being. It is a sign of humanity's divine origin (1 Pet 1:23) that human beings can be present to one another in a way that other forms of creation cannot. That way of being present, being with, being for, is love. The supreme nondualistic reality of God that makes God the creative origin of all that is and of all that is coming to be (Jn 1:3) consists in the fact that primarily God is present to God in the interbeing of the three divine Persons. Human beings share the presence of God as they develop the gifts of the Spirit by their turning from themselves to one another in the mutual attentiveness of love (Phil 2:5).

St. Irenaeus said that the human being cannot know God as an object, as something outside, but only by participation in God's own being. All presence is necessarily reciprocal and personal. I can be present to a tree, but a tree cannot be present to me in a reciprocal way. Divine presence is knowable to a person only to the degree that that person is present to his or her self. A distracted person cannot be present to another. A fully attentive person is "all there" and is present to all. Thus true self-knowledge (not to be confused with mere knowledge about oneself or with self-consciousness) is the natural and necessary precondition and context for knowledge of God (1 Cor 2:11).

Presence is manifest in the turning of attention. Attention is the direction of consciousness. This conversion—the turning from the limited realm of sin and egoism to the unlimited reality of God—is the means of entering the presence of God. Jesus is the embodiment in human consciousness (i.e., body, mind, and spirit) of God's total attention toward us. "We believe that the divine presence is everywhere," St. Benedict said (RB 19:1), and only that which is totally attentive can be everywhere simultaneously. Thus God loved the world in

eternity by being totally attentive to it in the Word and later in history in the incarnation. The call of Jesus to repent (*metanoia*) and to realize the immediacy of the kingdom expresses this nature of the divine presence as being knowable to us when we reciprocally turn toward it.

Conversely, we become most freely present to ourselves when we turn from ourselves (our egoism). Our greatest good is found beyond (and within) ourselves in being present to God. The free realignment of our attention is the work of faith and expresses love as the basic energy of all human growth. The presence of Christ in us through his gift of the Spirit (Jn 14:16) is what empowers this free gift of ourselves to be with God. The Spirit is in a special sense the presence (or self-knowledge) of God, being the love that flows between Father and Son (Jn 15:26).

We are most present to God, not through thought or emotion, although these have their value in maturing our capacity for divine experience, but when in love we reflect God's own glory back to God, "as in a mirror" (2 Cor 3:18, NRSV). Rather than being a state of passivity, this is fully to realize human potential by participating in the economy of the Trinity. The reciprocal presence of the divine Persons is simply the love of their undistracted attention to each other in perfect self-knowledge.

It is the entire interbeing and mutual presence of the three divine Persons that constitutes redemption. We can salvifically enter this presence through any one of the Persons, because each Person is always and everywhere present distinctly, but never without the total presence of the other two. It is in exploring the Trinitarian mystery of redemption that theology will come to perceive the relevance of Christ to the entire human family and to all human experience of God. The presence of God transfigures duality into communion and is therefore the basis of all ecumenism, interfaith dialogue, and the work for peace and justice (Jn 1:27).

When a human being perceives the interbeing of all creation, either experientially through our relationship with others and with nature or conceptually in the exploration of the subatomic universe, this perception is an early stage of participating in the presence of God. God is present in creation in and through the Trinitarian presence in which we participate. There are as many signs or icons of God's presence as there are existent beings. The Eucharist exemplifies the many dimensions in which we become present to the divine presence: in community, Scripture, sacrament, for example.

In prayer the focus is essentially on the presence of God within the spirit of the one praying. As this focus clarifies consciousness through the different stages of the spiritual journey, which includes all aspects of human development, the person becomes present to all creation. A privileged medium of this presence to God in creation is that of human poverty, in which condition human beings are more likely to be empty of pride and humble in recognizing their need of God. Hence the beatitudes (Lk 6:20ff.) reveal the paradoxical inversion of worldly values by which our presence to ourselves is united to the interbeing of the divine presence.

Again, it is in prayer that these abstractions become truths of personal and communal experience. As Meister Eckhart said, if we pray to God for anything except God, we are praying to an idol (*Sermon 70*). "Finding God consists in endlessly seeking God" (Gregory of Nyssa, *Life of Moses*). Christian life is a continuous dynamic of self-transcendence, an essentially timeless adaptation of the human mode to the divine through Christ, who is the incarnate sacrament of God's presence. The "day of Christ" (Phil 1:10) is the presence of God, and where presence is total, time is transcended. God is always present now: I AM (Exod 3:14).

See also ATTENTION, ATTENTIVENESS; CHRIST; CHURCH; COMMUNITY; CONSCIOUSNESS; DIVINIZATION; GOD; HOLY SPIRIT; PRAYER; SACRAMENTS.

Bibliography: S. Weil, *Waiting on God* (London: Collins, 1959).

LAURENCE FREEMAN, O.S.B.

PRIDE

See DEADLY SINS.

PRIESTHOOD, PRIESTLY SPIRITUALITY

See FRENCH SCHOOL OF SPIRITUALITY; MINISTRY, MINISTERIAL SPIRITUALITY.

PROPHECY

A spirituality that is in any way prophetic is characterized by a distinctive relational quality. Like all spirituality, it is born of human response to God's self-communication. However, it is unlike many other spiritualities in two significant ways. While it is the fruit of a very personal relationship with God, it is basically mediatorial and, therefore, primarily communal in its concerns. Secondly, it is always bound to some aspect of the community's understanding of itself as a people in covenant with God. A spirituality that is prophetic develops out of an individual's experience of having been called by God to proclaim something of fundamental importance to the community.

This kind of spirituality is not something that can be assumed. One must be called to be an intermediary between God and the community. A prophetic spirit grows out of such a call. It requires openness to God as well as unselfish commitment to the community. Since an authentic prophetic message is not only faithful to the heart of the religious tradition but also always relevant to the historical moment, this type of spirituality issues from perceptive insight into the religious implications of the "signs of the times."

"Signs of the Times"

A spirituality that is prophetic is rooted in social, economic, and political reality. One cannot be ignorant of or removed from the needs, aspirations, movements, and accomplishments of society and presume to be prophetic. It is within this reality that God is revealed, either reassuring the people of divine compassion and care or warning them of God's indignation and justice. Human history with all its possibilities, challenges, and risks is the matrix within which the reign of God takes shape. Its dynamism and novelty can be neither repressed nor ignored, for it mirrors the creativity of God.

It is precisely within this reality that a prophetic spirit is fashioned, a spirit enlivened by the energies of the day. It is not a spirit of the past but of the present. It is rooted in the belief that God is immanent and continually involved in the lives and history of people. No event, no moment in time is beyond the realm of divine activity. A spirituality that is prophetic flourishes by means of genuine involvement in the contemporary world.

Perceptive Insight

As important as contemporaneity may be, without religious insight it can hardly be considered prophetic. It is this insight and not merely relevance that engenders spirituality. The dynamics set in motion by human endeavor do not necessarily enhance life, nor are the aspirations of women and men always in their own best interests. Just as people have the ability to enrich their lives and the lives of others, so they can also manipulate and exploit, undermine and destroy. Human history contains a record of misunderstanding, indiscretion, and malice as well as of learning, achievement, and virtue.

Prophetic insight is forged in the flame of passionate attachment to the religious tradition. It is not critical for the sake of being critical; it is critical for the sake of the word of God. Attuned to this word, it perceives when believers are faithful to their religious responsibilities and when they are not. It encourages people to embrace whatever within society can serve to deepen their commitment to life and to God, and it warns them to avoid whatever might threaten it. A spirituality that is prophetic values contemporary society, but with eyes of discerning faith.

Communal Perspective

One is prophetic for others, not for oneself. Therefore, a spirituality that is prophetic is distinguished by its other-centeredness. Its mediatorial nature requires an accessibility both to God and to the community. Personal ambition, inclinations, or fears must be put aside when the reign of God is in jeopardy or the good of the community is at stake. Courage to speak or to act for the sake of righteousness is the hallmark of this spirit. The particulars of the actual situation will dictate whether righteousness will take the form of a cry for justice or for peace or for forgiveness or for reform, but the concerns will always be for others.

This other-centeredness is not separation from others. The one with a prophetic spirit is not a stranger to the community. Quite the contrary. The prophet is a member of the group, called to speak to that group from within it. The prophetic insight comes from the religious tradition that everyone holds in common, and the societal circumstances that are critiqued is the life setting of all. A prophetic spirit does not acquit one of the responsibilities of membership in the community. Instead, it frequently heightens the sense of communal inadequacy and guilt.

In summary, a compassionate understanding of society, a fervent devotion to religious faith, and an unselfish dedication to others mark a spirituality that is in any way prophetic.

See also COVENANT; JUSTICE; PREACHING; SCRIPTURE.

Bibliography: D. Dumm, *Flowers in the Desert: A Spirituality of the Bible* (New York: Paulist, 1987). C. Stuhlmueller, *Thirsting for the Lord: Essays in Biblical Spirituality* (New York: Alba House, 1977).

DIANNE BERGANT, C.S.A.

PROTESTANT SPIRITUALITIES

The Protestant Understanding of the Christian Life

The term *Protestantism* refers to that sector of Christianity that traces its origins to the Protestant Reformation of 16th-century Europe. The use of the term *Protestant spiritualities* to designate Protestant understandings of Christian life is problematic. In contemporary speech, *spirituality* refers loosely to strivings toward self-knowledge and self-development that are focused on nonmaterial aspects of human existence. Consequently, to many Protestant ears the term *spirituality* carries with it theological and anthropological implications that are antithetical to classical Protestant premises.

Spirituality as a term for the Christian life lends itself too easily to the following affirmations: The full realization of the Christian life and of human personhood is:

—a matter of developing an inner, nonmaterial aspect of human existence rather than an orientation that encompasses all of finite, bodily existence in interaction with the world;

—more readily achievable for a religious elite rather than for the ordinary person;

—a way to gain acceptance from God rather than the outgrowth of thankfulness toward God for the free gift of salvation.

Protestants would object to these statements because they contradict the following classical Protestant premises:

1) Justification by faith: Salvation is not by works but by faith. Because the Christian life is not something that earns God's favor, there can be no first- and second-class Christians or degrees of spirituality.

2) The sanctity of secular callings: All believers are priests before God. Spirituality or the Christian life is the birthright of all believers. Each individual has direct access to God and is not dependent on the Church, priests, or the sacraments for salvation. Clerics and religious are not more spiritual than lay people and do not have a head start toward salvation.

3) The goodness of all of created reality: The goodness of creation implies that all aspects of human life are basically good and potentially redeemable. Nonmaterial aspects of human existence are not to be understood as essentially religious or as bringing one closer to God. Thus the Christian life is not merely a matter of developing the spirit, if spirit is understood as the nonmaterial aspects of human existence, as it usually is.

In addition, *spirituality* fits better those contemporary theologies that see religious experience as the unfolding of universal, preconceptual aspects of the human person. It fits less well with those theologies that see religious experiences as structured by culturally and communally developed categories, not as diverse expressions of a universal human spirituality.

Overview of Historical Developments in Protestantism

Contemporary Protestant understandings of the Christian life have historical roots in the four branches of the Protestant Reformation of 16th-century Europe:

1) the Lutherans—followers of Martin Luther (1483–1546);

2) the Reformed—followers of John Calvin (1509–1564);

3) the Anabaptists—various groups on the continent who thought that neither Luther's nor Calvin's reforms of the Roman Catholic Church went far enough;

4) the English Reformation or the Anglican Church, originating in Henry VIII's denial of papal authority over the English Church (1534), seeing itself as a middle

way between the continental reformers and the Roman Church.

In addition, subsequent offshoots from these four branches have left lasting impressions on some Protestant denominations:

5) the English Puritans—English Protestants who objected to the English Reformation's retention of some Roman practices and its emphasis on Church authority and tradition instead of the sole authority of the Bible. Some Puritans established communities and churches in America and were thus a major force in shaping American Protestantism.

In the 18th century, three Protestant movements aimed to revitalize Churches that increasingly emphasized right belief and ignored the need for believers to have a vital experience of the presence of God that made a difference in their lives:

6) the Pietists, with leaders such as Philip Spener (1635–1705), August Francke (1663–1727), and Count Zinzendorf (1700–1760), who reacted against Lutheran orthodoxy in Germany;

7) the Methodists, founded by John Wesley (1703–1791), who reacted against the increasingly rationalistic religion of the Anglican Church;

8) the Great Awakenings in America, under the preaching of Jonathan Edwards (1703–1758), William Tennent (1673–1745), Gilbert Tennent (1703–1764), and George Whitefield (1714–1770), which were a reaction to a Puritanism that had lost its emotional power.

Luther

Luther's discovery of the concept of justification by faith and the experience that went along with this discovery are central to the Lutheran and most other Protestant ways of understanding the Christian life. Luther was a conscientious Augustinian friar who could not find a satisfactory answer to the question, How do I get right with God? No matter how scrupulously he practiced the Church's remedy for sin—confessing to a priest, receiving absolu-

tion, and performing prescribed penances—he was tormented by unconfessed sins, which began to accumulate immediately after he had confessed, and the possibility that he might be committing sins of which he was not even aware. Luther's difficulty in finding peace drove him to wonder whether God was even just. As a lecturer on the Bible, he was led by his study to the understanding that when Paul said in his Epistle to the Romans that God's righteousness is expressed in the gospel, he meant that God justifies sinners through his grace and sheer mercy. For Luther, this biblical understanding was like a new birth—a dramatic experience of God in Christ that led him to see the Bible and everything else in a new light.

For Luther, the main feature of Christian life was that the justified believer is always, in this life, also a sinner. The Christian life is *not* a matter of doing works that earn God's favor or achieve salvation. One way of expressing this in theological terms is to say that justification (God's declaration of a sinner as just through the sinner's faith in God's gracious forgiveness in Christ) is not based on sanctification (the process in which God makes human beings good and repairs the damage caused by sin). Instead, sanctification is based on, and is the natural outgrowth of, justification. Thus good works are the result of God's acceptance of a person; God's acceptance is not the result of anything that the person is or does.

Virtually everything else that Luther taught was related to this central understanding. Luther is probably best known for the ninety-five theses that he posted on the door of the Castle Church in Wittenberg in 1517, protesting the abuse of indulgences. His objections to the Church's sale of indulgences as a means for purchasers to obtain remission of years in purgatory for departed relatives was based on his conviction that no matter what the papal authorities said, the Bible teaches that God's acceptance cannot be bought or earned.

Luther's enunciation of the principle of the priesthood of all believers was an affirmation that the Christian life is the birthright of all believers. If justification is by faith, and faith comes by hearing the promise of God in his word, then all human beings have equal and direct access to God. Individuals are not dependent on the Church, priests, or the sacraments for their salvation. Luther admired the mystics and their emphasis on the individual's personal and direct experience of God, but he also emphasized the need for believers to depend on other believers, i.e., the Church, to attend worship services, and to make use of the two sacraments authorized by the New Testament—baptism and the Eucharist. He also emphasized the sacramentality of the preaching of the word of God.

Luther's teaching on the sanctity of secular callings is linked to the principle of the priesthood of all believers. If individuals are not dependent for their salvation on the Church, priests, or the sacraments, then those who have a religious calling do not have a head start toward salvation. There are no first- and second-class Christians. The cloister, asceticism, and disciplined religious practices are of no avail with regard to getting right with God. In addition, religious activities are no better than secular ones and do not necessarily please God more.

The other branches of the Protestant Reformation and the later offshoots reintroduced, in varying degrees and each in its own way, the notion that progress in the Christian life is possible and even necessary. From a strictly Lutheran point of view, normative descriptions of Christian life run the danger of compromising the principle of justification by faith and may be a return to the medieval view of the Christian life as a progressive striving toward God.

The Reformed Tradition

The Calvinist or Reformed understanding of Christian life differed from the Lu-

theran one primarily in that for Calvin the law (to be understood here as the moral teachings of the Bible, including the teachings of Jesus) could have a positive, guiding function for the believer, whereas for Luther it could not. Calvin and Luther agreed on the importance of the biblical concept of justification by faith. For both, the law reveals to individuals their bankruptcy before God and the need for God as savior. Even the moral teachings of Jesus are not consoling but rather terrifying because of the impossibility of their demands. The law reveals to humans their total depravity, not in the sense that each human is as sinful as he or she could possibly be, but in the sense that sin is all-pervasive. Union with Christ provides power to live a Christian life that includes good works. Christ's presence in the life of the believer transforms the believer, but in this life the believer always remains a sinner in need of justification by faith. The difference was that Calvin acknowledged the believer's need for the law as instruction in Christian living, whereas for Luther the law has no positive function, only the negative function of convicting of sin and, on the level of the state, of restraining from sin. Consequently, Calvin was willing to speak about progress in the Christian life, whereas Luther was not.

Both Luther and Calvin emphasized God's initiative and power in the work of salvation. Both accepted the Pauline teaching that those who are saved are predestined by God for eternal salvation in Christ. Calvin, however, was willing to follow his belief in the complete sovereignty of God to the conclusion that God also predestines those who are not saved to eternal damnation.

The Anabaptists

The Anabaptists called for an emphasis on discipleship and a radical return to New Testament principles, a return that they thought had not been effected by Luther and Calvin. Although many Anabaptists would not have denied the principle of justification by faith, their emphasis was on obedience and the newness of life in Christ. Most Anabaptist groups acknowledged the authority of the Bible, but the foundation of the Christian life and of the Christian Church was the presence of Christ through the Holy Spirit.

The Anabaptists thought that the Church should follow only those practices specifically prescribed by the New Testament. Although Luther and Calvin both simplified the Roman liturgy and eliminated what they saw as idolatrous, e.g., the use of images in worship, they did not eliminate all extrabiblical practices. Luther, in particular, thought that there was no harm in practices not authorized by the New Testament, such as confession, as long as they did not contradict any biblical principles.

The Anabaptist practice of rebaptizing adults (the name *Anabaptist* means "rebaptizer") highlights the difference between the approach of the Anabaptists and that of Luther and Calvin to the Church and to the Christian life. The Anabaptist groups believed that infant baptism is no baptism at all, not only because they thought that the New Testament clearly advocates adult baptism but because they understood the Church to be a voluntary association—a purified community gathered from the world at large. Baptism was seen as the believer's witness to faith in Christ, a sign of forgiveness and new life in Christ, a choice to join the community of Christian believers, and a commitment to live a holy life. Thus the Anabaptists emphasized the voluntary nature of entering the Christian life and the Christian community. For Luther and Calvin, the believer's dependence on God's initiative and on the support and nurture of the Christian community was reflected in the practice of infant baptism, as the helplessness of the infant made clear that the effectiveness of the sacrament was dependent on neither the will nor the actions of the infant.

The Anabaptists stressed the holiness and purity of both the Church and the individual believer. This purity was maintained by strict discipline within the Church and by means of the inclusion of only true believers in the Church.

The Anabaptist view of the Lord's Supper was similar to their view of baptism, i.e., neither was seen as a sacrament. While both Luther and Calvin denied the Roman Catholic teaching of transubstantiation, they acknowledged the real presence of Christ in the Eucharist (the traditional Reformed view of the Eucharist as a visible sign through which the Church remembers Christ's redemptive actions comes from Zwingli). The Anabaptists, on the other hand, believed that in partaking in the Lord's Supper, believers celebrate and express fellowship and communion with God and other believers.

The Anabaptist groups also disagreed with Calvin and Luther about the relationship of Church and state. Calvin and Luther challenged the authority of the Roman Church, but neither objected to what had been a basic premise for the medieval Church—that the state should guarantee the authority of the true Church, if necessary, by the use of arms. Most Anabaptist groups thought that the Church's fall dated from Constantine's declaration of Christianity as the state religion of the Roman Empire. For the Anabaptists, any Church that relied on secular rulers was thereby corrupt and, as an established Church, could not maintain its purity as an association of true believers.

Some extremist Anabaptists believed that they had direct access to God through the Spirit and that the Bible is not necessary for salvation. Some also carried out the principle of the priesthood of all believers to its logical conclusions in the political realm and were revolutionaries. Many Anabaptists were pacifists and set precedents for nonviolent civil disobedience, but some attempted to bring the kingdom of God by force.

The English Reformation

The English Reformation's view of the Christian life was characterized by breadth and inclusiveness and by a determination to steer a middle course between the Roman Church and the continental Reformation. Henry VIII, driven by his desire for a male heir, broke ties with Rome, declaring himself the supreme head of the English Church. Initial reforms under Henry were not extensive. A doctrinal statement referred to the authority of the Bible and justification by faith. The influence of the continental reformers was mediated more effectively through Thomas Cranmer, whom Henry had appointed archbishop of Canterbury.

Under the rule of Queen Elizabeth I, a religious settlement attempted to include all but the most radical Protestant and Catholic elements. Although Anglicanism was influenced by the continental Reformers, it rejected the doctrinal rigidity of the followers of Luther and Calvin. Uniformity in worship was considered essential, whereas the Thirty-nine Articles, which set forth basic beliefs, were used as a guide rather than as a strict doctrinal test. The Book of Common Prayer, a collection of prayers, Bible readings, and liturgical forms, has had a great influence on Anglican worship.

The English Reformation accepted the episcopacy as a legitimate structure for ruling the Church and attempted to maintain legitimate lines of succession even after the break with Rome. Thus Anglicans still considered themselves true Catholics and, through the episcopacy, traced their tradition to the beginnings of the Christian Church.

In contrast to the continental Reformers, the Anglicans set the authority of the Bible alongside the authority of the Church's tradition and the authority of reason. Although the theology of the English Reformation was Protestant in tone, the religious life of Anglicans has been dominated more by concerns for continuity with the true Catholic tradition and for proper order than by theological concerns.

The Puritans

The Puritans reacted strongly against the Anglican Church's appeal to the authority of tradition and reason alongside the Bible. For the Puritans, the Bible is the only proper basis for structuring the life of the individual believer and of the Church. The Puritans did not agree among themselves as to what the New Testament teaches about the organization of the Church (they included Presbyterian, Congregationalist, and Baptist groups), but they agreed that the New Testament, without the addition of tradition and reason, is the sole authority. Puritans thought of Calvin's theocratic government in Geneva as a model, but they also believed that no earthly power is absolute and beyond criticism. Their belief in the authority of God and the Bible and in the inevitable depravity of all humans led them to challenge misuse of power by the state and the Church, thus providing a foundation for the development of democratic structures.

For the Puritans, who exhorted believers to better themselves by leading disciplined, serious lives, the Anglicans represented a lukewarm, watered-down version of the Christian life. As Calvinists, the Puritans believed that God predestined some to salvation and others to damnation. They emphasized God's continual control of their lives through his providential activity, but this awareness led them to assiduous efforts rather than complacency. They shared Calvin's view that the Bible should be used for instruction in how to lead the Christian life, as well as to convict people of their sinfulness before God. They believed that if God had elected a person for salvation, then this election would be manifested by signs of God's grace in this person's life. Because they believed that justification by faith would always be evidenced by changes in a person's life, the teaching that had been the source of peace for Luther was for the Puritans the basis for much anxious introspection and self-examination.

John Bunyan's *Pilgrim's Progress,* a classic of Puritan literature, represented the Christian life as an allegorical quest in which the hero, Christian, overcomes great temptations and difficulties. Puritan preaching often used the metaphor of warfare to characterize the seriousness and single-mindedness of the Christian life. Trivial or frivolous pursuits had no place in this life. Pleasure, recreation, and even rest were permissible only when they promoted a life that glorified God. If God had elected you, you were responsible to do his work and to order everything in your life toward that end.

The Quakers, founded by George Fox, were related to Puritanism in that they shared the Puritan ethos, stressing the need for Christians to live simple, disciplined, and ethically pure lives. In contrast to the Puritans' emphasis on human sinfulness, however, Quakers believed that human beings are essentially good and that each person has the light of Christ and God within. Called "the Quakers" because they quaked at the word of God, they nevertheless emphasized the individual's direct experience of God.

The Quakers were known for distinctive patterns of worship and practice. They rejected the use of ordained ministers, special church buildings, and liturgy. Decisions at Quaker gatherings were made by reaching a consensus that included the whole group. Quakers have also traditionally advocated nonresistance as a means for social reform and have practiced philanthropy.

Most of the early Reformation movements included in their vision of the Christian life the experience of God's presence through the Holy Spirit. They also believed that their own reforms of the Church were guided by the Holy Spirit. As the vitality of some of the early Reformation movements

waned and some groups increasingly emphasized correct doctrine to the exclusion of the experience of the Spirit, three 18th-century movements attempted to revive the original emphasis of the Reformation on the believer's experience of the living Christ.

The Pietists

In Germany, Philip Spener and August Francke, leaders of the Pietist movement, organized small groups (*collegia pietatis*) of Lutherans who met in private homes to pray, read the Bible, and encourage one another in the faith. Each individual was also supposed to cultivate a daily time of prayer and Bible reading. The Pietists were convinced that believers must not only be justified but must also show progress in the Christian life. They were optimistic about the extent to which believers could overcome sin in their lives. They were impatient with the worldliness of many Church members and dismissed theological disputes as irrelevant to their main concern—the loss of vitality in the Church.

The Methodists

In England, John and Charles Wesley and George Whitefield tried to revitalize the Anglican Church, whose theology had become increasingly rationalistic. After having worked as a minister and missionary for years, John Wesley experienced a conversion at a religious meeting where Luther's preface to Paul's Epistle to the Romans was being read. In his own words, he felt his "heart strangely warmed" and experienced the assurance that Christ had died for his sins. Wesley's conviction that believers should experience Christ personally and that faith should express itself in a Christian pattern of life was also shaped by contacts with the Moravians, a continental Pietist group. Although John Wesley had no intention of forming his own Church, his movement eventually broke away from the Anglican Church to form the Methodist Church.

Wesley's theology emphasized the empowering presence of Christ. He held that believers could achieve "Christian perfection," perfection to be understood as full devotion to Christ, expressing itself in every act. He believed in justification by faith but was also convinced that the presence of Christ could effect a "simplicity of intention and purity of affection."

Wesley traveled throughout England and gathered audiences not only in churches but also in open fields, thus reaching working people who might otherwise never have entered a church. He preached a Christianity that could make a difference in the lives of believers. He had a genius for organization and set up classes, small groups of twelve with a leader, providing a way to collect funds as well as to nurture and supervise the growth of believers.

The Great Awakenings

The Great Awakenings, a series of revivals in America, were a reaction to the formalism of Puritan Churches. They shared the Pietist and Methodist emphasis on an experienced and lived Christianity. Jonathan Edwards was one of its leading preachers and theological commentators. A brilliant philosopher and theologian, Edwards' understated preaching often met with extreme emotional responses. Theologically a Puritan and Calvinist, Edwards approved of the revivals and affirmed the authenticity of conversion experiences and the appropriateness of emotion as a response to the Christian message.

Recent Developments

Beginning with the Great Awakenings, most influences on Protestant conceptions of the Christian life have cut across denominational lines. Since the 19th century, liberal theology (which accepted historical-critical methods as applicable to the books of the Bible and welcomed a critical reexamination and reinterpretation of basic Christian doctrines) has affected most mainline Protestant denominations.

So has the "social gospel," which called attention to the need for Christians to react religiously to social and economic changes. Fundamentalist Churches and denominations have developed in reaction to liberal trends in mainline Protestant denominations. The charismatic movement has been a contemporary revival movement within mainline Protestant denominations, emphasizing the experience of baptism in the Holy Spirit and the gifts and fruits of the Spirit. Since the 1960s, Protestant understandings of appropriate Christian responses to contemporary problems in the world have been affected by the black power, feminist, and ecological movements, as well as by Latin American liberation theologies.

See also ANGLO-CATHOLIC SPIRITUALITY; CHARISMATIC RENEWAL; FAITH; FUNDAMENTALISM; GLOSSOLALIA; GRACE; JUSTICE; PIETY; REFORMATION AND CATHOLIC REFORMATION SPIRITUALITIES.

Bibliography: J. Dillenberger and C. Welch, *Protestant Christianity: Interpreted Through Its Development* (New York: Scribner's, 1954). F. Senn, ed., *Protestant Spiritual Traditions* (New York: Paulist, 1986).

TIINA ALLIK

PROVIDENCE

Providence is that name of God which brings the motions of human existence into meaning. This definition takes the theological dialogue on providence into the realm of spirituality. The word *motions* denotes human experiences of loss/gain, chaos/design, abandonment/care, disorder/order, irrational/rational, or exile/homecoming and allows the blending and blurring of one motion into another to create the whole that is life. The wayfarer can identify in the motions the directing benevolence of providence and, in faith and with time's perspective, assess the providential meaning hidden in events.

Meaning has a twofold origin: God's gracious power revealing meaning and humanity's evolving insights in assessing meaning. The attribution of meaning allows faithful humanity to experience divine care in the negative moments of personal or corporate histories as well as in those moments that are experienced as ordered and rational. A spirituality of providence necessitates the inclusion of the negative motions of human existence into providence.

Providence is often articulated only as a design for the universe in which all is ordered and formed as care for lilies and sparrows. The problem arises when the experiences of the unpredictable, the disordered, and the misshapen dominate, or seem to dominate, existence, and humanity feels alone in a disordered universe. Is there a God? Does that God care for us? How is there providence if evil prevails and the innocent suffer? There is no one who has not asked these questions of life. A proper theology of providence allows that the motions of chaos and design be factored into the definition of providence, or the concept becomes useless for the spiritual journey.

The dialectic is to be grasped as a whole, that is, one does not "tough out" the chaotic while awaiting the advent of the designed. The chaotic is within the designed and the designed within the chaotic in both the physical and the metaphysical worlds. Mathematicians and scientists have been able to measure the presence and the regularity of the chaotic in the natural order. The secret of holiness is a graced ability not to polarize reality but to embrace the whole as providence—all of it care and all of it governance.

The child in all people wants to be cared for and demands that the caring take the shape of a particular human plan. Life, however, escapes controls. A proper spirituality of providence enables women and men to understand becoming whole in brokenness or to perceive design in utter chaos. Such meaning does not make events rational but allows the recognition that irrationality is not outside a caring providence. When hows and whys or words of explanation fail, the intimation of providence remains, a suggestion, a presence, a confirmation of meaning in the dialectic. Order is to be found right within disorder, form in the chaotic, and care right within the pain. Believers know the entirety to be providence and that divine caring always has a human face.

Care for the earth, evident in works of continued creation rather than wasteful destruction, belongs within a spirituality of providence. The time is now for citizens of the planet to assume its care and to insist on and carry out a proper economy of living that uses the gifts of the earth, water, air, plants, and animals with newly awakened appreciation, one born of greater understanding of the providential governance of the universe as that work has been entrusted to humanity.

Providence summons one to abandonment, not to an arbitrary plan calculated to test human endurance, but to a surrender to mortality that Christians in faith know is loved, held, and redeemed. The person who sees reality permeated by the providence of God gradually becomes welcomed as a wisdom teacher. Equanimity, born of time and grace, becomes evident to passersby. The terrible beauty of the earth, with its calms and its storms, its gentle breezes and its hurricanes, its new life and its deaths, seems somehow to be within the providence person.

Foresight (*providere,* "to see beforehand") occasionally replaces hindsight in the assessment of historical events. Because the providence of God not only acts within life but also invites participation, the providence person can often serve as prophet, a role among the people of God closely connected with a spirituality of providence. The providence person is able to name the way that is ahead for the community rather than only being able to respond to prior happenings. Such foresight can truly be called prophecy when prophecy is defined as an accurate interpretation of the present that shapes and directs the future. Because providence is experienced in the warp and woof of history, governed and designed with eternal care, the providence person touches and interprets events with an exquisite sensitivity and is thus often able to chart a possible future.

A spirituality shaped by a theology of providence is perfectly suited to the demands of the 21st century. The motions of history in which humanity currently finds itself invite submission to a wise and governing providence as well as endless reflection and action as humanity is called to participate in the divine ordering of the universe.

See also CREATION; ECOLOGICAL CONSCIOUSNESS; GRACE; HISTORY, HISTORICAL CONSCIOUSNESS.

Bibliography: T. Berry, *The Dream of the Earth* (San Francisco: Serra Club, 1990). L. Gilkey, *Reaping the Whirlwind* (New York: Seabury, 1976). J. Gleick, *Chaos* (Providence, R.I.: Janson, 1989).

BARBARA DOHERTY, S.P.

PRUDENCE

See CARDINAL VIRTUES.

PSYCHE

See CONSCIOUSNESS; MIND; SELF; SOUL.

PSYCHOLOGY, RELATIONSHIP AND CONTRIBUTION TO SPIRITUALITY

I. Background and Context

The Christian spiritual tradition arguably has always been deeply if unsystematically engaged with the phenomena of human interiority (affect, insight, memory, and imagination). For example, Evagrius Ponticus, writing as early as the 4th century, offers in his *Praktikos* a careful typology of the "passionate thoughts" that afflict the human person at prayer. From Richard of St. Victor in the 12th century to Ignatius of Loyola in the 16th century, Christian spiritual texts have frequently offered nuanced accounts of psychological data interpreted according to the theological worldview common to the time. The problematic of the relationship of spirituality to psychology arose as psychology emerged in the 19th century as a discrete positivist science that studies and interprets this same data on its own terms, without reference to a transcendent dimension or the hypothesis of a spiritual order to reality.

How one conceives, then, of the relationship between the secular, scientific investigation of human mental life (psychology) and the study and practical exploration of that self-transcendent dimension of human living that orients the person toward God (spirituality) will reflect one's foundational theological assumptions. There is a profound theological tradition, originating in certain themes found in Augustine but continuing into the present day through such Reformers as Luther and Calvin, which, in emphasizing the primacy and priority of God's salvific action and initiative, has concomitantly stressed the essential depravity or "fallen" character of human beings. Such a perspective would see the radical subordination of human nature to the divine, the psychical to the "spiritual." From this theological position, psychology would appear to have rather little to offer Christian spirituality, except perhaps to provide a more nuanced account of that human nature which stands in need of redemption and thus to more thoroughly convict the human race of sin. Exposing our penchant for idolatry and illusion, psychology is held to contribute something to a diagnosis of the pathology of the human condition for which only divine revelation can prescribe an adequate cure. Contemporary Protestant theologian Jürgen Moltmann was perhaps writing in the spirit of this theological tradition when he lauded psychoanalysis as "a bulldozer in the way of the Gospel."

There is, however, another emphasis to be found in the Catholic Christian tradition with roots in patristic spirituality and development in the thought of Thomas Aquinas. It assumes an essential continuity between the human and the divine, and hence speaks of grace "building upon" or "working through" nature. In contemporary Roman Catholic theology, Karl Rahner's "theological turn to the human" is a modern expression of this conviction that there is still in human persons a fundamental capacity for God, a readiness to be "hearers of the Word." This capacity may be obscured but is not destroyed by sin. From this perspective, the social sciences in general and psychology in particular may be regarded as potentially valuable partners in working out a "theological anthropology," an account of how it is that human beings bear this receptivity for divine revelation.

This is not to say that the Catholic Christian tradition has been uncritically open to the insights and perspectives of psychology, but its cautions are typically different. Where the tradition of the Reformers is concerned with the psychological diminution or reduction of God to the level of the human, the Catholic Christian response to psychology generally has been guarded about tendencies in the psychological sciences to reduce the human, that is, to explain away the human hunger for the divine in terms of some other, more primary need or drive.

The discussion of the relevance of psychology for spirituality follows this Catholic emphasis by (1) identifying the contribution of selected contemporary schools of psychology to a normative vision of the human person that would ground the dynamics of the spiritual life in the processes of human development and consciousness, and (2) specifying some of the techniques and methodologies of these schools that may most directly contribute to the theory and practice of Christian spirituality.

II. Psychoanalytic Psychology: The Tradition of Freud

A. *Normative View of the Human*

Psychoanalysis, the distinctive intellectual creation of Viennese physician Sigmund Freud (1856–1939) may variously refer to (1) a particular method of long-term individual psychotherapy, (2) that therapeutic practice as a general research instrument for the study of the psychic life of individuals, or (3) a family of related theories of human personality that may be generalized into a theory of culture and society.

Freud's theorizing about human nature changed and developed considerably over his long and active professional life, with some metapsychological models of the psyche never repudiated even as alternative versions were advanced. Moreover, the "psychodynamic tradition" that built upon but also significantly modified Freud's views reveals on inspection that "psychoanalysis" is no single unified body of psychological doctrine. Nevertheless, amidst considerable substantive disagreements, theorists in this tradition are broadly agreed upon these core principles.

1) *Historical determinism.* This principle holds that early childhood interpersonal experience, both real and imagined, exerts a lasting impact upon the form and content of psychic life—in a phrase, that "the child is the parent of the adult." The patterns developed by the young child in response to situations of desire and of conflict in the original family constellation persist into adult life and, for better or worse, manifest themselves in the structure of present-day relationships. The phenomenon of *transference* simply describes the fact that these earlier fears, motivations, and means of adaptation are brought or "transferred" into the relationship with an individual's analyst or other significant persons in present time.

2) *Exceptionless psychic causality.* From this perspective, all psychic events are re-

garded as "psychically caused" and hence "meaningful" as expressive of an intentionality and a motivation, albeit one that the individual himself or herself may not be aware of (i.e., unconscious). Thus psychoanalytic psychology finds significance in dreams and such everyday life events as slips of the tongue. Such occurrences are clues to the deep structure of an individual's inner life.

3) *Unconscious motivation and mental life.* Basic to the foregoing principles is the reality of the dynamic unconscious. This holds that human beings are not the masters of their own mental houses but are moved by motives, wishes, and intentions that begin outside conscious awareness and may or may not pass into consciousness. The method that Freud developed for the uncovering of the unconscious origins of conscious mentation was free association, the agreement between the analysand and the analyst that the former will verbalize without self-censorship whatever thoughts, feelings, or wishes come to mind as these arise in the analytic hour.

4) *Conflicting unconscious motives.* The primary dynamism in what Freud called the "psychical apparatus" is supplied by the effort of the human organism to manage the anxiety that attends the conflict between certain fundamental wishes and needs and the external and internalized social and cultural reality that sets limitations on the expression or gratification of these wishes. As Freud himself originally conceptualized these wishes, they were derived from the instinctual drives, primally sexual and aggressive. The most significant theoretical developments within the psychoanalytic tradition have had to do with rethinking drive theory and thus reconceiving the foundational motives for human behavior, but the general principle still stands. Human character reflects how one manages to live the vicissitudes of conflict around desire.

The analysts and scholars who have followed Freud have picked up different emphases or in some cases have substantially reconsidered the nature of the psychoanalytic project itself. *Ego Psychology,* represented by the work of Anna Freud, Heinz Hartmann, Erik Erikson, and Margaret Mahler shifted emphasis from an investigation of psychopathology to an examination of normality and health and the construction of a general developmental psychology based on the psychoanalytic principles described above. The notion of innate conflict is downplayed, and there appears instead a profound appreciation for the reciprocal, mutually enhancing relationship between the human and the "average expectable environment."

Object Relations Theory and Self Psychology, the former identified with such British writers as Melanie Klein, D. W. Winnicott, and W.R.D. Fairbairn, the latter the work of American analyst Heinz Kohut, presuppose and extend modern ego psychology in a direction that further moves beyond the classic psychoanalytic understanding of the human person as constituted to be inevitably in conflict with the restrictions of social life. Stephen Mitchell has argued that the normative vision of the human person that emerges in these developments within psychoanalysis, convergent with current research on infancy and early childhood, is a view of the human person as essentially constituted from birth to seek relationship as a primary and irreducible value. The underlying motive force in the psychic system is thus the desire for the interpersonal recognition that constitutes the individual's core sense of being a self-in-relationship. Such conflict as characterizes psychic life, therefore, has less to do with the vicissitudes of the instincts than with the consequences of the myriad failures of the interpersonal world to adequately mirror and respond to the human infant. These failures "live on" and are memorialized in what analysts call the "inner representational world," the way in which certain patterns of affective self-experience become linked with the multiple conscious and unconscious images and memories of significant persons in the individual's past.

Particularly in Europe, from the forties into the sixties, Catholic psychologists and theologians like Albert Plé, Louis Beirnaret, Marc Oraison, Ignace Lepp, Roland Dalbeiz, and Gregory Zilboorg entered into dialogue with classical Freudian psychoanalysis and examined critically but appreciatively its value for spiritual directors and pastors. With Jacques Maritain they insisted, however, on making a distinction between Freudian theory and Freudian "philosophy," by which they meant the presumptive atheism that declared that God could be "nothing but" a projection of the human desire for the security of a cosmic parent.

Over the last twenty years this dialogue has entered a new phase as it has engaged the paradigm shifts within psychoanalysis described above. William Meissner, Jesuit psychoanalyst, has written extensively on how contemporary or "post-modern" psychoanalysis, with its sensitive exploration of the lifelong role in health of the capacity for imaginative construction, has broken through the naive positivism of the original Freudian worldview. The result is that psychoanalysis, though taking no stand on the ontological reality of God, is able to offer an account of the functional value of human creativity in both religion and the arts that opens the door to a deeper understanding of the spiritual dimension of human experience. The leading edge of this dialogue, as reflected for example in the writings of Benedictine theologian Sebastian Moore, is to work out the positive contribution of contemporary psychoanalysis to a revitalized spiritual theology. Certainly an adequate psychological understanding of the human person as essentially and irreducibly constituted by the internal experience of being-in-relationship may be necessary to appreciate how human beings are constituted by the processes of their very development to "seek the face of God."

B. Techniques and Methods

A great many spiritual directors and pastors, perhaps without being fully self-conscious of doing so, already listen to their directees and parishioners with an ear tutored by the assumptions of depth psychology. For example, such directors are alert to the possible levels of intended and unintended meaning in any given communication; they look for the way in which individuals' past history of relationships, including their relationship with God, shapes and conditions how they experience the divine in present time; they are aware that much of potential value may be disclosed in the content of dreams.

Some contemporary psychoanalytic researchers have looked carefully and more systematically at the way in which an individual's psychic representations of God may be formed and transformed by the history of the individual's patterns of interaction with the significant other persons past and present. Ana-Maria Rizzuto's groundbreaking clinical investigation of the origin and function of the representation of God has been a model for such studies. The value of such studies for the practice of Christian spirituality is that they provide a framework within which to begin to understand how our actual experience from earliest life may deeply condition, for better and sometimes for worse, how it is we come to imagine the God of our prayer. The "soft" determinism of such a perspective allows that while early experience does shape present perception, new things can and do happen in our relationship with God, even as they happen in our ongoing relationship with our parents. A spirituality informed by this psychological perspective will be attentive to the movements in prayer of memory, of the emergence of long suppressed affective responses to parents and to a God-image modeled on certain aspects of parental experience, and of the healing power of contemporary experiences of being loved and accepted in the manner one's "inner child" had earlier needed and missed.

III. Analytical Psychology: The Tradition of Jung

A. *Normative View of the Human*

Analytical psychology is the creation of the Swiss psychiatrist Carl Jung (1875–1961), one of Freud's earliest and most brilliant collaborators. The son of a Reformed pastor, Jung broke with Freud in 1912 over the dynamics of the unconscious and the definition of libido. The dispute had also involved their respective approaches to the psychic function of religious or spiritual experience. For Jung, religion could not simply be analyzed back to the defensive distortions of the individual's libidinal (i.e., sexual) energies. "Libido" for Jung stood for a desiring that included far more than the discharge of instinctual energies. Since the concept comprehended a fundamental intentionality toward the experience of all potential dimensions of psychic life, it might be equally well realized in religious strivings and spiritual self-expression. Jung was eventually to say that all psychological healing potentially includes a "religious dimension." This greater apparent openness to the value of religion on the part of Jung should not, however, be mistaken for an uncritical endorsement of religious life and Church practice in the modern West. On the contrary, Jung saw himself as something of a prophetic voice raised against the way in which he felt the Christian Church in particular had squandered its spiritual capital by a literalist and legalist mentality that failed to understand the psychic depths and implications of its own symbols and doctrines.

The key to appreciating Jung's complex and often unsystematic insights is to understand that from first to last Jung and those who have followed his direction work from a profound reverence for what he termed "psychic reality" or "psychic objectivity." For Jung, the productions of the human psyche, whether in dreams, waking fantasies, or free associations, must be respected as having their own *sui generis* depth, authority, and autonomy, and as such could ultimately not be analyzed back to some putatively more basic impulse or drive system. For Freud, the human psyche is tragically set against itself by the vicissitudes of an instinctual life implicated in the traumata of early childhood experience. People fall ill of the lies and distortions of reality that they unconsciously fabricate to hide the reality of their past and present condition. Thus analysis cures, according to Freud's original formulation, by the skillful deciphering of the "hidden" miscommunications of the unconscious. Not so for Jung. The apparent irrationality of the psyche, or "soul," as Jung was willing to call it, defies scientific reduction and explanation but is not without its own inner logic, which Jung recognized as its drive toward "wholeness." The Jungian psyche is "whole" in at least these three important senses:

1) *The psyche is intrinsically healthy.* The natural trajectory or conatus of human psychological maturation is toward completion or the realization of the individual's essential being, a lifelong process that Jung termed "individuation." The manifest as well as the latent content of dreams for analytical psychologists is to be taken seriously and trusted as offering reliable clues as to the necessary direction of this process for any given individual. The psyche is thus seen as having its own inherent self-corrective dynamic that attempts to bring to consciousness the requirements of individuation.

2) *The psyche is composite.* There is an "inner manyness" to human beings that typically organizes itself in patterns of opposite but complementary personal char-

acteristics, functions, or capacities. These universal innate patternings of psychic energy, common across the human species though various in its manifold cultural expressions, are what Jung meant by the "archetypes." Two of the primal archetypal organizations of psychic life are according to the "male" and "female" principle, potentialities in all human beings regardless of gender. Since, for Jung, psychological development over the life span involves the balancing out and gradual integration of these various polarities (the *coniunctio oppositorum*), he gave particular attention to the countersexual archetypes: the *anima* in males, the *animus* in females.

3) *The psyche is collective in nature.* The psyche is not only formed by the layering of personal experience (the "personal unconscious") but is from birth endowed with these innate potential patterns for psychic organization described above as the archetypes. It is this dimension of the psyche that Jung called the "collective unconscious." It is manifest cross-culturally in the great myths, fairy stories, and certain collective rituals.

A number of Catholic thinkers, prominent among them the Dominican theologian Victor White, early responded to Jung's apparently more irenic approach to religion, and in particular the respect he had for certain Catholic rituals and doctrines that he felt more deeply manifested the realities of the objective unconscious. Subsequent writers on Christian spirituality similarly have found in Jungian psychology sympathetic resonances with the Christian spiritual tradition and resources for the revitalization of that tradition. For example, Jung's emphasis on the graciousness that is to be found in courageously facing and integrating the dark or shadow aspects of personality is viewed as a helpful corrective to tendencies in Christian spirituality that encourage the individual to deny and disavow such enduring aspects of self and society. At the same time, Jung's

treatment of the general problem of evil is one of the continuing points of critical dialogue between analytical psychologists and Christian theologians.

Perhaps the most significant contribution and challenge of analytical psychology to Christian spirituality is its insistence on making the privileged locus of the divine-human interaction the unfolding processes of individual psychic growth and transformation. On the one hand, this has returned to many believers a renewed and vivid sense of the numinous significance of their own most inner world. "Spiritual experience" is not isolated as the preserve of a few gifted adepts but is seen as the common inheritance of every human person who will attend seriously and responsibly to the communications of the unconscious. On the other hand, this view, if exclusively pursued, is criticized as promoting an individualistic, ahistorical and, in its own fashion, ultimately elitist theological anthropology that runs counter to the intuitions of main currents of spirituality in the Jewish-Christian tradition. The ongoing conversation between analytical psychology and Christian spirituality, like that with psychoanalysis, continues to be a lively and productive one.

B. *Techniques and Methods*

There are two principal ways in which the theoretical ideas and therapeutic approaches of analytical psychology have been appropriated as relevant to Christian spiritual practice.

1) Because of the greater confidence analytical psychologists typically have in the revelatory power of the psyche, they have introduced into the therapeutic process a wide range of methods to encourage exploration of spontaneous psychic creativity. These include music, creative writing, dance and movement, painting, and sculpting. Additionally, Jung developed a technique for expanding the imagery of dreams and waking fantasy termed "active

imagination." All these approaches have been variously adapted by Christian spiritual directors to facilitate the processes of prayer, meditation, and indepth personal engagement with the images and stories of Scripture. The journaling methods developed by Jungian analyst Ira Progoff have in particular found wide use in retreat centers and centers for spiritual formation.

2) The other analytic tool deriving from Jung's work that has been picked up widely by spiritual directors is the Myers-Briggs Type Inventory (MBTI). This personality test provides scores along bipolar dimensions: two attitudinal orientations of the personality (extraversion and introversion); two modes for processing perceptions of reality (sensing and intuition); two ways of coming to judgment (thinking and feeling); and two ways in which persons typically prefer to organize their lives (in a decisive, planned manner, i.e., "by judgment," or in a spontaneous, flexible fashion, i.e., "by perception"). Numerous writers have attempted to coordinate personality profiles from the Myers-Briggs Inventory with preferred approaches of spiritual discipline in order to more systematically prescribe modes of prayer congruent with the individual's own personality preferences.

More promising perhaps than this static and categorical use of the Jungian typologies is an approach that views these types in their dynamic function and employs them to help an individual understand, not who he or she is (as though this were a hard and unchanging self-description), but rather who he or she is becoming. Since Jung held that the spiritual challenge of the second half of life involves the development of aspects of personality that were secondary or submerged in the first half, the Myers-Briggs may help an individual identify where the spiritual growing edge of life may be found, and where the most difficult challenges and possibilities for living will locate themselves.

IV. Cognitive Developmental Psychology: The Tradition of Piaget
A. *Normative View of the Human*

Whereas both Freud and Jung developed their models of the psyche by the observation of the mental suffering of human beings in a therapeutic relationship, the Swiss psychologist Jean Piaget (1896–1980) constructed his theories by close observation and conversation with normal children and young adults under ordinary circumstances. His theories, therefore, are primarily accounts of the nonpathological development of the cognitive capacities of human beings as they go about the business of making sense of their multiple environments: physical, social, and interpersonal.

Piaget often spoke of himself as a "genetic epistemologist," meaning one who traces the way in which persons come to knowledge through the biological endowments of the senses and the intelligence. Over his long career Piaget investigated how a child develops capacities for play, logic, time, space, number concepts, and the ability to understand social rules. He was interested in the way human beings make sense of their experience by construing various "cognitive maps" of increasingly greater sophistication and complexity. The "cognitive developmentalists" who have followed in Piaget's path often speak of these various maps as "stages," more or less stable cognitive constructs to which new information is fit in or "assimilated" until such time as the adequacy of that stage is challenged by new experience and new data and must be reworked to "accommodate" this new material.

Contributions of cognitive developmental theory to a theological anthropology have been made by way of the work of certain post-Piagetian thinkers who began to examine higher order mental functioning than Piaget himself investigated. One such theorist was Lawrence Kohlberg of the Harvard Graduate School of Education, who looked at the "stages" of moral development by examining the way in which children and adults reasoned about hypothetical moral dilemmas. His research traces a normative trajectory of moral development from preconventional (reward-punishment) reasoning, through conventional reasoning (social relationships and shared rules), to a postconventional (principled) mode of ethical reasoning. Kohlberg's work has been critically expanded by subsequent researchers, such as his colleague Carol Gilligan, who have challenged the gender bias of his data and his formulation of moral decision-making. In the main, however, it was Kohlberg's work that was the inspiration for Protestant theologian James Fowler, who wed cognitive developmental theory to H. Richard Niebuhr's understanding of faith to create a model of "faith development" across the life cycle. Fowler's model has most often been taken up by religious educators, but it is not without potential application to spiritual direction, particularly as it may be useful in understanding the formal way in which persons interpret authority and relate to received symbol systems.

Another psychologist whose highly original research has been influential on spiritual writers is another of the "Cambridge School" of cognitive developmentalists, Robert Kegan. Kegan's "stages" are accounts of the progressive development of the individual's sense of what constitutes "the self" and what counts for "the other," with particular attention to the inner affective dimension of the process of "losing" and reconstituting the self. Joann Wolski Conn and Elizabeth Liebert are among the theologians who have found in Kegan's work a rich resource for looking at the dynamics of spiritual development.

The normative view of the human that proceeds from this family of psychology theory is one that sees the person preeminently as a "meaning maker" and a "knower" whose natural, if unobstructed, intellectual drive is toward coherence and consistency, and an ever-widening and more inclusive account of reality. In contrast to psychoanalytic theory's emphasis on the enduring impact of past history, cognitive developmental theories prize the active, present-oriented capacities of the human person to respond to current challenges to meaning. Correlated with a theological perspective, these theories yield a vision of a God whose signature on our nature is read in our irrepressible intentionality toward understanding ourselves in relationship to everything and everyone that is, while still experiencing our own individual distinctiveness and self-agency.

B. Techniques and Methods

When the spiritual director's listening perspective is informed by cognitive developmental theories, attention to the "content" of the directee's discourse is balanced with attention to the formal characteristics of the self-presentation, i.e., how the individual puts together his or her moral and spiritual worldview and not just what is said. There are no special methods developed out of this perspective, but every conversation in which a person is invited to articulate his or her view of God is seen as a developmental intervention insofar as it offers an occasion to more critically and self-reflectively appropriate one's own experience and examine one's own reality construction.

V. Other Psychologies

There are a range of other schools or approaches within contemporary psychology that have productively informed the work of spiritual writers in the Catholic tradition. *Existential Psychology* is less a discrete and coherent school of theory and therapy than it is a general approach to thinking about human nature shaped by European philosophers such as Tillich, Jaspers, Husserl, Buber, Heidegger, and Marcel. Such philosophers resisted the effort in other psychologies to give an account of human behavior in terms of putatively more basic biological drives or underlying biosocial motivations and insisted instead on the distinctively and irreducible human experience of "being-in-the-world." A handful of existential psychiatrists, including Ludwig Binswanger and Eugene Minknowsky, have drawn from this philosophical approach principles for the conduct of psychotherapy. It is an approach that broadly influenced Carl Rogers, Eugene Gendlin, Gerald May, and Thomas Hora, all of whom have in their own ways helped shape the thought and practice of pastoral counselors and spiritual directors. In this same wide-ranging family of existentialist thinking, one would also have to locate Adrian van Kaam, a Dutch priest and psychologist at Duquesne University, who has elaborated his own distinctive method of spiritual direction called "Formative Spirituality" and established a center for the training of spiritual counselors and teachers.

Transpersonal Psychology, identified initially with the work of Abraham Maslow, claims to trace its philosophical lineage back to the investigations of William James at the turn of the century. Like James, transpersonal psychologists are interested in studying higher or altered states of consciousness and potentialities that extend beyond what can be experienced or accounted for by the operation of ordinary or personal consciousness. It is thus an approach that takes seriously mystical experience and much of the phenomena historically described in the literature of saints and adepts both East and West. Ken Wilbur has made one of the most systematic efforts to bring together the insights of the transpersonalists with the work of depth psychologists to construct a comprehensive model for psychospiritual development. Also important to note for its potential significance in the area of spirituality is the effort to bring Eastern psychology, principally Buddhist, into constructive conversation with Western psychology (Wilbur and others, 1986).

See also AFFECT, AFFECTIVITY; ANTHROPOLOGY, THEOLOGICAL; ATTENTION, ATTENTIVENESS; CONSCIOUSNESS; JOURNEY (GROWTH AND DEVELOPMENT IN SPIRITUAL LIFE); PERSONALITY TYPES; SELF; SOUL; TRANSFORMATION; TRUST.

Bibliography: PSYCHOANALYTIC PSYCHOLOGY: J. Jones, *Contemporary Psychoanalysis and Religion: Transference and Transcendence* (New Haven, Conn.: Yale Univ. Press, 1991). J. McDargh, *Psychoanalytic Object Relations Theory and the Study of Religion: On Faith and the Imaging of God* (Lanham, Md.: Univ. Press of America, 1983). W. Meissner, *Psychoanalysis and Religious Experience* (New Haven, Conn.: Yale Univ. Press, 1984). A.-M. Rizzuto, *The Birth of the Living God* (Chicago: Univ. of Chicago Press, 1979).

ANALYTICAL PSYCHOLOGY: R. Moore, ed., *Carl Jung and Christian Spirituality* (New York: Paulist, 1988). A. Ulanov, *Primary Speech: A Psychology of Prayer* (Atlanta: John Knox, 1982). M. Wolff-Salin, *No Other Light: Points of Convergence in Psychology and Spirituality* (New York: Crossroad, 1986). M. Stein, *Jung's Treatment of Christianity: The Psychology of a Religious Tradition* (Wilmette, Ill.: Chiron, 1985).

COGNITIVE DEVELOPMENTAL PSYCHOLOGY: J. Wolski Conn, *Spirituality and Personal Maturity* (New York: Paulist, 1989). W. Conn, *Christian Conversion: Development Perspectives on Autonomy and Surrender* (New York: Paulist, 1986). E. Liebert, *Changing Life Patterns: Adult Development in Spiritual Direction* (New York: Paulist, 1992).

OTHER PSYCHOLOGIES: E. Gendlin, *Focusing* (New York: Bantam, 1981). G. May, *Will and Spirit: A Contemplative Psychology* (New York: Harper & Row, 1983). A. van Kaam, *Formative Spirituality,* 5 vols. (New York: Crossroad, 1983–1992). K. Wilbur, J. Engler, and D. Brown, eds., *Transformations of Consciousness* (Boston: Shambhala Press, 1986).

H. JOHN McDARGH

PURGATION, PURGATIVE WAY

The purgative way is the framework used by spiritual authors in describing the prayer experiences that mark beginners in the journey to spiritual maturity. Growth in the awareness of God's saving presence and activity, which is the goal of all prayer, begins with the individual's willingness to take seriously the call to discipleship. In the process of purgation the Holy Spirit seeks to bring the believer into deeper participation in the mystery of Christ crucified and risen.

The task of the purgative way is to come to an accurate knowledge of one's self and to a true understanding of God's call to ever new life in Christ so that one can leave behind whatever attachments keep the individual from a deeper commitment to the Christian life. Meditation, in which one tries to reflect on Scripture and to allow the word of God to be the horizon within which attitudes and patterns of behavior are reformed in accord with the gospel, is understood to be the principal means to this end.

The attempt to put on the mind of Christ toward one's life and one's world involves the constant struggle to overcome the attitudes and patterns of behavior that tend to draw the individual away from a life of holiness and service. Fidelity to meditation and the sacramental life of the Church provide the mainstay for the attempts that a person, aided by grace, makes to reform his or her life. Fidelity to meditative prayer will eventuate in affective prayer in which both the mind and the heart are drawn more deeply into union with Christ.

Beginners in the spiritual life who are faithful to prayer often experience consolation, joy, and a sense of peace emerging in their lives. However, the goal of prayer is not the enjoyment of consolations but union with God. Hence the joy that a beginner initially has in prayer soon comes to be replaced by tedium, boredom, and a sense of helplessness. Although they are profoundly painful, these experiences of dryness and fatigue in prayer indicate that the purgative work of God, before which the person is necessarily passive, is now aiding the active efforts of the individual to reform his or her life.

The active and passive process of purgation for beginners, called the night of the senses, involves a realignment of values and a letting go of the sinful and superficial through a series of experiences that bring spiritual suffering and seem like night in comparison with one's previous enjoyment of the daylight of God's presence in prayer. The consolation in prayer given to beginners provides the impetus for undertaking the active purgation that is necessary for deeper life in Christ. There are, however, obstacles to growth in the spiritual life which cannot be removed by the individual alone, even when he or she is aided by grace, but which will yield only to the active role of God in the process of purgation.

Prayer for those in the purgative way is experienced as an alternation between consolation and desolation. God grants consolation in prayer to give the individual courage to continue the work of conversion that is still necessary. But God also allows the person to experience the reality of human weakness through desolation so that one learns to trust not in his or her own strength but solely in God's redemptive work in Christ's death and resurrection.

Since the path to spiritual maturity requires the growth of faith, hope, and love in the life of the individual, the purgative activity of God is aimed at deepening one's practice of the theological virtues. By God's grace faith is deepened, so that even amidst the darkness of the work of purification, the individual believes in the loving presence of God within his or her own life and in the lives of others. Since the presence of God is still hidden in the darkness of faith, hope becomes essential so that a person may wait trustingly in poverty of spirit and a sense of helplessness while the purifying work of God unfolds in one's life. Continual surrender to the purifying action of God flows from the increase of love that the Holy Spirit enkindles in the believer as he or she becomes increasingly more open to the mystery of God's loving presence.

Discursive meditation, which has previously served as the basis for growth in the awareness of God's presence in the purgative way, becomes increasingly difficult as one is drawn ever more deeply into union with God through the purifying work of the

Holy Spirit conforming the person to Christ. Instead of the diversity of words and images that had characterized meditative prayer up to this point, one is now invited simply to be in the divine presence and to gaze in faith upon a single interior image, which serves as the symbol of God's loving presence.

The prayer that comes at the end of the purgative way is known as the prayer of simplicity or the prayer of loving regard. The person now experiences prayer as a loving gaze of faith upon the mystery of God's love in Christ. Although the alternation between consolation and desolation continues, since the process of purgation is ongoing, the individual surrenders peacefully in the prayer of simplicity to the work of the Holy Spirit. The trusting surrender to the mystery of God's plan of salvation in one's own unique call to holiness, a surrender that comes at the end of the purgative way, is the threshold that leads to the illuminative way.

In the purgative way one has been taught to listen attentively and to respond in faith, hope, and love to the word of God as it beckons the individual to greater maturity in the following of Christ. In ever simpler forms of prayer, culminating in the loving gaze, the person has learned to surrender to the will of God as divine love begins the arduous process of freeing one from all the obstacles that hinder full union with the triune God. Purified by the sanctifying activity of the Holy Spirit in the exterior aspects of life, one is now ready to move forward to the experiences of infused prayer and the interior purifications that constitute the illuminative way and the dark night of the spirit.

See also ABANDONMENT; ASCETICISM; DARKNESS, DARK NIGHT; DETACHMENT; ILLUMINATION, ILLUMINATIVE WAY; MEDITATION; RECOLLECTION; THREE WAYS; UNION, UNITIVE WAY.

Bibliography: B. Groeschel, *Spiritual Passages: The Psychology of Spiritual Development* (New York: Crossroad, 1983). J. Lozano, *Praying Even When the Door Seems Closed: The Nature and Stages of Prayer* (New York: Paulist, 1989).

THOMAS D. McGONIGLE, O.P.

PURGATORY

See AFTERLIFE.

PURITY OF HEART

See APATHEIA; BEATITUDE(S); DETACHMENT; HEART; SIMPLICITY.

Q

QUIETISM

In general, quietism refers to any contemplative spirituality that proscribes human effort, particularly active ascetical practice, in favor of complete passivity and abandonment to God. More specifically, quietism was a 17th-century contemplative movement, found largely in Italy and France, which taught that human perfection is made possible only through the inner quiet of a totally passive mental prayer. This prayer of surrender in obscure faith was thought to permeate every aspect of one's life, even one's sleep. All other forms of prayer and spiritual practice, including meditations on the humanity of Jesus as well as acts of virtue, adoration, and devotion, were thought to be obstacles to the perfect prayer of contemplation. The soul was obliged to remain absolutely passive in interior annihilation in order not to disturb its contemplative gaze. Even temptations were not to be resisted, since objectively evil actions were thought not to be sinful as long as the soul remained passive and resigned. The moral consequences of their doctrines eventually led to the condemnation of quietism's leading proponent, Miguel de Molinos, by Pope Innocent XI in 1687.

Quietism is a persistent danger whenever contemplation is disengaged from virtuous action, or the sacred humanity of Jesus is obscured by a preoccupation with his divinity. When these distortions occur in the life of prayer, both creation and humanity tend to be devalued, and the human person can seem powerless to act, even by way of response, in relation to the saving grace of God.

See also ABANDONMENT; CONTEMPLATION, CONTEMPLATIVE PRAYER; PRAYER.

Bibliography: L. Dupré, "Jansenism and Quietism," *Christian Spirituality: Post-Reformation and Modern,* ed. L. Dupré and D. Saliers (New York: Crossroad, 1989) 121–142. P. Pourrat, *Christian Spirituality: Later Developments, Part II: From Jansenism to Modern Times* (Westminster, Md.: Newman, 1955).

KEITH R. BARRON, O.C.D.S.

R

RAPTURE

The word *rapture* is derived from the Latin *raptus,* meaning "seized," thus highlighting passivity, the hallmark of this and other forms of ecstasy. In 2 Cor 12:2-4 St. Paul testifies that he experienced rapture. However, the *locus classicus* of the description of rapture and its effects is St. Teresa of Avila's *Life,* chaps. 18 and 20, and *Interior Castle,* Sixth Mansions, chaps. 4–6. Teresa distinguishes several kinds of rapture, the best known being "flight of the spirit." She defines rapture as a sudden, forceful, and irresistible "manifestation of the tremendous power of the Lord" (*The Collected Works of St. Teresa of Avila,* 3 vols., trans. K. Kavanaugh and O. Rodríguez, Washington, D.C.: Institute of Carmelite Studies, 1976–85, 1:130), by which he draws the soul outside itself, sometimes to himself, at other times to heaven.

As is often the case, Teresa's iconic descriptions of this mystical favor are the most memorable. The saint images rapture as a cloud: ". . . the Lord gathers up the soul, let us say now, in the way the clouds gather up the earthly vapors and raises it completely out of itself. The cloud ascends to heaven and brings the soul along, and begins to show it the things of the kingdom that He prepared for it" (*ibid.,* 1:129). Flight of the spirit is "like a fire that is great and has been getting ready to start blazing, so the soul, through the readiness it has from God does suddenly begin to blaze and shoot forth a flame reaching high in the air" (*ibid.,* 1:357; see 1:118–119).

In the context of the evolution of the mystical life set forth in the *Interior Castle,* rapture pertains to the sixth mansions of spiritual betrothal; the soul is granted this favor by its Spouse to fortify it for the suffering it undergoes on earth and to increase its desire for the spiritual marriage of the seventh mansions. The physical effects of rapture include weightlessness, lifelessness, and the suspension of the senses. The test of whether rapture is authentic, i.e., its source is God and not the devil or the imagination, is, Teresa insists, that "from here on the soul desires nothing for itself; it wants its actions to be in complete conformity with [the Lord's] glory and His will" (*ibid.,* 1:137).

See also ECSTASY; EXTRAORDINARY PHENOMENA; MYSTICAL THEOLOGY; MYSTICISM; REVELATION(S); VISION(S).

Bibliography: J. Aumann, *Spiritual Theology* (Huntington, Ind.: Our Sunday Visitor, 1980) 348–349.

JOSEPH F. CHORPENNING, O.S.F.S.

READING, SPIRITUAL

The term *spiritual reading* refers to a practice much honored in the Christian heritage and set off from other kinds of reading as much by its methods as by its content. It is the reading of sacred texts done "in the Spirit." Long regarded as one of the indispensable means of nourishing the spiritual life, it has at times even been prized as a form of prayer in itself. Although certain schools, notably the *devotio moderna,* distinguished it from the monastic *lectio divina* because of its supposed weighting of the intellectual over the affective, most of the tradition has treated the two as the closest of cousins because of their nearly identical goals and means.

Linked to the Jewish practice of ruminatively vocalizing the sacred books (Deut 30:14), Christian spiritual reading has always aimed to savor rather than analyze the holy words and to dwell upon, rather than critique, their inner connections to the one Word (Rom 10:8). Slow perusal, peaceful penetration, recitation with all the senses, learning by heart, meditative encounter, remaining within the book, docile listening—such frequently used descriptions capture the difference between this holistic style of reading and other more narrowly cognitional types. Its distinctive methods of seeking quiet surroundings, repeating key phrases, attending to inner stirrings while reading, and surrendering to the meanings of the text point to the underlying intent to "circle back on the words" (Origen, *Homily on Genesis,* 10:2) again and again in order to touch the silent ground out of which they all spring.

Because pondering the sacred words connects the learner with a channel of wisdom stretching all the way back to the apostolic witness, spiritual reading is an eminently ecclesial act. The monastics especially gave pride of place to the Bible, that "great library of the monk," and regarded all later classics as streams flowing from this one source. The discipline has also occupied a prominent niche among the themes and certainly the methods of spiritual (ascetical and mystical) theology. Spiritual reading is prescribed repeatedly as a road to virtue, to deeper prayer, to the correction of faults and the initiation of right action, to emancipation from cultural blindness, and in general to all levels of conversion.

In our time, insights from the interpretative sciences have shed further light on the reason why spiritual reading has held such a privileged place. The reader is seen to move into the hermeneutical circle and there begin to recognize biases, surrender to the "enchantments" of the text, and become attentive to new meanings shaken out of the work as it encounters present culture. The individual sounds the religious depths of the classic when he or she stands trustfully in that fertile space between the text and its audience, and listens for the voice behind the words, for that wider event out of which the language on the page was born. In this way, for instance, not just the directives of a Vincent de Paul for helping the poor but also the poor's enshrinement for him as other Christs, not only the prayer instructions of a Teresa of Avila but her longings for union, and not simply the discernment techniques of an Ignatius Loyola but also his ardor for the kingdom of God transform the reader.

Thomas Merton considered spiritual reading a form of worship, a "homage to the God of all truth." His characterization gets to the heart of the matter. Genuine spiritual reading leads the practitioner to hear in the written and spoken words an echo of that much fuller Word in which all forms of genuine communication live and move and have their being.

See also CONTEMPLATION, CONTEMPLATIVE PRAYER; LECTIO DIVINA; MEDITATION; PRAYER; STUDY.

Bibliography: J. Leclercq, *The Love of Learning and the Desire for God,* 2nd ed. rev. (New York: Fordham Univ. Press, 1974). S. Muto, *A Practical Guide to Spiritual Reading* (Denville, N.J.: Dimension Books, 1976). J. Rousse, H. Sieben, and A. Boland, "Lectio Divina et Lecture Spirituelle," *D.Spir.,* vol. 9, cols. 470–510.

THOMAS F. McKENNA, C.M.

RECOLLECTION

The word *recollection* itself indicates the kind of spiritual action in question wherein persons once again "collect" themselves around a unifying center. Using certain disciplines, individuals grounded in the Spirit reassemble the scattered aspects of their personal world and draw them into a tighter whole. The recollected person has come to lay more conscious hold of that core which anchors him or her in existence.

Historically, the term referred to both this general process of regrouping and also to various practices and stages of growth which help that movement along its way. In a revealing pre-Christian usage, Plato touched upon its generic meaning. In *Phaedo* (83, 7), he saw in the story of Dionysus-Zagreus, a hero who was cut to pieces by the Titans and subsequently put back together again by Apollo, a symbol of the soul struggling to regain its unity, which was lost when its powers were dispersed in the body. To recollect was to reconstruct that original state and so regain the missing integrity.

Various Church writers recast the religious intuition behind the myth into Gospel motifs. Athanasius portrayed Antony of Egypt as recollecting his spirit to prepare for renouncing the world (*Life of Antony,* chap. 2). John Climacus advised the initiate to "gather together within yourself your vagabond mind" (*Scale of Perfection,* IV, 101). Augustine confessed that it is God who "brings together what is scattered" within himself (*Confessions,* X, 40). Gregory the Great not only attached moral conditions to the recollective project but identified it as the first stage on the contemplative ascent (*Homilies on Ezekiel,* II, hom. 5, 8-9).

The *Imitation of Christ* gave the notion a utilitarian slant by proposing it as an especially effective method for dispelling distractions in prayer (I, 21, 2; III, 48, 5). It was Francisco de Osuna, however, a Spanish Franciscan of the 16th century, who produced the fullest treatment of recollection. In his *Third spiritual Alphabet,* he assigned both general and particular meanings to the concept, viewing it in the overall as the calming needed in the three powers of intellect, will, and memory if they are to attend to the image of Christ within, and specifically as the different stages on the contemplative journey. Teresa of Avila was indebted to his insight that the dynamisms in the human faculties are not to be shut down and eradicated, but rather tapped at their deepest level. In addition, she adopted the main structures in Osuna's prayer of recollection for her own treatment of contemplation (*The Interior Castle,* Fourth and Seventh Mansions). Whether in its acquired form as the highest instance of active contemplation or in its infused state as the initial degree of mystical union, the process of reassembling the dispersed self around its true nucleus, the indwelling spirit of Jesus Christ, is essential to spiritual growth.

In recent times, recollection themes have surfaced in the various types of centering that attempt to sensitize the disciple to the resonance between his or her praying and the unifying Spirit of Christ who prays within. On the one hand, these techniques consist in efforts to create a tranquil outer and especially inner space so that the heart can unburden itself of the compulsivities of modern life and become a quiet cell where God can dwell. On the other, they recognize the gentle receptivity needed to let the Father of Jesus Christ be reborn into the consciousness of the believer. Something like the recollective process will be part of every prayer as discipline and conditioner, as anticipatory stage, and fundamentally as a religious experience in its own right, revealing the drawing near of the Spirit of Christ who gathers in all things.

See also ATTENTION, ATTENTIVENESS; BREATH, BREATHING; CENTERING PRAYER; CONTEMPLATION, CONTEMPLATIVE PRAYER; MEDITATION.

Bibliography: H. Nouwen, *The Way of the Heart* (New York: Seabury, 1981). F. de Osuna, *The Third Spiritual Alphabet,* trans. M. Giles (New York: Paulist, 1981). H. Sieven and S. Lopez Santidrian, "Recueillement," *D.Spir.,* vol. 13, cols. 248–268.

THOMAS F. McKENNA, C.M.

RECOVERY

See ADDICTION.

REDEMPTION

Redemption is the process by which the human race, separated from the communion with God for which it was created, is restored to that communion through the salvific work of Jesus Christ, a work especially effected in the paschal mystery of his suffering, death, resurrection, and glorification. From the beginning of the revelation of God's dealings with the human family, a twofold reality was recognized: that men and women had been created in the divine image and for intimate communion with God, as recounted in the creation story and the tale of Adam and Eve in the Garden of Eden (Gen 1-3). Alongside this reality, however (though clearly secondary to it and hence later in the account of Genesis), is the rupture of that relationship through sin, with its individual and corporate significance. Resolving the conflict between these realities was the promise of a restoration through a descendant of the first human family, the interpretation later generations gave to the Lord's words to the serpent after the temptation of Adam and Eve: "I will put enmity between you and the woman, and between your offspring and hers; he will strike at your head, while you strike at his heel" (Gen 3:15).

The history of God's dealings with the patriarchs and the people of Israel is understood theologically as a history of the salvific process leading to, and culminating in, the redemptive life, death, resurrection, and glorification of Jesus Christ, in which the longed-for restoration of com-

munion between human and divine was accomplished. The reality of this salvation was at the heart of the Church's proclamation of the Good News. The manner of its accomplishment, lying as it does in the realm of divine mystery, has been understood in a variety of ways through the centuries. Some of these focused on the sacrificial or propitiatory aspects of the death of Jesus on the cross. Others attended more to the fact of the incarnation itself as beginning the restoration of humanity and its elevation to a divinized state.

Although redemption—the notion of ransoming a captive or buying back a slave from someone—is a metaphor for the saving action of God, understanding of the redemptive process often took elements of the nonreligious notion of redemption and sought to apply them to the divine mystery in such a way that God was understood as somehow paying Satan for sinful humanity or wrathfully punishing Jesus as a substitute victim for the demands of justice. Such an approach had a definite impact on spirituality because it emphasized God's justice, understood in a narrow sense as commutative justice, over mercy. It also emphasized the physical suffering of Jesus on the cross and failed to take into account adequately the fact that salvation is accomplished through the entire paschal mystery, which includes not only the suffering and death but also the resurrection and glorification of the Lord.

The Second Vatican Council speaks of redemption in terms of the transformation of the human person through the union of human nature to the divine Son and through his death and resurrection (LG 7). This is an example of the more recent appreciation of the redemption as effected by the entire mystery of Jesus: incarnation, life, death, resurrection, glorification. It also reflects the positive emphasis on what redemption accomplishes in the person rather than a negative emphasis on the prior state and speculation about hypothetical proprietary rights by the devil. Redemption is understood as part of the mystery of the Trinity, as the Son fulfilling the universal salvific will of the Father by pouring out the Holy Spirit on believers to unite them to the Son and through the Son to the eternal Father. Redemption thus is part of the interpersonal dynamic between the human person and the human family and the divine mystery, not a cryptoeconomic transaction between God and Satan.

Growing interest among liberation theologians in the significance of redemption as liberation from sin and sinful social structures is also part of contemporary theological discussion and in recent years has led to further reflection on the spirituality implied in such an understanding of redemption as affecting human and Christian life in the here and now. Gustavo Gutiérrez is an example of a liberation theologian who finds in the traditional Catholic spirituality of figures such as John of the Cross a way of entry into the mystery that is meaningful for this line of development.

See also BLOOD; CHRIST; DIVINIZATION; INCARNATION; JUSTICE; LIBERATION THEOLOGY, INFLUENCE ON SPIRITUALITY; MERCY; PASCHAL MYSTERY; RESURRECTION.

Bibliography: D. Edwards, *What Are They Saying About Salvation?* (New York: Paulist, 1986). John Paul II, *The Redeemer of Man* (Washington: USCC, 1979).

MICHAEL DODD, O.C.D.

REFLECTION

Reflection, meaning literally "to bend back," refers generically to the act of reconsidering what one knows and loves, and most basically to the underlying processes out of which these movements spring. While its most technically developed analysis is given in the philosophical disciplines, the concept has its deepest grounding in the dynamics of the spiritual life and has been regarded as an indispensable ingredient of any inner journey.

Taking his lead from the Neoplatonist notion that the mind in knowing any particular object simultaneously knows itself, Augustine traveled down into his own self-awareness and found at its font the vestiges of the indwelling Trinity. From another angle, Aquinas also commented on how it is that all knowledge is radically self-knowledge. By a more ontologically directed reflection, he arrived at that foundational reality whose essence it is to exist. In modern times, Kant's investigation of the universal requisites for cognition was taken up by certain theorists who developed an increasingly refined appreciation for the infinitely receding backdrop against which all knowing and loving happen. This horizon of mystery rises to awareness, at least in an implicit way, through a reflection on the transcendental conditions necessary for knowing and desiring. A final historical contribution comes from existentialist thinkers who have highlighted the indispensability of sincere reflection as a road to that sense of personal authenticity which is given only when the individual disengages from the automaticisms of mass culture in order to catch sight of the genuine self.

In our time, Thomas Merton pulled a number of these threads through the Christian spiritual tradition. He observed how the attainment of authentic personhood requires that special kind of reflection called contemplation, which alone can loosen the chains of social conformism. Only through such activity can the disciple hope to break through the pretenses of the flimsy "smoke-self" constructed by the false ego and draw up the genuine inner person "like a jewel from the bottom of the sea" (*New Seeds of Contemplation,* New York: New Directions, 1972, p. 38).

Merton also underscored the essential difference between shallow, narcissistic kinds of reflection and that more holistic type that has been taken up into God's own Self-awareness. Even if a disciple succeeds in reaching that imaginary inner window that opens onto the divine, that individual, warns Merton, has not yet entered that farland which contains the real roots of love. "Unless God speaks God's name in your soul, you will no more know God than a stone knows the ground upon which it rests in solitude" (*New Seeds,* p. 39). In the last analysis, the reflective process comes to full term only in faith, in that graced act of bending all the way back to its own wellsprings.

See also ATTENTION, ATTENTIVENESS; CONTEMPLATION, CONTEMPLATIVE PRAYER; MEDITATION; RECOLLECTION.

Bibliography: R. Schmidt, "Reflection," *New Catholic Encyclopedia,* vol. 12, pp. 166–169.

THOMAS F. McKENNA, C.M.

REFORMATION AND CATHOLIC REFORMATION SPIRITUALITIES

Background

Despite the criticisms that contemporaries and subsequent historians leveled against it, the religious devotion of many Christians in Western Europe had reached an almost unprecedented intensity by the beginning of the 16th century. This situation was the culmination of a number of factors operative in medieval and late-medieval society, factors so numerous and complex as to defy summary. The intensity manifested itself in the life and writings of mystics like Catherine of Siena and the Rheno-Flemish school; in movements like the *devotio moderna,* and its widely disseminated masterpiece *The Imitation of Christ;* in the renewal of the mendicant orders through the so-called observantist reforms; in greater emphasis on the necessity of sacramental confession and in various forms of veneration of the Eucharist; in a passionate seeking of the patronage especially of local saints through the cult of their relics and pilgrimages to their shrines; in the proliferation of lay confraternities and other voluntary associations noted for

their penitential practices or sometimes unruly celebrations of holy days, but also for their corporate works of mercy toward the sick, foundlings, and bereaved.

Contributing to the religious intensity of the period were conditions in society at large. The plagues and epidemics that swept through Europe even after the Black Death of the late 14th century, and then the outbreak of syphilis at the end of the 15th century, focused people's attention on their mortality and promoted interest in the passion and death of Christ and in the "art of dying" well. The devastation wrought by war, flood, and famine did the same. Among leaders of society the scandal of the Great Schism was not forgotten, kept vivid by the continuing financial exactions of the Roman Curia, which pointed to its failure to reform itself and seemed to mirror the worldly lives of local prelates. A newly acute historical consciousness highlighted the discrepancy between these realities and the simplicity of the early Church.

This situation gave impetus to widespread and variously defined calls for "reform" which had been in the air especially since the Council of Constance (1415–1418) and which generated a powerful rhetoric related to areas as diverse as ecclesiastical discipline, theological method, pastoral practice, schooling, public morality, and the exercises of piety. The invention of the printing press provided a vehicle for this rhetoric to reach all literate persons.

Efforts to address deficiencies in all these areas were under way in certain localities by the beginning of the 16th century, but they would not achieve definition and coordination until the middle decades. Surely of capital importance in this regard would be the outbreak of the Reformation and reactions to it, but those phenomena must be regarded as only the most dramatic manifestations of the hunger for a more genuine and heartfelt religious experience which antedated them and which to some extent would continue to develop almost independently of them.

Desiderius Erasmus (1469–1536)

The medieval and late-medieval traditions mentioned above would continue as powerful forces, especially in Catholicism, but the freshest and most articulate voice addressing the areas of greatest concern that would have impact in different ways and degrees upon both Catholicism and Protestantism was that of Desiderius Erasmus and the Humanist movement that he represented. Long recognized for his importance in shaping modern Western culture, Erasmus has become recognized only in the past few decades for his major contribution to *pietas,* his favorite term to describe the central concern of his life. By it he meant the godly or Christian life in all its aspects.

Erasmus' first major statement on the subject was his *Handbook of the Christian Soldier,* published in 1504 and republished numerous times in both a revised Latin text and vernacular translations. In 1516 he published the first critical edition of the Greek New Testament, the first volumes of his ongoing critical editions of the Fathers of the Church, and his *Education of the Christian Prince,* in which he articulated the Humanist conviction that through education *pietas* could be instilled and fostered in the young, thus laying the foundations for reform of the Church and society. Until his death he continued to publish a vast quantity of works dealing with prayer, preaching, confession, matrimony, widowhood, theological method, Christian death, the respective merits of virginity and martyrdom, the role of grace and free will, as well as a catechism, a prayer book, a sample liturgy, and commentaries on Scripture in the form of homilies and paraphrases. These and his many other writings, even those ostensibly on unrelated subjects, provided him with ample opportunity to address all the religious issues of his day.

To some of his contemporaries and to subsequent generations, Erasmus came to be best known for his criticisms of prevailing practice. Although those criticisms were uttered from his own particular standpoint, they articulated grievances felt in many quarters and pinpointed issues that would continue to preoccupy the era. He satirized the excesses and superstition in popular devotion to the saints and to their relics and shrines, and he criticized the arithmetical and mechanical character of certain supposedly grace-winning prayers, rituals, routinized liturgies, and religious talismans. He challenged the assumption that the profession of religious vows guaranteed greater sanctity than could be attained in other vocations, especially marriage. He questioned the notion that a just war was ever possible for a Christian society, and he ridiculed popes and bishops in armor. Imbued with a strong sense of morality, he leveled harsh words at lasciviousness in dress, frivolous pastimes, and excesses in food and drink.

Perhaps most important, Erasmus criticized the by then established Scholastic theology for the aridity of its speculation, its proof-texting use of the Bible, and its divorce from spirituality. The "modern theologians" were thus largely responsible, he proposed, for the situation of his day in which spiritual practice and theory were largely unrelated to the Scriptures and to the central mysteries of the Christian faith, particularly as expressed in the Pauline letters.

Erasmus' criticisms along these lines won him many enemies among Catholics, as did his later criticisms of Luther among Protestants. The prejudices he thereby aroused caused later generations to lose sight of the positive side of his message, reiterated though it was by him so insistently and persuasively. Nonetheless, both his criticisms and his solutions had an immense impact on his age, even on some of those who more or less explicitly repudiated them. In recent years his insights have become increasingly recognized by Catholic scholars for their consonance with the teachings and style of discourse of Vatican Council II, and therefore notably relevant for contemporary spirituality.

Erasmus often referred to his spiritual teaching as "the philosophy of Christ." This philosophy, or love of wisdom, was based on the Bible, the devout reading of which was meant to be the center of Christian devotion. The Fathers of the Church were, according to him, the best expositors of the Bible, for they combined teaching derived directly from study of the text with a literary style that led to its personal appropriation. Their style rendered their teaching accessible to all and led to a "theological *life*," the goal of every genuine theology. Christ's "philosophy" avoided the arid disputes and the trivial and irrelevant questions of his contemporaries and provided a model for a spirituality-theology-ministry newly centered on the paschal mystery.

The new way of approaching the Bible advocated by Erasmus and many of his Humanist colleagues had other consequences for spirituality. It meant an enlargement of the emphasis on the suffering and death of Christ to give full consideration to Christ's resurrection and glorification, or it sometimes placed emphasis on the incarnation as the best expression of the full mystery of Christ. Both these shifts tended to counter the morbid preoccupations with death in much late-medieval piety and significantly qualified the familiar theme of "contempt of the world."

The "return to the sources"—the Bible and the Fathers—provided criteria for excising unsuitable accretions to the practice of piety and for simplifying it. Translation of the "philosophy of Christ" into one's life meant that one despised riches, did not avenge wrongs, came to the aid of the poor, detested war, cherished others as members of the same body, put one's trust in God. The philosophy was sustained and expressed in relatively few practices like conversation with devout persons, the hearing of sermons, reception of the Eucharist, the repeated recall of one's baptism and the paschal mystery, prayerful reading especially of the Bible and the Fathers, and using appropriate remedies to resist temptation.

Especially with the passing of the years, Erasmus showed more respect for pious usages sanctioned by the longstanding tradition of the Church when they were not discordant with the simplicity of the philosophy of Christ and undue weight was not attributed to them. While Erasmus saw the philosophy of Christ to be affective in its basic orientation, he has little to say about the mystical aspects of spirituality that were of such great concern to many Catholics in his century.

Like many of his Humanist counterparts, Erasmus believed that the ethical content of the Greek and Latin classics correlated to a large extent with Christian teaching. While he rejected many presuppositions of Scholastic theology, he entertained a conviction similar to Aquinas's in this regard, and thus at least implicitly assumed that "grace perfects nature." This assumption opened the philosophy of Christ to religious and ethical truth outside the Christian tradition and strengthened its more positive and world-affirming aspects.

Martin Luther (1483–1546)

The issue of the relationship between grace and free will brought Erasmus into open conflict with Martin Luther. Stung by Luther's bitter criticism of his position, Erasmus defended himself, but as a result of the exchange he took care to give the Pauline doctrine of grace more adequate expression in his writings on *pietas*.

The free will-grace issue had already become the burning theological question of the day, but it was for Luther first and foremost the foundation for his spirituality, although he would not have conceded this distinction. Like so many of his generation, he sought to overcome the dichotomy between spirituality and theology. In a different and even more radical way than that of Erasmus, he sought to ground that theology/spirituality in the Bible.

Erasmus had been immersed in the Church Fathers and the classics from his earliest years. Luther came out of a much less cosmopolitan tradition and, as a member of the Augustinian Order, had been formally trained in Scholastic theology. After his appointment to the theological faculty of the newly founded University of Wittenberg in 1513, he began to read more widely, and was surely influenced to some degree by the "new learning" of the Humanist movement. Many of the issues related to spirituality for which he would do battle after the publication of the Ninety-Five Theses in late 1517 are, in fact, remarkably similar to those named by Erasmus, but this coincidence derives more from the general preoccupations of the era than from the direct influence of Erasmus or other Humanists. In any case, although the issues might have been similar or even the same, their resolution was often different, and, more important, they were encased in a quite different emotional and cultural frame of reference.

No record exists of any dramatic religious conversion in Erasmus, just as it is lacking for Aquinas and some other revered religious figures. Luther's two great conversions—the first "to become a monk" in 1506 and then the "Tower Experience" some years later—must, however, be the starting point for understanding his spirituality. In this regard he represents a common phenomenon of his age, in which analogous experiences are attested to for persons as different as Gasparo Contarini, Ignatius Loyola, Teresa of Avila, and Charles Borromeo.

As Luther described both of his conversions, he saw them as peremptory, instantaneous, and without premonition. The fact that even today scholars cannot altogether agree on a precise dating of the

"Tower Experience" indicates, however, that that event, in which he saw that we are saved not by "works" but by "faith alone," was longer in the making than Luther himself perceived. It was preceded by a long period of spiritual distress marked by intense feelings of powerlessness over his sinful inclinations, an inability to induce in himself the contrition requisite for forgiveness in the sacrament of penance, and a further inability to confess adequately his real or supposed sins.

This conversion experience was preceded as well by careful study of the Epistle to the Romans, which provided him with the theological categories to interpret the experience when it occurred. He saw with blinding light that he had been trying to save himself by "doing what he could"—by his "works"—whereas Paul taught that what was distinctively Christian was to acknowledge one's powerlessness and to let God, the only true Savior, do the saving by abandoning oneself to his gracious favor (or grace). It was the fallacy of the Jews and pagans to think that one could win or deserve that favor by one's own efforts. It was also the heresy of Pelagianism. "Let God be God!"

As the controversies first aroused by the Ninety-Five Theses continued to swirl around him and threaten his very life, Luther became convinced that the theologians of his day and even the whole "papal Church" were infected with Pelagianism. This led him to an outright rejection of the method and much of the content of medieval theology and to a reluctant but absolutely firm farewell to that Church itself.

In Luther's interpretation, the teaching of Scholastic theologians on grace and salvation was inextricably bound up with Aristotle's ethics, which taught that one saved oneself from the consequences of lower inclinations by the acquisition of good habits. Paul taught that one was saved from them by the utterly gratuitous grace of God alone, responded to by faith. Thus Luther's cry of "Scripture alone" was, in its negative aspect, a repudiation of "philosophy," the wisdom of this world, which was altogether misleading and false on the great question of one's salvation. In other words, there was no correlation between "nature and grace," between "free will and grace."

Upon this base he began to build a spirituality whose center rested on a powerful proclamation of "the gospel," for faith comes "by hearing." The gospel was a "shout," a "war cry" of the "good news" that God loves us as we are, not for our achievements or "works" or our ability to fulfill "the Law." For the devout Christian, the hearing of sermons concerning this message was a paramount exercise of piety, as, consequently, was the direct reading of the text. The "Law"—the Decalogue and the commandment to love God and one's neighbor as oneself—could be fulfilled only when one truly loved it in one's heart, which was altogether due to "grace alone."

Luther did not, therefore, eliminate good works from the life of the Christian, as he was often accused of doing. He insisted, however, that they were the result of grace, not its precondition. In his "Freedom of the Christian," perhaps his most eloquent and adequate expression of his position (1520), he stated clearly that he did not oppose good works themselves, which was unthinkable for a Christian, but opposed "false opinions" concerning them.

Nonetheless, Luther's conflict with the theological and ecclesiastical establishment, and his study of the Bible and other early Christian sources, led him to reject a number of medieval practices of piety and the assumptions that undergirded them, but not so radically as some of his followers and other Protestant reformers did. The "works" of piety and charity that he commended bear a generic resemblance to those commended by Erasmus.

Luther saw baptism and the Eucharist as the only sacraments warranted by the New Testament. He firmly believed in the Real Presence. While he retained the traditional structure of the Mass, he defined it as a communal celebration of the Last Supper rather than as a sacrifice offered by a priest. He enriched the service with beautiful hymns in the vernacular that he either composed himself or translated from the Latin. Other hymns, such as those on the Decalogue, were used especially during catechetical instruction.

Luther strenuously opposed obligatory celibacy for the clergy and was only slightly less opposed to the traditional vows of religion. He often commended prayer, especially in its communal forms in the church and home, and composed a prayer book, but, compared with many of his Catholic contemporaries, left few detailed instructions as to how the individual might engage in meditation or contemplation. Some scholars argue that he reoriented prayer away from being a pathway to a mystical vision of God to being a bulwark against trials and temptations. Despite the power of grace, the Christian is, according to Luther, in constant battle against "the world, the flesh, and the devil."

John Calvin (1509–1564)

Although John Calvin, who was Luther's much younger contemporary, adopted his most basic insights, he had a much different personality and had been trained in law and the humanities rather than Scholastic theology. Luther's "conversion to the gospel" was a powerful emotional experience, of which he left ample testimony. Only with difficulty can we trace Calvin's "conversion" around the years 1532–1534, and it seems to have been reasoned and primarily intellectual. All this means that despite a substantially identical doctrinal framework, Calvin's spirituality is of a different texture than Luther's.

It is significant, for instance, that, unlike Luther, who never composed a professed synthesis of his theology-spirituality, Calvin published his "handbook of piety," *The Institutes of the Christian Religion,* as a young man in 1536. He amplified it in several subsequent editions, culminating with the much expanded Latin edition of 1559 and the beautiful French translation of the next year. He also left behind a number of homilies and biblical commentaries.

Especially in the heat of controversy, Calvin came to express the devastating results of original sin in ever more pessimistic terms. This also provided him with a not often recognized opportunity to celebrate the power of grace. He came to differ with Luther somewhat on the Eucharist and certain other doctrines, but he especially criticized him for his failure to stress the importance of personal and public discipline in Christian life. When, therefore, Calvin began to preside over the Church of Geneva in 1541, he imposed a strict code of public conduct that became Geneva's hallmark. By force of the paradox that often seems to characterize close adherence to an Augustinian doctrine of grace, probity in external deportment assumed great significance, a development that in Calvinism opened the way for a dour and puritanical moralism, as happened in Catholicism with Jansenism.

The Anabaptists

With the so-called Anabaptists or "radical wing" of the Reformation, spirituality moved somewhat away from the biblical text and preoccupation with the Pelagian issue to greater emphasis on the free action of the Spirit within the individual, "believer's baptism," and radical stances on issues of social morality, ranging, for instance, from absolute pacifism to aggressive use of the sword for their cause, usually accompanied by a vivid millenarianism. These positions immediately won for them the fear and enmity of both Catholics and other Protestants.

The socially milder forms of Anabaptism as found in the Swiss Brethren, Mennonites, and others cultivated an inwardness and a simplicity in lifestyle, doctrine, and Church organization to the extent that they almost became their self-definition.

Although the Quakers, or Society of Friends, founded in the 17th century, are not their lineal descendants, there are certain congruences in spirituality among them.

The Council of Trent (1545–1563)

The Council of Trent was the corporate and institutional response of the Catholic Church to the many issues raised by the Reformation. While it never spoke of itself as dealing with spirituality, its many decisions concerning doctrine and morals had an immense, if generally indirect, influence on it. Trent's failure to make an explicit correlation between spirituality and the content of its doctrinal decrees gave unwitting support to the distinction between "theology" and "spirituality" that would continue in later Catholicism.

The centerpiece of Trent's doctrinal pronouncements was the decree of the sixth session on justification (1547). Within the framework of a cooperative understanding of the relationship between grace and free will, the decree is surely anti-Pelagian. From a pastoral viewpoint, it was perhaps not worded dramatically enough to forestall in every instance teachings that, even if they might pay lip service to orthodoxy, were untainted by Pelagianism or Semi-Pelagianism. The idea that one's worth is constituted by one's achievements was too deeply ingrained in Western culture to be eliminated in the religious sphere simply by an official decree.

Trent's protracted treatment of the doctrine of the seven sacraments assured their place in Catholic piety. In its disciplinary decrees the council concentrated on the pastoral obligations of bishops and pastors of parishes, especially insisting on their duty to preach. Contrary to what is often thought, sermons played as large a role in the spirituality of the Catholic Reformation as they did in Lutheranism and Calvinism. Their purpose was often construed differently, however, as is betrayed by Trent's injunction that they treat "vices and virtues, punishment and reward." The severe morality that marked the spirituality of certain Protestant confessions had its counterparts, therefore, in the Catholic Reformation, of which the preaching and disciplinary program of St. Charles Borromeo (1538–1584) as archbishop of Milan is a good example.

Trent never forbade the reading of the Bible by the faithful. Nonetheless, forces outside the council, perhaps encouraged by Trent's cautious reverence for the Vulgate and its other legislation about the publication of Scripture, cast suspicion on that traditional practice in many quarters, and the first papal *Index of Prohibited Books,* issued by Pope Paul IV in 1559, forbade all vernacular translations. The decree was soon mitigated, but for the next four centuries reading of the Bible by the ordinary Catholic would rarely be explicitly commended in works of piety. Even so, the New Testament continued as the basis for such fundamental works as the *Spiritual Exercises* of Ignatius Loyola.

Important though they are, the documents of Trent cannot be interpreted, therefore, as providing a comprehensive vision of the spirituality of the Catholic Reformation. The council's emphasis on the parish as the locus where Catholics were primarily to find their spiritual refection takes little account of the bustling activity of the churches of the religious orders, and Trent never mentions confraternities and other voluntary associations, perhaps the most important centers of piety for devout Catholics at least until the French Revolution. These organizations, in fact, took on a new vigor during the period. They also underwent some changes in character, gradually coming under more direct clerical control and codifying more precisely the spiritual obligations of members.

Given its agenda, Trent of course made no mention of the powerful movements toward a deeper interiority that during this period would move the history of spiritual-ity in Catholicism into a new era and almost give spirituality a new definition. For the most part, these movements began in Spain, even though they were greatly influenced in their earlier stages by spiritual writers from Italy, the Low Countries, and elsewhere.

Roman Catholic Spiritualities

The Benedictines and particularly the mendicant orders played pivotal roles in the elaboration of spiritual doctrine and practice. Three Franciscans of the observantist movement were among the first to write influential works: the *Arte para servir a Dios* by Alonso de Madrid (1521), the *Tercer abecedario espiritual* by Francisco de Osuna (1527), and the *Subida del monte Sion* by Bernardino de Laredo (1535). While orthodox in their religious beliefs, their interest was less in Scripture and dogma than in providing instruction on how to achieve internal silence and recollection in order to permit the penetration of divine action into the soul.

Analysis of religious experience was thus the basis of the teaching of these Franciscan masters and of others. It was in this climate that the mystical tendencies of 16th-century Spain began to develop. Their heterodox manifestations were found in the *Alumbrados,* and their greatest orthodox manifestations in the special form of Carmelite spirituality found in Teresa of Avila and John of the Cross. The importance Teresa attributed to spiritual direction in her many writings helped to popularize the persuasion of its importance and to move it to a new degree of sophistication in early modern Catholicism.

More generally accessible spiritualities were proposed by other Spaniards. In his *Ejercitatorio de la vida espiritual* (1500), Garcia Jiménez de Cisneros, the Benedictine abbot of Montserrat, introduced the practice of daily mental prayer for his monks. The *Ejercitatorio* was one element in a vast movement fostering such prayer, which found expression, for instance, in the Franciscan Peter of Alcántara, in the Dominican Louis of Granada, and especially in Ignatius Loyola.

Ignatius would also be one of the first ardent promoters of more frequent reception of the Eucharist than had been customary, even up to once or twice a week. It would become a key element of Jesuit spirituality and eventually of modern Catholicism. Ignatian spirituality would also be more fully imbued with pastoral concern and less wedded to the cloister than many of the others originating in Spain at this time, and would thus become one of the classic expressions of apostolic spirituality. The Jesuits would be especially important for creating and popularizing the retreat as we have come to know it. Among the major Catholic spiritualities to emerge in this period, Jesuit spirituality would be in some respects the most consonant with that of Erasmus, even though the Jesuits entertained some reservations about him.

During the 16th century Italy produced little that was original in spirituality, but it served as a matrix for movements begun elsewhere, especially in Spain. The Oratory, founded by Philip Neri (1515–1595), was of course important, but it left no major document articulating its positions. An internationally influential handbook of spiritual doctrine and practice, however, was *The Spiritual Combat* (1589) by the Theatine Lorenzo Scupoli (1530–1610). Intended for Christians in all walks of life, it foreshadowed works like Francis de Sales' *Introduction to the Devout Life*.

By the beginning of the 17th century, the center of Catholic spirituality had moved to France, where the so-called French School emerged. That school in its many articulations was not unaffected by Quietism and in one way or another even by Jansenism. The Baroque culture that was then coming into being in Italy seems to have influenced spirituality there in more optimistic, less introspective directions.

Conclusion

The period we have been considering was a major turning point in the history of spirituality, and its issues, failures, and achievements continue to have impact today. Although the period was marked by an immensely rich and often confusing diversity, it in general called for a deeper interiority than seemed to many of the leading figures to have been operative earlier. At the same time it witnessed some notable attempts to correlate spirituality with broader social issues.

This period witnessed heroic efforts to correlate spirituality more directly with the Bible and theology, a venture that was more successful with Humanists and Protestants than with others. It witnessed among Catholics in Spain and France a desire to reflect in a newly systematic way upon personal religious experience and the direct action of God within the soul. This resulted in a burgeoning of literature on mysticism and the higher forms of prayer, as well as the production of more highly developed instruments of spirituality such as retreats, spiritual direction, and methods of meditation and contemplation than had been known before.

Practically all the spiritualities of the period wrestled implicitly or explicitly with the crucial issue of the relationship between nature and grace. Even those that opted for a stronger statement about the role of the latter were often unable to free themselves from the persistent moralism that dogged the era and that too frequently resorted to fear of punishment to achieve its ends.

Protestants and Catholics alike insisted that a deep spirituality was available outside the cloister and in the married state. Even though Catholics postulated a special advantage for those living under religious vows, in their confraternities and similar organizations they employed an effective instrument for fostering a deeper spirituality in the laity and the diocesan clergy. Almost without exception, both Protestants and Catholics sought to effect a greater simplicity in the theory and practice of spirituality, but they often had great difficulty in achieving or maintaining it.

See also CARMELITE SPIRITUALITY; FRENCH SCHOOL OF SPIRITUALITY; IGNATIAN SPIRITUALITY; JANSENISM; MODERN SPIRITUALITY; PROTESTANT SPIRITUALITIES; QUIETISM; RHENO-FLEMISH SPIRITUALITY.

Bibliography: L. Châtellier, *The Europe of the Devout: The Catholic Reformation and the Formation of a New Society* (Cambridge: Cambridge Univ. Press, 1989). H. O. Evennett, *The Spirit of the Counter-Reformation* (Cambridge: Cambridge Univ. Press, 1968). M. Lienhard, "Luther and the Beginnings of the Reformation," *Christian Spirituality: High Middle Ages and Reformation,* ed. J. Raitt, World Spirituality 17 (New York: Crossroad, 1987) 268–299. J. O'Malley, "Introduction," *Spiritualia,* Collected Works of Erasmus 66 (Toronto: Univ. of Toronto Press, 1988) ix–li, and "Some Distinctive Characteristics of Jesuit Spirituality in the Sixteenth Century," *Jesuit Spirituality: A Now and Future Resource* (Chicago: Loyola Univ. Press, 1990) 1–20. M. Marcocchi, "Spirituality in the Sixteenth and Seventeenth Centuries," *Catholicism in Early Modern History: A Guide to Research,* ed. J. O'Malley (St. Louis: Center for Reformation Research, 1988) 163–192. L. Richard, *The Spirituality of John Calvin* (Atlanta: John Knox, 1974).

JOHN W. O'MALLEY, S.J.

REIGN OF GOD

See KINGDOM OF GOD.

RELIGION

See CARDINAL VIRTUES; DEVOTION(S), POPULAR; PIETY.

RELIGIOUS LIFE

In most general terms, religious life is a distinctive lifestyle, seen as countercultural in relation to that of the majority, embraced by men and women through a long-term or life dedication for a transcendent end—divinization.

Religious life is a global, cross-cultural phenomenon, not restricted to one historical period or location, existing in pre-Christian and non-Christian history in communities such as the Pythagoreans, Jains, Buddhists (beginning in the 6th century B.C., the latter two continuing to the present). Similar developments appear in Judaism just prior to the Christian Era among some celibate Essenes and the monks of Qumran. In each succeeding historical period for 2,500 or more years, men and women have been perceived in various cultures as set apart from the mainstream of humanity, precisely by choosing to stand outside the natural family with its activities devoted to meeting the needs of daily life, in view of a particular transcendent end. In Jainism and Buddhism this end is freedom from the otherwise endless cycle of rebirth; in Judaism it is preparation for the messianic era.

In this context religious life is the public and so institutionalized recognition of the fact that human experience includes a dimension that goes beyond history. It is thus fundamentally a phenomenon of hope, that is, of dissatisfaction with what one now has and of confidence in something better going beyond the present. Since it is a *life,* it can never be exhaustively described; here the considerations will be limited principally to a discussion of changes stemming from legislation of the Second Vatican Council.

Religious life in the Catholic tradition will be discussed with reference to (1) its definition, (2) its biblical foundation, (3) its charismatic and evolutionary character, (4) its reinterpretation and transformation since Vatican II, and (5) some outcomes of this process with respect to the understanding and future of religious life.

Definition

In the Catholic tradition, the term *religious life* has a general and a specific, canonical sense that is itself part of a theological and historical process as well as a conditioned outcome of that process.

General Sense

In a broad sense, religious life is a particular form of following Christ in celibacy, embraced under the inspiration and gift (charism) of the Holy Spirit as an expression of the gospel counsels and approved by Church authority as an authentic expression of Christian vocation. Religious life as such is neither clerical nor lay. This way of life is called "religious" (from the Latin *religare,* meaning "to bind") because one binds oneself to God through the evangelical counsels by a sacred promise, in virtue of which one is "totally dedicated to God by an act of supreme love, and is committed to the honor and service of God under a new and special title" (LG 44).

The modes in which this call has been and is being expressed, however, are so personal, diverse, and historically conditioned that the phenomenon continually escapes efforts to codify its manifestations, as the Code of Canon Law illustrates. In the Code, the term "institutes of consecrated life" refers to religious institutes (can. 607), secular institutes (can. 710), the eremitical life (can. 603), and to the order of virgins (can. 604), each of which includes a profession of the evangelical counsels of chastity, poverty, and obedience, either by vows or other sacred bonds, and is approved by Church authority (can. 573). Communities that observe a common life and share an apostolic purpose, but without religious vows, are called "societies of apostolic life," though some of these also embrace the counsels by a bond defined in their constitutions (can. 731).

Specific Sense

In the particular, canonical sense, the term *religious life* refers to one form of consecrated life, characterized by public profession of gospel counsels, observance of common life, and some form of "separation from the world" (can. 607 § 3). The latter is a technical phrase intended to distinguish religious life from that of secular institutes, a form of consecrated life meant for the faithful "living in the world" (can. 710).

Biblical Foundation

Religious life is rooted in the word of God understood in the Hebrew sense (*dabar*) as acting powerfully in personal and historical events.

1) The religious life sees its model as Christ himself, the Word made flesh, who lived a celibate, poor life (Lk 9:58), sharing a community of prayer and ministry with the disciples, totally open and obedient to the mission of redemption, even to death on a cross.

2) The guide of religious life is the teaching of Jesus, the Word of God, about detachment and dispossession of material goods (Mt 19; Lk 12:32-34) as a way of union with Christ and of availability for ministry (Lk 10:1-5), celibacy for the kingdom of God (Mt 9), and commitment to the will of God (Jn 4:32-34; 6:38-39), as well as vulnerability to persecution in the confidence of eternal life (Mk 10:28-31).

3) Religious life recognizes the ideal vision of Christian community described in Acts 2:42-47 and 4:32-37 as a model of communal response to the mystery of the Church, not only with respect to its form—common life, sharing of prayer, and worship—but also with respect to its source, namely, the outpouring of the Holy Spirit, whose gift effects the self-dedication of, and mutual relationships among, believers.

4) Religious life understands the nature of its organic development under the influence of the Holy Spirit in keeping with perceived conditions of the time in the teaching of Paul on virginity and his counsel of celibacy to widows, and recognizes the role of the apostles and bishops in interpreting and directing the expression of these gifts (1 Cor 7:25-40; 1 Tm 5:11-12).

In these early developments of Christian life and teaching, we see the word of God (*dabar*) living and acting in history, and

---

can discern the essential features of religious life as it has unfolded: personal response to the gospel recognized, proclaimed, and celebrated in the Church, emerging spontaneously as a gift of the Spirit, distinct from the vocation of the apostles and their successors, evolving organically within the community of faith in response to a particular stage of development within the Church, involving a distinct lifestyle and commitment discerned and directed by authority, engaged in upbuilding the Church and participating in its witness.

Charismatic Character

The religious vocation and life is thus essentially charismatic and prophetic both in origin and mode of operation. Although it appears as a permanent gift in the Church, it is distinguished precisely by its deeply personal, spontaneous, grass-roots character and the diversity of its manifestations. It is, moreover, historically conditioned. Men and women experience, discern, and respond to a divine call within specific political, economic, and social conditions that, when illumined by faith, act as a catalyst.

Each order or congregation grows out of the personal vocational response of individuals as it is experienced and responded to in faith and develops in its characteristic form. The importance of this personal response to the call of grace cannot be overestimated. When genuine, it not only leads to individual conversion and holiness but, in that individual response, opens a path for others. Thus the desert movement emerged in the person of Antony of Egypt and his response to the word of God at the end of the period of persecution. The lives and teachings of the Eastern Fathers and Mothers shaped the monastic life of men and women, and Benedict gave it form in the West. With the resurgence of urban life in the 12th and 13th centuries, the mendicant orders appeared in the calls of Dominic, Francis, and Clare. And with the

discovery of the New World, the period of explorations, the reforms of the Council of Trent, and the rise of modern industrial society, there arose reform groups and numerous apostolic congregations and societies, associated with such names as Ignatius of Loyola, Teresa of Avila, Vincent de Paul and Louise de Marillac, and Jane Frances de Chantal.

Each inspired expression rooted in the paschal mystery and comprising a total way of life flowing from, and directed to, the love of God finds in Scripture and sacrament certain themes and symbols peculiarly suited to its inspiration and psychology. As men and women draw on these symbols to interpret and direct their lives, a characteristic spiritual gift can be identified and becomes available to the Church as a whole in the form of a distinctive spirituality. Thus the monastic life emphasizes the themes of desert and conversion, the apostolic communities that of mission, and the evangelical life that of solidarity in love.

This organic diversity, however, is subject to a process of theological and canonical definition that is mediated by historical consciousness. Patristic spirituality, influenced by Neoplatonism, for example, perceived human activity with respect to its ends within a hierarchic value scheme and saw the monastic life as embodying a Neoplatonic ideal of contemplation requiring separation from the world of action and material reality through ascetical practice. Consequently, later apostolic orders that found inspiration in the life of the apostles sent to preach and heal came to be interpreted by contrast as active. Thomas Aquinas, recognizing the need for new categories, introduced the term *mixed life,* calling it the most perfect, since it embodied both the contemplative and active dimensions. The evangelical charism, as exemplified in Francis of Assisi, cannot be assimilated to either the apostolic or the monastic ideal, but simply involves living the gospel life in solidarity and openness in witness to the presence of the kingdom of God.

Gender also became a determining factor. While male observances regulating departures from a monastery underwent organic development often related to the ordination of monks and their ecclesial functions, female communities were subject to increasingly strict laws of cloister, which became universal in 1298. These laws limited the development of the female branches of the older orders while imposing monastic observance on modern congregations and depriving them of full status as religious to the 20th century.

Such definition gives rise to an inevitable tension because it tends to create certain conceptual frameworks and dichotomies that are nonbiblical in origin, e.g., contemplative/active, male/female, higher/lower, thereby imposing static categories that inhibit persons from perceiving and responding to the gift of the Spirit. Secondly, historical lifestyles became idealized, identified with the essence of religious life, and made normative. New charisms are then required to justify themselves in terms of definitions alien to their inspiration, while older forms tend to become rigid as they adapt to definition rather than to the ongoing call of grace. In the process religious life loses its vitality, thus depriving the Church of a prophetic witness.

Reinterpretation Since Vatican II

In the 20th century, following two world wars, economic crises, and unparalleled scientific developments, these tensions reached a stress point formally recognized by Pope Pius XII. Calling attention to the disparity between the charisms and structures of religious communities, between their lifestyles and the conditions of the times, and between formation given to candidates and the needs of their ministry in the mission of the Church, he summoned not only apostolic congregations but cloistered communities to adaptation according to the distinctive charism of each (*Sponsa Christi,* 1950) and promised new developments in the form of secular institutes (1947).

These same conditions, along with a renewed ecclesiology as expressed in the Dogmatic Constitution on the Church (*Lumen Gentium*) and the Pastoral Constitution on the Church in the Modern World (*Gaudium et Spes*), led the bishops of Vatican II to call for the renewal of religious life by "two simultaneous processes: (1) a continuous return to the sources of all Christian life and to the original inspiration behind a given community and (2) an adjustment of the community to the changed conditions of the times" (PC 2). Most important, religious were to regard the following of Christ according to the gospel as the supreme law and fundamental norm of religious life; to preserve the special character or charism of each community; to participate in the objectives of the Church in all major fields: Scripture, liturgy, doctrine, and the pastoral, ecumenical, missionary, and social areas. They were to make themselves aware of contemporary human conditions so as to respond to human needs in the light of faith. Profound spiritual renewal was to undergird all else (PC 2). In short, the council challenged and freed religious by recognizing with highest authority their true nature as charismatic, rooted in the word of God, prophetic and called to participate in Christ's mission within a very changed 20th century, understood in the light of a renewed ecclesiology.

Because this call touched the heart of religious vocation, it released unprecedented spiritual energies. General chapters of renewal, with processes that involved grassroots initiatives and consultation, were held, bringing every aspect of religious life to discerning prayer, dialogue, and analysis, and allowing religious to test their call by appropriate experimentation. Religious took new responsibility for their own lives, moving from a conforming to a reforming mode and bringing their own vocational experience and judgment to bear on the expression of their charism and the decisions that affected their lives. The process clarified personal values and gave priority to the gospel over mere custom. Relationships in community and among congregations were established at a more personal level; those beyond communities were expanded, and those with Church authorities matured. The history of evolution of the Conference of Major Superiors of Women to the Leadership Conference of Women Religious illustrates this transformation.

The pressures and struggles within communities during this process, though profound, were no cause for amazement, given the radical nature of the challenge. What proved surprising was that the task pushed all concerned into uncharted territory so quickly, proving the framework for renewal inadequate in many cases. This was particularly true for contemplative communities of women, which, unlike the apostolic communities, were given no direct permission to experiment. The urgency of the call of grace seemed to outdistance the interpretive framework, as confrontation with the needs of the Church and the world showed religious the profound demands of the gospel counsels.

Religious responding to the call to mission in emerging nations, particularly Latin America, were radicalized by confrontation with poverty and oppression rooted in unjust economic and political structures involving the industrialized nations of which they were citizens. Throughout, the renewed liturgy and communal prayer centered in the Scriptures proved normative. True worship in the renewed liturgy proved impossible without a commitment to relieve this suffering.

The Dogmatic Constitution on the Church had redefined the very notion of Christian vocation in the context of the universal call to holiness, affirming each as gift of the Spirit (LG 40-42), and thus eliminating the concept of higher/lower in relation to states of life. This radically adjusted the way religious perceived themselves and were perceived in the Church. As the sacramental character of married vocation was appreciated and lay ministries emerged, religious began to see themselves as inserted among the People of God.

In this process came also an experience of sin and the mystery of the cross. Resistance to renewal appeared and revealed obstacles to grace in self, community, the governing structures of the Church, and in society. In the effort to respond to the gospel demands celebrated in liturgy, heard in prayer, centered in meditation or the Scriptures, and experienced in ministry and relationships, religious underwent profound psychological growth and moral development discovering the meaning of *metanoia*—change of heart, attitude, consciousness, identity—as all previous certainties were challenged.

Large numbers of religious who discerned a different call to be their proper gift left religious life; many transferred to other institutes. Some communities merged; others discerned a call to new, nontraditional ministries in keeping with their charism. The elderly witnessed the death of many institutions they had built and served, while facing a new insecurity as membership declined. Externally, the drastic reduction of applicants to traditional religious life appeared to signal its demise. To accept such an interpretation, however, would be to miss the significance of what has been and is taking place.

Outcomes and Future

Efforts to renew have led religious to rediscover their biblical and charismatic vocation. As the laity assume responsibility for many established apostolates, religious have moved beyond existing institutions to respond to unmet needs of people in personal service and social advocacy. This work is begun in faith without financial means and often in collaboration with lay persons and members of other Churches. New beginnings among apostolic and monastic groups, often unnoticed, have multiplied. In these small groups a sense of purpose, openness, faith, and joy signal an unmistakable Pentecost. In situations of political and economic injustice, such responses expose those involved to persecution and death.

As has been the case historically, it is difficult to fit many responses into familiar categories. Religious continue to challenge and surprise human authorities in the Church, as they have throughout history. New ministries have brought religious into the public and political arena, which many see as unsuitable to the "nonsecular" vocation of religious, even though the fact of institutional injustice lies at the root of human suffering that religious feel called to alleviate.

The distinction in law between religious called to "separation from the world" and the vocation of those in secular institutes is not clear at the level of experience. These tensions merely witness to the limitation of human beings to adapt mental categories to new experience, as they summon all to greater dependence on, and openness to, the Spirit who is ever creating something new.

What seems clear at present is that religious of the future will find their place in solidarity with the oppressed apart from political, economic, and social security. The vocation to celibacy is being realized as a way of life rooted in love that seeks not to justify itself in perpetuating institutional forms, but only to remain open to the complete self-dedication to God to which one is always summoned anew. Obedience understood as attentiveness to the word of God in historical context is seen as a dynamic process. Religious authority itself is being called to profound listening to the Spirit at work in persons. Women in particular have discovered in their reflection on lived experience that a hierarchic structure that mediates the vow of obedience is not adequate to serve personal and communal discernment of, and response to, the word of God.

The vision of Christian community is being realized in the many associations, affiliations, friendships, and sharing in prayer, worship, and ministry among congregations and nonreligious, married and single, often nurtured by common sharing in a particular spirituality.

As North America moves away from a position of economic dominance in a redefined international community, new adjustments await religious. Religious communities in newly nationalized countries are developing within their own traditions and uncovering in the process new insights into the gospel. Especially important for the future is the relationship of these religious to the spiritual traditions of non-Christian religions dominant in their own cultures, witnessing as they do to a universal search of humankind for a transcendent destiny. Here the monastic and evangelical communities may play a vital role and find themselves called to provide a meeting ground for encounter between persons and groups of diverse spiritual backgrounds.

See also APOSTOLIC SPIRITUALITY; CHARISM; CONTEMPLATION, CONTEMPLATIVE PRAYER; DESERT; EASTERN (ASIAN) SPIRITUALITY; BENEDICTINE SPIRITUALITY; CISTERCIAN SPIRITUALITY; FRANCISCAN SPIRITUALITY; IGNATIAN SPIRITUALITY; LIBERATION THEOLOGY, INFLUENCE ON SPIRITUALITY; SECULAR INSTITUTES; THIRD ORDERS; VIRGINITY; VOWS.

Bibliography: M. de Carvalho Azevedo, *Vocation for Mission: The Challenge of Religious Life Today,* trans. J. Diercksmeier (New York: Paulist, 1988). K. Rahner, *The Religious Life Today* (New York: Seabury, 1976). *Review for Religious* 49, no. 2 (March–April 1990). S. Schneiders, *New Wineskins: Re-imaging Religious Life Today* (New York: Paulist, 1986). D. Steinberg, M. O'Hara, and H. Coughlan, eds., *The Future of Religious Life: The Carondolet Conference* (Collegeville, Minn.: The Liturgical Press, 1990).

M. CLARE ADAMS, O.S.C.

RENEWAL, PROGRAMS OF RENEWAL

The Church is "at the same time holy and always in need of being purified, and incessantly pursues the path of penance and renewal" (LG 8). Such renewal "essentially consists in an increase of fidelity to her own calling" (UR 6) by a continuous returning to the spirit of Christ, her founder, and responding to contemporary needs, recognizing the "joys and hopes, the griefs and anxieties" of the world and humankind to be Christ's and her own (PC 2; GS 1). The Second Vatican Council commended "the biblical and liturgical movements, the preaching of the word of God, catechetics, the apostolate of the laity, new forms of religious life and the spirituality of married life, and the Church's social teaching and activity" as manifestations of renewing life and pledges of ecumenical progress in the future (UR 6).

The years since the council have seen spirituality, the lived experience of faith, emerge as a central concern of the People of God. The charismatic renewal, cursillo, Marriage Encounter, and the retreat and spiritual direction movements focused the attention of serious Christians on the intensifying of their personal relationship with God in a way that embraced the whole of one's daily experience. For some, spiritual development grew to encompass the whole of personal living, emphasizing the body and the emotions in a holistic integration of experience that theology and morality had tended to denigrate. Others expressed a deepening Christian commitment to social and political justice, world peace, and ecological cooperation, sometimes through active participation in a variety of social action groups, e.g., the Fellowship of Reconciliation, Bread for the World, Pax Christi, Greenpeace. Through such movements many experienced powerful second conversions that moved them from an obligation-centered performance of requirements for Church membership into a committed adult spirituality.

Laity, professional religious, and clergy alike engaged in deepening ecumenical dialogue, action, and relationship with Jews and members of Eastern religions, particularly Buddhists, and more recently, with native African, native American, and the goddess or wiccan traditions of the ancient Indo-European worlds. The implementation of revised rites, particularly the Rite of Christian Initiation of Adults, the development of adult, family, and parish-centered education programs like RENEW, and the development of collaborative efforts to respond to social needs and action have strengthened the Church as community and brought increasing participation of laypersons in liturgical, evangelization, and social ministries, and the development of Church teaching. Acting out of conscience, many are assuming a responsibility for moral decisions in matters of divorce and remarriage, abortion, and homosexuality, sometimes involving dissent from traditional Church teaching and calling for just action against sexism, heterosexism, racism, and classism in the Church itself.

While some perceive renewal to be limited to guarding and transmitting traditional Church teaching, formulations, and practice, the experience of oppression in the light of the resources of Scripture and theology, particularly in Latin America, Asia, Africa, and feminist communities, has brought believers, professional theologians, and Church leaders together in developing local and liberation theologies. Processes for developing pastoral letters and actions in response to local, national, and world needs have provided laity and clergy at many levels within the Church with significant experiences of collaboration and partnership. Biblical scholarship has shown that the earliest Christian community was a renewal movement within Judaism and a "discipleship of equals" (Schüssler Fiorenza, pp. 140ff.). Many laywomen and men, realizing Vatican II's affirmation of the call of all to the same holiness and, by baptism, to ministry, experience a Christian feminist consciousness as an essential dimension of an emerging "lay-centered Church."

Continuing renewal invites laity and clergy to increasing partnership in the Spirit and continued restructuring of Church life and ministries to embody justice and equality for all the people of God and to continuing dialogue and action with other religious traditions, contributing to the fashioning of balanced relationships among earth's peoples and of humankind with the earth itself.

See also CONTEMPORARY SPIRITUALITY; VATICAN COUNCIL II.

Bibliography: L. Doohan, *The Lay-Centered Church: Theology and Spirituality* (Minneapolis: Winston, 1984). E. Schüssler Fiorenza, *In Memory of Her: A Feminist Theological Reconstruction of Christian Origins* (New York: Crossroad, 1983). R. McBrien, *Catholicism* 2 (Minneapolis: Winston, 1980) 691–729, 1077–1099. S. Schneiders, "Theology and Spirituality: Strangers, Rivals, or Partners?" *Horizons* 13 (Fall 1986) 253–274.

SUSAN E. HAMES, C.S.J.

REPENTANCE

See PENANCE, PENITENCE.

RESENTMENT

See FEELINGS.

RESPECT FOR LIFE, DIGNITY OF LIFE

See CONFRONTATION AND PROTEST; ECOLOGICAL CONSCIOUSNESS; ENVIRONMENT; JUSTICE; PEACE; PREGNANCY; WAR, IMPACT ON SPIRITUALITY.

RESPONSIBILITY

The word *responsibility* implies response to someone or something. The Book of Genesis implies that all human beings, as partners and images of God, are responsible for infrahuman creation (Gen 1:26ff.; 3:9; 4:9). Even though the theology of the time stressed collective responsibility, whereby guilt was to be borne by all subsequent generations, Jeremiah (31:1-34) emphasized individual responsibility in reference to covenant.

Responsibility did not emerge in philosophical terms until the 17th century. One of the earliest appearances was in 1656, when Pascal had a Jesuit superior declare that the "whole Society takes responsibility for a book written by any one of our members." In philosophical and political literature, the general connotation has been either of imputability or of accountability, notions always related to moral obligation, and freedom. Since the late 19th century, responsibility has been part of philosophical ethics. Levy Bruhl in 1883 distinguished two notions: the objective notion of legal responsibility and the subjective notion of moral responsibility.

Since, then, the word *responsibility* has been applied to practically all areas of human activity—professional responsibility, legal responsibility, political responsibility, social responsibility, and, for religious moralists, even an ethic of responsibility. Yet the existentialists, especially Heidegger and Sartre, have gone beyond such special fields of responsibility to apply it to the self. One is responsible for creating, projecting, making oneself. But as Niebuhr points out, this idea of responsibility for choosing the self one wishes to become is as old as Aristotle: "For the Greek philosopher ... man is the being who makes himself ... for the sake of a desired end. ... we act upon ourselves, we fashion ourselves" (Niebuhr, p. 49). Buber also proposed that responsibility move into the larger arena of lived life. Heidegger argued that moral responsibility is derived from human ontological responsibility.

Some theorists of developmental psychology also emphasize responsibility to and for one's self and others. Erikson indicates that a sense of responsibility develops in adulthood so that the integrity of old age involves an acceptance of one's responsibility for one's own life. Gilligan expands on Kohlberg's morality of justice to include a morality of care and responsibility for one's self and for others, usually with the emphasis on responsibility to and for others.

Conn has united the notions of responsibility for one's self with the ethical notion of responsibility for others as the basis for understanding Lonergan's notion of conversion. Responsibility for the Christian is response to God's call to each person to develop fully for God, self, and others. One can become a genuine self only insofar as one is true to others, through understanding, critical judgment, responsible decision-making, and genuine love.

Thus, when seen in relation to Catholic spirituality, responsibility is the unique response to God's personal call to become fully human by a life of self-transcendence in loving care for others and for all creation—a modern statement of God's call in Genesis and Jeremiah.

See also CONSCIENCE; OBEDIENCE; SELF.

Bibliography: W. Conn, *Conscience* (Birmingham, Ala.: Religious Education Press, 1981). A. Jonsen, *Responsibility in Modern Religious Ethics* (Washington: Corpus, 1968). R. McKeon, "The Development and the Significance of the Concept of Responsibility," *Revue International de Philosophie* 11 (1957) 2–32. H. R. Niebuhr, *The Responsible Self* (New York: Harper & Row, 1963).

MARGARET GORMAN, R.S.C.J.

RESURRECTION

The Christological and pneumatological starting point of Christian spirituality is the Easter event, which proclaims the resurrection of Jesus Christ, the crucified one. The integral paschal mystery is maintained by a theological understanding of the inseparability of cross and resurrection. In the NT the resurrection narratives focus on the resurrection appearances as experiences of the disciples, who encounter the eschatological reality of the risen Jesus, now manifest in history. The bodily resurrection of Jesus communicates both continuity and transformation, without being reduced to the phenomenal. The disciples experience the presence of the risen Christ, who is victorious over death because God's Spirit has raised him up. The Gospels are emphatic in insisting upon the identity between the crucified one and the risen one, as illustrated by the proclamations at the empty tomb (Mk 16:6; Mt 28:5; Lk 24:5-8) and Thomas's insistence that he had witnessed the crucifixion (Jn 20:25-29).

What the resurrection ratifies, particularly in the Synoptic tradition but likewise in John's Gospel, is the viability of the historical life and ministry of Jesus. The inauguration of the reign of God in Jesus' public ministry, on behalf of the poor, the outcast, and marginal, and in protest against injustice and for human dignity, met both acceptance and rejection. The apparent defeat of Jesus' cause in the abandonment of the cross is reversed by God's initiative in the resurrection. What flows from the resurrection narratives is the imperative for mission. Because God has vindicated Jesus' ministry and because suffering and death are not final, the disciples are empowered by the Spirit to witness to this salvific mystery by proclaiming the reign of God. When the resurrection is seen from this perspective, the pneumatological moment is simultaneous with the Christological.

The reforms of the Triduum liturgy, prior to the Second Vatican Council, reintroduced to the Church a more complete integration of this theology. When experienced as a single action of death-resurrection-mission, the paschal mystery promotes a spirituality that is nurtured by resurrection faith, and seeks to make a commitment to the transformation of the world. Resurrection faith speaks a word of hope, connecting human persons with God's future. Every Christian community is called to discern how God's fidelity to

Jesus empowers the baptized to live as the Body of Christ by a fidelity to the abandoned, the damaged, the poor, the outcast, and those deprived of justice and human dignity. Resurrection ultimately points the gathered assembly of believers to the power of God's Spirit to animate our human potential as co-creators of the reign of God's new life in every contemporary history. This hope, grounded in the events of the cross and the resurrection, repeatedly witnesses to God's cause as the cause of the defenseless.

See also BODY; CHRIST; HOLY SPIRIT; HOPE; INCARNATION.

Bibliography: L. Boff, *Jesus Christ Liberator* (Maryknoll, N.Y.: Orbis, 1978). R. Fuller, *The Formation of the Resurrection Narratives* (Philadelphia: Fortress, 1980). G. O'Collins, *Jesus Risen: An Historical, Foundational, and Systematic Examination of Christ's Resurrection* (New York: Paulist, 1987). P. Perkins, *Resurrection* (New York: Doubleday, 1984). E. Schillebeeckx, *Jesus: An Experiment in Christology* (New York: Seabury, 1979) 320–544; *Christ: The Experience of Jesus as Lord* (New York: Seabury, 1980); *Church: The Human Story of God* (New York: Crossroad, 1990).

GEORGE KILCOURSE

RETREAT, RETREAT MOVEMENT

A retreat is a period of time apart from one's normal activities spent in focusing on one's spiritual life. The practice of withdrawing from one's usual routine for the purpose of nourishing the inner life has ancient roots. The example of Jesus, who spent nights in prayer and withdrew into the desert, grounds the practice in the Christian tradition. In monasticism, legislation for the observance of Lent (RB 49) called for an intensification of one's usual spiritual exercises during the Lenten season and so underscored the importance of times for spiritual renewal. Pilgrimages were a medieval expression of this need to concentrate more radically on seeking God. Ignatius Loyola, in his *Spiritual Exercises,* provides a format for a retreat experience which aims at personal reform and which significantly shaped subsequent approaches to retreats.

In modern times annual retreats have been required of clergy and religious and are a standard part of formation programs. Vatican II encouraged the practice of retreats for laity as well as clergy. The renewal issuing from the council created a climate very favorable to the retreat movement.

Types of Retreat

Retreats are of varying lengths and diverse types. Some last only a day; others may extend even beyond a month. Quite common in the contemporary period are weekend and week-long retreats. The private retreat is a type in which an individual takes some time alone for spiritual renewal. Time is spent in quiet solitude, with opportunity for prayer, meditation, reading, and reflection. In the directed retreat the retreatant meets with an experienced spiritual director, who typically guides the individual through a series of meditations on the Scriptures. The retreatant meets with the director regularly to discuss the meditations and to discern the direction in which the individual is being called. Often the directed retreat is based on the model provided in the Ignatian *Spiritual Exercises.*

The preached retreat involves a retreat director giving conferences to a group gathered for that purpose. Often retreatants are encouraged to maintain an atmosphere of silence and are given opportunities to meet with the director individually. The retreat may have a specific theme relating to some aspect of ecclesial life, to the particular nature of the group, or to some contemporary problem. Thus, for instance, there are Holy Week retreats, retreats for married couples, and retreats focused on social justice. Part of the retreat agenda may include dialogue on the theme of the retreat by the participants. Retreats sometimes are designed to respond to a particular spirituality, such as the charismatic or the contemplative.

The retreat movement in the past several decades has promoted retreats for laity as well as clergy and religious, and has led to the establishment of retreat facilities in most areas. These facilities are under the auspices of either the local diocese or some religious congregation. As in past centuries, monasteries and religious houses also continue to be places where people go for retreat. Opportunities for retreat are a standard feature of current parish and campus ministry programs.

See also CURSILLO MOVEMENT; DEVOTION(S), POPULAR; RENEWAL, PROGRAMS OF RENEWAL; SPIRITUAL DIRECTION.

Bibliography: T. Dubay, "Retreats," *New Catholic Encyclopedia,* vol. 12, pp. 428–429; vol. 17, pp. 583–584. M. Jurado, "Retraites spirituelles," *D.Spir.,* vol. 13, cols. 423–434.

RAYMOND STUDZINSKI, O.S.B.

REVELATION(S)

Revelation, which according to its Latin etymology means "to remove the veil," has been an explicit theme in theology only in recent times. Nevertheless, the notion is crucial to the whole biblical tradition as well as to the development of modern spirituality.

In the Hebrew Scriptures, Yahweh manifests himself as Lord of creation and history through his actions in the world as interpreted by Moses and the prophets. The NT understands Jesus as the full revelation of God (Mt 11:25-27), the Word who manifests the Father (Jn 8:26), and the risen Lord who sends the Spirit to complete his own teaching (Jn 16:7-16). In Rom 1:19, Paul speaks of a revelation through nature but distinguishes this from God's self-manifestation in Jesus (1 Cor 1:17-2:16).

Early in the formative years of the theological tradition, Augustine (354–430) described revelation primarily as the inner light or divine illumination that enables believers to recognize and accept the God within who is the source of all truth. In the Middle Ages, Thomas Aquinas (1225–1274) put more emphasis on the objective character of revelation. As our teacher, God imparts to us the supernatural knowledge we need for salvation, especially through the life and teachings of Jesus Christ. By the time of Suarez (1548–1617), revelation was understood as a divinely given deposit of truths that tended to be identified with the propositions of faith. This propositional understanding of revelation persisted until the Second Vatican Council.

In the modern period, the Church responded to the attacks of agnostics and rationalists by insisting that revelation is supernatural knowledge necessary for salvation and is freely given to us through divine interventions interpreted by the prophets and authenticated by miracles. The First Vatican Council, in its Dogmatic Constitution on the Catholic Faith (1870), officially adopted this defense of supernatural revelation and also insisted against the fideists that acceptance of revelation in faith is a fully reasonable act.

Some theologians sought greater accommodation with modernity. Friedrich Schleiermacher (1764–1834) and liberal Protestants grounded revelation in subjective feelings such as absolute dependency and a taste for the infinite. Catholic modernists, represented by Alfred Loisy (1857–1940), described revelation as an acquired consciousness of our relationship with God elicited by moral sentiments of the heart. The Church hierarchy reacted by condemning modernism in the decree *Lamentabili* (1907), the papal encyclical *Pascendi* (1907), and the oath against modernism prescribed by Pope Pius X in 1910. After World War II, Catholic scholars such as Henri de Lubac, incorporating ideas from the Greek Fathers and modern biblical studies, developed a dynamic understanding of revelation rooted in God's revelatory action in history. Vatican II's Dogmatic Constitution on Divine Revelation (1965) adopted this general approach, thereby opening the way for further contributions from various sources, including liberation and political theology.

The models of revelation as doctrine, history, inner experience, dialectical presence, new awareness, and liberation proposed by Avery Dulles in his *Models of Revelation* suggest a close relationship between fundamental theological positions and styles of spirituality.

1) The neo-Scholastic tendency to identify revelation with Church doctrines fosters a traditional spirituality that emphasizes loyalty to the Catholic heritage and engenders a sense of security and solidarity.

2) The conviction that revelation is rooted in God's great historical interventions, especially the Christ-event, supports a biblical spirituality that promotes a personal relationship with God and finds nourishment in the scriptural narratives.

3) An understanding of revelation based on an inner experience of God's grace mediated through Christ fosters a mystical spirituality that draws on a reflective prayer life and takes seriously the personal religious experiences of others.

4) The model of revelation as dialectical presence, represented by Karl Barth and Protestant neo-Orthodoxy, grounds a Christocentric spirituality that has a strong sense of divine transcendence and the need to challenge sin in the world.

5) The contemporary theology of revelation as new awareness or an expansion of faith-consciousness sustains an incarnational spirituality that encourages a journey toward greater self-awareness, freedom, integration, as well as involvement in the task of humanizing the world.

6) Finally, the conviction that revelation is rooted in the struggle to emancipate the poor and oppressed leads to a liberation spirituality, which emphasizes following Jesus Christ the liberator, recognizing social sin, and finding solidarity in faith-sharing groups.

Systematic theology, as represented by Karl Rahner's *Foundations of Christian Faith,* relates revelation to existential concerns and to the faith as a whole. For Rahner, we human beings are potential hearers of the word who search for meaning and purpose in the evolutionary process and in history, as well as in our communal and personal experience. Christianity professes belief in the triune God who addresses to all human beings a fulfilling and integrating word that provides ultimate meaning to life in all its dimensions. God as the Holy Mystery remains forever beyond total comprehension and control. Sin and guilt radically threaten our ability to hear and respond to the word of the Lord. God's divinizing self-communication or uncreated grace affects human consciousness, producing a universal revelation heard in the call of conscience. From the beginning of human history, this universal revelation has been objectified by individuals and communities through various forms of symbolic communication, such as myths and rituals. For Christians, the biblical witness to divine revelation is normative for judging and interpreting all these objectifications.

God's self-communication and human responsiveness reached an unsurpassable high point in Jesus Christ, the definitive Word of God. The early Church preserved the memory of Jesus and his message in the NT, which provides normative guidance for believers in interpreting their grace-filled experience. The Church continues to witness to the risen Christ's abiding presence by celebrating the liturgy and living the law of love, always in the hope that this revelatory process will be fulfilled in the beatific vision.

Within this comprehensive theological framework, private revelations appear as historically and psychologically conditioned personal perceptions of interior grace, which must be judged for genuineness according to the normative Christ-event witnessed in the Scriptures and proclaimed by the Church. Private revelations such as those connected with Lourdes and the great mystics often enrich the spiritual lives of individuals but do not bind everyone to belief.

See also DISCERNMENT OF SPIRITS; EXTRAORDINARY PHENOMENA; FAITH; HOLY SPIRIT; INSPIRATION; PROPHECY; VISION(S).

Bibliography: A. Dulles, *Models of Revelation* (Garden City, N.Y.: Seabury, 1978). R. Latourelle, *Theology of Revelation* (Staten Island, N.Y.: Alba House, 1966). K. Rahner, *Foundations of Christian Faith* (New York: Seabury, 1978).

JAMES J. BACIK

RHENO-FLEMISH SPIRITUALITY

Rheno-Flemish spirituality refers to the specific spiritual movement that flourished in Belgium and the Rhineland during the 13th century. The Rhineland mystics characteristically sought God in the center of their being rather than in the affective devotion that characterized later spiritual movements.

This movement was strongly influenced by the Beguines, who, along with their male counterparts, the Beghards, originated as a lay association in northern France, Belgium, and the Rhineland during the 13th century. With no single founder or legislator, these spontaneous religious groups intended to recover the simplicity of the primitive Church in or out of enclosure. Beguines were urban women from various social classes whose lives were adapted to the particular conditions and society of the local area. While many maintained their own homes, they still lived a communal life of prayer, asceticism, almsgiving, and service. Beguines took no vows and did not renounce the possibility of marriage, but they submitted to a grand mistress, who was aided by a council of mistresses. The organization of their daily life and religious practices resembled that of the monastery, and after six years of formation, they could obtain permission to live as recluses. Openly attacked for their use of the vernacular for Bible reading and interpretation of Scripture, they were officially condemned by the Council of Vienne in 1311. However, Beguine communities survive to this day at Bruges, Louvain, Lier, and Diest.

Mechtild of Magdeburg (1210–1297)

Mechtild lived most of her life as a Beguine but went to live in the Benedictine monastery at Helfta when her writings provoked serious opposition. Mechtild was the first of the Rhineland mystics to write in German. Her principal work, *Das fliessende Licht der Gottheit* (*The Flowing Light of the Godhead*), is a collection of her teachings and experiences, a compendium of medieval mystical piety. Its first six books were written while Mechtild was a Beguine, and the seventh at Helfta. As its title expresses, Mechtild was incapable of suppressing her personal inner experience of God. Using a variety of literary techniques—dialogue, allusions to folk songs and dance motifs, as well as images that seem to leap off the page—Mechtild treats all aspects of the mystical journey. Her work is more apocalyptic and prophetic than that of her contemporaries and more characteristically emphasizes suffering. All we know of her life is gathered from scattered references in her writings. Aware of ecclesial corruption in her day, Mechtild's direct references to it made her the target of persecution during her forty years at Magdeburg. Blind and weakened by age and illness, she died in 1297 at Helfta.

Gertrude of Helfta (1256–1302)

Gertrude, received into the monastery school at Helfta when she was five years old, discovered the mystical life twenty years later. Her "conversion" was precipitated by a living encounter with Jesus and the revelation of a bond of love between them, an example of nuptial mysticism (*Brautmystik*) characteristic of the women mystics of the Rhineland. Her extant works include *The Herald of Divine Love* and the *Spiritual Exercises,* spiritual reminders of the basis of Christian life: baptism, investiture, spiritual espousals, monastic profession, praise of God, and preparation for death. Lost works are thought to include vernacular commentaries, paraphrases and explanations of obscure passages of the Scriptures, a treatise on Esther, and a hymn in honor of the passion of Christ.

Hildegard of Bingen (1098–1179)

Hildegard, who is often grouped with the Rheno-Flemish mystics because she is a representative of the mystical tradition from the same geographic area, actually stands apart from the other Rheno-Flemish mystics. Not only did she live a century before them, but her work represents a much more global attitude and aptitude than were characteristic of those mystical writers.

A native of the Rhineland who lived with the anchoress Jutta from the time she was eight years old, Hildegard was clothed as a nun in 1116 and became abbess in 1136. Between 1147 and 1152 she founded a Benedictine convent in Rupertsberg, near Bingen, and another near Rudensheim. Although she reported experiencing the power of God overshadowing her life even as a young child, Hildegard did not begin recording these visions and insights until she was forty years old. When these writings came under attack, she sought the advice of Bernard of Clairvaux, through whose intervention her writings were presented to the Council of Trier in 1147–1148, where she was defended by the Cistercian Pope Eugene III.

Hildegard's writings present a unique combination of spiritual revelations, scientific knowledge, and prophetic insight. Along with a collection of three hundred letters (*Briefwechsel*), she left her principal work, *Scivias,* which contains thirty-six of her visions and commentaries on them, and forms the basis for subsequent vol-

umes. These other works include *Liber Physicae Elementorum,* on nature, *Liber Compositae Medicinae,* on health, a theological work on St. Athanasius, a commentary on the Gospels, and an exposition on Benedict's Rule. Critical German editions of her other books include *Liber Vitae Meritorum,* which deals with the co-creative accountability of humankind; *De Operatione Dei,* which focuses on the influence of God on humankind; and a collection of songs and canticles (*Lieder*). Hildegard died at Rupertsberg on September 17, 1179.

Hadewijch of Antwerp

Little is known of the life of Hadewijch of Antwerp, but the corpus of her writings was discovered by three Belgian scholars in 1853. She is thought to have written them between 1225 and 1250, and her literary style has led scholars to conclude that she was of noble lineage. She also gives evidence of having had extensive knowledge of Scripture, liturgy, and theology. Clues from her writings lead us to believe that she either founded or joined a beguinage and became its mistress. Later accused of teaching Quietism, she was evicted from her community and exiled.

Hadewijch's visions, letters, and poetry develop the theme that the soul can attain union with God only through ecstatic love, expressed symbolically in the mystical marriage, a theme common to the Rheno-Flemish mystics. She is also one of the foremost representatives of *minnemystiek* (love mysticism), another contribution of 13th-century women.

Jan van Ruysbroeck (1293–1381)

Jan van Ruysbroeck (also spelled Ruusbroec), the best known of the Flemish mystics, was born in Ruysbroeck, near Brussels, in 1293. Virtually nothing is known of his early life but that at age eleven he went to live with a relative, John Hinckaert, a canon of the large collegiate church of St. Gudula. There, it is presumed, he studied grammar, logic, and rhetoric, as was common in the Middle Ages, but we know nothing more of his education before his ordination to the priesthood in 1317. For the next twenty-six years he served as a chaplain at St. Gudula, where he was intent upon opposing certain heretical teachings of his time, as his early treatises testify, in particular the heresy of the Brethren of the Free Spirit. While not a clearly delineated sect as such, the Free Spirits believed that a person is capable of total identification with God on earth, and that this identification can be lasting, not transitory.

The Kingdom of Lovers, Ruysbroeck's first work, was probably written in the early 1330s while he was still chaplain at St. Gudula. Ruysbroeck himself questioned the value and orthodoxy of the work and did not intend for it to be published, but through his secretary's indiscretion the book found its way into circulation. Later in his career he wrote an explanatory treatise entitled *The Little Book of Clarification* in order to elucidate further some points that were not clear in his earlier work.

His next work, *The Spiritual Espousals,* which took up some of the same themes, was widely known and read during his lifetime, and is generally regarded as his principal work. In it he divides the spiritual path into three stages: the active life—the minimum necessary for anyone who wants to be saved; the interior life, or the life of yearning for God; and the life of contemplation of God.

The Sparkling Stone was written shortly after *The Spiritual Espousals* and is similar to it in that it also treats the active, interior, and contemplative life, but with a stronger emphasis on questions related to the contemplative life. This work gives evidence of the evolution of Ruysbroeck's thought, with growing attention given to the common life, not as an attribute apart from contemplative life but inherent in it. Ruysbroeck's later treatises, *The Four Temptations* and *The Christian Faith,* are

ascetical and catechetical works, and *The Spiritual Tabernacle* is a lengthy allegorical treatise that gives Christian interpretations of many of the ritual details of the Book of Exodus and other Old Testament writings.

In 1343 Ruysbroeck left Brussels, accompanied by John Hinckaert and Francis van Coudenberg, with the intention of establishing a model community at Groenendael, a "green valley" ten kilometers outside the city. Joined by others, the community adopted the Augustinian Rule and became a vital spiritual center. There Ruysbroeck spent the remaining thirty-two years of his life, continuing his literary activity as well. He wrote *The Seven Enclosures* for a new community of Poor Clares, describing for them how they ought to lead religious life in the cloister. *A Mirror of Eternal Blessedness,* which contains a long section on the Eucharist, was also written for the Poor Clares. *The Seven Rungs in the Ladder of Spiritual Love* describes the rungs that lead one to the kingdom of God: good will, voluntary poverty, purity, humility, zeal in God's service, contemplative union with the Trinity, and immersion in the simple being of the Godhead. After writing *The Little Book of Clarification,* noted earlier, he did the last of his work in *The Twelve Beguines,* an awkward compilation of several treatises.

During his time at Groenendael, Ruysbroeck, venerated as a spiritual teacher, welcomed two visitors of note: the Rhenish mystic John Tauler and Gerard Groote, commonly regarded as the father of the *devotio moderna.* Jan van Ruysbroeck died peacefully at Groenendael in 1381. Buried in the monastery chapel, his remains were later moved to St. Gudula when the monastery was suppressed under Emperor Joseph II. He was beatified in 1909, and his feast day is observed on December 2.

There has been much debate as to whether Ruysbroeck stands at the end of the Rhineland school or at the beginning of the *devotio moderna.* While linguistically and culturally he belongs to the latter, his concern with contemplation and union with God places him more in the company of the Rheno-Flemish mystics.

Gerard Groote (1340–1384)

An influential spiritual movement that flourished in the following century was later labeled *devotio moderna*. Gerard Groote is regarded as the founder and leader of this movement, which spread as far abroad as Switzerland and northern Germany. Although much influenced by the Rhineland mystics, it eschewed the speculative intricacies of the German and Flemish writers, preferring instead to stress the practice of simple piety and asceticism. It regarded the true spiritual life to be the imitation of Christ. Only by meditating on his sacred humanity would the Christian be able to contemplate his divinity and attain that union with God which liberates the soul.

Thomas à Kempis (1380–1471)

Thomas à Kempis is the name most commonly associated with the spiritual tradition of the *devotio moderna*. Born of humble origin in Kempen in the Rhineland, he was sent to study at the monastery school at Deventer and joined the monastery of the Canons Regular of St. Augustine at Zwolle in 1399.

The *Imitation of Christ,* regarded as the finest example of the spirituality of the *devotio moderna* and generally attributed to Thomas à Kempis, is focused on the interior life and the Eucharist. Its four books, written separately and circulated independently, have had an immense impact on subsequent centuries. It insists on separation from the world and places a consistent emphasis on repentance and conversion. His other writings include *Soliloquy of the Soul* and biographies of Gerard Groote and St. Mydwina of Schiedam.

See also BRIDAL MYSTICISM; MARRIAGE, MYSTICAL; MYSTICISM; QUIETISM; SPIRITUALITY, CHRISTIAN (CATHOLIC), HISTORY OF; WESTERN MEDIEVAL SPIRITUALITY.

Bibliography: E. Zum Brunn and G. Epiney-Burgar, *Women Mystics in Medieval Europe,* trans. S. Hughes (New York: Paragon House, 1989). L. Cognet, *Introduction aux mystiques rheno-flamands* (Paris, 1968). Hildegarde of Bingen, *Scivias,* trans. C. Hart and J. Bishop, Classics of Western Spirituality (New York: Paulist, 1990). E. McDonnell, *The Beguines and Beghards in Medieval Culture* (New York: Octagon Books, 1969). John Ruusbroec, *The Spiritual Espousals and Other Works,* trans. J. Wiseman, Classics of Western Spirituality (New York: Paulist, 1985).

JULIA UPTON, R.S.M.

RITUAL

The word *ritual* is derived from the Latin *ritus,* meaning "structure." Ritual is a structured activity that facilitates personal and social transactions. Varieties of ritual behaviors enable humans to feel at home with themselves, with others, and with life's environment in general. Humans learn ritual behaviors as part of the process of socialization.

Religious rituals, like social rituals, are intended to be formative and expressive of personal and communal identity. This identity is one that requires initiation into the meanings of the rituals, for the form or structure of a ritual conveys meaning greater than the sensible form. In other words, religious rituals are symbolic actions that unify the doer with the sacred.

Christian rituals are formative and expressive of communion in the new covenant with and through Christ Jesus. The incarnational nature of Christianity presumes that there may be some changes in the forms of Christian rituals, for ritual expressions are influenced by sociocultural as well as religious factors. This is evidenced through the changing expressions of Christian sacraments on the one hand and the constancy of sacramental symbols on the other. It is the universality of the Christian Church that grounds and enriches the ritual potential of the reign of God among us.

See also CELEBRATION; CULTURE; DANCE; LITURGICAL PRAYER; LITURGY; PASCHAL MYSTERY; PRAYER; SACRAMENTS; WORSHIP.

Bibliography: R. Grimes, *Beginnings in Ritual Studies* (Lanham, Md.: Univ. Press of America, 1982). K. Rahner, ed., *The Concise Sacramentum Mundi* (New York: Seabury, 1975).

SHAWN MADIGAN, C.S.J.

ROSARY

A rosary is a string of prayers represented by knots or beads. Originating in Brahamanic India, the rosary was soon used by Buddhists, Muslims, and Sikhs to count repetitious prayers. Christian desert monks were using beads or pebbles to count prayers by the late 2nd century. Varieties of rosaries have existed in religious traditions, including Christianity.

The most familiar form of rosary for Roman Catholics had its origin in the 12th century. Devotion to Jesus and Mary was popular at this time. Christians who could not read the 150 psalms of the Divine Office often substituted "the beads." *Beda* in medieval English means "prayer." The substitute prayers could be Our Fathers, some liturgical Marian antiphons, or combinations of both.

Recitation of these prayers was accompanied by a meditation on the lives of Jesus and Mary as they unfolded in the liturgical seasons. In the 15th century the Carthusian Henry Kalkar bracketed the beads into sets of ten (decade), separated by a larger bead. By 1480 a rosary of fifteen meditations replaced an earlier rosary of fifty mysteries.

In the 16th century a petition was added to the Marian antiphons to form the Hail Mary. A crucifix and five beads joined the two ends of the rosary. Today the five-decade rosary is the most familiar form for many Roman Catholics.

See also DEVOTION(S), POPULAR; LITURGY; MARY; PRAYER; VATICAN COUNCIL II.

Bibliography: M. O'Carroll, *Theotokos* (Wilmington, Del.: Glazier, 1986). R. McBrien, *Catholicism* (Minneapolis: Winston, 1981).

SHAWN MADIGAN, C.S.J.

RULE OF LIFE

See BENEDICTINE SPIRITUALITY; FRANCISCAN SPIRITUALITY; MONASTICISM, MONASTIC SPIRITUALITY; SPIRITUAL WRITING, GENRES OF.

S

SABBATH

See LEISURE; LITURGY; PEACE.

SACRAMENT OF THE PRESENT MOMENT

See ABANDONMENT; ATTENTION, ATTENTIVENESS.

SACRAMENTS

When the Constitution on the Sacred Liturgy of the Second Vatican Council (*Sacrosanctum Concilium*) stated that the liturgy is the summit and source of the Church's activity, it went on to speak of worship as a communion in holiness, a renewal of covenant, and a mediation of grace, as well as glorification of God (SC 10). Clearly these statements pertain to the sacraments in a special way. In the chapter on the sacraments, the constitution speaks of the sanctification they work as a participation in the mystery of Christ's passion, death, and resurrection (SC 61). It is the intention of the constitution to make worship, and sacramental worship in particular, more central to the lives of Christians. In noting the split that has existed between popular devotion and liturgy, it suggests that these former be brought into closer conformity with the liturgy (SC 13). It also remarks on the complementarity between liturgy and other spiritual exercises (SC 12). From these latter two paragraphs, it is

evident that the council did not see liturgy, or, in particular, sacrament, as the sole nourishment of the spiritual life. It did, however, wish to make liturgy and sacrament central to it.

A similar line of thought is pursued in the introductions to the ritual revisions of sacramental liturgy made in the years following the Second Vatican Council. The general introduction to the revision of the rites of Christian initiation, first published in conjunction with the new order for infant baptism but pertinent also to adult initiation, notes how the three sacraments of initiation bring the faithful "to the full stature of Christ" and prepare them for their mission as Christians (*De Initiatione Christiana, Praenotanda Generalia* 2). The revision of the order for the preparation and initiation of adult candidates is based entirely on a concept and model of conversion. The new liturgy of penance sees conversion, or *metanoia,* as a profound change of the person, involving a totally new way of seeing and living one's life based on the reception of God's mercy and love (*Ordo Paenitentiae* 6). In a similar vein, the introduction to the rites of anointing spells out the change that takes place through the sacrament in the sick person's attitudes to health, pain, and suffering precisely because it is a participation in Christ's passion, death, and resurrection (*Ordo Unctionis Infirmorum* 6). The introduction to the new liturgy of marriage puts particular stress on the ecclesial dimension of the holiness of married life to which the sacrament gives initiation (*Ordo Celebrandi Matrimonium* 1).

This way of expressing the nature and grace of the sacraments is much more spiritually focused than the post-Tridentine doctrinal and catechetical explanation of sacraments as instruments of grace. This belonged to a period when Christians were much more conscious of the obligation and necessity of the sacraments than they were engaged in their celebration. Unfortunately, over several centuries the Church experienced a split between sacraments and spirituality. While the reception of sacraments was deemed necessary to the life of grace and to membership in the Church, the life of the spirit was nourished through other means. On the one side, the popular devotions that sustained popular piety took place alongside the sacraments and did not constitute a clear unity with them, even when they overlapped, as in the case of the Eucharistic devotions to which people were encouraged in the course of the celebration of Mass. On the other side, schools of spirituality, with their different accents on meditation, contemplation, asceticism, and mysticism, attended to the spiritual aspirations of religious, clergy, and the devout laity. Such spiritualities usually endorsed regular attendance at Mass and frequent confession and communion, without however attending much to the liturgies of these sacraments. Within this perspective sacraments were adapted to fit either the needs of common piety or the devotions of schools of spirituality. In short, rather than being taken as expressions, manifestations, and realizations of Christ's mystery, they belonged among the tools used to nourish faith and devotion, fitting differently into different spiritualities or different forms of common piety.

Elements of this attitude remain even today, to the extent that the ecclesial nature of sacrament is bypassed. The administration of child baptism or of the sacrament of the sick, for example, may be seen to cater to the needs of individual persons, with scant attention given to the way in which these sacraments express the celebration of Christ's Pasch as a mystery of ecclesial presence and communion. Magisterial advice and canonical regulations on such matters as the frequency of Eucharistic reception, Mass attendance, and sacramental confession sometimes read like counsels to the devout, tailored to personal piety.

All this medieval and contemporary development is certainly in contrast with early Christian centuries, when the whole spiritual life of Christians centered around the gathering for liturgy and was marked by participation in the mystery of Christ and the Church through the Eucharist and other sacraments. It is important, however, to grasp the real nature of the Second Vatican Council's retrieval of an earlier mentality. To present the practices of the past few centuries and those fostered by the Second Vatican Council as a contrast between a privatization of sacrament and a more communal focus is too limited in its perspective.

In the Western Middle Ages and pre-Reformation centuries, what was often done individually was deeply social. Baptism, penance, occasional Communion, regular Mass attendance, marriage in church, and a death comforted by the Church's sacraments were the ways whereby persons belonged to the social reality of the Church and became participants in the community of grace. This is still a social use of sacrament, but what it represents is the vision of a Church as a social, pastoral, and magisterial organization, looking after the needs of its members. This is in contrast with a vision of the Church as a living organism, the Body of Christ, sustained in its cohesion and unity by the life of the Spirit.

A strictly understood privatization, in which sacramental participation becomes a matter of personal choice and personal need, is more the result of a contemporary sense of the self, affected by the consumerist attitudes of Western society that are brought even to the sacraments. In effect, it represents a third view of the Church as an organism that caters to personal spiritual needs, with scant enough attention to the factors of social belonging and common ethic.

What is perhaps emerging today, not merely in the new sacramental texts but more in the efforts to implement sacramental renewal, is a fourth image or conception of Church. This is related to an organic rather than mechanistic vision of human life in its relation to the world. It centers around a postmodern rather than a classical view of the human person and promotes the participatory forms of ecclesial life.

The different views of the Church reflected in sacramental practice are, however, vital to the relation between sacrament and spirituality. This is so because at the root of the question about sacrament and spirituality is the representation of the Church and of the economy of grace that permeates sacramental celebration. It is rightly said that in recent liturgical reforms the Church is being called back to a sense of the sacramental that prevailed in early Christian centuries, though it should not be thought that this means reviving all that was then done, since general social and cultural realities were so different from what they are today. What is important is the realization that the Church comes to be as Church in sacrament, where it commemorates the paschal mystery of Christ, and that the economy of grace is inherently sacramental. The abiding presence of Christ's mystery in the world is mediated and expressed through the sacramental economy, wherein the Church is united with Christ as his Body through the gift and action of the Spirit.

It is, then, ideally from within a sacramental economy that the Christian's participation in the life of the Spirit and in the economy of grace is generated and that attitudes to the whole of reality are given fundamental expression. What is done with the ordering of Eucharistic celebration, the adult catechumenate, penance, anointing of the sick, the relation between baptism and confirmation obviously has a deep impact on the way in which the life of the Spirit flows. It also has a relation to how Christians envisage persons, society, the earth, and how they live the Christian life in present engagement and future expectation.

A good part of the difficulty in recent centuries in seeing the connection between sacrament and spirituality came from the fact that the grace of each sacrament was stated in rather abstract terms, and as far as celebration was concerned, all attention was given to the positing of the correct matter and form. As a result, the forms of celebration that had emerged as vital to sacrament in early centuries were neglected. With the revision of rites today, it is possible to retrieve these forms and hence to discern the contours of a sacramental spirituality by attending to the ways in which the gift of grace and the confession of faith are expressed.

The Paschal Mystery

The reforms of the Second Vatican Council have given an élan to a sacramental spirituality by putting to the fore the commemoration of the paschal mystery, as well as a sacramental and ecclesial vision of the entire economy of grace. Yet it is obvious that participation in the sacraments does not give rise to the same universal spirituality and that different perceptions of the Church are still functioning in today's congregations. A simple retrieval of a liturgy centered around the paschal mystery is not in effect possible. In reality, liturgical paradigms of Pasch and of the economy of grace have not been identical throughout the liturgical history of the first millennium and so present diversified models to current liturgical renewal. Furthermore, sacramental worship occurs within cultural context, and the cultural paradigm of world and human reality that prevails among people today is not that of the classical world of antiquity and the Middle Ages. The implications of all this for a sacramental spirituality need attention.

Since it is taken as key to the reform of the sacramental rites, the way in which belief in the Pasch is expressed is obviously vital to a spirituality rooted in sacrament. In effect, it does not have the univocity that the reforms and some liturgical writers appear at times to give to it. Historical studies on the origins of the celebration of the Pasch and on the relation of sacraments, especially those of initiation, to the Pasch are important. Since the blessing of oils for chrismation and for the sick and the reconciliation of penitents have been historically drawn into the annual paschal commemoration, clearly their meaning is also affected by paschal images.

While it has other features as well, the dispute over the date of the annual paschal celebration between the Quartodecimans and those favoring the Sunday vigil is in its own way significant of two different ways of commemorating Christ's death and resurrection. The one tradition accentuates Christ's suffering, culminating in his descent among the dead, celebrating it as the conquest of sin and death or of the whole world of darkness. Christ's rising from the dead is the dawn of a new era, the inauguration of a new creation. This tradition is associated with Syria, and eventually with the school of Antioch, in its emphasis on commemorating and representing the Pasch of Christ as his suffering and that conquering death, which ushered in a new era of grace and light.

The second tradition is less liturgically rooted and indeed gives moral or mystical interpretations even to sacramental rites. This is associated with the great writers of Alexandria, Clement and Origen, and indeed with the school of Alexandria. The interpretation given to the Pasch by these writers starts with an ideal of moral and mystical conversion whereby spiritual persons, though living in this world, look to the things of the spirit. Moral and mystical conversion become the paradigms for the Pasch of Christ, which is thus represented as a passage or transition from this world through death to life with God. The incarnation and the mystery of the Word Incarnate are a model for the Christian's turning from the things of this world to the things of God, and for the passage from the life of the old sinful creatures to life in Christ. Scripture and Eucharist are together in their invitation to the contemplation of the divine mystery, the soul being made ready for grace by an asceticism fostered even by liturgical rites.

This moral interpretation of the Pasch, which represents both Christ's death and Christian initiation as a passage to new life, took on more universal prominence in the catechesis of the great period of adult catechumenate and initiation in the 4th and 5th centuries. It is found, for example, in the mystagogical catechesis of Cyril of Jerusalem, Ambrose of Milan, Theodore of Mopsuestia, and John Chrysostom, alongside the earlier image of Christ's death, descent into hell, and rising as a conquest of evil and the dawn of a new creation. The more this catechesis becomes moral exhortation, however, the more the image of passage dominates, even giving rise to a tendency toward allegorical interpretation of rites. Augustine is credited with making the synthesis between the commemoration of Christ's Pasch and the renewal of the life of grace in the Christian by using the image of passage to interpret the redemptive power of the mystery of the incarnation as a descent and ascent of the Word. According to Augustine, the Word took on the humanity that had to be saved from the power of sin and brought this renewed humanity with him in his passage from this world to the bosom of the Father, ascending whence he had descended.

This paradigm of passage thus became applicable to an interpretation of sacrament, both as representation of Christ's Pasch and as renewal of Christian life. The conversion of the Christian, begun in baptism and perfected in all the sacraments, could be viewed as a living participation in the Pasch of Christ, a configuration to Christ and an imitation of his example. It was not, however, the exclusive image used, either in the sacramental rites and texts themselves or in preaching and catechesis. Often the sacramental ritual had to be amended or allegorically interpreted in order to fit this paradigm.

The development of the blessing of the baptismal water is a good example to illustrate this. Extant early Christian texts are developed around the image of the descent of the Spirit, which configures Christian rebirth, as proclaimed in Jn 3:1-6, to the baptism of Christ in the Jordan. The imagery is of the dawning of a new era, a new creation, a rebirth of humanity and of the world, through the gift of the Spirit. This concords with the commemoration of Christ's death and descent into hell as a conquest of sin and death and the release from the captivity of Satan, which makes room for the new age in which the life of the Spirit prevails. Exorcism of the water is later introduced into the blessing of the font for the purpose of driving out the evil spirits that infect human life and creation itself. This goes with a conversion morality that sees life as a struggle against sin in the midst of a still sinful world. It is connected with greater attention to the death-mysticism of Romans 6, in which Christian regeneration is presented as a death to the body of sin and a present participation in the life of the risen Lord, in the hope of the final resurrection. Hence in the liturgy of baptism, as in the liturgy of other sacraments, there exist side by side images of Christ's Pasch as the beginning of a new era through a victorious struggle and as a passage of the head of the body from a world of sin and death to a life with the Father, in which the redeemed now share in imitation and in anticipation.

The medieval West's emphasis on Christ's death as a vicarious and redemptive sacrifice for sin is an evolution of this concept, fitted more to a model of reality as an order of justice in which sin must carry the burden of reparation. This accent grew stronger as penitential practice, with more frequent sacramental confession and absolution, took a larger place in Christian life and was fitted to the need to reform the morals of Christian society. The Protestant Reformation in turn, with its strong persuasion of human sinfulness, followed the paradigm of Christ's death as satisfaction for sin, but it changed the medieval conception of sharing with Christ in making this satisfaction, through participation in his grace, to a conception of the need to receive the mercy of God, invoked by the Son's death, in pure faith and acceptance.

This evolution in the imagery of Christ's death and resurrection cannot be properly understood unless seen in the context of the moral contingencies of the Christian life and the influence on these of variant social and cultural factors. In a world of which they were but a small part, Christians could find in the Church the inaugural reality of the new creation in the Spirit. In the world that had become Christian, candidates for baptism were in a position that imposed a struggle with the sinful mores not left behind with the espousal of Christianity by social powers or with the conversion of northern peoples to Christianity. In the Middle Ages, justice emerged from the dialogue with philosophies as a dominant norm and one that was likely to challenge the evils of the time. In the Protestant Reformation, at one and the same time the presumptions of human endeavor were challenged and the focus on the life of the individual person was regained by the accent on mercy and on a justification given only through faith in Christ.

From this brief historical survey of the imagery of the death and resurrection of Christ, it may be seen that retrieving the imagery of paschal mystery as central to a sacramental spirituality is neither straightforward nor possible simply to mandate. As in the past, it has to develop through a faith and interpretation that affect the place of the Christian within the whole of reality and before the great dilemmas of good and evil, of life and death, as these affect the contemporary world and particular cultures. Today's remembrance of the Pasch is connected with the social and cultural realities that affect the Christian community as much as it was in the past. Because social and cultural perspectives are in fact more diversified than they were in the past, the Churches are actually witnessing a liturgical and sacramental pluralism that defies total comprehension. If the paschal mystery is too narrowly tied to a particular spirituality or to a particular way of seeing the place of the Christian people in the world, it may vanish from sacramental celebrations that interpret Christian involvement along different lines. If its imagery is left to the dynamic movement of the *lex orandi,* it may be incorporated into Christian remembrance in rather different ways as communities relate themselves to the prevailing cultural ideals and take their position on key questions of social order.

The Economy of Grace

Following this survey of the imagery of paschal mystery, and at the risk of simplification, some contrasts can be made as to how sacraments express the economy of grace. There are those sacramental celebrations in which it is the taking on of human flesh by the Word that is the key. Whether celebrated as incarnation or as epiphany (and there is a difference between these two perceptions), it is in that moment that humankind is fundamentally renewed in the Spirit and the struggle against evil is undertaken. The death of Christ becomes the supreme moment of conflict and of victory, or the price to be paid for the proclamation of the truth. There are other sacramental celebrations in which the sacrifice of the cross is the redemptive act whereby the fault of sin is satisfied and wiped out. Incarnation is the necessary prelude, and resurrection the return to the Father of the Son who came to do his will. There are also orderings of sacrament in which humanity's enduring and present sinfulness, with its constant need to be redeemed by Christ's blood, holds center. This can have the more Catholic ordering of communion with Christ in the offering of his sacrifice, prepared for by due repentance and sacramental reconciliation, or the more Protestant ordering around the faith in which the offer of mercy and grace is to be received, while the pleading of Christ's blood is continued in his heavenly intercession.

Bringing out these different perceptions of the economy of grace, which coincide with the divergent expressions of the Pasch, shows how spiritualities rooted in sacrament are not identical. The different modes of sacramental celebration, while they have in common that they are commemorations of Christ, engender different perceptions of worldly and human reality, and so ask for different ways of living through the Spirit in this world. In that, they are no different from the different schools of spirituality. Attention to sacrament, however, as participation in Christ and in the mystery of the Church allows for a spirituality that escapes the divorce between sacrament and other exercises of spirituality. It also introduces a common factor to all Christians, which is that they see in the sacraments the central expression of a common participation in the one mystery, however diversely represented this may be. On the other hand, much of the currently heard lament that liturgy seems to have little bearing on issues of justice has to do with the tendency to neglect the way in which sacraments evolve in relation to social and cultural factors.

The Dynamism of the *Lex Orandi*

In some interpretations, attention is given to the *lex orandi* by way of seeing it as a primary expression of faith that precedes or accompanies doctrinal explanation. Fuller insight, however, may be gained by attending to it as a canon of prayer and rite, setting out the forms within which faith is expressed in worship. While the particular way of envisaging sacramental communion with Christ and Church may change with the social and cultural context, this change takes place within traditional though always developing forms of ritual and prayerful expression. Bypassing narrow attention to matter and form, much more can be understood about how spirituality is engendered in sacrament by attending to the dynamic laws of the *lex orandi,* or styles of prayer and ritual. The mystery of the Church and the presence of Christ in his Pasch are indeed realized in the sacraments, but this comes about according to specific forms of faith expression, into which variant human concerns can be woven as the mystery transforms human life.

Through these forms the commemoration of the death and resurrection of Jesus Christ can assume a variety of human concerns and orient human life to God in the communion of this mystery. This is basic to the distinction between different sacraments, worked out in the Middle Ages to the number seven. Even within that numerical differentiation one can see different ways in which human life has been incorporated. In adult initiation it is the call to conversion and a reorientation of life that is taken into the memory of Christ. In infant baptism it is the need for this reorientation as it appears within the family and society as they are faced with the fact of human birth. In penance the continued experience of sin and fault is incorporated rather differently into the mystery of the Body of Christ according to the changing canonical norms that govern the demand for reconciliation. In the anointing of the sick, in some ages the experience in which persons are sanctified in the commemoration of the Pasch has been a rather wide one of human debility and sickness, whereas in others it has been the narrow experience of imminent mortality. In marriage it is the desire for a partnership that perfects the human person that is illumined, but very obviously the Church's way of relating this to the memory of Christ has varied according to the measure in which it has or has not accepted prevailing social perspectives.

What is foundational to sacrament is that these human realities, however much they have changed in the course of centuries, are drawn into the commemoration of Christ's death and resurrection, and it is this that both shows how they are intrinsic to redemption and transforms them into a new reality. Quite clearly, if sacramental rites do not develop in relation to the cultural and social modes in which people experience these realities, the connection with the commemoration of Christ is weakened and indeed may be spoken of in purely causal terms, with little or no attention to the actual ritual.

Seven features of the *lex orandi* can be noted in order to see how the life of the Spirit is bestowed through sacramental celebration.

Word and ritual. The proclamation of God's word is the initial sacramental action. This is not accidental to sacrament nor a mere preliminary. The sacramental blessing and ritual action flow out of the proclamation of the word. Sometimes they are seen as a response to it, but they might be better appreciated as motivated and prompted by it. The rite carries what is proclaimed and promised in the word over into blessing and ritual. All the revisions of sacramental rites since the Second Vatican Council have taken great care to ensure that each sacramental celebration has an appropriate liturgy of the word. The lectionaries in the rituals for baptism, confirmation, penance, marriage, and anointing of the sick are quite rich and nurture a faith that places the human realities involved within the paschal mystery of Christ and the life of the Church as a communion in the Spirit. Hence, through an ecclesial sacramental celebration, faith and the life of the Spirit are constantly nourished by the Scriptures.

Blessing. Once the centuries of its original evolution had passed, even in the Eucharist the power of the prayer of blessing, with its memory of Christ and its invocation of the Spirit, was little understood in ecclesial life and Christian spirituality. Yet it was one of the deepest and most compelling faith expressions which the Christian Church inherited from Judaism and which it still possesses in common with Judaism. Most people, when they think of blessing, probably think of a sign of the cross or a formula muttered over holy water or over objects of devotion to guarantee them some protective efficacy. Even this, however, is only a truncated outgrowth from a fuller blessing, which in being the blessing of God is blessing of persons and things.

It is well known that the celebration of the sacrament of orders contains a consecratory prayer and that marriage is completed by a nuptial blessing, but these are often seen as adornments to these sacraments rather than intrinsic to the ritual. They belong, however, to a blessing tradition that is foundational to sacramental celebration, and they have a similarity in structure and content to the Eucharistic Prayer, a fact that may not be often noted. Oils for chrismation, the catechumenate, and the anointing of the sick have always been prepared by a blessing, even if this blessing was not a part of the actual celebration of the offer of these sacraments to particular persons. Liturgical revisions have placed a blessing of the oil in each celebration of the sacrament of the sick. The one sacrament that still lacks an adequate

blessing prayer is penance, though the traditional services of Holy Thursday for the reconciliation of penitents provide models for this. Taking all these factors into account, we see that the approach to God in sacrament is always through blessing.

This blessing has its roots in Jewish worship, though it has undergone modification over the centuries and allows for considerable variation. The basic structure is that of a communal commemoration of God's salvific action, which motivates thanksgiving and praise as well as intercession. In the Christian tradition the focus of thanksgiving is on the mystery of Jesus Christ and the Church. That of intercession is on the gift of the Spirit, which God bestows on the assembled people and on the things of bread, wine, oil, and water, through which they commune in Christ's mystery and which are transformed through this gift. Remembrance of Christ, thanksgiving, intercession, and a confident trust in the power of the Spirit are thus imprinted on the Christian heart in face of God and become that in which persons are united as a Christian community. This is the hallmark of a spirituality which is ecclesial and which is conscious of God's saving action in history and in human life.

The power of the Spirit. As remarked, trust in the power of the Spirit is intrinsic to a spirituality nourished by sacrament. The Spirit enlivens and unites the Body and is mediated to the participants in sacramental celebration. The ritual actions serve to locate the action of the Spirit in community and in human life, since they show, as it were, those junctures at which the Spirit operates most powerfully. While the action of an ordained minister is essential to Christian sacrament, the spirituality of many centuries focused the action of grace too exclusively in his words and actions. When we note how blessings place the power of the Spirit in the things that are commonly shared or the actions that are commonly performed, we recognize that it is in these that the Spirit is present and through these that the Spirit is mediated. While the priest must bless the bread and wine or the oil and water, it is in the common table, the bath immersion, and the salving unction that the Spirit is given to participants. Similarly, in marriage it is in the communion of the couple in their dedication to each other and before the witness of the congregation that the Spirit abides, as in orders it is in the covenant between the community and the minister being ordained. In short, the rites of the sacraments manifest how the Spirit acts within the community of faith, in the bonding of human relation and in human action, and in the sharing together of the things of the earth.

Earthly realities. This last point is extremely important to Christian spirituality. It is one of its features that needs to come more to the fore in a time when people must globally face issues of international justice and ecological concern. Early Christian writers such as Tertullian and Augustine often remarked how God had chosen the most commonly needed and the simplest of the things of the earth for Christian sacrament. Unfortunately, because of certain doctrinal and devotional trends, they came to be used in very niggardly fashion. At times, as in the case of wafered Eucharistic bread or putrefying baptismal water, their very form was camouflaged. Some theologians even wrote that the choice of these particular items was arbitrary and simply a matter of divine command, not appreciating what God was expressing by incorporating them into the celebration of Christ and of God's covenant with humankind.

In the observance of their religious traditions, Jewish people are much more prone than Christians to bless God at meals and in the use of all the things of daily and of festive life. A similar spirit of blessing ought to flow over from the sacraments into the whole of Christian life. Because of the sacraments, this spirit of blessing can center on these very common things and make Christians mindful that it is by communion with them, and in a common and mutual sharing of them, that the power of the Spirit of Christ takes root in their existence and carries over into human affairs with rich blessings of peace and justice.

Time and place. Cultural studies suggest that there is a human instinct that motivates societies to carve out separate and distinct times and places for divine worship. These take on a sacred character that separates them from the profane. They are the sacred time and place into which people enter to encounter the divine, to hear or to do reverence to God. While Christian peoples have always determined special times for gathering, especially the Sunday, and while they have designated buildings for communal worship, this was done in the beginning in such a way as to suggest that in themselves time and place had no sacred character other than that given to them by the fact of Christian assembly. Some symbolic or commemorative meaning is indeed often attached to the Sunday or to Christian feasts, and there are many treatises working out the symbolism of building, altar, and sanctuary. However, Christians were at first careful not to let their places of gathering look like temples but chose instead homes or places of public gathering, such as the Roman basilica. They were likewise careful in their choice of time not to take any time that seemed in itself to have a sacred character but chose instead a time that was marked by salvific event, observant of the freedom of God's intervention.

All this makes the Christian mindful of the fact that the primary location of the holy is in the holy people, sanctified by Christ's blood, and that grace is not attached to special times but to the gratuitous and surprising intervention of God in human history and in human life. This is liable to generate a special way of relating to time and place, to any time or place, to all times and places. While assembly is vital to Christian identity, the advent of grace is tied to no time or place, and indeed opens every moment and every location to the *kairos,* or acceptable time, of God's love and saving action.

Human experience. Recent sacramental theology has taken an anthropological turn, that is, it attempts to understand the grace offered in the sacraments by starting with the human experiences to which sacraments relate it. The tendency of devotional history has been to attach sacraments to the human realities of birth (baptism), the age of reason (first confession and Communion), maturation to adulthood (confirmation), marriage (matrimony), and death (extreme unction). The suggested dispensation of recent ritual revisions, however, even while uneven in its approach, reminds us that of their nature sacraments do not fit into the human life cycle in this way.

Like the symbols of time and place, the human experiences and actions to which sacraments relate do not fit into what human instinct seems to dub the specifically sacred. Fundamental sacramental initiation through baptism, chrismation, and Eucharist marks conversion and perfects any moment of life at which the call of God and of Christ gratuitously enter a person's life. While it is unlikely that infant baptism will be abandoned entirely, there is nonetheless much wrestling with ecclesial and human realities to detach them from any given age and to ensure that Communion table, penance, and confirmation fit more readily into each child's individual settling into family, society, and Church through a development of the child's own faith. Along these lines, the most striking example of all, of course, was to allow a recovery of anointing as sacrament of the sick, whenever sickness occurs, rather than the sacrament of preparation for death.

None of this takes away from the vital relation of sacrament to human experience but simply dislocates it. It calls attention to the interpersonal and to a sense of being part of society and of history, as well as opening the eyes to each and every event of a human life that awakens a person to the struggles and hopes of existence or to its radically graced nature. Faith always arises in the midst of human experience, but the experience is less structured and less determined than the division of life through the periodization of the life cycle.

In conjunction with this, one can again recall to what experience the sacramental things open the eyes in their invitation to grace: a bonding in community and in love, a readiness to share a common table and to break the usual human boundaries of family and intimacy, a plunging witnessed by others into the rich springs of human and earthly life, a taking issue with the limitations of human debility as they obstruct one's desired independence and life together. These are the moments singled out for grace, as bread, wine, oil, and water are the things singled out. It is in these moments and over these things that the name of Christ is invoked in faith and the gift of the Spirit awaited, as people call out in unison to God the Father, whose motherliness impinges on the name itself of Father.

When ritual is too closely attached to the life cycle, furthermore, it is easy to exclude the historical quality of experience from sacrament. Within the memory of Christ, not only does the Church remember the experiences of each human life but it is mindful of historical events and prospects. The blessing prayers that are vital to sacrament, especially the Eucharistic Prayer, which is the central one, have not sufficiently evolved to include a broader human history. That they do so is important to the Church's stance in face of larger human issues and in making Christians conscious of their mission to witness to Christ and gospel in the midst of evolving cultural and social interests. It is by incorporating them into the memorial of the Pasch that Christians find a way of taking stock of such matters as humankind's failure to steward the earth, the sufferings of many under oppressive power structures, dominant human tragedies such as the Holocaust, and discriminations such as that against women, which have affected even the Church's own internal history. When such events and realities are recalled as Christ is remembered and the Spirit invoked, they are opened to the saving power of God's grace, and sacraments inspire action that is moved simultaneously by repentance and hope.

Cultural religious and devotional forms. Sacraments have not evolved through the centuries without relating to cultural and social realities or to the devotions that arise among people outside the liturgy. On the one hand, they seem to have been too much influenced by other religious traditions in their attachment of symbolism to time, place, and life cycle. On the other hand, their evolution has separated devotion and liturgy, and in non-Western cultures the Church has often taken an adversarial attitude to all that is religious in them. The attentiveness to human experience, however, as conditioned by history, culture, and society, as well as the offer of grace to human persons in the key moments of awakening to the holy in their lives, cannot be adequately incorporated into sacraments without dialogue with all that bespeaks the religious in human societies, cultures, and subcultures. It is often from prevailing social patterns of ritual observance and from devotions that become popular among the people, or among segments of the people, that we learn their sense of what needs to be redeemed and of the immediacy of God's presence in human life.

Consequently a sacramental liturgy and practice that is fully attentive to the human and to the ways of God's grace will allow forms of devotion and observance that arise outside its scope to have part in its own development. The full range of the partnership between sacramental liturgy and popular devotion augured by the Second Vatican Council has not yet been discerned, but its pursuit belongs to a genu-inely sacramental spirituality, to which nothing human is alien.

Conclusion

It could be asked how each sacrament in particular influences the life of the Spirit and marks the contours of Christian spirituality. In this entry, however, attention has been given to the expression of the mystery that is central to worship and to common sacramental structures. When these play a part in bringing Christian people together in the commemoration of the Pasch, the communion of the mystery of the Church, and the hope of the Spirit, they forge the distinctive and common marks of a Christian spirituality. At the same time, they allow for a diversity within this unity as different groups or individual persons pursue, in their own ways of remembering Christ, the life of grace that is a participation in this common mystery.

See also BAPTISM; CELEBRATION; CHRIST; CHURCH; DEVOTION(S), POPULAR; EUCHARIST; EXPERIENCE; GRACE; HOLY SPIRIT; LITURGY; MARRIAGE; PASCHAL MYSTERY; PENANCE, PENITENCE; RITUAL; VATICAN COUNCIL II.

Bibliography: L. Johnson, ed., *Called to Prayer: Liturgical Spirituality Today* (Collegeville, Minn.: Liturgical Press, 1986). L. Bouyer, *Liturgical Piety* (Notre Dame, Ind.: Univ. of Notre Dame Press, 1978). G. Braso, *Liturgy and Spirituality,* trans. L. Doyle (Collegeville, Minn.: Liturgical Press, 1971). A. Cunningham, *Prayer: Personal and Liturgical,* Message of the Fathers of the Church 16 (Wilmington, Del.: Glazier, 1985). I. Dalmais, "Theology of the Liturgical Celebration," *Principles of the Liturgy,* The Church at Prayer 1, ed. A. Martimort and trans. M. O'Connell (Collegeville, Minn.: Liturgical Press, 1985) 227–280. R. Duffy, *Real Presence: Worship, Sacraments and Commitment* (San Francisco: Harper & Row, 1982). T. Halton and T. Carroll, *Liturgical Practice in the Fathers,* Message of the Fathers of the Church 21 (Wilmington, Del.: Glazier, 1988). K. Irwin, *Liturgy, Prayer and Spirituality* (New York: Paulist, 1984). J. Jungmann, *Pastoral Liturgy* (New York: Herder, 1962). S. Madigan, *Spirituality Rooted in Liturgy* (Washington: Pastoral Press, 1988). A. Schmemann, *For the Life of the World: Sacraments and Orthodoxy* (Crestwood, N.Y.: St. Vladimir's Seminary Press, 1973). C. Vagaggini, *Theological Dimensions of the Liturgy,* trans. L. Doyle and W. Jurgens (Collegeville, Minn.: Liturgical Press, 1976).

DAVID N. POWER, O.M.I.

SACRED

See GOD; HOLINESS; MYSTERY.

SACRIFICE

The term *sacrifice* (Latin *sacer,* "holy," and *facere,* "to make") has referents in theology, liturgy, and spirituality; a commonsense understanding, grounded in images of animal sacrifice, further complicates efforts to achieve conceptual clarity for what is basically a symbolic act. The classical theological meaning—the death of Christ as the supremely efficacious offering to God—is explicated on the paradigm of OT sacrifices, surpassed by that of Christ. It includes in varying degrees an offering to God, the destruction of the offering, and the depriving of the self for the sake of the offering; in the explication of these elements, however, Christ's violent death is sometimes seen as required by a vengeful Father.

The liturgical referent is the claim that Eucharistic worship has a sacrificial character, derived from its nature as the sacramental representation of the sacrificial death of Christ. The Reformation effort to assert the efficacy of faith over works extended to the assertion that the only sacrifice offered in the Lord's Supper was that of praise and thanksgiving; redemption had been wholly accomplished by Christ's once-for-all sacrificial act. Catholic liturgical theology, focused on "the holy sacrifice of the Mass," dealt indirectly with this dimension through a consideration of the offertory rite, distinguishing offertory, consecration, and communion as the "principal parts of the Mass." But the parts were poorly articulated to one another and to the governing concept of sacrifice.

In spirituality, the goal of union with God suggests *oblation* as the more appropriate term for the self-offering by which the union is sought; the difficulty here has been the tendency to identify sacrifice or oblation entirely with a passive acceptance of suffering, in imitation of the suffering Christ.

The term also has secular usages with the connotation of self-deprivation for a stated purpose, noble or ignoble.

The OT does not have a single term for sacrifice, nor does it present a clear system of the myriad sacrificial practices it records; neither does it undergird them with a coherent theology. Furthermore, it records a constant prophetic polemic against sacrifice. The NT uses the term *thysia* to speak of the sacrifice of Christ three times (Heb 10:12; 1 Cor 5:7; Eph 5:2) and to speak of the life and works of Christians as sacrificial five times (Rom 12:1; Phil 2:17; 4:18; 1 Pet 2:5; Heb 13:15). Theological claims regarding the sacrificial character of the Eucharist rest on covenantal or paschal symbolism rather than explicit assertion.

A further unclarity in the referent for this term lies in the fact that while the cross of Christ often functions as a symbol of his sacrifice, it can only do so as the instrument of his death. It has no symbol of the resurrection, which is essential to the work of redemption, and is firmly linked to the death in the liturgical celebration of the paschal triduum. Likewise, the assertion of an ongoing heavenly sacrifice in the Letter to the Hebrews is a neglected scriptural insight (Heb 7:24-25). In Paul, the cross is an image of transformation, signaled through the lowly death *and* exaltation of Christ (Phil 2:6-11; Rom 6:9-11).

For Catholic theology, the Eucharist has been the central arena for the discussion of the sacrifice of Christ, soteriology being far less developed than Christology. The lack of sustained reflection, together with the acceptance of a normative notion of sacrifice against which Christ's death could be measured, has taken its toll; in the strictest sense, it must now be said that Christ's death is sacrifice only in an analogous sense. Its substance lies in the intensity and totality of his surrender to the Father, both in life and in death. But post-Tridentine theology, asking how the Eucharist could be considered a sacrifice, used a grammar of priest, victim, altar, and blood; inevitably the graphic aspects of Christ's death were emphasized. As a consequence, devotional writers found much material for construing Christian life in terms of abnegation and self-sacrifice. The more positive dimensions of the NT's description of all Christian life and works as sacrificial were eclipsed. The liturgical renewal's stress on the Eucharistic *action* (as opposed to the elements) provides a richer foundation for a spirituality of self-oblation in union with Christ's self-gift.

Early assertions that the Eucharist was an "unbloody" sacrifice are an implicit declaration that while the shedding of blood is essential for a "true sacrifice," that norm was not operative in this case. Nevertheless, the affinity between images of bloody ritual sacrifice and incidents of violence continues to be a source of problems. Early Christians had to be forbidden to seek martyrdom deliberately. Today it is recognized that the positive value given to the crucifixion makes the sacrifice of Christ vulnerable to ideological interpretations through which the Church can legitimate the violence of ordinary life. Liberation theologians, reacting to the institutionalized violence of Latin America, point out that a spirituality of co-suffering with Christ can legitimate the suffering caused by unjust social structures. They work to retrieve a theology of the cross (sacrifice) that sees it as a symbol of the freedom, love, and self-surrender with which Jesus met both life and death. Likewise, feminist theologians have recognized that the call to surrender and oblation has served to reinforce the patriarchal situation that limits women's expectations to passive, subordinate, and auxiliary roles, equates "becoming Christlike" with having no self of one's own, and insinuates guilt about even the smallest move toward self-affirmation. It is noteworthy, however, that Thérèse of Lisieux, unable to seek the priesthood because of her sex, found her vocation in the heart of the Church as love and offered herself as a "victim of Merciful Love." Seemingly, she grounded her spirituality in this oppressive woman's role, but recent scholarship tends to vindicate the powerful and healthy personality who chose a "little way" to live out this oblation.

See also ASCETICISM; EUCHARIST; MORTIFICATION; PASCHAL MYSTERY.

Bibliography: E. Underhill, "The Oblation," *The Mystery of Sacrifice* (New York: Longmans, 1938) 14–27. L. Boff, *Passion of Christ, Passion of the World* (Maryknoll, N.Y.: Orbis, 1987).

MARY BARBARA AGNEW, C.PP.S.

SADNESS
See FEELINGS; TEARS, GIFT OF.

SAINTS, COMMUNION OF SAINTS

The origin of the word *saint* is the Latin word *sanctus,* which means "holy." Saints are holy ones whose lives manifest the holiness of God. In Jewish and Christian traditions, the holy ones are those in communion with the living God. In the Jewish Scriptures, only God is the fullness of holiness (Isa 5:19; 6:3; 41:14; Lev 21:18-21; 33:20). For Christians, Jesus Christ is the holy one (Mk 1:24; Lk 4:34; Jn 6:69; Acts 3:14; 4:27, 30). In both traditions, the communion of saints are the People of God.

What it means to be holy is conditioned by sociocultural and religious factors. Because human holiness is always a partial expression of the holiness of God or of Jesus Christ, there is room for a great diversity of expressions of sanctity. A brief overview of Christian sainthood can illustrate some of this diversity. It cannot adequately deal with the pluralities of holiness in every age, but it can illustrate some sociocultural and ecclesial factors that condition the naming of public saints.

Christian Saints in the 1st Through the 6th Century

In the NT accounts, Jesus Christ is the source of holiness, the center of the communion of saints. Trinitarian communion is revealed through the Son, who invites others to be one with the holiness of God (Jn 2:19; 5:21; 10:17; 14–17). The communion of saints has a threefold meaning in the NT. First, those who share holy things, the sacraments and faith, are the communion of saints. Second, those united to Jesus Christ and, in him, to one another are the communion of saints. Third, those who share their lives and who show active concern for the poor and less fortunate are the communion of saints (Jn 13:14; 14:4-10; 17:1-21; Acts 2:44; 1 Cor 1:9; 10:16; 11-13; 2 Cor 8:13; 13:13).

The celebration of the Lord's Supper was formative and expressive of the meaning of the communion of saints. The Christian community that met at the table of the Lord were both critiqued and challenged by the call to "Do this. . . ." The measure of holiness would be the extent to which they gave over their lives to the urgency of the kingdom and to the formation of the new creation. Baptism into the new creation was baptism into the responsibility for the world.

As the communion of saints expanded to diverse cultural settings, there would remain a constancy in the holiness set forth in the Scriptures. At the same time, the incarnational nature of Christian holiness supported ongoing discernment of meanings in the power of the Spirit. The circumstances of the Christian community throughout the world necessarily affects the vision of what must be done to witness to the reign of God. Some cultural visions and practices may also serve as vehicles for the reign of God, while other aspects will require a new interpretation or a rejection by Christians. Early veneration of Christian saints can illustrate these principles.

The cosmology that dominated the early centuries of the Church influenced an eventual restriction of the word *saint* to mean only those who died in the Lord. How did the cosmology influence beliefs, and how did Christians reinterpret these beliefs?

In the early Christian era, it was thought that heaven was separated from the earth by a vast fault that ran between the moon and the earth. The starry lights of the Milky Way, between the moon and the earth, were the steppingstones to heavenly space. The vigil lights placed at the gravesites of the dead represented the Milky Way. The family that kept vigil at the gravesite provided lights to aid the journey to the heavens.

The graves of Christians were also set with vigil lights, but the interpretation differed from that of the pagan world. The Christian saint did not leave the earth for the heavens. The gravesite of the saint, the *loca sanctorum,* was a cultic place where the power of Jesus Christ through the saint was manifest. In other words, the saint did not journey to the heavens but rather brought the heavens to the earth. That was one reason why the celebration of the Lord's Supper over the burial place of the saint was a common practice. The "saint" was now someone who was empowered by Jesus Christ to manifest that power for the sake of those on earth.

By the middle of the 2nd century, the commemoration of all the dead was one manifestation of the communion of saints. By the 3rd century, such a commemoration was part of the form of remembrance and praise within the Eucharist. However, some of those who died in the Lord were already being set above the rest of the saints, due to the public manifestation of their witness to the death and resurrection of Jesus Christ.

The earliest cult of the saints was the cult of the martyrs. According to Roman law, a martyr gave witness to facts. For Christians, the martyr witnessed to the truth that Jesus Christ alone was Lord. The life given as testimony to this truth made the martyrs special symbols of holiness, for they witnessed physically to the death as well as the resurrection of Jesus Christ.

During centuries of persecution of Christians, the dominance of the martyr paradigm is understandable. In these centuries of persecution, the community would gather at the burial place on the anniversary of death. A brief account of the life of the martyr (*legenda*) would be read and the Eucharist celebrated. The earliest martyrologies listed the names of these saints on a calendar that identified their date of death. Local communities eventually exchanged calendars, so the local calendar grew in the number of listed martyrs.

When the persecution of Christians ended in the 5th century, there was a gradual change in the paradigm of holiness. The new age called for Christian witness or confession of faith, but the emphasis shifted to the interior martyrdom of ascetics and monks and to the confession of faith given by bishops, teachers, and missionaries. Many of these names were added to martyrologies by the late 6th century. A brief account of the life of the saint was now formally read on the day of celebration. At least by the 6th century, Christendom formally celebrated a festival of All Saints.

In the 2nd through the 6th century, the community of believers with their local leaders acclaimed certain witnesses to the Lord as saints. The cult of the saints expressed the awareness that heavenly saints could aid their sisters and brothers. The celebration of the Eucharist at the burial places of the saints was a reminder of the communion of saints.

The 7th Through the 20th Century

The popularity of the cult of the saints grew rapidly through the Middle Ages. Pilgrimages to tombs of saints, stories of miraculous cures, special favors, and answers to prayers were all part of a growing religious imagination. The so-called barbarian invasions added some questionable cultic practices to the veneration of saints. The pluralities of cults, the diversity of religious imagination regarding holiness, and a growing centralization of the Church all contributed to a gradual formalization of the process and affirmation of official sainthood.

In the 7th through the 9th century, the local bishop was the ultimate decider of sainthood. When a person was declared a saint, the body was exhumed and transferred to an altar. The bishop would then publicly declare the person a saint, and a particular day would be assigned on a local calendar for yearly liturgical celebration. On that day a brief legend would be read as part of the celebration. During these centuries the presence of a pope at a local canonization lent prestige to the event. However, the pope did not evaluate or affirm the local bishop's judgment. Saints were still named by a local bishop with the community.

It was not until the late 10th century that a pope officially canonized a saint. In 993 Pope John XV (985–996) declared Uldaric (Ulric) a saint. In the 12th century, Pope Alexander III (1159–1181) decreed that the pope alone could canonize saints. Local bishops could still use their power to acclaim saints, but now they had to obtain explicit permission and approval of the pope.

The mixture of superstition and devotion, of pious and questionable cultic practices, the political and ecclesial issues connected with canonizing some saints while ignoring others, and a growing centralization and uniformity were all currents contributing to papal control of canonizations. In 1588 Pope Sixtus V (1585–1590) divided the work of the Roman Curia, making the Congregation of Rites responsible for the identification of saints. Pope Benedict XIV (1740–1758) decided that all canonizations would occur at St. Peter's in Rome, for Rome symbolized the unity and universality of the Church.

The turbulence of the 16th through the 20th century, the gradual change of vision from national to world community, the evangelizing efforts of missionaries, and the power struggles and wars between some official Church leaders and heads of state influenced new paradigms of official sanctity. Official canonizations were dominated by popes, cardinals, bishops, priests, and male religious who either defended or furthered the Catholic Church.

Vatican II and the Communion of Saints

Though the documents of Vatican II reflect theological compromise, there is a clear call to all Christians to grow into the fullness of holiness, that is, to be saints. All the baptized are responsible for witnessing to the love of Jesus Christ for all. The Dogmatic Constitution on the Church states this in a number of ways (LG 1, 5, 8, 9, 11, 12, 13, 19, 20, 24, 28, 30, 32, 33, 36, 38, 40, 41, 42, 51).

The global contours of holiness are sketched in the Pastoral Constitution on the Church in the Modern World. The paschal mystery somehow touches the heart of everyone, and world transformation is its challenge (GS 38, 39, 40, 93). If world transformation is at the heart of Christian holiness today, then action for justice, care for the liberation of all peoples, uniting with the joys, sorrows, trials, and hopes of the world's people mark Christian holiness (GS 3, 10, 11, 16, 22, 25, 26, 27, 28, 30, 37, 39, 42, 43, 44, 45, 58, 75, 88, 91, 93). If this is true for the communion of saints, it is true for those who are to be formally declared saint in this age.

The revision of the universal calendar of saints was done with guidelines that included setting forth models of holiness for people of this age. The work on the revision was completed in 1969, the year Pope Paul VI (1963–1978) promulgated the calendar. Why is a calendar of saints set forth at all?

A liturgical calendar of saints functions as a part of the larger ecclesial symbol system that mediates the meanings of the paschal mystery. As a symbol system, the liturgical calendar of saints will express a Christology, ecclesiology, and spirituality. The way a saint is thematized by prayers and readings will convey some aspect of the paschal mystery. Insofar as a saint is an ecclesial symbol, the self-understanding of the holiness of the Church will condition the thematization. It will also condition the selection of saints for the universal calendar.

It was fitting for Vatican II to set forth some contours of holiness for this age. Though the council did not produce an explicit document on saintliness today, there are descriptions of saintliness that can be drawn from its reflections. The Dogmatic Constitution on the Church and the Pastoral Constitution on the Church in the Modern World are examples of this.

There is a clear assertion about the universality of the call to holiness. There is a call for Christians to be consciously global in their vision, to work for justice, to be renewed and empowered through the liturgy of the Church, and to live in the universal love of Jesus Christ. Does the revised calendar of saints reflect the universality of response to the call? Paul VI claimed that the revised universal calendar of saints reflects this universality. However, a glance at the official occupants of the revised calendar reflects the following. First, the geographical universality of the saints of universal significance is questionable. European saints make up 66 percent of the list, while some entire continents are unrepresented. Vocational universality is invisible, as well as proportionate gender occupancy. Celibate white male saints with ecclesial rank are overwhelmingly dominant. The few women saints are virgins, martyrs, or religious. There is an overabundance of socioeconomic middle-and upper-class saints. Saints of color, saints who were economically poor, and saints whose holiness grew through married life are invisible as saints of universal significance. Does official heaven still reflect the interests and ideals of a socially conditioned Church?

The Communion of Saints in Retrospect and Prospect

There is a constant in the identification of Christian saints, namely, the witness to the intimate and infinite love of Jesus Christ. The communion of saints has been grounded in that reality, celebrating and remembering the challenge whenever the community gathers to "Do this." The meaning of a life given for all has been embodied in many ways by many saints. Each age in history testifies to the holiness of Jesus Christ, but the contours of that holiness can change as the needs for various forms of witness change.

The saints in any age are transparent in their pointing to the new creation in Christ. Grasped by the urgency of the kingdom of God, a saint is one who inspires and evokes a response from others. The response may be positive or negative on the part of society and on the part of the Church.

In an age when there is a renewed awareness of the sufferings of innocent people, the saints will be those whose lives are spent working tirelessly to alleviate suffering. In an age when Christians must literally choose between life and death for the sake of the gospel, the saints will boldly choose life though the cost is death. In an age when there is a clash between the human dignity of all and the restrictive power of a few over all, the saints will name the sin. In an age when classism operates in society and in the Church, the saints will again proclaim the reign of God that is a communion of slave and free, Jew and Gentile, male and female. In an age when there is an ecclesial restriction of gifts of the Spirit to some groups but not to others, the saints will witness to the freedom of the Spirit to give gifts as the Spirit chooses, regardless of restrictive laws about use of the gifts.

Because the nature of sainthood is an incarnational reality, the contours of sanctity may change from age to age and culture to culture. For this reason, revisions of calendars of saints will always be necessary; the diversity of models of holiness will never be exhausted. What the Spirit has yet to say to the Church is not known. What is known by those who believe in the communion of saints is that the promise of the Spirit has been made, and the One who has made the promise shall remain true to his word.

See also BODY OF CHRIST; CHRIST; CHURCH; CONTEMPORARY SPIRITUALITY; HOLINESS; INTERCESSION; MARY; PETITION; VATICAN COUNCIL II.

Bibliography: L. Cunningham, *The Meaning of Saints* (New York: Harper & Row, 1980). C. Duquoc and C. Floristán, eds., *Models of Holiness,* Concilium 129 (New York: Seabury, 1979). S. Madigan, *Models of Holiness Derived from the Saints of Universal Significance in the Roman Calendar* (Ann Arbor, Mich.: Univ. Microfilms, 1984). Paul VI, *Mysterii Paschalis,* AAS 61 (1969) 222–226.

SHAWN MADIGAN, C.S.J.

SALESIAN SPIRITUALITY

The Salesian spiritual tradition began with St. Francis de Sales (1567–1622), as its name suggests, and St. Jane Frances de Chantal (1572–1641). Traditionally Francis alone has been regarded as the originator of Salesian spirituality, and Jane has been consistently seen, Pygmalion fashion, as Francis's chief handiwork. Recently it has been demonstrated that although Francis and Jane shared a common vision and employed the same religious language to articulate that vision, they were very different personalities and brought to their shared views their own distinctive life histories, capabilities, and religious perceptions.

University educated in law, theology, philosophy, and rhetoric, Francis was a man of the world intensely engaged in public life as a bishop of a diocese, spiritual director, writer, preacher, correspondent with people in all walks of life, reformer, and advocate of lay devotion. In the course of her life, Jane was a baroness, wife, mother, widow, foundress, and religious superior; her world was feminine, monastic, and contemplative in a way that Francis's was not. Francis's personality was characterized by equilibrium, patience, and gracefulness; Jane's, by anticipation, compassion, and ardor.

Salesian spirituality, then, may be said to be embodied in two primary historical forms. One is in Francis's person and writings, the most important and well known being the *Introduction to the Devout Life* (1609) and the *Treatise on the Love of God* (1616). The other is found in the person of Jane and the religious community of the Visitation of Holy Mary, which was co-founded by the two saints. Although the Visitation was inspired by Francis's initial vision and sustained by his conscientious but periodic spiritual direction, actual presence, and writings, responsibility for its ongoing nurturance fell to Jane, who survived Francis by nineteen years. Consequently the Visitation bears the imprint of Jane's personality and religiosity in a unique way.

The leitmotif of Salesian spirituality is the motto "Live Jesus!" which appears at the head of each of the letters Jane wrote and throughout the writings Francis penned. For Francis and Jane, this exclamation was an emphatic statement about how they saw themselves and what they were about in the world. The imitation of Christ is, of course, central to the entire history of Christian spirituality; however, each variety of Christian spirituality has its own distinctive understanding of, and manner of realizing, this imitation. This is true of Salesian spirituality, the goal of which is to make the gentle and humble Jesus live in the hearts of humankind. Unlike some spiritual traditions, Salesian spirituality teaches that the imitation of Christ does not require withdrawal or flight from the world or human society. One is to live Jesus in the circumstances of one's state of life, whatever it may be.

The *Introduction to the Devout Life* is the manifesto of this fundamental conviction of Salesian spirituality. In this work's preface Francis defines the originality of the *Introduction*'s contribution to the history of Christian spirituality: "Almost all those who have hitherto written about devotion have been concerned with instructing persons wholly withdrawn from the world or have at least taught a kind of devotion that leads to such complete retirement. My purpose is to instruct those who live in town, within families, or at court, and by their state of life are obliged to live an ordinary life as to outward appearances" (trans. J. Ryan, Garden City, N.Y.: Image Books, 1972, p. 33). Something of this notion of integrating devotion and society is also evident in Francis's original plan for the Visitation, which was that it be an unenclosed community of women devoted to love of God in prayer and to service to others, specifically visiting the poor. However, in 1618 Francis yielded to the demand of the archbishop of Lyons that the Visitation become cloistered, thus converting it into a formal order.

References to the human heart or the heart of God or of Jesus, as well as affective language associated with the image of the heart, are ubiquitous in the writings of Francis and Jane. It is virtually impossible to turn to a page in their works that does not contain such references or language. The Salesian spiritual world is a world of hearts. In Salesian thought God is love, and the divine heart is the source of that love. Jesus makes visible who God is and who we are in light of that revelation. The Salesian Jesus is the Jesus of Mt 11:29, who invites all: "Take my yoke upon you and learn from me, for I am meek and humble of heart."

The human heart has an innate capacity to love with a "pure love" that is modeled on the unconditional love of God for humankind. But human nature is wounded by sin, and hence much discipline and serious formation are required to recover the ability to love purely. The gentle, humble heart of Christ is the mediator between the worlds of divine and human hearts, and the model for the transformation of the human heart into a heart that pulses in union with God. To "Live Jesus," Francis avers, is to have the name of Jesus engraved on one's heart (*Introduction*, p. 124). Thus the vital core of one's being—one's heart, as understood in the holistic biblical sense—is to be surrendered to the living presence of Christ. This surrender means bringing to birth, and being animated by, humility in one's relationship with God and gentleness in one's relationship with neighbor.

In Salesian spirituality humility is synonymous with truth. Humility entails the awareness and affective appropriation of the truth about who God is—the Creator—and who the human person is—not the Creator but a creature made in God's image and likeness, and endowed with an innate divine dignity and with the capacity for union with God. Thus God touches each individual with grace, a gratuitously given invitation to divine union, for which the human person is created. This invitation is extended to everyone—layperson or cleric, man or woman, celibate or married. Anticipating Vatican II's universal call to holiness (LG 39-42) by four centuries, Salesian spirituality insists on the religious value of all states of life and affirms that union with God can be realized not only in the desert or monastery but anywhere. In fact, the vast majority of Christians are called to this union in the busyness of the world and amidst the obligations of marriage and family life.

The Christian lives between what Francis describes as the "two wills of God": God's will to be done, "how it should be," and the will of God's good pleasure, "the way it is." God's will is manifest not only in the received inspirations of either individual or community but also in the events,

facts, and existing realities of one's immediate situation—in the present and often painful reality in which one lives. Union with God means the creature's active, continual, and creative obedience to the Creator's will. Francis calls this union, which is cultivated by prayer, the sacraments, and spiritual direction and which is expressed by service to neighbor, "devotion": the "prompt, active, and faithful . . . observance of God's commands" and doing "quickly and lovingly as many good works as possible, both those commanded and those merely counselled or inspired" (*Introduction*, pp. 40-41). Jesus' earthly life is the pattern for this union: "My food is to do the will of the one who sent me and to finish his work" (Jn 4:34). Jesus was obedient to his Father's will, "becoming obedient to death, even death on a cross" (Phil 2:8). While God invites all to actualize the potential within for union, it is up to each person to respond. God absolutely respects human freedom.

Gentleness toward neighbor flows from the awareness of one's own divine dignity. It recognizes others as good and worthy of respect, even reverence, because they, too, bear God's image and likeness. In Salesian spirituality the inner beauty that is the divine image is to be manifested exteriorly by gentleness, gracefulness, graciousness, and charity. Relationships are central in the Salesian context; they are neither inimical nor peripheral to the love of God. It is in human relationships that one lets Jesus live. Jesus lived out his union with his heavenly Father among people as a compassionate presence, an agent of reconciliation, and an advocate for the marginalized. Both Francis and Jane showed this face of the gentle Jesus in their lives. Francis's biographers record numerous episodes from his life that earned him the title "the gentleman saint." One of the most famous recounts Francis's response to a man who had often made ribald comments about the saint in public: "Then one day [Francis] met him in the street, went up to him and spoke to him as kindly as ever. 'You bear me a grudge,' he said, 'as well I know, so don't try to deny it. But you know, if you put out one of my eyes, the other wouldn't bear you malice'" (*St. Francis de Sales: A Testimony by St. Chantal*, trans. E. Stopp, Hyattsville, Md.: Institute of Salesian Studies, 1967, pp. 90–91).

Likewise, Jane's maternal and compassionate guidance of her spiritual daughters stands out. Her primary concern was that the Visitandines be brought to spiritual maturity not through fear or servile duty but through love. Jane conceived of the entire process of formation within the Visitation as "winning the hearts" of the sisters by showing forth the qualities of the gentle, humble Jesus in governing and spiritual direction.

In human relationships one seeks to awaken in others an awareness of their divine dignity by the respect and reverence one demonstrates for their person, individuality, and liberty. In Salesian thought each person is unique and unrepeatable. For example, Francis says that when Jesus accomplished our redemption on the day of his passion and death, he "knew all of us by name and by surname" (*Treatise on the Love of God*, 2 vols., trans. J. Ryan, Rockford, Ill.: TAN Books, 1975, 2:280). Paralleling the centrality of human freedom in the divine scheme of things, each person's liberty is to be respected in human relationships, which should be characterized by detachment from one's own expectations. The ideal Salesian relationship is a God-centered union of hearts that enfleshes the living presence of Jesus in the world.

Francis's and Jane's vision of the kingdom of God that is realized, however imperfectly, in human society is one of the continually emerging presence of Jesus— the coming to birth of the humble and gentle heart of Christ in the hearts of human beings. The love that flows from the heart of the Salesian Jesus is a love that suffers and dies. So too the Salesian heart of humankind is the crucified heart of pure love that is broken, pierced, and dies to self-serving and self-satisfying love. From this death Jesus is born and lives in the human heart.

In her important St. Basil's Day colloquy (1632), Jane describes this process of death and birth as a martyrdom of love. She instructs the Visitandines as to how this martyrdom would be realized: "Give your absolute consent to God and you will experience it. What happens ... is that divine love thrusts its sword into the most intimate and secret parts of the soul and separates us from our very souls.... this is intended for generous hearts, who, without holding themselves back, are faithful to love" (quoted by Wright, "'That is what it is made for,'" p. 154). This martyrdom of love is clearly in continuity with the spirit of the early Christian martyrs, who, confident in the hope of the resurrection, sought union with Christ through participation in his passion and death.

The Visitation was the only religious community founded by Francis and Jane. Francis also wanted to found a community of priests but died before he could realize this desire. Subsequently numerous religious communities of men and women were inspired by the Salesian tradition. The best known are the Salesians of St. John Bosco, the Missionaries of St. Francis de Sales, and the Oblates of St. Francis de Sales, all of which were founded in the 19th century.

See also CHRIST; COMPASSION; DETACHMENT; DEVOTION(S), POPULAR; DISCIPLESHIP; FRENCH SCHOOL OF SPIRITUALITY; FRIENDSHIP; HEART; HEART OF CHRIST; HOLINESS; HUMILITY; LAY SPIRITUALITY; LOVE; MARTYRDOM; VATICAN COUNCIL II; VOCATION.

Bibliography: J. Chorpenning, "The Court, Monastery, and Paradise in St. Francis de Sales' *Introduction to the Devout Life*," *The Downside Review* 107 (1989) 22–33. W. Wright, *Bond of Perfection: Jeanne de Chantal & François de Sales* (New York: Paulist, 1985). W. Wright and J. Power, "Introduction," in Francis de Sales and Jane de Chantal, *Letters of Spiritual Direction*, trans. P. Thibert (New York: Paulist, 1988) 9–86. W. Wright, "'That is what it is made for': The Image of the Heart in the Spirituality of Francis de Sales and Jane de Chantal," in A. Callahan, ed., *Spiritualities of the Heart* (New York: Paulist, 1990) 143–158.

JOSEPH F. CHORPENNING, O.S.F.S.

SANCTITY

See HOLINESS.

SATAN

See DEMON(S), DEMONIC, DEVIL(S); EVIL; TEMPTATION.

SCHOOLS OF SPIRITUALITY

See SPIRITUALITY, CHRISTIAN (CATHOLIC), HISTORY OF; WESTERN MEDIEVAL SPIRITUALITY.

SCIENCE

See TECHNOLOGY, IMPACT ON SPIRITUALITY; WORLD.

SCRIPTURE

The Foundational Role of Scripture

Scripture has singular importance in Christian life. This central role of Scripture is part of Christianity's heritage from Judaism. For three thousand years believers have preserved the story of God's actions; for the greater part of that period the written word has been revered as sacred and honored as God's word.

The Word of God

"Word of God" is a rich concept in the Bible and in the spiritual life. The Hebrew term *dabar* connotes both "word" and "event." It is by the word that God created in Genesis 1 (e.g., Gen 1:3, 6, 9; Ps 33:6). The word or promise of God initiated the covenant with Abraham and his descendants (Gen 15:1, 4), and Abraham believed God (Gen 15:6). It was God's word that initiated the Exodus event (Exod 4:29-31). The Ten Commandments, the charter of the Sinai covenant, are known as the Ten

Words (Exod 34:28; Deut 4:13; 10:2, 4). God promised that this word of the law would not be remote but rather would be "something very near to you, already in your mouths and in your hearts" (Deut 30:11-14). It was the word of God that sustained Israel in the desert (Deut 8:3). The land was given to the people according to the word of the Lord (Josh 21:43-45).

But because leaders and people strayed from the word given by God, God sent prophets as special messengers of the word. God put the divine word in their mouths (see Jer 1:9; Ezek 2:8-9; 3:1-3), and they in turn proclaimed: "Thus says the word of the Lord" (or "The word of the Lord came to me thus . . ."). The word of God spoken by the prophets called the people to repentance, warned them of exile, and comforted them with the promise of God's undying love and fidelity to them.

After the Exile in the 6th century B.C.E., the word of God came to Israel through sages as well as prophets. The sage distilled the wisdom that had grown from the community's experience. The sage revealed to Israel the personification of God's wisdom, the Wisdom Woman who "[came] forth from the mouth of God" (Sir 24:3) and through whom God created all things. Thus the word of God appeared personified in the Wisdom Woman.

In the NT, John the Baptist came preaching the word of God that was spoken to him in the desert (Lk 3:2-3). He announced the arrival of Jesus, the One who was to come. In Luke, Jesus began his ministry by reading a Scripture passage and announcing its fulfillment (Lk 4:16-21). He told parables about the word of God (Mk 4:3-12, 14-20). People were amazed at the power and authority of Jesus' word (Lk 4:36).

The greatest leap in understanding, however, is found in the prologue to the Gospel of John. The prologue begins with the personification of the word of God at creation. "In the beginning was the Word, and the Word was with God, and the Word was God" (Jn 1:1). The climax, however, is the startling announcement: "The Word was made flesh and pitched his tent among us" (Jn 1:14, Greek translation). The Word of God became incarnate and wore human flesh.

From Oral to Written Communication

It is in the context of the development of the concept of the Word of God that the written word must be understood. Israel's earliest Scripture was certainly oral. The stories circulated orally; the ancient poems of Exodus 15 and Judges 4 were performed orally. The Christian Scripture began with preaching and telling the story. Only after the development of the story in the faith community did it begin to be written down.

The oldest written versions of the story of God's action with people may date to the 10th century B.C.E., to the flourishing of literary activity during the reigns of David and Solomon. As centuries passed, the story continued to be told and to be written in ways meaningful to each generation. During the Babylonian Exile in the 6th century B.C.E., various written versions of the foundational story were combined and edited, forming what is now called the Torah or Pentateuch, the five books from Genesis to Deuteronomy. The historical work that stretches from Joshua to 2 Kings and the preaching of the prophets were also edited and began to circulate. The people of God began to recognize the written word as the word of God.

Already in the 7th century B.C.E., when the Book of Deuteronomy was found in the Temple, King Josiah and the priests and scribes took to heart the words of the prophet Huldah, who proclaimed that this written work contained the word of God. In the 4th century, after the Exile, Ezra read "the book of the law of Moses," i.e., the Pentateuch, to the assembled people (Neh 8). The written book was reverenced as the law of God. Ben Sira indicated that the works of the prophets had been collected and that even the scroll of the Twelve

Prophets (Hosea to Malachi) was complete (Sir 48:20–49:10). New Testament authors refer to "the law [the Pentateuch] and the prophets [Joshua to 2 Kings and Isaiah to the Twelve]" (Mt 7:12; 22:40; Lk 16:16). Works of the sages were also collected in writing in the last centuries before the Common Era.

The same movement from oral to written communication of God's word occurred in the Christian tradition. The earliest Christian writings are the letters of Paul, written of necessity to exhort and encourage early faith communities. Initially they were a supplement and support to the oral preaching. As the generation of eyewitnesses began to die, believers also began to write the Gospels, the story of Jesus' life, death, and resurrection. Luke declared his purpose thus: "I too have decided, after investigating everything accurately anew, to write it down in an orderly sequence for you ... so that you may realize the certainty of the teachings you have received" (Lk 1:3, 4).

The Canon

The period in which the biblical books were written and edited was characterized by a double movement. Works that were valued by earlier generations as authentic accounts of God's will and works were preserved, read, and pondered by later generations. The same later generations, however, also continued to interpret God's word in the light of their own experience and to retell the story in writing to fit the needs of their own times. Thus, gradually a collection of books grew that was recognized as the genuine word of God. The believing community gathered and preserved the collection. The believing community pronounced the validity of the books as authentic revelation.

The end result of this gradual process was the development of a list of books that came to be recognized as inspired by God. The list is called the "canon" of Scripture. The word *canon* comes from the Akkadian word *qaneh,* which means "reed," and, by extension, "rule" or "measure." The canon or list developed slowly. A primary criterion was use by the worshiping and teaching community. The collection of books found at Qumran (the Dead Sea Scrolls) indicates that the Jewish community in the last few centuries before the Common Era had neither a standard list nor a final editing of the books. The Hebrew canon, the final list, was determined, at the earliest, toward the end of the 1st century C.E.

Initially Christians simply added their developing list of sacred books to the collection they already had. In the 2nd century C.E., however, a priest named Marcion declared that the Jewish Scriptures were useless for Christians in the face of the new revelation in Christ. He also decided that one version of the gospel story (primarily Luke) and a few of the letters of Paul were sufficient as Christian Scriptures. The Church community eventually declared the teaching of Marcion to be heresy and officially listed the books inherited from Jewish tradition, which they named the Old Testament, along with a NT list, including four Gospels. The OT list, however, included seven books that were not included in the final Hebrew canon: Judith, Tobit, Esther, the Wisdom of Solomon, Ben Sira, Baruch, and 1–2 Maccabees, as well as additions to Esther and Daniel. The NT list did not arrive at its present form until the 4th century; it is found in an Easter letter of Athanasius.

One further development of the Christian canon came in the 16th century. Luther, followed by the rest of the non-Roman traditions, listed only the books of the Hebrew canon in the Christian OT. The Roman Church at the Council of Trent declared the longer list, including the seven books previously mentioned, as the OT canon for the Roman Church. The seven books that are in the Roman canon of the OT but not in the Jewish canon or other Christian canons are sometimes called "deuterocanonical books." All Christian traditions agree on the NT canon.

Thus the Bible truly belongs to the believing community. The oral tradition was preserved and passed on in the community. The written works were produced in and for the community. It is the community that kept and copied the written works, the community that prayed and preached from the written works, and the community that made the final selection of written works that constitute today's Bible.

History of Interpretation

From the beginning of biblical tradition the faith community has also interpreted the written word. The earliest evidence of this is within Scripture itself, as each generation retold the story to fit its own situation. For example, the primary version of the Exodus-wilderness story is found in Exodus and Numbers. Psalmists, however, used the same story to emphasize different points. Psalm 78 tells the story of the plagues and the desert in a wisdom setting "so that the generation to come might know . . . that they should put their hope in God." Psalm 105 tells the story as a primary example of God's fidelity to the covenant. Psalm 106 tells the desert story in a psalm of repentance as an example of Israel's sin. The 1st-century author of the Book of Wisdom uses five examples of the Exodus-wilderness story to illustrate the theme: "By the things through which their foes were punished they in their need were benefited" (Wis 11:5).

Postbiblical interpreters also sought a way to relate the biblical text to the situation of their times. Already in the early centuries, however, there was a movement toward secondary or hidden meanings, especially in texts that seemed to have no immediate relevance to faith-filled life. By the medieval period four meanings were expected from a text: (1) the literal meaning; (2) an allegorical meaning, in which each element in the text was given symbolic significance; (3) a tropological or moral meaning, in which examples for right living were found; and (4) an anagogical or eschatological meaning, which related the text to the coming kingdom of God.

By the time of the Reformation, however, the emphasis in biblical interpretation began to shift. Several elements contributed to this shift in emphasis: a developed method for studying other ancient texts; the movement to translate the Scriptures into the vernacular; the rise of Protestantism, which brought both greater freedom of interpretation and greater attention to Scripture. The development of a scientific approach to history and the growth of archaeological investigation also affected methods for interpreting Scripture.

The 20th century has reaped the benefit of these developments. The chief goal of modern biblical study is an understanding of the original meaning of the text and the relationship of that original meaning to the life of contemporary believers. The primary method is the historical-critical method, in which questions of text, form, literary style and technique, historical background, source, and context are addressed. The method first began to flourish in the Protestant tradition. In the Roman tradition the encyclical *Divino Afflante Spiritu* (1943) of Pius XII marks the beginning of modern biblical scholarship and interpretation.

This beginning in the scholarly world was opened to the whole believing community through the Second Vatican Council. The Dogmatic Constitution on Divine Revelation (*Dei Verbum*), encourages Catholics to study the Bible and to recognize the Bible as a privileged revelation of God and God's will. The "sacred Scripture of both the Old and the New Testament are like a mirror in which the pilgrim Church on earth looks at God, from whom she has received everything, until she is brought finally to see Him as He is, face to face (cf. 1 Jn 3:2)" (DV 7).

Several developments flowed in the wake of Vatican II. New translations were done, notably the New American Bible and the Jerusalem Bible. A new Lectionary for the Eucharist with a three-year cycle of Sundays specifically designed to open the treasures of the word of God to God's people was adopted. Bible study groups and prayer groups arose and flourished. Scholarly and popular journals such as *The Catholic Biblical Quarterly* (since 1938) and *The Bible Today* began to grow. Commentaries such as *The New Jerome Biblical Commentary* and *The Collegeville Bible Commentary* were written and have been revised.

The word of God, written and preserved in the community, interpreted by the community, cherished by the community as a source of prayer and wisdom, continues in this new age to nourish the community.

Various Types/Genres of Scripture

Two Testaments

Christian tradition divides the biblical books into two testaments: the first or Old Testament, which Christians share with Jews and which contains the story of God's work in the world from creation to the period of the Second Temple (built in 515 B.C.E. and destroyed by the Romans in 70 C.E.); and the second or New Testament, which begins with the story of Jesus and contains documents and letters and visions of the early Christian community in the 1st century C.E.

There has been some attempt to designate the two testaments as the Hebrew Scriptures and the Christian Scriptures in order to indicate the significance of each. There is a problem in this designation for Roman Catholics, however, since the Roman canon of the OT includes seven books not found in the Hebrew Scriptures. It has also been suggested that the two testaments be called the First and the Second Testament.

Forms

The various biblical books are written in different forms or genres, and even within books there are a variety of forms. The Constitution on Divine Revelation instructs the interpreter as follows: "Since God speaks in sacred Scripture through men in human fashion, the interpreter of sacred Scripture, in order to see clearly what God wanted to communicate to us, should carefully investigate what meaning the sacred writers really intended, and what God wanted to manifest by means of their words. Those who search out the intention of the sacred writers must, among other things, have regard for 'literary forms.'... The interpreter must investigate what meaning the sacred writer intended to express and actually expressed in particular circumstances as he used contemporary literary forms in accordance with the situation of his own time and culture" (DV 12).

Narrative prose is a primary vehicle for the biblical story. The stories in the Pentateuch are generally short prose episodes loosely connected by chronology. The stories of the primeval history in Genesis 1–11 are mythic in character, that is, they speak of origins and the essential nature of things from the beginning. The patriarchal stories have the nature of saga, that is, they are heroic tales about the ancestors. The central theme of the patriarchal stories is God's choice of a people and the covenant-making between them.

Another genre of material found chiefly in the Pentateuch is *prescriptive law.* Large sections of Exodus and Deuteronomy and almost the whole of Leviticus are made up of law. Biblical law is found in two forms: absolute or apodictic law, and case or conditional law. The absolute form, which is virtually unique to Israel, consists of laws that state an unconditional demand, for example, "You shall not kill; you shall not steal." The conditional form, common in the rest of the Ancient Near East and in our modern law codes, consists of laws that state conditions and then prescribe a specific course of action. An example of conditional law is the following: "When [people] quarrel and one strikes the other with a stone or with his fist, not mortally, but enough to put him in bed, the one who struck the blow shall be acquitted, provided the other can get up and walk around with the help of his staff. Still, he must compensate him for his enforced idleness and provide for his complete cure" (Exod 21:18-19).

The whole Pentateuch is sometimes referred to as "the Law." This is an inadequate translation of *Torah,* which properly means "instruction." Law in biblical tradition is seen as a gift for life, the way to be like God. In that sense, both prescriptive law and prose episodes are law. Prescriptive law is *halakah,* "the way to walk." The narratives are *haggadah,* "the telling of the story." Both are guides for living.

The books that follow the Pentateuch are classified by Christians as *historical books.* There are two major "histories," one that includes the books Joshua–Judges, 1–2 Samuel, and 1–2 Kings; and the other that includes Ezra–Nehemiah and 1–2 Chronicles. The first of these, known in Jewish tradition as the Former Prophets, is sometimes called the Deuteronomic History, because the history is told in such a way that it illustrates major principles of Deuteronomy. Deuteronomy repeatedly asserts that obedience will result in blessing and disobedience will result in punishment. Both in single incidents, such as battles won and lost, and in overall sweep, such as exile as a result of disobedience, this history illustrates that principle. Deuteronomy also points out the importance of the true prophet. In the Deuteronomic History the word of the prophet does not fail.

The Chronicler's History (1–2 Chronicles, Ezra–Nehemiah) opens with a long genealogy beginning with Adam and ends with the period after the Babylonian Exile. Like the Deuteronomic History, the

Chronicler's History is an attempt to deal with the reasons for the Exile. The Chronicler's main focus is the worshiping community and cultic law. The proper pattern for worship was set in the Jerusalem Temple under David and Solomon. Israel's hope for the future is in the continuation of that pattern of worship. A major portion of the last two books is concerned with the rebuilding of the Temple and the reestablishment of the worshiping community.

In the NT the Acts of the Apostles is a historical book. It is a second volume to the Gospel of Luke and tells the story of Jesus' ongoing work in the world through the disciples. Its message is that God, through the Holy Spirit, continues the work of redemption in the Church.

Biblical histories, then, are interpreted history. They report not only events but a specific meaning underlying events. They are told from a theological perspective. Their intent is to describe God's actions in the world and among people.

Another major section of the Bible consists of *prophetic works,* e.g., Isaiah, Jeremiah, Ezekiel, the twelve minor prophets. These books record the preaching of Israel's prophets from the 8th to the 5th/4th century B.C.E. A prophet is called to be a messenger of God, one who "speaks for" God, and so prophetic speeches regularly begin with a messenger formula: "Thus says the Lord." A prophet's function is to call God's people to a fuller participation in covenant life. In speaking this call, the prophet both criticizes and energizes. The prophet criticizes abuses and sins, areas in which the people have fallen away from the covenant. The prophet also energizes by enabling the people to envision the wonder of God's plan for their future and the fidelity of God to promises made in their behalf. (See W. Brueggemann, *The Prophetic Imagination,* Philadelphia: Fortress, 1978.) Thus prophetic speeches are made up of judgment oracles, in which the people are told the consequences of their sins; lawsuits, in which God calls the people to trial for breaking the covenant; and oracles of salvation, in which the people are encouraged to believe in the possibility of faithful life with God.

Because the prophets are God's messengers to a specific people, their major focus is their own present and immediate future. They address the circumstances of their own time and the institutions of their own time, e.g., the monarchy, the priesthood, the military, the economic establishment. They portray a future for the people of their own time, a future characterized by God's fidelity and their own faithful response.

The books of Proverbs, Job, Qoheleth, Sirach, and the Wisdom of Solomon are usually classified as *wisdom literature.* The goal of wisdom is the good life. These books reflect the distillation of common human experience and teach principles for successful living in areas reaching from public relations and family life to the most profound questions of life and death. The rewards of wisdom are expected in this present life. The wise person looks forward to wealth, peace, honor, and a long life. Experience teaches, however, that sometimes this expectation is frustrated. Sometimes the wicked prosper and the wise suffer. The wisdom literature, in spite of this seeming contradiction, consistently advises fear of the Lord as the basic principle for living and consistently maintains the justice of God. The most recent book of the collection, the Wisdom of Solomon, arrives at the insight that only in life after death are wisdom's expectations fully realized.

The forms that appear in the wisdom literature are the basic forms used everywhere to convey common human experience, chiefly the proverb, the exhortation, and the speculative essay. Proverbs are short, easily remembered sayings that capture the "wisdom of many in the wit of one." Exhortations are longer pieces that give advice, often in the form of a speech from a parent or teacher to a child. The speculative essays debate the questions of innocent suffering, the justice of God, the frustrations of life.

A major contribution of the wisdom literature to biblical theology is the portrait of the Wisdom Woman. She is introduced in the Book of Proverbs (chaps. 1–9, 31), and as her description develops, it becomes evident that she participates intimately in the life of God. She was present at creation as designer of the world. Through her, creation came to be. She comes from the mouth of God, suggesting God's word or spirit. She is God's delight, and her delight is in human beings. Through her, humans become friends of God. She is the law; she is the mirror of God's glory. Those who find her find life; those who miss her find death.

The *psalms* are the prayer book of the Bible. The Book of Psalms is a collection of relatively brief poems intended primarily for use in worship. The book is actually a collection of collections, somewhat in the style of a modern hymnal. Many psalms are identified as belonging to the collection of Asaph or David or Korah.

There are two major categories of psalms: hymns and laments. The function of the hymn is praise of God. All praise, however, is insufficient in the face of God's goodness and greatness. The hymn, therefore, is usually addressed to others—all creation, all nations, the people of God—to join in the praise. After this call to praise, the hymn proceeds with the reasons for praise. The lament is an expression of distress and a cry for help. Laments are ordinarily addressed directly to God. After the cry to God, laments continue with complaint, a description of distress, hope for vindication and vengeance on enemies. Laments usually end with an expression of confidence in God and assurance that the prayer has been heard. Thus simple prayers of confidence such as Psalm 27 are often classified with laments.

There are some smaller categories of psalms classified by content: songs of Zion, royal psalms, wisdom psalms.

Perhaps the most difficult psalms for modern believers are the laments in which the prayer for vengeance is clearly expressed. Worshipers cringe at such graphic prayers for destruction. The focus of these psalms, however, is the victory of God's justice and the eradication of evil. The intent corresponds to the prayer "Thy kingdom come." Understood in this way, these psalms can function as a prayer for justice and peace in the world and as a prayer for the elimination of evil both within the worshiper's heart and in the larger society.

The Book of Psalms does not contain all the prayers of the Bible. Other hymns and laments are found scattered throughout the OT and the NT, e.g., Exodus 15, Deuteronomy 32, Judges 4, Ephesians 1, Philippians 2. These poetic prayers are usually called "canticles."

Some biblical books are properly recognized as biblical fiction. Primary examples are the books of Ruth, Jonah, Tobit, Esther, and Judith. These books have a dual purpose: to teach and to entertain. They clothe basic truths about God and human life in a story that, as it entertains, also shapes the lives of its readers. The plot may be based on historical events or the creation of the author. The NT parables are an example of shorter fictional creations that function to teach as well as to entertain. Within other biblical books are found some lengthy prose sections that exhibit the characteristics of carefully constructed plot and developed characters, e.g., the Joseph story (Gen 37–50) and the succession narrative (2 Sam 9–20; 1 Kgs 1–2), in which the controlling question is: "Who will succeed David on the throne?"

A kind of literature that developed in the last two centuries B.C.E. and the first two centuries C.E. is called *apocalyptic literature*. Apocalyptic literature arose in a situation of persecution. Because of the terrible distress of God's people, the conviction grew that history was too corrupt to be redeemed. God's victory and the vindication of the righteous would come fully only at the end of history. Evil is seen as greater than human power. Thus there will be a final battle between superhuman powers of good and evil, angels and demons, in which the world and history will be destroyed. Then the kingdom of God will arrive in its fullness, and the just, risen from the dead, will share in God's victory. The primary message of apocalyptic literature is the encouragement to persevere because God will win in the end.

Because it grew in a context of persecution and because it is largely visionary, apocalyptic literature is cryptic and mysterious. Much of it seems to be written in code. There are highly symbolic systems of colors and numbers. Impossible visions are portrayed that must be explained to the visionary (and the reader) by an angel. Apocalyptic literature, however, like prophetic literature, is addressed to the contemporaries of the author. The fantastic visions symbolize the present distress of the author's community. The intent of apocalyptic literature is not to predict a distant future but to proclaim to present believers the certain victory of God.

There are two major biblical apocalypses: the Book of Daniel and the Book of Revelation. Apocalyptic sections appear in other books, e.g., Isaiah 24–27; parts of Joel; Mark 13.

A new genre in the NT is the *gospel*. The first time the word *gospel* appears in reference to a written work is at the beginning of the Gospel of Mark. The Greek word *euaggelion,* which is translated "gospel," means "good news." The term indicates the purpose of a gospel, which is to persuade the hearers of something profitable to themselves. Thus gospels do not claim to be history but persuasion. The Gospel of Mark opens: "The beginning of the gospel of Jesus Christ [the Son of God]" (Mk 1:1). The evangelist intends to present the events of Jesus' life, death, and resurrection in such a way that the readers are convinced that Jesus is good news for their lives. The presentation, the sequence, and

the selection of stories are all ordered to that end.

Thus the four Gospels, while they present essentially the same story, differ in order to shape the story for the needs of differing audiences. Matthew, Mark, and Luke are often called "Synoptic Gospels" because their similarity allows one to "see them together" (Greek *synoptikos*). They tell many of the same stories in the same sequence, often with the same words. The Gospel of John differs significantly from the other three both in content and in sequence.

The Pontifical Biblical Commission reminds believers regarding Gospel study that the development of the Gospels took place in three stages: (1) events in the life of Jesus; (2) oral tradition, the telling of the story; and (3) the writing of the Gospel (*Instruction on the Historical Truth of the Gospels,* 1964). It is the result of the third stage that is present in the Bible. The Gospels represent a developed and interpreted tradition, shaped to encourage and to instruct believers in the Good News.

Another NT category is the *letter.* There are letters attributed to Paul and addressed to specific people and the so-called Catholic (i.e., universal) Epistles of James, 1–2 Peter, 1–3 John, and Jude. The letter opens with the address to the audience and frequently indicates the content of the letter. The main body of the letter contains instruction and exhortation. This is followed by a conclusion, which often contains final instructions and personal greetings.

Various Uses of Scripture in Christian Life
Liturgical Readings

Scripture is a central element in Christian liturgy. The Liturgy of the Word is a major section of the Eucharistic celebration. Since Vatican II the Roman Church has developed a Lectionary whose main purpose is to open the Scriptures more fully to the believing community. The Constitution on the Sacred Liturgy instructed: "The treasures of the Bible are to be opened up more lavishly, so that richer fare may be provided for the faithful at the table of God's Word" (SC 51). To that end a three-year Sunday cycle of readings was developed to replace the one-year Sunday cycle in the Tridentine Missal. A two-year daily cycle was also developed. The Tridentine Missal did not have a daily cycle except for the special seasons of Advent–Christmas and Lent–Easter.

The Sunday cycle is organized around the Gospel readings. In Year A, Matthew is read; in Year B, Mark; and in Year C, Luke. The Gospel of John is read in the seasons of Christmas, Lent, and Easter. The Gospel readings are semicontinuous, that is, selections are read in order from the beginning to the end of the Gospel. This arrangement of the Sunday gospels provides an opportunity for the Church to spend a whole year steeped in the spirituality of a specific Gospel.

The first reading of the Sunday liturgy is an OT reading except during the Easter season. During Ordinary Time this OT reading is chosen because of some relationship to the gospel. This arrangement allows for a thematic emphasis and for an ongoing awareness of the integral relationship between the OT and the NT. The second reading is ordinarily taken from one of the NT letters. These letters are also read in a semicontinuous fashion and thus may relate to the OT reading and the gospel only indirectly.

During special seasons and on feast days all the readings are chosen to highlight some aspect of the season or feast. In the weekday Lectionary an attempt is made to read a substantial portion of each of the Gospels every year and to read at least a part of the other biblical books (with a few exceptions) over a period of two years.

This arrangement of readings in the 1970 Lectionary achieves the purpose of opening a far richer selection of Scripture readings to the worshiping community.

It has also achieved an ecumenical purpose. Within six years of its introduction a great many of the Christian denominations that have a set cycle of readings had adopted the 1970 Lectionary with slight modifications. Thus in two major ways the 1970 Lectionary has enriched Christian spirituality.

There are some flaws in the 1970 Lectionary. The use of the OT in Sunday celebrations is limited to passages that relate closely to the gospels. While this is one significant approach to the OT, it eliminates major sections that have a more tenuous relationship to the NT, for example, the story of beginnings in Genesis 1–11 or the story of David and the ark in 1–2 Samuel. As a result, only about four percent of the OT is included in the Sunday Lectionary. In addition, some of the connections indicated by the selection of OT readings are forced or stilted.

The list of possible readings for the sacraments has also been significantly increased. Particularly rich selections are found for the sacrament of reconciliation and for anointing of the sick.

In the revised Roman Liturgy of the Hours, the readings for the Office of Readings have been expanded. They are organized in a semicontinuous fashion and include Scripture readings which are more difficult and which therefore have not been included in the Lectionary for Mass. Thus the faithful who share in the daily prayer of the Church are led through a significant portion of both the OT and the NT, which is supplemented with commentaries from ancient and modern sources. Monastic houses have developed their own cycle of Scripture readings for the Liturgy of the Hours following the same basic principles.

Preaching and Catechesis

The Lectionaries for Eucharist, the sacraments, and the Liturgy of the Hours have an essential effect on preaching and catechesis in the Church. The introduction to the Lectionary instructs that the homily should ordinarily be based on the Scripture readings for the day. "By means of sacred scripture, read during the liturgy of the word and explained during the homily, 'God speaks to his people, revealing the mystery of their redemption and salvation and offering them spiritual nourishment'" (I.1; see GIRM 33).

The arrangement of the 1970 Lectionary has given preachers a full set of texts and the possibility of significant and continuous biblical instruction over a period of several weeks. The development of the historical-critical method of analyzing and interpreting biblical texts has given preachers skills to deal with the texts. Many preaching aids built on solid biblical methods are published regularly. The faithful not only hear the word of God, but preachers aid them in breaking open the word and applying it to the circumstances of daily life.

The model for catechesis is the Rite of Christian Initiation of Adults. That rite is intimately linked to the Scripture readings of the Lenten Sundays. Thus catechesis is based on biblical material. Catechetical series that use the Sunday Lectionary as primary content and organizing principle are also beginning to appear.

Personal Prayer

Finally, Christians use the Bible as a chief source for less formal prayer. Prayer groups and study groups depend on Scripture for their material. The monastic art of *lectio divina,* or holy reading, has always been based on Scripture. A biblical text is chosen, read carefully and slowly, "chewed," and pondered. Other forms of meditation as well use Scripture as the primary text.

Conclusion

Thus Christians at the end of the 20th century have the wealth of the Bible opened for them in a way granted to no previous generation. The advance of biblical scholarship and the publication of new

translations and commentaries have made understanding of an accurate text a possibility. The great increase in the use of Scripture for liturgical and private prayer has brought the word of God into the daily and weekly life of the faithful. These circumstances have led to the growing awareness that God's word is living and alive, a two-edged sword that pertains to every area of Christian life. When the risen Christ appeared to the disciples on the way to Emmaus, he nourished them both in the breaking of the bread and by opening the Scriptures to them. The word of God continues to nourish the lives of Christians today.

See also COVENANT; EARLY CHRISTIAN SPIRITUALITY; INSPIRATION; JEWISH SPIRITUALITY; LECTIO DIVINA; LITURGY; MYTH; NARRATIVE; PREACHING; PROPHECY; REVELATION(S); TEACHING.

Bibliography: D. Bergant and R. Karris, eds., *The Collegeville Bible Commentary* (Collegeville, Minn.: Liturgical Press, 1989). L. Boadt, *Reading the Old Testament: An Introduction* (New York: Paulist, 1984). R. Brown, J. Fitzmyer, R. Murphy, eds., *The New Jerome Biblical Commentary* (Englewood Cliffs, N.J.: Prentice-Hall, 1990). W. Brueggemann, *The Message of the Psalms* (Minneapolis: Augsburg, 1984). R. Cabié, *The Eucharist,* The Church at Prayer 2, ed. A. Martimort, trans. M. O'Connell (Collegeville, Minn.: Liturgical Press, 1986). J. Hayes and C. Holladay, *Biblical Exegesis: A Beginner's Handbook* rev. ed. (Atlanta: John Knox, 1987). R. Keifer, *To Hear and Proclaim* (Washington: National Association of Pastoral Musicians, 1983). J. Newsome, *The Hebrew Prophets* (Atlanta: John Knox, 1984). K. O'Connor, *The Wisdom Literature* (Wilmington, Del.: Glazier, 1988). P. Perkins, *Reading the New Testament: An Introduction,* 2nd ed. (New York: Paulist, 1989).

IRENE NOWELL, O.S.B.

SECULAR INSTITUTES

Secular institutes are societies whose members, lay or clerical, dedicate themselves to lives of apostolic work and the observance of the evangelical counsels while living in the world. Unlike members of religious institutes, they do not make public vows or wear distinctive habits. Their ancient precursors were those ascetics and virgins who did not withdraw from the world but lived consecrated lives in their own homes.

Although a few societies and sodalities of this kind were formed during the late 18th through the 19th centuries as a new form of religious life, secular institutes as such did not receive pontifical approval until 1947 with the issuance of the apostolic constitution *Provida Mater Ecclesia* by Pope Pius XII.

In general, members of secular institutes do not live in common but support themselves in the pursuit of the profession to which they are called. They commit themselves to lives of Christian perfection by embracing the evangelical counsels of poverty, chastity, and obedience to the best of their ability in what would otherwise seem to be an ordinary secular life.

Persons do not change their canonical condition when becoming members of a secular institute, that is, priests remain clerics and laypersons remain laypersons. The growing number of secular institutes, in all their rich diversity, attests to the creative inspiration of the Spirit in the lives of those Christians who are seeking a life of service to others "which is both in the world and, in a sense, of the world" (PC 11).

See also APOSTOLIC SPIRITUALITY; VOCATION; WORLD.

Bibliography: J. Haley, ed., *Apostolic Sanctity in the World* (Notre Dame, Ind.: Univ. of Notre Dame Press, 1957). G. Reidy, *Secular Institutes* (New York: Hawthorn, 1962).

KEITH R. BARRON, O.C.D.S.

SECULARISM

Secularism, from the Latin *saeculum,* meaning "the span of a human lifetime," is a movement in which attention and energies are directed toward this world and away from any other world or form of existence. Arising during the Renaissance, secularism celebrated human cultural achievements and sought fulfillment in this world, in this life. Secularists believed that Christianity's belief in resurrection and heavenly reward led to a lack of development of the potential of human life in the here and now. In reaction to that perception, they were generally anti-Christian and antireligious.

In recent years many religious groups in the United States have become alarmed at what they term "secular humanism," which embodies many of the tenets of secularism described above. They contend that this has taken on the nature of a religion, claiming to explain all of reality and yet effectively denying the existence of God and of transcendent spiritual values. They are concerned that this pervasive attitude is actively taught in the educational systems. These discussions often lead to debates about the separation of Church and state and the question of whether a purely secular state is by that fact antireligious.

Others advocate a "secular Christianity" and seek to bridge the gap between secularism and faith. They seek to promote Christian values in society, not accepting the values of the world uncritically. Basing their reflections on an understanding of God who created the world, who communicates within history, and who becomes incarnate in the world, they believe Christians must live out the mystery of salvation in that same world. Harvey Cox is perhaps the person most associated with this movement. A reading of Vatican II's Pastoral Constitution on the Church in the Modern World (*Gaudium et Spes*) is essential for a balanced Catholic understanding of the value and limits of the secular society in relationship to the gospel of Jesus Christ.

See also AFTERLIFE; CHURCH; CREATION; FUTURE; KINGDOM OF GOD; MILLENARIANISM; PEACE; TECHNOLOGY, IMPACT ON SPIRITUALITY; VATICAN COUNCIL II; WORK; WORLD.

Bibliography: H. Cox, *Religion in the Secular City* (New York: Simon and Schuster, 1984).

MICHAEL DODD, O.C.D.

SELF

"Then Jesus said to his disciples, 'If anyone wants to be a follower of mine, let him renounce himself and take up his cross and follow me'" (Mt 16:24, JB).

"You shall love the Lord, your God, with all your heart, with all your being, with all your strength, and with all your mind, and your neighbor as yourself" (Lk 10:27; see Deut 6:5; Lev 19:18).

No one, surely, has ever thought that these central passages of the Christian spiritual tradition suggest that Christians should renounce their neighbors. Nonetheless, even leaving aside linguistic and exegetical aspects, the passages present difficulties for the Christian interpreter. How, for example, does one both love and renounce oneself? Further, what exactly does it mean to love oneself—and one's neighbor as oneself? Answers to these kinds of questions require a precise understanding of the self. We shall return to the questions after considering basic aspects of the self as understood in three disciplines: philosophy, theology, and psychology. We begin with a historical overview of contributions in these areas.

Historical Overview

While the meaning of the term *self* is too elusive to allow us to begin with a definition, we can start with a clue resulting from the close connection between self and interior subjectivity. In his *Confessions,* St. Augustine explicated his entry into himself in his search for a God who was more intimate to him than he was to himself. But it would be more than a millennium before interiority began to be plumbed again in a systematic way. Until the modern period, the individual was dealt with less in the subjective, first-person terms of "self" and more in the objective, third-person terms of "person." A grasp of the Christian meaning of person, therefore, is essential background for reaching a balanced understanding of "self" adequate for Christian spirituality.

The English word *person* reaches back to the Latin *persona* (*personare,* "to sound through") and the Greek *prosōpon* ("face," "actor's mask"). As a technical term it was first used in early Christian reflection on the Trinity and the incarnation (Tertullian). Boethius provided the first philosophical definition: "Persona est naturae rationalis individua substantia." With certain modifications this definition moved through medieval thinkers like Thomas Aquinas, Richard of St. Victor, and Duns Scotus and into modern thought as "the actual unique reality of a spiritual being, an undivided whole existing independently and not interchangeable with any other.... belong[ing] to itself and ... therefore its own end in itself. . . [with an] inviolable dignity" (M. Müller and A. Halder, "Person," in *Sacramentum Mundi,* ed. K. Rahner et al., New York: Herder, 1969, 6:404).

This basic meaning of person emerged from the interaction of Jewish and Christian religious experience with Greek philosophy. At the core of this religious experience is the person's free decision to respond to God's invitation to an intimate relationship. The Christian attempt to use Greek philosophical concepts such as nature and substance for its understanding and articulation of this experience gradually effected a transformation of these concepts. From a metaphysics of being, with its notion of the human individual as an infinite spirit trapped in a finite body, there developed a Christian theology of historical experience, with its understanding of the person as an embodied spirit of absolute significance and destined for resurrection. In this sense, a person is an essentially social being, constituted precisely as person through its relationship with other free, independent, historical beings. A person is a concrete unity of individuality and universality, of immanence and transcendence; it subsists in itself but is open to all reality.

It is in this meaning of person that the Christian tradition has designated the absolute mystery that is God as "personal." Divine life is understood as the immanent perfection of God's being realized in a multiple personal act of knowing and loving. It is the personal God to whom Christians are related in faith. And it is in this sense of personal as relational that the tradition has understood women and men to be created in God's image and likeness. Indeed, it was the tradition's attempt to understand the human and divine dialectically in terms of each other that led to a meaning of person not only as independent and intellectual but also as relational and free in self-creative love.

Still, despite the significant development in the meaning of person from Greek philosophy to medieval Christian theology, the approach remained basically one of treating an essentially first-person, subjective reality in third-person, objective terms. It was not until the early modern period that the Augustinian theme of interiority was resumed in a significant way by philosophers like Descartes and religious thinkers like Pascal.

Descartes, though aware only of his thinking, assumed that it required a thinker, a self, which he understood as a spiritual substance. This thinking self became his first principle of philosophy. Pascal further identified the self with all striving, including feeling and willing as well as knowing. Locke pressed Descartes's doubt to include even the substantial nature of the self, which he understood to be the person as perceived by himself or herself: "I am a self only for myself and a person for others." The existence of the self, the seat of personal identity, requires continuing consciousness of oneself from past into present. Hume also challenged the substantial nature of the self, finding it impossible to intuit a permanent self. Beyond intuition of self with particular percep-

tions, inference of a permanent self has only subjective validity.

Further emphasis on subjectivity came from Kant, Hegel, and Kierkegaard. Kant distinguished between the phenomenal self, which, like other phenomena, can be known, and the noumenal self, which can only be inferred as a basic condition of knowing. Only in moral consciousness of freedom and duty does Kant's true ethical self know itself. For Hegel, the self was revealed through a process of differentiating self from non-self and discovering its presence in the non-self. Self-consciousness is reached only by the self externalizing or alienating itself. Kierkegaard also focused on alienation, but alienation of the self from God. The self constitutes itself by freely accepting its dependence on God; despair comes from estranging oneself from God. "Pugno, ergo sum" best suggests the reality of the self constituted through the will's struggle to reach the authentic, religious level of existence.

Later authors understood the self to have several aspects. William James understood the self as the sum of all that one knows oneself to be. Self-awareness reveals two aspects: an "I," or stream of consciousness, and a "me," which includes many selves rooted in bodily existence. G. H. Mead also understood the self as twofold: the selves of the "me," which result from social interaction, and the fictitious "I," which is always offstage. Martin Buber saw the self constituted in the same dialogic way but extended the dialogue to include nature and God. H. Richard Niebuhr rooted his theology of the responsible self in a similar triadic pattern of dialogue.

Mainstream empirical psychology did not follow James in his interest in the self. Existential humanistic psychology has focused on the self, however, and certain psychoanalytic theorists have given major attention to the related concept of the ego and, most recently, even to the self. Existential humanists like Abraham Maslow, Carl Rogers, and Rollo May see the self as a set of radically human potentials, which must be actualized, realized, or fulfilled through striving for an immanent ideal. Neo-Freudians like Karen Horney, Heinz Hartmann, and Erich Fromm helped move a more fully personal ego than Freud's to the center of the psychoanalytic stage. And Erik Erikson has not only traced the psychosocial development of ego-identity but has also distinguished and related the unconscious ego, which integrates experience, and the conscious "I," the live, numinous center of awareness. Object-relations theorists and self psychologists such as D. W. Winnicott, Ronald Fairbairn, Otto Kernberg, and Heinz Kohut have focused on the development of the true self in the context of supportive interpersonal relationships, especially that between infant and nurturing parent. Victor Frankl, an existentialist with a psychoanalytic background, centers on meaning as the constitutive reality of the conscious person. In his view, self-actualization is not something that can be successfully sought after; self-actualization is only possible as a side effect of striving for self-transcendence. We shall see this concept of self-transcendence again as a central category in the philosophy and theology of Bernard Lonergan.

With this historical overview completed, we turn to five contributors to the understanding of self in theology, philosophy, and psychology who are significant for Christian spirituality: Teresa of Jesus, C. G. Jung, Robert Kegan, Bernard Lonergan, and Thomas Merton.

Major Contributors

Teresa of Jesus

For several reasons, Teresa of Jesus (of Avila) (1515–1582) has a detailed description and interpretation of self. Both her personality and concept of mysticism result in a spirituality that has a strong empirical, psychological focus. Teresa's extroverted character leads her not to introversion but to introspection. That is, in all of her writings (e.g., *Life, Spiritual Testimonies, Way of Perfection, Interior Castle*), she engages in clear interior self-analysis in which she objectifies herself, giving narrative descriptions of her interior states as she grows in relationship to God. Often she speaks of herself in the third person, which was not a literary device of the time. In other words, Teresa reduplicates her self in her writing.

Another reason why Teresa has such a thorough treatment of self is that her spirituality is essentially mystical and her mystical theology is essentially autobiographical. Having had no formal theological education, Teresa has no metaphysical theory of the divine-human relationship. Rather, her teaching about mysticism or the experience of the divine is generalization based on her own case. The mystical life, for her, is deduced from the way God led her, a way characterized by the experience of the permanence of two distinct persons in a union of love. Consequently her primary metaphors are those of relationship such as friendship and marriage; in contrast, Rhineland mysticism of "nothingness" would be foreign to her. The primary object of Teresa's attention, then, is not the divine essence but rather her own interior states of profound loving relationship to God in Christ.

Teresa describes the spiritual growth of a self that is aware of gender, class distinction, and cultural expectations. Although these categories are modern, the descriptions are Teresa's own. Embedded in 16th-century patriarchal culture, she assumes that being a woman makes her particularly subject to passions, weakness, and delusion. She accepts the expectation of her Spanish culture's myth of honor yet transposes it from an external code of respectability into an internal identification with Christ's code of conduct.

Teresa's spirituality of self can be approached through three central experiences: entering self, self-knowledge, self-surrender.

"The truth is," she says in *The Interior Castle* (V.1.2), "the treasure lies within our very selves." Her central experience is entering herself to be with God, who favors her with profound contemplative union. Imaging the self as a garden that is watered by God in four different ways or as a castle of diamond that one walks into seeking the central room, Teresa describes the feelings, insights, struggles, and favors of God that characterized each phase of her journey within. Although the move within is the focus of her narrative, connection to all that is beyond her is the ultimate goal. For example, she records in her *Spiritual Testimonies* (no. 14) that she "heard the words: 'Don't try to hold Me within yourself, but try to hold yourself within Me.' It seemed to me that from within my soul—where I saw these three Persons present—these persons were communicating themselves to all creation without fail, nor did they fail to be with me." Again, in *The Interior Castle* (VII.4.6), she insists, "This is the reason for prayer ... the purpose of this spiritual marriage: the birth always of good works, good works."

Self-knowledge, for Teresa, is a disposition that is necessary for every level of contemplative life. Basically it means absolute honesty about both our weakness and our gifts; it is an awareness of our goodness as derived solely from God's free and constant affirmation of us. As such, it is as indispensable as "bread which must feed all palates no matter how delicate"; that is, however sublime the contemplation, Teresa advises in *The Way of Perfection,* "let your prayer always begin and end with self-knowledge" (39.5). If awareness of our miserable limitations produces fear, Teresa warns, it is a sign that we really do not understand ourselves completely. Self-knowledge should generate freedom from self-preoccupation because it gives a realization that we have no good of our selves but all good from God.

Like all the saints, Teresa surrendered herself to God; unlike some, she struggled for twenty years before she could do it fully. Not long after this conversion experience she began the strenuous work of leading the reform of Carmel. Consequently her discussion of surrender is usually connected to issues of worry and concern for this significant ministry. In every case the emphasis is on peaceful trust in the midst of demanding responsibilities. In her *Spiritual Testimonies* (no. 10) she reveals that she was "anxiously desiring to help the order" when the Lord told her: "Do what lies in your power; surrender yourself to me, and do not be disturbed about anything; rejoice in the good that has been given you, for it is very great." Again, she stresses that surrender does not mean passivity but active partnership in the reforming work that God is directing: "It shouldn't be thought that this abandonment to God in necessities means I don't try to procure them, but I mean I don't do so with a concern that makes me worry" (no. 1).

Teresa makes a significant contribution to understanding self and religious experience through her detailed description and interpretation of her own experience of entering herself to find God. Later the Church confirmed the orthodoxy of this interpretation by declaring her a Doctor of the Church, and current scholarship evaluates her interpretation positively in terms of psychological theories such as Jung's.

Carl Jung

Because Jung (1875–1961) departed from Freud's negative evaluation of religion as neurotic and infantile, and instead viewed religion as a necessary source of human meaning and a requirement for psychological health, he is often used as a resource for spirituality. His most significant contributions include the relativization of the ego in relation to the Self (psychic wholeness) and attention to what he calls the masculine and the feminine aspects of humanity that must be integrated in order to realize the Self.

These notions are best understood in the context of Jung's theory of personality development. Picturing the psyche (totality of all psychic processes, conscious as well as unconscious) as a circle, the ego could be imaged as the center of the upper (conscious) area and the Self as a point midway between conscious and unconscious. In Jung's view, this Self is not only the source of the personality but also the power that seeks to be revealed through the choices and experiences of the ego, to which it has given birth. The ego stands in relation to the Self as the object to the subject.

According to Jung, the undiscovered Self is always, even in childhood, trying to manifest itself in a lifelong journey into wholeness: the process of individuation. In the first half of life the task is initiation into outward reality, while the task of the second half is initiation into the inner reality, a deeper self-knowledge and knowledge of humanity. Jung devoted the greater part of his study to the second half of this process, using his own experience as the primary initial data for his study.

Individuation requires that we confront and befriend two aspects of ourselves: the shadow and the contrasexual (masculine or feminine). Because the contrasexual aspect of Jung's theory has received the most thorough reevaluation in order to make it usable for spirituality, that topic will receive more development here. In order to achieve integration, one first confronts the shadow. Briefly, the shadow stands for the contents (sometimes positive) that have been rejected and repressed or less lived in the course of our conscious existence. It is the counterpart of our conscious ego, growing in pace with it. It is not bad, merely somewhat inferior, primitive, unadapted, and awkward. This "dark" mass of experience that is seldom or never admitted to our conscious lives bars the way to the creative depths of our unconscious.

In the second stage of the individuation process one encounters what Jung calls the complementary, contrasexual part of the psyche (*animus* in the woman and *anima* in the man). This aspect of Jung's view of the Self is so controversial in regard to its consequences for women that it deserves particular attention in two ways: first, we should be aware of the feminist negative critique and, second, we should notice the feminist positive reevaluation.

Naomi R. Goldenberg's view has become a classic critique of Jung on two counts. First, although Jung values "the feminine," his theory actually restricts women. Despite his warnings not to take his intuitive concepts too literally, Jung declares that women are characterized by Eros, an ability to make connections, while men are oriented toward Logos, analytical thinking. While Jung genuinely values woman for her Eros, he also confines her to this sphere. Moving into Logos, he maintains, is unnatural for her. Some professions are masculine, he says, and some feminine; therefore, being a nursemaid, for example, would result in psychic injury for a man. Jung goes beyond speculation to make dogmatic statements about roles that are claimed to be natural to women and men. The roles assigned to women, we notice, are those that support and promote the interests of men.

In addition, the *anima-animus* model clearly favors men. Postulating a contrasexual personality in each sex, Jung uses these terms without clear definitions and with different connotations. What is clear, however, is that the *animus* in women is deduced from Jung's notion of the opposite in men and is never developed to the same extent. What is also clear is that Jung is primarily concerned with the integration, according to the myth of the androgyne, of the feminine into the masculine psyche; that is, the masculine personality is fulfilled and completed by the feminine. For women, Jung's model militates against social change. For men, however, it allows control of all Logos activities while still sanctioning men to appropriate whatever Eros they need. We notice that it is this unequal notion of complementarity that pervades Roman documents dealing with women in the Church.

In order to use Jung's psychology with feminist therapy, analysts such as Polly Young-Eisendrath and Florence Wiedemann have revised some of his concepts in ways they believe are consistent with Jung's own revisions in later life. Pertinent concepts here are the archetype Self and the *animus* complex. As in Jung's theory, feminist revisions define "complex" as a collection of images, ideas, feelings, and habitual actions that is compelling or motivating in a nonrational way. Some complexes are partly conscious (e.g., body-image complex in most adults); others, such as the *animus* complex in women, are wholly unconscious. Unlike Jung, who understands the *animus* in women to be related to qualities foreign to their nature, feminist revisionists understand it as a complex organized around excluded aspects of one's gender identity. They are excluded as a result of the interaction of biological, social, and psychological influences which cannot be clearly separated and which research demonstrates are dependent on socialization in a male-centered culture. Gender (e.g., feminine) is a socially constructed reality, while sex (e.g., female) is a biological fact. The actual content of any woman's *animus* complex depends upon four things: the influences of her social group, what she knows about her own gender identity, her perceptions of the opposite sex, and the progress of her own personality development. Encountering this *animus* is necessary in the process of attaining the Self.

With Jung, feminist revisionists agree that the reason why a complex is so compelling and so difficult to manage intentionally is that it is organized around an archetype, that is, a universal tendency to respond to a typical human situation of instinctual-emotional arousal by forming affective images, organizing cores of meaning. Agreeing with Jung, they call the universal striving for coherence the archetype of Self and capitalize the word to distinguish it from a person's experience in a particular life context. Because of current social conditions, women struggle to achieve a consistent identity, frequently experiencing themselves as fragmented or divided in their development of a female self (consistent gender identity).

Because every known society has some scheme that creates social differentiation based on biological difference, revisionists understand gender to be founded on a basic archetype of difference. This is viewed as an archetype of opposites, or the instinctive tendency to discriminate between self and not-self. Because the means for establishing gender identity within cultures are so varied, any psychological study of women must include their specific social contexts. Revisionists, therefore, depart from Jung and do not accept universal archetypes of feminine and masculine; instead, they study gender themes that are typical in North American society. For example, adult women experience the excluded aspects of their gender identity in a developmental scheme that moves from "alien other" in an immature phase to "partner within" at a more mature phase. Through a successive integration of these unconscious complexes over a life span, women may reach individuation, a coherent female self.

Robert Kegan

Robert Kegan (b. 1946) of Harvard University and the Massachusetts School of Professional Psychology presents a theory of personality in which the term self is equivalent to ego in mainstream psychology. Kegan's theory is being used in contemporary spirituality because it can assist interpretation of the two basic human desires expressed in all religious literature: for relationship and for independence.

Sympathetic to the way feminist psychology values attachment, Kegan pays attention to the way it functions for both men and women. It can assist Christian feminism's inclusive vision because Kegan examines the advantages and limitations of both attachment and autonomy as they occur within the life-span development of women and men.

In *The Evolving Self* Kegan explains his view of human development as meaning-making activity. This activity unifies and generates thought and feeling as well as self (subject) and other (object). Emotion, in this perspective, is the experience of the motion of defending, surrendering, and reconstructing a center of meaning. Human evolutionary activity involves creating the other (differentiation) as well as our relating to it (integration). Self-other relations emerge out of a lifelong process of development: a succession of more adequate differentiations of the self from the world in which it is embedded, each creating a more complex object of relation. Maturity in each phase of the process is a relative triumph of "relationship to" rather than "embeddedness in."

Whereas psychoanalytic theory looks to infancy for its basic themes and categories, Kegan, in his constructive-developmental approach, regards infancy as qualitatively no different from any other moment in the life span. What is basic is meaning-making evolution. The distinctive features of infancy (fusion, differentiation, belonging) are activities that are necessary throughout a person's life. These same features recur in new forms at each phase of development as a person makes the meaning of "self" and "other" over and over again.

Kegan explains five developmental stages that may describe—but not necessarily be—everyone's life history. Each phase involves a certain kind of balance between the universal longing for both autonomy and inclusion. Each balance is a temporary solution to the lifelong tension between the yearnings for inclusion and distinctness; one phase will tip slightly toward autonomy, while the next will favor inclusion. One of the most distinctive features of Kegan's theory is his emphasis on development beyond the stage of autonomous self-direction, the stage that has the strength of independence but also a serious weakness. In the autonomous phase, control rather than mutuality is ultimate. This inhibits mature relationships and is still far from intimacy. The achievement of human maturity is characterized, rather, by *having* control, not *being* control, as in the previous phase, which is commonly considered the goal of maturity in most developmental theories. For Kegan, the most mature stage is one in which there is a self to be freely brought to others in equality and mutuality. There is a self that can surrender its controlling independence for freely chosen interdependence. The implications for relationship to others and to God are obvious.

Kegan's view supports an experience of maturity that is the outcome of a process of balancing the lifelong tension between the yearnings for inclusion and distinctness. Spiritual maturity, using this perspective, becomes a matter of deep personal openness, which comes from having an independent identity yet recognizing the personal limitations of independence as the goal of development. Valuing, instead, the intimacy of mutual interdependence, the mature person is one who can freely surrender herself or himself, who can risk a genuinely mutual relationship with others and with God.

Bernard Lonergan

In our historical overview of person and self, and in our consideration of the contributions to the meaning of self by Teresa, Jung, and Kegan, we have seen the shift from the third-person, objective approach focused on substance to the first-person, subjective approach emphasizing interiority. Self differs from person precisely in this point of subjectivity or interiority, which is to say consciousness. We have also seen that while modern philosophers and psychologists have paid considerable attention to the self, they have at the same time found it the cause of much perplexity and difference of opinion. Bernard Lonergan (1904–1984) saw this difficulty as rooted in a failure to understand the precise nature of conscious subjectivity as both cognitive and constitutive.

Lonergan follows the general lines of the distinction between "I" and "me" characteristic of modern philosophy and psychology. Within this interior duality, however, he introduces a distinctive understanding of the "I" that adequately complements the clarity philosophers and especially psychologists have given to the "me" as socially constructed. This meaning of "I" is rooted in an understanding of consciousness as the self's constitutive presence to itself, which had proven so elusive.

Lonergan focuses his analysis on such distinctively personal activities as understanding, judging, and deciding, all operations that are *essentially* personal in the sense that whenever they are performed the self is aware of, is present to, or experiences, itself operating. Such operations not only intend objects, then, but also render the operating self conscious. Thus, by their intentionality, personal operations make objects present to the self, and in the same act, by their consciousness, they simultaneously make the operating person present to itself—make it a *self*. A person may, for example, be most intensely conscious, present to self while absorbed, or, as we say, "lost," in a powerful film. Such experience seems paradoxical if we identify consciousness, not with the subject's self-presence in intentional activity, but rather with reflexive knowing. But reflexive knowing is a second act that, for example, a film viewer may perform, when, leaving the theater, she or he perhaps thinks about her or his own life in the light of the film. In this case, a person is simultaneously present to self in two different ways: as subject (an "I") by

consciousness, and as object (a "me") by the intentionality of the reflexive act.

Consciousness, according to Lonergan's distinctive theory, not only reveals the self-as-subject, but also *constitutes* it as such. The self experienced in consciousness does not exist without consciousness (e.g., in a coma). The "I" who understands, judges, and decides is not only revealed to itself in consciousness but is capable of understanding, judging, and deciding only through consciousness. The self is constituted as an "I" by consciousness. In short, consciousness is not only cognitive, it is also constitutive of the very reality of the self-as-subject.

If the self is constituted by consciousness, it is constituted as *this* self only through the concrete specifics of its own personal history, a history of meaning and value. As the self discovers and constructs a world of meaning and value, it also constitutes itself in some specific concrete shape. The self-as-object, in other words, is gradually created as this particular self through personal discoveries, decisions, and deeds. This constitution of the self-as-object through meaning and value occurs because the core of conscious subjectivity, the "I," is itself a radical, self-creating drive for meaning and value.

In Lonergan's understanding, then, the self is a personal reality constituted by a radical drive to move beyond itself for meaning and value, and, especially, to reach out to others in love. At bottom, the self is a fundamental desire for self-transcendence. This is another way of stating the basic point we noted in the section on Kegan: at root, the self is moved by two desires—for independence and for relationship. In Lonergan's view, self-transcendence is the desire for relationship with reality, especially human and divine reality. But self-transcendence requires a self capable of transcendence, an independent self, in other words, with the cognitive and affective power necessary to move beyond itself in realistic knowing, responsible deciding, and generous loving.

If the self is constituted by consciousness, however, it is rooted in the full reality of the whole person. One's sense of self at the object pole (one's self-image, self-esteem) includes a perception of one's body as well as a grasp of one's emotions. At the subject pole of the self, the drive for self-transcendence is likewise rooted in the images that trigger intelligent questioning and in the spontaneous empathy that sparks interpersonal love. Though the self reflects conflict at every level of personal reality, the drive for self-transcendence is truly a radical drive that heuristically unifies the self in its dynamism and integrates it in its fulfillment.

As the drive for self-transcendence unfolds, the empirically conscious self becomes, successively, the intelligently, rationally, and responsibly or existentially conscious self. According to Lonergan (*Method in Theology,* p. 240), the self's capacity and desire for self-transcendence meet joyful fulfillment when "religious conversion transforms the existential subject into a subject in love, a subject held, grasped, possessed, owned through a total and so an other-worldly love." The self-transcendence of such other-worldly love constitutes the fullness of authentic self-realization. And as we shall see with Thomas Merton, this culmination of the self-transcending process is an orientation toward mystery because, although conscious, it is not objectified. In mediating a return to immediacy, as Lonergan puts it, the contemplative self withdraws from objectification into a prayerful cloud of unknowing.

Thomas Merton

More than any other contemporary Catholic, Thomas Merton (1915–1968) stands at the center of Christian spirituality. Chronologically linking pre– and post–Vatican II perspectives, he also geographically bridges the orientations of East and West, even as he related the secular and monastic worlds. Beyond the self's prominence in modern philosophy, psychology, and theology, then, the fact that it is at the center of Merton's spirituality makes the self a primary reality in contemporary spirituality.

Merton's account of his conversion, *The Seven Storey Mountain* (New York: Harcourt, Brace, 1948), written in his early thirties, is the story of a journey of discovery. His *Seeds of Contemplation* (Norfolk, Conn.: New Directions, 1949) explicated this journey in universal terms as an escape "from the prison of our own selfhood." But this must be understood in light of Merton's paradigmatic distinction between the true and false self. The prison is the false self, the illusion of egocentric desires that wants to exist outside God's will and God's love, outside life and reality. One must escape the prison of the false self to discover one's true self and God. Because the false self is an illusion, the journey of discovery is paradoxical: "In order to become myself I must cease to be what I always thought I wanted to be" (*Seeds of Contemplation,* p. 38).

Because God is love, says Merton, to be made in God's image is to have love as the reason for one's existence. God is found in others, and the truth of life is the law of self-transcendence. A person "cannot enter into the deepest center of himself and pass through that center into God, unless he is able to pass entirely out of himself and empty himself to other people in the purity of selfless love." In self-transcendence, God and self are not opposed. Indeed, Merton maintains, "If I find [God], I will find myself and if I find my true self I will find [God]" (*Seeds of Contemplation,* p. 29). This is the ultimate truth of the spiritual life.

A dozen years later, in the radically revised *New Seeds of Contemplation* (Norfolk, Conn.: New Directions, 1961), Merton further characterizes the false self as the superficial consciousness of the external self, which is irreducibly opposed to the "deep transcendent self that awakens only in contemplation" (p. 7). Contemplation, according to Merton, is precisely the awareness that the superficial "I" of this external self is really "not I," the awareness that occurs in "the awakening of the unknown 'I' that is beyond observation and reflection" (*ibid.*). Being "born in sin" means that we come into the world with a false self and are alienated from our inner self, which is the image of God. Our true inner self must be saved from that "abyss of confusion and absurdity which is our own worldly self" (*ibid.*, p. 38), the external, empirical self, the ego.

Merton is not always clear, however, on the precise relationship between the true and false self. The spatial images of inner and outer are not entirely helpful. At times, for Merton, the true self, though hidden, already exists and must be discovered. This true self is not merely an imagined, ideal self. Still, in Merton's view, one must actively create, with God, the true self. In "The Inner Experience" (1959), Merton offers a clue to understanding the relationship between the true and false self by stressing that the inner self is not a part of our being but "our entire substantial reality itself, on its highest and most personal and most existential level" (CS 18, no. 1 [1983], p. 5). This suggests a correlation with Lonergan's self-transcendence; that is, the true self exists as drive for self-transcendence, but is still to be fully created as an actually self-transcending person. The false self, then, is a person viewed as failing in self-transcendence.

Merton's interest in Zen gave him further insight into the self. In contrast to the objectified, concept-dominated, reflexive consciousness of the isolated Cartesian ego, Zen, for Merton, is the ontological awareness of pure being beyond subject and object. Zen awareness is not "consciousness of" but "pure consciousness," in which the false self disappears. Like Lonergan's self-as-subject and Teresa's self whose faculties are sometimes "asleep" in deep prayer, Merton's true self emerges on its own terms of pure consciousness only in contemplation. For Merton, pure consciousness is a steppingstone to an awareness of God that lies beyond the inner "I." Despite the infinite metaphysical gulf between God and the true self, in spiritual experience each exists in the other, and in this identity of love and freedom there appears to be but one Self. In this transcendent experience the true self is indeed conscious, but conscious as "no self" because it is lost in God, where it finds its true identity. Through a contemplatively oriented process of self-transcendence, then, one may withdraw from the humanly constructed (false) self-as-object and be the originating (true) self-as-subject, where in nonobjectified conscious subjectivity God, too, may be experienced as Subject. For Merton, of course, this contemplative movement into the true self and God is never individualistic but always through the selfless love of others.

Conclusion

Now, to end at the beginning, we return to our opening questions. The answers lie, we suggest, in an understanding of the self-as-subject reaching out beyond itself to others. Loving ourselves-as-objects is the path to selfishness. We can and must love ourselves-as-subjects, however, and we do this only by loving others. We love others when we act for their true good, but this loving action is also acting for our own true good, the realization of our capacity for self-transcendence. The self we are called to renounce is not the true self-as-subject but the false self-as-object: the egocentric self-interests that are obstacles to the self-transcending love of others and our selves to which the Gospels call us.

See also ANTHROPOLOGY, THEOLOGICAL; CONSCIOUSNESS; CREATION; EXPERIENCE; GRACE; IMAGO DEI; INTERIORITY, INTERIOR LIFE; MIND; PSYCHOLOGY, RELATIONSHIP AND CONTRIBUTION TO SPIRITUALITY; SOUL; TRINITARIAN SPIRITUALITY.

Bibliography: *The Collected Works of St. Teresa of Avila,* 2 vols., trans. K. Kavanaugh and O. Rodriguez (Washington: ICS, 1976, 1980). W. Conn, *Christian Conversion* (New York: Paulist, 1986). N. Goldenberg, "A Feminist Critique of Jung," *Women's Spirituality,* ed. J. Conn (New York: Paulist, 1986). M. Gorman, "Self," *New Catholic Encyclopedia.* R. Kegan, *The Evolving Self: Problem and Process in Human Development* (Cambridge, Mass.: Harvard Univ. Press, 1982). B. Lonergan, *Method in Theology* (New York: Herder, 1972). P. Young-Eisendrath and F. Wiedemann, *Female Authority* (New York: Guilford, 1987).

JOANN WOLSKI CONN AND WALTER E. CONN

SELF-CONTROL

See FRUIT(S) OF THE HOLY SPIRIT.

SELF-KNOWLEDGE

See CONSCIOUSNESS; EXAMINATION OF CONSCIENCE; KNOWLEDGE; SELF.

SERVICE

Etymology

Service, in Greek usage, could refer to service as a slave, service for payment, service in public office, a willingness to serve, each designated by different terms. *Diakoneō* ("to serve") and *diakonia* ("service") indicate personal service, such as waiting on table or providing and caring for another, often identified with the service of women. Service lacked dignity unless it was service to the state. Greek thought focused on the development of the individual and the place of rulers, with little emphasis on self-sacrifice and service of one another.

Judaism developed a deeper understanding of *diakonia,* seeing nothing demeaning in service. It accepted the relation of slave to master and used similar language to describe the relationship of a person to God. In Lev 19:18 love of neighbor includes a readiness for, and commitment to, service of neighbor, but later developments emphasized service as meritorious work rather than as sacrifice for others. Interestingly, the OT uses the designation "servant" for varied religious leaders, prophets, and priests.

We discover another term, *leitourgia* ("service," "ministry"), which in Greek thought was used primarily in the political sense with minor cultic connotations, and in cultic contexts in the Septuagint. Num 16:9-10 reflects priestly ministry, setting the tone for its later usage in Judaism as the service of God by priests and laity. The NT uses *leitourgia* only six times (Lk 1:23; 2 Cor 9:12; Phil 2:17, 30; Heb 8:6, 9:21), preferring *diakonia* for its understanding of service.

New Testament Roots

Jesus presents an astonishing model of service when he challenges particular roles by speaking of a leader or master who serves (Mt 20:25-28; Lk 22:25-27; Mk 10:42-45). In John's Gospel, Jesus serves at table and washes the feet of his disciples, dramatically portraying the model of service he suggests for his followers (Jn 13:4-16). Many examples of the personal commitment of Christians to service, as a concrete way of following Christ's example and teaching, emerge in the pages of Scripture. Notable examples are service at a meal, associated with table fellowship (Lk 10:40; Jn 12:2); the service of individuals, prophets, and apostles (Acts 19:22; 2 Tm 1:18; 1 Pet 1:10; 2 Cor 3:3; Rom 1:1); and gifts of service within the community (1 Cor 12:4-12, 28; 2 Cor 4:1; Rom 11:13; Acts 1:17-25), demonstrating the inclusiveness of service and its connection with discipleship.

The command to love one's neighbor becomes Christian love in action, the mark of a true disciple; gifts within the community become the ministries or services that build up the Body of Christ. New patterns emerge that contradict the Greek idea of service as demeaning and transcend the popular Jewish understanding as well. Jesus reinstates the sacrificial element from the early biblical tradition (Mk 10:45) and gives concrete examples by which disciples will be judged (Mt 25:42-44). This service to others, the least of the brothers and sisters, is a service to Christ himself.

The NT also uses the term *diakonos* ("servant," "deacon") to describe Christians and apostles, since both are servants of Christ (Jn 12:26; 2 Cor 11:23) and all must serve one another (Mk 9:35; Mt 20:26). Paul is a servant of the Church (1 Cor 3:5; Col 1:25) and calls his coworkers servants (Col 1:7; 1 Thess 3:1-2). Occasionally *diakonia* is used for deacons (Phil 1:1; 1 Tm 3:8, 12), who contribute to the community through their service. Paul acknowledges women, such as Phoebe, who serve in this way (Rom 16:1).

Historical Development

The NT offers lists of ministries or services in 1 Cor 12:4-12; Rom 12:4-8; Eph 4:11-14 as gifts of the Spirit for the building up of the community. A close relationship exists between the *kerygma* ("proclamation"), *koinōnia* ("community"), and *diakonia* ("service"). Baptism into Christ results in an ecclesial experience of celebration and service. Responsibility for the building up of the community resides within the community, and the gifts of administration, teaching, prophecy, mercy, hospitality, leadership, etc., are examples of Christian service. Faith leads to service, service according to gift. Community, charism, and service provide a clue to the dynamic growth of the early Church, for we see no officials, organizations, offices, or hierarchy in this early period. The pastoral letters to Timothy and Titus indicate presbyters and local leaders who appoint others for particular services (1 Tm 5:22), but the formal offices have not yet developed. However, *1 Clement* calls the office of *presbyteros-episkopos* a divine institution (42-44). Writings such as the *Didache* (9 and 10) and *Letter of Barnabas* indicate functions of prophets and teachers at liturgical celebrations and introduce *episkopoi*

and *diakonoi* to share the burdens of teachers and prophets.

Beyond the NT period we see a number of specific changes regarding *diakonia* as service within the community and by the community. Early in the first millennium, documents reflect an ecclesial view of ministry, with the Council of Chalcedon (451) speaking of ordaining priests and deacons only when they have a community assigned to them. A connection between Eucharistic celebration and community leadership existed in this period, so it was theologically impossible not to have celebrations of Eucharist, since this was the prerogative of a leader chosen by the community. Ministry was eventually brought together under the bishop and collegial in form, but emphasis on the cultic dimensions of ministry emerged.

The 12th and 13th centuries brought us the medieval image of the priest that persists throughout the second millennium. The Third and Fourth Lateran Councils (1179 and 1215) stated that the Eucharist must be celebrated by a priest validly and legitimately ordained. Lost is the emphasis that the community appoints as ministers those it calls forth as leaders, who then preside at the Eucharist. In the 15th century there was a marked separation of priest and people, with a renewed emphasis on celibacy. A narrow theological view of ministry persisted in the Council of Trent, with its emphasis on the priest as mediator, separation of priest and laity, and celibacy for clergy. While changes can be attributed to changing times, the concept of service shifted to an exclusive focus on the ministry of the ordained, contrary to the earliest ecclesial tradition.

With the Second Vatican Council the expansion of ministry received new emphasis, and the term is used for the service performed by Christians because of baptism. However, theology distinguishes ecclesial ministry from the Christian's presence in the world in daily life and specifies "formal" and "informal" ministries in the Church. Perhaps we need to examine the terminology of service and ministry, since these expressions have changed significantly in usage over the centuries. However, ministry in the post–Vatican II Church is beginning to sound more like its biblical counterpart.

Meaning

The development of the meaning of service from NT times to Vatican II indicates a narrowing of the concept and practice of Jesus and the early Church. Service associated with baptism, charisms, and community becomes associated with ordination, authority, and office. The spirituality changes for the minister and for the community. The responsibility of building up the community in service and love falls on designated leaders and permanent ministers in the Church rather than on all believers. Contemporary Christian spirituality recognizes the earliest tradition of the Church, inviting all the baptized to address human needs, to build up the faith community, to pray and celebrate together.

If ministry or service in a spirit of love is the mark of a true disciple, then it engages the entire person and is not simply a task within the Church. The Christian attitudes of service, humility, and sacrifice replace status, power, and honor. Sensitivity to the Spirit, whose charisms generate service, becomes a requirement for local communities. Likewise, the emphasis on local Church seems appropriate, for here we readily identify what should be reflected in the universal Church. The association of service with charism challenges us to identify sexist limitations in Church policy.

Scripture gives us a broad base to interpret ministry today. In addition, we need to examine the Church's history and practice for the development of a separatist attitude regarding ministry. Selective remembrance of the tradition violates the gospel challenge and the model of Jesus as one who serves and who urges disciples to do the same. The passivity of Christians today

is an expected outcome of the narrow focus on ministry in so many centuries of Church life. Vatican II challenged this complacency by rightly focusing on the responsibility of all the baptized to live out their faith through service. These services in the Church are charisms for the building up of the faith community. The discussion of what particular service should be called ministry in a formal sense is a moot point until we regenerate the charism/service equation of the early Church.

Believers, accustomed to using gifts and competencies, to discussion and dissent, to participation and shared responsibility in their personal and social lives, are hungry for similar opportunities within the Church. The earliest understanding of service is a realistic foundation on which to build.

See also APOSTOLIC SPIRITUALITY; HUMILITY; KENOSIS; MINISTRY, MINISTERIAL SPIRITUALITY.

Bibliography: E. Schillebeeckx, Ministry: Leadership in the Community of Jesus Christ (New York: Crossroad, 1981). T. O'Meara, Theology of Ministry (New York: Paulist, 1983). W. Beyer, "Diakonia," Theological Dictionary of the New Testament 11, ed. G. Kittel (Grand Rapids, Mich.: Eerdmans, 1964) 81–93.

HELEN DOOHAN

SEXUALITY

The Traditional View

That a dictionary of Catholic spirituality would devote a special article to human sexuality is in itself a sign of the changing perceptions of the sexual dimensions of the human person as well as of the role of the body in the spiritual lives of Christians.

The fact is that much of Catholic morality and spirituality is affected by how we view our bodies and what story we tell ourselves about their role in an authentically human and Christian life. There was a time not too long ago when the majority of Catholics believed that we are in this world as a kind of trial to see whether we are good enough, holy enough, pure enough, to be allowed to live with God for all eternity in another world, called heaven. Our earthly sojourn is but a passing phase, an unreal phase of what we are told is an eternal life, and to achieve it in its fullness, we must obey God's laws, advance in goodness and virtue, and ultimately die in the state of grace. Our chief enemies during this trial and sojourn on the earth are, of course, the world and the flesh. They distract us from the spiritual and root our attention on the crasser and less noble elements of human life.

In the most influential pre–Vatican II book on Catholic spirituality, sexuality is treated under the heading "The Concupiscence of the Flesh" (Adolphe Tanquerey, *The Spiritual Life,* Tournai: Desclée, 1923, pp. 101–103). Tanquerey rehearses the traditional view succinctly and accurately. Pleasure is not in itself evil. God *allows* it when it is directed toward a higher end. He has attached pleasures to certain acts to facilitate the doing of them and to draw us to the fulfillment of our duties. To will pleasure without any reference to the end that makes it lawful, that is, to will pleasure as an end in itself, is disordered and leads to further moral evils. And of all the pleasures, the most dangerous are sexual pleasures, because they make us cherish our bodies so that we forget our souls. According to this account, "body" is the antithesis of "spirit," and hence is *always* an obstacle to the spiritual life.

This view, and various less rigid modifications of it, is counterintuitive and does little justice to the sexual experiences of the faithful. Arising as it does out of Stoic and spiritualistic worldviews, it cannot take into account a well-known truth revealed by the communally funded sexual experiences of generations of married Christians. Clearly, sexual activity *is* (or at least at its best *can be*) an authentic kind of spirituality. But in order to understand how that can be, one has to come to a new understanding of the relation of the human spirit to the human body.

The View of Thomas Aquinas

It is ironic that this "new" understanding turns out not to be so new but rather is an overlooked aspect of the thought of a 13th-century thinker, Thomas Aquinas.

According to the Platonic account, which became the Christian account, since all of the Church Fathers were Platonists, matter lies completely outside the domain of spirit. Even when they are joined, it is only by accident, that is, because of a fall of some sort on the part of spirit. And so the war between them goes on. The human soul/spirit is hampered and at risk all the while it is in matter, and so death is the liberation of the human spirit from the prison of the body. Given this view of human ontology, how could sexuality be anything more than a threat to spirituality?

Aquinas saw it otherwise. For him, human beings are neither spirits imprisoned in matter nor animals evolved from nature, not even "rational" ones. Though he accepted the Aristotelian definition of the human person, he did not think that "animal" was our proper genus, metaphysically speaking. If one wants to classify humans metaphysically, one has no alternative but to invoke the ontological genus "spirit." The specifying difference distinguishing human beings from "pure" spirits, that is, God and angels, is that we are "incarnate," that is to say, "enfleshed" spirits.

For Aquinas, human beings are totally, albeit imperfectly, spirit. That is to say, we human beings are so low in the order of spirits that, unlike angels, we must be incarnated, enfleshed, immersed in matter, precisely in order to perfect ourselves as spirits. Far from being a hindrance to the life of the spirit, physical matter is humankind's unique and special means of reaching spiritual perfection. For us, there simply is no other way (*De spir. creat.* I, 5).

Soul and body are joined in so intimate a union within the human person that Aquinas says not only does the human soul make the body live, it makes the body live by the soul's own spiritual life. So despite all appearances to the contrary, there is none other than a spiritual life in human beings. And in that one life the role of the human body is precisely to enable the human spirit to do the work of spirit (2 *Sent.* 3, 1, 6).

Since the human soul is an imperfect spirit, apart from its body it is impotent and unable to operate at all. The human soul is not, after all, an angelic spirit. The separation of the soul from the body at death puts the soul in a totally static and impoverished condition. Without body, the human soul cannot operate as spirit at all, cannot do the work of spirit, and so Aquinas taught that at death God makes up to the impoverished human soul for the lack of its body by a divine influx of some sort so that it can operate as spirit in the absence of its body until they are reunited at the final resurrection (ST I, q. 89, a. 1).

Aquinas identifies the "work of spirit" as knowing and loving. That is what spirits do, that is what it means to be spirit. On his hypothesis, it follows that we humans can do neither without body. All attempts by humankind at a purely spiritual knowing or loving are not only wrongheaded but futile. If we aspire to know and love one another, if we aspire to really be present to one another, then we must understand that as incarnate spirits we can only do that physically, incarnately, enfleshedly. More than that, if we aspire to know and love God, even then we can only do so incarnately, through our bodies. That is the price we pay for being lowest in the order of spirits. But the human body was created and fashioned as it is precisely to enable and empower us to be fully human and to do the very work of spirit. The human body is marvelously suited to its spiritual vocation. It is not only a biological wonder, it is a spiritual marvel as well.

But there is a deadly trade-off built into the bargain. We humans are the only spirits that face death precisely because of the fragile and unstable nature of our bodies. Aquinas asked why it was that an immortal soul should be joined to an organic body. Wouldn't it be better if it were joined to matter that more closely resembled it in indestructibility? Why not an inorganic body of granite, of diamonds? His answer was that in order for the lowest sort of spirit to know and to love, not any old body will do. A body is needed that is suited to its spiritual vocation, that is, a body equipped with sense organs, even sex organs. As a consequence, the human body is very fragile and has only the most precarious of holds on existence (ST I, q. 76, a. 5; *De anima* I, 8). So the paradox of a spirit having to face death is itself the direct result of that spirit's need to be incarnate in order to be about the work of spirit.

Given what has been said, we humans have only two things at our disposal with which to do the work of the spirit, to do the work of relatedness, love, and solidarity, to do the work of the kingdom. And when Jesus was among us, God though he be for Christians, he too, as human and an incarnate spirit, had only those same two things with which to accomplish his mission of reconciliation among us. And what are these two things? Our words and physical presence, of course. And to this day those are the only things we humans have, both for mediating to one another the superabundance of God's unconditional love for humankind and for having what traditionally has been called a "spirituality." We make an abiding mistake and sorely deceive ourselves whenever we think otherwise.

Aquinas's position is so radical and revolutionary that to this day it has not gained anything like widespread acceptance. Spiritualistic Platonic influences have prevailed into our own times. How different the history of Catholic spirituality would have been had the institutional Church given up its Platonic ways and followed Aquinas's lead in the 13th century. Undoubtedly sex would not have been viewed exclusively in terms of generative procreation and as the major moral problem with which people of faith must cope. Also, we would not have had to wait until the post–Vatican II era to begin to see human sexuality treated as an essential element in, rather than as a liability to, the spiritual life.

Toward a New Understanding

The spirit of Vatican II, which promised to update the thinking of the Catholic Church and to take more into its theological accounts the findings of the social and behavioral sciences, gave impetus to the desire for a renewed view of human sexuality as well. The documents of the council spoke of the human person holistically and seemed to invite Catholics to take a more positive attitude toward their own sexuality. Many accepted the invitation, only to find themselves criticized by the magisterium for having done so. And thus it was that deep divisions have developed between the teaching Church and its believing members on this issue of the meaning of human sexuality. After the promulgation of Paul VI's *Humanae Vitae* in 1968, always at issue is this matter of the relationship between human sexuality and biological procreation.

Across this planet, people who know little else about the Catholic Church know at least this one thing: the Catholic Church vigorously proclaims and authoritatively teaches that sex is for procreation. All other dimensions of human sexuality and all other ends properly achieved thereby are subordinate to that. So committed to that position is the Church of Rome that it goes on to say that to engage in sexual activity for whatever other legitimate purpose in such a way as to willfully and voluntarily preclude the possibility of procreation is a violation of sexuality's intrinsic meaning and hence is always immoral.

From the point of view of Catholic spirituality, the raging battles over sexual morality within the teaching Church between the magisterium and its moral theologians are for the most part uninteresting. However, some parties to that conversation have said and are saying things that are helpful in understanding how it is that human sexual activity at its best can be an authentic spirituality.

The Catholic Theological Society of America commissioned a study of human sexuality, which appeared in 1977 under the title *Human Sexuality: New Directions in American Catholic Thought* (New York: Paulist). Because it begins by briefly giving an account of sexuality in the Old and New Testaments, in the Christian tradition, and in the behavioral sciences of today, it remains a valuable resource for anyone interested in breaking into that discussion. For our purposes, it is helpful to note the richer and broader concept of sexuality that emerged from this study.

In human beings, sexuality is not so much an activity or function in which we participate periodically due to physiological factors but rather the *human* way of being present to the world and to each other. We always exist, function, and relate as sexed persons; at no time are we able to act independently of our sexuality. Not operative only in the restricted area of generativity and procreation, sexuality is at the core and center of a human being's total life-response. It is an inescapable ontological determinant of our existence and our personality.

Human sexuality, then, is no mere biological phenomenon. It is the living, concrete manifestation in us of a divine call. As such, it has an intimate relationship to both our human and our Christian vocation. It summons each one of us to both interpersonal and intrapersonal growth. Intrapersonally, our sexuality exhorts us to make of ourselves the woman or man we were meant to be. Interpersonally, our sexuality urges us to give up solipsistic individualism and to reach out to the other, to be present to the other, to relate. It is through our sexuality, then, that we are present to ourselves, to one another, and to the great Other who has pledged to be always with us.

In 1979 the Sacred Congregation for the Doctrine of the Faith roundly criticized the Catholic Theological Society of America study and urged the authors to reconsider their position. Nothing definitive has emerged, and both sides in this controversy continue to dialogue. Human sexuality remains a burning issue for our times.

Sex Primarily Relational

Several points can be made to support the idea that human sex is primarily relational, having less to do with biological procreation than with human bonding. First of all, if human sex were primarily procreational, then we would expect that humans would become sexually aroused only at times of fertility, much as happens among the animals. But as we have seen, the human person is fully and totally spirit, albeit an impoverished one. So to limit human sexuality to its biological function is to overlook the fact that in humans the most significant ends, or *teloi,* for human sexuality must be of a spiritual nature. If, as we have seen, the primary work of body is knowing and loving presence, then sexual arousal must be viewed in relation to these primary ends of an inspirited, sexed body.

We find this same conclusion in the everyday experiences of people as well as in our everyday language. Language doesn't arise for no reason. What were the original framers of language trying to tell us when they coined the happy phrase "to make love" when speaking of human sexual intercourse? The truth has been there from the start, and human experience corroborates it. Anyone can "have sex," but for human sexual intercourse to be lovemaking, it must be the work of the spirit. And as we have seen, that is precisely what it is, that is precisely what God means it to be.

Consider the excessive amount of psychic energy it takes for sex to remain casual. Once sexually active, how careful one must be. For it is the nature of human sex to make love, to bond one to his or her lover. Everyone knows this, and that is why those pleasure-seekers who are into promiscuity must hit and run, for should they tarry the least bit, they could well be caught up in the mystery of human sexuality—the spiritual bonding of persons, something no libertine wants anything to do with.

Consider that human beings are the only species—or so I am told—that copulates "face to face." How significant that is. The human face. What a mystery, what a precious part of the body for "making love." In the human face one encounters the mystery of incarnation, the wonder of spirit. The smile, the look, the glance—all revelatory, all disclosing the preciousness of the beloved, and bonding spirits. Libertines must look away lest their own eyes betray them, or they inadvertently make love, succumbing to the power of spirit incarnate.

The fact is that sexual activity, when it is truly lovemaking and the work of spirit, is the antithesis of self-indulgence. It is the height of asceticism. Those who have looked at sexually active people as self-indulgent and not pure and undefiled enough to be spiritual have perpetrated a horrendous untruth. While it may be true that pleasure-seekers use sex for their own interests, that is not the nature of human sexuality. That is a rejection of truly human sexuality, which is always spiritual, in favor of a lesser reality.

Those are some of the things that experience teaches us about human sexuality, and those who are sexually active in lovemaking ways have no difficulty recognizing it as an authentic spirituality. For in the end, what is spirituality? It is nothing less than the life of spirit, open and gracious, giving and caring, loving and sharing. As incarnate spirits, we can only do all that through the mediation of our bodies.

Human sexuality at its best, *is* spirituality. That truth has been known to believers for centuries. They have learned it from their own sexual experiences but have remained silent about it. They have remained silent because if they had spoken, they would have suffered recriminations and rejection from the Church, and because it is so precious and personal a truth, they felt it would be cheapened in the speaking.

Undoubtedly the simplest and most powerful account of how human love, when it is authentically love, is God-filled can be found in that marvelous fourth chapter of the First Letter of John. "Whoever is without love does not know God, for God is love" (4:8). "No one has ever seen God. Yet, if we love one another, God remains in us, and his love is brought to perfection in us" (4:12). "God is love, and whoever remains in love remains in God and God in him" (4:16).

John is obviously talking very concretely in this letter. Surely he never envisioned that Christians of later ages would interpret his words in a Platonic sense, that is, that the love that God is, can only be, an infinite, disembodied, totally spiritual love. How could he have foreseen that? He says just the opposite. So the concreteness of the love that God is and its identification with human love go all the way back to the earliest days of our faith. However, it is one thing to affirm that God is love, and quite another to affirm that sexual intercourse, when it is truly human, "makes love" and hence in some sense participates in God and in the love that God is. That is offensive to pious ears. God is so perfect, so dispassionate, so beyond the physical, that it seems sacrilegious to suggest that something as earthy, as passionate, as irrational and biological as sexual activity could incarnate his loving presence. Yet that is precisely what the sexual experience of two millennia of Christians reveals.

This is a profound mystery, so even those who have experienced it can't quite put it into words. But we know when our sexual activity "makes love" and when it doesn't. And there is something very special about those times when it does, so special that once one has experienced it, one finally understands what human sexual relations are *really* all about. They are about the work of spirit, the work of presence, the work of understanding, the work of love. One feels in solidarity with the beneficent Presence that transcends and yet dwells in our world. One feels gifted and graced. One, for however briefly, feels no need to dominate, no need to assert oneself, no need to manipulate, so delicious is the taste of being and of being loved. One feels forgiving and forgiven, at one with God and all of humankind, face to face with not only what is truly good but with the Goodness that is the hidden source of every other good. One feels oneself to be in a truly saving place and thinks to oneself, "This surely must be what salvation is all about!" With Julian of Norwich one becomes convinced that "all will be well, all will be well, all manner of things will be well."

But let us not deceive ourselves—sexual lovemaking is one of the most difficult of the spiritual arts. Though natural to us, it doesn't seem to come naturally to us; we must learn to do it. To have one's sexual activity "make love" and not simply pleasure oneself or one's partner involves an "unselfing" that we tend to avoid. Like all the other things of the spirit, it takes practice. But when it happens, it is always a very powerful spiritual experience with profound aftereffects. I am energized, I feel better able to love, I find myself more generous, more giving, more open, less self-conscious, more in touch with the wisdom of my body, more in touch with the God who has chosen to be incarnate in human life.

Spiritualism, puritanism, and fundamentalism have plagued the Christian faith throughout its history. Each has tried to overspiritualize the faith enterprise out of fear—fear of life, fear of love, fear of bonding, fear of emotions, fear of body. Fear causes them, following the lead of Plato and the ancient Stoics, to set up two worlds, one of body and matter the other of soul and spirit. But there is only one God. And there is only one world. In fact, there is only one reality—Spirit in the World, to use Karl Rahner's happy phrase. Perhaps the term *spiritual life* is misleading. Rather, the focus should be on *human life* (which, after all, is totally spiritual) and on the God who is incarnate there, revealing to us in our experience all we need to know in order, like God, to be truly present to one another and to our world. For if there is such a thing as Christian spirituality, it is the "spirituality of presence," and is, thanks to our sexed bodies, readily available to everyone regardless of state or station.

See also ABSTINENCE; BODY; CELIBACY; CHASTITY; DUALISM; ECSTASY; HOLISTIC SPIRITUALITY; HOMOSEXUALITY; INCARNATION; INTIMACY; LAY SPIRITUALITY; LOVE; MARRIAGE; VATICAN COUNCIL II; VIRGINITY.

Bibliography: Sacred Congregation for the Doctrine of the Faith, *Declaration on Certain Questions Concerning Sexual Ethics* (Washington: USCC, 1975). D. Goergen, *The Sexual Celibate* (New York: Seabury, 1974). P. Keane, *Sexual Morality: A Catholic Perspective* (New York: Paulist, 1978). M. Kelsey and B. Kelsey, *Sacrament of Sexuality: The Spirituality and Psychology of Sex* (Warwick, R.I.: Amity House, 1986). E. Kennedy, *A Time for Love* (New York: Doubleday, 1987). A. Kosnik et al., *Human Sexuality: New Directions in American Catholic Thought—A Study Commissioned by the Catholic Theological Society of America* (New York: Paulist, 1977). J. Nelson, *The Intimate Connection: Male Sexuality and Masculine Spirituality* (Philadelphia: Westminster, 1988); "Reuniting Sexuality and Spirituality," *The Christian Century* (Feb. 25, 1987) 187–190. D. Westley, *A Theology of Presence* (Mystic, Conn.: Twenty-Third Publications, 1988). E. Whitehead and J. Whitehead, *A Sense of Sexuality: Christian Love and Intimacy* (New York: Doubleday, 1989).

DICK WESTLEY

SILENCE

The theme of silence within spirituality and worship suggests first of all the practice of the cessation of speech for the sake of prayer, reflection, and greater attentiveness to God. This traditional and conventional understanding of silence implies an opposition between silence and word, which, though partially true, can also be misleading. Its truth lies in the ironic fact that although speech manifests the distinctive spiritual self-possession and presence-to-others of human personhood, it may also be degraded into a flight from self, others, and God. One may observe many forms of speech that amount to a diversion from reality and a literal waste of time: compulsive talking for the sake of talking, whether or not one has anything to say; gossiping; the doublespeak of mass media and propaganda; and what Heidegger has called the average understanding or account of things that discourages rather than encourages real thought about them.

This note of opposition between perceptive silence and empty speech also has a historical background in the development of monasticism, in which silence came to be equated with withdrawal from "the world." The historical success of Christianity—its evolution from a small persecuted sect to the socially dominant religion of the Roman Empire—posed the then new problem of the merely nominal believer versus the seriously devout. The merely nominal Christian lives in "the world" with its material, pragmatic, time-bound concerns and everyday chatter. But the seriously devoted Christian withdraws from this world to seek the life of perfection in contemplation and silence. Although monasticism was originally a lay movement, this differentiation was eventually subsumed under the broader, if not canonically accurate, distinction between those seriously concerned with religious life (monks, religious, and clergy) and those only indirectly and sporadically so (the laity). Consequently, in its historical development, silence is not only an ascetical practice but a countercultural gesture, a symbol of an alternative lifestyle. It records that thirst for uncompromising devotion to God that has in various ways always sought to differentiate itself from nonintentional or superficial religiousness.

Against this backdrop, the opposition of silence to word, which is undoubtedly a valid part of the meaning of silence, can nevertheless be overplayed. For silence as cessation of speech presupposes silence as the positive ground or horizon of speech. Silence and word are not only opposites but, paradoxically and more fundamentally, correlatives. If one avoids speech, it is not ultimately because speech is bad or less perfect than silence but because speech is nourished by silence. Silence is, as it were, the natural milieu of speech, and speech is unthinkable without silence. This positive dialectic of silence and word can be illustrated both theologically and anthropologically.

From a theological point of view, the Word or Logos issues forth from the silent mystery of God as God's own self-expression in and to humanity. Similarly, the words and deeds of Jesus issue forth from his own silent integrity, which consists in his openness to the Father, other people, and the entire cosmos. There are even those pivotal moments in which it is precisely the silence of Jesus that speaks—his silence before his accusers, his silent suffering. With this we have already begun to touch upon the anthropological dimension, since *Christos* is *anthropos*. Every human person experiences word, whether in speaking or hearing, from out of an ultimately incommunicable center of personhood that is graced by God's self-communication. And through word, each person moves with others toward the silent mystery of God before which words ultimately fail.

Beyond the traditional treatment of silence, whether as a way of life, an ascetical practice, or a component of worship and Christian living, there are other, less positive contexts in which silence comes to the fore and takes on importance for spirituality. What might be called the dark side of silence has not generally received the attention and careful analysis it deserves, especially within the academic study of spirituality. For in the life of the Church as well as elsewhere, silence can mean repression—a withdrawal from the full complexity of reality in favor of some partial and easier truth. When this occurs, whether on the personal or institutional level, certain zones of reality and even human voices are "silenced" in order to promote some particular ideologization of the faith. Silence, furthermore, can mean a lack of courage to act and speak out in the face of injustice and suffering. Masking as religious detachment, silence may well amount to an incapacity for communion and the refusal of charity.

Finally, silence can signify voicelessness and disempowerment. For example, a prominent feature of Vatican II's liturgical reforms was the restoration of the people's spoken and sung parts at worship after centuries of silence. These "centuries of silence" were not simply an aural phenomenon but a social-political one. The council recognized that having a public voice means having power and agency; in contrast, voicelessness is equivalent to passivity and powerlessness. When people are denied their own voice at their own liturgy as the Body of Christ, they are denied agency in their own religious histories. This strikes at the very core of spirituality and alienates one from religiousness. In a way, Vatican II's restoration of voice summarizes the entire spiritual challenge of ministry in our age: to bring the great body of believers from passivity to agency, from voicelessness to self-expression and self-donation, from "silence" to participation. And yet such participation cannot be more than a superficial phenomenon if it does not involve the renewed practice of silence, in the positive sense of receptive openness to God's mysterious presence.

See also CENTERING PRAYER; CONTEMPLATION, CONTEMPLATIVE PRAYER; DETACHMENT; INTERIOR-

ITY, INTERIOR LIFE; MEDITATION; MONASTICISM; MO-
NASTIC SPIRITUALITY; MYSTERY; NEGATIVE WAY; REC-
OLLECTION; REFLECTION; SOLITUDE; WAITING.

Bibliography: M. Picard, *The World of Silence* (Chicago: Regnery, 1952). H. U. von Balthasar, "The Word and Silence," *Explorations in Theology* (San Francisco: Ignatius Press, 1989) 127–146. A. Wathen, *Silence: The Meaning of Silence in the Rule of St. Benedict* (Washington: Consortium Press, 1973).

BOB HURD

SIMPLICITY

Though nearly every culture and religious tradition presents simplicity in some form as an ideal, few attempt to define precisely what it means to be "simple." Within the Christian spiritual tradition itself, for example, the notion of simplicity has been variously applied not only to the virtuous individual but also to God, mystical prayer, certain styles of liturgical celebration, and ordinary living. Ironically, then, Christian simplicity is perhaps not the simple concept one might expect but rather a cluster of interrelated themes.

In the Bible

Commentators often note that the OT concepts most closely associated with simplicity are integrity, perfection, and sincerity of heart (see Bauer, pp. 847–848; de Andia et al., cols. 892–897). Among OT figures, Noah (Gen 6:8-9; Sir 44:17), Abraham (Gen 17:1), Jacob (Gen 25:27), and Job (Job 1:1, 8; 2:3; 9:20-22) are described as *tam* ("perfect"), numbered among those who walk in *tamîm* ("integrity"), terminology often rendered as *haplous* ("simple") or *haplotēs* ("simplicity") in ancient Greek translations of the Hebrew Scriptures and perhaps ultimately derived from a cultic context requiring sacrificial victims that are whole, without fault or blemish. In the same spirit the psalmist calls upon Yahweh to "do me justice . . . because I am just, and because of the innocence that is mine" (Ps 7:9), elsewhere observing that only the one who "walks blamelessly" (*tamîm*) and "does

justice" (*tsedeq*) can "sojourn in your tent" and "dwell on your holy mountain" (Ps 15:1-2). In the Greek OT, those who "judge the earth" are urged to "seek [the Lord] in integrity (*haploun*) of heart" (Wis 1:1; see 1 Macc 2:37, 60; Dan 13:63). By contrast, simplicity in the derogatory sense of "immaturity" or "foolishness" appears relatively rarely in the OT (see Prov 1:22; 7:7; 8:5; 14:15; 22:3), and then usually conjoined with the observation that the "decree of the LORD is trustworthy, giving wisdom to the simple" (Pss 19:8; 119:130; see Ps 116:6; Prov 1:4; 9:4; 21:11).

A key passage for the NT and later Christian understanding of simplicity is the saying of Jesus that "if your eye is *haplous* (literally "simple," though often translated as "sound"), your whole body will be filled with light" (Mt 6:22; Lk 11:34), in contrast to the darkness of those whose eye is "evil." By placing this text within the Sermon on the Mount, amid admonitions to "store up treasures in heaven" (Mt 6:20) and "seek first the kingdom of God" (Mt 6:33) rather than attempting to "serve two masters . . . God and mammon" (Mt 6:24), Matthew seems to indicate that the "simple" or "sound" eye should be understood as a metaphor for purity of heart and total dedication to God. Similarly, the Lukan arrangement suggests an antithesis between the "simple eye" and all "doublemindedness," with the saying placed immediately before Jesus' denunciation of the Pharisees and scholars of the Law for their preoccupation with externals to the neglect of "judgment" and "love for God" (Lk 11:37-52). Not surprisingly, therefore, later patristic authors and spiritual writers have interpreted this text as wholly in keeping with Jesus' constant message: to be "simple as doves" (Mt 10:16), "clean of heart" (Mt 5:8), and "like children" (Mt 18:3; see Mt 19:14; Mk 10:15; Lk 18:17). Paul, too, confirms the relation between *haplotēs* ("simplicity") and total generosity in his appeal for contributions to the Church in Jerusalem (2 Cor 8:2; 9:10-13) and elsewhere (Rom 12:8), while in Jas 1:5 it is God who is said to give "generously and ungrudgingly" (*haplous*) to those who ask.

In short, biblical simplicity is first and foremost a matter of the complete surrender to God of all that one has and is, and includes the life of integrity and love that follows from such a dedication. Simplicity also figures as the supreme virtue in the *Testament of the Twelve Patriarchs,* where it is contrasted with duplicity, any tendency to be "double" (*diploun*) in mind and heart.

In Christian Tradition

A brief review of postbiblical developments (necessarily incomplete at least in part because, ironically, "simple" believers are those least likely to leave documentary evidence behind) shows how the Christian understanding of simplicity has evolved over centuries, sometimes narrowing the original biblical notion, sometimes expanding it or adding new layers of meaning. Simplicity, in the sense of individual and ecclesial integrity in faith and love, is a common theme in Christian writings of the apostolic and subapostolic period (e.g., *Didache, Letter of Barnabas, Letters of Clement*), and is even personified in *The Shepherd of Hermas*; moreover, the contrast between simplicity, on the one hand, and hesitation (*dipsychia*), lack of faith, and duplicity in thought, word, and deed, on the other, becomes increasingly associated with the choice between the "two ways" of life (good or evil) presented to human beings, and authors begin to explore further the need for "discernment of spirits," a critical issue in the later history of Christian spirituality (see de Andia et al., cols. 897–899).

In the patristic literature of the Latin Church, the terms *simplex* and *simplicitas* appear frequently, though not always with precisely the same meaning as *haplous* and *haplotēs*, but sometimes used instead in a more pejorative sense conveying ignorance and naiveté. Still, Augustine among others retrieves the OT contrast between "the simple heart" and "the double heart," noting, as Aquinas would later emphasize (ST I, q. 3, a. 7), that only God is altogether "simple" (see de Andia et al., cols. 901–903).

In the Eastern monastic tradition simplicity is associated with such themes as temperance, the true wisdom of faith, wholeheartedness (as opposed to hypocrisy), prudence in avoiding evil, childlike innocence, naturalness, and charity. In Western monasticism simplicity is often presented as among the most characteristic of monastic virtues, in contrast to the complex studies and concerns of Scholasticism. But both traditions recognize the gradual "simplification" that occurs in contemplative prayer as one is gradually divested of all particular thoughts and attachments and becomes illuminated by what Symeon the New Theologian calls the "simple light" of God (see de Andia et al., cols. 903–910).

Among the mendicants, *The Salutation of the Virtues* by Francis of Assisi (whom Innocent III called "simplicissimus") hails "Queen Wisdom . . . with your sister, holy pure Simplicity" that "destroys all the wisdom of this world and the wisdom of the body" (*Francis and Clare: The Complete Works,* trans. R. Armstrong and I. Brady, New York: Paulist, 1982, pp. 151–152; see Plus, p. 35). Some of the Beguines (e.g., Margaret Porete, in *The Mirror of Simple Souls*), as well as Meister Eckhart and his followers, explore in a far more radical way the metaphysical and mystical connection between the insights that "God is infinite in his simplicity and simple by reason of his infinity" (Sermon XXIX in *Meister Eckhart: Teacher and Preacher,* ed. B. McGinn, Mahwah, N.J.: Paulist, 1986, p. 223) and that if the soul "is to be united with God, she must be simple as God is simple" (Sermon 85 in *Meister Eckhart: Sermons & Treatises,* vol. 2, trans. and ed. M. O'C. Walshe, Longmead: Element Books, 1979, p. 264). According to Eckhart, it is in returning to the ultimate simplicity of being itself, beyond all modes and distinctions, that we find the point of union with God.

For Jan van Ruysbroeck, simplicity is "full of faith" and "embraces hope and charity." Relating simplicity to the will and not merely to the contemplative intellect devoid of imagery and concepts, he notes that "simplicity of intention gathers into the unity of the spirit the scattered forces of the soul, and unites the spirit itself with God" (see Plus, p. 73). "Simplicity of attention" reappears in a famous statement from *The Imitation of Christ* that the human person "is borne up from earthly things on two wings: simplicity and purity," and that "simplicity is in the intention" while "purity is in the love" (Bk. 2, chap. 4). Tauler, Ruysbroeck, and others of the Rheno-Flemish tradition likewise contrast inner simplicity with the unnecessary multiplication of spiritual practices and devotions.

Among the 16th-century mystical authors of the Iberian peninsula, John of the Cross, with his usual talent for synthesis, brings together much of the preceding discussion of simplicity. He rhapsodizes, for example, about "the infinite unity and simplicity of [God's] unique being" (*The Living Flame of Love* 3.17), and his explanation of the imagelessness of advanced mystical prayer is that "transformation in God makes [the soul] so consonant with the simplicity and purity of God, in which there is no form or imaginative figure, that it leaves her clean, pure, and empty of all forms and figures, purged, and radiant in simple contemplation" (*The Spiritual Canticle* 26.16). But John is equally concerned about the multiplicity of attachments and desires that impede the will from a pure and single-hearted love of God (*The Ascent of Mount Carmel*, III.16-45). He likewise notes that authentic spiritual experiences engender humility and simplicity (*The Ascent*, III.29.5), and warns that the multipli-

cation of petitions and liturgical ceremonies can be contrary to "the simplicity of faith" (*The Ascent*, III.43-44).

In the 17th-century French school of spirituality, Francis de Sales, Vincent de Paul ("For myself, God has given me so great an esteem for simplicity that I call it my Gospel"), and others closely identify simplicity with truth, purity of intention, humility, and the lack of all pretense. For the Carmelite John of St. Sampson, who dedicated five treatises to this virtue, simplicity seems at times to encompass everything else needed for the spiritual journey to God, whom he sometimes characterizes as "the Simple" (see de Andia et al., cols. 913–918; Plus, pp. 15–16, 56–57).

While Jane de Chantal and others practiced "the prayer of simple regard," a contemplative style of praying, without images or words, learned from Barbe Acarie (Marie of the Incarnation) and the French Carmelites, Madame Guyon speaks of a "prayer of simple presence," by which one engages in a "simple and continuous act" of total abandonment to God, without meditation, reflection, or the intervention of other particular acts of the will. Because of the condemnation of quietism, doubts about the very possibility of a continuous *act* (as opposed to habit) of prayer, and the failure to sort out terminological difficulties, later authors tend to be more cautious in their discussions of simplicity, shifting the focus back from the advanced stages of mysticism to simplicity in ordinary prayer, speech, action, and lifestyle. Still, simplicity is explicitly treated by such authors as de Caussade and Grou, and it is implicit throughout the "little way" of St. Thérèse of Lisieux, though she seldom uses the word itself except to agree that "the closer one approaches to God, the simpler one becomes," adding that "for simple souls there must be no complicated ways" (*Story of a Soul*, trans. J. Clarke, Washington: ICS Publications, 1976, pp. 151, 254).

The Contemporary Period

Simplicity shows up relatively rarely in the documents of Vatican II, except in the famous directives of the Constitution on the Sacred Liturgy that "the rites should be distinguished by a noble simplicity" and should be "short, clear, and unencumbered by useless repetitions" (SC 34; see 50, 66, 117). In retrospect, many now admit that this call to renew the traditional sobriety of the Roman Rite has too often been misused as a rationale for dull, unimaginative, and overly verbal ceremonies. As we are coming to realize, liturgy can be simple without becoming boring or uninspired.

Despite, or perhaps in response to, its oft-noted consumerism and materialism, North American culture has its own tradition of simplicity. The call to plain and simple living has found diverse expressions in U.S. history, from colonial Puritanism, the idealization of rural and agrarian life, Thoreau's cry in *Walden* that "our life is frittered away by detail . . . Simplify, simplify!" and the words of the familiar Shaker hymn, "Tis a gift to be simple," down to the blunt Twelve-Step maxim "Keep it simple, stupid!," the hippie movement of the late sixties, Jimmy Carter's famous description of modern consumerist America's "spiritual malaise" as he summoned the nation to resolve its energy crisis, and the current reaction against the "conspicuous consumption" and "meism" of the Reagan years. Today "the simple life" is often used "as an omnibus label to characterize such activities as the back-to-the-land movement, arts and crafts revivals, organic gardening, environmental conservation and recycling, anti-nuclear demonstrations, urban cooperatives, wilderness expeditions, consumer frugality and the like" (Shi, p. 3). Some, perhaps many, of these movements have at least distant religious roots or have drawn direct or indirect inspiration from the biblical tradition.

On another front, contemporary North Americans show continued interest in Eastern methods of meditation that essentially foster some form of calm, imageless attention, not unrelated to the loving union with divine Simplicity, beyond all forms and figures, of which many Christian mystics speak. At the same time, there are ongoing controversies about the degree of similarity among mystic states of different religious traditions and the legitimacy of using non-Christian techniques to help foster Christian contemplative experiences of the God of revelation (see the Congregation for the Doctrine of the Faith, *Letter to the Bishops of the Catholic Church on Some Aspects of Christian Meditation,* Washington: USCC, 1989).

In short, these varied traditions offer plentiful resources for a retrieval and contemporary understanding of simplicity while raising important questions. First, whether expounded on the basis of biblical insights or Neoplatonic philosophy, it is clear that, for believers, authentic Christian simplicity finds its source and inspiration in God. In both the OT and NT, people are called to a generous, wholehearted, and integral response toward God who has first loved us wholeheartedly, and toward others out of love for, and in imitation of, this same God. Jesus reaffirms the absolute priority of God and God's kingdom over all other concerns, thus proclaiming a radically simplified vision of life's purpose, often hidden from the rich and learned yet open especially to the simple and lowly.

For the followers of Jesus, then, simplicity in personal prayer, communal worship, conversation, dress, food, possessions, and all the other areas usually considered in the manuals of ascetical theology (or propounded anew today by the contemporary advocates of "simple living") become but so many expressions of the deeper simplicity of wholehearted dedication to God and neighbor. Everything is reprioritized around the coming of the reign of God. At the same time, "inner simplicity" means little without some practical outward manifestation; recent movements for social justice and ecological responsibility have reminded us that the cultivation of a simple lifestyle is no merely private spiritual exercise to increase personal holiness but a necessary component of responsible Christian stewardship for God's creation.

With regard to mystical prayer, some of the Christian tradition's more speculative analyses of higher contemplative states in terms of flight from the manifold world into an absolutely simple union with the pure undifferentiated "One" or "naked Godhead" may be difficult to sustain today apart from their underlying philosophical (and sometimes Neoplatonic) presuppositions. Contemporary scholars argue whether *any* conscious mystic state is ever so completely "pure" that it can be separated even from its subject's own belief system, within which the experience is interpreted and given meaning. In any case, the pursuit of "pure consciousness without particular content" often strikes modern believers as overly individualistic, dualistic, and escapist, as if the chief goal of Christian living were to avoid the world and flee our own creaturehood. Certainly no creature *as creature* ever becomes totally simple in every respect, and even the classic notion of God's absolute simplicity has been challenged in modern times by process theologians.

Yet from a phenomenological and psychological perspective, it is a fact of experience across all religious traditions that certain kinds of "simplification" predictably occur as one spiritually matures: conflicting energies and desires are calmed, reconciled, and focused on "the one thing necessary"; a multiplicity of devotions, discursive prayers, and pious thoughts gradually give way to a simple loving attention; and one surrenders more and more to the transforming activity of God in every aspect of one's life. It should not surprise Christians that the process is analogous to what one finds in any healthy love relationship, as the many words, gestures, and conflicting thoughts and feelings of early infatuation evolve into a silent, loving presence to each other. From such a perspective, the pursuit of authentic Christian simplicity becomes no longer an effort to escape our creaturehood but rather, as the Scriptures affirm, a readiness to walk with God in the simple human integrity that the Creator intended from the beginning.

See also ASCETICISM; CARMELITE SPIRITUALITY; CONTEMPLATION; DETACHMENT; DISCERNMENT OF SPIRITS; ECOLOGICAL CONSCIOUSNESS; EXPERIENCE; JUSTICE; MONASTICISM, MONASTIC SPIRITUALITY; MORTIFICATION; MYSTICSIM; PRAYER; QUIETISM; UNITY.

Bibliography: Y. de Andia, V. Desprez, and M. Dupuy, "Simplicité," *D.Spir.,* vol. 14, cols. 892–921. J. Bauer, "Simplicity," *Sacramentum Verbi,* ed. J. Bauer (New York: Herder, 1970) 3:847–848. R. Plus, *Simplicity* (Westminster, Md.: Newman, 1951). D. Shi, *The Simple Life: Plain Living and High Thinking in American Culture* (New York: Oxford Univ. Press, 1985).

STEVEN PAYNE, O.C.D.

SIN

Sin is an axial category in Christian life. The word is weary but the reality is energetic and destructive. As sin recedes to the periphery of modern consciousness, there appears a loss of confidence in its traditional images, models, and themes. Many regard guilt as mental malaise, when it might be symptomatic of their true moral condition. Hence the effort to restore intensity to the language of sin to revitalize its reality.

Only a being who is both nature's culmination and its transcendence has a capacity for sin. Sin is a mystery that arises in the ambiguity of the heart and defies definition. Sin "hates the light." Though freely chosen evil is a basic datum of experience, access to its irreducible opacity is gained through metaphor and simile. The language of sin is analogous. Whatever its models, it must speak of sin less as infraction of law than as betrayal of a relationship with God, of freedom and the lack thereof experienced in turning from God, and of the way that sin cripples the will. For sin is a notion that marks convergence between revealed religion and morality, spheres sundered in modern culture. As such, it transcends the ethical and points to the bonding of person and community to a self-communicating God. Sin menaces the health or survival of that bond. Hence it is more than unethical or illegal, it is unholy.

Christian concern with sin is not morbid fascination with the heart's darkness. Christianity's central proclamation is the "good news" of God's triumph over sin through Christ. Talk about sin, which is indispensable to talk about salvation, is subordinate to talk about grace. The mystery of iniquity must be understood in light of God's eschatologically victorious grace. In the sin-grace dialectic, two forces dispute the same terrain. The world is sin-ravaged; yet the battle does not hang in the balance. "Where sin increased, grace overflowed all the more" (Rom 5:20). The evil introduced by disobedient freedom finds healing in the obedient freedom of Jesus, whose acceptance of the evils humans inflict conquers the evil humans endure. Salvation, however, is good news only for those who admit a need for salvation. "Those who are well do not need a physician" (Mt 9:12). A theology of sin articulates the conviction that humanity ails and needs a physician. Hamartiology is inseparable from, and in function of, Christology.

Sin is parasitic. It is of concern not because of its intrinsic worth but because it eats away the life communicated in Christ. Christology is the axis of soteriology, not sin. Christ's significance does not derive from sin, but sin's significance derives from Christ, for sin is a measure of one's distance from what one is called to be—an image of the Son. Sin is less lost innocence than incompleteness. The egoism of sin that distances from God is initially revealed in the Law but radically in the Cru-

cified. There the personal and social drama of sin as self-crucifixion is laid bare.

In the Hebrew Scriptures

The concept of sin is not univocal in the Scriptures. There is no one Hebrew equivalent for "sin." Several words, none originally religious, are translated as "sin." Their use in religious discourse was originally metaphorical, and their unique overtones elude translation. The word most commonly rendered as "sin," *ḥeṭ* and its cognates, signifies "missing the mark" or "failing" and implies not just intellectual error but action that does not achieve its goal. While the word can be used without religious or moral connotations (e.g., Judg 20:16), it is usually part of the biblical language of morality, signifying failure in discharging a duty or satisfying a legitimate claim. Hence it implies the violation of a right, an offense against the holder of the claim, who may be human or divine: "If a man sins against another man, one can intercede for him with the LORD; but if a man sins against the LORD, who can intercede for him?" (1 Sam 2:25). The same verb occurs in both clauses. Moral usage presupposes norms governing the relationship, so that sin is an infraction entailing betrayal. In this sense sin can be unintentional, as when ignorance impedes or threatens the relationship (e.g., Num 22:31, 34).

The second most frequent Hebrew terminology for sin is more consistently metaphorical. Terms cognate with *'āwôn*, usually translated "iniquity," carry literal reference to crookedness, contrasted pejoratively with straightness or uprightness. The terminology indicates a defect not only of behavior but also of character, an inner deformity, painful and shameful, and is translatable therefore in terms of guilt, the distortion that remains as a result of the iniquitous act. "My iniquities . . . are like a heavy burden, beyond my strength" (Ps 38:5). This burden is transferable to a scapegoat (Lev 16:22). Of the Suffering

Servant it is said that "he bore the sin of many" (Isa 53:12, RSV).

The third most frequent terminology for sin presupposes a relationship secured by obligations. Words related to *pāša'* focus on the relationship and on rupturing contractual ties, e.g., when rebellion against a political superior is seen as a treaty violation (2 Kgs 8:20, 22). In religious discourse this terminology connotes a breach of covenant between God and the chosen people and the dissolution of community. The vassal-overlord tie in the ancient world was personal, not purely political. Hence sin as a covenant breach or violation of Yahweh's law (Hos 8:1) is less legal transgression than personal disloyalty, an insult to the sovereign whose beneficence initiated covenant and ruled out conflicting allegiances.

These three groups of terms point up respectively the offense sin does to another, the damage it does to the sinner, and the destruction it brings to relationships whose demands are not met. Other Hebrew terms point in similar and related directions, adding subtlety and richness. *'Awel* ("twisted") indicates distortion, lack of proper form, lameness. *Šeker* ("lie") applies not only to mendacity but to any sin, for sinners act deceitfully, pretending to be what they are not. The lie denies reality by speech, sin denies it by action. Plato's "lie in the soul" is more insidious than the lie on the tongue, for sinners believe their own lies. Sin is also *'awen* ("trouble"), which also signifies sorrow, affliction. Sinners are troublemakers for others and for themselves.

The origin of sin is approached on two fronts: the psychological and the historical. The psychological origin is refusal to acknowledge the reality of God (Hos 2:8; 4:1, 6). Sin wells up from the evil heart (Jer 7:24) as a deliberate, willful act for which humans are accountable. There is no indication that psychic or social aberrations excuse it. In fact, sin, the prophets frequently remind us, undermines society.

The historical question reduces to the question of how sin can enter a world governed by God's saving power. The Hebrew Scriptures provide no solution. The Adamic myth (Gen 3) distinguishes the origin of evil from the origin of being, yet it affirms that sin is as old as humanity. Sin corrupts a good creation. Goodness is primordial. Sin enters through human choice, though the origin of sin is not absolutely reducible to conscious choice. Adam and Eve find evil lying in wait and are lured by an external agent of evil. The serpent is the already-thereness of evil.

With psychological deftness the storyteller reveals how and why the couple succumb: they desire something not theirs—to be as gods. All sin is an idolatrous attempt to replace the Creator with self or another creature. The result is alienation from God, from each other, and from their own selves. This is not strictly a myth of falling, for Adam is no superman but the archetype of every human. In light of Genesis 3, Augustine saw sin as both pride and covetousness, aversion from God and conversion to creatures, "estrangement from the Creator, the highest good, for the sake of inferior goods" (*To Simplicianus* 2.2.18).

Genesis 3 must be read in conjunction with Genesis 4–11, which it prefaces. This anecdotal mélange shows how sin, once admitted, leaves its tracks everywhere, until all is corrupt (Gen 6:12). The trail of evil marches to the deluge, for Yahweh must destroy sinful humanity. After the deluge Yahweh appears resigned to the fact that "the desires of man's heart are evil from the start" (Gen 8:21) and resolves against further destruction. Yahweh's wrath is tempered by mercy, and so God is absolved of responsibility for evil.

Yet the conviction that sin carries in its wake death and disaster remains. The wisdom writings graphically describe the disaster that overtakes sinners (e.g., Job 18:5-21), as do the penitential psalms (e.g., Ps 38). The historical books tell the tragic tale of men whose sins unleash forces that destroy them: Abimelech (Judg 9), David (2 Sam 12–20), Ahab (1 Kgs 21–22). This theology of sin and personal responsibility culminates in the prophets, who construe Israel's fall as the inevitable consequence of its being a nation of sinners. All personal and social disasters are attributable to personal and corporate sin. In the Book of Job this retributive penal vision of reality shatters against a wall of suffering innocence.

Between the later writings of Judaism and the earlier books of the Hebrew Scriptures, a difference emerges. Judaism, in some sectors, sought security in law. In some Pharasaic circles the real malice of sin was obscured. Sin became more a transgression of law than a betrayal of Yahweh. Perfection in observance of law as interpreted by the Pharisees became the ideal. Dialogical encounter with God yielded to a moralism of submission to detailed demands of divine law made dense and complex in rabbinical interpretation. The religious ground of sin eroded as law pulled away from covenant; morality degenerated into legalism, sin into rule-breaking, self-assessment into sophistry or scrupulosity. Sin as code violation is different from sin as infidelity. Moreover, in Rabbinic Judaism humans were thought to be hobbled by an inclination to evil, *yetzer ha-ra,* which explains the fault of the Edenic pair. Yet *yetzer* is not evil; it also inclines to good. Without it no one would take a wife or tend a garden.

Thus the Scriptures view sin as the inverse of the divine initiative of love. Essentially it is infidelity, refusal to enter and maintain covenant with God, though this bond is constitutive of life, progress, and prosperity. Israel's history chronicles untiring attempts by the divine Lover to restore the bond that humanity breaks. As marriage became a metaphor for covenant, sin became adultery and prostitution (Hos 1:2). Further, as covenant is an alliance of people, obligations that assure social coherence are inseparable from those that assure communion with the Lord; betrayal of the Lord is betrayal of the community and vice versa. Loyalty to God and to neighbor are of a piece. Antisocial conduct and irreligious conduct are the same. Transition to the two loves that constitute the total law in the Christian Scriptures was easily made.

Another, more elusive biblical category that may not strictly pertain to the domain of sin yet is closely linked and not always easily distinguished from it is the category of defilement, the power of evil impinging from without, making one unclean before a wrathful and holy God. It is often alluded to in cultic contexts and associated with taboos about blood, sexual functions, skin diseases, and certain foods. With sin it shares the idea of overstepping boundaries when the secular touches the sacred, and it must be removed to regain a socially acceptable condition. Its roots are inaccessible, yet even today they lie dormant in the archaic layers of consciousness. Defilement is linked figuratively to sin. Ritual and figurative cleansing is connected to the removal of both. Yet even within the Bible, the two stand apart. Uncleanness may not be interpreted in moral terms as conscious and willful, while sin ultimately must be.

In the Christian Scriptures

The Christian Scriptures most commonly designate sin by the Greek terms *hamartia* and *hamartēma,* whose classical use signified a physical missing, or failure to reach, a goal. Hebrew notions of sin are assumed and sublated as sin comes to be viewed as act, state, and power, and God as conqueror of sin through Jesus. In the Synoptic Gospels sin appears most frequently in conjunction with the forgiveness brought by Jesus, friend of sinners, whom he calls to *metanoia.* Jesus asserts that sins come from the heart and that they alone defile a person (Mt 15:18-19; Mk 7:20-22). Sin is the wandering of a son from his father's house (Lk 15:18, 21). The posture assumed toward sin, forgiveness, and even works of righteousness in the parable of the prodigal son are paradigmatic. The sinner need but ask for forgiveness; there is joy in heaven at the return of the sinner (Lk 18:13f.; 15:7, 10). Sin is implicit in any failure to do right by one's neighbor (Mt 25:31-46; Lk 16:19-31) or to use God-given ability (Mt 25:14-30; Lk 19:12-26). The most heinous sins are done with hypocrisy, especially by religious persons (e.g., Mt 23).

In John the malice of sin is more stark and less privatized. Sin is lawlessness, unrighteousness (1 Jn 3:4; 5:17). The sinner is from the devil and a slave of sin (1 Jn 3:8; Jn 8:34) who prefers darkness to light (Jn 3:19f.). "Sin" appears more often in John than in the Synoptics and more commonly denotes not personal acts but a condition induced by sinful acts. Sin indwells the sinner. As in the Hebrew Scriptures, sin is a lie and its consequence is death. John provides the sole passage in the Christian Scriptures that explicitly differentiates deadly sins from those that are not death-inflicting (1 Jn 5:16), though this is hardly equivalent to the later distinction between mortal and venial sin. Most likely the lethal sin is unbelief, refusal of forgiveness in one blessed with faith. For John, Jesus is the sinless victor over sin, the Lamb who takes away the sin of the world, the atoning sacrifice (Jn 8:46; 1:29; 1 Jn 2:2). John's use of the singular indicates that sin is transpersonal more than it is conscious decision. It is a state of hostility that infects and seduces. John crushes the arrogance that thinks sin can be denied: "If we say, 'We are without sin,' we deceive ourselves, and the truth is not in us. . . . We make [God] a liar and his word is not in us" (1 Jn 1:8-10).

Paul provides the fullest theology of sin in the Christian Scriptures, almost all of it in the Letter to the Romans. Sin permeates the Gentile world due to its refusal to acknowledge God, who has abandoned the Gentiles to their destructive desires (Rom 1:18-32). Yet Paul does not divide the world between sinners and Jews. Possession and observance of Torah does not assure triumph over sin and cannot merit righteousness. Torah can only make one conscious of sin. Jew and Greek alike are "under sin"; all are idolaters and fall short of the glory of God (Rom 1:18-3:20). Paul sees sin woven into the human condition; it is not merely immoral acts or merely a state of the individual. Sin reigns in the world. It is a state of enmity toward God, a personified, cosmic power from which no one escapes. Yet no one is excused (Rom 5-8).

How sin became endemic to the human predicament is the concern of Rom 5:12-21. Paul traces the ever-present condition to the sin of Genesis 3. The sin of Adam severed harmonious ties with God for the entire human family. In Jewish belief sin brings death, and since all die, Paul infers, all have sinned. He does not assert that all share Adam's guilt, but all do share the condition ensuing upon his rebellion and become enemies of God (Rom 5:10). Crucial is Paul's Jewish belief in human solidarity and the representative personality of key figures. He attempts no explanation of the mystery of solidarity, but without it redemption could not be as total as the scourge of sin. The universality of God's deliverance is his primary concern; the curse of sin is its foil, as the first Adam is the second Adam's. If death is the effect of sin, sin is conquered by the death of Jesus. Dying and rising with Christ, Christians are liberated from sin. The enslaving reign of sin is vanquished by the reign of Christ (Rom 6:1-23; 1 Cor 15:3, 17). The locus of sin is the flesh, the total person hardened against God. Sin is a pseudo-law in the flesh over against the Mosaic Law. Enslaved, sinful humans cannot do the good they will. They lack resources to free themselves, and only Christ can liberate them (Rom 7:1-25). Herein is a basis for later teaching on concupiscence, what Paul refers to as *epithymia*.

For all this, Paul teaches neither determinism to sin nor classical Greek fatalism, whereby fallibility, not irresponsibility, dooms humans to blunders of every kind. The paradox of inevitability and responsibility, the involuntary in the voluntary, stands. Paul knows of a war between the law of the spirit and the law of the flesh. Nowhere does Scripture teach a doctrine of original sin, but cumulatively it does point to the universality, even the inevitability, of sin, from which the race cannot extricate itself. Victory comes only by the grace of Christ's Spirit (Rom 8:1-17).

Theological Reflection

The human person's capacity to close in on itself is a possibility for death, "a return to nothingness" (Athanasius, *On the Incarnation* 34.4-5). Freedom can negate itself in sinful choice. Yet sin is more than immoral choice. Freedom concerns not merely choice expressed in atomized acts; freedom primarily concerns being. Choosing sin, one becomes a sinner. Freedom is less concerned with the choice of objects than with the foundational orientation by which one defines and situates oneself in a relationship to or against God. The capacity for sin touches the absolute at the heart of freedom.

Theology has resorted to a triple registry of affirmations about sin: moral, eschatological, and ontological. In its moral dimension sin has been viewed in relation to law and construed as transgression of divine law, reflected in the light of reason and the precept of love of God and neighbor. Thus the classic definition of Augustine: "Sin is an action, word, or desire opposed to the eternal law. This eternal law is divine reason or will, which orders, maintains, and safeguards the natural order" (*Against Faustus* 2.27; see ST I-II, q. 71, aa. 2 and 6). Law expresses a duty to be done and implies a capacity to freely do it. In sinning, one contradicts one's own being by acting contrary to the law.

In eschatological affirmations, sin is viewed in reference to its consequences. Sin provokes justified chastisement by the order it violates. At the end of history, personal and collective, in the judgment of God the intrinsic malice of sin is definitively revealed and punished. The sanction is not extrinsic and arbitrary but is the unmasking of sin for what it is—an offense against God and an unraveling self-contradiction. Anticipating the end of history, the Church's penitential practice sought a discipline to restore the violated order and to free from sin. Origen and the East viewed penitential practices as purifying inner fires; Cyprian and the West saw them as expiation. Moral and eschatological affirmations are related: the culpable act brings chastisement. Only in the eschaton is sin fully revealed in its personal, social, even cosmic consequences.

A third set of affirmations touches upon Christian freedom in its theological reality. Sin is the loss of grace, an assault on the seal of baptism. Beyond the moral act is its transcendent ground: dialogical relationship in which God reveals Godself in the depths of personal being, where one receives oneself always anew in the divine transforming gift. Sin ruptures this communion and reduces freedom to non-freedom. More than transgression of law, sin is offense against God. At this level sin's social dimension is more fully revealed. The Spirit that sin rejects is the Spirit that unifies Church and society. Every sin, no matter how private, weakens the Church as the Body of Christ and communion in the Spirit. Hence reconciliation with God must also be reconciliation with the Church. Through the mystery of the Church in relation to the world, the interpersonal character of sin is magnified by reason of the sinner's corresponsibility for the injustice that savages the world.

While viewing the Church as the spouse of Christ and temple of the Spirit, the Fathers did not hesitate to hurl against it threats that the Hebrew prophets addressed against Israel for its injustice to the poor. Though avoiding the expression "sinful Church," Vatican II speaks of a Church that embraces sinners in its bosom (LG 14). The Church is at once *sponsa Verbi* and *casta meretrix,* holy by reason of the Spirit's indefectible presence yet needing purification, the dispenser of reconciliation and its subject.

The Irenaean View of Sin

As to the origin and place of sin in Christian life, there has been a diversity of views. The Irenaean vision takes an instrumental view of sin. Creation and redemption are a single order. Humans are created as children, imperfect and immature. Their sin is not the incomprehensibly perverse choice of those who can know and do better but the understandable straying of ignorant, weak children. The contest between good and evil is less the result of a fall than part of a natural order, an environment divinely appointed to allow humans made in God's image to grow into God's likeness in Christ. Sin is unaccomplishment of destiny, retardation, not deterioration; it is a *felix culpa,* a necessity abetting personal development, not forfeit of an original quality. History is testing-ground, person-making pedagogy. God's ordination of sin is in view of an ordination to salvation. Eden is dream, not memory. If the Irenaean perspective makes sin intelligible, it may be at the price of compromising the goodness of creation, for sin appears inevitable, given human imperfection. Creation is for redemption and subordinate to it.

The Augustinian View of Sin

In the anti-Gnostic myth of the Augustinian tradition, God created Adam and Eve good in an idyllic garden. Though finite, their goodness was perfect. Yet as creatures they were mutable, defectible. Eating forbidden fruit, they failed the test of obedience and chose a lower good than God. Self was absolutized. That choice is the origin and essence of sin. Rebelling against God, they experienced the unleashing of concupiscence, a flood of riotous appetites against reason and will. Their guilt

and concupiscence were transmitted to all their posterity. The result is a self-imposed shackling, social disharmony, persons at odds with one another because at odds with themselves.

Humans are not able to not sin; indeed, without grace they can only sin. Freedom is not indifferent before evil. The corruption of sin entails a predisposition to evil. The heart of the matter is character, not choice; freedom has an acquired nature encumbered by habit and history. Yet in the Augustinian view humans are not fundamentally evil. The fall of Adam and Eve was not caused by finitude as such. Further, though sin perverted their created goodness, it did not efface it. The sinner remains creature, and thus the image of God. But the universal proclivity to sin is now a second nature, entailing a "cruel necessity of sinning" (*Perfection of Justice* 9). Thus sin requires the double language of freedom and inevitability, contingency and universality, responsibility and tragedy.

This tradition maintains the moral impotence of humans and the universality of sin without impugning God or human nature. It confronts a double exigence. Against Manichean ontological dualism it asserts the negativity of sin, indeed, its nothingness; against Pelagian moralistic reductionism it asserts the positivity of sin as a power that lays siege and enslaves. Sin is not event or substance; it is not being but its privation, due to a style of life in which freedom is used contrary to its innate dynamism. It is the choice of vacuum instead of value. Such insanity has no explanation aside from a failure in the will to reasonably respond to an obligatory motive. Explanation seeks the cause of something. But sin does not conduce to being; it is an irrational forfeit of being, "a return to nothingness." Nonexistence needs no cause. "To try to discover the cause of such defection, which is deficient, not efficient, is like trying to see darkness or hear silence" (*City of God* 12.7). Excuses there may be, but not reasons. For basic sin is not yielding to reasonableness but failing to do so.

Yet, paradoxically, sin is more than mere privation, a failure of self-transcendence. It is positive revolt. The liberty that was a capacity for God is turned against itself and becomes a power for enslavement and death. For God "to purify the soul is a greater work than to create it out of nothingness, for the contrarieties of sin, its desires and affections, are more completely opposed to and offer greater resistance to God than does nothingness which offers no resistance" (John of the Cross, *The Ascent of Mount Carmel,* I.6). Sin is unreal, but its consequences are devastatingly palpable.

The Augustinian tradition does not assert that Adam and Eve were inclined to evil from the outset, lest evil and finitude coincide and God be accountable for creating them sinful. To avoid tracing sin to God or an essentially flawed nature, Augustinians posit a fall that radically injures human nature. The doctrine of original sin affirms the collective responsibility of the race, the ubiquity of sin, a universal need for redemption. Often the damaging use of this doctrine—for example, to keep people resigned to injustice—is counter to its intent and inner logic. Frequently, however, natural good dimensions of finitude have been tagged sinful by many espousing this doctrine. And too often the goodness of finitude is compromised as something to be lamented as impeding "higher values," to be fought, transcended, or accepted with reluctant resignation. To some extent, too, Augustinians render the fall incomprehensible by making it a fall of finite but perfect creatures. This is the price of sustaining the goodness of creation. Creation is intrinsically good; it is no mere means to redemption, by which God restores, even betters, the glory of creation.

In the Irenaean approach, God creates humans imperfect, which leads to sin as preparation for redemption; in the Augustinian approach, redemption is response to the fall. Neither Irenaeans nor Augustinians directly deny the goodness of creation. Yet Augustinians tend to identify dimensions of finitude as unruly children of the fall rather than as aspects of a good creation. The Irenaean tradition tends to identify dimensions of finitude as ingredient to immaturity and to be vanquished in the process of divinization rather than as integral to a good creation. Both endanger the goodness of human creatureliness.

Sin in Modern Thought

Though there is no developed orthodox doctrine of sin, the Augustinian vision dominated Western imagination. Critical biblical study and advances in the natural and social sciences show its lyricism, biologism, and juridicism to be flawed. Sin is either impossible because of the gift of righteousness or inescapable due to a constitutive defect in nature. The first alternative is counterfactual, the second Manichean. How then explain the origin of sin so as to avoid the Augustinian vision's pitfalls while retrieving its genuine insights, the proclivity of the heart to self-inflation or self-deflation, the solidarity of the race in evil, the weight of temporality? How hold together freedom and the tragic estrangement that makes humans chronically ineffectual in realizing moral ideals without equating finitude with sin? How skirt the naive optimism of neo-Pelagian moralism and saturnine pessimism of neo-Manichean fatalism? With insights from modern philosophy and social science, theology better fathoms the symbolic richness of humanity's dark underside.

Several factors elucidate the heart's waywardness. The human spirit is at once self-transcendent and bounded, finite and open to infinity. Herein resides the possibility of creativeness and destructiveness. Of transcendence and finitude angst is born. A dizzying infinity of possibilities must be restricted by choice. Frantically anxious to become all its possibilities, the self in its hubris may become forgetful of finitude and make of self a god. Or fearfully anxious for security, the slothful self may retreat from freedom to mediocrity. Either way, by hubris or *acedia*, exploitative self-assertion or lack of any self-assertion, lies alienation, incoherence, surrender of the true self in a failure to balance the polarities of existence.

From the depths of angst-ridden spirit rises endless active and passive aggression toward self and others. Angst is good, not sinful; it is a precondition of creativity as well as sin. Where love of God and neighbor are one's fundamental option, angst wears another face as a goad to creative personal and social achievement. Freedom as transcendence is undetermined yet hedged by a constitutive fallibility due to the rift between the infinity and finitude of human being, which is thus vulnerable to sin. Fallibility and angst are not penalties for a primal fall but ontological constituents of existence. Moreover, the difficulty of integrating finitude and infinity is compounded by humanity's epistemic distance from a God not immediately experienced but grasped only anticipatorily in a night of faith and hope. Goodness does not overwhelm; anxious human loves will be misplaced. For disproportion bedevils humanity; it desires totality yet approaches it only fragmentarily. Thus sin knows a tragic inevitability.

In Romans 7 Paul voices experience of a divided self trapped between appetites irresistibly luring to evil and ineffectually summoning to good. Spiritual aspirations outrun achievements; an unbridgeable gap separates "I want" and "I ought" from "I can." The clamoring appetites that defy truth and goodness are concupiscence. Psychoanalytic theory illumines the phenomenon of the unintegrated self. The id, a pool of unconscious libidinal energies, is controlled by the "pleasure principle" and spontaneously clamors for satisfaction. The emergent ego, aligned with the "reality principle," polices the id, not always with success. The similarities of the id and its operations to concupiscence are patent.

The id-ego tension is one facet of the modern theological person-nature tension. Sin is not the genesis of the tension. It is a natural developmental phenomenon; neither the id nor concupiscence is sinful or a consequence of sin, though they can be a precondition for sin, which in turn makes them even more divisive. Humans are born "fallen," alienated from their essential being and unity. The challenge is not to eliminate one polarity, which would result in a half-person, but to unify and integrate this manifold in love of God and neighbor.

The reservoir of spontaneous appetites labeled as "id" or "concupiscence" holds creative as well as destructive stirrings. The concupiscence that leads to evil is the same erotic drive that leads to passionate love of God. The Rabbinic *yetzer*, Freud's libido, theology's concupiscence all denote basically good psychic energies that can be directed in morally opposite ways and are not as such an ethico-religious liability. To bank the fires of passion is to extinguish the lights of civilization. Struggle for integration is a normal growth pattern, not a penalty for sin, and it is facilitated or aggravated by parents who transmit to offspring their own and the culture's values. A child's psychic shape is the parent's second legacy, and it takes hold in the superego, which internalizes parental and cultural values and, for weal or woe, becomes a powerful prevolitional moral orientation. The superego as a kind of prereflective conscience stores up aggression once vented on external authorities and visits it upon the ego. Thus guilt is born.

Finally, concupiscence ought not be reduced to sexual libido. It is also unbridled lust for power, wealth, even holiness, which is far more destructive. Anxiety and concupiscence feed a radical ineptitude—not so much that humans are biased toward evil but that they are unable to love the great good that beckons. "Our hearts are not in our power," said Augustine (*Gift of Perseverance* 13).

The Communal Nature of Sin

Social science affords a deeper understanding of the transhistorical, communal character of sin. Persons are socialized in solidarity with sinful societies. Sin is not a static, purely private reality but a snowballing social force that intensifies the spiritual ineptitude of individuals. The sin of the world shapes freedom prior to choice. Inserted into an environment contaminated by collective evil, persons are infected by the contagion before being able to resist. In their historicity they are inextricably situated in a web of greed, pride, inertia, and hostility. Evil is choice, but more, it is transsubjective, other. The sin of all is the sin of each, the sin of each the sin of all. The beguiling serpent is within but also without, always already there, waiting. Evil finds humans and they continue it.

Humans are agents but also victims. They are what they choose to be, but also what others decide for them. Coming to freedom is a social as well as personal adventure. A tangle of sinful persons, deeds, and institutions weaves a history of betrayal of God, self, and others. To be is to be willy-nilly complicit in a network of sin. No wall isolates the self from its culture; the currents of sinful history flow through humans, not around them. Being is being-with (*Mitsein*).

What people do with freedom depends on what they are; what they are is what they have become socially and is largely conditioned by their milieu. As Augustine put it, there may be free choice (*liberum arbitrium*) but not freedom (*libertas*)— (*Spirit and Letter*). Freedom is fettered. As Paul knew, sin is a demonic power of mythical magnitude. It "enters" the world, "inhabits," "abounds," "reigns." Before being ethical and juridical, it is ontological. Sin and freedom are antithetical. Freedom is proximity to God, harmony with divine purposes; sin is distance from, ineptitude for, God's presence and purpose. Self-possession and alienation are more fundamental than choice.

Unmanageable anxiety and concupiscence, epistemic distance from God, and situated freedom inevitably conduce to actual and habitual sin and make for the "realism of sin." Sin is the person's true situation before God. "Before God," not consciousness, is the measure of sin. Prophets must denounce sin to consciousness, which connives with evil by self-deceit and bad faith. Sin is more than sins; it is a radical mode of being, Ezekiel's "heart of stone." It runs deeper than conscious intention and choice; it hides at the level of what one spontaneously loves, which shapes what one is and does. Even in the converted lurks a kind of will not to love the good, a dark involuntary, a *curvitas,* an egoism. Captivation becomes a captivity freely willed. Each one feels the undertow of an evil that is one's own and not one's own. Each one is *simul iustus et peccator.* Conversion reveals the bitter fact that even good acts are marked by a coefficient of ambiguity, for the best heart's love ever falls short. "All our righteous deeds are like a filthy cloth" (Isa 64:5).

Further, anxiety, concupiscence, and sin-laden worlds lead to deformation of truth. The basic form of alienation is disregard for the transcendental precepts of self-transcendence: be attentive, intelligent, reasonable, responsible. Bias sets in motion a distortion of the situation, a dynamic of decline. The psychic bias of the neurotic flees from insight to affect. The individual bias of the egoist attends only to insights conducive to personal advance. The group bias of collective egoism, jealous of its privileges, rejects threatening insights calling for transformation. Lastly, the general bias of common sense rejects the searching insights of theory as nonsense.

Bias blocks personal and social growth. While bias manifests itself in inattentiveness and obtuseness, its roots are volitional. One is willing to attend to and understand only what one is willing to accept and choose. Antecedent unwillingness to respond to or create value strangles the capacity to understand. Lacking will to give free reign to the unrestricted desire to know, one stifles freedom as one's own, or the group's "knowledge" becomes coextensive with the knowable. Broader considerations calculated to upset the narrower coherence of biased individuals and groups must come from another.

In light of this depth analysis, the quality of an action may not indicate the basic character of its agent, for the act may not be in continuity with the self. A distinction is in order between origins of behavior that are relatively total, or central, and those that are relatively partial, or peripheral, between transcendental and categorical freedom. To love yet to act unlovingly are not always mutually exclusive. The moral badness of an act does not necessarily negate the basic goodness of a person.

Traditional theology evolved a distinction between two levels of actual sin—lethal, or mortal, and everyday, or venial (ST I-II, q. 88, aa. 1 and 2). The former leads to radical alienation from God and eternal damnation if not remitted; the latter does not. Mortal sin was identified by three necessary and sufficient conditions: gravity of matter, sufficiency of deliberation, full consent. Gravity of matter refers to the seriousness of the obligation violated and the extent of its violation. Preparing ministers for the confessional, where, by Tridentine prescription, sins had to be labeled and totaled, theology was given to cataloging and measuring the relative seriousness of the obligations of divine law and the extent of violations by reason of circumstance and psychological disposition. The mode of thought was casuistic, legalistic. A taxonomy of sins categorized them much as crimes and misdemeanors are sorted out and set guidelines for assessing guilt.

The Fundamental Option

Modern theologians found it difficult to reconcile this traditional view of sin with the experience that basic moral goodness may persist even in a person whose acts occasionally conflict with that goodness. If one assumes that mortal sins occur with frequency and are coped with by equally frequent recourse to the sacrament of reconciliation, one must also assume that humans frequently and abruptly reorient themselves and lightly pass back and forth from basic goodness to total estrangement from God. Because mercurial conversions appear contrary to experience, modern theology stresses what it calls the "fundamental option," the basic moral tonality of a person's life. This exercise of core freedom can deepen or reverse itself. But commitment to a vision of life and its values can survive sporadic deviations. Contrary commitment is not ruled out; neither is it assumed because of instances of erratic conduct.

An option for or against God cannot be eluded (ST I-II, q. 89, a. 6). Once made, such an option orients the story line of one's life. Foundational self-determinations provide the true basis for talk of a life of grace and its negation by mortal sin. It is unlikely that so profound a reversal as changing the prevailing trajectory of one's life can simplistically be identified with one of those acts traditionally classified as mortal sins. An act may be seriously sinful without being mortally so. There are degrees of gravity if not of mortality. Descent into mortal sin is usually an extended, subtle process. Though it may climax in one concrete evil act or omission, it cannot be simply identified with it.

Focus on the fundamental option, generally prereflexive, brings sins of omission, often overshadowed, into view. Too often conscience tallies its sins using traditional act-analysis while totally unmindful of the parable of final judgment, where condemnation is levied against those who "did not do for one of these least ones, [hence] did not do for me" (see Mt 25:31-46). When the focus is on atomized sinful acts, life-long selfish apathy can parade as inno-cence, even virtue. This newer perspective does not scuttle mortal sin but prefers to view it as a basic self-determination rather than as a class of isolated acts. An "up-right" life may cloak a deep-seated option that deifies self.

Social Sin

Due largely to the Church's penitential practice, sin became excessively priva-tized, individualistic. But sin always trans-lates into interpersonal relationships. A dualism dividing interiority from history is wrongheaded. In Scripture there is per-sonal sin, knowingly and freely chosen, and social sin accompanied by group blindness and egoism that is unconscious (e.g., Mt 13:13-15). The two are interrelated. A cul-ture, through its institutions, creates con-sciousness, and the injustice woven into them falsifies the consciousness of those they socialize. This is a corrective to the liberal mind that thinks individuals are born into a neutral environment where good is available to those who choose it.

Social sin is not a precise category. Yet it calls attention to important realities. So-cial sin is not merely an evil act of one or several persons that adversely affects soci-ety. What is proper to social sin is that it is organized sin; its subject is a collectivity. Its evil is born less of conscious delibera-tion and choice than of blindness. It issues in destructive consequences but no guilt in the ordinary sense.

Social sin embodies itself at several lev-els. It is found in dehumanizing behavior patterns of institutions that incarnate col-lective life. Destructiveness is masked; consciousness does not recognize it until its negative features slowly emerge over a long period. Even then, people are slow to acknowledge the systemic evil in their midst. Bias obstructs sight. The sheer massiveness of a social system creates a consciousness that conspires with it and looks upon it as irreplaceable, especially when one's own purposes are served by it. Inertia reigns.

Secondly, social evil permeates cultural, including religious, symbols that grip im-agination, fire hearts, and reinforce unjust institutional arrangements. Bias again be-gets blindness as symbol systems become ideologies that rationalize moral entropy and social devastation.

Thirdly, social sin is at work in the false consciousness created by institutions and ideologies that allows people to participate in a network of oppression with self-righteousness. False consciousness varies in intensity and runs from unconscious identification with the dominant culture to defensive rationalization of it. Only a values-inversion in consciousness leads to *metanoia*.

Finally, social sin surfaces in the collec-tive decisions and consent generated by distorted consciousness. Such choices and collusion with them, while appearing free and deliberate, may simply be logical, me-chanical consequences of a perversion built into oppressive institutions and skewed symbols and reflected in the illu-sions of consciousness.

Thus a dialectic exists between personal and social sin. Sinful social structures are created and maintained by sinful persons, and personal sin makes alienating institu-tions worse by reinforcing and magnifying their impact. The sinful use of power by an individual or group with authority may be-long to the category of personal sin. But the structures produced by corporate decision assume a logic of their own, inflict aliena-tion by molding consciousness, and be-come anonymous agents of social sin. Social sin in turn produces an environment in which personal sin is all but inescapable. Sin spirals; the irrational accumulates. Thus the need for a double analysis, per-sonal and sociopolitical.

The theology of sin, like all theologies, is a political hermeneutic. This becomes increasingly clear as the constitutive interdependence of humans intensifies. Intricate national and international structural arrangements facilitate and extend sinful behavior, though no person or persons may have set up an organization precisely to increase the world's evil. People do not sin to sin, but they sin for specious good reasons. Any organization is for creating or increasing a gratification to be pursued by moral and/or immoral means.

In the case of social sin, searching out sinfulness where alone it can be found—in free wills—is problematic. An institution is not one person but many, whose wills affect its behavior. Moral responsibility is shared, diffused to a degree that defies analysis. Persons come and go; the evil impact of institutions perdures in structure and function. There is no easy path from a perception of sinfulness to a fingering of particular sinners. The category "social sin" attempts to recognize the wrongness of the situation without exaggerating the personal responsibility of individuals complicit at various levels.

Most of what is meant by "social sin" cannot be disposed of by a simple change of individual hearts. Society with its institutions is more than the sum of its component individuals; social sin is more than the sum of personal sins. It is individuals, not *qua* individuals but in their togetherness, who are the subject of society and its objectifications and are collectively responsible for its good and evil. Social sin derives from individuals in their associated existence, and its consequences transcend individual, even collective, intentions. What they are not accountable for as separate individuals they are responsible for as associated individuals.

Social sin thus presents an enormous practical problem: structural reform, a task difficult to initiate, more difficult to persevere in, impossible to complete. Yet total liberation demands conversion not only of individuals but of the network of their relations. Changing structures is requisite for changing hearts. The challenge is insuperable. In its belief in humanity's perfectibility and its search for innocence, enlightened modernity cannot recognize its own radical moral impotence but only pallid, limited evils that technology can manage. It cannot entertain the ineradicability and destructiveness of personal and social sinfulness, and therefore cannot ultimately sense a need for forgiveness.

Yet the mystery of iniquity yields to the anomaly of good. Sin is but one vector of existence; a graceless world or human person has never been. History is perdition, but more so salvation. God's salvific will may flower in apocatastasis as divine purpose outstrips human folly. Humanity crucifies God and itself, but God continues pursuit on the cross, where "the banality of evil" is embraced in unconditional forgiving love, transformed into sin, and sin into grace. "In [Christ] all the fullness was pleased to dwell, and through him to reconcile all things for him, making peace by the blood of his cross [through him], whether those on earth or those in heaven. And you who once were alienated and hostile in mind because of evil deeds he has now reconciled in his fleshly body through his death, to present you holy, without blemish, and irreproachable before him" (Col 1:19-22).

See also CONSCIENCE; CONVERSION; DESIRE; EVIL; FREEDOM; GRACE; PENANCE, PENITENCE; REDEMPTION; TEMPTATION; VIRTUE; WILL.

Bibliography: S. Duffy, "Our Hearts of Darkness: Original Sin Revisited," TS 49 (1988) 597–622. G. Quell et al., "Hamartanō," *Theological Dictionary of the New Testament,* ed. G. Kittel (Grand Rapids, Mich.: Eerdmans, 1964) 1:264–316. S. Lyonnet and P. Gervais, "Péche-Pécheur," *D.Spir.,* vol. 12, cols. 790–853. A. Min, *Dialectic of Salvation: Issues in Theology of Liberation* (Albany, N.Y.: State Univ. of New York Press, 1989). R. Niebuhr, *The Nature and Destiny of Man* (New York: Scribner's, 1941-1943). P. Ricoeur, *The Symbolism of Evil* (New York: Harper & Row, 1967).

STEPHEN J. DUFFY

SINGLE LIFE

The single life is one way to foster intimacy with Christ; marriage is another. It is a misconception to identify the single vocation mainly in relation to the marital life, as if singleness had no identity of its own. This line of reasoning places singleness below marriage or conventual life, unfairly relegating it to a second-class position. Clearly, before anyone is married, vowed, or ordained, he or she is single. If a marriage ends because of separation or the death of a spouse, one is single again. While singleness predates marriage or community membership, it must not be defined negatively in relation to them but as a state of life to be celebrated in its own right.

Both Christian celibacy and Christian marriage are calls from God. Both are vocations requiring commitment to people entrusted to one's care as members of Christ's Body. Both are providential forms of life in which men and women consecrate themselves to unfold, with the help of grace, God's redemptive plan for all ages.

One must not allow oneself to drift halfheartedly into marriage or the single life without reflecting upon and praying about what path one is called to take. Singlehood as well as the married life may become a meaningless burden, devoid of life-giving possibilities, unless one periodically rekindles and renews the commitment to give oneself to Christ and others in joyful surrender. Otherwise being single can open one to the traps of self-centered preoccupation or sensual indulgence.

Pursuit of a celibate calling enables a person to be more abidingly present to all who need care. In married life this outreach of love to others is somewhat restricted by the obligation to meet primary responsibilities to the family. When one is single, one's expression of love and service has to embrace whomever God sends one's way, wherever the need for care arises in the course of a day, a month, a year. To be sure, this availability can be lived out in many ways. Some single people may be called to ministry among the homeless; others may become artists, scientists, manual laborers, entertainers, technicians, teachers.

Even when personal options are limited by circumstances—e.g., finding oneself single by virtue of "not meeting the right person" or suddenly losing a spouse—one has a choice to make: to celebrate being single in joyful surrender to God or to grow bitter because of it.

If we can see that both Christian marriage and Christian singleness are expressions of love for the risen Lord, then both states become deeply meaningful. Whether we marry or stay single, we can freely decide to incarnate our love for God and humanity in the situation in which Holy Providence places us. Lacking this vision and commitment, singlehood may become more of a burden than a basis for celebrating the Christian life. No matter how surrendered to the single state one may be, one is not free from suffering. To conform to Christ means to conform to the cross. This suffering is less a matter of what one gives up than of what one takes up in Christ's name. Choosing to live as a single person following the call of Christ necessarily promotes greater availability for ministry. This means in turn exposing oneself to the possibility of greater hurt and pain.

Christian single persons can be signs of God's love in the world only if they remain humble in the face of their calling. A holier-than-thou attitude obstructs the channeling of God's love to others. It corrupts celibacy and renders it worthless in the eyes of God. It destroys the basic meaning of self-giving love lived in the light of Jesus' own commitment to singlehood, for he himself was a single person in the world.

Single Christians who strive to remain faithful to God's call may be tempted not to pursue excellence, to maintain the status quo, to put their own interests and material needs above what is spiritually right and at times countercultural. They may be inclined to forget what their commitment to Christ really entails. They may want to conform only to their environment to avoid being hurt or feeling lonely. Peer pressure may triumph over intimacy with the Lord.

When single persons find themselves alone, laughed at, isolated from the "in" crowd, at odds with a society that does not welcome their efforts to witness to the value of singlehood in Christ, they may feel overwhelmed by the desire to escape it all. Even if the time is not right or the person they meet is wrong, they may jump at the chance to start a family of their own. To base a calling to marriage on a crisis of loneliness or to despair is unwise, to say nothing of the risk one takes of being unfaithful to one's divine life-call. At such times, under pressure, some people may make a premature decision, one they may live to regret for a lifetime. They listen to their own fears and confused voices or to the "me only" input of a secular culture. Silenced are the whispers of the Spirit.

To be sure, something similar may happen to married people. In moments of marital tension, when honeymoon bliss is gone, a husband or wife may fantasize about the comforts and freedoms enjoyed by single friends and colleagues, little realizing that they, too, are going through similar times of turmoil and confusion. The truth is that both states of lay life enjoy benefits and burdens. As experience teaches, this is by no means the whole story. Both states share not only in the joy of the resurrection but in the lonely sadness of Christ's agony and death.

The single Christian strives despite suffering to disclose God's divine generosity in a wounded world. It does not matter whether one is a nurse, machinist, teacher, administrator, fireman, cook, artist, dancer, or author. Every field implies some routine aspects that in and by themselves may seem meaningless from the viewpoint of a higher calling to share in Christ's transformation of the world.

In the light of their commitment to Christ, sexual expression for single Catholics means much more than mere "sex." The single male and female who live with the Christ as their center witness to the wholeness of the masculine and of the feminine, to the way in which these two sides of being human sustain each other. Empty sexual experiences are demeaning and out of touch with what it means to be male or female in Christ. In the light of God's love for us, single persons try to love others in a nonpossessive, nonmanipulative, self-giving, compassionate way. The key to such quality relationships is charity—a human attempt to love others with the love with which we have been loved by God.

Single Catholics are called to set high standards that exemplify the art of loving. This means rising above the tendency to get involved with others and truly befriending them. Such loving includes the risk of falling into emotional exclusiveness and consequent envy and jealousy. It also includes the risk of betrayed trust, mutual strife, and power struggles. But what is the alternative? A selfish, little life, isolated and withdrawn, that casts a shadow over the single vocation as such. Too often single men and women end up without any friends because they fear the risk of loving.

To embrace Christ as the center of one's life is to embrace everything and everyone in him. The relaxed detachment from exclusivity characteristic of such affectionate, inclusive loving enables others to witness in single women and men the transforming effect of a firm commitment to Christ. To imitate him is to attain the grace of loving others as God has loved us.

Detached yet committed loving is attained only by opening one's heart and soul to the all-inclusive love of Christ. The single vocation grants one the freedom to be flexible. While one's life reflects a definite direction, one must be open to the grace of the moment, ready to give up futile attempts to control life so that one can flow with the gifts and challenges of every new day.

It helps to try continually to take a wider view of things, a more transcendent perspective that enables one to trust in a Power greater than oneself and one's necessarily limited vision. Only in surrender to God's will, written in the directives of the daily situation, can single Catholics become peaceful, reconciling persons in the family and community that God calls them to serve.

In conclusion, Christian singles represent, in a special style and intensity, the receptivity every human being bears to the transcendent horizon of all that is. Human hearts, as St. Augustine said, are restless until they rest in God. All people are called to commitment and consecration. Because we live in a civilization in which the sense of ego satisfaction outstrips the sense of responsibility to foster the spiritual transformation of life and world, this call stands in danger of neglect. More than ever Christians need to celebrate the witness of committed single women and men who, by their very lives, participate in the transforming and redeeming plan of God for every creature on earth.

See also CELIBACY; COMMUNITY; FRIENDSHIP; INTIMACY; LAY SPIRITUALITY; MARRIAGE; MARRIAGE, MYSTICAL; RELIGIOUS LIFE; SEXUALITY; SINGLE PARENT; SOLITUDE; VIRGINITY.

Bibliography: S. Muto, *Celebrating the Single Life: A Spirituality for Single Persons in Today's World* (New York: Doubleday, 1982; rpt. New York: Crossroad/Continuum, 1989). S. Muto and A. van Kaam, *Commitment: Key to Christian Maturity* (Mahwah, N.J.: Paulist, 1989). A. van Kaam, *The Woman at the Well* (Denville, N.J.: Dimension Books, 1976).

SUSAN MUTO

SINGLE PARENT

Spirituality, once almost exclusively monastic in orientation, has been enriched in recent years by both lay and feminist spiritualities. While both may touch tangentially on the single state, single parenthood is an area as yet significantly overlooked. There have always been single parents, usually by circumstance, not by choice. They were often ostracized (in cases of out-of-wedlock births) or taken in by the extended family (in cases of death, divorce, or abandonment).

The sexual revolution, the feminist movement, soaring divorce rates, two-career families, economic necessity, political oppression, and numbers of abandoned or neglected children have effectively reduced the prevalence of nuclear families since Vatican II to a ratio of one in twenty-one in the United States. The myth of the nuclear family, however, continues to influence attitudes toward single parents; they are considered to be relatively rare or are somehow put at fault.

Sexual violence against women appears at an all-time high, figuring not only in the breakup of families but also in the reluctance of increasing numbers of women to enter into marriage, or at least to delay it until they feel emotionally and financially secure.

Ministering to the pastoral and spiritual needs of this group demands an awareness of its complex makeup. Single-parent families tend to be less well off economically because most are headed by women who earn less than men and who are also likely to lack job skills and the education necessary for advancement. Of those single by choice, not all became pregnant by choice and so may not have had the desired financial and educational security enjoyed by professional people who delay parenthood until later. The person single by choice is, at least theoretically, spared the emotional pain often central to the struggle of the person single by circumstance, who may initially receive support and sympathy from the community in dealing with abandonment, death, or divorce. But people soon forget and the pain lingers on. The previously joint venture and challenge of raising a child or children now becomes the total responsibility of one parent, who must deal with both his or her personal grief and that of the children.

While a Post-Cana support group may exist for those who have been married, little or nothing usually exists on the parish level for adoptive or foster parents or for unmarried parents. One must look further. In a society with few built-in supports for the single parent, parenting puts tremendous demands on the individual to be mother, father, homemaker, wage earner, friend, and companion to the child or children. Physical or economic limitations or the fact of being divorced can restrict one's sphere of socializing when one most needs adult contacts. In addition to a sense of emptiness, other pain is inevitable. Sooner or later children may get into trouble, have academic or social problems, be injured, or express anger or deprivation because they lack a father or a mother and blame the parent or themselves.

When such crises arrive, one's spirituality is sorely tested. Unless it is vibrant and healthy and can rely on a strong support system, the single parent risks either being overwhelmed by the moment or "toughing it out," possibly at the expense of the children.

There can be no one spirituality for such a diverse group, but it is clear that only an abiding trust in a provident God can carry a single parent through the difficult times, because there is no spouse to lean on, to use as a "sounding board," to share the same love and commitment toward the children. Friends can be a big help, but they can never share the same sense of responsibility for the spiritual and human development of a unique child of God.

Prayer ought to be the warp and woof holding the single-parent family together, for as the children grow, the dangers to their spiritual well-being increase. Materialism is perhaps the greatest corruptive influence faced by such families. In divorce the child often plays off parent against parent to see how much can be gotten in exchange for a rather shallow concept of love.

Similar risks arise when a parent overindulges to compensate for a sense of guilt or inadequacy in failing to provide the child with the "normalcy" of the nuclear family: two parents, brothers and sisters. Only a person deeply rooted in God will accept that more is not necessarily better. If he or she lives this, hopefully the children will also, and together they will find value in the more profound realities of care and concern for the needs of each other and of the broader community.

What should constitute the prayer life or spirituality of single parents? It should be rooted in a faith community. For Catholics, regular celebration of the Eucharist is certainly the ideal, but daily prayer and spiritual reading from Scripture or other sources are an essential goal for both parent and children, especially once the latter are of school age. Living the liturgical year in the home helps develop traditions and a spirituality that will further bind the family together and can even foster deeper family discussions.

The single parent, more than the married couple or single person, must often contend with Church, family, social, and/or professional disapproval. In outlining a spirituality, one needs to encourage the discovery of God's presence in all things. One finds God especially in the highs and lows of the single-parent experience, in learning to trust one's experience as prayerful and holy in itself. This means learning to make time for self and God, seeking out silence to listen for God's guidance in family decision-making and to refresh one's interior life. The ultimate challenge is an unceasing increase in receptivity, simplicity, and gentleness in dealing with children and self. Single-parent spirituality necessarily grows out of the limitations and needs of each individual, but always in the context of the broader community to which one belongs and in which one must feel a vital part with a genuine contribution to offer. This contribution may simply be the example of fidelity to one's specific responsibilities.

Everyone makes mistakes. One should learn from them but not dwell on them. A healthy spirituality is future-oriented, hope-filled, trying to create a more God-centered future in the present moment for self and child. This means that there are definite social and political dimensions to this spirituality. Sooner or later these social and political considerations need to play a more active role if one is to help create that better future for oneself and one's children. With God's help, a social and political agenda will emerge to ameliorate conditions for future single parents, to facilitate their parenting, to enhance their possibilities for spiritual and personal growth.

Single parents and their birth, adopted, or foster children must not be allowed to "fall through the cracks" of Church and society. These children will be the parents of tomorrow. Today they learn the meaning of God, Church, community, and family. The entire community and its pastoral ministers should be concerned lest they grow up with stunted or distorted notions of the meaning of God, Church, community, and family.

See also CHILD, CHILDREN; FEMINIST SPIRITUALITY; LAY SPIRITUALITY; MARGINALIZED, THE; MARRIAGE; SINGLE LIFE.

Bibliography: J. Wolski Conn, ed., *Women's Spirituality: Resources for Christian Development* (New York: Paulist, 1986). V. Finn, *Pilgrims in This World: A Lay Spirituality* (New York: Paulist, 1990). J. Lechman, *The Spirituality of Gentleness: Growing Toward Christian Wholeness* (San Francisco: Harper & Row, 1987). S. Muto, *Celebrating the Single Life* (New York: Crossroad, 1989).

SONYA A. QUITSLUND

SLOTH

See ACEDIA; DEADLY SINS.

SOCIAL JUSTICE

See JUSTICE.

SOCIAL SIN

See SIN.

SOLIDARITY

As used in theological writings and Church documents, the term *solidarity* refers to the empathetic foundation of Christian love. In order to truly serve the neighbor, that love must be born out of an identification or solidarity with the neighbor in his or her joys, suffering, and struggles. The call to solidarity is a call to affirm in one's life the interdependence and unity of humankind before God; what happens to one happens to all. As a response to the reality of human interdependence, solidarity is a moral virtue that promotes the common good and affirms the intrinsic value of all persons, who share filial bonds as children of the Creator.

The human community is a reflection of the divine community, the Trinity; the practice of solidarity is a response not only to other persons but also to their Creator. To exclude others from full participation in society is thus not only to commit an injustice against other human beings but also to commit a sin against God (John Paul II, *On Social Concern* 38-40).

If solidarity implies an affirmation of human community, then it implies a special affirmation of those persons who have historically been excluded or ostracized from the human community: the hungry, the naked, the sick, the "least ones" (see Mt 25:31-46). Chapter 25 of Matthew's Gospel speaks of Jesus Christ's identification with the powerless; hence the Christian's identification with Jesus Christ is verified by his or her own identification with the powerless. Solidarity with the powerless and an identification with their suffering reveal the many ways in which human beings continue to deny and undermine the unity of the human family, thereby denying the Creator.

Commitment to solidarity with the powerless, then, impels the Christian to join them in their struggle for justice, i.e., their struggle to be recognized as full members of the human community (John Paul II, *On Social Concern* 39; *On Human Work* 8). Solidarity with one's brothers and sisters is the verification of one's unity with God (Isa 58:6-7; Jer 22:13-16; Amos 5:21-24; Mt 25:31-46; 1 Jn 2:3-11; 4:7-21).

See also CATHOLIC ACTION; CATHOLIC WORKER MOVEMENT; COMMUNITY; COMPASSION; CREATION; JUSTICE; LIBERATION THEOLOGY, INFLUENCE ON SPIRITUALITY; LOVE; MARGINALIZED, THE; POOR, THE; POWER; PRAXIS; SERVICE; UNITY.

Bibliography: Pope John Paul II, *On Human Work—Laborem Exercens* (Washington: USCC, 1981); *On Social Concern—Sollicitudo Rei Socialis* (Washington: USCC, 1987). G. Baum and R. Ellsberg, eds., *The Logic of Solidarity* (Maryknoll, N.Y.: Orbis, 1989).

ROBERTO S. GOIZUETA

SOLITUDE

Solitude refers to the time and space wherein a person is alone for the purpose of realizing greater union with God. In Christian spirituality the examples of Jesus seeking solitude for prayer are basic to the various ways solitude has been understood as integral to a maturing prayer life. The Gospel of Luke gives special prominence to those prayer times of Jesus. "He would withdraw to deserted places to pray" (Lk 5:16).

Early centuries of Christian experience included Desert Fathers and Mothers whose lifestyle spoke powerfully to the role of solitude for persons devoted to the ways of prayerful union with God. Gradually monasticism developed as a prayerful way of life with a strong community emphasis. Nevertheless, the personal dedication of each member of the community was highlighted in the word *monastic*. To this day a monastic is one whose life is consecrated to God alone. Consequently, even though this personal consecration is lived out in a community, a monastic spends much time in solitude.

Aloneness with God, which is the reason for the Christian attraction to solitude, is not a matter of loneliness. Genuine solitude is rooted in each person's uniqueness. In limitless love God created each human person with a possibility for sharing divine life in a personal way that can never be duplicated. This absolute uniqueness of each person testifies beautifully to the unique tripersonal life of a Trinitarian God, in whose image and likeness each person is created. At the same time, this Trinitarian image and likeness moves each person to fulfillment in community.

Experiences of solitude can be cherished as privileged times of preparation for the culminating moment of solitude, the hour of death. Then and there, in that final moment of aloneness, God brings to fulfillment the union desired and deepened in each solitary experience throughout life.

Making room for experiences of solitude presents new challenges in modern technological societies. The rapid pace of life, the urbanization process with its crowded living conditions, and the constant communication provided by the media often present almost insurmountable difficulties to Christians longing for periods of solitude in some regular patterns. In the midst of continual hurry and noise, the human spirit continues to cry out for the stillness and quiet found in solitude.

Since the Second Vatican Council many Christians have begun to find new ways to make time and space for God in their lives. Retreat houses continue to flourish and include many laypersons among their retreatants. Individual directed retreats have become more available and more appreciated. New hermitages have been erected for private retreats. Places of prayer are beginning to emerge in neighborhoods and parishes. Prayer spaces are being inserted into lives busy with household tasks and with myriad forms of work responsibilities. There is every reason to hope that in the constantly maturing prayer life of the Church, Christian men and women in all cultures will continue to cherish periods and places of solitude.

See also DESERT; EREMITICAL LIFE; MONASTICISM, MONASTIC SPIRITUALITY; LAY SPIRITUALITY; PRAYER; RETREAT, RETREAT MOVEMENT.

Bibliography: C. F. Jegen, "Space and Time for the Spirit," *Lutheran Woman Today* 2 (January 1989) 3-6.

CAROL FRANCES JEGEN, B.V.M.

SORROW

See COMPUNCTION; TEARS, GIFT OF.

SOUL

The human individual's inherent capacity for selfhood, self-awareness, and subjectivity, the principle of human knowing and responsible freedom, has in Christian tradition and much of philosophical history been called "soul." Post-Enlightenment authors have used such terms as "infinite striving" (Lessing), "self-explication of the Idea" (Hegel), "the difference between ego and superego" (Freud), "existentiality" (Jaspers), "thereness" (Heidegger), "primordial realization of the future" (Bloch). Vatican II, in contrast to most earlier official Church documents, referred more often to "person" than to "soul," emphasizing that the human person is one, "though made of body and soul" (GS 14). Nevertheless, later in the same article we read that we are "not being mocked by a deceptive fantasy springing from mere physical or social influences" when we recognize in ourselves "a spiritual and immortal soul," but are "getting to the depths of the very truth of the matter."

Whatever the term, what is agreed is that human beings are spirit as well as flesh. Yet we have no experience at all of this spiritual aspect of ourselves except as rooted in our physicality, in our bodies. The theory of how soul and body, the spiritual and the physical, are joined in the human person has fascinated philosophers and religious thinkers for at least as long as history and literature have been recorded. The practical implications of the question are pivotal to an integrated spirituality.

Christian theology prior to the modern era sought understanding of the question predominantly in Greek philosophy. The explanation for this fact lies to a great extent in the spread of Greek power and culture in the Mediterranean region just prior to the beginning of the Christian era. Greek dominance led to the translation of the Hebrew Scriptures into Greek (the Septuagint), the adoption of current Greek philosophical terminology into that translation and into the Jewish and Christian Scriptures that would follow, and the strong influence of Platonic and Aristotelian reasoning on the interpretation of the Scriptures and on related theological questions for centuries to come.

Plato, building on the work of his master Socrates, argued that the soul (*psychē*) as the principle of life is both preexistent and immortal. He described the soul as simple, spiritual, and divine, though imprisoned for a time in a material body. This soul knows spiritual things (the forms) only through memory from its spiritual preexistence. It is destined to be released from the material through death and subsequent rebirths and deaths, eventually to become one again with God, with the eternal and unchanging good, true, and beautiful.

In Aristotle's thought, the human person is by definition *both* soul and body, not merely, as for Plato, soul imprisoned in and using body. The soul is the form, the "livingness" of the body. On this concept Thomas Aquinas in the 13th century built his presentation of soul as the body's form (ST I, q. 76).

On the question of human immortality, Aquinas departed from Aristotle. In the Aristotelian scheme only the supra-individual world-soul, not the individual soul, is immortal. But because Aquinas defined the soul as an individual spiritual substance, he saw it as capable of living on independently after the body's death. His interpretation has largely shaped official Catholic teaching up to the present in regard to afterlife.

Karl Rahner, however, has pointed out that treatment of the soul as form ("livingness") of the body is a philosophical approach whose implications would preclude ever dealing with either soul or body independently of the other, in life or in death. If these implications had been fully appreciated by Aquinas himself and by his disciples, Christian thinking might have been led away from Platonic dualism. But the dualistic emphasis, the dichotomy and even opposition between soul and body characteristic of Platonism and Neoplatonism, in fact prevailed in Catholic theology and spirituality until the biblical renewal of the 20th century converged with post-Cartesian anthropology to bring new insights and raise new questions still unanswered, the latter particularly in regard to individual eschatology.

Biblical Understandings

The human person as presented by the OT is an undivided unity of flesh and spirit. Two terms are used in Hebrew to refer to the human spirit: *nephesh* and *ruach*.

Nephesh, often inaccurately translated "soul," is the inner being of the human creature, intimately linked with breath and blood, and seen as the seat of the emotions and passions. Though it springs from the life-breath or spirit (*ruach*) of God, in our flesh (*bāsār*) it is inherently subject to death. In primitive Semitic thought and in some OT references, *nephesh* is imaged as a kind of diminutive version of the body that escapes in death through the mouth or nostrils or other opening, such as a wound. When God breathes into Adam's nostrils, Adam becomes a "living *nephesh*" (Gen 2:7). In death this *nephesh* dies (as in Num 23:10: "May my *nephesh* die the death of the just"), and it continues in existence as a "dead *nephesh*" (as in Num 6:6, where the nazirite is not to enter a place where there is a "dead *nephesh*").

The reality expressed by the term *ruach* is often very close to that expressed by *nephesh*. However, *ruach* does not have the same physical overtones, though its most literal sense is that of wind or breath. It usually implies intense activity and energy: the life-breath or spirit of God, or the inner strength and vitality of a human being.

These two Hebrew terms passed into the Septuagint and then into the NT as the Greek *psychē* and *pneuma* respectively. But in the NT the centrality of the Pentecostal experience brings about a new coalescence between them. Both are now gathered into a concentration on life in the Spirit of Christ as the only true life.

Psychē in the NT does not carry the physical connotations inherent in the Hebrew *nephesh*. Thus one is cautioned by ancient superstition to guard one's *nephesh* from escape by not sleeping with one's mouth open and to avoid sorceresses who snare *nephashot* in their magic wristbands (Ezek 13:18). But Jesus proposes that to safeguard one's *psychē*, one must surrender it to God's care (Mt 6:25) and even be ready to lose it (Mt 16:25; Mk 8:35; Lk 9:24; Jn 12:25). Yet it *is* to be safeguarded in this paradoxical way, for it is more precious than the whole world or anything else that might be offered in exchange for it (Mt 16:26; Mk 8:36f.). *Psychē* is thus intimately associated with the concepts of selfhood and of that life that has eternal value.

As with the Hebrew *ruach, pneuma* in the NT refers to the human spirit and principle of action as well as to the divine. However, a new complexity is introduced. Though OT reference to *bāsār* ("flesh") implies weakness and mortality in contrast to God's might and eternity, it involves no moral judgment. In the NT, especially in the Pauline and Johannine texts, "spirit" (*pneuma*) and "flesh" (*sarx*) come to be morally opposed, and "flesh" becomes a symbol not simply of weakness and mortality but of legalistic and even sinful obstruction of the Spirit of God. As the Spirit of God (*ruach*) had rushed upon David and entered into the prophets, so the Spirit (*pneuma*) comes upon Jesus at his baptism, is given to the disciples when Jesus breathes on them after the resurrection, and fills them at Pentecost according to Jesus' promise. Thereafter the Christian is to live no longer as *sarx* (nor even merely as *psychē*) but as *pneuma,* in the very specific sense of living according to the holy Spirit of God in Jesus. It is to be stressed that "flesh" and "spirit" are not opposed here in a dualistic sense of body and soul; their opposition in NT thought as expressions of human nonresponse or response to God's Spirit continues to assume the Hebrew view of human beings as indivisibly body and spirit.

The Human Person: Physical and Spiritual

Neither the OT nor the NT attempts a philosophical analysis of human nature, and such an analysis should not be read out of either the Hebrew/Aramaic or Greek terminologies as used there. The Bible does witness to a view of the human person as a being at once bodily and spiritual, and different generations of biblical writers wrestled in their own contexts with the meaning of that reality. There is, however, no biblical base for the dichotomy between soul and body that very early began to characterize Christian thinking under the influence of Platonism. In this respect, modern anthropology is nearer to biblical thought than the intervening nineteen centuries of Christian tradition.

Our experience of the spiritual is derived only through bodily behavior. We cannot even think about the spiritual without language, which in turn is utterly dependent upon physical experience. An independent reality known as "soul" can no more exist than a purely mechanical, unconsciously acting body can. Both "soul" and "body"

are abstractions, mere crutches to our thinking about ourselves.

An integrated spirituality cannot address the soul without addressing bodiliness as essential to humanness and holiness. Pauline and Johannine themes of opposition between "spirit" and "flesh" need to be reclaimed in their original intent, rescued from a flawed tradition that identified "flesh" with everything physical rather than with all that is not filled with, and driven by, the Spirit of God. It is, after all, the same Letter to the Romans that develops the spirit-flesh opposition and sings of the redemption of all creation in freedom.

See also AFTERLIFE; ANTHROPOLOGY, THEOLOGICAL; BODY; DUALISM; SELF.

Bibliography: A. Pegis, *Saint Thomas and the Problem of the Soul in the Thirteenth Century* (Toronto: Pontifical Institute of Medieval Studies, 1983). W. Pannenberg, *Anthropology in Theological Perspective* (Philadelphia: Westminster, 1985).

SUZANNE NOFFKE, O.P.

SPIRIT
See HOLY SPIRIT.

SPIRIT, HUMAN
See CONSCIOUSNESS; EXPERIENCE; SOUL.

SPIRITS

The meanings of the word *spirit,* whether in biblical, philosophical, or everyday usage, are many. The boundaries between them are frequently hazy. Used in the plural, however, *spirits* can at least be contrasted, on the one hand, with that spirit which, apart from materialist views, is a constituent of every living creature, especially every human being, and, on the other hand, with the one Spirit of God. Further specification is difficult, depending as it does on the context in which the term is used or implied.

The biblical words translated as "spirit" (Hebrew *ruach*; Greek *pneuma*) can both be used as well where English speakers would say "breath" or "wind." Hence the wordplay in Jn 3:8, which also suggests two of the characteristics often associated with spirit(s) in general: invisibility and unpredictability. Spirits, although they may be present at particular times and in particular places, are not themselves material bodies; and they are not ordinarily subject to human control. Indeed, the Bible sometimes speaks of spirits as if they were personal beings in their own right, able to enter human minds and hearts, which they imbue with their own goodness or evil. Such are the "lying spirit" that enticed Ahab (1 Kgs 22:21-23) and the "unclean spirits" cast out by Jesus (e.g., in Mk 5:1-13). Sometimes, however, as in phrases like "the spirit of jealousy" (Num 5:14, RSV) or "a spirit of compassion and supplication" (Zech 12:10), what is meant seems to be a change of feelings itself rather than someone or something that brings the change about. In any case, it is always a mistake to force upon biblical language about spirits the sharp (and debatable) separation drawn by certain modern philosophers between the "objective" and the "subjective," and it is wise to keep the same caution in mind when reading the many spiritual writers who have adopted a scriptural manner of speaking.

Among the effects of spirits on the human spirit, *inspiration* ("in-breathing") is especially important. Thinking, understanding, believing, confessing, and the like can all be prompted by, and thus be manifestations of, good spirits but also of evil ones (1 Jn 4:1), and the ability to distinguish between these is itself, according to Paul (1 Cor 12:10), a spiritual gift. Christian traditions of spirituality have by and large put greater emphasis on such discrimination, on testing the genuineness of inspirations, than on the speculative question whether the reality of the spirits involved is ontological or psychological.

Ignatius of Loyola, for example, uses descriptions of both kinds, so that in his *Spiritual Exercises* "various spirits" and "various thoughts" appear to be interchangeable expressions. The important thing is that they happen as though of themselves, in contrast to mental activities that result from one's own deliberate choosing. There occur, as conscious experiences, pulls and counterpulls that are to be interpreted, directly or indirectly, in light of Ignatius's meditation on the Two Standards.

Traditional talk of good and evil spirits can sound hopelessly archaic and no doubt lends itself to exaggeration and misunderstanding. The mainstream of the tradition, however, has never separated the good or evil *source* of dispositions, desires, and affections from the good or evil *end* they head toward. The notion of spirits, in other words, has been firmly tied to theology in general and to theological ethics in particular. Because much that once fell under the rubric of spirits is now discussed, quite legitimately, in the more recent language of the psychologists, there is need for maintaining this larger theological perspective. Holiness has as much—or as little—to do with psychological health as grace has with nature.

See also CHARISM; CONSCIOUSNESS; DISCERNMENT OF SPIRITS; EVIL; INSPIRATION; TEMPTATION.

Bibliography: H. Bacht, "Good and Evil Spirits," *The Way* 2 (1962) 188–195. J. Guillet et al., *Discernment of Spirits* (Collegeville, Minn.: Liturgical Press, 1970).

CHARLES C. HEFLING, JR.

SPIRITUAL CHILDHOOD

See CARMELITE SPIRITUALITY; CHILD, CHILDREN; SIMPLICITY.

SPIRITUAL DIRECTION

An Age-old Relationship

After two million years of sensing the dynamism of the unseen that pervades all of life, human beings continue to wonder about this mysterious dimension of reality. What ultimately can we know about life, death, and what lies beyond? Is the Mystery to be trusted or not? What is the best way for individuals, families, and nations to keep alive the peculiarly human capacity called "spirit" that yearns for more than the merely visible? This ability for being present to the unseen has given rise to a variety of spiritualities—faith-based ways of living in response to specific namings of the mysterious aspect of life. Teachers of wisdom, shamans, gurus, sages, pirs, soul-healers, prophets, zaddiks, and a variety of spiritual guides with "listening hearts" continue to be called upon to establish a relationship with seekers concerned about the spiritual direction of their human journey.

These guides attempt to make connections between an ultimate direction or "flow of all that is" and the concrete life circumstances of both themselves and the people who seek them out. If spiritual counseling is the goal, they focus in on the longing human spirit as it struggles for meaning in its personal life field. If, however, spiritual *direction* is sought, they aim further at awakening the heart to participation in the Mystery's self-communication within the guidelines laid down by a specific revealed tradition. Thus spiritual direction in any place or time is always nuanced by cultural differences as well as by a potential variety of faith and form traditions.

Specifically, foundational Christian spiritual direction, which traces its roots to the revelation of the Hebrew Scriptures and tradition and which emerged with the fullness of revelation in Christ, continued through the apostles and the life of the early Church. It began to take on diversified forms beginning with the 4th-century Desert Fathers and Mothers. By the 6th century this highly individualized charism had undergone many changes. This is seen in the more settled monastic communities, where, abiding by an objective rule for everyone, those living the monastic life concerned themselves with passing on directives for a gospel-based way of life. As the centuries passed, more active, non-monastic types of direction came into being, fluctuating between individualized and institutionalized models in tune with developing theologies of grace and of what it meant to "do God's will."

Christian directors were called upon to help people make sense of their daily struggles and/or religious experiences assisting them in discovering, not only in prayer but also in all of their lived experience, directives and meaningful evocations of the "more than," in this case the Holy Otherness revealed by Christ. In spite of post–15th-century appearances to the contrary, the basis of the Church's traditional understanding of spiritual direction has always been an appreciation of human freedom and of the inbuilt directedness toward the Divine Presence underlying all of life's events. Growth in self-knowledge, by bringing to the surface abiding tendencies and dispositions of heart, and discernment, the art and gift of recognizing the movements of the Holy Spirit in one's life, are intended to encourage this freedom.

Christian direction, then, is rooted in Christ as revelation of the Mystery, as being himself the way, the truth, and the life; the ultimate source of spiritualization, interiorization, and sanctification; the one who from his fullness pours God's love into human hearts by giving us the Holy Spirit. Scripture reveals Christ as director par excellence in one-to-one relationships with a variety of persons, including Nicodemus, Nathanael, the Samaritan woman, and the rich young man. However, both he and members of the early Church took for granted that individuals were meant to listen for the unfolding image of God existing in their depths in a multitude of other ways as well. These included receiving direction in a group, reading the works of spiritual masters, sharing in liturgical celebrations, and participating in the ongoing life of a viable Christian community—all recommended in the restored Rite of Christian Initiation of Adults.

The foundational assumption underlying the entire endeavor is that all creation is involved in a longing to attain its spiritual direction. We can trust God's transforming death-resurrection activity already taking place within the universe, leading it as well as all human beings in the direction of new birth. The communal reality of baptism introduces us into the life of graced participation in the Trinitarian life. However, due to a natural tendency toward entropy, to ignorance about our primary goal of eternal life in God, and to our sinful tendency toward idolatrous clinging to much that is not of God, we need divine grace as well as human guidance in order for such a radical transformation to take place.

An intentional relationship of Christian spiritual direction is not so much a matter of one person having authority to direct another; rather, both parties in the relationship are expected to become attentive listeners to the Holy Spirit, who continually provides providential direction in the life of each man and woman whether they are aware of it or not. Gradually individual blocks and resistances to spiritual growth will be uncovered and brought to consciousness. With increasing depth the desires of the true or core self are revealed when compulsive reactions of the false self give way to positive, truly free responses to divine initiatives. The essentially social goal of the liberation of the world from fear, oppression, and evil finds an energy source in these intentional relationships, grounded as they are in God's love.

In a Contemporary Climate

Changing views of world, self, others, and God appear in each new generation. Spiritual directors need to recognize how, particularly since the Renaissance, the ongoing explosion of physical and human sciences (philosophy, psychology, sociology, medical ethics, social anthropology, subatomic physics, economics, psychiatry, computer sciences, etc.) have broken up what had been a more or less agreed upon worldview among Western Christians. Instead of reality being a unified whole, it now appears divided. A multitude of partial and frequently conflicting theories present themselves in answer to the questions of human seekers.

Spiritualities now offer a bewildering plurality of possible life directives. In light of continual and unremitting advances in human knowledge, we find ourselves hungering for an integrative method of guidance and direction, foundational enough to incorporate the various psychological, sociological, socioeconomic, and anthropological discoveries that daily offer themselves to every man or woman searching for the spiritual direction of their life in the 21st century. No longer able to live a spirituality that sets them apart from their world and other persons in an isolated realm of mere interiority, contemporary seekers tend to view themselves as always in relation to, as inextricably connected with, the lived realities of their world.

In a manner somewhat different from that of former times, today's direction is explicitly concerned with pointing to connections between all beings, to our involvement with the whole of life rather than with just some of its parts, with what some are calling the "web of life," the dialogue we humans are with all aspects of our life field. Direction now involves not only one's relationship to the Sacred Otherness that underlies and upholds life; it is also concerned about one's openness to the environing universe and to cultural and social contexts. It questions us on issues of global justice and peace as well as on our response to immediate commitments embodied in family, work, and civic responsibility.

Thanks to the interreligious dialogue between the great world faith-traditions opened in this century, Christians are currently recovering the more contemplative and mystical aspect of Western Christianity, a dimension somewhat obscured during the course of the past five centuries. However, exposure to a plurality of new religions and sometimes misleading mystical approaches has left some seekers understandably confused. Contemporary direction inevitably involves the challenge of distinguishing modern forms of gnosticism from the incarnational approach so basic to the Christian gospel. It also recognizes that authentic mystical experience, closely related to the religious and social context in which it occurs, happens to more people than was formerly acknowledged.

A brief overview can only indicate a few aspects of the contemporary climate that provides a current context for most Western Christian spiritual direction. For example, a "systems view" of the universe and of the family comprises only one of the dynamic psychological orientations shaping the awareness of the Western consciousness. In recent centuries the rise of an analytic secular scientific mentality has contrasted, sometimes jarringly, with the more holistic spiritual traditions that saw human persons as *participants* in the cosmos and culture rather than as isolated observers set apart from it. In addition, the emergence of positive regard for the genius of feminine sensibility and potential is helping to counterbalance the rationalistic mentality of domination that has prevailed in the West for so many generations. The recovery of the "receptivity dynamics" common to all great religious traditions could contribute much toward alleviating the stress in everyday living that plagues most members of our individualistic, competitive culture.

Another positive source of discernment regarding the human condition lies in a recently discovered ability to appreciate the soul's journey as embedded in the changing context of the human developmental process. In understanding how the shell of a false self gradually comes to conceal the true image of God in each person, we are beginning to grasp the connection between human growth patterns and early emotional investments that may block later spiritual receptivity. Although maintaining a clear distinction between chronological and spiritual maturity, directors are more likely now to see the importance of relational and psychosexual development as they affect spiritual life. Viewed as opportunities for spiritual growth, adult commitments in love for others and work for the common good, significant life transitions (especially those that involve loss and detachment), and the aging process itself are now being disclosed as appropriate material for reflection during the direction process.

Current insights into the interrelation of body, mind, and spirit have put directors more in touch with areas like self-responsibility, nutritional awareness, stress management, physical fitness, environmental sensitivity, regular meditation practice, and the phenomenon of daily life as spiritual exercise. We are more familiar with the natural resistance to growth invitations hidden in the narration of everyone's "story." We know something of the hermeneutic process involved in understanding and interpreting what a person may or may not be expressing. We have a growing appreciation of the necessity of respectfully starting from what a person says about the events of his or her lived experience rather than trying to apply abstract principles and rules to individual cases.

In the endeavor to help people tap into the uncreated power of the Mystery pushing to be released in them, the director cannot ignore what we now know about new forms of idolatry—addictions, compulsions, wounded emotions, codependence, the confusion that attends shifting norms in moral guidance and family life, and the all too prevalent depression, fear, and loneliness that characterize loss of sensitivity to the self-communication of the Divine Other. The positive faith of the undivided

Church in our universe as a living field brimming over with created and uncreated energy that flows forth from the Trinitarian heart of the Mystery is needed now more than ever. We must become reconnected with our deepest roots as we pursue the adventure of being formed by, and giving form to, both our world and the unique "immortal diamond" concealed at the core of each human life.

Although much of the newer knowledge may be, by its very complexity and volume, outside the domain of the average director's attainment, he or she, besides learning to make competent referrals, must continue to study and also to grow in intuitive knowledge led by the ever-available Spirit. All the counseling skills and techniques in the world will not make up for lack of a "listening heart." Nor can they provide a sense of compassionate solidarity with another or trust in the self-communicating initiation of grace.

Today's Christian Spiritual Director

Rather than being someone who willfully makes things happen or controls another person, today's spiritual director is more likely to allow the Spirit to take the lead. As co-listener for the already existing direction in which the Spirit is leading directees, he or she has the task within that intentional relationship of paying attention to God's presence in the life of this other person, of attempting to make conscious the ongoing dialogue with God that gives meaning to that life. Within the context of contemporary pluralism and mindful of the delicate interdependence of complex factors in today's society, directors aim at integrating prayer and life, contemplation and action, faith and justice, in their own lives as well as in the lives of the directees. They know that when the dialogue between gospel values, life-shaping directives from the culture, and one's own embodied self becomes conscious, people become truly free to channel energy into more loving decisions and actions.

During a directee's experiences of dryness and dark nights, of aridity and of being called to further surrender, the director must sometimes admit his or her limited ability to do other than pray and make a wise referral. A more experienced director will recognize these genuine states of prayer and be able to sustain the directee, preventing discouragement and the temptation to give up on the spiritual journey. As a "wounded healer," the director with faith consistently relies on the Divine Other who has entered the direction process, permeating the entire life field with the transforming power of grace attuned to each unique individual.

Realizing that neither therapeutic counseling nor classic prayer-guidance is sufficient in itself, today's directors are opting for a more foundational approach that, while incorporating one faith tradition as ultimate, has links to other cultures and traditions as well. With its distinctive aims, perspectives, methods, and sources, this foundational approach remains grounded for Christians in an anthropology of the human person whose vital functional, sociohistorical, and transcendent image is open to the indwelling of the Holy Spirit. It is "being in touch" with this spiritual or pneumatic self that characterizes the depth dimension of the process of spiritual direction.

Directors recognize themselves as called to this work when sought out by others or missioned by the Church itself. Spiritual friends or companions, they are nevertheless "sent" and thus represent the sacred order of reality rather than just their own inner subjective illumination. Authentic directors throughout history have valued spiritual guidance as a work of love. Faithful and objective "others," they freely choose to stand in the Lord's place as both a prod and a source of light. Having themselves known the difficulty of laying bare their secret aspirations and resistances to grace in the presence of another, they realize the importance that the knowledge of God's mysteries and a simultaneous knowledge of human hearts have for their task.

They also understand the centrality of the sacred revelations, stories, or myths that make the Mystery meaningful and challenging for the faith community to which their directees belong. They are aware of how distortions can occur in a person's unique, possibly one-sided dialogue with divine revelation, particularly in regard to his or her image of the ultimate Source of that revelation. They perceive conversion, the shifting of one's personal fulcrum from sinful self-preservation to a renewed fidelity to one's deepest self, as always experienced for Christians as dying and rising with Christ in the fullness of God's love.

Distinctively Christian appraisal and appropriate decision-making, then, will take into account the Spirit's activity on all polarities of the life field as the directee begins to let go of obstacles and to live by faith and a realistic knowledge of self-in-relation. Here again, today's director may have greater or less access to the biospiritual self, to the dispositions of this person's heart, to both positive and negative ways he or she uses the powers of mind (imagination, memory, and anticipation) and to the directee's preferred style of exercising personal power. The discerning director remains convinced that evidence of the new covenant is to be found not in exterior acts of reformation alone but in the transformed intentionality of the human heart.

Rightly understood, the post–Vatican II reforms, especially as regards the relation of liturgy and spirituality, have reopened original Christian sources of scriptural, contemplative, and communal formation. Today's spiritual directors have a fresh opportunity to help searching men and women discover the deepest treasure of their hearts, the purpose for which they came to be, the depths of faith, hope, and love with which they are already gifted. To be helpful in this way, directors themselves

must first be awake to delight and trust in the Mystery. And then they must find themselves personally moved, to some degree at least, by the dynamics of that delight.

See also CONTEMPORARY SPIRITUALITY; DETACHMENT; DISCERNMENT OF SPIRITS; DISCRETION; EXPERIENCE; FRUIT(S) OF THE HOLY SPIRIT; GIFTS OF THE HOLY SPIRIT; HOLISTIC SPIRITUALITY; HOLY SPIRIT; JOURNEY (GROWTH AND DEVELOPMENT IN SPIRITUAL LIFE); LITURGY; PRAYER; PSYCHOLOGY, RELATIONSHIP AND CONTRIBUTION TO SPIRITUALITY; SELF; SIN; TRUST.

Bibliography: "Direction spirituelle," *D.Spir.,* vol. 3, cols. 1002–1214. C. Gratton, *The Art of Spiritual Guidance* (New York: Crossroad, 1992). K. Leech, *Soul Friend* (San Francisco: Harper & Row, 1977). A. van Kaam, *Formative Spirituality,* 5 vols. (New York: Crossroad, 1983–1992).

CAROLYN GRATTON

SPIRITUAL EXERCISES

See DISCERNMENT OF SPIRITS; IGNATIAN SPIRITUALITY.

SPIRITUAL THEOLOGY

See ASCETICAL THEOLOGY; MYSTICAL THEOLOGY; SPIRITUALITY, CHRISTIAN.

SPIRITUAL WRITING, CONTEMPORARY

The extraordinary growth of interest in Christian spirituality is reflected in the increase in the number of persons enrolled in courses in spirituality, in the commitment to a deep and sustained prayer life on the part of Christians of all walks of life, and in the growing number of participants in support/study groups focused on assisting participants develop toward an ever more mature spirituality. These currents, especially apparent since the Second Vatican Council, have been accompanied by a burgeoning of publications in the area of Christian spirituality.

"Christian spirituality" here refers to both a lived experience and an academic discipline. In the first instance, the term describes the whole of the Christian's life as this is oriented to self-transcending knowledge, freedom, and love in light of the ultimate values and highest ideals perceived and pursued in the mystery of Jesus Christ through the Holy Spirit in the Church, the community of disciples. That is to say, spirituality is concerned with everything that constitutes Christian experience, specifically the perception and pursuit of the highest ideal or goal of Christian life, i.e., an ever more intense union with God disclosed in Christ through life in the Spirit. At a second level, Christian spirituality is an academic discipline, increasingly interdisciplinary in nature, that attempts to study religious experience and to promote its development and maturation.

As an academic enterprise, Christian spirituality is an emergent and immature discipline. Though scholars have agreed on some common vocabulary, issues of concern, and methods of investigation, there is not as yet a commonly recognized theory regarding the precise limits and scope of this discipline. Noteworthy among the contributors to such a generalized theory regarding the nature of Christian spirituality are Sandra Schneiders and Walter Principe. It is also important to note here the contributions of several scholars who bring clarity to the discipline of Christian spirituality by making connections between systematic theology and spirituality. The work of Tad Dunne and Vernon Gregson is an example of this effort within a Lonerganian framework, while James Bacik, Annice Callahan, Harvey Egan, J. Norman King, and Robert Masson attempt to spell out the implications of the work of Karl Rahner for Christian spirituality in a systematic fashion.

Types of Writing

In an effort to develop a discipline recognized as such in the academy, scholars have profited immensely from a great number of contemporary publications that serve as reliable tools. The celebrated *Dictionnaire de spiritualité ascétique et mystique,* edited by Marcel Viller, assisted by Ferdinand Cavallera and Joseph de Guibert (Paris: Beauchesne, 1932–), is undoubtedly the most helpful and generally reliable encyclopedic dictionary in the field of Christian spirituality. In preparation since 1932, the *Dictionnaire* has, at this writing, arrived at the letter *S.*

Other significant contributions to the field of Christian spirituality are encyclopedic dictionaries, such as the *Dictionnaire de la vie spirituelle,* adapted by François Vial (Paris: Cerf, 1983). Helpful introductory volumes include such noteworthy publications as *The Study of Spirituality,* edited by Cheslyn Jones, Geoffrey Wainwright, and Edward Yarnold (New York: Oxford Univ. Press, 1986), and the *Compendio de teologia spirituale* (Rome: Gregorian University, 1976). Then there are extensive bibliographical tools such as the *Bibliographia Internationalis Spiritualitatis* (Rome: Pontificium Institutum Spiritualitatis, 1966–). *The Way, Studies in Formative Spirituality,* and *Nouvelle revue théologique* regularly publish bibliographies and review articles in the field of spirituality.

In addition, there are introductions and translations of classic texts, e.g., Michael Glazier's 12-volume series entitled The Way of the Christian Mystics, the Spiritual Classics series of Crossroad Publishing Co., as well as a number of series of critical texts and translations of spiritual classics. Especially noteworthy is the monumental 60-volume series Classics of Western Spirituality published by the Paulist Press and its new series Sources of American Spirituality.

Writing in the field indicates that interest in spirituality has moved well beyond the province of Catholicism and Christianity. There is now a deeper recognition that other religious traditions have their own spirituality, which until rather recently was thought to be a predominantly Catholic concern. To give an indication of just how widespread the interest in spirituality has become, one need only mention the 25-volume series World Spirituality: An Encyclopedic History of the Religious Quest, edited by Ewert Cousins (New York: Crossroad, 1985–), only three volumes of which are devoted to Christian spirituality. And it is within the treatment of Christian spirituality more generally that a treatment of issues germane to a specifically Catholic spirituality are addressed.

In addition to the aforementioned scholarly works and research tools, a number of journals are devoted to advancing scholarly pursuits in the field of spirituality. Here some of the most noteworthy are La vie spirituelle, Carmelitanus, Christus, Geist und Leben, Studia Mystica, and Cîteaux. It is also important to note here that Concilium regularly devotes one of its issues to spirituality, edited by Christian Duquoc and Casiano Floristán. And then there are journals and magazines that publish articles of a nonscholarly and popular sort.

But in addition to these there is a third category that consists of journals published for English-speaking readers which provide essays and reviews at once the fruit of sound academic discipline and at the same time accessible to nonspecialists interested in growing to Christian maturation. These journals make the findings in the academic discipline of spirituality accessible to educated, mature, and responsible Christians who seek to develop in the life of the Spirit. In this category are included such journals as Spirituality Today (ceased publication in 1992), The Way, Studies in Formative Spirituality, and Spiritual Life. The evolution of this third type of journal in terms of the issues treated and the contributing authors may itself serve as a gauge of the course of Christian spirituality since the Second Vatican Council. Similarly, the astonishing rise in the number of subscriptions to such journals

among laypersons is itself an indication of the acceptance of the council's challenge to growth and maturation in Spirit among all the baptized. Remarkable though it may seem, 58 percent of the subscriptions to Cistercian Studies Quarterly, a review of monastic and contemplative spirituality devoted primarily to issues pertinent to the Cistercian tradition, are taken by laypersons.

The American Benedictine Review and Worship address issues of concern to those in the field of spirituality, though this is not their primary focus. Journals such as Horizons, Theological Studies, and Theology Today have devoted essays and review essays to the subject of Christian spirituality. Entire volumes of Listening: The Journal of Religion and Culture, and Église et Théologie (a bilingual French-English publication) have been devoted to the subject of spirituality. Though many of their readers are interested in substantial issues of Christian spirituality, Review for Religious, Sisters Today, Weavings, Living Prayer, Desert Call, and Carmelite Digest tend to be devoted to issues of a more popular and practical sort.

In addition to resources and research tools for those working in the academic field of spirituality, scholarly journals, journals devoted to making the findings of such research more accessible to an educated readership, and journals and magazines of a more popular and practical sort, attention must be drawn to the growth in the number of books published in the area of spirituality. These range from the scholarly and esoteric to the "pop," "thin," and "fluffy," from critical editions of the classics to self-help manuals for coping with grief and handbooks for living with integrity through separation and divorce. Authors include priests, monks, nuns, religious, and laypersons, male and female, married and single. It would be impossible to provide an exhaustive survey of the various types of contemporary spiritual writings, though it is important to note that there continues to be an abiding interest in particular spiritualities, and there is a great deal of writing on these: spiritualities of the priesthood, religious life, married life. Suffice it to say that whether the subject be spirituality in general or particular spiritualities, there are some distinctive currents in the enormous flood of contemporary literature in the field.

Significant Currents

A brief survey of the currents in contemporary spiritual writing may provide indication of the shape or direction of spirituality on the brink of the third millennium.

First, much of the renaissance in contemporary spirituality has been given impetus by the Second Vatican Council. As a result, many of its fundamental orientations and convictions undergird a good measure of contemporary writing in Christian spirituality, though it must be acknowledged that there have remained signs of a defensive reaction to the reforms and renewal occasioned by the council.

Because the council stressed the reciprocal relationship between liturgy, especially the Eucharist, and Christian life (SC 1, 10), as well as the singular importance of Scripture and its formative role in the spiritual life, a great deal of contemporary spiritual writing rests on the premise that Christian spirituality is a liturgical and scriptural spirituality. In addition, the council's universal call to holiness (LG 40-41) has dealt a fatal blow, at least in theory, to the tightly held conviction that the fullness of the Christian spiritual life is reserved for an elite (usually vowed religious and clergy). All the baptized are called to fullness of life in the Spirit. Expressions of Christian spiritual life among the faithful cannot be understood or explained simply by extension or comparison with paradigms of mature spirituality appropriate to clergy and religious.

Since the council there has been sustained attention to a more holistic understanding of spirituality. Rather than beginning with doctrinal formulations or theoretical explanations of Christian life, contemporary writings in spirituality tend to begin by stressing the singular importance of the concrete experience of searching for God and of finding appropriate ways to live out one's response to the divine initiative. This has been coupled with attention to the importance of the specific context within which one lives out one's relationship with the other, others, and God, and the significance of culture as it shapes these relationships. There has been a deepening appreciation for the particular, the specific, and for differences as expressed, for example, in the attention given to the need to retrieve and/or develop approaches to prayer appropriate to persons in a great variety of life forms.

The attention given to the experiential and the contextual has been accompanied by an effort to undercut dualisms of all sorts. Hence there has been a sustained attempt to distinguish rather than unduly separate soul and body, spirit and flesh, Church and world, sacred and profane. To this has been joined a concern to focus on the "ordinary" and the "everyday," and the opportunities therein for the baptized to be a corporate witness and sign, or sacrament, in and to the world. With the setting aside of subtle and not so subtle dualist convictions and the embrace of a more incarnational and sacramental approach to spirituality, there has been a deeper appreciation of the value of interpersonal relationships, inclusive of intimacy and sexuality, with particular attention to the sacredness of marriage as the paradigmatic human relationship that discloses the divine. In highlighting the relational as disclosing the holy, great attention has been given to the significance of life in community, particularly communities of self-help and mutual help, whether these be parish renewal groups, prayer groups, study groups, Marriage Encounter, Cursillo, *communidades de base,* or 12-step groups.

This focus on the relational, interpersonal, and communal is related to another current in contemporary spiritual writing, which, though certainly not novel in the history of Christian spirituality, has been given unique emphasis in the postconciliar period. In the perennial search for the true, authentic self, contemporary writing reflects a reliance on interdisciplinary methods, drawing from biblical studies, psychology (especially developmental psychology), theology, history, and pastoral experience. Resources often extend beyond the author's particular religious tradition, reflective of the ecumenical and interreligious sensibility characteristic of religious and theological studies since the council.

The attempt to bring interdisciplinary and ecumenical/interreligious insights to bear on the subject of Christian spirituality might be exemplified in the writings of those who attempt to use personality-type indicators from the investigations of Myers-Briggs or the Enneagram, which has its roots in the tradition of the Sufis, in the process of Christian growth and development. Such approaches to the quest for true self are grounded in the conviction that human and spiritual development are not opposing, competing dynamics but are rather interrelated and complementary. The authentic self is one that is given by nature and developed by grace and Spirit. Such development requires commitment to ongoing self-scrutiny and willingness to risk and change. But this self-scrutiny extends beyond the province of the individual to include a mature critical consciousness vis-à-vis the social-symbolic order with its dominant ideology. Without such critical consciousness there is a tendency to overlook the truth that any authentic Christian spirituality is intrinsically relational, social, and, indeed, political.

Just as much contemporary spiritual writing assumes that human and spiritual development are interrelated and complementary, so too there is a sustained conviction that prayer and action are two dimensions of the human person that are to be held together in a noble tension in an ever-deepening integration. This must be understood against the background of a long tradition that tended to separate the "active life" and the "contemplative life." Without prejudice to the complexity of the issue, it may be said that there is a deeper recognition today that prayer and action are rooted in one same source, the human person, who is called to the prayer of loving attention, gratitude, and praise for the presence and action of God in human life, history, world, and Church, and to the activities whereby God's reign is advanced, especially through the works of prophetic service and the promotion of peace and justice. This is to recognize the importance of praxis in Christian life and spirituality. In contemporary spiritual writing, praxis does not refer to any and all action or practice. It is the practice of the gospel through which persons and communities do the truth in love freely, and in so doing enable others to do the truth in love freely, thereby participating more fully in the mystery of Christ who is contemplated in Christian prayer.

The recognition of the demands of justice in the Christian spiritual life has drawn greater attention to the rights of women in Church and society and to the struggle to work for the equality of women in all spheres of life. Indeed, the emergence of a specifically feminist spirituality is arguably one of the most significant, albeit unanticipated, results of the council. The place of women's experience and the significance of women's contributions in Christian tradition have been given a good measure of attention in contemporary spiritual writing, undoubtedly one of the most notable developments in the field. Similarly, the struggle for peace and justice has drawn attention to the experience of persons and groups at the margins of social and religious bodies, be they persons of color, the physically and mentally disabled, the divorced and remarried, persons in the Third World, gays and lesbians, or the economically oppressed. The experience of such persons and of the countless women who have often been invisible and powerless in Church and society has become an increasingly important, indeed, indispensable source for reflection on the nature of authentic Christian experience and praxis.

On the brink of the third millennium, there is ever-increasing attention to the implications of authentic Christian spirituality for the protection, preservation, and care of the earth and its resources. The threat of nuclear annihilation and the destruction of the ecological balance through systematic ravaging of the earth's resources have caused some to remind of the value and dignity of other forms of life, and to invite to a just and nonviolent way of living with other species and the whole of creation, upon which humans depend for their very existence.

Finally, contemporary spiritual writings evidence a strong commitment to find solutions to the problems that Christians face today by retrieving the riches of the past. This requires much more than recovering insights from former epochs and applying them uncritically as solutions to current problems. Rather, it demands a deep appreciation of the particular historical context within which the formulation of a given insight or truth took place, so that the fundamental orientations and motivations of a given historical age that underlie such a formulation might be brought to bear upon a very different context and set of circumstances marked by very different modes of being and perceiving.

Conclusion

Literature in the field of Christian spirituality in the years since the Second Vatican Council includes critical editions and translations, encyclopedic dictionaries, introductions, historical surveys, entire series of volumes devoted to spirituality, and bibliographies. All these have supplied helpful research tools for students and scholars. Journals ranging from the scholarly to the more popular have served a wide variety of persons interested in spirituality. Most notable is the orientation of many journals in the direction of educated but nonspecialist readers who wish to have access to the findings in the field of spirituality, but in an idiom more readily accessible to them.

In the category of published books there is a vast array, but with certain characteristics shared by the best of them. There is a focus on a holistic understanding, rooted in experience. Great attention is given to the contextual and relational dimensions of spirituality, inclusive of intimacy and sexuality. There is stress on the liturgical and scriptural foundations of spirituality as well as on the universal call to holiness, thereby undercutting the notion of a spiritual elite. Writing on particular spiritualities for clergy and religious usually reflects this sensibility. As in every age, attention is being given to the search for the true self, but with greater appreciation for the complementarity of human and spiritual development.

In this quest for the true self, self-scrutiny and the development of critical consciousness vis-à-vis the sources of oppression and injustice go hand in hand. This is related to the attempt to find modes of integrating prayer and prophetic service through forms of emancipatory praxis appropriate to the urgent demands of the age. Among these urgent demands are the promotion of the full equality of women in Church and society and the recognition of those who have been marginalized and, consequently, whose alternative experience has been rendered voiceless and insignificant by the dominant social-symbolic order in Church and society. At the brink of the third millennium, more but still insufficient attention is being given to the appropriate Christian response in the face of the possibility of nuclear annihilation and the probability of ecological crises of proportions heretofore unimagined. Finally, there is a fuller recognition of both the riches and the shortcomings of the Christian tradition for answering the problems to be faced in the third millennium.

See also CONTEMPORARY SPIRITUALITY; SPIRITUALITY, CHRISTIAN; SPIRITUAL WRITING, GENRES OF.

Bibliography: S. Schneiders, "Theology and Spirituality: Strangers, Rivals, or Partners," Horizons 13/2 (1986) 253–274; "Spirituality in the Academy," TS 50/4 (1989) 676–697.

MICHAEL DOWNEY

SPIRITUAL WRITING, GENRES OF

Literary genre is a specific form of writing that differs according to species or type. Distinct form and structure in literature are adapted to content and purpose. The literary form, or genre, is, in itself, a part of the communication of the intended meaning. Since 1900 the study of biblical literary genres has contributed to an understanding of the different traditions contained within the biblical texts. These same principles apply to any body of literature, including the different sources of Christian spirituality.

Vitae and Hagiography

Already in the early Christian literary experience, differences in genres of spiritual writing become apparent. In the apostolic age apologetic writing, which was polemical in nature in order to defend the truth of the Christian message, had a distinctly different character than the passiones, or the Acts of the martyrs. Initially these Acts, based on records of trials and executions, were simple narratives recounting the testimony and execution of the martyrs, e.g., Polycarp (d. ca. 155), Justin (d. ca. 166), and the Scillitan martyrs (d. ca. 180). Subsequent Acts were enriched with dialogues and visions which teach that the disciple of Christ is one who is ready to go to the cross. Christian spirituality involves a form of death. The Passion of SS. Perpetua and Felicity developed this spirituality in a motivating and edifying way.

From the veneration of the martyrs it was a natural step to compose stories about the lives of other exemplary Christians, particularly ascetics. After the persecutions of Diocletian had ceased, a new genre of literature developed—the vitae sanctorum, or lives of the saints. This development featured a new kind of heroic martyrdom in the tradition of the Acts of the martyrs, but it was developed within the Greek and Latin classical genre that treats the life of the hero or sage. St. Athanasius's Life of Antony, written in Greek in 357, one year after Antony's death, inserted into this tradition and model classic biblical themes and motifs taken from the prophets and the apostles. It was a form that demonstrated a new imitatio Christi. St. Athanasius wished to provide an example for other monks and to teach Christian identity and purpose. He also had in mind the broader community in his cultivation of the imagination in order to inspire Christians and to interest pagans.

With this work a new Christian literary genre was born. St. Jerome's Life of Paul the Hermit (376) and Sulpicius Severus's Life of St. Martin of Tours (397) became paradigmatic for subsequent Christian writing, which employed the heroic lives of saints to inspire and illustrate and to teach the biblical principles operative in the spirituality of Christian living. For many subsequent centuries these basic texts were primary formation texts for Christian life, particularly monastic life, and for the new Christian literary tradition known as hagiography, or lives of holy men and women. With his Life of Antony, St. Athanasius formed a new genre of spiritual writing, one very different in tone and content from his doctrinal tract On the Incarnation of the Word of God, which ultimately earned him the title "Father of Orthodoxy" in the Greek ecclesiastical tradition.

The *Dialogues* attributed to St. Gregory the Great (590–604) contributed to the medieval development of hagiography. The first three books of the *Dialogues* contain accounts of the lives and miracles of various Italian saints; the second book treats the life of St. Benedict. The early medieval writing accents miracles to illustrate that God is concretely manifested in historical figures, descendants of the patriarchs and apostles: "They [the Lombards] came at night while the community was asleep and plundered the entire monastery, without capturing a single monk. In this way God fulfilled His promise to Benedict, His faithful servant. He allowed the barbarians to destroy the monastery, but safeguarded the lives of the religious. Here you can see how the man of God resembled St. Paul, who had the consolation of seeing everyone with him escape alive from the storm, while the ship and all its cargo were lost" (*Dialogues* II.17).

Although the authorship of Gregory the Great is questioned, the *Life of Benedict* brought a new dimension and literary significance to the genre of the literature on the lives of the saints. It "provided the golden legend and the title deeds of the new Benedictine movement" (Clark, p. 283), which flourished in the early to middle 8th century, a time in which the *Dialogues* became widely known. The *Life of Benedict* provided a spirituality and a hermeneutical context for the interpretation and application of the Rule of Benedict.

Although the *Life of Antony* and the *Life of Benedict* can both be classified as belonging to the genre of hagiography, each has a different twist. The former teaches the monk about ascetical life, while the latter interprets a rule and supports a specific monastic movement. The *Life of Benedict* was a development in the genre of hagiography. This continued to be the case when the lives of the saints became official ecclesiastical documents on the occasion of their canonization. Thomas of Celano's *First Life of Francis* is a case in point. This life of St. Francis, written at the request of Pope Gregory IX on the occasion of Francis's canonization in 1228, was written to promote the cult of St. Francis and to demonstrate his universal appeal to the entire Church. Thomas's *Life* is very different from the *Life of St. Francis* written by St. Bonaventure some thirty years later. St. Bonaventure wrote this *Life* at the request of the general chapter when he was minister general of the Franciscans. He wrote as a teacher and theologian, and composed a "theological biography," in which the theological, ecclesiological, and eschatological significance of St. Francis and the Franciscan Order developed into a highly structured and specialized theological treatise.

Later in the Middle Ages these various hagiographical forms were known as "legends" (*legendae*) and were intended to be read aloud during the Divine Office. They were organized according to the calendar of saints' feast days and collected into a volume called the *Legendarium*. The most famous example of a popular medieval legendary of this type is *The Golden Legend* of Jacob of Voragine (d. 1298). This work served as the bible of saints' lives for the common people. For this reason it was the best known, most influential, and most imaginative writing connecting the concrete, lived Christian experience of the high and later Middle Ages with the earlier tradition of holiness.

In all these various forms of hagiography, there is consistency in that this literary genre actualizes the memory of the spiritual dynamic as developed in the life of a holy man or woman. This lived dynamic is a primary source for reflection and theological interpretation of the work of the Spirit of God. Hagiography and any form of spiritual biography provide primary texts for spirituality. This form of literature teaches the Christian faith through the method of providing individual example. A good workable definition of this literary genre within spirituality is as follows: "Sacred biography, as understood here, refers to a narrative text of the *vita* of the saint written by a member of a community of belief. The text provides a documentary witness to the process of sanctification for the community and in so doing becomes itself a part of the sacred tradition it serves to document" (Heffernan, p. 16).

Journal and Autobiography

The journal and the autobiography are other ways in which the lived dynamic of the Spirit in the development of the spiritual journey of a holy man or woman is expressed. These two literary genres are considered together because both provide a privileged personal form of spiritual literature. These forms of writing focus neither on the external witness nor on the social aspects of a holy life; rather, they take their origin from the inner voice within the heart and soul of the author. Whereas hagiography is written to illustrate and teach the *imitatio Christi,* the journal expresses the interior experience of the Christ who dwells within. It is written as a spiritual discipline in order to articulate and grasp the interior voice of the Spirit speaking in the heart. The spiritual autobiography is written to share one's own interior and personal journey with others. It is an abbreviated and more systematic or consistent form of the journal, recording the experience of the interior movement of the heart toward union with God. Conversion, internal conversation, soul searching, and the personal process of involvement in God provide the general literary structure.

The classic example of both these forms is the writings of St. Augustine. In his *Soliloquies,* Augustine responded to a voice deep within himself to search out and to write his personal and deepest thoughts that he might experience deeply his desire for God and activate his passionate search for truth. His *Confessions,* once *the* literary classic in Western spirituality, demonstrates the fruit of his constancy in the practice of journal writing. Augustine became deeply attuned to what God was doing to draw him to himself: "You have made us for yourself, O Lord, and our hearts are restless until they rest in you" (I.1).

The journals of Anne Frank, Pope John XXIII, and Dag Hammarskjold, as well as the autobiographies of Thomas Merton (*The Seven Storey Mountain*) and Dorothy Day (*The Long Loneliness*) demonstrate the renewed interest in this ancient form of spiritual writing. The work of Ira Progoff in developing a methodology for journal writing promises further development and broader use of this genre of spiritual writing.

Letters

The literary genre operative in letter writing is as varied and diverse as the writers, the recipients, and the relationships sustained. Sometimes letters were written for the public forum and for publication. St. Jerome, the prolific letter writer of the early Church, seems to have composed some of his letters with a larger audience in mind, beyond those to whom his letters were addressed. Their literary excellence and theological content made them the most copied letters throughout the Middle Ages. Many of Jerome's letters treat scriptural interpretation in view of various questions presented to him. However, there is variety, and all address the spiritual journey. He wrote to Paulinus on how a priest should live. He wrote letters to encourage zeal for study, to embrace virginity, and to accept widowhood. Jerome also wrote to St. Augustine and to Pope Damasus, but a third of his extant letters were written to women. Marcella was the woman most often addressed.

St. Francis of Assisi employed the use of letters to teach and preach in various ways. In the more public forum he addressed the clergy, the faithful, the whole Order of Friars Minor, and the rulers of people. In these letters he applied his spiritual vision of the gospel in different ways. He encouraged that his letters be copied: "Those who make copies of this writing so that it may be better observed should know they will be blessed by the Lord God" (*A Letter to Clergy* 8). A more personal letter, such as the one to his friend Brother Leo, an autography preserved yet today, reveals the freedom and the dynamic of the spiritual experience into which St. Francis led his friend Brother Leo: "In whatever way it seems best to you to please the Lord God and to follow His footprints and His poverty, do this with the blessing of God and my obedience." These letters and the relationships themselves offer basic principles of Franciscan spirituality. To these letters should be added the more elegant and even more theologically profound letters of St. Clare. Her letters to Blessed Agnes of Prague and to a sister named Ermentrude of Bruges demonstrate the power of mutually shared contemplative love these nuns experienced in "the ineffable charity that led Him to suffer on the wood of the Cross" (*Fourth Letter to Blessed Agnes* 22).

Some of the most celebrated letters of a man and a woman in Western spirituality are the letters of St. Francis de Sales and St. Jane de Chantal. The letters are classic in that they demonstrate spiritual orientation and principles radically influenced by a deep, long-term relationship. On June 24, 1604, Francis wrote to Jane: "Dear Madam, you can see clearly enough to what extent you may call on me and trust me. Make the most of my affection and of all that God has given me for the service of your soul. I am all yours; give no more thought to the role or to the rank I hold in being yours. God has given me to you; so consider me as yours in Him" (*Letter* 223). This experience of mutual trust, shared in and through their written correspondence, was extended by Jane de Chantal in the same way to others. In 1634 Jane wrote to Noel Brulart, "Really, as imperfect as I am, God has willed to unite my heart inti-

mately with yours, and for this I shall ever bless His goodness" (*Letter* 1297).

These letters and many others are an important source of spirituality. Letters are spontaneous, personal, and often written more freely than other genres of spiritual writing. Although they contain elements of the journal and the autobiography, letters are unique in that they illustrate a spirituality formed in the experience of personal relationship, and thus they manifest a spirituality formed in dialogue. Letters are intensely relational, and they thereby offer an understanding of the manifold interpersonal dynamics of various spiritual experiences. St. Catherine of Siena wrote to Pope Gregory XI, her sweet "Babbo," or "Daddy," and Hildegard of Bingen wrote to St. Bernard of Clairvaux concerning her preoccupation "on account of a vision." These two letters, of a slightly different genre than the letters mentioned above, provide a glimpse of mystics in action and of personal prophetic struggle.

Sermons and Scripture Commentaries

Primary literary sources for Christian spirituality include homilies and scriptural commentaries. Both of these are exegetical writing. Often both of these genres are included under the category of *sermones.* More strictly speaking, a sermon has a definite liturgical context or a specific exhortatory moral scope. St. Augustine left in his legacy about eight hundred sermons. His five commentaries on Genesis, his commentaries on the Psalms, on the Gospels, on the Epistles, and his concordance of the Gospels constitute an important corpus of spiritual literature. In all these, the spiritual focus and content are the expounded word of God.

Notes taken down during the course of a sermon was a common composition technique. St. Gregory of Nyssa in his *Commentary on the Song of Songs* explained that the final draft of the commentary was composed from written notes of his hearers. The scriptural writing of St. John

Chrysostom was composed in somewhat the same way. The method of Greek grammarians, who analyzed Greek classical texts word by word, was taken up by these two preachers.

Origen introduced allegorical method into exegetical writing. Allegory consisted of a fourfold sense: literal, messianic, moral or tropological, and eschatological. With Origen, Philo's use of hidden and divine meaning in the Hebrew Scriptures entered into the interpretation of the Christian Scriptures. The spiritual meaning of the sacred text offered the deeper revelation. This approach made possible a typological exegesis that connected the OT and the NT, in view of the future eschatological reality. The use of the spiritual sense of the text opened various attractive approaches to the Scriptures, and medieval authors, particularly monastic authors, creatively used this method to teach a Christian spirituality grounded in extensive use of the Scriptures.

Underlying any exegetical or scriptural homily, commentary, or sermon during the Middle Ages was the profound and mystical sense that the OT and the NT tell the same story of salvation. They are not two different collections of books; they are two different periods mutually revealing each other: *tempus legis* and *tempus gratiae*. These two periods, and more properly the first period of anticipation and desire in the OT, are ordered toward the final consummation.

In monastic circles, the Canticle of Canticles, also known as the Song of Songs, was widely read. It captured the monk's desire for intimate union with God. Many commentaries were written on this biblical text, and these commentaries developed into a popular literary genre in medieval monastic spirituality. St. Bernard of Clairvaux's *Commentary on the Song of Songs* is the masterpiece in monastic biblical commentary. This commentary is divided into eighty-six sermons, each of which treats different themes on union with and love of

God. Thus the terms "commentary" and "sermon" in this work of Bernard suggest a different usage than that mentioned above. In this case a commentary is a collection of sermons. The sermons in St. Bernard's *Commentary on the Song of Songs* are not liturgically designated; rather, in this instance, they are treatises connected to various themes within the biblical text of the Canticle of Canticles. They may or may not have been publicly read or preached. "A close study of the style of the *Sermons* shows an evident difference between certain passages which are subtly nuanced theological dissertations and could not have been delivered in spoken form and others which still have the sound of the spoken word" (Leclercq, p. xxiv).

Other uses of commentary on the Scriptures in the medieval period should be noted. Within monasticism commentaries were used to move and to touch the heart. The rhythm and fervent style were highly ordered toward the affective. Especially for the Cistercians, a scriptural commentary was a treatise on the love of God and on God's relationship with each soul, while Scholastic commentaries on the Scriptures, which developed in the cathedral schools and later in the universities, emphasized God's relationship with the Church and the divine truth revealed by the presence of God in the incarnation. Scholastic commentaries carefully covered the entire sacred text and gave attention to each "letter" found therein. Monastic scriptural commentaries, a primary genre of spirituality, were often incomplete. In these texts, once the love of God had been communicated, the task was complete. St. Bernard's *Commentary on the Song of Songs,* for example, was written over a span of eighteen years. He reached only the beginning of the third chapter, and it is considered a finished work.

During this same period, a literary genre known as *sententiae,* or sentences, developed. This literary form had different meanings, according to whether it was monastic or scholastic. In monastic circles *sententiae* were brief texts that gave a résumé or outline of a preached sermon. *Sententiae* were commentaries on a text. For example, commentaries on the rule were known as *sententiae.* These *sententiae* offered eminently practical direction for living the monastic life. The emphasis in these monastic books of sentences was on common sense, and little attention was given to literary style. In a sense, these collections continued the tradition of the *verba seniorum* of ancient monasticism.

In the scholastic circles the *sententiae* had the specific form of question and disputation, and they included the text that was to be commented upon. While the monastic usage accented principles of ordered living, the scholastic method developed principles of ordered thinking. Scholastic commentaries on the sentences are therefore of an entirely different genre than the monastic sentences. In each case, "sentences" and "commentary" had different meanings. In monasticism, sentences were the commentary; in scholasticism, sentences were the statements developed to be commented upon. In these cases, the same term, *sententiae,* bespeaks entirely different literary genres (Leclercq, pp. 107, 209).

Religious Rules

"The term 'rule' does not designate a well-defined literary form, but it has been used to cover a number of works differing substantially from one another. What these texts have in common is an intent to regulate the life of monks living in a *coenobium.* This legislation normally includes, on the one hand, theoretical spiritual teaching and, on the other, practical regulations to govern the daily life of the monastery" (Fry, pp. 84–85). Although the 6th-century Rule of St. Benedict was definitely conceived and received in or near Rome (Monte Cassino), it found wide and universal acceptance throughout the Western Church in the 9th century. This Rule thereby shaped medieval European mo-

nasticism. Its success is found in the fact that it captured and adapted both the oral and written monastic tradition inherited largely from the East. This Rule, like all religious rules, drew from the traditional deposit of monastic teaching in a way that is appropriate for given circumstances and concrete conditions in a given community. A rule regulates the religious life of the monk by teaching a spiritual vision. "Therefore, we intend to establish a school for the Lord's service. . . . as we progress in this way of life and in faith, we shall run on the path of God's commandments, our hearts overflowing with the inexpressible delight of love" (RB, Prol. 45, 49).

Because of their interest in the intrinsic value of the tradition, monastic writers borrowed much from one another. They were not much interested in who had formulated the tradition in any specific way. The Rule of St. Benedict and the many other rules that developed in the West between the 5th and 9th centuries drew from the spiritual teaching of Pachomius (d. 346), St. Basil (d. 379), John Cassian (d. 435), and St. Augustine (d. 430). St. Basil, in his *Asceticon parvum* and his later *Asceticon magnum,* left a written collection of ascetical principles and spiritual advice for those living the common life. This teaching became part of the monastic tradition later incorporated into rules. In fact, these texts by St. Basil even came to be called the Shorter and Longer Rules.

John Cassian wrote the *Institutes* for beginners in monastic life, and in his most influential book, the *Conferences,* he studied the ideal of the Egyptian monk. The first four books of the *Institutes* were later codified into a monastic rule. Thus the literary genre of rule has diversity of form and intention. One thing is clear: a rule is an introduction to a tradition. It offers neither the beginning nor the end of any given way of life. The concluding chapter of the Rule of St. Benedict points the monk beyond the Rule: "For anyone hastening on to the perfection of monastic life, there are the teachings of the holy Fathers. . . . What book of the holy catholic Fathers does not resoundingly summon us along the true way to reach the Creator? Then, besides the *Conferences* of the Fathers, their *Institutes,* and their *Lives,* there is also the rule of our holy father Basil" (RB 73.2, 4-5).

The Second Council of the Lateran (1139) recognized three rules: those of St. Benedict, St. Basil, and St. Augustine. Hence subsequent founders were to choose a rule already recognized. St. Dominic (d. 1221), for example, chose the Rule of St. Augustine. The great exception came from Assisi. Although it was a longer and more tedious task for St. Clare (d. 1153), both she and St. Francis (d. 1226) introduced a new literary genre of rule into the Church. Their rules drew from the monastic tradition, but they accented Gospel texts and incorporated the developing canonical discipline of the medieval Church. Thus the opening words of the Rule of St. Francis: "The rule and life of the Friars Minor is this: to observe the holy Gospel of our Lord Jesus Christ. . . . Brother Francis promises obedience and reverence to the Lord Pope Honorius and his canonically elected successors."

The Gospel texts throughout St. Francis's Rule incorporate a fresh focus on an obedient, humble, and poor Christ. The Poor Man from Assisi envisioned the friars as "pilgrims and strangers" called to live a life "in the world." The Rule of St. Clare, the first official rule written by a woman for women and approved after long years of struggle as she lay on her deathbed, stresses the human poverty of Christ as the central vision of life and contemplation. For example, even in a simple matter of dress, she wrote: "I admonish, beg, and exhort my sisters to always wear cheap garments out of love of the most holy and beloved Child Who was wrapped in such poor little swaddling clothes and laid in a manger and of His most holy Mother" (chap. 2).

Connected with the genre of rule is that of constitutions. Orders and congregations founded after the 16th century generally do not have a rule; rather, they have constitutions. St. Ignatius Loyola (d. 1556) spent years of thought developing a new form of religious life unencumbered by any facet of monasticism, even communal celebration of the Divine Office. All apostolic action is guided by love of the Church and obedience to the pope. This text gives active and practical apostolic direction in a spirituality of action. Unlike ancient rules, the later constitutions focused on the spirituality of the apostolic task at hand.

Treatises

The treatise as a genre in spirituality differs from the life, letter, sermon, and rule. Explicitly didactic in character, the treatise is systematic throughout, organized, and intended to present a comprehensive vision of specific principles of the spiritual life. It therefore has a speculative point of departure. But because it is a spiritual treatise, it also has a practical application to prayer, contemplation, and the moral life. An important early treatise that influenced many subsequent treatises in spirituality is *The Mystical Theology* of Pseudo-Dionysius. This work had great influence on both Victorine and Franciscan spiritual treatises.

A classic treatise of spirituality of the Middle Ages is St. Bonaventure's *Journey of the Soul to God.* In this intricate and exacting literary text, Bonaventure incorporates traditional theological and philosophical elements in order to lead the reader to contemplate systematically the vast scope of creation. He shows that creation is a book in which we can read God. Speculation is swept up into praise: "Therefore, open your eyes, alert the ears of your spirit, open your lips and apply your heart so that in all creatures you may see, hear, praise, love and worship, glorify and honor your God lest the whole world rise against you" (I.15).

Another classic example of a treatise in spirituality is *The Cloud of Unknowing.* The unknown author of *The Cloud* carefully leads the reader in the ascent to that high point where God lives in the dark cloud of mystery. In this treatise one learns of the importance of centering all affection in God. On a much more practical level, St. Ignatius Loyola, in *The Spiritual Exercises,* offers four weeks of carefully directed exercises in meditation in order to contemplate the whole mystery of salvation and to discern therein the divine will for oneself. *The Introduction to the Devout Life* by St. Francis de Sales is a comprehensive guide in practical principles of finding God in the ordinary daily life in the world.

Apocalyptic and Visionary Literature

Apocalyptic, based on the Greek word for "revelation," is a form of eschatology that places accent on the proximity of the end of time. Apocalyptic literature in Christian spirituality manifests the desire of the human heart to find a place for itself in the history of salvation, a history begun and to be ended by God. The Calabrian abbot Joachim of Fiore (d. 1202), in his *Exposition on the Apocalypse* and *Book of Concordance,* wrote in view of a received revelation of the Apocalypse and of a vision of the internal accord between the OT and NT. He then addressed the crisis of his age out of his new understanding of the Scriptures. His writing is filled with the use of revealed symbolic forms that find their base in an exegesis of the canonical apocalypses.

Joachim's legacy subsequently found new impetus in the Franciscan conviction that St. Francis embodied a new "advent" of Christ in history. Franciscan Spirituals saw Franciscan poverty as key to the last stage of history, the establishment of the contemplative Church. Ubertino of Casale (d. 1330) wrote the classic masterpiece of the Franciscan apocalyptic genre in spirituality, *The Tree of the Crucified Life of Jesus,* and from this work Franciscan Spirituals were able to find meaning in their own trials. This same literary genre was employed by Savanarola (d. 1498) in his famous *Compendium of Revelations.*

Apocalyptic is one form of visionary literature. The other, not directly connected to an exegetical method, moves forth from a variety of psychic intuitions and an intense devotional life of meditation. The most powerful visionary literature of the Middle Ages expresses the welling up of a profound female experience and inspiration. Medieval women mystics generally sensed themselves to be compelled by God to write their visions, and they did so with confidence, authority, and a sense of urgency. Their visions tended to be cosmic in scope, and they tended to apply the history of revelation and doctrinal affirmations to the individual soul. Hildegard of Bingen (d. 1181), for example, wrote a trilogy of visionary books: *Scivias, Book of Life's Merits,* and *The Book of Divine Merits.*

Hildegard inspires and teaches not so much by moving the affections of her reader or by explaining doctrine but by providing a picture of interconnecting symbols that allow the reader to understand. Thus her visionary literature should be read in a way that is connected with her music, paintings, and poetry. In a much simpler way, Julian of Norwich (d. between 1416 and 1423) recorded her *Revelations* (*Showings,* as she more often called them) as "bodily visions" and "corporal sights" that stimulated her search for symbolic understanding: "And in this he showed me something small, no bigger than a hazelnut, lying in the palm of my hand, and I perceived that it was as round as any ball. I looked at it and I thought: What can this be? And I was given this general answer: It is everything which is made" (Short Text, chap. 4).

Poetry, Prayers, and Meditations

Poetry formed the genre for hymns that entered Christian spirituality in the early liturgical experience. This initial development out of the tradition of Hebrew psalmody added devotion and variety to singing during vigil services. Later, nonliturgical poetry developed in its own right as a literary genre and thereby provided another poetic source for spirituality. Hadewijch, a Beguine of the mid-13th century, in her *Poems in Stanzas* and *Poems in Couplets,* moved the genre of poetry into the genre of mystical love lyrics. She used the poetry of courtly love to express ardent and emotional longing for God. In doing this, she drew on the sequences of the Latin liturgy and the common scriptural responses. Another poet of the Middle Ages, Jacopone da Todi (d. 1306), in his defense of Franciscan poverty against his own Franciscan Order and the papacy, found himself caught in conflict with the authorities of both the Church and the order. The best of his poetry was written while he was in prison. It moves dramatically in contrasting images as he defies arrogant power and brute hypocrisy. Yet the gentle poetry of St. Francis of Assisi, especially the *Canticle of Brother Sun,* remained an inspiration for Jacopone as he wrote his collection known as *The Lauds.*

Poetry also developed as a form of prayer. In his classic *Prayers and Meditations,* St. Anselm of Canterbury (d. 1109) created a poetry of intimate personal devotion. He brought poetry into the genre of private prayer. It was longer, more personal, and more daring theologically and affectively, and therefore unsuitable for liturgical use. His texts, which constituted a new form of private prayer, went beyond simple extracts from the psalms. Basic to this development was a life of continued meditation on the Scriptures and the lives of the saints. *Meditatio,* the art of remembering and associating various texts of the Scriptures, impregnated the heart with the words of the Scriptures. This, too, found expression in literary form. A more contemporary example of this genre is the *Meditations on Mary, the Mother of God* composed by John Henry Newman (d. 1890). In this meditation he compares and contrasts Mary with the outstanding biblical personalities who prefigured her.

Conclusion

The many different forms of literary genre that comprise the rich and varied sources of Christian spirituality are different from the sources of dogmatic and systematic theology. These latter sources draw upon the ancient creeds, decrees of synods and councils, and philosophical principles, with a view toward clarity and precision of thought and understanding, while the former are ordered toward devotion and spiritual experience. In fact, the different literary genres in spirituality reveal, in themselves, a specific form of practiced spirituality or devotional experience. Both genres, either of systematic/dogmatic or of spirituality, however, find a basis and a direction in that which is fundamental in Christian life—the Scriptures and the liturgy.

See also ASCETICISM; BENEDICTINE SPIRITUALITY; DESERT; EARLY CHRISTIAN SPIRITUALITY; FRANCISCAN SPIRITUALITY; HOLINESS; MYTH; NARRATIVE; PATRISTIC SPIRITUALITY; SAINTS, COMMUNION OF SAINTS; WESTERN MEDIEVAL SPIRITUALITY.

———

Bibliography: F. Clark, *The Pseudo-Gregorian Dialogues* (Leiden: Brill, 1987). H. Delehaye, *The Legends of the Saints* (Notre Dame, Ind.: Univ. of Notre Dame Press, 1961). T. Fry, ed., Introduction, *The Rule of St. Benedict* (Collegeville, Minn.: Liturgical Press, 1981). T. Heffernan, *Sacred Biography: Saints and Their Biographies in the Middle Ages* (New York: Oxford Univ. Press, 1988). J. Leclercq, Introduction, *Bernard of Clairvaux on the Song of Songs,* vol. 2 (Kalamazoo, Mich.: Cistercian Publications, 1983); *The Love of Learning and the Desire for God* (New York: Fordham Univ. Press, 1961). E. Petroff, *Medieval Women's Visionary Literature* (Oxford: Oxford Univ. Press, 1986).

J. A. WAYNE HELLMANN, O.F.M. CONV.

SPIRITUALITY, CHRISTIAN

Terminology

The word *spirituality* derives from the Latin *spiritualitas,* an abstract word related to *spiritus* and *spiritualis,* which were used to translate Paul's *pneuma* and *pneumatikos.* In Pauline theology "spirit" (*pneuma*) is opposed to "flesh" (Greek *sarx;* Latin *caro*), and "spiritual" (*pneumatikos*) is set over against either "fleshly" (Greek *sarkikos;* Latin *carnalis*—Gal 3:3; 5:13, 16-25; 1 Cor 3:1-3; Rom 7:14-8:14) or "animal" (Greek *psychikos;* Latin *animalis*—1 Cor 2:14-15), but, significantly for later developments, they are contrasted neither with "body" (Greek *soma;* Latin *corpus*) or "bodily" (Greek *somatikos;* Latin *corporalis*) nor with "matter" (Greek *hylē;* Latin *materia*). For Paul, the "pneumatic" or "spiritual" person is one whose whole being and life are ordered, led, or influenced by the "Spirit of God" (Greek *Pneuma Theou;* Latin *Spiritus Dei*—see 1 Cor 2:12, 14), whereas the person who is "sarkic," that is, "carnal" or "fleshly," or who is "psychic" or "animal," is one whose whole being and life are opposed to God's Spirit. The opposition, for Paul, is not between the incorporeal and the corporeal or between the immaterial and material, but between two ways of life. Thus one's body and one's psychic soul (Greek *psychē;* Latin *anima*) can, like one's spirit, be spiritual if led by the Spirit, and one's spirit, mind, or will can be carnal if opposed to the Spirit.

Spiritualitas, as first evidenced in the 5th century (Pseudo-Jerome, *Epist.* 7; PL 30:114D-115A: "So act as to advance in spirituality"), referred to the Pauline sense of life according to the Spirit of God. This use was continued in subsequent centuries, but in the 12th century *spiritualitas* began to be opposed to *corporalitas* or *materialitas.* This changed the Pauline religious meaning so as to now express something of the entitative order; the new meaning prepared for a later widespread view that con-

fused spirituality with disdain for the body and matter. Together with this philosophical meaning, the earlier Pauline view continued in authors such as Thomas Aquinas. Still further meanings appeared later: persons exercising ecclesiastical jurisdiction were called the *spiritualitas,* or "lords spiritual," as opposed to those exercising civil jurisdiction, the *temporalitas,* or "lords temporal"; next, ecclesiastical property came to be called *spiritualitas,* and the property of the civil ruler *temporalitas.*

Only in the 17th century did the philosophical senses of *spiritualitas* appear in the French and English cognates. At that time *spiritualité* was used in French for the devout life, but it was sometimes applied pejoratively by authors speaking of *la spiritualité* of Fénélon, Madame Guyon, and Marie de l'Incarnation, suspected of Quietism or fanaticism. After being used relatively rarely in the following centuries, *spiritualité* became widely used through its appearing in titles of two influential works, Auguste Saudreau's *Manuel de spiritualité* (1917) and Pierre Pourrat's four-volume *La spiritualité catholique* (1918-1928). English usage, from the 1920s on, saw more frequent examples of "spirituality" as a result of translation of Pourrat's work and that of other French authors. Since the 1950s the term has become very popular, frequently replacing terms such as "devotion," "piety," "interior life," "life of the soul," "spiritual life," "spiritual theology."

Although originating within a Catholic context, the term has more recently been adopted by many Protestants, by scholars of other religions, and even by secularists and Marxists. Assuredly, Christian spirituality must have at least a Christian ecumenical dimension, but this is insufficient. The increased meeting of Christians with diverse religious traditions means that Christian spirituality, whether experiential or the object of study, must not be isolated from these other traditions and must take account of their diverse "spiritualities," whether they be those of the "great" world religions or of native peoples whose rich spiritualities are being increasingly recognized (e.g., their awareness of divine presence, their rituals, their concern for all creation).

Three Levels of Spirituality

The Real or Existential Level of Lived Experience

Several different but related levels of spirituality can be distinguished. The first and most basic level is that of a person's lived experience, that is, the real or existential level. For Christian spirituality, the renewal of biblical theology and greater awareness of pneumatology in the West have led to an increasing link of this lived spirituality with the Pauline notion, that is, Christian life as guided or influenced by the Holy Spirit, who is given by the Father and the risen Christ in order to make persons sisters and brothers of Christ and children of the Father, as well as to fashion both women and men into images of Christ (Rom 8:29, 16-17). All this happens by the Spirit's leading them to advance in Christ to the "praise of the glory of [God's] grace" (Eph 1:6). The Holy Spirit gives individuals and the community the gifts of faith, hope, charity (1 Cor 13:13), wisdom, understanding (Col 1:9), and liberty (Rom 8:21; Gal 5:13; 2 Cor 3:17), fruits such as love, joy, peace, patience (Gal 5:23-24), and charisms of different kinds that build up the Christian community (1 Cor 12:4-11, 28-30; Rom 12:6-8; Eph 4:11-13).

These gifts of the Spirit and the person's mystical union with Christ mean that Christian life in the Spirit takes place in an ecclesial context, in which celebration of word and sacrament culminates in the Eucharist (here occur important variations in Catholic and Protestant spiritualities). At the same time this experiential level of Christian spirituality embraces the whole human person (body, soul, spirit), who is part of a constantly changing material created order (physical, plant, animal), who is a symbolizing, ritualizing being, who learns and uses language for communication and self-expression; a person who is both an individual and a member of society, who is inculturated in place and time and so is affected by his or her social and personal history; a person, finally, who is called to serve others in the social, political, and economic orders. Although Christians may not always consciously thematize their lived spirituality in this way—indeed, too often in the past many of these elements have not been related to Christian spirituality—their spirituality does involve all these elements. Thus their attitude toward them, whether positive or negative, or even if they are unaware of their spiritual import, affects their growth in tending toward God.

Since by baptism every Christian is plunged into the lived experience of life in the Spirit, spirituality on the existential level must include this experience of all Christians. Nevertheless, "spirituality" is often used especially of those who, guided and empowered by the Holy Spirit, consciously seek to further their going out of and beyond themselves and their limitations by intensifying their life in the Spirit and in Christ for the Father; or, to use other language, "spirituality" is often referred to those who of set purpose perseveringly seek "union with God" or "perfection" or "divinization."

Spirituality of Groups and Varying Spiritual Traditions

Although Christian spirituality as a lived experience must be personal, this experience is neither received nor lived in isolation. Each person is introduced into a particular social and inculturated spirituality, which presents Christian ideals and approaches to those ideals in a unique way. Hence a second level of Christian spirituality is that of a group, the family in the first instance and often the parish, but also for many the spirituality of a specialized group, e.g., Latin or Eastern Catholic spirituality; Anglican, Lutheran, Methodist, Baptist, Mennonite spirituality; the spirituality of different religious communities and increasingly of lay associates of religious communities; the spirituality of lay faith-communities, of cursillo, charismatic, or other movements. This second level often revolves around the formulation of teaching, or the development of symbols, rituals, artistic and other expression, or guidance about the lived reality or experience and how this is to be intensified. Sometimes the life, example, or teaching of an outstanding person (e.g., Francis of Assisi, Catherine of Siena, Julian of Norwich, Martin Luther, Teresa of Avila, John Wesley, Thérèse of Lisieux, Dorothy Day, Dietrich Bonhoeffer, Thomas Merton) becomes a pattern for others; sometimes such influence comes from writings by persons judged to be gifted with insight into spiritual development.

Historically, the dynamics of this second level has meant the rise of many varying traditions or schools of Christian spirituality. The varieties of Christian spirituality have their origin in the Christian Scriptures themselves. In addition to the Pauline doctrines, the four Gospels represent four different approaches to Jesus and his life and teaching: Mark's emphasis on the coming of the kingdom of God, reaching its climax in Christ's passion and death; Matthew's ecclesial interests and his presentation of Christian life in the challenging Sermon on the Mount; Luke's attention to the compassion of God revealed in Jesus; John's attention to Jesus as God's Word calling for faith in himself and offering life and the Spirit. Other texts bring out further aspects. For example, the doctrine of 1 Peter of the person's sharing the divine nature or of all Christians as the People of God sharing Christ's priesthood has been influential in past and present Christian spirituality; again, the Letter of James has provoked controversy about the relation between faith and works, a question already raised by Paul.

Each spiritual tradition or school seeks to model itself on the gospel but emphasizes different aspects of the gospel in teaching, practices, and forms of expression. Thus the many strands of reflection on Jesus and his gospel in the Bible called forth different emphases and responses as the gospel was preached, received, and inculturated in various regions in the early Church. The most striking variations were those between the West and the East, e.g., Eastern stress on liturgy and the resurrection of Christ, and Western stress on moral doctrine, original sin, and the passion of Christ. Further differences have grown within these larger traditions, e.g., Syrian versus Byzantine spirituality in the East, and Celtic or Germanic versus Latin spirituality in the West. Within these, still further variations took place within history. The most significant of these in the West was the split between Protestant and Catholic spiritualities, especially in relation to the doctrines of grace and works, different emphases on word and sacrament, and sharp divergences concerning ecclesiology. A recent clear example of such historical developments is the shift in Western spirituality in this century, the spirituality derived from the Second Vatican Council being a major although not exclusive component.

The Study of Spirituality

Past studies. Distinct from the first and second levels of spirituality is the study, practical or academic, of spirituality in programs or schools. In the Fathers, spirituality was generally interwoven with their theology, itself richly biblical, replete with symbolism and typology, often expressed in rhetorical fashion in their liturgical homilies. But, it has been noted, authors such as Clement of Alexandria, Tertullian, Origen, Ambrose, and Augustine wrote practical treatises to help promote the personal life of Christians (Solignac, col.

1156). The theology of the great medieval commentators or summists such as Bonaventure or Aquinas was of one piece. The articulations of their works did not represent distinct theological disciplines like the later divisions into dogmatic and moral theology. Their doctrine on life in the Spirit was interwoven with the whole fabric of their unified theology: the doctrines of God, the Trinity, creation, Christ, grace, sin, sacraments, etc., were as much a part of their spirituality as their discussions of virtues, prayer, etc. One of their main teaching offices was commentary on Scripture, in which application to life in the Spirit was prominent. The later demarcation of moral theology from dogmatic theology, the excessive multiplication of subtle questions, and the emphasis on a morals of obligation and casuistry robbed theology of its spiritual dynamism. Reaction against this deadening of theology led to the growth of separate treatises of spiritual theology or of ascetic and mystical theology. These continued to flourish in theological schools well into the 20th century.

Recent changes. The development of spiritual theology or of ascetic and mystical theology tended to focus narrowly on prayer, mortification, virtues and vices, rules of spiritual progress, and spiritual direction. The recovery of biblical, patristic, and liturgical theology; awareness of the all-embracing unity of theology for the great medieval masters; and recognition of the importance of Christian experience, personal and social, have broadened the theological context of studies in spirituality. Joann Wolski Conn has noted five distinctive trends in recent spirituality studies: "sustained attention to feminist issues, concern for the link between prayer and social justice, reliance on classical sources for answers to current questions, recognition of the value of developmental psychology and its understanding of the 'self,' and agreement that experience is the most appropriate starting point" (Conn, p. 31). These currents in the study of spirituality

are now often developed within new practical and academic programs specializing in spirituality. At the same time, the greater opening of theology itself to Christian experience, together with its greater use of new philosophies, hermeneutics, linguistics, anthropology, aesthetics, psychology, sociology, political science, and economics, has led theology to take a much broader approach to spirituality than was the case in earlier "spiritual theology." The conjunction of these developments in spirituality programs and in theology has raised the question of how the study of spirituality stands in relation to theology and religious studies as well as to the philosophical and other human sciences.

Religious studies and Christian spirituality. It should be noted that in academic circles there are two distinct approaches to spirituality. One operates within a community of faith responding to a revelation accepted as normative, although its conceptualization and verbal expression are subject to constant scrutiny and development. The other is the approach of secular religious studies, which examines spirituality without such a faith commitment. Such an approach, found in many secular universities, seeks to produce a description of different spiritualities, a presentation derived from the sources, widely conceived, that have been studied. These sources frequently include a faith-content and the response to it as an important and perhaps decisive element, but these are analyzed descriptively and are not judged in terms of a theology elaborated within a faith community. A further step is comparison of different spiritualities within the same religious tradition or as found in different religious traditions. This in turn can lead a scholar using these methods toward discovery of fundamental principles common to all the spiritualities studied and toward finding reasons for variations in spiritualities.

Such research has great value for Christian spirituality, even for those who work within a context of Christian faith. The results of this research can broaden the perspectives of committed students of Christian spirituality, can challenge assumptions and conclusions accepted too easily, and can suggest avenues and methods of research that might occur less readily to Christian scholars. However, there is room for a hermeneutics of suspicion when scholars using the methods of secular religious studies claim complete objectivity. It is necessary to examine the philosophical, psychological, sociological, linguistic, hermeneutic, and other methodologies being used by such scholars. These are sometimes made explicit but sometimes are assumed with inadequate self-criticism, and one must examine their application in order to see if reductionism is at work. For example, in the history of spirituality, why is some evidence selected as more crucial or influential than other evidence? Such selectivity inevitably involves the scholar's judgment of causalities by analogy with what the scholar considers decisive in the development of spirituality. The same is true with the application of other human sciences. Similar questions must, of course, be asked of the Christian scholar using these sciences in studying spirituality.

With respect to the first method, that used by scholars working within a Christian faith-commitment, the relations between the study of spirituality and theology are still subject to discussion, with no clear consensus existing at present. For some, the traditional notion endures, that is, that theology, sometimes conceived rather narrowly, should dominate the study of spirituality, providing principles that will guide practical applications to life in the Spirit. For others, theology itself must today use the resources not only of philosophy but of all the human sciences. Hence theology, when focused on Christian life in the Spirit, must take account of all these aspects in a multidisciplinary dialogue; further, it must have as part of its data not only

the revealed word of God as developed in authentic tradition but also the range of human experience, historical and especially contemporary.

Spirituality as a specialized field of study. Many regret the past split between theology and spirituality, and, wishing to maintain the fundamental unity of theological study, would want to unite spirituality, together with biblical, historical, liturgical, pastoral, and canonical studies, within one theological view in which each of these would provide insights for an integrating vision. But just as the demands of specialization have required that each of these areas of study develop its own method and programs, so it seems necessary for the academic study of spirituality to organize itself as a specialized field of study. Since the first two levels of spirituality, the very matter of study, are personal or social in particular rather than in universal ways, studies in spirituality concentrate on the particular more than does theology, even when theology has become more attuned to experience and to multidisciplinary dialogue. In a distinction without separation of theology and spirituality, Christian experience could be seen as a common "stock" (*souche*) for theology and spirituality, with theology examining the various components of this experience and spirituality investigating the way this experience becomes particular or personal according to different emphases in living the gospel (Laguë, pp. 350–351).

Increased specialization in biblical, historical, and other areas has, however, brought the danger of isolation and lack of communication with theology and other disciplines. The same danger could threaten spirituality studied as a distinct discipline. Christian spirituality must, like theology, be multidisciplinary, incorporating the outlook of anthropology, psychology, sociology, and other disciplines; it must also be ecumenical and in dialogue with non-Christian religions. But it must also remain in intimate contact with Christian theology and the other Christian areas of study.

Within these relationships a fundamental question is that of the criteria used to judge particular or group experiences of life in the Spirit. For some, a theology that is itself in intimate relationship with the other appropriate disciplines would be that which exercises final judgment of authentic Christian spirituality; for others, the judgment would come within the interplay of theology and the human sciences in their examination of the particular religious experience in question.

One of the most serious analyses arguing for spirituality as a distinct discipline is that by Sandra Schneiders, who has elaborated the methods and criteria of judgment she sees operative in its academic study. For her, "spirituality is the field of study which attempts to investigate in an interdisciplinary way the spiritual experience as such, i.e., as spiritual and as experience" (Schneiders, p. 692). She describes four characteristics that, for her, distinguish the discipline of spirituality from related fields of study. First, it is interdisciplinary, so that spirituality must use whatever approaches are relevant to the reality being studied; for Christian spirituality these include at least biblical studies, history, theology, psychology, and comparative religion. Second, it is "a descriptive-critical rather than prescriptive-normative discipline," that is, it "is not the 'practical application' of theoretical principles, theological or other, to concrete life experience. It is the critical study of such experience" (p. 693). Third, spirituality is "ecumenical, interreligious, and cross-cultural." The context for study of spiritual experience is "anthropologically inclusive," since Christianity is not presumed to exhaust or include the whole of religious reality (p. 693). Fourth, "spirituality is a holistic discipline" because it does not limit itself to "explorations of the explicitly religious" but examines all the elements integral to spiritual experience, e.g., "the psychologi-

cal, bodily, historical, social, political, aesthetic, intellectual, and other dimensions of the human subject of spiritual experience" (p. 693).

It might be observed that Schneiders often seems to speak of theology in a rather narrow sense. Most contemporary theologians would maintain that at least the first, third, and fourth characteristics must be true of theological method today if theology is to seek understanding of revelation and to inculturate it in today's world. Thus it would appear that the difference between theology and spirituality might be found in the second characteristic and in the ways the study of spirituality is practiced, although even here most contemporary theologians seek to begin from, and relate to, experience much more than did those using deductive methods (Laguë, pp. 347–349).

Perhaps the specificity of spirituality is better clarified by the description Schneiders gives of its practice (pp. 693–695): spirituality examines the individual as opposed to the general; it involves participation by the student of spirituality as opposed to an objective self-distancing (here she acknowledges the complications involved in the relation of praxis and personal self-involvement to the discipline); its procedures are by way of description, critical analysis, and constructive appropriation, in which theology and the human and social sciences play a part and in which hermeneutical theory governs the process; it seems to have an irreducibly triple finality, that is, accumulation of knowledge, assistance of the students in their spiritual lives, and help for them to foster spiritual life in others.

Schneiders' valuable contribution to the discussion seems to be open to further questioning about how to identify the ultimate criteria for critical judgment of Christian spiritualities as authentically human and Christian. Theology and the human and social sciences, it is said, are of particular importance to the analytical and critical second phase of study "leading to an explanation and evaluation of the subject" (p. 695; see p. 692), whereas "the third phase is synthetic and/or constructive, and leads to appropriation [in Ricoeur's 'sense of the transformational actualization of meaning' (note 68)]. Hermeneutical theory governs this final phase" (p. 695). Again, "while making use of a plurality of specific methods, the discipline has no one method of its own. Rather, methods function in the explanatory moment of the hermeneutical dialectic between explanation and understanding" (p. 694).

It seems, then, that in this view, after the contributions of theology and the other sciences have been heard, the application of hermeneutical theory provides the ultimate criterion for judgment. While it is true that theology itself must apply hermeneutical science self-critically, it could be asked how a Christian spirituality can be judged as authentic on grounds other than those of a broadly conceived Christian theology. Would hermeneutical theory, as expounded by the individual scholar, not become the final judge of authentic Christian spirituality and the ways of its development? And although "a theologically critical moment is integral to the study of the experience under investigation" (p. 692, n. 62), the final judgment is left to other methods and theories. Could it not be asked whether this ultimacy of hermeneutical criteria in fact leads spirituality thus conceived and practiced finally to approach the method of secular religious studies?

Problem Areas in Spirituality

The developing study of spirituality raises other questions and problems besides those already mentioned. The preceding discussion of interrelated disciplines evokes the serious problems raised by the pluralism of theologies, philosophies, anthropologies, hermeneutics, linguistic theories, etc. A multidisciplinary approach necessary to studies of spirituality will inevitably confront these pluralities, just as these theologies and the human sciences themselves meet analogous problems in their attempts to be multidisciplinary. The solution must lie in the recognition that there is no simple uniformity in any of the dialogue partners; rather, there are groups within each discipline whose variety can be enriching and challenging for those who listen to them all, even if integration is thereby made more difficult.

Second, there is the problem of training assistants or guides for those seeking to intensify their life in the Spirit. Although there are now a number of faculties of spirituality or departments within faculties of theology that have established solid standards for study and research, some of the more practical, rather brief programs are in danger of giving false confidence in their competence to those completing them. Those giving spiritual assistance in Christian spirituality run the risk of making erroneous judgments if they lack a thorough training in all aspects of theology as well as in other related disciplines such as psychology and anthropology. Christian spirituality must be guided by sound theology of the Trinitarian God, of creation, of the human person and human destiny, of sin, of Christ and his saving work, of the interplay of grace and human effort, of the sacraments—in a word, of all the mysteries of faith. Competence is also needed regarding principles of moral life and moral decisions together with knowledge of the theology of prayer, virtues, gifts of the Spirit, etc. Any Christian spirituality involves theological positions in these areas either explicitly or implicitly (Principe, p. 138). If these positions are not recognized or examined critically, assistance can be inadequate and possibly dangerous. Brief programs in practical spirituality can hardly equip persons to become competent assistants to others in their spiritual journey.

Third, spirituality as a discipline will have to examine more carefully whether it should take as its object only those who are consciously striving for a more intense life in the Spirit or whether it should examine manifestations of spirituality in all Christians. Here in particular the relevance of popular religion or popular devotion must be considered. The study of popular religion has become an important new field of religious studies, involving debates about its meaning and about methodology. This question is especially important if the discipline of spirituality wishes to examine the spirituality of social or cultural groups in the present or past.

Finally, the question of inculturation within catholicity, which has become increasingly important for theology and missiology, must likewise concern the study and indeed the lived experience of individual and group spiritualities. The past varieties of spiritualities are themselves products of inculturation of the gospel and of Christian lived experience of the gospel in differing historical cultures. Such inculturation has produced a catholicity of spiritual experience that provides a rich variety within a fundamental Christian unity of faith. The spread of the gospel throughout the world and the awareness of the need for more inculturation and true catholicity mean that study of spirituality and pastoral service of spiritual development will have to be even broader in scope than is the case at present. This increased multiplication of distinctive spiritualities, each striving to live the gospel, together with a disciplined study of them, should lead to an ever-richer worldwide "praise of the glory of God's grace."

See also APOSTOLIC SPIRITUALITY; ASCETICAL THEOLOGY; AUGUSTINIAN SPIRITUALITY; CELTIC SPIRITUALITY; CONTEMPORARY SPIRITUALITY; CULTURE; DEVOTION(S), POPULAR; DIVINIZATION; EARLY CHRISTIAN SPIRITUALITY; EASTERN CHRISTIAN SPIRITUALITY; ECOLOGICAL CONSCIOUSNESS; ECUMENISM, SPIRITUAL; HISTORY, HISTORICAL CONSCIOUSNESS; HOLISTIC SPIRITUALITY; HOLY SPIRIT; INCARNATION; LAY SPIRITUALITY; MODERN SPIRITUALITY; MYSTICAL THEOLOGY; PATRISTIC SPIRITUALITY; PROTESTANT SPIRITUALITIES; QUIETISM; REFORMATION AND CATHOLIC REFORMATION SPIRITUALITIES; WESTERN MEDIEVAL SPIRITUALITY.

Bibliography: *Dictionnaire de spiritualité:* A. Solignac, "Spiritualité: Le mot et l'histoire," vol. 14. fasc. 95-96 (1990), cols. 1142–1160. M. Dupuy, "Spiritualité: La notion de spiritualité," vol. 14, fasc. 96 (1990), cols. 1160–1173.
Nuovo dizionario di spiritualità, ed. S. De Fiores and T. Goffi (Rome: Edizioni Paoline, 1982); French adaptation by F. Vial (Paris: Cerf, 1983): G. Moioli, "Esperienza cristiana" pp. 536–541. S. De Fiores, "Spiritualità contemporanea," pp. 1516–1543. G. Moioli, "Teologia spirituale," pp. 1597–1609.
H. U. von Balthasar, "Das Evangelium als Norm und Kritik aller Spiritualität," *Spiritus Creator: Skizzen zur Theologie* 3 (Einsiedeln: Johannes Verlag, 1967) 247–267. J. Wolski Conn, *Spirituality and Personal Maturity* (New York: Paulist, 1989). M. Laguë, "Spiritualité et théologie: d'une même souche: Note sur l'actualité d'un débat," *Église et Théologie* 20/2 (1989) 333–351. W. Principe, "Toward Defining Spirituality," *Studies in Religion/Sciences Religieuses* 12 (1983) 127–141. S. Schneiders, "Spirituality in the Academy," TS 50 (1989) 676–697.

WALTER H. PRINCIPE, C.S.B.

SPIRITUALITY, CHRISTIAN (CATHOLIC), HISTORY OF

Jewish Antecedents

Christian spirituality arose within the Jewish spiritual tradition of God's abiding presence, faithful covenant love, the living word of Scripture, the supremacy of divine law, the necessity of worship, and the practice of remembrance. Refined by centuries of development, Jewish belief in God's manifold self-disclosure came to be understood as principally mediated by the inner word within the human spirit—consciousness, memory, will, and dreams. Public worship remained the focus of national identity, but personal spirituality centered on recollection or attentiveness—the practice of the presence of God.

Early Christian spirituality continued in a new and more inclusive way the line of development begun with Abraham, Moses, the prophets, and inspired sages. Discontinuity with Jewish law and custom occurred slowly and partially, beginning with Jesus.

Jesus and the Apostolic Community

Known for his teaching and miracles, Jesus preached reliance on God and love of neighbor mainly to the middle and lower classes, many of whom saw him as the promised Messiah. He healed the sick, blind, lame, and those afflicted with mental and spiritual disorders, even raised the dead. After his execution by the ruling class, his disciples' faith came to rest on Jesus' resurrection, which was proved to them by many appearances and confirmed by the bestowal of the Holy Spirit at Pentecost.

Early Christian spirituality centered on God's presence in Jesus himself, in the body of believers who unite in Jesus' name and teaching, and in each person not only as a disciple but as a human being. The goal and meaning of Christian spirituality is the recognition and enhancement of the Divine Presence, which is at once both hidden and manifest, that is, a mystery.

For early Christians, the transcendent Christ is no less the immanent Spirit who lives among and within us, present in the mysteries of baptism and Eucharist but also in the needs of the suffering, oppressed, and poor (Mt 25:40). Christ's Spirit is present as well in those who believe in the mystery of the Church as Christ's Body and among those who pray and work for the coming of God's reign on earth as it is in heaven (Mt 28:20). Eschatological in intent, early Christian spirituality looked forward to the return of Jesus in final glory.

Local communities developed around apostles and evangelists who preached a distinctive understanding of the teachings of Jesus and the meaning of his life, death, and resurrection. Tension between extreme Jewish Christians and those more open to pagan converts led to an uneasy compromise at the Council of Jerusalem. Another challenge arose from within the primitive Church itself—spiritual elitism based on extraordinary charisms such as ecstatic speech, healing, and prophecy (see 1 Cor 14). Simply "gifts" to Paul and "wonders" to other writers, such manifestations were interpreted as signs of God's favor, special forms of grace intended to strengthen the early community. They did not so much realize the presence of God as dramatically announce it.

Paul and his disciples tempered belief in the immanent parousia with an emphasis on sanctifying life in the present world to prepare for the life of glory yet to come, recognizing even in marriage a sacrament of Christ's love for, and presence in, his Body, the Church (Eph 5:16). With the destruction of Jerusalem in 135 and the disappearance of Jewish Christianity, subsequent spirituality was largely Pauline in character: moderate, missionary, and receptive toward the non-Jewish world.

The Early Church

Postapostolic spiritual writing emphasized simplicity or single-heartedness (*haplotēs*) as the Christian ideal. Its opposite, double-mindedness (*dipsychia*), was seen to lead to compromise and catastrophe, especially during persecution.

The earliest spirituality of the Church was liturgical, centered on identification with Christ in baptism and Eucharist. Essential forms were adopted from Jewish custom, although distinctive hymns, art, and architecture developed. Like private prayer, public prayer in the morning and evening was a widespread custom. Family Bible reading was common. Much early spirituality centered on ministry, especially by deacons and deaconesses, who took the Eucharist to sick or imprisoned Christians, distributed food and clothing, and otherwise attended to the needs of the community. Charitable institutions were founded to provide for the poor, widows and orphans, and the sick.

The Apologetic Period

Much early spiritual, dogmatic, and moral writing by "apologists," or defenders of the faith, such as Irenaeus, Justin Martyr, and Clement of Rome, resulted from efforts to refute opponents as well as unorthodox or extreme forms of Christian teaching. Gnostic sects, which flourished from the middle of the 1st century to the beginning of the 3rd, held that salvation could only be attained by means of secret insight into the mysteries of God, knowledge found only within the confines of an inner circle of initiates. In the 2nd century, Montanism, a dissident sect of ecstatic and morally austere Christians, spread from Phrygia into North Africa under the influence of the brilliant apologist Tertullian of Carthage. Anti-intellectual, millenaristic, and intolerant, Montanists demanded that Christians everywhere accept their teaching. Temperance was carried to an extreme in Encratism, a denial, especially by Tatian, of the sanctity of marriage and sex. By upholding marriage, orthodox Christianity protected the rights of women and children as well as the integrity of life as a whole.

During the 1st century several varieties of spirituality had arisen from different movements within Jewish tradition in the Diaspora as well as in Palestine. But the main current of early Christian spirituality, and the first explicit "school," had its source in the Wisdom tradition among the Jews in Egypt, particularly as shaped by Philo (ca. 20 B.C.–A.D. 50).

After the destruction of Jerusalem in 135, Syrian Antioch and especially Alexandria became the major centers of Christian theology and spirituality, followed by Rome, Ephesus, Damascus, and cities in Cilicia and Phrygia. The second capital of the empire, Alexandria had a large Jewish population, for whom the Bible had first been translated into Greek. There, according to tradition, St. Mark the Evangelist had founded a Church, and in the 2nd century Pantaenus began the first catechetical school. His successor, Clement (150–ca. 215), was the first Christian philosopher and theologian. Like the apologists, Clement opposed to Gnosticism the "true gnosis" of faith. Like Philo, his attitude toward philosophy was receptive; through his influence the conceptual framework of Middle Platonism was secured for Christian reflection. Clement was succeeded by Origen (ca. 185–254), the first Christian biblical scholar, who contributed significantly through his sermons and writing to the growing heritage of mystical spirituality.

The Age of Persecutions

Local and imperial persecutions during the late 2nd and 3rd centuries evoked a spirituality of peaceful resistance and encouragement. Early Christians believed that the suffering and death of martyrs effectively realized the presence of Christ, and such champions of faith earned special honor in memory and ritual. The spirituality that enabled them to endure suffering and death rather than forsake faith in Jesus became a model for all. Exhortation and consolation thus comprise the major part of relevant spiritual writings of the period—the Acts of the martyrs, letters and pastoral writings of Ignatius of Antioch, Polycarp, Tertullian, Cyprian of Carthage, and others. But extreme resistance toward reconciling Christians who had temporarily lapsed out of fear led to schism in the 3rd and 4th centuries, when Novatianists and Donatists rejected the tolerant attitude of Rome and Carthage as a betrayal of the martyrs.

The Patristic Period: Monasticism and Mysticism

Under Constantine, imperial toleration followed by the adoption of Christianity led to court interference in doctrinal disputes and the emergence of a "curial" spirituality based on Christ as sovereign, liturgical splendor, and hierarchical control. As partisans of Antiochene Arianism, emperors hindered or even persecuted orthodox Alexandrian theologians and bishops, e.g., Athanasius, John Chrysostom. But the mystical spirituality of Alexandria was fostered by the introduction of monasticism and further developed by a succession of brilliant and holy writers.

Monasticism arose as men and women turned to the deserts of Syria, Palestine, and especially Egypt to prove and increase their love of God through a life of simplicity and prayer. Guided by the example and rules of Antony, Pachomius, Mary, and Basil, Desert Fathers and Mothers (*abbas* and *ammas*) gathered both hermits and communities (cenobites) around them. The homilies, stories, and pithy sayings (apothegms) of monks such as Diadochus (ca. 475–550), Evagrius Ponticus (346–399), Macarius the Great (ca. 400), and Isaac of Antioch (fl. 350) formed the first specifically spiritual literature. By 415, John Cassian (360–435), a Scythian influenced by Evagrius, had established two monasteries in the West near Marseilles. His *Institutes* and *Conferences* greatly influenced the Benedictine tradition.

In sermons and writings, the great Cappadocian Fathers (Gregory of Nazianzus, Basil the Great, Gregory of Nyssa) first presented the spiritual doctrine of the period in systematic form, aided by their training in Neoplatonic philosophy, medicine, and science. Through them the tradition of *agnōsia*, "unknowing," founded on Scripture and developed by Philo, Athanasius, and Clement, entered spirituality as a whole. Such "negative knowledge" of God (apophatic spirituality) was distinguished from but correlated with "positive knowledge" (kataphatic spirituality), based on concepts and images.

At the end of the 5th century, as Antioch and Alexandria drifted further apart into Nestorianism and Monophysitism, the main currents of Eastern spirituality were ably synthesized by the pseudonymous author known as Dionysius the Areopagite. His four short books and ten letters gained acceptance because of their attribution to the disciple of St. Paul, but also because of their wisdom. Endorsed by Maximus the Confessor and Pope Gregory the Great in the 6th century, the Dionysian corpus became a major and lasting influence on both Eastern and Western spiritualities, especially in the 14th century.

Also in the 6th century, the Jesus Prayer (prayer of the heart) was promoted by Diadochus of Photike in northern Greece. Already found in the writings of Evagrius of Pontus and the Macarian homilies, devotion to Christ and sorrow for sin were expressed by constant repetition, sometimes with rhythmical breathing. This evoked an awareness of God's presence and a state of tranquillity (*hesychia*), which, developed in Syria, Palestine, and Egypt by Barsanuphius and John, Dorotheus, Abba Philemon, and St. John Climacus, gave its name to a major school of mystical spirituality, hesychasm. Despite the disruptions of the Moslem conquest and the Iconoclast heresy, Byzantine spirituality flourished for six more centuries as the empire recaptured areas lost during the Dark Ages, influencing large areas of Italy and Spain.

Latin Spirituality

By the 5th century the centers of Christian spirituality and theology shifted from Egypt and Syria to Africa and Italy, where the official language of the Church had changed from Greek to Latin. Augustine of Hippo (354–430), the greatest of the Latin Doctors, exercised a definitive spiritual influence on the West. For Augustine, a promoter of cenobitic monasticism, friendship and justice were primary values. Despite a negative attitude toward both the body and pleasure in his later writings, Augustine's spirituality was egalitarian, humane, and urbane, the only purpose of asceticism being for him the development and perfection of human and divine love.

By 360 Martin of Tours had established Pachomian monasticism in Gaul. As barbarian invasions began to threaten the Western empire, many patrician Christians also withdrew from civil administration into contemplative solitude under the influence of the ascetical spiritualities of Jerome, Pelagius, and Martin. But the greatest spiritual force of the period emanated from the monasticism developed by Benedict of Nursia (ca. 480–550). Benedictine spirituality fostered meekness, obedience, and humility. Hierarchical, authoritarian, and pastoral, the abbeys flourished in the wilderness rather than the city. The monks performed manual work as part of their spiritual discipline but also copied and preserved manuscripts. Daily reading of the Bible and the works of the Fathers were prescribed, and soon the abbeys became the schools of Europe.

The Celtic Church and Carolingian Reform

Christian Churches were founded in Celtic Britain as early as the 2nd century. Monasticism arrived by the 4th century, probably started by refugees or pilgrims from Gaul or Egypt near Roman outposts in Cornwall, Wales, and southern Scotland. Ireland was successfully evangelized by Patrick (ca. 390–460) and his followers, with monasteries being founded from Britain and Gaul in the following century.

Irish Christianity and its monastic tradition produced generations of saints and scholars who led the effort to reconvert Europe after the age of invasions, among them Brendan (484–583), Columba (521–597), Aidan (fl. 651), Brigid (ca. 450–523), Ita (fl. 570), and Hilda of Whitby (614–680). Columban (543–615) founded monasteries from Belgium to Italy. In its prime, Celtic spirituality was robust, learned, and uncomplicated, greatly resembling the Egyptian desert tradition. Sublime works of decorative art were achieved on a very small scale.

As waves of Celtic monks moved south and east, Benedictine missionaries approached England and France from Italy. Monks such as Boniface (680–754) evangelized pagan areas of Germany. The reconquest of barbarian Europe by Christian kings was also followed by the establishment of new monasteries and abbeys, where faith as well as agriculture and education flourished.

With the accession in 800 of Charlemagne (ca. 742–814) as emperor of the West, the Dark Ages came to an end. The following Frankish renaissance ushered in a century of growth in scholarship and the arts. Spirituality also flourished under Alcuin (735–804), Benedict of Aniane (750–821), Hilduin (fl. 835), Rabanus Maurus (776–856), Walafrid Strabo (808–849), other scholarly monks, and nuns such as the Saxon canoness Hrosvit of Gandersheim (ca. 940–1002). John Scotus Erigena (ca. 810–870) successfully translated the works of Dionysius into Latin, preparing for the medieval development of apophatic spirituality.

The Middle Ages: Scholasticism and Mysticism

Reforms associated with the abbeys of Cluny and Bec revitalized monastic spirituality in the 11th and 12th centuries with the foundations of the Camaldolese, Carthusian, and Cistercian orders. Their "desert" spirituality, together with the mystical, apophatic tradition of Dionysius and Benedictine Scholasticism, formed the third dominant school of the early medieval period. The outstanding influence of the era was the Cistercian Bernard of Clairvaux (1090–1153), whose preaching and commentaries promoted the theme of bridal mysticism. Other outstanding figures within Bernard's ambit included Hildegard of Bingen (1098–1179), William of St. Thierry (ca. 1085–1148), and Aelred of Rievaulx (1109–1167). The anti-intellectualism of the Cistercian tradition climaxed in the writings of a former abbot, Joachim of Fiore (1132–1202), which exacerbated the eschatological fever of southern Europe in the 13th century and were condemned at the Fourth Lateran Council (1215).

A more intellectual tradition was favored in the cathedral centers and houses of canons regular, such as that of St. Victor in Paris, which led in the introduction of apophatic spirituality, notably through the works of Hugh (ca. 1080–1142) and Richard (d. 1173). In the 13th century, academic theology triumphed over monastic theology through the dominance of the universities. Urban spirituality flourished with the coming of the friars, who quickly gravitated to the new centers of learning. The Dominicans and Franciscans especially attempted to balance apophatic and kataphatic elements, learning and devotion, eschatology and realism, contemplation and action, and radical poverty and effectiveness. Outstanding examples were provided in Bonaventure (1217–1274) and Thomas Aquinas (1225–1274)—mystics, saints, and professors.

Social, intellectual, and spiritual ferment during the 12th and 13th centuries led to the proliferation of radical, sometimes heretical cults and sects, followed by stern reprisals from both state and Church. Desiring a return to apostolic simplicity, many laywomen and laymen joined groups of Beguines and Beghards, self-supporting, noncanonical communities of high spiritual character. At first tolerated, such groups became suspect to Church authorities and were suppressed in the 14th century.

Notable women in this period include Mechtild of Magdeburg (ca. 1210–1282), Gertrude the Great (1256–1302), and Bridget of Sweden (ca. 1303–1373). Others ran afoul of authority, such as Marguerite Porete, who was executed for heresy in Paris in 1310. Many found refuge in Dominican convents, where the confluence of Scholasticism and mysticism under the influence of Meister Eckhart (ca. 1260–1328), Henry Suso (ca. 1295–1366), and John Tauler (1300–1361) ignited a mystical movement in the Rhineland that endured until the Reformation. Mysticism also flourished in the Low Countries, England, and Italy, inspired by the writings of Jan van Ruysbroeck

(1293–1381), the author of *The Cloud of Unknowing* (fl. 1380), Angela of Foligno (ca. 1248–1309), Jacopone da Todi (1230–1306), and Catherine of Siena (1347–1380), among others. In the East, Gregory Palamas (1296–1359) brought the mystical tradition of hesychasm to its highest development.

Decline and Reform

Devastated by the Black Death and the Hundred Years' War, and demoralized by the Great Western Schism, the witchcraft mania, and the advance of Islam, Europe in the late 14th and 15th centuries witnessed the dissolution of the medieval synthesis and its exuberant spiritualities. Widespread corruption in Church life was opposed by radicals like John Wycliffe (1330–1384) in England and Jan Hus (1372–1415) in Bohemia, but the oppression of the Lollards and the treacherous execution of Hus at the Council of Constance, like that of Savanarola (1452–1498) at Florence at the end of the century, could not stem the tide of reform.

Jean Gerson (1363–1429) and Nicholas of Cusa (1401–1464) exemplify the shift in spiritual paradigms leading toward the Protestant Reformation. Gerson held that contemplation is a form of ecstatic love, guided by will rather than intellect. He also divorced action from contemplation, denying that all are called to contemplative union with God. Most people, he believed, are capable only of active life in the world, being saved by faith and virtuous works apart from any consciousness of God's presence. Influenced by the Rhineland mystics, Cardinal Nicholas of Cusa was a mathematician, scholar, diplomat, and reformer. In the apophatic tradition, he affirmed divine incomprehensibility, the possibility of union with God through love and justice, and the universal impetus toward the reconciliation of all oppositions in the unifying nature of God.

Spirituality at this time favored personal experience over institutional authority as the otherworldliness, individualism, and emotionalism of the *devotio moderna* displaced the high mysticism of the Rhineland. Extolling feeling over thought and viewing the world negatively, this "new devotion" focused on the suffering Christ. The most representative and popular work of the period was *The Imitation of Christ,* attributed to Thomas à Kempis (1380–1471), an Augustinian canon of Agnietenberg.

Inspired by the "new devotion," Renaissance humanists such as Lorenzo Valla, Phillip Paracelsus, Giovanni Pico della Mirandola, John Colet, Thomas More, and Desiderius Erasmus added to the movement toward reform. But neither devotion nor humanism ultimately proved able to prevent open conflict between radical Reformers and resistant Roman authorities.

The Catholic Reformation

Spiritual thirst for a return to simple, apostolic Christianity, coupled with outrage over Church corruption, led to violent confrontation in the 16th century. Throughout northern Europe the long dominance of the monastic spiritual tradition ended in suppression. But as Catholic reform efforts finally commenced, new spiritualities appeared, especially in Spain. Methods of prayer and meditation known as "spiritual exercises" replaced the simple, organic, and often unstructured practices of classical patristic, monastic, and medieval spiritualities with systematic procedures, definite content, tight structure, and uniform regularity. In Spain, Italy, and France such practices were especially successful in the ministry of Ignatius Loyola (1491–1556) and Francis de Sales (1567–1622), who adapted the new practice to the needs and situation of laypersons. The Spanish Carmelite reform favored the medieval tradition of contemplation, but systematic meditation was also encouraged by Teresa of Avila (1515–1582) and John of the Cross (1542–1591).

Other Spanish spiritual reformers included García Jimenez de Cisneros (1455–

1510), St. Peter of Alcántara (1499–1562), Luis de León (d. 1591), St. John of Avila (d. 1569), St. Francis Borgia, St. John of God, Francisco de Osuna (1492–1540), and St. Bernardino of Laredo (1482–1540), whose *Ascent of Mount Sion* profoundly influenced Teresa of Avila. But the undeniably major spiritual writers of the period were Teresa of Avila and John of the Cross, both later declared Doctors of the Church. Positive, warm, and unsystematic, Teresa's description of the stages of the spiritual life are unequaled in depth and intensity. An apophatic theologian, John of the Cross was also original in his syntheses of the great traditions of Christian mysticism and more sweeping in his vision of the whole than previous writers.

The Modern Era

As events in Germany and Spain had dominated Catholic spirituality in the 16th century, developments in France prevailed in the 17th. During the period of conflict with Calvinism, spiritual writers were divided between traditional and Reformed influences. Jansenism, a stark and pessimistic spirituality, exerted far-reaching influence despite its condemnation in Paris and Rome. Mainstream spirituality was represented by saints and mystics such as Francis de Sales, Jane Frances de Chantal (1572–1641), Vincent de Paul (1580–1660), and Louise de Marillac (1591–1660). Less mystical influences included the French Oratorians; Cardinal Pierre Bérulle (1575–1629); Jean-Jacques Olier (1608–1657), founder of the seminary of St. Sulpice; Charles de Condren (1588–1647); St. John Eudes (1601–1680), Bérulle's disciple and successor; and Louis Grignion de Montfort (1673–1716)—the "French School."

Near the end of the century, the promotion of a suspect form of passive contemplation and the disinterested love of God by Miguel de Molinos (ca. 1640–1697) and Madame Guyon (1648–1717) caused orthodox spiritual writers to retreat even further from mysticism toward an asceticism that cultivated sentiments of human unworthiness, abasement before the supreme majesty of God, and a preoccupation with acquiring virtues, especially humility and obedience. "Abandonment" to the will of God became an increasingly popular practice. Gradually the term *spiritualité* replaced "devotion" for a life of methodical prayer and active service as distinct from both contemplation and enthusiasm.

Catholic spirituality was profoundly disturbed by the upheavals of the 18th and 19th centuries, especially the suppression of orders, monasteries, and other religious institutions during the French Revolution. With the restoration of the old order in 1848, however, new orders and congregations appeared and old ones began to return. Monastic life revived. Social reform in Europe and missionary work in the Americas, Africa, and Asia appealed to a new generation eager to bridge the gap between the Catholic past and the modern world. But condemnations of liberalism by Popes Gregory XVI in 1832 and Pius IX in 1869 brought the movement to a halt. Outstanding thinkers such as John Henry Newman (1801–1890) and Lord Acton (1834–1902) could not offset the reactionary tendency of Rome and the hierarchy as a whole, which culminated in the First Vatican Council (1869–1870).

In the second half of the century, spirituality tended to remain static and defensive. Popular piety turned increasingly to supernaturalism. Apparitions of the Virgin Mary in 1830 to St. Catherine Labouré, in 1846 at La Salette, and especially in 1858 at Lourdes polarized Catholic and secular opinion. Miracles and visions of other saints were widely reported. Stigmatics such as Louise Lateau (1850–1883), Catherine Emmerich (1774–1824), and St. Gemma Galgani (1878–1903) attracted widespread attention. But despite the publication of the writings of John of the Cross and a flurry of interest in medieval mystics, the situation was largely moribund.

Twentieth-Century Spirituality

Despite exceptions (e.g., von Hügel), Catholic spirituality in the early 20th century was not influenced by further conflict between modernists and conservatives. Until the Second Vatican Council, most teaching and practice remained traditional. But a vital lay spirituality was being fostered by Catholic Action groups such as the Young Christian Workers (Jocists) in Belgium and France, the Legion of Mary in Ireland, the Grail Movement in Holland, the Cursillo movement in Spain and Latin America, and the Catholic Youth Organization, the Christian Family Movement, and the Young Christian Students in the United States.

Between the First and Second World Wars, social reform and pacifism were represented by the communal mysticism of the Catholic Worker Movement in the United States and radical evangelical efforts such as the worker-priest movement of the 1940s in Belgium and France. After the Second World War a revival of the monastic life in the United States and elsewhere found thousands of men and women joining the contemplative orders, the diocesan priesthood, and less austere forms of religious life. Changes in Catholicism following the Second Vatican Council led to a reversal of interest in religious life and the departure of large numbers of clergy. Traditional forms of spirituality were also jettisoned for more perceivably relevant beliefs and practices.

Among other postconciliar spiritual developments, ecumenical cooperation, begun among Protestant Churches in the period after the First World War, slowly influenced Catholic attitudes, although emphasis abruptly shifted from interreligious dialogue and reunion among Christians to forms of joint protest against war and social injustice in the civil rights, peace, and feminist movements.

Entering Catholicism at the time of the council, Pentecostalism has remained a fundamentally popular movement. Supported by many bishops and the Vatican itself, charismatic renewal affirms traditional values, obedience to ecclesiastical and civil authority, strong devotion to Jesus, belief in miracles, reliance on prayer, and a confident expectation of God's immediate and particular assistance in every area of life. Many Catholic Pentecostals also tend toward millenarianism.

Some Catholics, including laity, clergy, and religious, have attempted to revive preconciliar spiritualities associated with the ultra-orthodox characteristics of the anti-modernist period, including clericalism, political conservativism, and a return to Latin and Tridentine liturgical practices. Contrary developments have included a new interest in the spiritualities of the Eastern Church, mysticism, and a greater appreciation of Asian religious belief and practice, especially forms of yoga and Zen Buddhism, emphases associated with the teachings of Pierre Teilhard de Chardin (1881–1955) and Thomas Merton (1915–1968). Contemporary interest in cosmology associated with New Age spiritualities is linked to the emancipation of Catholic belief from a creationist view of the universe. Lay spiritualities continue to develop through Marriage Encounter programs, Alcoholics Anonymous groups, women's conferences, and other special interest organizations.

Recent emphasis on health, conservation, and simpler ways of living has led to the emergence of holistic and ecologically concerned ("green") spiritualities. A similar humanistic approach on the part of secular organizations such as Amnesty International, Bread for the World, Food First, Friends of the Earth, Greenpeace, Oxfam, the Worldwatch Institute, and other voluntary organizations has fostered the growth of nonsectarian spiritualities in the tradition of the Catholic Worker Movement, Catholic Action, and the distributist movement associated with G. K. Chesterton and Hilaire Belloc in the 1930s.

Stimulated by an emphasis on God's "preferential option for the poor," Latin American liberation theology has recently produced its own liberation spirituality, a radical, grass-roots movement centered in small communities dedicated to social justice. The preaching of Jesus, especially the beatitudes, animates such spiritualities, which have great appeal to the poor and other marginalized victims of social oppression and injustice. Opposed to the concentration of wealth and power among ruling elites, the struggle against political and economic oppression of peoples of color and of developing nations in the Southern Hemisphere is substantially transforming the sense of the presence of God and the role of the Church in historical process and personal experience throughout the world.

See also AFFIRMATIVE WAY; APOSTOLIC SPIRITUALITY; ASCETICISM; AUGUSTINIAN SPIRITUALITY; BENEDICTINE SPIRITUALITY; CAMALDOLESE SPIRITUALITY; CARMELITE SPIRITUALITY; CARTHUSIAN SPIRITUALITY; CELTIC SPIRITUALITY; CISTERCIAN SPIRITUALITY; CONTEMPORARY SPIRITUALITY; DESERT; DOMINICAN SPIRITUALITY; EASTERN CHRISTIAN SPIRITUALITY; ENGLISH MYSTICAL TRADITION; EREMITICAL LIFE; FEMINIST SPIRITUALITY; FRANCISCAN SPIRITUALITY; FRENCH SCHOOL OF SPIRITUALITY; GNOSIS, GNOSTICISM; HESYCHASM; HOLISTIC SPIRITUALITY; IGNATIAN SPIRITUALITY; JANSENISM; JEWISH SPIRITUALITY; LAY SPIRITUALITY; MARGINALIZED, THE; MARTYRDOM; MILLENARIANISM; MODERN SPIRITUALITY; MONASTICISM, MONASTIC SPIRITUALITY; MYSTICISM; NEGATIVE WAY; PATRISTIC SPIRITUALITY; QUIETISM; REFORMATION AND CATHOLIC REFORMATION SPIRITUALITIES; RHENO-FLEMISH SPIRITUALITY; SALESIAN SPIRITUALITY; VATICAN COUNCIL II; WESTERN (LATIN) SPIRITUALITY; WESTERN MEDIEVAL SPIRITUALITY.

Bibliography: J. Aumann, *Christian Spirituality in the Catholic Tradition* (San Francisco: Ignatius Press, 1985). L. Bouyer et al., *A History of Christian Spirituality,* 3 vols. (London: Burns & Oates, 1968). C. Jones, G. Wainwright, and E. Yarnold, eds., *The Study of Spirituality* (New York: Oxford Univ. Press, 1986). B. McGinn and J. Meyendorff, eds., *Christian Spirituality: Origins to the Twelfth Century,* World Spirituality 16 (New York: Crossroad, 1985). J. Raitt, ed., *Christian Spirituality: High Middle Ages and Reformation,* World Spirituality 17 (New York: Crossroad, 1987). R. Woods, *Christian Spirituality: God's Presence Through the Ages* (Chicago: Thomas More, 1989).

RICHARD WOODS, O.P.

STATIONS OF THE CROSS

See DEVOTION(S), POPULAR.

STIGMATA

In Christian usage, *stigmata* (Greek for "marks," especially those branded on cattle and slaves) are signs on a person's body of the passion of Christ, usually wounds on the hands, feet, and side, appearing without external causes. Liturgical texts and spiritual literature often refer to Paul's expression about the marks of his sufferings for Christ: "I bear the marks of Jesus on my body" (Gal 6:17). This text, however, refers to wounds inflicted by others, not to stigmata in the technical sense.

The earliest documented case of stigmata is that of Francis of Assisi (d. 1226), who, according to his contemporaries, bore the marks of Christ's passion on his body in the last years of his life. At his death these wounds, inspected by witnesses, were acclaimed as signs of his special conformity to Christ.

Stigmata have been attributed, with varying evidence, to several hundred persons after Francis. These have included Veronica Giuliani (d. 1727) and Padre Pio of Pietralcina, Italy (d. 1968).

Various studies of the phenomenon have yielded contradictory conclusions: stigmata are the effect of religious hysteria; they are psychosomatic expressions of deep religious fervor; or they are a divine gift to be classified among the extraordinary phenomena of mysticism. Official Church authorities have generally expressed cautious reserve about the authenticity of cases of stigmatization.

For the study of spirituality, the appearance of stigmata testifies at least to a person's strong identification with the suffering of Jesus and is ordinarily accompanied by ecstatic experience.

See also ASCETICISM; BLOOD; BODY; CHRIST; ECSTASY; EXTRAORDINARY PHENOMENA; PIETY.

Bibliography: H. Thurston, *The Physical Phenomena of Mysticism* (Chicago: Regnery, 1952). I. Wilson, *Stigmata* (San Francisco: Harper & Row, 1988).

WILLIAM J. SHORT, O.F.M.

STORY

Human experience, whether individual or shared, is inherently durational. It must be understood in a narrative genre. To tell of human experience, then, is to tell a story. When we narrate the saga of Christianity, we place ourselves as a people of God located between the creation and the consummation. When I inscribe my own autobiography, I tell a story that declares who I am (as St. Augustine did in the *Confessions*). When we seek to find paths we can walk to achieve the spiritual goal of fullness of life, we use models that are explicit or implicit narratives.

The stories of Jesus provide primary models for the Christian life. To be a disciple is to walk in Jesus' path, to conform one's own life story to his. The notion of primary stories (of Jesus) and dependent narratives (of his people) provides a way to think of the relationship between the stories of Jesus and the models of the spiritual life. The stories of Jesus are irreducibly multivalent. Each of the spiritual traditions provides models that show numerous ways of letting "the same mind be in you that was in Christ Jesus" (Phil 2:5, NRSV). Indeed, the multiple accounts of the spiritual life can be understood as many ways of translating these stories from their original context in 1st-century Palestine into the many contexts in which Jesus' disciples seek to incarnate Jesus' story.

Story is also a genre that facilitates the recognition of the real union of spiritual and academic theology. With the peaking of the academic tradition in Christian theology in the High Middle Ages, spiritual theology tended to become separated from the theological enterprise. Spiritual theology was often construed either as merely the application to life of the truths delivered by rational theology or as a discipline separate from academic theology. Yet insofar as doctrines are crystallizations of human experience and thought—even the experience and thought of revelation—and as human experience and thought must be understood in a story, so doctrines receive their basic meaning in and from a narrative. To understand doctrines, then, one must understand both the stories in and from which they arose and how the insights those doctrines symbolize are properly translated into other narratives.

Once this inherent narrativity of doctrines is recognized, theological arguments between conservatives and progressives can be understood as disagreements not so much over doctrines as, more fundamentally, over how the Christian story may be incarnated in different contexts. For instance, the primary dispute between proponents of traditional spiritualities and supporters of "creation spirituality" is not so much about the doctrine of original sin, but about how the insight into human nature that this doctrine brings to linguistic expression can properly be integrated into the various stories of Christian life and Christian lives. Recognizing the centrality of story enables one to see that the ultimate purpose of all theology is practical and spiritual: the understanding, transformation when necessary, and proclamation in life of the stories that constitute Christian life and spirituality.

If story is the necessary genre for understanding human experience, then all spiritual direction must be based not in abstract principles or doctrines but in knowing how to understand stories. Christian spiritual discernment is the understanding and judgment of whether the true story of a shared or individual life is faithful to a primary Christian model. If my story, alas, distorts such a primary story, a spiritual director must enable me to reshape the life my story narrates. But such discernment and empowerment require not only know-

ing the primary stories but also understanding how they are told and lived well in remarkably varying contexts.

Hence, in practice, good spiritual direction requires understanding stories. And understanding the stories of Christians presupposes a solid background in the disciplines of biblical, historical, and philosophical theology, for one way of doing theology is learning how to understand the ways in which the primary stories of Christianity have shaped and can still configure the stories that inscribe the shapes of authentic spirituality.

See also MYTH; NARRATIVE; PREACHING; SCRIPTURE.

Bibliography: T. Tilley, *Story Theology* (Wilmington: Glazier, 1985). R. Krieg, *Story-Shaped Christology* (New York: Paulist, 1988). J. Shea, *Stories of Faith* (Chicago: Thomas More, 1980).

TERRENCE W. TILLEY

STUDY

Study is a prime means of acquiring knowledge, which in turn is integral to human and Christian wholeness. Thomas Aquinas, assuming a need for moderation of the thirst for knowledge in relation to other responsibilities, subordinated study to the cardinal virtue of temperance, a perspective that Sertillanges carried through in his treatment of the intellectual life. Lonergan placed the concept of study within a continuum of learning and appropriation of truth extending from the spontaneous and self-correcting accumulation of insights to the most deliberate and systematic processes of scientific investigation, in view of an integrated human development that is attentive, intelligent, reasonable, and responsible. Within the realm of spirituality several roles of study merit specific consideration.

Study and Prayer

While prayer is essentially and ultimately a matter of love, and while study in any formal or academic sense is certainly not prerequisite to union with God in prayer, religious study that is consonant with one's general intellectual formation undoubtedly enhances the understanding with which one enters prayer and sustains the integration of one's faith and prayer with life as a whole. Monastic traditions have in varying degrees incorporated sacred study into their way of life as a direct preparation for *lectio divina,* meditation, and contemplation, on the principle that love follows upon knowledge and that increasing one's knowledge of the things of God increases also one's potential for love. None of this is to deny the primacy of the action of God in prayer, but only to underline the necessity of human collaboration in the work of grace.

Study and Conscience

Conscience is the personal moral consciousness that ideally dictates responsible and reasonable decisions. Though the individual's conscience is the supreme rule of conduct in any given situation, the obligation remains constant throughout life to form one's conscience to the extent that one is able in the light of objective truth. Law, as a civil or religious society's attempt to articulate applications of value, is a guide in this. But even law must be judged in each concrete circumstance by the values on which it is or ought to be based. Therefore, mere knowledge of the norms of law cannot be a sufficient education of conscience for the mature adult. In proportion to his or her capacity, ability, and opportunity, each person needs to study the questions of value underlying the moral issues he or she faces. Judgment of the rightness or wrongness of action hinges ultimately on whether one has followed one's conscience. Nevertheless, how responsibly one has formed that conscience must also be considered in the assessment.

The concerns of spirituality, however, move beyond merely avoiding the wrong in one's moral decisions. Because love follows upon knowledge, the refinement of moral consciousness must be seen as requisite to the pursuit of holiness in love. Here again study comes into play (always in proportion to one's capacity and opportunity) as deepening love sharpens conscience, and sharpened conscience seeks to know more intimately the truth that dictates loving conduct.

Study and Ministry

As truth in the Christian tradition is necessarily linked with love, so study for a Christian must bear an ultimate relationship to ministry, which is the service of love. A Christian is not allowed the selfish luxury of studying truth, even the truth that is God, in isolation from the concerns of the rest of humankind. For the truth that is God is love.

The service of love, however, is surely augmented by specific study related to that service. It is possible and even commendable that some Christians should work to meet immediate needs or problems. But in today's world it is more and more clear that ministry must address also the causes of needs and problems if those needs and problems are to be eliminated. For this the study of issues and systems is essential. At least some individuals involved in any given ministerial effort must therefore engage in such study in depth in order to convey even a basic understanding of the issues and systems in question to others in the ministry, or the ministry will risk shallowness and even counterproductiveness.

In conclusion, while study cannot be interpreted as a universal Christian obligation or as generally essential to growth in love, its role in an integrated spirituality must be said to increase in importance in proportion to one's general intellectual capacity and formation.

See also DOMINICAN SPIRITUALITY; KNOWLEDGE; LECTIO DIVINA; MIND; PRAYER; READING, SPIRITUAL; TRUTH.

Bibliography: A. Sertillanges, *The Intellectual Life: Its Spirit, Conditions, and Methods* (Westminster, Md.:

Newman, 1948). B. Lonergan, *Insight: A Study of Human Understanding* (New York: Longmans, 1957).

SUZANNE NOFFKE, O.P.

SUFFERING

Suffering may be defined as any experience that impinges on an individual's or a community's sense of well-being. Synonyms include pain, grief, distress, disruption, affliction, imposition, oppression, discrimination, and any sense of loss or of being victimized. The negative experience may be physical, psychological, interpersonal, or spiritual, though in most instances it involves a combination of these. Suffering, then, is one's consciousness of life's dark side, the human experience that all is not peaceful and harmonious in our bodies, in our souls, in our relationships, in the cosmos.

Suffering is linked inevitably to the problem of evil (theodicy)—where it comes from, who or what causes it, and why. There is no single explanation of the origin and purpose of evil, nor is there any unanimous agreement as to the appropriate response to the suffering it entails. Evil is explained and suffering is assessed in light of one's worldview. For believers, this involves one's concept of human nature (anthropology) as well as one's image of God (theology). For Christians, one also incorporates the message and person of Jesus (Christology) and one's notion of redemption (soteriology).

In this meantime, between the "already" arrival but "not yet" fulfillment of the kingdom of God, what role does evil play? If God is omnipotent and benevolent, how can such a God cause and/or permit humans to suffer? How and why does a good God permit birth defects, epidemics, earthquakes, famines, and hurricanes? How should individuals or communities assess and respond to life's hurts and disappointments? The popularity of Rabbi Harold Kushner's book *When Bad Things Happen to Good People* attests to the fact that the origin of evil and the meaning of suffering continue to elude full human understanding. The Hebrew and Christian Scriptures as well as the broader Judeo-Christian tradition reflect the diversity of approaches to theodicy and the concomitant problem of suffering.

Theological Approaches to Evil and Suffering

One of the oldest models for conceptualizing the meaning of evil and suffering is *dualism,* whereby the forces of light are locked in an ongoing cosmic struggle with the forces of darkness. There may be two countervailing deities, as in the ancient myths of the Middle East, or one benevolent God may be opposed by the created powers of evil (fallen angels, devils, Satan, Beelzebub). Free-willed humanity is caught up in the midst of this eternal struggle. This approach finds expression not only in the myths of antiquity but also in John's Gospel and the Book of Revelation, Dante's *Divine Comedy,* and the apocalyptic writings of any era. It is primarily in the more fundamentalist branches of the world's religions that this neat separation of the world into opposing camps is fostered today.

A second approach traces the origin of evil to human choices and is commonly called the *classical, Augustinian,* or *free-will* theodicy. From the story of Adam and Eve (Gen 2–3), through the stories of the various infidelities of the chosen people, to the teachings and parables of Jesus concerning reward and punishment in the kingdom of God (e.g., Mt 6–7; 13), there has been considerable support for the belief that evil, and the suffering it entails, is humanly caused. Human vices, manifest in destructive human choices, reap their own negative consequences. The OT and NT abound with exhortations to turn away from sin (Deut 8:11-20; Jer 18:8; Ezek 18:30; Mt 3:2; Mk 1:15; Acts 2:38; Col 3:8) and to love God, neighbor, and self (Mt 22:34-40; Mk 12:28-34; Lk 10:25-28).

Augustine (354–430) is credited with systematizing the free-will theodicy, especially in chapters 4–7 of his *Confessions,* while Thomas Aquinas (1225–1274) and other medieval theologians largely refined it. In this century C. S. Lewis has given popular expression to it, while Paul Tillich has developed it in more academic terms.

A variation on this theme, the third approach, might be labeled the *punishment* or *retribution* model. Its proponents attempt to incorporate into the free-will motif those experiences of suffering that are not the result of conscious free choice—acts of nature as well as accidental or unintended acts of humanity. God is seen as the arbiter of all justice, exacting retribution for all human sins. If the consequences of one's actions do not redound to the perpetrating person or community in negative consequences, then God will exact vengeance through "natural" calamities of weather, disease, etc. The OT stories of the great flood and the plagues in Egypt reflect this interpretation. The Hebrew concept of Yahweh as the Lord (i.e., cause) of all history, its curses as well as its blessings, which later was adopted and adapted by John Calvin (1509–1564), finds expression in this century in the writings of Karl Barth and others of the Reformed tradition.

However, the poignant response of Job, the faithful one who suffered despite his innocence, attests to the fact that not all human suffering is the result of human choice and sin, whether as direct consequence or divine punishment. Jesus' defense and cure of the man born blind (Jn 9) similarly affirms that, at times, the innocent do suffer. Some evil and the suffering that it brings seem to be the result of caprice or chance.

A fourth option finds its OT expression in the four Suffering Servant Songs of Isaiah (chaps. 40–55) and its fullest embodiment in the suffering and death of Jesus Christ. Variously called *redemptive suffering, atonement,* or the *ransom myth,* this approach shifts from the question of the origin of suffering to its subsequent meaning. At least some human suffering is seen as an expiatory payment on a debt, whether one's own or that of others. The suffering servant in Isaiah, who serves as an archetype for Christ, the one who accepts abuse unto death, is really guiltless, nobly accepting punishment in behalf of others. This view of evil and suffering presupposes both a God or a cosmic ordering force that demands satisfaction as well as some measure of human solidarity, whereby a one-for-all atonement sacrifice will suffice.

A fifth approach to theodicy has been called the *Irenaean* model. It can be found in the writings of Irenaeus (ca. 130–202) and remained a strong theme in the Spirit-oriented Fathers and tradition of the Eastern Churches. It also has been called the *process, developmental,* and *evolutionary* model, because it finds expression to varying degrees in scholars as diverse as Charles Hartshorne, John Hick, and Teilhard de Chardin. The world was created unfinished. It is in the process of becoming, as are all its creaturely inhabitants. Evil and suffering are the natural spin-off, the inevitable growing pains of matter and spirit evolving from fetal immaturity into fullness of being (Rom 8:22-23). Life's "frictional phenomena"—finitude, laws of nature, the food chain, the birth-life-death cycle—are inevitable, a natural and in some sense essential dimension of the rhythm of life, the coming to be of God's kingdom in its fullness.

A variation on this theme, which attempts to combine it with the divine retribution motif, is to conceive of human suffering as *remedial,* imposed by God to test human stamina or to refine humanity as one fires pottery in a kiln to make it strong (Mal 3:2; 1 Cor 3:13; 1 Pet 1:7; Rev 3:18). Thus many so-called evils—exercise that is painful to unused muscles, study that taxes one's energy and concentration, and interpersonal tensions that call for commitment and fidelity—are in fact beneficial, paths to greater strength, wisdom, and virtue. Pious practices of self-mortification within the spiritual tradition (e.g., fasting, abstinence, tithing), although fundamentally related to the atonement tradition, find added justification and meaning in this medicinal model.

A final approach to evil and suffering, the one adopted by Job, is commonly called the *faith solution.* It also finds expression in Second Isaiah as well as in such 20th-century writers as transcendental Thomist Karl Rahner, process theologian John Cobb, and mystic Simone Weil. Ultimately, after all other approaches to the origin and purpose of evil are deemed more and less adequate, one must come face to face with the ultimate mystery of evil and the incomprehensibility of God. Confronted by all other "theories" about the meaning of suffering, innocent Job proclaimed, "Naked I came forth from my mother's womb, and naked shall I go back again. The LORD gave and the LORD has taken away. Blessed be the name of the LORD!" (Job 1:21-22). And amidst all his suffering Job wailed his lament, but he committed no sin nor uttered any insult to God.

Christian Response to Evil and Suffering

In the face of inexplicable evil and horrendous suffering (e.g., serious birth defects, the Holocaust, Hiroshima), believers in a loving God can but wring their hands in grief while still clinging to hope. Christ's agony in the garden serves as *the* paradigm. After anguishing over the bitter cup of suffering that he felt compelled to drink, after praying that it might pass away through divine intervention, Jesus ultimately accepts it, trusting in God: "Not my will, but thine be done" (Mt 26:36-46; Mk 14:32-42; Lk 22:40-46).

In this century three phenomena—the Holocaust, Third World liberation movements, and the feminist struggle—point

the way to a multifaceted response to suffering. Dorothee Soelle, in her groundbreaking work *Suffering,* challenges the "faith solution" for its tendency to promote what she calls "Christian masochism." By this is meant the passivity or false otherworldly asceticism that has too often plagued the "acceptance" response to suffering.

Soelle suggests a three-step process for responding. In the first phase, at the time of the initial evil with its concomitant suffering, one is frequently mute, dumbfounded, expending all energy merely to survive. In the second phase, one brings to explicit consciousness the horror that has been experienced. Whether merited or unmerited, caused by human agency or by fluke of nature, intentional or accidental, personal or social, we can feel the suffering in solidarity with others and give voice to our anguish. The Scriptures are rich with illustrations of "out of the depths" lamentations. Even Jesus cried out in anguish from the cross, echoing Psalm 22: "My God, my God, why have you forsaken me?" (Mk 15:34). Is this the sin of despair? Is this an act of infidelity to God? No, not if lamentation is seen as a middle phase, a necessary acknowledgment of suffering and loss that empowers one to act. Political theologians of Europe (Metz, Schillebeeckx, Moltmann) join liberation theologians (Sobrino, Boff, Boesak) in proposing the "dangerous memory of suffering" as the proper starting point for praxis, the interaction of theology or faith with lived experience.

In the third phase, the call to action, multiple approaches seem apropos. (1) Confronted by those evils, those sources of suffering that can be alleviated or even eradicated, justice demands that we reform, liberate, and right the wrong. Where disease, pestilence, famine, illiteracy, poverty, and oppression can be altered by human endeavors, there is no excuse for *apatheia,* passively accepting these sufferings. Personal, political, economic, and social change for the good is part of Christ's ongoing redemptive work, the bringing about of the reign of God here as well as hereafter. (2) In some instances, what at first may appear to be pure suffering can become personally or socially productive. Where this is the case we are called to "carry our cross," to allow the suffering to transform us, to cope in this meantime with the intention of fostering personal and communal growth and virtue. (3) Finally, and only in those situations where the evil faced is insurmountable and the suffering experienced seems ultimately meaningless, ought one to adopt the *faith solution,* defined as "active endurance," not passive acceptance.

Many contemporary theologians (Metz, Schillebeeckx, Moltmann, Sobrino, and Boff, as well as Pope John Paul II) call for human *solidarity* amidst suffering, confident that if we are made in God's image, then God enters into and shares palpably all human suffering. In a special way, those who suffer injustice remain indelibly etched in God's memory and ought to be inscribed in human consciousness. In the living memory of Christ Jesus there is hope, even in the face of inexplicable human suffering. No single response to suffering suffices. The origin of evil and the meaning of suffering defy simplistic categories.

See also AGING; ASCETICISM; COMPASSION; DARK-NESS, DARK NIGHT; DISABILITY, THE DISABLED; EVIL; HOLOCAUST; MORTIFICATION; PRAXIS; PURGATION, PURGATIVE WAY; REDEMPTION; SIN; SOLIDARITY; WAR, IMPACT ON SPIRITUALITY; WEAKNESS AND VULNERABILITY.

Bibliography: J. Moltmann, *The Crucified God* (New York: Herder, 1974). K. Rahner, "Why Does God Allow Us to Suffer?" *Faith and Ministry,* Theological Investigations 19 (New York: Herder, 1983) 194–208. D. Soelle, *Suffering* (Philadelphia: Fortress, 1975).

RICHARD SPARKS, C.S.P.

SUFFERING AND PASSION OF CHRIST

See CHRIST; SUFFERING.

SYMBOL

The etymology of the word *symbol* (Greek *symballein,* "to throw together or place together") suggests the notions of revelation and complementarity that forms a union. In its Greek noun form, symbol was made as two matching parts of a ring, staff, tablet, or coin were joined to form a unity. The holder of each part could then verify the identity or the legitimacy of the holder of the other part. Symbol thus revealed and united through a complementarity.

These general functions of the ancient symbol are still true today. A symbol is a sensible reality that mediates or reveals a meaning related to, but not limited to, its form. There must be a reception of the meaning if a symbol is to function. The function of any symbol is to evoke and invite a participation that facilitates both revelation and union. What is true for symbols in general is true for religious symbols in particular.

Perspectives on Symbols in General

A symbol includes a sensible element that mediates meaning and invites a participation in the meaning. The meaning may have some relationship to the form, but it is not limited to the form only. Some kind of initiation into symbolic meaning is required so that there can be authentic participation in the meaning. A symbol dies when it no longer evokes participation.

A distinction is often made between two kinds of representative forms or symbols. The basic distinction is between a representative form with a fixed meaning and a representative form that evokes an accumulation of meaning. The first is called a "sign"; the second is called a "symbol."

A sign is a representative form that has a one-to-one correspondence between form and meaning; that is, a sign has a communally understood and fixed meaning. There is need for an initiation into the meaning, but once learned, that meaning will remain basically unchanging. A stop sign, sign language, objects, actions, or anything else that humans commonly name and understand with fixed meanings are examples of signs. Context will not change the meaning. For example, regardless of whether a stop sign is pictured in a book, operative on a street corner, or imagined in one's head, the meaning will remain the same.

The representative form called symbol mediates a meaning, but the mediation is also an invitation and evocation. A symbol's form is somewhat complementary to the meaning conveyed, but the meaning goes beyond the limits of the form. A symbol functions within the paradox of truth; that is, a symbol reveals and conceals, mediates an absence as well as a presence, and invites the initiated into a participation in a fullness that cannot be conveyed through the sensible form.

Though the distinction made between sign and symbol may help to illustrate differences, it is possible that what is a sign for one can be a symbol for another. For example, a child may see and buy a ring because it looks nice. The ring is simply a piece of decorative wear that others will also name as a ring. An elderly couple, married for many years, may look at a similarly named object, a ring. However, the object may be a wedding ring. The meanings that this ring evokes will go beyond that of one-to-one correspondence. The wedding ring as a symbol mediates the paradox of truth. For example, the wedding ring can reveal a presence of love but also an absence of the fullness of love, assuming that love is still in process. The ring can identify their relationship to others on the "outside," but simultaneously the ring conceals the depth of the relationship on the inside. Religious symbols function like this latter example.

The Nature and Function of Christian Religious Symbols

For Christians, Jesus Christ is the primary symbol of meaning. The entire Christian symbol system has its meaning in him, with him, and through him. In Jesus Christ everything is held together (Col 1:17). How can the paradox of truth be considered operative if Jesus Christ is looked at as a core or primary symbol?

Jesus Christ is the presence of God for us, but he is also an absence. Jesus Christ is not fully experienced by the Church, which is one reason why the Church prays "Come, Lord Jesus." Though Jesus Christ reveals the fullness of God's love for the world by his life, death, resurrection, and sending of the Spirit, the fullness of that love has been only partially received.

There is an "inside" as well as an "outside" to symbols. Jesus Christ, truly God and truly human, is the inside and outside of God's Trinitarian life, which is beyond human understanding. The inside and outside nature of Christian symbols is manifest in the notion of sacrament. For Christians, Jesus Christ is the one sacramental symbol that mediates the triumph of life over death, of love over isolation, and of a new creation over the old.

The Christian Church is a sacramental symbol of Jesus Christ and his triumphant compassion. There are ritualized affirmations of the presence of Jesus Christ with us that are mediated through a symbol system called "sacraments." Though some communal sacramental moments have become fixed and formally named sacraments, such moments are not limited to these communally ritualized events.

Christian symbols are rooted in the incarnational essence of Christian faith. Jesus Christ is the core symbol of the faith of Christians. His whole life was sacramental. The Christian Church is a symbol of Jesus Christ. The whole of its life ought to be sacramental, but its life is not yet that which it is called to be. Its sacraments reveal the best of its life.

Each local church is a symbol of the Church catholic. At their best, Christian communities reveal the intimacy and infinity of the liberating love of Jesus Christ.

But symbols can also conceal. A Christian community can mediate presence but can also testify to absence.

It is possible for a Christian symbol to lose its power to invite and evoke participation in the reality it mediates or reveals. Christian symbols can lose power when they become domesticated. The symbol may become idolatrous on one extreme or meaningless at the other extreme. How might this occur, given the outer and inner meaning of symbols? One example could be the following. The Christian Church could be described as a sacramental symbol of the life-giving love of Jesus Christ for all. How could the symbol lose power to mediate this saving presence?

Looking at Christian symbols from the perspective of the outside and the inside, two extremes of lost power could be presented. Considering the Christian Church as symbol from the outside, the visible form or structure of the Church could become an idol. This happens when the outside or sensible reality is invested with a power it does not have. The outside is linked to divinity, as if the visible element were identical with the invisible. For example, someone might rigidly assert that only those people visibly identified with the structure of the Christian Church will be saved by Jesus Christ. This is identifying the Church with the fullness of Jesus Christ, something that is contrary to the universality of the paschal mystery. That judgment gives the sensible form of a symbol a power it does not have.

At the other extreme, considering the Christian Church from the inside nature of symbol, only an absence might be communicated through the sensible form. For example, the triumphant compassion of Jesus Christ for all may not be the experience that is mediated through the Christian Church. In this case the experience of an absence without a complementary presence becomes emptiness.

It may be apparent enough that what is mediated by a sacred symbol system does require an initiation into the meanings of the symbol system. These meanings have some relationship to the representative forms but extend beyond the forms. This raises the issue of the inculturation that testifies to the universality of the Christian tradition.

What is intended by symbols and what is received by diverse cultures and peoples requires ongoing discernment to avoid two extremes. The first is the imposition of a Eurocentric cultural domination of the symbol system. The second is the possibility of a total contextualization of symbols that ignores Christian traditions. The challenge for the future involves discerning intercultural and multicultural dialogue that furthers the evocative and participative power of the kingdom of God among us.

See also ART; BAPTISM; BODY OF CHRIST; CREATION; EUCHARIST; LITURGY; MYTH; NARRATIVE; PASCHAL MYSTERY; RITUAL; SACRAMENTS; STORY.

Bibliography: D. Power, Unsearchable Riches: The Symbolic Nature of Liturgy (New York: Pueblo, 1984). K. Rahner, "The Theology of the Symbol," More Recent Writings, Theological Investigations 4 (Baltimore: Helicon, 1966) 221–281.

SHAWN MADIGAN, C.S.J.

SYSTEMIC SIN
See SIN.

T

TEACHING

Teaching is most simply taken to mean the passing on of knowledge from one person or more to another person or more—whether that knowledge be information or wisdom, both of which have their place in the spiritual life. As St. Augustine correctly observes at the very beginning of his work *The Teacher,* all discourse of any kind whatsoever somehow falls under the rubric of teaching, but here teaching will be considered as it is more narrowly understood.

Teaching may theoretically be distinguished from the teacher, and in most cases perhaps it should be, but in the moral and spiritual realm such a distinction is, practically speaking, difficult and not always advisable. Following the words of Jesus in Mt 23:2-3, where reference is made to the hypocrisy of the scribes and Pharisees, an immoral teacher may hold a teaching office legitimately and may impart information, or facts, correctly, but such a person should not ordinarily be taken as a model in matters of wisdom, or correct living.

Immoral behavior on the part of someone merely imparting information about the spiritual life, however, is often sufficient to raise the resistance of those who are being taught and to cast the veracity of the information itself into doubt. Hence, a good moral life is necessary for a teacher of spiritual things, not only for the sake of the one teaching but also for that of those being taught. Spiritual writers have emphasized this crucial point throughout the Christian tradition, and they have not infrequently declared that immoral teachers will be held responsible for the immorality of their charges. At the same time, while a moral person can sometimes make up with the example of his or her life for what may be lacking in informational knowledge, moral goodness of itself is no guaranteed substitute for a command of facts, and an ethically good and well-intentioned but ill-informed teacher can pose a danger to the Christian community.

It is clear, then, that a good teacher will both present the truth and embody it, particularly when it is a question of the spiritual life. Furthermore, the good teacher will perform both tasks in an attractive and thus persuasive way, realizing that truth not perceived as beautiful will hardly move those to whom it is offered (H. U. von Balthasar, *The Glory of the Lord: A Theological Aesthetics,* vol. 1: *Seeing the Form,* trans. E. Leiva-Merikakis, New York: Crossroad, 1982, p. 19).

The character and skill of its teachers are important in Christianity because, like other religions, it depends for its continued existence on teaching that is humanly mediated rather than directly revealed by God. The Bible itself, albeit the word of God, was written in human language and must be interpreted by human beings. Indeed, without someone to explain its meaning, and especially to illuminate the OT by means of the NT, much of the Bible will necessarily remain incomprehensible on its deepest level (see Acts 8:26-35).

That knowledge about spiritual things, and ultimately about any things whatsoever, should have to be imparted in this way—that is, mediately by human beings rather than immediately by God—is an issue St. Augustine addresses in the prologue to his important treatise *On Christian Doctrine*. There he discusses two significant reasons as to why (spiritual) teaching has been relegated to human beings. First, it honors the human condition; God could have communicated the elements of the message by angels, but to have ignored human beings in this way would have been tantamount to declaring them unworthy to bear God's word. Secondly, teaching is a form of communication, and communication fosters love between individuals.

The teacher, although the primary communicator, must be receptive not only to what students may communicate in their turn but also to learning from other sources, never forgetting that he or she had to study before beginning to teach. Even the magisterium occurs in some sort of dialogical process. This suggests, ideally, a humility on the part of the teacher that is often at odds with the exalted way in which teachers are viewed in most cultures. Only God has the right to teach unilaterally, without, as it were, taking counsel of others, although God, too, hears others (see, e.g., Ps 4:3). Hence St. Augustine can say that while in one respect his episcopal office has set him over his congregation as a teacher, in another respect "we are students along with you, under that one Teacher [Christ], in this school" (*Enarr. in Ps.* 126.3).

See also KNOWLEDGE; PREACHING; STUDY; TRADITION(S); TRUTH.

Bibliography: St. Augustine, *On Christian Doctrine* (available in numerous translations).

BONIFACE RAMSEY, O.P.

TEARS, GIFT OF

A complex physico-psychological phenomenon, tears expose the intimate, profound relationship of body, emotion, mind, and spirit in the individual human being and the social group. As a mode of communication, tears express to oneself and others feelings and levels of experience that escape or go beyond verbal expression.

Biblical texts witness to tears as an expression of natural human emotions but also of deep sentiments of compunction (*penthos*), gratitude, and love related to the experience of grace as it affects the whole person concretely responding to God at all stages of the faith journey. As such, tears are seen as a gift (*to charisma tōn dakryōn—De virginibus*, attributed to St. Athanasius, PG 28:272), having their source in the action of the Holy Spirit and their fruit in holiness (see Lam 2:11; Pss 6:9; 39:13; 42; 126). Jesus wept over Jerusalem's resistance to grace (Lk 19:41-44). Mourning and tears are the subject of a beatitude; they bear fruit in joy at the triumph of grace (Mt 5:4; Lk 6:21).

Because tears are undifferentiated in their physical manifestation, they are the object of spiritual discernment with regard to their source (grace or weakness and melancholy) and their fruit (see Teresa of Avila, *Mansions* IV and VI).

A rich, unbroken tradition of the Christian East and West up to the recent past sees tears as a normal feature of spiritual life. The gift is seen as purifying and perfecting loving union with God and neighbor under the action of the Holy Spirit. (For historical sources, see Adnès, "Larmes.") Absence of tears is seen as signifying resistance to grace, e.g., Peter's tears (Mk 14:72) and Judas's lack of tears (Mt 27:5).

The gospel beatitude manifests itself today in experiences of personal and communal mourning in face of institutionalized injustice and in solidarity with vulnerable, powerless, oppressed persons. In celebration of Word and Eucharist, the fruits of the beatitude come to be realized in unshakable hope and joy amid persecution. Also, acknowledgment of psychological experiences related to, for example, addiction or childhood abuse or the breakthrough in therapeutic process experienced and recognized as a gift given in the very owning of weakness and loss, often through the agency of unconditional love and care by others, is frequently marked by profound weeping that marks an opening to the healing process and gradually becomes an expression of gratitude and freedom. Such tears are a gift and a deeply personal expression of the transforming action of God within the individual and the community.

See also COMPASSION; COMPUNCTION; PENANCE, PENITENCE.

Bibliography: I. Hausherr, *Penthos: The Doctrine of Compunction in the Christian East,* trans. A. Hufstader, Cistercian Studies 5 (Kalamazoo, Mich.: Cistercian Publications, 1982). P. Adnès, "Larmes," *D.Spir.,* vol. 9, cols. 287–303. M. A. Karasig, "Affective Self-Transcendence in Catherine of Siena's Beatitude of Tears," *Review for Religious* 49 (May-June 1990) 418–429.

M. CLARE ADAMS, O.S.C.

TECHNOLOGY, IMPACT ON SPIRITUALITY

From the Greek *tekhnē* ("skill" or "art"), the term *technology* refers not only to the application of science to commercial and industrial objectives but also to a source and sustaining power of the world in which we live. "Technological" may describe a state of mind, a worldview that has brought about significant achievements in our age. It also presents enormous risks and perils.

Technology has formed the frame of mind in which we live. It is all-embracing, giving rise to a civilization characterized by the domination of machines, electronic gadgets, and computers over human beings, standardization over spontaneity, means over ends. If there is one distinguishing characteristic of the technological age, it is the emphasis on calculation and means. The technological worldview is sustained by the pursuit of quantitative calculation of the one best means in every area of human life. The world and everything in it is viewed in terms of what works, how it may be used to bring about the most efficient results. The natural order and all forms of nonhuman life are viewed as means to serve human ends. Consequently, nonhuman life forms may be manipulated and controlled at will in an effort to assure their effective use in service of human goals and purposes. Since the technological mindset judges success and failure only by its own standards and aims, it lacks any higher perspective or ethical base by which the developments in this science of means and calculation might be evaluated.

The concern of technology is with how things can be used, with what works, and with how pressing problems might be fixed. Its concern is with immediate, prompt solutions. Overarching problems are deflected and long-range resolutions continue to be postponed. The peril of modern nuclear warfare is the most obvious and most problematic outcome of the technological mindset. In this view, it is more efficacious to solve problems of conflict and aggression by military force and nuclear war than it is to concentrate efforts in the creative and intelligent pursuit of peace by other, more painstaking processes. For peace there is no technology. Lasting peace can only be brought about through persons and nations committed to ongoing relationship, dialogue, trust, mutuality, and reciprocity.

Whatever the abuses of the technological age and the wrong turns taken in the civilization of technique, technology is not without merit. The first great achievement of the technological age is the greater measure of freedom human beings have in relation to nature. The second great achievement lies in the area of communications. Never before have human beings had such an array of quick and reliable networks of communication. Even its greatest gains, however, have brought untold risk to human life and the human psyche. While technology has freed human beings from some of their subjection to the forces of nature, it has had the net effect of enslaving them in turn to the dehumanizing processes of technology. Its perils are evident in the massive depersonalization that has resulted from precisely those forms of technology aimed at more effective personal communications. Technology has indeed made possible the quick transmission and reception of information, but it has done little to assure real interpersonal communication and communion, for which there is no technology.

A technological worldview, a science of means, this mindset of calculation, is altogether at odds with the priority of God's grace and the human response to the divine initiative in human life, history, world, and Church. It flies in the face of the riches of the Christian tradition and its wisdom regarding prayer, meditation, contemplation, mysticism, and union with God. Christian living by the power of the Holy Spirit entails attentiveness, receptivity, the discipline of gazing long and lovingly at the traces of God's grace and presence in the world, history, and human personhood. This prayerful stance, living the contemplative dimension of the life of grace through baptism, cannot be brought about by manipulation. It is altogether gratuitous. Prayer cannot flourish in a life propelled by technique and calculation. Life in Christ by the power of the Spirit rules out relationships built on domination and control. And it demands that human beings and nonhuman life be respected and appreciated because of their inherent value rather than used as means to ends, no matter how lofty or necessary these ends may seem to be.

See also CONSUMERISM; CREATION; ECOLOGICAL CONSCIOUSNESS; ENVIRONMENT; HOLOCAUST; MA-TERIALISM; NUCLEAR AGE, IMPACT ON SPIRITUALITY; PEACE; WAR, IMPACT ON SPIRITUALITY; WORLD.

Bibliography: J. W. Douglass, *The Non-Violent Cross* (New York: Macmillan, 1966). J. Ellul, *The Technological Society* (New York: Knopf, 1965).

MICHAEL DOWNEY

TEMPERAMENT
See PERSONALITY TYPES.

TEMPERANCE
See CARDINAL VIRTUES.

TEMPTATION

The word *temptation* comes from the Latin *temptare,* which means "to handle, test, or try." This root indicates the active nature of temptation as something with which we are engaged, along with its passive nature as something that "tests" us. It is not simply an experience we undergo passively and without responsibility, as long as our will is not incapacitated. As the Letter of James notes, God tempts no one, "rather, each person is tempted when he is lured and enticed by his own desire. Then desire conceives and brings forth sin" (1:14-15). It is not the same thing as suffering, though we often say we "suffer" temptation.

The Christian paradigm of temptation can be found in two classic stories in Scripture—that of Adam and Eve in the garden in Genesis and that of Jesus in the desert in Mt 4:1-11. Both of these contain in kernel the fundamental issue of temptation, the desire to be other than human. Evil is ever able to play on that desire. Human being is mortal and contingent. It demands for its maturity reasonableness, relationality, and responsibility. As relational creatures, we are required to communicate with others and to experience dependence upon others. The experience of being human has a spiritual dimension in which grace plays an elemental role.

This is the experience of the gratuitous nature of life, that the source of life and being is other than ourselves.

In the Book of Genesis, Adam and Eve are urged by the serpent to eat the fruit of the forbidden tree and to "be like gods who know what is good and what is bad" (3:5). They succumb to the temptation, and the fruit of this is to experience ever more painfully their human contingency and mortality.

In the Gospels, especially in Matthew, Jesus, at the start of his ministry, goes into the desert, where he is tested. Toward the end of his experience Jesus is hungry—he experiences human need, the human condition. Immediately "the tempter" comes to him, offering those conditions under which Jesus would not truly experience being human: power, possessions, and pride. These "temptations" underline the root of all temptations: to be free of contingency and dependence; to be nonrelational, irresponsible, and unreasonable; to reject mortality and refuse grace.

The temptation of sin is always to be other than human, to flee God, to act as if one were absolute. The result entails endless suffering and evil, as history attests.

See also DEMON(S), DEMONIC, DEVIL(S); EVIL; SIN.

Bibliography: W. Molinski, "Temptation," *Sacramentum Mundi: An Encyclopedia of Theology*, ed. K. Rahner, with C. Ernst and K. Smyth (New York: Herder, 1970) 6:210–213.

BENJAMIN BAYNHAM, O.C.S.O.

THANKSGIVING, THANKFULNESS
See GRATITUDE.

THIRD ORDERS

Third Orders are associations of the faithful who seek Christian perfection by following a papally approved rule in affiliation with a religious institute. Its members are called "tertiaries." These orders are given the designation "third" to distinguish them in order of establishment from First and Second Orders, to which male and female religious respectively belong. Third Orders can trace their origin in the 12th century to communities of laypersons who sought to live in close association with particular religious orders.

St. Francis of Assisi was the founder of the Franciscan Third Order and author of its original rule, now lost, which was approved by Pope Honorius III in 1221. This Third Order was highly successful, and other orders followed suit, although formal approval for a number of them was not given until the 15th century or later, including the Augustinians (1400), Dominicans (1406), Servites (1424), and Carmelites (1452), among others.

Originally, Third Orders were societies of laypersons living in the world under the guidance of First Order superiors. Eventually, however, some Third Order groups began living vowed lives in common and were then granted the status of religious institutes. These became designated as "Third Orders Regular." They contrast with the original constitution of Third Orders as societies of men and women, both lay and clerical, who live according to the charism of the religious order on which their rule is based, but who do not leave their secular state of life.

Secular order tertiaries understand their commitment to be a vocation in the deepest sense of the word. Entry into a Third Order requires a prescribed period of formation, followed by profession, which includes promises or vows, usually of chastity and obedience. Members in most orders are required to recite some portion of the daily Office in addition to other prayers and apostolic works, according to the rule they follow.

See also LAY SPIRITUALITY; VOCATION; WORLD.

Bibliography: P. Foley, *Three Dimensional Living: A Study of Third Orders Secular* (Milwaukee: Spiritual Life Press, 1962).

KEITH R. BARRON, O.C.D.S.

THIRD WORLD, SPIRITUALITY OF

In many respects the spirituality of Christians in the Third World is like that of Christians everywhere. As Jon Sobrino states, "Spirituality is purely and simply the actualization of the Spirit of Jesus in our own times" (Sobrino, p. x). What this noted Central American theologian is saying is that spirituality is a contemporary expression of a very old endeavor: to live according to Jesus' Spirit and to reflect on that experience of discipleship. Spirituality is not so much a set of abstract ideas or a collection of words as it is a response to God's liberating presence among us. It is a reflection on the power of God's grace, which transforms and challenges the individual disciple and the human community.

The spirituality of Third World Christians does have certain special qualities, however, because it is shaped by a particular social context. Christians in the Third World live in societies marked by economic injustice, political oppression, racism, and violence against women. These social ills are present in more developed countries as well, but rarely in the raw and unmitigated form they often assume in the Third World. Faced with such destructive manifestations of social sin, Christians in the Third World have given deep thought to the meaning of the gospel and produced a spirituality that responds to their environment in an innovative way. For some of them, living the gospel means being subjected to persecution and even death. To be a disciple under such circumstances obviously requires a clear understanding of Christian faith and the spiritual stamina to live it fully.

The spirituality of Christians in the Third World is modeled on Jesus' life. Like him, they proclaim the Good News in societies where powerful elites resent and resist their message because it challenges their authority. Like Jesus, they experience hostility and are sometimes put to death, but they are convinced that God's grace will triumph. Their conviction flows from the mystery of Jesus' resurrection. It is central to their spirituality and Christian praxis on behalf of justice. Third World Christians are fully aware of the consequences of sin. They see its effects in their daily lives, yet they refuse to admit that it is the last word on the human condition. As believing people, they celebrate the transforming power of God's grace operative in their commitment to one another in the Christian community and to the world at large. Their spirituality, just like their lives, is marked by realism and optimism, by daily struggle, and by intense faith in the God who raised Jesus from the dead.

The spirituality of Third World Christians can be found not only in books but, just as importantly, in stories, songs, and dance. These vital forms of expression often speak of life's deeper meaning viewed from the perspective of poor but believing people. Stories about courage, songs that commemorate small victories and instill hope, as well as dances that celebrate the joy of existence, express a belief in the reality of God-given liberation. For many people in the Third World, spirituality is understood as a mix of words, gestures, and actions that flow from a powerful belief in God's presence in the struggles and joys of daily life.

The spirituality of Christians in the Third World has been profoundly influenced by liberation theology. Like most Christians, liberation theologians understand theology as "faith seeking understanding," and spirituality as a reflection on discipleship. But liberation theologians are especially conscious of the injustice and suffering that surround them. They recognize that if theology and Christian spirituality are to have any meaning in Third World countries, they must address the question of injustice and oppression. The men and women who make up the Christian community may be poor and oppressed, but their faith is remarkably rich and powerful. What liberation theologians try to do is give voice to their beliefs and collective spirit. They write and "do" theology in the world of the poor. Using the experience and language of ordinary people to reflect on the meaning of discipleship, they have created a "liberating spirituality." It is an expression of poor and oppressed people's faith in the possibility of justice, denied them by a sinful society but promised by Jesus' preaching of God's reign.

Liberation spirituality pays special attention to the believing Christian as someone with unique personal qualities. To be a peasant, a member of an oppressed cultural minority, or an impoverished woman is not an accident but a significant event that shapes a person's self-understanding and faith. Each person is a unique and special participant in the construction of God's reign. Each person is a manifestation of God's grace. Precisely for this reason, liberation theologians and the spirituality they advocate denounce injustice in uncompromising terms. Injustice destroys human beings and the spirit that resides in them. It is an affront to human dignity and to God's plan for creation. A sound spirituality must galvanize people to address the injustice and oppression that deny their uniqueness and dignity. If it does not, it is deficient and may even reflect a distorted notion of faith.

Since the early 1980s, liberation theologians have made a special effort to create a strong and articulate spirituality that can sustain Christians in the Third World. In Latin America, Asia, and Africa the persecution of Christians is a common event rather than a distant memory. The spirituality of the Third World Church reflects the experience of martyrdom. It celebrates the courage of bishops, priests, religious, and, most importantly, tens of thousands of laypersons whose commitment has led them to witness to the gospel, sometimes at the price of imprisonment and death.

A striking example of how the experience of people in the Third World has influenced Christian spirituality can be found in the work of Gustavo Gutiérrez. His *On Job: God-Talk and the Suffering of the Innocent* is considered to be a masterpiece of contemporary spirituality. Other theologians have also produced texts on spirituality, writing from their particular vantage points in Latin America, Africa, and Asia. A growing number of these theologians are women who are adding a feminist dimension to Third World spirituality. These theologians represent a wide and diverse segment of the Christian community. They write to give courage to the victims of oppression and to celebrate their continued commitment to Jesus' vision. They also write to rouse the conscience and convictions of Christians in the First World. By doing so, they are making the spirituality of Third World Christians a universal force in the Church. In the last decade of the 20th century, these men and women are producing what will become the classics of spirituality in the 21st century.

See also AFRICAN SPIRITUALITY; AFRICAN-AMERICAN SPIRITUALITY; EASTERN (ASIAN) SPIRITUALITY; FEMINIST SPIRITUALITY; HISPANIC-AMERICAN SPIRITUALITY; JUSTICE; KINGDOM OF GOD; LIBERATION THEOLOGY, INFLUENCE ON SPIRITUALITY; POOR, THE; PRAXIS.

Bibliography: D. Dorr, *Integral Spirituality: Resources for Community, Peace, Justice, and the Earth* (Maryknoll, N.Y.: Orbis, 1990). G. Gutiérrez, *On Job: God-Talk and the Suffering of the Innocent* (Maryknoll, N.Y.: Orbis, 1986). J. Sobrino, *Spirituality of Liberation: Toward Political Holiness* (Maryknoll, N.Y.: Orbis, 1988).

CURT CADORETTE, M.M.

THOMISTIC INFLUENCE ON SPIRITUALITY

See DOMINICAN SPIRITUALITY; WESTERN MEDIEVAL SPIRITUALITY.

THREE AGES

The traditional stages of "beginner, proficient, and perfect" reflect OT and NT accounts of growth in faith, especially in later wisdom literature (e.g., Hebrew *kelach* = Greek *telios*, "mature," "perfected"; see Job 5:26; cf. 30:2). In the NT, Synoptic, Johannine, and Pauline characterizations typically employ a child-to-adult metaphor of physical, cognitive, emotional, and moral maturation, often in patterns of three: *brephos, nepios* (babe); *teknon* (small child), *paidos* (young child), *neaniskos* (youth); *pater/mater* (adult), *telios* (mature adult). See especially 1 Cor 14:20; 1 Pet 2:2-31; Jn 2:12-14, 18 (cf. Mt 2:18; 11:25; Mk 7:27; Lk 1:17; 10:21; Jn 8:39; 11:52; Acts 7:1; Rom 2:20; 8:16; 1 Cor 2:6; 3:1; 14:20; Eph 4:13-16; Heb 5:12b-14).

Favored by Origen and, in the West, by Augustine and Gregory the Great, the traditional formula was largely displaced by the functionalist-constructivist approaches (three ways) of Evagrius Ponticus, Didymus the Blind, the Cappadocian Fathers, and Dionysius the Areopagite, until recalled in the Middle Ages by Thomas Aquinas and especially Bonaventure. Various efforts were made to reconcile the maturational "three ages" model and the constructivist "three ways" models, mainly by amalgamation and largely unsatisfactorily, by John of the Cross and others, including in this century Reginald Garrigou-Lagrange. Recent promising attempts utilize a method of correlation based on a psychological interpretation of stages of development.

See also THREE WAYS.

Bibliography: J. Fowler, *Stages of Faith: The Psychology of Human Development and the Quest for Meaning* (San Francisco: Harper & Row, 1981). D. Helminiak, *Spiritual Development: An Interdisciplinary View* (Chicago: Loyola Univ. Press, 1986). K. Rahner, "Reflections on the Problem of the Gradual Ascent to Christian Perfection," *Theology in the Spiritual Life,* Theological Investigations 3 (Baltimore: Helicon, 1967).

RICHARD WOODS, O.P.

THREE WAYS

The three ways—purgative, illuminative, and unitive—are constitutive elements within the broad framework of interpretation that has traditionally been used to discuss diverse prayer experiences of the spiritual journey as these have been described by different individuals over the centuries. The NT idea of ever-deepening life in Christ through the Holy Spirit's work of conforming believers to the pattern of the Lord's death and resurrection, found in the text of Eph 4:11-24, formed the scriptural basis for subsequent reflection on the experiential dimensions of this process of spiritual growth.

The application of the paradigm of human growth to the spiritual life, already present in the text of Heb 5:13-14, provided a framework for thinking about the process by which one attained maturity in Christ. Early Christian writers such as Origen (185–254) laid the groundwork for speaking of the three ways, which found its patristic completion in the work of Evagrius Ponticus (346–399), who spoke of beginners, proficients, and the perfect, and Pseudo-Dionysius (ca. 500), who described purgation, illumination, and union as the constitutive elements of the spiritual journey.

The threefold conceptual framework for thinking about growth in the spiritual life provided by patristic authors found a new level of development in the imagery used by medieval authors, such as Bernard of Clairvaux (1090–1153), who preached about the threefold kiss of the beloved, and Catherine of Siena (1347–1380), who wrote of the three stairs of ascent to Christ crucified. The idea that growth in the spiritual life embraced the purgative, illuminative, and unitive ways had become so common in Roman Catholic spirituality by modern times that Pope Innocent XI in 1687 condemned the teaching of the quietist writer Miguel de Molinos, who held that the concept of the three ways was absurd (DS 2226 [1246]).

Discussion of the concept of the three ways within contemporary spirituality has asked questions regarding (1) the use of language and imagery in describing various religious experiences; (2) the successive or repetitive nature and the ascetical or mystical character of purgation, illumination, and union; (3) the relationship between growth in the spiritual life and the stages of human development.

Language and Imagery

Any experience of the presence of God, which touches human minds and hearts, always transcends any form of expression. Yet Christians also believe that God has inspired the authors of the various books of the Bible to choose the words and images that would, insofar as possible, reflect the truth of God's work among humankind. Christian spiritual writers have always seen in biblical language and images, especially as they find their center in the mystery of the incarnation, the great reservoir from which they could draw words and symbols that would seek to express in some way the mystery of human encounter with the living God.

The language and images surrounding courtship and marriage have been the most significant source for describing various aspects of profound religious experience. The beauty and intimacy of human love expressed in the Song of Songs have caused it to serve as the scriptural basis for centuries of writing and speaking about the experiences of God's absence and presence. Other images drawn from patterns of relationship in human life have included those of parenting and friendship. Powerful symbols in nature, such as light, fire, water, clouds, and night, have also been used by spiritual authors, since Scripture itself makes use of such images in describing the divine-human relationship.

Mystics and spiritual writers have drawn upon images from the world of daily experience—a garden, a castle, a mountain, or the desert—when they wished to represent meeting places between God and humankind or to indicate the journey motive within religious experience. In using language and images to describe various human encounters with the transcendent, which are part of the paradigm of the three ways, spiritual writers constantly emphasize the analogical character of their use of words and symbols. They also indicate the inadequacy of any human mode of communication to grasp or express the wonder of God's love as it seeks to draw human beings more fully into the mystery of the divine life.

Nature and Character

Over the centuries spiritual writers have differed in their opinions about the successive or repetitive nature of the three ways. Basing their views on the testimony of individuals about personal spiritual experiences, some authors, in the tradition of St. Teresa of Avila, have concluded that one successively passes through the purgative, illuminative, and unitive ways as distinct stages of the spiritual journey. Other writers, however, also relying on the witness and experiences of the saints and mystics, in the tradition of St. Bonaventure, have judged that purgation, illumination, and union are not successive stages. Rather, they are three diverse aspects of a single process of sanctification that is repeated in the lives of believers in accord with their varying needs for purgation, illumination, and union at different points in their own journey to spiritual maturity.

The conclusion one can draw from this diversity of opinion among spiritual authors is that there is no absolute pattern of coming to the fullness of life in Christ but that each individual experiences purgation, illumination, and union within the uniqueness of his or her own mysterious call to holiness. The freedom of the God who calls and the freedom of the person who responds constitute an essential horizon for any interpretation of the three ways.

The horizon of divine and human freedom is especially significant as one discusses the concrete meaning of the universal call to holiness. Are mystical experiences open to all within the broad framework of the three ways, as theologians in the tradition of Juan Arintero (1860–1928) and Reginald Garrigou-Lagrange (1877–1964) would maintain, or is the call to the fullness of union with God characterized by two paths—the ascetical and the mystical—as the tradition of Joseph de Guibert (1877–1942) and Adolphe Tanquerey (1854–1932) would teach? Although contemporary spirituality favors the view that the mystical way is open to all as the flowering of baptismal grace, there is also the recognition that the graces of the spiritual life require human cooperation. Thus the number of believers who respond fully to the divine invitation to pass beyond ascetical experiences to truly mystical experiences is probably small. In actuality, then, there are two paths to God, the ascetical and the mystical, not by divine design but by the failure of most to respond to the purgation that is necessary to experience illumination and ultimately union with God.

Psychological Development and Spiritual Maturity

The past two decades have seen the growth of interest in the psychological stages of adult development. Reflection on the crises and insights associated with the passage from one psychological stage to the next has occasioned questions about the relationship between the stages of adult development and the call to grow in Christian maturity associated with the concept of the three ways.

There is certainly no necessary relation between the psychological experiences associated with different passages that are part of adult development and the spiritual experiences that pertain to purgation, illumination, and union within the journey to fullness of life with God. However, humans are unitary beings whose psychological development and spiritual growth have a significant relationship to each other. It would seem, from the example of the lives of the saints, such as Teresa of Avila, that the crises associated with psychological development can also be a time for a new graced invitation to deepen one's relationship to God amidst the struggles that accompany a new stage of human growth.

The paradigm of the three ways offers the opportunity to discuss the diverse aspects that seem to constitute the process of sanctification necessary for every person in order to attain spiritual maturity. It also leads to the recognition of the unique paths, within the broad threefold pattern of spiritual growth, that God invites individuals to walk as they are transformed into a new creation through the Spirit's work of conforming them to the mystery of Christ's death and resurrection.

See also AFFIRMATIVE WAY; ASCETICAL THEOLOGY; BRIDAL MYSTICISM; DIVINIZATION; HOLINESS; ILLUMINATION, ILLUMINATIVE WAY; JOURNEY (GROWTH AND DEVELOPMENT IN SPIRITUAL LIFE); MYSTICAL THEOLOGY; MYSTICISM; NEGATIVE WAY; PURGATION, PURGATIVE WAY; THREE AGES; UNION, UNITIVE WAY.

Bibliography: B. Groeschel, *Spiritual Passages: The Psychology of Spiritual Development* (New York: Crossroad, 1983). J. Lozano, *Praying Even When the Door Seems Closed: The Nature and Stages of Prayer* (New York: Paulist, 1989).

THOMAS D. McGONIGLE, O.P.

TIME, RHYTHMS OF

See LEISURE; LITURGY.

TIME, SANCTIFICATION OF

See LITURGY; SACRAMENTS.

TOLERANCE

See FRUIT(S) OF THE HOLY SPIRIT.

TRADITION(S)

Tradition, from the Latin *tradere,* meaning "to hand on," is in its essence simply something that has been handed on. As a matter of course, however, it refers to a teaching that has been handed on over a certain period of time, whatever form that teaching may take. For this reason, for instance, a particular object may be called traditional because its manufacture conforms to a design that has been taught by masters to apprentices from one generation to another. Precisely because *tradition* implies a teaching that has been handed on, and has therefore presumably been proven, over a period of time, it carries greater weight than mere teaching per se.

In the Catholic Church the notion of tradition is central. Here a distinction is occasionally made between *tradition* and *Tradition.* The former term connotes such beliefs and practices as can in certain circumstances be dispensed with and even be allowed to lapse because, however good they may be and however long they may have endured, their goodness is determined by circumstances that can change. Among these may be counted particular devotions and ascetical practices. The latter term, *Tradition,* connotes what is indispensable and essential, e.g., belief in the Trinity and the administration of the sacraments. This distinction, which is valid for the Church as a whole, is also valid, *mutatis mutandis,* for groups within the Church, such as religious congregations. A further distinction must be made between authentic and inauthentic tradition. An inauthentic tradition is an accretion that somehow distorts an authentic tradition or renders vague its true intent; such tradition is illustrated and condemned in Mt 15:1-7.

The value of authentic tradition in the Church consists in the fact that it places the receiver of that tradition in contact with the original source of a given teaching (ultimately with Christ himself, but via a medium, e.g., the charism and history of a religious congregation) and with subsequent legitimate elaborations of that teaching. This contact, as is suggested with respect to religious congregations in PC 2, is the guarantor that all present activity and future development of a given person or group will be legitimate. To be out of contact with the authentic tradition is to place oneself in danger of deviating from the original source. It is taken for granted that such contact is life-giving and liberating. Hence great care has always been taken in defining the authentic tradition and in handing it on, although, ironically, this process has itself sometimes given rise to inauthentic traditions.

The authentic tradition of the Church exists in diverse manifestations, each one being a legitimate elaboration of the one teaching of Christ. The existence of these varying manifestations allows us to use the plural and to speak of traditions, which are ideally not in conflict with one another but which complement one another. Even in the NT one can see the emergence of several different approaches to the one teaching of Christ, e.g., Matthean, Johannine, and Pauline.

In the Church at large two major traditions have established themselves along geographical (and linguistic) lines virtually from the beginning—that of the East and that of the West. These traditions are marked by variations in temperament, theology, and liturgy, among other things. There are further subdivisions within these two great traditions, constituting traditions within traditions. Thus in the West over the course of nearly two thousand years numerous different spiritualities have arisen in numerous different places (Spain, France, the Rhineland), each having its own history, each emphasizing a particular method and laying stress on particular key concepts, although each had or has as its goal the knowledge and love of God. Cutting across the tradition(s) of spirituality as Eastern or Western are other traditions, e.g., married, unmarried, monastic, clerical.

It may be argued that tradition is so comprehensive a concept as somehow to touch upon all human activity, however apparently anarchic or innovative. That is, for every human activity there is a precedent that exerts an influence; nothing stands utterly by itself. It is certainly true that in the Church no activity of any value can stand apart from authentic tradition. Hence any spirituality of value must be located within the authentic tradition, both of the Church in general and of a more particular grouping within the Church. To suggest otherwise is to imply that spirituality has need of neither truth (from the broad tradition) nor specificity (from the more particular tradition). Spirituality is never simply in the Christian tradition but is qualified as belonging in some way to still another and more specific tradition.

See also CULTURE; HISTORY, HISTORICAL CONSCIOUSNESS; TEACHING.

Bibliography: Y. Congar, *Tradition and Traditions: An Historical and a Theological Essay*, trans. M. Naseby and T. Rainborough (London: Burns & Oates, 1966).

BONIFACE RAMSEY, O.P.

TRANSCENDENCE

See ANTHROPOLOGY, THEOLOGICAL; EXPERIENCE; GOD; GRACE; HOLY SPIRIT.

TRANSFORMATION

Transformation literally means "a change of form," but the word can be used in many different ways to indicate many types of change. Economies of countries can undergo a transformation from centrally controlled to market; nations can undergo a transformation in cultural attitudes; persons can undergo a transformation of character or clothing style or, more fundamentally, of consciousness.

In every case transformation denotes change. In the realm of spirituality this change is often referred to as a "conversion," although in Scripture and devotional writings it can also refer to the transformation of our world under the reign of God, for example, or our and our society's transformation in the City of God (Augustine). The messianic hope of Israel was, and still is, hope for the transformation of humankind. This is often portrayed as a time of feasting with God (Isaiah, Ezekiel). The eschatological vision of the early Christian Church, especially under the aegis of Paul, was of an imminent transformation of the world under the lordship of the risen Christ (1 Cor 15:51-52). This expectation of imminent total transformation is itself transformed gradually into a patient expectation of future transformation in God's time (2 Pet 3:8ff.), and its final flowering is described in the Book of Revelation.

Personal transformation or conversion for the early Christians was expressed by the request for baptism and was linked with manifestations of the Holy Spirit. This conversion entailed the transformation of one's moral life, internal and external, and consequently the transformation of one's social life. Conversion was understood as a unique occurrence that could not be repeated, and so the sacrament of penance was often postponed until death appeared imminent. This understanding of the role of confession underwent a transformation when the Irish monastic missionaries brought the practice of private auricular confession and "graded" penances to continental Europe, which allowed for repeated absolution under a set form of penances considered sufficient for the sin. Here we can see the gradual transformation of practice in regard to Christian sacramental rites and popular understanding.

"Transformation of consciousness" is a modern term used to constellate changes undergone in one's psychological, intellectual, and spiritual horizons, changes that can be as radical as embracing a wholly new worldview and a wholly new self-understanding. Consciousness in this sense entails one's intellectual, moral, psychic, and religious understanding, and its transformation can be understood as the heart of conversion (Lonergan, pp. 130, 267).

In prophetic terms we are promised a "new heart," a "heart of flesh" in place of the unconverted "heart of stone" (Ezek 36:26), and this is to be the gift of God. The experience of such a gift is commonly understood as a religious conversion, whether or not it is accompanied by commitment to a specific religion or Church. It can be termed an awakening to the element of "mystery" in life and often entails a new awareness of a reality that transcends the immediate. The explicit acknowledgment of Jesus and an understanding of the role of the Church in salvation history are a further differentiation of religious conversion and the transformation of one's understanding on many levels.

Transformation of consciousness is the work of the Holy Spirit (Jn 16:13f.), and its progress and usual "stages" are traced in the spiritual traditions of the Christian Church and in the writings and lives of its holy men and women. It is the awareness of the call to a radical transformation that is at the heart of the eighth chapter of St. Paul's Letter to the Romans. In recent times depth psychology has added its own contribution to our understanding of the process of transformation with its focus on the role played by symbol, myth, and story. Our personal transformation and that of our society and world are not separate, privatized events but are rather closely linked. Our own transformative journey is also that of the whole of God's people.

See also CONSCIOUSNESS; CONVERSION; GRACE; PSYCHOLOGY, RELATIONSHIP AND CONTRIBUTION TO SPIRITUALITY.

Bibliography: W. Conn, *Christian Conversion* (Mahwah, N.J.: Paulist, 1986). R. Haughton, *The Transformation of Man: A Study of Conversion and Community* (London: Chapman, 1967). B. Lonergan, *Method in Theology* (New York: Herder, 1972).

BENJAMIN BAYNHAM, O.C.S.O.

TRINITARIAN SPIRITUALITY

Preliminary Considerations

All authentic Christian spirituality is *ipso facto* Trinitarian. As such, it is greatly enriched by an appropriate understanding of this central Christian doctrine which lies at the foundation of Christian faith and practice. In much the same vein as the Second Vatican Council's affirmation that the Eucharistic liturgy is the source and summit of Christian life (SC 10), the doctrine of the Trinity, with its far-reaching practical implications, constitutes the heart and soul of Christian spirituality.

Spirituality considered from a Trinitarian perspective is not anything other than Christian life in the Spirit: being conformed to the person of Christ, and being united in communion with God and with others. Because redemption through Jesus Christ and deification by the Holy Spirit comprise the Christian life, an adequate understanding of Christian spirituality must be grounded in the doctrine of the Trinity. This doctrine functions as the summary of Christian faith, expressing the essential truth that the God who saves through Christ by the power of the Spirit lives eternally in the communion of persons in love.

Spirituality is not merely an aspect of Christian life, it *is* the Christian life in response to the Spirit. Different responses to the presence and activity of the Holy Spirit give rise to different forms of life, which may be recognized as diverse spiritualities. The various elements of spirituality, such as prayer, meditation, contemplation, and ascesis, are properly understood as means of response to the Spirit, that is, means of bringing about ever fuller participation in God's saving acts in God's providential plan for creation.

The connection between the Trinity and the spiritual life has not always been clear or strongly drawn. The general irrelevance of the doctrine of the Trinity in the West since the 5th century meant that it lost its footing as the central and unifying Christian mystery. This resulted in an impoverished because theoretically ungrounded Christian spirituality, as well as a theology cut off from the wellsprings of spirituality. Current efforts to retrieve and rethink the doctrine of the Trinity in light of the riches of the tradition and in view of contemporary insights and exigencies has been required, not merely desirable, for an authentic and appropriate contemporary Christian spirituality to flourish.

In this entry, the focus is not on biblical origins or the historical development of the doctrine of the Trinity, but on the contours of a spirituality rooted in a theology of God that is altogether Trinitarian. However, several connections between spirituality and Trinity are made, and a description of a contemporary Trinitarian spirituality is offered, in view of the biblical sources and the historical development of this central Christian doctrine.

We proceed in five steps. First, attention will be given to the close connection between the doctrine of the Trinity and Christian spirituality. Second, the doctrine of the Trinity will be described in very broad outline. The third step is to point the way toward an authentic Trinitarian spirituality. Fourth, we shall describe how different understandings of the Trinity affect Christian spirituality. Particular attention is given to the deleterious effects that result from Western Christianity's predilection to focus on the intradivine life of God. Finally, we will list fifteen principles of a thoroughgoing contemporary Trinitarian spirituality that is at once consonant with the riches of the Christian tradition and responsive to contemporary ecclesial needs and pastoral exigencies.

Trinity and Spirituality

The connection between the triune God and the Christian spiritual life is not as clear as it should be because of the margin-alization of the doctrine of the Trinity. Current efforts to retrieve the centrality of this doctrine in light of its practical implications have made it possible to see the whole Christian life quite differently. What is this doctrine at its heart, at its best? The doctrine of the Trinity affirms that it belongs to God's very nature to be committed to humanity and its history, that God's covenant with us is irrevocable, that God's face is immutably turned toward us in love, that God's presence to us is utterly reliable and constant. The basis for these affirmations is the self-revelation of God in the economy of salvation history, specifically, for Christians, in the economy revealed in Jesus Christ. Christian faith is the Spirit-assisted response to the incarnate Word of God, Jesus Christ, who reveals the face of the invisible God.

The affirmation that God is triune stands in sharp contrast to all unitarian or unipersonal notions of God. To say that God is triune does not substitute tritheism (belief in three gods) for monotheism (belief in one God); rather, the one God is affirmed to be "differentiated" in personhood. To put it another way, both Jesus Christ and the Spirit are essential to salvation; only God can save; therefore God, Christ, and the Spirit are divine. Different images and metaphors have been used to depict the triune nature of God, for example, source-river-stream, or memory-intellect-will, or lover-beloved-love. A more primordial image in the tradition is communion (*koinōnia*), which expresses the inherent diversity yet equality and interdependence of the divine Persons.

A Christian spirituality rooted in the triune God emphasizes community rather than individuality. The goal of the spiritual life is holiness, attained through the perfection of one's relationships with others rather than through an ever more pure gaze of the mind's eye on some eternal verity. Trinitarian spirituality naturally connects with the ethical demands of the Christian life, which is seen as the increase of communion among persons rather than personal sanctification achieved by a journey inward.

The Doctrine of the Trinity

The doctrine of the Trinity originated in the effort to think through the implications of the roles of Christ and the Spirit in salvation. In general, early Christian theologians concentrated on how God's saving acts were accomplished in the economy of redemption (*oikonomia*), and what this suggested about the nature of God's eternal being (*theologia*). Because of certain questions raised by Arius and others, particularly about whether Jesus Christ was of the same nature as God and how the suffering of Jesus Christ could be reconciled with an impassible God, Christian theologians were moved to answer these questions on the basis of a metaphysics oriented to an analysis of God's intradivine life. This approach shifted the focus from the diversity and uniqueness of the divine Persons within the economy of salvation to the equality of Persons within God's eternal Trinity. Among other things, this had the effect of diminishing the central role of economy in theological reflection on God, thereby signaling the "defeat" of the doctrine of the Trinity.

Augustine's theology of the Trinity had a deep and lasting influence on Western spirituality. He focused his theological reflection on the structure of God's "intradivine" life, that is, the relationships of Father, Son, and Holy Spirit to one another. Augustine favored images of the Trinity drawn from the psychology of the human person, understood to have the faculties of intellect, will, and memory. He believed that the structure of the individual human soul was a mirror image (vestige) of the Trinity. By knowing oneself, one would know God. Whether Augustine intended it or not, his version of contemplation and ascent to God through descent into the self muted the communitarian dimensions of the Chris-

tian life. In contrast, the Eastern tradition was loath to consider God "in Godself," apart from the economy of salvation, that is, apart from God's concrete existence as Father, Son, and Spirit with us.

Much contemporary reflection on Christian spiritual life is rooted in an approach to the Trinity emphasizing the intradivine life, mirrored in the inner life of the individual person. Knowing God means knowing the self in itself, in an ever deeper journey inward. There is always the danger that an unchecked pursuit of a personal spirituality will amount to nothing more than a narcissistic self-absorption and self-preoccupation. A revitalized doctrine of the Trinity provides just such a check, dispelling distorted notions both of the human person and of God. A thoroughgoing Trinitarian theology provides a radical critique of the approach that sees either the human being or God as "individuals," knowing and loving themselves in and of themselves. Augustine was certainly correct that the human person is a unique locus of the divine self-disclosure. And, given that we are created in the image and likeness of God, it is natural to look for the contours of that image within ourselves. However, Genesis 2–3 suggests that the image of God is to be found in the relationship between female and male, which gives the divine image in us a dimension beyond the solitary self. Persons, by definition, come into being through another and require others to exist as persons.

Rethinking Trinitarian Spirituality

A revitalized doctrine of the Trinity, rooted in the biblical, creedal and liturgical, and Greek patristic tradition confutes the solitary spiritual quest by deemphasizing the concern for "nature" and "substance" in favor of an emphasis on "person" and "relationship" and "communion." In this view, the primary and ultimate ontological category is person rather than substance. God is primarily personal, not a substance or a nature. This has vast implications for metaphysics as well as for the main concern of this entry, Trinitarian spirituality. In brief, since reality originates in personhood, existence itself is personal. Second, God, as personal, is intrinsically related to another; God does not exist as an isolated or self-sufficient being. A person, by definition, cannot exist by itself.

Since human beings are created in the image of an inherently relational God, human beings are not created as selves in isolation, but they are who they are, and come into being as what they are, through and for others. This is the central mystery disclosed in the economy of salvation in the incarnate Word. Christian living is not about solitary salvation, introspection, self-absorption, but about ever-fuller participation in communion with God and with others. Human persons are made for loving communion with others. Because God is not solitary, or self-sufficient, but lives eternally in ecstatic, outgoing love, human persons created in the image of this God find their personhood realized not in autonomy or self-sufficiency or isolation but in self-donation; we come to ourselves through others. Autonomy (the measure of oneself is oneself) and heteronomy (the measure of oneself is entirely the other) are balanced by theonomy, which is to say, the measure of one's personhood derives from, and is ordered to, the divine personhood of the absolutely personal triune God.

Understandings of the Trinity: Effects on Spirituality

The shift in focus from the diversity and uniqueness of divine Persons within the economy of salvation to the metaphysical equality of the Persons within God's eternal being affected the way Christians imaged and lived the Christian life, that is to say, spirituality in all its dimensions. Several of these dimensions are discussed below, with attention being paid to the ways in which a proper understanding of the Trinity might serve as a basis for an authentic Christian spirituality.

Holiness

We arrive at an understanding of God by contemplating the way God is for us and by participating in God's providential plan for the world, in other words, through the economy of salvation history. The notion that God is a self-subsistent community of selves constituting an intradivine Trinity no longer is persuasive. A God unaffected by human life and history, especially by human suffering, a God who lives in eternal simplicity and tranquility, withdrawn from history, has given rise to quite peculiar understandings of holiness that have prevailed throughout Christian history. Indeed the very notion of Christian holiness as being "set apart" is due in no small measure to an understanding of a God who is conceived of as existing apart from human history in intradivine communion.

The holy person has often been understood as the one who, by virtue of a "higher calling," is set apart and above others for nobler purposes. He or she is set apart geographically or enclosed behind cloister walls, distanced from the everyday concerns of life "in the world" and from the ordinary pursuits of domestic and civil life. This notion of holiness is rooted in the idea of a God who is withdrawn into the solitary simplicity of the intradivine life, dwelling in light inaccessible, unmoved by the contingencies of human history and who, because unchangeable, remains unaffected by human suffering and human development through history. The notion of a God unmoved by the tragedies and triumphs of human history is in part responsible for a vision of holiness in which persons flee the city and turn their backs on the world, in order to live for God alone, whose being is understood to be removed from the contingencies of human life. Even though the monastic (from *monos* = "alone") tradition gives particular attention to the common life, monastic life is properly understood as the solitary life pursued together with others.

If God is understood to exist on a separate plane apart from the way God is *for us* in the economy of salvation, then the holiness of God will be understood to be mirrored most perfectly in the Christian who is self-sufficient, who lives alone, and who remains unaffected by the actual historical circumstances that involve the great masses of human beings. On the other hand, if God is understood as God for us, then the holiness of God, and the holiness of Christians, will be understood differently.

In this alternative view, holiness rests in setting aside or standing apart from the self, moving beyond self-preoccupation, self-indulgence, self-fixation, and becoming persons conformed to the image of God in us through being toward others. God's very nature can be said to be ecstatic and fruitful. God's own personal movement is away from being a self-subsistent self, through self-donation and self-communication. God, by nature, stands apart from Godself in ecstatic and fecund love.

In this view, holiness does not reside primarily with those who are set apart to pursue nobler and loftier purposes, and who remain unmoved by daily concerns and the vicissitudes of life in the world. Rather, authentic Christian holiness is realized by living in Christ through the Spirit who enables our own ecstasis in response to God's loving ecstasis. Through the power of the Spirit, self-preoccupation and self-absorption become the real grist for the mill of Christian asceticism. We find the deepest gift of personal becoming not in removing ourselves from the affairs of human life but by entering into personal communion with the God who is for us and into communion with all those for whom Christ died.

Spiritual Life as Journey

Whatever merits the focus on the solitary self may have had, it is out of step with a renewed understanding of Trinitarian doctrine. The image of the solitary self in search of the true, hidden, deepest inner self as the paradigm of the Christian spiritual life is in no small measure the result of wrong turns taken in the development of the doctrine of the Trinity. For example, Augustine's approach to the Trinity gave rise to forms of Christian life that focused on the solitary quest for personal holiness by means of the inner journey through self-scrutiny and personal sanctification. God is not sought by looking first and foremost to God's redemptive acts in the providential plan of salvation. Just as the focus of Augustine's Trinitarian theology is the mystery of God in Godself, so the focus of spirituality becomes the mystery of the human person in itself, as vestige of the Trinity. The result was the proliferation of forms of Christian life that emphasized turning inward through withdrawal from the world, from human concerns, from domestic and affective relationships, and, by implication, from ethical responsibility for the transformation of the world through participation in the word and work of Jesus Christ in history. The world and culture were judged to be depraved, debauched, and decadent. The hermit and later the monk emerged as the paradigm of authentic Christian holiness.

Much contemporary reflection on the Christian spiritual life remains rooted in this approach to the Trinity. Union with God means knowing God in oneself, in an ever-deepening journey inward. It is ironic that the current emphasis on the close connection between psychology and spirituality has given rise to a great deal of narcissistic preoccupation with an individual's spiritual life. Due largely to this one-sided emphasis, much writing and discourse in the field of contemporary spirituality is judged by others in the wider Church and academy as nothing more than dilettantism and frivolity. The criticism is not without warrant. Much that passes for "spirituality" is a gross distortion that stands in need of a radical critique that a thoroughgoing Trinitarian theology can provide. At the same time, given that the human person is created in the image and likeness of God, it is not altogether without merit to emphasize the human person as a unique locus of the divine self-disclosure.

Discussion of a Trinitarian spirituality necessitates greater attention to the reality of personhood. The doctrine of the Trinity, rooted in the economy of salvation, shows that the primary and ultimate ontological category is *person*; existence itself is personal. This means that we are not selves in isolation but our very being is constituted and oriented toward and for another. The central mystery disclosed in the incarnate Word is that Christian salvation entails ever-fuller participation in communion with God and with others.

Human personhood is iconic of divine personhood. Created in the image of a God who is not solitary or self-sufficient but lives eternally in ecstatic, outgoing love, human persons created in the image of this God find our personhood realized not in autonomy or self-sufficiency or isolation but in self-donation. We come to ourselves through others; we come from others and are directed toward others. In this lies the truth of the Christian spiritual journey. Life in the grace of the Holy Spirit impels the journey to ever more complete communion between persons both divine and human. Human personhood can be described as theonomous, that is, derived from, and ordered to, divine personhood.

Prayer

Understandings of Christian prayer have been profoundly influenced by the historical and theological development of the doctrine of the Trinity. Those Christian traditions marked by a strong sacramental and liturgical approach to worship have managed to keep to the fore the communitarian nature of all authentic Christian prayer. Be that as it may, prayer has also been understood as an essentially private and individual exercise, even within the context of worship. The image of prayer as communication in the manner of conversation has occupied a central place in many Christian traditions of prayer. Prayer is seen as a conversation between the individual human person and God. Spiritual exercises and strategies of spiritual direction were conceived largely in light of the "one-to-one" model, and this remains true even in our own day. Prayer continues to be associated with the journey inward, figuring out God's will for oneself, what it means to be a disciple of Christ, invoking God's blessing for oneself and those held dear, examining one's failures and making amends for what one has done wrong. Such an approach to prayer and spiritual direction reflects an understanding of a God who is the other partner in personal dialogue, and who discloses hidden purposes and plans in the secret of the individual's heart.

While this dialogical model of prayer preserves its essentially personal nature, a Trinitarian approach to prayer highlights the communal, social, and indeed public character of all prayer. Prayer is more than an activity relegated to specific times and places in which one human being talks to God. Prayer disposes us and enables us to participate in the contemplative dimension of everyday living, and to recognize the presence and action of the Holy Spirit who dwells within us at every moment. All authentic Christian living is properly understood as doxological. Life in Christ is an expression of the praise and thanks given to God by the baptized. Every dimension of life in Christ participates in the ongoing economy of salvation. Prayer, then, is to be understood not only as conversation and communication in dialogue but as ongoing participation in the communion of persons which comprises God's providential plan for all of humanity. Indeed, above all, prayer is that which enables the Christian people to see the ordinary and the everyday as the arena of God's presence and action.

This Trinitarian perspective casts light not only on prayer but also on the related notions of meditation, contemplative prayer, the relationship between contemplation and action, and mysticism. Prayer describes the movement of the human heart toward ever-fuller participation in the life of God. It is the response of one's whole person to the divine initiative as this is apprehended and appropriated in the economy of salvation. The term "human heart" does not refer to the region of private, individual feelings or emotions as opposed to other dimensions of the person. The heart describes the deepest, most fundamental center of the person, and as such is found in the Hebrew and Christian Scriptures as well as in the history of Christian spirituality to describe the whole person. Indeed, the person *is* the heart. "Heart" is the word for *affectus,* or affectivity, which is the openness of the human being to be touched by another, by others, and by God. It names the human capacity to be toward the other. As such it is inclusive of communal and social realities. To have a heart is to possess the capacity to be in relationship. The heart describes the human being's openness to relate to the real, that is, to the claim of the other upon oneself. Thus "heart" is the human dynamic toward the good. Prayer is the deeply personal movement of the heart thus understood. Consequently prayer is never a private or isolated activity. It finds its fullest expression in interpersonal communion in and through communication with others and with God.

Prayer as the response of the whole person to the divine initiative disclosed in the economy of salvation cannot be understood properly if it is thought to exist in opposition to action. Prayer is the praxis of desire, that is, the effort of the human heart to be, precisely by being in relation to another in love. The openness to relationship that is the constitutive dimension of human beings is itself indicative of an absence, a longing for completion and fullness in and through another person.

Because human personhood is both given and achieved, prayer of the heart is expressed in simple loving attention to the gift of God's presence and action in human life, history, Church, and world, as well as in human self-expression through those activities by which we seek to participate more fully in establishing an authentic communion among persons. Loving attentiveness (contemplation) and establishing rightly ordered relations among persons (action) are coefficients in the praxis of desire.

From this Trinitarian perspective, prayer is not an exercise of the mind's undisturbed gaze upon eternal, unchanging truth. Nor is it methodical, organized discursive meditation designed to gain a glimpse of God's hidden purpose. Prayer does not spring from or nourish one's "spiritual life," as if such a life existed in a separate compartment of the self, mirroring in some vague way the true nature of God above human grasp. Rather, prayer is the movement of the attentive human heart to participate in the very life of God, to respond to the myriad ways that God comes in Christ through the power of the Spirit. This view of prayer opens one to see that the distinctions and fast separations between spiritual life and secular life, between sacred and profane, Church and world, rest on an overdrawn distinction between the immanent and economic Trinity. Just as there are not two trinities, immanent and economic, God *ad intra* and God *ad extra,* but one God who is precisely God *for us,* so the human person is a unity, and the realm of the human spirit is one. There is in each of us a single heart called to respond to the one triune communion of divine Persons made manifest in the presence and action of Jesus Christ and the Spirit.

A Trinitarian spirituality thus serves to correct skewed notions of the relationship between action and contemplation. Informed by the doctrine of the Trinity, action and contemplation do not pertain to separate spheres—the sacred and the secular, Church and world, spiritual life and the domain of the mundane and profane. The one God who providentially guides the economy of salvation is not only *for us* but *for the world.* Prayer awakens human consciousness to the contemplative dimension of everyday living and leads to the recognition that "God is so thoroughly involved in every last detail of creation that if we could truly grasp this it would altogether change how we approach each moment of our lives. For everything that exists—insect, agate, galaxy—manifests the mystery of the living God" (C. M. LaCugna, *God for Us: The Trinity and Christian Life,* p. 304).

As the fullest expression of Christian prayer, mysticism has been understood, for the most part, in terms of unmediated union with God. The individual soul meets, and gradually and progressively is united with, the one God. The goal of the mystical journey is the immediate experiential apprehension of the deepest recesses of divine life. The mystic is usually a solitary, often eccentric figure, someone not in any way like the ordinary Christian. Classical approaches to mystical experience affirmed that the mystical life was not the normal outcome of the baptismal call to the life of holiness and the pursuit of virtue. The mystical life was judged to be an extraordinary life, made possible by special graces. But the very notion of an immediate experience of God can undercut the priority of the economy of salvation wherein the providential plan of God for human beings and for the whole world is revealed, mediated through the incarnate Word, and made concrete in the work of the Holy Spirit who brings about the reordering of all of creation.

An approach to mysticism rooted in Trinitarian theology requires attention to the panoply of human experiences in history, world, culture, personality, and Church, wherein God's presence and action are discerned. Union with God is to be found in every form of communion: affective, sexual, familial, artistic; the intellectual pursuit of truth, the apprehension and pursuit of the good, the appreciation of the beautiful. All forms of authentic communion are potential avenues for union with the triune God.

At this juncture it may be useful to draw attention to the question of whether and to what degree Christian mystics are Trinitarian. The mystical writings of Catherine of Siena, The Victorines, and the Rhineland mystics in the West, and the Cappadocians, Maximus the Confessor, and Gregory Palamas in the East, to name just a few, clearly represent a spirituality informed by the symbols and narrative of the Christian tradition. On the other hand, *The Cloud of Unknowing,* or the writings of Pseudo-Dionysius, Thérèse of Lisieux, or especially Meister Eckhart, do not obviously exhibit the symbols of the Christian narrative. Since the affirmation of God as triune is central and essential to Christian faith, the question arises as to why so many mystical writings seem to rely so little on Trinitarian symbolism. It is conceivable that there is a particular way that mystics perceive the basic truth that the doctrine seeks to articulate, but that it is expressed in a way that requires skillful and careful translation. Or, it may be that the prevailing Christian doctrine of God had by a certain historical point so marginalized the Trinitarian dimension (because of its esoteric and speculative character) that Christian mystics gravitated toward a more generic monotheism. Whatever the reason, we affirm that Christian mysticism is a path through the economy of redemption, in which God is revealed through Jesus Christ and the Holy Spirit. Thus it is to be expected that Christian mystical experience in some way or another reflect the particularities of symbols and events important in Christian faith.

Vocation

In traditional Christian spirituality, vocation was restricted to mean a particular form of life, namely, religious life or ordination to the priesthood. Both of these had as an intrinsic component abstinence from sexual relations and the foregoing of marriage and children. Religious life and priesthood were regarded as the true Christian vocations, and therefore forms of life higher than marriage and the single life. And yet, from the perspective of a Trinitarian theology of God, because of the sacramental efficacy of baptism, by which a person is incorporated into a community of believers who constitute the Body of Christ, all the various ways that Christians respond to the call of Christ constitute authentic vocations. This diversity is properly understood in light of the universal call to holiness, rooted in baptism, strengthened in chrismation, and renewed in frequent celebration of the Eucharist. Of particular importance is the recognition of many kinds of vocations, for example, those whose call is to be reconcilers and healers in Church and world. Marriage and orders are merely two ways of sacramentalizing two of the many life forms among the various vocations and ministries in the Church.

Lamentably, even in our own day ordained ministry is still seen by many as setting the ordinand apart from, and above, the women and men he is ordained to serve. The ordained priest is understood to possess a special ontological character that entitles him to dispense grace and sacrament. But since ordained ministry is a participation in the life of Christ the servant, and since all ministries, ordained and nonordained, are rooted in the mission of Christ manifest in the economy of salvation (e.g., Jn 10:10), the ordained cannot properly be envisioned as a dispenser of grace, since grace is the prerogative of the Spirit who cannot be possessed and does not need safeguarding.

In the past the religious vow of obedience was understood as the conformity of one's life and decisions to the will of God expressed in the directives of the religious superior. Although it was presupposed that the individual superior voiced the will of God in and through the community, this was not always the case in either theory or practice. One could refuse the directive of a superior only on the grounds of grave violation of conscience. From a Trinitarian perspective, *obedire*, to listen to, to hear the word of God, requires attention to the free operation of the Spirit heard in a multiplicity of voices, institutions, and in the lives of various Christians who by their lives testify to the gospel. All Christians are called to obedience to God, not just those who are in religious life.

Asceticism

In the history of Christian spirituality, virginity and celibacy quickly developed as superior forms of life. Celibacy in particular was understood as a form of solitary life that precluded sexuality, marriage, and affective relationships. Virginity and celibacy were regarded as components of the *authentic* Christian life. Any survey of Christian history will show that the spirituality of the laity was understood as derivative and lesser because of the priority given to virginity and celibacy, again rooted in a particular understanding of God. Ascesis was understood narrowly as mortification of the flesh and rarely was applied to other demanding aspects of the Christian life such as the rigorous sacrifices entailed in marital and family life, especially caring for one's children; the uncertainties of agrarian life and daily struggles for sustenance; complex decisions about the use and disposition of goods; the chaste exercise of sexuality for noncelibates; responsibility for the earth; the discipline of education and study; proper care and exercise of the body (nutrition, diet, balance of leisure and work); the tedium of too much work.

Discernment and Spiritual Direction

Living the Christian life as a "professional" was seen to be the province of those in religious life or orders. It was assumed that a greater burden lay on those who had undertaken the "real" form of the Christian life signified by virginity and celibacy. Spiritual direction emerged as a need for the clergy, not for the laity, who were thought to be consumed by "worldly" rather than lofty spiritual matters. Spiritual direction amounted to charting the action of the Spirit in an individual's life, in consultation with a spiritual mentor. Regularly scheduled retreats, designed to feed the spiritual life, were a luxury of the clerical class, who did not have to care for families or worry about salaries.

All this stands in contrast to a different understanding of discernment as the task of the Christian community at large. Beholding the glory of God and deepening in the life of communion requires seeing the whole world, and every activity within it, as a locus for the Spirit's presence and action. Figuring out what it means to be a disciple of Christ "in the world" entails a clear perception of the purpose of one's life and the shape of one's destiny in view of God's providential plan for all of humanity. The dualisms between sacred and secular, between clergy and lay, between the professional and lay Christian are untenable if we adhere to the principle, drawn from Trinitarian theology, that all creation is the arena in which God is working out the providential plan of salvation. God is to be discovered as much in the ordinary, mundane, routine dimensions of life and work as in sacred times and spaces set aside for contemplation of God. Prayer is well thought of as awakening to the divine presence in *every* dimension of everyday living. Prayer need not be restricted to an activity that takes place during a specific time frame, in a certain place, offered by select persons.

Healing and Wholeness

The Christian tradition has paid a great deal of attention to the spiritual and corporal works of mercy. Concern for the healing of the body as well as of the soul is expressed in the Church's sustained commitment to the care of the poor, the sick, the suffering, and the dying. This commitment has taken the form of the early Church's care for the widow and the orphan, the response of communities of apostolic sisters to the pressing needs of their day, the ministry of educating generations of poor immigrants and refugees, and the continuing struggle of religious sisters to meet healthcare needs in the midst of crumbling economies and the medical profession's shifting values.

The enormous value of the Church's commitment in this domain notwithstanding, it must be recognized that many previous approaches to healing and wholeness rested on a dualist anthropology. Indeed, the very distinction between corporal (of or relating to the body) and spiritual (of or relating to the spirit or soul) works of mercy belies this. In the Church's practice, if not in its theory, spiritual works of mercy were accorded superior status. The groundswell of interest in pentecostalism and healing in the Roman Catholic Church in the postconciliar period, to say nothing of similar eruptions at various points in the history of Christian spirituality, indicate that this dualism is misleading and unsatisfactory in the quest for an integrated and holistic sense of Christian life. Contemporary approaches to healing and wholeness informed by a Trinitarian doctrine of God would give singular attention to the human person as a unity, indeed a mystery of quite complex dimensions uniting body, psyche, mind, intellect, will, personhood, and so forth. In such a perspective, greater emphasis would be given to the interrelationship between the various dimensions of person, and a greater recognition that healing and wholeness occur in the context of one's whole embodied personhood, especially in one's relationship with self, beloved, family, community, and God.

This wider view of healing and wholeness is reflected in the *Rite of Anointing and Pastoral Care of the Sick* (released on December 7, 1972, to be implemented by January 1, 1973), a high watermark in overcoming dualist anthropology. This rite replaces the sacramental rite of extreme unction, and reflects an altogether different view of human sickness, suffering, dying, and death. No longer is the sacrament viewed primarily in terms of readying the soul for its passage through death at the final moments of life; rather, anointing is understood within the context of the larger concerns of pastoral ministry to the sick. The rite provides a theological rationale for anointing that views it as part of the Church's struggle to overcome suffering and illness of all kinds. Where they are not overcome they can bear positive significance through participation in the mystery of the cross and resurrection of Christ.

Ministry to the sick is viewed as the responsibility of all men and women who serve the sick in any capacity. All baptized Christians are responsible for ministering to the sick, although the specific responsibilities differ according to the gifts given to each person. Particular focus is placed on the family and friends of the sick person, and the priest who is the proper minister of the sacrament of anointing. Visiting and caring for the sick is not simply the responsibility of priests; it is the mission of the entire Christian community.

The communal and relational context for the ministry and anointing of the sick is clearly reflected in the movement from the earlier practice of a private, final anointing to the possibility of a communal service within a liturgical setting involving community, family, and friends, as well as for the anointing of several persons at once. Group anointing may take place within the Eucharistic liturgy after the proclamation of the word as a distinct ritual for the sole purpose of anointing or within the context of a communion service. This rite more clearly expresses the purposes of anointing and pastoral care of the sick: to offer the Church's support and what it might lend to recovery and health; to strengthen the spirit to sustain the person with hope in the resurrection, even and especially if the illness and suffering lead to death.

Understanding of Church and World

The understanding of the nature of the relationship between Church and world was also marked by the historical and theological development of the doctrine of the Trinity. The view of God that has prevailed in Western Christianity has sometimes been referred to as Christocentric monotheism. Prominence was given to the person of Christ to such an extent that the importance of the Holy Spirit was eclipsed. The Spirit became something like the proverbial "middle child," inadvertently neglected and overshadowed because of the attention given to others. This had the lamentable effect of subordinating the Spirit to Christ.

By and large, classical definitions of the Church maintained that its foundation lay in the person of Jesus Christ and in his mission entrusted to the Twelve. In this view, Christ himself established the Church and entrusted its keys to Peter. The bestowal of the Spirit at Pentecost signaled the birth of the Church, but even more it marked the beginning of the mission to preach the Good News to the ends of the earth. Much reflection about the nature of the Church was focused on the role of Christ in the Church, particularly its institutional structure, while discourse about the Church's mission to the world focused on the pneumatic and charismatic. It was an easy theological move, then, to assert that the successors of the Twelve and those who through ordination share in their ministry, along with those who have an explicit ecclesiastical affiliation (through public profession of religious vows), are entrusted with the life of the Church *ad intra,* while all the others, the laity, share in the mission of the Spirit given in baptism for the sanctification of the profane, secular realm, i.e., the mission of the Church *ad extra.*

The theological problem with this conception of the Church-world relationship is that it rests on an unsatisfactory understanding of the reciprocity between Christ and the Spirit. It is precisely in and through the Spirit that Christ established the Church as the community of disciples. When they preach, teach, heal, and live lives of mercy and compassion, they do this in the presence and by the power of the Spirit of Christ. Envisioning the Church-world relationship in terms of sacred and secular, institution and charism, Christic and pneumatic, ministry *ad intra* and *ad extra,* rests on a bifurcation of Christ and Spirit that finds little justification in a proper understanding of the doctrine of the Trinity. It is unfortunate that even in much contemporary discussion about ministry, some argue that the ordained and the vowed religious serve the life of the Church *ad intra,* whereas the mission of laity is properly understood *ad extra.* Just as God does not live first *ad intra* and then *ad extra,* but lives one divine life shared and poured out in human history, so there is a *perichoresis,* a continuous dynamic interaction in the Church-world relationship. This is appropriately expressed in the Second Vatican Council's image of the Church as sacrament *in* and *to* the world.

Christian spirituality rooted in a revitalized doctrine of the Trinity rejects the subordination of Spirit to Christ, world to Church, lay to ordained and religious, secular to sacred. Moreover, the Church is not the exclusive realm of Christian living. A vast array of Christian life-forms emerge in response to the Spirit who enlightens, enlivens, guides, sanctifies, and heals in human life, history, world, and Church. The Spirit is the Spirit of God, Spirit of Christ in history and personality. There is no denying the Spirit's presence "outside" the Church.

Spirituality and the Social Order

One of the most deleterious effects of the focus on individual sanctification was the neglect of sociopolitical issues. Commitment to the spiritual life generally took the form of being charitable to those in one's immediate family and/or community and, by extension, being charitable to others in the world at large. Responsibility for the sociopolitical-economic order was not thought to be an essential part of Christian spiritual life and growth. Ethics was virtually synonymous with sexual ethics. While charity was thought to be required by the call of the gospel, justice—rendering to each person according to his or her need; creating a world in which all might grow; establishing rightly ordered relationships in accord with the providential plan of God for humanity—was regarded as desirable but not required.

A thoroughgoing Trinitarian spirituality entails the recognition that God's providential plan for the world involves absolutely every dimension of existence. Every inch and ounce of creation is embraced by the loving God through Jesus Christ. A Trinitarian ethic is at once personal and relational, and is inclusive of every human concern and commitment, with particular attention to the "last and the least" in Church and world. Even and especially those who are often judged to be nonpersons, as well as all forms of nonhuman life, are unavoidably the concern of a Trinitarian Christian ethic that looks to all creation, human personality, and indeed the whole world as iconic of the triune God.

Principles of Contemporary Trinitarian Spirituality

1. God comes to be known and loved in the course of a saving history. God's initiative toward all creation establishes the basis for any relationship between human beings and God. Consequently, prayer, reli-

gious discipline, celebration in word and sacrament, spiritual growth and maturation all rest on the prior initiative of God for us.

2. Christian spirituality, to be Christian, must be firmly rooted in the Christian economy of salvation where God is revealed to be the God of Jesus Christ by the power of the Holy Spirit. The symbols, images, and concepts appropriate to a Christian spirituality emerge from the record of this saving history and ordinarily will be drawn from the Scriptures and from other spiritual writers.

3. Christian spirituality concerns the invitation to participate in the very life of God through communion with the incarnate Word by the power of the Holy Spirit who is love. Such participation brings the believer into the heart of the mystery of God's triune life. The call to ever-deeper communion with God is at the same time the call to ever-deeper communion with others.

4. Christian spirituality develops through the life of prayer, which is the ongoing cultivation of relationship with God rooted in the divine initiative. The spiritual life is sustained and flourishes by the continuing call of the God who is recognized as active in history and present to creation, and by gradual appropriation of the salvific gift offered in the life and ministry, crucifixion and resurrection of Christ.

5. Christian holiness involves growth in conformity to our true natures as human beings created for union with the triune God. We are oriented in the very depths of our being to this union. Deification, or being made divine, according to the Greek Fathers, arises out of conformity to our true humanity.

6. Spirituality rooted in a renewed understanding of the triune God involves attention to the many dimensions of the human person and of the God-world relation, not just the "interior" dimension or the "inner life" of the human person. A contemporary Trinitarian spirituality ineluctably entails greater attention to a wide range of factors that together constitute the human being's relationship with self, others, and God. It is inclusive of the social, political, and economic realms; in a word, every dimension of personal and communal life is altogether involved in a Trinitarian Christian spirituality.

7. Because the mystery of the triune God grounds the communion among all persons, the spirituality to which it gives rise is singularly attentive to the quality of relationship between and among human persons, as well as their relationship to various other creatures and goods of the earth. Everything that exists originates from a relational God, and exists in relation to the whole and its various parts, so that relational interdependence is a hallmark of this spirituality.

8. The triune God is the paradigm of all human relationships. The divine Persons exist in a relationship of diversity, equality, mutuality, uniqueness, and interdependence. Theological reflection on the mystery of the triune God, in the form of the doctrine of the Trinity, is critical of modes of relationship built on domination/submission, power/powerlessness, or activity/passivity. Since the relational pattern of divine life is the norm of human life, relationships that respect difference, nurture reciprocity, and cultivate authentic complementarity are iconic of divine life.

Because both diversity and unity characterize the divine Persons, the Christian community welcomes equitable relationships between and among persons who may appear vastly unequal in terms of economic, social, mental, or physical ability. While the ideals of mutuality and reciprocity among persons lie at the heart of the doctrine of the Trinity, this should not be construed in a "privileged" way that excludes those whose personhood is broken, wounded, needy, or disabled by physical or mental handicaps. By virtue of their participation in the very life of God, human persons are theonomous, that is, each and every person possesses a dignity that goes beyond social standing or function.

9. Trinitarian spirituality is one of solidarity between and among persons. It is a way of living the gospel attentive to the requirements of justice, understood as rightly ordered relationships between and among persons. This entails working to overcome obstacles to full human flourishing posed by evil and sin. Sin may be understood as the failure to discern and build a community of rightly ordered relationships, the inability or unwillingness to respect the interdependence of all human and nonhuman life, and as the divisiveness that ruptures the harmony between God and human beings. A Trinitarian spirituality entails a commitment to live in rightly ordered relationship with self, others, and God. The restoration of such rightly ordered relationship is the meaning of salvation and does not involve only the individual but has wide-ranging implications for social forms of life.

10. A Christian spirituality informed by a proper understanding of the Trinity is wholly oriented to the God who is its source and end. It is a way of living through participation in the very life of God by communion with the Word of God in the power of the Holy Spirit, and communion with all creatures. Prayer, ascetical discipline, study, apostolic activity, the rigors of marriage and family life, the works of mercy, and especially the celebration of the paschal mystery in word and sacrament—all increase participation in divine life. Deeper participation in the life of God is, of course, recognized in the fruits borne in our being for others as God is for us.

11. The traditional contrast between active and contemplative forms of spirituality can no longer be sustained. Contemplation of God should lead to loving action on the behalf of others, and Christian action should be rooted in the insights of contemplative life.

12. The God who "dwells in light inaccessible" is, strictly speaking, unknowable and incomprehensible. Apophasis and the *via negativa* are important means of recognizing the ineffability of divine mystery. Even so, the God of salvation history is a self-revealing God who desires communion with all creatures. Thus, even though the mystery of God is in some sense unspoken and unspeakable, what we do know or say of God rests on how God exists for us, how God manifests and shares divine life in human history, personality, and society.

13. The mystery of God cannot be controlled or dissected by Christian theology nor fully grasped within a Christian spirituality. The mystery of God is the magnet for a contemplative gaze and the prayer of quiet repose rather than the object of analysis, systematic scrutiny, or theological assertion.

14. Similarly, the mystery of God cannot be controlled or thoroughly analyzed within any one religious tradition. Hence the importance of recognizing the insights of various religious traditions in order to come to a fuller understanding of the mystery of God. Although the doctrine of the Trinity is the specifically Christian way of speaking of God, it is looked upon by many as the most fertile domain for ecumenical, interfaith, and interreligious dialogue, precisely because it is an attempt to speak the truth about the ultimate mystery of God. In the interfaith and interreligious dialogues, consideration needs to be given to the question of whether doctrinal differences among religious traditions can be or ought to be reconciled by finding convergences in mystical experiences. One of the most important questions here is to what extent the particularities of the symbolic structure of a specific religion—for our purposes the Trinitarian structure of Christian faith—ought to inform mysticism.

15. A Trinitarian theology of God applied to the order of creation gives rise to a lively sense of stewardship for the goods of creation. A Trinitarian Christian spiritual-

ity provides fertile ground for exploring the relationship between human and nonhuman life in such a way as to throw light on current ecological themes such as the interdependence of various forms of life.

See also CHRIST; DIVINIZATION; GOD; GRACE; HOLY SPIRIT; MYSTICISM; SELF.

Bibliography: Y. Congar, *I Believe in the Holy Spirit*, 3 vols. (New York: Se/abury, 1983). D. Hardy and D. Ford, *Praising and Knowing God* (Philadelphia: Westminster, 1985). C. M. LaCugna, *God for Us: The Trinity and Christian Life* (San Francisco: Harper-Collins, 1991). C. M. LaCugna and K. McDonnell, "Returning from 'The Far Country': Theses for a Contemporary Trinitarian Theology," *The Scottish Journal of Theology* 41 (1988) 191–215. K. Leech, *Experiencing God: Theology as Spirituality* (New York: Harper & Row, 1985). V. Lossky, *The Mystical Theology of the Eastern Church* (Crestwood, N.Y.: St. Vladimir's Seminary Press, 1976). A. Louth, *The Origins of the Christian Mystical Tradition: From Plato to Denys* (Oxford; Clarendon, 1981). K. Rahner, *The Trinity* (New York: Herder, 1970). W. Rusch, *The Trinitarian Controversy* (Philadelphia: Fortress, 1980).

CATHERINE MOWRY LaCUGNA
MICHAEL DOWNEY

TRUST

Trust denotes a confidence or a sense of security in the reliability of someone else. It results in a state of being certain or secure. The term is thus a relational one, describing the quality of a relationship among two or more persons.

The Hebrew word for *trust* derives from the root *bth,* which means "to be certain or secure." It occurs nearly two hundred times in the OT, most often in prayers and songs. Forty percent of its occurrences are in the psalms. It refers most often to trust in God (e.g., Pss 28:7; 44:7ff.; 141:8; 144:2). God is the one in whom to put trust. God is a source of strength and refuge who protects those who put their trust in God. It is foolish to put one's trust in other gods or in human beings (see Jer 17:5f., Ps 146:3).

Trust also can include a sense of hope of future rescue (see Job 11:18) and a sense of faith in God that gives courage (Ps 23:4).

The NT subsumes trust under faith, especially faith in Jesus, both in his works and in the legitimacy of his message. The trust of those present is a presupposition for Jesus' working deeds of power (Lk 8:25) and for healing (Mk 5:36; Lk 8:50). And he demands trust in his message. Trust is, in a word, the fundamental attitude Jesus requires of his followers. This is carried on by his disciples, who require trust in the name of Jesus in their own acts of healing (Acts 3:16).

The NT writings continue this theme of trust as a sign of faith. Paul expands it at one point (1 Cor 13:7) to show that it is a fruit of love. Echoing the OT, the NT insists that trust is to be placed in God alone (Heb 10:23; 11:11); one should not put one's trust in flesh (Phil 3:3).

In the subsequent tradition of the Church, trust is linked with both faith and hope. Trust (Latin *fiducia*) has traditionally been seen as a particular quality or attitude by means of which we believe (the *fides qua*). This aspect of faith (as contrasted to the *fides quae,* the things believed) received special emphasis from Luther and the Reformers, thereby pointing to the proper attitude of the believer toward God. Trust thus understood is something to be cultivated as an index of one's union with God.

Thomas Aquinas and others emphasized the relation of trust to the virtue of hope. Trust has within its certainty an element of the unknown; were that not the case, trust would be replaced by utter certainty. Thus hope is inextricably linked with trust. Aquinas deals with trust under the virtue of magnanimity (ST II-II, q. 129, a. 6), where he calls trust a "strengthened hope" (q. 129, a. 6, ad 3). Trust is not itself a virtue but is a condition for the virtue of hope. It is this line of thought that influenced subsequent Catholic spiritual writers, who saw trust as providing the intentionality of hope that made possible growth in the life of God.

Trust has taken on new definition in contemporary spirituality through the work of psychology. Alfred Adler saw a lack of trust as the basis of neurotic disorders. More importantly, Erik Erikson saw the achievement of a level of basic trust as the foundation for further ego development. This has been adapted to the understanding of spiritual growth, especially by James Fowler in his work on faith development. Trust is seen as foundational for further growth in the spiritual life, both in one's relation to the unseen God and to one's visible neighbor.

See also FAITH; FRUIT(S) OF THE HOLY SPIRIT; HOPE.

Bibliography: E. Erikson, *Childhood and Society* (New York: Norton, 1963). J. Fowler, *Stages of Faith* (San Francisco: Harper & Row, 1981).

ROBERT J. SCHREITER, C.PP.S.

TRUTH

Reality, human knowing, and truth have been variously defined and interrelated by different philosophies. In all of them, though, truth lies in some sort of conformity between knowledge and reality. For the purposes of this entry, we are accepting the basic approach of the Scholastic tradition, in which truth is being (reality, what is) as knowable, in the same way that goodness is being as desirable. Knowability implies that truth, while intrinsic to being, has meaning solely and wholly in terms of our consciousness of it. Thus truth is in one sense a property of reality. In another sense it lies in the conformity of our conscious experience with that reality, and in yet a further sense, in the conformity of our words and behavior with our knowledge.

If human consciousness could receive and give expression to reality as simply as a mirror receives and reflects the light that strikes it, it would be comparatively easy to assess objectively the truth of a given proposition or the truthfulness of a given action. One would need only a sufficient quantity of data. But human consciousness must both receive and express the data of reality through the medium of language and through the filters, all the inherent limitations and acquired assumptions and biases, of our personal and social history.

An animal simply perceives a sensible reality and adjusts to it. What we human beings perceive is, as for the animal, only the sensible. But what we apprehend, what enters our consciousness, goes far beyond what is sensibly perceived. We know that we are perceiving, and therefore we apprehend it. We receive it and reflect on it through our particular personal, social, and linguistic filters and through our dispositions of feeling and will; we relate it to what is already present to our consciousness (and subconsciously to much more); we bestow our own peculiar value and meaning on it in view of all that; and we give it, at least mentally, more or less adequate expression in language. The potential for distorted apprehension exists in every phase and aspect of the process. And the potential for distortion is multiplied as what has been apprehended is communicated between individuals, within and across cultures and across history.

Thus we face the constant necessity for interpretation of what has been asserted as true. Every assertion is made within the contexts described above, and all these contexts are relevant to its interpretation and to any assessment of its truth or falsity. Also, every interpretation is made in a context of its own, so that persons who interpret out of radically different bases of understanding may come to radically opposing, though apparently equally logical, conclusions.

Individual human beings, then, and all humankind together must be forever in quest of a fuller grasp of truth, while acknowledging that that grasp will always be limited and conditioned. We will always need to be wary of the possibilities of distortion, for one distortion leads to further distortions. Positively, our particular distortions may, if we ask, find correction in the insights of other individuals, cultures, and ages. Every true insight leads to further insight and expansion of consciousness. As Paul Ricoeur has pointed out, each human person within the current of history is invited to ask a question no one else can ask (*History and Truth,* trans. C. Kelbley, Evanston, Ill.: Northwestern Univ. Press, 1965, p. 50).

Truth and God

Not every philosophy (e.g., Hegel, Marx) admits of the existence of ultimate, absolute, transcendent being. Those that do have variously named and attempted to describe that reality. "God" has in this sense been used both generically and, in our tradition, as a proper name. Following still a Scholastic approach, God as ultimate, absolute, transcendent being is intrinsically ultimate, absolute, transcendent goodness and truth. All else that is good and true is so only in a relative and inherently limited sense.

As inherently limited and relative beings, we may apprehend concepts about God, but we can never comprehend God. We can never comprehend infinite and absolute Truth. God must forever, even in an eventual resurrected life, be mystery for us.

God, absolute Truth, can never cease to be mystery to the individual human searcher, even at the deepest, purest, stillest point of mystical union. What Eric Mascall writes of mystery in general is preeminently true of confrontation with the mystery that is God: "[W]e are conscious that the small central area of which we have a relatively clear vision shades off into a vast background which is obscure and as yet unpenetrated. We find, as we attempt to penetrate this background . . . that the range and clarity of our vision progressively increase but at the same time the background which is obscure and unpenetrated is seen to be far greater than we had recognized before. . . . Thus, in the contemplation of a mystery there go together

in a remarkable way an increase both of knowledge and of what we might call conscious ignorance" (*Words and Images,* London: Longmans Green, 1957, p. 79).

Nor will God, absolute Truth, ever cease to be mystery to the whole sum of human knowledge. God is, in Nicolas Berdyaev's words, "Truth which has to be unriddled in the course of the whole of history" (*Truth and Revelation,* trans. R. M. French, London: Geoffrey Bles, 1953, p. 22).

But what of faith? What of grace? The infinite God might well reveal the face of absolute Truth to us, and we indeed believe this has been done and continues to be done in the person of Jesus Christ. But even infinite Truth fully revealed can be apprehended by us only through human filters and within human contexts that are never other than limited and limiting. Nor, to look at the question from the other side, is the mystery of God ever exhausted by our searchings.

Truth in the Church

The Christian Churches, including the Roman Catholic Church, are built upon the belief that God has been and continues to be revealed in history, most centrally in Jesus Christ. The primary witness to that revelation is seen as expressed in the Hebrew and Christian Scriptures. Therefore the understanding of truth articulated in those Scriptures ought to be foundational to Christian life.

The concept of truth in the Hebrew Scriptures is conveyed in the word *'emeth* (from *'āman:* "confirm," "support," "nourish"). The word connotes a sense of being true to oneself and others: faithful, trustworthy, constant, sincere. A word, human or divine, that is faithful to its speaker is true (2 Sam 7:28; Prov 14:25; Dan 10:21; Mal 2:6). God is true, faithful (Ps 54:7; 71:22; Isa 38:19), an attribute often associated in God with loving kindness (*ḥesed*) (Exod 34:6; Ps 86:15; Isa 16:5). God's people are to be faithful in return (1 Kgs 2:4; 3:6; Isa 38:3; Ps 26:3). The concepts of belief (because the source is trustworthy) and affirmation ("amen") are linguistically and theologically related.

The NT *alētheia* carries forward some of these same meanings (e.g., Rom 3:3; 2 Cor 4:2; Gal 5:7; 1 Tm 2:6-7). But here there is greater stress on truth as conformity with reality. And here truth is clearly Christological, especially in the Johannine texts. To do the truth, to walk in truth, is to live according to Christ rather than according to the former law (Jn 3:21; 1 Jn 1:6; 2 Jn 4; 3 Jn 3-4). Jesus' teaching is truth (Jn 3:31f.; 12:47f.). The truth Jesus preaches is the source of freedom (Jn 8:32) and of holiness (Jn 17:17ff.). Jesus' truth comes from God alone (Jn 1:18; 2:11; 5:17), and it is in Jesus that God's truth is revealed (Jn 1:14-16; Col 1:15; Phil 2:6; Heb 1:3; 2 Cor 3:17). Life in Christ demands that we live in truth, that we live in fidelity to the reality of God revealed in Jesus, that we live sincerely, without hypocrisy.

One must also ask in what sense the Scriptures are a source of truth for the Christian. The Scriptures are not themselves the revelation, but only the primary written witness to a belief over centuries of history that God is indeed a self-revealing God and that the revelation is couched in this particular history, culminating in the saving life, death, and resurrection of Jesus Christ. The witness of the Scriptures, therefore, is as subject to the principles of interpretation (hermeneutics) as the rest of human communication. The difference lies only in the faith that these writings do comprise a holy witness to a genuine divine revelation.

Any organized religion tends to generate, beyond its most basic sources, a tradition of orthodox and normative teaching to explicate those sources. Vatican II's Dogmatic Constitution on Divine Revelation refers to "the preaching of those who have received through episcopal succession the sure gift of truth" (DV 8). Roman Catholic tradition has from the patristic era placed great emphasis on the role of normative

teaching. Beginning in the 11th century, this normativeness became more and more centralized in the papacy, even to the point of proclaiming in the 19th century a dogma of papal infallibility.

More recently, however, it has been recognized that dogma, too, is within the realm of the human search for truth and subject to development. The same article cited above goes on to state that "as the centuries succeed one another, the Church constantly moves forward toward the fullness of divine truth until the words of God reach their complete fulfillment in her." The Pastoral Constitution on the Church in the Modern World set forth a practical guide: "[L]et there be unity in what is necessary, freedom in what is unsettled, and charity in any case" (GS 92). What is essential is that the individual Christian search for truth not in isolation but within the community of believers.

Not to be overlooked in this ecclesial search for truth is the role of ritual, of sacrament. In ritual a people expresses its belief and hope in ways that transcend words alone. Ritual embodies in its symbolism more than intellectual propositions about the reality in which we believe; in ritual, individual and community enter through actions and material signs into the wisdom of an entire people and history regarding God, self, and the universe.

The search for truth finds expression in a very particular way in mysticism, in the intimate personal experience of the divine in contemplation. In mystical prayer one strives for freedom from the usual modes of consciousness in order to be open to the direct revelation of, and union with, ultimate reality, ultimate truth—God. But as intimate and individual as it is, mystical prayer for the Christian is also inherently ecclesial and social, and its insights and intuitions must develop in mutuality with the ecclesial and social dialogue.

That ecclesial and social dialogue in turn must continue to use every resource of reason and experience in its search. The community of the Church has long basically trusted reason's contribution in the modes of philosophy and theology. The Second Vatican Council, especially in its Declaration on Religious Freedom, strengthened that respect for reason with the significantly new recognition that assent to "the truth [human beings] have discovered or think they have discovered" cannot be coerced (DH 3). We as Church are only beginning, however, to trust the insights derived from the full range of human experience in theological reflection.

Living in Truth

The truth of propositions and assertions lies in their conformity with objective reality. Personal truthfulness lies in conformity of our words and behavior with our apprehension of reality. We may, and in fact always will to some extent, be ignorant. We will, as a result of our ignorance or misapprehension, sometimes be in error. But as long as our words and behavior are consistent with our knowledge, there is no question of untruthfulness in the sense of mendacity, dissimulation, or hypocrisy.

Truthfulness, however, is deeper than this minimal consistency commonly referred to as honesty. It is an authenticity that is faithful to one's own conscious, free, responsible self and to all else that is. Authentic truthfulness is open to and actively pursues truth wherever it may be found. It knows that no individual or society or institution has yet exhausted or ever will exhaust the questions to be asked. It is not afraid of the conflicting understandings that are bound to characterize a human search in which there is so much inherent limitedness and potential for distortion. Truthfulness would rather risk being mis-

taken for a while than close off roads to new insight. It listens to and tests the voices of the prophets and the mystics who may have perceived a truth as yet unseen by society in general.

Living in truth is not a purely intellectual function. It requires that our intellectual search for, and fidelity to, truth be integrated with love. Mere consistency with fact, isolated from love, is not only cold but in the end must even be untrue, for goodness and truth are one in what is. An integrated spirituality strives, therefore, to love ever more truthfully and to discover and speak the truth with ever more genuine love.

To the extent that we expand and deepen our commitment beyond the specific truths and loves of the moment to the quest of ultimate, absolute truth, we learn to appreciate that everything is relative to that one Absolute and to order our values accordingly. Thus focused, we are increasingly freed from the blindness that would ensnare us in what is unimportant, dissipating, or destructive, freed to be transformed into the very truth and holiness of God.

See also AUTHORITY; CONSCIOUSNESS; FAITH; INTERPRETATION; KNOWLEDGE; MIND; MYSTICISM; REVELATION(S).

Bibliography: B. Lonergan, *Insight: A Study of Human Understanding* (New York: Philosophical Library, 1957). L. Dewart, *Religion, Language and Truth* (New York: Herder, 1970). E. Schillebeeckx and B. van Iersel, eds., *Truth and Certainty* (New York: Herder, 1973).

SUZANNE NOFFKE, O.P.

TWELVE STEP PROGRAM(S)
See ADDICTION.

U

UNDERSTANDING

See GIFTS OF THE HOLY SPIRIT.

UNION, UNITIVE WAY

The unitive way is the framework used by spiritual authors in describing the prayer experiences that mark those who have attained maturity in the spiritual journey. At the conclusion of the illuminative way, the person has been graced with prayer experiences conforming the mind and heart to Christ and has been initially purified at the core of her or his personality. The individual is now ready for the activity of the Holy Spirit in transforming union.

The desire for ever-deepening union with the triune God, enkindled in the illuminative way, and the existential realization of one's absolute poverty and helplessness in the face of the consuming desire for God's presence constitute the threshold of transforming union. The visits of God the Beloved in the experience of infused prayer serve to make the person increasingly aware of the greatness of God's love and of his or her total inability to respond adequately to these wondrous manifestations of divine love. Each new experience of the presence of God makes the individual yearn more deeply for total transformation in Christ, while at the same time convincing one that only the Holy Spirit can pro-vide the new heart that is necessary for full union with God.

The growth in faith, hope, and love, wrought in the dark night of the soul, opens the person to the divine initiative that is symbolized in the metaphor of betrothal at the beginning of the unitive way. The person experiences God's promise of total transformation already being realized as he or she is drawn outside of self and carried into the embrace of Divine Love. Although the ecstatic prayer of betrothal is transitory, the individual senses that he or she has truly been given a new heart and that, in truth, it is Christ who is the deepest reality at the center of one's being and activity.

The life of the individual, subsequent to betrothal itself, continues to be the alternation of the presence and absence of the Beloved that one has already known in the purgative and illuminative ways. But the purifying work of the Holy Spirit that is readying the person for the fullness of union with God, symbolized in the metaphor of marriage, is painful at times but is also marked by patient trust and peaceful waiting. One now knows experientially that God is faithful and will fulfill the promise of the fullness of transforming union made through the exchange of hearts in betrothal.

Each new visit of God the Beloved makes the individual more capable of sharing in the fullness of divine life. When the Holy Spirit has finished the work of purifying the mind and heart of the person, the grace of the mystical marriage is given through an experience of infused contemplation, which often includes an intellectual vision of the Trinity. In the mystical marriage one knows that by the grace of God she or he is irrevocably made one with Christ and shares, by the grace of transforming union, in his own relationship with the Father and the Holy Spirit.

The sufferings of the dark night of the soul now yield to a sense of profound peace because one understands that his or her own woundedness has now surrendered to the healing power of God's transforming love in the mystery of Christ's death and resurrection. The weariness of the long search for the Beloved in the spiritual journey gives way to the deep joy of being always in the presence of the merciful love of the triune God that is ever renewing and recreating one's life in Christ.

The experiential awareness in faith of sharing in the very life of the Trinity leads one to enter more fully into the mission of the Church to proclaim the gospel. Transformed in Christ and ablaze with the fire of the Holy Spirit, the person is guided by the gift of wisdom in knowing how to put herself or himself totally at the service of others in the activities of daily life. Zeal for the salvation and sanctification of all people so that they too will know the wonders of divine love constantly motivates the person to undertake whatever is necessary for the growth of the kingdom of God. The interests of God the Beloved and the human person have become so completely one that he or she allows the redemptive work of Christ and the sanctifying activity of the Holy Spirit to flow out to others in a new way through a life of humble service.

The experience of transforming union does not totally remove the human frailty or moral weakness of the person, but it does enable one constantly to plunge his or her own woundedness into the mystery of Christ's death and resurrection as the source of transformation in love. The individual is no longer painfully preoccupied with self but now is only joyful and thankful at being constantly graced by the ever-new mercies of God. Forgetfulness of self in the experience of the divine love, which flows from the presence of the triune God, frees the person to be present to others as sacrament of God's merciful love and forgiveness.

As any marriage ceremony itself is only the doorway to a life of growing together in love and unity, so too the mystical marriage of transforming union is not a static end but a dynamic beginning. Throughout the rest of his or her life the person will be asked to surrender again and again to the mystery of God's unfolding plan of salvation, which remains hidden in faith. One will know sorrow and suffering, but it will now be experienced as part of the living out of the truth of being one with Christ the Servant in his dying and rising. Sustained by the gifts of the Holy Spirit, the believer constantly lives in the hope-filled expectation that the transforming union experienced now is but a foretaste of the marriage feast of the kingdom. The individual in the unitive way waits peacefully amidst a life of humble service for the call of love, which will free her or him at last to enter joyfully into the fullness of eternal life, where truly God will be all in all.

See also BRIDAL MYSTICISM; ECSTASY; ILLUMINATION, ILLUMINATIVE WAY; MYSTICISM; PRAYER; PRESENCE, PRESENCE OF GOD; PURGATION, PURGATIVE WAY; THREE WAYS.

Bibliography: B. Groeschel, *Spiritual Passages: The Psychology of Spiritual Development* (New York: Crossroad, 1983). J. Lozano, *Praying Even When the Door Seems Closed: The Nature and Stages of Prayer* (New York: Paulist, 1989).

THOMAS D. McGONIGLE, O.P.

UNITY

Unity is the quality, condition, or state of being one or being whole. It is an important concept in Christian spirituality, since it describes the oneness of the triune God as well as the union and integrity of the person of Jesus Christ, who is both divine and human. Unity is also ascribed to the Church, humanity, and the totality of creation.

The oneness that unity denotes is not opposed to diversity but to division within that which is one. Within the one God there exists a diversity of Father, Son, and Holy Spirit, who are distinct Persons in one divine nature or essence (DS 75, 112, 800). This unity with diversity stands opposed to any type of monism of being or acting. The unity of God is revealed in and through the one person Jesus Christ, who has a divine and a human nature in union without confusion, change, division, or separation (DS 76, 301-302). The unity of Christ is the foundation and source of the unity of the Church.

Jesus' desire for the unity of his followers is poignantly expressed in his prayer to the Father "that they may all be one, as you, Father, are in me and I in you" (Jn 17:21).

Christians are incorporated into the one Body of Christ and united to the one Church through the sacraments of baptism and Eucharist, which communicate the Trinitarian life to them. Unity in the Church is not uniformity, however, as evidenced by the multiplicity and diversity of rites, languages, and theological interpretations of doctrine. While the unity of the faithful and, in a certain way, of the cosmos itself has been inaugurated in Jesus Christ, the full realization of unity awaits its eschatological fulfillment in the age to come.

See also BODY OF CHRIST; CHURCH; COMMUNITY; GOD; UNION, UNITIVE WAY.

Bibliography: J. Macquarrie, *Principles of Christian Theology,* 2nd ed. (New York: Scribner's, 1977). E. Mersch, *The Theology of the Mystical Body* (St. Louis: Herder, 1952).

KEITH R. BARRON, O.C.D.S.

UNSELFISHNESS

See FRUIT(S) OF THE HOLY SPIRIT.

V

VALUE

The notion of value, rarely the subject of systematic theology (with the stunning exception of Anselm's ontological argument for the existence of God), is central to spirituality. Worth, the meaning of *value*, is more fundamental than the content of any specific Christian value derived from the narratives of Christ's life or the mediations of value used in Christian formation. If virtues are understood as habits acquired to realize values, then value appears as the teleological referent of the virtues.

The use of the term *value* has expanded enormously in modern times. Before the 19th century it was restricted to economic applications indicating the worth of a commodity. Continental philosophers, notably F. Nietzsche and R. Lotze, were the first to use the concept of value to develop their ethics and aesthetics. The notion of value was subsequently incorporated into the emerging social sciences, especially psychology. The expanded use of *value* facilitated interdisciplinary dialogue, but at some cost to the clarity of the term. To make value a more precise concept and to accommodate its new meanings, general philosophies of value began to appear in the 20th century (R. B. Perry and J. Dewey).

The meaning of *value* is often put in terms of an alternative between objectivist and subjectivist presuppositions. For the objectivist, value is an inherent quality, present even when unrecognized or inadequately appreciated. The evaluator responds to value. For the subjectivist, value is a matter of personal assessment or convention. The evaluator assigns value. Objectivists assume the existence of universal moral norms and often adopt a deontological approach to moral decision-making. Subjectivists, to the contrary, view values as claims to value. Their approach to decision-making tends to be pragmatic and consequentialist.

The problem for objectivists is the way their notion of value as well as its particular contents is grounded. Substantiation by appeals to natural law must be on guard against physicalism and cultural bias. An alarming variation of natural law resting on the assumptions of sociobiologists argues that evolution has engineered an innate genetic printing of values (G. E. Pugh). Grounding values by appeals to divine or institutional authority or other heteronomy must negotiate the critiques of revelation, intuition, and loyalty to a tradition.

The problem for subjectivists is how to ground the notion of value at all. Postmodernity faces the limit case of an unrestricted pluralism of values, a self-contradictory notion. Arbitrariness is the absence of value. Behaviorists, for example, view value as whatever is rewarded. Relativism may only mask the failures of skepticism, voluntarism, or individualism. If the objectivist threatens to dominate the other, the subjectivist may suffer antinomian manipulation without limit.

The division of value into the objectivist and subjectivist perspectives may be found in Adam Smith's *Wealth of Nations*. Market pressures may drive value in exchange high above normal value in use. When the new social sciences posed the question of the relationship of the natural sciences to the human sciences, A. Ritschl posited an antithesis between judgments of fact and judgments of value, and then exploited the latter to subsume and protect the Christian faith from positivist critique. In Ritschl's view, religious affirmations and practice made no claim to scientific or historical truth. Ritschl's disjunction between fact and value, naive from the perspective of modern critical theory, became a central problem for the general theories of value in the following century. R. B. Perry's option, for example, was clearly subjectivist. He defined value as any object of any interest.

In the contemporary discussion a foundational contribution has been made by Bernard Lonergan, who elaborated a general theory of value that avoids subjectivism. For Lonergan, the apprehension of values is given in feelings. This approach allows him to identify values as the content of a person's consciousness in deliberative responsible activity. But what one person perceives as value may be disvalue. The validity of value judgments—true worth—is, for Lonergan, adjudicated like other truth claims and rests on the same criterion, authentic subjectivity. True value is affirmed by the morally self-transcending subject. The notion that objectivity is the practical achievement of authentic subjectivity is derived from Lonergan's general empirical method. Its application to a theory of value insists that value judgments are objective if they are the result of moral self-transcendence. The "if" is important. The exigence for authenticity is spontaneous, but it may be distorted, resisted, ignored. Valid value judgments presuppose conversion and moral education.

See also CONVERSION; DECISION, DECISION-MAKING; POSTMODERNITY; VIRTUE.

Bibliography: B. Lonergan, *Method in Theology* (New York: Herder, 1972). S. Happel and J. Walter, *Conversion and Discipleship: A Christian Foundation for Ethics and Doctrine* (Philadelphia: Fortress, 1986). D. Mieth and J. Pohier, *Changing Values and Virtues,* Concilium 191 (Edinburgh: T. & T. Clark, 1987).

KRISTOPHER L. WILLUMSEN

VATICAN COUNCIL II

The word *spiritualitas* appears but once in the index to the Latin original of the documents of Vatican II. The reference is to the Decree on the Up-to-Date Renewal of Religious Life (*Perfectae Caritatis*), where religious are encouraged to nourish their prayer from "the authentic sources of Christian spirituality" (PC 6). However, other synonymous and near-related words do figure prominently in the index, and it is misleading to say, as does Josef Sudbrack, that "in matters of spirituality, Vatican II merely worked over old questions such as 'the state of perfection'" ("Spirituality," *Sacramentum Mundi: An Encyclopedia of Theology,* ed. K. Rahner et al., New York: Herder, 1970, 6:156).

Our purpose here is not to assess the actual depth and extension of the Second Vatican Council's influence on spirituality over the past quarter of a century or so. It is still too early for a full assessment of an influence that, in any case, is far from uniform in intensity or extension. The focus here will be, rather, on the documents themselves insofar as they have a bearing on spirituality.

The Bible and the Liturgy in the Mainstream

While the Bible and the liturgy have always been at the center of the Church's life, it was the professed aim of the Second Vatican Council to position them squarely in the mainstream of the spiritual lives of all the members of the Church to a greater degree than had been the case for centuries.

Further, it wished to ensure that all the Church's members would accept the Bible and the liturgy as the main sources of nourishment and regulation of their spiritual lives.

A point of some importance is the mutual interdependence of the Bible and the liturgy, in the sense that it is in the liturgy that the Bible is potentially most effective in the life of the Church and in the sense that the Bible is normative for the liturgy and is its source. As J. M. R. Tillard puts it, "Scripture does not come fully alive except when joined with the liturgy. This is not merely because the liturgy is the official prayer of the Church, uniting all the faithful in the same praise and the same petition, but also because in the liturgy the words of the Bible become again the words that God's people address to the Lord or become the words that the Lord once more addresses to his people. In the Divine Office the words written on the pages of psalters and lectionaries become once again words pronounced, chanted, proclaimed. The return to the priority of the Scriptures implies, then, a return to the liturgy" ("Les grandes lois de la rénovation," *L'Adaptation et la rénovation de la vie religieuse,* Paris: Cerf, 1967, p. 145).

This mutual interdependence of the Bible and the liturgy is acknowledged by the Dogmatic Constitution on Divine Revelation (*Dei Verbum*) and by the Constitution on the Sacred Liturgy (*Sacrosanctum Concilium*). Thus: "The Church has always venerated the divine Scriptures as she venerated the Body of the Lord, in so far as she never ceases, particularly in the sacred liturgy, to partake of the bread of life and to offer it to the faithful from the one table of the Word of God and the Body of Christ" (DV 21). Later this same document describes the liturgy as being "full of the divine words" (DV 25). The Constitution on the Sacred Liturgy points out that Scripture is the source not just of the Scripture readings but for all of the liturgy: "For it is from it that lessons are read and explained in the homily, and psalms are sung. It is from the Scriptures that the prayers, collects, and hymns draw their inspiration and their force, and that actions and signs derive their meaning" (SC 24; see also SC 35). The Constitution on the Sacred Liturgy accepts that, in consequence, if worshipers are to derive maximum profit from the liturgy, they need to know the Scriptures. It asserts that "sacred Scripture is of the greatest importance in the celebration of the liturgy" and it urges a "sweet and living love for sacred Scripture" (SC 24). Those who pray the Divine Office are urged to "take steps to improve their understanding of the liturgy and of the Bible, especially of the psalms" (SC 90).

Josef Jungmann comments that it is the "special intention" of article 24 to ensure that the nonbiblical texts do not depart from the spirit and language of the liturgy. Liturgical and biblical renewal must go hand in hand (Vorgrimler, 1:20). It is easier to conceive of the liturgy and the Bible as being fully in the mainstream of the spiritual lives of all the members of the Church if the Church itself is conceived of not in juridical but in spiritual terms, or more accurately as both earthly and spiritual, the primordial sacrament. Thus the Constitution on the Sacred Liturgy describes the Church as "essentially both human and divine, visible but endowed with invisible realities ... so constituted that in her the human is directed toward ... the divine, the visible to the invisible, action to contemplation, and this present world to that city yet to come, the object of our quest" (SC 2). Jungmann comments that many of the bishops who took part in Vatican II "were astonished at this manner of speech about the Church, which differs from the view developed especially by Bellarmine during the struggle of post-Tridentine theology with the Reformation. For the Church is described here not in its juridical structure, but in its sacramental character, as the primordial sacrament, a notion which the Constitution on the Church later elaborated in greater detail" (Vorgrimler, 1:9).

The Bible and the Spiritual Life

In keeping with the assertion of the Constitution on Divine Revelation that "access to sacred Scripture ought to be open wide to the Christian faithful" (DV 22) and that "the entire Christian religion should be nourished and ruled by sacred Scripture" (DV 21), the Constitution on the Sacred Liturgy made provision for a more plentiful use of the Scriptures in the liturgy: "In sacred celebrations a more ample, more varied, and more suitable reading from sacred Scripture should be restored" (SC 35). It encouraged Bible services (SC 35), and in its chapter on the Eucharist it decreed: "The treasures of the Bible are to be opened up more lavishly so that a richer fare may be provided for the faithful at the table of God's word" (SC 51).

The Constitution on Divine Revelation twice draws attention to the importance for the Church's spiritual life of the increased availability of the Scriptures: "And such is the force and power of the Word of God that it can serve the Church as her support and vigor, and the children of the Church as strength for their faith, food for the soul, and a pure and lasting fount of spiritual life" (DV 21). It ends with the following pronouncement: "Just as from constant attendance at the eucharistic mystery the life of the Church draws increase, so a new impulse of spiritual life may be expected from increased veneration of the Word of God, which 'stands for ever'" (DV 26).

The Liturgy and the Spiritual Life

Among its "particularly cogent reasons for undertaking the reform and promotion of the liturgy," the Constitution on the Sacred Liturgy lists the fact that "it is the liturgy through which ... 'the work of our redemption is accomplished,' and it is through the liturgy, especially, that the faithful are enabled to express in their lives

... the mystery of Christ and the real nature of the true Church" (SC 2). It adds: "The liturgy daily builds up those who are in the Church, making of them a holy temple of the Lord, a dwelling-place for God in the Spirit, to the mature measure of the fullness of Christ" (SC 2).

If Vatican II made the "full and active participation by all the people" in the liturgy the primary aim of the renewal of the liturgy, this is because the nature of the liturgy demands it and also because the liturgy is "the primary and indispensable source from which the faithful are to derive the true Christian spirit" (SC 14). Later this document states that the liturgy "contains much instruction for the faithful. For in the liturgy God speaks to his people, and Christ is still proclaiming his Gospel. ... Not only when things are read 'which were written for our instruction' (Rom 15:4), but also when the Church prays or sings or acts, the faith of those taking part is nourished" (SC 33).

The council's concern that the liturgy be a more accessible source of spirituality is reflected in its decision to have its rites simplified and clarified and brought "within the people's power of comprehension" (SC 34; see also SC 50, 62) and in its insistence that if the liturgy is to "produce its full effects," those taking part in it must be receptive to it, their minds "attuned to their voices ... fully aware of what they are doing ... and enriched by it" (SC 11). When taking part in the celebration of the Eucharist, "this mystery of faith," the faithful "should not be there as strangers" but should have "a good understanding of the rites and prayers ... conscious of what they are doing .... They should be instructed by God's word" (SC 48). Describing the Divine Office as "a source of piety and a nourishment for personal prayer," the Constitution on the Sacred Liturgy urges those who take part in it to "attune their minds to their voices when praying it" (SC 90).

The normative function of the liturgy in the spiritual life has to do with the proper gradation of the importance of its various elements; the restoration of emphases, such as that on baptism during Lent (SC 108), which had become obscured over the centuries; and the spirit of simplicity with which the council would have the liturgy imbued. The importance accorded to the Eucharist (SC 47ff.) and the primacy of the celebration of the Lord's resurrection every Sunday and at Easter (SC 102, 106) have obvious implications for the spiritual lives of individual Christians. "The minds of the faithful should be directed primarily toward the feasts of the Lord . . . . the Proper of the Time should be given due preference over the feasts of the saints" (SC 108). The same is true of the provision that greater importance be assigned to the commemoration of "the very mysteries of salvation" than to the celebration of the feasts of the saints (SC 111), a sentiment also reflected in the ruling that the number of sacred images in churches "should be moderate and their relative positions should reflect right order" (SC 125).

This last provision reflects a rejection of the pretentious and a preference for the uncluttered, which is a feature of the Constitution on the Sacred Liturgy and which finds expression in its ruling that the revised liturgical rites "should be distinguished by a noble simplicity. They should be short, clear, and free from useless repetitions" (SC 34); and "in encouraging and favoring truly sacred art," ordinaries "should seek for noble beauty rather than sumptuous display," and they should reject what smacks of "mediocrity or pretense" (SC 124).

The Bible and the Liturgy: Schools of Spirituality

In the Dogmatic Constitution on the Church (*Lumen Gentium*), hearing the word of God and participating in the liturgy are recommended to all the faithful "if charity is to grow and fructify in the soul like a good seed" (LG 42). In the Decree on the Apostolate of Lay People (*Apostolicam Actuositatem*), active participation in the liturgy is described as the chief help for lay people in maintaining the "life of intimate union with Christ" (AA 4). The Decree on the Training of Priests (*Optatam Totius*) urges priests "to seek Christ in faithful meditation on the word of God and in active participation in the sacred mysteries of the Church" (OpT 8).

During their deliberations on the religious life the council Fathers discussed the nature and the sources of spirituality at some length (see Tillard, *op. cit*, pp. 129ff.). Their discussions led them to transcend a canonical distinction between active and contemplative religious life, and they recommended that religious "should join contemplation, by which they cleave to God by mind and heart, to apostolic love, by which they endeavor to be associated with the work of redemption and to spread the kingdom of God" (PC 5). They also came to reject an earlier draft of the decree, which had spoken about "pious exercises," by which was meant, Tillard remarks, "that heterogeneous collection of all the devotions, litanies, formulas, novenas and little offices which encumbered the prayer books and, alas, the lives of so many religious communities. In its definitive version, the Decree went back to the essentials: the religious life must draw nourishment from the two traditional sources of grace, the word of God and the liturgy, culminating in the common celebration of the Eucharist" (*op. cit.*, p. 144).

The relevant text of the Decree on the Up-to-Date Renewal of Religious Life (*Perfectae Caritatis*) is worth quoting in full: "Members of [religious] institutes should assiduously cultivate the spirit of prayer and prayer itself, drawing on the authentic sources of Christian spirituality. In the first place, let them have the sacred Scripture at hand daily, so that they might learn 'the surpassing worth of knowing Christ Jesus' (Phil 3:8) by reading and meditating on the divine Scriptures. They should perform the sacred liturgy, especially the holy mystery of the Eucharist, with their hearts and lips, according to the mind of the Church, and they should nourish their spiritual lives from this richest of sources" (PC 6). In his commentary on this passage, Friedrich Wulf says of the spirituality that religious would need in the future that it "will have to be quite different in many points from anything we have known hitherto. It will have to gather up all of past tradition, in a sense supersede it, and carry it further." He adds: "The overladen devotional systems, especially characteristic of modern congregations, are to be avoided. One of the marks of present-day spirituality is a simplicity and transparence that seeks to return to essentials" (Vorgrimler, 2:348).

If Vatican II invited religious to conduct their quest for holiness more in the mainstream of the Church's spiritual life, it also did much to spread awareness that the path to holiness is open to all members of the Church without exception. The very title of the chapter of the Dogmatic Constitution on the Church that deals with holiness is an indication of this: *De Universali Vocatione ad Sanctitatem in Ecclesia*, "On the Universal Call to Holiness in the Church." In that fifth chapter we read that "all Christians in any state or walk of life are called to the fullness of Christian life and to the perfection of love" (LG 40) and that "the forms and tasks of life are many but holiness is one" (LG 41).

Twenty-five years or more from now we may be less aware of what a momentous change had taken place, but this was not true of commentators closer to the event. Friedrich Wulf writes: "We catch sight here of an astonishing process. The Church is in the process of a portentous transformation. She is changing her whole countenance and bearing. One has to search the Constitution on the Church prepared for the First Vatican Council with care indeed to find so much as an implicit reference to the vocation all Christians have to holiness" (Vorgrimler, 1:261).

Twenty-five years ago no theologian and perhaps no layperson would have said explicitly that lay people are not called to holiness in the Church. It was, however, implicitly assumed, especially by lay people, almost at an unconscious level, that it was primarily priests and religious who were called to holiness and lay people only secondarily, if at all. And even then it was a matter for them of making do with hand-me-down versions of the spirituality of religious. A crucial text is article 41 of the Dogmatic Constitution on the Church: "The forms and tasks of life are many but holiness is one—that sanctity which is cultivated by all who act under God's Spirit and, obeying the Father's voice and adoring God the Father in spirit and truth, follow Christ, poor, humble and cross-bearing, that they may deserve to be partakers of his glory."

Out of the Fortress into Mission

It is accepted that Vatican II, and especially its Pastoral Constitution on the Church in the Modern World (*Gaudium et Spes*), ended a more fearful, defensive relationship between the Church and the rest of the world, a relationship that had given rise to an almost claustrophobic interpretation of the phrase *fuga mundi*, "flight from the world." The emphasis on the Bible and the liturgy as the mainstream sources of Christian spirituality, coupled with the universal call to holiness, have aided the members of the Church as, in a manner of speaking, they set out from the mental fortress, unarmed and with a greater consciousness of mission and of making their own "the joy and hope, the grief and anguish of the [people] of our time" (GS 1).

This was and is true of religious, especially of apostolic religious, no less than of diocesan priests and lay people. As the Council of General Delegates to the Pontifical Missionary Union put it in 1976: "The style of life which was rightly conceived for the living out of the monastic ideal was so strongly identified with the ideal of consecrated life as such that, later, the different religious foundations had to struggle considerably to find and to be allowed to develop structures and styles of life which would be attuned to their new and essentially different functions in the Church. This applies in a special way to modern apostolic foundations and—more especially—to our modern apostolic institutes of women.... The final breakthrough in this field has been achieved only by the Second Vatican Council and the evolution which has followed it. Only now has it been fully understood that, in our religious apostolic communities, the entire life of our members should be penetrated by an apostolic spirituality (PC 3). This implies, of course, that whatever appertains to the religious life of our congregations whould be discerned anew and renewed and adapted in such a way that our style of life is in perfect harmony with and promotes our apostolic and missionary activity" ("Orientations for an Apostolic Spirituality in Our Religious Congregations," *Religious Life Review,* July-August, 1976, p. 59).

A discussion document published by the Conference of Major Religious Superiors of Ireland in 1989 put it succinctly: "Formerly, monastic structures dictated the prayer forms and life-style of all religious. Now, the prayer forms and life-style of many of them are arising from and responding to the apostolate" ("Reflections on Our Journey: Being a Religious in Ireland Today," p. 41).

Diocesan priests and lay apostles have been engaged in a like quest. Cardinal Francis Marty put it as follows in 1984: "In the perspective of Vatican II, one may not any longer view the life of a priest as an existence filled with spiritual exercises, which belong to him alone, and from which proceed, as a sort of surplus, pastoral activities. Rather our very ministry is itself the norm of our lives, the source and the place of our sanctification" (*La documentation catholique,* no. 1874, p. 534).

Lay people are encouraged to take advantage of the spiritual helps common to all the faithful, and they are reminded that "family cares should not be foreign to their spirituality, nor any other temporal interest." Further, they are told that "lay spirituality will take its particular character from the circumstances of one's state in life ... from one's state of health and from one's professional and social activity" (AA 4).

Justice

Vatican II gave an impetus to a quest for justice which found expression later in the 1971 Synod of Bishops and in Pope Paul VI's *Evangelica Testificatio* and which has led to a quest for a spirituality fully alive to the demands of justice. The synod said that "action on behalf of justice and participation in the transformation of the world fully appear to us as a constitutive dimension of the preaching of the gospel" (*Justice in the World,* no. 6). John Grennan recalls that Enda McDonagh identifies both justice and prayer as two of the realities that people are passionately engaged with in today's world, and he comments: "Independent of one another, they can be dangerous: a passion for prayer without justice can create the religious fanatic. A passion for justice without prayer 'could and has led to vengeance.' Together they are 'mutually reinforcing, indeed mutually critical and corrective.' ... Whatever form such action [for justice] takes, it needs to be carried out with love, love not only for the poor but also for the oppressor" ("Approaches to Prayer," *Religious Life Review,* March-April, 1991, p. 75).

See also APOSTOLIC SPIRITUALITY; HOLINESS; JUSTICE; LAY SPIRITUALITY; LITURGY; MINISTRY, MINISTERIAL SPIRITUALITY; MISSION, SPIRITUALITY FOR MISSION; RELIGIOUS LIFE; RENEWAL, PROGRAMS OF RENEWAL; SCRIPTURE; WORLD.

Bibliography: A. Flannery, ed., *Vatican Council II: The Conciliar and Post Conciliar Documents* (Collegeville, Minn.: Liturgical Press, 1984); *Vatican Council II: More Post Conciliar Documents* (Collegeville, Minn.: Liturgical Press, 1982). H. Vorgrimler, ed., *Commentary on the Documents of Vatican II*, 5 vols. (New York: Herder, 1966–1969).

AUSTIN FLANNERY, O.P.

VIA NEGATIVA

See NEGATIVE WAY.

VIA POSITIVA

See AFFIRMATIVE WAY.

VICE

See SIN; TEMPTATION; VIRTUE.

VIRGINITY

Virginity, the abstinence from marriage and from all sexual relations, has been observed to some degree in most religious traditions, e.g., premarital virginity, cultic virginity. Christianity follows the teaching of the virgin Christ: perpetual virginity is a charism given to some women and men "for the sake of the kingdom of heaven" (Mt 19:12). Christian marriage, too, is a charism (1 Cor 7:7). Both of these charisms are mysteriously and freely bestowed by the Spirit.

Virginity for the sake of the kingdom can be a gift for a love of God so absorbing, so eschatological, that it precludes all other exclusive unions such as marriage, and is experienced as mystical/nuptial union with Christ. This has given rise to powerfully expressive lifestyles and spiritual literature, especially in patristic and medieval times. Virginity for the kingdom can also be a gift for such unreserved apostolic availability for the service of the whole People of God that it, too, precludes marriage. Likened to martyrdom, it is also apostolic in being a sign to the whole Church of the eschatological destiny of all: "At the resurrection they neither marry nor are given in marriage" (Mt 22:30).

By renunciation of a supreme benefit in human life—marriage—consecrated virgins witness to that faith and hope of the whole pilgrim Church in the grace of God which overcomes the corruptions of this world and bestows eternal union with God in the heavenly community. Consecrated virginity was the original element of institutes of consecrated life and remains their distinguishing mark today. Canon law provides for both a vow of chastity for religious institutes and for a rite of consecration for the "order of virgins" (CIC, cans. 599-604).

Vatican II's universal call to holiness (LG 39-40) corrects a tendency prevailing since patristic times to proclaim virginity as the "best" means to holiness, whereas it is the best means for those to whom the charism is given, as are marriage and single life in the world for those called to those states. All practice the chastity appropriate to their state.

See also BRIDAL MYSTICISM; CELIBACY; CHARISM; CHASTITY; MARRIAGE, MYSTICAL; VOWS.

Bibliography: W. Molinski, "Virginity," *Encyclopedia of Theology: The Concise Sacramentum Mundi*, ed. K. Rahner (New York: Seabury, 1975). S. Schneiders, "Non-Marriage for the Sake of the Kingdom," *Widening the Dialogue* (Ottawa: Canadian Religious Conference of Women Religious, 1974). K. Rahner, "On the Evangelical Counsels," *Further Theology of the Spiritual Life 2*, Theological Investigations 8 (New York: Crossroad, 1971) 133–167.

CARITAS McCARTHY, S.H.C.J.

VIRTUE

The idea of the virtues comes from an understanding of a human being as having a tremendous capacity both for good and for evil. Men and women are creatures who can go to extremes: they can become heroic in goodness, but they can also become tragically depraved. As an approach to the moral and spiritual life, the virtues respect one's potential to grow in the beauty of goodness, but they also take seriously that there is a promise in one that can be lost. In the Christian moral life, all stand poised between possibilities for greatness or awfulness. It is through the virtues that one grows in the promise of life, and through the vices that one self-destructs. In a Christian schema of the moral and spiritual life, virtues make one godly, and vices, their opposite, make one wicked.

What a Virtue Is

A virtue is a characteristic way of behavior which makes both actions and persons good and which also enables one to fulfill the purpose of life. When anyone both possesses and exercises the virtues, that person is brought to the wholeness proper to human nature; conversely, a lack of virtue constitutes a deprived nature and a diminished self. What might this understanding of the virtues entail?

First, it tells us that a virtue is a quality that accrues to a person through repeated activity. Virtues are possessed not externally but internally, for they represent how a person has been characterized by his or her most consistent behavior. Virtues are qualities of character acquired through corresponding actions. For instance, one takes on the character of generosity by practicing generosity; the quality of the behavior eventually becomes a quality of the self. That is why virtues—and vices too—are not ornaments of the self but the deepest expression of the self. Virtues capture what one's most consistent behavior has made of him or her.

Second, virtues are qualities that change a person. Thomas Aquinas, the foremost proponent of an ethics of virtue in the Catholic moral tradition, speaks of them as bringing about a "modification of a subject" (ST I-II, q. 49, a. 2). Through the virtues one takes on qualities one did not have before and loses some qualities one did have: generosity replaces selfishness, courage overcomes timidity or recklessness. Virtues are transformative activities that involve the restructuring of the self. That is why they are central to Christian spirituality. Christianity involves the reconstruction of the self from sinner to saint. That is the work of grace, but it is also the work of virtue. The effect of any habit is a change of self, and through the habits of virtue the self is changed unto goodness.

Third, the change or the modification achieved by virtue is not arbitrary but is measured according to a specific understanding of human excellence. A man or a woman acquires the virtues in order to grow into the fullness of human nature. The power of the virtues is that through the possession and exercise of them persons reach the intended purpose of their lives. The virtues are habits that bring a person to his or her fullest development, and that is why their meaning is derived from whatever good or set of goods represents the highest possible human excellence.

The word for this view of the moral life is *teleological.* It is derived from the Greek *telos,* which means "goal," "purpose," or "end." For instance, in the virtue ethics of both Aristotle and Aquinas, to be human is to have a purpose on which to make good. Aristotle called this the *telos,* or goal, of human nature and argued that one's authentic humanity is measured in proportion to one's participation in it. For both Aristotle and Aquinas, this purpose is not arbitrary; in fact, to ignore or neglect it is not just to become something different but to fail at the very thing for which life is given.

In this approach to the moral life, to be human is to be born into the world with something to achieve, namely, the fullness of one's human nature, and it is through the virtues that one does so. The virtues are precisely the activities that work the changes necessary for growth. Thus the connection between the *telos* and the virtues is that the *telos* represents the goal or purpose of life, whether that is seen as goodness, holiness, or fullness of life with God, and the virtues are the means through which it is achieved. Men and women move to their end through the virtues, but the movement is not a change of place but a change of person, which is why conversion is a fitting name for what the virtues do.

Fourth, the purpose of a virtue is to dispose one to what is best. There is nothing middling about the virtues. They are powers that work for the ultimate enhancement of the person in goodness, which in the Christian life is the achievement of sanctity. Christian virtues work to make everyone a saint, because that reconstruction of the self constitutes everyone's optimum potential in goodness. That is why the virtues can be called the preeminent humanizing activities. Moral development takes place through the virtues because they are the activities by which the self is reconstituted in its most fitting goodness. Christians call this goodness holiness and see it to be commensurate with one's fullest possible development. From a Christian perspective, the virtues are humanizing because the virtues are sanctifying.

Why the Virtues Are Needed

The most basic reason why human beings need the virtues is that they can, through the choices and decisions they make, become something other than human; they can end up with a life they ultimately regret. It would be different if human beings were unswervingly directed to what is best for them, but that is not the case. In this respect, human beings are not like other creatures. For instance, a horse cannot help but be a horse. It can grow, it can become bigger, faster, or stronger, but it cannot choose to be something other than a horse. With human beings it is different. They can choose to become something other than human by the behavior they adopt. Unlike other creatures, they do not by nature have an appropriate relationship to what most befits them. They can develop improperly. They can foster attachments that diminish more than enhance. They know, for example, that they can use

their freedom to turn away from God in sin. Thus it is not only the case that everyone needs the virtues to grow but more precisely that they need them to grow in a way that promotes the proper development of themselves. Put differently, if the virtues are needed because there is a gap between who persons are now and who they need to be in order to realize the purpose or goal of their humanity, it is also true that they need the virtues to focus and direct their lives to that which is genuinely best.

No one is determined to what is best; rather, because of free will one can choose to act against what is good or seek the good in the wrong way. Lives can be disordered. Virtues are needed to cultivate an appropriate relationship to all the goods that develop human nature. No one has this relationship to appropriate goods instinctively, because no one by nature is predetermined to any one good instead of others. The human will is pulled in a variety of directions. The virtues recognize the need to develop habits that incline one to whatever is best; otherwise there is nothing to prevent a person from ending up a lifetime away from where he or she ought to be. From a Christian perspective, the virtues are the only guarantee against a wasted life.

This suggests a second reason why the virtues are needed: a human nature wounded by sin needs to be rehabilitated through virtue. There is a realism implicit in any ethic of virtue. Human beings are a mixture of frailties, rebel angels whose tendencies to goodness are impaired by equally powerful tendencies to sin. Traditionally original sin has been the theological concept used to explain not only a diminished capacity for goodness but also all the elements within men and women that work against genuine well-being. The doctrine of original sin accounts for the inner contradiction often experienced between recognition of the good that needs to be done and an inability to do it. The category of original sin captures not only the need for virtue but also how difficult it can be to acquire virtue. With the concept of original sin, the full truth of what it means to live after the Fall is grasped.

Original sin describes the disorder suffered by human nature as a consequence of the loss of original justice. To speak of that state of innocence as original justice means that before sin entered the world, all lived in perfect harmony with God, others, and themselves. In Aquinas's parlance, original justice means that everything was perfectly subjected to God. But sin wrecks the harmony between God, others, and the rest of creation. With the loss of that harmony comes a disintegration that spreads through every aspect of life. Instead of having a perfectly ordered human nature and universe, human beings and their world are painfully disordered.

Aquinas uses an analogy to health. Prior to the Fall, human nature was perfectly healthy; however, with the fall from grace, that nature became ill. It is not completely infirm, but neither is it completely healthy. That is why Aquinas, following Augustine, speaks of original sin as "a sickness of nature" (ST I-II, q. 82, a. 1). As Aquinas sees it, the effect of original sin on human nature is like living with a low-grade flu. No one is so infirm that he or she cannot do any good, but a weakened human nature makes doing good difficult. Also, it is not just that original sin debilitates one or other dimension of existence, but that with it human nature is infirm throughout. With the loss of both inner and outer harmony, disintegration takes hold. It is experienced through inner turmoil and conflict. It is felt when one lives with a divided heart. And its power is known when a life stands in rebellion against God. As Aquinas says, "Once the harmony of original justice is shattered, the various powers of the soul strain toward conflicting objectives" (ST I-II, q. 82, a. 2).

The corruption of nature through original sin tempers one's possibility for goodness. A key principle in traditional Catholic moral theology states that "as a thing is, so does it act" (agere sequitur esse). A person's actions flow from his or her nature, but that nature must be taken into account when estimating potential for virtue. Original sin does not completely take away a capacity for virtue, but it does condition it. Aquinas expresses this when he says that "some bent toward disordered activity is a consequence of original sin" (ST I-II, q. 82, a. 1).

Human beings live with conflicting tendencies. On the one hand, they retain a bent toward virtue; on the other hand, they suffer opposing tendencies. Prior to the Fall there was what Aquinas calls a "connatural inclination" to virtue; however, that is no longer the case. There may be tendencies to virtue, but they have to be developed because there are tendencies to vice as well. Human beings are a mixture of tendencies, each of which offsets another. The picture Aquinas gives is of a human nature that needs to be healed, an insight that stands behind his remark that original sin is a "congenital defect" that does not destroy but does diminish capacity for virtue. In short, because nature is infirm, there is a need to develop virtue, but that is both difficult and tenuous.

Virtue works to restore a nature wounded by sin. Traditionally there have been four wounds to nature attributable to sin, each of which corresponds to a dimension of the person (ST I-II, q. 85, a. 3). First, there is the wound of ignorance. This wound represents how one can turn away from truth and seek refuge in misunderstanding. Second, there is the wound of malice. This wound settles in the will and describes how one can grow hardened to the good. Third, there is the wound of weakness, which depicts how a person can avoid what is right on account of difficulty or fear. Finally, there is the wound of concupiscence or disordered affection. This impairment of nature represents how one can be so driven by passion as to forget what is genuinely good and lovely. Collectively these four wounds portray how sin debilitates human nature. It affects the desire for truth, it weakens love for the good, it deprives one of the capacity to deal with difficulty or temptation, and it can make one lose one's freedom to pleasure.

Virtue works to heal these wounds to nature, while vice or sin deepens them. Sin increases the diminishment brought to human nature through original sin. That is why the ongoing effect of sin is always further debilitation. If patterns of sinfulness are embraced, the understanding grows darkened, the will becomes hardened, and it is increasingly difficult to be engaged in virtue and to avoid vice. Aquinas gives a more poetic depiction of the cumulative effect of sin when he describes it as a loss of the soul's refulgence (ST I-II, q. 86, a. 1). He says that every sin further stains a soul that has lost its original luster. Aquinas argues that sin, like virtue, is a kind of loving; the difference is that sin is disordered loving. To love anything is to cleave to it as if touching it. If what is loved is truly good and beautiful, then coming in touch with it enhances; that is why virtuous people shine in goodness. Virtue increases the radiance of goodness. What happens with sin is that through a misguided love something is clung to in the wrong way. Such a love does not befit but diminishes a person. Thus through habits of sinfulness the light of goodness is dulled and can be completely extinguished.

A third reason why the virtues are needed is to overcome vice. The best way to understand the vices is to realize that they are the opposite of virtue in every way but one: like the virtues, they are habits. If virtues are habitual ways of acting by which both actions and persons are perfected, the vices are habits that make both deeds and persons bad. Similarly, if the virtues turn one to what is best, the vices dispose one to what diminishes and destroys. Vices are habits that actively work against virtue. As habits, they are not dormant. As powerful tendencies to corrupting behavior, they will weaken and eventually overcome virtues unless the virtues are vigilantly set against them. Vices grow with the passage of time unless uprooted through the skilled practice of virtue. The image here is of a subject under fire. Everyone is composed of an array of tendencies, many of which conflict. Some strengthen, others are clearly dehumanizing. Vices are habits that dehumanize, and they are hardly inert; indeed, unless acted against and weakened, they will overcome virtues.

For instance, why does it take time and effort to become good? Or more pointedly, why is being good so difficult sometimes? Perhaps one reason why developing virtue is toilsome is that often the cultivation of a good habit requires overcoming a vice. The initial task of virtue is not so much the doing of good but the healing of a nature wounded by vice. Acquiring virtue involves, if not the uprooting of a particular vice, at least the weakening of a tendency to vice. The moral anthropology of an ethic of virtue argues that virtues come where vices either used to be or readily can be. Justice works against selfishness. Temperance works against debasing behavior. Courage wars with cowardice. Men and women are a blend of conflicting forces. Virtue always has an opposite, either in the form of an already acquired habit or its inclination. Therefore, even as virtue grows, there remains a tension to the moral life; for instance, when one strives to be good, the hold of sin can still be powerfully felt.

The impediments to virtue are especially powerful if they have developed into vices, because vices, like the virtues, are ingrained, characteristic ways of acting. Virtue is acquired by taking on the quality of a good act, such as justice; however, the same is true of a vice. Vices are acquired by taking on the quality of a bad act, such as cruelty, and the longer a vice has characterized a person, the deeper it grows, becoming part of the fabric of the person's personality. This explains why it can be so hard to change bad habits. Like virtues, vices are hardly superficial; rather, they are qualities of the self. Furthermore, if virtues are energies that work for the good, vices are energies too—they simply have an opposite focus. The strategy of vice is to overcome virtue. Vices will not acquiesce meekly to virtue, because, like the virtues, they are entrenched patterns of behavior that struggle to survive. The picture is of a human nature full of complex, conflicting tendencies, each fighting to gain sovereignty over the self.

Virtue must be more vigilant than vice, but what if it is not? What happens if sin becomes habitual? The peril of sin is not so much the evil of particular acts—though that cannot be taken lightly—but that sinning can become a habit. If that occurs, the behavior that should be disdained is found pleasing. Aquinas notes that everyone "chooses readily those things which habit has made congenial" (ST I-II, q. 78, a. 2). When it comes to the good, that is a blessing, but when it comes to sin, it is a danger. Aquinas's point is that all choose according to that with which they have grown comfortable. The odyssey of the Christian life illustrates that it is easy to grow comfortable with sin, so much so that a sinful act may hardly be recognized as such. What is frightening about sinning regularly is that an abhorrence for evil can be eventually lost. It is possible to grow accustomed to certain vices; worse than that, it is even possible to find sin more congenial than virtue. It is a terrible perversion to be corrupted to the point of finding sin more fitting than virtue, but it is possible once an act of sin becomes a habit of sin.

The Development and Growth of Virtue

Though human beings have a capacity for virtue, that capacity has to be developed. Virtues represent the development of inclinations and tendencies into habits. Like any habit, virtues are acquired through repeated activity. For instance, someone may have a disposition or tendency to patience but not yet have acquired the virtue of patience. A disposition is like an undeveloped virtue. To be disposed to a certain kind of behavior means that one occasionally practices the behavior, but not regularly or predictably. To do the good by chance but not by habit means that one is not yet virtuous. A person who does an act of justice may not yet have the virtue of justice. To possess a virtue, the good acts one does must flow from the good person one has become.

Habits, then, are different from dispositions. To possess a habit is to be so qualified by a particular way of acting that it is expected of a person. Unlike a tendency or disposition, a habit is a firm and predictable way of acting rooted in a quality of the person. If not developed into habits, inclinations can be lost; however, once dispositions become habits, they are much less likely to be lost, because they are characteristics of the self. For example, though one may be disposed to actions such as kindness, patience, or forgiveness, none is yet a virtue until it becomes so much a part of a person that it is truly a quality of the self; this is precisely why people expect the virtuous to be kind, patient, and forgiving.

Dispositions to virtue develop into habits of virtue by practice. Aquinas says that it is "by similar and repeated activity" that virtues are acquired (ST I-II, q. 51, a. 3). A habit is an expected way of behavior because it captures a correspondence between what one does and who one has become. If something is a habit, it means that repeated activity has made it part of who a person is, which explains why virtue seems to flow from the being of a person and why virtuous people are able to do the good with a certain ease, skill, and delight. There is a unity between their actions and their selves because through repeated activity the quality of the action has become a quality of their character, thus transforming them in a virtue's particular goodness.

The development of virtue takes time. As a habit, a virtue is not fickle and sporadic but firm and predictable. To possess a habit is to have taken on the quality of a certain kind of behavior so thoroughly that one really has been determined to it. Put more strongly, to be virtuous means that a person has been mastered by goodness, so much so that doing good is second nature. A single action is not enough to produce a virtue, but it begins a process by which one is gradually shaped in the goodness of a virtue. It is one thing to be shaped by that goodness, though, and another to actually possess it. In his treatise on the virtues, Aquinas says that the virtues are possessed only when practicing the good has "eroded the opposing conditions to virtue" and when a person has been so "impressed with the likeness" of a virtue's goodness that he or she begins to act that way with ease (ST I-II, q. 51, a. 3). Those "opposing conditions" to virtue are many, whether they be vices, personal weaknesses, or conflicting inclinations, and they explain why initially there is a strangeness to doing good. At first there is a clumsiness to being virtuous, because a person is not yet practiced in a virtue's goodness. Acquiring virtue is a matter of carving in oneself the quality of goodness, but that can take a very long time; in fact, Aquinas says it is like water "hollowing out a rock" (*De Virtutibus,* art. 9).

The growth of the virtues registers one's history with the good. No one becomes good instantaneously but only little by little. Aquinas captures this reality of the moral and spiritual life when he distinguishes three stages in the growth of virtue. For instance, when focusing on the virtue of charity, he speaks of the virtue of beginners, the virtue of those on their way, and the virtue of those who have finally arrived (ST II-II, q. 24, a. 9). In the first stage ("beginners"), virtue works not directly to do good but to overcome vice. As Aquinas puts it, "To begin with, he must devote himself mainly to withdrawing from sin and resisting the appetites, which drive him in the opposite direction to charity. This is the condition of beginners, who need to nourish and carefully foster charity

to prevent its being lost" (ST II-II, q. 24, a. 9). In this first stage of virtue a rehabilitation takes place. A nature weakened by sin tries to grow stronger in the good by rooting out vice. In the second stage ("those on their way"), the energy of virtue is directed to doing good, but the moral life is still seen as a kind of convalescence. In this second stage the person is an apprentice of virtue. He or she learns about the good and progresses in virtue but is not yet a moral virtuoso. The task in the second stage is to live in a way that allows one to be rooted more deeply in a virtue's goodness, though not yet possessing the virtue completely. The third stage of virtue applies to those "who have finally arrived." Aquinas says that in this stage "a man applies himself chiefly to the work of cleaving to God and enjoying him, which is characteristic of the perfect who 'long to depart and to be with Christ'" (ST II-II, q. 24, a. 9).

If virtues can grow, in what way do they grow? Virtues grow not extensively but intensively, which means that they grow not so much in themselves but in the person who possesses them. For instance, how can justice increase? The growth of justice occurs not in the virtue itself but in the degree that a person has the virtue of justice. The growth of any virtue is measured in terms of the qualification of the self by the virtue's goodness. Thus, to talk about the growth of justice is not to suggest that justice grows by justice being added to justice but that justice grows as one becomes more just.

But virtues can also be lost. Just as certain behavior develops virtue, certain behavior weakens virtue. Virtues are primarily lost through the practice of their opposite behavior, the vices. What happens is that the quality of one action, the vice, weakens and gradually uproots the quality of virtue. This is the principal way in which virtue can be destroyed. It will be destroyed if it is acted against by its contrary vice, for then the quality of the virtue is lost, and one is redefined by the quality of the vice. For instance, a person can lose the virtue of justice if he or she makes a habit of selfishness. Similarly, one can lose the virtue of courage if he or she is controlled by the desire to please others, which is a kind of cowardice. At first the virtue will only be weakened, but if the vice is practiced continually, the virtue will be destroyed because it cannot endure the quality of the vice.

But virtues can be lost not only by lack of exercise but even, Aquinas hints, by behavior that falls short of the quality of virtue one has already acquired. In other words, if one does not practice a virtue to the degree he or she is capable of doing, it will be weakened. It is not only actions contrary to virtue that weaken it but also actions that fall short of a goodness already there. Virtues have to be practiced in order to be kept, but they also need to be practiced in proportion to one's virtuosity. They must be practiced because they are habits, and habits are activities; the very meaning of a virtue is to act, so not to exercise a virtue is to weaken one's skill in the virtue. But virtue is also diminished, Aquinas suggests, when it is not practiced in proportion to one's possession of it: "If, on the other hand, the strength of the action is proportionally less than the strength of the corresponding habit, then the action does not help the habit to grow stronger but rather prepares for its decay" (ST I-II, q. 52, a. 3).

Perhaps what Aquinas suggests is that mediocrity in the moral and spiritual life is not benign. Everyone has to be vigilant about carelessness in the Christian life, and no one can afford to grow complacent about goodness, because it is not only bad actions that hurt one by weakening virtue but also actions that fall short of the goodness one already has. If being good is a matter of doing good, not being as good as one can be means that the goodness already possessed will be lost. In the moral life, a virtue that is not exercised in proportion to its possession will begin to decay. Therefore no one can afford to take chances with

goodness, and no one can ever be too secure in virtue. In an ethic of virtue, complacency is the first stage of deterioration.

The Cardinal Virtues

Besides the theological virtues of faith, hope, and charity, the four principal virtues are the cardinal virtues: prudence, justice, temperance, and fortitude or courage. As the word *cardinal* (Latin *cardo,* "hinge") suggests, these virtues form the hinge or axis on which the moral life turns. Why are these virtues prominent? First, these are the virtues needed to get through life. Without them a person cannot sustain the journey to the good. If progress is to be made in the moral life, one must be prudent, just, temperate, and courageous; these are the skills needed to navigate successfully all the situations and challenges one can confront.

Second, these are called the cardinal virtues because every virtue, except the theological virtues, is in some way derived from them and in some way manifests them. The cardinal virtues express some aspect or ingredient of every virtue, so that every virtue shows itself in some way as prudence, in some way as justice, in some way as temperance, and in some way as fortitude. The cardinal virtues mark four qualities an act must have if it is to be virtuous. If something is virtuous, it is prudent inasmuch as it is right judgment about what needs to be done; it is just insofar as it does what needs to be done in the way it needs to be done; it is temperate because it displays the right amount of passion in the doing of good; and it is courageous because it is not deterred by fear or hardship.

The most important cardinal virtue is prudence. Because a virtue is a characteristic way of acting, it is sometimes thought that it refers to rote, mechanical ways of behaving, almost as if virtue overrides any ingenuity or flexibility in human behavior. But that is not so. A virtue is a moral skill that enables a person to fathom in a situation precisely how the good can be done or needs to be done. Ethics is a practical science, dealing with concrete, everyday behavior; however, given the vast array of human situations, it is difficult to predict in advance exactly how the good ought to be done. Rules and principles help, but they cannot always tell how to capture the good. That requires discernment and wisdom, and this is what prudence supplies. Prudence comes first in the formation of every virtuous act because prudence is right judgment about what needs to be done.

There are certain situations in which a literal application of a rule does not allow the good to be achieved as it needs to be achieved. In these instances there is something about the situation that the principle or rule does not adequately address. It is in such moments that the need for prudence is felt. A prudent person is one who sees what a situation demands, who knows that the more concrete and particular a situation becomes, the harder it can be to know what ought to be done. Some discernment is required, and this is what prudence supplies.

Prudence is practical wisdom. It asks, "What shape must the good take in this situation if one is not to fall short of achieving it?" In other words, prudence strives to figure how one must act if he or she is not to misfire in the desire to do good. When in a situation in which there are many possibilities of action, a prudent person discerns what best enables the flourishing of the good. It is a virtue of moral astuteness that helps one to see how the good is fittingly practiced. Not a virtue of caution or restraint, prudence gives ingenuity to love.

Not even charity is enough for the Christian life. It is preeminent and essential, but it is not sufficient. Charity needs to be guided by prudence. In morals, good intentions are not enough. Charity supplies the best of intentions because it is the virtue that directs all one's behavior toward God; however, a person must also know how to make good on that intention, and that is

the work of prudence. A prudent person knows how to find the right means for a good end.

Nonetheless, even though charity needs prudence to bring wisdom and ingenuity to love, prudence, like all the virtues, is at the service of charity. Prudence is moral wisdom with a specific focus. Its interest is knowing how to act so that one can accomplish the basic intention of one's life, that of growing in friendship with God. Aquinas captures this relationship between prudence and charity when he writes, "Prudence is of good counsel about matters regarding a man's life in its entirety, and its last end. . . . Those only are such who are of good counsel about what concerns the whole of human life" (ST I-II, q. 57, a. 4).

Prudence connects the everyday with the ultimate. It is moral wisdom not only about the particular action before one but also about life taken as a whole. Prudence knows how to make everything one does serve the overall purpose of life, namely, moving more deeply into God. Standing in the service of charity, prudence supplies a special vision. If charity needs the moral acuity of prudence, prudence always has charity in mind. It is not a stodgy virtue, not a virtue of caution or restraint; on the contrary, it reads the everyday in light of the future a Christian wants his or her behavior to achieve.

The second cardinal virtue is justice. If prudence is the ability to know what needs to be done, justice is doing what needs to be done in the way it needs to be done. What distinguishes justice from prudence is that prudence is right judgment about what needs to be done while justice is right action (ST I-II, q. 61, a. 4). Prudence discerns, justice enacts.

The cardinal virtues of fortitude and temperance are related. Both pertain not directly to actions but to impediments to action. Their focus is the emotions, particularly when they make doing good more difficult instead of facilitating the doing of good. For instance, one can be persuaded to turn from the good on account of fear or difficulty. It is in such moments that courage or fortitude is needed to enable one "to be steadfast and not turn away from what is right" (ST I-II, q. 61, a. 2). Sometimes people are tempted to turn away from what is good because of adversity. They suffer setbacks, they are victims of misfortune, they know the scourge of tragedy. There are periods of darkness, times, as Faulkner writes in *The Sound and the Fury,* when "life looks like pieces of a broken mirror." If the Christian life is pictured as a journey to God through love, the importance of courage is clear. As with any journey, the human pilgrimage is speckled with difficulties and moments of deep discouragement. A person needs to know how to continue on through adversity, and this is the skill that courage gives. Aquinas quotes St. Augustine, who said that "courage is 'love readily enduring all for the sake of what is loved'" (ST II-II, q. 123, a. 4). Given the temptation to flee what is right when doing it is threatening or hard, it is not surprising that Aquinas says that "the chief activity of courage is not so much attacking as enduring, or standing one's ground amidst dangers" (ST II-II, q. 123, a. 6). Courage is the virtue by which one perseveres in what one loves and knows to be good even when doing so is costly; indeed, Aquinas sees martyrdom as the supreme manifestation of courage.

Like courage, the focus of temperance is the emotions, particularly when they obstruct virtuous behavior. This can happen in two ways. Sometimes the emotions can grow so powerful that they make one rash or careless, but at other times a person can feel so listless as to lack the energy to act at all. As its name suggests, temperance "tempers" the emotions either up or down. If the emotions are too strong, they need to be "tempered down," or subdued; if they are too weak, they need to be "tempered up," or aroused. Virtue depends on well-ordered affections, and this is what tem-

perance achieves; it gives the proper expression of feeling to actions. Thus temperance does not suppress the emotions but shapes them into their most appropriate expression, using them to empower virtuous behavior instead of obstructing it. In this sense temperance is like courage inasmuch as both virtues come into play whenever human beings are confronted with something that could "render them unreasonable" (ST II-II, q. 141, a. 2).

There are two parts to temperance: shame and honor or beauty. To speak of shame suggests that there is a nobility to being human beneath which no one should fall. Aquinas captures this when he describes intemperance as a puerile emotion. To be intemperate is to fall beneath the true dignity of a human being. Someone who is puerile has lost control of self and is a slave to the emotions. His or her life is not well-ordered, it is chaotic. An intemperate person is a creature of excess soon to become a creature of compulsion.

Intemperance can be debasing. When one's emotions are out of control, they govern the person instead of the person governing them. If this occurs, the emotions are not only destructive, they can also bring shame. Some things should not be done because they are repugnant to the nobility human beings have as creatures made in the image of God. A sense of shame is essential in order to appreciate the preciousness of human life. To debase oneself through intemperate behavior is to mock one's dignity as beloved of God. Aquinas says, "Intemperance is shameful ... for it debases a man and makes him dim. He grovels in pleasures well-described as slavish ... and he sinks from his high rank" (ST II-II, q. 142, a. 4).

To become slaves to the emotions is degrading. Aquinas speaks of intemperance as a "darkening of one's splendor and beauty" and as a "dulling of one's true dignity" (ST II-II, q. 142, a. 4). Sensitivity to shame, fear of being dishonored, uneasiness about losing a good reputation are all valuable qualities to have. To be sensitive to shame is to be anxious about possible disgrace, and this is a moral strength. Disgrace should be feared, as well as the loss of a good reputation. All this is part of temperance. A sense of shame is crucial in order to alert a person to things that are debasing. Aquinas realizes this when he writes, "Sentiments to shame, when repeated, set up a disposition to avoid disgraceful things" (ST II-II, q. 144, a. 1). This sensitivity to shame, which Aquinas also calls "a healthy fear of being inglorious," is an extremely valuable moral quality because it protects one from debasing and destructive behavior.

The importance of shame can be grasped if one considers what would happen if a person had no shame. Aquinas says that shame comes from "a horror of dishonor" (ST II-II, q. 144, a. 4). Shame protects a person from thoughtlessly risking integrity; it is a sentry before all that dishonors. What if a sense of shame is lost? The danger of intemperance is that it deadens sensitivity to what is debasing. A single intemperate act may be relatively harmless, but cumulatively it represents a deadening of moral sensitivity. One can grow numb to what is debasing about certain behavior because it has become so much a way of life that it can no longer be seen for what it is. As Aquinas warns, "Accordingly a man may lack a feeling of shame . . . because what is really shame-making is not apprehended as such, and accordingly a man sunk in sin may be quite shameless; indeed, far from being shamefaced, he may be brazen about it" (ST II-II, q. 144, a. 4).

The second part of temperance is honor or beauty. What makes anyone honorable is virtue, for honor stems not from possessions or power or fame but from moral excellence (ST II-II, q. 145, a. 1). Similarly, temperance is a virtue of the beautiful because it gives a proper measure or proportion to actions. A virtuous person is one who not only does the good but does it fittingly. For an act to be virtuous, what

matters is not simply what is done but how it is done. This is the function of temperance. Temperance shapes behavior into a proper balance of intelligence and passion. With temperance, every moral act is a thing of beauty; even the simplest act of kindness is something beautiful when done with style and grace. There are people whose acts of thoughtfulness, gestures of forgiveness, and everyday kindnesses display graciousness. There is an artistry to virtue, and it comes through temperance. Far from being a virtue that chastises, temperance arranges all the parts of an action so that the entire act, however small, is beautiful and noble.

See also CARDINAL VIRTUES; CONVERSION; DECISION, DECISION-MAKING; EVIL; FAITH; GOODNESS; HOPE; JUSTICE; LOVE; PRAXIS; SIN; VALUE.

Bibliography: Thomas Aquinas, Summa Theologiae I-II, qq. 49-67; 71; 85. Aristotle, Nichomachean Ethics, trans. M. Ostwald (Indianapolis: Bobbs-Merrill, 1962). S. Hauerwas, Character and the Christian Life: A Study in Theological Ethics (San Antonio: Trinity Univ. Press, 1975); "The Virtues and Our Communities" and "Character, Narrative, and Growth in the Christian Life," A Community of Character (Notre Dame, Ind.: Univ. of Notre Dame Press, 1981) 111–128; 129–152. A. MacIntyre, After Virtue (Notre Dame, Ind.: Univ. of Notre Dame Press, 1981). G. Meilaender, The Theory and Practice of Virtue (Notre Dame, Ind.: Univ. of Notre Dame Press, 1984). J. Pieper, The Four Cardinal Virtues (Notre Dame, Ind.: Univ. of Notre Dame Press, 1966). P. Wadell, "A Look at Aristotle's Ethics," Friendship and the Moral Life (Notre Dame, Ind.: Univ. of Notre Dame Press, 1989) 27–45.

PAUL J. WADELL, C.P.

VISION(S)

A vision is the supernatural perception of something or some person not naturally visible to the one having the vision. While people have reported visions of events occurring at great distances or visions of a symbolic nature, more common are reports of visions of the Lord, of Mary or another of the saints, of angels, or of someone deceased.

When the vision is perceptible to the eyes, it is called a corporeal vision or apparition. If it is perceived by the imagination, understood as an interior faculty of sense, it is called an imaginative vision. This does not imply that the vision is an illusion but refers only to the faculty of perception, noting that nothing is seen with the bodily eyes. Appearances of angels in dreams in Scripture would fall under this latter category.

Mystical writers also speak of intellectual visions, in which simple intuitive knowledge is communicated supernaturally without any impression in the external senses or in the imagination. John of the Cross and Teresa of Avila treat this last form of communication with higher regard than the others because there is no sensory element attached to it through which one could be deceived.

In the Bible angels and others appear without fanfare in dreams and to people in the waking state. This does not imply that visions were common occurrences but flows from the notion that God reveals himself to humankind in history. Growing appreciation of the transcendence of God in the OT led to a presentation of that revelation mediated through angels, who appeared where earlier traditions would have assserted that the Lord personally appeared in a vision. The utter otherness of God came to be understood as rendering a vision of God impossible in this life. This ambivalence about the possibility of seeing God can be found in the Book of Exodus. In Exod 33:18–34:9, Moses asks to see the glory of God. God refuses to show the divine face but agrees to appear and show his back to Moses. Yet in Exod 24:11, Moses and seventy elders ratified the covenant with God, who "did not lay his hand on the chief men of the people of Israel: they beheld God" (RSV). Although these stories represent different layers of the tradition, the intent in each case is to affirm the reality of God's self-revelation.

In the history of Christian spirituality, visions and locutions, or spoken revelations, occur often in the accounts of the lives of saints. This has sometimes led to the mistaken idea that such extraordinary events are signs of sanctity, whereas the experience falls generally into the category of charisms, which are for the benefit of others. Spiritual writers are unanimous in pointing out that visions and other extraordinary phenomena may have their origins in the human psyche or may be of diabolical rather than heavenly origin. That is why John of the Cross, for example, tends to place little emphasis on these experiences and teaches his followers to take the more certain though obscure path of pure faith, hope, and love. Teresa of Jesus places more confidence in such experiences, and her own life was marked by many visions and locutions. Yet she also counsels caution and explicitly rejects the idea that such phenomena are of the essence of Christian spiritual development or of sanctity.

Apparitions of Mary have a special place in understanding visions in the context of spirituality. Accounts of her appearing, often to children or to other marginalized individuals such as women or a Native American such as Juan Diego at Tepeyac, often result in intense outpourings of devotion. The Church does not affirm the reality of such appearances as being of divine faith, yet those that are compatible with the gospel and Christian tradition have often been supported and recommended. These messages consistently include calls to conversion of heart and to prayer, coupled with an assurance of the love of Mary and of God.

The more biblical and liturgical spirituality of the period following Vatican II often has had little use for the extraordinary accounts of visions and other revelations. These seem to some people to be a remnant of the 19th century and indications of a credulity that does no credit to contemporary Catholics as they move into the mainstream of American culture. A reasonable caution about such things is quite consistent with the tradition itself, yet a total rejection of the possibility of such events would seem to intrude on the fundamental notion of God revealing himself to people personally in history. The experience of many people in the charismatic renewal, as well as continued interest in Fatima and in the events reported at Medjugorje, is a sign that this element of Catholic devotional life is still present.

See also ANGELS; CARMELITE SPIRITUALITY; CHARISMATIC RENEWAL; DREAMS; ECSTASY; EXTRAORDINARY PHENOMENA; MARY; MYSTERY; MYSTICISM; PARAPSYCHOLOGY; PROPHECY; RAPTURE; REVELATION(S).

Bibliography: Gabriel of St. Mary Magdalen, *Visions and Revelations in the Spiritual Life* (Westminster, Md.: Newman, 1950).

MICHAEL DODD, O.C.D.

VOCAL PRAYER

See PRAYER.

VOCATION

The notion of vocation, or call, lies at the heart of Christian spirituality. A pervasive theme in both the Hebrew and Christian Scriptures, the concept of vocation is central to understanding the relationship between divine initiative and human response.

The term *vocation* comes from the Latin *vocare* ("to call"), which carries several connotations not apparent in the English derivative. In the simplest sense, *vocare* means "to summon," "to call someone over." It is also used in the sense of "to invite." Further, *vocare* sometimes refers to the act of naming or designating, often alluding to the deepest dimension of the act of naming. For example, in calling a child Brian, parents name the baby. In the deeper sense, the parents give the baby its very mode of existence, its status or place in the world. They call the child forth as a particular person by naming it. In calling their baby Brian, the Kellys actually constitute a unique person, i.e., Brian Kelly. So in a certain sense the act of creation is not complete until a child has been named.

From beginning to end, Sacred Scripture draws heavily upon the notion of vocation or calling to describe God's interaction with humankind. In the opening lines of the Hebrew Scriptures, humankind is called to dwell in the Garden of Eden (Gen 2:15). And in the closing lines of the Christian Scriptures, the faithful are beckoned or called to enter the New Jerusalem (Rev 21:2). Vocation, then, is an essential feature of the traditional interpretation of God's interaction with creation.

In the Hebrew Scriptures vocation refers first to God's calling humankind into existence, calling forth man and woman by name. It also refers to God's inviting humankind to share in the ongoing process of creation. This is symbolized by God's inviting humankind to name the animals (Gen 2:19). Just as God created humankind by calling it forth, humankind was to cooperate with God by calling forth the potentialities of God's initial creation. In naming the animals, humankind responded to God's call to participate in the creative process. In short, humankind was called to be God's partner.

The partnership between God and humankind finds expression in the theme of covenant: "I will be your God, and you will be my people." Here God the Creator explicitly *called* his people Israel into a covenant relationship. In calling for the inauguration of God's kingdom in Israel, God was specifying and amplifying the initial call. Through Israel humankind is called into a deep, interpersonal relationship with the caring Creator.

The theme of call or vocation also plays an important role in the Christian Scriptures. Here vocation is linked to the Greek term *kalein,* which, though usually translated as "to call," may also be rendered as "to name" or "to invite." For example, Jesus describes his mission as the calling of humankind to God. Men and women had forgotten that they were called to be creatures, cocreators, and partners in covenant. In Jesus, God repeated the call to humankind, offering the opportunity to repent, to be reconciled, to recall their original "vocation." Jesus was the call incarnate. Thus St. Paul refers to Jesus as the *kalon,* the one who calls. Those who accepted the call of Christ were referred to as *kalloumenoi,* those who are called. And the *kalloumenoi* formed the *ekklesia,* the assembly of those who have been called.

In Mt 4:21 we find Jesus calling disciples, inviting them to follow him in his calling. Here we have the birth of the Christian vocation, which is referred to as the *kleisis,* the "calling." Jesus called his disciples, and by implication all Christians, to continue his revelation of God's call to creation. The Christian is called to reiterate the *Verbum incarnatum,* to go forth to the whole world and proclaim the Good News to all creation. In other words, the Christian vocation demands that one join Christ in calling humankind back to the Father, back to the Creator. Men and women are to be reminded of their fundamental vocation: responsible cocreation and fidelity to a covenant of love with their Creator.

Placing the notion of vocation in this broad scriptural context reveals the inadequacy of the notion of vocation that had developed before the Second Vatican Council. Vocation had been generally understood as a call to the priesthood or the religious life. In the common parlance, "to have a vocation" meant to have a "religious" vocation, to be called to the religious sisterhood or brotherhood or to the ordained ministry. Although this understanding of vocation was not wrong, it was narrow and exclusive when contrasted with the fuller meaning of call as set down in Scripture and tradition. The consequence of this narrow view of vocation was the tendency to exaggerate the relative significance of the call to religious life and/or priesthood, while overlooking the authentic call character of other modes of Christian living.

Since the Second Vatican Council, a broader understanding of vocation has emerged. All human beings are called, and everyone responds according to his or her own capacities. As Vatican II emphasized: All persons "are *called* to be part of [the] catholic unity of the People of God, which is harbinger of the universal peace it promotes. And there belong to it or are related to it in various ways, the Catholic faithful as well as all who believe in Christ, and indeed the whole of mankind. For all . . . are called to salvation by the grace of God" (LG 13, italics added).

All men and women thus receive God's general call, and each responds in a specific way, depending upon his or her personal history. Those outside so-called revealed religions respond in a general way through responsible cocreation, even if it is not recognized and called such. Adherents of some revealed religions respond more specifically through a covenant relationship with the one God whom they serve in particular ways. The Christian, who believes that God's general call becomes fully articulated in Christ, the *Verbum incarnatum* or *Kalon,* responds by entering the Church of Christ through baptism. And, having entered the Church, the Christian further specifies his or her response by accepting responsibility for various aspects of the Church's mission, whether as a layperson, a religious, or a priest.

In summary, then, one's calling emerges toward specificity in humankind's corporate history as well as in the personal history of individuals. There are no special vocations, only specific states in life that are not predetermined but actively chosen through the creative response of individuals at whatever stage of specificity—creation, covenant, or the Christian Church—they encounter God's call.

See also BAPTISM; DISCIPLESHIP; GRACE; MINISTRY, MINISTERIAL SPIRITUALITY; VATICAN COUNCIL II.

Bibliography: L. O'Connell, "Towards a Theology of Vocation," *Chicago Studies* 18, no. 2 (1979) 147–159.

LAURENCE J. O'CONNELL

VOWS

The concept of vow is an ancient one. The OT speaks often of the offering to God of objects, persons, or the self as promises made consciously and voluntarily to perform good works (Num 15:1-10; Lev 27). Though vows were not required of the pious Jew, once made they were to be carried out with precision and rigor (Deut 23:22-24).

Nazirites were those Israelites who consecrated themselves to the service of God in specific ways for limited periods of time or for life (Num 6:1-8). Though abuses concerning vows were common and were denounced by the prophets, nevertheless the practice of taking vows was not repudiated by the early Church and, in fact, remained a time-honored one that continued to be common. Paul himself, on his last journey to Jerusalem, took a temporary nazirite vow (Acts 21:22-26).

Monastic life in the early Christian tradition was also based on a commitment to renunciation and virginity. Monastics of the 4th and 5th centuries, though not bound by formal, public vows, committed themselves to virginity and life according to a specific rule. Furthermore, both the Greek Fathers of the Church (Origen and Gregory of Nyssa) and the Latin Fathers of the Church (Cyprian and Augustine) recognized the validity of solemn promises made to God and the sacred obligations they incurred.

The vow consists of a public commitment to do a specified good for the sake of religious dedication or "divine service," the giving of the self to God. It is both a public contract and a public witness, the value of which does not lie in choosing good over bad in life but in choosing good above good. To vow poverty, for instance, is not to despise the goods of creation but to commit oneself to dependence on God and the just distribution of the goods of the earth in order to be free from the burdens which come with the amassment of wealth and which may distract a person from the development of the spiritual realities of life. A person does not take the vow of virginity because sexual expression is bad but because the control of passion and total consecration to God in the spiritual life is itself a good. The vow of obedience is not designed to curb human decision making, the supreme act of humanity, but to point to the presence and demands of a law above human law.

Though this type of obliging dedication was assumed from the time of the earliest monastic groups, the term *vow* itself came upon the scene later. The Latin concept of *propositum* ("promise"), the Spanish term *pactum* ("contract"), and St. Basil's *homologia* ("commitment") all connoted a vocational decision but not a matter of ecclesiastical contract. This desire to serve God in a particular monastery by following a specific rule is a form of commitment that promises in public a pledge of fidelity to a given way of life in a given group. In its earliest understandings, however, these commitments were not seen as public promises to fulfill a public pious act for the sake of a greater good in quite the same spirit that characterized the vows made in the Hebrew Scriptures.

As time went on and religious life took on a more formal character in the Church, the understanding of commitment itself changed. Since the choice of a lifestyle—marriage or religious life—is a social act with ramifications for the rest of society, its public declaration is both significant and customary. These obligations to God, in other words, affect a person's relationship to humankind as well. Consequently, society has a right to call vowed persons to accountability and has a corresponding responsibility to support them, since in binding themselves to the service of God, they also bind themselves in a special way to the needs of humanity. A public vow, therefore, is a public gift to the Church that the Church, through an official agency, recognizes, accepts, and affirms in an equally public fashion by receiving the vow and authorizing the compact.

The theology of vows that was developed by Thomas Aquinas was reiterated and emphasized in the rebuttal of the Council of Trent to the position of the Protestant Reformers that vows are contrary to the nature of baptism. This Tridentine theology of the vows stressed individual asceticism and withdrawal from the secular world. The Vatican II theology of the vows, in contrast, rejected the dualism of the 18th century for the sake of a more Trinitarian and communal notion of the vowed life and its role in society.

The chief witness value of religious vows lies in the fact that vows promise the future of the individual as well as the present. Vows are more than isolated good works done under a particular set of circumstances. Vows oblige the person to long-term dedication to a specific good. They are, then, public acts of faith in the eternal goodness and fidelity of God. Though they may be commuted under special circumstances and for special reasons or even taken for temporary periods of time, the vows of religious life are normally taken for a lifetime. This conscious commitment to a lifetime effort and single-minded dedication make for constancy in times of whim or stress if for no other reason than the seriousness with which they have been taken and the public dimension of their character. Not taken lightly, vows are not normally dismissed lightly.

Vows, then, differ from precepts because they promise more than moral law obliges. They give perpetual emphasis, strength, and embodiment to a particular facet (counsels) of the Christian life. Everyone is to live with the poor in mind, of course, but those who take a vow of poverty bind themselves to make that quality present in the Church. Everyone, married or single, is to live chastely according to his or her state in life, but the vow of chastity obliges the religious to attest to the fact that chastity and celibacy are possible. Everyone is to obey the gospel mandate, but the vow of obedience requires the religious to put the law of the gospel above every other law in life.

Precepts command but they do not oblige under law. The counsels are based on the life of Christ but differ from the commandments or the vows in that they are spiritual directives but not legal prescripts. The vows, unlike either precepts or counsels, have an expectation of the fulfillment of specific conditions, can only be dispensed by the proper authority, and take on a public responsibility to a greater good.

Vows signal the total giving over of one's life to the God of history as well as of eternity in order to live in the image of Christ and bring the kingdom of God. The vows are not signs of what life is to be in another world but of what life can be in this one.

See also CANON LAW, SPIRITUALITY IN; COVENANT; FIDELITY; LAW; RELIGIOUS LIFE; VOCATION.

Bibliography: W. Kaschmitter, *The Spirituality of Vatican II: Conciliar Texts Concerning the Spiritual Life of All Christians* (Huntington, Ind.: Our Sunday Visitor, 1975). J. Lozano, *Discipleship: Towards an Understanding of Religious Life,* Religious Life 2 (Chicago: Claret Center for Resources in Spirituality, 1983). J. Martos, *Doors to the Sacred: A Historical Introduction to Sacraments in the Catholic Church,* rev. ed. (Tarrytown, N.Y.: Triumph, 1991).

JOAN CHITTISTER, O.S.B.

W

WAITING

Hebrew and Greek terms for "waiting," both in the passive sense of "remaining" and the active sense of "hoping" or "looking for," appear often in the Bible and are variously translated. In the OT, while the wicked "lie in wait" for blood (Deut 19:11; Pss 10:9; 59:4; 119:95; Prov 1:11; Mic 7:2), the just wait above all on the Lord (Pss 37:7; 38:16; 130:6-7; Isa 33:2) with intense yearning for God's saving action (Jdt 8:17; Pss 25:5; 27:14; 33:20; Isa 33:2), placing all their hope in the Lord and "keeping God's way" (Pss 37:34; 39:8; 119:166). The Lord in turn hears the cry of those who wait and stoops to rescue them (Ps 40:1-4; Isa 64:3; Lam 3:25; Isa 30:15, 18). They are not "put to shame" (Ps 25:3; Isa 49:23) but "shall possess the land" (Ps 37:9) and rejoice in the Lord's salvation (Isa 25:9).

Jesus himself, and the salvation available through him, is the focus of NT waiting. He comes as the hope of those awaiting the reign of God (Mt 11:3; Mk 15:43; Lk 2:25, 38; 23:51) and teaches his disciples constant eschatological vigilance, "like servants who await their master's return from a wedding" (Lk 12:36). Put to death and raised up, Christ "now ... waits until his enemies are made his footstool" (Heb 10:13). Meanwhile, as we await his return in glory (1 Cor 1:7; Phil 3:20; 1 Thess 1:10; Tit 2:13; Heb 9:28) and "wait for adoption, the redemption of our bodies" (Rom 8:23), all creation "awaits with eager expectation the revelation of the children of God" (Rom 8:19).

It has often been noted that those immersed in today's culture of instant gratification find it difficult to wait. We also recognize that appeals for patience have too often been used in the past to protect the status quo. But in the wake of chastened post-Vatican II dreams of rapid social and ecclesiastical renewal, Christians are rediscovering the biblical value of "waiting on God." Contemporary psychologists and theologians are reaffirming what the spiritual tradition has known all along: that "passive purifications," experiences of impasse and frustration, and apparently fallow periods in our intellectual, emotional, social, and spiritual lives are often the seedbed for insights and breakthroughs that can only be received, not achieved. "The attitude that brings about salvation is not like any form of activity," observes Simone Weil, but "the waiting or attentive and faithful immobility that lasts indefinitely and cannot be shaken" (Weil, p. 196).

See also ATTENTION, ATTENTIVENESS; DESIRE; HOPE; SILENCE; TRUST.

Bibliography: B. Throckmorton, Jr., "Wait," *New Interpreter's Dictionary of the Bible,* vol. 4 (Nashville: Abingdon, 1962). S. Weil, *Waiting for God* (New York: Harper, 1973).

STEVEN PAYNE, O.C.D.

WAR, IMPACT ON SPIRITUALITY

Early Christianity and Warfare

War did not pose a major problem for the early Christian Church. Since Christians were a fringe social group, there was little demand upon them to volunteer for military service. A few apparently did, but the writings of Sts. Clement of Rome, Justin, and other Church Fathers of the period deny any general Christian responsibility to engage in warfare. Neither do we find in these writings any clear spirituality of pacifism.

After A.D. 180, however, the problem of Christians in the military developed into a major controversy in the Church. Christianity had experienced significant growth in numbers. And as the Roman Empire faced the increased threat of invasion by foreign forces, pressures mounted on the Christian community to contribute to its defense. More and more Christians were responding to this call of national service, thus forcing the Church to grapple seriously with the relationship between faith in Christ and participation in military service.

There were no official ecclesiastical instructions to guide Church Fathers in solving this new dilemma. The 3rd century did witness, however, the growth of a strong pacifist spirituality among some Christian writers, a trend that was corroborated to some extent by the influential *Apostolic Tradition* of St. Hippolytus. Tertullian was definitely the most outspoken of the new advocates of a pacifist spirituality as the only authentic expression of Christian faith. His position blended doctrinal principles with practical fears that the Roman military lifestyle seriously clashed with basic Christian moral commitments. However, Origen emerged as the most logical and consistent of the Christian pacifists of the period. While assuring the emperor that Christians were always behind him with their prayers, Origen proclaimed a strict pacifist spirituality, whose roots, he strongly maintained, were to be found in the teachings of Jesus himself.

Other prominent spokespersons for pacifist spirituality at that time were Cyprian and Lactantius. The former considered war an inherent evil from the standpoint of Christian spirituality, though he remained willing to condone the necessity of the Roman armies for the safety of the empire. Lactantius went beyond Cyprian, approaching the absolute reserve of Origen regarding Christians and warfare. He argued that Christian spirituality prevented participation in military service, for the biblical tradition clearly commands that we should not kill.

The 3rd century, therefore, was essentially marked by contrasts in the Christian community. On one hand, a growing number of ordinary Christian believers were accepting the premise that service in defense of the empire could be reasonably combined with Christian spirituality. On the other hand, an increasing number of Christian writers were insisting that warfare was inherently incompatible with Christian spirituality.

The whole tenor of the discussion on Christian spirituality and warfare abruptly changed at the beginning of the 4th century when Constantine declared Christianity to be the state religion of the empire in 313. The strong commitment to pacifism, rooted in the gospel itself, suddenly disappeared as a prominent feature of Catholic spirituality, not to reappear again with any seriousness until the 20th century. "To fight for the emperor is to fight for God"— that became the core of Christian spirituality in the 4th century and for centuries thereafter.

The Just War Theory

Sts. Athanasius, Basil, Ambrose, and Augustine set about clarifying and laying the theological foundations for the new spirituality of national defense. It was Augustine who gave this perspective its permanent shape in a decisive way, developing what has come to be known as the "just war" tradition.

Augustine took all those to task who were critical of either the Hebrew Scriptures or the NT with regard to war. In the Hebrew Scriptures, warfare was a direct disposition of God. Hence anyone who would dare call Moses or the Israelites impious or immoral for their actions would in fact be indicting God, who ordered these actions. The NT, in Augustine's judgment, refrained from any condemnation of war. In fact, it was possible, in his view, to generate positive support for the soldier's profession from the Gospels and Epistles.

The Augustinian doctrine on war and Divine Providence accented the all-wise designs of God, emphasizing how even war might play a constructive role in the divine governance of the world. Both the just and the unjust are meant to derive some profit from what admittedly is a plague on humanity. For the just, war enhances their patience, humility, and general discipline. For the unjust, it can serve as a spur for a reform of their immoral ways. An unqualified pacifism would represent, in Augustine's eyes, a form of spiritual haughtiness, because it would imply that creatures could fully comprehend the ultimate divine plan for the world.

Augustine wrote on all aspects of warfare from a moral and spiritual viewpoint. Since he considered war as inherently contrary to the natural order, he developed a set of criteria to determine when it was morally justifiable to go against the natural order. The morality of war could not be presumed, according to Augustine; the ruler had to establish a just cause. Augustine also added guiding norms for the conduct of war once it was launched. He likewise devoted considerable time to the qualities that should mark a "spirituality of national service," as it were, highlighting the virtues that should characterize the true Christian soldier.

Finally, Augustine's ideas on peace were the crowning point of his teachings on war.

That was the goal of his entire spirituality of warfare. In fact, there is so much lively antiwar rhetoric in parts of Augustine that, taken in isolation, he might appear an ardent supporter of a pacifist spirituality. For Augustine, peace was such a good thing that a Christian ruler, under certain conditions, could wage a war in order to restore or preserve peace. His just war spirituality was not intended as a guide for ordinary believers but rather for Christian kings. Since not only Augustine but Christian theology at large lacked any notion of human rights, authentic Christian spirituality permitted the ordinary believer little option but to serve, once the Christian ruler decided a war was just. Spirituality would come into play for ordinary Christians only in terms of their conduct while in the service of their country.

The Reemergence of Nonviolence

Clearly, a spirituality based on just war predominated in Catholic Christianity from the time of Constantine until the mid-20th century. The earlier nonviolent tradition was not totally lost, surfacing, for example, in parts of the monastic world during the Middle Ages. But few theologians or Church leaders gave it much credence.

A totally new situation opened up, however, with the Nazi onslaught against Jews, Poles, Gypsies, homosexuals, and others, and with the dropping of atomic bombs on Japan during World War II. The rapid escalation in the destructive potential of modern weaponry forced Catholicism into a major reconsideration of its almost singular commitment to just war spirituality. Pope John XXIII made a dramatic contribution to this rethinking in his plea for a new ethos of peacemaking in the Catholic community and within all humankind. In his encyclical *Pacem in Terris* (1963), he wrote that "in this age of ours, which prides itself on its atomic power, it is irrational to believe that war is still an apt means of vindicating violated rights." Pope Paul VI picked up on this same theme in many addresses on the subject of war, including his call at the United Nations for a total end to the arms race. Paul VI also clearly recognized that if the arms race is to be ended, there is need to develop structures for nonviolent resolution of conflict. Pope John Paul II has followed much the same path in his comments on issues of war and peace.

The United States bishops have followed the lead set in recent papal statements. Cardinal John Krol, testifying at a hearing of the Senate Foreign Relations Committee in the name of the National Conference of Catholic Bishops, stressed that in a nuclear era the morality of war has taken on an entirely new cast. Catholic morality must now be totally oriented toward arms control and disarmament. And in their historic pastoral letter on peace entitled *The Challenge of Peace* (1983), the bishops, while maintaining the primacy of the just war perspective for governmental leaders, called for a deep national commitment to arms reduction and peacemaking. They also revalidated pacifism as a moral option for individual Catholic believers and affirmed the principle of conscientious objection as authentically Catholic.

Even more striking have been the recapturing of the early Catholic spirituality of nonviolence by groups of grass-roots Catholics and the increasing attention given by biblical scholars to the strong proclivity toward peace apparent in Jesus' teachings. Evidence of a pacifist outlook first appeared in Catholic America in the early 19th century. Two Catholic converts, Isaac Hecker and Orestes Brownson, prolific writers in their period, showed strong traces in their works of their pacifist experiences with the Brook Farm commune in Massachusetts. In the 20th century the coming of World War I and the consequent introduction of nationwide conscription produced several Catholic pacifists, such as John Dunn and Ammon Hennacy. The Catholic Worker Movement, founded in 1933 by Dorothy Day and Peter Maurin,

introduced the first enduring pacifist group in American Catholicism. Hennacy joined the movement as a regular columnist for its newspaper. It was out of the Catholic Worker Movement that the first sustained American Catholic spirituality of nonviolence arose. And in 1936 a Catholic Pax group was born, strongly influenced by the pacifist strain in Russian Christianity, such as that found in the writings of Leo Tolstoy. The Pax version of pacifism was strongly tied to the belief that capitalism lay at the root of all wars.

During the Second World War a number of conscientious objectors came to the fore. Prominent among them was Gordon Zahn. He has been responsible for helping introduce U.S. Catholicism to the Pax Christi international movement, based in Europe, which in recent years has become the principal locus for the development of a Catholic spirituality of peace and related activities. While not formally pacifist in outlook, the American branch in particular is strongly inclined in that direction.

The Vietnam era produced a flurry of Catholic peace activities and writings and further development of a peace spirituality. The Catholic Peace Fellowship was born, Catholics such as the Berrigan brothers participated in nonviolent direct action on behalf of peace, and several bishops became prominently involved. Archbishop Raymond Hunthausen of Seattle held back tax payments to protest military spending, the bishop of Juneau testified on behalf of Catholics charged with trespassing on military installations, and the bishop of Amarillo set up a fund to assist workers who quit their jobs at military installations or munitions plants. And one of contemporary Catholicism's leading interpreters of spirituality, Thomas Merton, gave strong impetus to peace as an indispensable ingredient of Catholic faith.

On the level of scholarship, several prominent NT scholars have emphasized the strong peace thrust, if not outright pacifism, in the teachings of Jesus. This thrust, they say, is especially evident in Jesus' absolute commitment to love of enemy, which Donald Senior, C.P., terms his "most scandalous teaching." And a significant number of Catholics have been deeply influenced of late by the pacifist spirituality found in the writings of Protestant scholars Stanley Hauerwas and John Howard Yoder. Yoder, out of his Mennonite pacifist tradition, is strongly committed to a vision of a nonviolent Jesus, while Hauerwas has stressed the need to develop the local Church as a model of the peaceful community anticipating the peaceable kingdom.

The peace spirituality of contemporary Catholicism clearly remains in transition. The commitment to the primacy of peace is much stronger than it was several decades ago, though the majority do not stand ready to abandon totally the just war tradition. The pacifist legacy of the Church Fathers has reemerged as an important factor shaping that spirituality. Recently a third element has interjected itself into the discussion. It is liberationist spirituality, coming primarily from Latin America. It often believes that a peace spirituality unconnected with a concrete commitment to political and economic change can, in the end, wind up supporting the status quo. Prominent spokespersons for each side, such as Daniel Berrigan and Ernesto Cardenal, have debated this issue at length. Liberation spirituality, though committed to the peaceful nature of the ultimate divine kingdom, nonetheless believes that violence may be justified and necessary to defend the oppressed against the existing violence of the status quo. In that sense, it bears some connections with the just war tradition, even though it would be quite critical of the spirituality traditionally undergirding that tradition.

In the end, the current debate about spirituality is not about ultimate ends but about means. What is permitted a Christian committed to the spirituality of Jesus in terms of helping achieve the kingdom?

The debate in Catholicism over this will likely continue for an extended period.

See also CATHOLIC WORKER MOVEMENT; CONFRONTATION AND PROTEST; HOLOCAUST; NUCLEAR AGE, IMPACT ON SPIRITUALITY; PATRISTIC SPIRITUALITY; PEACE; WARFARE, SPIRITUAL.

Bibliography: R. Musto, *The Catholic Peace Tradition* (Maryknoll, N.Y.: Orbis, 1986). J. Pawlikowski and D. Senior, eds., *Biblical and Theological Reflections on "The Challenge of Peace,"* including full text of U.S. Bishops' 1983 pastoral letter on peace (Wilmington, Del.: Glazier, 1984). G. Weigel, *Tranquillitas Ordinis: The Present Failure and Future Promise of American Catholic Thought on War and Peace* (New York: Oxford Univ. Press, 1987). T. Merton, *Faith and Violence: Christian Teaching and Christian Practice* (Notre Dame, Ind.: Univ. of Notre Dame Press, 1968).

JOHN T. PAWLIKOWSKI, O.S.M.

WARFARE, SPIRITUAL

The subject of spiritual warfare or combat needs to be seen against the backdrop of Christian Gnosticism, which perceives the world as a hostile place against which one must fight. The world is regarded as full of temptations and evils, the source of all sin. A spiritual person must seek interior strength to combat these evils. This attitude is found in the Scriptures, especially in the Pauline letters. Comparing the Christian life to an athletic contest, Paul compares the Christians to soldiers who must arm themselves with the armor of discipline (Eph 6:11). In order to be on permanent guard against the enemy, which may be exterior or interior to the person, the Christian is called to a life of asceticism. Paul warns Christians to be on guard against the struggle between the spirit and the flesh.

Among the great spiritual writers in the early Church, the attitude of spiritual warfare is most evident in the writings of the Alexandrians, due to the influence of Gnosticism. Clement of Alexandria and Origen owe much of their thought to this Gnostic intellectual formation. They see redemption as a conflict, a victory won in a battle by the Creator, who comes to fight against the powers of hatred, which the fallen angels had birthed through their disobedience. Origen held that life is a spiritual combat in which one must struggle with demons. Spiritual perfection consists in achieving detachment from the inherently evil world through asceticism. As long as one can resist temptation to evil, the enemy powers can be overcome. God provides the necessary battleground where temptations cannot be put to death and destroyed. God authorizes the adverse powers in some way, so that one may be victorious over them (see *In Jesu Nave hom.* 14).

Origen's theory of Christian living drew from the thought of the Desert Fathers in Egypt and Syria. These monks withdrew from the world as hermits to devote themselves wholly to spiritual combat. According to St. Athanasius, Antony looked upon monastic life as a warfare in which the chief enemy was the devil and the demons. "Living this life, let us be carefully on our guard and, as is written, 'with all watchfulness keep our heart' (Prov 4:23). For we have enemies, powerful and crafty—the wicked demons; and it is against these that our wrestling is" (*Life of Antony*, no. 21).

In the 4th century, Evagrius Ponticus codified the notion of spiritual warfare in his Greek writings, later translated into Latin by John Cassian. In this monastic context, the goal of the Christian is to develop discipline, which leads to union with God by loving contemplation. In a Platonic sense, the kingdom of God is associated with contemplation, but sin is the distraction brought about by the created order. Spiritual combat requires that one practice *ascesis* in order to turn the mind back to its proper alignment. The discipline is twofold: moral and intellectual. In the moral order, one disciplines the will and the character, leading to the purgation of evil and the cultivation of good. In the intellectual order, one disciplines the mind as well as the senses through contemplation. The highest contemplation is *gnōsis* (the summit of knowledge) and *sophia* (wisdom). Prayer is a means for discipline, passing in a progressive fashion through the stages of petition, requests for virtues and graces, intercessions, and thanksgiving. Prayer and contemplation are closely joined, and in the Eastern tradition the goal is purity of heart (hesychasm) and perpetual prayer (the Jesus Prayer).

In the 16th century Lorenzo Scupoli, a priest of the Theatine Order, wrote his famous book *The Spiritual Combat* (1589). First published anonymously, this work is a classic of spirituality of the Counter-Reformation period. Addressing a pupil, he dedicates twenty-four chapters to the idea of the interior, unseen warfare. Many of these ideas are echoed in the 20th century in the manual of spirituality by Adolphe Tanquerey. Life is a struggle between our lower faculties, which tend naturally toward pleasure, and our higher faculties, which are drawn toward moral good. Pleasure is not always morally good, and reason must conquer hostile tendencies to establish order. This is depicted as a struggle between the spirit and the flesh, between the will and passion (Tanquerey, p. 30).

See also APATHEIA; ASCETICISM; DEMON(S), DEMONIC, DEVIL(S); DESERT; DETACHMENT; DUALISM; EVIL; GNOSIS, GNOSTICISM; HESYCHASM; MORTIFICATION; PASSION(S); PATRISTIC SPIRITUALITY; TEMPTATION; WORLD.

Bibliography: L. Scupoli, *The Spiritual Combat and a Treatise on Peace of the Soul*, Spiritual Masters Series (New York: Paulist, 1978). A. Tanquerey, *The Spiritual Life: A Treatise on Ascetical and Mystical Theology* (Tournai: Desclée, 1930).

MICHAEL S. DRISCOLL

WEAKNESS AND VULNERABILITY

The significance of weakness and vulnerability in Christian life will be treated here in light of empirical, scriptural, ontological, and practical considerations.

Empirical Considerations

Weakness is properly understood in relationship to strength, its opposite. When applied to human beings, the term describes a lack or deprivation in mind, body, or character. Those who are weak are those who lack the ability or the power to bring about change in their own lives or in the lives of others. Those whom society sees as weak, be it socially, mentally, or physically, have little or no measure of self-determination by the canons of the prevailing social-political order. From this perspective, the weak are powerless and voiceless. In itself, weakness is not a virtue and is not to be relished either in the self or in others. Be that as it may, the weak may become strong by recognizing and accepting human weakness rather than by ignoring or denying it. No matter how strong one may be or become, however, vulnerability remains a permanent factor of human existence.

Vulnerability is often thought to refer to a weakness that places one in a position of being forced to give in indiscriminately to any and all powers and forces. In this view, vulnerability causes one to be adversely affected by persons, events, and circumstances beyond one's own control. Properly understood, however, the term describes the fundamental openness of the human being to be affected by life, persons, and events. To be human is to be vulnerable, indeed defenseless, in the face of so many of the events and persons that affect us, for good or ill. At the most fundamental level, human vulnerability is part and parcel of being a person, of having a body. Our bodies, our selves, are really quite defenseless in the face of disease, sickness, suffering, accident, and finally death, which claims the life of each human being. From this vantage point, vulnerability is an anthropological constant. No matter how strong a person or group may be, there are the never-ending reminders that human life is very fragile, a gift, and the forces that bear upon it cannot be predicted or con-

trolled. Whatever precautionary and preventative measures human wisdom may require in order to assure human integrity and flourishing, human beings are fundamentally defenseless if life is to be lived on life's own terms. This fundamental vulnerability is often overlooked or flatly denied by individuals and by whole societies wherein cults of the young and of youth flourish, where the advertising industry exalts physical perfection and longevity, and where pain, impairment, and limitation are to be avoided at all costs.

Scriptural Considerations

The positive significance of human weakness and vulnerability in the spiritual life finds clear expression in Paul's affirmation that it is in human weakness that God's strength is found (2 Cor 12:9). Weakness here is not understood as that which in the human being easily succumbs to temptation or sin. Nor is it the weakness of the flesh as opposed to the strength of the spirit. One also finds a positive appreciation of weakness and vulnerability in the beatitudes (Mt 5:3-12; Lk 6:20-26), wherein the blessed are those who are defenseless and broken by human tragedy, those who sorrow and mourn, those persecuted by evil forces, those who are belittled and rendered insignificant by the strong and robust. Indeed, the whole history of Christian spirituality is a testimony against the folly of asserting one's strength and power to grow in the life of holiness, and an invitation to the life of wisdom and grace that can result from the recognition that human weakness and vulnerability can be a blessing rather than a curse.

Understanding the significance of weakness and vulnerability in the Christian spiritual life rests on an appreciation of the weakness and vulnerability of Jesus, particularly in his infancy and in his agony, passion, and death. This is perhaps best expressed in the *kenosis,* the self-emptying, of Jesus Christ described by Paul. The kenotic Christ, whose lordship is disclosed pre-

cisely in his self-emptying (Phil 2:6-11), refused to lay claim to exercises of authority,
power, and control of "the world." Refusing a type of power that controls and dominates, and embracing instead human weakness and vulnerability, is the very manifestation of Christ's power and lordship.
Jesus' refusal of external, "worldly" power
and his acceptance of the human condition
enabled him to enter the lives of others at
their most vulnerable point. But this differs greatly from the power of "the world."
This is the power of a displaced and unknown infant at Bethlehem and a crucified
minister and teacher of mercy on
Golgotha. The power of this *kenosis* differs
completely from that which brings about
change by control, domination, or manipulation. It manifests itself in care, compassion, self-sacrifice, reciprocity, and
mutuality.

Ontological Considerations

The roots of human weakness and vulnerability lie in finitude and contingency.
That is to say, all human and nonhuman
life, by virtue of its dependency upon the
Creator and because of its participation in
the created order, is subject to influences
and forces, both positive and negative, that
are ineluctably a part of creaturely existence. Finitude and contingency entail dependency upon the other, others, and God
for fulfillment and completion. This is true
not just of certain individuals or groups,
such as those who are physically or mentally disabled or infants and children.
There is, rather, a weakness and vulnerability common to all, rooted in finitude and
contingency. The possibilities for gaining
strength and for achieving human purpose
and fulfillment do not lie in the avoidance
or denial of the weakness and vulnerability
common to all but in finding the sources of
strength and power therein.

To be weak is to stand in need, to be dependent on another, others, and God. This
is to recognize that strength and power, indeed life itself, is not of one's own making

but is the gracious gift of the Creator to all
creatures. To accept and celebrate one's
life as a creature involves an admission
that one cannot exist independently of the
other, others, and God, and that one stands
in need of them for any growth and development in life with others and God.

From this vantage, vulnerability may be
understood as the human capacity to be
open, to be attracted, touched, or moved
by the draw of God's love as this is experienced in one's own life or in the lives of
others. It is vulnerability that enables one
to enter into relationships of interpersonal
communion and communication with others who recognize their own weakness and
need. Vulnerability requires the integrity
and strength, indeed the power, to risk
enormous pain, to bear the burdens of the
darkest hour without avoidance, denial, or
deception. It demands the stamina to open
oneself up in order to be touched in one's
fragility. In short, vulnerability implies the
willingness to lose oneself in the hope of
finding one's true self, the readiness to die
to oneself so that one might truly live.

Practical Considerations

Caution must be exercised in the face of
tendencies to romanticize human weakness and vulnerability, as well as related
notions such as "littleness" and "spiritual
childhood." A proper view of weakness and
vulnerability in the spiritual life gives little
room to laziness, irresponsibility, or,
worse, indifference. But balanced perspectives have not always been maintained, and
naive views of human weakness and vulnerability have provided the basis for refusing responsibility and cooperation in
the life of growth in grace and holiness.
And overly sanguine views of human weakness and vulnerability have sometimes
been advanced and supported as part of a
strategy to push the powerless further
under the control of their oppressors, to
keep those who are vulnerable to adversity
brought on by sociopolitical injustice con-

tent in the face of hardships and negative influences.

There are several implications of a positive appreciation of weakness and vulnerability for Christian spirituality. First, life in Christ by the power of the Spirit calls for a recognition of the vulnerability of all, often in the face of social and cultural pressures to ignore or deny this. Second, it must be recognized that those who are physically, mentally, or socially weak often find strength in human and spiritual resources that are deeper than human descriptions, thus inviting the strong and robust of this world to recognize the spiritual resources that are found in weakness, not in strength. Third, the entire meaning and message of Jesus may be considered in light of the revelation of God's presence and grace in the vulnerability of Christ on the cross and in the weak of this world.

See also AFFECT, AFFECTIVITY; AGING; COMPASSION; DISABILITY, THE DISABLED; MARGINALIZED, THE; POWER; SUFFERING.

Bibliography: E. Janeway, *Powers of the Weak* (New York: Knopf, 1980). M. Downey, *A Blessed Weakness: The Spirit of Jean Vanier and l'Arche* (San Francisco: Harper & Row, 1986). D. Soelle, *The Window of Vulnerability* (Minneapolis: Augsburg/Fortress, 1990).

MICHAEL DOWNEY

WESTERN (LATIN) SPIRITUALITY

This entry examines the fundamental influences and emphases in Western spirituality during the patristic period and in the early Middle Ages. The common factors are the use of the Latin language, the conscious identification with antecedent tradition, and the continuance of certain basic dispositions that owed their origin to the classical period.

Three factors governed the evolution of this fund of beliefs and values. First, just as ancient Rome had borrowed from Greece, so the Latin Church continued to adapt Eastern wisdom for its own profit. Many significant spiritual movements in the West coincided with a renewed interest in the Christian East, though the encounter resulted in a typically Western product, perhaps subtly influenced by Latin attitudes and philosophies. Second, doctrine often developed not by the evolution of an internal logic but as a pastoral response to changing social conditions and movements within the Church. Third, as the centuries passed, the Latin tradition gained depth by reflecting on itself.

The Church of North Africa

Although the West produced noteworthy spiritual writers such as Clement and Hermas (author of *The Shepherd*) and competent theologians such as the Apologists Hippolytus and Irenaeus of Lyons, the language of discourse was Greek. Christian literature in Latin seems to have begun in North Africa with the *Acts of the Martyrs* and with the works of Tertullian (ca. 160–225) and Cyprian (ca. 205–258).

Tertullian was a deeply religious man with a strong bent for asceticism and renunciation. This is clear even in his most positive works, the treatise *On Patience* and his commentary on the Lord's Prayer. Progressively he became more severe, especially in sexual matters and in issues that involved participation in public life. The result was a stern religious system that made many demands, including martyrdom, and offered few possibilities for repairing mistakes. Although his espousal of the heresy of Montanism diminished his subsequent influence, Tertullian was a significant figure in setting the agenda and framing the language of Latin tradition.

Cyprian left a distinguished forensic career in Carthage to become a Christian and eventually bishop of that city and a martyr. The letters written during the ten years of his episcopacy show that he dealt skillfully with a range of pastoral problems and was particularly zealous in defending the unity of the Church. Like Tertullian, he wrote a commentary on the Lord's Prayer and a treatise *On Patience*. Cyprian was held in high esteem by Augustine and, at least indirectly, influenced Benedict.

The themes of the Church as pilgrim and heaven as *patria* were strong in North Africa, perhaps reflecting the colonial mentality of those who lived there. As developed by Augustine and Gregory, this resulted in a "devotion to heaven" common in the West during the next thousand years.

Acts of the Martyrs

The accounts of the deaths of Christian martyrs had an important formative influence on Latin spirituality, specifically in their warm, affective tone and in their Christocentric piety. The narratives were framed to provide encouragement in the living of the virtues, particularly patience. This spirituality animated the domestic ascetics of the 2nd and 3rd centuries, Origen (ca. 184–254), and the Benedictine tradition.

Origen of Alexandria

The school of Alexandria was the westernmost outpost of Hellenistic thought and a meeting place with Jewish traditions. Many of the significant themes in later Western thought derive from this school and from Origen, its most famous member. These include teaching on the multiple levels of scriptural interpretation and on the five spiritual senses, Word mysticism, and the use of nuptial imagery. His treatise *On Prayer* and his many scriptural commentaries were particularly influential in both the East and the West. His practical teaching was ascetic. In line with standard Stoic approaches, the goal of spiritual attainment was described in terms of *apatheia*. Although Origen was condemned and some of the originals of his works were destroyed, many survive in the Latin translations of Jerome and Rufinus.

John Cassian

John Cassian (360–435) was an important means by which the teaching of Origen and Evagrius Ponticus (345–399) was funneled into the mainstream of the monastic West. Thirteen years after the death of Martin of Tours (316–397), Cassian founded twin monasteries at Marseilles, regulating the monastic life there according to what he had observed during his youthful sojourn in the Egyptian desert. He summarized his teaching in two influential works, the *Institutes* and the *Conferences*. In the first he describes external observance and offers a strategy for dealing with the "eight vices of monks" as a means of gaining purity of heart. The second is composed of twenty-four discourses supposedly given by the great Desert Fathers on various questions, the whole series constituting a systematic treatment of the spiritual life. These works exercised a clear influence in the West during the next thousand years.

Leo the Great

Pope Leo I (400–460) proved a good administrator and a competent advocate of orthodoxy against heretics. His significance for spirituality lies in his liturgical sermons, parts of which were later inserted in the cycle of readings for the Night Office. Two themes recur in these brief homilies. The first is the *hodie* ("today") of the liturgy. In celebrating the sacred cycles, we do more than commemorate: even today we have the opportunity to participate in the mysteries celebrated. This is the great *sacramentum* ("sacrament") given to Christians. The second emphasis is reflected in his frequent admonition "Imitate what you celebrate." The liturgy has moral consequences; its reality is complete only when it is an agent of evangelization of daily behavior.

Leo's name is loosely associated with the emergence of the Latin Sacramentary, which was beginning to coalesce during the period from the 5th to the 7th century. The prayers of the Missal were carefully crafted not only as an address to God but also as a means to instruct the faithful and to form their moral and spiritual attitudes. Many of these early collects are still in use today.

Ambrose of Milan

Ambrose (339–397) became bishop of Milan in 374, having previously been governor in that city. He was a strong opponent of Arianism and fearlessly intervened in public affairs. His pastoral zeal was expressed especially in his prolific writings. He quarried deeply in the Greek Fathers, adapting their vision to the situation of his congregation. He is credited with the writing of theological works, sermons, letters, and hymns, but it is his books of biblical commentary and his moral and ascetic writings that were widely read in later centuries. His work on ecclesiastical virtues, which is a baptized version of Cicero's *De officiis,* was especially popular. Several of his books deal with the state of consecrated virginity. He was later revered because of his relationship with Augustine.

Jerome

Jerome (331 or 347–420) lived a stormy life and was personally involved in many of the crises of the contemporary Church. His greatest contribution to spirituality was the immense labor of producing an authoritative Latin version of the Bible, subsequently known as the Vulgate. This was buttressed by a grand series of biblical commentaries not only explaining points of exegesis and history but attempting a spiritual interpretation also. Some of these found their way into the liturgy, and Jerome was the author most consulted about obscurities in the Scriptures. His teaching on monastic life, including some of his fiery outbursts against abuses, is often echoed in subsequent reformist texts. One of the influences on Jerome and on many later Western monks was the *Life of Antony* by Athanasius of Alexandria (326–373).

Augustine of Hippo

In Augustine (354–430) many of the spiritual attitudes of the previous centuries became more patent. Augustine knew no Greek; his direct sources were all Western or at least Westernized. Beyond theological polemic and ecclesiastical politics, Augustine is revealed as a contemplative seeker of God, a tireless proponent of divine grace, and a preacher of practical morality in daily life. Many of the characteristic elements of Augustine's spirituality will continue in the West for many centuries. These include the following: his basing of spirituality on the Scriptures, his emphasis on the conformity of inner life and external activity, his teaching on desire for God, and his conception of the spiritual life within an anthropological framework.

There are many contradictory veins in Augustine's thought. On the one hand, his spirituality was strongly affective, with many passages conveying his personal experience of the delight of God's love. On the other hand, his moral doctrine is often body-denying and rigorist, unconsciously drawing elements from Stoicism, Manicheism, and Neoplatonism and fed by the residue of guilt left by his own experience. His great work *The City of God* was profoundly influenced by the breaking up of the Roman Empire. It had the effect of propagating two polarities that were sometimes exaggerated in succeeding centuries. One was the sharp distinction between the Church and the world; the other was a tendency to contrast the present life unfavorably with the next. Texts marked by these tendencies were later used to deny legitimacy to the worldly involvement of Christians. The most important texts for spirituality are the *Confessions,* his writings on the Gospel of John and the Psalms, and his sermons, especially those that were read liturgically.

Benedict of Nursia

Benedict (480–547) is given the title "Patriarch of the West." Through the monasteries he founded and the Rule he compiled, he was a dominant force in the formation of Western monasticism and in the spirituality that animated it. His Rule is an adaptation of an existing Italian text known as the Rule of the Master. Benedict's great knack was in combining the asceticism, self-knowledge, and separation from the world evident in the Desert tradition with the complementary values of *humanitas,* discretion, moderation, community, and a sense of Church typical of his other sources—Augustine, Basil, Clement, and Cyprian. The result was a flexible and dynamic institution capable of adaptation to changing circumstances that invited monks to go beyond external observance to the assimilation of the beliefs and values on which monastic life depended. This resulted in a love for tradition and a zeal to keep alive the wisdom of the past. This "love of letters" served the Church well in the centuries of social decline that followed the collapse of the Roman Empire in the West.

Gregory the Great

Pope Gregory I (540–604) lived in a period of great turbulence due to barbarians, plagues, and natural disasters. He was well educated and a skilled administrator. At age thirty-five he established a monastery on the family estate and was shortly afterward ordained deacon and sent as an envoy of Pope Pelagius II to Constantinople. He was elected pope in 604.

For Gregory, who knew little Greek, to be Christian was to be Roman. Although he was profoundly influenced by Origen, Ambrose, Cassian, and especially Augustine, his spiritual synthesis was peculiarly his own. It was strongly biblical in tone, stressing the monastic virtues, particularly patience in time of trial. His key work in this respect is his *Moral Commentary on Job.* His *Gospel Homilies* reveal the scriptural foundation for his teaching, and his *Commentary on Ezekiel* not only provides a mirror of the times in which he lived but

contains solid teaching on contemplation. His *Pastoral Rule* reveals a keen insight into human behavior; it was widely read in the Middle Ages and, more recently, recommended by Pope John Paul I to any bishops who visited him during his brief tenure. In the three books of the *Dialogues,* Gregory describes the edifying lives of a number of Italian saints. The second book is devoted to St. Benedict. From this it was concluded that he was himself a disciple of Benedict, and his authority among later monks increased greatly as a result. Gregory was particularly appreciated by the 12th-century Cistercians.

Bede the Venerable

Bede (672–735) was a Benedictine monk of Jarrow in England who devoted his life to Christian scholarship, especially in works of history and biblical commentary. He seems to have combined Celtic piety with Roman monastic customs, taking his main theological stances from Augustine and Gregory. Together with the writings of Isidore of Seville (ca. 560–636), his works were appreciated and read as a compendium of traditional wisdom.

Penitentials

Penitentials were introduced into Europe by waves of Celtic monks following in the wake of St. Columban (540–615). These noncanonical manuals for confessors presupposed the frequent reception of private penance rather than the public practice favored earlier. The books contained detailed listing and grading of sins, together with appropriate penances. The effect of such usage was to inculcate a morality of limits, often with detriment to a more fundamental moral stance. The idea that works of penance could offset the malice of sin was also potentially dangerous, especially when machinery was provided for the commutation of penances into something less costly. It has also been suggested that such manuals may have been instruments of social control rather than aids to pastoral care.

Reformed Monasticism

As Europe changed, the monastic institution accommodated itself to a variety of different situations. Under Charlemagne, Benedict of Aniane (745–821) began a movement to unify the scattered monasteries of the Benedictine observance. With the foundation of Cluny in 910, the principle of a wider organization to complement autonomous local monasteries seems to have been established, and the way was prepared for the emergence of religious orders operating within the Church under a universal mandate and somewhat exempt from local control.

In the 11th century many reforms appeared under the guidance of charismatic leaders such as Peter Damian (1007–1072). The spirit of renewal received an impetus during the papacy of Gregory VII (1021–1085), resulting in the formation of many new orders, including the Cistercians and Norbertines, and the revitalization of many existing groups.

The 12th century marked a high point in Western spirituality in the group clustered around Bernard of Clairvaux (1090–1153) and in the school of St. Victor. An increasing appreciation of the self meant greater profundity in treating of spiritual experience and more sensitivity in mapping the rhythms of personal growth.

Later Middle Ages

As Western society began to change rapidly, new religious orders evolved, each with a distinctive spirituality to match a particular social layer. The 13th century witnessed the activities of Dominic (1170–1221) and Francis (1181–1226). There was a new interest in the writings of Pseudo-Dionysius. In Flanders and Germany centers of mysticism flourished, and the movement known as *devotio moderna* produced *The Imitation of Christ*. The 14th century was a period of great spiritual

energy in England with figures such as Richard Rolle (ca. 1300–1349), Walter Hilton (d. 1395), Julian of Norwich (1342–ca. 1420), and the authors of the *Ancrene Riwle* and *The Cloud of Unknowing*.

Progressively, however, spirituality was becoming privatized; the general level of spiritual life in the Church was declining. There were many reasons for this. Some were social, for example, the impact of the Black Death on morale in general. Human weakness undoubtedly played a role. Other factors were the result of a slow accumulation. The liturgy had ceased to be a source of vitality. Theology was reduced to a dialectic that developed the mind but did not feed the spirit. There was a drift toward clericalism, with the consequent alienation of the masses. Moral teaching was distorted, with the result that the practical challenge of the gospel was undermined by an unrealistic idealism on the one hand and by the search to escape excessive guilt on the other, for instance, by seeking the security of comprehensive legal structures. Finally, the official Church did not visibly implement the principles it inculcated in others. Meanwhile, the problems were so apparent that much pastoral energy was expended in solving them, often at the price of losing contact with the positive sources of renewal within the spiritual tradition.

Counter-Reformation

If we accept Cardinal Poole's assessment that the Reformation was brought about by people who sought "a religion of the heart," it follows that the crisis of the 16th century had spiritual components as well as divergent theologies. The spirituality that evolved in response to the division of the Church was often defensive, its agenda determined by current "errors" to be refuted and by the erosion of continuity evident in the 14th to the 16th century. Rationality, consistency, and organization were fostered; individual direction and various spiritual techniques assumed an importance hitherto unknown. The great teachers such as Ignatius Loyola (1491–1556), Teresa of Avila (1515–1582), John of the Cross (1542–1591), Francis de Sales (1567–1622), and Cardinal Bérulle (1575–1629) personally transcended these limitations, but not all their followers succeeded in doing so. To a large extent, the link with the ancient Western tradition of spirituality was broken. Schools of spirituality tended to multiply with every new religious order, each based on a particular devotion or activity. To some extent this situation lasted until the Second Vatican Council, and its effects are still tangible.

Liturgy was marginalized. Contemplative prayer was reserved for an elite. Belonging to a community became more a matter of submitting to an institution than of communion between persons. Private morality (especially in sexual matters), obedience to the hierarchy, and attention to detail became paramount virtues. Lay people were not taken seriously. Freedom and spontaneity became suspect. Creativity and innovation were interpreted as subversion, the body and the emotions were treated as hostile, art was considered irrelevant.

The outcome was a generalized approach to spirituality that was rational, institutional, and controlled. Human values ceded priority to law, identified with God's will. Although generosity was often high, spiritual transformation was not universally evident. High levels of immaturity, alienation, and resentment beset many of the most fervent, inhibiting their progress and sometimes exploding in a radical change in life's direction.

Without the benefit of a living tradition, ancient authors were read and quoted in such a way that they seemed to support this ideology. As a result, they are today often bundled together and dismissed as proponents of a dehumanizing approach to religion. The problem is more accurately located during the last four centuries.

Since Vatican Council II

Inevitably the search for an authentic spirituality in the Roman Catholic Church has led in many directions: to experimentation, to a baptism of contemporary social movements, to the adoption of other traditions: Protestant, Eastern Orthodox, and non-Christian. The potential of the ancient spiritual traditions of the West is not, however, widely recognized.

The formulation of a spirituality that does not involve denial of Western identity and culture is an urgent task facing the Church. It can be difficult to find spiritual guidance in the writings of the distant past. Not all elements of the ancient syntheses are applicable today. Some conclusions owed more to Stoicism and Neoplatonism than to the gospel. The static view of world order typical of Augustinianism has been superseded. Any form of dualism is not acceptable. There is a particular problem with certain terms that have in subsequent centuries assumed connotations foreign to their original meaning. Often modern readers find difficulty in appreciating the rhetorical conventions followed by the Fathers, particularly when using a translation.

Despite these difficulties, contact with the Latin tradition can help. The first principle is to offset the privatizing of religion that has been occurring in the past four hundred years. In the best phases of Western spirituality we find a profoundly biblical approach to Christian life, one that entered into dialogue with contemporary philosophies and sought to ground the spiritual life in a broadly based anthropology. There was a recognition of the need for involvement in community, an appreciation of culture and human values, and a constant challenge to incarnate what was experienced inwardly with the reality of daily behavior in both public and domestic spheres. At the same time there was a depth of understanding of rhythms of inner experience, a capacity to discern what was authentic, and a general approach which was not problem-centered but which understood the whole range of spiritual activities to be a natural expression of one aspect of human reality.

The council advocated a spirituality that was scriptural and liturgical, that had sufficient self-understanding to enable it to enter into dialogue with other traditions, and that confronted the problems associated with interaction with the real world and the creation of a culture responsive to Christian values. The only way that such an enterprise will be successful is for the West to own its historical roots. Understood in its own context, the distinguished past of Western spirituality can be instrumental in generating a contemporary synthesis that is both ancient and modern.

See also AUGUSTINIAN SPIRITUALITY; BENEDIC-TINE SPIRITUALITY; BRIDAL MYSTICISM; CARMEL-ITE SPIRITUALITY; CELTIC SPIRITUALITY; CISTER-CIAN SPIRITUALITY; DOMINICAN SPIRITUALITY; ENGLISH MYSTICAL TRADITION; FRANCISCAN SPIR-ITUALITY; FRENCH SCHOOL OF SPIRITUALITY; IGNATIAN SPIRITUALITY; JOURNEY (GROWTH & DE-VELOPMENT IN SPIRITUAL LIFE); MARTYRDOM; PATRISTIC SPIRITUALITY; REFORMATION AND CATH-OLIC REFORMATION SPIRITUALITIES; RHENO-FLEMISH SPIRITUALITY; SALESIAN SPIRITUALITY; SPIRITUALITY, CHRISTIAN (CATHOLIC), HISTORY OF; VATICAN COUNCIL II; WESTERN MEDIEVAL SPIRITUALITY.

Bibliography: P. Brown, *The Body and Society: Men, Women, and Sexual Renunciation in Early Christian-ity* (London: Faber, 1989). C. Butler, *Western Mysti-cism: The Teaching of SS. Augustine, Gregory, and Bernard on Contemplation and the Contemplative Life: Second Edition with Afterthoughts* (London: Consta-ble, 1926). M. Colish, *The Stoic Tradition from Antiq-uity to the Early Middle Ages,* 2 vols. (Leiden: Brill, 1985). E. R. Elder, ed., *The Spirituality of Western Christendom,* Cistercian Studies 30 (Kalamazoo, Mich.: Cistercian Publications, 1976). B. McGinn and J. Meyendorff, eds., *Christian Spirituality: Origins to the Twelfth Century,* World Spirituality 16 (New York: Crossroad, 1985). C. Mohrmann, *Etudes sur le latin des chrétiens,* 4 vols. (Rome: Edizioni di storia e letteratura, 1961–1977). N. Ryan, ed., *Christian Spir-itual Theology: An Ecumenical Reflection* (Melbourne: Dove, 1976).

MICHAEL CASEY, O.C.S.O.

WESTERN MEDIEVAL SPIRITUALITY

Medieval spirituality will be examined here according to three levels that may be distinguished: (1) the real or existential level of individual spiritual experience; (2) the spirituality of social groups and varying spiritual traditions; (3) spirituality as the object of study and reflection. This article will confine itself to Western Catho-lic spirituality.

The Existential Level of Individual Spiritual Experience

Since it is impossible to survey here the spiritual experience of medieval individu-als on this existential level, this section will examine the medieval *sources* that can be used for studying this first level. Autobiog-raphies are scarce: examples are those by Othlo of St. Emmeram and Guibert of Nogent, Ramon Lull's *Vita coaetanea,* the *Vita* of Henry Suso, *The Book of Margery Kempe.* Such works sometimes need to be read critically because of possible interpo-lations by scribes or later copyists. Allu-sions to the author's own experiences, as in the works of Richard Rolle, can provide in-sight. Among the most useful sources are personal accounts of spiritual experiences such as those by Hildegard of Bingen, Francis of Assisi, Hadewijch of Antwerp, Mechtild of Magdeburg, Juliana of Liège, Ramon Lull, Gertrude the Great, Angela of Foligno, Bridget of Sweden, Catherine of Siena, Julian of Norwich, and Margery Kempe. Written lives of saints that de-scribe their lived spirituality must be read with caution. For the most part, authors of such lives select materials according to their own or a generally received view of holiness (e.g., taking consecrated religious as almost exclusive models); also, they gen-erally confine themselves to edifying state-ments or accounts.

A more profound insight into a person's spiritual life may be gleaned from personal letters in which one person assists another in spirituality or discusses spiritual matters, e.g., the letters of Leander of Seville, Columbanus, Bernard of Clairvaux, Peter the Venerable, Clare of Assisi, Abelard and Heloise (if they are authentic), Hildegard of Bingen, Hadewijch of Antwerp, Catherine of Siena, Henry Suso, Jan van Ruysbroeck, John Gerson. Homilies or sermons can provide information insofar as they reveal the personal traits and spirituality of the preacher, as with Gregory the Great, Bede, Peter Damian, Bernard, Abelard, Aelred of Rievaulx, Bonaventure, Meister Eckhart, John Tauler, and others.

Prayers composed by authors such as Anselm, Bonaventure, Aquinas, and Gertrude the Great are one of the better sources, as are the vast variety of religious poems or hymns produced throughout the Middle Ages, such as those of Columba, Venantius Fortunatus, Bede, Alcuin, Theodulf of Orléans, Rabanus Maurus, Hroswitha of Gandersheim, Peter Damian, Abelard, Hildegard of Bingen, Adam of St. Victor, Philip the Chancellor, Hadewijch of Antwerp, Thomas Aquinas, Jacopone da Todi, John Gerson, Denis the Carthusian, and many others. Liturgies composed by individuals can provide similar indications when it is clear that the liturgy in question reflects the author's own spirit. For the lived spirituality of individual laypersons, wills or testaments, if they are not merely repeated formulae, may furnish evidence of how such persons viewed and lived their Christian life; the same is true of donations or commissions of works of art. Similar indications may sometimes be found in court rolls and other sources of social history. Finally, much may be gleaned indirectly about the spiritual experience of an author from his or her treatises on life in the Spirit.

Varying Spiritual Traditions and the Spirituality of Social Groups or Schools

Although spirituality as a lived experience must be personal, this experience is neither received nor lived in isolation. Each person is spiritually embedded in the culture of social groups as small as the family and the parish and as large as the universal Church. Hence medieval spirituality should also be considered in its communitarian or corporate aspects. Different forms of medieval spirituality on this level will be examined in three ways: (a) as developing within varying cultural backgrounds; (b) as influenced by and expressing different theological trends; (c) as taught and practiced by particular schools of spirituality.

Cultural Backgrounds of Varying Medieval Spiritualities

In contrast with recent developments, the varieties of medieval spirituality grew within societies basically united in one Catholic faith and in one Church. A major exception to this unity was the schism that separated Eastern and Western Christendom, so that, except for a few Oriental groups remaining united with Rome, Eastern spirituality was represented by various branches of Orthodoxy.

Sometimes the unity of Western Christendom was also disturbed by spiritual movements judged heretical, such as the Bogomils, the Cathars (including the Albigensians), the Waldensians, some followers of Joachim of Fiore, some Beguines and Beghards. As Jewish intellectual schools developed, Judaism influenced Christian authors such as Andrew of St. Victor but also challenged some accepted Christian views. Although the Muslims were a constant threat, they at the same time influenced Western technology, philosophy, and theology; they seem, however, to have had less impact on spirituality, except in Spain.

Within this general homogeneity, however, inculturation of the gospel led to varying emphases in spiritual traditions and schools of spirituality. This phenomenon is probably better named "acculturation," that is, the interaction between the preaching of the gospel and the different cultures leading to changes on both sides.

This interaction and mutual change often took place under the leadership of charismatic persons.

In the East, an evident example of such acculturation was the central role given to expression of the gospel through liturgical rites, icons, hymns, and devotional practices developed in various art forms and in languages such as Greek in the Byzantine Church, Old Slavonic in the Russian and Ukrainian Churches, and Syriac, Coptic, Georgian, and Armenian in other areas. A further example of such interaction is the variety in monastic traditions that prevailed in different parts of the East, e.g., the different monastic communities gathered on Mount Athos or the distinct types of cenobitic or idiorhythmic monastic life in the Russian tradition. These monastic spiritualities often influenced lay spirituality.

In the West, Christianity, including its forms of spirituality, was likewise shaped by the way diverse cultures received the gospel. If the Roman Latin outlook, with its tendency to moralism and legal structures, was dominant, the deeper roots of other cultures such as the Celtic, Gallican, Germanic, and Iberian produced significant variations in spiritualities within the acculturation process. These deeper roots beneath the Latin cultural overlay must be recognized, especially for understanding lay spirituality; the fact that the teachers of spirituality were usually clerics trained in Latin might foster an illusion of uniformity and obscure the presence of such deeper sources of varying spiritualities. In fact, Western Catholic spirituality in the Middle Ages exhibits no uniform pattern.

In the West, these culturally adapted variations in spirituality manifested themselves in many ways. Within the liturgy, tropes, verses, and hymns gave expression to and formed corporate spirituality; thus the later *Stabat Mater* and *Dies irae* exhibit a more personally affective spiritual attitude than do the earlier *Vexilla Regis* and *Victimae paschale laudes,* with their noble and sober spiritual intensity.

Architectural and artistic products, whether of high quality or not, give some indication of the spiritualities of different times and places. On the one hand, medieval enthusiasm for building cathedrals evidences both clerical and lay spirituality. On the other hand, the separation of the laity from the altar by large choirs and/or rood screens reflects a strongly hierarchical view of the Church as well as a failure to see the Eucharist as active celebration by the whole People of God. The development of private chapels, oratories, and chantries indicates the loss of a sense of corporate worship and a sometimes excessive concern for prayers for the dead. Eucharistic devotion may also be seen in various forms of artifacts such as ciboria, pyxes, tabernacles for reservation, monstrances, vestments, etc. The development, first of crosses, then of crucifixes and other depictions of Christ's passion, provide evidence of growing concentration on this aspect of spirituality. Statues of Mary and the saints run the gamut of spiritual moods.

Historical accounts and literature about the Crusades (1095–1396) give a picture of the vagaries, sound or disordered, of medieval spirituality. They demonstrate, for instance, growth in medieval devotion to the human Christ, and so to the places where he lived, as well as enthusiasm for relics of all kinds brought back to the West for veneration. They express the ideal of martyrdom as well as a more practical concern for indulgences (an important part of medieval spirituality), but they also reveal hostile judgments about the religion and spirituality of non-Christians. This hostility is, of course, most evident with regard to the Muslim ("infidel") opponents of the Crusaders, but it shows itself as well in the sufferings inflicted on Jews met on the way. Indeed, anti-Semitism must be reckoned a case of disordered, misdirected medieval "spirituality," as is clear from accounts of disputations, repression, and the evidence of sermons, writings, liturgy, art, etc.

Evidence of pilgrimage piety and popular devotion to various saints witnesses to trends in the spirituality of different groups of people. Dedications, donations, inscriptions, and treatises or manuals of piety may also yield information about the spirituality of differing times and places. Widely read literary works such as Boethius's *Consolation of Philosophy,* Dante's *Divine Comedy,* William Langland's *Piers Plowman,* and Chaucer's *Canterbury Tales* provide insight into varieties of spiritual outlook that might remain unknown if one were to rely only on explicitly spiritual treatises. A very fruitful way of access to medieval spirituality is through study of medieval religious drama. Begun within the liturgy, such drama moved outside the church building in order to present more elaborate plays about creation, Christ's passion, miracles, and morality. Since these plays were usually performed in the vernacular, they probably affected attitudes of people as intensely as do films or television today.

Rules for monasteries and religious orders, together with accounts of visitations, may indicate the spiritual ideals that were sought. Canonical collections or synodal decrees also show, sometimes only indirectly by their opposition to disorders, the spiritual views of their authors. Records of preaching in churches or in public, while revealing frequent allegorization of Scripture, exhibit attitudes about vices to be avoided and examples of spiritual ideals. Treatises on pastoral care present both the spiritual concerns and ideals of their authors as well as of those for whom they were written. Although penitentials, books used by confessors, deal mainly with sin, they point to different levels of medieval spirituality by the judgments they make about the kind and seriousness of sins.

Some Theological Trends Influencing and Expressing Spiritualities

Because the Scriptures were used so much in preaching, instruction, and guidance in the spiritual life, the way they were read and interpreted was important to the spiritual life of the people, and especially to the spirituality of monks and nuns, whose lives were deeply formed by their practice of *lectio divina.* It also affected theological inquiry and therefore spirituality to the extent that Scripture informed theology (this was less the case from the 14th century on). Medieval readers of Scripture generally paid less attention to the literal-historical sense and stressed patristic methods of spiritual interpretation, often systematized into three "senses" or meanings: the typological and/or allegorical, the tropological or moral, and the anagogical or eschatological. Although exegetes such as Andrew of St. Victor and Thomas Aquinas insisted that the literal-historical sense should be the solid basis for such spiritual interpretation and application, medieval spirituality by and large used the three spiritual senses.

Theology influenced spiritual attitudes about *God* by examining, among many other questions, the relation between the justice of an awesome, dreaded God (thought by many to be at work in the Black Plague) and the mercy of a tender, forgiving God. God's presence in and to all creation was widely felt. The doctrine of Trinitarian vestiges in all creatures and the clearer image of God or the Trinity in the human person were key elements in some spiritualities. Augustine's doctrine of human deification by grace, although often neglected, nevertheless had some influence, especially when it was later combined with the Eastern theme of *theōsis.* These doctrines provided a theological basis for understanding how a person's spiritual life may progress on the way to mystical union with God.

Despite this teaching of Augustine on the positive effects of grace, his doctrine of the deep wounding of human nature through *original sin,* itself transmitted through sexual intercourse, together with his pessimism about the number of the predestined, strongly penetrated theology and spirituality and led to discouragement about the human condition. Anselm and Aquinas did indeed alter this doctrine significantly by locating the essence of original sin in the disordered human will rather than in disordered sensual concupiscence. Nevertheless, Augustine's doctrines continued their influence, evoking constant concerns about predestination, grace, free will, and human meriting of salvation.

In Christian *anthropology,* Neoplatonic dualism and Stoic disdain of the passions, channeled into the West by the Church Fathers, produced fear and downplaying of the good aspects of the passions or emotions, the body, sexuality, and spontaneous human activity. Aristotle's influence led Albert the Great and Thomas Aquinas to positive, integrated views of the role these elements play in spirituality. Their doctrine, however, did not prevail. Medieval spirituality therefore continued to stress suppression of the emotions by the will, severe mortification of the body, morbid fear of sexuality, and watchful reserve concerning human activity, especially activity in a world judged dangerous and sinful.

With respect to human *moral-spiritual activity,* if Augustine and Aquinas stressed Christian freedom guided by the Holy Spirit within the New Law, the stronger tendency in spirituality was toward a moralism emphasizing obedience to laws and commands. In contrast with Eastern spirituality, the Holy Spirit's role was often forgotten or downplayed. In the later Middle Ages nominalism reinforced a moralism of obligation by teaching that moral right or wrong depends on an arbitrary divine will rather than on God's "reasons" reflected in the natures and finalities of creatures. Spiritual guidance or assistance generally followed this pattern, stressing obedience to another person (hence the phrase "spiritual *direction*"). This contrasts with Aquinas's view that a person, because created in the image of God and assisted by the Holy Spirit, should exercise self-counsel and discernment as a preparation for personal prudential judgments.

The dominant Augustinian *interiorism* affected medieval spirituality by advocating a journey from the external beauty of God's creation to the interior of the human mind and thence upward to the Trinity. Monastic liturgy and contemplative experience applied this interiorism in a search for the anticipated joy of heaven. This spirituality of interiority, so fruitful in many ways, was reflected in earlier centuries not only by monastic withdrawal from the world but also, at least partially, by the theme of contempt for the world (*contemptus mundi*); it undoubtedly led to the common view that the loftiest spirituality is that lived by religious. Lay spiritualities thus often tended to be watered-down versions of religious life.

While Bonaventure used Augustinian interiorism in a masterful way, the foundations for genuine lay spirituality were laid by Aquinas's revival of Irenaeus's theme that God is most perfectly glorified when each creature and all creatures together reach the ends for which God created them. For Aquinas, even if human persons by reason of their very being can find their absolutely final end and perfect happiness only in the beatific vision, they also glorify God by achieving other ends within the world rather than apart from it. Further research may show whether and to what degree Aquinas's views influenced the nonmonastic spiritualities of laypersons involved in the guilds or confraternities that flourished in the later Middle Ages.

Images of *Jesus Christ* and attitudes toward him influenced spirituality. In earlier centuries the image of Christ as all-powerful *Pantokrator* was sometimes tempered by portrayals of him as the Good

Shepherd or as the Good Samaritan healing the wayfarer robbed of grace and wounded in nature. Although medieval theology generally embraced a "descending" Christology (the divine Word "coming down" to become human), in the 12th century the "*assumptus homo*" theory expounded an "ascending" Christology (this man being "taken up" to be God). At the same time, Augustine's view of Christ as Head of the Body that is the Church played a role in ecclesiology and popular piety. (The term "*Mystical* Body" is not Augustinian; first applied to the Eucharist, it was afterward used to refer to the Church.)

Also, in the 12th century Bernard and his fellow Cistercians increasingly dwelt on Christ's humanity within a more affective spirituality. This trend was further intensified through the example and teaching of Francis of Assisi, the Franciscans, and the Poor Clares, whose piety increasingly focused on Christ's passion and death. Increased attention to Christ's wounds followed, leading some 13th-century mystics and writers to develop, within their spiritual experience, devotion to the heart of Jesus. Among these writers were Gertrude the Great; her novice mistress, Mechtild of Hackeborn; and a Beguine, Mechtild of Magdeburg. Bonaventure (*Lignum vitae* 8:30) and Thomas Aquinas (*In Ps.*21[22]: 15) also speak movingly in their writings of the heart of Jesus. The Black Death, together with the travails of frequent warfare, led to apocalyptic emphasis on Christ as the feared Judge coming to separate the sheep from the goats, as in the *Dies irae;* other eschatological themes, already present in earlier periods, grew stronger in the later Middle Ages.

Theological and popular presentations of *Christ's saving work* deeply affected medieval spiritualities. Earlier theories of Christ battling and overcoming the devil, including the medieval interpretation of the harrowing of hell, kept the devil and his temptations prominent in a combative type of spirituality. Anselm's merit-satis-

faction theory of redemption shifted attention to relations between human persons and God, to Christ's love and obedience as infinitely meritorious and as fully satisfactory of the infinite debt owed to God because of sin. Later theology and spirituality, however, sometimes deformed this into a "satis-passion" theory, as if Christ's sufferings in and of themselves were saving. This outlook twisted some spiritualities into the unhealthy direction of excessive penitential practices aimed at subduing the body and imitating Christ's sufferings. Stress on satisfaction, even when viewed correctly as active love and obedience expressed in penance, nevertheless led to emphases on works of satisfaction, including those for sins confessed, and to greater concern about purgatory and indulgences—serious concerns of later medieval spirituality. Christ's resurrection, although discussed by theologians, did not have the spiritual impact in the West that it had in the East.

When Christ, like his Father, was perceived as a stern judge, medieval devotion tended to turn to the *saints,* and especially to Mary, viewed as closer, more sympathetic helpers or even as mediators with Christ and the Father. The honor paid to Mary, the angels, and the saints in earlier medieval times developed into active invocation of them. Feast days and paraliturgical Offices, visits to Marian and other shrines, accounts of revelations and favors granted by Mary or other saints, dedications of churches and religious orders, the rosary, litanies, and other prayers, artistic presentations, legends, poetry, and hymns honoring Mary and the saints all combined to shift a great deal of medieval spirituality from centering on Christ to excessive focusing on Mary and on other saints, e.g., the archangel Michael, the apostles Peter and James (pilgrimages to Rome and Compostela), Mary Magdalene, Martin, Thomas à Becket, and others.

For monks and nuns, the community's *Eucharistic celebration* and choral Office centered their spirituality on Christ and his saving work made present in the Eucharist. For most of Christ's faithful, however, ignorance of Latin, together with physical separation from the sanctuary in larger churches, combined with lack of instruction to exclude them from active participation in these liturgies. Allegorical explanations of the ceremonies, such as those of Amalarius of Metz, related each liturgical action to some part of Christ's life and passion. These commentaries may have helped popular piety, but they deflected it from a soundly based Eucharistic spirituality.

Diminished appreciation of the centrality of the Eucharistic celebration also resulted from theological disputes about the presence of Christ's Body and Blood in the consecrated elements. Devotion increasingly centered on this presence and miracles associated with it. This devotion expressed itself in a fervent desire to view the consecrated species at the elevation of the Mass, and even more by the liturgical feast of Corpus Christi, with its attendant processions and singing. Further evidence of this shift was the increased practice of reserving the Eucharist in more elaborate tabernacles; sometimes placed in special chapels, these became the main focus of Eucharistic piety.

The devotion and spirituality of the faithful were fostered by *other liturgical exercises* such as processions within the liturgy, blessings for every kind of material object, exorcisms, and Rogation Days, which included processions in the fields with sung litanies and prayers for good crops.

Frequency of *confession* spread in early centuries from the monasteries to the people through the exhortations of monks engaged in apostolic work. The development of sacramental theology in the 12th century included much discussion about the sacrament of penance and led to the production of penitential books to guide confessors. By prescribing annual confession

to one's pastor, the Fourth Lateran Council (1215) fostered use of this sacrament. Following this council, the mendicant orders enthusiastically encouraged the people to confess more frequently and to perform many satisfactory penitential works or to lessen their rigor by the easier way of gaining indulgences.

Schools of Spirituality

Monasteries and religious orders. One of the main sources of the various schools of medieval spirituality was the rise of different monastic traditions and, later, of religious orders. Two monasteries near Marseilles, influenced by Cassian's experience of Eastern monasticism and by his *Institutes* and *Conferences,* had a strong ascetical flavor that may have been responsible for the spread of Massilianism (later called Semi-Pelagianism). This movement emphasized human effort at the beginning of justification (*initium fidei*). The monastery on the island of Lérins, founded by Honoratus, was also influenced by Eastern monasticism. The famous monastery of Iona in the Inner Hebrides, founded by Columba, became the center of Celtic spirituality. The strongly ascetical character of this spirituality continued in the forceful, controversial Columbanus, who, despite opposition, extended Celtic views and practices to the continent and finally established the influential monastery of Bobbio, located in northern Italy south of Pavia. Both Iona and Bobbio were important for including study and learning within monastic spirituality.

An exceptionally influential monastic movement was that derived from Benedict of Nursia, whose famous Rule became the guide for most Western monks from the 9th century onward. Drawing on earlier monastic guides, his Rule, written around 540, urged the following of Christ through obedience to fairly detailed prescriptions rather than attention to more general spiritual maxims, as with other monks. This obedience was guided by a patriarchal abbot. Benedict's Rule was tempered by prudence and by recognition of the vagaries of human nature. Although severe enough to overcome obstacles to spiritual growth, this way of life was less rigorous than others and spread rapidly. Benedictine spirituality owed much to Cassiodorus, who influenced subsequent Western monasticism by introducing into Benedictine life a dedication to learning that made monasteries repositories of classical and patristic literature. Although his foundations were absorbed into the Benedictine movement, they modified it by this acceptance of learning within the spiritual life.

Gregory the Great greatly helped the spread of Benedictine monasticism and spirituality because, as pope, he linked the Benedictine movement to the See of Rome. When clerical orders were introduced within Benedictine monasticism, apostolic service was joined to the original search for contemplative union with God. So strong was the Benedictine movement that in Gaul it eventually replaced or modified the monasticism based on the Rules of Caesarius of Arles and Columbanus. Parallel to monasteries of men were those of Benedictine women, where many outstanding spiritual persons flourished, such as Hroswitha, Heloise, Hildegard of Bingen, Gertrude of Hackeborn, and Gertrude the Great. In some cases abbesses governed monasteries that included sections for men as well as for women.

The 9th-century systematization of the Benedictine Rule achieved by Benedict of Aniane influenced the reform movement of Cluniac Benedictinism that began in the 10th century and continued for several centuries under a succession of impressive abbots. The monastery of Cluny, with hundreds of monasteries under its authority, became a powerful leader in Christian life and spirituality. Encouraging strict but adapted conformity to the Rule and a personal spiritual life oriented toward mystical contemplation, it emphasized an ever more splendid choir celebration of the liturgy as a way to combat evils in society and to give a foretaste of heaven on earth. While decorative arts and study flourished, the time devoted to manual labor decreased. Outstanding persons of distinctive character within the Cluniac family included Odo, Odilo, Peter the Venerable, Anselm of Bec (or Canterbury), and Rupert of Deutz.

Cistercian spirituality, furthered by its most famous representative, Bernard of Clairvaux, reacted strongly against the Cluniac version of spiritual life and adopted an austere regimen that clung to the original letter of Benedict's Rule. Like all monks, the Cistercians sought contemplative union with God but emphasized utter simplicity in architecture and liturgy, strict silence, sparse diet, and extensive manual labor as means to that union. The debates between Bernard and Peter the Venerable about Benedictine life are an outstanding example of discussions concerning spiritual ideals. The kind, temperate Peter appears more favorably in these debates than the rather fiercely judgmental Bernard. Some important Cistercians were William of St. Thierry, Aelred (Ethelred) of Rievaulx, Guerric of Igny, Isaac of Stella, and Joachim of Fiore, whose apocalyptic predictions deeply affected the spiritual outlook of many in subsequent centuries.

The eremitic tradition, so common in the East, found its most important Western representatives in the Carthusians, founded by Bruno. They combined a solitary life with gatherings on feast days for choral Office, Eucharistic celebration, and meals. The order maintained its fervor throughout the Middle Ages, especially in Spain, Italy, France, and also in England, where the Charterhouse provided a number of martyrs at the time of Henry VIII.

Another type of solitary life was that of anchorites and anchoresses. Since for Benedictines the life of a recluse was a higher spirituality, monks who were judged to be called to complete solitude were allowed to have cells separate from but near the monastery on the same property. In the later Middle Ages cells of recluse women and men were often attached to parish Churches. The *Ancrene Riwle* (or *Ancrene Wisse*), a guide for anchoresses, is an important witness to this type of spirituality, as are letters to recluses by such authors as Peter the Venerable and Aelred of Rievaulx.

The spirituality of the secular clergy often suffered from their being poorly educated and from abuses such as simony, lay investiture of unworthy persons, and other forms of control by feudal lords. The Gregorian reform of the late 11th century fought the sources of this decline, sought to establish clerical celibacy, and began to promote clerical life in communities of canons regular guided by the Rule attributed to Augustine. In addition to the influence of the Premonstratensian canons founded by Norbert, outstanding contributions to spiritual life and doctrine came from the canons regular of St. Victor in Paris. A series of outstanding mystical authors, including the theologians Hugh and Richard of St. Victor, the exegete Andrew of St. Victor, and the poet Adam of St. Victor, helped medieval spirituality by combining ascetic life and lofty contemplation with theological and spiritual writings.

Hugh and Richard spread knowledge of the important works of Pseudo-Dionysius the Areopagite in the West. This late 5th-century Eastern author wrote of God as the One and the Good above being and intelligibility, so that in his view union with God is better reached by the negative way of apophatic spirituality, that is, by denying names of God more than by proclaiming them in the affirmative way. He presented God's goodness as continually self-diffusive. His analyses of good, evil, and beauty entered later theology and spirituality, and his descriptions of angelic and ecclesial hierarchies—the latter including the sacraments—affected the whole outlook of later centuries, especially in ecclesiology. He provided influential teachings on symbolism and on the threefold levels of spiritual growth (purgation, illumination, and perfection) that lead to union with God when the person reaches a high state of perfection. This author profoundly affected the spiritual theology of Albert the Great, Bonaventure, and Aquinas. Albert was the source of this doctrine as used within the so-called speculative mysticism of his fellow Dominicans, Meister Eckhart, John Tauler, and Henry Suso, and of Jan van Ruysbroeck and others. As its title suggests, the anonymous 14th-century English work *The Cloud of Unknowing* was heavily indebted to Pseudo-Dionysius.

Although drawing on elements of the spirituality of the canons regular and the Benedictines, the mendicant orders that sprang up in the 13th century presented a new way of life in the Spirit. Franciscans, Dominicans, Carmelites, and Augustinians all shared the goal of contemplative mystical union with God fostered by choral Office, asceticism, and, in varying degrees, contemplative study. What was new was that they forsook Benedictine insistence on monastic stability, which often confined monks to one monastery in the countryside, in order to move about, especially in the growing towns and cities, doing apostolic work flowing from their contemplative experience. Whereas monasteries were independent unless they were grouped like the Cluniacs, the mendicants were tightly organized orders under general superiors, so that their members could move from one house to another. The spiritualities of each order varied according to the example and ideals of their founders and their distinct traditions. Second orders of mendicant women led cloistered contemplative lives and supported their brothers in the first orders by lives of prayer and penance.

In the 12th and 13th centuries the great theologians incorporated spiritual doctrine within their theology. In subsequent centuries, however, theological investigations, frequently neglecting Scripture, became so encumbered by endless disputations about the nature of theology or about what God can or cannot do by his absolute or well-ordered power that those seeking deeper life in the Spirit turned to more practical forms of spirituality.

Lay spirituality. Beguines (women) and *Beghards* (men) were mostly middle- or upper-class persons from northwestern European cities who led lives of chastity, poverty, and devotion without belonging to a religious order. Beguines first appeared in the late 12th century and were much more numerous than their male counterparts, the Beghards, who first appeared in the early 13th century. In fact, the movement was not only predominantly female but is noteworthy for being the only medieval female religious movement not inspired or guided by men. Some lived at home, others—especially the women—gathered in beguinages, which were either houses or walled-in settlements. Some Beghards practiced wandering mendicancy. The spirituality of these women and men seems to have been analogous to that of the mendicant orders, that is, it grew from a desire to follow the gospel ideal by lives of simplicity and piety without cloistered separation from the world. Many beguinages were centers of intense mystical experience, from which emerged writings such as those of Beatrice of Nazareth, Hadewijch of Antwerp, and Marguerite Porete. Suspicion, charges of heresy, and inconsistent ecclesiastical policy often troubled the Beguines and Beghards, but for the most part they continued in existence.

A very important, mainly lay movement called *devotio moderna* grew especially around the school of Windesheim. Gerard Groote and Florens Radewijns were leaders in the formation of a group called the Brethren of the Common Life, who assisted a similar group called the Sisters of the Common Life. Theirs was a practical devout life, without legal formal status or vows—for one reason, because founding new religious communities had been forbidden. They lived in a manner suited to the growing number of literate, self-conscious bourgeoisie uninterested in a speculative type of mysticism. Important authors of this school were Gerlach Peters, Hendrik Mande, and Thomas á Kempis, generally thought to be the author of *The Imitation of Christ.* This popular book stressed interior contemplative themes but tended to look down on speculation in favor of intense practical piety.

Third orders were another manifestation of lay spirituality. In the 12th century, lay penitential groups sought Christian perfection and a life of penance while carrying on their life and work in the world. With the rise of the Dominicans and Franciscans in the 13th century, some of these groups sought links with these orders for spiritual guidance and help. They were gradually organized into third orders of Dominicans and Franciscans, sharing the spiritual benefits of these communities, seeking to live their spirit, and imitating their practices as much as they could while remaining in the world.

Another important source of lay spirituality was the movement to form *guilds,* associations of merchants or craftsmen. These existed in some form in the earlier Middle Ages but became stronger throughout Europe from the 11th century on with the expansion of economic life in the growing cities. Although organized mainly for economic, educational, and social purposes, the guilds fostered spiritual values among the members. They usually had a patron saint who inspired their work or trade and whose feast the members celebrated in the saint's chapel in the local church; they also gathered there for commemorations of deceased members. Guilds were at times religious confraternities and burial societies, as well as agents of charity toward the widows and orphans of former members and toward the poor of the city. Some guilds took on responsibility for producing the religious dramas that expressed and formed much of later medieval lay spirituality.

The formation of *confraternities* of lay people is further evidence of the interest of the faithful in spirituality. Already present in the 12th century, they grew in the 13th century, when, for example, the desire to share in the Corpus Christi processions led guilds to form such religious unions. Helped in some cases by the religious orders, confraternities flowered greatly in the 14th and 15th centuries. Often linked with guilds, their spirituality penetrated human work, the family, and social life. Confraternities were organized to care for all human misery, especially the suffering of the poor and the sick. If the rules of some of these confraternities seemed to focus on externals, they did seek to stimulate a deeper spiritual life. This was especially true of the confraternities devoted to penance, the passion of Christ, and the Eucharist. One special form of confraternity developed in many Italian cities to sing *laude*—nonliturgical musical hymns of praise. These hymns may have been inspired by Francis of Assisi's canticle of praise, which he urged his friars to sing publicly in order to instruct and edify the people.

Spirituality as the Object of Study and Reflection

Although instruction in the spiritual life was regularly given in monasteries, religious orders, and lay associations in the Middle Ages, spirituality as such was not studied formally as it is today in academic faculties or programs. Medieval studies of spirituality must therefore be sought either in practical treatises seeking to help others advance in their spiritual lives or within theological works.

Practical Treatises

Practical treatises vary greatly; only a few examples can be indicated. Gregory the Great's *Moralia in Job* furnished extensive moral and spiritual teaching, together with considerable imagery—for example,

his teaching on the seven capital vices or his commendation of contemplation, which he allegorized through the biblical figures of Rachel and Mary in contrast to Leah and Martha, allegories of the active life. About the year 830, Jonas of Orléans wrote a work called *De institutione laicali,* which sought to give a spiritual teaching adapted to the faithful, especially married persons. Peter Damian contributed a number of treatises on spirituality for both monks and secular priests. Bernard's influential commentaries on the Song of Songs see the individual Christian as a bride of Christ; this work and his *De consideratione* are rich in practical advice and in descriptions of lofty mystical experience. William of St. Thierry's "Golden Letter" gained influence both because of its own merits and because it circulated under Bernard's name. Aelred of Rievaulx authored a *Speculum caritatis* as well as the remarkable *De spiritali amicitia,* which integrates Cicero's views of friendship within his own experience of Cistercian spirituality. Carthusian spirituality was admirably expressed in the works of Abbots Guigo I and Guigo II.

Hildegard of Bingen's *Scivias* is an early source of later Rhenish speculative mysticism. The discussions of religious life in the letters between Heloise and Abelard, whether this correspondence is authentic or not, reveal among other things a feminist challenge to some aspects of a male-oriented rule of life.

Numerous spiritual treatises by Hugh and Richard of St. Victor functioned as outstanding guides. Richard's *Benjamin minor* and *Benjamin major,* as well as his other works on the degrees of charity and interior states, established him as "la plus grand théoricien de la mystique au moyen âge" (Cayré 2:388). Bonaventure's *Itinerarium mentis in Deum,* together with his more practical treatises, made him an outstanding spiritual teacher throughout the later Middle Ages. Thomas Aquinas's *De perfectione vitae spiritualis* and his theological works stress the centrality of charity for spiritual perfection. The defense of mendicant religious life by Aquinas and Bonaventure was important to that aspect of medieval spirituality.

Spiritual writings in the vernacular began to appear. The Majorcan mystic Ramon Lull wrote a number of mystical works in Catalan; his *Book of the Lover and the Beloved* is, he says, modeled on the mysticism of the Muslim sufis. Eckhart's German works include, in addition to his many sermons outlining spiritual growth, the *Liber benedictus,* which despite its title was written in German. Henry Suso also wrote in German; his *Little Book of Eternal Wisdom* is more practical, whereas his *Little Book of Truth* is a speculative treatise about mysticism. Jan van Ruysbroeck's eleven spiritual treatises in Flemish had considerable influence.

English writers include the following: Richard Rolle of Hampole, whose *Incendium amoris* and *Emendatio vitae* were later translated into Middle English; the anonymous author of both *The Cloud of Unknowing* and *The Book of Privy Counselling;* Walter Hilton, who wrote his *Scala perfectionis* in English.

Later Latin treatises include the anonymous 14th-century *De adhaerendo Deo* and, in the 15th century, numerous works on mystical contemplation by Denis the Carthusian.

Theological Works

Too often neglected by students of spirituality are theological works that integrate spirituality within theology. Such works were produced by the 12th- and 13th-century commentators on Peter Lombard's *Sentences* and by writers of theological summae, who also treated issues of the spiritual life in their numerous commentaries on Scripture. Thus the 12th-century commentaries on Scripture by Gilbert of Poitiers and Peter Lombard had a continuing influence. Hugh of St. Victor's *De sacramentis,* written in the 12th century, is

an example of a work integrating theology and spirituality. Such integrated works increased in number in the 13th century, including commentaries on Lombard by Hugh of Saint-Cher, Richard Fishacre, Odo Rigaldus, Albert, Bonaventure, Thomas Aquinas, and others, together with the *Summa Fratris Alexandri* and the summae by William of Auxerre, Albert, Aquinas, and others.

Although these theological works may lack the affective warmth of spiritual treatises, they give solid theological principles in the many areas that affect life in the Spirit, for example, teachings on God's graciousness and call to a graced life, the missions and indwelling of the Trinitarian Persons, the gifts and fruits of the Holy Spirit, creation, the image of the Trinity in human persons, free will, the effects of sin, Christ's saving work, the Church and sacramental life, growth in grace, the theology of prayer, final beatitude, etc. The extensive scriptural commentaries of these same authors, too little studied, are rich in spiritual teaching and practical application.

A theologian whose writings come closer than others to modern studies of spirituality is John Gerson. In the early 15th century he consciously tried to give a proper theological basis for spiritual life. Seeing so many of his contemporaries neglect the Bible and patristic sources in favor of endless subtle disputes, he tried to offset the separation of spirituality from theology by composing several works—*De mystica theologia speculativa, De mystica theologia practica,* and *De vita spirituali*—in which spirituality was explicitly linked with theology. His attempt, however, failed to produce lasting results. Succeeding generations experienced increasing separation of "mystical" and then of "spiritual" or "affective" theology from their roots in the great truths of faith studied in theology. With this separation there came an impoverishment of spiritual writing through works examining spirituality in relation to a limited number of practical themes. Only in the present century have renewed efforts been made to link spirituality more intimately with the whole of theology.

See also AFFIRMATIVE WAY; APOCALYPTICISM; APOSTOLIC SPIRITUALITY; AUGUSTINIAN SPIRITUALITY; BENEDICTINE SPIRITUALITY; CAMALDOLESE SPIRITUALITY; CARMELITE SPIRITUALITY; CARTHUSIAN SPIRITUALITY; CELTIC SPIRITUALITY; CISTERCIAN SPIRITUALITY; DEVOTION(S), POPULAR; DOMINICAN SPIRITUALITY; EASTERN CHRISTIAN SPIRITUALITY; ENGLISH MYSTICAL TRADITION; EREMITICAL LIFE; EUCHARISTIC DEVOTION; FRANCISCAN SPIRITUALITY; ISLAMIC SPIRITUALITY; JEWISH SPIRITUALITY; LAY SPIRITUALITY; LECTIO DIVINA; MARY; MILLENARIANISM; MONASTICISM, MONASTIC SPIRITUALITY; MYSTICISM; NEGATIVE WAY; RELIGIOUS LIFE; RHENO-FLEMISH SPIRITUALITY; SAINTS, COMMUNION OF SAINTS; SPIRITUALITY, CHRISTIAN; SPIRITUALITY, CHRISTIAN (CATHOLIC), HISTORY OF; THIRD ORDERS; WESTERN (LATIN) SPIRITUALITY.

Bibliography: See articles on movements and persons in the following: Dictionary of the Middle Ages; Dictionnaire d'histoire et de géographie ecclésiastiques; Dictionnaire de spiritualité ascétique et mystique; New Catholic Encyclopedia. F. Cayré, Patrologie et histoire de la théologie, vol. 2, bks. 3 and 4 (Tournai: Desclée, 1955). J. Leclercq, F. Vandenbrouke, and L. Bouyer, The Spirituality of the Middle Ages (New York: Seabury, 1968). B. McGinn and J. Meyendorff, eds. Christian Spirituality: Origins to the Twelfth Century, World Spirituality 16 (New York: Crossroad, 1985). E. Petroff, ed., Medieval Women's Visionary Literature (New York: Oxford Univ. Press, 1986). W. Principe, "Christology," Dictionary of the Middle Ages (1983) 3:319–324; Introduction to Patristic and Medieval Theology, 2nd ed. (Toronto: Pontifical Institute of Mediaeval Studies, 1982); "Philosophy and Theology, Western Europe: Twelfth Century to Aquinas," Dictionary of the Middle Ages (1987) 9:590–606. J. Raitt, ed., Christian Spirituality: High Middle Ages and Reformation, World Spirituality 17 (New York: Crossroad, 1987). A. Vauchez, La spiritualité du moyen âge occidental: VIIIᵉ–XIIᵉ siècles (Paris: Presses universitaires de France, 1975). S. F. Wemple, "Women's Religious Orders," Dictionary of the Middle Ages (1989) 12:682–689.

WALTER H. PRINCIPE, C.S.B.

WILL

Will is a concept so central to moral anthropology that it is used by various and conflicting schools of thought. For all theorists, however, will implies a self, autonomy, agency, goals, and energy. The self wills; this is an expression of the self's autonomy. This will constitutes agency whereby the self interacts and cooperates with others for the sake of predetermined goals out of a flow of energy conceived precisely for the sake of attaining those goals. For many it is will that constitutes the fundamental difference between human and nonhuman forms of life; for others it is intelligence, and the will is the executive force of intelligence.

The fundamental notion underlying will is that it is a form of appetite: the reaching out of an imperfect being for something capable of perfecting it. To be human is to be hungry—for what sustains physical life, for what delights the senses, for what satisfies curiosity about fundamental meanings of life, for companionship, for self-expression, and for ultimate happiness. In all these many forms, humans find themselves imperfect or incomplete, needing assistance from outside themselves to sustain and stimulate them. All these forms of appetite are expressive of desire, which is an interior motion of feeling and wishing for an element capable of enhancing the self's sense of well-being.

Humans share appetite with the rest of the animal world. Will, however, is properly applied only to that form of appetite that pertains to humans. Animals possess physical and sense appetites, including hunger for food, companionship, and sexual gratification. Humans, in addition to these sense appetites, experience curiosity about, and desire for, objects that pertain to intellectually and spiritually conceived goals, for example, freedom, equality, and beauty.

Some, like Aquinas, held that the will is a passive power, understood in the sense that it is an appetite that seeks to obtain goods or goals offered to it by intelligence; thus intelligence (or discernment) plays the crucial role of determining the interest or object of the will. This view does not diminish the centrality or executive force of will but rather places will in reference to human knowledge and reflection as its cause. The classical dictum of Aquinas, "Nil volitum nisi praecognitum" ("Nothing is willed unless known ahead"), summarizes this.

Others, like Duns Scotus, held that the will is absolutely active: the will is the total cause of its own willing. From this view and its consequent development in nominalism and Enlightenment philosophy derives the understanding of human appetite as will-as-decision. Both of these positions require as psychological postulates the notion of distinct faculties of the soul—a notion generally dismissed as nonempirical and unprovable by contemporary philosophers and psychologists.

Usages

The term *will* can refer to distinct aspects of the human person:

1. *Will as act.* Here will refers to desiring, resolving, determining, choosing, and the like. All are forms of willing.

2. *Will as faculty.* This means the power or tendency within the person that tends toward acts of will. Since the will is a spiritual reality, it has to be conceived by analogy, and thus we can talk of a "seat" or "faculty" of willing as a human capacity.

3. *Will as subject.* The ego or the person is thought of as the subject "who wills." Since the will reaches out for union with spiritual reality, for God even, the will belongs uniquely to a subject capable of intersubjective relation with other spirits, and the human person must be so conceived in order to sustain a viable concept of will.

4. *Will as content or object of the willed act.* The law speaks of "a last will and testament," a concrete example of specified actions that pertain to the disposition of human will. One's will is often described in terms of its principal goals or objectives.

Will is related to freedom, since will is the origin of the problem of moral indetermination and responsible choice. While current legal usage presupposes the moral accountability of human choices for particular actions, freedom and free will are by no means universally respected as defensible notions. Various forms of determinism are dominant in psychological and social theories, including the physical determinism of behaviorism, which completely identifies the psychic with the physical, thus destroying the context for a meaningful interpretation of freedom.

Freud is usually interpreted as a biological determinist who, like certain behaviorists, reduces all human activity to reflex responses in the end. Psychological determinists either claim (like Socrates and Leibniz) that the will is coerced to accept the greatest value or the strongest motive, or claim (like Alfred Adler) that intellectual processes are so dominant in forming human character that will is merely acquiescence before these cognitive factors.

Christian humanist theories generally avoid the problem of determinism by holding on to two complementary dynamics: first, the will is the appetite of human intelligence and as such is moved by the knowledge offered by intellect; but, second, choice is still a matter of free self-determination, which touches precisely what, whether, when, and how deeply one wills that which intelligence has identified as good. There is hardly ever a moment when the human task is to choose one clearly denominated good in the presence of clearly evil alternatives. Most moral decisions embody the weighing of competing goods. Thus freedom of will engages not simply the resolution of conflicting claims but also the formation of character. Will has as its task not simply the resolution of dilemmas but also the spiritual deepening of the person. "For where your treasure is, there also will your heart be" (Mt 6:21).

Will and Character

Developmental psychology shows will to be foundational to one's moral evolution as a person. The infant who comes to life in a climate devoid of trust risks ending up in the limit situation of *autism*, a condition in which psychic life is completely enclosed

tion without acknowledgment of interpersonal relations. This is a condition in which the capacity to will is negated, symbolized by complete withdrawal from intersubjective exchange. Progress can rarely be made with children marked by severe autism, so fundamental is the need for will to human development. In parallel fashion, children who for various reasons feel unacknowledged or unaffirmed can develop manipulative traits that make real human exchange difficult. This is a condition in which will is imagined to be a domination over interpersonal reality rather than a force for dialogue and reciprocity. Adults who manifest such manipulative dispositions usually have severe difficulty in enjoying peer relationships.

Gerald May distinguishes between *willingness* and *willfulness* by contrasting fundamental attitudes that they manifest (*Will and Spirit*). Willingness is a surrendering of separateness and an entering into the forces of life itself; this demands a contemplative vision of the world as a Creator's gift. Willfulness is attempting to master, direct, control, or manipulate existence; this is based on a narcissistic reference to the impulses of the self. May's "contemplative psychology" refers to *wonder* as the differential experience that either allows "willing" persons to become part of a larger, mysterious universe of love and being or fails to move "willful" persons to release their grasp on attachment and their conscious or unconscious claim to absolute power over life. It is not surprising that May, as a psychotherapist, conceives of will as the moral core of the human person. The major therapeutic problems of our culture are situated around the capacity for free exchange among adult peers in cooperative interaction, unburdened of the threat of manipulation.

Changing Images of Will

The history of ideas has seen an endless exchange between those who see reality as dominated by "nature" and those who see it dominated by "freedom." One consequence has been the great multiplicity of definitions of will offered through the centuries. Paul Ricoeur uses as a central theme in his phenomenology of will the reciprocity between the voluntary and the involuntary. In human reflection, we must deal with equal integrity with both the "given" (nature) and the "desired" (freedom). To overcome the reductionism of those who would limit themselves to purely empirical accounts of reality, the thinker must weigh sympathetically both the whole scope of involuntary reality as part of an objective world and the full force of possibilities and images that erupt in the world of self-conscious reflection. This entire enterprise draws upon the resources of the will.

In moral theology, the ability to discriminate between voluntary and involuntary moments of thought and action is crucial. Recent moral theology has acknowledged the multiplicity of obstacles to complete moral freedom in ordinary situations. In pastoral practice, the continuing formation of adults in attitudes of responsibility is a needed and important aspect of Christian education. In addition to helping people to analyze what is objectively correct, pastoral practice must also help initiate individuals into habits and patterns of experience that expose them to, and sustain them in, familiarity with good, beautiful, and true realities, especially as these are shared with loved and admired friends.

Will and Contemplation

The dominant power of the will can be seen in the relation between the willing person and the object desired. Once some reality is intended as the goal of human willing and action, the willing person enters into a relation with the object that is specified not by his or her limited understanding and agency but by the reality of the object in its own domain.

Even if one imagines that willing demands knowledge as its basis, love of that which one wills may work reflexively on our knowledge, impelling us to greater study and deeper investment in that which we desire. Love seeks union. The will recognizes that the object of its intention will be joined to itself. In this way the will's tenacity in seeking God in prayer and contemplation is central to the transformation of the Christian's faith life.

By seeking the divine Other in accord with its own status of absolute simplicity, the devotee is drawn by love into increasingly simple, quiet forms of prayer and silence. The complacency of the believer's will in this kenosis of simplicity is a sign of grace and of the action of God's transforming power in the interior life of the believer. It is the nature of love to urge us on to deeper knowledge. This truer knowledge is destined to lead us also to fuller love by awakening us to the hidden mysteries of the one we love. Thus, in its fullest expression, will is seen to be so intimately linked to knowledge that the distinction between them appears to be artificial. Yet even so, the effort to distinguish can often clarify most helpfully the scope of human agency and so encourage us to persevere in the pursuit of both truth and goodness.

See also ANTHROPOLOGY, THEOLOGICAL; CONTEMPLATION, CONTEMPLATIVE PRAYER; DESIRE; MIND; SELF; SOUL.

Bibliography: G. May, *Will and Spirit: A Contemplative Psychology* (San Francisco: Harper & Row, 1982). P. Ricoeur, *Freedom and Nature: The Voluntary and the Involuntary,* trans. E. Kohak (Evanston, Ill.: Northwestern Univ. Press, 1966).

PAUL J. PHILIBERT, O.P.

WISDOM

Wisdom (Latin *sapientia*), as used in Scripture, liturgy, and theology, is a word with many rich meanings.

In Scripture

In Scripture, "Wisdom" is the title of a deuterocanonical book in the Greek Bible, or Septuagint (frequently referred to as the Old Testament by Christians). In this book, as in other sapiential books of the Bible, wisdom is presented as an attribute of God, an "effusion of the glory of the Almighty . . . the refulgence of eternal light . . . the image of [God's] goodness" (Wis 7:25-26).

Wisdom is also used to speak of God himself, the eternal Wisdom, and more specifically of the second Person of the Blessed Trinity, the Son of God, who as the Word is the total and adequate expression of the wisdom of God and who in his incarnation brought that wisdom to dwell among us. Jesus, "the wisdom of God" (Lk 11:49; 1 Cor 1:24), "in whom are hidden all the treasures of wisdom and knowledge" (Col 2:3), came as the authoritative teacher of wisdom.

Wisdom is also personified as a woman, born of God before all ages and active with God in the work of creation (Prov 8:22-30).

In the Liturgy

Liturgical texts attribute by accommodation some of the wisdom texts from the sapiential books to Christ, the Wisdom of God, and to Mary, the Seat of Wisdom, whom God called to collaborate in bringing the divine Wisdom into this world through the incarnation.

In Catholic Theology

In Catholic theology wisdom is one of the gifts of the Holy Spirit. The human person is raised up by baptism of water or desire to become a partaker of the divine nature and life. In order to function at this higher level of being, God endows the baptized with a new set of faculties called "the gifts of the Holy Spirit"—"gifts" because they are freely given to all at baptism; "of the Holy Spirit" because it is through them that the Holy Spirit, who is given to us at baptism to be our spirit, is able to act in our lives. By an accommodation of the text of Isa 11:2, "On him will rest the spirit of the Lord, the spirit of wisdom and understanding, the spirit of counsel and fortitude, the spirit of knowledge and piety, and the fear of the Lord will rest upon him," Catholics have traditionally spoken of the seven gifts of the Holy Spirit, numbering among them the gift of wisdom.

The Latin word *sapientia* comes from the word *sapere,* meaning "to savor," "to taste." Through the gift of wisdom the Holy Spirit enables us to taste and see how good the Lord is, to have a taste for the things of God, to sense the divine in all things. It bespeaks an experiential knowledge of God and of God's presence in all. As St. Paul says, "We have a wisdom .... This God has revealed to us through the Spirit. For the Spirit scrutinizes everything, even the depths of God" (1 Cor 2:5-10).

Wisdom is also understood as being an intellectual virtue that judges things in their highest causes and therefore is the noblest of the intellectual virtues. The person who considers maturely and without qualification the first and final cause of the entire universe will come to know God, as St. Paul attests (Rom 1:19). Hence wisdom appears in St. Augustine as knowledge of divine things (*De Trinitate* 12.14; PL 42:1009).

Theology, which is faith seeking understanding, goes to God most personally as deepest origin and highest end, not only because of what can be gathered by means of human wisdom but also because of what God alone knows about God's own self and yet discloses to us through revelation. Consequently theology, when it includes a true experiential knowledge of God through that love who is the Holy Spirit and when it contains an affective dimension as well as an intellectual one, is in itself a true wisdom.

Finally, prudence, insofar as it rules all the other moral virtues, is sometimes called "practical wisdom."

In Christian Life

The goal of Christian life is to think, understand, and act according to who we truly are as men and women who have been baptized into Christ. "Have among yourselves the same attitude that is also yours in Christ Jesus" (Phil 2:5). This is true wisdom.

Practically speaking, the Christian can seek to grow in wisdom by listening to the Sacred Scriptures. This listening, traditionally called *lectio divina,* should be grounded in solid, up-to-date Scripture studies. But it does not end there. Under the influence of the Holy Spirit and with the guidance of the Fathers of the Church and other men and women of the Spirit, this listening is open to the deeper meanings or senses of Scripture—the allegorical or mystical, the moral, and the analogical.

We also foster the practical growth of wisdom in our lives by opening ourselves to the activity of the Holy Spirit in the gift of wisdom through the practice of contemplative prayer. God, who made us and respects us more fully than all others, knows that our greatest gift is our freedom, because therein lies the power to love. God never violates our freedom. If we wish to always function at the level of our own very limited human reason, God will allow us to do that, but then we will never sense God and the things of God in the way that God does, in the way that is consonant with our divinized humanity. We can do this only through the activity of the Holy Spirit. Through the practice of contemplative prayer we abandon the use of our reason with its ideas, concepts, and images, and open the way for the Holy Spirit to act in us through his gifts, leading us into the fullness of divine wisdom.

See also CONTEMPLATION, CONTEMPLATIVE PRAYER; GIFTS OF THE HOLY SPIRIT; HOLY SPIRIT; MYSTICAL THEOLOGY; MYSTICISM; SCRIPTURE; VIRTUE.

Bibliography: K. Conley, *A Theology of Wisdom: A Study in St. Thomas* (Dubuque, Iowa: Priory Press, 1963). Thomas Aquinas, ST I, q. 1; II-II, q. 45.

M. BASIL PENNINGTON, O.C.S.O.

WITNESS

See MARTYRDOM.

WORK

The term *work* has had a great variety of meanings and connotations in the history of humankind. Greeks and Romans, though valuing agriculture, soldiering, and certain crafts from their earliest days, came to equate work, especially manual labor, with that of their slaves and to disdain it. Among the pagan Celts, by way of contrast, the *aes dana,* an entire class of workers that included skilled craftsmen, historians, lawyers, physicians, even poets and storytellers, held a status in many ways equal to that of the kings and warriors of the tribes. Germans and Anglo-Saxons associated their word for work, *Arbeit,* with hardship, suffering, and fatigue, while the French *travail* means toil, pain, and great difficulty.

In contemporary Western culture, definitions of work seem to reflect some of the same ambivalence as that of earlier cultures. Work is defined as physical or mental effort exerted to do or make something; as purposeful activity; as an occupation, business, trade, craft, or profession in which one's knowledge and skills are utilized. It is also defined as simply a means of employment or as labor or toil done in order to pay bills or meet expenses—in other words, as a "job" which, as necessary as it may be, a person often does with the hope of "moving on" to something else.

Many people are confused by these mixed messages from contemporary culture, and, perhaps most of all, by the religious and familial formation they received, often on an unconscious level, affirming, disdaining, or merely tolerating work. Ways are sought to bridge the gap between spirituality and work, between what is valued as sacred and meaningful and that aspect of life that can involve, for those who are employed or attempting to find employment, so much time and energy. A spirituality of work that is Christian begins with a return to those spiritual traditions that continue to influence ideas and feelings about work. When critically examined, they might provide resources for developing a more genuine and meaningful spirituality.

Work and the Jewish Heritage

The Jewish Scriptures contain a wealth of references to human work and individual professions that were highly valued by the Jews, such as that of farmer, builder, craftsman, doctor, artist, scholar, musician, fisherman, teacher, rabbi. The great myth of creation found in the Book of Genesis, however, has probably had, for good and for ill, the greatest influence upon modern Western culture's understanding of work. Important theological lessons about work are given in the powerful images and evocative language of this myth.

The opening words of the creation myth reveal everyone's experience of darkness and chaos that precedes any creative work: "In the beginning, when God created the heavens and the earth, the earth was a formless wasteland, and darkness covered the abyss, while a mighty wind swept over the waters" (Gen 1:1-2). As the story unfolds, a continuing process of creation is described in which, one day at a time, the transforming power of God is echoed in the command "Let there be . . . ." In the first five days of creation, light and darkness are separated, and dry land, plants, sun, moon, sea monsters, and flying birds are brought into existence. All of this God affirms as "good." On the sixth day God creates humankind "in the divine image . . . male and female he created them." God blesses them, saying, "Be fertile and multiply, fill the earth and subdue it. Have dominion over the fish of the sea, the birds of the air and all the living things that move on the earth." And God "found it very good." On the seventh day God completes "the work he had been doing" by resting and blessing the day, making it holy through inactivity, as the preceding six days were made holy by God's activity (Gen 1:1-2:4).

A number of insights regarding work emerge in this initial version of the creation story found in the Book of Genesis. The first is that the work of God is in fact the work of creation, a creative process that is holy and good because the Creator is holy and good. A second insight is that humanity is the culmination of that creation, and that everyone, made in God's image, shares the same power to create. There is implicit in the myth an invitation and challenge to be creative as God is—in other words, for all of humanity to become cocreators and co-workers with God. Though theologians sensitive to patriarchy and environmental issues would rightly blame the passage of Gen 1:28, in which God commands the first man and woman to "subdue" the earth and to "have dominion over . . . all the living things," for much of Western culture's disregard of the earth's ecological rights and of its conquest mentality, the story in its entirety emphasizes humankind's responsibilities to the earth and to all of its inhabitants.

The theme of humanity's being co-creators with God is reinforced by the use of the number six, for in mythological language it has a specific meaning and significance. Six is considered an imperfect number, and by describing creation as having occurred in six days, the Book of Genesis is clearly stating that creation itself is not complete, that humanity must continue the creative process begun by God. This is a major principle from Genesis that applies to any spirituality of work: the recognition that work, creativity, and human efforts continue what God has begun. Work is a sacred realm, the Jewish Scriptures clearly state, and our work is the realm where the Holy One dwells and where we share in the Holy One's creative power.

The number seven also has special meaning, for in myths it is considered a perfect number, a symbol of wholeness. Its use in the Book of Genesis teaches a third lesson regarding the Jewish understanding of work with implications for contemporary spirituality. According to that myth, the creative process of God was not completed or brought fully to fruition until the rest on the seventh day. This pattern of the interconnectedness of work and leisure reveals a rhythm of work and creativity that necessarily includes in human life—made as people are in God's image—time away from work. The theological message of the myth is that days of activity must be complemented by days and times set aside for rest, relaxation, prayer, and contemplation in order to restore creative powers and rekindle a sense of gratitude. For leisure is the mother of gratitude, and without leisure there will be no gratitude for any work that is done. This perspective on God's work and human work is revealed in this first version of the creation myth, a version that focuses on the *blessing* of God upon all of creation, especially humanity and the work of humankind.

While this more positive understanding of work has formed a significant part of the Judeo-Christian spiritual heritage, a second version of the creation myth, found in Gen 2:5-25 and linked with the story of the expulsion of Adam and Eve from the Garden of Eden in 3:1-24, has contributed to a very different perception of work. This version tells of Yahweh's planting a garden, creating "man," and realizing that "it is not good for the man to be alone" (Gen 2:18). God *then* creates the wild beasts, the birds of heaven, and finally, from one of the ribs of the man, a woman who is named Eve. Together the first man and woman are tempted by the serpent, and together they experience the consequences of eating the fruit from the tree of the knowledge of good and evil. The woman will experience pain in childbearing and constant conflict with her husband, while the man is promised: "Cursed be the ground because of you! In toil shall you eat its yield all the days of your life. Thorns and thistles shall it bring forth to you, as you eat of the plants of the field. By the sweat of your face shall you get bread to eat, until you return to the ground, from which you were taken" (Gen 3:17-19).

This second account, at least as it has been interpreted through the centuries, gives a much different view of work and of creation, not at all the positive view presented earlier, in which all creation is "good." Here human work is portrayed as a curse, a punishment inherited from our first parents, and the only relief from it is death itself. Whether one is a believer or not, this negative interpretation of work lies deep within Western humanity's collective and personal psyches. It continues to color modern perspectives and attitudes, and thus many people's ambivalence toward work. How can work be welcomed and embraced as a holy dimension of human life if it only produces brambles, thistles, resentments, and pain? How can anything be loved or appreciated that is perceived as a curse or a punishment?

Besides those found in the Book of Genesis, there are over five hundred references to work in the Jewish Scriptures. As God's goodness is reflected in the work of creation and humankind, so also is the work of God manifest in the history of Israel and the life of God's people (Deut 3:24; Judg 2:7). Salvation is God's work (Isa 29:33; 45:11), and to be aware of God's work through the gifts of creation and salvation is to be filled with gratitude and great joy. As the psalmist sings, "The heavens declare the glory of God, and the firmament proclaims his handiwork" (Ps 19:2). This happiness is itself "a gift of God" (Eccl 3:13). Above all, work done in imitation of God has an inherent dignity to it and leads to wisdom—a wisdom compared to the work of laying a foundation, building a house, and filling its rooms "with every precious and pleasing possession" (Prov 24:3-4). This wisdom, given to us by a loving God (Prov 2:6), is manifest in our care for the poor and our desire to follow the way of righteousness, that is, intimacy with God

(Prov 3:9, 27; 10:9; 22:9; 28:27; 29:7; Wis 10:10ff.). Work that leads to wisdom will be rewarded: "He who confers benefits will be amply enriched, and he who refreshes others will himself be refreshed" (Prov 11:25). The hardworking person's plans "are sure of profit" (Prov 21:5); "the kindly man will be blessed for he gives of his sustenance to the poor" (Prov 22:9).

These passages, and others like them, affirm human work and put it in the context of a spirituality of loving care and wisdom, attributes that necessarily include respect and care for the poor, the forgotten, the abused, the *anawim*. Still, the earlier interpretation of work as a curse seems to persist, sometimes subtly manifest in merely tolerating work as something to "get through until Friday," because deep down it is really seen only as a means to an end (i.e, making money, being "successful") rather than as a blessing and call to continue what God has begun.

Work in the History of Christian Spirituality

If the Jewish spiritual tradition contains mixed messages regarding work, the heritage from Christianity is also ambiguous. A dualism that negates the body, women, matter, this world, and, in effect, the incarnation of God has haunted Christian spirituality for centuries. Among Christians, the models of holiness presented for emulation have consistently been the martyr, the ascetic, the ordained leader, or the member of a religious community, suggesting that the most worthwhile kind of spirituality is that which denies the ordinary, the physical, the sexual, and the layperson. This has affected and continues to affect many Christians' understanding and appreciation of work, for when only one lifestyle is presented as heroic or worthy of emulation, the others (and the work associated with them) remain invisible, unrecognized, and undervalued. While this pattern persists in the Christian Churches, the history of the People of God is also rich in traditions and wisdom figures that reveal a spirituality which honors "ordinary" work and provides further insights into the Christian understanding of it.

Jesus, of course, is the Christian's first model of holiness, and in the NT he is portrayed as a person intimately acquainted with his own spiritual heritage. He even speaks of a God who is continuing to work: "My Father is at work until now" (Jn 5:17). Jesus believed that all work was meant to express a person's love for God and solidarity with one another in order to bring about God's reign. Identified by his own townspeople as a craftsman, a worker (e.g., "Is he not the carpenter, the son of Mary ..." [Mk 6:3]), he is attentive to the ordinary as the realm where God works and plays. Walking through fields of wheat, fishing on clear days, sitting down to meals with friends, praying alone on the mountain in the early waking hours, pointing to the lilies of the field, enjoying a wedding, crying at the death of a friend, he tells stories that reflect an appreciation of work. In his parables the sower sows a field (Mt 13:3), laborers work in a vineyard (Mt 13:30), the wise man builds a house (Mt 7:24ff.), a woman sweeps the floors of her home (Lk 15:8), the prodigal son takes care of pigs before reconciling with his father (Lk 15:11ff.), and fields of wheat are white for harvesting (Jn 4:35). He preaches about his dream, the reign of God, on which his friends' hearts are to be set (Lk 12:31), and he values highly work done in service of others: "The greatest among you must be your servant" (Mt 23:11). He tells his disciples that "your light must shine before others, that they may see your good deeds and glorify your heavenly Father" (Mt 5:16). Jesus is especially hard on the lazy servant who hides his talents, and he warns us that ultimately our life and work will be judged in terms of our loving service to one another: "Whatever you did for one of these least brothers of mine, you did for me" (Mt 25:40). Jesus' life and ministry reveal a rhythm of holiness in which work, prayer, and leisure each have their place.

After Jesus, the Christian understanding of work continued to evolve, influenced to a great degree by certain wisdom figures who reflected upon their experience of work in light of Jesus and the Judeo-Christian Scriptures. Though we have no systematic treatise on the subject of work written by the apostolic Fathers and those who followed them, the topic emerges in their writings on Christian life and responsibilities. Sts. Peter and Paul, for example, speak of the value of work united with the suffering of Christ (1 Pet 2:18ff.) and of the need for every Christian to contribute to the life of the Christian community through his or her work (2 Thess 3:6ff.). They and the early Church Fathers consistently advise that any Christian spirituality of work must also include generous and loving support of the poor and companionship with the saints. According to Clement of Rome, Christians are to support themselves by their own labor, and Ignatius the Martyr, in his letter to Polycarp, expresses the patristic ideal of Christian life: "Toil together, wrestle together, run together, suffer together, rest together, rise together, since you are stewards in God's house, members of His household, and His servants."

Clement of Alexandria counsels moderation when it comes to work: "We should not be idle, yet we should not become completely exhausted by our labor either." Like others, Origen discusses the dignity and necessity of work, and relates it to God's work of creation and to Jesus and his disciples, commending to us "Paul the tentmaker, and Peter the fisherman, and John who left his father's nets." Tertullian refutes the pagan charge that Christians are too otherworldly by arguing: "We are sailors along with yourselves; we serve in the army; we engage in farming and trading; in addition, we share with you our arts; we place the product of our labor at your service." Ambrose of Milan speaks eloquently of the dignity of the person who works, and he admonishes Christians to pay just wages to their laborers: "Give the hired servant his reward ... and do not defraud him of the price of his labor, because you too are a hired servant of Christ." Augustine links work and contemplation in his writings, and in his essay "Greatness of the Soul" he states his appreciation for "all the arts of craftsmen, the tilling of the soil, the building of cities. . . . Great are these achievements and distinctly human" (no. 72). A Christian's work, he writes, is made holy through Christ and through charity toward Christ's poor.

This theme of our kinship with the poor is a recurring one among these early writers, including John Chrysostom, who articulates a profound sense of justice, communal and social, which is the Christian's moral responsibility. Chrysostom speaks of the community of all Christians, which links them to Christ the Worker and the apostles and, as a result of that kinship, to the poor who work: "Think of these things ... [and] count the tentmaker as your brother. . . . Whenever you see someone driving nails, smiting with a hammer, covered with soot, do not therefore hold him cheap, but rather for that reason admire him" (Homily 20, *On First Corinthians*). While the ancient pagan world, following the example of the Romans, had come to consider manual labor the lot of slaves, and therefore degrading and unworthy of free men, the emerging Christian tradition as exemplified in Chrysostom's writings increasingly contradicted those attitudes. According to that tradition, all people are equal in the sight of God and have a responsibility toward one another; work is a manifestation of their care. Though it would take centuries before slavery was condemned and then abolished by Christian nations, the seeds of the awareness that slavery is inherently evil can be found in this evolving understanding of work.

Besides these individual writers in the early Church, the monasteries are another vital source that sheds light on a Christian understanding of work, especially those identified with the Desert, the Celtic Christians, and the later Benedictines. In the earliest centuries most of the members of these monasteries were lay people who had a great respect for work, manual and intellectual. Their major contribution was their belief that work is fundamentally holy, but also that it must be balanced with times of relaxation, solitude, and prayer. Other insights about work can be discerned when we briefly examine each.

The Desert Christians of the 3rd, 4th, and 5th centuries in Egypt, Syria, and Palestine manifested a healthy and deeply insightful appreciation of work. It was from them that Western culture, in particular, received the interpretation of work as a sacred reality. One of the great wisdom figures of this Desert tradition was St. Antony (251–356), who, though obviously valuing manual labor, linked it with the important work of meditation and prayer. Among the wisdom sayings associated with him is one in which he advises: "When you sit in your cell, be perpetually solicitous of these three things, namely, the work of your hands, the meditation of your psalms, and prayer." Promoting an ascetic lifestyle that definitely included work with one's hands, Antony also recognized the importance of leisure, as a story about him suggests: Once while Abbot Antony was conversing with some of the brothers, a hunter who was after game in the wilderness came upon them. Seeing Abbot Antony and the brothers enjoying themselves, the hunter disapproved. Abbot Antony said: "Put an arrow in your bow and shoot it." This the hunter did. "Now shoot another," said Abbot Antony. "And another, and another." The hunter said: "If I bend my bow all the time it will break." Abbot Antony replied: "So it is also in the work of God. If we push ourselves beyond measure, the brethren will soon collapse. It is right, therefore, from time to time, to relax our efforts."

As monasticism developed, the obligation to work was reflected in the monastic rules. The principal work of these early monasteries was, of course, agriculture, but tailors, carpenters, smiths, shoemakers, copyists, dyers, tanners, and even camel drivers contributed their services. When the monasteries became important centers of learning, such as those found in the Early Celtic Churches, the work of educating future leaders, lay and clerical, also became an important aspect of monastic life, along with offering hospitality to pilgrims, comfort to the sick, care for orphans, and spiritual guidance to those seeking it.

This Early Celtic Church of Ireland, England, Scotland, and Wales valued work and prayer as part of a daily routine. Those early saints believed that work is love made visible and, because of their pagan animist traditions, had a sense of the sacred all around them when they performed such simple tasks as lighting the morning fire, milking the cows, and caring for the sick and elderly. We find in the Rule of Columcille (named after one of the great Irish missionaries) that work, study, and prayer are ways to express a person's love of God: "Three labors in one day: prayers, work, and reading." In the later Rule of the Celi De, a reform movement in the Early Irish Church, we can discern how much the Celtic monasteries valued intellectual work: "The kingdom of heaven is granted to the person who directs study and to the one who studies and to the one who supports the pupil who is studying." And in poetry attributed to St. Columcille is expressed many of our own yearnings: "To work without compulsion, / That would be delightful."

In the Benedictine monastic tradition, the prayer of the monks was called the *Opus Dei,* "the Work of God." This prayer of praise to God throughout the day and night was considered the chief work of the monks, as well as the place where God worked on them. Within this context of individual prayer and communal singing of the Divine Office, manual labor and intellectual activities formed an overall rhythm of life in the monastery. The Rule of St. Benedict affirms a basic tenet regarding work from Christianity's earliest days: Work is an important antidote to idleness. As the Rule expresses it: "Idleness is the enemy of the soul. Therefore, the brothers should have specified periods for manual labor as well as for prayerful reading" (RB 48:1). The Rule of St. Benedict offers an example of a Christian spirituality that sees work, prayer, study, and contemplation as intertwined, all directed to praising God. It also contains a guiding principle that eventually made it one of the most popular of the Middle Ages and from which we might learn: "All things are to be done with moderation . . . " (RB 48:9), including one's work.

Work in 20th-Century Roman Catholicism

Because work is so intimately related to human life, culture, and religion, the topic continues to be a major theme in the social and political history of humankind, as well as in the history of Christian spirituality. In many ways, Christianity was split at the Reformation precisely over the theological issue involving work or works and how significant they are in the life of faith. Since that time, of course, the Enlightenment and the Industrial Age arose, casting aspersions upon the existence of God and the religious and spiritual dimensions of life. Further historical developments in the 20th century, such as technological advances, two world wars, the exploration of space, the rise and fall of communism, have had their effect on how individuals and societies perceive and value work. If it is true, as Thomas Aquinas said, that there can be no joy in life without joy in one's work, many individuals as well as countries, businesses, corporations, and Churches are discovering that without an awareness of the spiritual dimension of work, something essential is missing in national, institutional, and personal life. People come to feel detached from their work and from themselves when they find little or no meaning in it. Or if they place too much emphasis on it, they frequently experience the ravages of what today is termed "burnout" or what the ancients would call the "loss of soul." Either state leads to the experience of life as a vast wasteland, described so well by the English poet T. S. Eliot in a poem by that name: a great emptiness pervades one's days, quickly filled by compulsive and unethical behaviors, addictions of all sorts, and ultimately despair.

Much of the responsibility for this ennui lies at the doorstep of the Christian Churches because they have too readily preached a gospel, implicitly dualistic, that divides faith and life, Church and world, spirituality and work. In the centuries preceding Vatican II in the Roman Catholic Church, almost all lay activity and work were considered to have little if any intrinsic worth. This world was understood to be passing away and to have nothing of lasting value to it, except, perhaps, as it interacted with Church life. Obviously, this theological interpretation had severe effects on the Church's appreciation of the laity, since so much of their life was spent in interaction with "the world." (This, of course, did not contribute to lay people's appreciation of their own work.) Still, among Roman Catholics and other Christians in this century, there have been important breakthroughs in which the insights of earlier spiritual traditions are being recovered and new forms of a Christian spirituality that values human work are being created.

Because of the Second Vatican Council, the Roman Catholic Church began to articulate a new appreciation for work, connecting it intimately with Christian faith. It refrained from speaking of the reign of God only in terms of future fulfillment and instead began to affirm earthly progress as having a religious dimension to it. In particular, the Pastoral Constitution on the Church in the Modern World (*Gaudium et Spes*), issued December 7, 1965, aligned the Church in solidarity with the entire human family and placed special emphasis on the Christian's responsibility for developing the world. It denounced the split between faith and daily life, and spoke of God's plan that through our work we are to restore the earth, develop it, and bring it to greater wholeness (GS 34, 57). Echoing the words of Christ about how we will be judged, this document warns of the eternal consequences for those who disregard their responsibilities: "The Christian who neglects his temporal duties neglects his duties toward his neighbor and even God, and jeopardizes his eternal salvation" (GS 43). As God's original creation was good, so too is the ongoing creativity and effort of lay people's daily work (GS 12).

Though one can point to Vatican II as being responsible for much of a new appreciation of work, the work of lay people and those who mentored them in the years preceding the council had the greatest effect on Vatican II's stated theology and its implementation. Besides the biblical research, liturgical experimentation, and the competence, education, and involvement of Christian lay people in the workplace and Church life around the world, the inspiration of such saints as Francis de Sales, John Henry Newman, Thérèse of Lisieux, and others had its effect on an emerging lay spirituality. Theologians Marie-Dominique Chenu, Yves Congar, Karl Rahner, Edward Schillebeeckx, and Teilhard de Chardin, writing on the topic of work, also contributed their insights. Dorothy Day and Peter Maurin of the Catholic Worker Movement helped the Churches reexamine their attitudes toward work and their responsibility to the poor, while Thomas Merton re-emphasized, as the earlier monastic traditions had done, the connection between work and prayer.

Popes also added their wisdom: Leo XIII's *Rerum Novarum,* John XXIII's *Mater et Magistra,* and Paul VI's *Populorum Progressio* developed a theology of workers' rights based on the inherent dignity of work. Since Vatican II, Pope John Paul II's encyclical *Laborem Exercens* is especially fine in its articulation of workers' rights to just salaries and to joining associations and unions that will represent and protect those rights. Although it refers to work almost entirely in terms of the male labor force, leaving women, for the most part, in the home, the document is commendable, above all, in its articulation of a spirituality of work. Reflecting upon the interpretation of work as a "curse" in light of Christ's death and resurrection, the Pope writes eloquently of the hope and possibility of transformation when our work is united with Christ's: "The Christian finds in human work a small part of the cross of Christ and accepts it in the same spirit of redemption in which Christ accepted his cross for us. In work, thanks to the light that penetrates us from the resurrection of Christ, we always find a glimmer of new life, of . . . the body of a new human family, a body which even now is able to give some kind of foreshadowing of the new age" (LE 27).

Laborem Exercens, influenced as it was by Vatican II and the work of the laity in society and Church, is a clear expression of the inheritance received from the Judeo-Christian faith: not only are Christians called, as the Book of Genesis suggests, to become co-creators with God but, as baptized members of Christ's Body, they are to share in his ongoing priestly activity: the work of redemption.

A Christian Spirituality of Work

To develop an authentic Christian spirituality in which work has its rightful place means both valuing the significant contribution work can make and acknowledging its inherent limitations. This is what the Judeo-Christian heritage teaches; what Jesus' life, in particular, reveals; and what life experiences confirm. There is a rhythm to all creation, including our own creativity and work. Like all creation, human work is good and is good for us. It can bring a sense of satisfaction to those who can perceive the difference, however subtle, their efforts have made in the life of families, communities, and nations. Work sustains people, helping them to make payments on homes, to provide for the security and education of their families, to reach out to the poor and forgotten in society. It can help them to develop intellectually, psychologically, and spiritually. Most of all, as Jesus and the saints reveal, work has great significance, for it is a way in which human beings prepare for their ultimate lifework: a happy death and union with God.

At the same time, while work is a vital dimension of humanity and an expression of creativity and spirituality, it is but one area of life. It is not meant to be everything. It is not meant to be obsessive or addictive. Most of all, it is not meant to replace the true God with the gods of success, ambition, honor, recognition, or power. Unless work is united with prayer (in which false gods are often discovered) and leisure, it can lead to burnout, despair, and certainly little if any gratitude. Thus prayer, meditation, contemplation, and leisure have a place, not at the sidelines of life, but at its center and heart, whether one works in corporate life or pastoral ministry.

See also CHARISM; CREATION; LAY SPIRITUALITY; LEISURE; MINISTRY, MINISTERIAL SPIRITUALITY; PRAYER; RESPONSIBILITY; SERVICE; VOCATION; WORLD.

Bibliography: M.-D. Chenu, *The Theology of Work* (Dublin: Gill, 1963). P. Palmer, *The Active Life: A Spirituality of Work, Creativity, and Caring* (San Francisco: Harper & Row, 1990). E. Schumacher, *Good Work* (New York: Harper & Row, 1979). D. Soelle with S. Cloyes, *To Work and to Love: A Theology of Creation* (Philadelphia: Fortress, 1983). S. Terkel, *Working* (New York: Avon Books, 1975).

EDWARD C. SELLNER

WORLD

World in relationship to spirituality is a very rich but bewilderingly broad theme. It will be examined here first historically, as we glean what we can from ancient philosophy and its cosmologies. The Scriptures of Israel and Christianity will then be probed for the various interpretations of world they contain. After this, some of the major Western interpreters of cosmology, starting with the Fathers of the Church, will be touched on. The contributions of modern science to our understanding of our world will also be given attention. And, finally, the analogous use of the term *world* prompted by the pluralism of modern life will be discussed.

Classical Cosmology

With the dawn of consciousness in a child, an "out there" begins to reveal itself as unmistakable, mysterious, and immense. Eventually the child will learn to name this out there "the world." So also in Western civilization, it took centuries before human beings named the out there "world." Whether done by child or by civilization, the world is hardly named as a simple, empirical object of observation, independently of the observer. It is named interpretatively, with the interpreters aware that they are a part of the whole they are naming "world," and that therefore there is a direct relationship between the world and themselves.

The first philosophers were Greek, from Miletos in Ionia, in the 6th century B.C.E. Their first and basic object of reflection was the world, or cosmology. They were particularly interested in finding out the primary matter from which all things were composed. Thales surmised that it was water, Anaximenes that it was air, and Heraclitus that it was fire. Since they had not arrived at the distinction between spirit and matter, they assumed the primary matter to be material. They called the whole of the universe as they knew it "the cosmos." Thales (585–546 B.C.E.) had a brilliant pupil, Anaximander, who concluded that the primary matter that constituted the universe and all things in it was an indeterminate boundlessness, which he saw as eternal and infinite. This indetermi-

nate boundlessness functioned as the material cause of all that is.

The next group to conjecture about the cosmos, the Pythagoreans, came a half century later. They felt the need to complement Anaximander's principle of boundlessness with boundary or limit in order to give form to the otherwise unlimited. They saw these limits in terms of numbers. Each existent had a number or was a number. Numbers gave things definition or confined what would otherwise be without boundary.

Plato (b. 428 B.C.E.) brought the notion of the cosmos into a more comprehensive whole, a universe that included heaven and earth, the gods and human beings, in a unity. But he also dichotomized this whole into two worlds, one of them illusory, the other "true." The illusory world was perceived by the senses, the true one was suprasensible; to the latter the human spirit alone had access. The illusory world was perceived in shadows and hence was misperceived. Plato encouraged his students to leave the cave of illusion and shake off their appetites in which they were imprisoned in order to come into the sunlight and commune with the invisible and passionless "Ideas," or Forms, like Justice, Beauty, and Goodness, which are part of this true world. These are eternal patterns of which the objects that our senses grasp are imperfect reflections or copies. A divine Demiurge as well as an eternal World Soul are also seen by Plato as part of the explanation of how the world has come to be what it is.

Aristotle rescued Plato's Ideas from their disembodied existence in the "true" world and brought them back to the real world. Since he saw all existents as a combination of matter and form, Aristotle grounded Plato's abstractions in what he called "natures," which operated in the real world. For Aristotle, God was Form without matter and, in addition, the ultimate end, which could have no end other than itself. Indeed, the world was full of natures, each of which had forms and matter as a limiting, specifying principle. The world and all that is in it reflected God insofar as each thing had a form, which enjoyed a kind of immutability, and matter, which delimited it and made it mortal.

The Old Testament

While Greece was developing a sense of the cosmos, a parallel sense of the whole was developing in Israel. But the Israelites did not have a term for "world." To convey their notion of the spatial whole they intuited, they spoke of "the heavens and the earth." This phrase, though, did not connote a whole in the Greek sense of a universe unified by a single principle; rather, it described the sphere within which there were always conflicting forces and potential chaos. It is only in the late books of the Old Testament—those written in Greek by writers influenced by Hellenistic philosophy, like Maccabees and the Book of Wisdom—that the term *world* (cosmos) appears in the Old Testament. This is not immediately apparent to the reader, since in the Septuagint version of the OT the translators frequently rendered the several Hebrew circumlocutionary expressions for the whole by the Greek term *cosmos*.

Judaism, whether Hellenized or Semitic, alleged things about the world that Greek philosophy never claimed. Thus God made the world (Wis 9:9). God was its Creator (2 Macc 7:23), its Ruler (2 Macc 12:15), its King (2 Macc 7:5). The Temple is honored over the world (2 Macc 3:12). Adam is the first formed father of the world (Wis 10:1); Noah is the hope of the world (Wis 14:6); the wise are the salvation of the world (Wis 6:24).

In Israel's cosmology God occupied a space beyond the realm of the world. But this God was highly invested in this world and intervened again and again on behalf of a chosen people, Israel, in an action of commitment called "covenanting." Long before there was a perception of God as Creator of the world, Israel believed in its specialness to God, who was bonded to Israel in covenant. Although Israel's God was wholly other than the world, Yahweh did not stand aloof or apart from the world or its history. Israel's God was rooted in the meandering history of a people; hence theirs was "the God of Abraham, Isaac, and Jacob." Their God, however, was also manifest in natural phenomena—both those that were awesome, like violent storms, and those that were predictable, everyday wonders of nature. "The heavens declare the glory of God, and the firmament proclaims his handiwork" (Ps 19:1). Because all created things bespoke their origins, the psalmist could exclaim: "Let all your works give you thanks, O LORD, and let your faithful ones bless you" (Ps 145:10). To Israel, the world of nature was the usual place for God's presence to manifest itself, but it was also God's instrument for executing both divine will and judgment. Yet God was not dependent on the world.

The vulnerability and ephemerality of the world are evident in the eschatological scenarios of the prophets. While many of their inspired futuristic imaginings are national in form, the prophets at times were cosmic in their eschatological scope. Jeremiah, for example, foresaw the world being reduced to the chaos it had before the mighty wind swept over the abyss (Gen 1:1-2; Jer 4:23-26). The supporting pillars between earth and sky will totter on the Day of Yahweh (Isa 13:3-10), but the chaos that ensues is the necessary condition for a new creation coming into being (Isa 65:17). Much of Israel's eschatology envisioned a future that was transcendently beautiful but that did not discard the world of nature and history. These would be transformed in ways the prophets could only imagine. But toward the end of the OT period, a new kind of eschatology called "apocalyptic" began to develop.

The Intertestamental Period

Between the years 300 B.C.E. and 100 C.E., the unique genre of eschatology called "apocalyptic" developed. While much of it lies outside the canon of the Bible, it influenced the NT considerably. A good example of the world picture conveyed by apocalyptic can be found in the Dead Sea Scrolls. The sectarian community described in the scrolls is in flight from the world, has disdain for the world, and lives in expectation of a divine posthistorical intervention in which the redeemed will be saved but all the rest of the human race will be lost. In apocalyptic the world is under the judgment of God, since it is the domain of evil. It will come to a sorry end after undergoing unspeakable horrors. God will save the just from this world of sin, shame, and horror, and, in the end, it will cease to be.

There is reason to believe that apocalyptic thinking came from the Persian culture as it was experienced by exiled Israelites, since Persian literature displays some of the emphases that show up in Jewish apocalyptic: the division of the world into periods, the resurrection of the dead, and a sharp dualism between spiritual light and darkness, and therefore between one part of humanity and the other.

A favorite apocalyptic way of imagining the world is to divide it into ages, a present and a future age, or "eon." This age is passing away. It will yield to the future age in which God will be sovereign and the just will be vindicated.

The World in the New Testament

In general, "world" is spoken of in four senses in the NT. It is seen, first of all, as that which God created. For example, "before the world began" (Jn 17:5); "before the foundation of the world" (Jn 17:24); "ever since the creation of the world" (Rom 1:20). Second, world is contrasted to heaven, so it means earth. Or world could refer to the whole of humanity: "God so loved the world that he gave his only Son . . . (Jn 3:16). And, finally, it is used in a pejorative sense, usually in an apocalyptic context.

In most of the Johannine and Pauline corpus, the term "world" is morally and theologically freighted. In John, for example, the devil is its prince (Jn 12:31); for this reason the Christian is hated by the world (Jn 15:18) just as Jesus was (Jn 7:7); this world cannot know God (Jn 17:25); it is explicitly excluded from Christ's prayer (Jn 17:9); his disciples are told they do not belong to it (Jn 15:19); even though they must still live in it, they are not of it (Jn 17:11); they must be comforted by the fact that he has overcome it (Jn 16:33).

For Paul, through Christ the world has been crucified to him and he to the world (Gal 6:14). With Christ, he has died to the world (Col 2:11); the world was condemned, even though God was in Christ reconciling the world to himself (1 Cor 11:32; 2 Cor 5:19); the spirit of the world is sharply contrasted to the spirit of God (1 Cor 2:12).

Many apocalyptic conceptions suffuse the NT. There is frequent allusion to the separation of this age from the age to come. This age has its own wisdom, which must be rejected (1 Cor 2:6). Satan and demonic powers are this age's rulers. True, Christ has dethroned these powers, but this dethronement only profits those who believe in him, not the age itself, which is still "under the power of the evil one" (1 Jn 5:19).

The two ages of Jewish apocalyptic are not simply repeated in the NT. They are creatively rewoven to express the dawning realization that to be one with Christ enables one to live in the age to come here and now, at this time, while the present age is still going on. "So whoever is in Christ is a new creation: the old things have passed away; behold, new things have come" (2 Cor 5:17). "For you have died, and your life is hidden with Christ in God" (Col 3:3). "The victory that conquers the world is our faith" (1 Jn 5:4). Those who believe already taste "the powers of the age to come" (Heb 6:4, 5).

Salvation, therefore, is not something reserved for the age to come or for another world. In Jesus and through his ministry, "today salvation has come to this house" (Lk 19:9). Luke is enamored of the "today" motif. Hence the early Christian communities were very different in soteriology and eschatology than the Qumran (Essene) community, which fled the world to await a wholly future salvation.

But the salvation that was won by Christ was to affect more than Christians, even more than people. It was to affect the physical world itself, according to Paul's insight. He claims that "creation itself would be set free from slavery to corruption and share in the glorious freedom of the children of God" (Rom 8:21). Here Paul is referring to "all creation," which has been "groaning in labor pains even until now" (Rom 8:22). There is consistency between this intuition of Paul and the Genesis account, which has God create an unfallen world and all the creatures of the earth, which God pronounces good. There is also consistency with the NT doctrine of the resurrection of the body.

The Cosmology of the Fathers and the Middle Ages

To understand the postapostolic age's conception of the world, one must first delve into Gnosticism, because the first theologians in the Church, who began to emerge after the death of the apostles, were up against Gnostic worldviews and, in some cases, were themselves susceptible to Gnostic thought. Gnosticism covers many different figures, schools, and sects that flourished between the 2nd and the 4th century C.E. The best known and most influential of the Gnostic sects was Manichaeism, which began with Mani, a charismatic Jewish seer of the 3rd century.

The common denominator of most Gnostic sects and teachings was an aspiration to be privy to a saving enlightenment that could be acquired independently of the Scriptures. Its bias was to be acosmic, distrusting the data of the senses and, by extension, the material world, which supplies this data. For much of Gnosticism, a Demiurge, not God, was seen to be the author of the material world.

Those Gnostic sects that claimed to be Christian usually boasted of enlightenments that were transmitted to their leaders after Jesus' resurrection. Their claim to special knowledge rendered the authoritative magisterium and its still-developing doctrines irrelevant to salvation.

Gnosticism disdained the world and entertained pity for those who were ruled by passion for its enticements or who were unenlightened by the saving knowledge the elect had attained to. Since the material world got in the way of this enlightenment, it was deemed an obstacle to the spiritualized way of life Gnostic Christians aspired to live. They removed all taint of the world from their Jesus, whose bodily form, therefore, was a mere façade for conveying the enlightenment needed for salvation. He didn't really die on a cross, since he was spiritual. Many of the texts of the NT were employed to prove that a spiritualized and intellectualized Christianity was the only way to interpret them and to attain to the salvation Christ promised.

Many of the Fathers of the Church, like Irenaeus, Tertullian, Clement of Alexandria, Origen, and Hippolytus, wrote telling denunciations of this seductive and misleading way of understanding Christ and the Gospels. In their repudiations of Gnosticism, they affirmed the world, the body, and the humanity of Christ and denied the authority of its heterodox teachings. The Fathers were not wholly successful in ridding Christianity of a preoccupation with this purportedly heavenly knowledge and the ascent of the soul to the divine realm, as became evident in the Middle Ages.

The most cosmic view and the one that influenced the Church more than any other was that of St. Augustine (354–430). He saw the world as divided into two societies existing side by side. This division was along the lines of love. The one society, the City of God, was made up of those whose object of love was God. The other, which he called the City of the World, was composed of those whose object of love was self and the world with all its baubles. Its population had a solidarity in the sin of pride, beginning with Adam. Augustine did not see these two societies, which are intermingled throughout history, as Church and civil society, since many who were in the Church did not love God and many who were not in the Church did. His philosophy of history was a spelling out of the drama and the destiny of these two different dynamisms alongside each other.

The Middle Ages achieved a blending of the heavenly and earthly orders into such a unitary whole that virtually no attention was given to the world as world. Belief in God's creation of the world managed to so capture the attention of theologians, Church leaders, and thinkers of this period that the world as such was not an object of speculation. Or when they riveted their attention on it, their reflections dwelt on two of the world's more obvious qualities—its fragility and its transiency. The literature of the Middle Ages was usually marked by an ascetical, "flight from the world" mentality. While the writers would have had to attest to the goodness of the world, since their texts testified that God had made it and all creatures and pronounced them good, these writers were even more conscious of the fallenness of human nature and its pervasive sinfulness in the "use of creatures." These emphases left underdeveloped the theme of God's presence pervading each creature and being mediated to people through them.

One exception to the usual view of the world taken during the Middle Ages was that of the Irish monk John Scotus Erigena (810–877). He had studied Dionysius and therefore had become acquainted with Neoplatonism, and he based his cosmology on a Christianized version of Neoplatonic anthropology. As John Scotus saw it, "humanity is a particular intellectual idea eternally created in the mind of God." This divine idea of humanity functioned as a cause, in fact, the first of the causes. Through this cause, which was Adam, God made every other creature so that through humanity, Adam, all creation was to become inseparably one. Adam was to be the "mediating term and unification of all creatures." The fall of Adam produced the bewilderingly differentiated, menacing, and divided world we now see. The new Adam, Christ, is leading all of this back into the unity God had in mind in the beginning.

Thomas Aquinas (1225–1274) began the breakthrough that was needed to bring about a theological synthesis and to prepare the Church for the secularization process that flowered in subsequent centuries. Aquinas began to entertain ideas about the worldliness of the world, notwithstanding its creatureliness, contingency, and dependency. He has been called the "father of modern atheism" because his philosophy supplied some of the conceptual handles future generations needed to let things be investigated and appreciated for themselves. Hence the rise eventually of a state that was free of the Church, a natural science that eschewed the surveillance of Church authority, and, in general, an increasingly confident secularity.

The Renaissance, which spanned roughly the 15th and 16th centuries, began a double movement. One thrust of this was a movement back to the classics and ancient philosophy. The other was forward toward an appreciation of nature and the human in and of themselves. The result was an emancipation that was especially propelled by natural scientists such as Copernicus, Kepler, and Galileo. Unlike the medieval thinkers who were much more tied to traditional texts, these early scientists laid great weight on observation and hypotheses. Instead of looking at the movements of heavenly bodies to confirm the Bible, they sought to discover the principles and laws that governed these bodies intrinsically. They also turned their attention to the minutest particles of matter they could isolate.

Cosmologies, Cosmogonies, and Science

A cosmology is a formal understanding of the nature of the cosmos. It can be mythic, religious, scientific, or a mixture of these. A cosmogony is an interpretation of how the world began. It, too, can be scientific, mythic, religious, or a mixture of these. A worldview (*Weltanschauung*) is a cosmic perspective that influences not only one's particular perceptions of the world but also of everything that happens in it.

Related to *Weltanschauung,* worldview, is the term "world picture." A world picture is a series of images about reality that serve to make a unified whole. This picture of the whole is comprehensive enough for all specific data to be fitted into it. A world picture cannot be merely the result of experience, since experience only conveys the particular. Nurture, upbringing, teaching, and conditioning would have to enter into any explanation for the particular optic one has of the world.

One's world picture can be wholly mythical, as it was with early civilizations. More often it will be preconceptual, informal, implicit, idiosyncratic, and evolving. Or it can be developed by many philosophers and theologians over time. For example, Scholasticism was able to give an account of the particulars of human existence using faith and reason interchangeably. Or it can be a sketch plan, systematically, critically, methodically thought through by one thinker (e.g., Immanuel Kant, from whom we get the term *Weltanschauung*). Teilhard de Chardin would be a more recent proponent of a world picture. His is less an attempt to explain phenomena in themselves

than an effort to see them in terms of their overall teleology and arrange them in a sequence of earlier and later, based on artifacts and physical evidence. In general, it can be said that archaeology, physics, astrophysics, mathematics, and astronomy are contributing far more to world pictures in recent times than philosophy or theology.

Efforts at developing a scientific cosmology go back as early as the 6th century B.C.E., when the Pythagoreans introduced the idea of a spherical earth and postulated that the motions of the heavenly bodies were governed by harmonious natural laws. There have been many moments of evolution about the world since then. To cite a few: Aristotle's cosmology in the 4th century B.C.E. was geocentric. The earth was surrounded by a number of spheres, with fixed stars on the seventh, the outermost sphere. Thomas Aquinas adopted, and at the same time adapted, Aristotle's cosmology in the 13th century. Copernicus in the 16th century postulated a heliocentric universe: the earth travels around the sun. Late in the following century a Newtonian universe, mechanistic and infinite, was hypothesized. Isaac Newton's cosmology held pride of place for the next three centuries. Newton's worldview saw the world and the universe operating with exquisite precision according to deterministic laws of motion and causality. Sense-observed physical events or natural occurrences were to be analyzed according to these laws.

In the 20th century a new worldview or picture of the world developed, starting from quantum physics. Instead of expecting Newtonian objectivity and determinism, scientists gradually realized that randomness and subjectivity are much closer to the truth about the way the physical world operates. The world picture of physicists and the sciences moved from a mechanistic to an interactive one that saw the world as if it were a living organism that called for synthetic theories and hypotheses to explain it. Consequently, in place of commonsense data, which mislead and misled, there was a new respect for imagination. And the most successful imaginer of the lot was Albert Einstein.

Einstein's focus was not the microworld that occupied most scientists but the macroworld. He was interested in the interaction of the elements and events of the universe on one another and the systematizing of their interrelationships in theories of relativity. He imagined the universe pulsating, expanding and contracting on the basis of the curvatures of the space-time continuum. Just as space determines the movement of matter, so matter in space determines the curvature of space. Observing the relationship of the velocity of light to the velocity of objects, Einstein developed his initial theory of the physics of special relativity, which focused on the relationship of the motion of the observer to these other motions. But it is his general relativity theory—concerning the relativity of all motions, even nonuniform motions—that changed the worldview of so many in the 20th century.

Thanks in large part to the impetus given it by more advanced technology and Einstein's theories, the 20th century has enjoyed an explosion of cosmological data, with no end to the cosmologies and cosmogonies stimulated by this data. We now see how solitary and minute earth is in the middle of a cosmic sea. Scientists have concluded from applying Einstein's discoveries that the universe is expanding because of dynamisms inherent within it and that it is probably uniformly curved. If the curvature is eventually found to be negative by probes into outer space, it will be concluded that the universe is open and space is infinite. If the curvature is found to be positive (spherical), the conclusion will be that the universe is closed and space is finite. The big bang theory is the favorite present hypothesis for explaining the origin of the universe. Rapid developments in astronomical technology have enabled

human beings on earth to detect extragalactic redshifts and nebulae that point to innumerable galaxies beyond the Milky Way. The unmistakable evidence of a continuing expansion leads to the idea that the universe originated in a congested state that blew apart some ten to twenty billion years ago.

Efforts at generating science-based cosmologies must face the paradox that the more knowledge that is accrued about the universe, the more we realize how little is known about it and how it works. For example, scientists now realize how very little is known about the gravitational dynamics within and between galaxies. Given the velocities of the seen stars, asteroids, planets, and the like, it is clear that they should have separated long ago. What keeps them together is an inexplicable "dark matter," which is neither gas nor dust, star nor planet. At least that is the present state of our knowledge as a result of using the instrumentalities presently available for detecting such things. Although it has the properties of a mass, dark matter is unseen and unnamed. This has led scientists and would-be cosmologists to the humbling conclusion that 97 percent of the matter that constitutes the universe is unknown. That this dark matter exists is certain because of its effects, but what it is, is still a mystery.

Cosmogonies are as ancient as cosmologies. There were innumerable mythic versions of how the universe came to be long before there were scientific accounts and hypotheses. One of the earliest and most influential of these cosmogonies, so ancient that it influenced Judaism's protological myths, was the Mesopotamian epic of creation, *Enuma Elish*. This myth is redolent of Thales' insight because it imagines that water was the primal element in the constitution of the universe. North American Indian tribes also had elaborate cosmogonies.

Early Christianity was content to accept Israel's cosmogony. Versions of it can be found in Gen 1; Isa 40:12-22; 45:5-7; Pss 33; 148. It was not long after Jesus' resurrection, however, that his followers began to associate him with the event of creation itself. He was retrofitted, so to speak, into Israel's cosmogony as it came to be understood that his relationship to God had an existence that in some way antedated his own history and history itself. "In the beginning was the Word . . . " (Jn 1:1). "There is one God, the Father, from whom all things are . . . and one Lord, Jesus Christ, through whom all things are and through whom we exist" (1 Cor 8:6). The Letter to the Colossians is even more clear about the peculiar identity of this Christ who was "the firstborn of all creation. For in him were created all things in heaven and on earth, the visible and the invisible, whether thrones or dominions or principalities or powers; all things were created through him and for him. He is before all things, and in him all things hold together" (Col 1:15-17).

Science and Religion

The two worldviews that have been most at loggerheads in the past four centuries are the scientific and the religious. The scientific worldview prescinds from viewing the world from a transcendent perspective. Its range of interest is immanent. The religious perspective on the world is a transcendent one; it claims the world is not autonomous but contingent and dependent. The most famous historical collision between the Church and science took place over Galileo, though many similar clashes preceded and followed this one. The distancing of these two worldviews from each other, though painful and still not wholly in the clear, has had some value for both. It has freed science and scientific method from an a priori bias that has skewed or rendered impossible many valid inquiries. The result has been an unleashing of a wealth of disciplines and their findings that have made the physical world so much more malleable and susceptible to human purposes. And the uncoupling of science from ecclesiastical surveillance has been invaluable for religious understanding and theology because it has served to clarify the very different kind of knowing that faith represents over against scientific knowledge.

The human race has come to a torrential amount of information about the world in the 20th century, both about the macrocosm, of which the human species is an infinitesimal part, and about the complex microcosm of the psyche, which views and interprets the world in all its parts. Interpretation of cosmological data, whether that data is acquired scientifically or by commonsense observation, has been a major function of the religions. While many still retain a bias against accepting any data that does not come through sense perception or is not obtained empirically and scientifically, most moderns appreciate the fact that such a rejection is itself flawed, unscientific, even prejudiced. As long as religion or a religious interpretation of scientific data is consigned to the pejorative trash bin of subjectivity and scientific interpretation is presumed to have the trustworthy character of objectivity, then science and religion will remain antagonists.

A growing sophistication about hermeneutics is equipping many to know that knowing is inappropriately reduced to the two categories of objectivity and subjectivity. The increasingly appreciated discipline of hermeneutics shows how all data, scientific or not, comes to us already interpreted. Interpretation itself becomes a more universally expected and honored activity. Interpretation is seen now as an essential part of any effort at understanding, including the scientific. Cosmological data, for example, has more than one way of being interpreted. These plural interpretations are always done by subjects who alone have the prerogative to interpret objects and to critique one another's interpretations.

Religious faith has been a major font for interpretation and critical thinking about earth, world, and the heavens for most of the human race for most of its history. Today there seems to be a general acceptance among those capable of being critically religious and religiously critical that religious knowing is a different way of knowing than scientific knowing, and that there is no necessary conflict between the two. Religious knowing and scientific knowing are complementary and not contradictory contents and ways of knowing. Gone, too, is the presumption that there is an inevitable linkage between being scientific and being secularist.

The World and Ecology

Most of the present attention being visited on the world as an explicit object of reflection is stimulated by a new concern—its survival. The evidence is irrefutable that the human species is making planet Earth less and less habitable, possibly bringing it to an early demise. This growing attention to the world is not usually religious or philosophical but pragmatic and ethical.

The Bible has been cited as one of the culprits deserving of blame for the ecological crisis. The indictment is that the careless exploitation of the earth by the faiths that adhere to the Jewish and Christian Scriptures derives in large measure from Gen 1:26-28, where Adam and Eve are given dominion over the earth. This and other texts, the indictment continues, imbued human beings with a sense of superiority over the rest of creation with the resultant exploitation of its resources. Having failed to see that they are part of, and dependent on, the same ecosystems as the created things they so carelessly use, human beings are guilty of hubris and arrogance. They are one with the rest of living things and the material creation.

There are grounds for such an indictment. The problem is not with the revelation itself but with its interpretation. Additionally, it is only in recent times that the human race has been able to know the disastrous effects of some of its living habits, and lifestyles and technologies. It is now known that the resources the human species uses are neither unlimited nor, in many instances, are they self-replenishing. Furthermore, the ecological consequences of their use must be taken into account, both for present and future generations. The vocation to dominion, which God extended to the first couple and which has been seen as an essential part of the vocation of every human being, is interpreted wrongly if it appears to endorse the domination or subduing of the earth without reverencing it or replenishing it. The negative consequences of mistaking domination for dominion was not evident until the Industrial Revolution and its aftermath.

A whole new worldview is beginning to develop as a result of the growing ecological crisis. This worldview places front and center care for the ecosystems or the biosphere within which the human species functions. A reverence for life in all its forms is developing, as well as an appreciation of the continuum between human life and the infrahuman. A whole new criterion for the use of things is gaining acceptance the world over, namely, the consequences on future generations of our present use or neglect of things rather than their utility to us now in this generation.

A Jewish or Christian interpretation of the ecological crisis would see the world, even the universe itself, in all its plenitude as both God's gift to humanity and humanity's moral responsibility. According to the Scriptures, there is an intrinsic worth in all God's creatures because they continuously, albeit unconsciously, give glory to God simply by being themselves and doing what they are scripted to do through the laws of their natures. These laws are, in large part, why the created world has the order it has and sufficient predictability to be counted on. The trustworthiness of nature and the laws that govern it reflect God's faithfulness. Part of the moral responsibility of the human race is an unending seeking to know the laws each nature obeys. Indifference to the laws internal to each species or a refusal to learn those laws is a failure in collective stewardship. This ignorance brings an end to any number of species each year and threatens the larger ecosystems within which the human species itself lives.

The Church and the World

The interaction between the Church and the world inevitably occupies the attention of believers. Obviously, a crude *fuga mundi* (flight from the world) mentality does not do this interaction justice. Nor will a naive accommodation of faith to the world. There must be a mean between these two extremes. The world is itself an object of God's love, as are each of the creatures with which it teems. Recall that Peter was warned by God to call nothing profane that God held to be holy (Acts 10:29). A real grasp of Christian spirituality, especially of the doctrines of creation, incarnation, and providence, leads to a reverence for the world and for the created realities in it, each of which is capable of mediating God's presence to the believer.

Any probing of the interaction between the Church and the world establishes their mutuality. The world forms the Church as surely as the Church attempts to form the world. There is also a mutual need. The Church presupposes the existence of the world and has no reality that is not in some sense worldly. The fact that life in the Church is a unique way of being in the world and that it encourages an idiosyncratic style of living and thinking in the world must not obscure the fact of its dependence on it and that it would not exist were it not for the world.

Conversely, the world needs the Church. It needs a purpose beyond itself. It needs signs that convey and celebrate the fact that there is a unity between God and people, and between people with one another.

The world needs to be constantly reminded of the dignity of persons, of their transcendental finality, of their rights, of justice, of freedom, and of the unity of the human race. The world needs the Church because, as creation, it was made subject to futility until now and is groaning in labor pains while it awaits with eager expectation the revelation of the children of God (Rom 8:19-22). As if it were a loaf, the world needs the yeast of the gospel to leaven it, to lighten it, and to make life in it more tolerable and palatable. The Church calls the world to open out to a fullness it cannot deliver with its own immanent powers.

Vatican II gave to Catholic Christianity many categories for discerning the complexity of the relationship between the world and the Church. Its handling of the theme of the cultures and their relationship to the Church is a case in point. In addition, it affirmed the autonomy of the secular against an integralism that had sought to read and lead the temporal order solely in terms of the Christian religion. Rather than preserving or distancing itself from the world, the council was emphatic about the responsibility of the Church, and the laity in particular, to seek the renewal of "the whole temporal order." The fact that the destiny of the world and all that is in it is somehow to be united in Christ Jesus requires that through the laity the Church seek "to perfect the temporal order in its own intrinsic strength and excellence" (AA 7).

A Plurality of Worlds

Most moderns live in a plurality of distinct worlds. They live in a world of work, a world of home, a social world, a religious world. Race, economic class, and gender are three factors that help create these separate or distinct worlds. These plural worlds are each real to the people who live in them. Each has something peculiar that makes it what it is. In these worlds one belongs either by choice or by necessity or by history or by nature. Some of these worlds are big and one fits into them; some are small and one helps to make them what they are. Some of these worlds make me or have made me who I am, for better or for worse.

One travels between these worlds with ease or reluctance, animating some, being conditioned by others. The roles one plays are different in each of these worlds. This pluralism makes a richness of identity possible. But it is also possible that one's identity can become diffused or confused when there are contradictory demands coming from one's plural worlds. Furthermore, if the self is constituted only by the several worlds one inhabits, it can experience anomie and a lack of real commitment to any one of them.

Used in this sense, "world" is constituted by one's personal experience of it. It seems legitimate to include this peculiar use of the term *world* in this entry because of the growing frequency of this way of speaking. It is obvious, therefore, that the term itself can be used analogously.

See also CHURCH; CREATION; CULTURE; ECOLOGICAL CONSCIOUSNESS; EXPERIENCE; HISTORY, HISTORICAL CONSCIOUSNESS; LAY SPIRITUALITY; VATICAN COUNCIL II; WORK.

Bibliography: D. Liderbach, *The Numinous Universe* (New York: Paulist, 1989). J. Haught, *The Cosmic Adventure* (New York: Paulist, 1984). A. Einstein, *Relativity: The Special and General Theory,* trans. R. Lawson (London: Methuen, 1946). S. Toulmin, *The Return to Cosmology, Postmodern Science and the Theology of Nature* (Berkeley, Calif.: Univ. of California Press, 1982). R. Weidner and R. Sells, *Elementary Modern Physics* (Boston: Allyn and Bacon, 1980). S. Stumpf, *Socrates to Sartre: A History of Philosophy* (New York: McGraw-Hill, 1966). *Five Great Dialogues of Plato,* ed. L. R. Loomis, trans. B. Jowett (Roslyn, N.Y.: Walter J. Black, 1942). M. Lugones, "Playfulness, World-Traveling, and Loving Perception," *Women, Knowledge, and Reality,* ed. A. Garry and M. Pearsall (Boston: Unwin Hyman, 1989). B. McGinn and J. Meyendorff, eds., *Christian Spirituality: Origins to the Twelfth Century,* World Spirituality 16 (New York: Crossroad, 1987). J. Raitt, ed., *Christian Spirituality: High Middle Ages and Reformation,* World Spirituality 17 (New York: Crossroad, 1987).

JOHN C. HAUGHEY, S.J.

WORSHIP

See SACRAMENTS; LITURGY.

Z

ZEAL

The word *zeal* comes from the Greek *zelos* and its verbal form meaning "to be hot," "to begin to boil." The Septuagint has thus translated the Hebrew *qana* and its derivatives, meaning "to be dyed dark red or black," to refer to a vehement intensity of emotion that often heightens skin color. In English Bible translations, *zelos* is usually rendered by "zeal" or "jealousy," thus denoting not only strong emotion but also the ambiguous nature of zeal, which can range from selfless love to obsessive envy.

In the OT, divine zeal or jealousy is bound up with God's uncompromising love for a covenant people (Exod 20:5; Ezek 16:38); it is expressed in wrath or in mercy. Various personages are zealous for the one true God (Num 25:11, 13; 1 Kgs 19:10, 14). In the NT, the term *zeal* occurs most frequently in the Pauline letters, where its negative connotation appears in lists of vices (2 Cor 12:20; Gal 5:20) and its positive meaning connotes an ideal (Tit 2:14). Unenlightened zeal led Paul to persecute the nascent Church (Gal 1:14); yet he urges the Christians in Corinth to be zealous for the gifts of the Spirit (1 Cor 12:31) and praises their zeal for the welfare of others (2 Cor 7:7).

Zeal is an expression of love (ST I-II, q. 28, a. 4). It is a love that acts in favor of the object of love—a cause, an idea, or a person—and actively opposes all that is to its detriment. Traditionally it has been described as the flame of love. The object of Christian zeal might be God, God's glory, the good of others, or one's own holiness.

See also APOSTOLIC SPIRITUALITY; LOVE.

Bibliography: B. Renaud and X. Léon-Dufour, "Zeal," *Dictionary of Biblical Theology* (New York: Seabury, 1973).

MARY MILLIGAN, R.S.H.M.

TOPICAL INDEX

In the arrangement of *NDCS* entries according to ten topics, a particular understanding of spirituality is expressed. The foundations of spirituality lie in the divine initiative disclosed in **the Christian mysteries.** The response of **the human person** to the divine initiative is given expression in **the moral life**, inclusive of every dimension of human living. A contemporary understanding of person in relation to God and to others cannot but give careful consideration to ecclesial and sociopolitical realities. Put otherwise, a contemporary spirituality must be attentive to **the person in relation to the world.** This wider focus also brings into view the role of history in human and Christian life, together with the contextual and concrete dimensions of spirituality as these emerge in actual life situations. Christian life, therefore, cannot be conceived of as static and immutable. Authentic Christian living ineluctably entails **growth and development in the spiritual life.** This growth and development calls for a sustained commitment to **prayer,** both individual and communal. **Liturgy and devotion** bring Christian prayer to fuller form. Since Christian living is always both gift and task, the spiritual life requires **discipline(s)** if it is to mature. Contemporary efforts to grow and develop in the spiritual life are properly understood only in the context of the **history** of Christian spirituality. Various **types and schools of spirituality**, historical and contemporary, serve as a constant reminder that Christian spirituality does not develop in isolation but is always an expression of the human desire to be in relationship of communion with another, others, and God. This desire for relationship, for communion of persons enlivened by the Holy Spirit, takes different forms in every age. The appropriateness of these various expressions of Christian spirituality is to be assessed above all in view of the central Christian revelation: God is love (1 Jn 4:8).

The Christian Mysteries

The Human Person

The Moral Life

Prayer

Liturgy and Devotion

Types and Schools
of Spirituality

INDEX OF NAMES

THE EDITOR

Michael Downey is a lay Roman Catholic theologian. He holds a Master of Arts degree in special education, and a doctorate in theology from The Catholic University of America (1982). Associate Professor of Theology at Bellarmine College, Louisville, Kentucky, his publications include several books and numerous articles and essays on Christian spirituality and worship, published in the United States, France, and Canada. Professor Downey's research interests lie in giving methodological form to the study and teaching of Christian spirituality, in developing a theology of the weak, and in making connections between liturgy and spirituality. A member of the editorial board of *Spirituality Today* from 1985 to 1992, he is an editor of the *Merton Annual* and serves as editorial adviser for *Cistercian Studies Quarterly* and *Listening: Journal of Religion and Culture.*